UNIVERSITY CASEBOOK SERIES

Family Property Law

Cases and Materials on Wills, Trusts, and Future Interests

THIRD EDITION

Lawrence W. Waggoner
Lewis M. Simes Professor of Law
University of Michigan

Gregory S. Alexander
A. Robert Noll Professor of Law
Cornell University

Mary Louise Fellows
Everett Fraser Professor of Law
University of Minnesota

Thomas P. Gallanis
Associate Professor of Law and History
Ohio State University

New York, New York
FOUNDATION PRESS
2002

395 Hudson Street
New York, NY 10014
Phone Toll Free 1–877–888–1330
Fax (212) 367–6799
fdpress.com

Printed in the United States of America

ISBN 1–58778–070–4

TEXT IS PRINTED ON 10% POST CONSUMER RECYCLED PAPER

Preface

We derive the title of this casebook on wills, trusts, and futures interests from family law and property law. More than ever, the law of the family intersects with the law of property in this area. Disputes involving family property often pit one family member against another. To be sure, transmission of family property usually occurs quietly, privately, and harmoniously. But not always. In this book, we will come across intensely personal disputes—siblings against siblings, children of a prior marriage against their deceased parent's surviving spouse, aunt or uncle against niece or nephew. We can safely imagine the aftermath in strained or even severed family relationships. In reading and discussing these sometimes dryly presented cases, the human dimension ought not be overlooked. Family property law can affect not only the wealth but also the emotional lives of real human beings.

Once a static area, family property law has entered a reform phase as it responds to a variety of social and legal developments. These developments include: changing notions of family and society; the acceptance of a partnership theory for assessing the financial aspects of a marriage; a growing recognition that the traditional rules and doctrines advertised as giving effect to intention can work to undermine it; and the need to reshape the law of donative transfers into a unity, thus departing from the status quo under which one set of rules governs wills and another set governs other property arrangements such as life insurance, pension benefits, and revocable trusts.

The casebook centers on the Uniform Probate Code (UPC) and the Uniform Trust Code (UTC). The UPC was promulgated in 1969 and was revised in 1990. The UTC was promulgated in 2000, and is the first effort ever to produce a comprehensive uniform act on trusts. We believe that the UPC and UTC will influence family property law deep into this century.

Following an introductory chapter that explores fundamental issues in family property law, we divide the materials into four divisions. Division One covers probate transfers—intestacy, execution and revocation of wills, ademption, abatement, and lapse. Division One also contains a chapter on the Changing American Family that addresses the implication of the changing definition of family on intestacy and constructional law. Division Two brings nonprobate transfers into the discussion. It covers taxation, revocable trusts and other will substitutes, elder law, protection of the family, will contracts, mistake, formation of trusts, spendthrift, discretionary, and support trusts, termination and modification of trusts, and charitable trusts. Division Three covers powers of appointment and future interests, including classification, construction, and the rule against perpetuities. Division Four covers estate and trust administration.

Code Book. The casebook is meant to be used with a companion code book (selected by the teacher) that contains the UPC, the UTC, and other relevant uniform acts. The casebook itself references but does not reproduce these uniform acts. We believe that much is to be gained by studying the statutory text and official comments in the context of a code or act as a whole.

Editorial Conventions. We adhere to the customary casebook convention of omitting footnotes from cases and other extracted sources without disclosure, but we also omit citations within cases without the customary disclosure by way of ellipses. For the most part, citations to precedent within court opinions are omitted except where the citation identifies quoted passages. We only use ellipses to disclose deletion of substantive material from cases or other extracted sources.

Acknowledgments. First and foremost, we want to record our continuing gratitude to Richard V. Wellman, our co-author on the first edition, our colleague, our mentor, our teacher, our friend. Although Dick has retired from active law teaching, he remains as active as ever in law-reform work, continuing to serve on the Joint Editorial Board for Uniform Trust and Estate Acts. We are also deeply grateful to two other co-authors on books that served as predecessors to Family Property Law. The books are Family Property Settlements and Trusts and Succession, and the co-authors are Olin L. Browder and the late George E. Palmer, both of the University of Michigan Law School. The work of both still appears in this edition of Family Property Law. Olin and George were wonderful and generous colleagues who were always willing to share with us their many profound insights in the field.

Special thanks are due to Barbara Zezulka Brown of the University of Michigan Law School, Jylanda Diles of the Cornell Law School, and Patricia Buenzel of the University of Minnesota Law School, whose diligent, sustained, and skillful use of computers and word processing produced complicated charts and transformed our text into pages, titles, and type of the right size, shape, and location.

The co-authors of the second edition take special pleasure in welcoming Thomas P. Gallanis as a co-author of this edition.

LAWRENCE W. WAGGONER
GREGORY S. ALEXANDER
MARY LOUISE FELLOWS
THOMAS P. GALLANIS

October 2001

Summary of Contents

Table of Contents

Page

Division Four: Administration

Table of Abbreviations

Am. L. Prop. . . . . American Law of Property (A. James Casner ed. 1952)

Atkinson on Wills . . . . Thomas E. Atkinson, Handbook of the Law of Wills (2d ed. 1953)

Bogert on Trusts . . . . . . George G. Bogert & George T. Bogert, Law of Trusts and Trustees (2d ed. 1984-88)

Former UPC . . . . Uniform Probate Code (1969)

Gray on Perpetuities . . . . John Chipman Gray, The Rule Against Perpetuities (4th ed. 1942)

IRC . . . . Internal Revenue Code of 1986

Palmer on Restitution . . . . George E. Palmer, Law of Restitution (1978)

Page on Wills . W. Page, Law of Wills (W. Bowe & D.Parker rev. eds. 1959-82)

Restatement 3d of Property . . . . Restatement (Third) of Property: Wills and Other Donative Transfers (Vol. 1, 1999; Tent. Draft No. 1, 1995; Tent. Draft No. 3, 2001) (additional volumes in process)

Restatement 2d of Property . . . . . . Restatement (Second) of Property: Donative Transfers (1983, 1986, 1988, 1992)

Restatement of Property . . . . Restatement of Property (1936, 1940, 1944)

Restatement 3d of Trusts . . . . Restatement (Third) of Trusts (in process)

Restatement 2d of Trusts . . . . Restatement (Second) of Trusts (1959)

Restatement of Trusts . . . . Restatement of Trusts (1935)

Scott on Trusts . . . . Austin W. Scott, Law of Trusts (William F. Fratcher ed. 4th ed. 1987-89)

Simes & Smith on Future Interests . . . . Lewis M. Simes & Allan F. Smith, Law of Future Interests (2d ed. 1956)

UPC (or Current UPC) . . . . Uniform Probate Code (1990, 1993, 1997)

UTC . . . . Uniform Trust Code (2000, 2001)

Table of Cases

The principal cases are in italic. Other cases are in roman.
References are to pages.

D

E

H

I

J

K

Q

R

S

Y

Z

Permissions

We acknowledge with thanks the following authors and publishers who have given us permission to reproduce extracts from their copyrighted works.

Alexander, Gregory S., The Dead Hand and the Law of Trusts in the Nineteenth Century, 37 Stan. L. Rev. 1189 (1985). Copyright © 1985 by the Board of Trustees of the Leland Stanford Junior University. Reprinted by permission of the author, the Board of Trustees of the Leland Stanford Junior University, and William S. Hein & Co.

American Bar Association, Formal Opinion 210, Opinions on Professional Ethics 498 (ABA 1967). Copyright © 1967 by the American Bar Association. Reprinted by permission of the American Bar Association.

———, ABA Committee Report, Developments Regarding the Professional Responsibility of the Estate Planning Lawyer: The Effect of the Model Rules of Professional Conduct, 22 Real Prop. Prob. & Tr. J. 1 (1987). Copyright © 1987 by the American Bar Association. Reprinted by permission of the American Bar Association.

———, Report of the ABA Special Study Committee on Professional Responsibility, Comments and Recommendations on the Lawyer's Duties in Representing Husband and Wife, 28 Real Prop. Prob. & Tr. J. 765 (1994). Copyright © 1994 by the American Bar Association. Reprinted by permission of the American Bar Association.

———, Model Rules of Professional Conduct (2001). Copyright © 2001 by the American Bar Association. Reprinted by permission of the American Bar Association. Copies of the ABA Rules of Professional Responsibility 2001 Edition are available from Service Center, American Bar Association, 750 North Lake Shore Dr., Chicago, IL 60611-4497, 1-800-285-2221

American Law Institute, Restatement (Second) of Trusts. Copyright © 1959 by The American Law Institute. Reprinted by permission of The American Law Institute.

———, Restatement (Second) of Property (Donative Transfers). Copyright © 1983, 1986, 1988, 1992 by the American Law Institute. Reprinted by permission of The American Law Institute.

———, Restatement (Third) of Property (Wills and Other Donative Transfers). Copyright © 1995, 1999, 2001 by The American Law Institute. Reprinted by permission of The American Law Institute.

———, Restatement (Third) of Trusts). Copyright © 1996, 1999, 2001 by The American Law Institute. Reprinted by permission of The American Law Institute.

———, What Law Students Should Know about The American Law Institute (1996). Copyright © 1996 by The American Law Institute. Reprinted by permission of The American Law Institute.

———, Principles of the Law of Family Dissolution. Copyright © 2001 by the American Law Institute. Reprinted by permission of the American Law Institute.

Australian Capital Territory Wills (Amendment) Act No. 67, 1991. Reprinted by permission of the Parliamentary Counsel's Office of the Australian Capital Territory.

Blattmachr, Jonathan, Blattmachr, Donald, and Manley, Robert, Alaska's Revision of Its Trust Act, Which Sets Out to Permit Trusts to Preserve Assets and Reduce Taxes, May Have Implications for Trust Planning Nationwide, National Law Journal B5 (June 16, 1997). Copyright © 1997 by the National Law Journal. Reprinted by permission of the authors and the National Law Journal.

Buck, Estate of, California Superior Court Opinion, 21 U.S.F.L. Rev. 691 (1987). Reprinted by permission of the University of San Fanncisco Law review.

Campbell, Carroll A., Jr., Letter to Lawrence W. Waggoner, February 29, 1996. Reprinted by permission of the American Council of Life Insurance.

Chester, Ronald, Essay: Is the Right to Devise Property Constitutionally Protected?—The Strange Case of *Hodel v. Irving*, 24 Sw. U.L. Rev. 1195 (1995). Reprinted by permission of the author, Professor at the New England School of Law, and the Southwest University Law Review.

Claypool, Allan J., Asset Protection Overview (Techniques in the United States and Offshore), 24 ACTEC Notes 302 (1999). Copyright © 1999 by the American College of Trust and Estate Counsel. Reprinted by permission of the author and the American College of Trust and Estate Counsel.

Cooter, Robert, & Freedman, Bradley J., The Fiduciary Relationship: Its Economic Character and Legal Consequences, 68 N.Y.U. L. Rev. 1045 (1991). Copyright © 1991 by the New York University Law Review. Reprinted by permission of the authors and the New York University Law Review.

Dawson, John P., Economics Duress–An Essay in Perspective, 45 Mich. L. Rev. 253 (1947). Copyright © 1947 by The Michigan Law Review Association. Reprinted permission of The Michigan Law Review Association.

Ellman, Ira Mark, ALI Family Law Report, September 11, 2000, available at www.ssrn.com. Reprinted by permission of the author.

Emanuel, Linda J., & Emanuel, Ezekiel J., The Medical Directive, originally appearing in The Medical Directive: A New Comprehensive Advance Care Document, 261 Journal of the American Medical Association 3288 (1989), and subsequently available on the website, www.medicaldirective.org. Copyright © 1990 Linda J. Emanuel and Ezekiel J. Emanuel. Reprinted by permission of the authors.

Fellows, Mary Louise, et. al., Public Attitudes about Property Distribution at Death and Intestate Succession Laws in the United States, 1978 Am. B. Found. Res. J. 319. Copyright © 1978 by the American Bar Foundation. Reprinted by permission of the University of Chicago Press.

———, The Case Against Living Probate, 78 Mich. L. Rev. 1066 (1980). Copyright © Mary Louise Fellows. Reprinted by permission of the author.

Fletcher, Robert L., Perpetuitics: Basic Clarity, Muddled Reform, 63 Wash. L. Rev. 791 (1988). Reprinted by permission of the author and the Washington Law Review.

Florida Bar Association, Florida Advisory Opinion 95-4 (May 30, 1997). Reprinted by permission of The Florida Bar.

Friedman, Lawrence M., A History of American Law (2d ed. 1985). Copyright © by Lawrence M. Friedman. Reprinted by permission of Lawrence M. Friedman.

Halbach, Edward C., Jr., Uniform Acts, Restatements and Other Trends in American Trust Law at Century's End, 88 Calif. L. Rev. 1877 (2000). Reprinted by permission of the author and the California Law Review.

Hansmann, Henry, The Economics and Ethics of Markets for Human Organs, 14 J. of Health Politics, Policy, and Law 57 (1989). Copyright © 1989 by Duke University Press. Reprinted by permission of the author and Duke University Press.

Hansmann, Henry, and Mattei, Ugo, The Functions of Trust Law: A Comparative Legal and Economic Analysis, 73 N.Y.U. L. Rev. 434 (1998). Copyright © 1998 by the New York University Law Review. Reprinted by permission of the authors and the New York University Law Review.

Hill, John Lawrence, What Does It Mean to be a "Parent"? The Claims of Biology as the Basis for Parental Rights, 66 N.Y.U. L. Rev. 353 (1991). Reprinted by permission of the author and the New York University Law Review.

Johnston, Gerald P., An Ethical Analysis of Common Estate Planning Practices—is Good Business Bad Ethics? Originally published in 45 Ohio St. L.J. 57 (1984). Reprinted by permission of the author and the Ohio State Law Journal.

Kaveny, M. Cathleen & Langan, John P., The Doctor's Call, N.Y. Times, July 15, 1996, at A13. Copyright © 1996 by the New York Times. Reprinted by permission of the New York Times.

Kessler, Ronald, The Season: Inside Palm Beach and America's Richest Society (HarperCollins 1999) Copyright © 1999 HarperCollins. Reprinted by permission of HarperCollins.

Kolata, Gina, "Passive Euthanasia" Is the Norm in Today's Hospitals, Doctors Say, N.Y. Times, June 28, 1997, at 10. Copyright © 1997 by the New York Times. Reprinted by permission of the New York Times.

Langbein, John H., Substantial Compliance with the Wills Act, 88 Harv. L. Rev. 489 (1975). Copyright © 1975 by the Harvard Law Review Association. Reprinted by permission of the author and the Harvard Law Review Association.

———, Living Probate: The Conservatorship Model, 77 Mich. L. Rev. 63 (1978). Copyright © 1978 by John H. Langbein. Reprinted by permission of the author.

———, The Nonprobate Revolution and the Future of the Law of Succession,

94 Harv. L. Rev. 1108 (1984). Copyright © 1984 by the Harvard Law Review Association. Reprinted by permission of the author and the Harvard Law Review Association.

Langbein, John H., & Waggoner, Lawrence W., Reformation of Wills on the Ground of Mistake: Change of Direction in American Law?, 130 U. Pa. L. Rev. 521 (1982). Copyright © 1982 by the University of Pennsylvania Law Review. Reprinted by permission of the authors, the University of Pennsylvania Law Review, and William S. Hein & Company, Inc.

Lindgren, James, Death by Default, 56 Law & Contemp. Problems 185 (1993). Copyright © 1993 by Duke University. Reprinted by permission of the author and Duke University.

Lohr, Steve, A New Breed of Sam Spade Trails Crook's Hidden Assets, N.Y. Times, February 20, 1992, at A1. Copyright © 1992 by the New York Times. Reprinted by permission of the New York Times.

Lovas, Sol, When Is a Family Not a Family? Inheritance and the Taxation of Inheritance Within the Non-Traditional Family, 24 Idaho L. Rev. 353 (1987). Reprinted by permission of the author and the Idaho Law Review.

Malamud, Deborah C., Class-Based Affirmative Action: Lessons and Caveats, 74 Tex. L. Rev. 1847 (1996) Copyright © 1996 Texas Law Review Association. Reprinted by permission of the author and the Texas law Review Association.

Megarry, R. E., Criticism, 81 L. Q. Rev. 478 (1965). Reprinted by permission of Sweet & Maxwell.

Palmer, George E., Dependent Relative Revocation and Its Relation to Relief for Mistake, 69 Mich. L. Rev. 989, 997-99 (1971). Reprinted by permission of the Michigan Law Review.

——, The Law of Restitution (1978). Copyright © 1978, Little, Brown and Company, assigned to Aspen Law & Business, a division of Aspen Publishers, Inc.

Paulus, John C., Ademption by Extinction: Smiting Lord Thurlow's Ghost, 2 Texas Tech L. Rev. 195 (1971). Copyright © 1971 by Texas Tech University School of Law. Reprinted by permission of the Texas Tech Law Review.

Petri, Estate of, New York Surrogate Court Opinion, N.Y.L.J., April 4, 1994, at 29. Copyright © 1994 NPL IP Company. All rights reserved. Reprinted with permission.

Pezzin, Liliana E., & Schone, Barbara Steinberg, Parental Marital Disruption and Intergenerational Transfers: An Analysis of Lone Elderly Parents and Their Children, 36 Demography 287 1999). Reprinted by permission of the authors and the Population Association of America.

Posner, Richard A., Aging and Old Age (1995). Copyright © 1995 by the University of Chicago Press. Reprinted by permission of the author and the University of Chicago Press.

———, Economic Analysis of Law (5th ed. 1998). Copyright © 1998 by Richard A. Posner. Reprinted by permission of Richard A. Posner.

Powell, Richard R., The Rule Against Perpetuities and Spendthrift Trusts in New York: Comments and Suggestions, 71 Colum. L. Rev. 688 (1971). Copyright © 1971 by the Directors of the Columbia Law Review Association, Inc. Reprinted by permission of The Columbia Law Review Association.

Provensano, Matter of, New York Surrogate Court Opinion, N.Y.L.J., Dec. 13, 1982, at 17. Copyright © NLP IP Co. Reprinted with permission from the December 13, 1982 edition of the New York Law Journal.

Quinn, Jane Bryant, Insurance Ploy Can Leave Spouse Penniless, released for publication November 16, 1995. Copyright © 1995 by the Washington Post Writers Group. Reprinted by permission of the author and the Washington Post Writers Group.

———, Beneficiaries Who Don't Benefit, Washington Post, January 23, 2000, at H02. Copyright © 2000 by the Washington Post Writers Group. Reprinted by permission of the author and the Washington Post Writers Group.

Ramo, Roberta Cooper, Joseph Trachtman, Lecture to the American College of Trust and Estate Counsel, Musings of a Family Lawyer, 22 Prob. Law. 1 (1996). Reprinted by permission of the author.

Rein, Jan E., An Ounce of Prevention: Grounds for Upsetting Wills and Will Substitutes, 20 Gonz. L. Rev. 1 (1984/1985). Reprinted by permission of the author and the Gonzaga Law Review.

Rhode, Deborah L., & Minow, Martha, Reforming the Questions, Questioning the Reforms, in Divorce Reform at the Crossroads (Stephen D. Sugerman & Herma Hill Kay eds. 1990). Reprinted by permission of the authors and Yale University Press.

Schanze, Erich, Interpretation of Wills—An Essay Critical and Comparative, in Comparative and Historical Essays in Scots Law (D. L. Carey Miller and D.W. Meyers eds. 1992). Reprinted by permission of author, editors, and Butterworths.

Scott, Austin W., and Fratcher, William F., The Law of Trusts, 4th edition, (1988). Copyright © 1988, Little, Brown and Company, assigned to Aspen Law & Business, a division of Aspen Publishers, Inc.

Simes, Lewis M., The Policy Against Perpetuities, 103 U. Pa. L. Rev. 707 (1955). Reprinted by permission of the University of Pennsylvania Law Review.

Thornley, Trent J., Note, The Caring Influence: Beyond Autonomy as the Foundation of Undue Influence, 71 Ind. L.J. 513 (1996). Reprinted by permission of the Indiana Law Journal.

Thurow, Lester C., Generating Inequality: Mechanisms of Distribution in the U.S. Economy (1975). Reprinted by permission of the author.

U.S. Trust Company, Durable Health Care Power of Attorney & Living Will, in Practical Drafting-Will and Trust Provisions. Reprinted by permission of the U.S. Trust Company.

———, Survey of Affluent Americans, available at www.ustrust.com. Reprinted with the permission of the U.S. Trust Company.

Van Dolson, Randall D., Medicaid Eligibility Rules and Trusts for Disabled Children, 133 Trusts and Estates 51 (1994). Reprinted by permission of the author and Intertec Publishing Company.

Verbit, Gilbert P., State Court Decisions in Federal Transfer Tax Litigation: Bosch Revisited, 23 Real Prop. Prob. & Tr. J. 407 (1988). Copyright © 1988 by the American Bar Association. Reprinted by permission of the author and the American Bar Association.

Viorst, Judith, Necessary Losses (1986). Adapted from Friends, Good Friends–and Such Good Friends by Judith Viorst. Copyright © 1977 by Judith Viorst. Originally appeared in Redbook. Adaptation is included in Necessary Losses by Judith Viorst. Published by Simon & Schuster. Copyright © 1986 by Judith Viorst. Reprinted by permission of Lescher & Lescher, Ltd.

Waggoner, Lawrence W., Reformulating the Structure of Estates: A Proposal for Legislative Action, 85 Harv. L. Rev. 729 (1972). Copyright © 1972 by the Harvard Law Review Association. Reprinted by permission of the author and the Harvard Law Review Association.

———, Perpetuity Reform, 81 Mich. L. Rev. 1718 (1983). Reprinted by permission of the author and the Michigan Law Review Association.

———, The Uniform Statutory Rule Against Perpetuities: The Rationale of the 90-Year Waiting Period, 73 Cornell L. Rev. 157 (1988). Reprinted by permission of the author and the Cornell Law Review.

———, Estates in Land and Future Interests in a Nutshell (2d ed. 1993). Copyright © 1993 by West Group. Reprinted by permission of the author and West Group.

———, The Uniform Probate Code Extends Antilapse-type Protection to Poorly Drafted Trusts, 94 Mich. L. Rev. 2309 (1996). Copyright © 1996 by The Michigan Law Review Association. Reprinted by permission of the author and The Michigan Law Review Association.

Wellman, Richard V., Punitive Surcharges Against Disloyal Fiduciaries: Is *Rothko* Right?, 77 Mich. L. Rev. 95 (1978). Copyright © 1978 by The Michigan Law Review Association. Reprinted by permission of the author and The Michigan Law Review Association.

Family Property Law

Cases and Materials on Wills, Trusts, and Future Interests

THIRD EDITION

Chapter 1

Introduction to Family Property Law

PART A. THE FAMILY PROPERTY LAWYER

FAMILY PROPERTY LAW is an unconventional title for a classroom book on wills, trusts, and future interests. We chose the title to emphasize the symbiotic relationship between the transmission of wealth and family. Rather than viewing family law and inheritance law as parallel regimes, we believe it's more accurate to see inheritance law as playing a crucial role in the creation and maintenance of families and family law playing a similar role in wealth transmission.

The connection between family and property, of course, isn't an idea unique to this book. The connection was the centerpiece of a lecture delivered by Roberta Cooper Ramo in 1996 when she was the President of the American Bar Association. She was invited to present the Joseph Trachtman Lecture to The American College of Trust and Estate Counsel. Here is an extract from her lecture, titled Musings of a Family Lawyer, 22 Prob. Law. 1, 11-13 (1996):

> We [trust and estate lawyers] have chosen to describe what we do and what we specialize in [by] focusing on the very wrong end of the spectrum. We call ourselves by the documents that we draft or the Tax rules that we painstakingly learn. We know ourselves by the description of the state of property or the legal process and we do not call ourselves based upon what we do for the people who are our clients. We say we are "estate planners" and "probate lawyers" or that we have a "tax focus" or "tax expertise". . . . It is my honest belief that what the best of us do is exactly what the truly successful lawyer of the 21st century

> must do. The best among us focus on the problems and opportunities of our clients, which in the case of our practices is by definition the entire family.
>
> It has been a terrible error for us to allow those who specialize in the dissolution of families to take the name "family law" or "family lawyer". In fact, it is trust and estate lawyers, especially in these days of enormously complicated relationships, who look after and usually represent the entire family, with all of the difficult ethical challenges and disclosures and explanation that true fact requires. What you and I do is listen to the desires, to the wishes, to the hopes, to the terrors and to the facts of the life and the death of members of a family unit as they define it. Which is very often beyond what the law allows and these days includes relationships for which there is no legal standing—for example, gay or lesbian partners, relationships between men and women, between friends, sisters, brothers, aunts, uncles, cousins, business partners and, most difficult often, between parents and their children. And we figure out, within the bounds of the law and the continually changing tax systems and our imaginations, how we can take the assets of that group that thinks of itself as a family and magnify those assets to provide for those people that our client or clients loves or feels some obligation to care for over the lives of many generations.
>
> But the best of us do more. . . . We ask terrible questions about children and grandchildren. We know everything. We bring comfort with our reality and clarity for these complicated times. We talk to people who know they are dying, we anguish when our clients sometimes do not know who they really are and who no longer recognize us. . . .
>
> We know something more sensitive than our clients' secrets. We are entrusted, we family lawyers, to make their dreams come true. Our practice is focused on both life and death. We have longer lives these days in America but perhaps with less quality of life and much more need for financial security and help. Death is always complicated because of the difficulty in planning in a financial way and because now we have serial relationships and we need to care for people in each of the layers of our clients' lives. . . . Also it is our job, our duty, our professional obligation to help with literal questions of death and when and how it should be allowed to come.

Through the joint exploration of property and family, this book strives to present the social and legal foundations of family property law. Our goal is to present the challenges that will face the "family property lawyer" in the twenty-first century.

PART B. SHIFTING DEMOGRAPHICS AND THEIR IMPLICATIONS FOR THE 21ST CENTURY FAMILY PROPERTY LAWYER

As suggested by the chart below[1] (younger people to left, older people to right), the baby boomers will provide an abundant client base for the family property lawyer well into the twenty-first century. The opportunities presented by the aging of the baby boomers are accompanied by new challenges in meeting their planning needs.

The great bull stock market of the late 1990s created an enormous amount of wealth. An article in *Barron's* reported that the number of millionaires rose to 7.2 million in 1999, up from 3.4 million five years earlier. Over the same period, the number of pentamillionaires (those with investable assets of $5 million or more) rose to 590,000, up from 90,000 in 1994. Households

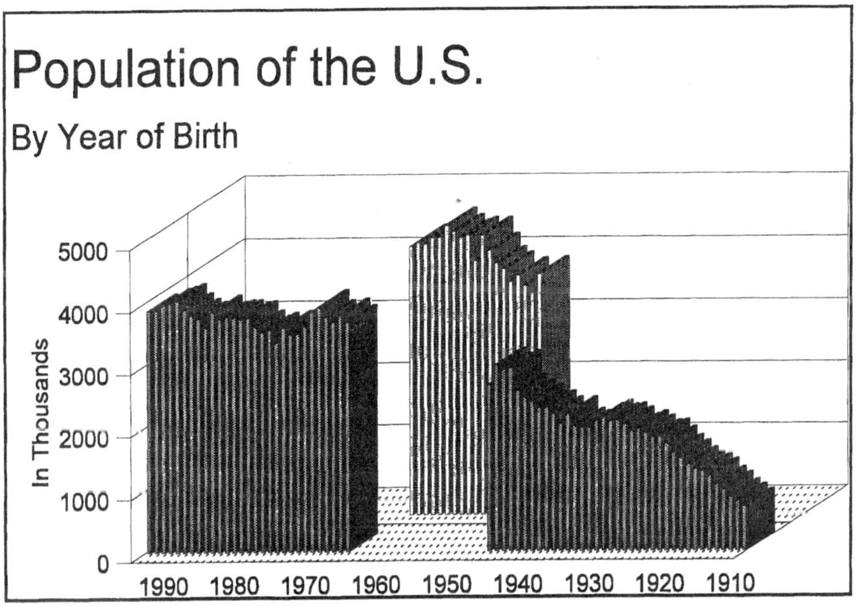

with liquid assets of $30 million or more rose to 55,000 in 1999, an increase of 18 percent from 1998. See Leslie P. Norton, The Wealth Revolution, Barron's, Sept. 18, 2000, at 33. A portion of this wealth has been lost, however, in the bear market that began in March 2000, with the bursting of the "dot-com bubble." As we write this in the Autumn of 2001, the economy was showing signs of stabilizing, but the long-term effect of the September

1. Based on data reported in U.S. Bureau of the Census, Statistical Abstract of the United States 1995: The National Data Book, 16, table 16 (115th ed. 1995).

11 terrorist attacks on the World Trade Center and the Pentagon remains to be seen.

Baby boomers are active participants in the stock market. A survey by the Investment Company Institute and the Securities Industry Association found that "the typical stockholder is 47 years old and lives in a household with annual income of $60,000 and total assets of $85,000. Most stock investors are married college graduates; 53 percent have individual retirement accounts and 80 percent have employer-sponsored pension plans." Robert D. Hershey Jr., Survey Says 78.7 Million Own Stocks in the United States, N.Y. Times, October 22, 1999, at C10. That same survey found that 48 percent of stockholders are baby boomers.

Although the general financial security of many baby boomers means that they are likely to need and want estate planning advice, it should be kept in mind that there is a substantial disparity in the economic well-being among baby boomers. Based on a survey conducted for AARP, boomers who are more likely to be concerned about their financial security during their retirement years are those who do not have college educations and who have lower annual incomes than their counterparts. See Roper Starch Worldwide, Inc. (written for AARP Research Group), Baby Boomers Envision Their Retirement: An AARP Segmentation Analysis (Feb. 1999).

Many baby boomers also stand to inherit unprecedented wealth from their aging parents. Predictions have been made that boomers are likely to inherit as much as $10.4 trillion (or $12-$13 trillion when adjusted for inflation since the time of the study) in inheritances from their parents. See Robert B. Avery & Michael S. Rendall, Wealth and Inheritance (Working Paper 1993) (hereinafter referred to as the Cornell Study, so named because the authors are Cornell professors). This estimate was based on the value of estates passing from heads of households who were fifty years of age or older and who had living children. The Cornell Study received wide attention in the press as well as in estate planning and financial advising circles. It also has generated critics who argue that this aggregate number is misleading. See, e.g., Andy Zipser, And Now, the Bad News: Baby Boomers Are Being Told to Expect Big Inheritances. Here's Why It Won't Work Out That Way, Barron's, Dec. 5, 1994, at 33-39. More recently, a Boston College study projects, based on 1998 dollars, that the amount of wealth transferred between 1998 and 2052 will be between $41 trillion and $136 trillion. The range results from different assumptions about the annual real growth rate. The amount is substantially greater than that estimated in the Cornell Study because it considers all persons in the United States who were at least age 18 in 1998. See John J. Havens & Paul G. Schervish, Millionaires and the

Millennium, in Planned Giving Design Center's Gift Planner's Digest, www.pgdc.net (Feb. 15, 2000).

The unprecedented wealth of the baby boomers' parents, as well as their own newly created wealth, leads some to predict "huge" increases in philanthropy in the United States. "Barring a prolonged economic crisis and stock-market collapse . . . [a] great deal of money will go to help the less well-off, particularly in health and education." "A Survey of the New Rich," The Economist, June 16, 2001, at 3, 4 [hereinafter Survey 2001]. The effect of the phase out of the federal estate tax[2] on charitable giving is uncertain. Some researchers believe that tax savings is only one, and not necessarily the most important, motivation for giving, and expect philanthropy to grow notwithstanding changes to the federal estate tax law. Survey 2001, at 15-16. Family property lawyers should expect to play an important facilitating role as their more wealthy clients consider their philanthropic goals.

The baby boomers also present family property lawyers with the challenge of addressing the needs of the changing American family profile. A few statistics suggest some significant trends. The marriage rate for unmarried women 15 years old and over fell 35 percent between 1970 and 1996, while the divorce rate for this population group increased by 31 percent during the same period. See U.S. Bureau of the Census, Statistical Abstract of the United States 1999: The National Data Book, 110, table 155 (119th ed. 1999). Over 32 percent of all births in 1996 were to unmarried mothers, compared with 18 percent in 1980. See id. at 76, 80, tables 93, 100. Although most children under the age of 18 are reared by both their parents, the percentage of children under 18 who are living only with their mother is steadily rising from 18 percent in 1980 to 23 percent in 1998. See id. at 67, table 83. The 2000 census data rcveal that more than two million grandparents are rearing their grandchildren. Eric Schmitt, Census Date Show a Sharp Increase in Living Standard, N.Y. Times, Aug. 6, 2001, at A1. In slightly more than 31 percent of all marriages that occurred in 1970, one of the spouses had been married previously as compared to 46 percent in 1988. See U.S. Bureau of the Census, supra, at 110, table 156. The numbers of unmarried cohabiting couples, both same-sex and opposite-sex, have also increased.[3] The changing demographics regarding unmarried couples, with

---

2. The phase-out of the federal estate tax is part of the Economic Growth and Tax Relief Reconciliation Act of 2001. See Chapter 7.

3. Due to data processing differences between the 1990 and 2000 censuses, however, "estimates of same-sex unmarried partners are not comparable between the 1990 and 2000 Census. We believe 2000 estimates of this category are better estimates than those produced in 1990. It should also be noted that estimates of opposite-sex unmarried partners, however, were not affected

and without children, are discussed in Chapter 3, Part A. Further information is provided in Chapter 3, Part B, about stepchildren, adopted children, nonmarital children, and the technological advances concerning children of assisted conception. The new family patterns and the new ways of creating families require family property lawyers of the twenty-first century to abandon old and comfortable assumptions about who their clients and their clients' families might be. The one thing we can predict about the future practice of estate planning (as well as about future law reform) is that it will consist of designing solutions to the yet unforeseen needs of the families of the baby boomer generation.

For example, the prevalence of divorce and remarriage may have a substantial effect on intergenerational transfers. A recent study concluded the following:

> Families containing only stepchildren have lower rates of financial and time transfers and lower rates of intergenerational coresidence than families that include biological children. . . .
>
> . . . Along several dimensions, widowed parents engage in more intergenerational transfers than divorced parents. Compared with their divorced counterparts, widowed individuals have significantly higher rates of coresidence and make cash transfers that are over twice as large. Parents who have experienced multiple marriages make significantly smaller transfers to their children than do parents who never remarried. Moreover, remarried parents are less likely to receive informal care from their children . . . and purchase significantly more hours of formal care than parents who were married only once.

Liliana E. Pezzin & Barbara Steinberg Schone, Parental Marital Disruption and Intergenerational Transfers: An Analysis of Lone Elderly Parents and Their Children, 36 Demography 287, 292 (1999).

The character of estate planning will also change dramatically because of predictable increases in the elderly population. By the year 2025, the number of people 55 and older is expected to increase 41 percent. See id. at 25, table 24. The Census Bureau predicts that the 85 and older population will grow from 4.2 million in 2000 to 7 million in 2025. See id. What all this means is that four living generations in a family will become the norm as the baby boomers become great-grandparents. The unprecedented numbers of the *oldest old,* as they are called, will require that the nation, as well as

---

by these editing procedures and changes, and are comparable between the two censuses." U.S. Bureau of the Census, Technical Note on Same-Sex Unmarried Partner Data From the 1990 and 2000 Censuses, www.census.gov/population/www/cen2000/samesex.html.

individual families, address the health, social, and economic problems of great-grandparents. The implications in family property law of increasing numbers of elderly are far-reaching. Family property lawyers will have to address the complexities raised by the four-generation family. A plan that considers only the needs of parents and children, without consideration of great-grandparents and grandchildren will no longer be satisfactory. In addition, to meet the needs of current clients and future clients, family property lawyers must be prepared to address elder law issues, many of which are raised infra Chapter 9.

INTERNET REFERENCES. Estate planning is on the Internet. The home page for the ABA Section of Real Property, Probate and Trust Law, with links to related sites, is at www.abanet.org/rppt. The home page for the American College of Trust and Estate Counsel (ACTEC) is at www.actec.org. Another site with links to a number of estate planning, tax, and elder law sites, as well as to selected articles from magazines, newsletters, and other periodicals dealing with these topics, is www.users.aol.com/dmk58/eplinks. A fee-charging site for lawyers is LawOnTheWeb.com.

If you're interested in seeing the wills of famous people, such as Jacqueline Kennedy Onassis, Chief Justice Warren E. Burger, President Richard Nixon, Benjamin Franklin, Samuel Johnson, Babe Ruth, Walt Disney, Jerry Garcia, John Lennon, Elvis Presley, and many others, see www.ca-probate.com/wills or www.courttv.com/library/newsmakers/wills.

PART C. DONATIVE FREEDOM

1. Cultural Tradition

The Restatement 3d of Property introduces its subject by stating that "[t]he organizing principle of the American law of donative transfers is freedom of disposition."[4] Freedom of disposition, or donative freedom, encompasses several distinct yet related ideas—the right to give your property away during life and to pass it on at death, the right to choose who gets it, the right to choose the form in which they get it, and the right to give another person the right to make those choices even after your death. Donative freedom has a strong cultural tradition in Anglo-American law.[5]

---

4. Restatement 3d of Property at 3.

5. See Ronald Chester, Inheritance In American Legal Thought, in Inheritance and Wealth in America 23, 23-32 (Robert K. Miller, Jr. & Stephen J. McNamee eds. 1998).

Is freedom of disposition socially and economically justified? As Professor Edward C. Halbach, Jr., asked: "What justifications are there for the private transmission of wealth from generation to generation? And how do we rationalize allowing only some individuals, selected by accident of birth, to enjoy significant comforts and power they have not earned?"[6] Therein lies the dilemma: The idea of freedom of disposition focuses on the right of the donor to transmit the wealth that he or she earned, but that right must be balanced against the right of the recipient to receive wealth that he or she did not earn. From the standpoint of the donor, the ability to pass property at death and choose who gets it plays a part in motivating industry, creativity, entrepreneurship, saving, and investment. According to a 1999 survey of the wealthiest one percent of Americans (defined as those with a net worth of $3 million or more or whose annual income is $225,000 or more) commissioned by the U.S. Trust Company, and available on its website, www.ustrust.com, 87 percent of the respondents said that the most important advantage of wealth was the ability to give advantages to your children, and 52 percent said that it was the ability to leave an inheritance.[7]

From the standpoint of the recipient, the following excerpt from Ronald Kessler's book, The Season: Inside Palm Beach and America's Richest Society (1999), suggests some of the detrimental economic and social consequences resulting from inherited fortunes.

> With only 9,800 residents, Palm Beach is inherently a very small town . . . . Here, on $5 billion worth of real estate, live some of the richest people in the world. . . . For the heirs of old wealth, Palm Beach offers a synthetic society that reveres lineage and breeding rather than accomplishment. . . .
>
> . . . . People brought up without the need to struggle bypass life's learning processes. . . . Existing on inherited funds, their sole decision each day is where they should go for lunch or dinner. . . . Inherently weak, they are susceptible to the constant pressure to drink. Many become alcoholics. . . .

Kessler, supra, at 6, 284.

Donative freedom would therefore seem, on the one hand, to be consistent with the philosophy of liberal individualism, which profoundly influences the relationship between the government and its citizens within the United States. On the other hand, to permit large transmissions of wealth would seem to

---

6. Edward C. Halbach, Jr., An Introduction to Death, Taxes and Family Property, in Death, Taxes and Family Property 3 (Edward C. Halbach, Jr., ed. 1977).

7. See also Christopher D. Carroll, Why Do the Rich Save So Much? (National Bureau of Econ. Research Working Paper No. 6549, 1998); Barbara Fried, Who Gets Utility from Bequests? The Distributive and Welfare Implications for a Consumption Tax, 51 Stan. L. Rev. 641 (1999).

contradict the foundation on which our capitalist democracy was built and the basic tenets of liberal individualism itself. Once the focus shifts from the donor to the recipient, vestiges of a class system become all too apparent. Acquiring significant amounts of family wealth by gift or by will is difficult to reconcile with liberal individualism's commitment to equality and its rejection of status by birthright. Although reliable statistics are hard to come by, the Cornell Study found that over 80 percent of the population doesn't expect to receive any inheritance at all or only a small inheritance.[8] Another 11 percent expects to receive a moderate inheritance. Only 5 percent expects to receive a large inheritance. The Cornell Study also found that inheritance accounted for 15 percent of household wealth across all age groups. This study found that the average (mean) household wealth of persons across all age groups who had never received an inheritance was $135,600, while the average (mean) household wealth of those who had received an inheritance was $316,800, $109,300 of which came from inheritance.[9] The U.S. Trust Survey supports the Rand Study. It reports that only 10 percent of the respondents indicated that the primary source of their wealth came from inheritances.

Whatever may be the truth regarding aggregates, disparity in inheritance on an individual basis can contribute to disparity in wealth even among persons with equal incomes, education, health, and marital status.[10] It is the consequence of wealth and its effect on inequality in American society that Deborah C. Malamud explores in her article Class-Based Affirmative Action: Lessons and Caveats, 74 Texas L. Rev. 1847, 1871-72 (1996):

---

8. See also James P. Smith, Unequal Wealth and Incentives to Save 15 (Rand Corp. 1995) (hereinafter referred to as the Rand Study).

9. The Rand Study, however, found that aggregate inequality in wealth is due to a variety of factors that are more important than inheritance, factors such as health, education, income, and marital status. See Rand Study, supra note 8, at 15.

10. Lester Thurow offers these comments about how large fortunes are made:

> Large instantaneous fortunes are created when the financial markets capitalize new above-average rate of return investments to yield average rate of return financial investments. It is this process of capitalizing disequilibrium returns that generates rapid fortunes. . . . To become very rich one must generate or select a situation in which an above-average rate of return is about to be capitalized. . . .
>
> Once great wealth has been created, the holder diversifies his portfolio and after that is subject to diversification and to earning the market rate of return. Because most holders of wealth eventually diversify their portfolios, great fortunes remain even after the underlying disequilibrium in the real capital markets disappears. . . .
>
> Once created, large fortunes maintain themselves through being able to diversify and through inheritance.

Lester C. Thurow, Generating Inequality: Mechanisms of Distribution in the U.S. Economy 142 (1975).

> Wealth is distributed far less equally than income in American society. Wealth barriers are strongly resistant to intergenerational mobility, and inequality in wealth has greatly increased in the United States since the mid-1970s. Wealth has a major impact on life chances, in that it diminishes the dependency of an individual's economic well-being upon occupation, income, educational attainment, or any of the other conventionally measured elements of relative economic position. Even the expectation of future wealth is highly significant in assessing an individual's economic circumstances. For example, a recent college graduate who expects to inherit wealth in the near future can accept a "meaningful" low-paying job in social services, the humanities, or the arts and can even create the appearance that he is living on his salary. But he knows that if he ever wants to buy a house, he need not save in advance for a down payment (an obstacle that would be insurmountable for nonwealthy people of his income); he knows that he need not save money for retirement, limit himself to jobs that provide health benefits, or worry that his choices will render him unable to afford to raise children. Wealth is thus a source of personal economic freedom in a broader sense: it is the freedom to take risks, to make mistakes, to be cushioned from market forces. To fail to consider wealth is to understate the extent both of economic inequality in the United States and of its intergenerational transmission.

The debate over freedom of disposition broke out in public preceding the phased-in repeal of the federal estate and generation skipping transfer taxes enacted by the Economic Growth and Tax Relief Reconciliation Act of 2001 (EGTRAA) (see Chapter 7). One commentator argued: "Th[e] instinct to leave your own money to your own children cannot be called selfish. Sociobiologists, in fact, would call it altruistic, for in their view the willingness of an organism—usually a gene—to sacrifice so that its offspring flourishes is the very definition of altruism. Whether or not one agrees with them, repeal of the estate tax taps into very strong family feelings."[11] Another commentator argued, however: "[T]he real danger is that if [estate] taxes are eliminated, the historic and unique character of American society and culture will be placed in jeopardy. From the start, we have been a nation struggling to balance two competing values: freedom and equality. . . . Individuals [are] entitled to personal wealth and property as the legitimate fruit of labor and reason. Entitlement by birth, however, [is] not inherently healthy; it [is] the distinguishing feature of an aristocratic society. . . . [T]he wealthiest Americans—those worth tens of millions to many billions—should not be allowed to pass on every penny of these riches to their children."[12]

---

11. Alan Wolfe, The Moral Sense in Estate Tax Repeal, N.Y. Times, July 24, 2000, at A23.

12. Leon Botstein, America's Stake in the Estate Tax, N.Y. Times, July 23, 2000, § 4, at 15.

2. Constitutional Protection?

Although donative freedom has a strong cultural tradition in Anglo-American law, it is not considered to be constitutionally protected against all forms of interference or limitation. Indeed, donative freedom is not completely unfettered in American law.[13] The Supreme Court has upheld the constitutionality of the federal transfer tax laws (infra Chapter 7, Part A), which curtail to some extent the right during life or at death to pass your property on above a certain amount. See New York Trust Co. v. Eisner, 256 U.S. 345 (1921) (federal estate tax); Bromley v. McCaughn, 280 U.S. 124 (1929) (federal gift tax). If you're married, state elective share law (infra Chapter 10, Part A) curtails to some extent the right to choose who gets your property. The Rule Against Perpetuities and other rules (infra Chapter 19) restrict the right to choose the form in which they get it. In Irving Trust Co. v. Day, 314 U.S. 556 (1942), the Supreme Court held that the Fourteenth Amendment does not prohibit a state from granting the decedent's surviving spouse an elective share in the decedent's estate. The Court stated:

> Rights of succession to the property of a deceased, whether by will or by intestacy, are of statutory creation, and the dead hand rules succession only by sufferance. Nothing in the Federal Constitution forbids the legislature of a state to limit, condition, or even abolish the power of testamentary disposition over property within its jurisdiction. Expectations or hopes of succession, whether testate or intestate, to the property of a living person, do not vest until the death of that person.

Id. at 562. See Daniel J. Kornstein, Inheritance: A Constitutional Right?, 36 Rutgers L. Rev. 741 (1984).

The view that "the dead hand rules succession only by sufferance" of the state, however, has been put into question by the Supreme Court's decisions in Hodel v. Irving, 481 U.S. 704 (1987), and Babbitt v. Youpee, 519 U.S. 234 (1997). *Irving* concerned the constitutionality of § 207 of the Indian Land Consolidation Act of 1983 (ILCA), which provided:

> No undivided fractional interest in any tract or trust or restricted land within a tribe's reservation or otherwise subjected to a tribe's jurisdiction shall descend by intestacy or devise but shall escheat to the tribe if such interest represents 2 per centum or less of the total acreage in such tract and has earned to its owner less than $100 in the preceding year before it is due to escheat.

---

13. Because the restrictions on donative freedom are fairly modest, the Restatement 3d of Property declares that "[p]roperty owners have the *nearly* unrestricted right to dispose of their property as they please." Restatement 3d of Property § 10.1, comment a (emphasis added).

The case was brought by the heirs or devisees of four decedents who were enrolled members of the Oglala Sioux Tribe. Justice O'Connor, writing for the Court, found that the government's restriction on a property owner's right to transfer property at death amounted to a taking without just compensation.[14]

> [T]he character of the Government regulation here is extraordinary. . . . [T]he regulation here amounts to virtually the abrogation of the right to pass on a certain type of property—the small undivided interest—to one's heirs. In one form or another, the right to pass on property—to one's family in particular—has been part of the Anglo-American legal system since feudal times. The fact that it may be possible for the owners of these interests to effectively control disposition upon death through complex inter vivos transactions such as revocable trusts, is simply not an adequate substitute for the rights taken, given the nature of the property.[15] Even the United States concedes that total abrogation of the right to pass property is unprecedented and likely unconstitutional. Moreover, this statute effectively abolishes both descent and devise of these property interests even when the passing of the property to the heir might result in consolidation of property—as for instance when the heir already owns another undivided interest in the property. Since the escheatable interests are not, as the United States argues, necessarily de minimis, nor, as it also argues, does the availability of inter vivos transfer obviate the need for descent and devise, a *total* abrogation of these rights cannot be upheld.
>
> In holding that complete abolition of both the descent and devise of a particular class of property may be a taking, we reaffirm the continuing vitality of the long line of cases recognizing the States', and where appropriate, the United States', broad authority to adjust the rules governing the descent and devise of property without implicating the guarantees of the Just Compensation Clause. See, e.g., Irving Trust Co. v. Day, 314 U.S. 556, 562 (1942).

Id. at 716-18. In 1984, while *Irving* was pending in the Court of Appeals, Congress amended § 207. In an 8-to-1 decision, the Supreme Court in *Youpee* held that the amended act was also unconstitutional. The Court considered the amendments to § 207 and held, in an opinion written by Justice Ginsburg, that they did not cure the constitutional infirmities identified in *Irving*.

---

14. Although the Court's decision was unanimous, no one joined Justice O'Connor in her opinion for the Court. Justice Brennan concurred joined by Justices Marshall and Blackmun. Justice Scalia concurred joined by Chief Justice Rehnquist and Justice Powell. Justice Stevens concurred joined by Justice White. For insight on the Court's deliberations and the Justices' competing views, which are revealed in the public papers of Justice Marshall, see Michael A. Heller, The Boundaries of Private Property, 108 Yale L.J. 1163, 1214 n.247 (1999).

15. Will substitutes, such as revocable trusts, are discussed infra Part E. Eds.

> Congress' creation of an ever-so-slight class of individuals equipped to receive fractional interests by devise does not suffice, under a fair reading of *Irving*, to rehabilitate the measure. Amended § 207 severely restricts the right of an individual to direct the descent of his property. Allowing a decedent to leave an interest only to a current owner in the same parcel shrinks drastically the universe of possible successors. And, as the Ninth Circuit observed, the "very limited group [of permissible devisees] is unlikely to contain any lineal descendants.' . . .
>
> The United States also contends that amended § 207 satisfies the Constitution's demand because it does not diminish the owner's right to use or enjoy property during his lifetime, and does not affect the right to transfer property at death through non-probate means. These arguments did not persuade us in *Irving* and they are not more persuasive today.

519 U.S. at 244-45. The Court's treatment of the takings issue as applied to American Indian law is disquieting. What is particularly pernicious about *Irving* and *Youpee* is that the Court chose to raise to the level of constitutional protection an individual property owner's right to devise when presented with cases involving property owners who objected to a statute designed to further collective tribal ownership. For a further discussion of why the Supreme Court's protection of the valuable property-held interest of descendibility inappropriately interfered with routine legislative attempts to develop "anti-fragmentation mechanisms," see Michael A. Heller, The Boundaries of Private Property, 108 Yale L.J. 1163, 1213-17 (1999).

Having applied the Anglo-American tradition to decide the constitutionality of § 207 and later amendments to it, the court left outstanding the question of what remains of the philosophical and historical tradition of "the dead hand rules succession only by sufferance." Professor Ronald Chester addresses this issue in Essay: Is the Right to Devise Property Constitutionally Protected?—The Strange Case of *Hodel v. Irving*, 24 Sw. U. L. Rev. 1195, 1209 (1995):

> *Hodel v. Irving* is not technically saying that the complete abrogation of the rights of descent and devise is in itself unconstitutional. What the Court is saying is that "complete abolition of both descent and devise of a particular class of property *may* be a taking" in circumstances such as those in *Irving*, where the Court felt alternative means of passing property at death were not realistically available. . . .
>
> Thus, the apparent damage that *Hodel v. Irving* does to the centuries-old positivist position of *Irving v. Day*, may, upon further reflection, be minor. . . .

PART D. TERMINOLOGY

Family property law uses a specialized terminology when identifying the principal actors involved in wealth transmission and their activities and documents. To be sure, some of the new legal terms you will encounter are ambiguous and have led to litigation requiring courts to interpret the meaning of a disposition found in a will or other type of document. They will be significant sources of discussion in the chapters that follow. Many of the terms, however, have well-accepted meanings, and it's those that we introduce you to here.

A person dying without a valid will has died *intestate* and is referred to as the *intestate*. A person who dies with a valid will is said to have died *testate* and is called the *testatrix* or *testator*. Conventional legal jargon distinguishes between the testator (if a man) and the testatrix (if a woman). This gendered grammar serves no legal purpose today and, therefore, we no longer consider this practice appropriate. In our text, then, we refer to all persons who died with a valid will as the testator. The Uniform Probate Code (UPC or Code) and most state statutes also adhere to this usage, but the term "testatrix" still shows up in court opinions. We haven't used our editing pen to change the term in the excerpts of opinions included in the book.

When a decedent's will doesn't dispose of all of his or her property, it's usually said that the decedent has died *partially intestate*, rather than *partially testate*. Whether a person dies partially or fully intestate (dies without any will), intestate property is distributed in accordance with intestate succession statutes. The American statutes on intestate succession are derived in part from two sources in English law: the common-law canons of descent, which determined inheritance of land, and the English Statute of Distribution, 1670, 22 Car. 2, ch. 10, which governed succession to personal property. The separate treatment of land and personal property in the English law of intestate succession gave rise to a special terminology. Inheritance of land was called *descent*. In fact, the word *inheritance* itself was reserved for intestate succession to land. Those who took land by intestacy were called *heirs*. Succession to personal property was often called *distribution* because of the fact that title to personal property passed to the personal representative, who made distribution to those entitled to share in an intestate's personal property after paying the debts and any other claims against the estate. As a consequence, statutes on intestate succession were (and still are) called *statutes of descent and distribution*. Those who took personal property by intestacy were called *distributees* or *next of kin*.

The history is somewhat the same in testate succession. In older usage, a disposition of land by will was a *devise*, and the one to whom the land was given was a *devisee*. A disposition of personal property was a *legacy* or *bequest*, and the recipient was a *legatee*. Today the words are commonly used almost interchangeably, especially devisee and legatee. The UPC § 1-201 defines the word "devise," when it appears in the Code, as "a testamentary disposition of real or personal property." Many lawyers have interpreted (misinterpreted?) this statutory definition as meaning that, in UPC states, the words "devise" and "devisee" are the proper words to use in wills for bequests of personal property as well as for devises of land. We have gone along with this newer usage and in this book we usually refer to testamentary dispositions of land or personal property as "devises" and the recipients as "devisees."

Although the rules for intestate succession to real and personal property have major points of difference in a few American jurisdictions, and minor ones in some others, the tendency from an early time in our legal history has been to eliminate such differences. Today, in well over two-thirds of the states, there is a single pattern of inheritance without regard to the nature of the property.

One important difference, however, remains in most states. In accordance with the traditions of English law, title to and the right of possession of land pass directly to the heirs, whereas title to and the right of possession of personal property pass to the *administrator*, a fiduciary who is now often called the *personal representative*. The same difference appears in the law of wills. Title to and possession of land disposed of by will vests in the devisee, whereas title to and possession of personal property goes to the personal representative, the *executor*, where the will names an executor. Where there is legislation on the point, however, title to both real and personal property usually passes directly to the heirs or devisees, subject to a right of possession in the personal representative for purposes of properly administering the estate. See, e.g., UPC §§ 3-101, -709. The old difference in concept can still be found in some states where they require the personal representative first to use the personal property found in the estate to pay estate creditors before using the real property. With the modern tendency to eliminate differences between succession of real and personal property, the old terminology is disappearing. Lawyers now often use the words "inheritance," "heirs," and "next of kin" without regard to the character of the estate. Nevertheless, disregard of the older usage is still dangerous as long as there is some reason for differentiating between real and personal property. For example, testators sometimes make devises to their own or somebody else's "heirs" or "next of kin." A devise of real property to "next of kin," or a devise of personal property to "heirs," may be ambiguous if the applicable law contains a different pattern for succession for real and personal property.

PART E. THE PROBATE/NONPROBATE DICHOTOMY

Division One (Chapters 2 through 6) of this book is devoted to family property law as it relates to a decedent's probate estate. As defined in section 1.1 of the Restatement 3d of Property, a decedent's probate estate "consists of property owned by the decedent at death and property acquired by the decedent's estate at or after the decedent's death." Chapters 2 and 3 focus on the distribution of the probate estate when a decedent dies without a will and Chapters 4 through 6 focus on the distribution of the probate estate when a decedent dies with probate's exclusive instrument—a valid will. Division Two (Chapters 7 through 15) brings nonprobate transfers into the discussion. Nonprobate instruments are plentiful and include the revocable trust, life-insurance contract, pension-account contract, and joint bank or stock account. Chapters 8 and 13 through 15 discuss the formation and operation of trusts in detail. Chapter 20 is devoted to the subject of fiduciary administration. It describes the powers, duties, and liabilities of fiduciaries, including both probate representatives and trustees. In other words, it establishes the legal contours of the term *fiduciary*.

Sometimes trusts are created by will. These trusts are referred to as *testamentary trusts*. Trusts can also be created by nonprobate instruments, which are referred to as *lifetime trusts*, *inter vivos trusts*, or *nontestamentary trusts*. However created, a trust is a fiduciary relationship with respect to property, in which title and beneficial ownership are separate. The trustee holds title to and manages the trust property for the benefit of another person or persons, who are called the beneficiary or beneficiaries. A lifetime trust can be irrevocable or revocable. If it remains revocable until the settlor's death, it operates as a will substitute and serves the function of avoiding probate.

A good deal of the discussion in this book is devoted to trusts because, as we shall see, they are used by family property lawyers to maximize flexibility and minimize administrative complexity as they accomplish their clients' family property goals. Although Chapters 8, 13 through 15, and 20 will go into more detail about the formation and operation of trusts, we present this conceptually simple fiduciary arrangement to you here so that at the outset you can begin to appreciate its usefulness as an estate planning tool. By addressing probate transfers first, we don't mean to indicate that they are more important than nonprobate transfers. Nor do we mean to suggest that intestate succession and wills are more important forms of transfer than other forms, such as lifetime trusts. On the contrary, our organization is designed to show that intestate succession is a statutory default mechanism that becomes operative when a property owner dies without having executed a will or without having executed any will substitutes, such as acquiring a life-insurance contract and designating a beneficiary to receive the proceeds. A will, in turn, operates as a default mechanism by controlling the distribution of property that isn't otherwise controlled by a nonprobate instrument. How and why nonprobate transfers have come to overshadow probate transfers is the subject of the following reading.

John H. Langbein, The Nonprobate Revolution and the Future of the Law of Succession

97 Harv. L. Rev. 1108, 1108-09, 1113-25 (1984)

The law of wills and the rules of descent no longer govern succession to most of the property of most decedents. Increasingly, probate bears to the actual practice of succession about the relation that bankruptcy bears to enterprise: it is an indispensable institution, but hardly one that everybody need use. . . .

I. The Will Substitutes

Four main will substitutes constitute the core of the nonprobate system: life insurance, pension accounts, joint accounts, and revocable trusts. When properly created, each is functionally indistinguishable from a will—each reserves to the owner complete lifetime dominion, including the power to name and to change beneficiaries until death. These devices I shall call "pure" will substitutes, in contradistinction to "imperfect" will substitutes (primarily joint tenancies), which more closely resemble completed lifetime transfers. The four pure will substitutes may also be described as mass will substitutes: they are marketed by financial intermediaries using standard form instruments with fill-in-the-blank beneficiary designations. . . .

Although the revocable trust is the fundamental device that the estate-planning bar employs to fit the carriage trade with highly individuated instruments, the revocable trust also keeps company with the mass will substitutes. Standard-form revocable trusts with fill-in-the-blank beneficiary designations are widely offered in the banking industry and were at one time aggressively promoted in the mutual fund industry. The Totten trust, an especially common variant, is simply a deposit account in which the beneficiary designation is thinly camouflaged under language of trust. The depositor names himself trustee for the beneficiary, but retains lifetime dominion and the power to revoke. . . . Either by declaration of trust or by transfer to a third-party trustee, the appropriate trust terms can replicate the incidents of a will. The owner who retains both the equitable life interest and the power to alter and revoke the beneficiary designation has used the trust form to achieve the effect of testation. Only nomenclature distinguishes the remainder interest created by such a trust from the mere expectancy arising under a will. Under either the trust or the will, the interest of the beneficiaries is both revocable and ambulatory. . . .

The "pure" will substitutes are not the only instruments of the nonprobate revolution; "imperfect" will substitutes—most prominent among them the common-law joint tenancy—also serve to transfer property at death without probate. Joint tenancies in real estate and in securities are quite common; joint tenancies in automobiles and other vehicles are also fairly widespread. Because they ordinarily effect lifetime transfers, joint tenancies are "imperfect" rather than "pure" will substitutes. When the owner of a house, a car, a boat, or a block of IBM common stock arranges to take title jointly, his cotenant acquires an interest that is no longer revocable and ambulatory. Under the governing recording act or stock transfer act, both cotenants must ordinarily join in any subsequent transfer. Yet like the pure will substitutes, joint tenancy arrangements allow the survivor to obtain marketable title without probate: under joint tenancy, a death certificate rather than a probate decree suffices to transfer title. . . .

II. The Hidden Causes Of The Nonprobate Revolution

The will substitutes differ from the ordinary "last will and testament" in three main ways. First, most will substitutes—but not all—are asset-specific: each deals with a single type of property, be it life insurance proceeds, a bank balance, mutual fund shares, or whatever. Second, property that passes through a will substitute avoids probate. A financial intermediary ordinarily takes the place of the probate court in effecting the transfer. Third, the formal requirements of the Wills Act—attestation and so forth—do not govern will substitutes and are not complied with. Of these differences, only probate avoidance is a significant advantage that transferors might consciously seek.. . . The probate system has earned a lamentable reputation for expense, delay, clumsiness, makework, and worse. In various jurisdictions, especially the dozen-odd that have adopted or imitated the simplified procedures of the Uniform Probate Code of 1969 ("[former] UPC"), the intensity of hostility to probate may have abated a little. There are, however, intrinsic limits to the potential of probate reform. As Richard Wellman, the principal draftsman of the [former] UPC, forthrightly declared: "The assumption that administration of an estate requires a judicial proceeding is as doubtful as it is costly." Because the Anglo-American procedural tradition is preoccupied with adversarial and litigational values, the decision to organize any function as a judicial proceeding is inconsistent with the interests that ordinary people regard as paramount when they think about the transmission of their property at death: dispatch, simplicity, inexpensiveness, privacy. As long as probate reform still calls for probate, it will not go far enough for the tastes of many transferors, who view probate as little more than a tax imposed for the benefit of court functionaries and lawyers.

The puzzle in the story of the nonprobate revolution is not that transferors should have sought to avoid probate, but rather that other persons whose interests probate was meant to serve—above all, creditors—should have allowed the protections of the probate system to slip away from them. Probate performs three essential functions: (1) making property owned at death marketable again (title-clearing); (2) paying off the decedent's debts (creditor protection); and (3) implementing the decedent's donative intent respecting the property that remains once the claims of creditors have been discharged (distribution). . . . Although the will substitutes are not well suited to clearing title and protecting creditors, a series of changes in the nature of wealth and in the business practices of creditors has diminished the importance of these functions. . . .

The probate court is empowered to transfer title to a decedent's real property and thereby to restore it to marketability under the recording system. The cautious procedures of probate administration have seemed especially appropriate for realty, because the values tend to be large and the financing complex. In theory, the probate court should exercise a similar title-clearing function for all personalty, down to the sugar bowl and the pajamas, because only a court decree can perfect a successor's title in any item of personalty. Of course, ordinary practice quite belies the theory. Beyond the realm of vehicles and registered securities, which are covered by recording systems and thus resemble realty in some of the mechanics of transfer, formal evidence of title is not required to render personalty usable and marketable.

The preoccupation of probate procedure with the transfer of title to single-tenancy real estate reflects the wealth patterns of the small-farm, small-enterprise economy of the nineteenth century that shaped our probate tradition. . . . Promissory instruments—stocks, bonds, mutual funds, bank deposits, and pension and insurance rights—are the dominant component of today's private wealth. Together with public promises (that is, government transfer payments) these instruments of financial intermediation eclipse realty and tangible personalty.

The instruments of financial intermediation depend upon an underlying administrative capacity that is without counterpart in the realm of realty and tangible personalty. Financial intermediation is, as the term signifies, intrinsically administrative. . . . Once a bureaucracy appropriate to such tasks is in operation, only a scant adaptation is necessary to extend its functions and procedures to include the transfer of account balances on death. The probate system nonetheless backstops the practice of financial intermediaries in important ways. The standard form instruments of the nonprobate system all but invariably name the transferor's probate estate as the ultimate contingent beneficiary. If, therefore, the named beneficiaries predecease the transferor or cannot be identified, the financial intermediary remits the fund to probate distribution. Messy heirship determinations are foisted off onto the courts. Likewise, if the proper course of distribution is for some reason doubtful, or if contest threatens, financial intermediaries can force the probate (or other) courts to decide the matter. . . . In this way the nonprobate system rides "piggyback" on the probate system. . . . In the nonprobate system, genuine disputes still reach the courts, but routine administration does not. . . .

The other set of changes that underlie the nonprobate revolution concerns another great mission of probate: discharging the decedent's debts. Many of the details of American probate procedure, as well as much of its larger structure, would not exist but for the need to identify and pay off creditors. These procedures are indispensable, but—and here I am asserting a proposition that has not been adequately understood—only for the most exceptional cases. In general, *creditors do not need or use probate*.
I have undertaken to verify this point within the retail and consumer credit industry. Without mounting a systematic empirical study, I have tried to inquire broadly among credit officers and credit information specialists and their lawyers. Among those I interviewed, I found unanimity both on the central proposition that probate plays an inconsequential role in the collection of decedents' debts, and on the reasons why.

In the vast majority of cases, survivors pay off decedents' debts voluntarily and rapidly. . . .

Creditors know that survivors behave in this way, and they rely upon voluntary notice from survivors as their primary means of learning about a debtor's death. . . . In the remainder of cases, which usually involve unmarried decedents, the creditor commonly discovers the death when the account becomes delinquent and collections personnel begin making inquiries. None of the large retail creditors with whom I spoke made any effort to take advantage of the formal notice-of-death procedures contained in the probate codes for their protection, nor did they have anyone assigned to read newspaper obituaries or inspect official death registers. . . .

Creditor protection is also intertwined with a variant of the principal will substitute, life insurance. So-called credit life insurance typically discharges an insured's account balance at death. . . .

Toward the upper end of the scale of consumer debt, where we encounter automobile finance, we find a different mode of creditor protection, the security interest. . . . This leverage over survivors ordinarily leads to out-of-court settlement of such debts. . . . When this formidable battery of out-of-court payment and collection practices fails to clear a debt, the creditor protection system of probate may also be unavailing. Although the safeguards of notice, court filings, hearings, adjudication, and so forth are meant to protect creditors, they are often self-defeating, because they make probate proceedings too expensive to be cost effective for collecting routine debts. Account balances are often so small that collection costs would exceed the likely recovery even if nonlawyers handled most of the filings and subsequent steps.

Nonetheless, creditors do use probate. The large creditors with whom I spoke were prepared to go to probate to attempt to collect debts of several thousand dollars when preliminary investigation by credit information agencies or in-house personnel revealed the likelihood of substantial assets in a probate estate. None seemed concerned to trace nonprobate assets. . . .

In the late twentieth century, creditor protection and probate have largely parted company. Had this development been otherwise, the rise of the will substitutes could not have occurred. If creditors had continued to rely significantly upon probate for the payment of decedents' debts, creditors' interests would have constituted an impossible obstacle to the nonprobate revolution. For—make no mistake about it—the will substitutes do impair the mechanism by which probate protects creditors. Even though the substantive law governing most of the major will substitutes usually recognizes the priority of creditors' claims over the claims of gratuitous transferees (life insurance is sometimes an exception), the decentralized procedures of the nonprobate system materially disadvantage creditors.

Notes and Questions

1. *Probate Administration.* Chapter 20 is devoted to a consideration of many probate administration issues. The purpose of this Note is to give you a general sense of the probate process and the responsibilities of the decedent's *personal representative* (p.r.). Any discussion of probate administration quickly becomes complicated because the probate laws are not uniform and the practices in local probate offices are diverse. Nevertheless, a general description of the probate process is possible. If a decedent dies without a valid will or if the decedent's will fails to name an executor, the court, in

accordance with statutory direction, will name an administrator for the estate. If the will names an executor who is willing and able to serve, that person will act as the p.r. of the estate. Executors and administrators have the same responsibilities. They are fiduciaries who are entrusted with the property of decedents. They are accorded powers that they must exercise on behalf of those persons who have claims to the estates of decedents—beneficiaries and creditors. In preparation for beginning the probate administration process, the p.r. should consult with the family and assist, as requested, with funeral arrangements. The p.r. should also ascertain surviving kin and obtain their addresses, notify the decedent's bank, employer, insurer, and annuity obligor of the decedent's death, identify and protect the decedent's moveable assets, and review records for business contracts, property transactions, debts, and credits. The p.r. is responsible for locating the decedent's will and obtaining copies of the decedent's death certificate.

Upon collecting this information and notifying the appropriate persons, the p.r. should file a petition for probate of the will and obtain court appointment as p.r. The will should be probated in the county in which the decedent was domiciled at death. If real property is located in another jurisdiction, the p.r. will also have to seek ancillary administration in that jurisdiction. The p.r. should arrange for probate bonds, if necessary, and give required notices to creditors of the estate.

A p.r.'s next responsibility is to collect, protect, inventory, and appraise all probate assets. All estate cash and checks payable to the decedent should be deposited in the p.r.'s estate account. This would include collecting and depositing insurance proceeds that are payable to the estate as well as any sums owed to the decedent. In addition, a p.r. is responsible for taking possession, storing, or otherwise securing tangible personal assets. Sometimes it's necessary to prepare an inventory of estate assets for court filing and to arrange for appraisal of estate assets as may be required by the court or dictated by federal and state tax rules. The p.r. should set up a record system to identify probate and nonprobate assets passing at death to surviving joint tenants and death beneficiaries. This information will be required for reporting on state inheritance and federal estate tax returns. Finally, the p.r. has a responsibility to investigate business arrangements that may require attention and make appropriate protective and managerial arrangements.

The p.r. must also consider all estate claims presented to him or her or to the court, by gathering the necessary information needed to reject or allow each of the claims. The United States Supreme Court held in Tulsa Professional Collection Services, Inc. v. Pope, 485 U.S. 478 (1988), that the due process clause requires that creditors of the decedent who are known to, or reasonably ascertainable by, the p.r. must be given actual notice of court proceedings serving to bar creditors' claims. The Court held that notice by publication is insufficient. For further discussion of this case and its impact on probate procedure, see infra Chapter 20, Part A.

The p.r. should discharge undisputed and minor obligations as soon as possible. In making these decisions, the p.r. should consider the amount of all known claims against an estate and an estate's liquidity. The p.r. is responsible for making sure that all taxes are paid and paid in a timely fashion. The p.r. must obtain all the information necessary to file necessary tax returns pertaining to federal and state income and transfer taxes. In addition to discharging claims, the p.r. should consider the other cash demands on the estate. These would include payments for family allowances, which are statutorily provided, see infra Chapter 10, Part B, administrative expenses, and legacies. The p.r. must make decisions about how needed cash may be best raised and what assets, if any, need to be liquidated. The p.r. must also make investment decisions, taking into consideration market conditions as well as the circumstances of estate beneficiaries. The p.r. has the responsibility for managing and investing the probate assets prudently pending distribution.

Finally, the p.r. must determine the respective rights of estate beneficiaries. The p.r. must prepare an accounting of receipts and disbursements. This accounting must indicate whether the receipts and disbursements are related to income or principal. The p.r. must also prepare a distribution plan for the court and obtain approval from the beneficiaries of the plan. The p.r. should consider whether to make partial distributions in cash or in kind. Those decisions will be influenced by tax consequences for the estate and for the affected beneficiaries. A final distribution will occur from the estate upon the issuance of an order by the court or upon the receipt by the p.r. of a release from the beneficiaries.

2. *Creditors' Claims.* Professor Langbein writes that creditors do not rely much on probate administration to secure discharge of debts owed them. His analysis, however, focuses exclusively on voluntary creditors. Do you think that persons who have tort claims or claims for child support arrearages against the decedent would rely on the protections afforded by probate administration? Do you think property passing by will substitutes, such as life-insurance proceeds and joint bank accounts, should be beyond the reach of tort claimants or claimants for child support? The question of creditors' rights to reach nonprobate property is discussed infra in Chapter 8, Part A. We'll see that the rights of creditors to reach nonprobate property are

frequently determined by statute and depend on the type of will substitute involved.

3. *The Right of Publicity.* Although descendibility is clear for most property interests, it has been disputed with regard to the right of publicity. The right of publicity is the legal recognition of people's interest in their own names, signatures, likenesses, or other indicia of identity. See Restatement (Third) of Unfair Competition § 46 (1995). The importance of the question of whether heirs can control the use of a person's identity after that person's death has increased in recent years as digital technology has increased the opportunities for commercial use of deceased celebrities.[16] Although the majority of jurisdictions that have considered this issue by statute or by court-made law recognizes the right of publicity to be descendible, all limit the duration of the right. The jurisdictions vary a great deal in the length of time that they recognize post-mortem publicity rights. See, e.g., Cal. Civil Code § 3344.1(g) (70 years);[17] Ind. Code § 32-13-1-8 (100 years); Va. Code Ann. § 8.01-40 (B) (20 years). For further discussion of the right of publicity, see Alice Haemmerli, Whose Who? The Case for a Kantian Right of Publicity, 1999 Duke L.J. 383.

4. *The Will/Will Substitute Distinction.* Professor Langbein writes that "[t]he owner who retains both the equitable life interest and the power to alter and revoke the beneficiary designation has used the trust form to achieve the effect of testation. Only nomenclature distinguishes the remainder interest created by such a trust from the mere expectancy arising

---

16. You may have seen the controversial TV commercials for Alcatel, the French telecommunications company, that used Martin Luther King, Jr. delivering his "I Have a Dream" speech to an empty Washington Mall and Lou Gehrig giving his "Luckiest Man" speech to an empty Yankee Stadium. The Washington Mall and Yankee Stadium were emptied digitally to make it appear at first that they gave their speeches to no one. King's name and likeness were licensed for an undisclosed fee to Alcatel by King's heirs through the Martin Luther King, Jr. Center for Nonviolent Social Change. Gehrig's name and likeness were licensed to Alcatel for a six-figure fee that will be donated to medical research by the estate of Lou Gehrig's widow. See Richard Sandomir, Gehrig's Digital Remake, N.Y. Times, May 12, 2001, at B16; Paul Farhi, King "Dream" Becomes Commercial, Wash. Post, March 28, 2001, at C01.

17. The California statute was amended in 1999 in response to the Ninth Circuit's interpretation of California law in Astaire v. Best Film & Video Corp., 116 F.3d 1297 (9th Cir. 1997), denying Fred Astaire's widow a right of recovery against a videotape manufacturer for using film clips of Fred Astaire's performances in a series of instructional videotapes. As amended, the California statute is titled the "Astaire Celebrity Image Protection Act."

In Hoffman v. Capital Cities/ABC, Inc., 255 F.3d 1180 (9th Cir. 2001), the Ninth Circuit relied on the First Amendment right of freedom of speech in reversing a district court judgment in favor of Dustin Hoffman for damages against Los Angeles Magazine for publishing an article that contained, without permission, a digitally-altered still photograph of Dustin Hoffman from the movie "Tootsie."

under a will." Langbein, supra, at 1113. That passage was probably particularly confusing when you read it because it seems to say that what the law calls a will and what the law calls a revocable lifetime trust has the same substantive consequences. If that is so, why distinguish the two instruments at all? The answer is that family property law is in a transitional stage, moving toward the elimination of the will/will substitute distinction. The twentieth-century nonprobate revolution has significantly affected family property law. Many important issues ignore the distinction. For example, statutory protections of spouses provide that nonprobate as well as probate property is reachable by disinherited spouses. See infra Chapter 10, Part A. Similarly, the federal and state income and transfer tax laws treat property passing by wills and will substitutes alike. See infra Chapter 7, Part B. Full integration of the law of wills and will substitutes, however, isn't yet complete. Many legal consequences still turn on whether an instrument is labeled a will or a will substitute. For example, a marital dissolution accompanied by a property settlement operates to void any devise to one spouse in the other spouse's will. The legislatures generally have failed to reform these statutes to make void will-substitute transfers made to former spouses. But see UPC § 2-804. Throughout the study of family property law, the will/will substitute distinction requires the following inquiries: Does this rule apply only to wills? Should the rule, or a variant of it, apply to will substitutes? A still further question is: Does, or should, the rule apply to *all* donative transfers, including lifetime transfers that are not will substitutes, such as irrevocable lifetime trusts?

Problem

Of the following asscts, which would be subject to probate administration at G's death, assuming that A survived G? Which of the assets are held in a form that, using Professor Langbein's term, would be considered a "pure" will substitute? Which of the assets are held in a form that, again using Professor Langbein's term, would be considered an "imperfect" will substitute? Which of the assets would be subject to probate administration if A predeceased G?

(1) Car: Title in G

(2) Bank accounts:

Checking account: Joint title in G and A

Savings account: Title in G

(3) LMN Mutual Fund: Title in G and A as equal tenants in common

(4) Certificate of Deposit: G and A as joint owners with right of survivorship

(5) Series EE U.S. Savings Bonds: Title in G, payable on death to A
(6) Home: Title in G and A as joint tenants with right of survivorship
(7) Group term life insurance on life of G with A named as beneficiary
(8) Qualified pension plan provided to G by G's employer with A named as beneficiary in case of death before retirement.

PART F. SOURCES OF FAMILY PROPERTY LAW

1. The Restatements

Throughout this book, you will find frequent references to the Restatement of Property and to the Restatement of Trusts. These two Restatements are central to family property law.

Both of these Restatements are currently undergoing revision. Volume 1 and a tentative draft of the Restatement (Third) of Property (Wills and Other Donative Transfers) (referred to herein as the Restatement 3d of Property) have been published.[18] Volume 1 covers intestacy, execution and revocation of wills, and post-execution events affecting wills. The tentative draft covers construction, reformation, and modification of donative documents.

Three tentative drafts of the Restatement (Third) of Trusts (referred to herein as the Restatement 3d of Trusts) have been published.[19] These tentative drafts cover the nature, characteristics, and types of trusts, the creation of trusts, the elements of trusts, and the nature of the beneficiaries' rights and interests. The previous editions of these Restatements have greatly influenced the development of family property law during this century. The current editions now in process are likely to continue to be influential.

As indicated below, the Restatements are issued in the name of the American Law Institute (ALI or Institute), and are formulated through an extensive deliberative process. What follows is a statement issued by the ALI in 1996 for the purpose of introducing law students to the workings of the Institute.

---

18. Lawrence W. Waggoner of the University of Michigan Law School is the Reporter and John H. Langbein of the Yale Law School is the Associate Reporter for the Restatement 3d of Property. The late A. James Casner of the Harvard Law School was the Reporter for the Restatement (Second) of Property (Donative Transfers) (referred to herein as the Restatement 2d of Property) and the late Richard R. Powell of the Columbia Law School was the Reporter for the first Restatement of Property (referred to herein as the Restatement of Property).

19. Edward C. Halbach, Jr., of the University of California at Berkeley School of Law is the Reporter for the Restatement 3d of Trusts. The late Austin W. Scott, Jr., of the Harvard Law School was the Reporter for the Restatement (Second) of Trusts and for the first Restatement of Trusts (referred to herein respectively as the Restatement 2d of Trusts and the Restatement of Trusts).

What Law Students Should Know About the American Law Institute (1996)

The American Law Institute [ALI] was organized in 1923 as a result of a study reporting that the two chief defects in American law were its uncertainty and its complexity. Produced by a group of prominent judges, lawyers, and law professors, the study called for the formation of a new organization whose mission would be to improve the law and its administration. According to the Institute's Certificate of Incorporation, its purpose is "to promote the clarification and simplification of the law and its better adaptation to social needs, to secure the better administration of justice, and to encourage and carry on scholarly and scientific legal work."

To this end, the Institute undertook to formulate a comprehensive series of Restatements of the common law. Between 1923 and 1944, Restatements were developed for Agency, Conflict of Laws, Contracts, Judgments, Property, Restitution, Security, Torts, and Trusts. In 1952, ALI started the Second series of Restatements, which included new editions of the original Restatements plus new subjects, including Foreign Relations Law and Landlord and Tenant Law. The Third Restatement series, now in progress, includes projects on the Law Governing Lawyers; Torts (Apportionment of Liability and Products Liability); Trusts; and Property (Donative Transfers, Mortgages, and Servitudes). . . .

A project is undertaken by ALI only after careful consideration by it's [sic] officers and Council (its governing body). A legal scholar with expertise in the field is designated the project's "Reporter." The Reporter submits drafts of "black-letter" text and explicating commentary to a carefully constituted group of Advisers. With most recent projects, drafts are also reviewed by a larger Members Consultative Group consisting of ALI members with particular interest in the subject. If approved by the Council, tentative and proposed final drafts are presented to the membership during an Annual Meeting of the Institute, where members may approve the drafts or recommit them for further revision or reconsideration. Over a period of years, this careful and deliberative process eventually produces the official text of an ALI Restatement . . . .

Members of The American Law Institute are selected on the basis of professional achievement and demonstrated interest in the improvement of the law. The Institute's membership consists of eminent federal and state judges, distinguished lawyers, and respected law professors. Elected membership is currently limited to 3000, which includes some members in foreign countries. The Chief Justice of the United States, Associate Justices of the Supreme Court, Chief Judges of the U.S. Court of Appeals, and chief justices of the highest state courts are ex officio members of the Institute, as are deans of law schools that are members of the Association of American Law Schools. The influence of the Institute's work is widespread, and many ALI publications have been accorded an authority greater than that of any legal treatise. This is largely due to the care with which the work is produced, the quality of the personnel involved in each project and in the ALI Council and membership, and the degree and deliberative consideration each draft is given. Over the years, there have been over 130,000 published court decisions citing the Restatements of the Law . . . .

2. The Uniform Trust and Estate Acts

Uniform Probate Code. For statutory law, this book centers on the Uniform Probate Code (UPC) and the Uniform Trust Code (UTC). The UPC was originally promulgated by the Uniform Law Commission[20] (ULC) in 1969. Richard V. Wellman, then of the University of Michigan Law School and later of the University of Georgia School of Law, was the Chief Reporter. The UPC has had a profound effect on American law. The UPC is the first effort, ever, at comprehensive codification of the law of estates and probate. Its major divisions cover the substantive and procedural law of intestacy, wills, donative transfers, guardianship, conservatorship, and estate and trust administration.

The UPC is not a static Code. Unlike nearly all other uniform acts, the UPC is constantly monitored by a supervisory body called the Joint Editorial Board for Uniform Trust and Estate Acts (until 1999, the board was known as the Joint Editorial Board for the Uniform Probate Code). The JEB is composed of nine members—three from the ULC, three from the American Bar Association, and three from the American College of Trust and Estate Counsel. Six of the nine members (including the chair, Malcolm A. Moore) are practitioners of national reputation; three are academic lawyers. There are, in addition, an Executive Director (David M. English), a Director of Research (Lawrence W. Waggoner), and three liaisons, one to probate judges and two to law teachers.

Throughout the twenty-plus years after the UPC's origination, the JEB has, with the approval of the ULC, revised a section here and a section there to eliminate unintended consequences and, in some cases, to reflect changed policy choices. But the supervisory process took a dynamic turn in the mid-1980s. The heightened activity culminated, in 1989, and again in 1998, in a thoroughly revised Article VI, dealing with multiple-party accounts and related areas, and, in 1990, in a dramatically revised Article II, the core

20. Short for the National Conference of Commissioners on Uniform State Laws.

substantive article of the UPC. The revised Article II makes significant changes in the law of intestacy, wills, elective-share law, and constructional law. Lawrence W. Waggoner of the University of Michigan Law School was the Chief Reporter for the 1990 Article II revisions. As revised, UPC Article II reflects four fundamental policy objectives: (1) to respond to the changes in the American family, especially the multiple-marriage society; (2) to extend the partnership theory of marital property, now recognized in divorce law, into the laws protecting surviving spouses from disinheritance; (3) to move toward unification of the law of probate and nonprobate transfers; and (4) to diminish the formalistic barriers to the implementation of transferors' intentions. Consistent with these objectives, major changes have been introduced into virtually every chapter of the law.

We believe that the current (revised) version of UPC Article II will influence American family property law into the new millennium. At the same time, you must bear in mind that the former version of UPC Article II or non-UPC law still constitutes the law in many states. The UPC revisions are so comprehensive that it will take significant periods of study before large numbers of states will move to enact them. Thus, in this book, we principally focus on the current (revised) version of the UPC, making references to the former version or non-UPC law as necessary.

Uniform Trust Code. In 2000, the ULC approved the Uniform Trust Code (UTC), which is the first comprehensive uniform codification of the law of trusts. The reporter for the UTC was David M. English of the University of Missouri-Columbia School of Law. Although a number of existing uniform acts relate to trusts, the importance of trusts in family estate planning, as well as the incompleteness of the existing acts, led to a recognition of the need for a uniform act that comprehensively addressed trust law issues. The initial model for the UTC was Division 9 of the California Probate Code, which contains an extensive trust statute. It was also drafted in close coordination with the preparation of the Restatement 3d of Trusts. As it does for the UPC, the JEB will monitor the UTC. Because we believe that the UTC will influence the development of trust law during this century, we focus on its provisions throughout the trust chapters of the book.

Statutory References. This book is meant to be used with a statute book containing the UPC, the UTC, and various other uniform laws that are germane to family property law. There is more than one such book available.

The casebook and the statute book are integrated by the freestanding captions in the casebook denominated Statutory References. These Statutory References direct you to the major statutory material reproduced in the statute book that you should examine in conjunction with the topic you are about to study.

Internet References. The Home Page for the American Law Institute can be found at www.ali.org. The Home Page for the Uniform Law Commission is at www.nccusl.org, which has links to the text of uniform laws, lists of enacting states, and drafts of uniform laws in process.

DIVISION ONE
PROBATE TRANSFERS

Chapter 2

Intestate Succession

PART A. INTRODUCTION

Statutory References: *UPC §§ 1-107, 2-104, 2-108*

WHO Is Likely to Die Intestate? Conventional wisdom is that most people die intestate. Conventional wisdom also is that the older and wealthier you are, the more likely you are to have a will.[1] An empirical study corroborated the points that age and wealth are good predictors of will-making, but cast some doubt on the notion that most people die intestate. See Mary Louise Fellows et al., Public Attitudes About Property Distribution at Death and Intestate Succession Laws in the United States, 1978 Am. B. Found. Res. J. 319, 336-39 (hereinafter 1978 Survey). The results of a telephone survey conducted in five states in 1977 revealed the following

1. There will always be exceptions. A striking one is Howard Hughes, who died intestate in 1976. In his case, however, he apparently once had a will, but it couldn't be found after his death and the proponent and principal beneficiary of the will, the Howard Hughes Medical Institute, was unable to probate it as a lost will. The story is told infra Chapter 5, Part B.

demographic characteristics of the respondents who said they had a will and those who said they didn't have one:

Demographic Characteristics	*Have Will*	*No Will*
Family income:[2]		
Under $67,500	34.6%	65.4%
$67,500 and above	65.4%	34.6%
Estate size:[3]		
$0-$134,999	27.7%	72.3%
$135,000-$269,999	50.2%	49.8%
$270,000-$1.35 million	69.0%	31.0%
Age:		
17-30	12.3%	87.7%
31-45	34.6%	65.4%
46-54	60.7%	39.3%
55-64	63.4%	36.6%
65 and over	84.6%	15.4%
Family status:		
No children	10.9%	89.1%
Some minor children	32.2%	67.8%
All adult children	72.6%	27.4%

Although, overall, nearly 55 percent of the respondents interviewed said they had no will, the above table shows that those without a will were young and unlikely to die in the near future. About 73 percent of the population dies between the ages of 65 and 95. See the chart opposite, which shows the percentage of people still living at birth through age 110.[4] If this survey is accurate for the country as a whole, and if 60.7 percent of the 46-54 population, 63.4 percent of the 55-64 population, and 84.6 percent of the 65-and-over

2. The family income and estate size figures presented above have been adjusted for inflation. Between 1977, when the survey was conducted, and 1998, the consumer price index indicates nearly a 270 percent decline in the purchasing power of the $1. The original figures have been adjusted accordingly. See U.S. Census Bureau, Statistical Abstract of the United States 1999: The National Data Book 882, table 1435 (119th ed. 1999).

3. See supra note 2. In U.S. Trust's survey of the top 1 percent of Americans based on wealth, two-thirds of whom had estates between $1 million and $10 million, 84 percent had a will. See ustrust.com.

4. The chart is based on Table 90CM, Treas. Reg. § 20.2031-7.

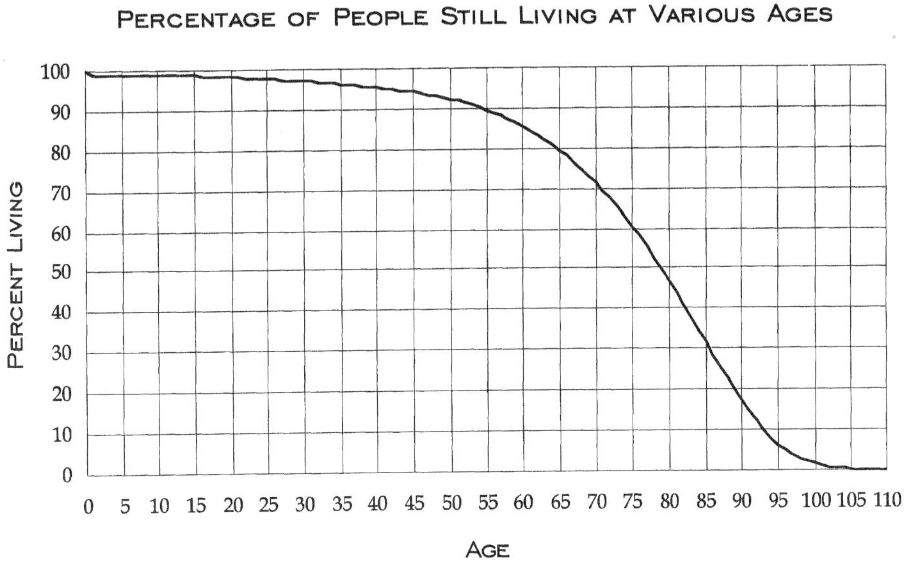

population have wills, the conventional wisdom that most people die intestate may be unfounded. Perhaps it's more accurate to suggest that most people who die prematurely die intestate.[5]

Besides age and income, what additional factors might explain why some people don't make wills? See John M. Astrachan, Why People Don't Make Wills, 118 Tr. & Est. 45 (Apr. 1979).

Of course, even for those people who die intestate, intestacy is often not the prevailing form of family property transfer.[6] Many decedents will die having provided for the disposition of at least some of their property through a will substitute, such as a joint tenancy with right of survivorship or a life insurance contract. Data gathered in a study of probate administration conducted in the 1970s show that life insurance and joint tenancy property is commonly found in decedents' estates. See Robert A. Stein & Ian G. Fierstein, The Demography

---

5. In 1997, the five leading causes of death for both males and females between the ages of 25 and 44 were cancer, accidents, heart disease, human immunodeficiency virus (HIV) infection, and suicide. See National Center for Health Statistics, National Vital Statistics Reports, June 30, 1999, at 27, 28, 30, table 8.

6. A state's intestacy statute may not be applicable for all property interests found in the decedent's probate estate. For example, California's statute on the right of publicity includes its own distribution scheme if the decedent fails to transfer the right during life or by will. See Cal. Civ. Code § 3344.1(d) (West). For further discussion of the right of publicity, see supra Chapter 1, Part C.

of Probate Administration, 15 U. Balt. L. Rev. 54, 102-04 (1985). The popularity of will substitutes is further demonstrated in a survey of same-sex partners in Minnesota conducted in 1996. Seventy-one percent of the respondents had joint bank accounts, 63 percent held their homes in joint tenancy with right of survivorship, and nearly 70 percent had a life insurance policy naming their partner as beneficiary of the proceeds. See Mary Louise Fellows, et al., Committed Partners and Inheritance: An Empirical Study, 16 Law and Ineq. J. 1 (1998).

Historical Roots of Intestacy Rules. The intestacy rules of modern America have their roots in medieval England. Under the English canons of descent (which developed from customary rules), only persons related by blood to the decedent could be heirs. Blood relatives were divided into three groups: (1) descendants (or issue), (2) ancestors, and (3) collaterals. See infra Section 3.

According to the English canons, the intestate's land was inherited by his descendants so long as any descendant was living at his death. This was true also under the English Statute of Distribution, 1670, which governed the succession of personal property, except that it made provision for surviving wives.

The English canons, which in fact were not uniformly applied throughout England, provided that a male descendant should be preferred to a female descendant and that, among male descendants, the eldest should take the entire estate (a rule of inheritance referred to as primogeniture). In a society such as England's, which was dominated by a landed and male aristocracy, one purpose of primogeniture was to preserve the unity of the patrimony, the large family estates, in the male line.[7] Primogeniture wasn't abolished until 1926 by the Administration of Estates Act, 1925, 15 Geo. 5, ch. 23, § 45. The English Statute of Distribution followed neither of these rules and basically codified well-established customary rules for dividing personal property equally among the decedent's children. See John H. Baker, An Introduction to English Legal History 321-22 (2d ed. 1979).

If the intestate died without leaving any living descendant, his land passed to collateral heirs; ancestors were completely excluded from inheriting land. The

---

7. The purposes and effects of the rule of primogeniture are subjects much debated among legal historians. English lawyers themselves did not agree on its purposes. Sir Matthew Hale, for example, defended primogeniture by making the improbable claim that it ensured socially useful occupations for younger sons, who otherwise would have "neglected the Opportunities of greater Advantage of enriching themselves and the Kingdom." Matthew Hale, The History of the Common Law of England 142 (Charles M. Gray ed., 1971) (first published in 1713). The great English legal historian, Sir Frederic Maitland, claimed that primogeniture obliterated class distinctions. See 2 Frederick Pollock & Frederic W. Maitland, A History of English Law 274 (1898).

exclusion of ancestors wasn't followed either by the English Statute of Distribution or in any U.S. jurisdiction.

In America, rejection of the preference for males to females and of primogeniture among male descendants began during the colonial period. Reform of intestacy law, including the elimination of primogeniture in virtually all of the states in favor of a rule that treated the children equally, reflected the influence of the political tradition of republicanism that animated the Revolution. The preambles to the Revolutionary and post-Revolutionary acts governing inheritance expressed the republican abhorrence of aristocracy, family dynasties, and large estates.[8] This ideology co-existed uneasily with the commitment to individual rights of ownership. The conflict between individual freedom of disposition and the prevention of dynastic wealth is one of the recurrent stories throughout American succession law. See supra Chapter 1, Part C.

Policy Bases of Intestate Succession. What objectives do and should guide policymakers in developing a system for succession of property upon the death of a person who lacked a valid will or will substitute? The rationale that today is commonly ascribed to intestacy laws is expressed in the following passage from the court's opinion in King v. Riffee, 309 S.E.2d 85, 87-88 (W. Va. 1983):

> Our laws concerning intestate succession are designed to effect the orderly distribution of property for decedents who lack either the foresight or the diligence to make wills. The purpose of these statutes . . . is to provide a distribution of real and personal property that approximates what decedents would have done if they had made a will. Spouses and children enjoy a favored position under the laws of intestate succession because, on statistical average, they are the natural objects of most peoples' [sic] bounty.

In the 1978 Survey, supra, at 324, the authors suggest that effectuating probable intentions of decedents is not the only objective of intestacy statutes:

> The alternative . . . rationale for adopting a particular distributive pattern in an intestacy statute is that it serves society's interests. There are four identifiable community aims: (1) to protect the financially dependent family; (2) to avoid complicating property titles and excessive subdivision of property; (3) to promote and encourage the nuclear family; and (4) to encourage the accumulation of

---

8. See, e.g., 2 Laws of the State of Delaware, ch. 53 (Samuel & James Adams pub. 1797); 1 Public Acts of the General Assembly of North Carolina, ch. 22 (James Iredell ed., Francis Xavier Martin rev. 1804). For further discussions of the relationship between early American inheritance law and republican political ideology, see Gregory S. Alexander, Time and Property in the American Republican Legal Culture, 66 N.Y.U. L. Rev. 273 (1991); Stanley N. Katz, Republicanism and the Law of Inheritance in the American Revolutionary Era, 76 Mich. L. Rev. 1 (1977).

> property by individuals. If society's well-being requires a distributive pattern different from the determined wishes of intestate decedents, the decedents' wishes should be subordinated.

To this list, we would add another objective: to produce a pattern of distribution that the recipients believe is fair and thus doesn't produce disharmony within the surviving family members or disdain for the legal system.

Requirement of Survival of the Decedent. Only persons who survive the decedent are entitled to succeed to the decedent's property by testate or intestate succession. See Restatement 3d of Property § 1.2. Unless altered by statute, survival by only an instant is sufficient. On occasion, decedents and their devisees or heirs die in circumstances—such as an automobile or airplane accident—in which it is impossible to determine the order of deaths. To meet this problem, almost all states had passed a statute identical to or closely patterned after the Uniform Simultaneous Death Act (1953) (USDA), § 1 of which provides:

> *No Sufficient Evidence of Survivorship*. Where the title to property or the devolution thereof depends upon priority of death and there is no sufficient evidence that the persons have died otherwise than simultaneously, the property of each person shall be disposed of as if he had survived. . . .

Why does it make sense to presume that the testator or intestate survived? Dissatisfied with the USDA, the former UPC provided that "any individual who fails to survive the decedent by 120 hours is deemed to have predeceased the decedent." Do you see the reason for the dissatisfaction with the USDA? The current UPC embraces the 120-hour requirement. UPC § 2-104. It explicitly requires, however, that survivorship of the decedent by 120 hours be "established by clear and convincing evidence." See also UPC § 2-702 (adopting the 120-hour requirement of survival for all donative dispositions, including life insurance, and for joint tenancies and joint accounts with a survivorship feature); Former UPC § 2-601 (adopting the 120-hour requirement for devises). In 1991, the Uniform Law Commission revised the USDA to adopt the UPC's 120-hour requirement of survival.

The Uniform Determination of Death Act (1980) defines death as follows:

> *Section 1. [Determination of Death.]* An individual who has sustained either (1) irreversible cessation of circulatory and respiratory functions, or (2) irreversible cessation of all functions of the entire brain, including the brain stem, is dead. A determination of death must be made in accordance with accepted medical standards.

Forty states and the District of Columbia have enacted the Uniform Determination of Death Act and, in 1991, the Uniform Law Commission incorporated it into § 1-107 of the UPC and the revised USDA.

The definition of death is crucially important for determining when organ retrieval should take place. Both the legal and medical communities have had to face the difficult policy questions raised by the dual goals of maximizing the availability of organs and preserving the rights and interests of patients and their families. Although ethicists have engaged in significant debate concerning a legal and medical definition that uses two different criteria for determining death, the Act has achieved widespread adoption. For further discussion of the question of determining death and its relationship to organ donation, see James M. DuBois, Non-Heart-Beating Organ Donation: A Defense of the Required Determination of Death, 27 J.L. Med. & Ethics 126 (1999); Jerry Menikoff, Doubts about Death: The Silence of the Institute of Medicine, 26 J.L. Med. & Ethics 157 (1998); John T. Potts, Jr. et al., Commentary: Clear Thinking and Open Discussion Guide IOM's Report on Organ Donation, 26 J.L. Med. & Ethics 166 (1998).

Relatives in Gestation at the Decedent's Death. For purposes of intestacy and for purposes of devises of any present interest in property, persons who are born after the decedent's death generally are not eligible to receive the decedent's property.[9] The common law treats children in gestation at the decedent's death as if they were alive at the decedent's death if they subsequently are born alive. This principle is codified in some states and in both the former and current versions of UPC § 2-108.

In administering this principle, there is precedent suggesting a rebuttable presumption that the date of conception was nine months prior to the date of birth. See, e.g., Equitable Trust Co. v. McComb, 168 A. 203, 207 (Del. Ch. 1933); In re Wells, 221 N.Y.S. 714, 724 (Sur. Ct. 1927). To be entitled to share in the decedent's estate, a child in gestation at the decedent's death must be born alive and probably must be born viable. See, e.g., Ebbs v. Smith, 394 N.E.2d 1034 (1979); Recent Developments, 70 Mich. L. Rev. 729, 735 (1972). Under UPC § 2-108, the child must survive birth by at least 120 hours.

---

9. Some exceptions to this rule can arise with regard to devises made to a class of persons. See infra Chapter 18, Part B.

PART B. GENERAL PATTERNS OF INTESTATE SUCCESSION

1. Spouse

Statutory References: *UPC § 2-102*

One of the major concerns in intestacy law is the appropriate share of the decedent's estate that the surviving spouse should receive. Consideration of the spousal share requires an evaluation of other relatives' claims to the estate. Under most state schemes, the surviving spouse inherits the entire estate if the decedent leaves no surviving descendants or parents. That is to say, that most states give priority to the claims of the surviving spouse over those of siblings, grandparents, and any other collateral relatives or ancestors.

But, if the decedent leaves descendants, in some states, the surviving spouse may have to share part of the estate with them. This is so even when some or all of them are minors, in which case any portion the minors inherit must be placed in what frequently can be a cumbersome and expensive guardianship form of ownership. See infra p. 54. It is also so even when some or all of the descendants are adults with adequate means of support and when the surviving spouse is in far greater financial need. That financial need may result from the spouse's dependency on a limited, fixed income source or because of health concerns or both.

If the decedent leaves no descendants but leaves a parent or parents, in some states, the spouse may have to share the estate with the parent or parents. This result might seem appropriate if the parent or parents have financial need and/or the couple have not been married very long. It seems more problematic if the parents are financially self-sufficient ("WOOPS," in newspeak, standing for well-off older people).[10]

What seems clear from the few of many variations in family situations just described is that family circumstances vary too much to think that any intestacy statute could be designed to achieve a fair result in every case. Moreover, a complex set of rules can add administration costs, as well as lead to public confusion and misunderstanding. See infra p. 73, considering the question of giving courts discretionary power in intestate succession. What also seems clear is that the question of fairness demands consideration not only of the decedent's likely intent, but also a consideration of the decedent's duties and obligations to family members.

---

10. Between 1980 and 1997, the percent of persons 65 years old and over living below the poverty level decreased by approximately one third. See U.S. Census Bureau, supra note 2, at 484, table 764.

Former Uniform Probate Code. As originally promulgated in 1969, § 2-102 of the UPC granted the decedent's surviving spouse the entire intestate estate if the decedent left neither surviving descendants nor surviving parents. If either a descendant or a parent survived the decedent, the surviving spouse received only the first $50,000 plus one-half of the remaining balance of the estate. If one or more of the decedent's descendants were not the surviving spouse's descendants, however, the former UPC did not give the spouse priority on the first $50,000. Instead, it limited the spouse's share to one-half of the intestate estate. Intestacy statutes had not typically addressed the question of step relationships.

The use of the lump-sum-plus-a-fraction-of-the-remaining-balance device enabled the former UPC to pay (or appear to pay) a proper obeisance to tradition while assuring the spouse the entire estate in the modest estates of $50,000 and under, and assuring the spouse the bulk of the estate if it did not have an appreciably greater value than $50,000. In a $100,000 estate, for example, the spouse's share was $75,000, with $25,000 going to the decedent's descendants or parents. In a $150,000 estate, the spouse took $100,000, with $50,000 going to the descendants or parents.

Non-Uniform Legislation. Contrasted with the intestacy patterns generally in effect when the former UPC was promulgated, the surviving spouse's share granted by former § 2-102 was quite generous. The UPC became a catalyst for legislatures to reconsider the share passing to the spouse. Currently, most non-UPC states now provide that the spouse receive a significant portion of the intestate estate both when the decedent is survived by descendants and when the decedent is not survived by descendants, but is survived by one or both parents. Also, following the lead of the UPC, many non-UPC states also address the issue of step relationships in their intestacy statutes.

Public Attitudes. Except perhaps for the wealthy, whose behavior should have very little relevance to the proper design of an intestacy law, studies have identified a strong social preference to give the entire estate to the surviving spouse, even when the decedent has surviving children or parents.[11] Some of these studies were based on an examination of the probated wills of similarly situated decedents who died during a particular time frame in a particular

11. In the U.S. Trust's Survey of Affluent Americans, 85 percent of the respondents indicated that they planned to leave the majority of their estates to their spouses. See ustrust.com.

locality.[12] Other studies were based on interviews with living persons.[13]

These empirical studies confirm that the former UPC was aligned more closely with public attitudes than the non-UPC laws in effect at the time. Although the former UPC retained the traditional approach of splitting the estate between the spouse and the descendant or parent, it used the lump-sum-plus-a-fraction device that, as noted above, made an actual split less likely, and made the spouse's share greater than 50 percent when a split did occur.

Uniform Probate Code. The UPC's approach in 1969 significantly increased the share of the intestate estate that passed to the surviving spouse. For medium to larger intestate estates, however, it still failed to reflect society's preference to have the surviving spouse receive the entire estate. In those estates, the former UPC still called for a split between the spouse and descendants and between the spouse and parents if there were no descendants.

The drafters rethought this approach and made significant revisions to the spouse's share in § 2-102. It continues the pattern of giving the surviving spouse the entire estate when the decedent is not survived by descendants or parents. It goes further, however, and provides that the surviving spouse also receive the entire estate when the decedent is survived by descendants under two conditions. The first condition is that the descendants must also be the descendants of the surviving spouse and the second is that the surviving spouse must have no descendants who are not the decedent's descendants.

The move to have the spouse inherit the entire estate is aligned with statutory reforms found throughout the United States, Canada, and Europe. In her book, Mary Ann Glendon has identified this trend, which she calls the "shrinking circle of heirs" phenomenon. See Mary Ann Glendon, The Transformation of Family Law 238 (1989). By this she means that, over time, throughout the United States and Europe, "the position of the surviving spouse has steadily improved everywhere at the expense of the decedent's blood relatives." Id. She goes on to point out that this trend "strikingly illustrate[s] the movement of modern marriage into the foreground of family relationships." Id. at 239. It recognizes "the gradual attenuation of legal bonds among family members

---

12. See, e.g., Marvin B. Sussman et al., The Family and Inheritance 86-87, 89-90, 143-45 (1970); Olin L. Browder, Jr., Recent Patterns of Testate Succession in the United States and England, 67 Mich. L. Rev. 1303, 1307-09 (1969); Allison Dunham, The Method, Process and Frequency of Wealth Transmissions at Death, 30 U. Chi. L. Rev. 241, 252-53 (1963).

13. Mary Louise Fellows et al., Public Attitudes about Property Distribution at Death and Intestate Succession in the United States, 1978 Am. B. Found. Res. J. 319, 351-54, 358-64, 366-68; Contemporary Studies Project, A Comparison of Iowans' Dispositive Preferences with Selected Provisions of the Iowa and [Former] Uniform Probate Codes, 63 Iowa L. Rev. 1041, 1089 (1978); U.K. Law Comm'n, Family Law: Distribution on Intestacy (No. 187) app. C, at 36-37, 40-45 (1989).

outside the conjugal unit of husband, wife, and children," id. at 238, and "[t]he tendency to view a marriage that lasts until death as a union of the economic interests of the spouses . . . ." Id. at 240.

As Professor Glendon noted, granting the surviving spouse the entire intestate estate comes "at the expense of the decedent's blood relatives." Notice the *categories* that lose out to the surviving spouse under § 2-102. Under § 2-102(1)(i), the losers are the decedent's collateral relatives and/or ancestors more remote than parents; under subsection (1)(ii), the losers are the decedent's descendants.[14]

As between these two categories, decedents presumably view their children as having greater claims to at least some portion of their property than the claims of their collateral relatives and/or ancestors more remote than parents. Section 2-102(1) appears, however, not to recognize any distinction between these two categories of claimants—after all, it grants a surviving spouse the entire estate to the exclusion of both. In fact, § 2-102(1) can be understood to distinguish between the two categories.

Section 2-102 is predicated on the notion that the decedent's children aren't losing. Rather, the surviving spouse is viewed as occupying two roles—one as the decedent's primary beneficiary and one as a conduit through which to benefit the couple's children. If decedents have died prematurely, at a time when their children were still minors, surviving spouses are seen as being in a better position to use the inherited property for the benefit of their children as well as for themselves.[15] For decedents who live out their life expectancies, surviving spouses are likely to be older and have greater economic needs than their children. By then, the children are probably middle-aged working adults with fewer financial concerns than a surviving spouse. That does not mean, however, that the conduit theory does not operate for adult children. The statute assumes that the adult children will inherit any unconsumed portion of the decedent's property at the surviving spouse's death.

The conduit theory does not apply to a decedent's collateral relatives and/or ancestors more remote than parents. Section 2-102 is predicated on the notion that their "loss" is permanent. When a decedent leaves a surviving spouse and collateral relatives and/or ancestors more remote than parents, a surviving spouse is the sole beneficiary of the estate. The statute assumes that the surviving spouse, while alive or at death, is unlikely to share any significant portion of the decedent's property with those other relatives.

---

14. The distribution pattern when the decedent is survived by a surviving spouse and a parent or parents is discussed infra pp. 45 and 59.

15. See infra p. 54, discussing the disadvantages of guardianships when minor children inherit property in their own right.

When there are other than joint children in the family, the conduit theory becomes problematic. If the state gives the entire estate to the surviving spouse of a decedent who leaves surviving descendants who are not the surviving spouse's, the risks of permanent "loss" to those descendants appear greater because the surviving spouse is related to them only by marriage. Similarly, if the state gives the entire estate to the surviving spouse who has descendants who are not the decedent's, the risk exists that the surviving spouse will share at least some of the decedent's property with the decedent's stepchildren and their descendants at the expense of the decedent's children and their descendants.[16] Thus, the dilemma facing the states in the stepparent situations becomes one of striking a reasonable balance between the objective of granting the surviving spouse an adequate share and the objective of providing for the economic needs of a decedent's minor children and reducing the risks that the decedent's adult children and their descendants are not permanently disinherited.

Section 2-102 resolves that dilemma by invoking the lump-sum-plus-a-fraction device for these situations. The intent isn't to restrict the share going to spouses to the bare minimum necessary to provide them with the basic necessities of life, but to grant a share that is commensurate with the size of the estate and family circumstances. In the typical intestate estate of small to modest size, this approach still allows the surviving spouse to take the entire estate. A factor that makes this even more likely is that, under the UPC scheme, the lump-sum portion of the formula is in addition to the probate exemptions and allowances, which also favor surviving spouses and amount to a *minimum* of $43,000. See UPC §§ 2-402 to -404.[17]

In the larger intestate estates, infrequent though they may be, the UPC approach is predicated on the notion that decedents would prefer some provision for their descendants once assured that surviving spouses would receive an adequate share. Economic security for a surviving spouse is likely to be further enhanced in most of these larger estates because the decedent is apt to have

---

16. The possibility exists that the same conflicts will arise after the decedent's death if the surviving spouse has more children. To take that possibility into account when designing an intestacy law would mean that the surviving spouse should usually receive a limited share. Moreover, surveys of public attitudes that favor surviving spouses receiving the entire estate suggest that the public believes that conjectural situations that might pose a conflict in the future should be disregarded. The generally accepted approach of intestacy law has been to make the decision about how much to award the surviving spouse based on the familial situation existing at the decedent's death.

17. See infra Chapter 10, Part B for further discussion of these provisions. Currently the UPC does not provide for cost-of-living adjustment for the dollar amounts stated in §§ 2-102, -402 to -404. The Joint Editorial Board for Uniform Trust and Estate Acts has approved a proposal that would account for inflation for these as well as other dollar amounts stated in the Code, but as yet it has not been presented to the Uniform Law Commission.

executed will substitutes providing for the spouse, such as joint tenancies with right of survivorship or joint money-market accounts. For large estates, the lump-sum-plus-a-fraction device has the advantage of assuring that the *decedent's* children receive some inheritance.

Section 2-102 recognizes the greater potential for conflicting loyalties when the decedent has children by a prior marriage than when only the surviving spouse has children by a prior marriage. In the latter case, the surviving spouse is granted the first $150,000 ($193,000 including the minimum probate exemptions and allowances) plus 50 percent of any remaining balance. In the former case, the surviving spouse is granted only the first $100,000 ($143,000 including the minimum probate exemptions and allowances) plus 50 percent of any remaining balance. Do you believe that the surviving spouse should receive the same amount regardless of whether the decedent was survived by any descendants who were also the descendants of the surviving spouse?

The approach taken is admittedly a crude solution to potential conflicting loyalties. Can you think of a more responsive solution? Would a statutory trust do the trick? Under this approach, the surviving spouse would be granted the *use* of all the property for life, but at death some portion of or all of the unconsumed property would be returned to the decedent's own children. The substantial shares passing to surviving spouses under § 2-102 make questions concerning the mutual acquisition of the marital estate moot. Regardless that title ownership may have been in the decedent, the intestate statute assures the surviving spouse retains ownership of most of the marital estate. If the statutory-trust approach were enacted, which would provide surviving spouses only funds necessary for their support and deny them the right to make gifts during life or at death of the property held in trust, then issues regarding ownership rights to the marital estate would have to be addressed.[18]

The final circumstance in which, if the estate is large, § 2-102 gives the surviving spouse less than the entire estate is when a decedent dies survived by a surviving spouse and parent, but no descendants. Here, § 2-102(2) grants the surviving spouse the first $200,000 ($243,000 including the minimum probate exemptions and allowances) plus three-fourths of the remaining balance. Since very few intestate estates exceed $243,000, and fewer still exceed this value by any substantial margin, the surviving spouse *in practice* will nearly always

18. For a more extensive discussion of the statutory-trust approach, see Lawrence W. Waggoner, The Multiple-Marriage Society and Spousal Rights Under the Revised Uniform Probate Code, 76 Iowa L. Rev. 223, 234-35 (1990). For discussion of the partnership theory of marriage and how it is implemented in community-property law, marital-property law, and separate-property law, see Chapter 10, Part A. For an historical consideration of maintenance trusts and their gendered implications, see Mary Louise Fellows, Wills and Trusts: "The Kingdom of the Fathers," 10 Law & Ineq. J. 137 (1991).

receive the entire intestate estate when a parent survives the decedent.[19] Why do you think § 2-102 does not provide that the surviving spouse receive the entire intestate estate when the decedent is childless, but leaves a surviving parent?

EXTERNAL REFERENCES. John W. Fisher, II & Scott A. Curnutte, Reforming the Law of Intestate Succession and Elective Shares: New Solutions to Age-Old Problems, 93 W. Va. L. Rev. 61 (1990); Martin L. Fried, The Uniform Probate Code: Intestate Succession and Related Matters, 55 Alb. L. Rev. 927 (1992); Lawrence W. Waggoner, The Multiple-Marriage Society and Spousal Rights Under the Revised Uniform Probate Code, 26 Real Prop. Prob. & Tr. J. 683 (1992).

2. Descendants

Statutory References: *UPC §§ 2-103, -106, -708, -709, 5-202, -423*

a. Descendants' Share

In the absence of a surviving spouse, the law of all states—UPC and non-UPC law, alike—gives the entire estate to the decedent's descendants, *i.e.*, to the decedent's children and descendants of deceased children. The descendants universally inherit to the exclusion of the decedent's ancestors, such as parents and grandparents, and to the exclusion of collateral relatives, such as brothers and sisters.

When a decedent dies leaving a surviving spouse as well as descendants, the descendants' share is determined in accordance with the applicable distribution patterns outlined above. Under some non-UPC statutes and under UPC law applying to small and modest estates, the spouse may receive the entire estate to the exclusion of the decedent's descendants. Under other non-UPC statutes and under UPC law applying to larger estates, the spouse and descendants share the estate.

---

19. Alaska, Colorado, Hawaii, Michigan, Montana, and North Dakota have followed the UPC recommendation, allowing parents to share with the surviving spouse. Other states that have otherwise enacted the UPC's general pattern of intestacy (Arizona, Minnesota, New Mexico, South Dakota, Utah, and West Virginia) provide that the surviving spouse inherits the entire estate when the decedent dies without surviving children but with a surviving parent or parents.

b. Representation Among Descendants

Any share that goes to the decedent's descendants is divided among them by representation.[20] The term "descendants" (or "issue") indicates a multiple-generation class, which includes not only children, but also grandchildren, great-grandchildren, and so on through the descending line.

To explore the idea of representation, we give you G, a 78-year-old widow who has just died, leaving some married surviving children in their late forties or early fifties, a somewhat greater number of surviving grandchildren in their twenties or early thirties, a few of whom are married with young children.[21]

G's four-generation family is depicted in the chart below, except that the chart does not show the descendants' spouses, G's ancestors, or G's collateral relatives. The parenthetical figures show each survivor's age.

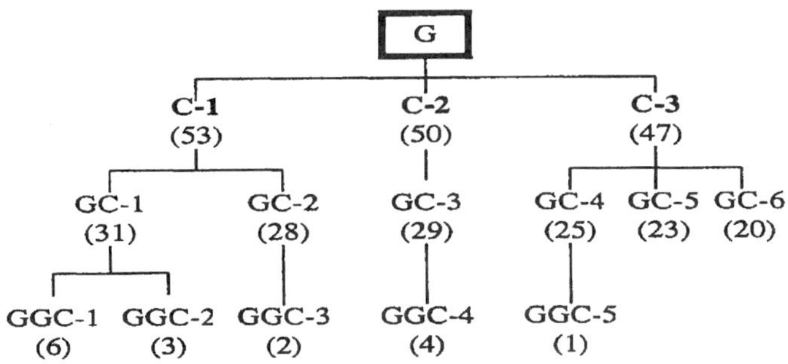

One of the principal features of representation is that the property is divided among the living persons who are nearest to the decedent in each descending line. A descendant is not an eligible taker if he or she has a living ancestor who is also a descendant of the decedent. Consequently, the only descendants who

---

20. The idea of taking by representation is traceable to the canons of descent, which provided that lineal descendants should represent their deceased ancestors in inheritance. The idea of taking by representation was also carried over into the Statute of Distribution. In one form or another, representation appears in all the American statutes.

21. With average life expectancy projected to be 77.4 years (80.6 for white women, 74.1 for white men, 75.5 for Black women, 65.1 for Black men) in 2010, three-generation families will be quite common and four-generation families, such as G's, are already not at all unusual. U.S. Census Bureau, supra note 2, at 93, table 127. Many people now live long enough to have grown grandchildren and young great-grandchildren.

We made all persons with children married in the hypothetical to avoid issues regarding the law's treatment of children whose parents are not married to each other. We will address those and other status questions in Chapter 3. For now, the purpose of the hypothetical is to help you understand the concept of representation and the different representational systems found in the intestacy statutes around the country.

share in G's estate are C-1, C-2, and C-3. Each child takes a 1/3 share.[22] G's grandchildren and great-grandchildren take nothing. The spouses of married descendants do not share in the decedent's estate.

Representation comes into play only if at least one child predeceases G. We want you to consider the division of G's estate in each of four variations. We give you the results in the following table, but you will have to work through each system to appreciate how these results are reached.

Variation 1: C-1 predeceased G.	• Under all systems, C-2 and C-3 take 1/3 each, and GC-1 and GC-2 take 1/6 each.
Variation 2: C-1, C-2, and C-3 predeceased G.	• Under the per-stirpes system, GC-1 and GC-2 take 1/6 each; GC-3 takes 1/3; and GC-4, GC-5, and GC-6 take 1/9 each. • Under all of the other systems, each grandchild takes 1/6.
Variation 3: C-1, GC-1, and GC-2 predeceased G.	• Under the per-stirpes and the per-capita-with-representation systems, GGC-1 and GGC-2 take 1/12 each and GGC-3 takes 1/6. • Under the former and current UPC systems, GGC-1, GGC-2, and GGC-3 take 1/9 each.
Variation 4: C-2 and C-3 predeceased G.	• Under the per-stirpes, the per-capita-with-representation, and the former UPC systems, GC-3 takes 1/3 and GC-4, GC-5, and GC-6 take 1/9 each. • Under the current UPC system (per capita-at-each-generation), GC-3, GC-4, GC-5, and GC-6 take 1/6 each.

Variation 1 presents the most straightforward application of the idea of representation. Where C-1 predeceased G, C-2 and C-3 would continue to receive their one-third shares, but C-1 would be represented by GC-1 and GC-

22. As noted in the text, intestate succession is limited to the first living person or persons in each descending line. Descendants of living descendants do not share in the estate, nor are they relevant in determining the shares of their parent. *Should* they be relevant? Should a child who has, say, three children receive a greater intestate share than a child who has fewer children or no children at all?

2. Under all of the systems of representation, GC-1 and GC-2 would divide C-1's one-third share equally, *i.e.*, each would receive a 1/6 share.

Representation becomes more complicated in *Variations 2*, *3*, and *4*, and the outcome depends on which system of representation the jurisdiction follows.

Per-Stirpes System. The per-stirpes system is unalterably faithful to the idea of representation. The per-stirpes system was used by the common law under the canons of descent for land,[23] and a minority of states in this country prescribe it for intestate succession of both land and personal property.[24]

The per-stirpes system operates in three steps:

> *Step One*: Divide the estate into primary shares at the generation nearest to the decedent (*i.e.*, at the children generation). This primary-share generation is often described by the courts as the generation at which the "stocks" or "roots" or "stirpes" are determined. The number of primary shares is equal to the number of children alive at the decedent's death plus the number of children who predeceased the decedent leaving descendants who survived the decedent. Any deceased children who have no living descendants are disregarded in determining the number of primary shares. The number of primary shares is determined at the children generation even if no children survive the decedent.
>
> *Step Two*: Allocate the primary shares. One share goes to each living member of the children generation, if any. One share also goes to the descendants of each deceased child with living descendants.
>
> *Step Three*: Divide and subdivide each primary share allocated to the living descendants of a deceased child. Each of these primary shares is divided and subdivided among the deceased child's descendants.

In *Variation 2*, where all of G's children predeceased her, the per-stirpes system stands alone in the way it divides G's estate. All of the other systems, discussed below, disregard the children generation and make the initial division of the estate at the grandchild generation.

Per-Capita-with-Representation System. With the exception of the first step, this system is identical to the per-stirpes system. *Step One* in this system is to divide the estate into primary shares at the generation nearest to the decedent

---

23. See 2 William Blackstone, Commentaries *218.

24. See, e.g., Fla. Stat. Ann. § 732.104; Ga. Code Ann. § 53-2-1; Ill. Rev. Stat. ch. 755, § 5/2-1; Va. Code Ann. § 64.1-3. Tennessee, which otherwise has adopted the former UPC's general pattern of intestacy, continues to use per stirpes. Tenn. Code Ann. § 31-2-106. Minnesota and South Dakota, which have otherwise adopted the UPC's general pattern of intestacy, continue to use per stirpes. Minn. Stat. § 524.2-106 (adopting the per-stirpes system for the descendants of the decedent, the per-capita-with-representation system for the descendants of the decedent's parents, and per capita without representation for the descendants of the decedent's grandparents); S.D. Codified Laws Ann. § 29A-2-106.

that contains at least one living member. Thus, if *all* of the decedent's children are dead, as in *Variation 2*, but at least one grandchild is alive, the primary shares are determined at the grandchildren generation rather than at the children generation. In a strict sense, then, the grandchildren take in their own right, *per capita,* and not as representatives of the decedent's deceased children.

If one of the grandchildren in *Variation 2* had also predeceased G, leaving living descendants, however, the descendants of that deceased grandchild would take in a representative capacity. Hence, the system is called "per capita *with representation*," a term that really means per capita at the nearest generation with a living member, with descendants of deceased members of that generation taking by representation. Because the second and third steps in this system and in the per-stirpes system are the same, this system is sometimes called "modified per stirpes." Indeed, it is sometimes employed under the statutory term "per stirpes."[25]

Former Uniform Probate Code System. As promulgated in 1969, UPC § 2-106 adopted a variation of the per-capita-with-representation system. Nineteen states had enacted the former UPC's representation system.[26] Although the statutory language could have been drafted more clearly, § 2-106 was meant to codify *Step One* of the per-capita-with-representation system and to fix the primary-share generation at the nearest generation to the decedent containing at least one living member.[27]

The former UPC departed from the per-capita-with-representation system at *Step Three*. Under the former version of § 2-106, each share allocated to the descendants of a deceased member of the primary-share generation was divided and subdivided "in the same manner." The same manner meant as if deceased members of the primary-share generation were decedents with respect to their primary shares. The same manner, therefore, required that a primary share be subdivided at the nearest generation to the deceased descendant containing at least one living member. Perhaps a useful way of describing the former UPC's system is that it is per capita with per-capita representation.

In contrast, the per-capita-with-representation system is in reality *per capita with per-stirpes representation. Step Three* of that system divides and subdivides

---

25. See, e.g., Ark. Code Ann. § 28-9-205; Ohio Rev. Code Ann. §§ 2105.06, .12, .13, as interpreted in Kraemer v. Hook, 152 N.E.2d 430 (Ohio 1958).

26. In New Hampshire, the enactment of the former UPC omitted § 2-106. Estate of Martineau, 490 A.2d 779 (N.H. 1985), however, judicially adopted the system prescribed by former § 2-106.

27. The statutory phrase "surviving heirs in the nearest degree of kinship" would have made this point more clearly had it said "surviving heirs in the nearest degree of kinship that contains one or more surviving heirs."

each of the primary shares as under *Step Three* of the per-stirpes system. The primary shares are divided and subdivided at the nearest generation to the deceased descendant regardless of whether that generation contains any living member.

Variation 3 illustrates this point. It poses the situation in which G is predeceased by C-1, GC-1, and GC-2. Under the former UPC, C-1's 1/3 primary share is divided equally among GGC-1, GGC-2, and GGC-3, giving each a 1/9 share. Under the per-capita-with-representation system, C-1's primary share would be subdivided at the deceased grandchildren generation, giving GGC-1 and GGC-2 a 1/12 share each and giving GGC-3 a 1/6 share.

Current Uniform Probate Code—Per Capita at Each Generation. UPC § 2-106 adopts yet another system of representation—the per-capita-at-each-generation system. The former version of § 2-106 neither assured equality among the children's families nor equality among members of the same generation whose parents had predeceased the decedent. The current version of § 2-106 assures equality among members of the same generation whose parents predeceased them. To see how it accomplishes this result, consider *Variation 4*, in which C-2 and C-3 predeceased G.

Both the former and current versions of UPC § 2-106 give a 1/3 share to C-1. Under the former version, however, the four grandchildren do not receive equal shares. GC-3 represents C-2 and gets a full 1/3 share. The other three represent C-3 and each takes a 1/9 share. Under the current version, however, equality among the four grandchildren is achieved. The current version achieves equality by the device of treating the four grandchildren as representing both C-2 and C-3. Another way to think about the operation of this representational system is that it treats C-2 and C-3 as if they were one person who had four children. This device gives each grandchild an equal 1/6 share.

The per-capita-at-each-generation system can be described by the following three operational steps:

> *Step One:* Divide the estate into primary shares at the nearest generation to the decedent that contains at least one living member. The number of primary shares is the number of living persons in that generation plus the number of deceased persons in that generation who have living descendants.
>
> *Step Two*: Allocate one primary share to each living member of the primary-share generation.
>
> *Step Three:* Combine the remaining primary shares, if any, into a single share and assume that the descendants already allocated a share (and their descendants) had predeceased the decedent. Then distribute that single share among the decedent's descendants in accordance with Step One.

This system consistently results in "horizontal equality," (*i.e.*, equality among members of the same generation) as distinguished from the "vertical equality" (*i.e.*, equality among children's families) consistently accomplished by the per-stirpes system. The per-capita-at-each-generation system is now in force in eleven states (Alaska, Arizona, Colorado, Hawaii, Maine, Michigan, New Mexico, New York, North Carolina, Utah, and West Virginia).[28] In 1988, the Canadian province of Manitoba adopted the per-capita-at-each-generation system, see Manitoba Statutes, c. I-85, Intestate Succession Act § 5, and in 1999, the Alberta Law Reform Institute recommended that system for the province of Alberta. See Alberta Law Reform Institute, Reform of the Intestate Succession Act, Final Report No. 78, at 144-47, 184 (1999), which can be found on the web at www.law.ualberta.ca/alri/. As recounted in the Official Comment to UPC § 2-106, the results of client surveys found that the public finds the per-capita-at-each-generation system considerably more to its liking than the other systems.[29]

Use of the Various Systems of Representation in Planning. Wills and trusts frequently rely on multiple-generation class gifts. For example: "to A for life, remainder to A's descendants who survive A." Good drafting entails supplementing this disposition by designating which system of representation the testator or grantor of the trust wants used. What system should be used in the absence of an express designation? See UPC § 2-708; Restatement 2d of Property § 28.2; infra Chapter 18, Part A.

Without doubt, the most frequently designated system in these types of gifts is per stirpes: "to A for life, remainder to A's descendants who survive A, per stirpes." Although the per-stirpes system has a commonly understood meaning, some courts have held that the phrase "per stirpes" invokes the per-capita-with-representation system. See, e.g., Kraemer v. Hook, 152 N.E.2d 430 (Ohio 1958); Estate of Dakin, N.Y.L.J., May 10, 1988, at 12 (Sur. Ct.). Therefore, the use of the term "per stirpes" without further clarification risks litigation over the term's meaning. See UPC § 2-709 for a statutory rule of construction defining "per stirpes." In the absence of such a statutory rule of construction,

---

28. See Restatement 3d of Property § 2.3, Statutory Note 4. Montana, which has otherwise adopted the UPC's general pattern of intestacy, uses the per-capita-with-representation system. Mont. Code Ann. § 72-2-116. North Dakota, another UPC state, inadvertently repealed its provision on representation without enacting a substitute. See supra note 24 (describing representational systems of Minnesota and South Dakota).

29. See Raymond H. Young, Meaning of "Issue" and "Descendants," 13 Prob. Notes 225 (Am. C. of Tr. & Est. Couns. 1988) (reporting a client survey in which 71 percent of the respondents chose the per-capita-at-each-generation system; 19 percent chose per-stirpes; 9 percent chose the former UPC system); Contemporary Studies Project, A Comparison of Iowans' Dispositive Preferences with Selected Provisions of the Iowa and [Former] Uniform Probate Codes, 63 Iowa L. Rev. 1041, 1108-16, 1135-37 (1978) (finding that in a survey of the public at large 87 percent of the respondents chose the per-capita-at-each-generation system; 12 percent chose per stirpes).

it is good practice to insert a clause in the will or trust that defines the term. For examples of litigation that could have been avoided by a definitional clause, see Rhodes v. First Alabama Bank, 699 So.2d 204 (Ala. Civ. App. 1997) (litigating meaning of "to the descendants of my other children per stirpes"); Trust Estate of Dwight, 909 P.2d 561 (Haw. 1995) (litigating meaning of "to such of the issue of my said adopted children as shall then be living in equal shares per stirpes"). It is essential to be clear whether the initial division into primary shares is to be made at the children generation of A, even when no member of that generation is living, or whether the initial division into primary shares is to be made at the nearest generation to A that contains at least one living member.

Litigation has arisen in a number of cases over the use of phrases such as "to my brothers and sisters, per stirpes," or "to my nieces and nephews, per stirpes." See, e.g., Hartford Nat'l Bank & Trust Co. v. Thrall, 440 A.2d 200 (Conn. 1981); Bennett v. Lloyd, 267 S.E.2d 3 (Ga. 1980); Will of Griffin, 411 So. 2d 766 (Miss. 1982); Wachovia Bank & Trust Co. v. Livengood, 294 S.E.2d 319 (N.C. 1982); Restatement 2d of Property § 25.1 comment i, illus. 14 (stating that "children" means issue); cf., e.g., Estate of Walters, 519 N.E.2d 1270 (Ind. Ct. App. 1988) (litigating meaning of "to my wife, Jessie E. Walters, per stirpes"); Estate of Johnson, No. C6-98-1883, 1999 WL 118639 (Minn. Ct. App. Mar. 9, 1999) (litigating meaning of "[t]o Bernice Mesick, if she survives me, per stirpes"). Surely language whose meaning is so doubtful that it has caused so much litigation is to be avoided in drafting legal documents.

Uncertainty about the primary share generation is not the only ambiguity contained in phrases such as "to my nieces and nephews, per stirpes." If one of the nieces dies leaving a descendant, should that descendant be able to share in the gift? How would you edit this language to provide that descendants of nieces and nephews share in the gift?

It would appear from the client surveys and other empirical studies referred to above that, if asked, most clients would prefer the horizontal equality accomplished by the per-capita-at-each-generation system. At the same time, surveys also indicate that the great majority of lawyers believe that most clients prefer the system that we have called per stirpes. See Young, supra (finding that 85 percent of lawyers surveyed indicated that most clients prefer this system). Why do you suppose this discrepancy exists?[30] How would you pose the

---

30. After the Alberta Law Reform Institute issued a preliminary report recommending the enactment of the per-capita-at-each-generation system, a practicing lawyer "questioned a few clients as to their preferences between the *per stirpes* approach and the per-capita-at-each-generation approach. He discovered that his clients preferred the per capita [at each generation] approach. He considered this surprising until he realized that he had never suggested such a scheme so why would clients consider it." Alberta Law Reform Institute, Reform of the Intestate

representation question to a client?

c. Guardianships for Minors

If an intestate decedent leaves heirs who are minors, a guardian, who is referred to as a "conservator" in some states, must be appointed to receive and manage the intestate assets passing to the minor or incapacitated heirs. A surviving parent becomes the sole guardian of a minor child but only of the child's person. A court appointment is necessary to give the parent responsibility over the child's property.

If there is no parent, a court will have to appoint someone to take responsibility for the heir's custody and care, a "guardian of the person." That appointment may include responsibility not only for the minor's person, but also for the minor's property. Often the appointment is unclear about the extent of the guardian's responsibility. It is generally assumed that a guardian is appointed for both the person and the property of a minor unless the terms of the appointment provide otherwise.

One of the major estate planning concerns of parents with minor children is to designate a particular person, usually a close friend or relative, to act as guardian of the child's person. The need arises if both parents die, together or separately, before the child reaches the age of majority. The need also arises when a minor child is reared by a single parent and that parent dies. In most states, a guardian may be designated by a will. Under the UPC, the appointment is made by probate of the parent's will and acceptance by the designated person. Court confirmation is unnecessary. See UPC § 5-202.

If the parents die intestate, obviously they have no say over who will be appointed guardian of their minor child or children. There must be a court proceeding, and the court will appoint a guardian from a list of available relatives. For parents with minor children, the opportunity to name a guardian for their children is a primary motivating factor for them to seek legal advice and execute a will.

Gay or lesbian parents with minor children cannot rely on courts to appoint their surviving domestic partner as guardian of the child's person if the surviving partner is neither the biological nor adoptive parent of the child. But see In re Pearlman, 15 Fam. L. Rep. (BNA) 1355 (Fla. Cir. Ct. 1989) (granting custody to surviving partner); In re Astonn H., 635 N.Y.S.2d 418 (Fam. Ct. 1995) (same). The legally recognized parent needs to execute a will naming the surviving partner as guardian. Executing a will is not a foolproof solution, however, because courts may nevertheless find that other persons with a

---

Succession Act 144 n.388 (Final Report No. 78, 1999).

biological and emotional relationship with the child have standing to contest custody based on the best interest of the child. See Axelrod v. Avery, No. 532395, 1994 WL 684736 (Conn. Super. Ct. 1994); see also McGuffin v. Overton, 542 N.W.2d 288 (Mich. Ct. App. 1995), appeal denied, 546 N.W.2d 256 (Mich. 1996) (denying the surviving partner named as the guardian of the children in the decedent's will standing to contest the grant of temporary custody to the biological father).

Procedures for appointment of the guardian, both of the person and of the property, have often been slow and expensive. Even after appointment, further judicial proceedings are usually needed, increasing the delay and cost of guardianship. This is especially so for guardianship of the ward's property. If there are multiple children, separate guardianships have to be obtained for each child, even though the same person is usually appointed guardian for each child. The guardian does not have title to the ward's property. Rather, the guardian is merely custodian of the property with limited powers. These powers are defined by statute, and historically statutes defined the powers inadequately, both in the sense of uncertainty of meaning and failure to grant certain important powers, particularly concerning investment of protected property. These deficiencies made it necessary in many instances for the guardian to obtain court authorization for actions in dealing with the ward's property, generating expenses that diminish the ward's assets. Required accounting and bonds further depleted the wealth available to the ward.

Many states have reformed the guardianship laws to ameliorate some of these problems. The Uniform Law Commission promulgated a Uniform Guardianship and Protective Proceedings Act (UGPPA) (1987), which was revised in 1997. Presently, the Joint Editorial Board for Uniform Trust and Estate Acts is considering incorporating the current version into the UPC. Under both Article V of the UPC and the UGPPA (1997) the appointed person, who is called a *conservator*, is accorded powers, duties, and liabilities comparable to those of a trustee. Under both statutory schemes, the conservator also receives substantial management powers that are exercisable without court order.

Several devices are available to avoid the problems associated with property guardianships or conservatorships, but they require predeath planning. These include a so-called contingent trust for minors. It can be created during life or at death in a will. The creation of a trust and consideration of a variety of the provisions it might contain are the subject of Chapters 13 and 14. An alternative device is the creation of a custodianship through a lifetime transfer to minors under the Uniform Gifts to Minors Act (1966) or lifetime or testamentary transfers to minors under the newer Uniform Transfers to Minors Act (1986) (UTMA). Under the UTMA, the custodian has substantial discretionary powers free of court supervision and for that reason is preferable to a conservatorship.

The UTMA is most useful for relatively small gifts while trusts are preferable if large amounts of property are involved.[31]

3. Ancestors and Collaterals

Statutory References: *UPC § 2-103*

2 William Blackstone, Commentaries on the Laws of England *202-05 (John L. Wendell ed. 1854)

Consanguinity, or kindred, is defined by the writers on these subjects to be . . . the connection or relation of persons descended from the same stock or common ancestor. This consanguinity is either lineal or collateral.

Lineal consanguinity is that which subsists between persons, of whom one is descended in a direct line from the other . . . . Every generation, in this lineal direct consanguinity, constitutes a different degree, reckoning either upward or downward . . . . This is the only natural way of reckoning the degrees in the direct line, and, therefore, universally obtains, as well in the civil and canon, as in the common law.

The doctrine of lineal consanguinity is sufficiently plain and obvious; but it is at the first view astonishing to consider the number of lineal ancestors which every man has, within no very great number of degrees; and so many different bloods is a man said to contain in his veins as he hath lineal ancestors. Of these he hath two in the first ascending degree, his own parents; he hath four in the second, the parents of his father and the parents of his mother; he hath eight in the third, the parents of his two grandfathers and two grandmothers; and, by the same rule of progression, he hath a hundred and twenty-eight in the seventh; a thousand and twenty-four in the tenth; and, at the twentieth degree, or the distance of twenty generations, every man hath above a million of ancestors, as common arithmetic will demonstrate.[32] This lineal consanguinity, we may

---

31. Other devices are available for adults who are legally incapacitated, including durable powers of attorney and statutory custodial trusts. See infra Chapter 9.

32. This will seem surprising to those who are unacquainted with the increasing power of progressive numbers, but is palpably evident from the following table of a geometrical progression, in which the first term is 2, and the denominator also 2; or, to speak more intelligibly, it is evident, for that each of us has two ancestors in the first degree; the number of whom is doubled at every remove, because each of our ancestors has also two immediate ancestors

observe, falls strictly within the definition of *vinculum personarum ab eodem stipite descendentium;* since lineal relations are such as descend one from the other, and both, of course, from the same common ancestor.

Collateral kindred answers to the same description; collateral relations agreeing with the lineal in this, that they descend from the same stock or ancestor; but differing in this, that they do not descend one from the other. Collateral kinsmen are such, then, as lineally spring from one and the same ancestor, who is the *stirps*, or the root, the *stirpes*, trunk, or common stock, from whence these relations are branched out. . . .

We must be careful to remember, that the very being of collateral consanguinity consists in this descent from one and the same common ancestor. . . . In short, as many ancestors as a man has, so many common stocks he has from which collateral kinsmen may be derived. And as we are taught by Holy Writ that there is one couple of ancestors belonging to us all, from whom the whole race of mankind is descended, the obvious and undeniable consequence is, that all men are in some degree related to each other. For, indeed, if we only suppose each couple of our ancestors to have left,

---

of his own.

Lineal Degrees.	*Number of Ancestors*	*Lineal Degrees.*	*Number of Ancestors*
1	2	11	2048
2	4	12	4096
3	8	13	8192
4	16	14	16384
5	32	15	32768
6	64	16	65536
7	128	17	131072
8	256	18	262144
9	512	19	524288
10	1024	20	1048576

A shorter method of finding the number of ancestors at any even degree is by squaring the number of ancestors at half that number of degrees. Thus, 16 (the number of ancestors at four degrees) is the square of 4, the number of ancestors at two; 256 is the square of 16; 65536, of 256; and the number of ancestors at forty degrees would be the square of 1048576, or upward of a million millions.

one with another, two children; and each of those children, on an average, to have left two more (and without such a supposition, that human species must be daily diminishing), we shall find that all of us have now subsisting near two hundred and seventy millions of kindred in the fifteenth degree, at the same distance from the several common ancestors as ourselves are; besides those that are one or two descents nearer to or further from the common stock, who may amount to as many more.[33] And if this calculation should appear incompatible with the number of inhabitants on the earth, it is because, by intermarriages

33. This will swell more considerably than the former calculation; for here, though the first term is but 1, the denominator is 4; that is, there is *one* kinsman (a brother) in the first degree, who makes, together with the *propositus*, the two descendants from the first couple of ancestors; and in every other degree the number of kindred must be the *quadruple* of those in the degree that immediately precedes it. For, since each couple of ancestors has two descendants, who increase in a duplicate *ratio*, it will follow that the *ratio*, in which all the descendants increase downward, must be double to that in which the ancestors increase upward; but we have seen that the ancestors increase upward in a duplicate *ratio*: therefore, the descendants must increase downward in a double duplicate, that is, in a quadruple *ratio*.

Collateral Degrees.	*Number of Kindred*	*Collateral Degrees.*	*Number of Kindred*
1	1	11	1048576
2	4	12	4194304
3	16	13	16777216
4	64	14	67108864
5	256	15	268435456
6	1024	16	1073741824
7	4096	17	4294967296
8	16384	18	17179869184
9	65536	19	68719476736
10	262144	20	274877906944

This calculation may also be formed by a more compendious process, *viz.*, by squaring the couples, or half the number of ancestors, at any given degree; which will furnish us with the number of kindred we have in the same degree, at equal distance with ourselves from the common stock, besides those at unequal distances. Thus, in the tenth lineal degree, the number of ancestors is 1024; its half, or the couples, amount to 512; the number of kindred in tenth collateral degree amounts, therefore, to 262144, or the square of 512. And if we will be at the trouble to recollect the state of several families, within our own knowledge, and observe how far they vary from this account—that is, whether, on an average, every man has more than one brother or sister, four first cousins, sixteen second cousins, and so on—we shall find that the present calculation is very far from being overcharged.

among the several descendants from the same ancestor, a hundred or a thousand modes of consanguinity may be consolidated in one person, or he may be related to us a hundred or a thousand different ways.

a. Parents and Their Descendants

Parents. The decedent's parents and their descendants inherit to the exclusion of more remote ancestors and their descendants.[34] The decedent's parents and their descendants inherit, however, only if the decedent leaves no surviving descendants. Under UPC §§ 2-102 and -103, parents of decedents with large estates inherit if the decedent leaves a surviving spouse but no descendants. The parents take one-fourth of that part of the probate estate, if any, that is in excess of $200,000 ($243,000 including the minimum probate exemptions and allowances provided for in UPC §§ 2-402 to -404). The former UPC gives the parents half of that part of the estate, if any, that is in excess of $50,000.

If the decedent leaves neither a surviving spouse nor surviving descendants, the decedent's parents inherit to the exclusion of the decedent's surviving siblings or their descendants under most intestacy statutes. This is the rule under both the former and the current versions of UPC § 2-103. In a few states, under various formulas, the decedent's parents, brothers, and sisters share in the estate.[35]

The parent-child relationship is unique among familial relationships because of the physical, emotional, and financial vulnerability of children while they are minors. The law and society place primary responsibility for their safety and well-being on parents. If parents fail to meet those responsibilities, should they be allowed to inherit from their child's intestate estate? This question has gained some public attention when minor children have died accidentally, and parents, who had previously abandoned them, claim a share of their estates, which include damages from a wrongful death suit. See, e.g., Margaret Gibbons, Court Asked to Decide Authority over Wrongful Death Suit, Legal Intelligencer (Suburban ed.), May 31, 2000, at 5; Nancy Plevin, Mother of Bus-crash Victim Demands Lawsuit Be Dropped, Santa Fe New Mexican, Mar. 26, 1999, at A1.

The issue of "worthy parents" is not necessarily limited, however, to

---

34. Under the English canons of descent, as condensed by Blackstone, an intestate's land "shall linearly descend to the issue of the person who last died seized, *in infinitum*; but shall never linearly ascend." 2 William Blackstone, Commentaries *208. Legal historians have not provided an adequate explanation for the preclusion of ancestors from inheriting land. The English Statute of Distribution allowed ancestors to inherit, as does every U.S. jurisdiction.

35. In Illinois, for example, parents, brothers, and sisters take equal shares; if only one parent survives, that parent takes a double share; if a brother or sister is deceased, the surviving descendants of that brother or sister take the deceased sibling's share, per stirpes. Ill. Rev. Stat. ch. 755, § 5/2-1(d).

situations in which the child dies while a minor and the estate includes property as a result of a child's wrongful death. UPC § 2-114(c) provides that neither a biological parent nor a parent's kindred can inherit from the child unless that parent "has openly treated the child as his [or hers], and has not refused to support the child." A minority of states denies inheritance rights to parents if they either have abandoned or have not supported their children.[36] No jurisdiction has considered denying a parent inheritance rights based on evidence of physical or emotional abuse. But see Robin L. Preble, Family Violence and Family Property: A Proposal for Reform, 13 Law & Ineq. J. 401 (1995) (proposing to deny inheritance to parents based on proof of abuse while a decedent was a minor). Given the increase of public attention to both child abuse and the failure of parents to provide court-ordered child support, we can expect legislative activity in this area. Inheritance statutes that ignore the misconduct of parents toward their children not only will not have public support, but policymakers are likely to seek an array of strategies to encourage parental responsibility and view reform of the intestacy laws as one of many solutions to a serious social problem.[37]

Ancestral Property. At common law, land returned to the branch of the family from which the decedent inherited it. See 2 William Blackstone, Commentaries *220. Some type of ancestral-property rule persists in only a few states.[38] Neither the former UPC nor the UPC contains an ancestral-property rule.

Descendants of Parents. If neither of the decedent's parents survives, the descendants of the decedent's parents inherit by representation. The system of representation employed in the jurisdiction most likely will be the same system employed in the jurisdiction for representation among the decedent's own

---

36. See Paula A. Monopoli, "Deadbeat Dads": Should Support and Inheritance be Linked?, 49 U. Miami L. Rev. 257 (1994) (reviewing the status of the law in this area); see also Anne-Marie E. Rhodes, Abandoning Parents under Intestacy: Where We Are, Where We Need to Go, 27 Ind. L. Rev. 517 (1994) (addressing the question of abandonment and failure to provide child support as a basis for barring a parent's right to succession from a child); Patricia G. Roberts, Adopted and Nonmarital Children—Exploring the 1990 Uniform Probate Code's Intestacy and Class Gift Provisions, 32 Real Prop. Prob. & Tr. J. 539, 568-69 (1998) (analyzing UPC § 2-114(c) and its limited impact on non-UPC inheritance statutes).

37. See infra Chapter 3, Part A (discussing misconduct of spouses); infra Chapter 8, Part D (discussing how killing of decedent can affect property succession).

38. See Ky. Rev. Stat. Ann. § 391.020 (applying only to real estate with different consequences depending on whether the decedent's parent who made the gift is alive and whether the decedent is a minor); La. Civ. Code Ann. art. 897 (applying only to gifts of real estate that an ancestor has given to a descendant and that descendant dies without issue); Nev. Rev. Stat. § 134.070-.080 (applying to both real and personal property that has been inherited by a child who dies as a minor and unmarried).

descendants. UPC § 2-106 applies the per-capita-at-each-generation system. But see Minn. Stat. § 524.2-106 (described supra note 24).

Relatives of the Half Blood. Today, the principle is generally recognized that relatives of the half blood are treated the same as relatives of the whole blood. This principle is codified in most states and in UPC § 2-107. A relative of the half blood is a collateral relative who shares one common ancestor. If, for example, the decedent's mother or father has children from a prior relationship, those children will be the decedent's half brothers or half sisters. Descendants of a decedent's half brothers or half sisters are also related to the decedent by the half blood. The term half blood should not be taken literally to mean that it applies only to biological relatives; it can also apply to persons who are adopted by a common ancestor. If, for example, a decedent's mother has an adopted son from a prior relationship, he also will be decedent's half brother.

Relatives by Affinity. Blood or adopted relatives of the decedent's spouse, such as the spouse's parents, siblings, or descendants of siblings, and spouses of the decedent's blood or adopted relatives, such as daughters- and sons-in-law, are relatives by affinity. Nearly all jurisdictions exclude them from inheriting under their intestacy statutes. See infra Chapter 3, Part B, discussing stepchildren.

b. More Remote Ancestors and Collaterals

Parentelic System. To summarize the preceding description of intestacy statutes, excepting the discussion of the share passing to the surviving spouse, we have identified the first two steps of the "parentelic system." The canons of descent and to a lesser degree the Statute of Distribution utilized this system. A parentela consists of an ancestor and that ancestor's surviving descendants. The parentelic system of inheritance is based on a preference for persons who are in the nearest parentela to the decedent. Thus, the parentelic system provides that the first parentela (the decedent's own surviving descendants) inherits first; if that parentela contains no surviving members, the second parentela (the decedent's parents and their descendants) inherit next; and so on.[39] The grandson of the intestate's sister, being a descendant of the intestate's parents, therefore, takes in preference to an uncle, who descended from the intestate's grandparents.

This procedure—going, step by step, up the ladder of ancestral seniority—can theoretically continue forever, but no state does that. Under the UPC, the parentelic system is carried out through the third parentela (grandparents and

39. As noted supra note 34, the canons of descent did not permit ancestors to inherit. So, under the canons of descent, the second parentela was only comprised of the descendants of the decedent's parents and did not include the parents themselves and so on.

their descendants).

The Table of Consanguinity, found on the following page, makes the parentelic system appear simpler than it is. Not depicted by the Table is the fact that each step up the ladder brings about a geometric increase in the number of ancestors at the head of each parentela. See supra note 33.

Under UPC § 2-103(4), the estate is first divided into paternal and maternal halves (if there is at least one grandparent or descendant of a grandparent in each half). If both of the grandparents on one side predeceased the decedent, that half is a separate parentela for purposes of representation among the descendants of the predeceased grandparents.[40]

Nearest Kindred—Determining Degrees of Kinship. Many American statutes (but not the UPC) provide that, if no member of any of the specifically designated parentela survives the intestate, the estate passes to the intestate's "nearest kindred" or "next of kin." The phrases "in equal degree" and "without representation" frequently accompany the kinship terms.

Statutes designating kin as heirs require a determination of degrees of kinship between the intestate and those kin claiming a share of the estate. Under the "nearest kindred" part of the statute, the relatives in the *lowest* degree of kinship, being the intestate's nearest living relatives, share the estate equally. This type of distribution is *nonrepresentational.* In other words, it might be described as "per capita without representation." Relatives must take, if at all, in their own right and not as representatives of deceased ancestors. Each heir takes an equal share, because all the relatives who are entitled to participate in the estate will be in the same degree.

In its primary sense, each degree reflects a difference of one generation. Thus, a great-grandparent of the intestate is related to the intestate in the third degree, a great, great-grandparent is in the fourth degree, and so on. The determination of the degree of relationship is somewhat more complicated when it comes to collateral relatives, as we shall see below.

The Civil-Law Method. For collateral relatives, the method for computing degrees of kinship used in American law relies upon the English judges' interpretation of "next of kindred in equal degree" found in the Statute of Distribution. They applied the civil-law method of computing degrees, which consists of counting generations under the following formula: count the number of generations (1) up from the intestate to the intestate's ancestor who is also an ancestor of the collateral relative and (2) down from that common ancestor to the collateral relative. The total of these two figures constitutes the degree of

---

40. If the surviving grandparents or descendants of a grandparent are all on one side, that side takes the whole.

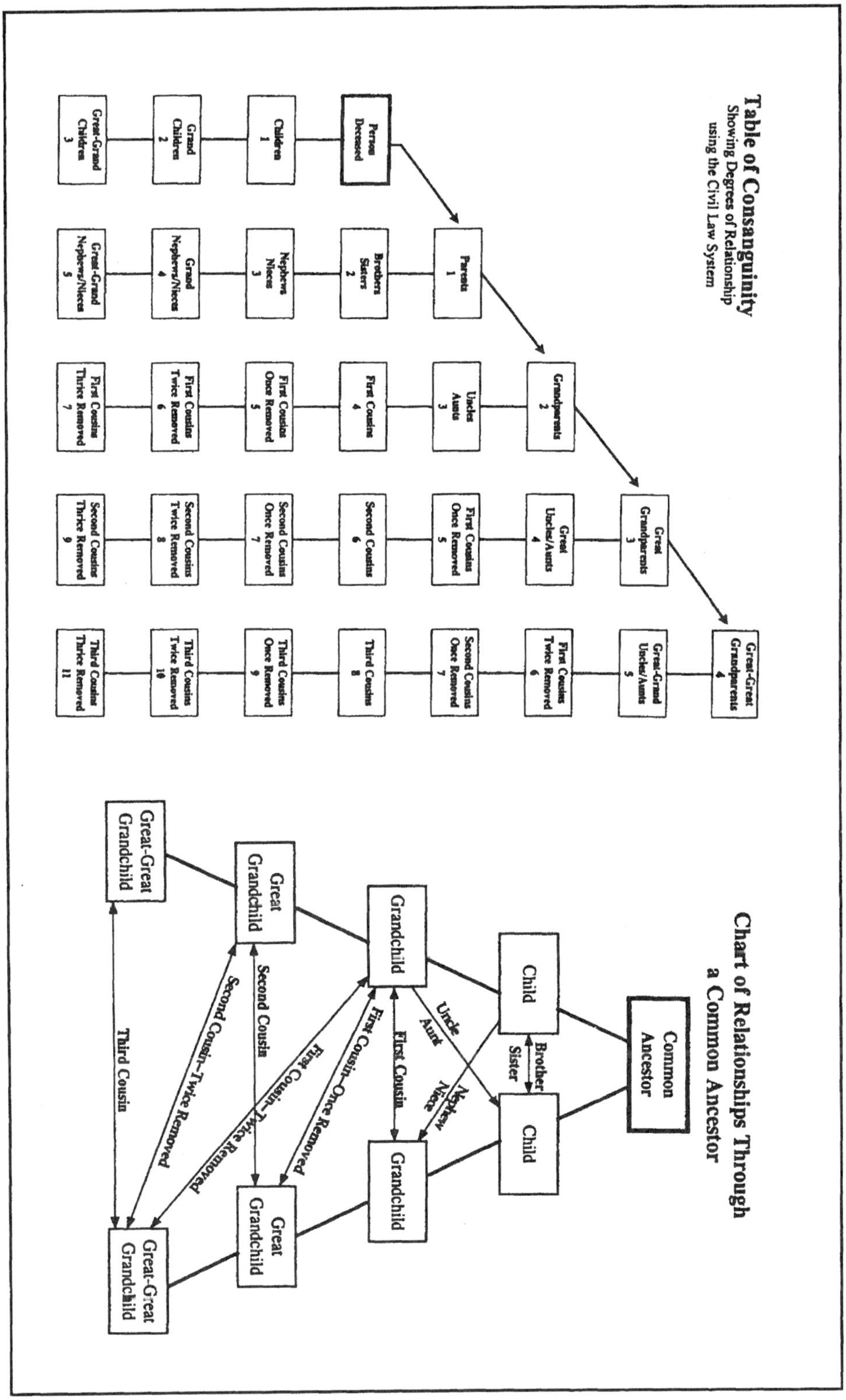
Table of Consanguinity
Showing Degrees of Relationship
using the Civil Law System
Person Deceased
Children 1
Grand Children 2
Great-Grand Children 3
Parents 1
Brothers Sisters 2
Nephews Nieces 3
Grand Nephews/Nieces 4
Great-Grand Nephews/Nieces 5
Grandparents 2
Uncles Aunts 3
First Cousins 4
First Cousins Once Removed 5
First Cousins Twice Removed 6
First Cousins Thrice Removed 7
Great Grandparents 3
Great Uncles/Aunts 4
First Cousins Once Removed 5
Second Cousins 6
Second Cousins Once Removed 7
Second Cousins Twice Removed 8
Second Cousins Thrice Removed 9
Great-Great Grandparents 4
Great-Grand Uncles/Aunts 5
First Cousins Twice Removed 6
Second Cousins Once Removed 7
Third Cousins 8
Third Cousins Once Removed 9
Third Cousins Twice Removed 10
Third Cousins Thrice Removed 11
Chart of Relationships Through a Common Ancestor
Common Ancestor
Child
Child
Brother Sister
Grandchild
Grandchild
Uncle Aunt
Nephew Niece
First Cousin
First Cousin–Once Removed
Great Grandchild
Great Grandchild
Second Cousin
First Cousin–Twice Removed
Second Cousin–Twice Removed
Great-Great Grandchild
Great-Great Grandchild
Third Cousin

kinship for each collateral relative.[41] See 4 Richard Burn, Ecclesiastical Law 538-43 (9th ed. 1842).

Under this formula, a sister or brother is related to the decedent in the second degree, a niece or nephew is related in the third degree, and an aunt or uncle is also related in the third degree. See the chart, supra p. 63. Many American statutes explicitly provide that degrees shall be computed according to the method of the civil law. When the statute has been silent on the point, most courts have used this method.

The Modified Civil-Law System. Under a fairly widespread statutory modification of the civil-law method, when there are two or more collateral relatives in equal degree who claim through different common ancestors, those claiming through the ancestor nearest to the decedent take to the exclusion of the others. Is this system any different from the parentelic scheme?

Problems

In the chart below, the decedent, D, died intestate without leaving a spouse or descendants.

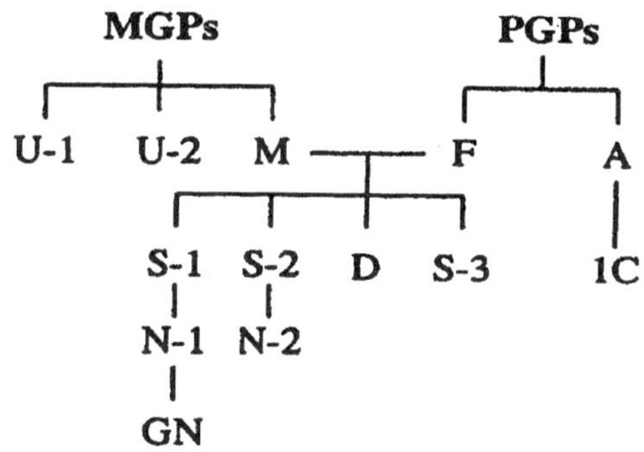

How is D's property divided under the UPC §§ 2-103, -106 under the following alternative circumstances?

---

41. At one time, another method, the canon-law/common-law method, had some following. This method differs from the civil-law method in one important respect. Instead of using the total of the two figures (the number of generations from the intestate to the common ancestor plus the number of generations from the common ancestor to the claimant), it uses only the larger of the two figures. The canon law employed this method for determining which marriages between relatives were prohibited and for limiting the number of successive donees in frankmarriage. See Atkinson on Wills § 7, at 45.

Although England never used this method for inheritance purposes, Blackstone erroneously reported that it was. 2 William Blackstone, Commentaries *204. Blackstone's error led to adoption of that method for inheritance purposes in a few American states. But it has now disappeared. The last remaining jurisdiction in which it was used for inheritance purposes, Georgia, repealed it in 1972.

1. All of D's relatives depicted in the above chart survived him.

2. All of D's relatives depicted in the above chart survived him, except for M, F, MGPs, PGPs, and the following relatives, all of whom predeceased him:

(a) S-1.

(b) S-1, S-2, and S-3.

(c) S-1, S-2, S-3, and N-1.

(d) S-1, S-2, S-3, N-1, N-2, and GN.

How do your answers change if the statute instead provides for property of intestate decedents to be distributed to their "nearest kindred" and uses the civil-law method? How do your answers change if the statute that refers to "nearest kindred" requires that they be determined by the modified civil-law method?

c. Limitations on Inheritance

Both the English canons of descent and the Statute of Distribution provided for inheritance by any blood relative no matter how remote the relationship. Through the first half of the twentieth century, nearly all of the U.S. jurisdictions adopted the same rule. The rule of unlimited inheritance, however, makes probate administration more complex. It increases the potential number of problems concerning proof of heirship under the intestacy statutes, and, even if the decedent dies with a will, it requires that all remote relatives be identified and located so that they might have the opportunity to contest any wills offered for probate.

The increased administrative costs are hard to justify when the potential takers of the probate estate are distant relatives with whom the decedent had no personal or social ties—so-called "laughing heirs." Indeed, the Sussman, Cates and Smith study revealed that such heirs "saw themselves as [unworthy takers]. They had rendered the deceased no service of any kind; they could not justify their windfall to themselves. Unlike Irish Sweepstakes winners, they did not even risk a shilling for their good fortune." Marvin B. Sussman, Judith N. Cates & David T. Smith, The Family and Inheritance 144-45 (1970).

A "Model Probate Code" was published in 1946 as the product of a research project carried on at the University of Michigan Law School in cooperation with a committee of the American Bar Association. That Model Code limited inheritance by collateral relatives to grandparents and those descended from grandparents. Legislation of several American states followed that recommendation and limited inheritance before the exhaustion of family lines. See In re Shumavon, 701 N.Y.S.2d 84 (N.Y. App. Div. 1999) (holding first cousins once removed were not eligible distributees under New York intestacy statute). Likewise, both the former and current versions of the UPC abandon the rule of unlimited inheritance. See UPC §§ 2-103, -105.

Internet References. The Internet has made it somewhat easier to locate long-lost heirs. Lexis-Nexis has a system called P-TRAK that attorneys can use in attempting to locate heirs. Two other sites are www.heirfinder.com and www.heirsearch.com. Genealogy on the Web, www.magpage.com, provides links to numerous genealogical sites. An ambitious genealogical project is USGenWeb, www.usgenweb.com. Online databanks of the National Archives www.nara.gov, of the Library of Congress, www.lcweb.loc.gov/rr/genealogy, and of the American Family Immigration History Center, www. ellisislandrecords.org, can also be used to search for long-lost relatives or ancestors. Another helpful resource is the National Genealogical Society, www.genealogy.org. Other sites include Ancestry.com, Inc., www.ancestry. com, FamilyHistory.com, www.familyhistory.com, Mormon Church Family Search site, www.familysearch.org, Genealogy Links for Historians, www.ucr.edu/h-gig/hist-preservation/genea, Genealogy Resources on the Internet, www.users.aol.com/johnf14246/internet, MyFamily.com, www. myfamily.com. Specialty sites include Afrigeneas, www.msstate.edu/ archives/history/afrigen/index, JewishGen, www.jewishgen.org, Treasure Maps, www.firstct.com/fv/tmapmenu.

Many other sites on the web offer search vehicles for locating persons by name, though the information tends to be incomplete and in some instances inaccurate or out of date. Search vehicles include AnyWho, www.anywho. com, InfoSpace US People Finder, www.infospace.com, InfoSpace People Search (Canada), www.206.129.166.101/canada, Locateme, www.locateme.com, Lookup USA People Directory www.lookupusa.com, Lycos People Find, www.lycos.com/pplfndr, Switchboard, www.switchboard.com/, Who Where?, www.whowhere.com/phone, and Yahoo People Search, www. yahoo.com/search/people/.

PART C. REARRANGING INTESTATE SUCCESSION

The intestacy statutes make it appear that decedents' estates must be distributed in accordance with the statutory rules unless the decedent executes a will. The statutes also make it appear that heirs have no power to vary an intestacy statute's operation. The following materials show that the situation is not as inflexible as it appears.

1. Agreement Among the Heirs

Statutory References: *UPC §§ 1-403, 3-912*

If an intestate's heirs aren't satisfied with the distribution under the intestacy statute, they normally can divide up the decedent's assets in a different way. UPC § 3-912 contains a provision authorizing private agreements among successors. Difficulties can arise in reaching these agreements.

Problem of Unascertained Successors or Successors Who Lack Capacity. If all the successors are competent adults, any agreement among the successors will be enforced. In many situations, however, successors include minors and/or persons who lack capacity to enter into agreements. UPC § 1-403, which was amended in 1997, provides (in the absence of a conflict of interest) for conservators to represent the protected persons whose estates they control, for trustees to represent trust beneficiaries, for parents to represent their minor children under certain conditions, and for the appointment of guardians ad litem to represent the interests of unborn and unascertained parties. It only applies, however, to "formal proceedings [and] judicially supervised settlements."

That limitation is a substantial one because formal judicial proceedings can result in delays and considerable expense. The challenge is whether a statute could be designed to allow issues arising under intestacy, wills, and trusts to be resolved by agreement without court approval. The key to the effectiveness and fairness of such a statute is to identify those instances in which minors or other persons under a disability, unborns, or unascertained parties can be represented adequately by others who have similar, and not conflicting, interests. If their interests cannot be adequately represented by others, the statute would have to provide for the appointment of a special representative who could negotiate on their behalf. Article 3 of the Uniform Trust Code (UTC) establishes criteria permitting representation of trust beneficiaries by fiduciaries (personal representatives, guardians, and conservators) and parents. See UTC § 303. It also permits an otherwise unrepresented "minor, incapacitated, or unborn individual, or a person whose identity or location is unknown or not reasonably ascertainable" to be represented "by another having a substantially identical interest with respect to the particular question or dispute." UTC § 304. Representation can only occur if there is no conflict of interest between the representative and the person represented. Article 3 only applies to trusts. The Joint Editorial Board for Uniform Trust and Estate Acts is currently considering how it might extend the UTC's approach to nonjudicial settlements to issues concerning intestacy and wills.

Potential Adverse Tax Consequences. Agreements can have adverse tax consequences to the parties. To the extent the agreed upon distribution differs from that which the intestacy laws would have directed, federal gift taxes may be incurred.[42] If an agreement under § 3-912 is not for the purpose of settling a bona fide controversy, the Service will treat it as the substantive equivalent of

---

42. The Economic and Tax Relief Reconciliation Act of 2001 (EGTRRA), which repeals the estate and generation-skipping transfer taxes, for the year 2010, retains the gift tax and makes the concerns expressed in the text of continuing relevance. See infra Chapter 7.

the heirs having received their inherited portions under the intestacy laws and then having made gifts of part or all of those assets to one or more of the other parties to the agreement. Cf. DePaoli v. Commissioner, 62 F.3d 1259 (10th Cir. 1995) (considering whether the settlement was a product of a bona fide will contest). If the heirs want to rearrange the intestacy pattern of distribution, a better course of action might be to utilize qualified disclaimers to accomplish the desired rearrangement. If executed properly, this approach avoids federal gift tax liability. Disclaimers are discussed below.

2. Disclaimers

Statutory References: *Unif. Disclaimer of Property Interests Act (1999) (UPC Art. II, Part 11)*

Disclaimers at Common Law. A disclaimer, sometimes called a renunciation, is the refusal to accept gratuitously transferred property. For lifetime transfers, the right to disclaim frequently is expressed in terms of the donee's nonacceptance of a gift. The acceptance requirement for a completed gift and the right to disclaim an inheritance or a devise are conceptually the same—both reflect a policy that ownership cannot be forced upon a transferee. The common law, which originated the disclaimer doctrine, broadly protected a transferee's right to just say no. The courts adopted a relation-back doctrine, under which a disclaimer was considered to relate back to the date of the transfer and operate as a nonacceptance. Under relation back, all claims of creditors and governmental taxing authorities seeking to attribute ownership rights to the disclaimant were ineffective. The only exception at common law was that heirs could not prevent title from passing to them by intestate succession.[43]

State Disclaimer Legislation. The breadth of the relation-back doctrine led to the growing popularity of disclaimers. Disclaimers have now become a matter of statutory law in most jurisdictions. In 1999, the Uniform Law Commission (ULC) promulgated the Uniform Disclaimer of Property Interests Act (UDPIA), which updates and replaces a number of uniform disclaimer acts dating back to 1973. The UDPIA abandons the relation-back doctrine and instead specifies the time when a disclaimer becomes effective and provides that a disclaimer "is not a transfer, assignment, or release." See UDPIA § 5(e), (f). In the near future, the ULC is expected to incorporate the UDPIA into the UPC as Part 11 of Article II (UPC §§ 2-1101 et seq.), replacing the UPC's former

43. See, e.g., Watson v. Watson, 13 Conn. 83 (1839); Coomes v. Finegan, 7 N.W.2d 729 (Iowa 1943). The theory was that intestate succession could not be refused because it arises by operation of law. See Christian M. Lauritzen, II, Only God Can Make an Heir, 48 Nw. U.L. Rev. 568 (1953).

disclaimer provision contained in § 2-801.

Although disclaimer statutes increase the formalities for accomplishing a disclaimer, they should not be interpreted as reflecting dissatisfaction with the common law. On the contrary, these statutes are designed to make disclaimers more useful to beneficiaries through regularization. Perhaps the clearest proof of legislative approval of the right to disclaim is the statutory extension to property passing by intestacy and to new types of nontestamentary transfers.

Federal Disclaimer Legislation. The delay in the effective dates of the repeal of the estate and generation-skipping taxes, the retention of the gift taxes, and the introduction of a modified carryover-basis rules, under the EGTRRA, suggests that disclaimers will continue to be used for many tax motivated purposes. See infra Chapter 7. State statutes are not uniform on a number of subsidiary questions, such as the time allowed after the decedent's death or after the date of the transfer to file the disclaimer. The Tax Reform Act of 1976 introduced provisions on disclaimers into the Internal Revenue Code (IRC) "to achieve uniform treatment" and to "provide a uniform standard . . . for determining the time within which a disclaimer must be made." H.R. Rep. No. 94-1380, 94th Cong., 2d Sess. 65 (1976). Disclaimers are a significant component of post-mortem estate planning. With federal tax savings a major motivating factor when a beneficiary considers a disclaimer, qualification under the federal statute inevitably becomes of primary importance.[44]

Under IRC §§ 2518, 2046, and 2614(c), a disclaimant incurs no federal transfer tax consequences if the disclaimer meets the IRC's definition of a "qualified disclaimer." Generally speaking, a qualified disclaimer must be "irrevocable and unqualified;" in writing and filed within nine months of the later of the time of the transfer or the disclaimant's twenty-first birthday; the disclaimant must not have accepted the interest or any of its benefits; and the interest must pass, without direction by the disclaimant, to either the transferor's spouse or a person other than the disclaimant.

The enactment of these federal provisions has diminished the significance of the state law requirements. State disclaimer statutes are now playing secondary roles as spoilers and facilitators of the federal tax law. A state's disclaimer law may affect the manner of obtaining qualification of a disclaimer for tax purposes if it contains more restrictive rules than the federal statute. In a few situations, a more restrictive requirement can prevent a disclaimer from being "qualified"

---

44. Beneficiaries have instituted malpractice claims for failure of attorneys to advise them on tax savings available through disclaimer. See, e.g., Linck v. Barokas & Martin, 667 P.2d 171 (Alaska 1983) (recognizing negligence claim); Barner v. Sheldon, 678 A.2d 717 (N.J. Super. Ct. App. Div. 1996) (refusing to recognize negligence claim).

for federal tax purposes.[45] State laws also indirectly affect federal taxation because they control the devolution of disclaimed property. By selecting devolution patterns that most frequently coincide with the disclaimant's dispositive intent, the state can remove a potential disincentive to disclaim and encourage its citizens to take advantage of tax-saving opportunities.

Creditors' Rights. The prevailing view in the United States is that a beneficiary can disclaim an interest to prevent creditors from reaching the property. Creditors' rights may be defeated even if the disclaimer would otherwise qualify as a fraudulent conveyance. See, e.g., Tompkins State Bank v. Niles, 537 N.E.2d 274 (Ill. 1989); Frances Slocum Bank & Trust Co., 666 N.E.2d 411 (Ind. Ct. App. 1996). The courts reason that, in the absence of explicit statutory direction to the contrary, the relation-back theory should apply and the disclaimer should be effective as against creditors.[46] In Drye v. United States, 528 U.S. 49 (1999), however, the Court held that a disclaimer of a son's right to take his mother's estate by intestacy was ineffective to defeat a tax lien against the disclaimant.

The appropriate treatment of disclaimers under the Federal Bankruptcy Code turns on the timing of the disclaimer. Disclaimers arise in two contexts under the Code. The first context concerns fraudulent conveyances. The Code creates a federal fraudulent conveyance statute. 11 U.S.C. § 548(a). This provision permits a bankruptcy trustee "to avoid any transfer of an interest of the debtor in property . . . made or incurred within one year before the date of the filing of the petition . . . if the debtor . . . received less than a reasonably equivalent value in exchange for such transfer . . . ." Section 548 presents the issue of whether a pre-petition disclaimer should be effective as against creditors. The second context concerns the inclusion in the bankruptcy estate of inheritances that occur within 180 days after a petition for bankruptcy relief has been filed. 11 U.S.C. § 541(a)(5). This provision raises the issue of whether a disclaimer of an inheritance, which occurs within 180 days of a bankruptcy petition, is an unauthorized post-petition transfer under 11 U.S.C. § 549(a).

In both contexts, the crucial question of statutory interpretation would seem

---

45. IRC § 2518(c)(3) provides that if the beneficiary transfers the property or interest to the person or persons who would have taken the property had the disclaimer been effective under local law, the disclaimer will qualify for federal tax purposes. Although this rule eliminates reliance on local law in the majority of disclaimer cases, it remains inadequate for interests that are not transferable. That can happen if the interest is subject to a spendthrift provision. See infra Chapter 14, Part A. The problem can also arise if local law does not permit a personal representative of a beneficiary who is dead or incompetent to make a disclaimer or a gratuitous transfer. But see UDPIA § 14 (providing that any disclaimer that is qualified for tax purposes is a valid disclaimer under the Act).

46. For examples of statutes protecting creditors' rights against disclaimers, see Fla. Stat. §§ 689.21(6), 732.801(6)(a); Mass. Ann. Laws ch. 191A, § 8(2).

to be whether a disclaimer should constitute a "transfer" under federal bankruptcy law. See Douglass G. Boshkoff, Bankruptcy in the Seventh Circuit: 1991, 25 Ind. L. Rev. 981, 983 (1992); George M. McCoskey, Death and Debtors: What Every Probate Lawyer Should Know About Bankruptcy, 34 Real Prop. Prob. & Tr. J. 669, 684-90 (2000). The courts, however, have not approached disclaimer issues in this way. In Jones v. Atchison (In re Atchison), 101 B.R. 556 (Bankr. S.D. Ill. 1989), aff'd, 925 F.2d 209 (7th Cir.), cert. denied, 502 U.S. 860 (1991), a case arising out of Illinois, the Seventh Circuit held that a pre-petition disclaimer was effective. It reasoned that the relation-back theory embraced by the applicable state law prevented the debtor from having a property interest to transfer. Accord Simpson v. Penner (In re Simpson), 36 F.3d 450 (5th Cir. 1994) (per curiam); see also Hoecker v. United Bank of Boulder, 476 F.2d 838 (10th Cir. 1973) (reaching same results in case decided under the 1898 Bankruptcy Act). It remains to be seen whether the Supreme Court's analysis in the *Drye* case of the interplay of federal and state law may be extended to the bankruptcy context. See McCoskey, supra, at 684 n.62.

In a case also arising out of Illinois, Williams v. Chenoweth (In re Chenoweth), 132 B.R. 161 (Bankr. S.D. Ill. 1991), aff'd, 143 B.R. 527 (S.D. Ill. 1992), aff'd, 3 F.3d 1111 (7th Cir. 1993), the bankruptcy court held that a post-petition disclaimer violated § 549 and the Seventh Circuit affirmed.[47] The bankruptcy court distinguished *Atchison* by reasoning that "[t]he 'entitled to acquire' language of § 541(a)(5)(A) results in a much broader definition of property of the estate for testamentary interests arising after bankruptcy and manifests Congress' intent to capture such interests for the trustee and the bankruptcy estate." 132 B.R. at 164. For other cases holding that post-petition disclaimers are avoidable, see In re Gilroy, 235 B.R. 512 (Bankr. D. Mass. 1999); Cornelius v. Cornell (In re Cornell), 95 B.R. 219 (Bankr. W.D. Okla. 1989); Geekie v. Watson (In re Watson), 65 B.R. 9 (Bankr. C.D. Ill. 1986); Flanigan v. Lewis (In re Lewis), 45 B.R. 27 (Bankr. W.D. Mo. 1984). See Adam J. Hirsch, Inheritance and Bankruptcy: The Meaning of the "Fresh Start," 45 Hastings L.J. 175, 183 n. 25 (1994) (reviewing the case law in this area).

An issue closely associated with creditors' rights concerns the effect of a disclaimer on eligibility for public assistance and Medicaid benefits. The

---

47. Should § 541(a)(5) apply if a testator conditions a devise on her not dying during the 180 days following the commencement of the devisee's bankruptcy case? The court in In re McGuire, 209 B.R. 580 (Bankr. D. Mass. 1997), presented with similar facts held the condition effective for bankruptcy purposes and that the property subject to the conditional devise did not become part of the bankruptcy estate. This case suggests interesting estate planning strategies for preventing creditors from reaching property intended for a debtor.

prevailing view is that a disclaimer causes a loss of eligibility for public assistance. See, e.g., Troy v. Hart, 697 A.2d 113 (Md. Ct. Spec. App.), cert. denied, 700 A.2d 1215 (Md. 1997); Molloy v. Bane, 631 N.Y.S.2d 910 (App. Div. 1995); see also Hinschberger v. Griggs County Soc. Serv., 499 N.W.2d 876 (N.D. 1993) (denying medical assistance benefits to a claimant based on his release for less than adequate consideration of his rights to his wife's estate, including his right to an elective share and family allowance); Tannler v. Wisconsin Dep't of Health & Soc. Serv., 564 N.W.2d 735 (Wis. 1997) (terminating Medicaid eligibility for surviving spouse's failure to make spousal election). Contra, e.g., Estate of Kirk, 591 N.W.2d 630 (Iowa 1999).

Disposition of Disclaimed Property. If the testamentary or nontestamentary instrument provides for an alternative disposition in the event of a disclaimer, that alternative disposition controls. See, e.g, Estate of Devlin, 259 N.Y.S.2d 531 (Sur. Ct. 1964); UDPIA § 6(b)(2). In the absence of an alternative disposition, a disclaimed interest passes as provided by the disclaimer statute or by the common law. In general, for property passing by will or by intestacy, the statutes apply the fiction that the disclaimant predeceased the decedent. See UDPIA § 6(b)(3). For property passing by a nontestamentary instrument, they apply the fiction that the disclaimant predeceased the date that the instrument became effective.

Representation Revisited. Can a disclaimer be used to manipulate shares under the various systems of representation? Notice the difference between a disclaimer statute that provides that the decedent's "estate" devolves as if the disclaimant predeceased the decedent and one that provides that the "disclaimed interest" devolves as if the disclaimant predeceased the decedent.

How does the language of UDPIA § 6(b)(3)(A) handle this problem?

Problems

1. G died intestate, survived by her son, A, and by three granddaughters, X, Y, and Z. X and Y are A's children. Z is the child of a predeceased son, B. A disclaimed all his interest in his mother's estate. What result under a statute providing that the decedent's "estate" devolves as if the disclaimant predeceased the decedent? Under a statute providing that the "disclaimed interest" devolves as if the disclaimant predeceased the decedent? Under UDPIA § 6(b)(3)(A)?

2. In Problem 1, suppose that A predeceased G but B survived G. B disclaimed. What result under these various statutes?

Internal Reference. For the effect of disclaimers by present-interest beneficiaries on remainder interests, see infra Chapter 17, Part B.

External References. Ronald A. Brand & William P. LaPiana, Disclaimers in Estate Planning: A Guide to Their Effective Use (1990); Adam J. Hirsch, The Problem of the Insolvent Heir, 74 Cornell L. Rev. 587 (1989); John H. Martin, Perspectives on Federal Disclaimer Legislation, 46 U. Chi. L. Rev. 316 (1979).

3. Formality versus Discretion in Intestate Succession

If the decedent's heirs can voluntarily rearrange intestacy patterns of distribution, should the courts have a power to vary the shares on the petition of one or more parties in interest? Under American law, as under the English canons of descent and the Statute of Distribution, intestate shares are determined mechanically. A surviving spouse's share, for example, is determined solely by reference to the decedent's other surviving relatives (or, under the UPC, by reference also to the surviving spouse's descendants). Traditional legislation does not authorize a court to inquire into the harmony or disharmony in the marital relationship. It does not allow for inquiry into the surviving spouse's contribution to the decedent's wealth.[48] It does not allow for any inquiry into the surviving spouse's needs, such as might be determined by the extent of the survivor's own assets and earning power.[49] All these issues are deemed irrelevant. In this sense, the current American law of intestate succession can be characterized as having a high degree of formality.

Although the former UPC was path breaking in important ways, it did not break with tradition on this point. The basic statutory scheme of the former UPC still looked to the decedent's surviving relatives to determine the share of any particular relative. When the UPC was revised in 1990, it still determined the shares passing to a relative by applying mechanical factors relating to the existence of a surviving spouse and descendants and their biological or adoptive ties to the decedent or the surviving spouse. No judicial discretion was introduced into the statutory scheme.

The question of formality versus discretion will come up again in several other areas of succession law. At this point, it will be useful for you to begin thinking about the reasons for and against discretion and formality and about

---

48. See infra Chapter 10, Part A, discussing the relevance of the length of the marriage for determining the spouse's share. See also Ark. Stat. Ann. § 28-9-214(2) (permitting a spouse of a childless decedent to receive the entire estate only if the decedent and spouse were married for three years or more).

49. Such information is relevant, however, under family allowance statutes that are in effect in most states. We will study these statutes in Chapter 10, Part B, but at this point we need to bear in mind that they permit a judge to make a discretionary support allowance out of certain assets of the estate for the needs of the surviving spouse and children during the period of estate administration. In practice, these discretionary allowances often consume a substantial portion or all of a small estate.

whether the cogency of these reasons varies from one context to another.

External References. Rosalind F. Atherton, Family Provision Legislation in Common Law Jurisdictions, in International Academy of Estate and Trust Law: Selected Papers 1997-1999, at 681 (Rosalind F. Atherton ed. 2001); S. M. Cretney, Reform of Intestacy: The Best We Can Do?, 111 Law Q. Rev. 77 (1995); Frances H. Foster, Linking Support and Inheritance: A New Model from China, 1999 Wis. L. Rev. 1199; Mary Ann Glendon, Fixed Rules and Discretion in Contemporary Family Law and Succession Law, 60 Tul. L. Rev. 1165 (1986).

PART D. ALTERING INTESTATE SUCCESSION BY MEANS OTHER THAN TESTAMENTARY DISPOSITION

In Part C, we learned that the heirs are not bound by the distributive pattern of the intestacy statute. What means are available to the decedent for altering the intestacy statute? The most obvious means is to make a valid will disposing of the decedent's entire estate. This is the topic of Chapter 4. Short of that, the decedent can alter the intestacy scheme by making an advancement, entering into a contractual agreement with a potential heir, and possibly by executing a so-called negative will.

1. Advancements and Related Doctrines

Statutory References: *UPC § 2-109*

Advancements. An advancement is a gift made during life to a family member. It is a gift, however, that has the effect of reducing the share of the probate estate that the donee receives by intestate succession upon the donor's death intestate.[50] The primary purpose of the advancements doctrine is to further the intestacy statute's distribution pattern that assures equal treatment among the decedent's children. By taking into account lifetime parental gifts to children, the advancement doctrine achieves more equal sharing by the children of their parent's wealth when the parent dies without a will.

Most jurisdictions originally modeled their advancement statutes upon the English Statute of Distribution, which provided only the manner for accounting for these lifetime gifts. The English courts apparently treated all gifts made

---

50. See infra Chapter 6, Part A for discussion of the related doctrine of satisfaction, having to do with gifts made to satisfy will devises.

during the life of the decedent as advancements, except gifts of small sums or gifts made for the purpose of maintenance or in satisfaction of the decedent's support obligation. Proof of whether a gift fell within one of the exceptions to the rule rested on objective evidence of the nature or purpose of the gift. See, e.g., Taylor v. Taylor, 20 L.R.-Eq. 155 (1875); Boyd v. Boyd, 4 L.R.-Eq. 305 (1867).

American statutes, following the English Statute of Distribution, made no attempt to define an advancement or to provide guidelines on the type of transfers to be treated as advancements. Unlike their English counterparts, however, the American courts generally refused to adopt any objective tests to identify advancements.[51] Instead, they interpreted the advancement statutes as authorizing an inquiry to determine if the decedent's specific intent was to make an advancement rather than an absolute gift. See, e.g., Holland v. Bonner, 218 S.W. 665 (Ark. 1920); Bulkeley v. Noble, 19 Mass. (2 Pick.) 337 (1824). Predictably, this judicial inquiry created a significant number of cases involving factual disputes that were made difficult by the inevitable unreliability of the evidence admitted to show the decedent's intent.

Disenchantment with the operation of the advancements doctrine led a number of nineteenth-century legislatures to restrict advancements to gifts accompanied by a writing expressing the decedent's intent to make an advancement. The general rule is that a decedent can avoid the operation of the intestacy statute only by executing a will. Why should a writing that does not meet the will formality requirements be sufficient to vary the intestacy law by having a gift treated as an advancement?

All American jurisdictions have statutes providing for advancements. See Restatement 3d of Property § 2.6, Statutory Note. Two common features found in the statutes are that they enlarge the scope of permissible recipients beyond the child and they require written evidence of an intent to make an advancement. UPC § 2-109 cxpands thc class of cligiblc advanceecs bcyond thc decedent's children to include all of the decedent's heirs. See Young v. Young, 979 P.2d 338 (Utah 1999) (holding, under a statute modeled on former UPC § 2-110, that a gift was not an advancement because there was no evidence that the required writing existed).

Releases and Assignments. Presumptive heirs (or devisees) can *release* their expectancy interests to the decedent. Presumptive heirs (or devisees) can also *assign* their expectancy interests to third persons. Contracts to release or assign

---

51. South Carolina is the only state in which the courts have held that the specific intent of the decedent is irrelevant. The objective circumstances surrounding the gift, such as the amount or purpose of the gift, are considered to determine if a court should treat a particular gift as an advancement. See, e.g., Heyward v. Middleton, 43 S.E. 956 (S.C. 1903); Rees v. Rees, 11 Rich. Eq. 86 (S.C. 1859); M'Caw v. Blewit, 2 McCord Eq. 90 (S.C. 1827).

expectancy interests are only enforceable in equity and only if the heir (or devisee) receives fair consideration. If releasors or assignors predecease the decedent, should their descendants be bound by their ancestor's dealings?

Should a release apply to devises in a will executed subsequent to the contract of release? In Ware v. Corwell, 465 S.E.2d 809 (Va. 1996), the court held that a release by a daughter to her mother prevented the daughter from taking under her mother's will, even though the will was executed subsequent to the release agreement. As a result of this holding the testator's son inherited the mother's estate to the exclusion of his sister. Two facts make the result in *Ware* not surprising. First, the release by its written terms applied to subsequently executed wills. Second, it was executed by the daughter and mother, as well as the son, as part of a settlement agreement over a dispute of ownership. The settlement agreement thus operated as an assignment by the mother's daughter to her son, as well as a release by the daughter to her mother. *Ware* serves as a warning to attorneys to ask their clients about prior transfers and agreements and consider how they should be taken into account in the estate plan.

EXTERNAL REFERENCES. William Wheeler Thornton, A Treatise on the Law Relating to Gifts and Advancements (1893); Harold I. Elbert, Advancements: I, 51 Mich. L. Rev. 665 (1953); Harold I. Elbert, Advancements: II, 52 Mich. L. Rev. 231 (1953); Harold I. Elbert, Advancements: III, 52 Mich. L. Rev. 535 (1954); Mary Louise Fellows, Concealing Legislative Reform in the Common-Law Tradition: The Advancements Doctrine and The Uniform Probate Code, 37 Vand. L. Rev. 671 (1984).

2. Negative Wills

Statutory Reference: *UPC § 2-101(b)*

Under prevailing court-made law in the United States, which relied on early English decisions, an intent to disinherit expressed in a will has no effect on the right of an heir to inherit any intestate portion of the estate. See Seeman v. Seeman, 858 S.W.2d 114 (Ark. 1993). English courts subsequently recognized negative wills so long as the testator leaves at least one heir to succeed to the property. See In re Wynn, [1984] 1 W.L.R. 227 (Ch. 1983); Lett v. Randall, 107 Rev. Rep. 26 (Ch. 1855); Bund v. Green, 12 Ch. D. 819 (1879).

The distinction between a testamentary provision directing that a devisee receive property and one directing that a devisee not receive property makes little sense if the purpose of a will is to provide the means of avoiding the effect of intestacy statutes and of achieving the testator's donative intent. UPC § 2-101(b) reverses the prevailing common-law rule because that rule "defeats a testator's intent for no sufficient reason."[52] UPC § 2-101(b) comment. Restatement 3d of Property § 2.7 also authorizes negative wills, contrary to the prevailing common-law rule. Under the UPC, if a testator writes a will that disinherits an heir, the heir is presumed to have disclaimed. The distribution of the presumed disclaimed share is therefore governed by the UDPIA.

UPC § 2-101(b) does not impose any qualification on the right of a testator to disinherit the testator's heirs. Nevertheless, the South Dakota Supreme Court in Estate of Jetter, 570 N.W.2d 26 (S.D. 1997), appeal after remand, 590 N.W.2d 254 (S.D. 1999), interpreted S.D. Codified Laws § 29A-2-101(b), which is the UPC provision, as adopting the English rule. After devising his entire estate to his brother, the testator states in his will, "I have intentionally omitted all of my heirs . . . who are not specifically mentioned herein, and I hereby generally and specifically disinherit each and all persons whomsoever claiming to be my heirs-at-law . . . ." 570 N.W.2d at 27. The court erroneously held that the disinheritance clause was ineffective because the statute did not authorize a clause disinheriting *all* of the testator's heirs when it resulted in an escheat.[53] The Restatement 3d of Property § 2.7 comment a takes a position opposite to *Jetter*, stating that "[t]he class to be disinherited need not be limited to a group constituting some but not all of the testator's heirs."

To make clear that a spouse cannot receive both a devise and also elect to take dower, an elective share, homestead allowance, or the like, a will sometimes includes a provision like that found in Waring v. Loring, 504 N.E.2d 644, 645 (Mass. 1987): "The provisions of this will for the benefit of my wife . . . are in lieu of dower and of all her statutory rights in or to any part of my estate." If the will partially fails, as it did in *Waring*, does this language

---

52. The UPC provision has been enacted in Alaska, Arizona, Colorado, Hawaii, Michigan, Minnesota, Montana, New Mexico, North Dakota, Pennsylvania, South Dakota, Utah, and West Virginia. See Martin D. Begleiter, Article II of the Uniform Probate Code and the Malpractice Revolution, 59 Tenn. L. Rev. 101, 114 (1991) (explaining how the UPC provision "should prevent any malpractice action based on a person who decedent desired would take nothing by intestacy").

Before the promulgation of § 2-101(b), New York had been the only state to overrule the common law. It alters the statutory definition of a will to include a direction by a testator as to how property "shall not be disposed of." N.Y. Est. Powers & Trusts Law § 1-2.19. If a testator disinherits an heir in a will, the effect of the New York statute is to treat the heir as having predeceased the testator for purposes of applying the intestacy statute. See, e.g., Cairo's Estate, 312 N.Y.S.2d 925 (App. Div. 1970), aff'd per curiam, 272 N.E.2d 574 (N.Y. 1971).

53. In Julia M. Melius, Note, Was South Dakota Deprived of $3.2 Million? Intestacy, Escheat, and the Statutory Power to Disinherit in the Estate of Jetter, 44 S.D. L. Rev. 49 (1999), the author concluded that "[t]he correct decision [in *Jetter*] would have allowed not only Jetter, but all future testators, to control the disposition of their intestate properties. Instead, under an erroneous application of the new statutory provisions in South Dakota, the court chose to follow the 'English Rule.'"

preclude the spouse from taking under the will *and* taking her share as an heir of the intestate portion of the estate? The court in *Waring* held that she could take both. The court reasoned that intestacy, unlike dower and the elective share, does not require the surviving spouse to make an election and does not disrupt the testator's distributive plan. The court limited its decision to the situation in which partial intestacy resulted from an ineffective provision in the will. Contra, e.g., Hills' Will, 191 N.E. 12 (N.Y. 1934). How would a *Waring*-type case be decided under UPC § 2-101(b)?

INTERNAL REFERENCE. For a further discussion of the doctrine of equitable election, see infra Chapter 8.

EXTERNAL REFERENCE. J. Andrew Heaton, Note, The Intestate Claims of Heirs Excluded by Will: Should "Negative Wills" Be Enforced?, 52 U. Chi. L. Rev. 177 (1985); Frederic S. Schwartz, Models of the Will and Negative Disinheritance, 48 Mercer L. Rev. 1137 (1997); Annot., Effect of Will Provision Cutting off Heir or Next of Kin, or Restricting Him to Provision Made, to Exclude Him from Distribution of Intestate Property, 100 A.L.R.2d 322 (1965).

Chapter 3

The Changing American Family

THE Changing American Family—From "Leave it to Beaver" to "The Brady Bunch." One of the most interesting stories, beginning in the 1970s and continuing into the present, is that of the changing American family. Unmarried same-sex and opposite-sex couples, including some with children, are increasingly prevalent in American society.[1] Although the traditional "Leave It to Beaver" family, consisting of a wage-earning husband, a housekeeping and child-rearing wife, and two or three joint children, hasn't disappeared, it is no longer the only noticeable and socially acceptable pattern. Approximately 53 percent of all married couples now have husband and wife working outside the home.[2] Divorce rates are higher than in the years before

1. See Jennifer Steinhauer, Living Together Without Marriage or Apologies, N.Y. Times, July 16, 1995, at A9.

2. U.S. Census Bureau, Household and Family Characteristics: March 1998 (Update), Current Population Reports (Series P20-515), tbl. 15, at 133.

1970,[3] and many married couples are more like "The Brady Bunch"—they have children from prior marriages on one or both sides.[4] Indeed, stepfamilies are so common that one researcher reports that "[o]ne out of every three Americans is now a stepparent, a stepchild, a stepsibling, or some other member of a stepfamily."[5] Families are also increasingly headed by single parents; approximately 28 percent of all children live in one-parent families, overwhelmingly families headed by mothers.[6] For a recent discussion of all of these trends, see Eric Schmitt, For First Time, Nuclear Families Drop Below 25% of Households, N.Y. Times, May 15, 2001, at A1.

The challenge facing courts and legislators is to provide a family property law that reflects the changing and diverse American household. This chapter reflects on how family property law is currently responding to different family arrangements and considers alternative approaches.

PART A. WHO IS A "SURVIVING SPOUSE"?

1. Formal Marriage

The rights accruing to a surviving spouse in probate law are based on status. These rights include the right to a share of the estate if the decedent dies intestate. See supra Chapter 2. States also provide a surviving spouse other statutory rights, such as a family allowance, protection against intentional disinheritance (traditionally referred to as an "elective share"), and protection against unintentional disinheritance by a premarital will that the decedent failed to revise after the marriage. In most states, these and other similar rights accrue only to a person who was lawfully married to the decedent when the decedent died. See infra Chapter 10.

---

3. In the 1950s and 1960s, the divorce rate never exceeded 2.6 percent. Since 1970, the divorce rate has never fallen below 3.5 percent. It reached a peak of 5.3 percent in 1979 and 1981, and was 4.3 percent in 1997. U.S. Census Bureau, Statistical Abstract of the United States: 1999, tbl. 91, at 75.

4. See Susan Chira, Struggling to Find Stability When Divorce Is a Pattern, N.Y. Times, Mar. 19, 1995, at A1.

5. Jan Larson, Understanding Stepfamilies, Am. Demographics, July 1992, at 36.

6. U.S. Census Bureau, Marital Status and Living Arrangements: March 1998 (Update), Current Population Reports (Series P20-514), tbl. A, at iii.

2. *Divorce, Separation, Misconduct*

Statutory References: *UPC § 2-802*

Not surprisingly, if the decedent's marriage is dissolved by divorce or annulment, the decedent's former spouse loses the status of surviving spouse. Likewise, if the decedent's marriage is void because it was bigamous, incestuous, or preceded by an invalid divorce decree, the decedent's would-be spouse doesn't have the status of surviving spouse. But what if the decedent's divorce or annulment is itself invalid? Or, what if the decedent and decedent's spouse separate but do not divorce? Or, what if a divorce suit is pending but not final at the time of the decedent's death?

UPC § 2-802 addresses some but not all of these status questions.[7] Note that § 2-802 isn't framed as a definition of "spouse." Instead, it gives a list of situations in which a person is *not* a surviving spouse. The most obvious of these is where the marriage ended by valid divorce or annulment. The others are where the survivor obtained or consented to a final decree or judgment of divorce or annulment, even though the decree later proves to have been invalid; where the survivor, following an invalid decree obtained by the decedent, participated in a marriage ceremony with a third individual; and where the survivor was a party to a valid proceeding purporting to terminate all marital property rights.

A few states, by statute, go farther and bar the surviving spouse from taking for desertion or adultery.[8] Although no state addresses the question of spousal

---

7. Section 2-802 appeared in the former UPC and was carried forward in the current UPC without substantive change.

8. See, e.g., Ky. Rev. Stat. § 392.090 (spouse barred if spouse "leaves the other and lives in adultery," unless the spouses "afterward become reconciled and live together as husband and wife"); Mo. Rev. Stat. § 474.140 (spouse barred "[i]f [he or she] voluntarily leaves his spouse and goes away and continues with an adulterer or abandons his spouse without reasonable cause and continues to live separate and apart from his spouse for one whole year next preceding his death, or dwells with another in a state of adultery continuously, or if any wife after being ravished consents to her ravisher . . . unless such spouse is voluntarily reconciled to him and resumes cohabitation with him"); N.H. Rev. Stat. Ann. § 560:19 (spouse barred if "at the time of the death of either husband or wife, the decedent was justifiably living apart from the surviving husband or wife because such survivor was or had been guilty of conduct which constitutes cause for divorce"); N.Y. Est. Powers & Trusts Law § 5-1.2(a)(5), (6) (spouse barred if spouse "abandoned the deceased spouse, and such abandonment continued until the time of death" or if the spouse "who, having the duty to support the other spouse, failed or refused to provide for such spouse though he or she had the means or ability to do so, unless such marital duty was resumed and continued until the death of the spouse having the need of support"); N.C. Gen. Stat. § 31A-1(a)(3), (b) (spouse barred if he or she "willfully and without just cause abandons and refuses to

abuse explicitly, courts may interpret physical and emotional abuse as constructive abandonment. See, e.g., In re Jellech, 854 S.W.2d 828 (Mo. Ct. App. 1993) (applying a Missouri statute to deny a husband a right to the decedent's estate based on evidence that his "abusive conduct, in conjunction with the evidence of his other actions, was such that . . . decedent could not reasonably have been expected to live with [the husband]"); see also Robin L. Preble, Family Violence and Family Property: A Proposal for Reform, 13 Law & Ineq. J. 401 (1995) (proposing a statute that would bar inheritance rights of a surviving spouse if there are court documents or arrest records showing a pattern of domestic abuse against the decedent within five years of the decedent's death).

A few courts, without statutory authority to vary the rights provided to surviving spouses, have denied claims against decedents' estates by persons who were lawfully married to the decedents. See, e.g., Estate of Abila, 197 P.2d 10 (Cal. 1948) (barring wife because an interlocutory decree of divorce, granted to the decedent before his death, terminated the decedent's obligation of support, though it did not dissolve the marriage).

3. Putative Spouses

The purpose of the putative spouse doctrine is to protect the financial and property interests of persons who enter into a marriage believing in good faith that it is a valid marriage. It is largely controlled by statute in the United States. But see, e.g., Walker v. Walker, 47 N.W.2d 633 (Mich. 1951); Annot., Rights in Decedent's Estate as Between Lawful and Putative Spouses, 81 A.L.R.3d 6 (1977).

Under the Uniform Marriage and Divorce Act § 209 (1973) (UMDA), a putative spouse "acquires the rights conferred upon a legal spouse."[9] A putative

---

live with the other spouse and is not living with the other spouse at the time of such spouse's death"); 20 Pa. Cons. Stat. § 2106 (a) (spouse barred "who, for one year or upwards previous to the death of the other spouse, has wilfully neglected or refused to perform the duty to support the other spouse, or who for one year or upwards has wilfully and maliciously deserted the other spouse"); Va. Code § 64.1-16.3 (A) (spouse barred if spouse "willfully deserts or abandons his or her spouse and such desertion or abandonment continues until the death of the spouse").

9. Section 209 goes on to declare:

> If there is a legal spouse or other putative spouses, rights acquired by a putative spouse do not supersede the rights of the legal spouse or those acquired by other putative spouses, but the court shall apportion property, maintenance, and support rights among the claimants as appropriate in the circumstances and in the interests of justice.

spouse is defined in the UMDA as "[a]ny person who has cohabited with another to whom he is not legally married in the good faith belief that he was married to that person." Courts have used the putative spouse doctrine to recognize a claim for an intestacy share by an unmarried cohabitor. See, e.g., Estate of Leslie, 689 P.2d 133, (Cal. 1984). They have also applied it to a claim for other spousal rights, such as rights under an omitted spouse statute. See, e.g., Estate of Sax, 263 Cal. Rptr. 190 (Ct. App. 1989).

Neither the former UPC nor the current UPC explicitly confers rights upon or denies rights to putative spouses. Courts in a UPC state are free to adopt the putative spouse doctrine, and legislatures can enact both the UPC and the UMDA.

The Restatement 3d of Property § 2.2 Comment e provides that "[u]nless precluded by applicable statute, a putative spouse is treated as a legal spouse for purposes of intestacy."

4. Common-Law Marriage

Most states have abolished common-law marriage by statute. See, e.g., Ga. Code Ann. § 19-3-1.1 (effective Jan. 1, 1997); Idaho Code § 32-201 (effective Jan. 1, 1996); Ohio Rev. Code Ann. § 3105.12 (effective Oct. 10, 1991). Negative judicial and legislative reaction to the concept of common-law marriage grew during the late nineteenth century. One criticism of the concept was that the informality of common-law marriages made them highly vulnerable to fraud and perjury. See, e.g., Wagner's Estate, 159 A.2d 495 (1960). Another was that common-law marriage undermined the sanctity of marriage. See, e.g., Sorenson v. Sorenson, 100 N.W. 930, 932 (Neb. 1904). See generally Michael

---

The Official Comment accompanying § 209 further explains:

> It is possible for a person to have more than one putative spouse at the same time, since good faith is the test. In addition, a putative spouse and a legal spouse may be able to claim from a single estate or from other funds legally available to a spouse. A common situation of the latter type might involve a bigamous marriage in which the second spouse was never married or had been divorced. In such cases, the court is instructed to apportion property and the other financial incidents of marriage between the legal and the putative spouse, or among putative spouses. A fair and efficient apportionment standard is likely to be the length of time each spouse cohabited with the common partner.

Eight states have enacted the UMDA (Arizona, Colorado, Illinois, Kentucky, Minnesota, Missouri, Montana, and Washington). Some states had adopted the putative spouse doctrine by statute before the promulgation of the UMDA. See, e.g, Cal. Fam. Code § 2251; Wis. Stat. § 765.24; see also 42 USC § 416(h)(1)(B) (adopting the putative spouse doctrine for purposes of qualifying for benefits under the Social Security Act).

Grossberg, Governing the Hearth: Law and the Family in Nineteenth-Century America 86-90, 95-97, 101-02 (1985).

Only eleven states (Alabama, Colorado, Iowa,[10] Kansas, Montana, Oklahoma, Pennsylvania, Rhode Island, South Carolina, Texas, and Utah[11]) and the District of Columbia still recognize common-law marriages. The requirements necessary to establish a common-law marriage are somewhat different from state to state, but can be summarized as follows:

> The jurisdictions which recognize common law marriages all require that the parties presently agree to enter into the relationship of husband and wife. Most jurisdictions also require cohabitation, or actually and openly living together as husband and wife. . . . Some jurisdictions further require that the parties hold themselves out to the world as husband and wife, and acquire a reputation as a married couple. However, other jurisdictions hold that cohabitation and reputation are not requirements of a valid common law marriage, but solely matters of evidence.
>
> Under all of these definitions, evidence that the parties have stated "We're not married, we're just living together" will destroy the claim of a common law marriage.

Sol Lovas, When Is a Family Not a Family? Inheritance and the Taxation of Inheritance Within the Non-Traditional Family, 24 Idaho L. Rev. 353, 361 (1987). New Hampshire has codified a statutory version of common-law marriage applicable only on death. The New Hampshire statute is set forth infra p. 101.

In some states where common-law marriage has been abolished, courts have applied a de facto common-law marriage doctrine to couples who lived together (or stayed overnight?) in a common-law marriage state. In Kellard v. Kellard, 13 Fam. L. Rep. (BNA) 1490 (N.Y. Sup. Ct. 1987), a New York woman and man, unmarried but cohabiting with one another, took an automobile trip to Disney World in 1978. During the trip, they stayed overnight in a motel in South Carolina where they registered as wife and husband, and engaged in sexual intercourse. They also stayed for two nights in a motel in Georgia. Some years later, in defense to a divorce suit filed in New York by the woman, the man claimed that no divorce was necessary because he wasn't married to the plaintiff. A New York court rejected his defense, holding that the couple's

---

10. But see Iowa Code § 595.11 (valid marriage but aiders and abetters required to pay $50 cash to state).

11. See Utah Code Ann. § 30-1-4.5 (recognizes marriage if meet certain statutory requirements, which are modeled generally on traditional common-law marriage requirements).

behavior en route to Disney World satisfied the common-law marriage requirements of South Carolina and Georgia.[12] This, along with the lengthy history of the couple's relationship, led the court to recognize them as married. Accord, e.g., Renshaw v. Heckler, 787 F.2d 50 (2d Cir. 1986); Metropolitan Life Ins. Co. v. Holding, 293 F. Supp. 854 (E.D. Va. 1968). Contra, e.g., Vandever v. Industrial Comm'n, 714 P.2d 866 (Ariz. Ct. App. 1985); Goldin v. Goldin, 426 A.2d 410 (Md. Ct. Spec. App. 1981); see also Gary Taylor, Increased Mobility Adds to Common Law Claims, Nat'l L.J., Aug. 14, 1989, at 24.

The Restatement 3d of Property § 2.2 Comment f provides that a common-law spouse is a spouse for purposes of intestate succession in states recognizing common-law marriage.

5. *Domestic Partnerships*

Demographics. According to the 2000 census, approximately 5.5 million of the nation's 105.5 million households (or about 5.2%) are headed by unmarried partners. Of the unmarried partner households, approximately 595,000 (or 10.8%) are headed by partners of the same sex. These figures were derived from state-by-state data on the Census Bureau's website, www.census.gov, and from an analysis in the New York Times. See Households Headed by Gays Rose in the 90's, Data Shows, N.Y. Times, Aug. 22, 2001, at A17.[13]

Data from earlier studies indicated that approximately 10 percent of the nation's couples were domestic partnerships, with about 28 percent (approximately 1.7 million) being lesbian or gay.[14] These studies also show that the number of opposite-sex partnerships has been growing more rapidly than same-sex ones. Opposite-sex households increased at a 28 percent rate between 1990 and 1994 as compared to just 4 percent for same-sex households.[15]

---

12. As noted in the text, Georgia subsequently abolished common-law marriage. See Ga. Code Ann. § 19-3-1.1 (effective Jan. 1, 1997).

13.The title of the newspaper article is somewhat misleading, as numbers from 1990 concerning same-sex partners cannot be directly compared with data from 2000 because the two censuses did not use the same method of collecting information about them. However, estimates of opposite-sex unmarried partners are comparable between the 1990 and 2000 censuses. See supra Chapter 1, Part B, n. 3.

14. See U.S. Census Bureau, Marital Status and Living Arrangements: March 1998 (Update), Current Population Reports (Series P20-514), tbls. B, 8, at iv, 71 [hereinafter CPS].

15. See American Demographics Inc., One-Third of Unmarried Partners Are Gay, The Number News (May 1996).

Moreover, the studies suggest that about 57 percent of domestic partners (same-sex or opposite-sex) are under age thirty-five. Only a relatively small percentage (between 9 and 10 percent) of same-sex partners have children under the age of fifteen living with them as compared to opposite-sex partners (36 percent).[16]

Larry Bumpass and James Sweet, sociologists who have conducted numerous studies on cohabitation that primarily focus on opposite-sex couples, have found significant attitude changes regarding cohabitation that they believe "have profound implications for future change."[17] Although 70 percent of persons over age seventy believe that cohabitation is unacceptable, the proportion of persons disagreeing with cohabitation declines as age decreases, with only about 25 percent of persons between the ages of twenty-five and twenty-nine finding cohabitation unacceptable.[18] Bumpass and Sweet also show that behavior is consistent with changing attitudes. According to their data "about half of the population under age 40 have lived with an unmarried partner—in ten years that will be true for the population under age 50."[19] What is striking about the data is that—across all age groups—the percent of unmarried couples cohabitating increased between the late 1980s and the early 1990s. For persons between the ages of thirty-five and thirty-nine, the percent of unmarried couples cohabitating increased from about 17 percent in 1987-88 to about 22 percent in 1992-94; for persons between the ages of forty-five and forty-nine the increase was less dramatic (13 percent as compared to 16 percent); for persons between the ages of fifty and fifty-four, however, the percentage went from about 4 percent to about 16 percent.[20]

Legal Rights. The respective rights of domestic partners upon dissolution of the partnership during life or at death are governed almost exclusively by court-made law. As one lawyer who specializes in gay and lesbian issues observes, "I used to say, 'Why do we want to get married? It doesn't work for straight people,' . . . . But now I say we should care: They have the privilege of divorce

16. CPS, supra note 14, tbl. 8, at 71.

17. Larry L. Bumpass & James A. Sweet, Cohabitation, Marriage and Union Stability: Preliminary Findings from NSFH2 (NSFH Working Paper No. 65) 6 (May 1995).

18. See id. at figure 1.

19. Id. at 7.

20. Id. at table 2, figure 4.

and we don't. We're left out there to twirl around in pain."[21] Why is this area left to the courts in an age of legislation?

The lawsuits that come to public attention frequently involve a defendant who is a wealthy celebrity, entertainer, or professional athlete. But less celebrated cases come to court also. These suits are sometimes grounded on a common-law marriage claim, but, when that claim is unavailable, they can still go forward as a "palimony suit."[22] The most famous of the "palimony" cases is Marvin v. Marvin, below.

Not surprisingly, most of the litigation involving domestic partnerships arises in the context of a dissolution during life. Claims arising at death are less common because, if the partners remain devoted to each other, the deceased partner probably provided for the survivor by will or other parts of an estate plan. Therefore, it's unusual for a surviving partner to claim legal rights to a share of a decedent's estate. When these claims do arise, however, they typically invoke theories of recovery based on contract or on status, or both.

a. Recovery Based on Contract?

Plaintiffs have no problem in stating a cause of action when they allege that they made a monetary contribution toward the purchase of specific property on the understanding that they would be the owner or part owner. The fact that the property isn't titled in the name of the plaintiff isn't a defense. A cause of action for the imposition of a purchase-money resulting trust or a constructive trust on the specific property is well established.[23] See, e.g., Estate of Eriksen, 337

---

21. Kirk Johnson, Gay Divorce: Few Markers in This Realm, N.Y. Times, Aug. 12, 1994, at A16.

22. The term "palimony" is misleading because the plaintiff is usually seeking a division of the couple's property, not an award of periodic payments similar to alimony.

23. The remedy is so well established that even same-sex couples have encountered little difficulty in stating a cause of action for the imposition of a purchase-money resulting trust or a constructive trust on specific property when plaintiffs allege or prove that they contributed monetary consideration toward the purchase of particular property. See, e.g., Bramlett v. Selman, 597 S.W.2d 80 (Ark. 1980). Indeed, this type of cause of action has been recognized even in states such as Georgia that have held that cohabitors' agreements based on services are unenforceable because the consideration is immoral. See Weekes v. Gay, 256 S.E.2d 901 (Ga. 1979). The Georgia Supreme Court has also upheld a written agreement by cohabiting lesbian partners based on promises regarding "the mutual contribution toward improvement of the real estate and sharing of expenses and assets." It reasoned that "[n]othing in the contract casts upon either of the parties the responsibility to perform any illegal activity" and "that the alleged illegal activity was at most incidental to the contract rather than required by it." Crooke v. Gilden, 414 S.E.2d 645, 646 (Ga. 1992). For a discussion of the constructive trust and the purchase-money

N.W.2d 671 (Minn. 1983) (holding that the surviving domestic partner was entitled to a constructive trust in her favor of a one-half interest in a home purchased with joint funds but titled in the decedent's name alone).

Once outside the realm of the constructive trust, however, it becomes more difficult for a plaintiff to state a cause of action based on a contractual understanding between domestic partners. Consider the following three cases.

Marvin v. Marvin

557 P.2d 106 (Cal. 1976)

[The plaintiff, Michelle Triola, brought a breach of contract action against the defendant, Lee Marvin. Because the trial court granted judgment on the pleadings for the defendant, the question on appeal was whether the plaintiff's complaint stated a cause of action or could be amended to state a cause of action.]

TOBRINER, J. . . . Plaintiff avers that in October of 1964 she and defendant "entered into an oral agreement" that while "the parties lived together they would combine their efforts and earnings and would share equally any and all property accumulated as a result of their efforts whether individual or combined." Furthermore, they agreed to "hold themselves out to the general public as husband and wife" and that "plaintiff would further render her services as a companion, homemaker, housekeeper and cook to . . . defendant."

Shortly thereafter plaintiff agreed to "give up her lucrative career as an entertainer [and] singer" in order to "devote her full time to defendant . . . as a companion, homemaker, housekeeper and cook;" in return defendant agreed to "provide for all of plaintiff's financial support and needs for the rest of her life."

Plaintiff alleges that she lived with defendant from October of 1964 through May of 1970 and fulfilled her obligations under the agreement. During this period the parties as a result of their efforts and earnings acquired in defendant's name substantial real and personal property, including motion picture rights worth over $1 million. In May of 1970, however, defendant compelled plaintiff to leave his household. He continued to support plaintiff until November of 1971, but thereafter refused to provide further support.

On the basis of these allegations plaintiff asserts two causes of action. The first, for declaratory relief, asks the court to determine her contract and property rights; the second seeks to impose a constructive trust upon one half of the property acquired during the course of the relationship. . . .

---

resulting trust, see generally infra Chapter 13.

2. *Plaintiff's complaint states a cause of action for breach of an express contract.* In Trutalli v. Meraviglia (1932) 215 Cal. 698, 12 P.2d 430 we established the principle that nonmarital partners may lawfully contract concerning the ownership of property acquired during the relationship. We reaffirmed this principle in Vallera v. Vallera (1943) 21 Cal.2d 681, 685, 134 P.2d 761, 763 . . . .

[W]e can abstract from [our prior] decisions a clear and simple rule. The fact that a man and woman live together without marriage, and engage in a sexual relationship, does not in itself invalidate agreements between them relating to their earnings, property, or expenses. Neither is such an agreement invalid merely because the parties may have contemplated the creation or continuation of a nonmarital relationship when they entered into it. Agreements between nonmarital partners fail only to the extent that they rest upon a consideration of meretricious sexual services. . . .

The principle that a contract between nonmarital partners will be enforced unless expressly and inseparably based upon an illicit consideration of sexual services not only represents the distillation of the decisional law, but also offers a . . . precise and workable standard . . . .

In summary, we base our opinion on the principle that adults who voluntarily live together and engage in sexual relations are nonetheless as competent as any other persons to contract respecting their earnings and property rights. Of course, they cannot lawfully contract to pay for the performance of sexual services, for such a contract is, in essence, an agreement for prostitution and unlawful for that reason. But they may agree to pool their earnings and to hold all property acquired during the relationship in accord with the law governing community property. . . . So long as the agreement does not rest upon illicit meretricious consideration, the parties may order their economic affairs as they choose, and no policy precludes the courts from enforcing such agreements.

3. *Plaintiff's complaint can be amended to state a cause of action founded upon theories of implied contract or equitable relief.* . . . Both plaintiff and defendant stand in broad agreement that the law should be fashioned to carry out the reasonable expectations of the parties. . . .[24]

---

24. We note that a deliberate decision to avoid the strictures of the community property system is not the only reason that couples live together without marriage. Some couples may wish to avoid the permanent commitment that marriage implies, yet be willing to share equally any property acquired during the relationship; others may fear the loss of pension, welfare, or tax benefits resulting from marriage. Others may engage in the relationship as a possible prelude to marriage. In lower socio-economic groups the difficulty and expense of dissolving a former marriage often leads couples to choose a nonmarital relationship; many unmarried couples may also incorrectly believe that the doctrine of common law marriage prevails in California, and thus

[A]lthough parties to a nonmarital relationship obviously cannot have based any expectations upon the belief that they were married, other expectations and equitable considerations remain. The parties may well expect that property will be divided in accord with the parties' own tacit understanding and that in the absence of such understanding the courts will fairly apportion property accumulated through mutual effort. We need not treat nonmarital partners as putatively married persons in order to apply principles of implied contract, or extend equitable remedies; we need to treat them only as we do any other unmarried persons. . . .

Although we recognize the well-established public policy to foster and promote the institution of marriage, perpetuation of judicial rules which result in an inequitable distribution of property accumulated during a nonmarital relationship is neither a just nor an effective way of carrying out that policy. . . .

We conclude that the judicial barriers that may stand in the way of a policy based upon the fulfillment of the reasonable expectations of the parties to a nonmarital relationship should be removed. As we have explained, the courts now hold that express agreements will be enforced unless they rest on an unlawful meretricious consideration. We add that in the absence of an express agreement, the courts may look to a variety of other remedies in order to protect the parties' lawful expectations.[25]

The courts may inquire into the conduct of the parties to determine whether that conduct demonstrates an implied contract or implied agreement of partnership or joint venture, or some other tacit understanding between the parties. The courts may, when appropriate, employ principles of constructive trust or resulting trust. Finally, a nonmarital partner may recover in quantum meruit for the reasonable value of household services rendered less the reasonable value of support received if he can show that he rendered services with the expectation of monetary reward.

---

that they are in fact married. Consequently we conclude that the mere fact that a couple have not participated in a valid marriage ceremony cannot serve as a basis for a court's inference that the couple intend to keep their earnings and property separate and independent; the parties' intention can only be ascertained by a more searching inquiry into the nature of their relationship.

25. We do not seek to resurrect the doctrine of common law marriage, which was abolished in California by statute in 1895. Thus we do not hold that plaintiff and defendant were "married," nor do we extend to plaintiff the rights which the Family Law Act grants valid or putative spouses; we hold that she has the same rights to enforce contracts and to assert her equitable interest in property acquired through her effort as does any other unmarried person.

Since we have determined that plaintiff's complaint states a cause of action for breach of an express contract, and, as we have explained, can be amended to state a cause of action independent of allegations of express contract,[26] we must conclude that the trial court erred . . . .

WRIGHT, C.J., and MCCOMB, MOSK, SULLIVAN and RICHARDSON, J., concur. CLARK, J. (concurring and dissenting).

Notes

1. *Subsequent History*. On remand, the plaintiff failed to prove the existence of an express or implied contract, but the trial court awarded her $104,000 for rehabilitation on the ground of an unspecified equitable theory. On appeal, the judgment granting this award was reversed for want of a "recognized underlying obligation in law or in equity." Marvin v. Marvin, 176 Cal. Rptr. 555 (Ct. App. 1981). See also Taylor v. Polackwich, 194 Cal. Rptr. 8 (Ct. App. 1983) ("rehabilitative award" reversed on appeal).[27]

2. *The Illegal Consideration Problem.* A few post-*Marvin* decisions have held that contracts between unmarried cohabitors are unenforceable on public policy grounds.[28] See, e.g., Rehak v. Mathis, 238 S.E.2d 81, 82 (Ga. 1977) ("It is well settled that neither a court of law nor a court of equity will lend its aid to either party to a contract founded upon an illegal or *immoral* consideration. Code Ann. § 20-501. . . . The parties being unmarried and the appellant having

---

26. We do not pass upon the question whether, in the absence of an express or implied contractual obligation, a party to a nonmarital relationship is entitled to support payments from the other party after the relationship terminates.

27. But compare Watts v. Watts, 405 N.W.2d 303 (Wis. 1987), in which the court stated:

> Many courts have held, and we now so hold, that unmarried cohabitants may raise claims based upon unjust enrichment following the termination of their relationships where one of the parties attempts to retain an unreasonable amount of the property acquired through the efforts of both. [Footnote citing cases from other jurisdictions omitted.]
>
> In this case, the plaintiff alleges that she contributed both property and services to the parties' relationship. She claims that because of these contributions the parties' assets increased, but that she was never compensated for her contributions. She further alleges that the defendant, knowing that the plaintiff expected to share in the property accumulated, "accepted the services rendered to him by the plaintiff" and that it would be unfair under the circumstances to allow him to retain everything while she receives nothing. We conclude that the facts alleged are sufficient to state a claim for recovery based upon unjust enrichment.

Watts is discussed in Leonard Wagner, Note, Recognizing Contract and Property Rights of Unmarried Cohabitants in Wisconsin: *Watts v. Watts*, 1988 Wis. L. Rev. 1093, 1113-15, 1117-18.

28. In a few states, it is a criminal offense for a man and a woman to cohabit without being married to each other. See Miss. Code § 97-29-1; N.M. Stat. § 30-10-2.

admitted the fact of cohabitation in both verified pleadings, this would constitute immoral consideration under Code Ann. § 20-501 . . . ."); Hewitt v. Hewitt, 394 N.E.2d 1204, 1208-09, Ill. 1979) ("Illinois' public policy regarding agreements such as the one alleged here was implemented long ago . . . , where this court said: 'An agreement in consideration of future illicit cohabitation between the plaintiffs is void.' . . . The issue, realistically, is whether it is appropriate for this court to grant a legal status to a private arrangement substituting for the institution of marriage sanctioned by the State. The question whether change is needed in the law . . . [is best left to] the legislative branch . . .").

Jones v. Daly

176 Cal. Rptr. 130 (Ct. App. 1981)

[The plaintiff, Randal Jones, brought an action against the estate of James Daly, who died in July 1978. Because the trial court sustained the defendant's demurrer without leave to amend, the question on appeal was whether the plaintiff's complaint stated a cause of action.]

LILLIE, J. . . . Plaintiff, Randal Jones, first met James Daly in December 1975. Between that time and March 1976, they "met on frequent occasions, dated, engaged in sexual activities and, in general, acted towards one another as two people do who have discovered a love, one for the other." In March 1976 plaintiff and Daly orally agreed that plaintiff would move into Daly's condominium with Daly, quit his job, go travelling with Daly and "cohabit with him [Daly] as if [they] were, in fact, married." They also entered into an oral agreement (referred to hereinafter, in the language of the complaint, as "cohabitors agreement") whereby each agreed: during the time "they lived and cohabited together," they would combine their efforts and earnings and would share equally any and all property accumulated as a result of their efforts, whether individual or combined, except that Daly would give plaintiff a monthly allowance for his personal use, and they "would hold themselves out to the public at large as cohabiting mates, and [plaintiff] would render his services as a lover, companion, homemaker, traveling companion, housekeeper and cook to Daly"; and "in order that [plaintiff] would be able to devote a substantial portion of his time to Daly's benefit as his lover, companion, homemaker, traveling companion, housekeeper and cook," plaintiff would abandon "a material portion" of his potential career as a model, and in return Daly would furnish financial support to plaintiff for the rest of his life. Pursuant to and in reliance on the "cohabitors agreement," plaintiff and Daly "cohabited and lived together continuously" from March 1976 until Daly's death, and plaintiff allowed himself to be known to the general public "as the lover and cohabitation mate of Daly." Plaintiff performed all of the terms and conditions required to be performed by him under the "cohabitors agreement." During the time that plaintiff and Daly "lived and cohabited together" they acquired, as a result of their efforts and earnings, substantial real and personal property (hereinafter, in the language of the complaint, "cohabitors' equitable property"). Plaintiff does not know the exact nature and extent of such property, but he believes it has a value in excess of $2 million and will amend the complaint to reflect the true value when it is ascertained. Under the "cohabitors agreement," all of the "cohabitors' equitable property" was to be shared and divided equally between plaintiff and Daly. All of such property is in the possession of defendant executors and under their control. Plaintiff has demanded that defendants recognize his interest in the "cohabitors' equitable property," but defendants refuse to do so. . . .

In determining whether the "cohabitors agreement" rests upon illicit meretricious consideration, we are guided by the following principles: "[A] contract between nonmarital partners, even if expressly made in contemplation of a common living arrangement, is invalid only if sexual acts form an inseparable part of the consideration for the agreement. In sum, a court will not enforce a contract for the pooling of property and earnings if it is explicitly and inseparably based upon service as a paramour." (Marvin v. Marvin, supra, 18 Cal. 3d 660, 672.) The complaint herein alleges: Following their initial meeting, plaintiff and Daly "dated, engaged in sexual activities and, in general, acted towards one another as two people do who have discovered a love, one for the other"; plaintiff orally agreed "to cohabit with [Daly] as if [they] were, in fact, married"; at the same time they entered into the "cohabitors agreement" whereby they agreed that during the time "they lived and cohabited together" they would hold themselves out to the public at large as "cohabiting mates" and plaintiff would render his services to Daly as "a *lover*, companion, homemaker, traveling companion, housekeeper and cook" (emphasis added); in order that plaintiff would be able to devote his time to Daly's benefit "as his lover, companion, homemaker, traveling companion, housekeeper and cook," he would abandon his career; plaintiff and Daly "cohabited and lived together" and pursuant to and in reliance on the "cohabitors agreement," plaintiff allowed himself to be known to the general public as the "lover and cohabitation mate" of Daly. These allegations clearly show that plaintiff's rendition of sexual services to Daly was an inseparable part of the consideration for the "cohabitors agreement," and indeed was the predominant consideration. . . .

Marvin states that "even if sexual services are part of the contractual consideration, any *severable* portion of the contract supported by independent consideration will still be enforced." That principle is inapplicable in the present case. There is no severable portion of the "cohabitors agreement" supported by independent consideration. . . . Neither the property sharing nor the support provision of the agreement rests upon plaintiff's acting as Daly's traveling companion, housekeeper or cook as distinguished from acting as his lover. The latter service forms an inseparable part of the consideration for the agreement and renders it unenforceable in its entirety. . . .

The judgment is affirmed.

SPENCER, J. and HANSON, J. concurred.

Questions

Why did the *Marvin* court find it easy to sever the sexual component of the parties' relationship and the *Jones* court find it impossible to do?

We know that Lee didn't want to "give a dime" to Michelle. An antagonistic attitude such as Lee's toward Michelle will typically prevail when the relationship terminates during the defendant's life. Should the court in cases such as *Jones*, where the relationship ended because of the death of one of the partners, assume a similarly antagonistic attitude by the decedent toward the plaintiff? Why didn't the court tell us whether James died intestate, or, if he died with a will, when that will was written? How might consideration of these factors have affected the analysis of the case, particularly with respect to *Marvin's* directive "to protect the parties' lawful expectations"?

Whorton v. Dillingham

248 Cal. Rptr. 405 (Ct. App. 1988)

[The plaintiff, Donnis G. Whorton, brought a breach of contract action against the defendant, Benjamin F. Dillingham, III. Because the trial court sustained the defendant's demurrer without leave to amend, the question on appeal was whether the plaintiff's complaint stated a cause of action.]

WORK, J. . . . The alleged facts include the following. At the time the parties began dating and entered into a homosexual relationship, Whorton was studying to obtain his Associate in Arts degree, intending to enroll in a four year college and obtain a Bachelor of Arts degree. When the parties began living together in 1977, they orally agreed that Whorton's exclusive, full-time occupation was to be Dillingham's chauffeur, bodyguard, social and business secretary, partner and counselor in real estate investments, and to appear on his behalf when requested. Whorton was to render labor, skills, and personal services for the benefit of Dillingham's business and investment endeavors. Additionally, Whorton was to be Dillingham's constant companion, confidant, traveling and social companion, and lover, to terminate his schooling upon obtaining his Associate in Arts degree, and to make no investment without first consulting Dillingham.

In consideration of Whorton's promises, Dillingham was to give him a one-half equity interest in all real estate acquired in their joint names, and in all property thereafter acquired by Dillingham. Dillingham agreed to financially support Whorton for life, and to open bank accounts, maintain a positive balance in those accounts, grant Whorton invasionary powers to savings accounts held in Dillingham's name, and permit Whorton to charge on Dillingham's personal accounts. Dillingham was also to engage in a homosexual relationship with Whorton. Importantly, for the purpose of our analysis, the parties specifically agreed that any portion of the agreement found to be legally unenforceable was severable and the balance of the provisions would remain in full force and effect.

Whorton allegedly complied with all terms of the oral agreement until 1984 when Dillingham barred him from his premises. Dillingham now refuses to perform his part of the contract by giving Whorton the promised consideration for the business services rendered.

Adults who voluntarily live together and engage in sexual relations are competent to contract respecting their earnings and property rights. Such contracts will be enforced "unless expressly and inseparably based upon an illicit consideration of sexual services. . . ." (Marvin v. Marvin). . . .

The holding in *Marvin* suggests the court determined that the contract before it did not *expressly* include sexual services as part of the consideration, and thus, it did not need to reach the issue of whether there were severable portions of the contract supported by independent consideration. The only reference to sexual services in *Marvin*'s alleged facts was that the parties agreed to hold themselves out to the public as husband and wife, which apparently the court did not interpret as expressly indicating sexual services were part of the consideration. . . .

Unlike the facts of *Marvin*, here the parties' sexual relationship was an express, rather than implied, part of the consideration for their contract. The contract cannot be enforced to the extent it is dependent on sexual services for consideration, and the complaint does not state a cause of action to the extent it asks for damages from the termination of the sexual relationship.

The issue here is whether the sexual component of the consideration is severable from the remaining portions of the contract.[29] . . .

Thus, the crux of our analysis is whether Whorton's complaint negates as a matter of law, a trier of fact finding he made contributions, apart from sexual services, which provided independent consideration for Dillingham's alleged promises pertaining to financial support and property rights. The services which plaintiff alleges he agreed to and did provide included being a chauffeur, bodyguard, secretary, and partner and counselor in real estate investments. If provided, these services are of monetary value, and the type for which one would expect to be compensated unless there is evidence of a contrary intent. Thus, they are properly characterized as consideration independent of the sexual aspect of the relationship. By way of comparison, such services as being a constant companion and confidant are not the type which are usually monetarily compensated nor considered to have a "value" for purposes of contract consideration, and, absent peculiar circumstances, would likely be considered so intertwined with the sexual relationship as to be inseparable. . . .

We hold that Whorton—based on allegations he provided Dillingham with services of a chauffeur, bodyguard, secretary, and business partner—has stated a cause of action arising from a contract supported by consideration independent of sexual services. Further, by itemizing the mutual promises to engage in sexual activity, Whorton has not precluded the trier of fact from finding those promises are the consideration for each other and independent of the bargained for consideration for Whorton's employment.

We believe our holding does not conflict with that in *Jones v. Daly* . . . .

Jones is factually different in that the complaining party did not allege contracting to provide services apart from those normally incident to the state of cohabitation itself. Further, Jones's complaint stated the agreement was premised on that they "would hold themselves out to the public at large as cohabiting mates. . . ." In contrast, Whorton's complaint separately itemizes services contracted for as companion, chauffeur, bodyguard, secretary, partner and business counselor. These, except for companion, are significantly different than those household duties normally attendant to non-business cohabitation and are those for which monetary compensation ordinarily would be anticipated. Accepting Whorton's allegations as true, we cannot say as a matter of law any illegal portion of the contract is not severable so as to leave the balance valid

29. Dillingham does not assert *Marvin* is inapplicable to same-sex partners, and we see no legal basis to make a distinction.

and enforceable, especially where it is alleged the parties contemplated such a result when entering into their agreement. . . .

The judgment is reversed.

WIENER, J. and BENKE, J., concur.

Notes

1. *Express Contract Required?* Some jurisdictions have taken the position that only an express contract concerning property division upon dissolution of a domestic partnership is enforceable. They don't recognize an implied contract. See, e.g., Levar v. Elkins, 604 P.2d 602 (Alaska 1980); Estate of Alexander, 445 So. 2d 836 (Miss. 1984); Dominguez v. Cruz, 617 P.2d 1322 (N.M. Ct. App. 1980); Morone v. Morone, 413 N.E.2d 1154 (N.Y. 1980). The *Alexander* court held that if a remedy is to be given to a surviving domestic partner in the absence of an express contract, "the Legislature should provide the remedy." A similar view was expressed in Carnes v. Sheldon, 311 N.W.2d 747 (Mich. Ct. App. 1981). Although prior Michigan cases had held that express contracts are enforceable to the extent they are based on independent consideration and had enforced contracts implied in fact for wages or for the value of commercial services, the court in *Carnes* refused to extend those equitable principles to a case involving a domestic partnership, reasoning that "recovery based on principles of contracts implied in law essentially would resurrect the old common-law marriage doctrine which was specifically abolished by the Legislature. . . . [J]udicial restraint requires that the Legislature, rather than the judiciary, is the appropriate forum for addressing the question raised by plaintiff. We believe a contrary ruling would contravene the public policy of this state 'disfavoring the grant of mutually enforceable property rights to knowingly unmarried cohabitants.'"

2. *Express Written Contract Required?* Should only express *written* contracts be enforceable? Premarital agreements are enforceable only if in writing. See Unif. Premarital Agreement Act § 2 (1983) ("A premarital agreement must be in writing and signed by both parties. It is enforceable without consideration."). Minnesota enacted a statute providing that an express written contract "between a man and a woman who are living together . . . out of wedlock" is valid, even if "sexual relations between the parties are contemplated." The statute also provides that, in the absence of an express written contract, any claim to another's earnings or property must be dismissed as contrary to public policy if it is "based on the fact that the individuals lived together in contemplation of

sexual relations and out of wedlock within or without this state."[30] Minn. Stat. §§ 513.075, .076.

Texas enacted a similar statute providing that "an agreement made on consideration of . . . nonmarital conjugal cohabitation" is enforceable only if it is writing. See Tex. Bus. & Com. Code Ann. § 26.01(b)(3) (effective Aug. 31, 1987). In Zaremba v. Cliburn, 949 S.W.2d 822 (Tex. Ct. App. 1997), the plaintiff, Thomas E. Zaremba, filed suit against Harvey Lavan Cliburn, Jr., aka Van Cliburn. Zaremba alleged that, on or about July 14, 1966, he and Cliburn became close friends and sexual partners and, in 1977, Cliburn asked him to move in with him. He further alleged that at the same time he moved in with Cliburn, he, either orally or impliedly, agreed to provide services like shopping, doing the mail, paying the bills, drafting checks, co-managing the household, and dealing with accountants, creditors, and real estate agents in exchange for a share in Cliburn's income. He contended that 17 years later, Cliburn dissolved their alleged partnership and he received no partnership assets or income. Relying on a Minnesota case applying the Minnesota statute, Hollom v. Carey, 343 N.W.2d 701 (Minn. Ct. App. 1984), the Texas court concluded that the similar Texas statute "bars all unwritten palimonial agreements concerning relationships that continued past the [new statute's] effective date."

The American Law Institute recently promulgated a document entitled The Principles of the Law of Family Dissolution (PLFD). As discussed in greater detail infra p. 106, this document addresses the rights of domestic partners at the dissolution of their partnership. The PLFD provides certain rights automatically to domestic partners who meet the document's definitions, but if the partners wish to alter the remedies available under the PLFD, they must do so in a written agreement signed by both parties. See PLFD §§ 7.01(2)(a),[31]

---

30. This statute does not prevent a cause of action for a constructive trust or a purchase-money resulting trust where the plaintiff contributed monetary consideration toward the purchase of specific property titled in the decedent's name alone. See Estate of Eriksen, 337 N.W.2d 671 (Minn. 1983).

31. Comment b to § 7.01 provides:

> *b. Scope.* . . . This chapter also applies to agreements between domestic partners that would avoid, alter, or augment legal consequences that would otherwise arise under Chapter 6 when their relationship ends. This chapter is not intended, however, to govern contracts between nonmarital partners in jurisdictions that do not follow the principles such as those in Chapter 6. That is because the chapter is designed for agreements that vary otherwise applicable legal norms, such as those that govern the obligations of married couples at divorce, or that govern nonmarital couples who acquire legal obligations to one another by operation of law, as under Chapter 6. This chapter is not intended to govern agreements between persons who have no obligations to one another except as they may create by their agreement. The requirements of this Chapter also do not govern contracts concerning financial claims that one spouse may have at the other's death. Such contracts are covered by the Restatement

7.04(1).

b. Recovery Based On Status?

We now turn to theories of recovery based on status. We first examine instances in which the status of spouse has been debated in such a way that would permit recovery only by opposite-sex couples. We then consider remedies that extend to same-sex partners.

(i) Opposite-Sex Couples Only

Dissolution During Life. Some state courts have held that a cohabitation relationship involving two persons of the opposite sex can have the same force and effect as a legal marriage.[32] For example, in Goode v. Goode, 396 S.E.2d 430 (W. Va. 1990), Martha and Carl Goode separated after having lived together for twenty-eight years. Although the couple had never formally married, they had constantly held themselves out to the public as wife and husband. They had four children. Martha, age forty-seven, filed a divorce action against Carl, age sixty-one, seeking an equitable division of the property they had acquired during their cohabitation. Although West Virginia isn't a common-law marriage state, the court held that Martha could recover, saying:

> [W]e hold that a court may order a division of property acquired by a man and woman who are unmarried cohabitants, but who have considered themselves and held themselves out to be husband and wife. Such order may be based upon principles of contract, either express or implied, or upon a constructive trust. Factors to be considered in ordering such a division of property may include: the purpose, duration, and stability of the relationship and the expectations of the parties. Provided, however, that if either the man or woman is validly married to another person during the period of cohabitation, the property rights of the spouse and support rights of the children of such man or woman shall not in any way be

---

Third, Property (Wills and Other Donative Transfers).

32. For cases providing for equitable division of property acquired while the couple cohabited before marrying or acquired while the couple cohabited after having divorced each other, see, e.g., Eaton v. Johnson, 10 Fam. L. Rep. (BNA) 1094 (Kan. Ct. App. 1983); Pickens v. Pickens, 490 So. 2d 872 (Miss. 1986); In re Marriage of Lindsey, 678 P.2d 328 (Wash. 1984). But see Davis v. Davis, 643 So. 2d 931, 936 (Miss. 1994) (distinguishing *Pickens*, supra, because the claimant had refused an earlier proposal of marriage, had not demonstrated that the $5 million accumulated during the couple's cohabitation was a result of the couple's joint efforts, and had been "well-compensated during and after the relationship"). Accord Malone v. Odom, 657 So. 2d 1112 (Miss. 1995) .

> adversely affected by such division of property.[33] The expectations of the parties under these circumstances would be equitable treatment by the other party in exchange for engaging in such a cohabiting relationship.[34]

A jurisdiction going perhaps even farther toward allowing unmarried plaintiffs to utilize the divorce laws is Washington. In Connell v. Francisco, 898 P.2d 831 (Wash. 1995) (en banc), the Washington Supreme Court relied on the state's marital dissolution statutes for determining the appropriate division of property upon the dissolution of an opposite-sex domestic partnership. Shannon Connell and Richard Francisco lived together from 1983 until their relationship ended in 1990. At the time that they began cohabiting, Connell owned only her own clothing and a leasehold interest in a New York apartment. Francisco had a net worth of approximately $1.3 million that included personal property, real property, and several companies. When the relationship ended, Connell had $10,000 of savings, $10,000 in jewelry, her clothes, an automobile, and her leasehold interest in the New York apartment. Francisco's net worth had increased to over $2.7 million. Connell filed a lawsuit against Francisco "seeking a just and equitable distribution of the property acquired during the relationship." Id. at 833. Based on earlier decisions, most especially Marriage of Lindsey, 678 P.2d 328 (Wash. 1984), the *Connell* court held that, upon a finding of a "meretricious relationship," a court should rely on the principles contained in the Washington statute that provided for a "just and equitable" division of community and separate property upon the dissolution of a marriage. It held, however, that in developing the common law to be applied to meretricious relationships, only some, but not all, of the principles of the marital dissolution statute should apply. Contrary to the rule applicable to married couples, the court held that the property owned by each party prior to

---

33. Under the facts of this case, the parties lived together for an extended period of time, considered themselves as husband and wife, and, in fact, pooled their resources to include taking property under three joint deeds. Therefore, in this case, the equities are more easily determined than in a relationship between two parties which was for a shorter duration, or where the parties did not consider themselves to be husband and wife, or where the parties did not pool their resources. Cases in other jurisdictions have noted that "[e]ach case should be assessed on its own merits with consideration given to the purpose, duration and stability of the relationship and the expectations of the parties." Hay v. Hay, 678 P.2d 672, 674 (Nev. 1984). [Footnote by the court. Eds.]

34. See Thomas v. LaRosa, 400 S.E.2d 809 (W. Va. 1990) (denying domestic partner any recovery and distinguishing *Goode* because her partner was married throughout the period of cohabitation and she knew he had not obtained a valid divorce). Contra, e.g., Koslowski v. Koslowski, 403 A.2d 902 (N.J. 1979); Mullen v. Suchko, 421 A.2d 310 (Pa. Super. 1980).

the relationship should not be subject to division. The court did agree that property acquired during the relationship should be presumed to be community-property-like (i.e., presumed to be owned by both parties regardless of title ownership) in accordance with the marital dissolution statute.

Dissolutions at Death. Although most of the litigation involving opposite-sex partners has focused on property disputes between living partners who have separated, some cases have involved claims by the surviving partner to a share of the decedent's estate. It is interesting to note that reliance on divorce laws (as in *Connell*, above) hasn't led courts to invoke inheritance laws when domestic partnerships end by death. In Peffley-Warner v. Bowen, 778 P.2d 1022 (Wash. 1989) (en banc), the surviving partner, Marilyn Peffley-Warner, appealed a decision of the Social Security Administration that had denied her widow's benefits under the Social Security Act when her opposite-sex partner of twenty-two years died. The Ninth Circuit certified to the Supreme Court of Washington the question of whether Washington law would treat Peffley-Warner as a wife with respect to its intestate statute. If the answer was yes, then Peffley-Warner could prevail because the Social Security Act provides that, even if the applicant was not validly married to the insured (the decedent), she could still qualify "if such applicant would, under the laws applied by such courts in determining the devolution of intestate personal property, have the same status with respect to the taking of such property as a wife . . . ." 42 U.S.C. § 416(h)(1)(A)(ii). The Supreme Court held that "[t]he division of property following termination of an unmarried cohabiting relationship is based on equity, contract or trust, and not on inheritance. . . . Peffley-Warner is neither a surviving spouse nor an heir to [the] decedent . . . . She is therefore not entitled to share in the decedent's estate under Washington laws of intestate succession." Id. at 1027.

However, complaints have also been held to state a cause of action when they sought the imposition of a constructive trust on specific property based on a confidential relationship between the domestic partners. See, e.g., Poe v. Estate of Levy, 411 So.2d 253 (Fla. Ct. App. 1982).

State Legislation. For opposite-sex couples, the doctrine of common-law marriage (discussed supra pp. 83-85) can sometimes turn domestic partners into spouses, thereby conferring the benefits of marriage. To refresh your recollection about common-law marriage, consider the following statutory version of the doctrine, enacted by the legislature of New Hampshire, which introduced a three-year, bright-line rule:

> *N.H. Rev. Stat. Ann. § 457:39. Cohabitation, etc.* Persons cohabiting and acknowledging each other as husband and wife, and generally reputed to be such, for the period of 3 years, and until the decease of one of them, shall thereafter be

deemed to have been legally married.

Federal Law. Congress has extended the definition of marriage beyond state law rules to determine eligibility under some of its entitlement programs. For example, the Supplemental Security Income for the Aged, Blind, and Disabled program, 42 U.S.C. § 1382c(d), provides that

> In determining whether two individuals are husband and wife for purposes of this subchapter, appropriate State law shall be applied; except that—
>
> . . .
>
> (2) if a man and woman are found to be holding themselves out to the community in which they reside as husband and wife, they shall be so considered for purposes of this subchapter notwithstanding any other provision of this section.

See also 20 C.F.R. § 416.1806(a)(3) ("We will consider someone to be your spouse . . . for SSI purposes if . . . "You and an unrelated person of the opposite sex are living together in the same household at or after the time you apply for SSI benefits, and you both lead people to believe that you are husband and wife."). Accord 20 C.F.R. § 1826(c).

(ii) Including Same-Sex Couples

Braschi v. Stahl and Its Progeny. One of the earliest cases involving the right of a same-sex domestic partner to be treated as enjoying the same status as a spouse was Braschi v. Stahl Assoc. Co., 543 N.E.2d 49 (N.Y. 1989). There, the New York Court of Appeals held that the surviving gay partner of a deceased tenant was entitled to the same statutory rent and eviction protections accorded the "surviving spouse of the deceased tenant or some other member of the deceased tenant's family who has been living with the tenant [of record]." The apartment owner argued that the term "family member" should be defined according to the state's intestacy laws. Id. at 52-53. The court rejected that argument, reasoning that

> [i]n the context of eviction, a more realistic, and certainly more valid, view of a family includes two adult lifetime partners whose relationship is long term and characterized by an emotional and financial commitment and interdependence. This view comports both with our society's traditional concept of "family" and with the expectations of individuals who live in such nuclear units . . . .

Id. at 53-54. The court went on to adopt objective standards to determine whether a family relationship existed that warranted statutory protection under the rent and eviction statute and accompanying regulations.

> The determination as to whether an individual is entitled to noneviction protection should be based upon an objective examination of the relationship of the parties. In making this assessment, the lower courts of this State have looked to a number of factors, including the exclusivity and longevity of the relationship, the level of emotional and financial commitment, the manner in which the parties have conducted their everyday lives and held themselves out to society, and the reliance placed upon one another for daily family services. These factors are most helpful, although it should be emphasized that the presence or absence of one or more of them is not dispositive since it is the totality of the relationship as evidenced by the dedication, caring and self-sacrifice of the parties which should, in the final analysis control.

Id. at 55.

In the wake of the *Braschi* decision, regulations were issued enlarging the definition of family member to include "[a]ny other person residing with the tenant . . . as a primary . . . residence . . . who can prove emotional and financial commitment, and interdependence between such person and the tenant." The regulation went on to specify a number of relevant factors that may be included but indicated that "no single factor shall be solely determinative" and "[i]n no event would evidence of a sexual relationship between such persons be required or considered." The listed factors included the sharing of household expenses, the intermingling of finances, participating in family-type activities, formalizing legal obligations toward each other, holding themselves out as family members, performing family functions, and other patterns of behavior demonstrating an intention to create a long-term, emotional committed relationship. N.Y. Comp. Codes, R. & Regs. tit. 9, § 2500.2[n].[35]

While the *Braschi* court showed flexibility in interpreting the word "family," subsequent New York decisions revealed that the same flexibility would not be extended to the word "spouse." In Estate of Cooper, 592 N.Y.S.2d 797 (App. Div.), appeal dismissed, 624 N.E.2d 696 (N.Y. 1993), the surviving gay partner of the decedent argued that he should be allowed to elect against the

---

35. The Division of Housing and Community Renewal (DHCR) indicated that the purpose of the regulations was "to clarify a non-traditional family member's right to remain in his or her home, particularly at a time when a significant percentage of these households may be vulnerable to the AIDS epidemic." Quote of DHCR found in Rent Stabilization Ass'n of New York, Inc. v. Higgins, 630 N.E.2d 626, 630 (N.Y. 1993), cert. denied, 114 S. Ct. 2693 (1994). The deceased tenant in *Braschi* had died of AIDS, but the court did not address the implications of this disease to its ruling. See Joseph G. Arsenault, Comment, "Family" but Not "Parent": The Same-Sex Coupling Jurisprudence of the New York Court of Appeals, 58 Alb. L. Rev. 813, 830-31 (1995).

decedent's will under the New York statute that gives a "surviving spouse" a personal right of election to take a prescribed fraction of the decedent's estate. The partner advanced two arguments to support his claim. The first argument, relying on *Braschi*, was that "surviving spouse" as used in the statute should be construed to include a domestic partner. However, the court rejected this argument, reasoning that the statute's reference to "husband and wife" showed a contrary intention. *Braschi* was distinguished because it construed the term "family member" rather than spouse and because treating a domestic partner as a family member furthered the purpose of the statutory protections regarding rent-controlled apartments. The surviving partner's second argument was that the spousal election statute violated the equal protection clause of the state constitution because it "directly derives from, and compounds, the State's unconstitutional conduct in . . . prohibiting members of the same sex from obtaining marriage licenses." Id. at 799. The court rejected this argument, too, relying on precedents from other states that had upheld the constitutionality of statutes prohibiting same-sex marriage.

In a later case, the surviving gay partner of a decedent challenged the constitutionality of New York's inheritance statute because it precluded him from inheriting the estate of his deceased partner. In re Petri, N.Y.L.J., Apr. 4, 1994, at 29. The *Petri* court held that the inheritance statute was not violative of the surviving partner's rights under either the state or federal constitutions, but it suggested that denying a marriage license to lesbian and gay couples may be unconstitutional:

> The state has a substantial, if not overwhelming, interest in having its descent and distribution scheme clear, simple, predictable and capable of determining heirs at the moment of death. Determination of distributees must be accomplished with a minimum of hearings, investigations and collateral litigation. This can only be accomplished by the establishment of a licensing procedure for the creation of the marital relationship. The Legislature recognized this when it abolished common-law marriages many years ago. . . .
>
> [T]hese considerations apply equally to heterosexual and homosexual couples. Mitchell's [the surviving partner] claim, at best, is that he and decedent had a common law marriage. This is a claim he would be required to establish at a hearing, which hearing would bring into play the same concerns and difficulties that existed prior to the abolition of common-law marriages. Mitchell can not be placed in a better position than any purported common law marriage partner in New York State which, with respect to the laws of intestacy, is no position at all, irrespective of gender or sexual orientation. Accordingly, he has failed to demonstrate any constitutional infirmity in the descent and distribution laws.
>
> The fact that petitioner and decedent could not have obtained a marriage license

> without, at least, recourse to a judicial proceeding does not warrant a different result. This court cannot conclude that no relief would have been available and none was sought here.
>
> Additionally, it should be noted that the requirement of a solemnized marriage may not be assumed to be based on sexual orientation. Section 13 of the Domestic Relations Law has no requirement that applicants for a marriage license be of different sexes. . . .
>
> With no clear precedent, the assumption that same sex marriages are prohibited in New York is premature. . . . It is questionable whether, in this era of domestic partnerships and alternative lifestyle education in grammar schools, it can still be said that marriage has one universal meaning which does not include couples of the same sex.[36]

In Vasquez v. Hawthorne, 994 P.2d 240 (Wash. Ct. App. 2000), petition for review granted, 11 P.3d 825 (Wash. 2000), the decedent, Robert Schwerzler, died intestate, survived by his partner of about 26 years, Frank Vasquez. The trial court awarded Schwerzler's entire intestate estate to Vasquez, but the Washington Court of Appeals reversed, saying:

> We hold that a same-sex [couple cannot] have a "quasi-marital" relationship. Same-sex persons may not legally marry and such a relationship is not entitled to the rights and protections of a quasi-marriage, such as community property-like treatment.

On October 11, 2000, the Supreme Court of Washington granted a petition for review of the Court of Appeals decision.

Recognition of Domestic Partnerships by Corporations, Universities, and Municipalities. While no jurisdiction in the United States gives domestic partners all of the benefits of marriage, a number of American cities have extended the same employee benefits such as health insurance to the domestic partners (of the same or different sex) of city employees that are extended to spouses of city employees. Berkeley, San Francisco,[37] Santa Cruz, and West Hollywood, California, Denver, Colorado, Ann Arbor and East Lansing,

---

36. But see Storrs v. Holcomb, 645 N.Y.S.2d 286 (Sup. Ct. 1996) (holding that marriage in New York is limited to opposite-sex couples and that the gender classification serves a valid public purpose). Eds.

37. In 1996, the San Francisco Board of Supervisors approved an ordinance prohibiting the city government from contracting with companies that do not make the same benefits available to employees' domestic partners that they do to spouses of employees. Similar ordinances have been enacted in Seattle and Los Angeles. See Roberto Ceniceros, Seattle, L.A. Pass Mandates on Partner Benefits, Dec. 6, 1999, at 1 (available in Lexis, News library, Curnws file).

Michigan, Ithaca, New York, and Seattle, Washington, are among the cities in the vanguard of this movement. See Mary P. Treuthart, Adopting a More Realistic Definition of "Family," 26 Gonz. L. Rev. 91, 101-05 (1990/91). Many businesses also offer benefits to employees' domestic partners, including IBM, Apple, Eastman Kodak, Hewlett-Packard, Microsoft, Sun Microsystems, Time Warner, Walt Disney, Xerox, Citigroup, J.P. Morgan, Goldman Sachs Group, Merrill Lynch, and the "big three" car makers, General Motors, Ford, and DaimlerChrysler. More than 70 of the top law firms also provide domestic partner benefits, as do many universities. For information about the employers offering these benefits, see the Human Rights Campaign's website, www.hrc.org.

In Tanner v. Oregon Health Sciences University, 971 P.2d 435 (Or. Ct. App. 1998), a court ruled for the first time in the United States that public agencies must extend medical, life, and dental insurance benefits to domestic partners of their employees on the same basis that the benefits are available to married spouses of their employees. The court based its decision on state constitutional grounds.

Recognition of Domestic Partnerships by the American Law Institute. As mentioned supra p. 98, the American Law Institute has recently approved the final version of The Principles of the Law of Family Dissolution (PLFD). Chapter 6 of the PLFD concerns domestic partners. Professor Ira Mark Ellman, the chief reporter, has summarized the approach of Chapter 6 as follows:

> Chapter 6's treatment of domestic partners does not adopt the contractual approach most often associated with the California Supreme Court's decision in *Marvin v. Marvin*, but instead follows more recent trends that treat persons as having entered a relationship with legal significance when they live together and share a life together for a sufficient period of time. These trends are most evident in the law of some foreign countries, particularly Canada and Australia. Under the formulation adopted by the Institute, parties who live together with their common child, for the required minimum time period, are deemed domestic partners. The required time period is left for the adopting jurisdiction to choose, but the commentary suggests that a two-year period would be reasonable. Unrelated parties who do not have a common child are presumed to be domestic partners if they share a common household for a separately-established minimum period, the commentary suggesting a three-year period as a reasonable choice. The resulting presumption is rebuttable by evidence that the parties did not "share a life together as a couple," a defined phrase that is elaborated upon in the commentary. Parties may also be treated as domestic partners if one of them shows that they shared a common household and a life together for a "significant period of time," even if that time is less than the minimum periods set in the other provisions. Once parties are considered domestic partners, the dissolution of their relationship triggers

> property and compensatory payment (alimony) remedies that overlap almost entirely with those available at the dissolution of marriage. It should be noted that Chapter 6 addresses only the legal claims that the domestic partners have against one another at the dissolution of their relationship. Nothing in the chapter requires third parties, such as employers or government agencies, to accord any special treatment of the domestic partners. The relationship of third parties to married couples, or unmarried domestic partners, is not within the scope of the ALI's Family Dissolution project. Chapter 6 makes no distinction between opposite-sex and same-sex couples, incorporating both within its rules.

Ira Mark Ellman, ALI Family Law Report, Sept. 11, 2000 (available at www.ssrn.com, abstract no. 241418).

The Restatement 3d of Property § 2.2 Comment g states:

> *g. Domestic partner*. . . . To the extent that a domestic partner is treated [by the PLFD] as having the status of a spouse, conferring rights on such a partner on the dissolution of the relationship, the domestic partner who remains in that relationship with the decedent until the decedent's death should be treated as a legal spouse for purposes of intestacy.

The Need for Legislative Solutions. Many legal scholars have urged state legislatures and the Uniform Law Commission to recognize and protect the property interests of domestic partners based on their status. For recent articles in this vein, see, for example, T.P. Gallanis, Default Rules, Mandatory Rules, and the Movement for Same-Sex Equality, 60 Ohio St. L. J.1513 (1999); Susan N. Gary, Adapting Intestacy Laws to Changing Families, 18 Law & Ineq. 1 (2000); E. Gary Spitko, The Expressive Function of Succession Law and the Merits of Non-Marital Inclusion, 41 Ariz. L. Rev. 1063 (1999). Scholars have also encouraged practicing lawyers to help domestic partners prepare and execute the documents necessary to protect themselves. See, for example, Jennifer K. Robbennolt & Monica Kirkpatrick Johnson, Legal Planning for Unmarried Committed Partners: Empirical Lessons for a Preventive and Therapeutic Approach, 41 Ariz. L. Rev. 417 (1999).

A Legislative Proposal. Compare the following proposal, drafted by Lawrence Waggoner, with the New Hampshire statute set forth supra p. 101 and with the factors mentioned by the court in *Braschi*:

Intestate Share of Committed Partner
(Working Draft, Jan. 20, 1995)[38]

(a) *[Amount.]* If an unmarried, adult decedent dies without a valid will and leaves a surviving committed partner, the decedent's surviving committed partner is entitled to:

(1) the first [$50,000], plus one-half of any balance of the intestate estate, if:

(A) no descendant or parent of the decedent survives the decedent; or

(B) all of the decedent's surviving descendants are also descendants of the surviving committed partner and there is no other descendant of the surviving committed partner who survives the decedent;

(2) one-half of the intestate estate, in cases not covered by paragraph (1).

(b) *[Committed Partner; Requirements.]* To be the decedent's committed partner, the individual must, at the decedent's death: (i) have been an unmarried adult; (ii) not have been prohibited from marrying the decedent under the law of this state by reason of a blood relationship to the decedent; and (iii) have been sharing a common household with the decedent in a marriage-like relationship. Only one individual can qualify as the decedent's committed partner for purposes of this section.

(c) *[Common Household.]* For purposes of subsections (b) and (e), "sharing a common household" or "shared a common household" means that the decedent and the individual shared the same place to live, whether or not one or both had other places to live and whether or not one or both were physically residing somewhere else at the decedent's death. The right to occupy the common household need not have been in both of their names.

(d) *[Marriage-like Relationship; Factors.]* For purposes of subsection (b), a "marriage-like relationship" is a relationship that corresponds to the relationship between marital partners, in which two individuals have chosen to share one another's lives in a long-term, intimate, and committed relationship of mutual caring. Although no single factor or set of factors determines whether a relationship qualifies as marriage-like, the following factors are among those to be considered:

(1) the purpose, duration, constancy, and degree of exclusivity of the relationship;

(2) the degree to which the parties intermingled their finances, such as by maintaining joint checking, credit card, or other types of accounts, sharing loan obligations, sharing a mortgage or lease on the household in which they lived or on other property, or titling the household in which they lived or other property in joint tenancy;

(3) the degree to which the parties formalized legal obligations, intentions,

---

38. An earlier version of this statute is found in Lawrence W. Waggoner, Marital Property Rights in Transition, 59 Mo. L. Rev. 21 (1994).

and responsibilities to one another, such as by one or both naming the other as primary beneficiary of life insurance or employee benefit plans or as agent to make health care decisions;

(4) whether the couple shared in co-parenting a child and the degree of joint care and support given the child;

(5) whether the couple joined in a marriage or a commitment ceremony, even if the ceremony was not of a type giving rise to a presumption under subsection (e)(3); and

(6) the degree to which the couple held themselves out to others as married or the degree to which the couple held themselves out to others as emotionally and financially committed to one another on a permanent basis.

(e) *[Presumption.]* An individual's relationship with the decedent is presumed to have been marriage-like if:

(1) during the [six] year period next preceding the decedent's death, the decedent and the individual shared a common household for periods totaling at least [five] years;

(2) the decedent or the individual registered or designated the other as his [or her] domestic partner with and under procedures established by an organization and neither partner executed a document terminating or purporting to terminate the registration or designation;

(3) the decedent and the individual joined in a marriage or a commitment ceremony conducted and contemporaneously certified in writing by an organization; or

(4) the individual is the parent of a child of the decedent, or is or was a party to a written co-parenting agreement with the decedent regarding a child, and if, in either case, the child lived before the age of 18 in the common household of the decedent and the individual.

(f) *[Force of the Presumption].* If a presumption arises under subsection (e) because only one of the listed factors is established, the presumption is rebuttable by a preponderance of the evidence. If more than one of the listed factors is established, the presumption can only be rebutted by clear and convincing evidence.

A recent empirical study based on a telephone survey found the following. When asked how they would divide the estate of a person survived by parents and a domestic partner, nearly 65 percent of persons in a same-sex committed relationship said they would give the entire estate to the person's partner. When the same question was asked of the general public, about 45 percent of the respondents said they would divide the estate equally between the partner and the parents and over two-thirds of the general public group would give the partner 50 percent or more. When asked how they would divide the estate of a person survived by a child from a prior relationship and a domestic partner, nearly 60 percent of the same-sex couples surveyed would divide the estate equally between the child and the partner. About a third of the general public respondents favored the estate being shared equally by the child and the partner and about a third of them favored the child receiving the entire estate. See Mary Louise Fellows et al., Committed Partners and Inheritance: An Empirical Study, 16 Law & Ineq. J. 1 (1998).

Same-Sex Marriage in the United States. One possible, but controversial, answer to discrimination based on sexual orientation is to allow same-sex marriage. This issue gained public prominence in the United States as a result of the Hawaii Supreme Court's decision in Baehr v. Lewin, 852 P.2d 44 (Haw. 1993). The Hawaii constitution provides that "no person shall . . . be denied the equal protection of the laws, nor be denied the enjoyment of the person's civil rights or be discriminated against in the exercise thereof because of race, religion, *sex* or ancestry." Haw. Const. art I, § 5 (emphasis added). The court held that the state was denying same-sex couples the right to marry based on the sex of the applicants. In accordance with its equal protection clause, the state was therefore required to demonstrate a compelling state interest why same-sex couples should be denied the right to marry. The court remanded the case for trial to hear evidence on that issue. The trial court postponed its hearing so that it might take into account the recommendations of the newly established Commission on Sexual Orientation and the Law. In the interim, the Hawaii legislature passed a bill in 1994 affirming marriage as intended for opposite-sex couples capable of procreation.[39] The Commission reported back in December 1995 that denial of a marriage license to same-sex couples was a denial of equal protection on the basis of the sex of the applicants. See David W. Dunlap, Panel in Hawaii Recommends Legalizing Same-Sex Marriage, N.Y. Times, Dec. 11, 1995, at A11. The trial court subsequently heard the case and ruled in late 1996 that the state had failed to meet its burden of showing that prohibiting same-sex couples from marrying was necessary to achieve a compelling state interest. See Baehr v. Miike, Civ. No. 91-1394, 1996 WL 694235 (Haw. Cir. Ct. Dec. 3, 1996). The court granted the state's motion to stay the ruling pending an appeal to the Hawaii Supreme Court.

In a preemptive effort to prevent having to recognize Hawaii same-sex

---

39. For cases upholding the state's power to limit marital status to heterosexual couples, see Jones v. Hallahan, 501 S.W.2d 588 (Ky. 1973); Baker v. Nelson, 191 N.W.2d 185 (Minn. 1971), appeal dismissed, 409 U.S. 810 (1972); Singer v. Hara, 522 P.2d 1187 (Wash. Ct. App. 1974). Except for *Baehr*, more recent cases have reached the same result. See Dean v. District of Columbia, 653 A.2d 307 (D.C. App. 1995); Storrs v. Holcomb, 645 N.Y.S.2d 286 (Sup. Ct. 1996).

marriages, several states enacted anti-same-sex marriage legislation.[40] See David W. Dunlap, Fearing a Toehold for Gay Marriages, Conservatives Rush to Bar the Door, N.Y. Times, Mar. 6, 1996, at A7. The federal government also took preemptive action. In a midnight signing ceremony, President Clinton signed the Defense of Marriage Act. See Todd S. Purdom, Gay Rights Groups Attack Clinton on Midnight Signing, N.Y. Times, Sept. 22, 1996, § 1, at 10. The Act allows states to refuse to recognize same-sex marriages of another state. It also provides that the term "marriage" as used in all federal statutes or agency rulings, regulations, or interpretations means "only a legal union between one man and one woman as husband and wife" and the term "spouse" means "only a person of the opposite sex who is a husband or a wife." See Pub. L. No. 104-199, 110 Stat. 2419, codified at 1 U.S.C. § 7.

In the end, Hawaii did not legalize same-sex marriage. Instead, the state legislature enacted the Reciprocal Beneficiaries Act, which became law without the Governor's signature on July 8, 1997. See Haw. Rev. Stat. § 572C-1. Under the Act, any "two individuals who are legally prohibited from marrying under state law" are permitted to register as reciprocal beneficiaries, thereby entitling them to many, but not all, of the benefits of marriage, including the right to create joint tenancies, to claim an elective share in the other's estate, to enjoy protections against unintentional disinheritance, to make health care decisions for the other, to file an action in the event of the other's wrongful death, and to claim the other's governmental pension benefits.

The same-sex marriage debate moved to Vermont in 1999, when the Vermont Supreme Court issued its pathbreaking decision in Baker v. Vermont, 744 A.2d 864 (Vt. 1999). In that decision, the court held that excluding same-sex couples from the benefits of marriage violated the "common benefits" clause of the Vermont constitution:

> May the State of Vermont exclude same-sex couples from the benefits and protections that its laws provide to opposite-sex married couples? That is the

---

40. Before the Hawaii controversy began, eight states already had language in their marriage statutes that precluded same-sex marriage (Arizona, Colorado, Indiana, Louisiana, Maryland, Minnesota, Texas, and Virginia). See Lesbian/Gay Law Notes, Summer 1996, at 102. As of Spring 2000, thirty-three states had laws denying recognition to same-sex marriages. See Human Rights Campaign, Law Briefs, Spring 2000, at 3. The Michigan statute, enacted in 1996, provides: "Marriage is inherently a unique relationship between a man and a woman. As a matter of public policy, this state has a special interest in encouraging, supporting, and protecting that unique relationship in order to promote, among other goals, the stability and welfare of society and its children. A marriage contracted between individuals of the same sex is invalid in this state." Mich. Comp. Laws Ann. § 551.1.

fundamental question we address in this appeal, a question that the Court well knows arouses deeply-felt religious, moral, and political beliefs. Our constitutional responsibility to consider the legal merits of issues properly before us provides no exception for the controversial case. The issue before the Court, moreover, does not turn on the religious or moral debate over intimate same-sex relationships, but rather on the statutory and constitutional basis for the exclusion of same-sex couples from the secular benefits and protections offered married couples.

We conclude that under the Common Benefits Clause of the Vermont Constitution, which, in pertinent part, reads,

> That government is, or ought to be, instituted for the common benefit, protection, and security of the people, nation, or community, and not for the particular emolument or advantage of any single person, family, or set of persons, who are a part only of that community,

Vt. Const., ch. I, art 7., plaintiffs may not be deprived of the statutory benefits and protections afforded persons of the opposite sex who choose to marry. We hold that the State is constitutionally required to extend to same-sex couples the common benefits and protections that flow from marriage under Vermont law. Whether this ultimately takes the form of inclusion within the marriage laws themselves or a parallel "domestic partnership" system or some equivalent statutory alternative, rests with the Legislature. Whatever system is chosen, however, must conform with the constitutional imperative to afford all Vermonters the common benefit, protection, and security of the law.

The Vermont legislature responded to the *Baker* decision by enacting legislation enabling same-sex (but not opposite-sex) couples to enter into civil unions. The legislation became effective on July 1, 2000. Under the new law, same-sex couples who enter into civil unions "shall have all the same benefits, protections and responsibilities under law, whether they derive from statute, administrative or court rule, policy, common law or any other source of civil law, as are granted to spouses in a marriage." Vt. Stat. Ann. tit. 15, §1204(a). The legislation further states that parties to a civil union "shall be included in any definition or use of the terms 'spouse,' 'family,' 'immediate family,' 'dependent,' 'next of kin,' and other terms that denote the spousal relationship, as those terms are used throughout the law." Vt. Stat. Ann. tit. 15, §1204(b).

As this casebook goes to press, the civil union law is relatively new, and it is too soon to ascertain its full impact. A year after the law was signed, 502 Vermont couples and 1,977 couples from out of state have entered civil unions, with women outnumbering men by about two to one. See Carey Goldberg, Quiet Anniversary for Civil Unions, N.Y Times, July 31, 2001, at A14. Initial reports also suggest that Vermont residents are deeply divided on whether the civil union law should remain in force. See Carey Goldberg, Vermont Residents

DH-PHS-CU-00

DEPARTMENT OF HEALTH

VERMONT LICENSE AND CERTIFICATE OF CIVIL UNION

LOCAL FILE NUMBER — STATE FILE NUMBER

TYPE OR PRINT IN BLACK INK. SEE MANUAL FOR INSTRUCTIONS.

106501

PARTY A

1. NAME (First, Middle, Last) | 1b. MAIDEN SURNAME (If Applicable) | 1c. DATE OF BIRTH (Month, Day, Year)

2. SEX | 3. MAILING ADDRESS (Street and Number or Rural Route Number, City or Town, State, Zip Code)

4a. USUAL RESIDENCE – STATE | 4b. CITY OR TOWN | 5. BIRTHPLACE (State or Foreign Country)

6a. FATHER'S NAME (First, Middle, Last) | 6b. BIRTHPLACE (State or Foreign Country) | 7a. MOTHER'S NAME (First, Middle, Maiden Surname) | 7b. Birthplace (State or Foreign Country)

PARTY B

8a. NAME (First, Middle, Last) | 8b. MAIDEN SURNAME (If Applicable) | 8c. DATE OF BIRTH (Month, Day, Year)

9. SEX | 10. MAILING ADDRESS (Street and Number or Rural Route Number, City or Town, State, Zip Code)

11a. USUAL RESIDENCE – STATE | 11b. CITY OR TOWN | 12. BIRTHPLACE (State or Foreign Country)

13a. FATHER'S NAME (First, Middle, Last) | 13b. BIRTHPLACE (State or Foreign Country) | 14a. MOTHER'S NAME (First, Middle, Maiden Surname) | 14b. Birthplace (State or Foreign Country)

APPLICANTS

We hereby certify that the information provided is correct to the best of our knowledge and belief and that we are free to form a civil union under the laws of Vermont.

15a. SIGNATURE | 15b. DATE SIGNED | 15c. SIGNATURE | 15d. DATE SIGNED

CERTIFICATION

I hereby certify that the above named persons have made oath to the truth of the facts stated in the foregoing declaration and complied with the civil union laws of the State of Vermont.

16a. DATE ON WHICH LICENSE WAS ISSUED (Month, Day, Year)

16b. TOWN CLERK (Signature)

16c. TOWN OR CITY

16d. THIS LICENSE IS VALID FROM ______ (DATE)

TO ______ (DATE) UNLESS WAIVED BY A VERMONT COURT

OFFICIANT

This license authorizes the establishment of a civil union IN VERMONT ONLY of the above named parties by any person duly authorized to certify a civil union.

17a. I CERTIFY THAT THE ABOVE PERSONS ESTABLISHED A CIVIL UNION ON (Month, Day, Year) DATE > | 17b. IN THE CITY OR TOWN OF

17c. SIGNATURE OF OFFICIANT

17d. NAME (Type/Print) | 17e. TITLE

17f. ADDRESS OF OFFICIANT (Street and Number or Rural Route Number, City or Town, State, Zip Code)

REGISTRATION

18a. CLERK'S SIGNATURE | 18b. DATE RECEIVED BY LOCAL REGISTRAR

19a. TRUE COPY – (Clerk's Signature) (To be signed by Registrar on copy only) | 19b. TOWN | 19c. DATE

Attest:

CONFIDENTIAL INFORMATION. THE INFORMATION BELOW MUST BE COMPLETED. IT WILL NOT APPEAR ON CERTIFIED COPIES OF THE RECORD.

PARTY A

20. NAME | IF PREVIOUSLY MARRIED OR IN A CIVIL UNION: LAST MARRIAGE OR CIVIL UNION ENDED BY — ☐ DEATH ☐ DISSOLUTION ☐ DIVORCE ☐ ANNULMENT (23a.) | DATE MONTH YEAR (23b.) | EDUCATION (Specify only highest grade completed) Elementary or Secondary (0-12) | College (1-4 OR 5+) (24.)

21. RACE – White, Black, American Indian, etc. (Specify) | 22. TOTAL NO. OF CIVIL UNIONS OR MARRIAGES INCLUDING THIS ONE

PARTY B

25. NAME | IF PREVIOUSLY MARRIED OR IN A CIVIL UNION: LAST MARRIAGE OR CIVIL UNION ENDED BY — ☐ DEATH ☐ DISSOLUTION ☐ DIVORCE ☐ ANNULMENT (28a.) | DATE MONTH YEAR (28b.) | EDUCATION (Specify only highest grade completed) Elementary or Secondary (0-12) | College (1-4 OR 5+) (29.)

26. RACE – White, Black, American Indian, etc. (Specify) | 27. TOTAL NO. OF CIVIL UNIONS OR MARRIAGES INCLUDING THIS ONE

Split Over Civil Unions Law, N.Y. Times, Sept. 3, 2000, § 1, at 14. Precisely what effect this law will have beyond the borders of Vermont remains to be seen.[41] Voters in Nebraska have already responded by approving a proposed constitutional amendment that reads in pertinent part: "The uniting of two persons of the same sex in a civil union, domestic partnership or other similar same-sex relationship shall not be valid or recognized in Nebraska." Pam Belluck, Nebraskans to Vote on Most Sweeping Ban on Gay Unions, N.Y. Times, Oct. 21, 2000, at A7; Veronica Daehn, Gay Activists: 416's Passage May Deter U. Nebraska Applicants, Daily Nebraskan Via U-Wire, Nov. 10, 2000 (available in Lexis, News library, Curnws file).

Many persons who are joined in their commitment to antidiscrimination policies for lesbians and gay men are divided on the issue of same-sex marriage. The high pitch of the public debate about the issue has made complex and nuanced exploration of its implications that much more difficult.[42] See David L.

---

41. In Matter of an Application for a Change of Name by Jill Iris Bacharach to Assume the Name of Jill Iris Bacharach-Bordman, ___ A. 2d ___ (N.J. Super. Ct. App. Div. 2001), the court, reversing a decision of the trial court, held that a name-change application by a New Jersey woman who had been civilly united with her partner in Vermont could not be denied. The court said:

> Appellant and her partner can exchange rings, proclaim devotion in a public or private ceremony, call their relationship a marriage, use the same surname, adopt and rear children. All these actions may be taken in full public view. None are offensive to the laws or stated policies of this state. To deny the applicant a statutory change of a portion of her surname . . . is . . . inherently discriminatory [,and] the denial of her request was a misapplication of judicial discretion . . . .

42. The issue of same-sex marriage has generated considerable scholarship. See John Boswell, Same-Sex Unions in Premodern Europe (1994); William N. Eskridge, Jr., The Case for Same-Sex Marriage (1996); Ruthann Robson, Lesbian (Out)law: Survival Under the Rule of Law (1992); Lesbian and Gay Marriage: Private Commitments, Public Ceremonies (Suzanne Sherman, ed., 1992); Thomas B. Stoddard & Paula Ettelbrick, Legalizing Lesbian and Gay Marriages: A Conversation for Many Voices (1989); Mary Becker, Strength in Diversity: Feminist Theoretical Approaches to Child Custody and Same-Sex Relationships, 23 Stetson L. Rev. 701 (1994); Jennifer Gerarda Brown, Competitive Federalism and the Legislative Incentives to Recognize Same-Sex Marriage, 68 S. Cal. L. Rev. 745 (1995); Craig W. Christensen, If Not Marriage? On Securing Gay and Lesbian Family Values by a "Simulacrum of Marriage," 66 Fordham L. Rev. 1699 (1998); William N. Eskridge, Jr., A History of Same-Sex Marriage, 79 Va. L. Rev. 1419 (1993); Steven K. Homer, Against Marriage, 29 Harv. C.R.-C.L. L. Rev. 505 (1994); Nan D. Hunter, Marriage, Law and Gender: A Feminist Legal Inquiry, 1 Law & Sexuality 9 (1991); Kathryn E. Kovacs, Recognizing Gay and Lesbian Families: Marriage and Parental Rights, 5 Law & Sexuality 513 (1995); Sylvia A. Law, Homosexuality and the Social Meaning of Gender, 1988 Wis. L. Rev. 187; Arthur S. Leonard, Lesbian and Gay Families and the Law: A Progress Report, 21 Fordham Urb. L.J. 927 (1994); Nancy Polikoff, We Will Get What We Ask For: Why Legalizing Gay and Lesbian Marriage Will Not "Dismantle the Legal Structure of Gender in Every Marriage," 79 Va. L. Rev. 1535 (1993); Robin West, Universalism, Liberal Theory, and the Problem of Gay Marriage, 25 Fla. St. U. L. Rev. 705 (1998); Evan Wolfson, Crossing the

Chambers, What If? The Legal Consequences of Marriage and the Legal Needs of Lesbian and Gay Male Couples, 95 Mich. L. Rev. 447 (1996).

Same-Sex Marriage Outside the United States. In September 2000, the Netherlands became the first and only country to give full marriage rights to partners in same-sex unions. Under the new law, effective in April 2001, gay and lesbian couples may marry at city hall, divorce in the same manner as heterosexuals, and adopt Dutch children. See Same-Sex Dutch Couples Gain Marriage and Adoption Rights, N.Y. Times, Dec. 20, 2000, at A6; Dutch Legislators Approve Full Marriage Rights for Gays, N.Y. Times, Sept. 13, 2000, at A4.

Although no other country grants such full equality, same-sex civil unions in Europe have existed for more than a decade. Denmark led the way in 1989, followed by Norway, Sweden, and Iceland in the mid-1990s. Hungary joined the group in 1996, as did Switzerland in 1998 and Germany in 2001 (although a constitutional challenge to the German legislation is pending). See Nicola Branch, The Struggle for Equal Status, The Guardian (London), May 22, 1999, at 19; Valentine Low, Ken's Late at the Altar: Europe Sets Trend for Gay "Marriages," Evening Standard (London), July 3, 2000, at 7; Harassment Goes Hand-in-Hand With New Freedom For Gays, Agence France Presse, Oct. 13, 1999 (available in Lexis, News library, Curnws file); German Constitutional Court Green Lights "Gay Marriage" Law, Agence France Presse, July 18, 2001 (available in Lexis, News library, Curnws file); Reuters, Same-Sex Partners Win Legal Status in Germany, N.Y. Times, Aug. 2, 2001, at A3. In each of these countries, same-sex couples who register are granted many of the same rights as opposite-sex couples who are married or (where this is available) who have similarly registered as domestic partners. One notable exception, however, is the right to adopt. None of these countries permits domestic partners to adopt, except Denmark, which enacted this reform in 1999. See Branch, supra, at 19.

In Italy and Spain, domestic partnership ceremonies are offered by some local governments, but not at the national level. See Harassment, supra.

In 1999, the French Parliament created the civil solidarity pact, a domestic

---

Threshold: Equal Marriage Rights for Lesbian and Gay Men and the Intracommunity Critique, 21 N.Y.U. Rev. L. & Soc. Change 567 (1994-95); Craig A. Bowman & Blake M. Cornish, Note, A More Perfect Union: A Legal and Social Analysis of Domestic Partnership Ordinances, 92 Colum. L. Rev. 1164 (1992); Alissa Friedman, Note, The Necessity for State Recognition of Same-Sex Marriage: Constitutional Requirements and Evolving Notions of Family, 3 Berkely Women's L.J. 134 (1988); William M. Hohengarten, Note, Same-Sex Marriage and the Right of Privacy, 103 Yale L.J. 1495 (1994); Note, The Legality of Homosexual Marriage, 82 Yale L.J. 573 (1973); Developments in the Law Note–Sexual Orientation and the Law, 102 Harv. L. Rev. 1508 (1989).

partnership arrangement for same- and opposite-sex couples. The pact (known by its French acronym, PACS) provides some benefits, for example in the areas of employment and taxation, but it provides no rights to inheritance or adoption. See Suzanne Daley, French Couples Take Plunge That Falls Short of Marriage, N.Y. Times, Apr. 18, 2000, at A1.

In June 2000, Brazil became the first Latin American country to offer partial recognition to same-sex couples, enabling them to inherit each other's social security and pension benefits, and to name a partner as a dependent for income tax purposes. See Larry Rohter, Brazil Grants Some Legal Recognition to Same-Sex Couples, N.Y. Times, June 10, 2000, at A3.

Countries shaped by the English common law have been much slower than their civilian counterparts to grant rights to same-sex couples. Still, there have been signs of change. Immigration regulations in Australia, New Zealand, Canada, and the United Kingdom allow entry and residency to be established on the basis of same-sex domestic partnerships. See Deb Price, Gays Need Equality on Dual-Passport Issue, Detroit News, Feb. 21, 2000, at A9. In 1999, British Columbia extended intestacy rights to domestic partners by allowing them to qualify as common-law spouses if they have "cohabited with another person, for a period of at least 2 years immediately before the other person's death, in a marriage-like relationship, including a marriage-like relationship between persons of the same gender." Estate Administration Act 1996 § 1(b), as amended by the Definition of Spouse Amendment Act 1999. Also in 1999, the Supreme Court of Canada ruled that Ontario's Family Law Act was unconstitutional because it limited the definition of "spouse" to heterosexuals. See M v. H, 171 D.L.R. 4th 577 (Can. 1999). How this decision will affect other statutes and other Canadian provinces remains to be seen.

Related Estate Planning Issues. All fifty states and the District of Columbia permit an individual to designate someone (a proxy) to make health care decisions when that individual is incapacitated. For an example of a health care proxy statute, see the Uniform Health-Care Decisions Act §§ 2-4 (1993) (UHCDA), discussed in Chapter 9. If an individual fails to make a designation, the statutes typically identify a class of persons who may serve as surrogate decisionmakers. The UHCDA lists in § 5(b) the following family members in descending order of priority who may act as surrogate: the spouse, an adult child, a parent, or an adult sibling. In § 5(c), it provides that "[i]f none of the individuals eligible to act as surrogate under subsection (b) is reasonably available, an adult who has exhibited special care and concern for the patient, who is familiar with the patient's personal values, and who is reasonably available may act as surrogate." The commentary warns that for "those in non-traditional relationships who want to make certain that health-care decisions are made by their companions[, they] should execute powers of attorney for health care designating them as agents . . . ."

Another issue that arises concerns the appointment of a guardian or conservator for persons who become incapacitated and who have otherwise failed to provide for the event of incapacity through use of a durable power of attorney. All states provide for the appointment of guardians or conservators who are given the authority to handle incapacitated persons' financial matters as well as to make other decisions necessary for their care. Here, the uniform law on point is the Uniform Guardianship and Protective Proceedings Act (1997) (UGPPA). Unfortunately, when listing the categories of persons who may serve as guardians, the UGPPA and the law of most states give low priority to domestic partners.

On the poor treatment of domestic partners in the UHCDA and UGPPA, see T.P. Gallanis, Default Rules, Mandatory Rules, and the Movement for Same-Sex Equality, 60 Ohio St. L. J. 1519 (1999).

Transsexual as Surviving Spouse? Can a transsexual who married the decent be the decent's surviving spouse for purposes of intestate succession in a state prohibiting same-sex marriage? See Estate of Gardner, 22 P.3d 1086 (Kan. Ct. App. 2001) (remanding case for trial to determine whether survivor was a female when the marriage license to the male intestate was issued).

External References. Writings on the topic of the legal rights of domestic partners are legion. Here are references to a few of them. Philip Blumstein & Pepper Schwartz, American Couples: Money, Work, Sex (1983); Geertje Else Wiersma, Cohabitation: An Alternative to Marriage? (1983); Mary S. Bruch, Cohabitation in the Common Law Countries a Decade After *Marvin*: Settled in or Moving Ahead?, 22 U. C. Davis L. Rev. 717 (1989); Robert C. Casad, Unmarried Couples and Unjust Enrichment: From Status to Contract and Back Again?, 77 Mich. L. Rev. 47 (1978); H. Jay Folberg & William P. Buren, Domestic Partnership: A Proposal for Dividing the Property of Unmarried Families, 12 Willamette L. Rev. 453 (1976); Harry D. Krause, Legal Position: Unmarried Couples, 34 Am. J. Comp. L. 533 (Supp. 1986); Sol Lovas, When Is a Family Not a Family? Inheritance and the Taxation of Inheritance within the Non-Traditional Family, 24 Idaho L. Rev. 353 (1987); Rebecca L. Melton, Legal Rights of Unmarried Heterosexual and Homosexual Couples and Evolving Definitions of Family, 29 J. Family L. 497 (1991); Brooke Oliver, Contracting for Cohabitation: Adapting the California Statutory Marital Contract to Life Partnership Agreements between Lesbian, Gay or Unmarried Heterosexual Couples, 23 Golden Gate U.L. Rev. 899 (1993); Susan W. Prager, Sharing Principles and the Future of Marital Property Law, 25 UCLA

L. Rev. 1 (1977); Maimon Schwarzschild, Same-Sex Marriage and Constitutional Privacy: Moral Threat and Legal Anomaly, 4 Berkeley Women's L.J. 94 (1988-89); Jana A. Singer, The Privatization of Family Law, 1992 Wis. L. Rev. 1443; Mary P. Treuthart, Adopting a More Realistic Definition of "Family," 26 Gonz. L. Rev. 91 (1990/91); William V. Veter, Restrictions on Equal Treatment of Unmarried Domestic Partners, 5 B.U. Pub. Int. L.J. 1 (1995); Stacey L. Boyle, Note, Marital Status Classifications: Protecting Homosexual and Heterosexual Cohabitors, 14 Hastings Const. L.Q. 111 (1986).

Internet References. The Nolo Press site, www.nolo.com/category/family.html, offers self-help legal products, including books such as A Legal Guide for Lesbian and Gay Couples and The Living Together Kit.

PART B. WHO IS A "DESCENDANT"?

Finding a satisfactory meaning of the term "descendant" is surprisingly vexing. The question of who qualifies as a descendant is treated as a status question in the sense that the inheritance rights of the decedent's descendants are linked to the identification of a legally recognized parent-child relationship: A decedent's grandchild *is* a grandchild because a legally recognized parent-child relationship exists between the decedent and a parent of the grandchild.

This Part examines the circumstances under which the law does or should recognize a parent-child relationship. The question not only arises for purposes of intestate succession but also for purposes of construing language in wills, trust instruments, life-insurance policies, and similar documents making gifts to classes such as "children," "descendants," or "issue."

1. Intestate Succession

Statutory References: *UPC §§ 1-201(5), 2-107, -113, -114*

a. Adopted Children/Stepchildren/Foster Children

Intestate Succession By, From, and Through Adopted Children. Formal adoption as a social institution has undergone substantial change within the past half century. Unknown to the English common law, which exhibited a strong preoccupation with blood ties,[43] adoption is now a widely accepted method of

43. The English aversion to adoption was initially transplanted to the American colonies, but diminished availability of alternatives produced a more favorable climate for legal recognition of adoption in the mid-nineteenth century. Following enactment of the first adoption acts between 1849 and 1850, the remaining states quickly authorized adoption, either by statute or judicial

creating familial relationships.[44] Of the children under 18 who were living with their married parents in 1990, the Census Bureau reports that 81.5 percent were living with their biological parents. Only 2.1 percent were adopted and living with their adoptive parents.

Legal reaction to adopted children has been far from uniform. In all states, either by statute or decision, adopted children inherit from their adoptive parents. There is less agreement, however, on inheritance by adopted children from their biological parents and from ancestors and collateral relatives of their biological and adoptive parents. What policy concerns are influencing the legislatures when they decide these issues? If a statute is silent on such issues, how should courts construe it? For a discussion of these matters, see Jan E. Rein, Relatives by Blood, Adoption, and Association: Who Should Get What and Why, 37 Vand. L. Rev. 711 (1984).

UPC § 2-114(b) and most non-UPC statutes treat adopted persons as children of their adoptive parents for all inheritance purposes. In other words, they abrogate the common law's "stranger-to-the-adoption" rule and allow a child not only to inherit from but also through the adoptive parent and allow adoptive family members to inherit from or through the adopted child. In MacCallum v. Seymour's Administrator, 686 A.2d 935 (Vt. 1996), Richard adopted his stepchild, Gail, who was his wife Anita's child by a former marriage. Subsequently, Richard and Anita had a biological child, Janet. Richard's brother, Philip, died intestate, without a surviving spouse and without any surviving descendants of his own. Richard predeceased Philip. The Vermont intestacy statute provided that Philip's only heir was Janet. Richard's adopted stepchild, Gail, was not included because the statute provided that adopted children inherit from their adopting parents but not from relatives of their adopting parents. The Supreme Court of Vermont held that this statute violated a state constitutional provision stating that the "government is, or ought to be, instituted for the common benefit, protection, and security of the people, nation,

---

ruling. See Michael Grossberg, Governing the Hearth 268-80 (1985).

44. Indeed, the federal government offers income tax incentives that encourage people to adopt. The Internal Revenue Code provides a 100% tax credit for adoption expenses up to a certain limit and an exclusion, up to the same limit, of employer-provided payments reimbursing adoption expenses. IRC §§ 23, 137. Currently, these limits are $5,000 ($6,000 for a child with special needs), and the limits phase out for single and married taxpayers starting with adjusted gross income of $75,000 and ending with adjusted gross income of $115,000. IRC §§ 23(a)-(b), 137(a)-(b). The Economic Growth and Tax Relief Reconciliation Act of 2001 has further expanded these benefits, increasing the phase-out range to between $150,000 and $190,000 (beginning in 2002) and expanding the credit and exclusion to $10,000 for all children (beginning in 2003). Pub. L. 107-16 § 202.

or community, and not for the particular emolument or advantage of any single person, family, or set of persons, who are a part only of that community." (This clause was also at issue in the same-sex marriage case of Baker v. Vermont, supra p. 111). The court declined to decide the case on the basis of the equal protection clause of the 14th Amendment of the U.S. Constitution. In Nunnally v. Trust Co. Bank, 261 S.E.2d 621 (Ga. 1979), the Supreme Court of Georgia upheld such a statutory scheme against a challenge based on the equal protection clause.

Another troublesome problem is, to what extent should or do adopted children retain inheritance rights from their biological families? The case of Estates of Donnelly, which follows, raises this question.

Estates of Donnelly

502 P.2d 1163 (Wash. 1973)

NEILL, J. May an adopted child inherit from her natural grandparents? Both the trial court and the Court of Appeals . . . answered "yes." We granted review . . . and disagree. In speaking of heirs and inheritance, we refer to the devolution of property by law in intestacy and not by testamentary or other voluntary disposition.

John J. and Lily Donnelly, husband and wife, had two children, a daughter, Kathleen M., now Kathleen M. Kelly, and a son, John J., Jr. The son had one child, Jean Louise Donnelly, born October 28, 1945. Jean Louise's father, John J. Donnelly, Jr., died on July 9, 1946, less than a year after her birth. Her mother, Faith Louise Donnelly, married Richard Roger Hansen on April 22, 1948. By a decree entered August 11, 1948, Jean Louise was adopted by her step-father with the written consent of her natural mother. She lived with her mother and adoptive father as their child and kept the name Hansen until her marriage to Donald J. Iverson. . . .

Lily Donnelly, the grandmother, died October 7, 1964, leaving a will in which she named but left nothing to her two children. All of her property she left to her husband . . . .

John J. Donnelly, Sr., the grandfather, died September 15, 1970, leaving a will dated October 16, 1932, in which he left his entire estate to his wife, Lily, who had predeceased him. He, too, named but left nothing to his two children, and made no provision for disposition of his property in event his wife predeceased him. His daughter, Kathleen M. Kelly, as administratrix with wills annexed of the estates of her parents, brought this petition to determine heirship and for a declaration that Jean Louise Iverson, the granddaughter, take nothing and that she, Kathleen M. Kelly, the daughter, be adjudged the sole heir of her mother and father, Lily and John J. Donnelly, Sr., to the exclusion of Jean Louise Iverson, her niece and their granddaughter.

The trial court decided that each was an heir. It concluded that Jean Louise Iverson, daughter of John J. Donnelly, Jr., and granddaughter of his father, John J. Donnelly, Sr., should inherit one-half of the latter's estate and that Kathleen M. Kelly, daughter of John J. Donnelly, Sr., should inherit the other half of the estate.

Kathleen M. Kelly, the daughter of decedent, appealed to the Court of Appeals which affirmed, and now to this court. With the issue recognized to be close and of general importance, we granted review . . . .

As the trial court in its memorandum opinion and the Court of Appeals noted, the issue is whether RCW 11.04.085, which says that an adopted child shall not be deemed an heir of his natural parents, cuts off the inheritance from the natural grandparents as well. The Court of Appeals put the question precisely . . . :

> In Washington, may a natural granddaughter inherit from her intestate grandparents, notwithstanding her adoption by her stepfather after the death of her natural father, the son of the decedent grandparents?

The sole beneficiary under his will having predeceased him, John J. Donnelly, Sr., died intestate. His estate would thus pass by the statutes governing intestacy according to RCW 11.04-.015, which says:

> The net estate of a person dying intestate . . . shall be distributed as follows: . . . .
>
> (2) . . . the entire net estate if there is no surviving spouse, shall descend and be distributed . . .
>
> (a) To the *issue* of the intestate; if they are all in the same degree of kinship to the intestate, they shall take equally, or if of unequal degree, then those of more remote degree shall take by representation.

(Italics ours.)

Issue "includes all the lawful lineal descendants of the ancestor." RCW 11.02.005(4). A descendant is one "who is descended from another; a person who proceeds from the body of another, such as a child, grandchild." Black's Law Dictionary 530 (Rev. 4th ed. 1968). Thus, both the daughter and granddaughter are descendants and issue of John J. Donnelly, Sr. The daughter under the descent and distribution statutes would take as the most immediate descendant, and the granddaughter being of more remote degree would take by representation as the sole issue of her deceased father who stood in the same degree of kinship to John J. Donnelly, Sr., as did Kathleen M. Kelly. RCW 11.04.015.

RCW 11.02.005(3) states:

> [E]ach share of a deceased person in the nearest degree shall be divided among those of his issue who survive the intestate and have no ancestor then living who is in the line of relationship between them and the intestate, those more remote in degree taking together the share which their ancestor would have taken had he survived the intestate.

Thus, a statutory right to inherit one-half of the grandfather's estate is vested in Jean Louise Iverson, the granddaughter, unless that right is divested by operation of RCW 11.04.085, which declares that an adopted child is not to be considered an heir of his natural parents:

> A lawfully adopted child shall not be considered an "heir" of his natural parents for purposes of this title.

When the question of the right of an adopted child to inherit from his natural parents came before us, the intent of the legislature was clear from the literal language of the statute. We held that RCW 11.04.085 prevents an adopted child from taking a share of the natural parent's estate by intestate succession. However, reference to the literal language of RCW 11.04.085 does not answer the instant question, *i.e.*, whether, by declaring that an adopted child shall not take from his natural parent, the legislature also intended to remove the adopted child's capacity to represent the natural parent and thereby take from the natural grandparent.

The purpose of statutory interpretation is to ascertain and give effect to the intent of the legislature. To decide whether RCW 11.04.085 also severs the right of the adopted child to inherit from a remote ancestor, we must first determine why the legislature terminated the rights of inheritance with respect to the natural parent. In so doing, we should be guided by the established principle of statutory interpretation which requires that:

> In placing a judicial construction upon a legislative enactment, the entire sequence of all statutes relating to the same subject matter should be considered.

Connick v. Chehalis, 53 Wash.2d 288, 290, 333 P.2d 647, 649 (1958).

The legislature has addressed itself to the inheritance rights of adopted children in both the probate and domestic relations titles of RCW . . . . For example, RCW 26.32.140 also directly affects the inheritance rights of an adopted child:

> By a decree of adoption the natural parents shall be divested of all legal rights and obligations in respect to the child, and *the child* shall be free from all legal obligations of obedience and maintenance in respect to them, and *shall be* to all intents and purposes, and for all legal incidents, *the child, legal heir, and lawful issue of his or her adopter or adopters, entitled to all rights and privileges, including the right of inheritance* and the right to take under testamentary disposition, and subject to all the obligations of a child of the adopter or adopters begotten in lawful wedlock.

(Italics ours.)

Since RCW 11.04.085 and RCW 26.32.140 each delimit the inheritance rights of an adopted child, the two statutes must be read in pari materia . . . .

It is clear that: (1) the adopted child cannot take from his natural parent because he is no longer an "heir" (RCW 11.04.085); and, (2) the adopted child enjoys complete inheritance rights from the adoptive parent, as if he were the natural child of the adoptive parent (RCW 26.32.140). Both statutes are in harmony with the fundamental spirit of our adoption laws—*i.e.*, that for all purposes the adopted child shall be treated as a "child of the adopter . . . begotten in lawful wedlock."

Legislative intent is to be ascertained from the statutory text as a whole, interpreted in terms of the general object and purpose of the legislation.

The question at bench should, therefore, be decided in the context of the broad legislative objective of giving the adopted child a "fresh start" by treating him as the natural child of the adoptive parent, and severing all ties with the past. We believe it clearly follows that the legislature intended to remove an adopted child from his natural bloodline for purposes of intestate succession.

The trial court and Court of Appeals, however, held that although an adopted child may not take *from* a natural parent dying intestate, the same child may take *through* the natural parent, by representation, if the natural parent dies before the natural grandparent. Little supportive reasoning is offered for this inconsistent result. In reaching its conclusion, the Court of Appeals reasoned that consanguineal ties are so fundamental that an explicit expression of legislative intent is required to deprive an adopted child of the bounty which would normally be his by reason of the "intuitive impulses" generated by the blood relationship. The Court of Appeals reasoned that had the legislature desired to remove an adopted child from its natural bloodline, it could have used the word "kin" in place of the word "parents" in RCW 11.04.085. Thus, since RCW 11.04.085 does not specify that an adopted child may not take from an intestate natural grandparent, this capacity is not lost.

However, where the literal interpretation of a particular word is repugnant to the intent of the legislature plainly manifested by the legislation taken as a whole, such interpretation ought not to prevail. . . .

Obviously, the legislature did *not* consider consanguinity to be of controlling importance where the blood relationship must be presumted [sic] to be strongest—the natural parent. Moreover, RCW 26.32.140 provides that an adopter and his kin shall inherit from an adopted child to the exclusion of the child's natural parents or kin. Thus, if respondent here had predeceased her natural grandfather, he would not have been permitted to inherit from his natural grandchild, any "intuitive impulses" of kinship notwithstanding. And, if consanguinity had *in fact* moved the grandparent to provide for respondent here, he could easily have done so by will.

The legislative policy of providing a "clean slate" to the adopted child permeates our scheme of adoption. The natural grandparents are not entitled to notice of any hearing on the matter of adoption. RCW 26.32.080. RCW 26.32.150 provides that, unless otherwise requested by the adopted, all records of the adoption proceeding shall be sealed and not open to inspection. Pursuant to RCW 26.32.120, a decree for adoption shall provide: (1) for the issuance of a certificate of birth for the adopted child, containing such information as the court may deem proper; and (2) that the records of the registrar shall be secret. RCW 70.58.210 declares that the new birth certificate shall bear the new name of the child and the names of the adoptive parents of the child, but shall make no reference to the adoption of the child. Thus, the natural grandparents have no assurance that they will know the new name or residence of the adopted child. Indeed, in the usual "out of family" adoption situation the administrator of a deceased natural grandparent's estate will be unable to locate—much less to identify—the post-adoption grandchild.

The consistent theme of the relevant legislation is that the new family of the adopted child is to be treated as his natural family. The only conclusion consistent with the spirit of our overlapping adoption and inheritance statutes is that RCW 11.04.085 was intended to transfer all rights of inheritance out of the natural family upon adoption and place them entirely within the adopted family.

Respondent suggests it is most probable that the legislature never considered the problem of inheritance by adopted persons from their remote natural kin when it passed RCW 11.04.085. Thus, respondent contends that the word "parents" should be strictly construed. We disagree.

> On numerous occasions this court has indicated that a statute should be construed as a whole in order to ascertain legislative purpose, and thus avoid unlikely, strained or absurd consequences which could result from a literal reading. That the spirit or the purpose of legislation should prevail over the express but inept language is an ancient adage of the law.

Alderwood Water Dist. v. Pope & Talbot, 62 Wash.2d 319, 321, 382 P.2d 639, 641 (1963).

As we stated in State ex rel. Spokane United Rys. v. Department of Pub. Serv., 191 Wash. 595, 598, 71 P.2d 661, 663 (1937):

> The rule that the expression of one thing will, under certain circumstances, exclude others, should be applied as a means of discovering the legislative intent, and its application should not be permitted to defeat the plainly indicated purpose of the legislature. [Citations omitted.]
>
> In determining the legislative intent, the purpose for which a law was enacted is a matter of prime importance in arriving at a correct interpretation of its parts, and "'A thing which is within the object, spirit and the meaning of the statute is as much within the statute as if it were within the letter.'" 2 Lewis' Sutherland Statutory Construction (2d ed.), §§ 369 and 379.

The broad legislative purpose underlying our statutes relating to adopted children is consistent only with the inference that RCW 11.04.085 was intended to remove respondent, an adopted child, from her natural bloodline for inheritance purposes. If the adopted child cannot take from her natural father, she should not represent him and take from his father.

The chain of inheritance was broken by respondent's adoption. Reversed.

HAMILTON, C.J., and STAFFORD, WRIGHT and UTTER, JJ., concur.

[The dissenting opinion of HALE, J., in which FINLEY, HUNTER, and ROSELLINI, JJ., concurred, is omitted.]

Notes and Questions

1. *Uniform Probate Code.* The UPC adopts the general principle of the Washington statute in *Donnelly* and places adopted persons exclusively in their adopting families for inheritance purposes. UPC § 2-114. The UPC anticipates cases like *Donnelly*, however, by providing an exception for stepparent adoptions.

2. *Other Statutory Approaches*. Pennsylvania has taken a functional approach to the question, at least as it arises with regard to family members other than the child's biological parents:

> *Pa. Cons. Stat.* § *2108.* An adopted person shall not be considered as continuing to be the child or issue of his natural parents except in distributing the estate of a natural kin, other than the natural parent, who has maintained a family relationship with the adopted person.

A more restrictive approach can be seen, for example, in Florida's statute, which states:

> *Fla. Stat. Ann. § 732.108(1)(b).* Adoption of a child by a natural parent's spouse who married the natural parent *after the death of the other natural parent* has no effect on the relationship between the child and the family of the deceased natural parent.

(Emphasis added). See also Minn. Stat. § 524.2-114 (a stepparent adoption does not terminate the parent-child relationship with the parent who is not the spouse of the stepparent if the adoption occurs after that parent's death).

3. *Grandparents' Visitation Rights.* In Troxel v. Granville, 120 S.Ct. 2054 (2000), Jennifer and Gary Troxel filed a petition for the right to visit their grandchildren, invoking a Washington state statute empowering courts to grant visitation rights to "any person" if doing so "serve[s] the best interest of the child." Revised Code of Washington § 26.10.160(3). The children's mother fought the grant of visitation all the way to the U.S. Supreme Court, which declared the statute an unconstitutional infringement on the rights of parents to rear their children. As the Court explained:

> The problem here is not that the Washington Superior Court intervened, but that when it did so, it gave no special weight at all to [the mother's] determination of her daughters' best interests. . . . In an ideal world, parents might always seek to cultivate the bonds between grandparents and their grandchildren. Needless to say, however, our world is far from perfect, and in it the decision whether such an intergenerational relationship would be beneficial in any specific case is for the parent to make in the first instance.

Id. at 2062.

4. *Discovering the Identity of Birth Parents.* Should adopted children have the right to discover the identity of their biological parents? In most states, no such absolute right exists, but the law may be moving in this direction. In 1998, Oregon passed the first voter-approved law giving all adult adoptees access to their birth records. A group of birth mothers asked the U.S. Supreme Court to block the law, but the Court declined to intervene. See Sam Howe Verhovek, Oregon Adoptees Granted Access to Birth Records, N.Y. Times, May 31, 2000, at A16.

5. *Termination Without Adoption.* In Estate of Fleming, 21 P.3d 281 (Wash. 2001), the Washington Supreme Court held that the biological family's right to inherit is severed by the termination of parental rights when a child is given up for adoption, not by the adoption itself. Thomas Fleming had no known father, and his mother surrendered him to Catholic Charities of the Diocese of Seattle,

terminating her parental rights so that Thomas could be adopted. But he was never adopted. Thomas died intestate at the age of 50, at which point his biological mother and brother sought to be declared his heirs. The state supreme court rejected their claims, holding that the termination of parental rights gave Thomas a "fresh start" (id. at 285).

Problems

1. F and M, a married couple with one child, X, were killed in an airplane crash. After the deaths of F and M, M's sister, A, and A's husband, B, adopted X. F's father, PGF, a widower, then died intestate. See S.D. Codified Laws § 29A-2-114 (maintains parent-child relationships for both biological parents if a child is adopted by a grandparent or descendant of a grandparent); Lisa A. Fuller, Intestate Succession Rights of Adopted Children: Should the Stepparent Exception Be Extended?, 77 Cornell L. Rev. 1188 (1992). The Restatement 3d of Property § 2.5 Comment f, illustration 3 provides that, unless precluded by clear statutory language, X should be treated as PGF's grandchild (F's child). Would the Restatement's solution be possible under the UPC?

2. M and F, a married couple, had two children, X and Y. M died, and F married M's sister, A. A adopted Y because Y was still a minor, but A did not adopt X because X was a self-supporting adult living in another city. M's mother, MGM, died intestate. Assume that the only relatives who might have survived MGM are the people mentioned in this problem. Who are MGM's heirs if A survived MGM? If A predeceased MGM? See UPC § 2-113.

Stepchildren and Foster Children. Unless adopted, stepchildren are usually not entitled to inherit from their stepparents or the stepparents' relatives. Similarly, foster children are not entitled to inherit from members of their foster families. See UPC § 1-201(5).

In California, a recent breakthrough has occurred. Under California Probate Code § 6454, stepchildren or foster children (and their descendants) are entitled to inherit from or through their stepparents or foster parents if "the relationship of parent and child" began "during the person's minority and continued throughout the [parties'] joint lifetimes" and if "it is established by clear and convincing evidence that the foster parent or stepparent would have adopted the person but for a legal barrier."

This statute has generated considerable litigation. Several cases have required the courts to interpret the phrase "but for a legal barrier." The question that has arisen is whether the refusal of a biological parent to consent to an adoption by a stepparent when the child was a minor is a sufficient legal barrier under the statute once the child attains the age of majority. After a split had arisen among the intermediate appellate courts on this issue, the California Supreme Court in Estate of Joseph, 949 P.2d 472 (Cal. 1998), held that the "but for" requirement was not met because adoption could have occurred once the child became an adult.

The California courts have also addressed the question of what constitutes a continuous relationship. See Estate of Stevenson, 14 Cal.Rptr.2d 250 (Ct. App. 1992) (the children lived with their stepmother from about 1953 until about 1959 at which time the couple separated; they reconciled seven years later and the children were reunited with their stepmother; the court held that the courts should consider the totality of circumstances to determine whether the statutory requirement was met and held that the circumstances in this case warranted a finding that the relationship was continuous); see also Estate of Claffey, 257 Cal. Rptr 197 (Ct. App. 1989) (raising the question of what it means to have a relationship of parent and child). For further analysis of the California statute, see Margaret M. Mahoney, Stepfamilies in the Law of Intestate Succession and Wills, 22 U.C. Davis L. Rev. 917 (1989) (viewing the statute as too restrictive); Thomas M. Hanson, Note, Intestate Succession for Stepchildren: California Leads the Way, But Has It Gone Far Enough?, 47 Hastings L.J. 257 (1995) (recommending a broadening of the eligibility requirements under the statute as well as a liberal interpretation of the existing statute); Robin Meadow & Jeffrey M. Loeb, Heir Unapparent, L.A. Lawyer, June 1994, at 34 (recommending repeal of what authors view as a misguided expansion of the rights of stepchildren and foster children).

Problems

A and B were married and had two children, X and Y. A and B got divorced and B was awarded custody of X and Y. B married C. A married D. B and C had a child, Z. A and D had a child, V.

1. C died intestate, survived by A, B, D, V, X, Y, and Z. Under UPC §§ 2-102, -103, and -114, who are C's heirs and what shares do they take? How would your answer differ if C had adopted X and Y?

2. X died intestate, survived by V, Y, and Z. A, B, C, and D predeceased X. Under UPC §§ 2-103 and -107, who are X's heirs? How would your answer differ if C had adopted X and Y?

External References. Margaret M. Mahoney, Stepfamilies and the Law (1994); Stepparenting: Issues in Theory, Research and Practice (Kay Pasley &

Marilyn Ihinger-Tallman eds., 1994); David L. Chambers, Stepparents, Biologic Parents and the Law's Perception of "Family" After Divorce, in Divorce Reform at the Crossroads 102 (Stephen D. Sugarman & Herma Hill Kay eds., 1990).

"Equitable Adoption" of Foster Children. Foster children who haven't been formally adopted by their foster parents may nevertheless obtain inheritance rights under a doctrine called "equitable adoption." Courts also refer to this doctrine as "virtual adoption," "de facto adoption," or "adoption by estoppel." Courts in over half the states have recognized such a doctrine, but a number of jurisdictions have rejected it. The strongest factual situation presented for applying the doctrine is where the foster parents expressly contracted to adopt the child but failed to complete the adoption procedures. Even if the child can't prove an express contract, courts have implied a contract under certain circumstances. However, the reliance on contract theory has sometimes operated to restrict the application of the doctrine. In Welch v. Welch, 453 S.E.2d 445 (Ga.), cert. denied, 115 S. Ct. 2617 (1995), for example, the court held the doctrine inapplicable because an agreement to adopt was invalid. The agreement was entered into between the foster parents and the juvenile court, but the juvenile court was not competent to contract for that adoption. See also O'Neal v. Wilkes, 439 S.E.2d 490 (Ga. 1994) (held that paternal aunt had no authority to enter into an adoption contract with foster parent and, therefore, doctrine was inapplicable).

In Wheeler Dollar Savings & Trust Co. v. Singer, 250 S.E.2d 369, 373-74 (W. Va. 1978), the Supreme Court of Appeals of West Virginia departed from the traditional requirement of either an express or implied contract to adopt:

> While the existence of an express contract of adoption is very convincing evidence, an implied contract of adoption is an unnecessary fiction created by courts as a protection from fraudulent claims. We find that if a claimant can, by clear, cogent and convincing evidence, prove sufficient facts to convince the trier of fact that his status is identical to that of a formally adopted child, except only for the absence of a formal order of adoption, a finding of an equitable adoption is proper without proof of an adoption contract.

The court described the circumstances that would satisfy this test as follows:

> The equitably adopted child in any private property dispute such as the case under consideration involving the laws of *inheritance* or *private trusts* must prove by clear, cogent and convincing evidence that he has stood from an age of tender years in a position *exactly* equivalent to a formally adopted child. Circumstances which tend to show the existence of an equitable adoption include: the benefits of love and affection accruing to the adopting party; the performances of services by

> the child; the surrender of ties by the natural parent; the society, companionship and filial obedience of the child; an invalid or ineffectual adoption proceeding; reliance by the adopted person upon the existence of his adoptive status; the representation to all the world that the child is a natural or adopted child; and the rearing of the child from an age of tender years by the adopting parents. . . . Of course, evidence can be presented which tends to negate an equitable adoption such as failure of the child to perform the duties of an adopted child, or misconduct of the child or abandonment of the adoptive parents; however, mere mischievous behavior usually associated with being a child is not sufficient to disprove an equitable adoption.

Id. at 373-74.

In Kisamore v. Coakley, 437 S.E.2d 585 (W. Va. 1993), the same court underscored both the high level of proof and the strictness of the requirement of showing that the child's "status is identical to that of a formally adopted child." In *Kisamore*, the foster parents, Vivan and Joy Kisamore, obtained custody in 1971 of their foster child, Susan, pursuant to an Adoptive Parents Agreement that indicated the couple's intention to adopt Susan. Before the adoption could become final, Susan was required to live in the couple's home for six months. Vivan died in an accident two months after obtaining custody of Susan, before he could finalize the adoption. Joy adopted Susan later that year. Vivan's father died intestate in 1991. The court denied Susan's claim for the right to inherit from Vivan's father:

> Obviously, the appellant [Susan] had not been formally or legally adopted during the time [the Adoptive Parents Agreement] was in effect; and thus, looking at this agreement and considering the rules to be obeyed by the Kisamores, it is difficult to say that the appellant was in a "position exactly equivalent to that of a formally adopted or natural child[.]" . . .
>
> It is unfortunate that Vivan Kisamore and the appellant only had [two months] together before Vivan Kisamore died. Due to the fact that Vivan Kisamore was a truck driver, it is unclear as to how much time Vivan Kisamore and the appellant really had together to form the bonds of father and daughter.
>
> Yet, even if we assume that Vivan Kisamore and the appellant spent those [two months] together, one could not conclude that Vivan Kisamore satisfied the requirements of establishing equitable adoption in the rearing or upbringing of the child from tender years or that the appellant was able to perform services for Vivan Kisamore. Furthermore, the sparse evidence we do have before us suggests, first, it would be difficult to assume that the appellant relied, at the time, upon the existence of the adoptive status, and second, that there was a representation to all the world that the child was a natural or adoptive child. . . .
>
> The heightened standard of proof and the strong language found in . . . *Wheeling Dollar* cast a demanding burden on the appellant to prove she was

> equitably adopted. However, the facts in this case fall far short of the standard followed in the above case[ ].

Id. at 588. See also Welch v. Wilson, 516 S.E.2d 35 (W.Va. 1999) (emphasizing again the heavy burden of proof required for equitable adoption but holding that the appellant, Glenell Welch, had satisfied it).

The cases are divided on whether an equitable adoption only qualifies the child to inherit from the child's foster parents or grants the child full status as a child of the foster parents for other purposes.[45]

Although California grants a foster child a right of inheritance if the child would have been adopted "but for a legal barrier" (see supra p. 127), California continues to recognize the need for the doctrine of equitable adoption. See Cal. Prob. Code § 6455 ("Nothing in this chapter affects or limits application of the judicial doctrine of equitable adoption for the benefit of the child or the child's issue.").

b. Children of Parents Not Married to Each Other

The Evolving Legal Status of Nonmarital Children. Historically, the common law labeled nonmarital children as "filius nullius"—the child of no one. These children formally lacked the right to inherit from or through either

---

45. For cases granting full status, see First National Bank v. Phillips, 344 S.E.2d 201 (W. Va. 1985) (allowed an equitably adopted child to inherit from a foster parent's other child); Foster v. Cheek, 96 S.E.2d 545 (Ga. 1957) (allowed an equitably adopted child to receive insurance benefits providing for a "child" on a policy insuring a foster parent); Bower v. Landa, 371 P.2d 657 (Nev. 1962) (allowed a suit under a wrongful death statute for the death of a foster parent); Estate of Radovich, 308 P.2d 14 (Cal. 1957) (an equitably adopted child had a right to favorable state inheritance tax treatment).

Contra, e.g., Reynolds v. Los Angeles, 222 Cal. Rptr. 517 (Ct. App. 1986) (denied a foster father the right to pursue a wrongful death action upon the accidental death of his equitably adopted son); In re Estate of Jenkins, 904 P.2d 1316 (Colo. 1995) (en banc) (denied an equitably adopted child the right to take under the testamentary trust of his foster grandfather); First National Bank v. People, 516 P.2d 639 (Colo. 1973) (denied favorable inheritance tax treatment to an equitably adopted child); Board of Education v. Browning, 635 A.2d 373 (Md. 1994) (denied an equitably adopted child the right to inherit from the foster parent's sister); McGarvey v. State, 533 A.2d 690 (Md. 1987) (denied favorable inheritance tax treatment to an equitably adopted child); Estate of Riggs, 440 N.Y.S.2d 450 (Sur. Ct. 1981) (denied family members of a foster parent the right to inherit from an equitably adopted child).

Courts have held that the doctrine has no effect on the child's right to inherit from the child's biological parents. See, e.g., Kupec v. Cooper, 593 So. 2d 1176 (Fla. Dist. Ct. App. 1992); Gardner v. Hancock, 924 S.W.2d 857 (Mo. Ct. App. 1996). Courts have also held that the doctrine isn't available to a person who claims to have been equitably adopted as an adult. See, e.g., Miller v. Paczier, 591 So. 2d 321 (Fla. Dist. Ct. App. 1991).

parent. The law in practice, however, was more complicated. Church courts and, later, common-law courts enforced a father's duty to support his children born out of wedlock, thus indicating some willingness to recognize the parent-child relationship between nonmarital children and their biological parents. See Richard H. Helmholz, Support Orders, Church Courts, and the Rule of Filius Nullius: A Reassessment of the Common Law, 63 Va. L. Rev. 431 (1977).

The number of nonmarital births has risen dramatically since 1970. According to the Census Bureau, 32.4 percent of births in 1997 were to unwed mothers, up from 10.7 percent in 1970. See U.S. Census Bureau, Statistical Abstract of the United States: 1999, tbl. 99, at 79; U.S. Census Bureau, Statistical Abstract of the United States: 1995, tbl. 94, at 77. Single motherhood is strongly correlated with low income and low education. According to the New York Times, 42.5 percent of unmarried women who had incomes of less than $10,000 had a baby between July 1993 and June 1994, whereas only 2.9 percent who had incomes of $75,000 and higher had a baby during that period. In addition, 45.6 percent of unmarried women who didn't graduate from high school had a baby during that period, compared to 30.3 percent who were high school graduates and 6.1 percent who had a college degree. See Margaret L. Usdansky, Single Motherhood: Stereotypes vs. Statistics, N.Y. Times, Feb. 11, 1996, § 4, at 4.

Inheritance Rights of Nonmarital Children. Insofar as the Uniform Probate Code is concerned, it completely reverses the common law: The general principle of the UPC is that individuals inherit from and through their biological parents regardless of their parents' marital status. UPC § 2-114(a).

As for non-UPC law, the statutes uniformly entitle nonmarital children to inherit from their mothers, but differences exist concerning the children's right to inherit from their fathers, ostensibly because of the greater difficulty of proving paternity. Pre-1977 statutes in many states allowed nonmarital children to inherit from their fathers only if the father had married the child's biological mother and acknowledged or recognized the child. In 1977, the United States Supreme Court in Trimble v. Gordon, 430 U.S. 762 (1977), held this type of statute to be an unconstitutional denial of equal protection. The statute at issue, from Illinois, provided:

> An illegitimate[46] child is heir of his mother and of any maternal ancestor, and of

---

46. Regarding this vocabulary, consider the following observation:

> [T]he court wishes to express criticism of the use of the word "illegitimate" as applied to children. Not only is this term, when used in connection with children, repugnant to this court but its use in any local

> any person from whom his mother might have inherited, if living; and the lawful issue of an illegitimate person shall represent such person and take, by descent, any estate which the parent would have taken, if living. A child who was illegitimate whose parents inter-marry and who is acknowledged by the father as the father's child is legitimate.

The State of Illinois argued that the statute served its interest of promoting family relationships, assuring accurate and efficient disposition of property at death, and mirroring the presumed intentions of its citizens. The Supreme Court held that none of the state's interests justified the statutory discrimination against nonmarital children. It held that the state cannot influence the conduct of parents by burdening their child. It refused to address "the question whether presumed intent alone can ever justify discrimination against nonmarital children," because it did not believe that the state enacted the statute for that purpose. The Supreme Court acknowledged that problems of proving paternity might justify a more demanding standard for nonmarital children to claim under their fathers' estates than that required for them to claim under their mothers' estates or than that required for marital children generally. It held, however, that this concern did not warrant "the total statutory disinheritance of illegitimate children whose fathers die intestate."[47]

The Supreme Court revisited the questions of proof and expeditious handling of estates in Lalli v. Lalli, 439 U.S. 259 (1978), in which it considered New York's legislative approach for assuring an accurate and efficient probate process. The New York statute provided:

> An illegitimate child is the legitimate child of his father so that he and his issue inherit from his father if a court of competent jurisdiction has, during the lifetime of the father, made an order of filiation declaring paternity in a proceeding instituted during the pregnancy of the mother or within two years from the birth of the child.

The decedent's son, Robert Lalli, contended that requiring an order of filiation

---

> law, ordinance or resolution or in any public or judicial proceeding or in any process, notice, order, decree, judgment, record, public document or paper, is a violation of law (*see* General Construction Law, sec. 59). Despite this fact judges, legal writers and others continuously use that term when writing about children born out of wedlock.

Estate of Leventritt, 400 N.Y.S.2d 298, 299 (Sur. Ct. 1977). Eds.

47. In Reed v. Campbell, 476 U.S. 852 (1986), the Court gave its decision in *Trimble* retroactive effect where at the time of the child's claim the statute barring inheritance had been declared unconstitutional and the father's estate was still open.

during the father's lifetime discriminated against him on the basis of his nonmarital-child status in violation of the Equal Protection Clause of the Fourteenth Amendment. The evidence showed that the father had acknowledged his paternity in a notarized document and that he had acknowledged openly and frequently that Robert Lalli was his son. Additionally, the evidence showed that the decedent had provided support to his son, vitiating the need to bring the paternity action that the statute contemplated. The Court concluded that the paternity adjudication requirement was tied to the state interest in an orderly process for wealth succession and found that the statute did not violate the Equal Protection Clause.

Following *Lalli*, the New York legislature amended the statute so that it now provides in part:

> *N.Y. Est. Powers & Trusts Law § 4-1.2(a). Inheritance by non-marital children . . . .*
>
> (2) A non-marital child is the legitimate child of his father so that he and his issue inherit from his father and his paternal kindred if:
>
> (A) a court of competent jurisdiction has, during the lifetime of the father, made an order of filiation declaring paternity or the mother and father of the child have executed an acknowledgment of paternity . . . , which has been filed with the registrar of the district in which the birth certificate has been filed or;
>
> (B) the father of the child has signed an instrument acknowledging paternity, provided that
>
> (i) such instrument is acknowledged or executed or proved in the form required to entitle a deed to be recorded in the presence of one or more witnesses and acknowledged by such witness or witnesses, in either case, before a notary public or other officer authorized to take proof of deeds and
>
> (ii) such instrument is filed within sixty days from the making thereof with the putative father registry established by the state department of social services . . . and
>
> (iii) the department of social services shall, within seven days of the filing of the instrument, send written notice by registered mail to the mother and other legal guardian of such child, notifying them that an acknowledgment of paternity instrument acknowledged or executed by such father has been duly filed or;
>
> (C) paternity has been established by clear and convincing evidence and the father of the child has openly and notoriously acknowledged the child as his own;[48] or
>
> (D) a blood genetic marker test had been administered to the father which

48. See Bruce A. Langer, Proving Paternal Kinship: The Lawyer as Detective, N.Y.L.J., Sept. 10, 1992, at 1 (describing the demands on an attorney representing a nonmarital child for the purpose of proving a putative father's open and notorious acknowledgment of the child).

together with other evidence establishes paternity by clear and convincing evidence.

(3) The existence of an agreement obligating the father to support the nonmarital child does not qualify such child or his issue to inherit from the father in the absence of an order of filiation made or acknowledgment of paternity as prescribed by subparagraph (2).

Proving "Open and Notorious" Acknowledgment. Requiring proof that a father "openly and notoriously" acknowledged "the child as his own" has raised some difficulty when the father died before the child was born. The Supreme Court of Iowa in Estate of Evjen, 448 N.W.2d 23 (Iowa 1989), was asked to consider the meaning of open and notorious acknowledgment in these circumstances. The Iowa statute provided that nonmarital children inherit from their fathers

> if the evidence proving paternity is available during the father's lifetime, or if the child has been recognized by the father as his child; but the recognition must have been general and notorious, or in writing.

The decedent's estate did not contest paternity. It argued that the statute required that the father also recognize the child as his own. Even though the doctor didn't perform a pregnancy test and confirm the pregnancy until after the decedent's death, and even though the decedent was killed in an automobile accident a week after the child's mother told the decedent that she believed she was pregnant, the court held that the father had openly and notoriously recognized the child. During the week that the decedent knew of the probable pregnancy, he told at least five people that the baby was his. The court held that this evidence was sufficient to find a recognition for the purpose of the inheritance statute.

Rather than relying on evidence showing how a father openly and notoriously held out a child as his own before the child's birth, California provides an alternative legislative approach. For inheritance purposes, California allows clear and convincing evidence to establish paternity when "[i]t was impossible for the father to hold out the child as his own." Cal. Prob. Code § 6453(b)(3).

The Doctrine of Virtual Legitimation. In the absence of a statutory provision allowing paternity to be shown by evidence that the father treated the child as his own, the Georgia Supreme Court established the doctrine of virtual or equitable legitimation to allow a nonmarital son to inherit from his biological father. In Prince v. Black, 344 S.E.2d 411, 412 (Ga. 1986), the court held that

> There may be cases in which there is such clear and convincing evidence that the child is the natural child of the father and that the father intended for the child

> to share in his intestate estate, in the same manner that the child would have shared if he had been formally legitimated, that equity will consider that done which ought to have been done. Thus the father's intentions will be fulfilled by allowing the child to inherit the property that was undisposed of by will as if the child was legitimate, although the child was not formally legitimated and cannot be considered legitimate in the eyes of the law.

The Georgia legislature has incorporated the reasoning of *Prince* into the state's probate code, which provides that nonmarital children may inherit from their fathers if there is "clear and convincing evidence that the child is the child of the father." Ga. Code Ann. § 53-2-3.

Uniform Parentage Act. In 1973, the Uniform Law Commission promulgated the original version of the Uniform Parentage Act (UPA), which has since been adopted in nineteen states. In August 2000, the Commission approved a revised version of the UPA. Both versions authorize actions to be brought to establish the identity of a child's biological mother or father. Original UPA §§ 3, 6; Revised UPA § 106, 201. In proving paternity, medical tests can be required. Original UPA § 11, 12 (blood tests); Revised UPA § 621, 622 (genetic tests). The Revised UPA relies heavily on genetic testing. If an individual refuses to submit to genetic testing, the court may, on that ground alone, determine parentage contrary to the position taken by that individual. Revised UPA § 622. The complete text of the Revised UPA is available at the Uniform Law Commission's website, www.nccusl.org.

Acknowledgment and Support Required in Order to Inherit from Nonmarital Children? Although Uniform Probate Code § 2-114(a) facilitates inheritance by a nonmarital child merely on proof of parentage, § 2-114(c) precludes a biological mother or father, or the kindred of either, from inheriting from a marital or nonmarital child unless the parent "has openly treated the child as his [or hers], and has not refused to support the child." See Estate of Ford, 552 So. 2d 1065 (Miss. 1989) (interpreting a statute similar to § 2-114(c)[49] and holding that a biological father's family was not entitled to inherit from a nonmarital child because the claimants failed to establish by a preponderance of the evidence that the father openly recognized the decedent as his child and that the father did not refuse or neglect to support her). But see Cal. Prob. Code § 6452 (allowing a relative of the parent as well as the parent

---

49. The Mississippi statute placed conditions only on a biological father's right to inherit from a nonmarital child. The former version of UPC § 2-109 had a similar rule. The current UPC neither distinguishes between biological mothers and fathers nor between marital and nonmarital children.

to acknowledge and contribute to the support of the child).

EXTERNAL REFERENCES. Ralph C. Brashier, Children and Inheritance in the Nontraditional Family, 1996 Utah L. Rev 93; Marsha Garrison, Law Making for Baby Making: An Interpretive Approach to the Determination of Legal Parentage, 113 Harv. L. Rev. 835 (2000); Peggy Cooper Davis, Contested Images of Family Values: The Role of the State, 107 Harv. L. Rev. 1348 (1994); Deborah L. Forman, Unwed Fathers and Adoption: A Theoretical Analysis in Context, 72 Tex. L. Rev. 967 (1994); John Lawrence Hill, What Does It Mean to Be a "Parent"? The Claims of Biology as the Basis for Parental Rights, 66 N.Y.U. L. Rev. 353 (1991); Mary Kay Kristhardt, Of Fatherhood, Families and Fantasy: The Legacy of *Michael H. v. Gerald D.*, 65 Tul. L. Rev. 585 (1991); Mary L. Shanley, Unwed Fathers' Rights, Adoption, and Sex Equality: Gender-Neutrality and the Perpetuation of Patriarchy, 95 Colum. L. Rev. 60 (1995); Robin West, The Ideal of Liberty: A Comment on *Michael H. v. Gerald D.*, U. Pa. L. Rev. 1373 (1991); Traci Dallas, Note, Rebutting the Marital Presumption: A Developed Relationship Test, 88 Colum. L. Rev. 369 (1988); Deborah A. Ellingboe, Note, Sex, Lies, and Genetic Tests: Challenging the Marital Presumption of Paternity under the Minnesota Parentage Act, 78 Minn. L. Rev. 1013 (1994).

Children Conceived by Assisted Reproductive Technologies. Medical technology allows for the conception of a child by means other than sexual intercourse. The development of assisted reproductive technologies challenges traditional notions of family, kinship, and parenting with far-reaching social and legal implications. One commentator underscores the complex issues we are likely to face in the future when he says:

> We now live in an era where a child may have as many as five different "parents." These include a sperm donor, an egg donor, a surrogate or gestational host, and two nonbiologically related individuals who intend to raise the child. Indeed, the process of procreation itself has become so fragmented by the variety and combinations of collaborative-reproductive methods that there are a total of sixteen different reproductive combinations, in addition to traditional conception and childbirth. This total is the product of varying the source of the male gametes (whether by husband or third-party donor), the source of the female gametes (whether by wife or third-party egg donor), the location of fertilization (whether in the wife, the laboratory, or the surrogate host), and the site of gestation (either in the wife or the surrogate).

John Lawrence Hill, What Does It Mean to Be a "Parent"? The Claims of

Biology as the Basis for Parental Rights, 66 N.Y.U. L. Rev. 353, 355 (1991). See, e.g., Jaycee B. v. Superior Court, 49 Cal. Rptr. 2d 694 (Ct. App. 1996) (gestational surrogacy case involving child conceived from sperm and egg of anonymous donors).

Inheritance Rights and Posthumous Reproduction. In general, existing statutes relating to inheritance laws weren't designed to address the question of a child conceived posthumously. For example, children conceived posthumously wouldn't qualify as heirs of their decedent fathers or mothers under statutes codifying the common law regarding children in gestation. They only apply to children who were conceived before the decedent's death.[50] See UPC § 2-108; supra Chapter 2.

The Restatement 3d of Property § 2.5, Comment 1, takes the position that, "to inherit from the decedent, a child produced from genetic material of the decedent by assisted reproductive technology must be born within a reasonable time after the decedent's death in circumstances indicating that the decedent would have approved of the child's right to inherit." Accord Estate of Kolacy, 753 A.2d 1257 (N.J. Super. Ct. Ch. Div. 2000) ("Given that [the] general legislative intent [is to enable children to inherit property from their parents], it seems to me that once we establish, as we have in this case, that a child is indeed the offspring of a decedent, we should routinely grant that child the legal status of being an heir of the decedent, unless doing so would unfairly intrude on the rights of other persons or would cause serious problems in terms of the

---

50. In Hecht v. Superior Court, 20 Cal. Rptr. 2d 275 (Ct. App. 1993), a case in which the court held that the decedent had testamentary power over frozen sperm that he had deposited with a sperm bank, the court said:

> [I]t is unlikely that the [decedent's] estate would be subject to claims with respect to any [children conceived after his death from his frozen sperm, which he had willed to his domestic partner]. The interest of heirs and courts in the finality of probate rulings was recognized by the committee which drafted the Uniform Status of Children of Assisted Conception Act, which has been adopted in various forms in North Dakota and Virginia. Section 4 of that Act provides in pertinent part that ". . . (b) An individual who dies before implantation of an embryo, or before a child is conceived other than through sexual intercourse, using the individual's egg or sperm, is not a parent of the resulting child." . . . The Committee Comment states that "Subsection 4(b) is designed to provide finality for the determination of parenthood of those whose genetic material is utilized in the procreation process after their death. . . . It is designed primarily to avoid the problems of intestate succession which could arise if the posthumous use of a person's genetic material could lead to the deceased being termed a parent."

Courts are beginning to grapple with the right to determine the disposition of frozen embryos when the parties, usually after divorce, disagree. In J.B. v. M.B., __ A.2d ___ (N.J. 2001), the court adopted the rule that an agreement entered into when in vitro fertilization is begun is enforceable, "subject to the right of either party to change his or her mind about disposition up to the point of use or destruction of any stored preembryos."

orderly administration of estates.")

The Revised UPA also addresses the question of posthumous reproduction. Section 707 provides that if a spouse dies before the placement of eggs, sperm, or an embryo, the deceased spouse is not considered the parent of any resulting children unless the deceased spouse had consented in writing to be the parent of children so conceived. In addition § 702 provides a blanket rule that the *donor* of the eggs or sperm is not the parent of any child conceived by any form of assisted reproduction.[51]

External References. See Lisa M. Burkdall, Note, A Dead Man's Tale: Regulating the Right to Bequeath Sperm in California, 46 Hastings L.J. 875 (1995); Ronald Chester, Freezing the Heir Apparent: A Dialogue on Postmortem Conception, Parental Responsibility, and Inheritance, 33 Hous. L. Rev. 967 (1996); Christine A. Djalleta, Comment, A Twinkle in a Decedent's Eye: Proposed Amendments to the Uniform Probate Code in Light of New Reproductive Technology, 67 Temple L. Rev. 335 (1994); Sherri Gilbert, Note, Fatherhood from the Grave: An Analysis of Postmortem Insemination, 22 Hofstra L. Rev. 521 (1993).

Spousal Consent to Assisted Reproduction. If both spouses are alive, must a husband consent to assisted reproduction in order to be considered the father of any children so conceived? Under the Revised UPA, the answer is yes. Section 703 treats the mother's husband as the father of the child only if the husband has consented in writing to, or provided sperm for, the procedure. In the absence of legislation, the husband of a married woman who has undergone donor insemination should be advised to adopt the child in order to clarify paternity. Care should be taken, however, to make sure that the state's adoption or inheritance statutes will not, upon adoption by the husband, terminate the relationship between the child and the mother.

The Rights of Gamete Donors. As noted above, the Revised UPA provides that a donor of eggs or sperm is not the parent of a child conceived through assisted conception. Revised UPA § 702. Are there instances when this rule might be too restrictive? For discussions of the ethical issues regarding anonymous gamete donors, see Jan Hoffman, Egg Donations Meet a Need and Raise Ethical Questions, N.Y. Times, Jan. 8, 1996, at A1; Peggy Orenstein, Looking for a Donor to Call Dad, N.Y. Times, June 18, 1995 (Magazine).

---

51. The Uniform Status of Children of Assisted Conception Act, promulgated by the Uniform Law Commission in 1988 and adopted in North Dakota and Virginia, similarly provides that a donor of egg or sperm is not the parent of a child conceived through any method of assisted conception. USCACA § 4(a). This rule is specifically applied to the case of posthumous reproduction. USCACA § 4(b).

Same-Sex Couples with Children: Adoption. Only a relatively small percentage (between 9 and 10 percent) of same-sex couples have children under the age of fifteen living with them. For opposite-sex couples, this figure is 36 percent.[52] However, for those same-sex couples that do have children, or that want to have children, there are considerable obstacles in obtaining legal recognition of parent-child relationships. Problems often arise when both partners seek to be recognized as parents of the child. Why? Because many of the state statutes regulating adoption, inheritance, and assisted conception rely on marital status to determine parent-child relationships. We have already seen examples of the well-accepted stepparent adoption, in which a child is adopted by the *spouse* of the child's existing parent. Second-parent adoption is the term used to refer to an adoption by the nonmarital partner of the child's existing parent. Whether states will allow a second-parent adoption is a matter of ongoing controversy.

Some courts have been willing to construe existing adoption statutes broadly to permit both partners to be recognized as the parents of the child. For example, in Matter of Adoption of Two Children by H.N.R., 666 A.2d 535, 538 (N.J. Super. Ct. App. Div. 1995), the court authorized the adoption of twins by the biological mother's lesbian partner. Many other courts presented with this issue in recent years have interpreted the adoption statutes to allow for second-parent adoptions. See, e.g., Adoption of Tammy, 619 N.E.2d 315 (Mass. 1993); Matter of Evans, 583 N.Y.S.2d 997 (Sur. Ct. 1992); Adoption of B.L.V.B., 628 A.2d 1271 (Vt. 1993). The issue, however, is far from settled. For cases refusing to allow such an adoption, see Adoption of T.K.J. & K.A.K., 931 P.2d 488 (Colo. Ct. App. 1996); In Interest Angel Lace M., 516 N.W.2d 678 (Wis. 1994); Adoption of Doe, 719 N.E.2d 1071 (Ohio Ct. App. 1998).

When allowing second-parent adoptions, the courts haven't distinguished between family situations in which one of the parents is biologically related to the child and those in which one of the parents had previously adopted the child. Compare In re M.M.D. & B.H.M., 662 A.2d 837 (D.C. 1995) (one of the gay partners had previously adopted the child; subsequently, the partners jointly petitioned the court for the right to adopt the child) with Adoption of Tammy, 619 N.E.2d 315 (Mass. 1993) (a lesbian partner was inseminated with semen from the other partner's biological cousin giving birth to a daughter; subsequently the partners jointly petitioned the court for the right to adopt the

52. CPS, supra note 14, tbl. 8, at 71.

child). See also In re Jacob, 660 N.E.2d 397 (N.Y. 1995) (one of the two cases joined for appeal concerned an opposite-sex cohabitating couple adopting the biological mother's child from a previous marriage).

The Uniform Adoption Act (UAA), promulgated by the Uniform Law Commission in 1994, is one of the few legislative attempts to facilitate joint parenting arrangements between unmarried couples.[53] UAA § 4-102 addresses the question of second-parent adoptions by providing:

> (b) For good cause shown, a court may allow an individual who does not [qualify as a stepparent], but has the consent of the custodial parent of a minor to file a petition for adoption under this [article]. A petition allowed under this subsection must be treated as if the petitioner were a stepparent.

UAA § 4-103(b) goes on to provide that

> An adoption by a stepparent does not affect:
>
> (1) the relationship between the adoptee and the adoptee's parent who is the adoptive stepparent's spouse or deceased spouse; . . .
>
> (3) the right of the adoptee or a descendant of the adoptee to inheritance or intestate succession through or from the adoptee's former parent; . . .

The UAA thus avoids defining a cohabitating partner and merely leaves it to the courts to determine whether "good cause" is shown to warrant treating a petitioning cohabitating partner as a stepparent.[54]

---

53. In contrast, a few legislatures have enacted statutes banning adoptions by lesbians and gay men. See, e.g., Fla. Stat. ch. 63.042(3) (banning adoption by any "person [who] is a homosexual") (upheld in Lofton v. Kearney, __ F.Supp.2d ___ (S.D. Fla. 2001)); Miss. Code § 93-17-3(2) (prohibiting adoption by "couples of the same gender"). These enactments probably are, in part, a response to the public's concern about lesbians and gay men raising children. See The Limits of Tolerance?, Newsweek, Feb. 14, 1994, at 47 (public opinion survey indicating only 29 percent of the public favor adoptions by lesbian and gay couples as compared to 65 percent who are against them).

54. That the drafters intended to reach the results found in cases like *H.N.R.* cannot be doubted. The commentary to § 4-102 cites Adoption of B.L.V.B., 628 A.2d 1271 (Vt. 1993), as well as Matter of Evans, 583 N.Y.S.2d 997 (Sur. Ct. 1992), to support the following statement:

> In addition to permitting individuals who are within the formal definition of "stepparent" to adopt a minor stepchild under this Article, Section 4-102 allows an individual who is a de facto stepparent, but is not, or is no longer, married to the custodial parent, to adopt as if he or she were a de jure stepparent. To file a petition under this Article, the de facto stepparent or "second parent" has to have the consent of the court and the custodial parent, whose parental rights will not be terminated by an adoption under this Article. In addition, for the court to grant the petition, the other requirements of this Article have to be met, including the court's determination that the adoption is in the minor adoptee's best interests.

Same-Sex Couples with Children: Assisted Conception. Under a literal interpretation of the Revised UPA, if one lesbian partner gives birth to a child as a result of donor insemination, the other partner is not treated as that child's parent. The Revised UPA's sections on assisted conception speak only of "husband" and "wife." See, for example, Revised UPA § 703.[55] It is not at all clear whether courts would be willing to treat a partner as the equivalent of a spouse under these types of statutes. See Emily McAllister, Defining the Parent-Child Relationship in an Age of Reproductive Technology: Implications for Inheritance, 29 Real Prop., Prob. & Tr. J. 55, 76-77, 109, 117-18 (1994) (proposing a statute that would acknowledge a parent-child relationship between the partner of the birth parent and the child).

A second issue concerning donor insemination is the legal relationship, if any, of the sperm donor to the child born of assisted conception. If a woman chooses anonymous donor insemination, questions concerning the father-child relationship are unlikely to arise. If a woman chooses a known donor, issues regarding a genetic father's legal obligations and rights can, and have, arisen. Similar questions could also arise regarding egg donors. Questions concerning the legal relationship of the sperm donor to the child and whether his rights are terminated can become an issue in second-parent adoption proceedings. Revised UPA § 702 precludes any relationship between the sperm donor and the child.

Much of the debate concerning the appropriate role of the known sperm donor in the rearing of the child has turned on the intentions of the birth mother, her lesbian partner, and the sperm donor at the time of conception and whether that understanding should be recognized by the courts through application of equitable estoppel doctrines. For purposes of considering inheritance law reform, the question becomes how much participation in the family life of a child should be sufficient, in combination with the genetic connection, to warrant recognition of inheritance rights of the child from or through the sperm donor and of the sperm donor from or through the child. The Restatement 3d of Property § 2.5, Comment l provides that "[i]n general, such a child should be treated as part of the family of the parent or parents who treat the child as their own and raise the child, one or both of whom might not be the child's genetic parent." A further question becomes whether an agreement or clear and convincing evidence of the mutual intention of the parties to prevent a child's right to inherit or to preclude mutual inheritance should override any

55. The Revised UPA's sections on assisted conception do not apply where there has been a "gestational agreement" (see Revised UPA § 701), but such agreements are limited to couples who are married. Revised UPA § 801.

statutory rules permitting inheritance. These and many other issues have not yet been resolved by legislatures or courts. Cf., e.g., Jhordan C. v. Mary K., 224 Cal.Rptr. 530 (Ct. App. 1986) (the sperm donor's parental rights were not extinguished under the state statute and led to the award of visitation rights of a child who was being raised by the birth mother and her lesbian partner); In re R.C., 775 P.2d 27 (Colo. 1989) (held that an agreement between a woman and the sperm donor could override a statute intended to protect the woman from a paternity claim of the donor and remanded the case to determine if such an agreement existed); Hartman v. Stassis, 504 N.W.2d 129 (Iowa Ct. App. 1993), cert. denied, 510 U.S. 1043 (1994) (ordered child support upon petition of a lesbian mother on behalf of her two children born to her as a result of sexual intercourse with defendant); Thomas S. v. Robin Y., 618 N.Y.S.2d 356 (App. Div. 1994) (awarded order of filiation to a sperm donor who was known to his child as her father over objections of the child's lesbian mothers); McIntyre v. Crouch, 780 P.2d 239 (Or. Ct. App.), cert. denied, 495 U.S. 905 (1989) (similar to *R.C.*, supra).

External References. Fred A. Bernstein, This Child Does Have Two Mothers . . . And a Sperm Donor with Visitation Rights, 22 Rev. L. & Soc. Change 1 (1996); Suzanne Bryant, Second Parent Adoption: A Model Brief, 2 Duke J. Gender L. & Pol'y 233 (1995); Marc E. Elovitz, Adoption by Lesbian and Gay People: The Use and Mis-Use of Social Science Research, 2 Duke J. Gender L. & Pol'y 207 (1995); Deborah Lashman, Second Parent Adoption: A Personal Perspective, 2 Duke J. Gender Law & Pol'y 227 (1995); Charlotte J. Patterson, Adoption of Minor Children by Lesbian and Gay Adults: A Social Science Perspective, 2 Duke J. Gender Law & Pol'y 191 (1995); Charlotte J. Patterson, Children of Lesbian and Gay Parents, 63 Child Development 1025 (1992); Nancy D. Polikoff, Brief, The Social Construction of Parenthood in One Planned Lesbian Family, 22 Rev. L. & Soc. Change 203 (1996); Nancy D. Polikoff, This Child Does Have Two Mothers: Redefining Parenthood to Meet the Needs of Children in Lesbian-Mother and Other Nontraditional Families, 78 Geo. L.J. 459 (1990); Jane S. Schacter, Constructing Families in a Democracy: Courts, Legislatures and Second-Parent Adoption, 75 Chi.-Kent L. Rev. 933 (2000); Elizabeth Zuckerman, Comment, Second Parent Adoption for Lesbian-Parented Families: Legal Recognition of the Other Mother, 19 U.C. Davis L. Rev. 729 (1986).

2. Rules of Construction for Class Gifts

Statutory References: *UPC §§ 2-701, -705, 8-101(b)(5)*

The Restatement 3d of Property§ 11.3, Comment a, provides that rules of construction "are devices that *attribute* intention to *individual* donors in particular circumstances on the basis of *common* intention. [They] are rebuttable upon a finding of a contrary intention. If there is no finding of a contrary intention . . . the meaning of the ambiguous portion of the document is controlled by the rule of construction . . . . Rules of construction . . . therefore operate as special purpose presumptions in the law of donative transfers."

a. Adopted Children/Stepchildren/Foster Children

Adopted Children. Wills, trusts, and other donative documents commonly include gifts to classes of persons, such as "to A's children" or "to A's descendants." Whether adopted children are included within these class gifts depends in the first instance upon the intention of the donor. The drafter should expressly address this matter in the instrument. If the instrument fails to indicate the donor's intent one way or the other, the law must provide an answer. Intestacy statutes aren't controlling in these circumstances, but they are often used as guides to what the donor likely intended and to public policy.

Courts and statutes usually treat an adopted child as a member of the class if the donor of the class gift adopted that child. See UPC § 2-705(a); Restatement 2d of Property § 25.4. The more difficult and controversial situation arises where someone other than the donor adopted the child. Suppose, for example, that Alice makes a gift to her nieces and nephews and Alice's brother adopts a daughter. According to the so-called "stranger-to-the-adoption" doctrine developed by the courts, Alice is presumed not to have intended to have her adopted niece share in the class gift. The rationale for this rule of construction is similar to that encountered as the basis for nonrecognition of the intestacy rights of adopted persons from the adopting parent's family, which is that the adopting parent shouldn't be permitted to determine the beneficiaries of a gift made by a person who didn't participate in the adoption. However, if circumstances indicate that the donor probably intended to include the adopted person (for example, where the donor knew that the adoptive parent was incapable of having children), then the presumption is rebutted.

Both UPC § 2-705(c) and Restatement 2d of Property § 25.4 abrogate the "stranger-to-the-adoption" doctrine. Under the UPC, the doctrine is abrogated if the adopted child lived while a minor, either before or after the adoption, as a regular member of the household of the adopting parent. Under the Restatement, the doctrine is abrogated if the adopted child has been or will be reared by the adopting parent.

Ohio Citizens Bank v. Mills, below, tells the story of one state's struggle to dislodge the stranger-to-the-adoption doctrine and raises the question whether laws that change or expand the rights of adopted children should apply to documents in existence on the effective date of the statute or only to documents executed subsequently.

Ohio Citizens Bank v. Mills

543 N.E.2d 1206 (Ohio 1989)

The facts, and procedural background, of this case are as follows. On September 21, 1944, Charles H. Breyman created an inter vivos trust which provided for the ultimate distribution of the trust assets to his "living grandchildren and to the living children of each deceased grandchild" upon the death of his daughter, Marie Breyman Mills. He also permitted his daughter to postpone the time of distribution beyond her death until after the death of her son, Robert E. Mills, Breyman's grandson. Prior to her death in 1973, Marie Breyman Mills did exercise the power of extension and postponed the distribution of the trust assets until 1985, the date of Robert E. Mills' death. Charles Breyman died in 1945. In 1957, Robert E. Mills married Esther K. Mills. Five years thereafter, Robert E. Mills adopted his wife's children from her previous two marriages, Roxanne Mills Pugh and Judith Lynne Muth. Later, [after Esther's death in 1963,[56]] Robert E. Mills remarried, and from that marriage emanated one natural child, Robert David Mills, appellant herein.

Following the death of Robert E. Mills in 1985, the trustee commenced a trust construction action to determine the beneficiaries of the Breyman trust. Named as defendants in that action were appellant, Robert David Mills, the natural child of Robert E. Mills, appellees, Roxanne Mills Pugh and Judith Lynne Muth, the adopted children of Robert E. Mills, and Elva Marie Bonser, an alleged illegitimate child of Robert E. Mills.

The matter was submitted to the trial court upon the stipulated facts and the parties' cross-motions for summary judgment. In two separate entries, the trial court entered judgment against Elva Marie Bonser and appellees Pugh and Muth, respectively. In the latter entry, the trial court relied upon the law in effect at the time Breyman created his trust and the "stranger to the adoption"

56. Reported by the appellate court. Eds.

doctrine to determine that Breyman did not intend to include adopted children in the designated class of trust beneficiaries. The court found as a matter of law that appellees are not beneficiaries of the Breyman trust.

Upon appeal by Pugh and Muth, the appellate court applied the adoption statute in effect at the time of review to determine that Breyman did intend to include adopted persons and reversed the decision of the trial court.

This cause is now before this court pursuant to the allowance of a motion to certify the record. . . .

HOLMES, J. The issue presented for our consideration is whether R.C. 3107.15(A)(2), which in effect abrogated the common-law "stranger to the adoption" doctrine, may be applied in construing wills or trust documents created prior to the effective date of such statute. We answer such query in the negative, and accordingly reverse the court of appeals.

In determining whether or not an adopted child is included within a class designation in a will or trust instrument, and where a reading of the "four corners" of such instrument does not give a reviewing court the appropriate clues, various additional considerations must be weighed.

First, it is axiomatic that the intent of the testator, grantor, or settlor will be ascertained and given effect wherever legally possible. The express language of the instrument generally provides the court with the indicators of the grantor's intentions, and the words used in the instrument are presumed to be used in their ordinary sense. In his trust instrument, Charles Breyman provided for the distribution of the trust assets to the "living children of each deceased grandchild." Appellant, Robert David Mills, the natural child of Robert E. Mills, is a living child of a deceased grandchild, and is obviously an intended beneficiary of this trust.

With respect to the adopted children of Robert E. Mills, the difficulty arises, of course, as to whether they are included within this class of "living children," where no such intent is stated. We then must look to the history of this area of the law, both the common law and statutory law, regarding the inheritance rights of adopted children.

Within the common law dealing with inheritance by adopted children, courts generally have treated an adoption by the settlor or grantor differently than adoptions by others. In the former situation, courts have readily concluded that the testator is presumed to have intended to include his child or children by adoption as well as his natural children. In the latter situation, the courts have been less likely to hold that an adopted child is to be included within a class in a testamentary gift or inter vivos trust. See, generally, Annotation, Adopted child as within class in testamentary gift (1962), 86 A.L.R.2d 12; Annotation,

Adopted child as within class named in deed or inter vivos trust instrument (1962), 86 A.L.R.2d 115.

Courts have traditionally looked to the specific words or terms utilized to designate the class, such as "heirs," "heirs at law," "child," "children," "issue," and "heirs of the body." The courts have tended to ascribe the common or ordinary meaning to such words, and have held that the terms "child," "children," "grandchildren," "heirs of the body," "issue," or "heirs" appearing in a will, trust or other instrument exclude an adopted child, absent a contrary intention within the instrument itself and the surrounding circumstances. In contrast, the term "heirs at law," when given its ordinary meaning, has been held to include an adopted child.

Various presumptions or rules of construction have been historically utilized by the courts in this area of the law. One of these presumptive rules is that of "stranger to the adoption," with which we deal herein. Such rule basically is to the effect that there is a presumption that a testator or settlor intended to include a child adopted by him within a generally stated class, but where the testator or settlor is a stranger to an adoption of another, such as where the adoption takes place after the testator's death, it will be presumed that he did not intend the adopted child to be included within the designated class, unless a contrary intention clearly appears.

The courts also must look to the circumstances surrounding the execution of the will or trust. The most important factor here would be the time of the adoption in relation to the execution of the will or trust, or to the death of the testator or settlor. If the facts show that the adoption took place within the lifetime of the testator or settlor, and he knew about and approved of such adoption, the adopted child may well be included within the class.

Also, of course, reviewing courts must look to the various statutes regulating the rights of an adopted child, including the current statutes and the legislative history of such statutes. Specifically, when construing an inter vivos trust, as here, a court should determine the intent of the settlor in light of the law existing at the time of the creation of the trust, since an inter vivos trust speaks from the date of its creation—not the date upon which the assets are distributed. In construing the words used by a settlor, it is a well-established presumption that the testator or settlor was acquainted with the relevant then-existing statutes, their judicial interpretation and the effect they might have on the devolution of his estate. In 1944, when Charles Breyman created the inter vivos trust at issue, the "stranger to the adoption" doctrine was recognized, and he set forth no provisions in the trust contrary to the presumption that adopted children were not included in a gift to "living children of each deceased grandchild."

However, appellees argue, and the court of appeals agreed, that the "stranger to the adoption" doctrine is no longer a rule of construction in Ohio, by virtue of R.C. 3107.15(A)(2), which "places adopted children on the same footing as natural children." That statute, effective January 1, 1977, provides:

> (A) A final decree of adoption and an interlocutory order of adoption that has become final, issued by a court of this state, shall have the following effects as to all matters within the jurisdiction or before a court of this state: . . .
>
> (2) To create the relationship of parent and child between petitioner and the adopted person, as if the adopted person were a legitimate blood descendant of the petitioner, for all purposes including inheritance and applicability of statutes, documents, and instruments, whether executed before or after the adoption is decreed, which do not expressly exclude an adopted person from their operation or effect.

The timeliness of the applicability of an adoption statute such as R.C. 3107.15, as it relates to the beneficiary rights of adopted children, is an important consideration for a reviewing court, and goes directly to the question of what law governs, in point of time. While the general rule, as stated above, is that the law existing at the time an inter vivos trust is executed is the law which applies, a subsequent legislative enactment which changes the rights of inheritance of adopted persons may apply, depending on the intent of the General Assembly.

In this regard, a statute will not be applied retrospectively unless a contrary intention clearly appears. Where a statute is to be applied prior to its effective date in such a manner as to entirely abrogate a longstanding common-law rule, the General Assembly must clearly state its intention in order to do so.

The adoption statute construed here, R.C. 3107.15, does not specifically state that it should apply retrospectively to all existing wills, but only that it shall apply to instruments, "whether executed before or after *the adoption is decreed.*" (Emphasis added.) Although the presumption embodied in the "stranger to the adoption" doctrine may no longer be applied subsequent to the effective date of the statute, the application of this doctrine has not been totally abrogated by the statutory change. The doctrine may still be utilized in the interpretation of certain wills and trust instruments executed prior to such effective date, January 1, 1977.

Reasonably interpreted, and given the absence of an express intention to apply its provisions retrospectively, R.C. 3107.15(A)(2) shall be applied prospectively, and subsequent to its effective date, January 1, 1977, to those documents, statutes, and instruments, whether executed before or after an adoption is decreed, which do not expressly exclude the adopted person from the law's or instruments' operation and effect. Provisions of an inter vivos trust shall continue to be governed by the law existing at the time of its creation, absent a contrary expression of intent within the trust instrument itself. . . .

Finally, appellees argue that, in any event, the adoption statute in effect at the time Charles Breyman created his trust also abrogated the "stranger to the adoption" doctrine. We are unpersuaded, since appellees' arguments reflect an erroneous reading of the legislative history of the adoption statute and of our cases construing such legislative changes.

Prior to 1932 the rights of adopted persons were set forth in G.C. 8030. That section provided, in pertinent part, as follows:

> . . . and the child shall be invested with every legal right, privilege, obligation and relation in respect to education, maintenance and the rights of inheritance to real estate, or to the distribution of personal estate on the death of such adopting parent or parents as if born to them in lawful wedlock; provided, such child shall not be capable of inheriting property expressly limited to the heirs of the body of the adopting parent or parents. . . .

In construing this statute, this court held that adopted children were enabled to inherit from but not through their adopting parents. The "stranger to the adoption" doctrine was a valid rule of construction.

The adoption statute was expanded with the enactment of G.C. 10512-19, effective January 1, 1932. That section added the following language to the prior statute after the limitation to the heirs of the body:

> . . . but shall be capable of inheriting property expressly limited by will or by operation of law to the child or children, heirs or heirs at law, or next of kin, of the adopting parent or parents, or to a class including any of the foregoing . . . .

We interpreted these provisions to overrule prior law and allow adopted children to inherit both from as well as through their parents. When G.C. 10512-19 was renumbered G.C. 10512-23 upon the establishment of Ohio's "Adoption Code", effective January 1, 1944, no substantive changes were made to the relevant provisions above. Thus, the law existing at the time of the execution of the Charles Breyman trust was restricted to the rights of inheritance of adopted children, by will or intestate succession, and did not speak to trust instruments. The law existing at this time also recognized the "stranger to the adoption" doctrine.

With the enactment of G.C. 8004-13, effective August 28, 1951, the rights of adopted persons were further expanded by omitting the inheritance rights stated above at G.C. 10512-19 and in lieu thereof adding the following provision:

> . . . For all purposes under the laws of this state, including without limitation all laws and wills governing inheritance of and succession to real or personal property and the taxation of such inheritance and succession, a legally adopted child shall have the same status and rights, and shall bear the same legal relationship to the adopting parents as if born to them in lawful wedlock and not born to the natural parents; provided:
>
> (A) Such adopted child shall not be capable of inheriting or succeeding to property expressly limited to heirs of the body of the adopting parent or parents . . . .

This provision, by its express language, was still not made specifically applicable to trust instruments.

G.C. 8004-13 remained basically unchanged as R.C. 3107.13 until 1972, when two significant changes were made. R.C. 3107.13 was amended effective January 26, 1972 to read, in pertinent part, as follows:

> . . . For all purposes under the laws of this state, including without limitation all laws, wills, and trust instruments governing inheritance of and succession to real or personal property and the taxation of an estate, a legally adopted child shall have the same status and rights, and shall bear the same legal relationship to the adopting parents as if born to them in lawful wedlock and not born to the natural parents; provided:
>
> (A) Such adopted child shall not be capable of inheriting or succeeding to property expressly limited to heirs of the body of the adopting parents. . . .
>
> Unless an express intention to the contrary appears in a will or trust instrument, "child," "children," "issue," "grandchild," or "grandchildren," includes a legally adopted child, for the purpose of inheritance to, through, or from the adopting parents of such child, irrespective of when such will was executed or such trust was created.

The provisions of the amended statute for the first time made the right to inherit under the adoption statutes applicable to trust instruments. These revisions also provided that when the term "children" is used in a trust instrument, such term includes a legally adopted child irrespective of when the trust was created.

Thus, it was only after 1972 that the "stranger to the adoption" doctrine began to be eroded. The final expansion of the rights of adopted children came with the enactment of current R.C. 3107.15, effective in 1977. This section removed the limitation prohibiting adopted children from inheriting property limited to "heirs of the body" and, thus, although prospectively, fully accorded adopted children the same rights of inheritance as natural born children. The abrogation of the "stranger to the adoption" doctrine has been a slow, deliberate process, and had not yet begun when Charles Breyman executed his trust in 1944.

Accordingly, based upon the law existing in 1944, we conclude that the presumption embodied in the "stranger to the adoption" doctrine is applicable to the Charles Breyman trust, consistent with the grantor's intent. Such intent was to include only natural children in the distribution of assets of his trust estate. The judgment of the court of appeals is reversed, and the judgment of the trial court is reinstated.

Judgment reversed.

MOYER, C.J., and SWEENEY, DOUGLAS, WRIGHT, HERBERT R. BROWN and EVANS, J., concur.

Notes and Questions

1. *Uniform Probate Code.* Had the UPC governed in *Mills*, the outcome would have been different. Section 8-101(b)(5) provides that "any rule of construction or presumption provided in the Code applies to instruments executed . . . before the [Code's] effective date unless there is a clear indication of a contrary intent." Consequently, § 2-705, which abrogates the stranger-to-the-adoption rule for all governing instruments, not merely for wills, applies to documents executed before the Code's effective date. If Roxanne and Judith lived while minors as regular members of Robert E. Mills's household (a fair assumption), they would have been included in the class gift and each would have taken a one-third share. Robert David Mills would have received only one-third of the corpus, not all of it.

2. *Policy of Pre-Effective Date Application.* As a matter of legislative policy, should statutory changes in rules of construction be expressly restricted to documents executed after the statute's effective date? What justifications are there for the UPC's approach of expressly extending application of its constructional rules to documents executed before the UPC's effective date?

Will of Hoffman, infra p. 156, demonstrates that a change in a common-law rule of construction often applies to documents executed before the court's decision. Is the case for application to pre-effective date documents stronger for common-law changes in rules of construction than it is for statutory changes in rules of construction?

3. *Remainder Interest to "Heirs."* If the remainder interest created by Charles Breyman's trust had been in favor of Robert E. Mills's "heirs" rather than his "children," the predominant rule of construction is that Robert's heirs should be determined by reference to the intestacy statute in existence at Robert's

death, not the statute in existence when Charles executed his trust.[57] See In re Dodge Testamentary Trust, 330 N.W.2d 72 (Mich. Ct. App. 1982) (set forth infra Chapter 18); UPC § 2-711; Restatement 2d of Property § 29.4.

4. *The 1972 Ohio Statute.* Had Robert E. Mills died between January 26, 1972, and January 1, 1977, would it have been more likely that the Ohio court would have held Roxanne and Judith were eligible to share in the class gift? If your answer is yes, should the fact he died after January 1, 1977, have produced a different result simply because the 1977 Ohio statute repealed the 1972 statute?

5. *Fact Variations of Mills.* Suppose, in *Mills*, that Esther had no children by a prior marriage and that Esther and Robert E. had adopted Roxanne and Judith as infants through an adoption agency. Suppose further that Robert E. hadn't remarried after Esther's death. Does the *Mills* precedent mean that Roxanne and Judith would be excluded from class membership under Charles's trust? If so, who would take the corpus of the trust?

Take a different variation of the original facts. Suppose that Esther hadn't died. Instead, Esther and Robert E. were divorced and Esther was awarded custody of Roxanne and Judith. Would or should Roxanne and Judith take as class members under Charles's trust?

6. *Legislative Response to Mills.* Effective May 30, 1996, the Ohio legislature amended Ohio Rev. Code § 3107.15 to provide that a final decree of adoption creates a parent-child relationship "for all purposes including inheritance and applicability of statutes, documents, and instruments, whether executed before or after the adoption is decreed, and whether executed or created before or after the effective date of this amendment, which do not expressly exclude an adopted person from their operation or effect." For discussion, see Fifth Third Bank v. Crosley, 669 N.E.2d 904 (Ohio Misc. 1996).

Adoption of Adults. Adoption statutes generally permit adoptions of adults.[58] An adoption of an adult devisee may be useful in preventing an anticipated will contest. By removing the testator's disappointed collateral relatives as heirs, the adoption prevents them from having standing to contest the will. See, e.g.,

---

57. But cf. Society Nat'l Bank v. Jacobson, 560 N.E.2d 217 (Ohio 1990).

58. A most extraordinary use of adult adoptions was posed in a biography of Huntington Hartford, heir to the A. & P. fortune. Wishing to rid himself of his first wife, he is reported to have suggested that his mother adopt her and make her his sister! Lisa R. Gubernick, Squandered Fortune (1991).

Collamore v. Learned, 50 N.E. 518 (Mass. 1898).[59] Will this planning technique work under the UPC? See UPC § 2-114(b). What further implications arising out of the adoption should be considered before an attorney advises a client to enter into an adult adoption? See UPC § 2-114(b); UAA §§ 1-102, -105, 5-101, -102 (1994). But see Cal. Prob. Code § 6451.

Can or should an adoption of an adult be used to qualify a person as a member of a class for purposes of sharing in a class gift? Will this technique work under the UPC? See UPC §§ 2-701, -705(c). In the absence of clarifying legislation or language in the governing instrument,[60] some courts have treated the adult presumptively as an adopted child for purposes of construing the dispositive instrument. See, e.g., Chichester v. Wilmington Trust Co., 377 A.2d 11 (Del. 1977) (gift to "issue" included stepchildren adopted as adults); Estate of Fortnoy, 611 P.2d 599 (Kan. Ct. App. 1980) (remainder to "heirs" of life tenant; at age 90, life tenant adopted wife's nephew, age 65); Hagaman v. Morgan, 886 S.W.2d 398 (Tex. Ct. App. 1994) (devise to "bodily issue" included adopted adult). In Davis v. Neilson, 871 S.W.2d 35, 39 (Mo. Ct. App. 1993), the court held that the presumption of inclusion can be overridden if evidence shows that adoption did not establish "family ties to the testator's family." By "restricting the presumption of inclusion to only individuals who are the natural objects of the testator's bounty," the court intended to "sift[] the bounty hunters from the class." The will provided that a grandson receive income until age 40, at which time the corpus and accumulated income was to be distributed to that grandson's issue. Immediately before his 40th birthday, the grandson adopted his secretary, her son, and three of his friends.

Other courts have refused presumptively to construe the dispositive instrument to include a child who was adopted as an adult. In Cox v. Whitten, 704 S.W.2d 628, 629 (Ark. 1986), for example, the court excluded a person adopted as an adult sixteen years after the testator died by holding that the testator's reference "to her brothers' children was not selected with the idea of including a person who was not adopted until long after her death." The excluded person was 48 years old when the testator's brother and his wife adopted him. See Victoria M. Mather, The Magic Circle: Inclusion of Adopted Children in Testamentary Class Gifts, 31 S. Tex. L. Rev. 223, 234-37 (1990);

---

59. But see Adoption of Sewall, 51 Cal. Rptr. 367 (Ct. App. 1966) (allowing disappointed collateral heir to attack adoption decree for fraud and undue influence).

60. It isn't unusual to find form books for wills and trusts that define class gift terms as including an adopted child "only if the individual was adopted under the age of 18 at the date of adoption." See, e.g., Mich. Will Manual p. XVI-22 (1990).

see also Harper v. Martin, 552 S.W.2d 690 (Ky. Ct. App. 1977) (allowing adopted adult to inherit under the intestacy statute from collateral relative of adoptive parent even though decedent was adjudged incompetent at the time of the adoption; court distinguished *Minary*, infra).

Adoption of a Legal Spouse or Domestic Partner. The Uniform Adoption Act expressly prohibits the adoption of a spouse. UAA § 5-101(a)(1). In the absence of an adoption statute prohibiting adoptions of spouses, the question arises whether the adopted spouse should be treated as a member of the class eligible to share in the class gifts other than those found in the adopting parent's donative documents. In Minary v. Citizens Fidelity Bank & Trust Co., 419 S.W.2d 340, 343-44 (Ky. 1967), a wife who was adopted by her husband under the state's adoption statute was not treated as a child for purposes of determining the takers of a class gift to heirs found in her mother-in-law's will.[61] The court focused on the question of achieving the testator's likely intent and did not address the question of the absence of a parent-child relationship between the husband and wife:

> It is of paramount importance that man be permitted to pass on his property at his death to those who represent the natural objects of his bounty. . . . Our adoption statutes should not be given a construction that does violence to the above rule . . . .

Accord In re Belgard's Trust, 829 P.2d 457 (Colo. Ct. App. 1991) (court recognized the wife's right to inherit from her husband as his child through the intestacy statute but denied her the right to be included in a class gift to her husband's children in a trust created by the husband's mother; court did not focus on husband-wife relationship but the fact that the adoption was of an adult).

Although the reasons for the adoptions may have been different than for adoptions of spouses, petitions for adoption of same-sex partners have also been controversial. In Adoption of Swanson, 623 A.2d 1095 (Del. 1993), Richard Sorrels, age 66, petitioned to adopt James Swanson, age 51, his lifetime partner. The purpose of the adoption was "to formalize the close emotional relationship that had existed between them for many years and to facilitate their estate planning," including preventing claims against their respective estates by family members and reducing inheritance tax liability under Delaware law. Id. at 1095. The court recognized that the adoption statute confers discretion on the

---

61. A challenge to the validity of the adoption was dismissed for lack of jurisdiction. See Minary v. Minary, 395 S.W.2d 588 (Ky. 1965).

family court to approve adult adoptions and that it would be against public policy to foster an incestuous relationship. It nevertheless held that

> where, as here, the petition contemplates an adoption that is not only within the scope of the statute, but which is also widely recognized as a proper exercise of the authority granted by the statute, we can divine no reason why this petition should be denied.
>
> Since the primary object of statutory construction is to reach a result in conformity with legislative policy, once that policy is determined we need only test the construction by the rules of reasonableness and conformity with that policy. In this case, our construction of the statute—permitting the adoption of one adult by another for economic reasons—is consistent with a policy promoting limited judicial inquiry into the purposes or motives behind such a relationship.

Id. at 1099.

In contrast, in a 4-2 decision, the New York Court of Appeals in Adoption of Robert Paul P., 471 N.E.2d 424, 425-27 (N.Y. 1984), denied the petition of a gay man to adopt his partner:

> [A]doption in New York, as explicitly defined in § 110 of the Domestic Relations Law, is "the legal proceeding whereby a person takes another person into the *relation of child* and thereby acquires the rights and incurs the responsibilities of *parent*." (Emphasis supplied.) It is plainly not a quasi-matrimonial vehicle to provide nonmarried partners with a legal imprimatur for their sexual relationship, be it heterosexual or homosexual. . . . Moreover, any such sexual intimacy is utterly repugnant to the relationship between child and parent in our society, and only a patently incongruous application of our adoption laws—wholly inconsistent with the underlying public policy of providing a parent-child relationship for the welfare of the child . . .—would permit the employment of adoption as the legal formalization of an adult relationship between sexual partners under the guise of parent and child. . . .
>
> While there are no special restrictions on adult adoptions under the provisions of the Domestic Relations Law, the Legislature could not have intended that the statute be employed "to arrive at an unreasonable or absurd result." . . . Such would be the result if the Domestic Relations Law were interpreted to permit one lover, homosexual or heterosexual, to adopt the other and enjoy the sanction of the law on their feigned union as parent and child.

The comment to UAA § 5-101 indicates that the drafters favor the approach adopted in *Robert Paul P.* The comment includes a cite to the case and the statement that "[i]f a relationship other than that of parent and child is intended, the adoption may be denied."

If adoption of domestic partners is allowed, questions about whether the adopted adult should be treated as a member of a class eligible to share in a class gift found in donative documents executed by someone other than the adoptive parent will have to be addressed. Cf. First Nat'l Bank of Dubuque, v. Mackey, 338 N.W.2d 361 (Iowa 1983) (settlor's daughter adopted her "friend" with whom she "shared an apartment" when she was 58 and the friend was 44; the daughter's purpose in adopting her friend was to make her friend the sole beneficiary of the trust; the court held that she should not be included as a member of the class named in the mother's trust absent evidence that the adopted adult had a *in loco parentis* relationship with the adopter).

Stepchildren and Foster Children. Usually courts don't construe class gifts to include stepchildren. See Restatement 2d of Property § 25.6. California, however, applies a constructional rule that includes as a member of a class eligible to share in class gifts some stepchildren and foster children (or their issue when appropriate to the class). See Cal. Prob. Code § 21115. The statute incorporates California's intestacy rule, see Cal. Prob. Code § 6454, which recognizes a parent-child relationship if it begins during the stepchild's or foster child's minority and continues throughout the parent and child's joint lifetimes and if it is established by clear and convincing evidence that the stepparent or foster parent would have adopted the child but for a legal barrier. See supra pp. 127-28 for further discussion of this provision.

Courts have refused to extend the doctrine of equitable adoption to presume that an equitably adopted child should be treated as a member of class in a donative instrument executed by a member of the foster parent's kindred. See, e.g., Matter of Estate of Jenkins, 904 P.2d 1316 (Colo. 1995) (en banc).

b. Children of Parents Not Married to Each Other

Will of Hoffman

385 N.Y.S.2d 49 (App. Div. 1976)

BIRNS, J. . . . Mary Hoffman, the testatrix died in 1951. Her will established a trust for the benefit of her two cousins and provided that when the first of the two should die, his one-half share of the income should be paid for the remainder of the trust term "to his issue."

One cousin is still living; the other died in 1965, survived by a daughter and a son named Stephen. Stephen died in 1972 leaving two children, the infants represented by respondent-appellant herein. Stephen never married the mother of these children nor was an order of filiation entered. The Surrogate, however, determined that the two children were indeed the children of Stephen.

Relying on precedent, the Surrogate ruled that . . . the term "issue" as used in the will meant lawful issue only, and absent an intention to the contrary it could not be assumed that the testatrix intended illegitimate descendants as the object of her bounty.

In this court, as she did below, respondent-appellant asserted that inasmuch as the word "issue" in the provision of the will under consideration was not qualified by the word "lawful," the question of legitimacy was not in decedent's mind when she made her will. In addition, the change in conventional attitudes towards illegitimates, as reflected in statutes and decisions, would warrant a construction of the word "issue" as including illegitimates, in the absence of contrary intent to exclude them.

Petitioner-respondent emphasizes that under settled case law, where the word "issue" appears in a will it will be interpreted to mean only lawful descendants in the absence of clear evidence of a contrary intent of a testator.

We recognize that precedents do hold that in the absence of an express intent to the contrary by a testator, the word "issue" presumes lawful issue and not illegitimate offspring. This presumption has its roots in an earlier society where there was no sense of injustice in the teaching that the sins of the fathers were to be visited upon their children and succeeding generations . . . .

Because of changes in societal attitudes and recent developments in constitutional law, we are of the opinion that, to the extent that precedents require this burden to be placed upon illegitimate claimants under a will, the law is not only outmoded, but discriminatory and should be rejected. We would reverse. . . .

Apparently the precise question before us has never been decided by the Court of Appeals or this court. . . .

Our statutes do provide continuing evidence of legislative concern for illegitimate children . . . .

While nothing in the [Estates, Powers, and Trusts Law] provides that illegitimate children are "issue" for the purposes of taking under a will, rights of illegitimates to share in the estates of their kin are expanding. In fact, present attitudes appear to reject an inferior social or legal status for illegitimates.

[Many] statutes, state and federal, . . . demonstrate significant changes in societal attitudes vis-a-vis illegitimate children, each of which was directed toward the elimination of disadvantages, legal and social, suffered by illegitimates. This parade of legislation was well underway, when in 1950, the testatrix executed the will before us.

The question raised is whether social and statutory changes require a reconsideration of the rule which presumed an intent by testatrix to exclude illegitimate descendants in sharing under her will.

Certainly, it cannot be said, as a matter of fact, that the testatrix was aware of these changes in societal attitudes as evidenced by the legislation referred to, or aware of community attitudes towards premarital sex or sex without marriage. Nor can it be said with any degree of assurance that at the time she executed her will she was provided with an explanation of the word "issue" which appeared on the type-written pages of that document. It is just as likely that the word "issue" in her mind had a meaning no different from "progeny" or "offspring".

The will itself supports the conclusion that the bequest to her cousins was of paramount concern in establishing the trust. It is most unlikely that she gave any more than passing thought to the children who now, 25 years after her death, claim under her will, particularly as to whether or not they would be legitimate.

The presumed intent of the testator with which all the precedents are concerned, although represented as rebuttable, is in fact, in most cases irrebuttable. The passage of time has made it impossible to establish that the testatrix did not intend to exclude illegitimate descendants from sharing under her will. . . .

To continue to rely upon these precedents and then declare that in using the word "issue" in her will, testatrix intended only lawful issue and not illegitimates is to attribute to her a frame of mind not at all supported by the facts. We recognize that the testatrix should possess the broadest freedom of choice in making known the objects of her bounty, and that it is the duty of the court to ascertain the testatrix's intent. Nevertheless, the court should not under the guise of determining the testatrix's intent substitute its own preference as to the legatees who shall take under the will. There should be a demonstrable relation between judicial interpretation of a will and the testatrix's actual frame of mind. . . .

We have been instructed that "[t]hat court best serves the law which recognizes that the rules of law which grew up in a remote generation may, in the fullness of experience be found to serve another generation badly, and which discards the old rule when it finds that another rule of law represents what should be according to the established and settled judgment of society, and no considerable property rights have become vested in reliance upon the old rule. It is thus great writers upon the common law have discovered the source and method of its growth, and in its growth found its health and life. It is not and it should not be stationary. Change of this character should not be left to the Legislature."

The Court of Appeals has stated, just recently: " . . . from the earliest times the doctrine of *stare decisis* did not require a strict adherence to precedent in every instance . . . ."

There are cases also where "the rule of adherence to precedent though it ought not be abandoned, ought to be in some degree relaxed." In the case before us, we are of the opinion that rigid adherence to precedent will produce a result not warranted by facts but rather by adherence to an anachronistic rule.

Therefore we reject the rule that where the word "issue," standing alone, appears in a will, it will be interpreted to include within its meaning only lawful descendants. We hold that the word "issue" should be construed to refer to legitimate and illegitimate descendants alike in the absence of an express qualification by the testatrix.

Further justification for our decision today can be found in expanding concepts of the Equal Protection Clause (U.S. Constitution, 14th Amendment). To construe "issue" in a will as excluding illegitimate children otherwise entitled to inherit thereunder, is, as stated before, nothing more than the substitution of judicial preference for a testator's intent. Such preference, under the guise of judicial construction, we believe, is state action. (See Shelley v. Kraemer, 334 U.S. 1.) State action is proscribed if it promotes discrimination based upon an unconstitutional classification. . . .

In holding that illegitimates are covered by the Equal Protection Clause, the Supreme Court of the United States [in Weber v. Aetna Casualty & Surety Co., 406 U.S. 164] struck down as discriminatory a statute which provided that illegitimate children did not have the same right to share in the death benefits under a Louisiana workmen's compensation statute as did legitimate children. . . .

Because of the expanding concept of equal protection we should not adhere rigidly to the rules enunciated in the cases cited as precedents herein. To do so would require us to hold that illegitimates enjoyed a lesser status than legitimate children before the law in cases such as the one before us.

In rejecting archaism, we do no more in this appeal than hold that the word "issue" as used by testatrix in her will should have no meaning other than that ordinarily and customarily imputed to persons in its usage in the absence of any manifestation of an intent to the contrary. . . . Accordingly, the law will not be required to discriminate against children labeled illegitimate through no fault of their own. . . . All concur.

Notes and Questions

1. *New York Legislation.* As amended in 1990, New York legislation codifies the *Hoffman* rule by providing that, "[u]nless the creator expresses a contrary intention, . . . a nonmarital child is the child of a mother and is the child of a father if the child is entitled to inherit from such father under section 4-1.2 of

this chapter [set forth supra p. 134]." N.Y. Est. Powers & Trusts Law § 2-1.3.[62]

2. *Rules of Construction Regarding Nonmarital Children.* The law is clearly moving away from the traditional constructional rule that children of unmarried parents are presumptively *excluded* from membership under class-gift terminology. The rule of construction that should replace the traditional rule is more controversial. Is it to be the opposite rule, as the *Hoffman* court held and the New York legislation provides, under which nonmarital children are presumptively *included* under class-gift terminology? Is some intermediate rule more appropriate, under which children of unmarried parents are included in some circumstances, but excluded in others? Keep in mind that rules of construction supply *presumptive* meaning to the language in a private instrument, such as a will or trust. Transferors are not bound by a rule of construction. Well-drafted documents expressly address whether nonmarital children are intended to be takers of gifts made to classes of beneficiaries. The function of the rule of construction is to reflect the likely intent of transferors who fail to indicate whether they want to include nonmarital children as members of a class.

Children of unmarried parents always presumptively included. The Restatement 2d of Property § 25.2 promulgates a rule of construction stating that nonmarital children are presumptively included in class gift terminology.[63] This approach has also been adopted by a number of recent judicial decisions in addition to *Hoffman*. In Powers v. Wilkinson, 506 N.E.2d 842, 848 (Mass. 1987), the Supreme Judicial Court of Massachusetts broke from prior Massachusetts precedent dating back about 150 years by holding that "the word 'issue,' absent clear expressions of a contrary intent, must be construed to include all biological descendants." This new Massachusetts rule of construction, however, is not to apply retroactively, but "only to trust instruments executed after the date of [the *Powers*] opinion." In Northwestern Nat'l Bank v. Simons, 242 N.W.2d 78, 80 (Minn. 1976), the Supreme Court of Minnesota, four justices dissenting, held that a nonmarital child of a granddaughter of the settlor of a trust created in 1921 was a beneficiary of the trust under a provision in favor of the settlor's "issue." The court said: "When there

62. Interestingly (in view of *Hoffman*), this statute only applies to wills of persons dying on and after September 1, 1991, and to lifetime instruments previously executed that on that date were subject to the grantor's power to revoke or amend, and to all lifetime instruments executed on or after that date.

63. The Restatement 3d of Property has not yet addressed the question.

is some doubt, either from family circumstances, the behavior or knowledge of a settlor, or from the trust instrument itself, this court will hold that illegitimate issue are to be included as issue."[64] In Estate of Dulles, 431 A.2d 208, 17 A.L.R.4th 1279 (Pa. 1981), the Supreme Court of Pennsylvania held that a codified rule of construction declaring that, in the absence of an explicit declaration to the contrary in the governing instrument, a person born out of wedlock is not included in class gift language (such as "grandchildren"), is in violation of the equal protection clause of the federal constitution.

Children of unmarried parents presumptively included under an agency concept. A competing approach utilizes an agency concept for documents of a transferor who is not the parent of the nonmarital child. Under this concept, Mary Hoffman would be presumptively deemed to have viewed Stephen as her agent: If Stephen had treated his nonmarital children as his own, they would be included in Mary's class gift to her cousin's "issue"; if Stephen had not treated them as his own, they would be excluded from the class. UPC § 2-705(b) adopts this agency approach. It states that, in construing a dispositive provision by a transferor who is not the natural parent, an individual born to the natural parent is not considered the child of that parent unless the individual lived while a minor as a regular member of the household of that natural parent or of that parent's parent, brother, sister, spouse, or surviving spouse.[65] The Supreme Court of Wisconsin also used the agency concept when it held in In re Trust of Parsons, 203 N.W.2d 40 (Wis. 1973), that the traditional presumption against inclusion of a child of unmarried parents is rebutted if the child was "a part of the family circle." California Probate Code § 21115(b) promulgates a similar rule.

A distinction is sometimes drawn in academic legal circles between "rules" and "standards." The distinction focuses on the degree of precision with which a legal proposition is formulated: Rules are more specific than standards. Both UPC § 2-705(b) and *Parsons* seek to establish the same agency-concept proposition, but § 2-705(b) formulates it as a rule and *Parsons* formulates it as a standard. What are the pros and cons of each method of formulation? See Isaac Ehrlich & Richard A. Posner, An Economic Analysis of Legal Rule-making, 3 J. Leg. Stud. 257 (1974); Duncan Kennedy, Form and Substance in Private Law Adjudication, 89 Harv. L. Rev. 1685, 1699-1701 (1976); Carol M. Rose, Crystals and Mud in Property Law, 40 Stan. L. Rev. 577 (1988).

---

64. Minnesota subsequently enacted UPC § 2-705, but omitted subsections (b) and (c). See Minn. Stat. Ann. § 524.2-705.

65. Note that § 2-705(b) applies to marital as well as nonmarital children.

3. *Adopted-Out Nonmarital Children.* After *Hoffman* was decided, a case arose in New York concerning a nonmarital child who, upon birth, was put up for adoption and shortly thereafter was adopted. The case is Estate of Best, 485 N.E.2d 1010 (N.Y. 1985), cert. denied sub nom. McCollum v. Reid, 475 U.S. 1083 (1986). In *Best*, the testator died in 1973, leaving a will that devised the residue of her estate in trust. The trustee was directed to pay income to the testator's daughter, Ardith, for life. On Ardith's death, the testator directed the trustee to pay the income to Ardith's issue for the life of each. Ardith was the mother of two children, David and Anthony. David was born in 1952, out of wedlock. David was immediately placed with an agency for adoption and shortly thereafter adopted by the McCollums. Ardith's second child, Anthony, was born in 1963, in wedlock.

The Surrogate applied the presumption established in *Hoffman*, held that it had not been rebutted, and concluded that David was entitled to share in the income from the testator's trust. See 455 N.Y.S.2d 487 (Sur. Ct. 1982). The Appellate Division affirmed, saying: "Because we agree with the reasoning set forth in the opinion of Justice Birns in Matter of Hoffman (supra), we hold that the Surrogate properly applied the presumption established therein in the case at bar." 477 N.Y.S.2d 431, 432 (App. Div. 1984).

The Court of Appeals reversed. Although the court accepted as a "rebuttable rule of construction" the proposition that "the unmodified term issue [refers] to children born both in and out of wedlock," the court held that adopted-out children posed a different question. As to adopted-out children, the court said: "Only if a child adopted out of the family is specifically named in a biological ancestor's will, or the gift is expressly made to issue including those adopted out of the family, can the child take." 485 N.E.2d at 1013. See also N.Y. Dom. Rel. Law § 117 (prevents severance of parent-child relationship for adopted-out children when they are adopted by certain family members); N.Y. Est. Powers & Trusts Law § 2-1.3(a)(1) (applies same rules to construction of documents); George B. Reese, Best Friends and Relations: Construing "Issue" in Instruments and Intestacy Statutes, 4 Hofstra Prop. L.J. 71 (1990) (reviewing *Best* and subsequent statutory enactments).

The Restatement 2d of Property promulgates a somewhat different rule of construction. Under § 25.5, an adopted-out child is presumptively excluded from a class gift if the adoption "removes the child from the broader family circle" of the biological parent.

How would the facts in *Best* be analyzed under the Restatement or under UPC §§ 2-701 and -705?

4. *Children Conceived by Assistive Reproductive Technologies.* The Restatement 2d of Property adopts the following rule of construction:

> § *25.3 Gifts to "Children"—Child Conceived by Means Other Than Sexual Intercourse.* When the donor of property describes the beneficiaries thereof as "children" of a designated person, the primary meaning of such class gift term includes a child conceived by means other than sexual intercourse who is recognized by the designated person as a child of him or her. It is assumed in the absence of language or circumstances indicating a contrary intent, that the donor adopts such primary meaning.

EXTERNAL REFERENCES. Edward C. Halbach, Jr., Issues About Issue: Some Recurrent Class Gift Problems, 48 Mo. L. Rev. 333, 347-50 (1983); Patricia G. Roberts, Adopted and Nonmarital Children: Exploring the 1990 Uniform Probate Code's Intestacy and Class Gift Provisions, 32 Real Prop., Prob. & Tr. J. 539 (1998).

Chapter 4

Execution of Wills

INTESTATE succession is a default regime that operates in the absence of a valid will. See Restatement 3d of Property § 2.1, comment c. Intestacy has not always operated as a default regime. It was once mandatory law. In early English law, property owners were deprived of the right to make a will. To be sure, the power to dispose of personal property by will was recognized early. The ecclesiastical courts asserted jurisdiction over succession to personal property on death, and encouraged bequests for religious and charitable purposes, as well as for the decedent's family. During the Anglo-Saxon period, both men and women could dispose of land at death, but recognition of testamentary transfers ceased within about a century after the Norman Conquest. The gift of land by will "stood condemned," Maitland wrote, "because it is a death-bed gift, wrung from a man in his agony. In the interest of honesty, in the interest of the lay state, a boundary must be maintained against ecclesiastical greed and the other-worldliness of dying men." 2 Frederick Pollock & Frederic W. Maitland, History of English Law 328 (2d ed. 1898). The church courts never gained jurisdiction over succession to land and the Crown courts weren't concerned with seeing that a man atoned for his wrongs by devoting a portion of his property to pious objects.

Land, during this early period, passed by inheritance to the eldest son. Nevertheless, landowners sought means to make provision at death for their other children, for pious uses, and perhaps for a general freedom of testamentary disposition. This became possible after equity began to enforce uses in the early part of the fifteenth century. A landowner would transfer land (enfeoff) to A, to hold to the use of the feoffor for life and then to such uses as the feoffor might appoint in his will. The Chancellor recognized the will appointing the use (for it was not a disposition of legal title to land) and compelled A to carry out the uses.

One of the purposes of the Statute of Uses, passed in 1536 (27 Hen. 8, ch. 10), was to eliminate testamentary disposition of land by way of use. The preamble to the statute condemned "wills and testaments, sometimes made by nude parolx and words, sometimes by signs and tokens, and sometimes by writing, and for the most part made by such persons as be visited with sickness, in their extreme agonies and pains, or at such time as they have scantly had any good memory or remembrance." But the demand for power of testation was strong and four years later, in 1540, the first English Statute of Wills was enacted, permitting testamentary disposition of land with certain limitations that are important only to the student of the English history of feudalism. Notably, three years later, another act was passed providing that a married woman's devise was invalid. See 34 & 35 Hen. 8, ch. 5, § 14.[1]

Probate Procedure. Procedurally, the determination about whether a particular decedent left a valid will is made in a proceeding in which the instrument is *offered* for probate by the *proponent*. If the instrument is found to be valid, it is *admitted to probate* as the decedent's last will. This procedure developed early in English law for wills of personal property but not for wills of real property, even after wills of land were authorized by statute in 1540. The ecclesiastical courts assumed jurisdiction over wills of personal property but not of land. Until a probate court was established in England in the mid-nineteenth century and given jurisdiction over the probate of all wills, there was no direct means of establishing the validity of a will of land. Instead, validity was usually put in issue by an action in ejectment or trespass brought to try the title to land.

---

1. For discussion of the development of women's property rights in the United States, including the right of women to make wills, see Norma Basch, In the Eyes of the Law: Women, Marriage, and Property in Nineteenth-Century New York (1982); Marylynn Salmon, Women and the Law of Property in Early America (1986); Elizabeth Bowles Warbasse, The Changing Legal Rights of Married Women 1800-1861 (1987); Richard H. Chused, Married Women's Property Law, 1800-1850, 71 Geo. L.J. 1359 (1983). See also Susan Staves, Married Women's Separate Property in England, 1660-1833 (1990).

Nearly everywhere in this country, some court is given jurisdiction to probate wills, whether the property involved is real or personal or both. In many states there are separate probate courts, although they may go by other names, such as surrogates' courts in New York, or orphans' courts in Pennsylvania. In other states, the court of general jurisdiction, such as a circuit or county court, exercises probate jurisdiction. Although there are many local differences in the jurisdiction of probate courts, in general they perform more functions than passing on the validity of wills. Probate courts appoint executors and administrators and exercise supervision over these personal representatives in the administration of decedents' estates, regardless of whether the decedents died testate or intestate. The appointment of a personal representative is traditionally described as the grant of *letters testamentary* or *letters of administration*.

The Relationship Between Substantive Requirements and the Statutory Formalities. Determining that a particular decedent left a valid will has been thought to require: (1) solid evidence of the existence and content of the decedent's directions; (2) some indication that the directions were not casually arrived at; (3) reason to think that the directions were the product of the decedent's free choice; and (4) reason to think that the decedent had the mental capacity to comprehend what property was owned and who were the so-called natural objects of the decedent's bounty at the time the dispository decisions were made.

Throughout American history, these objectives—frequently called the evidentiary, cautionary, and protective functions—have been partly achieved through the establishment of statutory formalities for the execution of a valid will. In broad form, the statutory formalities have remained unchanged. They are that the will must be: (1) in *writing*; (2) *signed* by the testator; and (3) *attested* by credible witnesses. The details of two of these three basic requirements—signature and attestation—vary considerably from state to state. These variations are largely attributable to the fact that, before the widespread adoption of the former UPC, American statutes were—and still are in non-UPC states—largely copied from one or the other (or, in some cases, partly from both) of two English statutes: the Statute of Frauds of 1677 and the Wills Act of 1837.[2]

---

2. In early law, wills of personal property weren't required to be in writing nor were wills of land when they were made through the device of a use. The Statute of Wills of 1540, 32 Hen. 8, ch. 1, seems to have established the requirement of a writing, though it wasn't necessary that the instrument be written or signed by the testator nor that it be witnessed. The hesitation in making a flat statement that a writing was necessary arises from the language of the statute giving power to any person who should "have" any lands as tenant in fee simple to "give, dispose, will and devise" the same "by his last will and testament in writing, or otherwise by any act or acts

Statute of Frauds, 1677, *§ 5.*[3] [A]ll devises and bequests of any lands . . . shall be in writing and signed by the party so devising the same or by some other person in his presence and by his express directions and shall be attested and subscribed in the presence of the said devisor by three or four credible witnesses or else they shall be utterly void and of none effect.

Wills Act, 1837, *§ 9.*[4] [N]o will shall be valid unless it shall be in writing and executed in manner hereinafter mentioned; (that is to say,) it shall be signed at the foot or end thereof by the testator, or by some other person in his presence and by his direction; and such signature shall be made or acknowledged by the testator in the presence of two or more witnesses present at the same time, and such witnesses shall attest and subscribe the will in the presence of the testator, but no form of attestation shall be necessary.

The later English statute, the Wills Act of 1837, increased rather than decreased the statutory formalities. Before the promulgation of the UPC in 1969, most American states had opted for a statute modeled on the Statute of Frauds provision with its relatively fewer formal requirements. The former UPC reduced the formalities still further in order to "validate the will whenever possible." Art. II, Part 5, gen. comment. Accordingly, former UPC § 2-502 required a will to be in writing, signed by a testator, and signed by two persons who witnessed either the testator's act of signing or the testator's acknowledgment either of the testator's own signature or of the will.

UPC § 2-502 generally continues the original set of formalities. It takes a further step, however, in the direction of upholding wills whenever responsibly possible by adding a new section, § 2-503. Section 2-503 sets forth a harmless-error rule under which a will that was not executed in conformity with § 2-502 is valid if the proponent can establish by clear and convincing evidence that the decedent intended the proffered document to constitute the decedent's will. Section 3.3 of the Restatement 3d of Property sets forth a similar harmless-error rule. See infra p. 181.

Military Wills. In October 2000, Congress made available an alternative set of formalities for military wills, called "military testamentary instruments." See Floyd D. Spence National Defense Authorization Act for Fiscal Year 2001 § 551, Pub. L. No. 106-398, 114 Stat. 1654 (codified as 10 U.S.C. § 1044d). The statute provides:

10 U.S.C. § 1044d. Military testamentary instruments: requirement for recognition

---

lawfully executed in his life . . . ." The authorities state, however, that a writing was required. See, e.g., 7 William S. Holdsworth, History of English Law 367 (1926).

3. Statute of Frauds, 1677, 29 Car. 2, ch. 3.

4. Wills Act, 1837, 7 Wm. 4 & 1 Vict., ch. 26.

by States.

(a) *Testamentary Instruments to Be Given Legal Effect.* A military testamentary instrument—

(1) is exempt from any requirement of form, formality, or recording before probate that is provided for testamentary instruments under the laws of a State; and

(2) has the same legal effect as a testamentary instrument prepared and executed in accordance with the laws of the State in which it is presented for probate.

(b) *Military Testamentary Instruments.* For purposes of this section, a military testamentary instrument is an instrument that is prepared with testamentary intent in accordance with regulations prescribed under this section and that—

(1) is executed in accordance with subsection (c) by (or on behalf of) a person, as a testator, who is eligible for military legal assistance;[5]

(2) makes a disposition of property of the testator; and

(3) takes effect upon the death of the testator.

(c) *Requirements for Execution of Military Testamentary Instruments.* An instrument is valid as a military testamentary instrument only if—[6]

(1) the instrument is executed by the testator (or, if the testator is unable to execute the instrument personally, the instrument is executed in the presence of, by the direction of, and on behalf of the testator);

(2) the instrument is executed in the presence of a military legal assistance counsel[7] acting as presiding attorney;

(3) the instrument is executed in the presence of at least two disinterested witnesses (in addition to the presiding attorney), each of whom attests to witnessing the testator's execution of the instrument by signing it; and

(4) the instrument is executed in accordance with such additional requirements as may be provided in regulations prescribed under this section.

---

5. The term "person eligible for military legal assistance" means a person who is eligible for legal assistance under 10 U.S.C. § 1044. Under § 1044, persons eligible for legal assistance are members of the armed forces who are on active duty; members and former members entitled to retired or retainer pay or equivalent pay; officers of the commissioned corps of the Public Health Service who are on active duty or entitled to retired or equivalent pay; and dependents of such persons.

6. 10 U.S.C. § 1044d(e) provides in paragraph (1) that, under regulations prescribed under this section, each military testamentary instrument shall contain a statement that sets forth the provisions of subsection (a), but also provides that paragraph (1) shall not be construed to make inapplicable the provisions of subsection (a) to a testamentary instrument that does not include a statement described in that paragraph.

7. The term "military legal assistance counsel" is defined as (A) a judge advocate (as defined in 10 U.S.C. § 801(13)); or (B) a civilian attorney serving as a legal assistance officer under 10 U.S.C. § 1044.

PART A. FORMALITIES OF EXECUTION: THE PROPONENT'S CASE

As indicated above, most non-UPC statutes in this country prescribe formalities for the execution of a will modeled on one or the other of the English statutes. In the majority of non-UPC states the legislation is based on the Statute of Frauds of 1677, except that only two witnesses are usually required.[8] Some states have added requirements not found in the English statutes, such as the requirement that a will be "published," by which it is meant that the testator must declare to the witnesses that the document is the testator's will.[9]

In addition to attested wills (wills subscribed by the prescribed number of attesting witnesses), a substantial and growing number of states also recognize the validity of certain types of unattested wills. Here we are principally speaking of holographic wills. The formalities prescribed for a valid holographic will are that the will must be written in the handwriting of the testator and signed, and, in some states, that it must be dated.

The goal of the statutory formalities—writing, signature, attestation (or, in the case of holographic wills, writing in the testator's hand, signature, and perhaps dating)—is to facilitate a reasonably reliable post-death determination of whether a decedent chose to exercise testamentary freedom and, if so, of the distributive plan. In addition to the evidentiary, cautionary, and protective functions, the formalities serve a channeling function. These functions are described in the Restatement 3d of Property § 3.3, comment a, as follows:

> *a. Purpose of the statutory formalities.* . . . The evidentiary function requires solid evidence of the existence and content of the decedent's directions. The cautionary function requires some indication that the decedent arrived at these directions with adequate awareness. The protective function attempts to assure that the contents and the execution of the will were the product of the decedent's free choice. The channeling function is meant to facilitate a substantial degree of standardization in the organization, language, and content of most wills, so that they can be prepared and administered in a fairly routine manner.

For greater elaboration of these functions, see John H. Langbein, Substantial

---

8. Three witnesses were once required in a few states, principally in New England. Of these, only Vermont still retains a three-witness requirement. See Vt. Stat. Ann. tit. 14, § 5.

9. The Statutory Note to Restatement 3d of Property § 3.1 lists Arkansas, Indiana, Iowa, Louisiana, New York, Oklahoma, Pennsylvania, and Tennessee as states that require a will to be "published." California does not require the testator to declare to the witnesses that the instrument is the testator's will, but does require that the witnesses understand that the instrument is the testator's will.

Compliance with the Wills Act, 88 Harv. L. Rev. 489, 492-97 (1975). The Restatement 3d of Property § 3.3, comment a, states that "[t]he purpose of the statutory formalities . . . is to determine whether the decedent adopted the document as his or her will. The formalities are meant to facilitate this intent-serving purpose, not to be ends in themselves." As we shall see, however, many courts seem to view the formalities as ends in themselves.

1. Attested Wills

Statutory References: *UPC §§ 2-502, -503, -506*

The Preferred Method for Executing a Valid Will. As indicated earlier, the statutes differ among the states as to various details of formality. Differences in the statutes create a potential for invalidity even if the testator complies with the formality requirements of the state in which the will is executed or where the testator is domiciled. If the testator changes domicile or if the testator owns real property in other states, the common-law rules of conflict of laws potentially could lead to the will being held partially or totally invalid. Most states, however, have enacted statutes that recognize a will executed outside the state. UPC § 2-506, for example, recognizes a will executed outside the state in accordance with either the law of the place of execution or of the testator's domicile. See Restatement 3d of Property, Statutory Note to § 3.1 (describing variations in choice-of-law statutes); Jeffrey A. Schoenblum, Multijurisdictional Estates and Article II of the Uniform Probate Code, 55 Alb. L. Rev. 1291 (1992) (analyzing UPC § 2-506).

The presence of the common-law rules and the lack of uniformity within the choice-of-law statutes suggest the advisability of complying with the maximum formalities called for by the law of any state.

Attestation Clauses. Attestation clauses are located immediately below the line for the testator's signature, and typically provide:

> The foregoing instrument, consisting of____ typewritten pages, including this page, was signed, published and declared by the above named testator to be his [her] last will, in the presence of us; we, in his [her] presence, at his [her] request, and in the presence of each other, have hereunto subscribed our names as witnesses; and we declare that at the time of the execution of this instrument the

testator, according to our best knowledge and belief, was of sound mind and under no constraint.

Dated at _________________, _____, this ____ day of __________, ____.

________________ ____________________________
Witness Address

________________ ____________________________
Witness Address

________________ ____________________________
Witness Address

Although no state requires the use of an attestation clause as a prerequisite to validity, lawyers routinely use them because they raise a rebuttable presumption that the events recited therein actually occurred. See Restatement 3d of Property § 3.1, comment q. In most states, the presumption is regarded as a presumption of fact. That means the presumption remains operative and is entitled to evidentiary weight notwithstanding the introduction of contrary evidence. See, e.g., Estate of Clark, 603 N.W.2d 290 (Mich. Ct. App. 1999); Jackson v. Patton, 952 S.W.2d 404 (Tenn. 1997); see also Estate of Johnson, 780 P.2d 692 (Okla. 1989) (holding will invalid where testimony of witnesses persuasively contradicted attestation clause). Even if the witnesses' testimony contradicts the events recited in the attestation clause, the presumption of regularity continues so long as that testimony is insufficient to show that the testator failed to comply with the statutory formalities. See Betts v. Lonas, 172 F.2d 759 (D.C. Cir. 1948) (upholding will on the basis of a presumption of regularity arising from fact that the will looked regular on its face).

On occasion, a will, regular on its face but without an attestation clause, has been denied probate when the witnesses couldn't recall whether the required procedures had been followed. For example, in Young v. Young, 313 N.E.2d 593, 597 (Ill. App. Ct. 1974), the court said, "where the purported will does not contain an attestation clause, the proponent of the will has the burden of proving its proper execution by other evidence. . . . The [proponent] has furnished no such evidence."

Lawyer Liability for Invalid Execution. A lawyer who supervises the execution of a will may be liable to the intended devisees if the lawyer caused the will to be invalidly executed. See, e.g., Biakanja v. Irving, 320 P.2d 16 (Cal. 1958); Licata v. Spector, 225 A.2d 28 (Conn. C.P. 1966); Guy v. Liederbach, 459 A.2d 744 (Pa. 1983); Auric v. Continental Casualty Co., 331 N.W.2d 325 (Wis. 1983); Martin D. Begleiter, First Let's Sue All the Lawyers—What Will We Get: Damages for Estate Planning Malpractice, 51 Hastings L.J. 325 (2000); John R. Price, Duties of Estate Planners to Nonclients: Identifying, Anticipating and Avoiding the Problems, 37 S. Tex. L. Rev. 1063 (1996); see also In re Grant, 936 P.2d 1360 (Kan. 1997) (censuring lawyer who, after the death of the decedent, altered a will to conceal the fact that it had been invalidly executed and submitted the altered will for probate). But see DeThorne v. Bakken, 539 N.W.2d 695 (Wis. Ct. App. 1995) (holding it was reasonable for the lawyer to believe that under the circumstances a witness giving assistance to the testator in signing the will complied with the law).

Should a lawyer be liable to a potential beneficiary of a will if the decedent dies before the lawyer completes preparation of the will or arranges for its execution? The court in Radovich v. Locke-Paddon, 41 Cal. Rptr. 2d 573 (Ct. App. 1995), held no. On June 21, 1991, the lawyer, Locke-Paddon, met with the decedent to discuss drafting a new will for her in which she would establish a testamentary trust that gave her husband, Radovich, the income from the trust corpus for his life. At this meeting, Locke-Paddon learned that the decedent had been diagnosed with breast cancer. He delivered a "rough draft" of the proposed new will to the decedent on October 8, 1991, declaring that "it was my understanding that the next move was hers; I could not proceed any further with the preparation of the new will until she communicated to me her comments and whether she was satisfied with its provisions. Moreover, [the decedent] told me she intended to confer with her sister . . . before finalizing the provisions of the draft of the proposed new will." Id. at 575. The decedent died on December 19, 1991, without having further communicated with the lawyer. Without deciding whether Locke-Paddon's performance had met the professional standard of care to his client, the court found that the lawyer had no duty to the potential beneficiary:

> [W]e see both practical and policy reasons for requiring more evidence of commitment than is furnished by a direction to prepare a will containing specified provisions. From a practical standpoint, common experience teaches that potential testators may change their minds more than once after the first meeting. Although a potential testator may also change his or her mind after a will is signed, we perceive significantly stronger support for an inference of commitment in a signature on testamentary documents than in a preliminary direction to prepare such documents for signature. . . .
>
> [I]mposition of liability in a case such as this could improperly compromise an attorney's primary duty of undivided loyalty to his or her client, the decedent. . . . Here, notwithstanding his inexplicable delay in preparing the draft will in the first place, Locke-Paddon did get the draft to the decedent more than two months before she died. Thus here the decedent . . . did have an opportunity to execute the testamentary document before death. Further, the undisputed facts make plain that it was the decedent's intent to give further thought to her testamentary plan and to consult with her sister. . . . "[I]mposition of liability would create an incentive for an attorney to exert pressure on a client to complete and execute estate planning documents summarily," without the additional consideration the decedent in this

> case said she intended to give them, and "[f]ear of liability to potential third party beneficiaries would contravene the attorney's primary responsibility to ensure that the proposed estate plan effectuates the client's wishes and that the client understands the available options and the legal and practical implications of whatever course of action is ultimately chosen." Krawczyk v. Stingle, 543 A.2d 733, 736 (Conn. 1988).
>
> We acknowledge that in the circumstances it would have been professionally appropriate, at least, for Locke-Paddon to have inquired of the decedent whether she had any questions or wished further assistance in completing the change of testamentary disposition she had discussed with him. But on weighing relevant policy considerations we conclude that Locke-Paddon and the law firm cannot be held to have owed a duty to Radovich to have done so.

Id. at 582-83. For other cases holding the lawyer not liable for delay in having the client execute the will, see Krawczyk v. Stingle, 543 A.2d 733 (Conn. 1988); Gregg v. Lindsay, 649 A.2d 935 (Pa. Super. Ct. 1994), appeal denied, 661 A.2d 874 (Pa. 1995). See also Michael G. Desmarais, Is the "Backover Defense" Now Viable in a Legal Malpractice Action for Negligent Estate Planning?, 22 ACTEC Notes 348 (1997) (critiquing *Radovich*).

Contrast the English case of White v. Jones, [1993] 3 All E.R. 481 (C.A.), where the English Court of Appeal, Civil Division, held a lawyer liable to the devisees named in the testator's letter to his solicitor giving directions regarding the preparation of a new will. Although the requested will was a simple will, preparation of it was unreasonably delayed, and the testator died before it was prepared. To the argument that the testator might have changed his mind before executing the will, Sir Donald Nicholls V-C said (id. at 493):

> I can see no reason to doubt that, if [the solicitors] had got on with the matter as they should have done, a new will under which each plaintiff would have benefitted, at least to the extent of the £9,000, would have been signed by [the testator] before he went on holiday.

a. The Writing Requirement

All the statutes, including the Uniform Probate Code, require a will to be in writing. The Restatement 3d of Property § 3.1, comment i, provides that:

> *i. The writing requirement*. . . . The requirement of a writing does not require that the will be written on sheets of paper, but it does require a medium that allows the markings to be detected. A will, for example, scratched in the paint on the fender of a car would be in writing, but one "written" by waving a finger in the air would not be.

A videotape or tape recording is not recognized as a writing and cannot operate as the will itself. See Estate of Reed, 672 P.2d 829 (Wyo. 1983) (court rejected a proffered tape recording as a holographic will). Videotapes have been admitted into evidence, however, for the purpose of proving a testator's testamentary capacity and freedom from undue influence. See, e.g., Geduldig v. Posner, 743 A.2d 247 (Md. Ct. Spec. App. 1999); Estate of Burack, 607 N.Y.S.2d 711 (App. Div. 1994); Estate of Kessler, 977 P.2d 591 (Wash. Ct. App. 1999); Ind. Code § 29-1-5-3(c). The opinions of estate planners differ on whether videotapes are useful. Compare William R. Buckley, Videotaped Wills: More Than a Testator's Curtain Call, 126 Tr. & Est. 48 (Oct. 1987) with Hanson S. Reynolds, The Impact of Probate Litigation, in Sophisticated Estate Planning Techniques, CA 39 ALI-ABA 735 (Sept. 7, 1995).

b. The Signature Requirement

All the statutes, including § 2-502 of the Uniform Probate Code, require the testator to sign the will. The UPC and many non-UPC statutes qualify the signature requirement by the rule that, if the testator does not sign the will, someone else can sign the testator's name if it is done in the presence and at the direction of the testator. A further requirement, sometimes imposed by non-UPC statutes, is that persons who sign for testators must also sign their own names and sometimes also give their addresses. See Restatement 3d of Property, Statutory Note to § 3.1.

Estate of McKellar, below, considered the validity of a will under a statute modeled on the English Statute of Frauds of 1677, supra p. 168.

Estate of McKellar

380 So. 2d 1273 (Miss. 1980)

BROOM, J. Execution and attestation of a purported Last Will and Testament are at issue in this case appealed from the Chancery Court of Lauderdale County. In that court Tiny Bell filed for probate a document said to be Greta Meador McKellar's true Last Will and Testament. The matter was contested and after hearing testimony the lower court found that the document was statutorily deficient and therefore invalid. . . .

The purported Last Will and Testament of Greta Meador McKellar (McKellar herein) is a five-page instrument [completely written out in McKellar's own handwriting and] dated August 23, 1977. McKellar died March 29, 1979. . . . According to the document at issue, several beneficiaries of McKellar's purported Will were persons not her heirs at law. Her heirs at law were stated to be Tiny Bell, named by the lower court as her administratrix, Nell Thrash and Jacqueline Field.

First paragraph of the purported Will is in the following language:

To Whom it May Concern

> *I, Greta Meador McKellar, being of sound mind and body, declare this to be my last Will and testimony [sic] concerning my real and personal property. . . .*

The document consists of five pages (four sheets of paper), the last of which is on the reverse side of page 1. Near the bottom of the last page, being page No. 5, is the following:

> *The following have witness [sic] my writing of this five page will—*
> *Luciana Brewer*
> *Lucille Jay*
> *Douglas Watkins.*

Nowhere on the instrument except in the opening paragraph does McKellar's purported signature appear.

Testimony adduced to the lower court included the three people whose names appear at the end of the document as witnesses. Douglas Watkins testified that she took the deceased McKellar to the hospital, and that while a patient in the hospital, McKellar called Watkins to her room and said, "Sign this." Watkins did not see McKellar write any part of the document; nor did she see McKellar sign her name, nor hear McKellar acknowledge signing the document. According to Watkins, McKellar did not tell her what the document was.

Another witness to the instrument, Luciane [sic] Brewer, stated that McKellar called her to McKellar's hospital room where McKellar handed Brewer one page to sign. She testified that in all McKellar had four or five pieces of paper, and that when she (Brewer) signed it, she saw no other names on the paper. Brewer's further testimony was that McKellar discussed the contents of the instrument with her but did not state that McKellar told her that McKellar had signed the instrument. Brewer did not read the instrument.

Lucille Jay testified that McKellar asked her to come to McKellar's room where McKellar said, "This is my Last Will and Testimony [sic]. . . ." Jay stated that when she signed the instrument as a witness, she didn't examine it but that Mrs. Brewer had already signed it when she, Jay, signed it.

The witness Watkins kept the controversial document until the day after the funeral when she opened the envelope containing the document.

The chancellor in his opinion held that the

> [P]urported will was not signed by the purported testatrix as is required by law and the cases in this jurisdiction. It is the opinion of this Court that the statements made to the witnesses by the purported testatrix did not carry with it any words signifying that the purported testatrix had signed the will.

Upon this record we cannot say that the decree against the purported Will was manifestly wrong or that the chancellor's finding was contrary to the law or the evidence. Careful analysis of the testimony establishes that none of the witnesses who testified stated that they saw or read or heard the entire document. None of the pages of the document except near the bottom of page five was signed by a witness, and McKellar's purported signature was at the top of page one. No testimony is in the record that any of the witnesses saw or observed McKellar either affix her signature on the document or heard her acknowledge that she had previously or at any time signed or affixed her signature to the document.

Under the case law of this state, the execution of a Will is a statutory privilege and not a constitutional or common law right. We have held many times that the intention of a testator is the paramount issue in the construction of Wills but one's intention does not become important nor the object of search by a court until there is first established a Will executed according to statutory requirements. Wilson v. Polite, 218 So. 2d 843 (Miss. 1969). *Wilson* dealt with a purported Will wherein the testatrix did not sign (subscribe) at the bottom. Accordingly we held it not to be a valid holographic Will. In *Wilson*, there were no attesting witnesses to the purported Will, and it could not be valid as a non-holographic Will so it was a nullity. *Wilson* made the following pronouncement concerning a non-holographic or attested Will (the type now at issue):

> [T]he name of the testator may be written at any place on the instrument, so long as it is declared to be his signature, and the instrument is published and signed in the presence of the witnesses.

Our statute applicable here is Mississippi Code Annotated § 91-5-1 (1972) which states in pertinent part that:

> [S]uch last will and testament, or codicil, be signed by the testator or testatrix, or by some other person in his or her presence and by his or her express direction. Moreover, if not wholly written and subscribed by himself or herself, it shall be attested by two (2) or more credible witnesses in the presence of the testator or testatrix. . . .

Upon this record we cannot say that the Will was properly executed . . . and therefore the lower court must be affirmed. Affirmed.

PATTERSON, C.J., SMITH and ROBERTSON, P.JJ., and SUGG, WALKER, LEE, BOWLING and COOPER, JJ., concur.

Notes and Questions

1. *Strict-Compliance Approach.* Writing in 1975, Professor Langbein observed:

> The law of wills is notorious for its harsh and relentless formalism. The Wills

> Act[10] prescribes a particular set of formalities for executing one's testament. The most minute defect in formal compliance is held to void the will, no matter how abundant the evidence that the defect was inconsequential. Probate courts do not speak of harmless error in the execution of wills. To be sure, there is considerable diversity and contradiction in the cases interpreting what acts constitute compliance with what formalities. But once a formal defect is found, Anglo-American courts have been unanimous in concluding that the attempted will fails.

John H. Langbein, Substantial Compliance With the Wills Act, 88 Harv. L. Rev. 489 (1975).

What formal defect caused Greta McKellar's will to fail? To what do you attribute the court's picky attitude? Was it because the court suspected that Greta's will was an unreliable expression of her true wishes?

2. *"Signature" in the Exordium?* When Greta McKellar wrote her name in the exordium, was she signing her will? The Restatement 3d of Property § 3.1, comment j, states:

> *j. Testator's signature. . . .* To be a signature, the testator must write his or her name with the intent of adopting the document as his or her own. A signature provides evidence of finality, and serves to distinguish the final will from a preliminary draft, an incomplete document, or scribbled thoughts about how the will might take shape in the future. The testator's handwritten name in freestanding form at the end of the document unquestionably satisfies the signature requirement. The testator's handwritten name in freestanding form at any other place on the document raises an inference that the testator "signed" the document.
>
> A person's name written in his or her own handwriting is not necessarily a signature. If the testator's name is not written in freestanding form, then there should be other evidence that the testator adopted the document as his or her will in order to count the handwritten name as a signature.

Courts going as far back as Lemayne v. Stanley, 3 Lev. 1, 83 Eng. Rep. 545 (K.B. 1681), have accepted a handwritten name in the exordium as the testator's signature, given other proof of finality. See Philip Mechem, The Rule in *Lemayne v. Stanley*, 29 Mich. L. Rev. 685 (1931). But see Estate of Wederberg, 589 N.E.2d 1000 (Ill. App. Ct.), appeal denied, 602 N.E.2d 453 (Ill. 1992) (the court held that the document handwritten by the decedent except for the signatures of witnesses was invalid as a will because the only place decedent's name appeared was at the top of the first page where the decedent wrote the words "Opal Wederberg's Will").

3. *Position of the Testator's Signature.* Unlike the English Statute of Frauds of 1677, supra p. 168, and the Uniform Probate Code, the English Wills Act of

---

10. See supra note 4. Eds.

1837, supra p. 168, requires the testator to sign "at the foot or end" of the will.[11]

In this country, a small minority of states requires the testator's signature to be at the end of the will. See Restatement 3d of Property, Statutory Note to § 3.1. For cases in which the will failed because the testator didn't meet the requirement of signing at the end, see, e.g., Winter's Will, 98 N.Y.S.2d 312 (App. Div. 1950), aff'd without opinion, 98 N.E.2d 477 (N.Y. 1951) (concerning a decedent and the proper number of attesting witnesses who signed their names underneath the dispositive provisions of the instrument but above a clause naming certain persons as executors);[12] Sears v. Sears, 82 N.E. 1067 (Ohio 1907) (concerning a decedent who, using a printed will form, failed to sign her name on the indicated dotted line but did write her name in the attestation clause below the signature line); Estate of Proley, 422 A.2d 136 (Pa. 1980) (concerning a decedent who, using a printed will form designed to be folded over, wrote her name on the back portion on a blank line below the printed words "Will of . . ."). Even if the will is upheld, the requirement can lead to litigation. See, e.g., Clark v. National Bank of Commerce, 802 S.W.2d 452 (Ark. 1991). The Restatement 3d of Property § 3.1, comment l, provides: "Depending on the facts and circumstances, [provisions of a will that appear below the testator's signature] might be given effect under the harmless-error doctrine (see § 3.3),[13] but if not, their existence does not invalidate the will and prevent the provisions appearing above the testator's signature from being given effect."

4. *The Sign-First Requirement.* Most courts assume that the testator must sign the will before the witnesses sign. See, e.g., Burns v. Adamson, 854 S.W.2d 723 (Ark. 1993). By substantial authority, however, the exact order of signing is not critical if the testator and the witnesses sign as part of a "single (or continuous) transaction." See, e.g., Bain v. Hill, 639 So. 2d 178 (Fla. Dist. Ct. App. 1994); Waldrep v. Goodwin, 195 S.E.2d 432 (Ga. 1973); Hopson v.

11. The rigidity of this requirement, or at least of its interpretation, was relaxed somewhat by an amendment in 1852 that permitted, *inter alia*, a signature "so placed at or after, or following, or under, or beside or opposite to the end of the will, that it shall be apparent on the face of the will that the testator intended to give effect by such his signature to the writing signed as his will. . . ." 15 & 16 Vict., ch. 24.

12. N.Y. Est. Powers & Trusts Law § 3-2.1(a)(1)(A) (providing now that the material above (but not below) the signature can be given effect). See Estate of Mergenthaler, 474 N.Y.S.2d 253 (Sur. Ct. 1984) (invalidating the residuary devise because a four-page will had been improperly stapled and paginated prior to execution, resulting in the testator signing page three rather than page four).

13. The harmless-error doctrine of Restatement 3d of Property § 3.3 is set forth infra p. 181. Eds.

Ewing, 353 S.W.2d 203 (Ky. 1961); Restatement 3d of Property § 3.1, comment m. A few courts have rejected the single-transaction idea. See, e.g., Barnes v. Chase, 94 N.E. 694 (Mass. 1911); Marshall v. Mason, 57 N.E. 340 (Mass. 1900); Estate of Hartung, 145 A.2d 798 (N.J. Super. Ct. App. Div. 1958).

Suppose a testator signs her will *before* the witnesses arrive. After the witnesses arrive, she asks them to sign her will as witnesses and tells them that she already signed it. But, she folds the paper in such a way that the witnesses never see her signature. If the case were governed by a statute modeled on the English Statute of Frauds of 1677, supra p. 168, the will would probably be valid. See Betts v. Lonas, 172 F.2d 759 (D.C. Cir. 1948).

But, would the will be valid if the case were governed by a statute modeled on the English Wills Act of 1837, supra p. 168, which requires that the testator's "signature shall be made or acknowledged by the testator in the presence of" the witnesses? See Hudson v. Parker, 1 Rob. Ecc. 14, 25, 163 Eng. Rep. 948, 952 (P. Ct. 1844), where the court said:

> What is the plain meaning of acknowledging a signature in the presence of witnesses?—what do the words import but this?—"Here is my name written, I acknowledge that name so written to have been written by me; bear witness;" how is it possible that the witnesses should swear that any signature was acknowledged unless they saw it?

Accord Patten v. Patten, 558 P.2d 659 (Mont. 1976) (will invalid). But see Norton v. Georgia Railroad Bank & Trust Co., 285 S.E.2d 910 (Ga. 1982), where the court held that a testator's acknowledgment of his signature to the witnesses "need not be explicit, but may be inferred from conduct." A witness testified that he was not in the house when the testator signed the will. The witness later entered the living room and sat at a table "right by" the testator and across from the lawyer who drafted the will. The lawyer asked the witness to witness the instrument, and the witness signed it in the presence of the testator. The court held that the testator's conduct was a sufficient acknowledgment of his signature to the witness.

5. *Crossed Wills.* H and W go to a lawyer for simple wills. At their request, the lawyer prepares a will for W devising her entire estate to H if H survives her, and if not, to the couple's children, A and B. The lawyer also prepares a will for H devising his entire estate to W if she survives him, and if not, to A and B. When W and H go to the lawyer's office to sign the wills, the lawyer confuses the wills and gives W's will to H to sign and H's will to W to sign. The mistake is not discovered until W dies, survived by H, A, and B. Does W have a valid will? In Estate of Pavlinko, 148 A.2d 528 (Pa. 1959), the court held that the will signed by H "could not [be] probated as [W's] will, because

it was not signed by [her] . . . [and that the will signed by W] is a meaningless nullity." But see In re Snide, 418 N.E.2d 656 (N.Y. 1981), described infra Chapter 12, Part B.

6. *Unsigned Will.* In Dalk v. Allen, 774 So.2d 787 (Fla. Dist. Ct. App. 2000), review granted, 789 So.2d 343 (Fla. 2001), Christel McPeak went to her attorney's office to sign her will and other estate planning documents. There were eight documents requiring her signature: four duplicate originals of the "Living Will and Designation of Health Care Surrogate," three duplicate originals of the "Durable Power of Attorney" and the original "Will." Christel reviewed all of the documents and expressed to her attorney that they met with her approval and complied with her wishes. The court then found:

> 9. On March 20, 1998 each of the duplicate original Living Wills and Powers of Attorney were fully executed, witnessed, and, in the case of the Powers of Attorney, notarized.
>
> 10. On March 20, 1998 the "Last Will and Testament of Christel D. McPeak" was witnessed and notarized in the presence of Mrs. McPeak and in the presence of Attorney Baker, Jemma Baker and Anne Dick. However, due to confusion in circulation of multiple original documents for signature and mistake, that document was not physically signed by Mrs. McPeak.
>
> 11. Nevertheless, during the joint meeting for signature of documents, Mrs. McPeak did declare in the presence of witnesses and the notary the "Last Will and Testament of Christel D. McPeak", necessarily including the typed signature affixed thereon, to be her Last Will and Testament.

The court held that Christel McPeak's will was invalid:

> It is clear from the record and the trial court's findings of fact, that the absence of a signature resulted from a mistake. The decedent apparently intended to sign the will, but clearly she did not. While we recognize that her intentions, as expressed in the purported will, may have been thwarted by operation of the statute, nevertheless the will is not entitled to probate for lack of her signature.

The court did, however, certify to the Florida Supreme Court, which granted review, the following question: "May a constructive trust be imposed over the assets of an estate in favor of a beneficiary named in an invalidly executed will, where the invalidity is the result of a mistake in its execution, and the invalid will expresses the clear intention of the decedent to dispose of her assets in the manner expressed therein?" The certification was based on Estate of Tolin (set forth infra Chapter 5, Part B), a case in which the Supreme Court had held that a constructive trust could be imposed to correct a unilateral mistake in attempting to revoke a codicil.

Restatement 3d of Property

§ *3.3 Excusing Harmless Errors*. A harmless error in executing a will may be excused if the proponent establishes by clear and convincing evidence that the decedent adopted the document as his or her will.

. . . .

[Comment] b. Excusing harmless errors. In applying [the harmless-error rule] to particular cases, a hierarchy of sorts has been found to emerge among the formalities. The requirement of a writing is so fundamental to the purpose of the execution formalities that it cannot be excused as harmless under the principle of this Restatement. Only a harmless error in executing a *document* can be excused under this Restatement.

Among the defects in execution that can be excused, the lack of a signature is the hardest to excuse. An unsigned will raises a serious but not insuperable doubt about whether the testator adopted the document as his or her will. A particularly attractive case for excusing the lack of the testator's signature is a crossed will case, in which, by mistake, a wife signs her husband's will and the husband signs his wife's will. Because attestation makes a more modest contribution to the purpose of the formalities, defects in compliance with attestation procedures are more easily excused.

Notes and Question

1. *The Current Reform Movement—The Harmless-Error Rule*. UPC § 2-503, which adopts a harmless-error rule by legislation, is quite similar to statutes in effect in Israel,[14] several Australian states (Australian Capital Territory, New South Wales, Northern Territory, Queensland, South Australia, Tasmania, Victoria, and Western Australia),[15] and several Canadian provinces (Manitoba, New Brunswick, Prince Edward Island, Quebec, and Saskatchewan).[16] During

---

14. Israel Succession Law, 5725-1965, in Ministry of Justice, 19 Laws of the State of Israel 62, ch. 1, § 25 (1965).

15. Australian Capital Territory Wills Act § 11A; New South Wales Wills, Probate and Administration Act § 18A; Queensland Succession Act of 1981, § 9; South Australia, Wills Act 1946, as amended by Wills (Miscellaneous) Amendment Act 1994, § 12; Tasmanian Wills Act § 26; Victoria Wills Act 1997; Western Australia Wills Act 1990, § 34. On the harmless-error rule in Australia, see Rosalind Atherton, Dispensing with Wills Formality in Australia: The Problem of the Draft Will in the Tranquil Revolution, (1994) Austl. Prop. L.J. 68; John H. Langbein, Excusing Harmless Errors in the Execution of Wills: A Report on Australia's Tranquil Revolution in Probate Law, 87 Colum. L. Rev. 1, 4 (1987); P. Vines, When is the Testator's Intention the Requisite Intention under the Dispensing Power?, (1995) Austl. Prop. L.J. 152.

16. Manitoba Statutes 1982-83-84, c. 31, Wills Act, § 23; New Brunswick Wills Act § 35.1; Prince Edward Island Probate Act § 69.2; Quebec Civ. Code § 714; Saskatchewan Wills Act 1996, § 37. A harmless-error rule is also adopted in the Uniform Wills Act of Canada § 19

the last several years, Colorado, Hawaii, Michigan, Montana, South Dakota, and Utah have adopted statutes modeled on UPC § 2-503.[17] For support of this approach, see Bruce H. Mann, Formalities and Formalism in the Uniform Probate Code, 142 U. Pa. L. Rev. 1033 (1994). For criticism of this approach, see Lloyd Bonfield, Reforming the Requirements for Due Execution of Wills: Some Guidance from the Past, 70 Tul. L. Rev. 1893 (1996); Melanie B. Leslie, The Myth of Testamentary Freedom, 38 Ariz. L. Rev. 235 (1996); C. Douglas Miller, Will Formality, Judicial Formalism, and Legislative Reform: An Examination of the New Uniform Probate Code "Harmless Error" Rule and the Movement Toward Amorphism (Pts. 1 & 2), 43 Fla. L. Rev. 167 (1991), 43 Fla. L. Rev. 599 (1991).

In the first appellate decision under UPC § 2-503, Estate of Brooks, 927 P.2d 1024, 1027-28 (Mont. 1996), the court held:

> Under the express language of [the Montana enactment of UPC § 2-503], the proponent of a document bears the burden of proving the decedent's intent that the writing constitutes his or her will. . . . It is axiomatic that for [the decedent] to have intended the document to be her will, she must have been [mentally] competent to execute a will at the time she signed the document on March 21, 1995. . . . Thus, unlike the situation in which a duly executed will is admitted to probate, no presumption that the decedent was [mentally] competent to execute a will exists where [the Montana enactment of UPC § 2-503] applies. . . . The District Court listened to testimony and accepted evidence and, thereafter, determined that [the proponent] had not proved by clear and convincing evidence that [the decedent] was competent when she signed the document . . . .

2. *Will of Ranney*. In Will of Ranney, 589 A.2d 1339, 1344-45 (N.J. 1991), the Supreme Court of New Jersey embraced a harmless-error rule. The result was that the court upheld a will signed by the attesting witnesses on the self-proving affidavit rather than on the will itself (see infra p. 201):

> Rigid insistence on literal compliance often frustrates [the] purposes [of the formalities]. . . . Compliance with statutory formalities is important not because of the inherent value that those formalities possess, but because of the purposes they serve. . . . It would be ironic to insist on literal compliance with statutory formalities when that insistence would invalidate a will that is the deliberate and voluntary act of the testator. Such a result would frustrate rather than further the purpose of the formalities. . . . Generally, when strict construction would frustrate the purposes of the statute, the spirit of the law should control over its letter. . . .

(1988).

17. Colo. Rev. Stat. § 15-11-503 (deviates from UPC § 2-503 by omitting clauses (ii), (iii) and (iv)); Haw. Rev. Stat. Ann. § 560:2-503; Mich. Comp. Laws Ann. § 700.2503); Mont. Code Ann. § 72-2-523; S.D. Codified Laws § 29A-2-503; Utah Code Ann. § 72-2-503.

> Accordingly, we believe that the Legislature did not intend that a will should be denied probate because the witnesses signed in the wrong place. . . .

3. *Electronic Will?* In Rioux v. Coulombe, 19 Est. & Tr. Rep. 2d 201 (Quebec 1996), the police found a suicide note with the decedent's body, directing them to an envelope that contained a computer diskette marked "this is my will/Jaqueline Rioux/February 1, 1996." The diskette contained only one file, which had been saved to memory on the same day that the decedent had noted in her diary that she had made a will on computer. The file, when later printed out, contained unsigned directions regarding the disposition of her property at death. Although the Supreme Court of Quebec held that the will did not satisfy the requirements for an attested or holographic will, the court upheld the validity of the will under the Quebec harmless-error statute. That statute, R.S.Q. § 714, provides:

> A holographic will or a will made in the presence of witnesses that does not meet all the requirements of that form is valid nevertheless if it meets the essential requirements thereof and if it unquestionably and unequivocally contains the last wishes of the deceased.

According to the English version of the headnote, the court stated:

> Great caution must be exercised by a court before validating a will recorded on computer memory. However, there was no doubt that the diskette and the text printed therefrom constituted the will of the deceased. In addition, even though the document entitled "will" is not signed, the computer diskette does bear the signature of the deceased. In the same way that a signature on an envelope has, in the past, been considered as sufficient, the signed diskette met the signature requirements of the Code.

19 Est. & Tr. Rep. 2d at 202. Does the fact that a file on a diskette indicates that it was saved to memory on a certain date preclude the possibility that the file was subsequently altered and saved to memory on a different date? Neither the Uniform Electronic Transactions Act (1999) nor the Electronic Signatures in Global and National Commerce Act applies to the "creation and execution of wills, codicils, or testamentary instruments." Uniform Electronic Transactions Act § 3(b)(1); Electronic Signatures in Global and National Commerce Act § 103(a)(1), 15 U.S.C. § 7003. The Reporter's Note to Restatement 3d of Property § 6.3 concludes that the requirement that a will be in writing and signed by the testator is not satisfied by an electronic record or electronic signature.

c. The Attestation Requirement

Statutory References: *UPC §§ 1-102, 2-502, -503, -505*

Signature Requirement. Nearly all statutes require two witnesses and require the witnesses to "sign" the will.[18] For cases treating a witness's handwritten name appearing in the body of a will as a signature, see Mossler v. Johnson, 565 S.W.2d 952 (Tex. Civ. App. 1978); Robinson v. Ward, 387 S.E.2d 735 (Va. 1990).

Presence Requirement. Non-UPC statutes commonly prescribe that the witnesses must sign the will "in the presence of" the testator. Signing by the witnesses outside of the presence of the testator, followed by an acknowledgment of the signature in the testator's presence, is generally not permitted. See, e.g., Chase v. Kittredge, 93 Mass. (11 Allen) 49 (1865); see also Atkinson on Wills § 72, at 344; Annot., What Constitutes the Presence of the Testator in the Witnessing of His Will, 75 A.L.R.2d 318 (1961). But see, e.g., Wade v. Wade, 195 S.E. 339 (W. Va. 1938) (a witness's acknowledgment and identification of his signature were equivalent to an actual signing of his name in the presence of the testator and the other witness).

Statutes modeled on the English Wills Act of 1837, supra p. 168, commonly impose additional signing-in-the-presence-of requirements: They require that the *testator* sign (or acknowledge the signature) "in the presence of" the *witnesses* and that the *witnesses* sign "in the presence of" *each other*.[19] The "presence" requirement has proved to be troublesome, in part, because of the narrow meaning many courts have given to the word.

Stevens v. Casdorph

508 S.E.2d 610 (W. Va. 1998)

PER CURIAM: . . .

I. Factual Background. On May 28, 1996, the Casdorphs took Mr. Homer Haskell Miller to Shawnee Bank in Dunbar, West Virginia, so that he could execute his will.[20] Once at the bank, Mr. Miller asked Debra Pauley, a bank employee and public notary, to witness the execution of his will. After Mr.

---

18. Notable exceptions are Vermont, which requires three witnesses (see Vt. Stat. Ann. tit. 14, § 5), and Pennsylvania, which does not require the witnesses to sign the will (see 20 Pa. Cons. Stat. Ann. § 2502).

19. The English Wills Act did not literally require the witnesses to sign in the presence of each other. It required the testator to sign or acknowledge the signature in the presence of the witnesses present at the same time. The witnesses were then required to sign in the presence of the testator.

20. Mr. Miller was elderly and confined to a wheelchair.

Miller signed the will, Ms. Pauley took the will to two other bank employees, Judith Waldron and Reba McGinn, for the purpose of having each of them sign the will as witnesses. Both Ms. Waldron and Ms. McGinn signed the will. However, Ms. Waldron and Ms. McGinn testified during their depositions that they did not actually see Mr. Miller place his signature on the will. Further, it is undisputed that Mr. Miller did not accompany Ms. Pauley to the separate work areas of Ms. Waldron and Ms. McGinn.

Mr. Miller died on July 28, 1996. The last will and testament of Mr. Miller, which named Mr. Paul Casdorph[21] as executor, left the bulk of his estate to the Casdorphs.[22] The Stevenses, nieces of Mr. Miller, filed the instant action to set aside the will. The Stevenses asserted in their complaint that Mr. Miller's will was not executed according to the requirements set forth in W.Va.Code § 41-1-3 (1995).[23] After some discovery, all parties moved for summary judgment. The circuit court denied the Stevenses' motion for summary judgment, but granted the Casdorphs' cross motion for summary judgment. From this ruling, the Stevenses appeal to this Court.

II. Standard of Review. This Court has held that "[a] circuit court's entry of summary judgment is reviewed de novo." Syl. pt. 1, Painter v. Peavy, 192 W.Va. 189, 451 S.E.2d 755 (1994). . . .

III. Discussion. The Stevenses' contention is simple. They argue that all evidence indicates that Mr. Miller's will was not properly executed. Therefore, the will should be voided. The procedural requirements at issue are contained in W.Va.Code § 41-1-3 (1997). The statute reads:

> No will shall be valid unless it be in writing and signed by the testator, or by some other person in his presence and by his direction, in such manner as to make it manifest that the name is intended as a signature; and moreover, unless it be wholly in the handwriting of the testator, *the signature shall be made or the will acknowledged by him in the presence of at least two competent witnesses, present at the same time; and such witnesses shall subscribe the will in the presence of the testator, and of each other,* but no form of attestation shall be necessary. (Emphasis added.)

The relevant requirements of the above statute calls for a testator to sign his/her will or acknowledge such will in the presence of at least two witnesses at the same time, and such witnesses must sign the will in the presence of the

21. Paul Casdorph was a nephew of Mr. Miller.

22. Mr. Miller's probated estate exceeded $400,000.00. The will devised $80,000.00 to Frank Paul Smith, a nephew of Mr. Miller. The remainder of the estate was left to the Casdorphs.

23. As heirs, the Stevenses would be entitled to recover from Mr. Miller's estate under the intestate laws if his will is set aside as invalidly executed.

testator and each other. In the instant proceeding the Stevenses assert, and the evidence supports, that Ms. McGinn and Ms. Waldron did not actually witness Mr. Miller signing his will. Mr. Miller made no acknowledgment of his signature on the will to either Ms. McGinn or Ms. Waldron. Likewise, Mr. Miller did not observe Ms. McGinn and Ms. Waldron sign his will as witnesses. Additionally, neither Ms. McGinn nor Ms. Waldron acknowledged to Mr. Miller that their signatures were on the will. It is also undisputed that Ms. McGinn and Ms. Waldron did not actually witness each other sign the will, nor did they acknowledge to each other that they had signed Mr. Miller's will. Despite the evidentiary lack of compliance with W.Va.Code § 41-1-3, the Casdorphs' argue that there was substantial compliance with the statute's requirements, insofar as everyone involved with the will knew what was occurring. The trial court found that there was substantial compliance with the statute because everyone knew why Mr. Miller was at the bank. The trial court further concluded there was no evidence of fraud, coercion or undue influence. Based upon the foregoing, the trial court concluded that the will should not be voided even though the technical aspects of W.Va.Code § 41-1-3 were not followed.

Our analysis begins by noting that "[t]he law favors testacy over intestacy." Syl. pt. 8, Teubert's Estate, 171 W.Va. 226, 298 S.E.2d 456 (1982). However, we clearly held in syllabus point 1 of Black v. Maxwell, 131 W.Va. 247, 46 S.E.2d 804 (1948), that "[t]estamentary intent and a written instrument, executed in the manner provided by [W.Va.Code § 41-1-3], existing concurrently, are essential to the creation of a valid will." *Black* establishes that mere intent by a testator to execute a written will is insufficient. The actual execution of a written will must also comply with the dictates of W.Va.Code § 41-1-3. The Casdorphs seek to have this Court establish an exception to the technical requirements of the statute. In Wade v. Wade, 119 W.Va. 596, 195 S.E. 339 (1938), this Court permitted a narrow exception to the stringent requirements of the W.Va.Code § 41-1-3. . . .

Wade stands for the proposition that if a witness acknowledges his/her signature on a will in the physical presence of the other subscribing witness and the testator, then the will is properly witnessed within the terms of W.Va.Code § 41-1-3. In this case, none of the parties signed or acknowledged their signatures in the presence of each other. This case meets neither the narrow exception of *Wade* nor the specific provisions of W.Va.Code § 41-1-3.

IV. Conclusion. In view of the foregoing, we grant the relief sought in this appeal and reverse the circuit court's order granting the Casdorphs' cross-motion for summary judgment.

REVERSED.

WORKMAN, J., dissenting: The majority once more takes a very technocratic approach to the law, slavishly worshiping form over substance. In so doing, they not only create a harsh and inequitable result wholly contrary to the indisputable intent of Mr. Homer Haskell Miller, but also a rule of law that is against the spirit and intent of our whole body of law relating to the making of wills.

There is absolutely no claim of incapacity or fraud or undue influence, nor any allegation by any party that Mr. Miller did not consciously, intentionally, and with full legal capacity convey his property as specified in his will. The challenge to the will is based solely upon the allegation that Mr. Miller did not comply with the requirement of West Virginia Code 41-1-3 that the signature shall be made or the will acknowledged by the testator in the presence of at least two competent witnesses, present at the same time. The lower court, in its very thorough findings of fact, indicated that Mr. Miller had been transported to the bank by his nephew Mr. Casdorph and the nephew's wife. Mr. Miller, disabled and confined to a wheelchair, was a shareholder in the Shawnee Bank in Dunbar, West Virginia, with whom all those present were personally familiar. When Mr. Miller executed his will in the bank lobby, the typed will was placed on Ms. Pauley's desk, and Mr. Miller instructed Ms. Pauley that he wished to have his will signed, witnessed, and acknowledged. After Mr. Miller's signature had been placed upon the will with Ms. Pauley watching, Ms. Pauley walked the will over to the tellers' area in the same small lobby of the bank. Ms. Pauley explained that Mr. Miller wanted Ms. Waldron to sign the will as a witness. The same process was used to obtain the signature of Ms. McGinn. Sitting in his wheelchair, Mr. Miller did not move from Ms. Pauley's desk during the process of obtaining the witness signatures. The lower court concluded that the will was valid and that Ms. Waldron and Ms. McGinn signed and acknowledged the will "in the presence" of Mr. Miller.

In Wade v. Wade, 119 W.Va. 596, 195 S.E. 339 (1938), we addressed the validity of a will challenged for such technicalities and observed that "a narrow, rigid construction of the statute should not be allowed to stand in the way of right and justice, or be permitted to defeat a testator's disposition of his property." 119 W.Va. at 599, 195 S.E. at 340-341. We upheld the validity of the challenged will in *Wade*, noting that "each case must rest on its own facts and circumstances to which the court must look to determine whether there was a subscribing by the witnesses in the presence of the testator; that substantial compliance with the statute is all that is required. . . ." Id. at 599, 195 S.E. at 340. A contrary result, we emphasized, "would be based on illiberal and inflexible construction of the statute, giving preeminence to letter and not to spirit, and resulting in the thwarting of the intentions of testators even under circumstances where no possibility of fraud or impropriety exists." Id. at 600, 195 S.E. at 341.

The majority's conclusion is precisely what was envisioned and forewarned in 1938 by the drafters of the *Wade* opinion: illiberal and inflexible construction, giving preeminence to the letter of the law and ignoring the spirit of the entire body of testamentary law, resulting in the thwarting of Mr. Miller's unequivocal wishes. . . .

The majority strains the logical definition of "in the presence" as used in the operative statute. The legal concept of "presence" in this context encompasses far more than simply watching the signing of the will, which is the technical, narrow interpretation of the word apparently relied upon by the majority. Where the attestation of the will by the witnesses occurred within the same room as the testator, there is, at the very minimum, prima facie evidence that the attestation occurred within the "presence" of the testator. See 20 Michie's Jurisprudence, Wills § 34 (1993); Annotation, What Constitutes the Presence of the Testator in the Witnessing of His Will, 75 A.L.R.2d 318 (1961). . . .

The majority embraces the line of least resistance. The easy, most convenient answer is to say that the formal, technical requirements have not been met and that the will is therefore invalid. End of inquiry. Yet that result is patently absurd. That manner of statutory application is inconsistent with the underlying purposes of the statute. Where a statute is enacted to protect and sanctify the execution of a will to prevent substitution or fraud, this Court's application of that statute should further such underlying policy, not impede it. When, in our efforts to strictly apply legislative language, we abandon common sense and reason in favor of technicalities, we are the ones committing the injustice.

I am authorized to state that Justice MAYNARD joins in this dissent.

Notes and Questions

1. *Line-of-Vision Test.* The prevailing interpretation of the "presence" requirement is that the witness must have signed within the testator's "line of vision." The line-of-vision test requires at a minimum "that the testator, without changing his position, might have seen the will being attested; it is not necessary that he actually saw it." See Newton v. Palmour, 266 S.E.2d 208, 209-10 (Ga. 1980); Estate of Ross, 969 S.W.2d 398 (Tenn. 1997), appeal denied (1998). One court even held that the will failed because the testator, ill in bed, could only see the backs of the witnesses as they signed, not their hands or the paper on which they wrote. Presence, the court said, means "'within view' . . . the thing to be seen, or to be within the power of the party to see, is the very act of subscribing by the witness." Graham v. Graham, 32 N.C. 219, 220 (1849). The line-of-vision test also wouldn't be met if a witness signs a will while on the telephone with the testator who is across town in his home affirming his intent to execute a will and have the witness sign it as a witness. Will of Jefferson, 349 So. 2d 1032 (Miss. 1977). Suppose the testator is blind. Under the line-of-vision

test, what result? See, e.g., Welch v. Kirby, 255 F. 451 (8th Cir. 1918) (will upheld).

2. *Conscious-Presence Test*. A respectable number of courts, and now the Restatement 3d of Property § 3.1, comment p, have interpreted the "presence" requirement more liberally. They have adopted the "conscious-presence" test, which recognizes that a person can sense the presence of another without seeing the other person. "If [the witnesses] are so near at hand that they are within the range of any of [the testator's] senses, so that he knows what is going on, the [presence] requirement has been met." See, e.g., Demaris' Estate, 110 P.2d 571 (Or. 1941).

3. *Uniform Probate Code*. Instead of codifying the conscious-presence test, the former UPC largely dispensed with the "presence" requirement. UPC § 2-502 substantially carries forward this approach. The only place the "presence" requirement is retained is where testators direct someone else to sign for them. Section 2-502 of the former Code required that person to sign the testator's name "in the testator's presence." The revised version requires the person to sign the testator's name "in the testator's *conscious* presence." (emphasis added).

The UPC doesn't require the *witnesses* to sign in the presence of the testator or in the presence of each other. It requires the witnesses to "witness" the testator's act of signing the will or "witness" the testator's act of acknowledging either the signature or the will. Presumably, the "witnessing" requirement means that they must observe the act. See Estate of Allcott, 912 P.2d 671 (Idaho Ct. App. 1995) (concerning two witnesses who did not witness the testator signing her will, acknowledging her signature, or acknowledging her will). The requirement would not be satisfied by showing simply that the act took place within their line of sight. Would the will in *Jefferson*, supra, have been validly executed under UPC § 2-502? See Estate of McGurrin, 743 P.2d 994 (Idaho Ct. App. 1987), review denied, 746 P.2d 85 (1987) (holding invalid a telephone acknowledgment under former UPC § 2-502 and also rejecting the harmless-error doctrine); cf. Will of Heaney, 347 N.Y.S.2d 922 (Sur. Ct. 1973), order aff'd, 355 N.Y.S.2d 569 (App. Div. 1974) (holding invalid a telephone acknowledgment under a non-UPC wills statute).

The UPC's abrogation of the requirement that the witnesses sign in the testator's presence raises a question about whether there is any time limit on when the witnesses must sign the will after they have witnessed the testator's signature or acknowledgment of the signature or of the will. Estate of Peters, below, which was decided under the former version of UPC § 2-502, addresses this question. It also addresses the question of whether courts should abandon the strict-compliance approach in favor of a harmless-error approach to the statutory formalities.

Estate of Peters

526 A.2d 1005 (N.J. 1987)

[Conrad Peters died on March 28, 1985. His wife, Marie, predeceased him by slightly more than five days. Conrad and Marie had no children by their marriage, but Marie had a son, Joseph Skrok, by a prior marriage. Marie's will devised her entire estate to Conrad if he survived her (which he did), but if not, to Joseph. Conrad's will devised his entire estate to Marie if she survived him (which she did not), but if not, to Joseph.

At Marie's request, her sister-in-law, Sophia M. Gall, an insurance agent and notary public, prepared the wills for Marie and Conrad. About two years before he died, Conrad suffered a stroke that put him into the hospital. The stroke affected him physically but not mentally. Marie, Sophia, and Sophia's husband (Marie's brother), came to Conrad's hospital room with Conrad's will. Sophia read the provisions of the will to Conrad, who then assented to it and signed it. None of the individuals who witnessed Conrad's signing of the will signed the will as witness, the apparent intention being to await the arrival of two of Sophia's employees, Mary Gall and Kristen Spock.

Later in the afternoon, after Mary and Kristen arrived, Sophia reviewed the will briefly with Conrad, who, in the presence of Mary and Kristen, indicated his approval and acknowledged his signature. Sophia then signed the will as a notary, but neither Mary nor Kristen placed her signature on the will. Sophia then folded the will and handed it to Marie. When Conrad died fifteen months later, the two witnesses, Mary and Kristen, had still not signed the will.

Joseph Skrok presented Conrad's will for probate. Its validity was disputed by the State of New Jersey, which would succeed to Conrad's estate if his will was invalid. Conrad left no surviving blood relatives.

At the probate proceeding, Sophia testified as to why the two intended witnesses never signed the will:

> As I say, just because of the emotional aspect of the whole situation, my sister-in-law was there, my husband, her brother was there, myself and the two girls. There were six of us. The other patients had visitors. It got to be kind of—I don't know how to explain it, just the situation, and the girls were in a hurry to get back to the office, because they had to leave the office.
>
> I honestly think in their minds, when they saw me sign the will, they thought that is why they were there. And we folded up the will, gave it [to] my sister-in-law. It was just that type of situation.

The trial court found the will validly executed, by treating Sophia's signature as notary as the valid signature of a witness and by allowing one of the other witnesses to sign the will. The Appellate Division reversed.]

HANDLER, J. . . . The operative statute governing the validity of the execution of a will is N.J.S.A. 3B:3-2. The statute prescribes the formalities necessary for the proper execution of a will. It requires (1) that the will be in writing and (2) that it be signed by the testator (or by someone in his presence and at his direction). It also requires that a will be signed by at least two persons who witnessed either (a) the signing or (b) the testator's acknowledgment of his signature or of the will. . . .

Wills are solely the creatures of positive law. "The right to make a will . . . is derived from the statute." A. Clapp, 5 New Jersey Practice, Wills and Administration § 41, at 173 (3d ed. 1982). . . . Historically, courts have held that, as statutory creations, wills must adhere to the requirements prescribed by the statute. Failure to comply with the statutory requirements has long resulted in a will being declared invalid, no matter how accurately the document may have reflected the wishes of the testator.

This policy of construing the wills statute's formalities strictly came to be criticized for producing inequitable results and for encouraging, in effect, the circumvention of the wills statutes through such means as conveyances in joint tenancy, revocable trusts, tentative or "Totten" trusts, and cash value life insurance policies. . . . The perception of inequitable results, coupled with the decline of wills, relative to other instruments, as means of devising property after death, led the National Conference of Commissioners of Uniform State Laws and the American Bar Association, in August 1969, to propose adoption of the [former] Uniform Probate Code. The [former] Code's approach was not to encourage courts to abandon their strict construction of the formalities prescribed, but rather to reduce the number and refine the scope of those formalities so that, if strict construction were employed, "inequities" in individual cases would occur less frequently and would be justified by the importance of the interests protected by the formal requirements that were retained. . . .

A second approach to reform was proposed in 1975 by Professor John Langbein, in "Substantial Compliance With the Wills Act," [88 Harv. L. Rev. 489 (1975)]. According to Professor Langbein, "[t]he finding of a formal defect should lead not to automatic invalidity, but to a further inquiry: does the noncomplying document express the decedent's testamentary intent, and does its form sufficiently approximate Wills Act formality to enable the court to conclude that it serves the purposes of the Wills Act?" Id. . .

The current statute, a variant of the [former] Uniform Probate Code, constitutes a significant statutory change from its predecessor with respect to how a will must be witnessed. In accordance with the [former] Uniform Probate Code, the thrust of the change is to reduce the number of formalities entailed in the witnessing of the execution of a will and, in doing so, to ease the difficulty of complying with the formalities that are prescribed for witnesses. . . .

Plaintiff argues that the repeal of N.J.S.A. 3A:3-2 and the elimination of the requirement that the witness sign in the presence of the testator indicate that the Legislature intended that a witness could sign a will as a subscribing witness at any time after the testator has signed or acknowledged the will, even after the testator's death. Plaintiff points to the lack of any other restrictions in the statute relating to when witnesses may sign a will. Plaintiff thus argues that the procedure employed here was within the contemplation of the statute. In the alternative, plaintiff argues that, in the absence of any allegation of fraud, the will should be validated as in substantial compliance with the statute. We treat first the argument that the procedure involved here—allowing the witness to sign the will some eighteen months after the will was witnessed, where the testator had died with the will unsigned by witnesses some fifteen months after the will was witnessed—complies with the statute.

It cannot be overemphasized that the Legislature, in reforming the Wills statute, did not dispense with the requirement that the execution of a will be witnessed. Indeed, it is arguable that as the number of formalities have been reduced, those retained by the Legislature have assumed even greater importance, and demand at least the degree of scrupulous adherence required under the former statute.

It is generally acknowledged that witnesses serve two functions, which can be characterized as "observatory" and "signatory." The current statute clearly requires the fulfillment of both functions; a testamentary writing proffered as a will, in the statute's terms, "shall be *signed* by at least two persons each of whom *witnesses* either the signing or the testator's acknowledgment of the signature or of the will."

The observatory function consists of the actual witnessing—the direct and purposeful observation—of the testator's signature to or acknowledgment of the will. It entails more than physical presence or a casual or general awareness of the will's execution by the testator; the witnessing of a will is a concomitant condition and an integral part of the execution of the will.

The signatory function consists of the signing of the will by the persons who were witnesses. The signatory function may not have the same substantive significance as the observatory function, but it is not simply a ministerial or precatory requirement. While perhaps complementary to the observatory function, it is nonetheless a necessary element of the witnessing requirement. The witness' signature has significance as an evidentiary requirement or probative element, serving both to demonstrate and to confirm the fulfillment of the observatory function by the witnesses. There is nothing, therefore, to suggest that in retaining the requirement that a will's execution be witnessed, the Legislature meant to imply that either witnessing function is dispensable.

The statutory policy to reduce the required formalities to a minimum should not, in our view, be construed to sanction relaxation of the formalities the statute retained.

Resolution of the issue of when the witnesses must sign the will in relation to their observations of the execution of the will by the testator follows from the purpose of the requirement that the will be signed. Because, as noted, the signatory function serves an evidentiary purpose, the signatures of the witnesses would lose probative worth and tend to fail of this purpose if the witnesses were permitted to sign at a time remote from their required observations as witnesses. Consequently, because the witnessing requirement of the statute consists of the dual acts of observation and signature, it is sensible to infer that both acts should occur either contemporaneously with or in close succession to one another.

We are thus satisfied that it would be unreasonable to construe the statute as placing no time limit on the requirement of obtaining two witnesses' signatures. By implication, the statute requires that the signatures of witnesses be affixed to a will within a reasonable period of time from the execution of the will. . .

The requirement of subscription within a reasonable time follows also from the consistent policy of this state that execution formalities are substantive requirements, and, therefore, that execution defects are substantive. Because the purpose of execution formalities is to prevent fraud and undue influence, they have consistently been held by our courts to be substantive requirements. The fact that the Legislature has reduced the number of execution formalities required does not diminish the significance of the formalities it retained; if anything, in our view, their significance is heightened. What this Court stated in Hale's Will, supra, 21 N.J. at 297, 121 A.2d 511, is no less true under the reformed statute: the purpose of execution formalities is to "forestall[ ] fraud by the living upon the dead [and to] discourage imposition on the unwary. . . ."

Given our conclusion that the witnesses must sign within a reasonable time from observation, the question is whether the time period involved here—in which the testator died with the will still unsigned by witnesses fifteen months after the will was witnessed—is reasonable. Two factors in this case affect our determination of reasonableness: (1) the fact that the witness signed after the testator's death; and (2) the fact that some eighteen months passed between the observatory and signatory functions of the witness. While there have been no New Jersey cases addressing the issue of whether a witness may sign a will after the testator's death, the problem has been treated in other jurisdictions. In Estate of Flicker, 215 Neb. 495, 339 N.W.2d 914, 915 (1983), the Nebraska Supreme Court observed that the purpose of the witnessing requirement is to prevent fraud or mistake, and that permitting witnesses to sign after the testator's death "would erode the efficacy of [this] safeguard. . . ." Thus, "[the witnesses'] signatures are the last acts in the ceremony required by the statute. By its terms, the statute requires a witness to sign." See also Matter of Estate of Mikeska, 140 Mich. App. 116, 362 N.W.2d 906, 910 (1985) ("We agree with the holding in *Flicker*, as well as with the rationale"); Rogers v. Rogers, 71 Or. App. 133, 691 P.2d 114 (1984) (a will, as an ambulatory instrument, takes effect at the time of the testator's death; failure to comply with the formalities of execution by the time the testator has died results in an invalid will).

In this case, the Appellate Division declined to adopt a bright-line rule under N.J.S.A. 3B:3-2 requiring witnesses' signatures before the death of the testator. It expressly left open the question raised by Leo's Will, 12 Fla. Supp. 61 (Fla. Dade Co. Cir. Ct. 1958), concerning the validity of a will where a testator has died moments after execution, but before the witnesses have had an opportunity to sign. We endorse this conclusion. There may indeed be cases in which the affixation of witnesses' signatures after the testator's death would be reasonable, particularly if the witnesses were somehow precluded from signing before the testator died. This case, however, does not present such a situation. Even if one accepts the testimony that the emotional trauma of the moment prevented the witnesses from signing the will while the testator was hospitalized, there is simply no adequate explanation of the failure to have obtained their signatures in the extended fifteen-month interval prior to his death. If the Legislature's retention of the signing requirement is to be at all effectual, signing must occur within a reasonable time of observation to assure that the signature attests to what was actually observed, and not to what is vaguely remembered. While this requirement does not necessarily entail subscription prior to the testator's death, the interval here between the observation and the testator's death was simply too long for subscription after death to have been reasonably within the contemplation of the statute.

Plaintiff argues in the alternative, however, that even if compliance with execution formalities was defective, this Court should validate the will in the absence of any allegation of fraud because it was in "substantial compliance" with the statute. Thus, given the historical trend toward liberalization of the wills statute described above, and the policy favoring validation of wills that "meet the minimal formalities of the statute," the ultimate question raised by this case is how courts should construe wills that fail to satisfy even the "minimal formalities" retained in the statute.

As Professor Langbein has explained, "[t]he substantial compliance doctrine would permit defective compliance with . . . ceremonials to be evaluated purposively. It would permit the proponents to prove that in the circumstances of the case the testator executed the will with finality and that the execution is adequately evidenced notwithstanding the defect." Langbein, "Substantial Compliance with the Wills Act," supra, at 521. The doctrine has been criticized, however, because it reduces predictability of wills:

> The argument in favor of the implementation of the substantial compliance doctrine is that, while it lacks the predictability of the [former] U.P.C., it does insist upon a higher degree of formality yet with the understanding that where the failure to comply with any formality is shown, proof may be received to demonstrate that the function of the formality has still been met. . . . The problem is that wills are unlike the world of contract where the demands of business often necessitate informality. . . . Wills are more often made without such demands of time pressure. The testator has every opportunity to comply with formality requirements. . . .
>
> A second problem is the ambiguity of "substantial compliance." . . . Does it mean that some formalities are more important than others and that substantial compliance involves completion of only the important formalities?
>
> [Nelson and Starck, "Formalities and Formalism: A Critical Look at the Execution of Wills," 6 Pepperdine L. Rev. 331, 355 (1979).]

In addition, the doctrine's reliability has been questioned because of its emphasis upon evidence of testamentary intention and the recollection of distant, indistinct events. Irmiston, "Formalities and Wills: A Plea for Caution," American/Australian/New Zealand Law: Parallels and Contrasts, A.B.A., 72, 74 (1980). This has led to rejection of the doctrine in some states, where it has been found to "lead to confusion and uncertainty." Hopkins v. Hopkins, 708 S.W.2d 31, 32 (Tex. Ct. App. 1986). . . .

The . . . New Jersey courts have generally rejected a rule of substantial compliance. . . .

To [adopt a substantial-compliance doctrine] on the facts of this case would, in our view, effectively vitiate the statutory requirement that witnesses sign the will.[24] We continue to believe that, as a general proposition, strict, if not literal, adherence to statutory requirements is required in order to validate a will, and that the statutory requirements must be satisfied regardless of the possibility of fraud in any particular case. . . .

Accordingly, for the reasons stated, the judgment below is affirmed.

Notes and Questions

1. *Probative Value of Witnesses' Signatures*. What is the probative value of the witnesses' signatures and why is that value lost if the witnesses don't sign at or within a "reasonable time" after the execution ceremony?

---

24. We are unwilling to foreclose consideration of the substantial compliance doctrine in a case where there is no question of fraud, and where, unlike this case, there has been a clear attempt to comply with a statutory formality but compliance is deficient. In this case, however, the statutory formalities contemplate at a minimum witnessing by two persons; the treatment of a notary's signature as that of a witness does not compensate for the absence of the signature of a second witness.

2. *Estate of Gerhardt*. In Estate of Gerhardt, 763 A.2d 1289 (N.J. Super. Ct. Ch. Div. 2000), the will of Mary Elizabeth Gerhardt was signed by one witness and a notary public. The court upheld the will by treating the notary public as a valid second witness, saying: "Although statutory compliance is essential to ensure a valid will execution, it would be inequitable to invalidate a will that is the deliberate and voluntary act of the testator. . . . To deny probate in this instance would frustrate rather than further the purpose of the formalities." Accord Estate of Friedman, 6 P.3d 473 (Nev. 2000).

3. *Sisson v. Park Street Baptist Church*. William and Lilian Taylor, husband and wife, residents of Ontario, Canada, arrived at their lawyer's office to execute their wills, which had been prepared in accordance with their instructions. Shirley Walton, a legal secretary, and William Lech, the drafting lawyer, were to act as attesting witnesses. Both witnesses were present when William and Lilian signed their wills. Both witnesses signed William's will in William's presence. Shirley also signed Lilian's will in Lilian's presence, but for some unexplained reason, Lech neglected to sign Lilian's will as a witness. So far as relevant to this case, the Ontario Succession Law Reform Act 1990, § 26, subsection 4(1), contains three requirements for executing a will: (1) the testator must sign the will; (2) the testator must sign the will in the presence of two attesting witnesses present at the same time; and (3) two or more of the attesting witnesses must subscribe the will in the presence of the testator.

Although other Canadian provinces, had adopted a harmless-error rule by statute, Ontario had not done so. See Note 1, supra p. 182. Nevertheless, the Ontario Court of Justice adopted a harmless-error rule, and upheld Lilian's will. Sisson v. Park Street Baptist Church, 24 E.T.R.2d 18 (Ont. Gen. Div. 1998). The judge found that Lilian had adopted the document as her will, that the purposes of the statutory formalities had been served, and that the first two of the three statutory requirements had been complied with:

> I am satisfied that the will actually reflects the intention of the testatrix. . . .
>
> I find that the . . . absence of legislation on point should not stop the court from developing the common law where, in circumstances like this, there has been substantial compliance, given that the dangers which two witnesses are to guard against does not exist here.

Accord Krause v. Toni, No. Penticton 17406, 1999 CarswellBC 2019 (B.C.S.C. June 28, 1999). But see Bolton v. Tartaglia, No. Vancouver L000554,2000 Carswell BC 799 (B.C.S.C. Apr. 12, 2000) (holding will invalid because of failure of an attesting witness to affix her signature and deferring to the legislature to adopt a harmless-error rule).

4. *Witnesses Signing after Decedent's Death*. The question of whether, under former UPC § 2-502, a will is valid if witnesses sign the decedent's will after

the decedent's death, having otherwise witnessed the decedent's signing or acknowledging of the signature or of the will arose in Estate of Royal, 826 P.2d 1236 (Colo. 1992) (en banc). The *Royal* court rejected the reasonable-time test advanced by *Peters*. Instead, the court adopted what it viewed as "a bright line rule" and interpreted the statute as requiring that the witnesses sign before the decedent's death. Whether the witnesses sign within a reasonable time of when the decedent signed or acknowledged the signing or the will is deemed irrelevant so long as it occurs before the decedent's death. It also rejected the lower court's approach that would have allowed witnesses to sign after the decedent's death upon a showing of exceptional circumstances. See also Gonzalez v. Satrustegui, 870 P.2d 1188 (Ariz. Ct. App. 1993) (refusing to recognize a post-death signature by a witness); N.Y. Est. Powers & Trusts Law § 3-2.1(a)(4) (requiring the two witnesses to attest the testator's signature and sign the will within one thirty-day period).

5. *Uniform Probate Code's Approach.* As revised in 1990, UPC § 2-502 altered the former version by introducing a reasonable-time standard for signing by the witnesses, but because of the harmless-error rule adopted in § 2-503, the failure of the witnesses to sign the will within a reasonable time or to sign it at all isn't necessarily fatal to the validity of the will. Should the witnessing requirement be abandoned altogether by eliminating it from the statutory formalities? The elimination of this requirement is proposed in James Lindgren, Abolishing the Attestation Requirement for Wills, 68 N.C. L. Rev. 541 (1990), but opposed in Langbein, Excusing Harmless Errors in the Execution of Wills: A Report on Australia's Tranquil Revolution in Probate Law, 87 Colum. L. Rev. 1, 52 (1987).

Problems

1. Suppose that, after G's death, there were found among her important papers a handwritten but unsigned draft of her will and a signed typewritten copy of the handwritten draft. Could either document be probated under the harmless-error rule?

2. Suppose instead that, after signing her will, G handed it to her nephew and asked him to "get it witnessed." The nephew took the will to two neighbors, one after the other, who signed as "witnesses." The nephew then returned the will to G. Under the harmless-error rule, what result?

3. Suppose that the nephew took the will to only one neighbor, who signed as a "witness." What result under the substantial-compliance doctrine? See, e.g., Taylor v. Estate of Taylor, 770 P.2d 163 (Utah Ct. App. 1989) ("A standard of substantial compliance would forgive no more than 'slight or trifling departures from technical requirements'. . . . [O]nly one witness . . . amounts to an absolute failure to comply—strictly or substantially—with even the most

liberal construction of [our statute requiring that a will be signed by at least two persons in the testator's presence and in the presence of each other]."). The Utah legislature subsequently enacted the harmless-error rule of UPC § 2-503. See Utah Code Ann. § 72-2-503.

Competency of Attesting Witnesses. The English Statute of Frauds of 1677, supra p. 168, required the witnesses to be "credible." In this country, most non-UPC statutes require the witnesses to be either "credible" or "competent." Today in almost all states the conviction of a crime no longer makes a person an incompetent witness to a will. See Page on Wills § 19.82. Mental incompetency, whether from mental deficiency, extreme intoxication, or the influence of drugs, remains a ground of disqualification as a witness. See id. § 19.83. Insofar as age is concerned, a few states specifically provide by statute a minimum age, such as eighteen, for attesting witnesses. See, e.g., Ark. Code Ann. § 28-25-102(a); Idaho Code § 15-2-505; see also Norton v. Hinson, 989 S.W.2d 535 (Ark. 1999) (rejecting harmless-error rule and holding decedent's will invalid because attesting witness was not 18 years old as required by statute). More commonly, however, no age is specified in the statute, and the cases usually allow minors who are old enough to observe, remember, and relate the facts occurring at the execution ceremony to be valid witnesses. See, e.g., Estate of Dejmal, 289 N.W.2d 813 (Wis. 1980); Atkinson on Wills § 65, at 320; Page on Wills § 19.81.

Interested Witnesses—Disqualified at Common Law. The Statute of Frauds of 1677 was construed to disqualify a witness who was a devisee under the will and, therefore, presumably interested in sustaining the will. At that time, a person who had an interest in the outcome of litigation was disqualified from testifying as a witness because of that interest. (Parties to a lawsuit could not testify in their own behalf.) In construing the Statute of Frauds, the courts carried over this incapacity of the "testimonial" witness to the attesting witness. See Alvin E. Evans, The Competency of Testamentary Witnesses, 25 Mich. L. Rev. 238 (1927). The result was that a will wholly failed where one of the necessary attesting witnesses was also a devisee.

Purging Statutes. After a time, it came to be thought in England that the invalidity of the entire will was unnecessarily harsh on the other devisees. To remedy the situation, a statute—sometimes referred to as a "purging statute"—was passed in 1752 that provided that the disposition to the attesting witness should be void, but the witness should "be admitted as a witness to the execution of such will." 25 Geo. 2, ch. 6, § 1. By eliminating the witness's interest, the witness was made "credible" and the will was saved.

In this country, as indicated above, most non-UPC statutes require attesting witnesses to be either "credible" or "competent." See Restatement 2d of Property, Statutory Note to § 33.1. Whichever word is used, the devise of a beneficial interest is usually regarded as disqualifying the witness, unless there is a purging statute similar to the English statute of 1752.

Almost all non-UPC states have purging-type legislation. Most American purging statutes go on to provide a partial exception for a devisee who is also an heir of the testator or a devisee under the testator's prior will.[25] Under this partial exception, heirs or devisees who are necessary witnesses forfeit only the portions of their devises that exceed the amount they would have taken by intestacy or under prior wills if the wills in question were invalid. Suppose, for example, that G's will devised $10,000 to X. X served as an attesting witness to G's will. G's prior will, which was not witnessed by X and which was revoked by the subsequent will, devised $8,000 to X. Under the heir/devisee exception, X forfeits $2,000 of the $10,000 devise contained in G's subsequent will. Are witnesses who are devised less than what they would have taken if the wills they witnessed were invalid "interested" witnesses? See Sparhawk v. Sparhawk, 92 Mass. 155 (1865), and cases cited in Atkinson on Wills § 65, at 315 n. 48.

Spouse of a Witness. The common-law disqualification of a witness who had an interest in the outcome of litigation extended also to the witness's spouse; and this same notion was applied in England to hold that the spouse of a devisee was not a credible witness to a will. Moreover, the 1752 statute did not save the will, because it invalidated a devise only to the attesting witness. The situation was remedied in the English Wills Act of 1837 by invalidating a devise to the spouse of an attesting witness as well as to the witness. See 7 Wm. 4 & 1 Vict., ch. 26, § 15.[26]

In this country, the purging statutes in about eight states expressly cover a devise to the spouse of an attesting witness. The spouse rule has survived constitutional challenge. See Dorfman v. Allen, 434 N.E.2d 1012 (Mass. 1982).

---

25. One court interpreted a purging statute to have the heir/devisee exception, though the statute expressed no such exception. See Manoukian v. Tomasian, 237 F.2d 211 (D.C. Cir. 1956), cert. denied, 352 U.S. 1026 (1957). (The position is now codified in D.C. Code Ann. § 18-104.) But see, e.g., Rosenbloom v. Kokofsky, 369 N.E.2d 1142 (Mass. 1977) (refusing to adopt the exception).

26. The same history appears in some of our states, though with a surprising time lag. Thus Illinois and New Hampshire enacted statutes at a fairly early date modeled on the English legislation of 1752. In 1892, the New Hampshire court held that the spouse of a devisee was not a competent witness to the will, that the statute did not apply to the devise, and that the will was not therefore properly executed. See Kittredge v. Hodgman, 32 A. 158 (N.H. 1892). In 1909, the same decision was reached in Illinois. See Fearn v. Postlethwaite, 88 N.E. 1057 (Ill. 1909). In 1911, each state amended its statute so as to invalidate not only a devise to an attesting witness but also a devise to the witness's spouse.

In the absence of an express provision in the purging statute voiding all or a portion of a devise to the spouse of an attesting witness, a number of decisions have held that spouses of devisees are not "interested" witnesses. See, e.g., Estate of Harrison, 738 P.2d 964 (Okla. Ct. App. 1987); Estate of Livingston, 999 S.W.2d 874 (Tex. App. 1999).

Time When Competency is Required. The competency or incompetency of the witness is determined when the will is executed. Thus, in Estate of Parsons, 163 Cal. Rptr. 70 (Ct. App. 1980), the court held that a witness who disclaimed her devise was not made disinterested.[27]

Uniform Probate Code—Interest of Attesting Witness Not Disqualifying. UPC § 2-505 charted a new course on the treatment of interested witnesses. Under § 2-505, interested witnesses are not disqualified as attesting witnesses and they do not forfeit any portion of their devises. Close to 40 percent of the states now follow this rule. See Restatement 3d of Property, Statutory Note to § 3.1. The rationale of the UPC drafters was that disregarding the interest of the witnesses simplifies the law, prevents unjust results for homemade wills in which family members innocently serve as witnesses, and doesn't appreciably increase the opportunity for fraud or undue influence. See the comment to UPC § 2-505.

d. Self-Proved Wills

Statutory References: *UPC §§ 2-504, 3-406*

A majority of the states authorize wills to be made self proved. See Restatement 3d of Property, Statutory Note to § 3.1. A self-proved will is a will for which the testator and the witnesses have executed an affidavit before a notary public or similar officer detailing the procedures followed in the execution of the testator's will. The effect of a self-proved will varies among jurisdictions. In some jurisdictions a self-proved will conclusively establishes that all formalities have been met. The UPC conclusively presumes that all the signature requirements imposed by its wills statute have been met and create a rebuttable presumption that all other requirements for a valid will have been met. See Estate of Stephens, 608 N.W.2d 201 (Neb. Ct. App. 2000) (holding that self-proved will statute adopted from the UPC conclusively presumes that signature requirements of execution were met). A self-proved will also serves

---

27. California subsequently changed its rule by adopting a modified version of the UPC. Under Cal. Prob. Code § 6112, "any person generally competent to be a witness may act as a witness to a will," but "the fact that the will makes a devise to a witness [who is a necessary witness] creates a presumption that the witness procured the devise by duress, menace, fraud, or undue influence."

to eliminate the need for having the witnesses testify upon the filing of the will to prove its authenticity. The current UPC carries forward the self-proved will provisions found in the former versions of UPC § 2-504(a) and (b) without substantive amendment. See also UPC § 3-406, detailing the effect of having a self-proved will.

Unfortunately, cases have arisen in which testators or witnesses, through their own confusion or through misdirection by lawyers or others assisting the parties during the execution procedure, have only signed the self-proving affidavits and not the wills themselves. Most courts have upheld wills signed on the self-proving affidavits. See, e.g., Estate of McKay, 802 P.2d 443 (Ariz. Ct. App. 1990); Will of Carter, 565 A.2d 933 (Del. 1989); Hickox v. Wilson, 496 S.E.2d 711 (Ga. 1998); Estate of Benson, 1996 WL 118367 (Minn. Ct. App. Mar. 19, 1996) (unpublished opinion); Estate of Cutsinger, 445 P.2d 778 (Okla. 1968); see also Will of Ranney, supra p. 183 (utilizing substantial-compliance doctrine). Other courts, however, have held the wills invalid. See, e.g., Estate of Sample, 572 P.2d 1232 (Mont. 1977); Orrell v. Cochran, 695 S.W.2d 552 (Tex. 1985); Estate of Ricketts, 773 P.2d 93 (Wash. Ct. App. 1989). The genius of the self-proved will idea is that it wasn't set up in the statutes as a requirement but rather as an option. In the hands of certain courts, however, it has turned out to have unfortunate consequences.

The 1990 revision to the UPC added a new subsection (c) to § 2-504 to respond to this potential execution mistake by providing that, if necessary to prove a will's due execution, a signature affixed to a self-proving affidavit will be considered to be a signature affixed to the will. For a similar legislative response, see Tex. Prob. Code Ann. § 59(b), interpreted by Bank One, Texas v. Ikard, 885 S.W.2d 183 (Tex. Ct. App. 1994) to apply to wills executed before the effective date of the amendment if the testator died after the amendment's effective date. For further discussion of self-proving affidavits, see Bruce H. Mann, Self-Proving Affidavits and Formalism in Wills Adjudication, 63 Wash. U. L.Q. 39 (1985); Annot., 1 A.L.R. 5th 965 (1992).

Military Wills. The federal statute providing an alternative set of formalities for military wills (see supra p. 168) authorizes a self-proving affidavit. The use of a self-proving affidavit provides prima facie evidence that the will was executed in compliance with the formalities. See 10 U.S.C. § 1044d(d).

INTERNET REFERENCES. To the surprise of virtually no one, you can now order up a custom-prepared will via the Internet. One such site is the LawGix site, lawgix.com. Robert L. Shapiro, Esq. (one of O.J. Simpson's defense lawyers) is co-founder of a website offering self-tailored wills and other legal documents. See www.legalzoom.com. Another site from which you can order self-help will-making products is the Nolo Press site, www.nolo.com/ category/ estate.

In Unauthorized Practice of Law Committee v. Parsons Technology, Inc., 1999 WL 47235 (N.D. Tex. 1999), the court granted summary judgment in favor of the Unauthorized Practice of Law Committee of the Texas State Bar and issued an order permanently enjoining Parsons Technology, Inc. from selling and distributing its software programs, Quicken Family Lawyer Version 8.0 and Quicken Family Lawyer '99 (QFL), within the state of Texas. QFL offers over 100 different legal forms, such as employment agreements, real estate leases, premarital agreements, and seven different will forms, along with instructions on how to fill out these forms. In Unauthorized Practice of Law Committee v. Parsons Technology, Inc., 179 F.2d 956 (5th Cir. 1999), the Fifth Circuit Court of Appeals vacated the injunction and judgment in favor of the plaintiff because after the district court decision the Texas Legislature enacted an amendment to its unauthorized-practice-of-law statute providing that "the 'practice of law' does not include the design, creation, publication, distribution, display, or sale . . . [of] computer software, or similar products if the products clearly and conspicuously state that the products are not a substitute for the advice of an attorney," effective immediately. H.B. 1507, 76th Leg., Reg. Sess. (Tex. 1999).

e. Statutory Wills

The term "statutory will" refers to two distinct concepts, the California Statutory Will and the Uniform Statutory Will Act. Both, however, have a feature in common, which is that they offer a state sponsored pattern or patterns of property distribution that differs from the state directed pattern of property distribution under the intestacy laws.

Both the California Statutory Will and the Uniform Statutory Will Act require that the will be executed in accordance with the state's rule for executing an attested will. The will forms supplied to the public under the California Statutory Will legislation provide explicit directions to the maker for the procedures required for valid execution. For discussion of statutory wills and consideration of ways to improve their effectiveness, see Gerry W. Beyer, Statutory Fill-In-the-Blank Will Forms, Prob. & Prop., Nov.-Dec. 1996, at 26; Gerry W. Beyer, Statutory Fill-in Will Forms—the First Decade: Theoretical Constructs and Empirical Findings, 72 Or. L. Rev. 769 (1993); Gerry W.

Beyer, Statutory Will Methodologies—Incorporated Forms vs. Fill-In Forms: Rivalry or Peaceful Coexistence?, 94 Dick. L. Rev. 23 (1990); Theresa A. Bruno, The Deployment Will, 47 A.F. L. Rev. 211 (1999); Herbert T. Krimmel, A Criticism of the California Statutory Will, 19 W. St. U. L. Rev. 77 (1991).

California Statutory Will. The California statutory will is a state sponsored and distributed will form. Cal. Prob. Code §§ 6200-48. Other states that have enacted the California Statutory Will are Maine, Michigan, and Wisconsin.

Uniform Statutory Will Act (1984). Rather than offer a state sponsored set of will forms, the Uniform Statutory Will Act follows a different approach, called the incorporation-by-reference approach. The pattern of distribution is set forth in the statute rather than in the will. The testator adopts (incorporates by reference) the statutory pattern by executing a will that states that all or a specified portion of the testator's estate is to be disposed of in accordance with the enacting state's Uniform Statutory Will Act. Only Massachusetts and New Mexico have adopted the Uniform Statutory Will Act. The Uniform Law Commission no longer promotes it as a recommended act.

2. Unattested Wills

Statutory References: *UPC §§ 2-502(b), (c), -503*

Unattested wills fall into two categories: holographic wills and nuncupative wills. By far, most of the litigation arises in connection with holographic wills.

Nuncupative Wills. A substantial minority of states, by statute, allows personal property (often with a maximum limit on value), and in a few instances real property, to pass under nuncupative or oral wills. "Soldiers in active military service" and "mariners or sailors at sea" traditionally have been excused from the more rigorous testamentary formalities. See Statute of Frauds, 1677, 29 Car. 2, ch. 3, §§ 19-21, 23; Wills Act, 1837, 7 Wm. 4 & 1 Vict., ch. 26, § 11. Some states allow persons in their "last illness"—"one so violent that the testator has not the time, opportunity, or means to make a written will in legal form"—to make oral wills, provided certain requirements are met. The testator must: (1) be dying and know it; (2) express orally the intent to make an oral will; and (3) call upon "competent" witnesses (usually at least two) to witness that the spoken words are testator's last will. The witnesses must put into writing their testimony within a prescribed time after the act, and generally the nuncupative act must take place within the testator's home, unless the testator was "surprised" by the "last illness" while on a journey. See Restatement 3d of Property, Statutory Note to § 3.2; Atkinson on Wills §§ 76-78; Page on Wills §§ 20.13-20.31; Kevin R. Natale, Note, A Survey, Analysis, and Evaluation of Holographic Will Statutes, 17 Hofstra L. Rev. 159 (1988).

Holographic Wills. A holographic will is one that is written entirely or materially in the handwriting of the testator. Although holographic wills weren't authorized in England (unless properly attested), a majority of American jurisdictions now statutorily recognize their validity. All of the statutes require that the testator sign the will and all of them dispense with witnesses to the execution. A few, however, contain a provision concerning the number of witnesses needed to prove the testator's handwriting. A number of the statutes also require that the will be dated. A few require that the will be signed "at the end."

Under statutes such as the California provision in effect in *Estate of Black*, below, courts have sometimes validated a holographic will containing some nonholographic matter under one of two theories—the *intent theory* or the *surplusage theory*. Both theories recognize that words or marks on a sheet of paper that are not in the testator's handwriting do not necessarily disqualify the handwritten portion as a holographic will. Under the intent theory, words or marks not intended by the testator to be part of the will need not be in the testator's handwriting. Under the surplusage theory, the portions of the document in the testator's handwriting are given effect as a holographic will if they make sense as a will standing alone, without regard to the portions of the document not in the testator's handwriting. The Restatement 3d of Property § 3.2, comment b, adopts the surplusage theory, but also provides that a jurisdiction committed to the intent theory should adopt a presumption that any portion that is surplusage—any portion not essential for the handwritten provisions to make sense as a will—was not intended by the testator to be part of the will.

Estate of Black

641 P.2d 754 (Cal. 1982)

RICHARDSON, J. Appellant Gene Ray Bouch appeals from the denial of probate of the holographic will of Frances B. Black, deceased, who died on September 6, 1977, a resident of Long Beach, California. [See infra p. 207 for] a copy of the instrument, which purported to leave the bulk of her estate to appellant and his family. . . . It may be seen from an examination that the instrument was handwritten on three pages of a partially preprinted stationer's form. It is conceded by all parties that all of the handwriting, including the date and her name, is that of the testatrix. Probate was denied because of her incorporation of some of the printed language on the stationer's form. Having found that none of the incorporated material is either material to the substance of the will or essential to its validity as a testamentary disposition, we conclude that the trial court erred in rejecting the holograph and reverse its order.

Testatrix used three copies of a stationer's form, which form obviously was intended to be used for a one-page will. In appropriate blank spaces in the exordium clause at the top of each page, and in her own handwriting, testatrix inserted her signature and the place of her domicile. Other printed language on each page of the form relating to residuary gifts, the appointment of an executor, attesting witnesses and a testimonium clause generally was either stricken or ignored by testatrix. At the bottom of her third and last page, however, following all of the dispositive provisions of the will, she inserted in the appropriate spaces of the preprinted form the name and gender of her executor. And although she dated the holograph entirely in her own hand at the top of the first page of her will, she also utilized pertinent blanks to insert the date of the instrument at the end of the last page and to identify the city and state in which she executed it.

Using virtually all of the remaining space on each of the three pages, testatrix expressed in her own handwriting a detailed testamentary disposition of her estate, including specific devises and legacies to individuals and a charitable institution and a bequest of her residuary estate. As noted, no handwriting of any other person appears on any of the three pages.

Probate was denied to the holograph apparently because testatrix was seen to have "incorporated" the indicated preprinted portions of the form "as part of her will," in violation of the presumed, implied prohibition of Probate Code section 53, which provides:

> A holographic will is one that is entirely written, dated and signed by the hand of the testator himself. It is subject to no other form, and need not be witnessed. No address, date or other matter written, printed or stamped upon the document, which is not incorporated in the provisions which are in the handwriting of the decedent, shall be considered as any part of the will.

Where, as here, there is no conflict in the evidence, "the validity of the holographic instrument must be determined entirely by reference to the applicable statutes and principles of law." (Estate of Baker, 59 Cal. 2d 680, 683, 381 P.2d 913, 31 Cal. Rptr. 33 (1963)) Unanimously in *Baker*, we stressed that "The policy of the law is toward a construction favoring validity, in determining whether a will has been executed in conformity with statutory requirements." (Ibid.) Moreover, we affirmed "the tendency of both the courts and the Legislature . . . toward greater liberality in accepting a writing as an holographic will. . . ." (Ibid.) "*Substantial compliance with the statute, and not absolute precision is all that is required. . . .*" (Id., at p. 685, 381 P.2d 913, 31 Cal.Rptr. 33 italics added.)

. . . In construing section 53 we bear in mind the primary legislative purpose of the holographic will statute which was identified by us in Estate of Dreyfus (1917) 175 Cal. 417, 418-419, 165 P. 941, as the prevention of "fraudulent

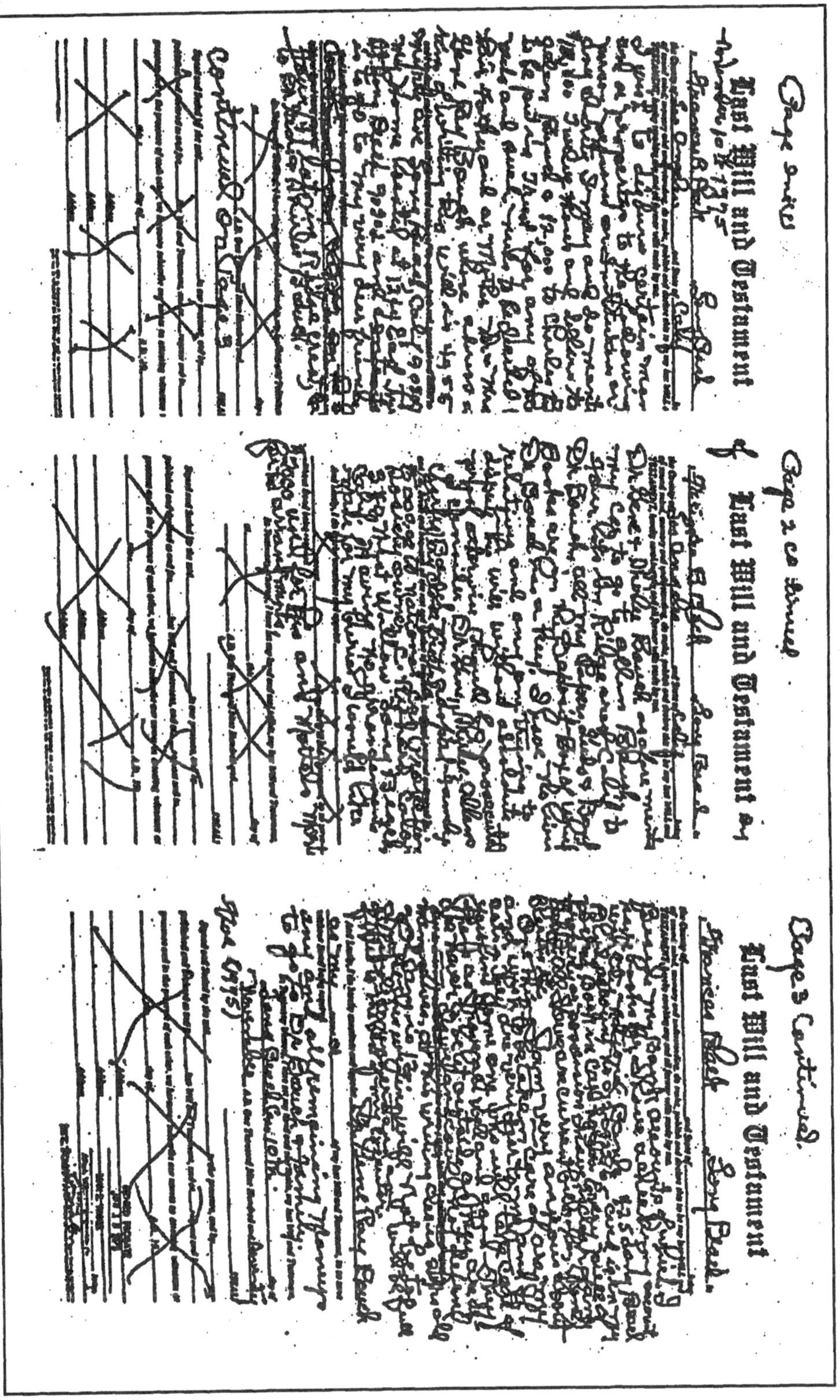
Page one
Last Will and Testament
Page 2 continued
Last Will and Testament
Page 3 continued
Last Will and Testament

will-making and disposition of property" by virtue of the recognized difficulty of forging an entire handwritten instrument. After reviewing the legislative history of the statute in Dreyfus we had "no doubt that (the holographic provision) owes its origin to the fact that a successful counterfeit of another's handwriting is exceedingly difficult, and that, therefore, the requirement that it should be in the testator's handwriting would afford protection against a forgery of this character." (Id., at p. 419, 165 P. 941.) . . . An overly technical application of the holographic will statute to handwritten testamentary dispositions, which generally are made by persons without legal training, would seriously limit the effectiveness of the legislative decision to authorize holographic wills. . . .

Read literally, section 53 requires only that a holographic will be "written, dated and signed" by the hand of testatrix, and that printed matter not incorporated in the handwritten provisions not be considered as any part of the will. . . . Frances Black's will fully satisfies the requirements of the statute. There is no question as to the authorship or authenticity of the handwritten document before us. To reiterate: There is no handwriting on any page of the holograph which is not admittedly that of testatrix. The will is dated both at its beginning and partially at its end in the handwriting of testatrix. She wrote her name on each page and we deem this a sufficient "signature." On each of the first two pages she referred to the instrument as her "will," and on the last page she expressed the hope that "this writing" would be given legal effect. The completeness and integrity of the testamentary disposition written in her own handwriting, in our view, is itself evidence of her intent to authenticate the document as her last will and testament by affixing her signature at the top of each page. We have repeatedly said that "It is settled in California that the signature need not be located at the end (of a holographic will) but may appear in another part of the document, provided the testator wrote his name there with the intention of authenticating or executing the instrument as his will." (Estate of Bloch 39 Cal. 2d 570, 572-573, 248 P.2d 21 (1952)).

No sound purpose or policy is served by invalidating a holograph where every statutorily required element of the will is concededly expressed in the testatrix' own handwriting and where her testamentary intent is clearly revealed in the words as she wrote them. Frances Black's sole mistake was her superfluous utilization of a small portion of the language of the preprinted form. Nullification of her carefully expressed testamentary purpose because of such error is unnecessary to preserve the sanctity of the statute. Moreover, rejection of the instrument as a will would have the unfortunate practical consequence of passing her estate through the laws of intestacy to the daughter of her excluding those whom she described in the holograph as "my very dear friends" and "my adopted family" and the charity which was apparently close to her predeceased husband by a former marriage—in fact, a stranger to her—thereby heart and which she specifically wished to benefit. The resulting frustration and defeat of her testamentary plan would be directly contrary to our Baker reasoning and would serve neither valid public policy nor common sense.

The order appealed from is reversed.

[The dissenting opinion of MOSK, J., is omitted.]

Notes

1. *First Generation Holographic Will Statutes.* Section 53 of the California Probate Code is a first generation holographic will statute. The essential characteristic of the first generation holographic will statute is that it requires a holographic will to be *entirely* written, signed, and dated in the testator's handwriting. Under this type of statute, most courts have held wills like that in *Black* invalid. See, e.g., Wolcotts' Estate, 180 P. 169 (Utah 1919). Contra, e.g., Fairweather v. Nord, 388 S.W.2d 122 (Ky. 1965); Estate of Teubert, 298 S.E.2d 456 (W. Va. 1982). Cases are collected in Annot., Requirement That Holographic Will, or its Material Provisions, Be Entirely in Testator's Handwriting, 37 A.L.R.4th 528 (1985); Annot., Requirement That Holographic Will Be Entirely in Handwriting of Testator as Affected by Appearance of Printed Matter or Handwriting of Another, 89 A.L.R.2d 1198 (1963).

2. *Second Generation Holographic Will Statutes.* The former UPC established the second generation holographic will statute. Former UPC § 2-503 retained the signature requirement, deleted the requirement that the will be dated, and replaced the requirement that the will be "entirely" in the handwriting of the testator with the requirement that the "material provisions" be in the testator's handwriting. After *Black* was decided, the California legislature replaced its holographic will statute with a provision nearly identical to former UPC § 2-503. Cal. Prob. Code § 6111(a).

Estate of Johnson, 630 P.2d 1039, 1040-41 (Ariz. Ct. App. 1981), was decided under former UPC § 2-503. The decedent, Arnold H. Johnson, died on January 28, 1978, at the age of 79. He was survived by six children. A printed will form was presented for probate. The italicized portions shown below were in the decedent's handwriting. In part, the will reads:

THE LAST WILL AND TESTAMENT

I *Arnold H. Johnson* a resident of *Mesa Arizona of Maricopa* County, State of Arizona, being of sound and disposing mind and memory, do make, publish and declare this my last WILL AND TESTAMENT, hereby revoking and making null and void any and all other last Wills and Testaments heretofore by me made. . .

Second—I give devise and bequeath to *My six living children as follows*

To John M. Johnson 1/8 of my Estate
Helen Marchese 1/8
Sharon Clements 1/8
Mirriam Jennings 1/8
Mary D. Korman 1/8
A. David Johnson 1/8

To W.V. Grant, Souls Harbor Church
3200 W. Davis Dallas Texas 1/8

To Barton Lee McLain)
and Marie Gansels)
Address 901 E. Broadway Phoenix) 1/8
~~*Az*~~ *Mesa)*

The trial court denied Probate of this document, and on appeal the appellate court affirmed, saying in part:

> Initially it is to be noted that Arizona has adopted the [former] Uniform Probate Code, the holographic will provisions being contained in § 2-503 . . . .
>
> The statutory requirement that the material provisions be drawn in the testator's own handwriting requires that the handwritten portion clearly express a *testamentary* intent. . . . In our opinion, the only words which establish this requisite testamentary intent on the part of the decedent are found in the *printed* portion of the form. . . .

Johnson would seem no longer to be good law after the decision of Estate of Muder, 765 P.2d 997, 1000 (Ariz. 1988), reversing 751 P.2d 986 (Ariz. Ct. App. 1988). The court said:

> We hold that a testator who uses a preprinted form, and *in his own handwriting* fills in the blanks by designating his beneficiaries and apportioning his estate among them and signs it, has created a valid holographic will. Such handwritten provisions may draw testamentary context from both the printed and the handwritten language on the form. We see no need to ignore the preprinted words when the testator clearly did not, and the statute does not require us to do so.

3. *Third Generation Holographic Will Statute*. The *Johnson* case and the lower appellate court decision in the *Muder* case prompted the drafters of the UPC to amend the former UPC's holographic will statute. Under UPC § 2-502(b), (c), only the "material portions of the document" need be in the testator's handwriting and portions of the document that are not in the testator's handwriting, along with other extrinsic evidence, can be used to establish testamentary intent. Arizona and California have enacted a similar provision regarding extrinsic evidence. Ariz. Rev. Stat. Ann. § 14-2502(B); Cal Prob. Code § 6111.5.

4. *Misreading of the UPC Holographic Will Statutes?* In treating that the printed portion of a holographic will written on a preprinted will form as extrinsic evidence, have the courts misread the statute? The Restatement 3d of Property § 3.2, comment c, points out that under the former and current UPC, "the nonholographic material on a preprinted will form is part of the holographic will, not extrinsic evidence."

PART B. GROUNDS OF CONTEST: THE CONTESTANT'S CASE

Statutory Reference: *UPC § 2-502(c)*

1. Testamentary Intent

Restatement 3d of Property

§ *3.1, Comment g. Testamentary intent.* To be a will, the document must be executed with testamentary intent, i.e., the decedent must intend the document to be a will or to become operative at the decedent's death. Whether the decedent executed a document with testamentary intent is a question of fact on which evidence of intention may be considered. A clear, unambiguous expression of testamentary intent in the document raises a strong (but not irrebuttable) presumption that the document was executed with testamentary intent. The presumption is rebuttable only by clear and convincing evidence.

§ *3.2, Comment c. Testamentary intent—holographic wills.* Holographic wills as well as attested wills must be executed with testamentary intent. See § 3.1, Comment *g*. Testamentary intent need not be shown from the face of the will, but can be established by extrinsic evidence. Extrinsic evidence can also be used to establish the meaning of a holographic will.

Estate of Kuralt

981 P.2d 771 (Mont. 1999)

LEAPHART, J. On July 4, 1997, Charles Kuralt (Mr. Kuralt) died in a hospital in New York City. His widow, Suzanna "Petie" Baird Kuralt (Petie), thereafter filed a petition in the state courts of New York for probate of his estate. On September 15, 1997, Petie, as the Domiciliary Foreign Personal Representative of the Estate of Charles Kuralt (the Estate), secured Montana counsel and filed a Proof of Authority pursuant to § 72-4-309, MCA (1995), in the Fifth Judicial District Court, Madison County, seeking to probate certain real and personal property owned by Mr. Kuralt in Madison County, Montana.

On September 30, 1997, Appellant Patricia Elizabeth Shannon (Shannon), an intimate companion of Mr. Kuralt for nearly thirty years, filed a Petition for

Ancillary Probate of Will. This petition challenged the application of Mr. Kuralt's New York will to the real and personal property in Madison County. In part, the basis for Shannon's petition was a letter, dated June 18, 1997, which she had received from Mr. Kuralt shortly before his death indicating that he intended Shannon to "inherit" 90 acres along the Big Hole River. Shannon claimed that the letter constituted a valid holographic will that entitled her to Mr. Kuralt's real property in Madison County and, therefore, that the property should not be allowed to pass under the antecedent terms of Mr. Kuralt's New York will.

The Estate filed a Response and Objections to Petition for Ancillary Probate on November 10, 1997. On December 5, 1997, a hearing on Shannon's petition was set for March 3, 1998. Deposition and written discovery ensued. On the day of the scheduled March 3, 1998, hearing, the Estate filed a Motion for Summary Judgment and accompanying brief, arguing that Mr. Kuralt's June 18, 1997 letter expressed, at most, only a future intent to make a will, but not a present testamentary intent to devise the Montana property to Shannon.[28]

Notwithstanding the Estate's pending motion for summary judgment, the evidentiary hearing on Shannon's petition began on March 3, 1998, with the presentation of Shannon's case in chief. Thus, on March 3 and 4, 1998, the District Court heard "extrinsic evidence" bearing upon Mr. Kuralt's intent in writing the letter of June 18, 1997. This evidence showed, *inter alia*, that Mr. Kuralt had already transferred 20 acres of his land along the Big Hole River to Shannon in 1997, and that although that transaction had been structured as a "sale," it had been in substance a gift because Mr. Kuralt had secretly supplied the $80,000 in purchase money to Shannon before the ostensible transfer took place. Further, this extrinsic evidence suggested that, prior to Mr. Kuralt's fatal illness, Mr. Kuralt and Shannon had planned to transfer the remaining 90 acres of Mr. Kuralt's property along the Big Hole River in the same manner—as a sham "sale"-gift transaction—in the fall of 1998.

On April 30, 1998, the District Court heard argument on the Estate's motion for summary judgment and thereafter, on May 26, 1998, entered an Order and Memorandum granting partial summary judgment to the Estate.[29] In this order,

---

28. It is undisputed in this case that Mr. Kuralt's letter of June 18, 1997, meets the threshold formal requirements for a valid holographic will: Mr. Kuralt was of sound mind and sufficient age at the time that he wrote the letter, and the letter is entirely in Mr. Kuralt's handwriting and was signed by him. See §§ 72-2-521 and -522(2), MCA. Thus, the only issue in dispute here is the question of whether Mr. Kuralt possessed the requisite testamentary intent in writing the letter.

29. The District Court denied the Estate's request for summary judgment with respect to certain items of personal property, about which the court held that there were contested issues of material fact. This aspect of the District Court's summary judgment ruling is not at issue on appeal.

the court agreed with the Estate's position and held that the June 18, 1997 letter "clearly contemplates a separate testamentary instrument not yet in existence to accomplish the transfer of the Montana property." Shannon appeals from the order of the District Court granting partial summary judgment to the Estate. We reverse the District Court and remand for trial because there are genuine issues of material fact.

Issues Presented. There are two issues on appeal:

(1.) Was the District Court correct in concluding that summary judgment was appropriate because the evidence raised no genuine issues of material fact?

(2.) Did the District Court err in concluding that the letter of June 18, 1997, was not a valid holographic will because it expressed no present testamentary intent?

Factual Background. Mr. Kuralt and Shannon first met in 1968 in Reno, Nevada, when Mr. Kuralt brought his CBS show "On the Road" to Reno to cover the creation and dedication of the "Pat Baker Park," a project which Shannon had spearheaded. During that weekend, Mr. Kuralt, a married man, invited Shannon to dinner. Thus began a protracted personal relationship between Mr. Kuralt and Shannon, lasting nearly thirty years until Mr. Kuralt's untimely death on July 4, 1997. Mr. Kuralt and Shannon took pains over the years to keep their relationship secret, and were so successful in doing so that even though his wife, Petie, knew that Mr. Kuralt owned property in Montana, she was unaware, prior to Mr. Kuralt's death, of his relationship with Shannon.

From 1968 to 1978, Shannon and Mr. Kuralt saw each other every two-to-three weeks for several days at a time. Indeed, Mr. Kuralt maintained close contact by telephone and mail, and spent a majority of his non-working time with Shannon during this ten-year period. Although Mr. Kuralt and Shannon spent less time together over the remaining twenty years of their relationship, they maintained meaningful personal and financial ties. The couple regularly vacationed together, frequently traveling around the United States, as well as Europe.

Mr. Kuralt also established close, personal relationships with Shannon's three children, acting as a surrogate father and providing them with emotional and material support which continued into their adult lives. For example, Mr. Kuralt paid the entire tuition for Shannon's eldest daughter to attend law school and for Shannon's son to attend graduate school. Over the years, in fact, Mr. Kuralt was the "primary source of support" for Shannon and her children, providing them with substantial sums of money on a regular basis—usually \$5,000 to \$8,000 per month.

In the 1980s, Mr. Kuralt and Shannon formed a limited partnership called "San Francisco Stocks," which packaged and sold frozen cooking stocks. Mr. Kuralt provided all the capital for the partnership, while Shannon and her two children ran the day-to-day operations of the business. San Francisco Stocks operated for approximately five years, closing in 1988. At that time, Shannon moved to London, England, where Mr. Kuralt paid for Shannon to study landscape gardening at the Inchbald School of Design. During this time period, Mr. Kuralt and Shannon traveled regularly around Ireland.

In 1985, Mr. Kuralt purchased a home in Ireland and then deeded the property to Shannon as a gift. That same year, Mr. Kuralt purchased a 20-acre parcel of property along the Big Hole River in Madison County, near Twin Bridges, Montana. On this parcel, Mr. Kuralt and Shannon constructed a North Carolina-style cabin. In 1987, Mr. Kuralt purchased two additional parcels along the Big Hole River which adjoined the 20-acre parcel, one parcel upstream and the other parcel downstream of the cabin. These two additional parcels constitute approximately 90 acres, and are the primary subject of this appeal. Also in 1987, Mr. Kuralt purchased the old Pageville Schoolhouse located on Montana Highway 41 between Twin Bridges and Dillon, and Mr. Kuralt and Shannon moved the old schoolhouse to one of the newly-purchased parcels with plans to renovate the structure and utilize it as a retirement home.

On May 3, 1989, Mr. Kuralt executed a holographic will, which stated as follows:

> *May 3, 1989*
> *In the event of my death, I bequeath to Patricia Elizabeth Shannon all my interest in land, buildings, furnishings and personal belongings on Burma Road, Twin Bridges, Montana.*
> *Charles Kuralt*
> *34 Bank St.*
> *New York, N.Y. 10014*

Mr. Kuralt mailed a copy of this holographic will to Shannon.

However, Mr. Kuralt thereafter executed a formal will, on May 4, 1994, in New York City. In this will, Mr. Kuralt proclaimed: "I, CHARLES KURALT, a resident of the City, County and State of New York, declare this to be my Last Will and Testament and revoke all my prior wills and codicils." With respect to real property owned by Mr. Kuralt, the will provided:

> TWO: I devise all my real property (including any condominium) which is used by me as a residence or for vacation purposes, together with the buildings and improvements thereon, if any, to my wife, PETIE, if she shall survive me.
>
> . . . .
>
> FIVE: All the residue and remainder of my property and estate, real and personal, of whatever nature and wherever situate, including any property not effectively disposed of by the foregoing provisions of this Will, but excluding any property over which I have any power of appointment or disposal which power I hereby expressly do not exercise (hereinafter referred to as my "residuary estate"), I

> dispose of as follows: [the will then proceeds to gift the entire residuary estate outright to Petie, except for a credit shelter trust benefitting the Kuralts' two children].[30]

The will makes no specific mention of the description or location of any of the real property, in Montana or elsewhere, that had been owned by Mr. Kuralt. The beneficiaries under Mr. Kuralt's Last Will and Testament are his wife, Petie, and the Kuralts' two children; neither Shannon nor her children are named as beneficiaries. In fact, Shannon was not even aware that Mr. Kuralt had executed his Last Will and Testament until institution of the probate proceedings at issue in this appeal.

On April 9, 1997, Mr. Kuralt deeded his interest in the original 20-acre parcel with the cabin along the Big Hole River to Shannon. Although Shannon ostensibly "paid" Mr. Kuralt $80,000 for this parcel, those funds in fact came from Mr. Kuralt, who, some time earlier, had begun sending Shannon installments of money to accumulate the necessary "purchase" price. It appears that Mr. Kuralt and Shannon dressed this gift up as a sale so as to keep their long-standing personal relationship a secret. After the filing of the deed to the 20-acre parcel, Shannon sent Mr. Kuralt, at his request, a blank buy-sell real estate form. Apparently, Mr. Kuralt's intent was to deed the additional 90 acres along the Big Hole River to Shannon. At Shannon's behest, however, Mr. Kuralt and Shannon agreed that this transfer should be accomplished in much the same manner as they had previously negotiated the "sale" of the 20-acre parcel with the cabin—by Mr. Kuralt providing the purchase money so that the gift-transaction could be disguised as a sale. They further agreed that the transaction would be consummated in September of 1997 when Shannon, her son, and Mr. Kuralt had agreed to meet at the Montana cabin.

Tragically, Mr. Kuralt became suddenly ill and entered a New York hospital on June 18, 1997. On that same date, Mr. Kuralt wrote a letter to Shannon in which he expressed grave concern for his health and arguably sought to devise the remainder of the Montana property to Shannon:

> *June 18, 1997*
> *Dear Pat—*
> *Something is terribly wrong with me and they can't figure out what. After cat-scans and a variety of cardiograms, they agree it's not lung cancer or heart trouble or blood clot. So they're putting me in the hospital today to concentrate on infectious diseases. I am getting worse, barely able to get out of bed, but still have high hopes for recovery . . . if only I can get a diagnosis! Curiouser and curiouser! I'll keep you informed.*

---

30. A "credit shelter trust" is a frequently used estate planning technique for saving transfer taxes. Eds.

> *I'll have the lawyer visit the hospital to be sure you inherit*[31] *the rest of the place in MT. if it comes to that.*
> *I send love to you & [your youngest daughter,] Shannon. Hope things are better there!*
> *Love,*
> *C.*

Enclosed with this letter were two checks made payable to Shannon—one for $8,000 and the other for $9,000. After this letter was mailed, Mr. Kuralt did not have any formal testamentary document drawn up devising the 90-acres of Montana property to Shannon. Thus, Shannon sought to probate the letter of June 18, 1997, as a valid holographic codicil to Mr. Kuralt's formal 1994 will, a claim which the District Court rejected in its summary judgment ruling. Shannon appeals.

Discussion. (1.) Was the District Court correct in concluding that summary judgment was appropriate because the evidence raised no genuine issues of material fact?

Summary judgment is appropriate only where there are no genuine issues of material fact and the moving party is entitled to judgment as a matter of law. Rule 56(c), M.R.Civ.P. We review a grant of summary judgment *de novo*, and, in so reviewing, this Court employs the same Rule 56(c), M.R.Civ.P., criteria as a district court. *Jarrett v. Valley Park, Inc.* (1996), 277 Mont. 333, 338, 922 P.2d 485, 487.

Shannon aptly labels the "strange procedural posture" of this case as "quixotic." From the outset of this dispute, Shannon and her attorneys pushed for an early resolution at trial because Shannon is presently experiencing "penurious circumstances." The Estate, in turn, sought to delay the institution of trial on the merits, repeatedly requesting additional time for preparation and discovery. At the start of the evidentiary hearing on March 3, 1998, the Estate again requested a continuance and, at that time, also filed its Motion for Summary Judgment. The District Court, while granting the Estate additional time in which to complete their anticipated discovery, denied the Estate's request for a continuance. In allowing Shannon to proceed with the presentation of her case in chief, the District Court stated:

> Well, I'm going to expedite this case; and I'm going to do it by first denying the motion to continue. But I'm going to grant the [E]state a right, after the evidence is introduced here today, which should be helpful to the [E]state, to complete their contemplated discovery. I'm going to permit them to recall any witnesses which the Petitioner puts on today for cross-examination; and of course, . . . to call any witnesses of their own. We're in a search for the truth, and we're going to pursue

---

31. In the original letter, Kuralt underlined the word "inherit." Eds.

it with dispatch if it takes all summer.

Then, during the "expedited" evidentiary hearing which ensued, counsel for the Estate objected to Shannon's presentation of "extrinsic evidence" bearing upon the question of whether Mr. Kuralt's letter contained the requisite *animus testandi* to render it a valid holographic will:

> We're here for a June 18, 1997, document, and whether or not that document is a holographic codicil to Mr. Kuralt's May 4, 1994, will. The letter speaks for itself. We believe that it's clear and unambiguous; and in that matter, because of that, extrinsic evidence is not permitted to be considered. Now, this appears to be in the form of extrinsic evidence; and I make a standing objection to these proceedings, to any further evidence, because of that.

In response, counsel for Shannon cited Montana case law and a Montana statute in support of the argument that, irrespective of ambiguity, "extrinsic evidence is allowed on holographic wills." The District Court apparently agreed with Shannon since it overruled the Estate's "standing objection" to the presentation of extrinsic evidence on Mr. Kuralt's intent.

Thus, the District Court allowed the presentation of extrinsic evidence relevant to the question of Mr. Kuralt's intent in writing the letter of June 18, 1997. Regardless of whether the court admitted that evidence because it found the letter to be ambiguous or whether the court allowed the presentation of extrinsic evidence because it agreed with Shannon's argument that such evidence may be discretionarily admitted in any holographic will dispute, the result is the same: extrinsic evidence was admitted showing that Mr. Kuralt had previously gifted 20 acres along the Big Hole River to Shannon while disguising the transaction as a sale; that evidence also suggested that Mr. Kuralt intended to do the same with the remaining 90 acres of his Madison County property.

The District Court, having allowed the introduction of extrinsic evidence on testamentary intent, erred in granting summary judgment because that evidence raised a genuine issue of material fact which precludes the granting of judgment as a matter of law. Our role in applying the criteria of Rule 56(c), M.R.Civ.P., like that of the District Court, is to first determine whether the Estate, as the moving party, has met its burden of demonstrating that no genuine issues of material fact exist which would preclude judgment as a matter of law. Here, the Estate has failed to sustain that burden and, accordingly, the court erred in granting summary judgment.

We disagree with the Estate's position that Shannon's extrinsic evidence is "immaterial" to the question of testamentary intent, and is merely "an insubstantial attempt to manufacture a material issue of fact." Rather, we agree with Shannon that the District Court improperly resolved contested issues of material fact when it found, in support of its conclusion that the letter "clearly contemplates a separate testamentary instrument not yet in existence," that:

> The extrinsic evidence—none of which is contested—confirms this conclusion. Petitioner herself testified during her deposition and at trial that decedent intended to "sell"—not "will"—the Montana property to her in the fall of 1998. While the extrinsic evidence substantiates a close and personal relationship between Petitioner and the decedent extending over 29 years, during which she and her children were apparently entirely housed, supported, educated and temporarily set up in business by the decedent, those facts are not sufficient to create a testamentary intent which the language of the letter clearly refutes.

When drawing all reasonable inferences in favor of Shannon, as the party opposing summary judgment, we conclude that the extrinsic evidence raises a genuine issue of material fact as to whether Mr. Kuralt intended to gift, rather than sell, the remaining 90 acres of his Madison County property to Shannon. The plain language of the letter of June 18, 1997, indicates, as Shannon points out, that Mr. Kuralt desired that Shannon "inherit" all of his property along the Big Hole River. While other language in the letter—"I'll have the lawyer visit the hospital . . . if it comes to that"—might suggest, as the Estate argues and as the District Court concluded, that Mr. Kuralt was contemplating a separate testamentary instrument not yet in existence, it is far from certain that that is the result Mr. Kuralt intended by the letter.

At the very least, when reading the language of Mr. Kuralt's letter in light of the extrinsic evidence showing the couple's future plans to consummate the transfer of the remaining 90 acres vis—vis a mock "sale," there arises a question of material fact as to whether Mr. Kuralt intended, given his state of serious illness, that the very letter of June 18, 1997, effect a posthumous disposition of his 90 acres in Madison County. Nor are the parties merely arguing different interpretations of the facts here; we have, in this case, a fundamental disagreement as to a genuine material fact which would be better reconciled by trial.

As this Court has firmly acknowledged, summary judgment "was not intended nor can it be used as a substitute for existing methods in the trial of issues of fact. . . ." *Kober v. Stewart* (1966), 148 Mont. 117, 122, 417 P.2d 476, 479. The very purpose of summary judgment is to determine whether any genuine issues of material fact exist. See Rule 56(c), M.R.Civ.P. However, it is not the function of a trial court to adjudicate genuine factual issues by way of summary judgment. In this case, the District Court improperly resolved a disputed issue of material fact on a summary judgment motion when it should have instead deferred the determination of that issue to the trier of fact at trial.

We hold that, because there is a genuine issue of material fact, the District Court erred in granting judgment as a matter of law. Accordingly, we reverse the court's grant of summary judgment and remand, for trial, the factual question of whether, in light of the extrinsic evidence, Mr. Kuralt intended the letter of June 18, 1997, to effect a testamentary disposition of the 90 acres in Madison County to Shannon.

Our holding obviates the need for this Court to reach the second issue on appeal. We note, however, that the parties spend a good deal of energy arguing, with respect to the second issue on appeal, whether extrinsic evidence on testamentary intent may be considered in any will dispute or only in those cases in which the alleged testamentary document is ambiguous as to intent. While we do not express any opinion with respect to the second issue on appeal, as we do not reach that issue herein, we deem it necessary, for purposes of guiding these proceedings on remand, to address the evidentiary question of whether a court may admit extrinsic evidence only when the alleged testamentary document is ambiguous as to intent.

In arguing to the District Court that extrinsic evidence may be admitted regardless of ambiguity, Shannon relied principally upon § 72-2-522, MCA,[32] which states in relevant part: "*Intent that the document constitute the testator's will may be established by extrinsic evidence*, including, for holographic wills, portions of the document that are not in the testator's handwriting." Section 72-2-522(3), MCA (emphasis added). The language of that statute does not admit of any exception or qualification, but clearly permits a court to discretionarily admit extrinsic evidence bearing on testamentary intent in any will dispute. As a practical matter, a court will generally turn to extrinsic evidence when the alleged testamentary document is ambiguous as to intent; however, a court "may" admit extrinsic evidence in any will dispute where that evidence is helpful in ascertaining testamentary intent or lack thereof. See § 28-2-905(2), (3), MCA ("This section does not exclude other evidence of the circumstances under which the agreement," including a will, "was made or to which it relates, as described in 1-4-102. . . ."); § 1-4-102, MCA ("For the proper construction of an instrument, the circumstances under which it was made, including the situation of the subject of the instrument and of the parties to it, may also be shown so that the judge be placed in the position of those whose language he [or she] is to interpret.").[33]

Nor is the language of § 72-2-522(3), MCA, inconsistent with our prior case

---

32. Montana Code Annotated § 72-2-522 is the same as UPC § 2-502(c), except that the Montana legislature's enactment substituted the word "may" for "can." Eds.

33. As the District Court itself noted in its summary judgment order:

> Generally, however, in giving effect to any will, some extrinsic evidence must be admitted to enable the court to apply the words of the will to the matters to which it relates. "This is true even though there is no ambiguity in the will, for what the courts mean when they say that extrinsic evidence is not admissible when the will contains no ambiguity is that such evidence will not be admitted to vary or contradict the unambiguous language of the will."

law. It has long been the general rule in this jurisdiction that:

> "All that is necessary to make an instrument testamentary is that it should show, when read in connection with surrounding facts and circumstances, a testamentary intention." If the paper propounded is clearly of a testamentary character, it speaks for itself; but, if the intention of the testator is left in doubt by the form of expression used, then the intention must be arrived at by considering it in the light of the surrounding circumstances, and the intention must clearly appear.

In re Noyes' Estate (1909), 40 Mont. 231, 240-41, 106 P. 355, 358 (citations omitted). More recently, this Court has restated this general rule as follows: "Whether sufficient testamentary intent is present in an alleged will should be determined by first looking to the writing itself. However, if the intent is not clear from the writing, then the surrounding circumstances may be considered." *Matter of Estate of Ramirez* (1994), 264 Mont. 33, 36, 869 P.2d 263, 265 (citations omitted).

We do not disagree with the Estate's position that "[e]xtrinsic evidence is not admissible to supply testamentary intent when such intent is clearly absent on the face of the writing." Consistent with the Estate's position, the aforementioned authorities suggest that "the determination of the testamentary intent is to be made from the writing itself,'" and "'the surrounding circumstances may be considered'" in making the determination whether an alleged testamentary document *itself* contains the requisite *animus testandi*. *In re Van Voast's Estate* (1953), 127 Mont. 450, 452, 266 P.2d 377, 378, quoting *In re Augestad's Estate* (1940), 111 Mont. 138, 140, 106 P.2d 1087, 1088. Under no circumstance, however, may extrinsic evidence be utilized to manufacture testamentary intent where the alleged testamentary document contains no indication of an intent by the testator to make a disposition of property effective on death.

We are of the opinion, however, that Mr. Kuralt's letter of June 18, 1997, does not reveal a clear lack of testamentary intent. The letter suggests, as previously noted, that Mr. Kuralt desired Shannon to "inherit" the remainder of his property along the Big Hole River. Of course, as the parties dispute, other language in the letter raises the question of whether that expression of Mr. Kuralt's desire embodies merely an intent to perform an act in the future (i.e., prospective intent to draft a formal codicil to his Last Will), rather than a present, testamentary intent to dispose of his property (i.e., intent that the very letter constitute a valid holographic codicil to his Last Will).

However, when viewed in light of the extrinsic evidence, which shows not only the history of gift-giving by Mr. Kuralt to Shannon and her children but also that Mr. Kuralt wrote the letter in dispute under circumstances of dire health, the question of whether that letter contains the necessary *animus testandi* becomes an issue suitable for resolution by the trier of fact. Because Mr. Kuralt's letter is unclear as to testamentary intent, the District Court properly admitted extrinsic evidence bearing upon Mr. Kuralt's intent in the summary judgment proceeding. The court should, therefore, also admit all extrinsic evidence relevant to the question of Mr. Kuralt's testamentary intent when the issue goes to trial.

In sum, we reverse the District Court's grant of summary judgment to the Estate because there are genuine issues of material fact which preclude judgment as a matter of law. Accordingly, we remand for trial the question of whether Mr. Kuralt's June 18, 1997, letter evinces testamentary intent. In resolving that question at trial, the District Court shall admit, for the benefit of the trier of fact, extrinsic evidence germane to the question of testamentary intent.

REVERSED AND REMANDED.

WILLIAM E. HUNT, SR., JIM REGNIER, and JAMES C. NELSON, JJ., concur.

Chief Justice J.A. TURNAGE dissenting.

I respectfully dissent and would affirm the District Court holding that the June 18, 1997 letter "clearly contemplates a separate testamentary instrument not yet in existence to accomplish the transfer of the Montana property."

Section 72-2-523, MCA, requires that a document or writing added upon a document can only constitute a decedent's will if the proponent establishes by clear and convincing evidence that the decedent intended the document or writing to constitute, in this case, decedent's holographic codicil.

The letter of June 18, 1997, and the record in this case does not meet the standard of clear and convincing evidence.

The June 18, 1997 letter, as set forth in the majority opinion, contains this—and only this—language relating to the question of a holographic will: "I'll have the lawyer visit the hospital to be sure you inherit the rest of the place in MT. if it comes to that." That language clearly indicates that decedent Kuralt did not intend the letter to operate as a holographic will but, rather, expressed his intent that at a future date he would have a lawyer visit him in the hospital to be sure that Patricia Shannon would, by a document thereafter to be executed, inherit "the rest of the place in MT." Such language is precatory and expresses only a desire or wish. It certainly does not constitute imperative, direct terms of bequest.

Notes

1. *Result on Remand*. On remand, the trial court found that Charles Kuralt's letter of June 18, 1997, was written with testamentary intent:

> This Court's careful review of the disputed letter, when considered with

> extrinsic evidence, leads this Court to conclude Kuralt intended, by the very letter, to dispose of his remaining Montana property to Shannon through inheritance. Prior to Kuralt's admission to the hospital, it is clear he intended to transfer the Montana property to Shannon via gift or sham real estate transactions. However, all of that changed when Kuralt accepted the fact his medical condition was serious and undiagnosed. . . .
>
> [The sentence] "I'll have the lawyer visit the hospital to be sure you inherit the rest of the place in MT. if it comes to that" (emphasis in original) . . . together with extrinsic evidence specifically informs Shannon that "you inherit the rest of the place in Montana."

Estate of Kuralt, No. DP-29-1997-3609 (Mont. Dist. Ct., March 22, 2000).

In Estate of Kuralt, 15 P.3d 931, 934 (Mont. 2000), the Supreme Court of Montana affirmed the judgment of the trial court, saying:

> The record supports the District Court's finding that the June 18, 1997 letter expressed Kuralt's intent to effect a posthumous transfer of his Montana property to Shannon. . . .
>
> The District Court focused on the last few months of Kuralt's life to find that the letter demonstrated his testamentary intent. The conveyance of the 20-acre parcel for no real consideration and extrinsic evidence that Kuralt intended to convey the remainder of the Montana property to Shannon in a similar fashion provides substantial factual support for the District Court's determination that Kuralt intended that Shannon have the rest of the Montana property.
>
> The June 18, 1997 letter expressed Kuralt's desire that Shannon inherit the remainder of the Montana property. That Kuralt wrote the letter in extremis is supported by the fact that he died two weeks later. Although Kuralt intended to transfer the remaining land to Shannon, he was reluctant to consult a lawyer to formalize his intent because he wanted to keep their relationship secret. Finally, the use of the term "inherit" underlined by Kuralt reflected his intention to make a posthumous disposition of the property. Therefore, the District Court's findings are supported by substantial evidence and are not clearly erroneous. Accordingly, we conclude that the District Court did not err when it found that the letter dated June 18, 1997 expressed a present testamentary intent to transfer property in Madison County to Elizabeth Shannon.

2. *Estate of Foxley.* Eileen C. Foxley executed a valid will on February 8, 1985. When she executed the will, she had six daughters and two sons. The will divided the bulk of her estate among her six daughters in equal shares. In December 1993, one of the daughters, Jane F. Jones, died and was survived by her only son, Hogan. The evidence at trial indicated that Foxley did not want her grandson, Hogan, to participate in her estate because she believed that he had abused his mother (Foxley's daughter).

Foxley died in October 1994. Upon her death, two of her daughters found a folder containing the original will and a photocopy of the will in the den of

Foxley's home. Foxley had made handwritten alterations on the photocopy of the will. In its original form, Article I provided:

> My only children are William C. Foxley, Sarah F. Gross, John C. Foxley, Winifred F. Wells, Elizabeth F. Leach, Sheila F. Radford, Mary Ann Pirotte and Jane F. Jones.

Foxley had lined through "Jane F. Jones," and written in her own handwriting: "her share to be divided to between 5 daughters. E.F. 1-7-94."

In its original form, Article III provided:

> I hereby give, devise and bequeath all of the rest of my proper [*sic*] to my six (6) daughters in equal shares.

Foxley had lined through "six," and written "5" below "(6)."

The trial court found that Foxley had substantially complied with the requirements of a holographic codicil and admitted the photocopy and original will to probate. The Court of Appeals affirmed, finding that Foxley's signature, the material provisions, and an indication of the date of signing were in her handwriting and that she had clearly demonstrated her intentions by her spoken words, her writings, and her actions.

In Estate of Foxley, 575 N.W.2d 150 (Neb. 1998), the Supreme Court of Nebraska reversed. The court held that the holographic codicil was invalid because the "handwritten words, standing alone, do not evidence a clear testamentary intent." The court also held that the handwritten portions, "[w]hen read on their own without reference to the original will, . . .cannot be understood (575 N.W.2d at 155):

> The statement "her share to be divided to between 5 daughters" does not express testamentary intent and is not clear without a handwritten reference to which daughter is to be excluded. Similarly, the line through "Jane F. Jones" is not sufficient because that line has no meaning unless read in conjunction with the typewritten names. Without the requisite testamentary intent, Foxley's handwritten words cannot be deemed material provisions.

The result was that one-sixth of Mrs. Foxley's estate went to her grandson.

3. *Restatement 3d of Property*. The Reporter's Note to Restatement 3d of Property § 3.2 said this of *Foxley*: "By refusing to treat the nonhandwritten portions of the original, attested will as extrinsic evidence that can be considered in determining testamentary intent and the meaning of the handwritten codicil, the court reached a manifestly unjust result."

4. *Sham Will Precedent*. The question of testamentary intent can also arise in the context of an attested will. Should a court allow extrinsic evidence to show that a decedent lacked the requisite testamentary intent even though the

proffered document is by all appearances a properly executed attested will? In Lister v. Smith, 3 Sw. & Tr. 282, 288-89 164 Eng. Rep. 1282, 1285 (P. Ct. 1863), the testator executed a codicil to his will, but extrinsic evidence was presented and the jury found that he never intended the codicil to be operative. His purpose in executing the codicil was to force a member of his family to give up a house that she occupied; the codicil revoked a bequest to the woman's daughter. The court held the evidence admissible, saying:

> The momentous consequences of permitting parol evidence . . . to outweigh the sanction of a solemn act are obvious. It has a tendency to place all wills at the mercy of a parol story that the testator did not mean what he said. On the other hand, if the fact is plainly and conclusively made out; that the paper which appears to be the record of a testamentary act, was in reality the offspring of a jest, or the result of a contrivance to effect some collateral object, and never seriously intended as a disposition of property, it is not reasonable that the Court should turn it into an effective instrument. And such no doubt is the law. There must be the *animus testandi*. . . . But here I must remark that the Court ought not, I think, to permit the fact to be taken as established, unless the evidence is very cogent and conclusive.

See also Vickery v. Vickery, 170 So. 745 (Fla. 1936) (denying probate to a will, regular on its face, when the evidence showed that the decedent executed it to satisfy a requirement for initiation into a Masonic order); Fleming v. Morrison, 72 N.E. 499 (Mass. 1904) (denying probate to a will, regular on its face, when the evidence showed that the decedent had told the drafting lawyer that it was a "fake" will made for the purpose of inducing Mary Fleming, who was named as the sole devisee in the purported will, to have sex with him). Cases are collected in Annot., Admissibility of Extrinsic Evidence Upon Issue of Testamentary Intent, 21 A.L.R.2d 319 (1952).

2. *Conditional Wills.* When persons are about to enter into life threatening situations, do the wills they execute in contemplation of this imminent danger remain valid if they survive? Would it make a difference if the life threatening activity is described in the will as the reason for executing the will? In Eaton v. Brown, 193 U.S. 411, 414-15 (1904), the decedent, Caroline Holley, wrote a will stating, "I am going on a Journey and may not ever return. And if I do not, this is my last request." She went on to make a specific devise to a church and leave the residuary of her estate to her adopted son. She returned to her home after her trip and died several months later.

Justice Holmes delivered the opinion of the Court, ordering that the will be admitted to probate. He reasoned that,

> [s]he was thinking of the possibility of death or she would not have made a will. But that possibility at that moment took the specific shape of not returning from her

> journey, and so she wrote "if I do not return," before giving her last commands. We need not consider whether, if the will had nothing to qualify these words, it would be impossible to get away from the condition. But the two gifts are both of a kind that indicates an abiding and unconditioned intent,—one to a church, the other to a person whom she called her adopted son. The unlikelihood of such a condition being attached to such gifts may be considered. And then she goes on to say that all that she has is her own hard earnings and that proposes to leave it to whom she pleases. This last sentence of self-justification evidently is correlated to and imports an unqualified disposition of property; not a disposition having reference to a special state of facts by which alone it is justified and to which it is confined. If her failure to return from the journey had been the condition of her bounty,—an hypothesis which is to the last degree improbable in the absence of explanation,—it is not to be believed that when she came to explain her will she would not have explained it with reference to the extraordinary contingency upon which she made it depend instead of going on to give a reason which, on the face of it, has reference to an unconditioned gift.

Eaton v. Brown exemplifies the general attitude of the courts, which is to resolve doubts in favor of validity. See, e.g., Estate of Mallett, 873 P.2d 715 (Ariz. Ct. App. 1994) (holding that a holographic will that stated that "if I should expire from this operation; I wish my wife . . . should inhert [sic] everything" was not a conditional will, but instead expressed the testator's inducement for writing the will); Albright v. Albright, 901 S.W.2d 144 (Mo. Ct. App. 1995) (rejecting the allegation that the will was conditional on residuary devisee being a minor at the time of the testator's death). Decisions denying probate to wills because the stated conditions fail do occur from time to time. See, e.g., Estate of Blankenship, 518 S.E.2d 615 (S.C. Ct. App. 1999), in which a husband and wife executed a joint will. The will stated that "in the event we should die simultaneously or within a short time of each other," we devise our property to all our children except our daughter, Anne. The wife died three years after her husband and the court held that her will was "clearly and unambiguously conditional." Id. at 616.

2. Testamentary Capacity

Statutory References: *UPC §§ 2-501, 5-411*

a. Age Requirement

Probate codes commonly establish a minimum age for the execution of a will. UPC § 2-501 and almost all non-UPC statutes set 18 as the minimum age. See Restatement 3d of Property § 8.2, Statutory Note.

The age requirement is purely a physical requirement and, as illustrated by Estate of Teel, 483 P.2d 603 (Ariz. Ct. App. 1971), can be over-inclusive and under-inclusive as compared with its purpose of assuring that only a person of mature judgment can execute a will. In *Teel*, the decedent, Marvin Teel, was approximately 54 years of age when he executed his will, but he was developmentally disabled and possessed the mental capacity of a 10- to 12-year-old. The will was upheld.

b. Mental Requirement

Mental Deficiency. UPC § 2-501 not only requires a person to be at least 18 years old when executing a wills, but also requires the person to be "of sound mind." It is usually thought that the mental capacity needed to execute a will is not as high as that needed to make an irrevocable lifetime gift. Why not? The Restatement 3d of Property sets forth the generally accepted standard for mental capacity to make (or revoke) a will:

> § *8.1 Requirement of Mental Capacity*. . . . (b) To have mental capacity to make or revoke a will, . . . the testator . . . must be capable of knowing and understanding in a general way the nature and extent of his or her property, the natural objects of his or her bounty, and the disposition that he or she is making of that property, and must also be capable of relating these elements to one another and forming an orderly desire regarding the disposition of the property.

The definition of mental capacity relates to mental *ability*, not actual knowledge. In Williams v. Vollman, 738 S.W.2d 849 (Ky. Ct. App. 1987), an elderly testator was held competent to execute a will at a time when his wife and one of his daughters were deceased, but he was unaware of their deaths because the news was kept from him for fear that it would weaken his resolve to live. The test, the court said, "does not require that the testator have actual knowledge of the objects of his bounty." The test only requires that he have "sufficient mind to know the objects of his bounty."

Fletcher v. DeLoach

360 So. 2d 316 (Ala. 1978)

TORBERT, C.J. The appellant, Mary Elizabeth DeLoach Fletcher, is the proponent of Ada B. Padgett's last will and testament, which was executed on April 15, 1970. [T]he testatrix died on October 31, 1975. . . . The appellees, a son and granddaughter of the testatrix, contested the probate of said will . . . , and moved that the contest of the will be transferred to circuit court for a trial by jury. See sections 43-1-70, 43-1-78, Code of Alabama 1975. The probate judge ordered the transfer of the cause to circuit court for trial by jury on April 2, 1976.

The trial . . . judge, after hearing the evidence, ruled that the will had been properly executed and that there was no evidence of undue influence or fraud in the case. Therefore, the only issue submitted to the jury was whether the testatrix possessed testamentary capacity at the time she executed the will of April 15, 1970. The jury found for the appellees (contestants) on the issue of testamentary capacity, and the trial judge ordered that Mrs. Fletcher was not entitled to have the will probated.

Mrs. Fletcher filed a motion for new trial . . . , alleging that the testimony and the evidence failed to support the jury's verdict. The trial judge denied this motion. . . . Mrs. Fletcher appeals from the denial of her motion for a new trial and from the jury verdict on a similar ground—whether the contestants satisfied their burden to prove the testatrix's lack of testamentary capacity. We hold that there was evidence before the jury which would tend to show that the testatrix lacked testamentary capacity at the time she executed the will of April 15, 1970, and we therefore refuse to overturn the verdict of the jury where it has not been shown to be clearly wrong and unjust.

The testatrix must have testamentary capacity in order to execute a valid will; I.e., she must have

> mind and memory sufficient to recall and remember the property she was about to bequeath, and the objects of her bounty, and the disposition which she wished to make—to know and understand the nature and consequences of the business to be performed, and to discern the simple and obvious relation of its elements to each other. . . .

Knox v. Knox, 95 Ala. 495, 503, 11 So. 125, 128 (1892). However, since it is presumed that every person has the capacity to make a will, the contestant has the burden to prove a lack of testamentary capacity. . . . Unless the contestant presents evidence that the testatrix suffered from a permanent type of insanity prior to the execution of the will (which was not shown in this case), the contestant's burden of proof is met when the jury is reasonably satisfied from the evidence that the testatrix did not have testamentary capacity at the time she executed the will.

When mental capacity is at issue, the factual inquiry must necessarily be of the broadest range. . . . Thus, evidence offered as to the mental and physical condition of the testatrix, either before or immediately after execution of the will, is admissible since it tends to indicate her condition when the will was signed. Likewise, testimony regarding the testatrix's "conversations, deportment, acts, and appearance" has been found to be competent on the issue of testamentary capacity. Batson v. Batson, [117 So. 10, 15 (1928)].

Also relevant to this issue is the character of the testamentary scheme; i.e., the reasonableness of the distributions made by the testatrix in her will. It is permissible for the jury to examine the will to see if its provisions are "just and reasonable, and consonant with the state of the (testatrix's) family relations," since this would reflect on her capacity to recall the natural objects of her bounty. Fountain v. Brown, [38 Ala. 72, 74 (1861)]. This court, in Councill v. Mayhew, 172 Ala. 295, 55 So. 314 (1911), has stated that:

> An *unequal* disposition of property per se raises no presumption . . . of testamentary incapacity, nor is it per se unnatural; but the unequal treatment of those who ostensibly have equal claims upon the testator's bounty, or the preference of one to the exclusion of another, may under the circumstances of a particular case, be deemed *unnatural*. In such a case, an *unnatural* disposition is a fact to be ascertained and considered by the jury [on the issue of testamentary capacity].

The pecuniary condition of the testatrix's heirs, when considered in the light of an unnatural disposition of property, would also reflect on the character of the will and would therefore be admissible.

There was sufficient evidence presented in this case for the jury to find that the testatrix lacked testamentary capacity when she signed her will on April 15, 1970. The testimony indicated that the testatrix became quite depressed after her eldest son died in January of 1970, and there was also evidence presented that she was disoriented when she went to Florida with relatives both before and after April 15, 1970. The evidence indicated a noticeable decline in the testatrix's attention to her appearance and to the cleanliness of her clothing immediately prior to the execution of the will.

The fact that the 1970 will left all of the estate to Mrs. Fletcher, the testatrix's daughter, thus making no provision for her son or granddaughter, could be evidence of an unnatural disposition of her property, and could be considered by the jury on the issue of testamentary capacity. This feature of the 1970 will is significant in that the 1970 instrument revoked the testatrix's prior will of 1959, which provided for the equal disposition of her estate among her three children.

The unnatural disposition manifested by the 1970 will and the pecuniary condition of the testatrix's heirs in 1970 (which did not show a great disparity between Mrs. Fletcher's financial condition and that of the testatrix's son and granddaughter), when considered with the evidence of the mental and physical condition of the testatrix before and after the execution of the will, supports the jury's verdict that the testatrix lacked testamentary capacity. In cases of this nature, the verdict of the jury cannot be overturned unless shown to be clearly wrong and unjust. The refusal of the trial judge to grant the appellant-proponent's motion for new trial strengthens this presumption in favor of the verdict. After a careful consideration of the record in this case, we feel that the jury's verdict is not clearly wrong and unjust, and the judgment entered in favor of the contestants is hereby affirmed.

BLOODWORTH, FAULKNER, ALMON and EMBRY, JJ., concur.

The Lucid Interval. The Restatement 3d of Property sets forth the well-accepted lucid-interval principle as follows:

> § *8.1, comment m. Lucid interval.* A person who is mentally incompetent part of the time but who has lucid intervals during which he or she fully comprehends the significance of a donative transfer can, in the absence of an adjudication or statute that has contrary effect, make a valid will or a valid inter vivos donative transfer, provided such will or transfer is made during a lucid interval.

In Lucero v. Lucero, 884 P.2d 527, 530, 533-34 (N.M. Ct. App. 1994), one of eight children, Patricio Lucero, who was favored in a previous will, contested the subsequent will executed by Carolina M. Lucero on the grounds of testamentary incapacity. Carolina was under a conservatorship at the time she executed the second will and was diagnosed as having senile dementia and cortical atrophy. The court nevertheless upheld the district court's finding that the decedent had sufficient capacity based on a finding that it was executed during a lucid interval.

> In spite of her medical diagnosis, Mrs. Lucero enjoyed numerous lucid intervals. In July 1988 Mrs. Lucero attended a branding at the neighboring ranch owned by her daughter . . . . Mrs. Lucero participated in the activities and engaged in normal conversations dealing with ranching. The testimony indicated that, although her mental status did vary, Mrs. Lucero visited with family members in person and by telephone both prior to and after the time she executed her will in August 1988, and at such times she recognized family members and engaged in appropriate conversations. . . .
>
> Numerous courts interpreting the UPC have found that generally senile, confused, or even mentally ill testators may possess sufficient capacity to execute a will during lucid moments. . . .
>
> The UPC specifically provides that the appointment of a temporary conservator shall not be evidence of incapacity. In the present case the district court found the record and findings in Mrs. Lucero's conservatorship proceedings created a rebuttable presumption that she lacked testamentary capacity. However, the district court found that presumption of a lack of testamentary capacity was overcome by "clear and convincing evidence that the decedent knew and recognized her issue, understood and acknowledged the general nature, character and extent of her estate and specifically requested the preparation of the Last Will and Testament at issue herein." There is substantial evidence in the record to support this finding.

See also Bye v. Mattingly, 975 S.W.2d 451 (Ky. 1998) (upholding validity of will, which the decedent's housekeeper who would take under a prior will challenged, based on the lucid interval doctrine notwithstanding that the decedent had been diagnosed with Alzheimer's disease and under a conservatorship).

Authority of Conservator to Make a Will for a Mentally Incapacitated Person. Courts have doubted that they have the power to authorize a conservator or guardian to make, amend, or revoke a will for a protected person unless a statute expressly authorizes that power. Such a power is now expressly authorized in UPC § 5-411. By contrast, the former UPC § 5-407(b)(3) had expressly precluded the court from authorizing the execution of a will by the conservator for a protected person.

Insane Delusion/Monomania/Partial Insanity. An insane delusion is a belief to which the testator adheres against all evidence and reason. "The subject-matter of the insane delusion must have no foundation in fact, and must spring from a diseased condition of mind. It does not mean merely a mistaken conclusion from a given state of facts, nor a mistaken belief of a sane mind as to the existence of facts." Dibble v. Currier, 83 S.E. 949 (Ga. 1914). Accord Jackson v. Austin, 1999 WL 760974 (Ark. Ct. App. Sept. 22, 1999) (upholding will) (unpublished opinion); Estate of Breeden, 992 P.2d 1167 (Colo. 2000) (en banc) (upholding will). In Boney v. Boney, 462 S.E.2d 725, 727-28 (Ga. 1995), for example, an adopted son contested his father's will, which named his stepmother sole beneficiary of his father's estate, claiming that the will was a product of his father's monomania. The son's claim was based on an incident in which his wife and children, once having sat down at the dining room table to eat at his father's and stepmother's home, left to dine at another relative's home. The evidence showed that after that evening the relationship between the son and his father was cool at best, the father stating that he believed the son's wife and children departed because she refused to eat food prepared by the son's stepmother. Evidence of the father's anger included his having cursed at the son's wife and having threatened "to slap her." Lifelong friends testified that they had never known the testator to curse at or threaten a woman. The court held that

> [w]hile the jury was authorized to find that the testator erroneously concluded that the departure was an insult, given the foundation in fact for the conclusion (food prepared by the propounder [the stepmother] had been available; the caveator's [son's] wife and children did leave without eating), the testator's belief that the departure was an insult to the propounder was, at most, "'the result of an erroneous conclusion based upon an illogical deduction drawn from facts as they really exist,'" which does not constitute the insane delusion that is necessary for monomania.

An insane delusion doesn't necessarily affect the validity of the will. As the North Dakota court stated in Kingdon v. Sybrant, 158 N.W.2d 863 (N.D. 1968): "[I]t is not sufficient to establish that the testator was the victim of [an insane] delusion, but the evidence must go further and establish that the will itself was the product of that delusion and that the testator devised his property in a way which, except for that delusion, he would not have done."

Problems

1. G came to believe that people were living in the trees on his farm. His will devised $40,000 so they could be fed and devised the residue of his estate to his wife, W. Is the $40,000 devise valid?

2. Pearl was elderly and suffered from a variety of medical problems, including diabetic seizures. Her physician recommended that she go into a nursing home where the seizures could be controlled. When her nephew, Henry, whom she had raised from infancy and who had been living in her house and caring for her, suggested that she abide by her physician's wishes, she went into a rage and eventually became convinced that he wanted her to go into the nursing home so he could steal her possessions. She executed a new will in favor of other relatives, with whom she had little contact, expressly revoking a former will that named Henry sole beneficiary. Is Pearl's new will valid? Compare Johnson v. Dodgen, 260 S.E.2d 332 (Ga. 1979), and Spruance v. Northway, 601 S.W.2d 153 (Tex. Civ. App. 1980), with Estate of Bonjean, 413 N.E.2d 205 (Ill. App. Ct. 1980). For an excellent discussion of the role of a lawyer when questions arise about a client's capacity, see Jan Ellen Rein, Ethics and the Questionably Competent Client: What the Model Rules Say and Don't Say, 9 Stan. L. & Pol'y Rev. 241 (1998).

3. In Estate of Koch, 259 N.W.2d 655 (N.D. 1977), Chris Koch and Elizabeth Koch were married in 1940 and divorced in 1974. They had five children. Chris died in 1976. In the 1960s, Chris came to believe that Elizabeth "was bad," that she "never did anything," and "was running around with other men." Chris expressed the view that no one cared for him and demonstrated suicidal tendencies. Doctors recommended extensive psychiatric treatment, but Chris only agreed to being admitted to a medical ward of the hospital for about a week. A few years later, he suffered a severe heart attack and was hospitalized for over a month. Following this episode, his children noticed further deterioration of his mind, and came to believe that he was sick mentally as well as physically. Chris continued to accuse Elizabeth of being unfaithful to him, and also of being an alcoholic. In 1973, Chris did undergo psychiatric care at various institutions. In that same year, Chris's two eldest daughters signed a petition to have him committed. The mental health board determined that Chris should not be committed. Shortly after the hearing, Chris wrote letters to two of his children telling them never to come home again. At a subsequent divorce hearing also held in 1973, three of the children testified on behalf of their mother.

In March 1974, Chris executed a will devising all of his property to his brother. Between 1974 and his death in 1976, Chris spent some time with each of his children, but efforts at reconciliation with Elizabeth failed. During this period, Chris was able to function well in society, and his neighbors thought he was mentally competent. Indeed, they had no knowledge of his mental problems and suicidal tendencies. Chris told several people that his children had sided with their mother, Elizabeth, at the commitment and divorce proceedings, and that he thought the commitment proceeding was commenced to get his money.

The court held that Chris's 1974 will was invalid, saying: "[D]ecedent's feelings toward his children were produced by beliefs held by the decedent which were unfounded in fact and . . . these beliefs were the reason the decedent excluded his natural objects of bounty from his will." Did Chris hold beliefs toward his children that were unfounded in fact?

Strike Suits. The foregoing discussion of testamentary capacity demonstrates that these types of will contests inevitably involve consideration of complex familial relationships and difficult medical judgments. The demanding factual circumstances surrounding will executions that arise in many of the cases make it difficult to assess how well the law achieves the goal of furthering testamentary freedom by protecting testators from themselves. The excerpt from Professor Langbein's article and *Crowley v. Katleman*, which follow, provide additional reasons for concern. The public's interest in having open access to courts must be weighed against assuring that the judicial process is not used as a coercive weapon. For further discussion of nonfinancial motivations of contestants and the effect of changes in family structure, divorce, and remarriage, see Jeffrey P. Rosenfeld, Will Contests: Legacies of Aging and Social Change, in Inheritance and Wealth in America 173 (Robert K. Miller, Jr. & Stephen J. McNamee eds. 1998).

John H. Langbein, Living Probate: The Conservatorship Model

77 Mich. L. Rev. 63, 64-66 (1978)

Although we do not have comparative data directly on point, the impression is widespread that [will contests alleging testamentary incapacity] occur[] more frequently in the United States than on the Continent or in England. We may point to several factors that bear upon the differential:

(1) In civil law countries, children as well as the spouse have a forced share entitlement in the estate of a parent. The disinherited child, who is the typical plaintiff in American testamentary capacity litigation, is unknown to European law. The European parent can leave his heir disgruntled with the statutory minimum, but that share will often be large enough by comparison with the

potential winnings from litigation to deaden the incentive to contest.

(2) Many Americans jurisdictions permit will contests on the question of capacity to be tried to a jury, which may be more disposed to work equity for the disinherited than to obey the directions of an eccentric decedent who is in any event beyond suffering. Civil jury trial has disappeared from English estate law; it was never known on the Continent.

(3) American law is unique among Western civil procedural systems in failing to charge a losing plaintiff with the attorney fees and other costs incurred by a defendant in the course of resisting the plaintiff's unjustified claim. In testamentary capacity litigation the American rule has the effect of requiring decedents' estates to subsidize the depredations of contestants. Put differently, the American rule diminishes the magnitude of a contestant's potential loss, which diminishes his disincentive to litigate an improbable claim.

(4) Civil law systems provide for the so-called authenticated will, which is executed before a quasi-judicial officer called the notary. This is not the only means of making a valid will in European countries, and because it is costly it is not widely used. But the notarial procedure does permit a testator who fears a post-mortem contest to generate during his lifetime and have preserved with the will evidence of exceptional quality regarding, *inter alia*, his capacity. The notary before whom the testator executes his will is not a judge; he does not adjudicate capacity. But his is a legally qualified and experienced officer of the state who is obliged to satisfy himself of the testator's capacity as a precondition for receiving or transcribing the testament. The authenticated will is, therefore, extremely difficult for contestants to set aside for want of capacity in post-mortem proceedings. . . .

A major reason that the impact of capacity litigation in America is so difficult to measure is that most of it is directed towards provoking pretrial settlements, typically for a fraction of what the contestants could be entitled to receive if they were to defeat the will. Especially when such tactics succeed, they do not leave traces in the law reports. Thus, the odor of the strike suit hangs heavily over this field. The beneficiaries named in the will are likely to be either charitable organizations whom the testator preferred to his relatives, or else those of his relatives and friends whom he loved most and who are most likely to want to spare his reputation from a capacity suit. They are typically put to the choice of defending a lawsuit in which a skilled plaintiff's lawyer will present evidence to a jury at a public trial touching every eccentricity that might cast doubt upon the testator's condition, or compromising the suit, thereby overriding the disposition desired by the testator and rewarding the contestants for threatening to besmirch his name.

Crowley v. Katleman

881 P.2d 1083 (Cal. 1994) (en banc)

[The plaintiff, Arthur Crowley, sued the defendant, Carole Katleman, and her attorneys for malicious prosecution for challenging a will. The decedent, Beldon Katleman, had executed a will prior to his marriage to the defendant. The will named Crowley, his long time friend, neighbor, and attorney, as the principal beneficiary. Crowley had not participated in the drafting or execution of the will, and the decedent never revoked or otherwise changed the will after his marriage.

In the will contest the defendant and her attorneys alleged the following six grounds for invalidating the will: "(1) Crowley exerted undue influence over Beldon Katleman; (2) Beldon Katleman revoked the will by destroying it; (3) the will was not in fact his last will; (4) he lacked testamentary capacity when he executed the will; (5) the will was not duly executed; and (6) Crowley defrauded Beldon Katleman to induce him to make the will." During the course of the litigation, Crowley twice offered to give Carole Katleman one-half the estate to settle the dispute. She refused. The probate court held the will valid, but also held that, notwithstanding the will's no contest clause, Carole Katleman qualified as an omitted spouse and accordingly awarded her all the community property and one-half of the decedent's separate property.[34]

Subsequently, Crowley filed the present action for malicious prosecution. In the complaint, he alleges that "Carole Katleman acted maliciously and without probable cause in contesting the will on the grounds that (1) it was not duly executed, (2) it was void for fraud, (3) Beldon Katleman lacked testamentary capacity, (4) it was not his last will, and (5) Beldon Katleman revoked the will by destroying it." He did not allege malicious prosecution regarding the ground of undue influence. In the complaint, Crowley also alleges that the attorney defendants "instigated and continued the will contest maliciously and without probable cause." The complaint goes on to allege that they "knew, or should have known, there was no probable cause for contesting the will on the grounds that (1) it was not duly executed, (2) it was not Beldon Katleman's last will, (3) it was void for fraud, and (4) Beldon Katleman lacked testamentary capacity . . . ." As against the attorneys, the complaint did not allege malicious prosecution regarding the grounds of either undue influence or revocation.

The Superior Court, Los Angeles County sustained the defendants' demurrer. Crowley appealed. The Court of Appeals reversed, and the Supreme Court granted review.]

MOSK, J. . . . Because the case is before us on a demurrer, the issue is

---

34. See infra p. 273 (discussing no-contest clauses); infra Chapter 10, Part C (discussing omitted spouse statutes). Eds.

whether the complaint properly pleads the element of probable cause. Specifically, the issue is whether a malicious prosecution action for bringing a will contest on multiple grounds may be maintained when the plaintiff does not allege that *all* the grounds asserted in the contest lacked probable cause. . . .

[T]he Court of Appeal was correct in concluding that "The holding in [*Betero v. National General Corp.*, 529 P.2d 608 (Cal. 1974)] is controlling." Under the rule of that decision, the complaint in the case at bar states a cause of action for malicious prosecution even though it does not allege that every one of the grounds asserted in the will contest lacked probable cause. . . .

Unable to distinguish *Bertero*, defendants ask us to overrule it. . . .

[After dismissing a number of the defendants' arguments, the court considers a statutory argument.] [D]efendants contend in effect that the *Bertero* rule is no longer necessary because the trial court now has statutory powers to deal with frivolous or delaying conduct that it lacked in 1974 when *Bertero* was decided and that provide a remedy superior to the cause of action for malicious prosecution in these circumstances. . . . [D]efendants particularly stress Code of Civil Procedure section 128.5, enacted in 1981 (hereafter section 128.5). That statute authorizes trial courts to award certain expenses, including attorney fees, resulting from "bad-faith actions or tactics that are frivolous or solely intended to cause unnecessary delay." . . . [I]t does not follow that the Legislature intended to substitute this remedy for the cause of action for malicious prosecution, less still to overrule *Bertero*.

The legislative history shows that the Legislature's intent was far more modest. . . .

There is still another reason to conclude that the Legislature did not intend either to substitute section 128.5 for the cause of action for malicious prosecution or to overrule *Bertero*: the remedies are not coextensive. Section 128.5 allows compensation only for out-of-pocket litigation costs, including attorney fees, that directly result from the objectionable conduct; the relief cannot include consequential damages. By contrast, *Bertero* stressed that a plaintiff who pleads and proves a case of malicious prosecution may recover not only litigation costs and attorney fees but also "compensation for injury to his reputation or impairment of his social and business standing in the community [citations], and for mental or emotional distress [citation]." (529 P.2d at 608, fn. omitted.) . . .

Lastly, defendants contend the *Bertero* rule is "particularly inappropriate" in a will contest. Their arguments, however, are primarily directed at showing that the tort of malicious prosecution itself is a "particularly inappropriate" remedy for will contests brought with malice and without probable cause. Defendants' main premise is that such a contest is not a new and separate action but the continuation of an existing proceeding, i.e., the petition to probate the will . . . .

They also stress that such a contest does not seek affirmative relief from the proponent of the will—e.g., money damages—but simply seeks to prevent the will from being admitted to probate. They point out that the contest is initiated by filing an "objection" to the petition, and they conclude that the grounds of the contest are therefore "analogous to affirmative defenses." Crowley disputes this characterization of a will contest, stressing that the pleading that initiates it, however denominated, is in the form of a civil complaint, that a summons issues on that complaint, directing the proponent of the will to file a responsive pleading and that the latter may then answer or demur. . . .

To be sure, a will contest cannot be initiated until the petition to probate the will has been filed, and to that extent it is dependent on the latter. The answer to the defendants' point, however, is not to be found in the technical niceties of will contest pleading, but in the reality of the matter. Whether they are called affirmative relief or affirmative defenses, the formal assertion of grounds to contest a will has the effect of injecting new factual and legal issues into the probate process, and of placing on the will's proponent the burden of mounting a defense to those issues. It is true the contest does not pray for money damages; but it ordinarily seeks to deny the beneficiaries their inheritances and to enrich the contestants pro tanto, and the case at bar illustrates that the dollar amount at stake can be substantial. As the case at bar also illustrates, the filing of such a contest can dramatically transform the probate of a will from a routine ex parte procedure, often conducted by simple affidavit, into sharply adversarial and hotly contested litigation, necessitating lengthy and expensive discovery and trial. . . .

"The elements of the common law malicious-prosecution cause of action have evolved over time as an appropriate accommodation between the freedom of an individual to seek redress in the courts and the interest of a potential defendant in being free from unjustified litigation." (*Oren Royal Oaks Venture v. Greenberg, Bernhard, Weiss & Karma, Inc.*, (1986) 42 Cal.3d 1157, 1169, 728 P.2d 1202.) When the prior action charged multiple grounds of liability and there was probable cause for some grounds but not for others, the question arises whether the malicious prosecution plaintiff has satisfied the requirement of showing that the prior action was brought without probable cause. . . .

As explained in *Bertero*, the cause of action for malicious prosecution . . . is . . . intended to redress two kinds of harm. (1) The *individual* who is sued "is harmed because he is compelled to defend against a fabricated claim which not only subjects him to the panoply of psychological pressures most civil defendants suffer, but also to the additional stress of attempting to resist a suit commenced out of spite or ill will, often magnified by slanderous allegations in the pleadings." (529 P.2d at 608.) And (2) "The *judicial process* is adversely affected by a maliciously prosecuted cause not only by the clogging of already crowded dockets, but by the unscrupulous use of the courts by individuals '. . . as instruments with which to maliciously injure their fellow men.'" (*Id.* at 608, italics added.)

. . . Defendants assert that the judicial burden caused by a subsequent malicious prosecution action is greater than the burden of defending against groundless theories of recovery in the original action. In some cases this may be true; but in other cases . . . to mount a defense against multiple baseless and malicious grounds may well be no less onerous than to mount a defense against separate causes of action. . . . [T]he most we can fairly say is that the . . . judicial cost of a subsequent malicious prosecution action is not necessarily greater than that of defending against multiple baseless and malicious grounds in the original action.

We are therefore remitted to . . . [deciding] which weighs more in this context—(1) the policy of encouraging free access to the courts . . . or (2) the policy of redressing the harm suffered by individuals compelled to defend against unjustifiable litigation . . . .

It is true that untrammeled access to the courts promotes social peace by providing the citizenry with an alternative to potentially dangerous self-help methods of redressing private grievances. But it is not an unmixed blessing: many of our courts are burdened by overcrowded dockets and long delays, and all litigation exacts both public and private costs. We are willing as a society to incur those burdens and costs when the litigation is well founded or, even when ultimately unsuccessful, was at least initiated with probable cause and without malice. In those circumstances the balance tips in favor of the policy of encouraging judicial access. That policy becomes counterproductive, however, when it operates to promote litigation that is groundless and motivated by malice; such litigation has no place in our judicial system, and we are therefore unwilling to bear its costs. After careful consideration, we see no reason to reach a different result when the litigation in question is the assertion of baseless and malicious grounds of liability in a single lawsuit: in both instances the balance tips in favor of the policy of making whole the individuals harmed by such abuse of our courts. . . .

For all these reasons we reaffirm the rule of *Bertero*, *supra*, as the law governing the issue presented by this case.

The judgment of the Court of Appeal is affirmed.

LUCAS, C.J. and KENARD, BAXTER, GEORGE, and WERDEGAR, JJ., concur.

[The dissent of ARABIAN, J., is omitted.]

3. Undue Influence/Duress

Restatement 3d of Property

§ *8.3 Undue Influence, Duress, or Fraud*

(a) A donative transfer is invalid to the extent that it was procured by undue influence, duress, or fraud.

(b) A donative transfer is procured by undue influence if the wrongdoer exerted such influence over the donor that it overcame the donor's free will and caused the donor to make a donative transfer that the donor would not otherwise have made.

(c) A donative transfer is procured by duress if the wrongdoer threatened to perform or did perform a wrongful act that coerced the donor into making a donative transfer that the donor would not otherwise have made.

(d) A donative transfer is procured by fraud if the wrongdoer knowingly or recklessly made a false representation to the donor about a material fact that was intended to and did lead the donor to make a donative transfer that the donor would not otherwise have made.

A contestant is not likely to discover direct evidence of undue influence/duress. The contestant's case must usually be based on circumstantial evidence. When cases are such that direct evidence of the truth is unavailable, the law generally responds by establishing presumptions. It is usually accepted that a presumption of undue influence arises if the alleged wrongdoer was in a confidential relationship with the donor and there were suspicious circumstances surrounding the preparation, formulation, or execution of the donative transfer. Although there is disagreement about the matter, the Restatement 3d of Property provides that the effect of the presumption is to shift to the proponent the burden of going forward with the evidence, not the burden of persuasion. See Restatement 3d of Property§ 8.3, comment f. On what constitutes a confidential relationship, the Restatement gives the following guidance:

> *Restatement 3d of Property* § *8.3, comment g. Confidential relationship—fiduciary, reliant, or dominant-subservient.* Traditionally, the single term "confidential relationship" has been used to describe a relationship that gives rise to a presumption of undue influence if coupled with suspicious circumstances. When examined more closely, the term "confidential relationship" embraces three sometimes distinct relationships—fiduciary, reliant, or dominant-subservient. For purposes of clarity, this Restatement refers to these relationships separately, although any one of them can be called "confidential" and give rise to a presumption of undue influence.
>
> A fiduciary relationship is one characterized as fiduciary by law, one in which the law imposes fiduciary duties on the fiduciary. Some fiduciary relationships are

between the donor and a hired professional. For example, an attorney is in a fiduciary relationship with his or her client, an institutional trustee is in a fiduciary relationship with the beneficiaries of the trust, and an institutional guardian or conservator is in a fiduciary relationship with his or her ward or protected person. Other fiduciary relationships are not necessarily between the donor and a hired professional. For example, an agent under a power of attorney is in a fiduciary relationship with his or her principal, but the donor's agent under a power of attorney frequently is a close family member or trusted friend who receives no fee for acting as agent. So also an individual trustee, guardian, or conservator might be a close family member or a trusted friend who might not receive a fee for acting in that capacity.

Whether a reliant relationship exists is a question of fact. The contestant must establish that, because of a family relationship or otherwise, there was a relationship based on special trust and confidence, for example, that the donor was accustomed to be guided by the judgment or advice of the alleged wrongdoer or was justified in placing confidence in the belief that the alleged wrongdoer would act in the interest of the donor. Examples might include the relationship between a financial adviser and customer or between a doctor and patient.

Whether a dominant-subservient relationship exists is a question of fact. The contestant must establish that the donor was subservient to the alleged wrongdoer's dominant influence. Such a relationship might exist between a hired caregiver and an ill or feeble donor or between an adult child and an ill or feeble parent.

In a particular case, these three relationships might overlap. That is, the alleged wrongdoer might be in a fiduciary, reliant, and dominant-subservient relationship with the donor. In another case, however, the relationships might not overlap. For example, an ill or feeble donor might be suspicious of the motives of a hired caregiver, but still be in a subservient relationship with that person, feeling that "I must do what he or she says."

Ramsey v. Taylor

999 P.2d 1178 (Or. Ct. App. 2000),
petition for review denied, 18 P.3d 1099 (Or. 2000)

DE MUNIZ, P.J. Defendants Melody Taylor and First Interstate Bank appeal from a judgment of the trial court setting aside in part the last will and testament and inter vivos trust of John C. Ramsey, Sr. (Senior) on the ground that Taylor exerted undue influence over Senior. Plaintiff John Ramsey, Jr., (John II), cross-appeals from several aspects of the court's decision as well. We review de novo, ORS 19.425(3),[35] and reverse on appeal and affirm on cross-appeal.

Plaintiff initiated this action to invalidate the terms of Senior's last will and inter vivos trust, to invalidate and set aside all transfers made by Senior in the

35. The court undoubtedly meant to cite Ore. Rev. Stat. § 19.415(3), which provides: "Upon an appeal from a decree in a suit in equity, the Court of Appeals shall try the cause anew upon the record." Eds.

final months of his life to Taylor, and to have those assets made a part of the intestate estate of Senior. Defendants include Taylor, the primary beneficiary under Senior's last will and trust, First Interstate Bank, the trustee of the trust, and the remaining trust beneficiaries: John Ramsey III (John III) and Ron Ramsey, both of whom are John II's sons, Leslie and Cody Ramsey, both of whom are great-grandchildren of Senior,[36] and Nan May, a niece of Senior's deceased wife. Plaintiff further sought a declaration that Taylor was not entitled to any share in Senior's estate pursuant to ORS 112.455, on the ground that Taylor had feloniously slain Senior by administering morphine to him.

After trial, the court issued an opinion concluding that Taylor did not feloniously kill Senior but that Taylor did exercise undue influence over him. The court set aside most of the transfers made by Senior to Taylor in the last months of his life and also invalidated Senior's last will and trust to the extent that it benefitted Taylor. The court, however, concluded that the last will and trust remained valid insofar as the remaining beneficiaries were concerned. The court therefore concluded that the bequests and transfers to Taylor should pass to John II pursuant to the laws of intestate succession but that the remainder of the estate should pass to the other beneficiaries pursuant to the terms of Senior's last will and trust.

On appeal, First Interstate and Taylor assign error to the trial court's conclusion that Taylor exercised undue influence over Senior in regard to the execution of his last will and trust and to the court's conclusion that Taylor exercised undue influence over Senior in regard to certain lifetime transfers made to Taylor. On cross-appeal, John II argues that the trial court erred in failing to set aside all lifetime transfers made to Taylor by Senior and in failing to invalidate the final will and trust in their entirety and to allow Senior's entire estate to pass to him through intestate succession.

On de novo review, we find the following facts pertinent to our legal analysis. For the most part, we recite the facts chronologically. Senior's wife died in 1984. At that point, he was living in California. After his wife's death, Senior suffered from depression and alcoholism but received treatment and greatly reduced his drinking. Shortly after his wife's death, Senior befriended a teenaged girl, Jill Brogdon, who provided housekeeping services for him and helped him with correspondence. He assisted Brogdon in paying for college and remained friends with her throughout the remainder of his life. At trial, Brogdon testified that, when she worked for Senior in the late 1980s, he had

36. Default judgments were entered against the Ramsey defendants. John III testified at trial that, although named as defendants, he and defendant Ron Ramsey have a verbal agreement with plaintiff John II that John II will split any money he receives as a result of this suit with John III, Ron and their children.

> a lot of negative things to say about his family. He was very bitter towards them. He said they were dishonest; that all they wanted was his money; that they had stolen from him in the past; and that they didn't come and visit him; and that he didn't trust them.

She further testified that Senior instructed her to hide his checkbooks and credit cards before his family came to visit, because his grandsons had stolen his checks and credit cards in the past. She indicated that Senior had received letters from family asking him for money and would dictate "nasty letters" to those relatives, sometimes providing them with funds, but also threatening to cut them out of his will or to reduce the amount of money he was leaving them. He was particularly angry at a granddaughter, Joanne Davis. Throughout the time Brogdon worked for Senior in the mid to late 1980s, he instructed her to write out revisions to his will on several occasions.

In 1989, Senior moved from California to Oregon. One of his reasons for moving was so that he could hunt and fish with his son and grandsons. Senior bought a house in which he lived with his grandson, John III, and John III's family. John III was under the impression that Senior was buying the house for John III, but then discovered that Senior intended to live there also. Senior lived in that house from 1989 to 1991. In 1990, Senior's granddaughter Joanne Davis also moved into the house with her family. Also in 1990, Senior was admitted to Ashland Community Hospital with gastrointestinal problems. Hospital records indicated: "Patient lives with his grandson. Apparently his grandson is quite disruptive, very demanding, threatening, and is a big emotional problem to the patient."

In late 1990, Senior executed a will leaving his estate to a trust created at the same time. Under the terms of that trust, 30 percent of the estate was to go to John II, 30 percent was to go to Ron, 20 percent was to go to John III, 10 percent was to go to Joanne Davis, and 10 percent was to go to his granddaughter Jeri Zabel.

John III and his family were unhappy with the living arrangements and wanted Senior and the Davis family to leave the house. Eventually Senior found another place for Davis and her family to stay, and, in 1991, also moved out himself, signing over the title of the house to John III and his wife.

Senior then bought the house in which he lived until his death. John II moved in with Senior, but they had trouble getting along. Senior was angry at John II because John II was not taking care of himself but was living off disability pay. Both John II and his half-sister, Betty Kasser, testified at trial that they believed that Senior had bought the house for John II. John II moved out of the house due to his disagreements with Senior.

In July 1991, Senior amended his trust to disinherit his grandsons John III and Ron, apportioning the 50 percent of the estate that previously had been bequeathed to them to the children of Joanne Davis and Jeri Zabel. In September 1991, shortly after John II moved out of the house due to their disagreements, Senior further amended the trust to disinherit John II as well, leaving the entire amount to his granddaughters Zabel and Davis and their children.

After John II moved out of Senior's house, Senior had a series of women companions who took care of the house for him and helped him with his business affairs, and/or had intimate relationships with him. Senior had his granddaughter Davis living with him for part of the time. Senior also gave money to his granddaughter Zabel. John III told Senior: "Why are you giving her money? She's ripping you off." Senior also gave a car to Jeannie Parker, who apparently was an illegitimate grandchild of Senior. After Parker wrecked the car, John III told Senior not to give her money to buy another car. Senior also befriended a woman named Karen Dixon, another woman named Mary Jo Estrada, and a woman named Philomena King. John III consistently advised Senior not to give money away to these women and indicated his belief that the women were taking advantage of Senior. Others, including his attorneys and one of his physicians, noted that Senior often bestowed valuable gifts on his female companions.

In mid-1993, Senior entered into a relationship with Mary Jo Estrada. In the course of his relationship with Estrada, Senior had a new will and trust prepared. Under the terms of that trust, Estrada was to receive 25 percent of the estate, Zabel was to receive 25 percent, John II was to receive 10 percent, John III and Ron were each to receive five percent, and the remainder was to be distributed among Senior's great-grandchildren. Those documents, however, were never executed.

In anticipation of Estrada moving into his residence with him, Senior transferred the title to real property and a mobile home to Estrada. Estrada testified that Senior wanted her added to the title of his property because "he had an attitude towards his family that he just didn't feel like they catered to him enough." In August 1993, Estrada and Senior went on a vacation together to Hawaii. Senior became annoyed with Estrada when she refused to sleep with him during that trip. When Estrada failed to move in with him, Senior hired an attorney to rescind the property transfers. Estrada reconveyed the property and mobile home to Senior. Senior's attorney also sought to recover $8,500 from Estrada after Senior had given her a check for that amount to have her teeth fixed. However, Senior later decided not to pursue recovering the $8,500 from Estrada.

Beginning in 1993, Philomena King worked for Senior as a housekeeper and bookkeeper. She assisted him until May 1995, when she was hurt in a car accident. During the course of their association, Senior gave her title to a car, paid a number of bills for her, and had a heat pump installed in her house. In total, Senior gave her approximately $50,000 in cash and gifts.

In late 1994, Senior executed a new will and trust, leaving 36 percent to John II, 14 percent each to John III, Ron, and Philomena King, three percent each to Joanne Davis and Nan May, and the remainder in various amounts to Senior's Davis and Ramsey great-grandchildren. John Curtis, the attorney who prepared the will and trust, testified that Senior was not pleased with John II, because John II had been asking Senior for large sums of money over the course of time and because John II was not working. Senior told his family about the bequest to King. John III asked him why he was giving King so much money.

Wendy Ramsey, wife of Senior's grandson Ron, testified that Senior liked to have women around and freely spent money on them and that she had told a police officer that Philomena King was using Senior for his money and not doing any housework. She further testified that Senior had tried to use his money to influence family members and had told the family on numerous occasions that he was changing his will. Senior's grandson, Ron, testified that he "didn't want to see [Senior] squander his money away, and didn't want him to get taken advantage of." Ron testified that he believed that Senior gave things to women who were not family members because he was senile.

Beginning in about August 1994, Senior received volunteer counseling services through the Age Wise program to help homebound seniors. His counselor, Gordon, stated that Senior was upset that his family did not help him with the house and yard and that they were only interested in his money.

During the winter of 1994 to 1995, Senior regularly went for coffee at a restaurant with John II and some of his friends. One of John II's friends testified that Senior and John II appeared to get along pretty well at first but later became more argumentative. He also testified that Senior's clothes were tattered and unsanitary and that his hygiene was poor. Senior told the Age Wise worker Gordon that the only reason John II took him to coffee "is because I pick up the tab."

In late spring 1995, Senior met Taylor's sister, Donaldson, at the restaurant where Senior had coffee with John II, some time after King had been injured in a car accident and was unable to help him with household tasks. When Senior told Donaldson that he needed a housekeeper, Donaldson mentioned that Taylor had a cleaning service and offered to have Taylor contact him. In early June, Taylor went to Senior's house to give a bid on cleaning services. Senior later recontacted Taylor and explained that King intended to do the cleaning and that Taylor's services would not be needed.

Shortly thereafter, Taylor invited Senior to her mother's birthday party. After the party, Senior told Taylor that he wanted her to do the cleaning after all, and she first cleaned for Senior on June 15, 1995. King testified that Senior had a sexual relationship with Taylor and no longer wanted King to visit him because he was afraid that Taylor would find her there and that she would not want King there. Taylor, on the other hand, testified that Senior had had a sexual relationship with King and that he was extremely hurt because he found out that she was living with another man.

From mid-June until late July, Senior spent a great deal of his time at Taylor's house and spent the night there once. Senior paid Taylor $150 for cleaning services in June. In early July, Senior and Taylor took a short vacation together to Brookings. In July, Senior paid Taylor several thousand dollars and also gave gifts of several hundred dollars each to Taylor's sister and mother. Senior also paid off Taylor's credit card debt of about $3,500. The Age Wise counselor, Gordon, noted that, during the period when Taylor was caring for Senior, the appearance of his house and yard was improved and that there was food available in the house. Gordon also testified that Senior had been depressed and unhappy but that his attitude became better after Taylor started helping him.

Throughout this time, Senior's health was deteriorating rapidly, and Taylor regularly took him to doctor's appointments, obtained prescriptions for him, and managed his bills for him. Senior reported weight loss, weakness, and angina problems to his physician, Dr. Gillette. Tests revealed anemia, renal failure and high calcium, which suggested to Dr. Gillette that Senior had multiple myeloma, a type of bone marrow cancer. Prostate and throat cancer also were indicated. Senior was referred to Dr. Traynor, who confirmed the cancer diagnoses. Dr. Gillette referred Senior to Southern Oregon Home Health Care, an agency that gives in-home care. Over the course of treating Senior for several years, Dr. Gillette recorded some social history of Senior, indicating that he lavishly spent money on his family, especially a granddaughter in California, but that "he felt that he'd given his other relatives a lot of money and had not gotten anything back from them." Dr. Gillette also was aware that Senior had a series of female companions for whom he bought many things.

On July 27, 1995, Senior made arrangements for his broker to sell a municipal bond and place the proceeds into his account, telling him that he planned to use the money for medical treatment. When he visited the broker's office, he introduced Taylor to the broker as his granddaughter. At trial, Taylor testified that Senior had not intended to use the money for medical treatment but had intended to buy a motor home and travel with her.

In August 1995, the Age Wise worker Gordon saw Senior on several occasions. He noted that Senior was in quite a bit of pain but that he seemed mentally competent and alert. Senior also indicated to Gordon that he was very pleased that Taylor was there. Gordon noticed that the house was clean and that Senior was clothed better than he had been previously. A Home Health Care aide, Keleman, who had given Senior assistance in 1994, also began assisting him again in August 1995. In 1994, she noted little furniture and food in the house, Senior's clothes were very ragged and old, and he seemed estranged from his son and grandsons over financial matters. In August 1995, she noted that Taylor had made the house much more homelike by decorating and providing home-cooked food for Senior. Senior also told Keleman that Taylor had bought him new clothing, and he was complimentary of her. Keleman thought Senior seemed very clear-headed when she saw him in 1995.

Also beginning in August 1995, Home Health Care nurses began visiting Senior in his home. On August 4, 1995, a nurse indicated in a written report:

> "10. Poor family dynamics—son came by during admit & son & pt. argued. pt. asking then demanding son leave—son left. pt stated 'I haven't talked to him in a long time and I don't want to talk to him now'—pt. in tears—sons visit. Lives alone & has x 5 yrs. 11. emotional—pt. depressed & unhappy—situation—son & grandson."

At trial, John II described his confrontation with Senior on August 4, indicating that Senior had told him that he would not receive the house when Senior died. John II was bothered "because the house was already mine, in my opinion; he bought it for me." John II denied that he and Senior were arguing but admitted that Senior was in tears. He stated that Senior would "go into tears when he wanted his way." He further testified that the nurse that was present at the time "sat there and patted his poor little hand like he was a poor little baby that couldn't do anything. I remember that. He was good at manipulating that." On cross-examination, John II indicated that he did not believe Senior's tears were genuine, that he was crying only to get sympathy from the nurse, and that the tears were unconvincing: "My two-year-old grandson does better than that." He stated that Senior wanted him and his family "to kiss his ass more than we did, and he didn't care too much that we didn't."

John III also visited Senior's home on August 4, 1995 and was made aware of Senior's cancer. However, he did not believe that Senior had cancer at that point and, in fact, stated at trial that he believed at that point that Senior "was too well to have anybody to come in and take care of him." Although he was aware that Senior was part of a hospice program, he did not understand that hospice services were provided to terminally ill people who wished to die at home. During his visit on August 4, John III met Taylor for the first time. During that visit, Senior showed John III some proposed changes to his will but John III refused to read them. John III argued with Taylor about her handling Senior's checkbook for him and told her that there was no reason for her to be in Senior's will. John III told Senior: "Don't do it; she's taking you for the money just like everyone else."

On August 7, Senior visited his attorneys, John Curtis and Mark Deems.

Senior recounted to them his confrontation with John II on August 4 that had culminated with Senior ordering John II from the house and told them he wished to modify his will and trust. Taylor brought Senior to their office but was not present during Senior's meeting with the attorneys. Senior informed the attorneys that he no longer wanted either John II or Philomena King to be a beneficiary and that he wanted Taylor to be a beneficiary. Other beneficiaries were to include Nan May and Senior's great-grandchildren. Senior described Taylor as somebody that he liked very much who had been taking care of him. He also expressed concern that his family would challenge the new will and trust. Senior described to the attorneys how he wanted his estate to be distributed but they had no witnesses available at the time, so they rescheduled an appointment for August 10 for the execution of the new documents. Also on August 7, Senior went to his bank and added Taylor's name to his checking account, making it a joint account with right of survivorship. At that point, the account had approximately $14,000 in it.

Senior returned to his attorneys' office on August 10 and read the documents that they had prepared. Again, Taylor brought him to the appointment but did not attend the meeting. Senior made numerous changes to the disposition of the trust at that point: $25,000 each to John II, John III, Ron Ramsey, and Nan May, $20,000 each to great-grandchildren Leslie and Cody Ramsey, and the residue of the trust estate to Melody Taylor.[37] Senior then executed the new will and trust. Senior also expressed concern that the "no contest" provision of the will would not prevent his family from challenging it and had the attorneys draft the following declaration, to which Senior subscribed and swore:

> "I, JOHN C. RAMSEY, SR., being first duly sworn on oath, depose and say as follows:
>
> "I have today executed a restatement of my Trust which was dated December 22, 1994. I am not under the influence of any drug medication and/or treatment which could diminish my abilities to appreciate the nature and consequences of this restatement. I am under no undue influence and/or coercion.
>
> "I have intentionally provided significant, yet smaller amounts for my son and grandsons because they have for several years alienated my affections by being irresponsible, contentious, and constantly seeking financial support from me rather than providing for themselves.
>
> "I have made provisions for MELODY J. TAYLOR in this restatement of trust. MELODY J. TAYLOR provides me care and support. In providing for MELODY J. TAYLOR instead of my sons and grandsons, I am recognizing her for providing for my needs."

37. Based on our review of the record, we would estimate that the residue would be about 60 percent of Senior's total estate.

Senior also had prepared and executed on that date an advance directive appointing Taylor as his health care representative and providing health care instructions indicating that he wished for no artificial feeding and life support. Both attorneys were of the opinion that Senior was mentally competent at the time he executed all of those documents. Curtis testified that, at the time the documents were executed, Senior knew who his next of kin was and also knew the extent of his property.

Also on August 10, Senior paid off another credit card bill for Taylor and paid off her home mortgage of approximately $38,000. He used the money that he had planned to use for the motor home. At trial, Taylor testified that Senior gave up his plans for traveling in the motor home when he realized that he was too ill to travel. When Senior's stockbroker saw the check for the home mortgage clear, he called Senior to ask about it. Taylor explained to him that the check had paid off her mortgage, that it was a birthday present, and that she was not Senior's granddaughter but his "significant other." The broker also talked to Senior, who confirmed that the mortgage payoff was a birthday gift.

On August 10, 1995, John III visited Senior and was told that Senior had kidney failure. He testified that he still did not understand that Senior was dying. Taylor was not present during their meeting. Senior again asked John III to read the changes Senior made in his will and trust, but John III refused to do so. Later that day, John III argued with Taylor and stated his belief that she did not care for Senior and was there only for his money. John III tried to order Taylor out of the house, but she refused to leave. This argument took place in front of a hospice worker, whose notes for that day indicate: "Family support absent due to dysfunctional relationships w/ son & grandson who live locally." Further notes from that day indicate that the hospice worker believed Taylor to be too inexperienced and immature to be Senior's primary caregiver and that attempts to explain the gravity of Senior's illness were unproductive. A Home Health Care nurse that visited Senior on August 10 indicated that he was mentally alert and competent but in a lot of pain. Some time after the meeting on August 10, John III told Taylor that Senior was only "faking" illness in order to get her attention and that he would get better if she left.

Beginning on August 13, Taylor stayed at Senior's home to take care of him. On August 15, 1995, Dr. Gillette made a house call on Senior because he was leaving town shortly and did not expect Senior to live much longer. Dr. Gillette found Senior to be in pain and unable to sit up but also found that Senior talked in his usual manner. Dr. Gillette believed that Senior understood that the disease was progressing rapidly and that he did not have long to live. Senior indicated to Dr. Gillette that he did not want any aggressive medical therapy to prolong his life but wanted only palliative measures. Dr. Gillette believed that Senior was competent to make that decision at that point. Dr. Gillette prescribed

Duragesic skin patches and Propacet for pain control. Dr. Gillette was of the opinion that Taylor was a concerned and compassionate caregiver.

Also on August 15, 1995, Senior saw Dr. Sandefur at the radiation oncology department at the Rogue Valley Medical Center for an evaluation for treatment of his cancer. Dr. Sandefur perceived that Senior was in excruciating pain. Dr. Sandefur determined that Senior's pain was caused by the multiple myeloma and that he was in profound renal failure. Dr. Sandefur described the pain from multiple myeloma as "some of the worst pain that we see." Dr. Sandefur told Senior that he had days to weeks to live. Senior told Dr. Sandefur that he did not want any form of treatment but that he wanted to be comfortable. Dr. Sandefur believed Senior to be mentally competent to make that decision. Dr. Sandefur gave Senior a shot of Demerol to control the pain before he left the medical center.

On August 16, 1995, John III came to Senior's house with a Jackson County sheriff's deputy, with the intention of having the deputy remove Taylor from Senior's home. He told the deputy that Taylor was "taking [Senior] for all he was worth." John II also was present but remained outside because it was understood that his presence would upset Senior. The plan was for the deputy to confront Taylor while John III went to get his grandfather. John III went through the house while the deputy confronted Taylor, and John III tried to pull Senior up from where he was lying down, which caused Senior a great deal of pain. John III therefore put him back down. Meanwhile, Taylor showed the deputy the advance directive for health care, and he determined that Senior had authorized Taylor to take care of him. Taylor and the deputy came into the room, and Taylor cursed and yelled at John III for jerking Senior out of bed and causing him pain. The deputy asked John III to leave, then asked Senior if he wished Taylor to remain there, and Senior indicated that he did. The deputy then explained to John III that he would need to get a lawyer to see about having Taylor removed.

On August 17, Senior's attorneys visited him at his home, in order to bring him paperwork necessary to fund the trust. At that time, Senior executed yet another declaration of intent, stating that he was aware that he was dying, that he was under no undue influence, and that he believed that his son and grandsons, for the previous several years, had "been more concerned with my wealth than my well being. I have intentionally made gifts and provisions for MELODY J. TAYLOR and others instead of my son and grandsons. I feel it is my money to do with as I please." At that time, Senior also signed a request expressing his wish "to be cremated and placed with the cremation of my deceased wife, Millie, and distributed to the Brookings, Harbor area which I showed to MELODY J. TAYLOR, and hereby request that MELODY J. TAYLOR be the distributee thereto."

While Senior's attorneys were visiting on August 17, John II's half-sister Kasser came to Senior's house with several of her friends. She testified that Taylor and her mother and grandmother were present, as was a hospice worker. She testified that Senior was "fine and healthy" and "very alert" during her visit. She further testified that Taylor and her grandmother smelled of alcohol and that Taylor interrupted her when she spoke with Senior. She was suspicious of Taylor. Taylor became angry with one of Kasser's friends and asked her to leave because the woman refused to tell Taylor her name. Kasser further testified that Senior had told her in the past that he had bought the house in which he was living for John II.

Around the same time, Senior had Taylor contact Jill Brogdon. Taylor told Brogdon that Senior was dying of cancer and wanted to see her. Taylor's mother picked up Brogdon at the airport and took her to see Senior four days before his death. Senior was glad to see her and was "very alert" but was in pain. She saw Senior again the day before his death and saw that he was noticeably more fatigued than he had been several days earlier. Senior's niece, Nan May, also was flown in to visit, as one of Senior's last wishes.[38]

On August 18, 1995, Dr. Gillette prescribed morphine elixir, one teaspoon to be taken every four hours as needed, for pain control. Dr. Gillette told Taylor that "she should use what was needed to help keep him out of pain." Taylor administered the medication according to the doctor's instructions.

On August 19, one of the visiting nurses contacted Dr. Hites, who was on call for Dr. Gillette, because Senior was still in pain. Dr. Hites increased the morphine dosage to one teaspoon every two hours, as needed. Taylor administered the medication according to the doctor's instructions. Also on that date, Taylor contacted Ron Ramsey's family and indicated that she did not believe that Senior would live much longer. She asked if they would come over that evening. Wendy Ramsey agreed that they would come over the following day.

On August 20, 1995, the visiting nurse assessed Senior's pain as 10 on a scale of 1 to 10 and again contacted Dr. Hites, who increased the morphine dosage to one teaspoon every hour, as needed. Again, Taylor administered the medication as prescribed. Wendy and Ron Ramsey visited that day, with their daughter Leslie. A Home Health Care nurse was present during part of their visit. Wendy described Senior as curled in fetal position and shaking. He woke up several times but would fall back asleep. She noted that he had blue liquid on the corner of his mouth. She also testified that Taylor and her mother were drinking beer and that Taylor offered her a beer, as well. Leslie Ramsey fed

---

38. May is a defendant in this action but did not testify at trial and, although named as a cross-respondent on John II's cross-appeal, has not appeared on appeal.

Senior a strawberry but he was unable to keep it down. Ron Ramsey first met Taylor on this occasion but did not speak to her very much. When he saw his grandfather's condition, he cried and held his hand. He had known of his grandfather's cancer but had not believed that the condition was serious.

Ron then called John II, who came over. John II argued with Taylor, stating that she was trying to take Senior's money and that he was going to get her kicked out of the house. John II believed that some of Senior's belongings had been removed from the house.

On the morning of August 21, Senior died. The same visiting nurse that had attended him the previous two days was present at the time. After his death, Senior's remains were taken to a funeral home. Shortly thereafter, Taylor notified the funeral home of Senior's cremation request and of his desire that she spread his and his wife's ashes. An employee at the funeral home told Taylor that she had no right to do that and that Senior's family would need to instruct the funeral home as to the disposition of his remains. . . . Senior's attorney, Curtis, also contacted the funeral home to try to make arrangements for disposition of Senior's remains according to his wishes but also was told that the funeral home would deal only with Senior's family. . . .

Another fact that came out at trial is relevant to our analysis, although it does not fit within the chronology as set forth above: The vast majority of the fact witnesses who testified at trial, for both sides, expressed the opinion that Senior loved power, liked to use money to manipulate people, and regularly changed his will or threatened to change his will in order to manipulate people. John II testified that Senior "loved his power; money was power." As noted above, John II expressed a belief that Senior wanted the family "to kiss his ass more than we did" but that John II was "not going to bow down and lick [Senior's] feet."

In a lengthy written opinion, the trial court concluded that Taylor was not precluded from benefitting from Senior's will on the ground that she took his life with felonious intent, given that the prescribed amounts of morphine, combined with Senior's renal failure, accounted for the amount of morphine in Senior's body at the time of his death. The court did, however, conclude that Taylor was precluded from benefitting under Senior's will on the ground that she exercised undue influence over Senior in the disposition of his estate. Following the formula for assessing undue influence set forth in In re Reddaway's Estate, 214 Or. 410, 329 P.2d 886 (1958), the court concluded that Taylor had a confidential relationship with Senior, that there were suspicious circumstances surrounding Senior's execution of his final will and trust, and that consideration of the various factors set forth in the *Reddaway* case led to a conclusion that Senior was unduly influenced by Taylor in the disposition of his estate.

Those factors are discussed in detail below. The court further concluded that Taylor unduly influenced Senior to pay off the mortgage on her house and to add her to his checking account with rights of survivorship and therefore also set aside those lifetime transfers to Taylor. The court also concluded that the cash payments and payments on Taylor's credit cards, amounting to some $19,000, bore a reasonable relationship to the economic value of the services Taylor provided to Senior in the final months of his life and declined to set aside those transfers. The trial court finally concluded that, although Taylor exercised undue influence in the execution of Senior's final will and trust, it should only be set aside insofar as it benefitted Taylor. The court therefore allowed the provisions to the other beneficiaries to remain intact.

We turn first to the primary issue raised by Taylor and First Interstate on appeal, as resolution of that issue is dispositive of most of the other issues presented. The issue is whether Taylor exercised undue influence over Senior in the payment of her mortgage, the assignment of a right of survivorship in his checking account, and the disposition of his estate under his final will and trust. Although we agree with the trial court that *In re Reddaway's Estate* provides the necessary framework for analysis of the undue influence claim, we reach a different conclusion than the trial court, primarily based on our assessment of the facts on de novo review, which differs somewhat from the trial court's assessment of the facts.

In *Reddaway*, the Supreme Court noted that there are two distinct approaches to analyzing undue influence. In one approach, the basic question is whether the testator was induced to execute an instrument that, in reality, did not express the testator's wishes but the wishes of another. 214 Or. at 418, 329 P.2d 886. The other approach, and the one the court ultimately adopted, focuses not on the testator's freedom of will but on "the nature of the influencer's conduct in persuading the testator to act as he does." Id. at 419, 329 P.2d 886. Under that approach, undue influence "denotes something wrong, according to the standards of morals which the law enforces in the relations of men, and therefore something legally wrong, something, in fact, illegal." Id., quoting Morris v. Morris, 192 Miss. 518, 6 So.2d 311 (1942) (internal quotations marks omitted). Under this "moral standard" approach, "the consequences of upholding the influenced gift are important. It would be expected that there would be less concern with the influencer's motive in a contest between him and the state claiming by escheat than there would be in a contest between him and the donor's deserving spouse." *Reddaway*, 214 Or. at 419, 329 P.2d 886.

The court went on to devise a test by which this "moral standard" could be applied in undue influence cases. First, a court must determine whether a "confidential relation" existed between the testator and the challenged beneficiary. Such a relationship is one "'such as to indicate a position of dominance by the one in whom confidence is reposed over the other.'" Id. at 421, 329 P.2d 886, quoting Doneen v. Craven, Executor, et al., 204 Or. 512, 522, 284 P.2d 758 (1955). The court specifically noted that such a relationship may exist where the testator is guided by the judgment and advice of another, and it may exist between a patient and a nurse. Id. If a confidential relationship exists and "suspicious circumstances" are shown, then "'the beneficiary [must] go forward with the proof and present evidence sufficient to overcome the adverse inference.'" Id. at 420, 329 P.2d 886, quoting In re Southman's Estate, 178 Or. 462, 482, 168 P.2d 572 (1946). The *Reddaway* court then enumerated seven criteria by which to evaluate whether "suspicious circumstances" are present: (1) whether the challenged beneficiary participated in the preparation of the will; (2) whether the testator received independent advice from an attorney in preparing the will; (3) whether the will was prepared in secrecy and haste; (4) whether the decedent's attitude toward others had changed by reason of his or her relationship with the challenged beneficiary; (5) whether there is "a decided discrepancy between a new and previous wills of the testator; and continuity of purpose running through former wills indicating a settled intent in the disposition of his estate"; (6) whether the disposition of the estate is such that a reasonable person would regard it as unnatural, unjust or unfair; and (7) whether the testator was susceptible to undue influence. Id. at 421-27, 329 P.2d 886. We turn to the application of these factors to the present case.

I. Confidential Relationship

We agree with the trial court that a confidential relationship existed between Senior and Taylor. Evidence in the record establishes not only that Taylor and Senior spent most of their time together in the last few months of his life but also establishes that Taylor took increasing responsibility over that time in managing all aspects of Senior's day-to-day life, including procuring and administering his medications, arranging and driving him to medical and business appointments, caring for his house and clothes, providing his food, and managing his checkbook. Taylor and First Interstate argue that no confidential relationship has been established because there is no direct proof that Taylor offered, or Senior accepted, business or financial advice from her. They further point out that an abundance of evidence demonstrates that Senior had strong opinions and ideas about what to do with his money. As to the question of direct evidence that Taylor gave business or financial advice, we disagree that direct evidence is necessary to establish a confidential relationship under these circumstances. Unrebutted evidence establishes that Senior reposed confidence in Taylor to handle most aspects of his daily life, including his finances. See Albright v. Medoff, 54 Or.App. 143, 145, 634 P.2d 479 (1981) (evidence that testator added beneficiary as authorized signatory to checking account was evidence of confidential relationship). The evidence also amply demonstrates that Senior made numerous financial decisions in the final months of his life that provided monetary benefits to Taylor. Moreover, evidence that Senior was strong-minded does not directly bear on the question of whether he had a confidential relationship with Taylor; that evidence is more properly considered in conjunction with the "susceptibility to influence" factor discussed below. Given the circumstances, we conclude that a confidential relationship existed between Senior and Taylor.

The question, then, is whether "suspicious circumstances" are present that would require Taylor to go forward with " 'evidence sufficient to overcome the adverse inference' " of undue influence. *Reddaway*, 214 Or. at 420, 329 P.2d 886, quoting Southman's Estate, 178 Or. at 482, 168 P.2d 572. We turn to each of the factors listed by the *Reddaway* court to evaluate "suspicious circumstances."

A. Procurement. This factor concerns whether the beneficiary participated in the preparation of the challenged will. There is evidence that, before Senior's meeting with his attorneys on August 7, Taylor assisted Senior in preparing a revision of the previous trust document, substituting herself for Philomena King as a beneficiary. It is undisputed that the documents that Senior actually signed on August 10 did not reflect the same changes in the disposition of his estate as did the changes that Taylor assisted in preparing. However, it also is undisputed that the documents actually executed on August 10 did, in fact, give a greater amount of Senior's estate to Taylor than did the revision that Taylor helped to prepare. In sum, we find that there is sufficient evidence of "procurement" to suffice as a "suspicious circumstance." More attention is given to this factor in the section below, concerning whether evidence was presented to overcome the "adverse inference" drawn from the presence of a confidential relationship and suspicious circumstances.

B. Independent Advice. This factor concerns whether Senior "had the benefit of the independent advice of his own attorney in drawing up the new will" that benefitted Taylor. *Reddaway*, 214 Or. at 422, 329 P.2d 886. Also relevant to this factor is whether the beneficiary was present during the meeting with the attorneys. Id. at 423, 329 P.2d 886. That a beneficiary made the appointment and escorted a testator to an attorney's office do not, in themselves, support an inference of undue influence. See Knutsen v. Krippendorf, 124 Or.App. 299, 309-10, 862 P.2d 509 (1993), rev. den. 318 Or. 381, 870 P.2d 221 (1994). Evidence in the record establishes that Senior met with his attorneys on two occasions to prepare his final will and trust and that Taylor was not present at those meetings. Although we have found it to be a suspicious circumstance where a testator is taken to a beneficiary's attorney rather than his or her own attorney to prepare a will, see Sangster v. Dillard, 144 Or.App. 210, 218, 925

P.2d 929 (1996), mod. on other grounds 146 Or.App. 105, 931 P.2d 815 (1997), it is undisputed that Senior consulted his own attorneys, who had previously prepared a will and trust for him. Moreover, one of the attorneys testified that Senior told him that Taylor had been of no help to him in deciding how to dispose of his estate. Also, the attorneys discussed with Senior his intent to benefit Taylor and the reasons why he was benefitting Taylor to a greater extent than he was benefitting his family. We conclude that no "suspicious circumstance" was present regarding whether Senior received independent advice concerning his last will and trust.

C. Secrecy and Haste. This factor concerns whether there was "secrecy and haste attendant on the making of the will." *Reddaway*, 214 Or. at 423, 329 P.2d 886. We do not find that there was any secrecy attendant on the making of Senior's final will and trust. As stated in the facts recited above, Senior attempted to talk to both John II and John III about the changes he planned to make to his will and trust on August 4, several days before consulting his attorneys. This precipitated the disagreement described above. Senior again attempted to discuss the changes with John III on August 10. There is no evidence from which it can be inferred that Senior's final will and trust were prepared in secrecy. Given Senior's history of threatening and following through on his threats to cut family members from his will, it is entirely consistent with Senior's past behavior that he would inform his family of his intent to reduce their prospective inheritances. As to haste, the evidence shows that Senior's final will and trust were prepared in relative haste, undoubtedly due to his deteriorating physical condition. We do not believe, however, that haste in preparing and executing a will because the testator understands that he is terminally ill is the type of haste that the court had in mind when it declared that "haste and secrecy" could be a "suspicious circumstance." We do not consider the relative haste with which Senior prepared and executed his final will and trust to be a "suspicious circumstance" in light of the fact that no secrecy was involved.

D. Change in Decedent's Attitude Toward Others. This factor concerns whether there has been an unexplained change in the testator's "attitude toward those for whom he had previously expressed affection[.]" *Reddaway*, 214 Or. at 423, 329 P.2d 886. The trial court found that, although Senior had had negative feelings toward his family before Taylor even met Senior, Senior "had been kept away from his family and friends by Ms. Taylor during the last two months of his life which had an effect on his attitude toward his family." On de novo review, we disagree with the trial court's factual conclusion. There was evidence that Senior spent a great deal of time with Taylor in June and July 1995 and therefore often was not at home. He also spent a great deal of time with Taylor in August during his final illness, when she stayed at his home with him. There also was evidence that Senior did not wish to see John II, as shown by his statement on August 4 to his nurse that "I haven't talked to him in a long time and I don't want to talk to him now." Further evidence is John II's behavior in choosing to remaining outside of Senior's house on August 16 while John III attempted to have the sheriff's deputy remove Taylor from the house, because the Ramseys understood that John II's presence would upset Senior.

There was evidence that Taylor was protective of Senior, that she was upset by John II's behavior in causing Senior to cry on August 4, and also when John III pulled Senior from his bed on August 16th, causing him pain. There is also evidence that Taylor was irate with guests such as Kasser and her friends when they were rude to her and that she engaged in verbal battles with John II and John III when they threatened her. However, there also was evidence that John II, John III, and Ron Ramsey all had occasion to be alone with Senior during the last month of his life without Taylor's interference (although there is no evidence that Ron Ramsey made any effort to visit Senior until the day before his death). There also was evidence that Taylor facilitated visits by Senior's friend Jill Brogdon and his niece Nan May during the final week of his life, at his request. The evidence does not support the trial court's conclusion that Taylor kept Senior from his family and friends during the final months of his life.

As to whether Senior's attitude toward others changed during the final months of his life when he was involved in a relationship with Taylor, there is some evidence that his relationship with his family, and in particular, his relationship with John II, deteriorated during this time. The question, however, is whether there was an "unexplained" change in attitude toward one for whom the testator "had previously expressed affection." *Reddaway*, 214 Or. at 423, 329 P.2d 886. As the trial court acknowledged, Senior's disaffection for John II had begun well before Senior even met Taylor. In fact, from the time that John II moved out of Senior's house in 1991 due to their disagreements, until Senior executed his 1994 will and trust, Senior had entirely disinherited John II. Even from that time in 1994 to mid-1995, when Senior's and John II's relationship arguably had improved, Senior expressed his dissatisfaction with John II to his attorney and also told the Age Wise worker Gordon that John II invited him to coffee only to get Senior to pay for it. Given the history of the stormy relationship between Senior and John II and the details of the argument between them on August 4 that culminated with Senior ordering John II from his house, it would be difficult to say that there was an "unexplained" change in Senior's attitude toward John II that can be attributed to Taylor's influence. Compare Sangster, 144 Or.App. at 217-18, 925 P.2d 929 (testator who underwent an "extreme change in attitude" toward the grandchildren to whom she intended to leave her estate up until the last month of her life was under "undue influence"); cf. Knutsen, 124 Or.App. at 309, 862 P.2d 509 (testator's "drastic change" in attitude toward new beneficiary and previous beneficiary shortly before will was executed was indicative of new beneficiary's dominance over testator).

E. Change in the Testator's Plan of Disposing of His Property. This factor concerns whether there is "a decided discrepancy between a new and previous wills of the testator; and continuity of purpose running through former wills indicating a settled intent in the disposition of his estate[.]" *Reddaway*, 214 Or. at 424, 329 P.2d 886 citing In re Estate of Elise Rosenberg, 196 Or. 219, 230, 246 P.2d 858 (1952). Frankly, the only continuity of purpose that can be gleaned from Senior's prior wills and trusts is his purpose of disinheriting beneficiaries with whom he had recently fought and disinheriting or reducing the inheritance of those to whom he had already given substantial gifts. To summarize: In the mid to late 1980s, Senior had Brogdon write out revisions to his will on several occasions after threatening to cut off family members who either asked for or received funds from him. In 1990, after buying a house in which he allowed John III's family to live, Senior executed a will leaving John III 10 percent less than he was leaving to John II and Ron Ramsey. After giving the house to John III in 1991, Senior disinherited him entirely in his next will. After John II moved out of Senior's new house in 1991 due to their disagreements, Senior disinherited him, as well. Evidence showed that Senior provided living accommodations to his granddaughter Davis around that time and that the next trust, the one prepared but never executed in 1993, disinherited Davis, but reinstated John II, John III and Ron Ramsey as minor beneficiaries. There was evidence that Senior gave money to his granddaughter Zabel and that she later was omitted from the 1994 will and trust. It is also notable that the will and trust benefitting Taylor was not the first to provide generous benefit to one of Senior's "significant others."

In short, over the last decade of his life, Senior's various wills and trusts did not reveal any settled intent as to the disposition of his estate. Although all of them, including the last, benefitted family members to some extent, which family members were benefitted varied greatly, apparently based on Senior's most recent dealings with them.

F. Unnatural or Unjust Gift. This factor was described by the *Reddaway* court as follows: If a testator "make[s] an unfair or unnatural disposition, it is a circumstance to be weighed in determining whether improper influence had been used." 214 Or. at 424, 329 P.2d 886. This factor is, perhaps, one of the most elusive. The *Reddaway* court indicated that a testator may "favor his mistress over his wife, or he may disinherit a deserving son," id., but that such a disposition would be considered "unnatural" and would constitute a circumstance to be weighed in determining if undue influence had been used.

Under the facts of *Reddaway*, the court clearly considered a disposition favoring a caregiver who apparently provided sexual favors to the testator and who had only known him a short time to be "unnatural," given that it was made "at the expense of a faithful son who has devoted a good share of his life to his father's business [.]" The court emphasized that influence gained "by kindness and affection" is not necessarily "undue influence" but that "the law does not disregard the donee's purpose or motive in eliciting the donor's affection." Id. at 425-26, 329 P.2d 886. The court stated that, "[i]f it is established that the donee generated the donor's affection for him solely for the purpose of inducing a gift, the court will ordinarily find a way to deprive the donee of the fruits of his deception." Id. at 426, 329 P.2d 886.

Here, the testator has chosen to favor a "significant other," or "mistress" as the *Reddaway* court would put it, to a greater extent than he has favored his family members. Moreover, the testator had known this "significant other" for only a little more than two months at the time of his death. Also, although there is no direct evidence that Taylor generated Senior's affection "solely for the purpose of inducing" him to make gifts, we can infer from the circumstances that Senior's generosity toward her may have had something to do with her willingness to show him affection. We take into account the fact that Senior was in his 80s at the time he met Taylor and clearly was not easy to get along with and the fact that Taylor was in her 30s. We also take into account that, within weeks of meeting Senior, Taylor took a vacation with him and began accepting very generous gifts of cash from him. We conclude that this evidence is sufficient to describe Senior's choice to benefit Taylor as a "suspicious circumstance" under the test of *Reddaway*. However, we will address this topic again in the section below concerning whether sufficient evidence was presented to overcome the "adverse inference" drawn from the presence of a confidential relationship and suspicious circumstances.

G. Donor's Susceptibility to Influence. Finally, the court must consider the "physical and mental condition of the donor" in determining whether a disposition of property was the result of undue influence. Id. at 426, 329 P.2d 886. The court in *Reddaway* concluded that, under the facts of that case, the testator's "mental and physical condition made him an easy mark for one who might wish to influence him." Id. at 427, 329 P.2d 886. The court did not, however, "think that it is necessary to recite this evidence." Id. Looking back to the statement of facts in that case, though, we can discern the evidence to which the court referred. The testator in *Reddaway* came under the care of the caretaker/mistress at a time when he was "almost helpless, due to a series of paralytic strokes." Id. at 414, 329 P.2d 886. Although there was evidence by a physician that the testator's mind was clear, id. at 415, 329 P.2d 886, there also was evidence that a written request was made to his attorney, ostensibly by the testator, at a time when he was unable to write without someone guiding his hand. Id. at 416, 329 P.2d 886. The court concluded that the evidence was "quite clear" that the testator "was emotionally unstable, probably senile, during the period that influence was alleged to have been exerted." Id. at 416-17, 329 P.2d 886. Similarly, in *Knutsen*, 124 Or.App. at 312, 862 P.2d 509, the court found that a testator who was "physically ill, on medication, confused, disoriented and suffering from memory loss" was susceptible to influence.

By comparison, the evidence in this case shows that Senior remained fairly physically active until the last few days of his life, when the pain of his cancer rendered him relatively immobile. Although he clearly was deteriorating quickly due to the rapid spread of his cancer, he was not physically helpless or feeble until after he executed his final will and testament. Concerning Senior's mental susceptibility to undue influence, we find no evidence of senility or instability or that his mental condition made him an "easy mark." *Reddaway*, 214 Or. at 427, 329 P.2d 886. Also, there is no evidence that he was confused, disoriented, or suffering from memory loss. Knutsen, 124 Or.App. at 312, 862 P.2d 509.

The testimony of a great number of the fact witnesses, and even the expert testimony of Dr. Luther who opined that Senior was susceptible to influence, convinces us that Senior was not, in fact, susceptible to undue influence. The evidence demonstrates that Senior had, for approximately the last decade of his life, consciously chosen to get attention, indeed homage, from others either by giving them generous gifts or promising them generous parts of his estate. He appears to have been fully aware that he was using his money to obtain attention from his family and friends. We do not agree with Dr. Luther's assessment that Senior's use of his money in this manner demonstrates vulnerability to undue influence. Rather, it demonstrates that Senior was intent on influencing others, not that he was influenced by others.

II. Did Taylor Overcome the Adverse Inference?

Under the rubric provided by *Reddaway*, we have concluded that Taylor had a confidential relationship with Senior and that two suspicious circumstances were attendant on the making of his final will and trust. The question, then, is whether there is evidence in the record to overcome the adverse inference that must be drawn from our findings thus far. We believe that there is.

The first suspicious circumstance that we found was that Taylor assisted Senior in drafting revisions to his 1994 trust before he consulted his attorneys in August 1995. In light of other evidence in the record, however, we find that any adverse inference to be drawn by this circumstances has been overcome. The record shows that Senior had, for about the last decade of his life, relied on his female companions to write down potential changes to his wills and trusts.

Taylor certainly was not the first companion to do so. Moreover, although Senior had assistance from his companions in drafting potential revisions, it is clear from the testimony of his attorneys that, at least for the 1994 and 1995 revisions, he sought and received independent advice from his attorneys, then made additional changes in the disposition of his estate before executing the documents. Furthermore, one of Senior's attorneys testified that, before Senior executed his final will and trust, Senior stated that Taylor had been of no help to him in deciding how to dispose of his estate. We conclude that Taylor has overcome any adverse inference to be drawn from her participation in preparing a preliminary draft of Senior's final will and trust.

The other suspicious circumstance that we have found to be present in this case is that Senior's choice to benefit a "significant other" whom he had known for only a few months rather than leave his entire estate to family members and that this may be termed an "unnatural" disposition under the *Reddaway* test. There are two facets to our analysis of whether a gift is, in fact, an "unnatural" one. The focus in our discussion above, in which we concluded that the disposition here qualified as "unnatural," was on Taylor's reasons for fostering a friendship and accepting large gifts from a much older man. Our focus in considering whether she has overcome the adverse inference to be drawn from those circumstances is on the other facet of the equation--did the testator, by making such a disposition, actually "disinherit a deserving" family member, *Reddaway*, 214 Or. at 424, 329 P.2d 886, or make the "gift at the expense of a faithful" family member? Id. at 425, 329 P.2d 886.

First, we note that this case is unlike many of the cases that find a gift to be "unnatural" when it deprives a family member of an amount that the child would have expected to take under previous dispositions. In this case, the record reflects that, under most of his previous wills and trusts, Senior wished John II either to receive nothing or to receive a relatively small portion of the estate. Even the previous will and trust most beneficial to John II allocated to him only 36 percent of the estate. There is no indication in the record that Senior ever intended John II to be the primary beneficiary of any will and trust.

Second, the record amply demonstrates that Senior did not perceive John II as either "deserving" or "faithful" for a long period of time before Taylor came on the scene. Clearly, Senior felt he was entitled to more attention and respect from his family, as shown by his numerous comments to others. John II, on the other hand, testified that Senior wanted him to "kiss his ass" and that he was unwilling to "lick his feet." The final disagreement between John II and Senior, which occurred only days before he executed his final will and trust, involved John II claiming an entitlement to Senior's home. Although we certainly do not pass judgment on the behavior of either John II or Senior toward each other, the record supplies ample evidence—and evidence that has nothing to do with any influence that Taylor had over Senior—that Senior had reason to conclude that John II was neither "deserving" nor "faithful" as those terms are used in *Reddaway*.

Finally, and perhaps most important to our analysis, we take seriously Senior's sworn declarations of August 10 and 17, in which he made it clear why he was choosing to benefit Taylor to a greater extent than John II: Senior declared that John II had been "irresponsible, contentious, and constantly seeking financial support" from Senior, whereas Taylor had been providing him with "care and support." Senior also declared that John II had, in recent years, "been more concerned with my wealth than my well being."

On this record, we feel compelled to honor Senior's wishes as to the disposition of his estate. Although Taylor was on the scene only for a short time, she provided Senior the care and comfort that he wanted and needed during the final stages of a very painful illness. The Ramsey relatives, on the other hand, and we refer specifically to John II and John III, provided Senior no support at the end of his life, expressed opinions that he needed no support or care and was only acting ill or upset to get attention from Taylor and his nurses, fought with him about his money and estate and, in general, acted exactly as Senior said: "more concerned with [Senior's] wealth than [his] well being." Senior's declarations on August 10 and 17, as supported by other evidence in the record, overcome any adverse presumption that his bequest to Taylor is "unnatural" or "unjust" under the circumstances.

We therefore conclude that the trial court erred in setting aside the portions of Senior's final will and trust that benefitted Taylor. For essentially the same reasons set forth above, we also conclude that the trial court erred in setting aside Senior's inter vivos gifts to Taylor.

III. CROSS-ASSIGNMENTS OF ERROR

Our disposition of the appeal renders moot John II's cross-assignment of error that the trial court erred in invalidating only the portions of the will and trust that benefitted Taylor. . . .

In his final assignment of error, John II argues that the trial court erred in failing to set aside all of the inter vivos transfers to Taylor. Although John II did not assign error to the trial court's conclusion that Taylor did not feloniously kill Senior by administering the prescribed morphine, John II argues that, as a matter of "equity and good conscience," Taylor should not be entitled to keep any money that she received from Senior because she "was the person who administered or directed the administration of the morphine." We reject John II's argument. We agree with the trial court's conclusion that Taylor administered the morphine in the amounts prescribed by Senior's physicians. We also agree with its conclusion that that amount of morphine was required to control the excruciating pain that Senior was experiencing during the last days of his life. The record shows that, although it was common medical knowledge that administering such an amount of morphine to a terminal cancer patient suffering from renal failure could lead to the result seen here, physicians are known to use morphine in these circumstances anyway, in order to ease the suffering of dying patients.

We have concluded that Taylor did not exercise undue influence over Senior when she received inter vivos gifts from him or when he made her a major beneficiary of his final will and trust. We do not find that "equity and good conscience" require us to deprive Taylor of those gifts on the ground that she and Senior's physicians carried out his wishes that he receive only palliative care during his final illness.

Reversed and remanded on appeal with instructions to administer John C. Ramsey Sr.'s estate in accordance with his final will and trust; affirmed on cross-appeal.

Notes

1. The Restatement 3d of Property § 8.3 comment h provides:

> *h. Suspicious circumstances.* . . . A testator's decision to leave a substantial devise or even the bulk or all of his or her estate to voluntary caregivers—relatives or other persons voluntarily caring for the testator—is not a basis for invalidating a will, in the absence of suspicious circumstances tending to show that the will was not the testator's free and independent decision.

2. *Expenses of Defending a Will Contest.* UPC § 3-720 provides that a personal representative who defends or prosecutes any proceeding in good faith, whether successful or not, is entitled to receive from the estate all necessary expenses and disbursements, including reasonable attorneys' fees.

3. *Lawyer Named as Beneficiary of the Will.* Rules of professional responsibility generally forbid lawyers from naming themselves as beneficiaries in wills that they draft. See, e.g., Estate of Auen, 35 Cal. Rptr. 2d 557 (Ct. App. 1994) (invalidating will on basis of undue influence); Conn. Bar Ass'n, Ethical Op. 97-1 (1997). The ABA Model Rules of Professional Conduct (2001) (MPRC) address the question as follows:[39]

> *Rule 1.8: Conflict of Interest: Prohibited Transactions . . .*
>
> (c) A lawyer shall not prepare an instrument giving the lawyer or a person related to the lawyer as parent, child, sibling, or spouse any substantial gift from

---

39. The Model Rules were approved by the American Bar Association's House of Delegates in 1983.

a client, including a testamentary gift, except where the client is related to the donee.

The American College of Trust and Estate Counsel (ACTEC) has issued Commentaries on the MRPC to provide guidance to estate planning lawyers in meeting their professional responsibilities [hereinafter ACTEC Commentaries].[40] With regard to Rule 1.8(c), the Commentaries state:

> *Gifts to Lawyer.* A lawyer may properly prepare a will or other document that benefits the lawyer, the lawyer's spouse, children, siblings or parents for a client who is closely related to the lawyer or the lawyer's spouse. However, the lawyer should exercise special care if a relative of either the lawyer or the lawyer's spouse proposes to make a gift that is disproportionately large in relation to gifts that the relative proposes to make to others who are equally related. Neither the lawyer nor anyone associated with the lawyer should assist a client who is not closely related to the lawyer or to the lawyer's spouse to make a substantial gift to the lawyer or to the lawyer's spouse, children, parents, or siblings. . . . For the purposes of this Commentary (1) a closely related person is a spouse or one who would be entitled to receive part or all of the client's estate if the client were to die intestate not survived by a spouse; and (2) the substantiality of a gift is determined by reference both to the size of the client's estate and to the size of the estate of the lawyer or the lawyer's spouse or children. The provisions of this rule extend to all methods by which gratuitous transfers might be made by a client to a lawyer including life insurance, joint tenancy with right of survivorship, and pay-on-death and trust accounts.

See also Section 127 of the Restatement (Third) of Law Governing Lawyers for a similar set of guidelines. For further discussion of the question of undue influence and professional responsibility, including extensive annotations of relevant case and statutory law, William H. McGovern, Jr., Undue Influence and Professional Responsibility, 28 Real Prop. Prob. & Tr. J. 643, 647-63 (1994).

4. *Lawyer Named as Fiduciary in Will.* The MRPC do not address the issue of lawyers being named as personal representatives of the estate or trustees in their clients' estate plans. Report of the Special Study Committee on Professional Responsibility, Preparation of Wills and Trusts that Name Drafting Lawyer as Fiduciary, 28 Real Prop. Prob. & Tr. J. 803, 808-13 (1994). The Restatement also gives little guidance in this area. Most ethics committees and the few courts that have considered the issue view the practice as permissible, although some decisions contain a strong note of caution. See N.Y. Sur. Ct. R. § 1850.6 (for wills naming lawyers as fiduciaries, affidavits are required by the

---

40. ACTEC, Commentaries on the Model Rules of Professional Conduct (3d ed. 1999). Updated annotations of the commentaries are available at www.actec.org.

testators indicating they understood lawyers would be entitled to fees and the reasons for nominating the lawyers; a failure to submit an affidavit warrants a hearing to determine whether an appointment was the product of undue influence); Joseph W. deFuria, Jr., A Matter of Ethics Ignored: The Attorney-Draftsman as Testamentary Fiduciary, 36 Kan. L. Rev. 275, 285-92 (1988) (detailed discussion of the authorities). But see Discipline of Martin, 506 N.W.2d 101 (S.D. 1993) (suspending lawyer for two years for misconduct, which included among other infractions naming himself as executor and trustee when that resulted in him being able to manage his own heavy debt to the estate). For further discussion of this issue, see A.B.A. Section of Real Prop. Prob. & Tr. L., Developments Regarding the Professional Responsibility of the Estate Planning Lawyer: The Effect of the Model Rules of Professional Conduct, 22 Real Prop. Prob. & Tr. J. 1 (1987); Frank Coolidge, New Avenue for Lawyers Boasts Old Tradition, 128 Tr. & Est. 20 (1989); deFuria, supra; Gerald P. Johnston, An Ethical Analysis of Common Estate Planning Practices—Is Good Business Bad Ethics?, 45 Ohio St. L.J. 57, 86-101 (1984); McGovern, supra, at 668-73; Edward D. Spurgeon & Mary J. Ciccarello, The Lawyer in Other Fiduciary Roles: Policy and Ethical Considerations, 62 Fordham L. Rev. 1357 (1994); Robert A. Stein & Ian G. Fierstein, The Role of the Attorney in Estate Administration, 68 Minn. L. Rev. 1107 (1984).

5. *Testamentary Appointment of Lawyer*. A provision in a will directing that the drafting lawyer be hired to represent the personal representative is usually held not binding on the personal representative. Clients have a right to hire their own lawyers, and in these cases, the client is the personal representative. See, e.g., Estate of Sieben, 128 N.W.2d 443 (Wis. 1964).

Suppose, in an effort to defeat the nonbinding effect of such an appointment, lawyers use the following provision for wills they draft:

> I hereby nominate X to be my personal representative subject to the condition that X agrees to employ [the drafting lawyer] as the lawyer for my estate; if X refuses, then Y is to be my personal representative, subject to the same condition; if both X and Y refuse, then the court is to appoint a personal representative who will agree to retain [the drafting lawyer].

Should the courts enforce this provision? Compare Estate of Deardoff, 461 N.E.2d 1292 (Ohio 1984) (provision held not enforceable) with Estate of Devroy, 325 N.W.2d 345 (Wis. 1982) (provision held enforceable). Binding or not, of course, Professor Johnston points out the practical effect of the testamentary appointment.

> [I]t is still likely that the specified attorney will be retained, since the [personal representative] and members of the testator's family generally want to carry out the desires of the decedent. This, too, can be deceptive when the testator had no

> preference in the matter, and simply acceded to the provision inserted by the drafting attorney in the belief that it was routine boilerplate.

Johnston, supra, at 106. See also Jean F. Powers, Testamentary Designations of Attorneys and Other Employees, 20 Golden Gate U. L. Rev. 261 (1990); ACTEC Commentaries, supra, Annotations to MRPC § 1.8.

6. *Devises to Spouses and Domestic Partners*. Courts recognize that spouses exert influence over one another regarding their estate plans. The courts, however, consider a spouse of a decedent to be a natural object and, therefore, they generally refuse to find undue influence when the spouse is the primary or sole beneficiary of the decedent's will. See, e.g., Estate of Mowdy, 973 P.2d 345 (Okla. Ct. App. 1998), cert. denied (1999) (upholding will contested by decedent's children against their stepmother).

Do courts consider a domestic partner to be a natural object of the testator's bounty? Do the courts extend the marital exception to unmarried, cohabitating partners? In Lamborn v. Kirkpatrick, 50 P.2d 542, 544 (Colo. 1935), the court invalidated the will of a childless widower that his partner wrote for him as she sat at his bedside twelve days before his death. The will, which devised over half of the decedent's estate to his partner, was contested by the decedent's sister on the ground of undue influence. Rather than using the fact of cohabitation as a reason not to find undue influence, the court used it as a basis for finding it.

> We deem it proper to attach to illicit cohabitation . . . [a] moral basis for requiring an affirmative showing against the existence of undue influence from one who is shown to be guilty of illicit cohabitation. . . . The unlawful intimacy of this meretricious relation between a testator and a beneficiary who is not related to him by blood or marriage usually assumes a clandestine form and, after the testator's death, would almost invariably render such undue influence as results therefrom incapable of proof except by the aid of the presumption . . . .

Accord Will of Kaufmann, 205 N.E.2d 864 (N.Y. 1965) (holding invalid a will that had left the decedent's entire estate to his domestic partner). But see Estate of Sarabia, 270 Cal. Rptr. 560 (Ct. App. 1990) (treating a will, which decedent's brother challenged, as not an "unnatural will" because it named the decedent's partner as a devisee); Evans v. May, 923 S.W.2d 712, 715 (Tex. Ct. App. 1996) (declining to hold that the devisee's "30-year relationship as the decedent's 'lifemate' constitutes undue influence as a matter of law").

The Restatement 3d of Property § 8.3 comment f provides:

> *f. Presumption of undue influence*. . . . [A] testator's domestic partner . . . is as much a natural object of the testator's bounty as a donor's spouse. So also is any other relationship entitling the donor's unmarried partner to intestacy rights under applicable law, such as a civil union relationship or a relationship based on the

partners' signed reciprocal beneficiary designation. A testator's decision to leave a substantial devise or even the bulk or all of his or her estate to his or her unmarried partner is no more a basis for invalidating a will on the ground of undue influence than a similar dispositive plan favoring the testator's surviving spouse. The dispositive plan in either case is not considered unnatural and thus to invalidate it on the ground of undue influence requires strong evidence that the will was not the result of the testator's free and independent judgment.

For further discussion of this issue, see Arthur S. Leonard, Sexuality and the Law: An Encyclopedia of Major Legal Cases 664-71 (1993); Joseph W. deFuria, Jr., Testamentary Gifts Resulting from Meretricious Relationships: Undue Influence or Natural Beneficence?, 64 Notre Dame L. Rev. 200 (1989); Ray D. Madoff, Unmasking Undue Influence, 81 Minn. L. Rev. 571 (1997); Jeffrey G. Sherman, Undue Influence and the Homosexual Testator, 42 U. Pitt. L. Rev. 225 (1981); E. Gary Spitko, Gone But Not Conforming: Protecting the Abhorrent Testator from Majoritarian Cultural Norms through Minority Culture Arbitration, 49 Case W. Res. L. Rev. 275 (1999).

The current law of undue influence raises particularly serious problems for the gay community, when a gay partner, who dies of AIDS, leaves a will devising a substantial portion of his estate to his surviving partner who cared for him during his illness. As one commentator put it, "acts of care become evidence of undue influence" under current law. Trent J. Thornley, Note, The Caring Influence: Beyond Autonomy as the Foundation of Undue Influence, 71 Ind. L.J. 513, 514 (1996). Thornley goes on to discuss how the law of undue influence is based on a theory of autonomy, meaning a view "of society as merely a collection of free-thinking, rational beings," and how that theory produces inappropriate results.

> [T]he primary problem with the law of undue influence . . . [is that] [i]t does not adequately account for acts of care. In fact, acts of care can be, and are, used against defendants during will contests. There are at least three ways in which this problem manifests itself.
>
> First, the current law of undue influence overemphasizes the role of reason as a proper basis for decisionmaking, to the exclusion of other human faculties like emotion. . . .
>
> Second, the current standard of undue influence improperly conceptualizes dependency. Since dependency is antithetical to the notion of self-rule, autonomy theory requires an almost radical independence of the individual. Likewise, the law discourages dependency by allowing evidence of such to support a claim of undue influence. For example, the presumption of undue influence may arise when evidence of dependency exists in the testator-beneficiary relationship. Because caring involves an element of dependency, the law has the effect of discouraging caring activity. . . .
>
> Third, the law of undue influence, based upon autonomy principles, suggests

> that a rights-based conception is the only adequate way in which to view relationships. The law endorses autonomy by protecting a person's "right" to be free from interference in testation. This quasi-contractual view of relationships manifests itself in the law of undue influence in factors of opportunity, motive, confidential relationship, and participation in the will-making process. These factors lead courts to inquire into whether an influencer has interfered with the testator's right to testamentary disposition. . . .
>
> [I]ntimate relationships, both inside and outside marital bonds, are not based entirely, or even primarily, on rights. The law may not always need to protect rights in the context of *some* intimate relationships because, by their nature, those relationships are based upon a caring concern and affection which is beyond the rigid, formulaic adherence to rights.

Id. at 529-31.

4. Fraud/Forgery

As applied to wills and succession, the concept of fraud is derived from the common-law tort action for deceit. See Atkinson on Wills § 56. Testators can be defrauded in a variety of ways. *Fraud in the execution* occurs when testators are defrauded about the nature or contents of the documents they are signing. Another type of fraud is called *fraud in the inducement*. This type of fraud occurs when testators are intentionally misled into forming a testamentary intention that they would not otherwise have formed.

In Carson's Estate, 194 P. 5, 8 (Cal. 1920), Alpha O. Carson died, leaving a will devising the residue of her estate to "my husband J. Gamble Carson." In a will contest, it was alleged that, although Gamble had gone through a marriage ceremony with Alpha a year before her death, and she believed that he was her husband, and made her will in that belief, he was not her husband because he was already married to a woman who was still living and from whom he had not been divorced. It was further alleged that Gamble knew he was not free to marry, and yet represented that he was, and that Alpha's belief that she was married to him was induced by these false representations. It was also alleged that solely because of this belief, she made the will in question, leaving the bulk of her estate to him. The court said:

> The gross fraud upon the testatrix is, of course, apparent. According to the evidence, she was seduced by a marital adventurer into a marriage with him which was no marriage in the eyes of the law because of the fact, which he concealed from her, that he had already had at least one, if not more, spouses, legal and illegal, who were still living and undivorced. There can be no question also that if the bequest to Carson were the direct fruit of such fraud, it is void. The only question in the case, assuming the contestants' evidence to be true, as we must, is, Was the bequest in fact the fruit of the fraud? This is a question of fact which it was for the jury to determine; and, unless it can be said that the jury could have

> reasonably reached but one conclusion concerning it, and that was that the bequest to Carson was not the direct fruit of his fraud, the evidence was sufficient to prevent a nonsuit.

The remedy for the fraud contemplated by the *Carson* decision was the denial of probate of the residuary clause. Fraud or other wrongful conduct can appear in a variety of circumstances surrounding the making or revoking of wills, and in some of these cases merely denying probate of the will or a part thereof will not adequately remedy the fraud. If a wrongdoer resorts to coercion to prevent a testator from executing a will or deceives a testator into believing that a devise to a person was included in the will when in fact it was not, no remedy is available in the probate court. The remedy must be by way of constructive trust.

5. Constructive Trust and Other Remedies

Statutory References: *UPC §§ 1-106, 2-517, 3-905, -1101 to -1102*

Constructive Trust as a Remedy for Wrongful Conduct. For centuries, Anglo-American courts, both law and equity, have been working out relief in wrongful-conduct situations to prevent unjust enrichment by ordering restitution of the benefit to the one at whose expense it was obtained.

The law courts developed a remedy usually called *quasi-contract*. For example, if the defendant steals the plaintiff's goods and sells them, the plaintiff, suing in quasi-contract, may recover a money judgment for the amount realized on the sale. The action developed out of the common-law action of assumpsit, which was used to recover for breach of express contract. In the theft case, there was, of course, no express contract by which the defendant was to pay over the proceeds to the plaintiff, but the court treated the situation as though there were and allowed the plaintiff to makc use of assumpsit. Although the history is somewhat more complicated than this, the process is illustrative of a tendency of lawyers (as well as other people) to make use of the familiar instead of developing a new set of ideas and techniques to meet the demands of the situations facing them. This development occurred in the law courts, and quasi-contract remains today a strictly legal remedy, seeking a money judgment.

While the law judges were working out quasi-contract, Chancery was developing its own remedies to prevent unjust enrichment, the principal one being *constructive trust*. If the defendant steals the plaintiff's money and uses the money to buy land, the plaintiff may sue in equity for a decree ordering the defendant to transfer title to the land to the plaintiff. The equity court treats the defendant as though the defendant were a trustee of the land for the benefit of the plaintiff. There is, of course, no express trust any more than there was an express contract in the first case.[41] The equity judge is giving relief to prevent unjust enrichment and is making use of a familiar idea for this purpose by "constructing" a trust. Unlike the law court's judgment in quasi-contract, this is not a money judgment but rather a judgment for specific restitution, requiring, that is, the transfer of title to a specific asset. The remedy is wholly in the province of equity.

If a wrongful act prevents a testator from making a will or a particular devise, courts have held that constructive trust relief is not available because the complaining party has been deprived only of an "expectancy," which is not a property interest. The prevailing view, however, is that such relief is available to protect "disappointed hopes and unrealized expectations." See, e.g., Latham v. Father Divine, 85 N.E.2d 168, 11 A.L.R.2d 802 (N.Y. 1949); Austin W. Scott, The Expectant Legatee, 63 Harv. L. Rev. 108 (1949). Plaintiffs, of course, have a considerable burden in proving that the wrongful act in fact prevented the making of the will or a particular devise. A claim for constructive relief based on the wrongful acts can be asserted against beneficiaries other than the wrongdoer.

The case of Pope v. Garrett, 211 S.W.2d 559, 561-62 (Tex. 1948), is typical on this point. Some days before her death, Carrie Simons requested a friend and neighbor, Thomas Green, to prepare a will for her, leaving all of her property to Claytonia Garrett. Simons and Garrett were unrelated. Green prepared the will as requested and read it to Simons. Simons then declared it to be her will and prepared to sign her name to it. Present in the room during this time were Garrett, the Reverend Preacher, Jewell Benson (a friend of Garrett), and several others, including Simons's sister, Lillie Clay Smith, and Simons's niece, Evelyn Jones. As Simons was about to sign the will, Smith and Jones—"by physical force or by creating a disturbance"—prevented her from carrying out her intention. Shortly after this incident, Simons suffered a severe hemorrhage, lapsed into a semi-comatose condition, and remained in that condition until her death a few days later. The court held that Garrett was entitled to the imposition of a constructive trust in her favor.

> Shall the trust in favor of Claytonia Garrett extend to the interests of the heirs who had no part in the wrongful acts? From the viewpoint of those heirs, it seems that they should be permitted to retain and enjoy the interests that vested in them as heirs, no will having been executed, and they not being responsible for the failure of Carrie Simons to execute it. On the other hand, from the viewpoint of Claytonia Garrett, it appears that a court of equity should extend the trust to all of the interests in the property in order that complete relief may be afforded her and that

---

41. Later, we will study the express trust, which is frequently used by transferors in disposing of their wealth. See infra Chapters 8 and 13.

none of the heirs may profit as the result of the wrongful acts . . . .

Accord White v. Mulvania, 575 S.W.2d 184 (Mo. 1978); Rogers v. Rogers, 473 N.E.2d 226 (N.Y. 1984); UPC § 1-106; Palmer on Restitution § 20.17.

Would Carrie Simons's will have been valid under the harmless-error rule of UPC § 2-503?

Tortious Interference with an Inheritance. A person who—by undue influence, duress, fraud, or other tortious conduct—causes a decedent to divert property from one who would otherwise have received it through gift, devise, or intestate succession may be liable for damages in tort for wrongful interference with inheritance or gift. It is a relatively new theory of tort liability. See, e.g., In re Marshall, 257 B.R. 35 (Bankr. C.D. Cal. 2000);[42] Henshall v. Lowe, 657 So. 2d 6 (Fla. Dist. Ct. App. 1995); Nemeth v. Banhalmi, 466 N.E.2d 977 (Ill. App. Ct. 1984); Doughty v. Morris, 871 P.2d 380 (N.M. Ct. App. 1994); Bohannon v. Wachovia Bank & Trust Co., 188 S.E. 390 (N.C. 1936); King v. Acker, 725 S.W.2d 750 (Tex. Ct. Civ. App. 1987); Restatement 2d of Torts § 774B (1979); see also Allen v. Hall, 974 P.2d 199 (Or. 1999) (en banc) (relying on tort of intentional interference with prospective economic advantage). Contra Labonte v. Giordana, 687 N.E.2d 1253 (Mass. 1997); Economopoulos v. Kolaitis, 528 S.E.2d 714 (Va. 2000). Courts have allowed these actions to be brought before the death of the testator. See, e.g., Carlton v. Carlton, 575 So. 2d 239 (Fla. Dist. Ct. App. 1991); Harmon v. Harmon, 404 A.2d 1020 (Me. 1979).

For actions brought after the testator's death, courts have held that a tort action for wrongful interference with inheritance will lie only if the claim for wrongful conduct could not have been asserted as part of the proceedings to admit a will to probate or in a will contest. See, e.g., Robinson v. First State Bank, 454 N.E.2d 288 (Ill. 1983); see also, e.g., Estate of Knowlson, 562

---

42. In the *Marshall* case, Vicki Lynn Marshall, also known as Anna Nicole Smith, *Playboy* Playmate of the Year 1992 and later a model for "Guess?" jeans, was 26 years old when she married J. Howard Marshall II, age 89 and said to be one of the richest persons in Texas. They were married in June 1994; he died in August 1995. Applying Texas law, the bankruptcy court awarded her $449,754,134 in a proceeding against her stepson for tortious interference with her expectancy of inheritance or gift. The court ordered the award to be reduced by any amount that she recovers in a probate proceeding then pending in Texas, which was based on an alleged oral agreement to give her half of his estate. She subsequently recovered nothing in the probate proceeding in Texas, and the court ordered her to pay $500,000 in legal fees incurred by her stepson. See Jury Gives Playmate Nothing, Associated Press, March 8, 2001; Payment of Fees is Ordered in Probate Dispute, Reuters, July 11, 2001. The bankruptcy award was subsequently vacated by a federal district court, holding that the bankruptcy court had non-core jurisdiction of the case. Consequently, the case must be heard in federal district court, where the bankruptcy court's award will be treated as a recommendation. See Edward J. Boyer, Judge Voids Big Award to Anna Nicole Smith, Los Angeles Times, May 25, 2001.

N.E.2d 277 (Ill. App. Ct. 1990) (concluding that summary judgment in favor of defendant was prematurely granted because the unavailability of probate relief remains speculative until contests over prior wills are resolved); Huffey v. Lea, 491 N.W.2d 518 (Iowa 1992) (holding doctrine of claim preclusion was inapplicable because the same evidence did not support the will contest and the tort action and because a complete remedy would not be provided in the will contest). Some courts, however, permit a plaintiff to bring the tort action at the same time as the will contest. See, e.g., Estate of Roeseler, 679 N.E.2d 393 (Ill. App. Ct. 1997).

Unlike for a will contest, consequential and punitive damages are available under a tortious interference claim. Even if a will contestant prevails, they can bring a subsequent tort action seeking punitive damages based on attorney's fees incurred during the will contest. Another major difference is that the presumptions for validity and higher standards of proof that probate law has developed in furtherance of testamentary freedom are inapplicable in a tort suit. For further discussion of this tort, see M. Read Moore, At the Frontier of Probate Litigation: Intentional Interference with the Right to Inherit, Prob. & Prop., Nov.-Dec. 1993, at 6; Annot., 18 A.L.R. 5th 211 (1994); Nita Ledford, Note, Intentional Interference with Inheritance, 30 Real Prop. Prob. & Tr. J. 325 (1995).

Living Probate. An 1883 Michigan statute unsuccessfully attempted to grant testators an option to "prove" or "validate" their wills while they were still alive.[43] The statute permitted the testator to petition the county probate court, which would then notify the presumptive heirs and others named by the testator of a hearing, at which the testator's testamentary capacity and freedom from fraud or undue influence would be determined. If these were established, the probate court would decree the validity of the will. Appeals from the decree and the testator's right to revoke or alter the will were expressly provided for by the statute. The Michigan Supreme Court, however, held that the statute authorized a proceeding beyond the scope of judicial power and declared it unconstitutional. See Lloyd v. Wayne Circuit Judge, 23 N.W. 28 (Mich. 1885). It ought to be noted that, when *Lloyd* was decided, declaratory judgments were quite unknown to the law.

Since this early unsuccessful attempt, only three states, Arkansas, North Dakota, and Ohio, have resurrected the idea of living probate.[44] Although the Ohio statute has generated some litigation, the other two statutes have not been

---

43. The Michigan statute is reprinted in Howard P. Fink, Ante-Mortem Probate Revisited: Can An Idea Have A Life After Death?, 37 Ohio St. L.J. 264, 268 n.8 (1976).

44. Ark. Code Ann. §§ 28-40-201 to -203; N.D. Cent. Code 30.1-08.1; Ohio Rev. Code §§ 2107.081-.085.

used. See Tracy Costello-Norris, Note, Is Ante-Mortem Probate a Viable Solution to the Problems Associated with Post-Mortem Procedures?, 9 Conn. Prob. L.J. 327, 338-44 (1995).

Considerable literature, however, exists advocating various forms of living probate. See, e.g., Gregory S. Alexander, The Conservatorship Model: A Modification, 77 Mich. L. Rev. 86 (1978); Gregory S. Alexander & Albert M. Pearson, Alternative Models of Ante-Mortem Probate and Procedural Due Process Limitations of Succession, 78 Mich. L. Rev. 89 (1979) (advocating an "administrative model," in which a guardian ad litem would conduct an independent investigation and report to the court; the court would hold a hearing and issue a binding judgment, without notice to affected persons); David F. Cavers, Ante Mortem Probate: An Essay in Preventive Law, 1 U. Chi. L. Rev. 440 (1934) (suggesting the appointment of a probate officer to determine the validity of a testator's will based on affidavits of the will drafter and disinterested witnesses as well as interviews of them and the testator); Howard P. Fink, Ante-Mortem Probate Revisited: Can An Idea Have A Life After Death?, 37 Ohio St. L.J. 264 (1976) (advocating a "contest model" of living probate, in which all affected persons would be notified and given an opportunity to contest the validity of the will in an adversarial proceeding; the court would then issue a declaratory judgment as to testamentary capacity, undue influence, and compliance with formalities of execution; this is the model that has been enacted in Arkansas, North Dakota, and Ohio); John H. Langbein, Living Probate: The Conservatorship Model, supra (advocating a "conservatorship model," in which all affected persons would be represented in an adversarial proceeding by a guardian ad litem); Aloysius A. Leopold & Gerry W. Beyer, Ante-Mortem Probate: A Viable Alternative, 43 Ark. L. Rev. 131 (1990) (advocating some form of ante-mortem probate); see also Gerry W. Beyer, Pre-Mortem Probate, Prob. & Prop., July-Aug. 1993, at 6.

Mary Louise Fellows argued in an article, The Case Against Living Probate, 78 Mich. L. Rev. 1066, 1080 (1980), that the living-probate proposals are seriously flawed.

> First, the proposals will fail to achieve their own stated objectives of improving the evidence available during probate and assuring testators that their dispository schemes will be carried out. Second, all three proposals [i.e., the "contest," "conservatorship," and "administrative" models] make the testator pay a high price for these ephemeral advantages. Finally, and perhaps most important, all three proposals are unfair to presumptive takers, and under the Administrative Model that unfairness may rise to the level of a constitutional due process violation.

Settlement of Will Contests. Will contests are frequently settled rather than tried. See Jeffrey A. Schoenblum, Will Contests—An Empirical Study, 22 Real Prop. Prob. & Tr. J. 607, 618-24 (1987). UPC §§ 3-1101 and -1102 (1990).

Interest is also growing in using mediation to resolve will contests. See Ronald Chester, Less Law, But More Justice?: Jury Trials and Mediation as Means of Resolving Will Contests, 37 Duq. L. Rev. 173 (1999); Susan N. Gary, Mediating Probate Disputes, Prob. & Prop., July-Aug. 1999, at 11; Robert N. Sacks, Mediation: An Effective Method to Resolve Estate and Trust Disputes, 27 Est. Plan. 210 (2000); E. Gary Spitko, Judge Not: In Defense of Minority-Culture Arbitration, 77 Wash. U. L.Q. 1065 (1999); E. Gary Spitko, Gone But Not Conforming: Protecting the Abhorrent Testator from Majoritarian Cultural Norms through Minority-Culture Arbitration, 49 Case W. Res. L. Rev. 275 (1999); see also Chapter 2, Part C (discussing settlements and their potential tax consequences).

In a highly publicized case, the children of Seward Johnson, an heir to the Johnson & Johnson pharmaceuticals fortune, charged that the will was a product of undue influence by Seward's third wife, Basia. The case settled before the jury came to a verdict, resulting in $40 million of the approximately $400 million estate being paid to the children. The estate also paid approximately $25 million of legal fees for all the parties. See Barbara Goldsmith, Johnson v. Johnson (1987); David Margolick, Undue Influence: The Epic Battle for the Johnson & Johnson Fortune (1993). Legal experts agree that the children's lawsuit was weak, but more importantly that Johnson's lawyers should have taken steps during the planning process to reduce the risk of contest. See John L. Carroll & Brian K. Carroll, Avoiding the Will Contest, Prob. & Prop., May-June 1994, at 61; John H. Langbein, Will Contests, 103 Yale L.J. 2039, 2045-47 (1994) (reviewing David Margolick, Undue Influence: The Epic Battle for the Johnson & Johnson Fortune (1993)). Some techniques for reducing the risk of will contests are considered by Professor Jan Rein below.

Jan E. Rein, An Ounce of Prevention: Grounds for Upsetting Wills and Will Substitutes

20 Gonz. L. Rev. 1, 64-68 (1984/1985)

Two common situations seem to invite a will contest. One is the so-called unnatural will scenario in which the testator either treats his children unequally or disowns his nuclear family in favor of a charity or a friend. The second is the stepparent scenario where the testator favors a spouse of his later years at the expense of his children by a prior marriage. In either case, the disappointed members of the family may become convinced that the decedent would not have made such a disposition had he not been either unbalanced or unduly pressured by the favored beneficiaries. Gifts between unpopular types of unmarried cohabitants (e.g., same sex friends; older woman-younger man) seem particularly vulnerable. Wills made by infirm or mentally impaired testators also invite contest.

It is not enough for a lawyer faced with such a situation to draft a technically perfect instrument. If it reasonably appears that the testator has capacity and he cannot be dissuaded from making the suspicious disposition, the lawyer who drafts a will which strongly suggests the possibility of a contest has a duty to take special precautions to ensure that the desired donative plan will survive the testator's death. . . .

No-contest clauses are frequently inserted to discourage will contests.[45] Such clauses (also called *in terrorem* or forfeiture clauses) purport to deprive any legatee or devisee who brings contest from taking his gift under the will. Although this device can be effective, in many cases it is of limited utility in discouraging contests. First, a potential contestant cannot be deterred by such a proviso unless the will leaves him a substantial gift. Second, many courts refuse to enforce such clauses when it appears that the contest was brought in good faith and on probable cause. This salutary exception is made out of concern that the device might otherwise be used by unscrupulous schemers as a weapon to secure the fruits of their misdeeds from challenge by scaring off those worthy contestants who should be encouraged to dispute a truly fishy-smelling will.

Several commentators have suggested the use of will substitute arrangements, particularly the revocable inter vivos trust. The theory is that lifetime transfers are "more resistant" to capacity and undue influence challenges even though the substantive capacity standard is higher for lifetime transactions than for wills. Of course, the effectiveness of this strategy depends on the type of will substitute employed and the atmosphere in which it is arranged. . . . Even trust agreements have been successfully challenged, particularly those drafted by an attorney selected by one of the major remainder beneficiaries and executed by an enfeebled, dependent settlor with no business experience. This suggests that lifetime property arrangements made by vulnerable transferors fare no better than wills executed by vulnerable testators. One also suspects the converse—that wills made by strong minded and active testators fare no worse than will substitutes arranged by strong minded and active settlors—also holds true.

Even if the devices and tactics just described are employed, the lawyer will want to take the precautions traditionally relied on by the estate planning bar to

---

45. UPC §§ 2-517, 3-905 and Restatement 3d of Property § 8.5 provide that no-contest clauses are unenforceable if probable cause exists for instituting the proceedings. For discussion of the meaning of probable cause, see Estate of Shumway v. Gavette, 9 P.3d 1062 (Ariz. 2000). For criticism of this provision, see Martin D. Begleiter, Anti-Contest Clauses: When You Care Enough to Send the Final Threat, 26 Ariz. St. L. Rev. 629 (1994); Dawn Koren, Note, No-Contest Clauses: Settlement Offers from the Grave, 12 Prob. L.J. 173 (1995). See also Jo Ann Engelhardt, In Terrorem Inter Vivos: Terra Incognita, 26 Real Prop. Prob. & Tr. J. 535 (1991) (advocating use of in terrorem clauses in lifetime trusts). Eds.

protect the donative plan. These center around the preparation and execution of the will itself.

All preliminary conferences with the testator should be held out of the presence of the prospective beneficiaries. Because even irregular wills tend to stand where a rational basis for the disposition is shown, it is a good idea to build a record of the reasons for the apparently unnatural will. The testator should be warned of the irregularity of the proposed plan and asked to explain his reasons for desiring such a disposition. The true reason should always be given because a fabricated explanation made to spare the feelings of an excluded heir may arm the potential contestant with a factual basis for claiming that the disposition was the product of an insane delusion. It may sometimes be desirable to include a statement of such reasons, albeit not necessarily in the will itself. Whether in the will or in a separate document, this memorialization should always be done in measured, factual terms, "without the use of extreme or bitter language." This is because hysterical language decreases the testator's credibility and also leaves the estate vulnerable to a suit for testamentary libel.

[L]ay testimony that the testator knew what he was doing often prevails over medical evidence of incapacity. This suggests that a carefully orchestrated execution ceremony is of prime importance. Too many lawyers select as witnesses anyone who happens to be around (usually secretaries) or, worse yet, send the client off with the will to have it witnessed on his own. The will should be attested by more than the minimum number of witnesses required by statute. Some of the persons selected should be acquainted with the testator (e.g., testator's neighbor, banker or clergyman) but all should be completely disinterested. Ample time should be allowed for the witnesses to chat with the testator and to form an opinion regarding the this [sic] testator's capacity on that day. Some lawyers have employed psychiatrists to render an opinion at some stage of the proceedings. This strategy may backfire by suggesting that those who were advising the testator entertained doubts as to his capacity. In special cases it may be desirable to make a videotape or sound recording of the testator's conversation with the witnesses and the execution ceremony itself. This might serve to deter disgruntled relatives from bringing a contest or, if a contest is brought anyway, might permit the triers of fact to form their own impression of the testator's mental state.

PART C. UNATTESTED DOCUMENTS AND EVENTS—INCORPORATION BY REFERENCE, INDEPENDENT SIGNIFICANCE, AND RELATED DOCTRINES

Statutory References: *UPC §§ 2-503, -510, -512, -513, -602*

Integration. Wills frequently are composed of multiple pages. No state requires each sheet of paper of a multiple-page will to be separately executed. Writings contained on separate pieces of paper can be effective as parts of a single document. The process of integrating separate papers into one will, however, like the process of integrating separate papers into one contract under the Statute of Frauds, involves some proof of intention that the parts be considered together—proof that would be supplied, for example, by relation of sense or by physical attachment.

Occasionally, a court suggests that either relation of sense or physical attachment is essential to integration, see, e.g., Seiter's Estate, 108 A. 614 (Pa. 1919), but the actual decisions tend strongly to support the view that any evidence will suffice so long as the court is satisfied that at the time of execution the separate papers were present and regarded by the testator as parts of the will. See, e.g., Cole v. Webb, 295 S.W. 1035 (Ky. 1927); Estate of Beale, 113 N.W.2d 380 (Wis. 1962); see also Estate of Benson, 1996 WL 118367 (Minn. Ct. App. Mar. 19, 1996) (unpublished opinion) (relying on doctrine to validate will when witnesses signed self-proving affidavit); Annot., Validity of Will Written on Disconnected Sheets, 38 A.L.R.2d 477 (1954).

Incorporation by Reference. In most jurisdictions, unattested papers—papers that weren't present when the will was executed—can be regarded as part of the will by incorporation. See Atkinson on Wills § 79; Alvin E. Evans, Nontestamentary Acts and Incorporation by Reference, 16 U. Chi. L. Rev. 635 (1949); Alvin E. Evans, Incorporation by Reference, Integration, and Non-Testamentary Act, 25 Colum. L. Rev. 879 (1925).

Restatement 3d of Property

§ *3.5 Integration of Multiple Pages or Writings Into a Single Will.* To be treated as part of a will, a page or other writing must be present when the will is executed and must be intended to be part of the will.

§ *3.6 Incorporation by Reference.* A writing that is not valid as a will but is in existence when a will is executed may be incorporated by reference into the will if the will manifests an intent to incorporate the writing and the writing to be incorporated is identified with reasonable certainty.

§ *3.4 Republication by Codicil.* A will is treated as if it were executed when its most recent codicil was executed, whether or not the codicil expressly republishes the prior will, unless the effect of so treating it would be inconsistent with the testator's intent.

Simon v. Grayson

102 P.2d 1081 (Cal. 1940)

WASTE, C.J. The question presented for determination upon this appeal involves the construction and effect to be given a provision in a will purporting to incorporate a letter by reference. Respondent's claim to certain of the estate's funds is based upon the terms of the letter. The appellants, who are residuary legatees under the will, contend that the attempted incorporation by reference was ineffectual. The facts, which were presented to the trial court upon agreed statement, are as follows:

S. M. Seeligsohn died in 1935. His safe deposit box was found to contain among other things, a will and codicil and a letter addressed to his executors. The will, which was dated March 25, 1932, contained a provision in paragraph four, leaving $6,000 to his executors

> to be paid by them in certain amounts to certain persons as shall be directed by me in a letter that will be found in my effects and which said letter will be addressed to Martin E. Simon and Arthur W. Green (the executors) and will be dated March 25, 1932.

Paragraph four also provided that any one having an interest in the will "shall not inquire into the application of said moneys" and that the executors "shall not be accountable to any person whomsoever for the payment and/or application of said sum . . . this provision . . . is in no sense a trust."

The letter found in the testator's safe deposit box was dated July 3, 1933, and stated:

> In paragraph VIII of my will I have left you $6,000—to be paid to the persons named in a letter and this letter is also mentioned in said paragraph. I direct that after my death you shall pay said $6,000 as follows: To Mrs. Esther Cohn, 1755 Van Ness Ave. San Francisco, Calif. the sum of $4,000— . . . If any of the said persons cannot be found by you within six months after my death, or if any of the said persons shall predecease me, the sum directed to be paid to such persons . . . shall be paid by you to my heirs as described in paragraph IX of my said Will. . . .

This letter was written, dated and signed entirely in the handwriting of the testator. No letter dated March 25, 1932, was found among his effects.

The codicil to the will was executed November 25, 1933. It made no changes in paragraph IV of the will and contained no reference to the letter, but recited,

"Except as expressly modified by this Codicil, my Will of March 25th 1932 shall remain in full force and effect." . . .

It is settled law in this state that a testator may incorporate an extrinsic document into his will, provided the document is in existence at the time and provided, further, that the reference to it in the will clearly identifies it, or renders it capable of identification by extrinsic proof. An attempt to incorporate a future document is ineffectual, because a testator cannot be permitted to create for himself the power to dispose of his property without complying with the formalities required in making a will.

In the case at bar the letter presumably was not in existence when the will was executed, for the letter bore a date subsequent to the date of the will. However, the letter was in existence at the time the codicil to the will was executed. The respondent points out that under the law the execution of a codicil has the effect of republishing the will which it modifies, and argues from this that Seeligsohn's letter was an "existing document" within the incorporation rule. . . . The principle of republication thus applied is unquestionably sound. In revising his scheme of testamentary disposition by codicil a testator presumably reviews and reaffirms those portions of his will which remain unaffected. In substance, the will is re-executed as of that time. Therefore, the testator's execution of the codicil in the present case must be taken as confirming the incorporation of the letter then in existence, provided the letter can be satisfactorily identified as the one referred to in the will. And this is true, notwithstanding the codicil made no reference to the letter and recited that the will should remain in full force "except as expressly modified by this codicil", for the letter, if properly incorporated, would be an integral part of the republished will.

We are also of the opinion that the trial court did not err in concluding that the letter found with the will was the letter referred to in the will. Conceding the contrary force of the discrepancy in dates, the evidence of identity was, nevertheless, sufficient to overcome the effect of that factor. The . . . informal document [need not] be identified with exact precision; it is enough that the descriptive words and extrinsic circumstances combine to produce a reasonable certainty that the document in question is the one referred to by the testator in his will. Here the letter was found in the safe deposit box with the will. It was addressed to the executors, as the will stated it would be. No other letter was found. Moreover, the letter is conceded to have been written by the testator, and its terms conform unmistakably to the letter described in the will. It identifies itself as the letter mentioned in the will and deals with the identical subject matter referred to in that portion of the will. All these circumstances leave no doubt that the letter of July 3, 1933, is the one that the testator intended to incorporate in paragraph four of his will. . . .

The judgment is affirmed.

SHENK, CARTER, CURTIS, and GIBSON, JJ., concur.

Notes and Question

1. *Incorporation by Reference—Recognition of the Doctrine.* A few states—notably Connecticut, Louisiana, and New York—refuse to recognize the doctrine of incorporation by reference. In Hatheway v. Smith, 65 A. 1058 (Conn. 1907), the Connecticut court reasoned that "the only power given by [the statute of wills] is that of disposing of . . . property by means of a writing containing in itself language by which the subject and object of the testamentary gift intended is therein expressed."[46]

2. *Incorporation by Reference—Common-Law Elements.* In formulating the necessary elements of an effective incorporation by reference, courts frequently say that the will must refer to the extrinsic writing as one in existence. Thus, in Wagner v. Clauson, 78 N.E.2d 203, 206, 3 A.L.R.2d 672 (Ill. 1948), the Illinois court described the essential elements of incorporation as follows:

> (1) the will itself must refer to the paper to be incorporated (a) as being in existence at the time of the execution of the will, (b) in such a way as to reasonably identify such paper in the will, and (c) in such a way as to show the testator's intention to incorporate such instrument in his will and make it a part thereof; (2) such document must in fact be in existence at the time of the execution of the will, and must be shown to be the instrument referred to in the will.

---

46. The rejection of incorporation by reference in Connecticut was presaged by a decision some three years earlier, in a case involving William Jennings Bryan. Bryan, a self-styled candidate of the ordinary American, lost three presidential elections as the nominee of the Democrat Party. He opposed the gold standard and delivered the famous "Cross of Gold" speech at the 1896 Democrat Party national convention. A religious fundamentalist, he fought against the teaching of evolution in the public schools and helped prosecute the teacher, John Scopes, in the famous 1925 Scopes Trial in Tennessee.

Bryan's Appeal, 58 A. 748 (Conn. 1904), involved the will of Philo S. Bennett. Bennett's will devised $50,000 to Bennett's wife, Grace Imogene Bennett, "in trust, however, for the purposes set forth in a sealed letter which will be found with this will."

In connection with the execution of the will, Bennett, with Bryan's help, prepared a letter to Mrs. Bennett directing her to pay the $50,000 to Bryan. Bennett's letter explained that he believed the welfare of the nation depended upon the triumph of the political principles for which Bryan stood and that he wished to help Bryan financially, "so that he may be more free to devote himself to his chosen field." The letter was enclosed in a sealed envelope addressed to Mrs. Bennett. Both the will and the envelope were placed in the testator's safe deposit box, where they remained until after his death. Mrs. Bennett refused to honor the letter, largely because Bennett's will, which Bryan had helped prepare, left $20,000 to Bennett's female companion.

Bryan sued to enforce the letter, but was unsuccessful. The court did not then pass on whether it would recognize the doctrine of incorporation by reference, but placed its decision on the ground that the requirements of a valid incorporation were not satisfied. In its view, the will did not contain "any clear, explicit, unambiguous reference to any specific document as one existing and known to the testator at the time his will was executed."

Requirement (1)(a) has sometimes led to the rejection of a writing that *was* in existence, for the reason that the testator failed to use the correct tense in describing the writing, a situation most likely perhaps to occur in instances of republication by codicil. Thus, in Durham v. Northen, [1895] P. 66, the will created a trust and directed the trustees to set apart properties "which the trustees will find noted by me for the purpose." A paper was found listing such properties, but it was dated later than the will. A codicil republishing the will was executed after the date of this paper. The court held that the paper was not incorporated because the will "does not refer to a document as existing." For an American case with a similar fact pattern and result, see Kellom v. Beverstock, 126 A.2d 127 (N.H. 1956). Problems can also be encountered with regard to requirement 1(b). See Estate of Norton, 410 S.E.2d 484 (N.C. 1991) (holding properly executed codicil failed to identify clearly and distinctly the pages to be incorporated even though the pages were stapled to the codicil).

3. *Statutory Recognition of the Doctrine.* The doctrine of incorporation is codified in twenty-four states, mostly along the lines of UPC § 2-510. See Restatement 3d of Property, Statutory Note to § 3.6. If the *Durham* or *Kellom* cases had been governed by UPC § 2-510, would the result have been different?

4. *Incorporation Into Holographic Wills.* The decisions are divided on the question whether a valid holographic will can effectively incorporate a writing that is not in the testator's handwriting if the statute requires the will to be "entirely" in the testator's hand. For cases upholding incorporation, see Plumel's Estate, 90 P. 192 (Cal. 1907); Johnson v. Johnson, 279 P.2d 928 (Okla. 1954). For cases rejecting incorporation, see Hewes v. Hewes, 71 So. 4 (Miss. 1916); Hinson v. Hinson, 280 S.W.2d 731 (Tex. 1955). Two leading writers have taken opposing positions on the issue. Compare Atkinson on Wills § 80, at 392 with Philip Mechem, The Integration of Holographic Wills, 12 N.C. L. Rev. 213, 225-29 (1934). Comment f of the Restatement 3d of Property takes the position that incorporation "does not affect the holographic character of the will."

5. *Incorporation of Defectively Executed Wills.* In Allen v. Maddock, 11 Moore P.C. 427, 14 Eng. Rep. 757 (P.C. 1858), Anne Foote attempted to execute a will, but it was invalid because it was attested by only one witness. Five years later, on her deathbed, she duly executed a codicil, which recited that it was "a codicil to my last will and testament." No other reference to the will was contained in the codicil, which merely disposed of a small amount of property to Anne's servant, Eliza.

By allowing the invalid will to be incorporated into the codicil, the court held that the will was entitled to probate along with the codicil. The court rejected the contention that "there is no such distinct reference to this paper in the codicil, as to enable the court to receive parol evidence in order to identify it. . . ." It is necessary, the court said, "and it is sufficient, that the description should be such as to enable the court, when the evidence is produced, to say what is the instrument intended."

6. *Incorporation of Defectively Executed Trust.* In Tyson v. Henry, 514 S.E.2d 564 (N.C. Ct. App. 1999), review denied, 540 S.E.2d 752 (N.C. 1999), the decedent, Tyson, died on October 16, 1996. In April of that year he had executed a will that contained the following provision:

> I bequeath and devise all . . . land which I own at the time of my death to VANCE B. TAYLOR, as Trustee under the provisions of a certain Trust Agreement executed on the ___ day of April, 1996, by me as the Grantor . . ., and I hereby direct that my interests in such . . . land so devised to such Trustee shall be added to and administered as a part of the trust estate created and established under the terms of the provisions of the said Trust Agreement for the benefit of beneficiaries . . . .

The trust agreement referred to in the will was signed by Tyson, but Taylor, the appointed trustee, never signed it nor did he ever receive any cash or property to be held as part of the trust. The court held, in accordance with prevailing law, which is discussed infra Chapter 13, Part B, that the trust could not qualify as a valid lifetime trust because the decedent never transferred property to the trustee during his life. The court went on, however, to hold that the trust was valid by virtue of the doctrine of incorporation by reference, because the trust instrument was in existence at the time of the will's execution and the will "clearly and distinctly" referred to it. For further discussion of techniques to coordinate a client's will and trust, see infra Chapter 8, Part C.

Republication. Republication of a will by codicil is usually thought of as the equivalent of *re-execution* of the will. This idea did not originate as a device to subvert the incorporation-by-reference requirement that only documents in existence when the will was executed can be incorporated. Instead, it originated as a device to subvert a different rule—the rule that a will could not dispose of land acquired after the will was executed.

From an early time, a will could bequeath after-acquired personal property, but it was not until the Wills Act of 1837, supra p. 168, that English law permitted a will to operate on after-acquired land. The church courts had jurisdiction over wills of personal property and borrowed from Roman law the concept that a will could dispose of after-acquired chattels. But general power of testation over land was first given by the Statute of Wills of 1540, 32 Hen. 8, ch. 1, which enabled any person who should "have" any land to dispose of it "by last will and testament . . . ." This language was soon construed as allowing disposition only of land owned by the testator when the will was executed. See Brett v. Rigden, 1 Plow. 340, 344, 75 Eng. Rep. 516, 523 (C.P. 1568); 7 William S. Holdsworth, History of English Law 365 (1926); 2 Frederick Pollock & Frederic W. Maitland, A History of English Law 315 (2d ed. 1898).

By § 3 of the Wills Act of 1837, the old rule as to land was changed in England so as to permit a person to dispose by will of "all real estate and all personal estate which he shall be entitled to, either at law or in equity, at the time of his death." In this country, the old rule as to after-acquired land has been everywhere eliminated, in most states by statute. See, e.g., UPC § 2-602.

Restatement 3d of Property

§ *3.7 Independent Significance.* The meaning of a dispositive or other provision in a will may be supplied or affected by an external circumstance referred to in the will, unless the external circumstance has no significance apart from its effect upon the will.

Acts Having Independent Significance. All jurisdictions give effect to devises that identify the property or the devisee by reference to acts and facts that have *independent* significance. The independent significance doctrine has been codified in some states. See UPC § 2-512; Restatement 3d of Property, Statutory Note to § 3.7.

One of the earliest applications of the independent significance doctrine occurred in Stubbs v. Sargon, 3 My. & Cr. 507, 511, 40 Eng. Rep. 1022, 1024 (Ch. 1838). The testator devised the premises in Little Queen Street to trustees to pay the rents to the testator's sister, Mary Innell, during her life, and after her decease, in trust to dispose of and divide the same unto and amongst the testator's partners who were in copartnership with her at the time of her death. The Chancellor upheld the devise, saying:

> In the present case, the disposition is complete. The devisee, indeed, is to be ascertained by a description contained in the will; but such is the case with many unquestionable devises. A devise to a second or third son, perhaps unborn at the time—many contingent devises—all shifting clauses—are instances of devises to devisees who are to be ascertained by future events and contingencies; but such persons may be ascertained, not only by future natural events and contingencies, but by acts of third persons.

The Chancellor's decision affirmed a decision by the Master of the Rolls, 2 Keen 255, 269, 48 Eng. Rep. 626, 632 (1837), who gave this explanation of the doctrine of independent significance:

> [If] the description be such as to distinguish the devisee from every other person, it seems sufficient without entering into the consideration of the question, whether the description was acquired by the devisee after the date of the will, or by the testator's own act in the ordinary course of his affairs, or in the management of his property, and I think that a devise to such person as may be the testator's partners or the disponees of his business may be good.

Examples of the many decisions approving references to circumstances having significance apart from their impact on the testamentary disposition include Dennis v. Holsapple, 47 N.E. 631 (Ind. 1897) (concerning the following disposition: "Whoever shall take good care of me and maintain, nurse, clothe and furnish me with proper medical treatment . . . shall have all of my property."); Gaff v. Cornwallis, 106 N.E. 860 (Mass. 1914) (concerning a devise of "the contents, if any, of a drawer in said safe . . ."); Brown v. Clothey, 79 N.E. 269 (Mass. 1906) (concerning a devise by a manufacturer of a product "which I may leave on hand at my decease"); Creamer v. Harris, 106 N.E. 967 (Ohio 1914) (concerning the following disposition: "I give to Sadie Harris . . . one bureau and contents . . ."); Reinheimer's Estate, 108 A. 412 (Pa. 1919) (concerning a devise to "the party . . . who may be farming my farm and taking care of me at my death").

In In re Robson, [1891] 2 Ch. 559, a devise of the testator's desk "with the contents thereof" was held to pass title to money found therein and debts due the testator evidenced by notes contained in the desk. A key in the desk unlocked a separate tin box containing securities. The court held that the devisee was not entitled to the contents of the box. Many of the cases noted above involved similar questions of intention.

If decedents in their wills devise their property in a manner that directs that property be distributed in accordance with the wills executed by other designated persons, courts will give effect to those devises as acts having independent significance. This is true even though the wills of those designated persons are not yet in existence at the time the decedents execute their own wills. The will of a third person is not a testamentary act of the decedent and therefore has independent significance. In re Tipler, 10 S.W.3d 244, 246, 249-50 (Tenn. Ct. App. 1998), appeal denied, (Tenn. 1999) adopts this view. Gladys S. Tipler in 1982 executed an attested will, in which she left most of her estate to her husband, James, upon the condition that he survive her. The will did not address the possibility that he might predecease her. Two days later, she executed a holographic codicil stating:

> *Should my husband predecesse* [sic] *me I hereby declair* [sic] *that his last Will and testament upon his death is our agreement here to four* [sic] *made between us . . . .*

> *With the exception Mr. Tipler or myself can elect to make any changes as we desire depending upon which one predeceasest* [sic] *the other. If no changes are made by either of us this will be our last Will and testament.*

Her husband executed his will in 1990 and he died six months later. Gladys Tipler died in 1994. Her heirs challenged the validity of the codicil, arguing first that the "codicil should not be enforced because it referred to a document not yet in existence." Second they argued that Tennessee law requires all material provisions of a holographic will to be in the testator's handwriting and that the husband's will was not in Gladys Tipler's handwriting. The court held that:

> the doctrine of facts of independent significance is applicable in this case to permit Testatrix' codicil to refer to Husband's will, provided the document is a valid holographic codicil. To determine whether the holograph contains all material provisions in Testatrix' handwriting, the trial court properly considered Testatrix' intent. . . . Since Testatrix wanted her estate to go to whomever Husband wished, the codicil contained all material provisions in Testatrix' handwriting, even though it stated only that her estate should go to the beneficiaries under Husband's will and did not specifically name beneficiaries.

Reference to Unattested Writing. UPC § 2-513 introduced a new idea into American probate law. As part of its policy of effectuating a testator's intent by reducing formalities, the UPC permits testators to dispose of their tangible personal property without having to meet the requirements of the doctrines of incorporation by reference or acts having independent significance. A handwritten document or a signed writing is sufficient so long as the will refers to it. It can be executed before or after the will was written and modified at any time.

This idea has proven to be popular and nearly half the states have enacted a provision similar or identical to either the former or current version of § 2-513. See Jones v. Ellison, 15 S.W.3d 710 (Ark. Ct. App. 2000) (holding that under a statute modeled after the former version of the UPC that a note found in the testator's jewelry box was sufficient to demonstrate her intent to give the devisee the items found in jewelry box).

Problem

G's will devised her antique desk to her granddaughter, A. It also contained the following clause:

> I might leave a written statement or list disposing of items of tangible personal property. If I do and if my written statement or list is found and is identified as such by my Personal Representative no later than 30 days after the probate of this

> will, then my written statement or list is to be given effect to the extent authorized by law and is to take precedence over any contrary devise or devises of the same item or items of property in this will.

After G's death last month, G's will was discovered in the top drawer of her antique desk. In the same drawer was a piece of paper in G's handwriting, dated about a year after the date of execution of her will that says: "Antique desk to granddaughter, B."

Under the original version of UPC § 2-513, who is entitled to G's antique desk, A or B, if the handwritten document is unsigned? What would be the result if UPC § 2-513 applies? Do your answers change if the handwritten document is signed by G?

PART D. JOINT REPRESENTATION OF HUSBAND AND WIFE IN ESTATE PLANNING

Lawyers frequently represent both spouses when designing an estate plan for a married couple. The joint representation occurs either because the spouses ask for joint representation in view of their shared mutual estate planning goals and their desire to avoid unnecessary legal fees, or because their lawyer encourages joint representation to assure that the plans are compatible in meeting the couple's needs. Lawyers are well aware, however, that joint representation carries the risk that neither spouse "will receive the representation a single individual might receive under the same circumstances." Nevertheless, many of them conclude that "family needs, tax incentives, and the very nature of marriage often make separate counseling unnecessary, and indeed, inappropriate." Report of the ABA Special Study Committee on Professional Responsibility, Comments and Recommendations on the Lawyer's Duties in Representing Husband and Wife, 28 Real Prop. Prob. & Tr. J. 765, 770 (1994) [hereinafter Special Study (Representing Husband and Wife)].[47]

In the early 90s, two national estate planning organizations engaged in major studies, that among other issues, addressed the question of joint representation of spouses. The result was the ABA's Section of Real Property, Probate and Trust Law publishing the Study (Representing Husband and Wife), supra, and ACTEC issuing its Commentaries on the Model Rules of Professional Conduct. See supra note 41. These two publications, along with the realization of the inadequate guidance provided under the states rules of professional conduct, led the Florida Bar Association's Real Property, Probate and Trust Law Section to

---

47. The reference to tax incentives generally concerns designing an estate plan that minimizes transfer taxes through use of the federal unified credit equivalent amount and the federal gift and estate tax marital deductions. See infra Chapter 7, Part A.

request an ethics advisory opinion on the question of joint representation of spouses. See Hollis F. Russell, Joint Representation of Spouses in Estate Planning: The Saga of Advisory Opinion 95-4, Fla. B.J., Mar. 1998, at 39. The Advisory Opinion 95-4, below, is representative of one view, among a range of views, regarding estate planning practice involving married couples.

Florida Advisory Opinion 95-4 (May 30, 1997)

In a joint representation between husband and wife in estate planning, an attorney is not required to discuss issues regarding confidentiality at the outset of representation. The attorney may not reveal confidential information to the wife when the husband tells the attorney that he wishes to provide for a beneficiary that is unknown to the wife. The attorney must withdraw from the representation of both husband and wife because of the conflict presented when the attorney must maintain the husband's separate confidences regarding the joint representation. . . .

Situation Presented. Lawyer has represented Husband and Wife for many years in a range of personal matters, including estate planning. Husband and Wife have substantial individual assets, and they also own substantial jointly-held property. Recently, Lawyer prepared new updated wills that Husband and Wife signed. Like their previous wills, the new wills primarily benefit the survivor of them for his or her life, with beneficial disposition at the death of the survivor being made equally to their children (none of whom were born by prior marriage).

Husband, Wife, and Lawyer have always shared all relevant asset and financial information. Consistent with previous practice, Lawyer met with Husband and Wife together to confer regarding the changes to be made in updating their wills. At no point since Lawyer first started to represent them did either Husband or Wife ever ask Lawyer to keep any information secret from the other, and there was never any discussion about what Lawyer might do if either of them were to ask Lawyer to maintain such a separate confidence.

Several months after the execution of the new wills, Husband confers separately with Lawyer. Husband reveals to Lawyer that he has just executed a codicil (prepared by another law firm) that makes substantial beneficial disposition to a woman with whom Husband has been having an extra-marital relationship. Husband tells Lawyer that Wife knows about neither the relationship nor the new codicil, as to which Husband asks Lawyer to advise him regarding Wife's rights of election in the event she were to survive Husband. Lawyer tells Husband that Lawyer cannot under the circumstances advise him regarding same. Lawyer tells Husband that Lawyer will have to consider Lawyer's ethical duties under the circumstances. Lawyer tells Husband that, after consideration, Lawyer may determine to withdraw from representing

Husband and Wife. Lawyer further tells Husband that, after consideration, Lawyer may determine to disclose to Wife the substance of Husband's revelation if Husband does not do so himself.

Issues Presented. The following ethical questions have been asked by the RPPTL Professionalism Committee:

1. Prior to Husband's recent disclosure, did Lawyer owe any ethical duty to counsel Husband and Wife concerning any separate confidence which either Husband or Wife might wish for Lawyer to withhold from the other?

2. Assuming that Husband does not make disclosure of the information [referred to in Issue 1.] to Wife:

a) Is Lawyer required to reveal voluntarily the information to Wife?

b) May Lawyer in Lawyer's discretion determine whether or not to reveal the information to the Wife? If so, what are the relevant factors which Lawyer may or should consider?

c) If Lawyer does not reveal the information to Wife, is Lawyer required to withdraw from the representation? If so, what explanation, if any, should Lawyer give to Wife?

3. May Lawyer continue to represent Husband alone if Lawyer notifies Wife that Lawyer is withdrawing from the joint representation and will no longer represent Wife? If so, is disclosure to Wife necessary in order to obtain her informed consent to Lawyer's continued representation of Husband?

4. Assuming that adequate disclosure is made to Wife, may Lawyer continue to represent both Husband and Wife if they both wish for Lawyer to do so?

The RPPTL Professionalism Committee views Lawyer's representation of Husband and Wife as a "joint representation." The committee concurs in this view in reaching the opinion expressed below.

Discussion. From the inception of the representation until Husband's communication to Lawyer of the information concerning the codicil and the extra-marital relationship (hereinafter the "separate confidence"), there was no objective indication that the interests of Husband and Wife diverged, nor did it objectively appear to Lawyer that any such divergence of interests was reasonably likely to arise. Such situations involving joint representation of Husband and Wife do not present a conflict of interests and, therefore, do not trigger the conflict of interest disclosure-and-consent requirements of Rules 4-1.7(a) and 4-1.7(b), Rules Regulating The Florida Bar.[48]

---

48. It is important to recognize, however, that some spouses do not share identical goals in common matters, including estate planning. For example, one spouse may wish to make a Will providing substantial beneficial disposition for charity but the other spouse does not. Or, either or both of them may have children by a prior marriage for whom they may wish to make different beneficial provisions. Given the conflict of interest typically inherent in those types of situations, in such situations the attorney should review with the married couple the relevant conflict of

In view of the conclusions reached in the remainder of this opinion, we conclude that, under the facts presented, Lawyer was not ethically obligated to discuss with Husband and Wife Lawyer's obligations with regard to separate confidences. While such a discussion is not ethically required, in some situations it may help prevent the type of occurrence that is the subject of this opinion.

We now turn to the central issue presented, which is the application of the confidentiality rule in a situation where confidentiality was not discussed at the outset of the joint representation. A lawyer is ethically obligated to maintain in confidence all information relating to the representation of a client. Rule 4-1.6. A lawyer, however, also has a duty to communicate to a client information that is relevant to the representation. Rule 4-1.4. These duties of communication and confidentiality harmoniously coexist in most situations. In the situation presented, however, Lawyer's duty of communication to Wife appears to conflict with Lawyer's duty of confidentiality to Husband. Thus, the key question for our decision is: Which duty must give way? We conclude that, under the facts presented, Lawyer's duty of confidentiality must take precedence. Consequently, if Husband fails to disclose (or give Lawyer permission to disclose) the subject information to Wife, Lawyer is not ethically required to disclose the information to Wife and does not have discretion to reveal the information. To the contrary, Lawyer's ethical obligation of confidentiality to Husband prohibits Lawyer from disclosing the information to Wife.

The lawyer-client relationship is one of trust and confidence. Rule 4-1.6 recognizes a very broad duty of confidentiality on the part of a lawyer. Save for a few narrow exceptions set forth in the rule, a lawyer is prohibited from voluntarily revealing any "information relating to the representation" of a client without the client's consent. Rule 4-1.6. The duty of confidentiality "applies not merely to matters communicated in confidence by the client but also to all information relating to the representation, whatever its source" and "continues after the client-lawyer relationship has terminated." Comment, Rule 4-1.6.

It has been suggested that, in a joint representation, a lawyer who receives information from the "communicating client" that is relevant to the interests of the non-communicating client may disclose the information to the latter, even over the communicating client's objections and even where disclosure would be damaging to the communicating client. The committee is of the opinion that disclosure is not permissible and therefore rejects this "no-confidentiality" position. The argument for a "no-confidentiality" approach— which is a departure from the usual rule of lawyer-client confidentiality—is premised on two bases: (1) that joint clients have an expectation that everything relating to

---

interest considerations and obtain the spouses informed consent to the joint representation.

the joint representation that is communicated by one client to the joint lawyer will be shared by the lawyer with the other client (i.e., that joint clients have no expectation of confidentiality within the joint representation); and (2) that the law governing the evidentiary attorney-client privilege sets (or should set) the standard for the lawyer's ethical duties in the joint representation setting. Both of these foundations, in the committee's opinion, are flawed.

Significantly, existing Rule 4-1.6(c)(1) allows the joint clients' lawyer to share information received from one client with the other client, without the need to obtain consent from the communicating client, when such disclosure is reasonably necessary to further the interests of the joint representation. Thus, a presumption of "no confidentiality" is not needed to facilitate representation of joint clients with a mutual goal. Rather, such a presumption would serve only to permit the lawyer to reveal an adverse separate confidence, against the communicating client's wishes and outside the parameters of Rule 4-1.6. At that point in time, it is clear that a conflict of interests has arisen and any "community of interests" has been damaged or destroyed. See Report of the Special Study Committee on Professional Responsibility prepared by the American Bar Association Section of Real Property, Probate and Trust Law, 28 Real Prop., Prob. & Tr. L.J. 765, 776-77 (1994) (hereinafter the "Study Committee Report") ("Because these expectations [of joint clients] may change, the lawyer must reassess these expectations as the representation progresses.").

Furthermore, accurately predicting the expectations of a typical client in a given situation is risky business. This would seem to be especially true concerning separate confidences imparted by one joint client to the lawyer that are in some way adverse to the other joint client. Even commentators who oppose maintaining the usual confidentiality rule in the joint client setting acknowledge that client expectations concerning confidentiality may be different in the case of separate confidences that are adverse to the non- communicating client than they are when the communication clearly furthers the objectives of the joint representation. See, e.g., Study Committee Report, at 788 ("Most [separate] confidences would not be imparted if the client were mindful of the lawyer's competing duty [of communication] to the other spouse."); Collett, Disclosure, Discretion, or Deception: The Estate Planner's Ethics Dilemma from a Unilateral Confidence, 28 Real Prop., Prob. & Tr. L.J. 683 (1994) (hereinafter, Collett), at 684 ("Absent agreement concerning the nature of the relationship, clients may have different expectations concerning the lawyer's obligation to maintain individual confidences."). Moreover, a leading case in the area of attorney-client privilege in joint representations states, "As between joint clients, there can be no 'confidences' or 'secrets' unless one client manifests a contrary intent." Brennan's, Inc. v. Brennan's Restaurants, Inc., 590 F.2d 168, 173 (5th Cir. 1979). The committee is of the opinion that it would be inadvisable to rely on such a speculative basis as "joint client expectations" to justify altering the usual lawyer-client confidentiality rule when applied to joint representation situations. This is especially true where confusion or misunderstanding on the part of the clients may be minimized or eliminated by means of a discussion between the lawyer and the clients at the outset of the representation. See Collett, at 738-39.

The second basis advanced for a no-confidentiality rule is the law governing the evidentiary attorney-client privilege. See Restatement of the Lawyer Governing Lawyers (Proposed Final Draft) (hereinafter the "Restatement"), sec. 112, comment I. Communications relevant to a matter of common interest between joint clients generally are not privileged as a matter of law. Case law cited in support of a no-confidentiality rule invariably is grounded in the law of attorney-client privilege.

It is important to note that the ethical duty of confidentiality is broader than the evidentiary attorney-client privilege. This distinction holds true even in a joint client setting. . . .

The ethical duty of confidentiality assures a client that, throughout the course of the representation and beyond, the lawyer ordinarily may not voluntarily reveal information relating to the representation to anyone else without the client's consent. In contrast, the evidentiary privilege becomes relevant only after legal proceedings have begun. The privilege is a limited exception to the general principle that, in formal legal proceedings, the legal system and society should have all relevant information available as part of the search for truth. Thus, there are different purposes underlying the concepts of confidentiality and privilege. The committee is of the opinion that the law of privilege does not, and should not, set the ethical standard of lawyer-client confidentiality.

It has been argued in some commentaries that the usual rule of lawyer- client confidentiality does not apply in a joint representation and that the lawyer should have the discretion to determine whether the lawyer should disclose the separate confidence to the non-communicating client. This discretionary approach is advanced in the Restatement, sec. 112, comment I. This result is also favored by the American College of Trusts and Estates in its Commentaries on the Model Rules of Professional Conduct (2d ed. 1995) (hereinafter the "ACTEC Commentaries"). The Restatement itself acknowledges that no case law supports the discretionary approach. Nor do the ACTEC Commentaries cite any supporting authority for this proposition.

The committee rejects the concept of discretion in this important area. Florida lawyers must have an unambiguous rule governing their conduct in situations of this nature. We conclude that Lawyer owes duties of confidentiality to both Husband and Wife, regardless of whether they are being represented jointly. Accordingly, under the facts presented Lawyer is ethically precluded from disclosing the separate confidence to Wife without Husband's consent.

The conclusion we reach is consistent with the Rules of Professional Conduct and with prior committee decisions. . . .

Additionally, in Opinion 92-5 we concluded that a lawyer who was faced with a federal law purporting to require the lawyer to disclose client information that was confidential under Rule 4-1.6, but not protected by the attorney-client privilege, could not disclose the information without client consent until compelled to do so by legal process.

Our conclusion is also supported by out-of-state authorities. Facing an issue quite similar to that presented by the instant inquiry, the Committee on Professional Ethics of the New York State Bar Association in its Opinion 555 concluded that the lawyer's duty of confidentiality to the communicating joint client (a partner in a two-partner partnership) must take precedence over the lawyer's duty to provide relevant information to the non-communicating joint client (the other partner). That committee reasoned that the mere joint employment of a lawyer does not imply consent on the part of the joint clients to reveal a communication to the non-communicating joint client where disclosure would be adverse to the communicating client. . . .

The committee further concludes that Lawyer must withdraw from the joint representation under the facts presented. An adversity of interests concerning the joint representation has arisen. This creates a conflict of interest. Many conflicts can be cured by obtaining the fully informed consent of the affected clients. Rule 4-1.7. Some conflicts, however, are of such a nature that it is not reasonable for a lawyer to request consent to continue the representation. The Comment to Rule 4-1.7 provides in pertinent part:

> A client may consent to representation notwithstanding a conflict. However, as indicated in subdivision (a)(1) with respect to representation directly adverse to a client and subdivision (b)(1) with respect to material limitations on representation of a client, when a disinterested lawyer would conclude that the client should not agree to the representation under the circumstances, the lawyer involved cannot properly ask for such agreement or provide representation on the basis of the client's consent.

In the situation presented, the conflict that has arisen is of an [sic] personal and, quite likely, emotionally-charged nature. Lawyer's continued representation of both Husband and Wife in estate planning matters presumably would no longer be tenable. Rule 4-1.16 thus requires Lawyer's withdrawal from representation of both Husband and Wife in this matter.

In withdrawing from the representation, Lawyer should inform Wife and Husband that a conflict of interest has arisen that precludes Lawyer's continued representation of Wife and Husband in these matters. Lawyer may also advise both Wife and Husband that each should retain separate counsel. As discussed above, however, Lawyer may not disclose the separate confidence to Wife. The committee recognizes that a sudden withdrawal by Lawyer almost certainly will raise suspicions on the part of Wife. This may even alert Wife to the substance of the separate confidence. Regardless of whether such surmising by Wife occurs when Lawyer gives notice of withdrawal, Lawyer nevertheless has complied with the Rules of Professional Conduct and has not violated Lawyer's duties to Husband. . . .

Notes

1. *Separate Representation*. The Advisory Opinion analyzes the lawyer's representation of the spouses as a joint representation. Some estate planning lawyers have advocated the notion of co-representation or separate representation of spouses. See, e.g., Jeffrey Pennell, Professional Responsibility: Reforms Are Needed to Accommodate Estate Planning and Family Counseling, 25 U. Miami Inst. Est. Plan. ch. 18 (1991); Special Study (Representing Husband and Wife). It's described as follows:

> In a separate representation, the lawyer may not disclose confidences and will not have duty to withdraw until the parties' interests actually become adverse and then only if they do not consent to continued representation. Nonetheless, there are certain activities that simply may not be undertaken in a separate representation. Examples of truly adverse representations are the assertion of differing rights to assets and concealment of assets belonging to the other spouse. Under the analysis employed for joint representation, there may in fact be no need for a written conflict letter unless the potential for conflict is apparent. Separate representation must, however, be created by agreement.

Special Study (Representing Husband and Wife), supra, at 794. The idea of separate representation has been severely criticized. See Reporter's Note to Restatement (Third) of the Law Governing Lawyers § 211 (Proposed Final Draft No. 1, Mar. 29, 1996); Geoffrey C. Hazard, Jr., Conflict of Interest in Estate Planning for Husband and Wife, 20 Prob. Law. 1 (1994).

2. *A v. B*. Disclosure questions can arise in situations other than one where one spouse separately confides to the lawyer representing both spouses. The manner a lawyer learns information about one spouse that might be material to the other spouse may justify different disclosure obligations, because one spouse did not communicate anything to the lawyer with an expectation that it would be kept confidential.

In A. v. B., 726 A.2d 924 (N.J. 1999), a law firm jointly represented spouses in the drafting and execution of wills in which they devised their respective estates to each other. The estate plans contemplated the possibility that the surviving spouse could ultimately devise the decedent spouse's estate to lineal descendants who were not lineal descendants of the decedent spouse. At the commencement of the representation, each spouse signed a letter explaining the possible conflicts of interests between the spouses and that information provided by one spouse could become available to the other. By signing the letter, each spouse "consented to and waived any conflicts arising from the firm's joint representation." Id. at 925. The letter did not contain an express waiver of confidentiality.[49]

Because of a clerical error, the law firm had accepted representation of a mother bringing a paternity action against the husband. DNA evidence ultimately proved paternity, but issues remained concerning child support. Once the firm recognized the conflict of interest, it withdrew from its representation of the mother. After the firm encouraged the husband to inform his wife of the existence of the child, it stated that if he did not do so, it would. The firm believed that it was obligated to inform the wife "that her current estate plan may devise a portion of her assets through her spouse to the child." Id. at 926. The husband took procedural actions in the paternity action to prevent the firm's disclosure.

The court analyzed the facts as presenting a conflict between a lawyer's duty of confidentiality and a lawyer's duty to inform clients of material facts. The court explicitly distinguished the hypothetical case set forth in Advisory Opinion 95-4 on three grounds: (1) the permissible disclosure rules differed, (2) the firm learned about the husband's paternity from a third party and not from the husband himself, and (3) the spouses had signed an agreement indicating their intent to share all information with each other.

The court concluded, under the New Jersey Rules of Professional Conduct, that the law firm was permitted to disclose the fact of the nonmarital child to the wife. It based its decision on a broad interpretation of the term "fraudulent act" that is found in the Rules. The court concluded that the husband's deliberate omission of the existence of the nonmarital child constituted a fraud on his wife, because in "discussing their respective estates with the firm, the husband and wife reasonably could expect that each would disclose information material to the distribution of their estates . . . ." Id. at 927. It went on to say that "[g]iven the wife's need for the information and the law firm's right to disclose it, the disclosure of the child's existence to the wife constitutes an exceptional case with 'compelling reason clearly and convincingly shown.'"Id. at 932.

---

49. See ACTEC, Engagement Letters: A Guide for Practitioners (1999). This publication can be found at www.actec.org/pubInfoArk/comm/engltrtoc.htm.

EXTERNAL REFERENCES: Naomi Cahn and Robert Tuttle, Dependency and Delegation: The Ethics of Marital Representation, 22 Seattle U. L. Rev. 97 (1998); Teresa Stanton Collett, Disclosure, Discretion, or Deception: The Estate Planner's Ethical Dilemma from a Unilateral Confidence, 28 Real Prop. Prob. & Tr. J. 683 (1994); Teresa Stanton Collett, The Ethics of Intergenerational Representation, 62 Fordham L. Rev. 1453 (1994); Teresa Stanton Collett, And the Two Shall Become as One . . . Until the Lawyers Are Done, 7 Notre Dame J.L., Ethics & Pub. Pol'y 101 (1993); Geoffrey C. Hazard, Jr., Conflict of Interest in Estate Planning for Husband and Wife, 20 Prob. Law. 1 (1994); Russell G. Pearce, Family Values and Legal Ethics: Competing Approaches to Conflicts in Representing Spouses, 62 Fordham L. Rev. 1253 (1994); Jeffrey Pennell, Professional Responsibility: Reforms Are Needed to Accommodate Estate Planning and Family Counseling, 25 U. Miami Inst. Est. Plan. ch. 18 (1991); John R. Price, Ethics in Action Not Ethics Inaction: The ACTEC Commentaries on the Model Rules of Professional Conduct, 29 U. Miami Inst. Est. Plan. ch. 7 (1995); Thomas L. Shaffer, The Legal Ethics of Radical Individualism, 65 Tex. L. Rev. 963 (1987); April A. Fegyveresi, Note, Conflicts of Interests in Trust & Estate Practice, 8 Geo. J. Legal Ethics 987 (1995).

Chapter 5

Revocation of Wills

A WILL is an inherently revocable document.[1] The methods of revoking a will are codified in all U.S. jurisdictions and are the subjects of Parts A and B of this Chapter. Part C covers situations in which a change in the testator's circumstances revokes a will. Parts D and E explore the circumstances under which a will that was previously revoked is nevertheless given effect at the testator's death.

The Restatement 3d of Property § 4.1 sets forth the methods of revoking a will, by providing that "[a] testator may revoke his or her will in whole or in part by subsequent will or by revocatory act."

PART A. REVOCATION BY SUBSEQUENT WILL

Statutory References: *UPC § 2-507*

All of the revocation statutes authorize a testator to revoke a will by validly executing another will that contains an express revocation clause.[2] See, e.g., UPC § 2-507(a)(1). A will drafted by a lawyer will typically contain an express revocation clause, such as "this will revokes all wills and codicils previously made by me."[3] Even a valid will containing an express revocation clause sometimes leads to litigation about whether a prior will should be given effect. See, e.g., Coussee v. Estate of Efston, 633 N.E.2d 815 (Ill. App. Ct.),

---

1. But compare infra Chapter 11 on Will Contracts.

2. Most courts hold that a holographic will can revoke a formal, attested will, even in a jurisdiction where the statute provides that a will can be revoked only by an instrument executed with the same formalities as the revoked will. Cases are collected in Annot., Revocation of Witnessed Will by Holographic Will or Codicil, Where Statute Requires Revocation by Instrument of Equal Formality as Will, 49 A.L.R.3d 1223 (1973).

3. The Restatement 3d of Property § 4.1, comment c, provides that "[a] clause providing that 'this will revokes all previous wills made by me' is effective to revoke all previous wills *and codicils*, since the term 'will' includes 'codicil.' See § 3.1, comment *a*."

appeal denied, 642 N.E.2d 1275 (Ill. 1994) (question arose about whether a revocation clause applied only to prior Greek wills and not to a previously executed Illinois will).

The UPC permits revocation by a subsequent will that contains only a revocation clause. Both the UPC and the Restatement 3d of Property define the term "will" as including a testamentary instrument that merely revokes another will. See UPC § 1-201(56); Restatement 3d of Property § 3.1, comment a. A testator obtaining legal advice is unlikely to execute an instrument that only revokes a previous will, because lawyers typically advise a client to replace one will with another.

The UPC and non-UPC revocation statutes also provide that, in the absence of an express revocation, a prior will is revoked by an "inconsistent" subsequent will. See UPC § 2-507(a)(1); see also Restatement 3d of Property § 4.1, comment d. *Revocation by inconsistency* (also called *implied revocation*) typically occurs when a testator, without the aid of an attorney, executes a will that fails to include an express revocation clause. When a testator dies with two or more wills and the latest one fails expressly to revoke the earlier ones, litigation can arise about whether the testator intended the subsequent will to replace the prior wills in whole or in part or merely to supplement the prior wills. This was the circumstance in Gilbert v. Gilbert, below.

Gilbert v. Gilbert

652 S.W.2d 663 (Ky. Ct. App. 1983)

PAXTON, J. This is an appeal from a judgment of the Jefferson Circuit Court determining that a holographic instrument, consisting of two writings folded together inside a sealed envelope, was a codicil instead of a second and superseding will. Appellees are a brother of the testator, a niece and three nephews of the testator, and two beneficiaries unrelated to the testator. Appellants are the testator's sisters and remaining brothers.

Frank Gilbert died testate on June 5, 1979. Two writings were offered for probate: an eight-page typewritten instrument, prepared by an attorney, dated April 2, 1976, and the holographic instrument dated December 8, 1978. The "codicil" was written on the back of a business card and on the back of one of Frank's pay stubs. The card and stub were found folded together in a sealed envelope. On the back of the business card, Frank wrote: "12/8/78 Jim and Margaret I have appro $50,000.00 in Safe. See Buzz if anything happens [signed] Frank Gilbert". On the back of the pay stub, Frank wrote: "Jim & Margaret $20,000.00 the Rest divided Equally the other Living Survivors Bro. & Sisters [signed] Frank Gilbert 12/8/78". Written on the envelope is the following: "This day 12/8/1978 I gave to Jim and Margaret this card which I Stated what to do". "Jim and Margaret" are James Gilbert (one of the appellees) and Margaret Gilbert, brother and sister-in-law, respectively, of Frank Gilbert, the testator. The typewritten instrument and the holographic instrument were admitted to probate on September 4, 1979, the holographic instrument being admitted as a codicil.

Appellants subsequently brought a will contest action in Jefferson Circuit Court seeking to have the holographic instrument interpreted as a second and superseding will. After a hearing, the circuit court entered a judgment construing the second instrument as a codicil affecting only the money Frank kept in his employer's safe. This appeal is from that judgment. We affirm.

Appellants argue . . . [that] the separate holographic writings should have been construed as a second and superseding will instead of a codicil. . . . This interpretation would eliminate James Gilbert from sharing in any portion of his brother's estate, except the $20,000.00 bequeathed to him and his wife, Margaret, in the "codicil". Appellees argue, of course, that the "codicil" pertains only to the money in the safe and that James takes both his share under the typewritten will and one-half of the first $20,000.00 of the money in the safe pursuant to the terms of the "codicil". . . .

The second instrument was probated as a codicil, but because it does not refer to the typewritten will, we prefer to characterize it as a second will. A testator can have more than one will effective at the same time, each distributing part of the estate. In such a case the subsequent wills "perform the office of codicils". Muller v. Muller, 108 Ky. 511, 516, 56 S.W. 802, 803 (1900). We believe that to be the situation in this case: the second will serves as a codicil because it does not contain a revocation clause and only distributes part of the residuary estate.

The holographic will does not revoke the typewritten one. We think it is very unlikely that Frank intended to supplant the elaborate distribution of his estate contained in the eight-page typewritten will with a single phrase scratched out on the back of a pay stub. Furthermore, there is no revocation clause in the second will and Kentucky courts have consistently held that one testamentary instrument revokes another only if it is the clear intent of the testator to do so, and even then the revocation is only to the extent necessary. The second will in this case need only re-distribute part of the residue.

We must resolve Frank's intent by looking at the four corners of the two wills, and harmonizing any conflicting provisions to give effect to every provision of each instrument. Here, it is easy to harmonize the two instruments. The only way to give effect to every provision of both instruments is to adopt the trial court's interpretation, to-wit: the two holographic writings comprise a second will that distributes only the money Frank kept in his employer's safe. It was not inconsistent for him to distribute, by a second will, a portion of his estate that would have passed under the residuary clause of the first will.

The judgment of the Jefferson Circuit Court is affirmed. All concur.

Notes

1. *Non-Uniform Probate Code Law.* Most non-UPC statutes fail to elaborate on how to determine whether a subsequent will is sufficiently inconsistent with a prior will to revoke it in whole or in part. As the Supreme Court of California stated, the fundamental question is whether the later will "was intended to wholly supplant the prior will." Danford's Estate, 238 P. 76 (Cal. 1925). But how is that question to be answered? The Restatement 3d of Property formulates the following principle:

> § *4.1, [Comment] d, Revocation by inconsistency.* If the later will makes a complete disposition of the testator's estate, it is presumed that the testator intended the later will to replace the earlier will. . . . Unless the presumption is rebutted by clear and convincing evidence, the earlier will is revoked and only the later will is operative on the testator's death.
>
> If the later will does not make a complete disposition of the testator's estate, it is presumed that the testator intended the later will to supplement rather than replace the earlier will. If this presumption is not rebutted by clear and convincing evidence, the later will revokes the earlier will only to the extent that the later will is inconsistent with the earlier will. Each will is fully operative on the testator's death to the extent that they are not inconsistent.

2. *Uniform Probate Code.* The same proposition is expressly adopted in UPC § 2-507.

PART B. REVOCATION BY REVOCATORY ACT

Statutory References: *UPC § 2-507*

The English Statute of Frauds of 1677, § 6, 29 Car. 2, ch. 3, permitted revocation of a will by "burning, canceling, tearing or obliterating the same." The UPC and nearly all non-UPC statutes have a somewhat similar provision.[4]

That the statutes recognize revocation by act to the document exemplifies how the law can be molded by the practices of the people whose affairs it regulates.

---

4. Some statutory lists are less comprehensive than the one contained in the English statute. See, e.g., Goode v. Estate of Hoover, 828 S.W.2d 558 (Tex. Ct. App. 1992) (holding the original will valid under a statute that included only acts of destruction or cancellation when the attempted revocatory act consisted of removal and substitution of the first page of the will). UPC § 2-507(a)(2) and many non-UPC statutes include "destroying."

One reason for recognizing revocation by burning, tearing, etc. is the fact that many people choose this method of revoking their wills.[5]

The law treats a will as revoked because its maker *intended* to revoke it. Just as the law requires a writing to furnish reliable evidence of an intent to make a will, the law also insists upon reliable evidence of a manifestation of intent to revoke. In the main, reliable evidence consists either of another duly executed writing (revocation by instrument) or of some act to the instrument that tends of itself to suggest that the testator meant to revoke the will or some part of it.

Among the prescribed methods of revoking by act, most of the litigation has concerned cancellation.[6] Cancellation occurs when the testator has crossed out or marked through the document or part of it or has written on the document words such as "canceled" or "null and void."

EXTERNAL REFERENCE. Verner F. Chaffin, Execution, Revocation and Revalidation of Wills: A Critique of Existing Statutory Formalities, 11 Ga. L. Rev. 297 (1977).

Kronauge v. Stoecklein

293 N.E.2d 320 (Ohio Ct. App. 1972)

CRAWFORD, J. Plaintiffs, the appellants herein, are the heirs at law of Helen L. White, deceased. Defendants are her executor and the beneficiaries under her will, the principal beneficiary being Jennifer L. Jones aka Jennifer L. Manson.

The will of Helen L. White was executed on October 4, 1968. It was drawn upon the stationery of her attorney, Robert J. Stoecklein, who was also one of the witnesses to the will. She never spoke to him thereafter about changing or revoking the will.

---

5. "The old law enabled a man to revoke his will by canceling it, and such was the habit of Englishmen." Edward B. Sugden (later Lord St. Leonards), Speech in the House of Commons upon the Law of Wills Bill 32 (1838). Sir Edward Sugden was criticizing the failure of the Wills Act of 1837 to include "canceling" as a method of revoking a will by act to the document. He suggested "a few simple rules by which we ought to be governed in the alterations of our law of property," one of which was: "Run not counter to the habits of the people."

6. But see, e.g., Southtrust Bank of Alabama v. Winter, 689 So.2d 69 (Ala. Civ. App. 1996), in which the testator placed her will and a codicil in a paper sack in a hallway closet area that the testator referred to commonly as "trash alley." The court held that "as a matter of law, the mere placement of the will in the paper sack did not 'materially and permanently destroy the efficacy of the document.' Accordingly, placing the will in the paper sack was not an act of cancellation or abandonment and did not constitute a revocation of the will." Id. at 72-73 (quoting Board of Trustees v. Calhoun, 514 So. 2d 895 (Ala. 1987)). See also Mattax v. Moore, 595 N.E.2d 969 (Ohio Ct. App. 1991) (admitting a will to probate notwithstanding page three of a three-page will was separated from the first two pages).

On the otherwise blank margin of the will, in the handwriting of the testatrix, but not touching any of the writing in the will, appear these words:

> *This will is void. We have never heard or seen Jennifer Jones or did she come to Jess' funeral so I do not leave her anything*
>
> *April 17, 1971*

Plaintiffs brought this action to contest the will. Defendants filed a motion for summary judgment. The facts upon the motion were stipulated.

The court sustained the motion and entered judgment for the defendants, the appellees and proponents of the will. Plaintiffs, the appellants and contestants, have appealed.

The parties agree that the single question before us on appeal is whether the writing on the margin revoked the will.

There is no inherent or common-law right to dispose of one's property by will. Such right depends upon statute. The law is quite specific as to the formalities required to make a valid will, or to revoke it. R.C. § 2107.33 provides the exclusive methods of revoking a will. These must be strictly complied with in order to make the revocation effective.

R.C. § 2107.33 reads:

> A will shall be revoked by the testator by tearing, canceling, obliterating, or destroying such will with the intention of revoking it, or by some person in such testator's presence, or by such testator's express written direction, or by some other written will or codicil, executed as prescribed by sections 2107.01 to 2107.62, inclusive, of the Revised Code, or by some other writing which is signed, attested, and subscribed in the manner provided by such sections. . . .

The intent of the testatrix here is not questioned.

It is conceivable that a writing might be so placed over the text of the instrument as to constitute [a cancellation]. Such is not the case here, where the writing does not touch any part of the wording in the will itself. It must therefore be classified as a writing which is not a canceling; and, of course, the writing does not purport to be "signed, attested and subscribed in the manner provided by such sections." (R.C. §§ 2107.01 to 2107.62.) . . .

Judgment affirmed.

SHERER, P.J. and KERNS, J., concur.

Notes and Question

1. *Invalid as a Revocation by Cancellation; Valid as a Revocation by Subsequent Instrument*. As the court suggested in the *Kronauge* case, a statement of cancellation, if properly executed, can be given effect as a revocation by subsequent instrument, regardless of whether the statement of

cancellation touches any of the words on the will. See, e.g., Kehr's Estate, 95 A.2d 647 (Pa. 1953). Doubtless this is most likely to occur in jurisdictions that recognize holographic wills. See, e.g., Estate of Nielson, 165 Cal. Rptr. 319 (Ct. App. 1980); Estate of Langan, 668 P.2d 481 (Or. Ct. App. 1983).

2. *Touching of the Words.* No touching of the words is required for revocation by burning or tearing. See, e.g., White v. Casten, 46 N.C. 197 (1853) (burning); Crampton v. Osborn, 201 S.W.2d 336, 172 A.L.R. 344 (Mo. 1947) (tearing).

In contrast, most authority is consistent with the *Kronauge* proposition that words of cancellation in the margin or on the back of the will fail to revoke a will by cancellation. See, e.g., Noesen v. Erkenswick, 131 N.E. 622 (Ill. 1921); Yont v. Eads, 57 N.E.2d 531 (Mass. 1944); Estate of Cox, 621 P.2d 1057 (Mont. 1980); Thompson v. Royall, 175 S.E. 748 (Va. 1934). Contra Kroll v. Nehmer, 705 A.2d 716, 716, 723 (Md. 1998); Warner v. Warner's Estate, 37 Vt. 356 (1864). In *Kroll*, the court simply assumed, without discussion, that a testator effectively revoked her 1985 will by writing on the back of the will the words "VOID—NEW WILL DRAWN UP 6-28-90." See also Estate of Dickson, 590 So.2d 471 (Fla. Dist. Ct. App. 1991), in which the court held that words of cancellation that touched the notarial seal of the self-proving affidavit attached to the will qualified as a sufficient act revoking the will.

UPC § 2-507(a)(2) eliminates the distinction between revocation by cancellation and revocation by burning or tearing. Regardless of the type of revocatory act, a touching of the words on the will isn't required. The position of the UPC is supported by the Restatement 3d of Property § 4.1, comment g.

Revocatory Act Performed by Another. Like most probate code provisions on revocation, UPC § 2-507 authorizes the performance of a revocatory act not only by the testator, but also by another person. The execution analogue of this procedure is the procedure under which someone other than the testator signs the testator's name. See supra Chapter 4, Part A. Not surprisingly, the question of whether the other person's act was done in the testator's "presence" arises in this context just as it did in the will execution context. Consider, for example, the case of Estate of Bancker, 232 So. 2d 431, 432 (Fla. Dist. Ct. App.), cert. denied, 238 So. 2d 111 (Fla. 1970). Adrian G. Bancker died in 1967, survived by his wife, three natural children, and a stepdaughter. Shortly before his death, Adrian became dissatisfied with the attorney who drew his 1966 will and who was named alternate executor therein. For the purpose of reviving a former will,[7] Adrian directed his wife, stepdaughter, and her husband to destroy the 1966 will. Adrian remained in bed while they went into another room, removed the will from a wall safe, and destroyed it by tearing it into pieces and flushing them down a toilet. The court held that the 1966 will was not revoked, saying:

> [The Florida] statute specifically provides the revocation must be made in the presence of the testator. Under this statute, such revocation must take place in the physical and mental presence of the testator. The requirements for a valid revocation of a will must be strictly observed.

Would the outcome of the *Bancker* case have been different if the case had been governed by UPC § 2-507? If a testator telephones her attorney who has custody of her will and directs the attorney to destroy it, would the will be revoked under UPC § 2-507? Would it matter whether the will was destroyed while the testator was on the telephone? Could the harmless-error rule of either UPC § 2-503 or the Restatement 3d of Property § 3.3 apply if the evidence clearly and convincingly shows that the testator intended to revoke the will? See Estate of O'Donnell, 803 S.W.2d 530 (Ark. 1991).

Ineffective Attempt to Revoke. If a testator intends to revoke a will by act to the document and the will isn't destroyed by physical act because another person fraudulently intervened to prevent the destruction, the will remains effective. Without the physical act, an intent to revoke is insufficient to revoke a will. The courts, however, will provide a remedy for any wrongful interference with an attempt to revoke and will accomplish a testator's intent through the constructive trust remedy. See supra Chapter 4, Part B. See, e.g., Brazil v. Silva, 185 P. 174 (Cal. 1919) (the related case of Estate of Silva, 145 P. 1015 (Cal. 1915) had held the will revocation ineffective and directed the contestants to seek relief in equity); White v. Mulvania, 575 S.W.2d 184 (Mo. 1978); Morris v. Morris, 642 S.W.2d 448 (Tex. 1982).

Generally the law of wills has limited the constructive trust remedy to situations in which a third party has wrongfully interfered with an attempt to execute or revoke a will.

---

7. In order to revive a former will in Florida, the testator must reexecute the former will or execute a codicil republishing the former will. See Fla. Stat. Ann. §§ 732.508(1), 732.511. Was the fact that the testator in *Bancker* did neither relevant to the outcome of the case?

Estate of Tolin

622 So. 2d 988 (Fla. 1993)

[On November 7, 1984, Alexander Tolin executed a will that devised the residue of his estate to his friend, Adair Creaig. The will was prepared by his attorney, Steven Fine, and executed in the attorney's office. The original will was retained by the attorney and a blue-backed photocopy of the original executed will was given to Mr. Tolin. On July 14, 1989, Alexander Tolin executed a Codicil to the Last Will and Testament that changed the residuary beneficiary from Adair Creaig to Broward Art Guild, Inc. This codicil was also prepared by his attorney, Steven Fine, at the attorney's office. Again, the attorney retained the original in his office and gave Mr. Tolin a blue-backed photocopy of the original executed codicil.

Alexander Tolin died on October 14, 1990. Approximately six months before his death, Mr. Tolin advised his neighbor, Ed Weinstein, a retired New York attorney, that he had made a mistake and that he wished to revoke the codicil and reinstate Adair Creaig as the residuary beneficiary. Mr. Weinstein advised him that he could accomplish his purpose by tearing up the original codicil. At a meeting at which Mr. Tolin and Mr. Weinstein were present, Mr. Tolin handed Mr. Weinstein a blue-backed document, which he represented was his original codicil. Mr. Weinstein looked at the document. It appeared to him to be the original codicil and he handed it back to Mr. Tolin. Mr. Tolin then tore it up and destroyed it. It is not disputed that this document was torn up and destroyed with the intent and for the purpose of revocation.

However, soon following Mr. Tolin's death, Mr. Weinstein spoke with Steven Fine and discovered for the first time that Mr. Fine had in his possession the original will and codicil. The document that Mr. Tolin tore up was actually the blue-backed photocopy that Mr. Fine had given to Mr. Tolin at the time of its execution. It is undisputed that this was an exact copy of the fully executed original codicil and was in all respects identical to the original except for the original signatures.

Steven Fine, the personal representative, petitioned the circuit court to admit the will and codicil to probate. He also filed a motion to determine the validity of the codicil. Additionally, Creaig filed a petition seeking revocation of the codicil. The circuit court entered an order revoking probate of the codicil and reinstating the provisions of the will.

On appeal, the district court reversed and held that destroying an unsigned copy of a will or codicil, even one containing a photo image of the original signature, is insufficient to revoke the original will or codicil. On rehearing, the district court certified the question raised by this case as one of great public importance, and the Supreme Court accepted jurisdiction.]

HARDING, Justice. The primary rule of construction in construing a will is ascertaining and giving effect to the testator's intent. Additionally, it is well settled that strict compliance with the will statutes is required in order to effectuate a revocation of a will or codicil. Estate of Dickson, 590 So.2d 471, 472 (Fla. 3d DCA 1991); Estate of Bancker, 232 So.2d 431, 433 (Fla. 4th DCA), cert. denied, 238 So.2d 111 (Fla.1970). Section 732.506 provides the procedure for revoking a will or codicil by physical act. Section 732.506 provides that

> [a] will or codicil is revoked by the testator, or by some other person in [the testator's] presence and at [the testator's] direction, by burning, tearing, canceling, defacing, obliterating, or destroying it with the intent, and for the purpose, of revocation.

Thus, in order for a testator to effectively revoke a codicil, there must be a "joint operation of act and intention to revoke." In re Dickson, 590 So.2d at 473; Stewart v. Johnson, 142 Fla. 425, 194 So. 869 (1940).

Creaig argues that section 732.506 does not specifically require the destruction of the original codicil, but allows a testator to revoke a will or codicil by intentionally destroying a copy. She focuses on the language of section 732.506 that the testator revokes the will or codicil by "destroying it with the intent, and for the purpose, of revocation." (Emphasis added). Creaig urges that the use of the pronoun "it" does not specifically require the revocation of the original document, and that the Legislature left open the question of whether the destruction of a copy would be adequate to revoke a will or codicil. Thus, she concludes that because the testator in the instant case intentionally revoked the codicil and destroyed a "correct copy," the testator effectively revoked the codicil.

We reject Creaig's argument and find that the plain language of section 732.506 requires the intentional destruction of the original will or codicil in order to effectuate a revocation. Section 732.506, which describes the manner for revoking a will or codicil by a physical act, uses the pronoun "it" in reference to the terms "will or codicil" contained therein. The terms "will or codicil" are specifically defined as instruments "executed by a person in the manner prescribed by this code." Section 731.201(35), Fla. Stat. (1989). Further, section 732.502, Florida Statutes (1989), prescribes the manner used to properly execute a will or codicil. The use of the terms "will or codicil", which have specific statutory definitions, shows a legislative intent that in order to effectively revoke a will or codicil by a physical act, the document destroyed must be the original document.

Applying the law to the instant case, it is clear that the testator did not effectively revoke the codicil. The parties' stipulation shows that the testator destroyed a document which "was an exact copy of the fully executed original Codicil and was in all respects identical to the original except for the original signatures." Because the testator destroyed a copy of the codicil rather than the original codicil, his attempted revocation was ineffective.

The next issue we address is whether a constructive trust should properly be imposed when a testator fails to effectively revoke a codicil because of a mistake of fact which prevented the testator from fulfilling the requirements of section 732.506. A constructive trust is properly imposed when, as a result of a mistake in a transaction, one party is unjustly enriched at the expense of another. Wadlington v. Edwards, 92 So.2d 629 (Fla.1957). Although this equitable remedy is usually limited to circumstances in which fraud or a breach of confidence has occurred, it is proper in cases in which one party has benefitted by the mistake of another at the expense of a third party. Holmes v. Holmes, 463 So.2d 578 (Fla. 1st DCA 1985).

In the instant case, . . . [i]t is clear that the testator's intent to revoke the codicil was frustrated by his mistake in destroying a copy of the codicil rather than the original. Further, the Broward Art Guild has benefitted from the testator's mistake at the expense of Creaig. Thus, we find that a constructive trust is appropriate under these unique and undisputed facts.

This case shows the importance of distinguishing an original document from a copy. The facts in the instant case show that the testator's mistake in destroying a copy of the codicil, rather than the original, was caused by the high quality of the copy, which made it indistinguishable from the original. As technology advances, the determination of whether an instrument is an original or a copy may become more difficult. Thus, it is advisable for attorneys preparing documents, such as wills and codicils, to consider designating which documents are copies. Such a designation would have aided in the disposition of this case.

Accordingly, we approve the holding of the district court that the testator's destruction of a copy of a codicil is not an effective revocation of the codicil. However, we remand the case to the district court with directions that upon remand to the trial court, a constructive trust shall be imposed on the assets conveyed by the codicil for Creaig's benefit.

It is so ordered.

OVERTON, SHAW and GRIMES, JJ., concur.

MCDONALD, J., concurs in result only with an opinion, in which BARKETT, C.J., and KOGAN, J., concur.

MCDONALD, Justice, concurring in result only.

Under the unique facts of this I conclude that the testator effectively revoked his codicil. I thus agree with the trial judge and the dissent in the case under review. The effect of the majority opinion is to accomplish the result of a revoked codicil. While I quarrel with the route it took, the majority reaches the correct destination and I therefore concur in the result.

BARKETT, C.J., and KOGAN, J., concur.

Note

Accord Restatement 3d of Property § 4.1, comment f. But see Estate of Charitou, 595 N.Y.S.2d 308 (Sur. Ct. 1993), where the court on similar facts rejected the imposition of a constructive trust because of the absence of wrongdoing. For further discussion of mistake and judicial reformation to prevent unjust enrichment resulting from mistake, see infra Chapter 12.

Presumption of Intent to Revoke. If a will contestant proves that the testator had custody of the will, a will that is found physically mutilated is presumed to be revoked. See, e.g., Bakhaus' Estate, 102 N.E.2d 818 (Ill. 1951). As demonstrated in *Estate of May*, below, this presumption is rebuttable. "Moreover, the presumption regarding a mutilated will must be tempered when the act is a blemish that could easily have occurred accidentally, such as a small tear across a corner or a singe mark that could have been caused by a dropped cigarette ash. Although insignificant acts such as these are technically sufficient as revocatory acts . . ., they must be shown to have been done by the testator with the intent to revoke." Restatement 3d of Property § 4.1, comment j.

Estate of May

220 N.W.2d 388 (S.D. 1974)

DUNN, J. . . . The decedent lived alone on a farm a few miles from Parker, South Dakota. He executed a document on December 28, 1967 entirely in his own handwriting purporting to dispose of his property upon his death. There was no question raised of undue influence or of testamentary capacity. The decedent told Victor Brandt on at least two occasions that he did have a will, the last time being approximately three days before his death. On February 14, 1973 John R. May died in Turner County, South Dakota.

Mrs. Eva Christensen, respondent and a sister of the deceased, searched the decedent's home and bank boxes thoroughly after his death but could find no will. Mrs. Christensen, the sheriff of Turner County and others went through the papers of the deceased in his home; some papers were destroyed and others piled into boxes and stored in a rented barn near the home of a niece, Eva Brandt. Later, Mrs. Brandt found the contested will with the papers moved to the barn and in a box of documents which also contained current receipts, bills, bank statements and current business records of the deceased.

The document purporting to be a Holographic Will is hereby set out in full [subsequently], showing where it was cut out of the book on the right margin, and where it was torn on the left margin.

There is no evidence to show what happened to the document from the date it was executed to the date it was found. It came from decedent's home and the inference would be that it was in decedent's possession at least until the date of his death. All of the witnesses testified that decedent's home was a mess with important documents as well as worthless scraps of paper piled around the house without any system or order. In the light of these facts the trial court ruled that the Holographic Will had been torn and obliterated by the decedent during his lifetime with the intent and for the purpose of revoking the same in accordance with SDCL 29-3-1 which states:

> Except in the cases in this chapter mentioned, no written will, nor any part thereof, can be revoked or altered, otherwise than:
>
> (1) By a written will or other writing of the testator, declaring such revocation or alteration, and executed with the same formalities with which a will should be executed by such testator; or
>
> (2) By being burnt, torn, canceled, obliterated, or destroyed, with the intent and for the purpose of revoking the same, by the testator himself, or by some person in his presence and by his direction.

In considering this statute we should also refer to SDCL 29-3-3:

> A revocation by obliteration on the face of the will may be partial or total, and is complete if the material part is so obliterated as to show an intention to revoke; . . . .

As there was no extrinsic evidence that decedent intended to destroy the will, the trial court of necessity in reaching its decision had to rely on the presumption generally set out in 57 Am. Jur., Wills, § 550, which reads as follows:

> It is generally agreed that if a will produced for probate, which is shown to have been in the custody of the testator after its execution, was found among the testator's effects after his death, in such a state of mutilation, obliteration, or cancellation as represents a sufficient act of revocation within the meaning of the applicable statute, it will be presumed, in the absence of evidence to the contrary, that such act was performed by the testator with the intention of revoking the instrument. . . . Whatever presumption arises from acts of cancellation or mutilation is rebuttable, but the burden of the rebuttal rests upon the proponent.

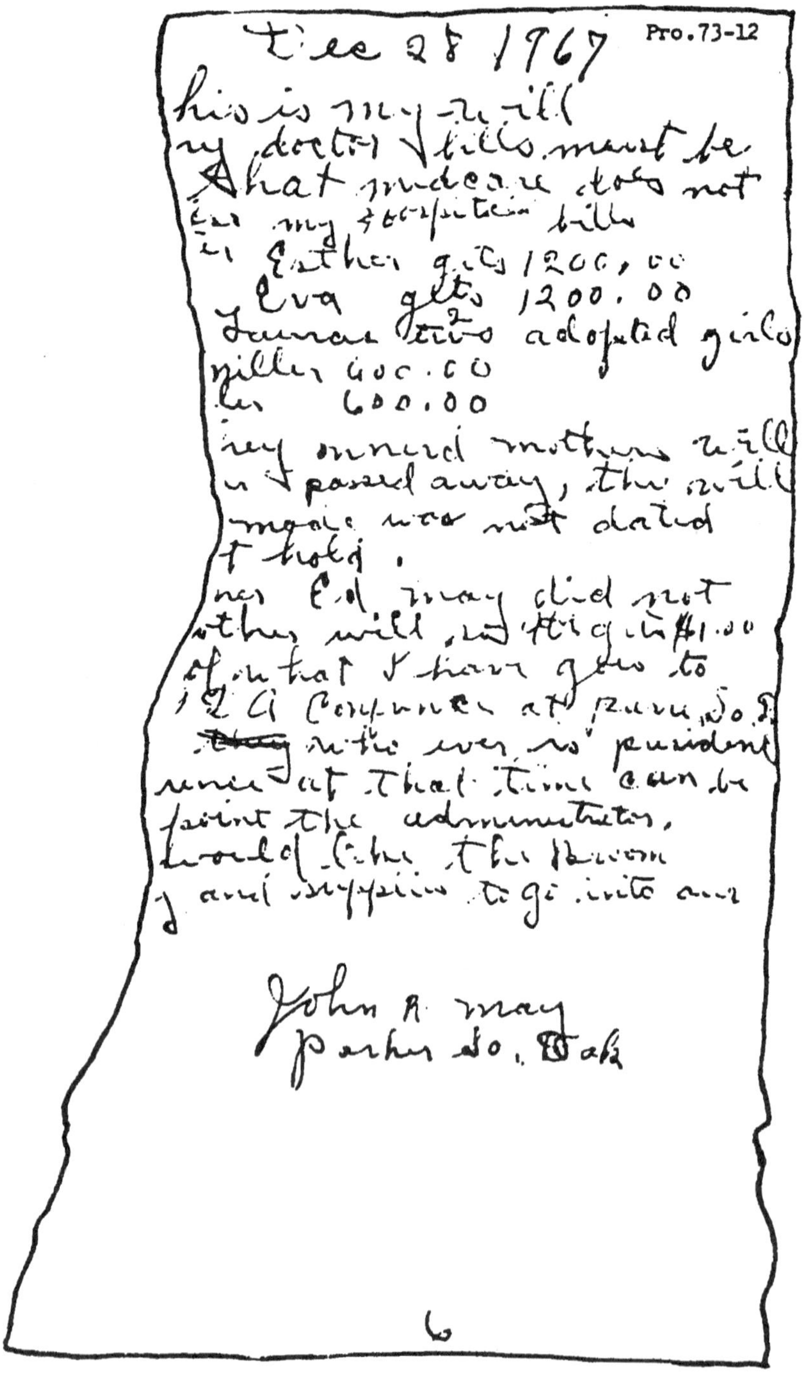
Dec 28 1967 Pro.73-12

his is my will
ny doctor bills must be
hat medicare does not
[illegible] my hospital bills
[illegible] Esther gets 1200.00
Eva gets 1200.00
[illegible] 2 two adopted girls
Miller 600.00
[illegible] 600.00
[illegible] mothers will
[illegible] passed away, the will
made was not dated
[illegible] hold.
[illegible] Ed May did not
other will, [illegible] $1.00
of what I have goes to
R C A Company at [illegible]
who ever is president
[illegible] at that time can be
point the administrator.
would like the broom
[illegible] and supplies to go into [illegible]

John A. May
Parker So. Dak

6

Proponent of the will rebuts this presumption by evidence that the decedent told Victor Brandt (husband of Eva Brandt, niece of decedent) that he had a will on two different occasions, the last time being some three days before his death. This testimony was corroborated by Mrs. Brandt to the extent that her husband had advised her of decedent's statements at the time that they were made. No other will was ever found. Mrs. Brandt would be an heir of the decedent if the will was not upheld and would take nothing under the will. Accordingly, the testimony of the Brandts on this subject is most credible and convincing and any presumption of intent to revoke the will arising from the tearing while in the possession of the decedent was effectively rebutted. In Fleming v. Fleming, 367 Ill. 97, 10 N.E.2d 641, it is stated:

> Any act of tearing of the paper on which the will is written, however slight, is an act of tearing within the meaning of this statute if done with intent to revoke the will, but it is likewise true that no act of tearing or cutting, unless it be with the intention to revoke the will, accomplishes such purpose. The intent with which the act is done governs. . . .

Thus the trial court's finding No. 6, that the will had been revoked "by tearing and obliterating same with the intent of revoking" is clearly erroneous under the evidence as there was no actual evidence of an intent to revoke, and the presumption of intent arising from the tearing was effectively rebutted. . . . [The court addresses the question of the proper disposition of the decedent's property under the will.]

It is concluded that the opponents of the will have not established that the Holographic Will executed by the testator on December 28, 1967 was ever revoked "By being burnt, torn, canceled, obliterated or destroyed with the intent and for the purpose of revoking the same. . . ." The presumption of intent to revoke arising from the torn document has been rebutted and the will effectively provides for the disposition of decedent's property. Every effort should be made by the courts to uphold a will that has been validly executed. As the only evidence here on earth to indicate decedent's desires as to the disposal of his property upon his death, the Holographic Will should have been upheld.

Judgment reversed. All Justices concur.

Lost or Destroyed Wills. What happens if the decedent is known to have executed a will, but it cannot be found after death? If the will remained in the decedent's possession after execution, there are many decisions that presume the decedent destroyed the will with intent to revoke. See Atkinson on Wills § 101, at 553; Annots., Sufficiency of Evidence of Nonrevocation of Lost Will Not Shown to Have Been Inaccessible to Testator—Modern Cases, 70 A.L.R.4th

323 (1989); Proof of Nonrevocation in Proceeding to Establish Lost Will, 3 A.L.R.2d 949, 952 (1949). Concerning this presumption, the Supreme Court of Iowa, in Estate of Crozier, 232 N.W.2d 554, 558 (Iowa 1975), remarked:

> There is good reason why the burden of proof on the part of a lost will proponent [where the will was traced to the testator's possession] should not be prohibitive. "Wills are carelessly lost and misplaced and a reasonable opportunity should be given to establish such a will. Likewise wills are sometimes suppressed or destroyed for an ulterior purpose. The defeat of that purpose ought not be made too difficult or impossible."

Crozier went on to hold, however, that the presumption is rebuttable only by clear and convincing evidence. See also Estate of Mitchell, 623 So. 2d 274 (Miss. 1993) (reversing the lower court that gave a jury instruction that the presumption could be rebutted "by a preponderance of the evidence" and holding that the proponents of the will had to rebut the presumption by "clear and convincing proof"); Barnett v. Oliver, 2000 WL 286715 (Tenn. Ct. App. Feb. 17, 2000), quoting Shrum v. Powell, 604 S.W.2d 869 (Tenn. Ct. App. 1980) (holding proponent met burden of showing by "'the clearest and most stringent evidence'" that the decedent did not revoke his will). But see Estate of Glover, 744 S.W.2d 939 (Tex. 1988) (held that the presumption is rebuttable by a preponderance of the evidence). The Restatement 3d of Property § 4.1, comment j, similarly provides that "the presumption [that the testator destroyed the will or performed some other revocatory act on it with intent to revoke] is not such a strong one that clear and convincing evidence is required to rebut it."

The Supreme Court of Mississippi in Estate of Leggett, 584 So. 2d 400, 403 (Miss. 1991), quoted Jarman's Treatise on Wills with approval, and took the position that the amount of evidence needed to rebut the presumption depended on the nature of testator's situation that might suggest either the likelihood or unlikelihood that testator intended to revoke the will.

Wills Executed in Duplicate. To execute a will in duplicate means that the formal procedures for executing a will were performed on two copies of the same will. The effect of duplicate execution is that the testator has two identical wills. If a will is executed in duplicate, an act of revocation performed with revocatory intent on one of the duplicates also revokes the other duplicate. This rule is sometimes codified, as in Cal. Prob. Code § 6121.

The presumption of revocation becomes a source of special difficulty for wills that are executed in duplicate. If one executed copy is retained by the testator and the other executed copy is retained by the testator's lawyer or delivered to another person (for example, the personal representative), and the copy retained by the testator cannot be found after death, courts have held that there is a presumption of destruction with intent to revoke. See, e.g., Horton v. Burch,

471 S.E.2d 879 (Ga. 1996); Estate of Fowler, 681 N.E.2d 739 (Ind. Ct. App. 1997), transfer denied, 698 N.E.2d 1186 (Ind. 1998). Yet, the fact that an executed copy of the will was safely in the custody of the lawyer or another might cause the testator to be careless with the retained executed copy. In these circumstances especially, the presumption rests on uncertain ground and its application could lead to a denial of probate in a case where the testator had no revocatory intent.

On occasion, the fact of duplicate wills was sufficient to conclude the will remains unrevoked. In Stiles v. Brown, 380 So. 2d 792 (Ala. 1980), for example, revocation of the will of Claude Stiles was avoided where Stiles' lawyer, James T. Tatum, Jr., twice gave Stiles the legal advice that "if he, Mr. Stiles, desired to revoke [the will], he would have to destroy both the duplicate original in his own possession and the one Mr. Tatum had in his possession." Although Stiles's copy couldn't be found after his death, the fact that Stiles had made no effort to destroy the duplicate retained by Tatum was considered strong evidence in rebutting the presumption of revocation.

Equally uncertain are the situations in which both executed copies were retained by the testator, but only one can be found after death. Courts have held that the presumption of revocation applies to these situations also. See, e.g., Phinizee v. Alexander, 49 So.2d 250 (Miss. 1950); Mittelstaedt's Will, 112 N.Y.S.2d 166 (App. Div. 1952), appeal dismissed, 109 N.E.2d 86 (N.Y. 1952). In Etgen v. Corboy, 337 S.E.2d 286, 291 (Va. 1985), however, the court held that:

> [W]here duplicate originals of a formally attested will are in the possession of the testator from the time of execution until discovery among his effects after death and one version is altered while the other is in its original condition, then neither will is entitled to a presumption that it is the true will of the testator. In such a situation, the proponents of the different versions of the will must prove that their version is the true will.

Leading writers on wills preach against duplicate execution. See, e.g., John R. Price, Contemporary Estate Planning 212 (1983); Alvin E. Evans, Testamentary Revocation by Act to the Document and Dependent Relative Revocation, 23 Ky. L.J. 559, 568-70 (1935). See also Atkinson on Wills § 86, at 443. Retention by the lawyer or another of a conformed or photostatic copy of the executed will is, of course, quite another matter and highly recommended.[8]

---

8. A copy of a will is conformed "if it has been clearly marked as a 'copy,' with the date and the names of the testator and witnesses inserted, preferably typed rather than printed or handwritten (e.g., */s/ Thomas T. Testator, /s/ Wilma W. Witness*)." Gerald P. Johnston, An Ethical Analysis of Common Estate Planning Practices—Is Good Business Bad Ethics?, 45 Ohio

Proof of Lost or Destroyed Wills. Rebutting the presumption of revocation isn't the only barrier to probating a lost or destroyed will. About half of the states, including those that have enacted the UPC, require the will's contents and due execution to be proved by clear and convincing evidence.[9] See, e.g., White v. Brennan's Administrator, 212 S.W.2d 299, 3 A.L.R.2d 943 (Ky. Ct. App. 1948) (holding evidence sufficient); Estate of Shaughnessy, 648 P.2d 427 (Wash. 1982) (holding evidence insufficient).

Restrictive Lost Will Statutes. A few states place further conditions on the probate of a lost or destroyed will. One type of restrictive statute is Ark. Code Ann. § 28-40-302, which provides:

> *Proving Will.* No will of any testator shall be allowed to be proved as a lost or destroyed will, unless the provisions are clearly and distinctly proved by at least two (2) witnesses, a correct copy or draft being deemed equivalent to one (1) witness, and:
>
> (1) The will is proved to have been in existence at the time of the death of the testator; or
>
> (2) The will is shown to have been fraudulently destroyed in the lifetime of the testator.[10]

This statute, like many others we study in this course, poses a dilemma for the courts. Taken literally, and applied strictly, the statute seems to impede rather than promote donative freedom. The statutory requirement that the will be "in existence at the time of death of the testator" or "have been fraudulently destroyed" would seem to mean that a court cannot probate an unrevoked lost will, even when the will's proponents can prove its contents. In such situations, many courts have interpreted the statutory language in such a way as to render it meaningless. The most popular approach has been to interpret "existence" to mean "legal existence." A will is in "legal existence" if it has not been revoked. Another approach has been to interpret the "fraudulently destroyed" part of the

---

St. L.J. 57, 131 n.473 (1984).

9. The UPC does not contain an explicit provision imposing special requirements of proof in formal testacy proceedings seeking probate of lost or destroyed wills. Hence, the general rules of evidence control proof.

The Code does make it clear, however, that lost or destroyed wills must be established in formal rather than informal probate proceedings. See UPC § 3-303, comment. Furthermore, the Code specifies that in formal proceedings the petition to establish a lost or destroyed will must "state the contents of the will, and indicate that it is lost, destroyed, or otherwise unavailable." UPC § 3-402. The Code also makes it clear that the petition must request an order finding the will valid. UPC § 3-405 governs the court's response to the petition, indicating that the judge may, but need not, "require proof of the matters necessary to support the order sought."

10. See also Nev. Rev. Stat. § 136.240(3); Okla. Stat. tit. 58, § 82; Wyo. Stat. § 2-6-207.

statutory language to include constructive as well as actual fraud. Are these interpretations of the statute supportable?

Fraud. If a person obtains access to a testator's will and wrongfully destroys it, the will is not revoked. The act to the document is ineffective because it is not accompanied by the testator's intent to revoke. Sadly, perpetrators of this type of fraud are difficult to catch. One was caught in Estate of Legeas, 258 Cal. Rptr. 858, 861-63 (Ct. App.), vacating 256 Cal. Rptr. 117 (Ct. App. 1989), which considered the question whether a fraudulent destruction of a will is a tortious act.

> The area of transfers from a decedent's estate has proven to be a fertile breeding ground for fraud. Courts have condemned fraud in a constellation of contexts. Its reported manifestations have been organized by commentators into these categories: (1) in inducing or preventing an inter vivos conveyance; (2) in the procuring of the execution of a will; (3) in the prevention of the execution of a will; (4) in causing the revocation or alteration of a will; (5) in the prevention of the revocation or alteration of a will; and (6) in the destruction, concealment, or spoliation of a will. Our concern is with the last grouping.
>
> Judicial aversion to testamentary-related fraud is not a recent phenomenon. The common law of Britain permitted equitable relief to recover a bequest which had been frustrated by the destruction or concealment of a will. . . . Traditional equitable remedies such as the imposition of a constructive trust were, however, deemed inadequate for complete redress. Beginning in 1834, the courts of eight states have explicitly recognized an independent tort action for damages caused in the intentional destruction, concealment, or spoliation of a will. . . .
>
> We believe it is fitting to augment these expressions of disapproving policy with a tort action for damages resulting from the fraudulent destruction, concealment, or spoliation of a will.

Ethics and the Safeguarding of Clients' Wills. Upon consideration of the practical and legal issues that arise when wills that were in the possession of their testators cannot be found at their deaths, the obvious question is how best to safeguard wills. The practice of many attorneys is to offer safekeeping of the will in the law firm's vault. Is this practice ethical? A preliminary report of an ABA Committee concluded that it was:

> The opinion of the committee is that the practice [of attorney safekeeping] ought to be regarded as ethical, assuming the attorney provides safekeeping merely as an accommodation and makes it clear that his safekeeping is only an alternative to safekeeping by the client, by the fiduciary-designate, or by the county clerk (where authorized by statute). The general theme of the ethics opinions is that attorney safekeeping is permissible if the testator expressly requests it but, if the attorney initiates the safekeeping, the prominent case of *State v. Gulbankian* [196 N.W.2d 233 (1972)] indicates that he may be subject to disciplinary sanction for solicitation. Further, retention of the will by the attorney may also be deemed to

increase his risk of malpractice exposure for failure to inform the client of changes in the law.

ABA Committee Report, Developments Regarding the Professional Responsibility of the Estate Planning Lawyer: The Effect of the Model Rules of Professional Conduct, 22 Real Prop. Prob. & Tr. J. 1, 28 (1987). See also Price, supra, at 212 (suggesting attorney safekeeping permissible "if requested by the client to do so"). Contrast Johnston, supra note 6, at 124-33, who suggests that the practice of attorney retention requires devisees or the executor to retrieve the will from the drafting attorney, thereby creating an appearance of soliciting probate administration business.

UPC § 2-515 authorizes testators or their agents to deposit a will with a court for safekeeping. After death, UPC § 2-516 imposes a duty on any person who has custody of a will to deliver it upon the request of an "interested person" (which is defined in UPC § 1-201(24)), to a person able to secure its probate or, if none is known, to an appropriate court. Section 2-516 also provides that a person is liable for damages for a failure to deliver a will.

Is There a Duty to Probate a Will? Must an unrevoked will be probated? Although any "interested person" can petition for probate of a will, the personal representative normally files the petition. If not, the self-interest of one or more of the devisees named in the will can usually be counted on to prompt the filing of a petition.

If, however, the affected parties wish to suppress the will and divide up the decedent's assets in a different way, they normally can do so. See Annot., Family Settlement of Testator's Estate, 29 A.L.R.3d 8 (1970). UPC § 3-912 (1990) authorizes private agreements among successors. See UPC § 1-201(48) (defining term "successors"). This agreement doesn't need the consent of the executor. Successors have the power to direct executors not to probate wills and, if they do so, the executors lose their standing to proceed. See UPC § 3-720, comment (1990). See supra Chapter 2, Part C for discussions of problems of obtaining agreement of unascertained successors or successors who lack capacity, potential adverse tax consequences, and disclaimers as an alternative to successors' agreements.

Partial Revocation by Revocatory Act. The English Statute of Frauds of 1677 provided that no devise "nor any clause thereof" should be revoked except in the manner specified, including various acts to the document. Under the Wills Act of 1837 the comparable language was "no will . . . or any part thereof." The English courts construed "clause" in the Statute of Frauds to mean "part," see Swinton v. Bailey, L.R. 4 App. Cas. 70, 85 (1878), and the same construction seems to have been taken for granted under American statutes patterned on the Statute of Frauds. See Patrick v. Patrick, 649 A.2d 1204 (Md. Ct. Spec. App. 1994); Brown v. Brown, 74 S.E. 135 (S.C. 1912). Section 2-

507 of the UPC allows a will "or any part thereof" to be revoked by revocatory act. Similar provisions appear in most non-UPC statutes. In all, or almost all, of these states, partial revocation by revocatory act seems to be recognized.

By necessity, a partial revocation by act to the document—if valid—has a double effect: it deprives someone of property and gives that property to someone else. Therefore, unless authorized by statute, courts have not recognized a partial revocation by act. See, e.g., Law v. Law, 3 So. 752 (Ala. 1888); Miles' Appeal, 36 A. 39 (Conn. 1896). Contra, e.g., Bigelow v. Gillott, 123 Mass. 102 (1877). This is true only of revocation by act to the document. It seems to be everywhere taken for granted that there can be partial revocation by subsequent instrument. See Law v. Law, supra.

In a state that doesn't allow partial revocation by act to the document, the result is that the will is probated as originally written. Complications arise, however, if the portion of the will that the testator attempted to eliminate cannot be read, and its contents cannot be established by other evidence. This was the circumstance presented to the court in Hansel v. Head, 706 So. 2d 1142, 1146-47 (Ala. 1997), in which the testators of a joint will obliterated the name of one member of a class that was to receive a devise of cash assets. It addressed the statutory dilemma as follows:

> On the one hand, it is clear that we should give effect to the testators' intent with respect to the disposal of their property. On the other hand, it is also clear that we may not give effect to their intent to revoke that portion of the bequest that it obliterated, but that we should, if possible, enforce the will in its original form.
>
> When the obliterated portion of a will is undiscernible, the question becomes one more of evidence than of intent. When the question concerning a portion of a will is a lack of evidence, the remainder of the will should be upheld. . . . Here, the evidence is sufficient as to all but one legacy. The will itself exists. . . .
>
> The attempted revocation of a portion of a will not material to the overall testamentary plan allows the will to be admitted to probate with the property that would have passed by the obliterated portion passing by intestacy. In this case, the obliteration of the name of one member of the class that is to receive one-half of the Heads' net cash assets is not material to the testators' overall testamentary plan. Thus, we hold that the will should be admitted to probate and the share allocable to the person whose name was obliterated should be disposed of through intestacy.

But see, e.g., Johannes' Estate, 227 P.2d 148 (Kan. 1951) (denying probate entirely).

In Wyoming, the court qualified partial revocations, limiting their validity only to those for which "the testamentary scheme [after the partial revocation] is basically the same as before." Seeley v. Estate of Seeley, 627 P.2d 1357, 1361 (Wyo. 1981). In *Seeley,* the testator cut a provision out of her will that granted her son an option to purchase certain property, leaving the rest of the dispository plan unchanged. The court held the partial revocation valid.

In Dodson v. Walton, 597 S.W.2d 814, 816 (Ark. 1980), the Arkansas court adopted a similar rule by limiting the effect of an interlineation or obliteration of part of a will to cases in which it "does not change the testamentary disposition provided for in the will." If it does operate to make such a change, the attempted partial revocation is ineffective and the will as originally drawn is to be given effect. In *Dodson*, the testator's will had devised her estate to six named persons who were to share equally. Subsequent to executing her will, she canceled the name of one of the devisees with the intent of excluding him from taking. The court held the partial revocation void and probated the will as originally executed. Justice Stroud dissented from the majority opinion in *Dodson* because it limited partial revocations only to wills containing no residuary clause or to some other provisions unrelated to property dispositions, such as the naming of an executor. 597 S.W.2d at 817. Accord Estate of Malloy, 949 P.2d 804 (Wash. 1998) (en banc); see also Patrick v. Patrick, supra, at 1112 (permitting some changes to the residuary clause but not if the revocation "changes the character of the will").

The Restatement 3d of Property disapproves of the approach taken by the courts in *Seeley* and *Dodson*:

> *Restatement 3d of Property§ 4.1, [Comment] i. Partial Revocation by act . . .* Even when partial revocation by act is authorized by statute, there still remains a measure of resistance to the practice. Although these statutes are held to permit revocation by act of a complete devise, it has sometimes been held that a partial revocation by act is ineffective if its purpose and effect would be to rearrange the shares within a single devise or otherwise to rewrite the terms of the will by deleting selected words.
>
> This Restatement disapproves any distinction between revocation of a complete devise and rearranging shares within a single devise or otherwise rewriting the terms of the will by deleting selected words. It is a classic example of a distinction without a difference. . . . In authorizing revocation of a will "or *any* part thereof" by act, the legislature has not limited the authorization to revocation of a complete devise. The legislature not only granted broad approval of deleting words but of the natural consequence of doing so—giving effect to the will as if the deleted words were not present.

Courts have held that a decedent can validly alter a holographic will by making handwritten changes thereon without signing the will again. See, e.g., Estate of Archer, 239 Cal. Rptr. 137 (Ct. App. 1987); Randall v. Salvation Army, 686 P.2d 241 (Nev. 1984); Stanley v. Henderson, 162 S.W.2d 95 (Tex. Comm'n Appeals 1942); Moyers v. Gregory, 7 S.E.2d 881 (Va. 1940);

Charleston Nat'l Bank v. Thru The Bible Radio Network, 507 S.E.2d 708 (W. Va. 1998).

Effect on a Codicil of a Revocation of the Will. The English Wills Act of 1837 provided:

> *7 Wm. 4 & 1 Vict., ch. 26, § 20:* That no will or codicil, or any part thereof, shall be revoked otherwise than . . . by another will or codicil executed in manner herein-before required, or by some writing declaring an intention to revoke the same, and executed in the manner in which a will is herein-before required to be executed, or by the burning, tearing, or otherwise destroying the same by the testator, or by some person in his presence and by his direction, with the intention of revoking the same.

In Goods of Turner, L.R. 2 P. & D. 403 (1872), the phrase "no will *or codicil* . . . shall be revoked otherwise than by . . . ." was interpreted to mean that a codicil can be revoked by act only if the act is performed on the codicil. An act performed on the will can revoke the will but not the codicil. This position became generally accepted in English law.

In this country, courts have taken a different tack. The question has usually been made to turn on the relation between the dispositive provisions of the will and codicil, summed up in the following statement of a New York court:

> If they are necessarily interdependent or so interinvolved as to be incapable of separate existence, the revocation of the will ipso facto revokes the codicil, otherwise not.

Francis' Will, 132 N.Y.S. 695, 703 (Sur. Ct. 1911). Accord Halpern's Estate, 224 N.Y.S.2d 58 (Sur. Ct. 1962); Ayres' Will, 43 N.E.2d 918 (Ohio Ct. App. 1940).

The Restatement 3d of Property usefully separates the question of revocation from the issue of construction when it states:

> *§ 4.1, [Comment] n. Revocation of will by act—effect on codicil.* The revocation of a will by act does not revoke a codicil to the will. If the codicil depends on the revoked will for its meaning, however, the codicil may have no effect as a matter of construction.

Suppose G performs a revocatory act on a codicil to her will but performs no revocatory act to the will itself. What issue does this raise? Does the revocation of the codicil revoke the will? See Estate of Hering, 166 Cal. Rptr. 298 (Ct. App. 1980) (discussed infra p. 331).

External Reference. Annot., Sufficiency of Evidence of Nonrevocation of Lost Will Where Codicil Survives, 84 A.L.R.4th 531 (1991).

PART C. REVOCATION BY CHANGES IN CIRCUMSTANCES—MARRIAGE, DIVORCE, REMARRIAGE

Statutory References: *UPC §§ 2-508, -804*

Restatement 3d of Property

§ *4.1 Revocation of Wills.*

(a) . . . .

(b) The dissolution of the testator's marriage is a change in circumstance that presumptively revokes any provision in the testator's will in favor of his or her former spouse. Neither marriage nor marriage followed by birth of issue is a change in circumstance that revokes a will or any part of a will.

Between the time that a testator executes a will and dies, the testator's family circumstances can change dramatically.[11] The purpose of this Part is to explore how the law does, and should, treat a will that a testator executed without considering the possibility of subsequent marriage, divorce, or remarriage. The legal issues take on a greater urgency in view of the changing American family profile. See Chapter 1, Part B and Chapter 3. The increasing incidences of divorce and remarriage heighten the likelihood that a testator's family circumstances will change after executing a will. If the law is to reflect the economic and social context in which it operates and is likely to continue to operate, it must incorporate changing family patterns into the law of will revocation.

Related to the issue of remarriage, of course, is the question of stepchildren. The *Spencer* case, below, is a case of remarriage by a widower. The case involves the common dispute pitting a decedent's children by a prior marriage against the decedent's second spouse. As Jane Bryant Quinn noted, "[When older people remarry,] your friends will be enchanted. But don't be surprised if your children aren't. It's usually not the 'pater' they worry about, but the patrimony." Jane Bryant Quinn, Making the Most of Your Money 83 (1991).

Automatic Revocation of Premarital Wills. At common law, premarital wills of women were revoked upon marriage and premarital wills of men were revoked upon marriage and birth of issue. The wills were revoked as soon as the

---

11. For further discussion of changes in circumstances that occur between the time that a testator execute a will and dies, see infra Chapter 6, which considers changes in a testator's property and changes in the circumstances of a testator's devisees, and infra Chapter 10, Part C, which considers the unintentional disinheritance of a surviving spouse and children.

operative event or events occurred. The fact that the spouse or the spouse and the couple's issue predeceased the testator was accorded no legal significance. See 1 Thomas Jarman, A Treatise on Wills 152 (2d Am. ed. 1849).

At one time in this country, more than half the states had statutes similar to the now-repealed Hawaii statute that was applicable in the *Spencer* case, below. Some of these statutes provided for revocation upon marriage alone, others for revocation upon marriage and birth of issue. A few states still have marriage-revocation statutes.[12] As we shall see in Chapter 10, modern probate codes invoke other means to protect the testator's new spouse and children against unintended disinheritance.

Estate of Spencer

591 P.2d 611 (Haw. 1979)

OGATA, J. Contestants-appellants (hereinafter appellants), who are children of the deceased testator, appeal from an Order Denying Motion for Declaratory Judgment and from an Order of Probate entered by the court below. The question presented to us on this appeal is whether a will in which the testator gives and bequeaths his entire estate to a woman by her maiden name, is revoked by the subsequent marriage of the testator to that woman by operation of HRS § 536-11 (1975 Supp.).[13] This section provided the following:

> By marriage. If, after the making of a will, the testator or testatrix marries and no provision is made in the will for such contingency, such marriage shall operate as a revocation of the will, and the will shall not be revived by the death of the (testator's) or testatrix's spouse.

We hold that the statute operated to revoke the will and reverse the orders entered by the court below.

The facts in this case are not in dispute. On October 17, 1974, the testator, Robert Stafford Spencer (hereinafter "testator"), then a widower, executed a will in which he left his entire estate to "Sandra Jean Cantwell, of 361 Laleih-

---

12. Those states are Georgia, Kansas, Maryland, Massachusetts, Nevada, Oregon, and Rhode Island. An Alabama statute that preserved the common-law distinction between a man's and a woman's premarital will, providing for the revocation of a woman's, but not a man's, will upon subsequent marriage alone, was held unconstitutional in Parker v. Hall, 362 So.2d 875, 99 A.L.R.3d 1014 (Ala. 1978).

13. HRS § 536-11 (1975 Supp.) was the applicable statute when the will was made and at the time of the testator's subsequent marriage. It was repealed by the [former] Uniform Probate Code, effective as of July 1, 1977. The [former] Uniform Probate Code provides for revocation of a will by divorce or annulment only and does not provide for revocation of a will by subsequent marriage.

oku Street, Wailuku, County of Maui, State of Hawaii." On December 28, 1974, testator married Sandra Jean Cantwell (hereinafter "appellee"). On January 10, 1975, the testator died, leaving as survivors, the appellee, his wife, and two children by a prior marriage, who are the parties involved in this dispute.

Appellee filed in the court below a petition for probate of the will executed on October 17, 1974. Appellants thereafter filed an appearance and contest of will, and about two weeks later, filed a motion for declaratory judgment requesting the court to declare that the will submitted for probate had been revoked by the subsequent marriage of their father to Sandra Jean Cantwell, the sole beneficiary. At the hearing on the motion, appellee, over objection by appellants, was permitted to introduce evidence that tended to indicate that, at the time testator executed his will, he intended to marry Sandra Jean Cantwell. This evidence showed that prior to the marriage, on August 21, 1974, testator had designated the testamentary beneficiary as the beneficiary of his interest in the State Employees' Retirement System, under the designation of "Sandra Tarlton Spencer," and had referred to her on such form as his wife; and, that on September 3, 1974, the parties had met with the Reverend Winkler to set a date for their marriage. Upon these facts, the court below found that the testator's will was not revoked by operation of HRS § 536-11 (1975 Supp.). The order denying the motion for declaratory judgment further stated:

> The Court further finds that HRS 536-11 does not automatically revoke a will made prior to marriage where such will names as beneficiary a person who later becomes the spouse of the testator, where there is clear evidence that the testator and such person intended to marry, even though there is no express provision in the will stating that it was providing for the contingency of such marriage;

HRS § 536-11 (1975 Supp.) must be given effect according to its plain and obvious meaning. We have said that this court is bound by the plain, clear and unambiguous language of a statute unless the literal construction would produce an absurd and unjust result and would be clearly inconsistent with the purposes and policies of the statute. . . . We think the language used in HRS § 536-11 (1975 Supp.) is explicitly clear and unambiguous, and the literal construction does not produce a result that is absurd and unjust and clearly inconsistent with the purposes and policies of the statute. The statute provides in clear terms that "[if,] after the making of a will, the testator . . . marries . . . such marriage shall operate as a revocation of the will," unless "provision is made in the will for such contingency." It is clear to us that "contingency" refers to a testator's marriage after having made a will. The will of the testator in the instant case does not contain any provision with respect to the marriage of the testator as the trial court so found in its order denying the motion.

Appellee argues that to revoke the will would produce a result that is absurd and unjust and clearly inconsistent with the purpose of the statute by reducing her share of testator's estate by two-thirds. Notwithstanding revocation of the will, however, the appellee, although no longer entitled to testator's entire estate, is protected by her dower rights under HRS Chapter 533. . . .

Moreover, merely designating "Sandra Jean Cantwell" as the beneficiary of his entire estate did not provide in the will for the contingency of subsequent marriage, for in doing so, the testator did no more than he would have done in leaving any testamentary gift and the statute requires more than this. . . .

The testator's will was revoked by operation of HRS § 536-11 (1975 Supp.) for failure to comply with the statutory requirement. The orders entered by the court below are reversed.

RICHARDSON, C.J., OGATA and MENOR, JJ. concur.

Notes and Question

1. *Question.* Suppose that Robert had died after he executed his will but before he and Sandra got married. What result?

2. *Scrivener's Error?* Erickson v. Erickson, 716 A.2d 92 (Conn. 1998), involved a similar set of facts and a nearly identical statute. On September 1, 1988, Ronald K. Erickson executed a will. At that time, he was a widower and had three grown children from his previous marriage. Two days later, on September 3, 1988, he married Dorothy A. Mehring, a widow with four grown children from her previous marriage. Ronald died on February 22, 1996. His will devised the residue of his estate "to Dorothy A. Mehring" and also named her executor of his estate. The decedent's daughters claimed that under Conn. Gen. Stat. § 45a-257(a),[14] a statute nearly identical to the Hawaii statute in the *Spencer* case, their father's will was automatically revoked upon his marriage to Dorothy. The trial court held that Ronald's will was not revoked because it provided for the contingency of marriage. The trial court reasoned (716 A.2d at 97):

> [The decedent's] will bequeathed all of his estate to the woman he was licensed to marry and did marry two days later. In his will, he named her executrix and designated her the guardian of his daughters, whose mother had previously died. The nature of these provisions, coupled with the extreme closeness in time of the marriage constitutes clear and convincing evidence of provision for the contingency of marriage. It would be preposterous to assume that [the decedent] was instead executing a will to make provisions that were to be revoked two days later.

---

14. This statute was repealed in 1996 and replaced with a statute based on the former version of UPC § 2-301, which we study infra Chapter 10, Part C.

On appeal, the Connecticut Supreme Court held that "[o]n the basis of existing case law, the question of whether a will provides for the contingency of a subsequent marriage must be determined: (1) from the language of the will itself; and (2) without resort to extrinsic evidence of the testator's intent." Consequently, the court concluded that "the will, in and of itself, did not provide for the contingency of the subsequent marriage of the decedent and, therefore, under existing case law, properly would have been revoked by that marriage pursuant to § 45a-257(a)." The court went on to hold, however, that "under the circumstances of this case, the trial court improperly excluded evidence of a mistake by the scrivener that, if believed, would permit a finding that the will provided for the contingency of marriage." Dorothy had made an offer of proof that the decedent's attorney would, if permitted, testify as follows (716 A.2d at 95 n.8):

> During the course of the execution of the wills there was no conversation whatsoever about the fact that the Saturday marriage would revoke the will that had been drafted on Thursday. . . . [He] would testify that the reason that he did not place in the will any specific mention of the marriage . . . was because in his view when a man executes a will two days before his marriage in which he leaves everything to the woman that he's about to marry, makes her guardian of his children, makes her administrator of the . . . estate, and if she should predecease him, leaves half of his estate to her kids . . ., that [clearly makes provision in the will for not just a contingency, but the imminent . . . of the marriage that's going to take place two days later.

The court concluded (id. at 101):

> [The extrinsic evidence offered, if believed, could prove clearly and convincingly that there was a scrivener's error that induced the decedent to execute a will that he intended to be valid despite his subsequent marriage. The offer of proof indicates that the evidence would be susceptible to an inference by the fact finder that there had been an implied assertion by the scrivener that the will would be valid despite the decedent's subsequent marriage.

On remand, the Connecticut Superior Court held that the decedent's widow failed to meet her burden of proof, which resulted in the decedent dying intestate. Erickson v. Estate of Erickson, 1999 WL 1063260 (Conn. Super. Ct. Nov. 4, 1999).

Revocation upon Divorce. Statutes in a large number of states once provided for revocation by operation of law in cases of "subsequent changes in the conditions or circumstances of the testator." Led by Lansing v. Haynes, 54 NW 699 (Mich. 1893), it was widely held that divorce coupled with a property settlement constituted a subsequent change in the circumstance of the testator sufficient to revoke provisions in a pre-divorce will in favor of the decedent's former spouse. A few states still follow this principle despite the absence of a statute on the subject. See, e.g., Rask v. Estate of Rask, 501 So. 2d 421 (Miss. 1987) (holding no revocation occurred under this principle in situation where the divorced couple continued to live together after the divorce and the couple apparently never carried out the property settlement agreement).

In the vast majority of states, the generally worded statutes have disappeared,[15] having been replaced by more specific statutory provisions similar or identical to the former version of UPC § 2-508, under which the statute specifically provides that divorce (or annulment) alone revokes any disposition of property made by the will to the former spouse. The statutes typically go on to provide that revoked devises pass as if the former spouse failed to survive the decedent. See former UPC § 2-508 But see current UPC § 2-804(d) (giving effect to revoked provisions as if the former spouse disclaimed).

Problem

A and B had no children by their marriage to each other, but each had adult children by a former marriage. During their marriage to each other, A executed a will devising all of his property to B if B survived A. If B failed to survive him, A devised one-half of his property to his children and one-half to B's children. (B also executed a will, which contained reciprocal provisions.)

A and B were subsequently divorced. A died soon after the divorce, survived by B, his children, and B's children. A had never revoked his will. How is A's estate to be distributed? Assume that the case arose in a jurisdiction that has a provision similar or identical to the former version of UPC § 2-508? See, e.g., Estate of Kerr, 520 N.W.2d 512 (Minn. Ct. App. 1994); Estate of Coffed, 387 N.E.2d 1209 (N.Y. 1979).

---

15. The District of Columbia and New Hampshire seem to be the last remaining jurisdictions. D.C. Code Ann. § 18-109 (see Luff v. Luff, 359 F.2d 235 (D.C. Cir. 1966) (holding that divorce coupled with a property settlement revokes provisions in a pre-divorce will in favor of former spouse)); N.H. Rev. Stat. Ann. § 551:14.

The generally worded statutes might be broad enough to revoke will provisions naming domestic partners as devisees when the testators fail to amend their wills after the domestic partnership terminates. Courts may not extend, however, the revocation statutes that specifically provide for revocation upon divorce to the domestic partnership situation. cf. Guaiacol v. Erle, 648 N.E.2d 539 (Ohio Ct. App. 1994), appeal denied, 646 N.E.2d 466 (Ohio 1995) (upholding devise to testator's former "live-in companion"). Extending the application of a revocation-upon-divorce statute would be particularly difficult in jurisdictions adopting a provision modeled after UPC § 2-508, which provides that, with the exception of the specific statutes enumerated, "a change of circumstances does not revoke a will or any part of it."

How would the outcome be changed if the case were governed by the current version of UPC § 2-804? See also UPC §§ 2-604, -801. Cf. Hermon v. Urteago, 46 Cal. Rptr. 2d 577 (Ct. App. 1995) (holding that the decedent's former stepchildren weren't eligible to take under a devise to "my spouse's children" and "my spouse's issue" subsequent to the divorce and urging the legislature to consider enacting a statute modeled after UPC § 2-804); In re Walker, 849 S.W.2d 766 (Tenn. 1993) (through strained interpretation of trust provisions, holding that the children of the testator's former spouse didn't take under a will that provided for them to take in the event "my wife [should] predecease me"). For further discussion of revocation by changes in circumstances, see infra Chapter 8, Part B, having to do with will substitutes.

PART D. REINSTATING A REVOKED WILL

Statutory References: *UPC § 2-509*

Restatement 3d of Property

§ *4.2 Revival of Revoked Wills*

(a) A will that was revoked by a later will is revived if the testator: (i) reexecuted the previously revoked will; (ii) executed a codicil indicating an intent to revive the previously revoked will; (iii) revoked the revoking will by act intending to revive the previously revoked will; or (iv) revoked the revoking will by another, later will whose terms indicate an intent to revive the previously revoked will.

(b) A will that was revoked by act is revived if the testator: (i) reexecuted the will; (ii) executed a codicil indicating an intent to revive the previously revoked will; or (iii) performed an act on the will that clearly and convincingly demonstrates an intent to reverse the revocation.

(c) A testamentary provision that was revoked by dissolution of the testator's marriage is revived if: (i) the testator remarried the former spouse, reexecuted the will, or executed a codicil indicating an intent to revive the previously revoked provision; or (ii) the dissolution of the marriage is nullified.

Consider G, a testator who had previously executed two wills. Will No. 2 expressly revoked Will No. 1. Shortly before her death, G revoked Will No. 2 by drawing a large "X" across each of its pages. Has G died intestate, or is Will No. 1 her valid will? In jurisdictions that follow the view that the execution of Will No. 2 revoked Will No. 1—this isn't the view universally followed, as we shall see—the question, framed in legal terminology, is whether Will No. 1 has been "revived" or "reinstated." A somewhat different way of thinking about the same question is: Did the revocation of the revoking document (Will No. 2) revoke the revocation (of Will No. 1)?

In England, prior to the Wills Act of 1837, there was no statutory provision on revival. Although the Statute of Frauds of 1677 provided for revocation by later instrument or by act to the document, that statute was silent on the matter of revival. Two approaches emerged in the English decisions: One came from the ecclesiastical courts, which had jurisdiction over succession to personal property; the other came from the common-law courts, which passed on questions of revocation (as well as of due execution) when an issue of title to land was raised.

The Ecclesiastical Rule. Under the ecclesiastical rule, whether G's Will No. 1 would be revived would depend on G's intent. In a lengthy opinion in Williams v. Miles, 94 N.W. 705 (Neb. 1903), then Commissioner Roscoe Pound (who later became Dean of the Harvard Law School) canvassed the state of English and American law on revival and described the ecclesiastical rule as follows:

> [T]he ecclesiastical courts . . . , endeavor[ed] in each case to ascertain the testator's intention, . . . making that intention the criterion. In a leading case the doctrine of those courts was stated thus:
>
>> The legal presumption is neither adverse to, nor in favor of, the revival of a former uncanceled [will], upon the cancellation of a later revocatory will. Having furnished this principle, the law withdraws altogether, and leaves the question as one of intention purely, and open to a decision either way, solely according to facts and circumstances.

94 N.W. at 708, quoting Usticke v. Bawden, 2 Addams (Eng. Eccle.) 116, [162 Eng. Rep. 238] (1824). In practice, of course, the proponent of the revoked will presumably has the burden of establishing an intent to reinstate that will. A court would deny probate of the will unless the proponent could produce some evidence of such intent.

The Common-Law Rule. The common-law rule would treat Will No. 1 as G's valid will, regardless of her intention. The common-law rule is sometimes referred to as a rule of "automatic revival." This is how Commissioner Pound, in *Williams* described it:

> Lord Mansfield announced a rule, which was followed by the common-law courts when questions as to wills disposing of real property came before them, to the effect that if the first will is preserved, and a subsequent will, revoking it expressly or by implication, is destroyed or canceled, the revocation is repealed, and the original will revived and continued in force, by virtue of these circumstances.

94 N.W. at 707-08. Strictly speaking, Commissioner Pound didn't get the common-law rule quite right. Lord Mansfield's actual view, enunciated in the leading case of Goodright v. Glazier, 4 Burr. 2512, 2514, 98 Eng. Rep. 317, 319 (K.B. 1770), was that the first will had never been revoked:

> A will is ambulatory till the death of the testator. If the testator lets it stand till he dies, it is his will: if he does not suffer it to do so, it is not his will. Here, he had two. He has canceled the second: it had no effect, no operation; it is as no will at all, being canceled before his death. But the former, which was never canceled, stands as his will.

The second will in *Goodright* apparently contained no express revocation clause, but Lord Mansfield later made it clear that the position he had taken would apply even though it had. See Harwood v. Goodright, 1 Cowp. 87, 98 Eng. Rep. 981 (K.B. 1774).

American Rules on Revival in the Absence of a Statute. In the minority of states in which revival isn't controlled by statute,[16] there appears to be a preference for the English ecclesiastical rule. See Hawes v. Nicholas, 10 S.W. 558 (Tex. 1889) (ruling that the destruction of a subsequent will was not itself sufficient to demonstrate intent to revive); Gould's Will, 47 A. 1082 (Vt. 1900) (placing burden of proof on proponent of a revoked will and further stating that careful preservation of the revoked will by testator can be counted as an indication of an intent to revive); May v. Estate of McCormick, 769 P.2d 395 (Wyo. 1989) (holding that, in the absence of evidence of an intention to revive, a revoked will is not revived by the destruction of a later will that expressly revoked all prior wills). The English common-law rule also has its adherents, however, as in Whitehill v. Halbing, 118 A. 454, 28 A.L.R. 895 (Conn. 1922); Succession of Dambly, 186 So. 7 (La. 1938). No decisions in the remaining states appear to exist on the question.

Statutory Rules on Revival. In England, the common-law rule of "automatic revival" and the ecclesiastical rule giving effect to intention however proved were abrogated in 1837. The Wills Act of 1837 replaced those rules by a so-called "antirevival" rule. Under the statutory "antirevival" rule, G's Will No. 1 would be revived only if G either reexecuted that will or executed a codicil showing an intention to revive that will.

In this country, statutes in fourteen jurisdictions maintain the antirevival stance of the English Wills Act and require either a reexecution of the revoked will or the execution of a codicil showing an intention to revive. See Statutory Note to Restatement 3d of Property § 4.2. The statutes in the remaining states

---

16. Those states are Connecticut, Louisiana, Mississippi, New Hampshire, Texas, Vermont, and Wyoming.

have liberalized the strict requirements of the English Wills Act and moved in the direction of the English ecclesiastical rule. Under early versions of these statutes, revival of Will No. 1 would occur if it "appears by the terms of" the revocation of Will No. 2 that it was G's intention to revive and give effect to Will No. 1 or if Will No. 1 was "republished." Today, this version exists in only five states (Indiana, Kansas, Nevada, Ohio, and Oklahoma). The other states have replaced the early version permitting revival with more liberal versions modeled after either the former UPC or the current UPC. See Statutory Note, supra. Estate of Boysen, below, applied the former UPC, which was then in effect in Minnesota.

Estate of Boysen

309 N.W.2d 45 (Minn. 1981)

PETERSON, J. Genevieve Thompson appeals from the order of a three-judge panel of the Dodge County District Court affirming the order of the county court, probate division, admitting to probate a will of decedent Chris Boysen. The issue raised by this appeal is whether decedent revived the will. Because we believe the relevant statute, Minn. Stat. § 524.2-509(a) (1980), was misapplied below, we reverse and remand for a new trial.

Decedent was the father of appellant Genevieve Thompson and respondent Raymond Boysen, proponent of the will in question. Decedent's wife predeceased him by 30 years. Appellant married and moved to Austin, Minnesota. After respondent married, decedent made his home with respondent and his wife in Hayfield, Minnesota. In 1964 respondent was appointed guardian of decedent's person and estate. In 1973 decedent moved from respondent's home to a residence for the elderly located in Hayfield. He lived there until his death in 1977.

Decedent executed the will on March 12, 1964, when he was 75 years old. In the will he devised all his real property—in large part a 200-acre farm near Hayfield—to respondent on the condition that respondent pay appellant $7,000. Decedent bequeathed his personal property to respondent and appellant in equal shares.

After its execution the will was filed with the Dodge County clerk of court. In 1972 the court removed the will from the courthouse vault in order to review it in connection with a proceeding for the dissolution of respondent's marriage. A few years later respondent learned the will had never been returned to the clerk of court's custody. When attempts by decedent's attorney to locate the will proved unsuccessful, decedent discussed the preparation of a new will with a paralegal employed by the attorney. At the probate court hearing the paralegal described their conversation:

> When he came in, he said that his will had been lost so it was necessary for him to make another will, . . . I had been present and witnessed the first will. He thought perhaps I remembered what was in it. I said too long a time had gone by. I didn't . . . could not remember the details of the first will and we had no copy. He said at that time that it was necessary to make one because he wanted the farm to go to Raymond. He said at the first will he had given money to Genevieve, the farm to Raymond and a sum of money to Genevieve. He was indecisive as to this amount of money that he should put in to her because he didn't know what money he'd have, you know, what money there would be left to divide for her. He didn't know what . . . valuations would be to . . . things have changed. So he . . . he did ask if this . . . We discussed and we said, well, how did you determine the first amount of money? And he said, well, he had thought that 3/4 to 1/4 would be a . . . set that sum of money. So we said, 'Well, you can use fractions; you don't have to use sums of money if you don't want to.' And that is why he made a fraction in place of a total sum of money.

Decedent executed the new will on May 13, 1975. It differs from its predecessor in one significant respect: it provides that in order to take decedent's real property respondent must pay appellant a sum equal to one-fourth the property's appraised value. The farm is worth approximately $600,000.

Decedent filed the new will with the clerk of court. He gave respondent an unsigned copy of the will. Respondent put the copy in a safe deposit box.

Efforts to determine the whereabouts of the old will continued. In June 1975 the clerk of court notified decedent's attorney that the old will had been found. In February 1976 the attorney, acting at decedent's direction, withdrew the new will from the court files.

Shortly thereafter, Raymond drove decedent to the attorney's office. The secretary gave decedent the new will and he signed a receipt for it. During the drive back to Hayfield decedent tore the new will in half. At the probate court hearing Raymond testified that decedent handed him the torn will and said:

> They maybe have lost it yet. This will give us . . . some sort of an idea on my likes . . . you take care of it.

Raymond placed the torn will in a locked box at his home. He removed the copy from the safe deposit box and returned it to decedent. Decedent tore the copy in half.

Decedent died in April of the following year. Raymond, as the executor of decedent's estate, filed a petition for probate of the 1964 will. Genevieve objected to the petition and sought an adjudication of intestacy. The probate court found that decedent revived the 1964 will and accordingly admitted the will to probate. A three-judge panel of the district court affirmed the probate court's order. We granted Genevieve leave to appeal to this court from the district court's determination.

Minn. Stat. § 524.2-509(a) (1980) [Former UPC § 2-509(a)] governs the question whether decedent revived the 1964 will. That statute provides:

> If a second will which, had it remained effective at death, would have revoked the first will in whole or in part, is thereafter revoked by acts under section 524.2-507 [Former UPC § 2-507], the first will is revoked in whole or in part unless it is evident from the circumstances of the revocation of the second will or from testator's contemporary or subsequent declarations that he intended the first will to take effect as executed.

The 1975 will expressly revoked all prior wills and codicils of decedent. The 1975 will was revoked when decedent tore it in half. Under section 524.2-509(a) the 1964 will is not revived unless from "the circumstances of the revocation" of the 1975 will or from decedent's "contemporary or subsequent declarations" it is evident that he intended the 1964 will "to take effect as executed."

The probate court found that decedent did so intend. The district court panel held the probate court's finding not clearly erroneous. Our review of a factual finding of a court sitting without a jury is likewise limited to the question whether the finding is clearly erroneous. . . . Here, however, we are presented with a case involving the application of a statute we have not previously had occasion to interpret. On this appeal we must initially determine the correct interpretation of section 524.2-509(a) and then decide whether the district court's application of the statute to the facts of this case was consistent with that interpretation.

Where a later will which would have revoked an earlier will is itself revoked, section 524.2-509(a) establishes a presumption against revival of the earlier will. That presumption is rebutted if "the circumstances of the revocation" of the later will or the "testator's contemporary or subsequent declarations" make evident his intent that the earlier will "take effect as executed." In the present case decedent made no declarations indicating such an intent. Our concern, then, is with the meaning of the phrase "the circumstances of the revocation." No court in another jurisdiction that has enacted the [former] Uniform Probate Code appears to have interpreted this phrase.

The question under section 524.2-509(a) is whether a testator, at the time he revoked a will, intended to die intestate or to revive an earlier will. We believe that in allowing the trier of fact to consider "the circumstances of the revocation" when deciding this question the legislature meant to permit an examination of all matters relevant to the testator's intent. Accordingly, the trier of fact should consider the following:

> 1. Did the testator, at the time he revoked the later will, know whether the earlier will was in existence?

2. If the testator did know that the earlier will was in existence, did he know the nature and extent of his property and the disposition made of his property by the earlier will, particularly with respect to persons with a natural claim on his bounty?

3. Did the testator, by action or nonaction, disclose an intent to make the disposition which the earlier will directs?

Only if these questions are affirmatively answered should the earlier will be admitted to probate. Because these questions were not addressed below, the district court's order must be reversed and this case remanded for a new trial. By remanding the case we do not intimate an opinion regarding the ultimate result.

Reversed and remanded.

[The dissenting opinion of SCOTT, J. is omitted.]

Notes and Questions

1. *Subsequent History*. On remand, the trial court applied the supreme court's directives and determined that the 1964 will was not revived. The trial court also, however, applied the doctrine of dependent relative revocation, which we study in Part E, as a way of giving effect to the 1975 will. On appeal, the Minnesota Court of Appeals held that the procedural rules of the prior appeal rendered this determination improper. See Estate of Boysen, 351 N.W.2d 398 (Minn. Ct. App. 1984). In the end, Chris Boysen died intestate.

2. *Boysen's Discrete Subrequirements Approach*. Is *Boysen* an example of a hard case making bad law? The court was surely correct in saying that "the legislature meant to permit an examination of all matters relevant to the testator's intent" in determining whether one of the statutory requirements for revival were met. Do you agree, however, that it is appropriate to translate that general statutory prescription into discrete subrequirements, all of which must be met? Such an approach surely makes the proponent's case harder than the legislature intended it to be.

3. *Disapproval of the* Boysen *Approach.* UPC § 2-509 continues to employ the same statutory language interpreted in *Boysen*. The Comment to the section, however, explicitly rejects the *Boysen* discrete subrequirements approach, but does not disapprove of the result that the 1964 will was not revived.

4. *Mistake in the Inducement?* The Restatement 3d of Property § 4.2, comment f provides that "[a]n intent to revive a former will is ineffective if it was the product of a mistake in inducement. The burden of proof is on the party claiming that it was the product of a mistake in inducement." Could Genevieve have carried that burden in *Boysen*?

5. *Revival of a Will That Was Revoked by Act.* Suppose that after G's death, an attested will, which earlier had been torn into a number of pieces, was found among G's important papers taped back together. Evidence shows that G was

at all times in control of the document. What result under UPC § 2-509? Should a court treat the will as having been revived? See Breathitt v. Whittaker's Executors, 47 Ky. 530 (1848). What standard of proof should be required to show revival in this type of case? See Restatement 3d of Property § 4.2(b), supra.

Revocation of a Codicil. In Estate of Hering, 166 Cal. Rptr. 298 (Ct. App. 1980), the decedent, Henry Hering, executed an eight-page typewritten will on October 21, 1976. Elaine Bockin was to receive a specific devise of the decedent's personal effects and rent-free use of certain premises. She was to be the income beneficiary of a testamentary trust, with the trustee also having power to invade the corpus of the trust for her benefit. At Elaine's death, any remaining corpus of the trust was to be distributed to the Braille Institute of America, Inc.

On January 13, 1977, Henry executed a typewritten three-page "First Codicil to Will of Henry Richard Hering." The codicil referred to the specific articles of the will containing Elaine's name and amended those articles by deleting her name and inserting the words "Evelyn Salib." The codicil also expressly confirmed and republished the will in all other respects.

On December 2, 1977, in the presence of his attorney and with intent to revoke the codicil, Henry made a large "X" through all of the writing on each page of the codicil and on each page wrote the words, "Revoked December 2, 1977 Henry R. Hering."[17] Henry's attorney testified that, shortly before Henry made these marks on the codicil, Henry stated that he thought that the X's would reinstate the provisions in the original will, devising the income interest to Elaine rather than Evelyn.

When the case was decided, the California statute on revival provided:[18]

> If, after making a will, the testator makes a second will, the destruction or other revocation of the second will does not revive the first will, unless it appears by the terms of such revocation that it was the intention to revive and give effect to the first will, or unless, after such destruction or revocation, the first will is duly republished.

---

17. As an alternative argument, Bockin argued that even if the antirevival provisions applied, the December 1977 writing was a valid holographic codicil that republished the original will. Estate of Hering, 166 Cal. Rptr. 298, 299-300 (1980). The court declined to address this issue once it found that the antirevival statute didn't apply to a revoked codicil. Id.

18. The California provision has now been repealed and replaced by the former UPC version of § 2-509. See Cal. Prob. Code § 6123.

The court gave effect to Henry's 1976 will as originally written but not on the theory that the revoked provisions of the 1976 will had been revived under the above revival statute. The above revival statute was, in fact, held inapplicable to cases of partial revocation by codicil. (Although UPC § 1-201 defines the term "will" as including a "codicil," California then had no similar statutory provision.[19]) With the legislation held to be inapplicable, the court applied the common-law rule on revival, under which a subsequent revocation of the codicil "leaves the will in force and effect as written." But see Estate of Lagreca, 687 A.2d 783 (N.J. Super. Ct. App. Div. 1997) (holding under an antirevival statute that a revocation of a codicil by act does not revive the revoked will provisions and therefore the decedent died partially intestate).

How would the *Hering* case be decided under UPC § 2-509 ? How would the *Hering* case have been decided under the court's approach and under the approach of the UPC if, just before he made the "X" marks on his 1977 codicil, Henry had said "Now neither Evelyn nor Elaine will get any of my property"?

PART E. DEPENDENT RELATIVE REVOCATION (INEFFECTIVE REVOCATION)

As we shall see, dependent relative revocation is a remarkable doctrine, ingeniously devised to give a testator results that come close to actual intention when actual intention, though established to a court's satisfaction, cannot be given effect. The Restatement 3d of Property seeks to rename the doctrine[20] and formulates it as follows.

Restatement 3d of Property

§ 4.3 Ineffective Revocation (Dependent Relative Revocation)

(a) A partial or complete revocation of a will is presumptively ineffective if the testator made the revocation:

(1) in connection with an attempt to achieve a dispositive objective that fails under applicable law, or

(2) because of a false assumption of law, or because of a false belief about an objective fact, that is either recited in the revoking instrument or established by clear and convincing evidence.

---

19. One was added in 1983. See Cal. Prob. Code § 88.

20. In Goods of Brown, [1942] P. 136, 138, the judge decried the term "dependent relative revocation," saying: "The name of this doctrine seems to me to be somewhat overloaded with unnecessary polysyllables. The resounding adjectives add very little, it seems to me, to any clear idea of what is meant."

(b) The presumption established in subsection (a) is rebutted if allowing the revocation to remain in effect would be more consistent with the testator's probable intention.

Although the development of the doctrine of dependent relative revocation (ineffective revocation) is commendable, it is still the law of second best. Of prime concern as you study the following materials is whether the law can do better.

External References. George E. Palmer, Dependent Relative Revocation and Its Relation to Relief for Mistake, 69 Mich. L. Rev. 989 (1971); Joseph Warren, Dependent Relative Revocation, 33 Harv. L. Rev. 337 (1920).

Callahan's Estate

29 N.W.2d 352 (Wis. 1947)

Eva Callahan died in June 1945 at the age of eighty-seven years as a result of an illness with which she was stricken on the preceding January 21st. Her husband, Dr. John L. Callahan, Sr., died on January 5, 1945 at the age of eighty-four. The Callahans were the parents of two children then living, John Jr. and Albert.

In July 1932 Eva Callahan and her husband executed wills almost identical in their provisions. In December 1936, September 1938, February 1940 and August 1944, further wills were drawn by each clearly evidencing common design and collaboration in their preparation. On the night of January 1, 1945 Quincy H. Hale, an attorney in the city of La Crosse who had drawn the various wills for the Callahans, visited them in the company of his wife. At the conclusion of the visit Dr. Callahan accompanied the Hales to the door and informed them that he and his wife had destroyed their 1944 wills for the purpose of reinstating their 1940 wills, and had done so because Albert had begun drinking heavily again and they desired to put him back in the position he occupied under their 1940 wills. Albert had been addicted to the excessive use of intoxicating liquor and had received less than equal treatment with John in the 1940 wills. In the 1944 wills his position was improved because he had at that time given up drinking. At the time of Dr. Callahan's statement Mrs. Callahan was in the room but said nothing.

The next day, January 2, Mr. Hale determined that the destruction of the 1944 wills did not reinstate the 1940 wills. He drew a new will for Dr. Callahan almost identical with his 1940 will and took it to him for execution. He then informed the doctor and Mrs. Callahan that their 1940 wills had not been revived by destruction of the later wills. He had not been requested to draw the new will by Dr. Callahan either on the preceding night or on the day following, but did so purely of his own volition. He stated that he acted in haste because he was convinced that the doctor would not live long. He did not prepare a similar will for Mrs. Callahan because she was in good health and he was not concerned about her. Dr. Callahan executed the will on January 2 and died three days later.

Mrs. Callahan was stricken on January 21. She was taken to the hospital immediately and died the following June. While she was at the hospital two additional wills were drawn. . . . Mr. Hale testified that Mrs. Callahan was incompetent [to execute a will] after she entered the hospital on January 21. . . .

[Mrs. Callahan's] will of 1940 [and] will of 1944 . . . were offered for probate in the alternative. The petition for probate was made by Mr. Hale who had retained a copy of the destroyed 1944 will. John and Albert objected to the probate. [A] decree was entered admitting the 1944 will to probate, from which John and Albert appeal. . . .

RECTOR, JUSTICE. The appeal of . . . Albert and John from the judgment admitting the 1944 will to probate raises the question whether the trial court properly applied the doctrine of 'dependent relative revocation'.

That rule is ordinarily applied in cases where a testator having executed one will thereafter revokes it by the execution of a later will which, for some reason fails to become effectual. In such cases revocation of the earlier instrument 'is treated as relative and dependent upon the efficiency of the later disposition, which was intended to be substituted.' Will of Lundquist, 1933, 211 Wis. 541, 543, 248 N.W. 410, 411. The revocation of the earlier document is held to be dependent upon the validity of the later one and the later one being invalid, the earlier one stands. The rule has been criticized by some courts and some textwriters, but it is the law in this jurisdiction.

The situation presented here differs somewhat from the usual case in which the doctrine is applied. Here we have a revocation of a later will with an announced intention of reinstating a former one. But the rule was applied to such a situation in Powell v. Powell, 1866, L.R. 1 Prob. 209. The reasoning upon which it is based applies to the same extent that it does in the typical case. Adherence to the rule requires that we apply it here.

It is argued that there is a distinction between this case and other cases in which the rule has been applied. It is said that here the testatrix was advised the destruction of the 1944 will did not reinstate the 1940 will, that she had an adequate opportunity thereafter to prepare a new will if she had desired to do so, and that her failure to prepare a will indicated that her destruction of the 1944 will was not conditioned but was accompanied by an intention to revoke the document absolutely. There is considerable force in the argument. The doctrine of dependent relative revocation is based upon the testator's inferred intention. It is held that as a matter of law the destruction of the later document is intended to be conditional where it is accompanied by the expressed intent of reinstating a former will and where there is no explanatory evidence. Of course if there is evidence that the testator intended the destruction to be absolute, there is no room for the application of the doctrine of dependent revocation. Failure to prepare a new will may or may not be significant. The inferences to be derived from such a failure will vary according to the circumstances. If it were due to lack of opportunity, it would be difficult to attribute any great significance to it. The inferences, as in other factual questions, are to be drawn by the trier of fact.

Here the trial court evidently did not consider the delay in preparing a new will sufficient to establish that the 1944 will was destroyed with the intent to revoke it absolutely. It was justified in arriving at that conclusion.

Three days after Mr. Hale's advice to Mrs. Callahan, her husband died and she was stricken sixteen days after his death with an illness which rendered her incompetent thereafter. Both she and her husband were advanced in years. She was eighty-seven and he was eighty-four. They had lived together for many years. Her grief at his death, the necessity for arrangements that were then required and the loss that she must have felt, constitute adequate explanation of her failure to discuss the matter of a new will in the short time before she became ill.

There is a further argument to the effect that Mr. Hale's testimony as to the testatrix's intention in destroying her 1944 will is incompetent and of no probative force. [The court then held that Dr. Callahan's statement to Mr. Hale was in the course of a social visit and that Mr. Hale's testimony was not incompetent under a statute prohibiting disclosure by an attorney of communications of a client made to him "in the course of his professional employment."]

So far as the matter of probative force is concerned, it strikes us that the circumstances are persuasive as to the testatrix' intention. We must bear in mind that prior to the doctor's statement to Mr. Hale he and his wife had each executed five wills and these wills carried the clearest indication that they were the result of collaboration and execution of a common design. The fact that they acted in concert in preparing these wills carries an inference that they collaborated in destroying their 1944 wills. Dr. Callahan's statement to Mr. Hale in the presence of Mrs. Callahan that they had acted together must be considered as the statement of one who without doubt had consulted with her in the matter. . . .

JUDGMENT AFFIRMED.

Notes and Questions

1. *Theory of Dependent Relative Revocation—Mistake or Conditional Revocation?* In the earliest English decision on the general problem, the court based relief partly upon the ground that the revocation "ought to be relieved against and the will set up again in equity, under the head of accident." Onions v. Tyrer, 2 Vern. 742, 23 Eng. Rep. 1085, 1 P. Wms. 343, 24 Eng. Rep. 418 (Ch. 1716). Recognition that the problem is essentially one of giving relief for mistake still appears in some of the cases, but the conventional analysis is the conditional-revocation theory. As the Restatement 3d of Property explains, neither theory is completely satisfactory.

> § *4.3, [Comment] a. Rationale and historical note.* . . . This Restatement treats the doctrine of ineffective revocation as one of independent integrity, grounded neither in a conditional-revocation analysis nor exclusively in a mistake analysis. . . . The conditional-revocation theory is thoroughly unsatisfactory as a basis of the doctrine. The notion that the testator actually intended to make the revocation conditional is a fiction . . . . The mistake theory is unsatisfactory as an exclusive basis of the doctrine. Equity only grants relief for mistake if the actor was laboring under an erroneous belief *at the time of the act* . . . . This restriction makes the mistake theory too limiting, and the doctrine of ineffective revocation has properly been extended to cases in which the testator was not mistaken when he or she revoked . . . .

2. *Giving Effect to the Testator's Intention.* As noted in the introductory text to this Part, dependent relative revocation is the law of second best. Callahan's intention was to revive her 1940 will. She didn't intend her destroyed 1944 will to stand unrevoked under the doctrine of dependent relative revocation. The 1940 will couldn't be given effect because the applicable Wisconsin legislation contained an antirevival provision similar to the one in the English Wills Act of 1837, requiring reexecution of the revoked will.[21] Dependent relative revocation in cases like *Callahan* should all but disappear in states adopting a liberal revival rule like the one found in UPC § 2-509.

Giving Effect to the Testator's Intention in Other Dependent Relative Revocation Cases. The factual pattern faced by the court in the *Callahan* case—revocation of a later will for the purpose of reviving a former one—is only one of several factual patterns that lend themselves to a dependent-relative-revocation analysis. Another typical situation in which courts have applied

---

21. The current Wisconsin statute on revival, Wis. Stat. Ann. § 853.11(6), tracks UPC § 2-509.

dependent relative revocation is where a testator revokes a will by revocatory act erroneously believing that a later will is validly executed. We will study these revocation-to-make a replacement-will cases below. As you study them, consider the extent to which adoption of a harmless-error rule would give family property law a mechanism by which to give effect to the testator's intention, the later will.

In fact, would it not be the case that a combination of the liberal revival rule of UPC § 2-509 and enactment of UPC § 2-503 or judicial adoption of the harmless-error rule of Restatement 3d of Property § 3.3 would pretty much make the doctrine of dependent relative revocation obsolete?

The widespread enactment of UPC § 2-503 or widespread judicial adoption of the harmless-error rule of Restatement 3d of Property § 3.3 is probably years away. Therefore, it is important to consider how the courts should administer the law of second best. The Restatement 3d of Property provides the following guidance:

> § *4.3, [Comment] a. Rationale and historical note.* . . .A revocation [that is made in connection with an attempt to achieve a dispositive objective that fails under applicable law] is only presumptively ineffective, not automatically ineffective. The revocation is still given effect when the court determines that the testator, if given the choice, would probably have preferred the revocation to remain in effect rather than to have it set aside. This is a question of fact, to be determined on the basis of relevant evidence. [A]n always relevant and often decisive factor on the question of probable intention is whether the outcome of treating the revocation as ineffective comes closer to the testator's failed dispositive objective than the outcome of allowing the revocation to remain in effect. If the outcome of allowing the revocation to remain in effect comes closer to the testator's failed dispositive objective, this tends to rebut the presumption. Consequently, if, from this comparison or from other relevant evidence, it is established that the testator's probable intention would have been for the revocation to stand, the presumption is rebutted and the revocation remains in effect. Otherwise, the presumption prevails and the revocation is nullified on the theory that, had the testator known that revoking the will would not facilitate intention, the testator would not have formed an intent to revoke. Under this doctrine, then, if the presumption is not rebutted, the will is valid and effective because it was never revoked.

See also George E. Palmer, Dependent Relative Revocation and Its Relation to Relief for Mistake, 69 Mich. L. Rev. 989, 997-99 (1971).

In Kroll v. Nehmer, 705 A.2d 716 (Md. 1998), Margaret Binco revoked her 1985 will by writing on the back of the will "VOID—NEW WILL DRAWN UP 6-28-90." After her death in 1994, a 1990 will and a 1994 will were found. Both wills were handwritten and apparently signed by Margaret, but neither will was validly executed because Maryland generally does not recognize holographic wills and neither will was signed by attesting witnesses. Consequently, the choice was between: (1) intestacy (allowing the revocation of the 1985 will to stand) and (2) the 1985 will (rendering the revocation of the 1985 will ineffective under the doctrine of dependent relative revocation).

The *Kroll* case was both difficult and unusual because a comparison of the pattern of distribution under intestacy with the pattern of distribution under the revoked 1985 will showed that neither approximated Margaret's failed dispositive objective as expressed in her invalidly executed later wills. In the end, the court chose intestacy because it appeared that Margaret's intention to disinherit the devisees of her revoked will was stronger than her intention to disinherit her sole heir in intestacy. The court said:

> [T]he fact is that, with the possible exception of the First Church of God, whose status under the 1990 will is, at best, unclear, none of the beneficiaries under the 1985 will were named in the 1990 will. The 1990 will replaced them all, indicating that Ms. Binco did not wish any of them (again with the possible exception of the First Church of God) to be benefitted. The effect of applying the doctrine and disregarding her revocation, however, is precisely to do what she clearly did not want done—to leave her estate to people she had intended to disinherit. We cannot fairly presume such an intent on her part . . . .

Estate of Patten

587 P.2d 1307 (Mont. 1978)

[Ella D. Patten died in 1973, survived by her two sons, Donald and Robert. In 1970, about three years before her death, she had attempted to execute a will that devised the bulk of her $200,000 estate to Donald. This 1970 will was found in her safe-deposit box after her death, and Donald presented it for probate. Robert, however, successfully contested its validity on the ground of improper execution. See Patten v. Patten, 558 P.2d 659 (Mont. 1976).

The 1970 will consisted of two pages. Ella Patten's signature appeared at the bottom of the first page. The second page contained only an attestation clause, with the signatures of three members of her doctor's office staff. The ineffective attempt at proper execution occurred on July 6, 1970. Ella Patten took the will with her to a doctor's appointment. After being attended by her doctor, "a request was transmitted to the office staff to witness her will." Ella, who one witness described as habitually secretive about her personal affairs, folded the document over so that only the second page was visible to the witnesses. Contrary to the will formality requirements of the then-existing Montana statute,[22] Ella neither signed in the presence of the witnesses nor acknowledged her signature to them.

After failing to get the 1970 will probated, Donald presented for probate a copy of a 1968 will. The original of the 1968 will had been given to Ella by her attorney after its proper execution, but could not be found after her death. The copy presented for probate was a copy retained by her attorney. The district court granted summary judgment to Robert, denying probate of the copy of his mother's 1968 will.]

HASWELL, C.J. . . . Both [the 1968 and 1970] wills left the bulk of decedent's estate, approximately $200,000, to Donald Patten. There are some differences between the wills. In the 1968 will, Robert Patten was named executor of the estate. In the 1970 will, this appointment was deleted. The 1970 will omits some specific bequests which were in the 1968 will. The remaining paragraphs in the wills are almost identical in language and in form. . . .

The doctrine [of dependent relative revocation] is applied with caution. The mere fact that a testator made a new will, which failed of effect, will not of itself prevent the destruction of an earlier will from operating as a revocation. The doctrine can only apply where there is a clear intent of the testator that the revocation of the old is conditional upon the validity of the new will. For the doctrine to apply, the new will must also not have changed the testamentary purpose of the old will and essentially repeated the same dispositive plans such that it is clear that the first will is revoked only because the second duplicated its purpose. Thus, while the doctrine may be widely recognized, it is narrowly applied. . . .

In deciding whether to apply the doctrine in a given case, the testator's "intent" is the controlling factor. The testator must intend that the destruction of the old will is dependent upon the validity of the new will. Thompson on Wills, supra. Evidence of this intent cannot be left to speculation, supposition, conjecture or possibility. The condition that revocation of a will is based upon the validity of the new will must be proved by substantial evidence of probative value. A showing of immediate intent to make a new will and of conditional destruction are required to re-establish a destroyed will under the theory of dependent relative revocation. [T]o prove this intent the proponents of the revoked will must show that the new will was executed concurrently with or shortly after the destruction of the old will and both wills must be similar in content. In the present case, Donald Patten, the proponent of the copy of the 1968 will, has not proven that decedent intended the destruction of the 1968 will to depend upon the validity of the 1970 will. . . . No one knows when the

---

22. In 1974, Montana enacted the former UPC, including § 2-502. In 1993, it enacted the current UPC, including §§ 2-502 and 2-503. See Mont. Code Ann. §§ 72-2-522, -523.

decedent destroyed her will or how she did it. The record does not show that the 1970 will was executed concurrently or shortly after the destruction of the 1968 will.

While the content of both wills is similar in some respects, the dissimilarities are such that they reveal decedent's revocation of the 1968 will was not conditioned on the validity of the 1970 will. In the 1968 will, decedent bequeathed $5,000 and $2,500 to her grandchildren, the son and daughter of Robert Patten. In the 1970 will, Donald Patten's name was written in by pen and ink as executor. In the 1968 will, Robert Patten was the named executor. These differences in the wills show that decedent may not have intended the same dispositive plan.

Here, the evidence that decedent intended the revocation of the 1968 will to depend upon the validity of the 1970 will is merely conjecture and speculation. As that is the case, the District Court was correct in granting summary judgment to Robert L. Patten. The doctrine of dependent relative revocation can only be applied where the evidence of the testator's intent is clear and convincing. Such is not the case here.

. . . . Here, we have no evidence that the revocation of the 1968 will depended upon the validity of the 1970 will. The doctrine of dependent relative revocation has no application under these circumstances. . . .

JUDGMENT AFFIRMED.

DALY, HARRISON, SHEA AND SHEEHY, J.J., concur.

Notes and Questions

1. Did intestacy come closer to Ella's dispositive plan exemplified by her invalidly executed 1970 will than her validly executed but revoked 1968 will? Section 4.3, comment c of the Restatement 3d of Property provides:

> § *4.3, [Comment] c. Revocation intending to make a replacement will. . .* After death, the only evidence available may be the ineffectively executed replacement will, and sometimes but not necessarily the revoked first will. Consequently, the doctrine of ineffective revocation would be too restricted if it required evidence of the time of revocation and of a contemporaneous intent to make a replacement will. There need not be affirmative proof of the time of revocation or that, at the time of revocation, the testator intended to replace the first will with a replacement will.

2. *Uncompleted Plan?* In Dougan's Estate, 53 P.2d 511 (Or. 1936), Dougan made numerous pen and pencil marks on her will and then took the mutilated will to her lawyer, together with an outline of the provisions of a new will, which she requested him to prepare. The will was prepared, but she suffered a stroke and died before she could get to the attorney's office to execute it. Estate of Ausley, 818 P.2d 1226 (Okla. 1991), involved similar facts. Ausley marked

up his will with "X's" and the words "void." He then hired an attorney to draft a new will for him. The attorney presented Ausley with a draft of a proposed new will on June 16, 1988. Some unspecified changes regarding some property in Oklahoma were required. Ausley died on June 20, 1988, before a new draft was presented to him. Both the *Dougan* and the *Ausley* courts held that the mutilated wills couldn't be given effect under dependent relative revocation. Why not? The Restatement 3d of Property states:

> § *4.3, [Comment] c. Revocation intending to make a replacement will*. . . If the testator never had a plan to make a replacement will, the doctrine of ineffective revocation is inapplicable. Similarly, if the testator intended to make a replacement will but never took steps to complete the plan, the doctrine cannot be applied. The testator's uncompleted plan to make a replacement will provides no benchmark against which to gauge whether the testator's probable intention would be to have the revocation stand or fall. The revocation stands. . . .
>
> Between an ineffective attempt to make a replacement will . . . and a wholly uncompleted plan to make a replacement will . . . is an intermediate case . . . in which the testator's actual intention, though not embodied in a defectively executed replacement will, is sufficiently provable to use as a benchmark against which to gauge whether or not the testator's probable intention would have been for the revocation to prevail.

In Trust Estate of Daoang, 953 P.2d 959 (Haw. 1998), the court held that the settlor of a revocable trust had "sufficiently manifested his intent to amend the trust" by "signing a letter sent by his attorney to confirm [the settlor's] plans to amend" the trust, "even assuming the subsequent execution of a more formal document was contemplated."

Ineffective Alterations. Testators sometimes attempt to alter their wills by marking them up—by crossing out attested language and inserting unattested substitute language. The purpose is usually to alter dispositions of property or designations of persons.

Schneider v. Harrington

71 N.E.2d 242 (Mass. 1947)

[Letitia Bliss's will provided that her entire estate was to be disposed of in the following manner:

> 1. To my niece Phyllis H. Schneider, of 2368 Washington Avenue Bronx, New York, one third (1/3).
>
> 2. One third (1/3) to my sister, Margaret J. Sugarman, of 177 West 95th Street New York City, New York.

3. One third (1/3) to my sister, Amy E. Harrington, of New York City, New York.

The will contained no residuary clause, but it did contain a provision stating: "I am intentionally omitting my other sisters and brothers for I feel that they are well taken care of." At some time after the execution of the will, Letitia used a pencil to cross out all of clause 3 and the figures "1/3" in clauses 1 and 2. She then inserted by pencil the figures ½ in clauses 1 and 2, leaving uncancelled in these clauses the words "one third."

Letitia left no husband or children. Her heirs were four sisters and twenty-two nieces and nephews.]

SPALDING, J. . . . The judge of probate entered a decree allowing the will with the exception of certain portions which had been crossed out by the testatrix. The case comes here on the appeal of Amy E. Harrington, a sister of the testatrix, who took one third of the estate under the will as executed, but nothing under the will as allowed. . . .

The decree of the court below provided that the will was to be allowed except for clause 3 and the figures "1/3" in clauses 1 and 2; it also provided that the figures "½" which had been substituted for the figures "1/3" in clauses 1 and 2 were not part of the will.

By the law of this Commonwealth a will can be revoked "By burning, tearing, cancelling or obliterating it with the intention of revoking it, by the testator himself or by a person in his presence and by his direction." G.L.(Ter.Ed.) c. 191, § 8. In the case before us there was clearly a "cancelling" of the third clause of the will which, if done with the requisite revocatory intent, would constitute a revocation pro tanto; a part of a will may be canceled, leaving the rest in full force. For reasons that will presently appear, it is not necessary to decide whether the canceling of the figures "1/3" in the first and second clauses, leaving the words "one third" intact, would, if coupled with the necessary intent, effect a revocation of the legacies therein provided.

The appellant argues that the cancellation of clause 3 was made conditional on the validity of the attempted substitutions in clauses 1 and 2, and that since these failed for want of proper authentication there was no revocation. The doctrine of conditional revocation (frequently, but less aptly, called dependent relative revocation) is recognized in this Commonwealth. In Sanderson v. Norcross, 242 Mass. 43, 45, 136 N.E. 170, 171, it was said, "The doctrine is widely established that a revocation of a valid will, which is so intimately connected with the making of another will as to show a clear intent that the revocation of the old is made conditional upon the validity of the new, fails to become operative if the new will is void as a testamentary disposition for want of proper execution. Revocation in its last analysis is a question of intent. A revocation grounded on supposed facts, which turn out not to exist, falls when the foundation falls." After recognizing the doctrine as part of our law, the court went on to say that "It is a principle to be applied with caution. . . . Courts have no power to reform wills. . . . Omissions cannot be supplied. . . . The only means for ascertaining the intent of the testator are the words written and the acts done by him." 242 Mass. at pages 45, 46, 136 N.E. at page 172. It has been held on the authority of Sanderson v. Norcross that where a testator cancels or obliterates portions of his will in order to substitute different provisions, and in such a way as to show a clear intent that the revocation is conditional on the validity of the substitution, and the substitution fails for want of proper authentication, the will stands as originally drawn. Thus in Walter v. Walter, 301 Mass. 289, 17 N.E.2d 199, the testatrix, after her will had been executed, obliterated the description of real estate in two devises, and then interlined different descriptions which were not properly authenticated. The decree of the Probate Court allowed the will, but disallowed the devises which had been obliterated. On appeal, this court reversed the decree, holding that the obliterations when considered with the interlineations disclosed an intent on the part of the testatrix to revoke only if the interlineations were valid as a substitute, and that parol evidence was admissible to prove the original wording of the obliterated clauses.

We think that the principle discussed above is applicable here. It is clear that the cancellations and the substitutions were inextricably linked together as parts of one transaction; and it is evident that the testatrix intended the cancellations to be effective only if the substitutions were valid. But the substitutions, inasmuch as they were not authenticated by a new attestation as required by statute, were invalid. Consequently the cancellations never became operative. Additional support for this conclusion, if any is needed, may be found in the fact that the will contained no residuary clause, and if the decree entered in the court below should stand there would be a partial intestacy—a result which we think the testatrix did not intend. It follows that the decree of the Probate Court is reversed, and a new decree is to be entered allowing the will as worded prior to the attempted changes. . . .

So ordered.

Notes, Question, and Problem

1. *Harmless-error Rule?* Under the harmless-error rule of the Restatement 3d of Property or the UPC § 2-503, could the words written on the will be given effect?[23]

---

23. Under conventional law, of course, the testator's actual intention couldn't be carried out because the alterations were unattested. Even under conventional law, however, the case would be open to proof that the will was in the altered form at the time of execution. See Cravens'

2. *Attempted Reduction of the Devised Amount.* In Ruel v. Hardy, 6 A.2d 753 (N.H. 1939), a clause of Ethel Smith's will provided: "To Frank . . . , and to Walter . . . and . . . Lilla . . . , I give five hundred dollars to each one." After execution, in an unattested act, Ethel struck out "five" and inserted "one." The residuary devisee was her husband, Benjamin. The court found dependent relative revocation inapplicable and held that legacies to Frank, Walter, and Lilla were revoked.

> A reduction of eighty per cent of the legacy tends more to show a preference on her part that her legatees should have nothing rather than that they should have the full sum . . . .

Accord Estate of Lyles, 615 So. 2d 1186 (Miss. 1993).

3. *Problem.* As originally executed, G's attested will devised $10,000 to her brother, A, and $20,000 to her brother, B. After G's death, G's will was found with "$10,000" crossed out and the figure "$12,000" written in above it and with "$20,000" crossed out and the figure "$3,000" written in above it. All of the alterations were in G's handwriting. What result?

Revocation Based on a Mistake of Fact or Law. Although most dependent relative revocation cases involve an attempt to achieve a dispositive objective that fails under applicable law, the category is not restricted to such situations. Consider how the doctrine of dependent relative revocation might apply to the following problems.

Problems

1. G, having been informed that her favorite nephew, N, a soldier, had been killed in combat, wrote across a $10,000 devise to him in her will the words "Canceled." Extrinsic evidence establishes that G revoked the devise because she thought N had died in combat. Shortly after G's death, N, who had not died in combat but had been taken prisoner of war, was released. What result? Compare Campbell v. French, 30 Eng. Rep. 1033 (Ch. 1797); Gillespie v. Gillespie, 126 A. 744 (N.J. Eq. 1924), with Witt v. Rosen, 765 S.W.2d 956 (Ark. 1989); Salmonski's Estate, 238 P.2d 966 (Cal. 1951).

2. G's will contains a $10,000 devise to his niece, N. G executed a codicil stating that he revoked the devise to N because G had made substantial gifts to

---

Estate, 242 P.2d 135 (Okla. 1952); and cases collected in Annot., Interlineations and Changes Appearing on Face of Will, 34 A.L.R.2d 619, 630 (1954). Recall also that there is authority holding that the decedent can validly alter a *holographic* will by writing changes thereon without re-signing it. See supra p. 316.

N. N can establish that G did not give her substantial gifts. See Witt v. Rosen, 765 S.W.2d 956 (Ark. 1989); Giddings v. Giddings, 32 A. 334 (Conn. 1894); Mendinhall's Appeal, 124 Pa. 387 (1889); Cummins's Estate, 37 Pa. Super. 580 (1908). Compare Whitlock v. Vaun, 38 Ga. 562 (1867); McCarthy v. Dillon, [1964] I.R. 259 (1963), with Goddard v. Overend, [1911] 1 I.R. 469 (Ch.).

Express Revocation by Subsequent Instrument. Can dependent relative revocation be applied if a will was *expressly* revoked in connection with an attempt to achieve a dispositive objective that fails under applicable law? Most courts have held that it can be. See, e.g., Linkins v. Protestant Episcopal Cathedral Foundation, 187 F.2d 357 (D.C. Cir. 1950); Kaufman's Estate, 155 P.2d 831 (Cal. 1945); La Croix v. Senecal, 99 A.2d 115 (Conn. 1953); Charleston Library Society v. Citizens & Southern Nat'l Bank, 20 S.E.2d 623 (S.C. 1942).

Crosby v. Alton Ochsner Medical Foundation, 276 So. 2d 661 (Miss. 1973) (5-to-4 decision), is one of the few cases in which the court refused to apply the doctrine. Hollis Crosby died leaving a will that devised one-half of the residue of his estate to his widow and the other half to the Alton Ochsner Medical Foundation. The devise to the Medical Foundation, having been made in a will executed within ninety days of Hollis's death, was void under the Mississippi mortmain statue. The will contained a clause expressly revoking all former wills.

Hollis's former will, executed more than ninety days prior to death, contained a similar devise to the Medical Foundation. The Medical Foundation argued that the doctrine of dependent relative revocation should be applied so as to render ineffectual the revocation of the devise in its favor in the prior will.

The court rejected the Medical Foundation's argument, saying in part:

> [In Hairston v. Hairston, 30 Miss. 276 (1855)], this Court . . . said: "[When] the will contains an express clause of revocation, . . . there is nothing from which it could be inferred that the testator intended only to revoke conditionally . . . . [I]t would be incompetent to introduce evidence to prove that the declaration was not designed to operate as an absolute, but only as a conditional revocation . . . ." (30 Miss. at 301-303). . . .
>
> We do not think that it can be maintained that *Hairston* was wrongly decided or that its results are detrimental to the public. In fact, we are of the opinion that the law announced therein is sound. A person has a right to make a will and so long as it is in conformity with the law, he or she may leave his or her property as desired. By the same token such person has the right to revoke a will for any reason he or she may have. Due to the construction we have placed on our revocation statute, the only way that a person may be sure that the revocation of a will is unequivocal and certain is by a declaration in writing either in another will

> or in a separate writing duly attested revoking the former will. When so revoked such a person is assured that after death no one will be heard to say that he or she did not intend to revoke the former will. We think this is a valuable right and should not be disturbed.

Is the Mississippi court's conclusion and reasoning persuasive? If not, how would you answer the court's point that a revocation that is unambiguously and unconditionally declared in a validly executed will cannot be rendered conditional by extrinsic evidence?

Partial Application of Dependent Relative Revocation. The court in Arrowsmith v. Mercantile-Safe Deposit & Trust Co., 545 A.2d 674 (Md. 1988), was asked to apply dependent relative revocation to only one will provision and to treat the rest of the will as revoked. George H. C. Arrowsmith died in 1983, leaving a will dated July 29, 1982. George's 1982 will expressly revoked all prior wills and exercised a testamentary power of appointment over some $7 million in assets of an irrevocable inter vivos trust created by his mother in 1953.

George's 1982 will did not contain a perpetuity saving clause, a device routinely used by lawyers to avoid violating the Rule Against Perpetuities. See infra Chapter 19, Part C. In the absence of the perpetuity saving clause, George's exercise of the power of appointment violated the Rule.

George had executed two prior wills, one in 1976 and the other in 1966. His 1976 will expressly revoked all prior wills and exercised his testamentary power of appointment in terms similar to those contained in the 1982 will. The 1976 will also failed to contain a perpetuity saving clause.

George's 1966 will exercised his testamentary power of appointment, but in terms quite dissimilar to the 1982 or 1976 wills. The 1966 will, however, contained a perpetuity saving clause.

The court was asked to apply dependent relative revocation to conclude that the revocation of the perpetuity saving clause in the 1966 will was conditioned upon the validity of the exercise of the power of appointment in the 1976 will and, in turn, in the 1982 will. The court declined to apply dependent relative revocation in this manner, saying:

> Plucking the perpetuities saving clause from the 1966 will and inserting it in the 1982 will is inconsistent with the theoretical justification for the doctrine. . . . [T]he doctrine's underlying theory of conditional revocation limits the relief which a court can grant. If a later will which expressly revokes earlier wills itself fails in whole or in part, the doctrine requires a court to decide whether the decedent would have preferred the prior will to the result under the later will, which may be partial invalidity or intestacy. . . . The doctrine . . . does not present a court with a menu. It is not the judicial function to select some provisions from column A and some provisions from column B in order to put together a valid will.

In contrast to *Arrowsmith*, the California Court of Appeal held in Estate of Anderson, 65 Cal. Rptr. 2d 307, 317 (Ct. App.), rev. denied (1997), that dependent relative revocation applied with regard to a provision in the testator's first will that was otherwise wholly revoked by her second will. As a result of an attorney error, the testator's second will failed to include a specific reference to a power of appointment that she had received under her husband's will. A valid exercise of the power depended on her will containing a specific reference to it. See infra Chapter 16, Part C. Extrinsic evidence established the testator's intent to exercise her power in the second will just as she had in article eighth of her first will. The court held that:

> On these facts, we conclude that a "question [has] arise[n] as to the effectiveness of the second instrument, . . . so that upon its failure to be operative for want of proper execution *or other cause*, the testator will be presumed to have intended the original instrument to stand *to the extent that the later proves ineffective*." (Estate of Salmonski, [38 Cal.2d 199, 212, 238 P.2d 966], italics added.) Because the second will did not effectively exercise the power of appointment, article eighth of the first will remained in effect under the doctrine of dependent relative revocation.

The result in *Anderson* is supported by Restatement 3d of Property § 4.3, comment e and illustration 18.

Internal Reference. See the discussion in Chapter 19 of UPC §§ 2-901 to -906, which incorporates the Uniform Statutory Rule Against Perpetuities (Uniform Rule) into the UPC. Generally speaking, the effect of the Uniform Rule is to insert a perpetuity saving clause into all trusts that contain a perpetuity violation. Had the *Arrowsmith* case been governed by the Uniform Rule, George's 1982 will would have been valid, and there would have been no reason to go into court to correct the mistaken omission of the perpetuity saving clause.

Chapter 6

Post-Execution Events Affecting Wills

THERE will always be some interval between the time when a will is executed and the time when it takes effect to transfer property. Sometimes the interval will be measured in decades. Older wills, sometimes called "stale" wills, are just as valid as "fresher" ones, but have the potentiality to do mischief because they are so out of date. A challenge for the estate planner is to draft a plan that can accommodate expected and unexpected changes in property and family circumstances. A challenge for the courts and legislatures is to develop rules and doctrines to respond to changes in a manner that is consistent with the testator's manifested estate plan. In this Chapter, we will study the law's response to changes in a testator's property and changes in the circumstances of a testator's devisees.

It is difficult to overemphasize the seemingly obvious point that many of these issues could—and should—be avoided by foresight and careful drafting. The doctrines studied in this Chapter operate as "default rules." They apply because, and only to the extent, the testator and the testator's attorney failed to address the issue in a will provision. As you study the cases, think about what type of will provision you would have advised the testator to have inserted when initially drafting the will or when reviewing the will in light of changed circumstances.

Formal Opinion 210 (March 15, 1941)[1]

Opinions on Professional Ethics 498 (ABA 1967)

An attorney may properly advise a client for whom he has drawn a will of the advisability of reexamining the will periodically and may from time to time send

1. The Canon referred to in this opinion is from the Canons of Professional Ethics, an antecedent of the Model Rules of Professional Conduct. Eds.

notices to the clients advising him of changes in law or fact which may defeat the client's testamentary purpose, unless the attorney has reason to believe that he has been supplanted by another attorney.

Canon Interpreted: Professional Ethics 27. A member calls attention to the effect on testamentary dispositions of subsequent changes in general economic conditions, of changes in the attitude or death of named fiduciaries in a will, of the removal of the testator to a different jurisdiction where different laws of descent may prevail, of changes in financial conditions, family relationship and kindred matters, and then inquires whether it is proper for the lawyer who drew the will to call attention of the testator from time to time to the importance of going over his will. . . .

The inquiry presents the question as to whether such action on the part of the lawyer is solicitation of legal employment and so to be condemned. Many events transpire between the date of making the will and the death of the testator. The legal significance of such occurrences are [sic] often of serious consequence, of which the testator may not be aware, and so the importance of calling the attention of the testator thereto is manifest.

It is our opinion that where the lawyer has no reason to believe that he has been supplanted by another lawyer, it is not only his right, but it might even be his duty to advise his client of any changes of fact or law which might defeat the client's testamentary purpose as expressed in the will.

Periodic notices might be sent to the client for whom a lawyer has drawn a will, suggesting that it might be wise for the client to reexamine his will to determine whether or not there has been any change in his situation requiring a modification of his will.

External Reference. For a discussion of a lawyer's duty, if any, to notify will clients of changes in the law that may require modifications of their wills, see Gerald P. Johnston, Legal Malpractice in Estate Planning—Perilous Times Ahead for the Practitioner, 67 Iowa L. Rev. 629, 655-58 (1982).

Classification of Devises. Many of the doctrines studied in this Chapter traditionally involve a two-stage analysis. The first stage is classifying the devise as one of four types of devises—specific, general, demonstrative, or residuary. The Restatement 3d of Property § 5.1 defines these classes as follows:

(1) A *specific devise* is a testamentary disposition of a specifically identified asset.

(2) A *general devise* is a testamentary disposition, usually of a specified amount of money or quantity of property, that is payable from the general assets of the estate.

(3) A *demonstrative devise* is a testamentary disposition, usually of a specified amount of money or quantity of property, that is primarily payable from a designated source, but is secondarily payable from the general assets of the estate to the extent that the primary source is insufficient.

(4) A *residuary devise* is a testamentary disposition of property of the testator's net probate estate not disposed by a specific, general, or demonstrative devise.

The second stage is to apply the doctrine based on the classification of the devise. In other words, the classification of the devise governs the legal outcome.

This two-stage analysis suggests that courts are involved in highly formalistic rule-making. Traditionally, this has been true, and to a great extent still is. The materials that follow, however, also show that courts and legislatures have now begun to erode that formalism by moving to a more generalized inquiry into intention.

PART A. POST-EXECUTION CHANGES IN THE ESTATE

1. Ademption Of Specific Devises By Extinction

Statutory References: *UPC §§ 2-606, 5-426*

Specific devises are normally used to pass on to particular relatives or friends property the testator holds specially dear. Often, these are items of tangible personal property—a particular piece of jewelry, the piano, a coin or stamp collection, a particular work of art. Also, a piece of real estate is sometimes specifically devised—the family farm, the family home, the vacation house, and so on. In addition, on occasion, testators devise specific financial assets, such as particular stocks or bonds or a savings account.

Although devises of specific financial assets sometimes prove troublesome, specific devises of tangible personal property or land do not, for the most part, raise many issues. Occasionally, though, the testator might give the piano or the diamond ring to the devisee in advance of death, might sell a particular painting and purchase another one in its place, or might sell the family home and move to another one. Also, as the population ages, more and more elderly testators eventually become incapacitated to some degree. As a testator's financial affairs are taken over by a guardian or conservator, or by an agent acting under a durable power of attorney, specifically devised property becomes more likely to be sold so that the proceeds can be used to pay for nursing care and associated expenses. Occasionally, also, specifically devised property is stolen in a burglary or destroyed in a fire. Finally, it is quite possible that a testator becomes annoyed with the devisee and disposes of the specifically devised property as a method of revoking the devise—revocation by act to the property, so to speak, as opposed to revocation by subsequent instrument or by revocatory act to the will.

Under the doctrine of ademption by extinction, a specific devise is adeemed—ineffective—if the testator no longer owns the specifically devised property at death. As Estate of Hume, below, shows, the generally accepted interpretation of the doctrine follows the so-called identity theory, which means that the court does not inquire into the reason why the specifically devised property is not found in the estate.

Dispositions by Guardians or Conservators. One type of situation in which the courts have been reluctant wholly to disregard the testator's intention arises where a guardian or conservator, acting on behalf of an incapacitated testator, sold or otherwise disposed of an item of specifically devised property.

In the leading case of Morse v. Converse, 113 A. 214 (N.H. 1921), the testator's guardian withdrew a savings bank deposit that had been specifically devised, and used part of the proceeds to buy a Liberty bond, which remained in the estate at the testator's death. The court awarded the Liberty bond to the devisee. As for the part of the withdrawal that had been spent by the guardian, the court held that the devisee had no claim, since "nothing has come to the executor's hands upon which the will can operate." The tendency of the guardianship cases has been in favor of the New Hampshire view,[2] and a few states have adopted that view by statute, so as to provide that the specific devisee "becomes entitled to receive any remaining money or other property."[3]

In Estate of Mason, 397 P.2d 1005 (Cal. 1965), the California Supreme Court refused to limit the devisee to the traceable proceeds of the sale. Several years after the testator had executed a will specifically devising her home to Fairbank, she became mentally incompetent and a guardian of her estate was appointed. The guardian sold the home for $21,000, deposited the proceeds into a special account, and spent all but $556 for the support of the testator. The court held that the amount spent should be paid to Fairbank out of the residuary

---

2. See, e.g., Stake v. Cole 133 N.W.2d 714 (Iowa 1965); Estate of Graham 533 P.2d 1318 (Kan. 1975); Walsh v. Gillespie 154 N.E.2d 906 (Mass. 1959); Estate of Warren 344 S.E.2d 795 (N.C. Ct. App. 1986); Estate of Swoyer, 439 N.W.2d 823 (S.D. 1989). Cases are collected in Annots., Ademption or Revocation of Specific Devise or Bequest by Guardian, Committee, Conservator, or Trustee of Mentally or Physically Incompetent Testator, 84 A.L.R.4th 462 (1991); Ademption or Revocation of Specific Devise or Bequest by Guardian, Committee, or Conservator of Mentally or Physically Incompetent Testator, 51 A.L.R.2d 770 (1957).

3. See, e.g., N.Y. Est. Powers & Trust Law § 3-4.4 (this is an amended version of an earlier statute that reversed the position adopted by the Court of Appeals in Ireland's Estate, 177 N.E. 405 (N.Y. 1931), a case in opposition to Morse v. Converse).

estate.[4] Any other result, Justice Traynor said, "would allow the guardian to destroy his ward's testamentary plan even though the guardian was acting to protect the ward's economic interests."

The UPC explicitly adopts a guardianship exception, adopting the Estate of Mason, rather then Morse v. Converse, view about the amount to which the devisee is entitled. UPC § 2-606(b). See also UPC § 5-426 (directing the conservator to take into account the protected person's estate plan when making investment and expenditure decisions and authorizing the conservator to examine the will).

Dispositions by Attorneys-in-fact Acting Under Durable Powers of Attorney. In recent practice, durable powers of attorney—powers of attorney that are not automatically revoked when the principal becomes mentally incompetent—have become popular substitutes for guardianships or conservatorships. See infra Chapter 8, Part C. At least one court has expressly extended the guardianship exception to dispositions made under authority of durable powers. See Estate of Graham, 533 P.2d 1318 (Kan. 1975). See also Hobin v. O'Donnell 451 N.E.2d 30 (Ill. App. Ct. 1983) ("[A]demption requires some act of the testator indicative of an intention to revoke. . . . If someone other than the decedent sold the stock without permission or if the decedent was incapable of forming the requisite intent, then there was no ademption."); Estate of Warren, 344 S.E.2d 795 (N.C. Ct. App. 1986); Annot., Ademption or Revocation of Specific Devise or Bequest by Guardian, Committee, Conservator, or Trustee of Mentally or Physically Incompetent Testator, 84 A.L.R.4th 462 (1991). But see Estate of Hegel, 668 N.E.2d 474 (Ohio 1996) (refusing to extend statutory exception for sales by "guardians" to a sale by an agent under a durable power of attorney).

UPC § 2-606(b) addresses this problem by explicitly extending the guardianship exception to sales by an agent on behalf of an incapacitated testator under a durable power. To ease the administrative burden of a post-death inquiry into the mental state of the testator, § 2-606(e) establishes a rebuttable presumption that a sale or other disposition by an agent is on behalf of a testator who is incapacitated.

Estate of Hume

984 S.W.2d 602 (Tenn. 1999)

ANDERSON, Chief Justice. We granted this appeal to determine whether the probate rule of ademption by extinction applies to the specific bequest of a house, where the house is sold at foreclosure before the testator's death and sales proceeds representing the testator's interest are identifiable after his death.

---

4. Accord, e.g., 20 Pa. Cons. Stat. Ann. § 2541(16.1), construed in Estate of Fox, 431 A.2d 1008 (Pa. 1981).

The trial court, emphasizing the testator's intent as reflected by the will, concluded that the bequest had not been adeemed because there were proceeds remaining from the foreclosure sale. The foreclosure sale proceeds were ordered to be distributed to the beneficiary of the specific bequest. The Court of Appeals affirmed.

After our review of the record and applicable authority, we conclude that the foreclosure of the house prior to the testator's death resulted in an ademption by extinction of the specific bequest and that the foreclosure sale proceeds should have been distributed to the residuary beneficiary of the estate. Accordingly, we reverse the judgment of the Court of Appeals and remand the case to the trial court for further proceedings.

Background. Foster Hume, III, a licensed attorney, executed a valid holographic will dated August 1, 1990. In addition to other bequests, Hume specifically devised his house in Atlanta to his niece, Meredith Klank ("Klank"), stating in his will, "my Atl. House to . . . Meredith. (Clank [sic] I believe)." Hume named the appellant, University of the South ("University"), residuary beneficiary.

Hume purchased the Atlanta house in 1986, subject to a mortgage in favor of NationsBanc. Hume faithfully made his mortgage payments to NationsBanc until the late summer of 1991. Because of Hume's delinquency, NationsBanc sold the house at foreclosure before Hume's death on November 12, 1991.

The surplus proceeds of $55,745.07, after satisfying the mortgage debt, were paid to the estate's Executrix, who took the position that the Atlanta house had been adeemed and that the proceeds should be paid to the University, the residuary beneficiary, and not to Klank, the beneficiary of the specific bequest. Klank, claiming the right to the surplus proceeds, filed an exception to the Executrix's final accounting in Davidson County Probate Court. The Executrix moved to have her final accounting approved.

The Davidson County Probate Court denied the Executrix's motion and ordered that the proceeds be paid to Klank. Relying on the lack of proof in the record to indicate Hume had actual knowledge of the foreclosure proceeding, the court reasoned that Hume had not voluntarily parted with his house and thus must have intended Klank to receive it, as indicated by the will.

The Court of Appeals affirmed the trial court, finding that an ademption by extinction had not occurred in this case for two main reasons. First, the court noted that "Testator's only contribution to the foreclosure was his inability or failure to pay the debt which cannot be presumed to be a voluntary act; and there is no evidence that it was deliberate or voluntary." Second, the Court of Appeals distinguished between cases in which the foreclosure sale was insufficient to satisfy the debt, where an ademption by extinction would occur, and cases in which the foreclosure sale resulted in surplus proceeds, where an ademption by extinction would not occur.

We granted the University's application for permission to appeal.

Analysis. The only issue presented for our review, whether the bequest of the Atlanta house has been adeemed by extinction, is purely a question of law; thus, our review is de novo with no presumption of correctness given the judgments of either the trial court or the Court of Appeals.

The parties dispute whether the specific bequest was adeemed by the foreclosure sale and whether the testator's intent is relevant to the issue. Noting that the specific bequest at issue involves Hume's "Atl[anta] house," not Hume's interest in the house, the University argues that the bequest to Klank was adeemed by the foreclosure sale and that even if Hume's intent could be discerned from the record, that intent is irrelevant. Conversely, Klank argues both that the Testator's intention is relevant to the present case and that the Testator's will transferred his interest in the house, which at the time of his death was represented by the proceeds remaining after the foreclosure sale.

We begin our analysis by noting that ademption is generally defined as "the extinction, alienation, withdrawal, or satisfaction of the legacy by some act of the testator by which an intention to revoke is indicated: the doing of some act with regard to the subject-matter which interferes with the operation of the will." E.g., American Trust & Banking Co. v. Balfour, 138 Tenn. 385, 198 S.W. 70, 71 (Tenn.1917). Implicit in Tennessee ademption cases is the notion that the two parts of this definition each respectively correspond to the two types of ademption recognized in Tennessee, ademption by satisfaction and ademption by extinction. See, e.g., Rhodes v. Kebke, 179 Tenn. 480, 167 S.W.2d 345 (1943) (ademption by satisfaction case). The present case involves the issue of ademption by extinction.

Ademption by extinction results because of "the doing of some act with regard to the subject-matter which interferes with the operation of the will." *Balfour*, 198 S.W. at 71. In these cases:

> [t]he rule [of ademption by extinction] prevails without regard to the intention of the testator or the hardship of the case, and is predicated upon the principle that the subject of the gift is annihilated or its condition so altered that nothing remains to which the terms of the bequest can apply.

Wiggins v. Cheatham, 143 Tenn. 406, 225 S.W. 1040, 1041 (1920) (emphasis added) (citation omitted). In other words, it only matters that the subject of the specific bequest no longer exists because of "the doing of some act;" it is irrelevant who or what initiates "the doing." *Balfour*, 198 S.W. at 71.

Ademption by satisfaction, on the other hand, refers to the situation in which the testator "gives in his lifetime to a legatee what he had left him in his will."

Rhodes, 167 S.W.2d at 348. In ademption by satisfaction cases, the testator deals with the legatee in such a way so as to result in an "extinction, alienation, withdrawal, or satisfaction of the legacy" during the testator's lifetime. *Balfour*, 198 S.W. at 71. In such cases, the testator's intent is relevant to determine whether the testator's action regarding the legatee "amounts to a withdrawal of the gift from the operation of the will." *Rhodes*, 167 S.W.2d at 348. Accordingly, a primary distinction between ademption by satisfaction cases and ademption by extinction cases is that the intent of the testator is relevant to the former but not to the latter, and that the act of extinction may be the action of anyone.

This rule that the intent of the testator is irrelevant in ademption by extinction cases is in harmony with the modern holdings found in the majority of states. E.g., McGee v. McGee, 122 R.I. 837, 413 A.2d 72 (R.I. 1980). In *McGee*, the Rhode Island Supreme Court defines the rule and persuasively analyzes the policy supporting it. The *McGee* court stated with respect to the "in specie" test:

> This test focuses on two questions only: (1) whether the gift is a specific legacy and, if it is, (2) whether it is found in the estate at the time of the testator's death. The extinction of the property bequeathed works an ademption regardless of the testator's intent.
>
> . . .
>
> Moreover, under the principles enunciated by Lord Thurlow . . . only the fact of change or extinction, not the reason for the change or extinction, is truly relevant. The vast majority of jurisdictions adhere to this rule. This "in specie" theory of ademption, although it may occasionally result in a failure to effectuate the actual intent of a testator, has many advantages. Significant among these advantages is simplicity of application, as opposed to ad hoc determination of intent from extrinsic evidence in each particular case. This theory further has the advantages of stability, uniformity, and predictability.

Id. at 76-77 (citations omitted).

The rule of ademption by extinction has been applied in several Tennessee cases similar to the case before us. For example, in Ford v. Cottrell, 141 Tenn. 169, 207 S.W. 734 (Tenn.1918), the testator specifically bequeathed certain interests in a house which he owned at the time he executed his will. Prior to testator's death, he sold the house. This Court found that "[a]t the death of the [testator] the specific property in question has [sic] been sold . . . and was not, therefore, in existence." Id. at 737. We held that the specific bequest had been adeemed or extinguished and that the proceeds from the sale of the property during testator's lifetime formed part of the general estate. Id.

Just a year earlier, in *Balfour*, this Court announced "the rule that a specific legacy is adeemed when there has been a material alteration or change in the subject-matter, and that the property into which it was converted in such change cannot be substituted as or for the specific bequest." Id. at 71. The testator bequeathed life insurance policy proceeds to his daughter. Prior to his death, the testator collected the cash surrender values of the policies which he later invested in real estate mortgage notes. Applying the rule, this Court held that the specific bequest of the life insurance policy proceeds had been adeemed. Id.

Applying the foregoing rule, we conclude that the specific bequest of the Atlanta property was adeemed in its entirety by the foreclosure sale regardless of Hume's presumed intentions. Much like the specific bequest in *Ford*, at Hume's death, "the specific property in question ha[d] been sold . . . and [i]s not, therefore, in existence." Id. at 737. The only difference between the sale in *Ford* and the sale in the present case is the identity of the seller. It is of no significance that a third party and not Hume initiated the sale in the present case because, as previously stated, the rule of ademption by extinction applies without regard to the testator's intentions. Thus, the foreclosure sale constituted "the doing of some act with regard to the subject-matter which interferes with the operation of the will." *Balfour*, 198 S.W. at 71. Accordingly, in our view, the foreclosure sale prior to Hume's death adeemed the specific bequest of the house.

We further conclude that the proceeds cannot be substituted for the specific bequest of the house because "a specific legacy is adeemed when there has been a material alteration or change in the subject-matter, and . . . the property into which it was converted in such change cannot be substituted as or for the specific bequest." *Balfour* 198 S.W. at 71. The change in form involved in this case is strikingly similar to the change in form which resulted in an ademption by extinction in *Ford*. Just as the proceeds resulting from the sale of the house in *Ford* formed part of the general estate, Id. at 737, so do the proceeds resulting from the sale of the house in the present case. Accordingly, we hold that the foreclosure sale resulted in such a "material alteration" to the subject matter of the specific bequest so that the proceeds "cannot be substituted as or for the specific bequest." *Balfour*, 198 S.W. at 71.

Conclusion. We conclude that the testator's intent is irrelevant in deciding the question of whether a specific bequest has been adeemed by extinction. We further conclude that a foreclosure sale so alters the form of the specific bequest of a house that an ademption by extinction results regardless of whether identifiable proceeds remain from the foreclosure sale. We therefore reverse the judgments of the trial court and the Court of Appeals and remand to the trial court for further proceedings. Costs of this appeal are taxed to the appellee.

DROWOTA, HOLDER, and BARKER, JJ., concur.

BIRCH, J., not participating.

Notes and Questions

1. *The Identity Theory vs. The Intent Theory. Hume* is a rather stark example of the application of the rule of Ashburner v. Macguire. That rule is sometimes referred to as the "identity" theory of ademption, in contrast to the "intent" theory. According to the identity theory, ademption depends solely upon whether the subject matter of a specific devise exists as part of the testator's estate at death, and the testator's intent concerning the continued validity of the devise is irrelevant. According to the intent theory, ademption depends upon the testator's subjective intent, determined on a case-by-case basis. What reasons do you suppose have led courts, in an area of law seemingly dedicated to carrying out the testator's intent, to adopt a rule that disregards intent? See John C. Paulus, Ademption by Extinction: Smiting Lord Thurlow's Ghost, 2 Tex. Tech. L. Rev. 195 (1971); John C. Paulus, Special and General Legacies of Securities—Whither Testator's Intent, 43 Iowa L. Rev. 467 (1958).

3. *Adoptions of the Intent Theory.* Although the identity theory of Ashburner v. Macguire has been generally accepted in this country, some courts have recently departed from that approach. See, e.g., White v. McCammant, 182 N.W.2d 147 (Iowa 1970); Wachovia Bank & Trust Co. v. Ketchum 333 S.E.2d 542 (N.C. Ct. App. 1985); Estate of Austin, 169 Cal. Rptr. 648 (Cal. Ct. App. 1980).

The Restatement 3d of Property also adopts the intent theory, placing the burden of proof on the devisee to show that failure of the devise would be inconsistent with the testator's intent:

> *§ 5.2 Failure ("Ademption") of Specific Devises by Extinction*
>
> (a) If specifically devised property, in its original or in a changed form, is in the testator's estate at death, the devisee is entitled to the specifically devised property.
>
> (b) If specifically devised property is not in the testator's estate at death, the devisee is entitled to any proceeds remaining unpaid at death of (i) any sale, (ii) any condemnation award, or (iii) any insurance on or other recovery for damage to or loss of the property.
>
> (c) Subject to subsection (b), if specifically devised property is not in the testator's estate at death, the specific devise fails unless failure of the devise would be inconsistent with the testator's intent.

UPC § 2-606(a)(6) also adopts the intent theory, placing on the devisee the burden of showing by clear and convincing evidence that "ademption would be inconsistent with the testator's manifested plan of distribution or that at the time the will was made, the date of disposition, or otherwise, the testator did not intend that the devise adeem." How would a court have decided *Hume* if subsection (a)(6) had applied? At least one non-UPC statute expressly adopts an intent approach. See Ky. Rev. Stat. § 394.360.

Avoidance of the Identity Theory. Even in jurisdictions that nominally follow the identity theory, there is no shortage of cases that find one way or another of effectuating intent. Three of the most common avoidance techniques are described below.

Reclassification of the devise. The doctrine of ademption by extinction applies only to specific devises. Especially in the case of devises of financial assets, the courts have exercised discretion in classifying the devises as specific or general. For example, in Will of Blomdahl, 257 N.W. 152 (Wis. 1934), the testatrix' will devised "one hundred (100) shares of the common stock of the Ohio Oil Company to Mr. Fred T. Woodford" and "one hundred (100) shares of the common stock of the Ohio Oil Company to the First Church of Christ Scientist, of Milwaukee, Wisconsin." The evidence indicated that the testatrix owned 200 shares of the common stock of the Ohio Oil Company at the time the will was executed, but not at the time of her death.

The court held the devises to be general and, therefore, not adeemed, saying in part:

> The language used by the testatrix in framing her bequest, when read by itself, clearly carries a presumption that she intended, upon her death, to provide the named legatees each with 100 shares of the Ohio Oil Company common stock. If that language in the will is read in connection with the fact that she owned, at the time of the execution of the will, 200 shares of that stock, it might reasonably give rise to the presumption that she was giving away the stock then in her possession. But will such a presumption, if acted upon, carry out the intention of the testatrix? In order to avoid the problematical as far as possible, and as an aid to the rules of law which now apply to the interpretation and construction of wills, we hold that words specifically identifying the property and indicative of possession are necessary in the making of a specific bequest. . . .
>
> It is a generally accepted rule that where the language of the will is clear and unambiguous, it must control and that rule must prevail in this instance. The gift of a certain number of shares of stock without words of identification and possession is a general legacy. The absence of such words in these particular bequests brings this will within the rule accepted by this court and they must be held to be general bequests.

But see, e.g., First Nat'l Bank v. Perkins Inst. for the Blind, 176 N.E. 532 (Mass. 1931) (a devise of "all of my stock in . . . Standard Oil Company of New Jersey" was held specific and adeemed, where the stock had been called during the testator's lifetime).

When courts find a devise similar to the one in *Blomdahl* to be general, a question arises whether the personal representative is required to purchase for the devisee an asset of the sort described in the will. Some courts have given the devisee an option to take the value of the asset in cash or to have the asset purchased on his or her behalf. See Annot., Right of General Legatee of Stocks, Bonds, or Other Securities, Where Testator Owns at Time of Death None Such as Are Described in Will or less than Bequeathed, 22 A.L.R.2d 457, 464-67 (1952).

Courts have also avoided ademption by classifying the devise as demonstrative rather than specific. See, e.g., Lavender v. Cooper, 285 S.E.2d 528 (Ga. 1982); Smith v. Estate of Peters, 741 P.2d 1172 (Alaska 1987).

Change in form. Courts sometimes avoid ademption of a specific devise by holding that, although the subject matter of the devise is not in the estate in its original form, it is in the estate in a changed form. In Goode v. Reynolds, 271 S.W. 600 (Ky. 1925), the testator's will made a specific devise to Reynolds of five shares of stock in the Third National Bank of Lexington. During the testator's lifetime, this bank consolidated with another bank in Lexington and, in place of his original five shares, the testator received five shares of stock in the consolidated bank, and also five shares of stock in a realty company organized to take over certain real estate holdings of the old Third National Bank that did not go into the consolidation.

In holding that these new shares were in the estate at death and that they went to Reynolds, the court said, in part:

> In 40 Cyc. 1921, we find:
>
> > A change in the form of a security bequeathed does not necessarily work an ademption. So there is no ademption where notes bequeathed are renewed, where stock bequeathed is exchanged for notes of the company, where stock in a consolidated corporation is accepted by testator in lieu of stock in a component corporation which he had bequeathed or where a state bank, stock in which has been bequeathed, is changed to a national bank.
>
> We believe the rule laid down by these authorities to be the correct one. The likeness of the new shares to the old is more important than their differences. Applying this rule, we think it plain that Miss Reynolds is entitled to the securities given in the consolidation for the securities surrendered.

Accord Stenkamp v. Stenkamp, 723 P.2d 336 (Or. Ct. App. 1986); UPC § 2-606(a)(5).

Ademption and the "time-of-death" construction technique. As an initial matter, under both the identity and intent theories of ademption, property that matches the testator's description normally will pass to the devisee whether or not it was the identical property that the testator owned at the time of execution. As stated in Paulus, 2 Tex. Tech. L. Rev., supra p. 358, at 206:

> Although it is commonly stated that "a will speaks at the death of the testator," normal rules of construction demand that the meaning of the words used will be determined in reference to the situation in which the testator finds himself when he executes the will. "The language of a will is to be construed in light of circumstances existing when the will is written; the will operates, however, upon the property existing when death occurs." From an ademption-prevention standpoint, however, it is often helpful to assume that the "words were spoken at death." The will is ambulatory and the testator's lack of revocation or modification suggests that he approves the language of the will in reference to the circumstances that exist at his death.

As indicated, courts sometimes use this time-of-death construction technique to avoid ademption. For example, in Milton v. Milton, 10 So.2d 175 (Miss. 1942), a devise of "my home place" was held applicable to the house and lot the testator owned at death, even though they were not the same assets owned when the will was executed.

The time-of-death construction technique applies to specific devises of securities as well as to devises of other kinds of property. Even if, after executing a will making a specific devise of securities, the testator sold the securities and later purchased new securities that fit the description of the will, there will normally be no ademption. In Estate of Russell, 521 A.2d 677 (Me. 1987), a devise of "my shares in the Putnam High Yield Trust" was held to pass to the named devisee all 1,527 shares in the fund held by the estate at death, notwithstanding that the testator purchased 610 of those shares after executing the will.[5]

EXTERNAL REFERENCES. Gregory S. Alexander, Ademption and the Domain of Formality in Wills Law, 55 Alb. L. Rev. 1067 (1992); Mary Kay Lundwall, The Case Against the Ademption by Extinction Rule: A Proposal for Reform, 29 Gonzaga L. Rev. 105 (1993/94).

---

5. The time-of-death construction technique originated in the Wills Act of 1837. Early common law allowed a testator to dispose of all his or her personal property owned at death but not land acquired after the will was executed. The 1837 Wills Act changed the old rule as to land by permitting a person to devise "all real estate and all personal estate which he shall be entitled to, either at law or in equity, at the time of his death." To make sure that the courts would not defeat the new rule, another section of the Act provided that a will shall be construed, with reference to the estate, to speak "as if it had been executed immediately before the death of the testator, unless a contrary intention shall appear by the will."

The old rule as to after-acquired land has been eliminated everywhere in this country, in most states by statute. See, e.g., UPC § 2-602.

2. Accessions and Accretions

Statutory Reference: *UPC § 2-605*

What rights does a devisee have to assets that were produced by a devised asset after execution of the will? This is a matter of "accessions" or "accretions." In most situations, the choice is between awarding the product to the devisee of the underlying asset or awarding it to the residuary devisees. Accession questions can involve many forms of wealth, including corporate stock, mortgages, promissory notes, oil and gas leases, and cultivated farm land.

In general, courts have held that specific devises transfer that specific asset together with accessions and accretions occurring *after the testator's death.* Thus, for example, rent becoming due after the testator's death goes to the devisee of the land. See Atkinson on Wills § 135, at 750-51. Specific devises do not bear interest, strictly speaking. If the specifically devised asset has not actually produced any income or interest, the devisee is not entitled to any interest. By contrast, general devises do bear interest, beginning ordinarily one year after the testator's death.

Specific devises of debts or obligations usually carry with them interest accrued but unpaid *at* the testator's death. Thus specific devises of mortgages or debts pass any accrued but uncollected interest to the devisees. See id. Similarly, courts have held that a specific devise of a bond passes to the devisee an overdue interest coupon that was attached to the bond at the testator's death. See id.

Post-Execution, Pre-Death Accessions and Accretions. What if the accession or accretion occurs after execution of the will but before death? It is well settled that collected interest on a specifically devised bond does not pass to the specific devisee even if the interest remained part of the testator's estate. The law has had more difficulty in analyzing the effect of post-execution accessions upon devises of corporate stock. This is especially so where the accession results from a corporate restructuring. Corporate restructuring of stock by means of stock splits or stock dividends may affect devises of the stock in fundamental ways, because they potentially alter the economic interests that will be received by the devisee.

Stock splits. A *stock split* occurs when a corporation amends its charter to increase the number of shares outstanding and issues these shares on a pro-rata basis to existing shareholders. For example, if a corporation has 1,000,000 shares of stock outstanding selling at $50 per share, a two-for-one stock split will increase the number of shares outstanding to 2,000,000. Existing shareholders will receive two shares for every share they own, but each share will now be worth only $25.

The traditional approach to resolving questions of stock accessions resulting from stock splits has been to pin the result on whether the devise is classified as specific or general. If the devise is classified as specific, then the virtually uniform result has been to give to the devisee the increase in the number of shares resulting from a stock split. If the devise is classified as general, the devisee does not receive the benefit of the stock split.

The former version of the UPC adhered to the traditional view concerning stock splits—that whether the devisee is entitled to the additional number of shares resulting from stock splits depends upon the specific-general distinction. Former UPC § 2-607. This approach has led to some interesting decisions on the classification of the devise at issue.

Fitch's Will, 118 N.Y.S.2d 234 (App. Div. 1952), illustrates how far some courts will go to allow the devisee of corporate shares to enjoy the advantage of any stock splits. A will contained a devise of 115 "shares of U.S. Steel Co. common stock." The testator owned 115 shares of U.S. Steel when the will was made, but later sold the stock and owned none at his death. After this sale, but before his death, United States Steel Corporation issued three shares of common stock in exchange for each share of the old stock. The court held that the devise was general, so that there was no ademption. The administrator was ordered to deliver to the devisee "three shares of common stock for each one stated in the will," on the theory that it was "the intent of the testator to bequeath Steel common stock equivalent to the stock that existed when he made his will." The court was not moved by the argument that this "in effect seems to regard the legacies as general legacies for the purpose of avoiding their loss by ademption, but . . . as specific legacies for the purpose of replacing the stock. . . ." Accord, e.g., McFerren's Estate, 76 A.2d 759, 22 A.L.R.2d 451 (Pa. 1950).

Watson v. Santalucia, below, illustrates how some recent courts have abandoned the specific-general distinction to determine who receives the benefits of stock splits.

Watson v. Santalucia

427 S.E.2d 466 (W. Va. 1993)

NEELY, J. The question before us is what happens when a stock splits immediately before the death of a testator, and the testator has left a specific number of shares to his heirs. Traditionally, we viewed such a question as turning on whether the bequest was "specific" or "general" and then applied the result thought to follow automatically from the chosen label. However, the problems created by the use of the distinction between "general" and "specific" legacies in the stock split situation far outweigh any advantages to be gained by relying on those classifications. Instead we adopt today the rule that, in the absence of anything manifesting a contrary intent, a legatee of stock is entitled to any additional shares received by a testator as the result of a stock split occurring in the interval between the execution of a will and the testator's death. Accordingly, we reverse the decision of the Circuit Court of Lewis County.

The facts are not disputed. Frank Cirigliano (testator) died testate on 15 May 1990. The testator's will, dated 30 June 1988, as modified by two codicils executed in February 1990, was admitted to probate on 21 May 1990. The appellants are John T. Law, Marino Paletti and Teresa Calabrese, each the legatee of 100 shares of stock in Citizens Bancshares, Inc. The appellees, plaintiffs below, Geraldine C. Watson and Virginia Paletti, are the co-executrices of the estate and the beneficiaries under the residuary clause of the testator's will.

On 30 June 1988, (as well on 27 February 1990 when the most recent codicil to the will was executed) the testator owned 2,000 shares of the capital stock of Citizens Bancshares, Inc. The following provisions are relevant to this case:

> FOURTH: I give and bequeath unto John T. Law 100 shares of the capital stock of Citizens Bancshares, Inc.
>
> FIFTH: I give and bequeath unto Marino Paletti 100 shares of the capital stock of Citizens Bancshares, Inc.
>
> SIXTH: I give and bequeath unto Teresa Calabrese 100 shares of the capital stock of Citizens Bancshares, Inc.. . . .
>
> NINTH: I hereby authorize, empower and direct the personal representatives of this, my Will, as soon after my death as my said personal representatives may consider it advantageous, to sell, convey and otherwise transfer and convert to money all my property and estate, real, personal and mixed, wheresoever situate, which at my death may not already be in the form of cash, except for and subject always to the provisions of Items 'Second' through 'Eighth', above, and any and all sales by my personal representatives, pursuant to the authority vested in said personal representatives by this item, may be made by my said personal representatives at private or public sale, at such time or times, at such place, or places, at such price or prices, and upon such terms and conditions as to cash or credit as may be fixed by my said personal representatives. . . .
>
> TWENTY-SEVENTH: I give and bequeath all of the rest, residue and remainder of my estate unto the following persons in the following proportions:
>
> Pasquale Cirigliano, my nephew, one-ninth (1/9th);
>
> Maria Cirigliano Covelli, my niece, one-ninth (1/9th);
>
> Angiolina Cirigliano, my niece, one-ninth (1/9th);
>
> Antonio Santalucia, my nephew, one-ninth (1/9th);
>
> Francesca Santalucia Petrocelli, my niece, one-ninth (1/9th);
>
> Teresina Santalucia, my niece, one-ninth (1/9th);
>
> Rosa Santalucia, my niece, one-ninth (1/9th);
>
> Pasquale Santalucia, my nephew, one-ninth (1/9th); and
>
> The children of Giuseppe Santalucia, my nephew, who are living at the time of my death, one-ninth (1/9th).

On 21 April 1990, the shareholders of Citizens Bancshares, Inc., at its regular annual meeting, caused a four-for-one split of the shares of the corporation. The par value of the stock was commensurately reduced from one dollar a share to twenty-five cents per share. This stock split became effective on 1 May 1990. On 15 May 1990, after a protracted illness that confined him to his home, Mr. Cirigliano died; at that time his 2,000 shares of stock in Citizens Bancshares, Inc., had become 8,000 shares as a result of the stock split.

On 11 December 1991, the Circuit Court of Lewis County entered its order that Mr. Law, Mr. Paletti and Ms. Calabrese are entitled only to the 100 shares mentioned in the will, as opposed to the same proportional interest in the bank, now represented by four hundred shares each, that they would have had if the testator had died fifteen days earlier. Mr. Law, Mr. Paletti and Ms. Calabrese appeal from that decision.

"The paramount principle in construing or giving effect to a will is that the intention of the testator prevails, unless it is contrary to some positive rule of law or principle of public policy." Syl. pt. 1, Farmers & Merchants Bank v. Farmers & Merchants Bank, 158 W.Va. 1012, 216 S.E.2d 769 (1975). However, in reaching his decision, the circuit court relied to a large extent on W.Va. Code 41-3-1 [1923], which states, in full:

A will shall be construed, with reference to the estate comprised in it, to speak and take effect as if it had been executed immediately before the death of the testator, *unless a contrary intention shall appear by the will.* [Emphasis added]

Code 41-3-1 [1923] is a codification of a common law rule. In construing similar statutes or the common law rule, most jurisdictions have concluded that this rule "relates to the effect and operation of the instrument, not to its construction." Egavian v. Egavian, 102 R.I. 740, 745, 232 A.2d 789, 792 (1967); Lee v. Foley, 224 Miss. 684, 689, 80 So.2d 765, 767 (1955). Indeed, a common sense reading of the "unless a contrary intention shall appear by will" exception to W.Va. Code 41-3-1 [1923] means that we need to determine the intent of the testator *before* this statute has any meaning. Weiss v. Soto, 142 W. Va. 783, 98 S.E.2d 727 (1957). Indeed, reference to W. Va. Code 41-3-1 [1923] in this situation merely serves to confuse the issue, not to clarify. Our mission is to follow our cardinal rule of will construction: We must determine the testator's intent.

Traditionally, most courts (including this Court) relied on the distinction between a "general" bequest and a "specific" bequest to determine to whom the shares of stock acquired in a split after the will was executed, but before the death of the testator, belonged: the named legatee or the residuary legatee. However, the general/specific distinction was not initially designed for use in this area, but only for purposes of ademption, abatement, or disposition of income earned on the principal of the bequest during administration of the estate.[6] Furthermore, most courts have found that relying on such a standard does not comport with the notion of effecting the testator's intent[.]

The two principal difficulties with the general versus specific classification approach are that it fails to consider the testator's intent with specific reference to the additional shares created by a stock split and that it also fails to recognize the basic nature of a stock split. Bostwick v. Hurstel, 364 Mass. 282, 287, 304 N.E.2d 186 (1973). We agree with the reasoning of the Bostwick court and adopt the rule that the distinction between a "specific" bequest and a "general" bequest is not applicable to a stock split.[7] A stock split is merely a bookkeeping adjustment on the part of the corporation; "it does not alter the pre-existing proportionate interest of any stockholder or increase the intrinsic value of his holding or of the aggregate holdings of the other stockholders as they stood before. The new certificates simply increase the number of shares, with consequent dilution of the value of each share." Eisner v. Macomber, 252 U.S. 189, 211, 40 S.Ct. 189, 194 (1920). Furthermore, a stock split is an event over which a testator rarely has control or advance knowledge. Therefore, our question becomes: When the testator bequeathed 100 shares of stock in Citizens Bancshares, Inc., did he intend to give the control over the corporation that 100 shares provided at the time of execution, or did he intend to give exactly 100

---

6. An excellent summary of the appropriate use of the general/specific legacy distinction is found in Re Estate of Parker, 110 So.2d 498, 500-501 (Fla. App. 1959), cert. denied, 114 So.2d 3 (Fla. 1959):

> A specific legacy is a gift by will of property which is particularly designated and which is to be satisfied only by the receipt of the particular property described. Income received during administration on property specifically devised shall become property of the specific devisee. A general legacy or devise is one which does not direct the delivery of any particular property; is not limited to any particular asset; and may be satisfied out of the general assets belonging to the estate of the testator and not otherwise disposed of in the will. Income received on the property which is the subject of a general bequest passes to the residue of the estate.
>
> It was held at common law that if the particular property described in a specific bequest is disposed of by the testator during his life, or cannot be located, the bequest must fail or adeem. It was also the rule at common law that if the subject of a bequest was described in general terms, it was considered to be a general bequest and disposition by testator during his life of all or a part of the property so bequeathed did not create an ademption. In such case the personal representative was required to obtain and deliver to the legatee property satisfying the general description of the bequest. If, however, the property designated in the will for payment of charges against the estate was insufficient for that purpose, general bequests would abate prior to specific bequests.
>
> The technical distinction between general and specific bequests becomes important only when considering situations involving ademption, abatement or disposition of income earned on the subject of the bequest during administration.

7. We express no opinion today on the applicability of the "specific"/"general" distinction to other events that may occur between the execution of a will and the death of the testator, such as dividend reinvestments or stock dividends; the issue is not before us.

shares, no matter what percentage of the corporation those shares represented at the time of his death?

In Cuppett v. Neilly, 143 W.Va. 845, 105 S.E.2d 548 (1958) (the only West Virginia case on point), this Court was presented with a situation where a woman left 100 shares of General Motors common stock to a legatee. General Motors then split its stock three-for-one two years after the testatrix executed her will, but two-and-a-half years before the testatrix died. After the split, the testatrix sold fifty of the shares and died owning 250 shares of General Motors common stock. The dispute was over whether the 150 shares of General Motors common stock that remained from the split would pass to the beneficiary of the stock bequest or to the residuary estate.

Although this Court could have relied on the intent of the testator to reach its decision, this Court instead relied on the general/specific bequest distinction. As we have seen above, however, reliance on this distinction is misplaced in the stock split situation. Therefore, to the extent that the Cuppett decision relied upon the general/specific bequest distinction to decide the distribution of the additional shares as a result of the stock split, it is overruled.

Without the general/specific fiction to rely on, we must now determine what this testator would have wanted done with the shares that accrued as a result of the stock split. A stock split is an occurrence that a testator has little reason to anticipate at the time he executes his will and one over which he has little or no control. Moreover, the intent of a testator in bequeathing stock rather than cash seems to imply that the testator intends to give a certain share of a corporation rather than a specific dollar value. The best way to effect the testator's intent, then, is to behave as if the stock split had never happened and to award to beneficiaries of specific stock bequests accretions as a result of stock splits between execution of the will and the death of the testator. Therefore, in the absence of anything manifesting a contrary intent, a legatee of stock is entitled to any additional shares received by a testator as the result of a stock split occurring in the interval between the execution of a will and the death of the testator. The result of this rule is that the interests are divided in the same manner as the testator intended; they are apportioned *as if the split had never occurred*.

In this case, we apply our presumption that the testator would intend that the same interests be given to the legatees of stock shares as if the split had never occurred. John T. Law, Marino Paletti and Teresa Calabrese, the legatees of 100 shares of stock in Citizens Bancshares, Inc. (each) in the will are to receive 400 shares each, with the balance of the stock passing, as per the will, to the residuary legatees.

Accordingly, the decision of the Circuit Court of Lewis County is reversed, and the case is remanded for further proceedings consistent with this opinion.

Reversed and remanded.

Notes

1. *Uniform Probate Code and Restatement 3d of Property*. UPC § 2-605 basically adopts the approach used in *Watson*. That approach is also now codified in Massachusetts, following the decision in Bostwick v. Hurstel, referred to in *Watson*. See Mass. Gen. Law c. 191, § 1A(3). The Restatement 3d of Property also adopts the *Watson* approach:

> § *5.3 Effect of Stock Splits, Stock Dividends, and Other Distributions on Devises of a Specified Number of Securities*. A devise of a specified number of securities carries with it any additional securities acquired by the testator after executing the will to the extent that the post-execution acquisitions resulted from the testator's ownership of the described securities.

2. *Stock Dividends*. A stock dividend is a distribution to existing shareholders of stock in lieu of a cash dividend. Usually, stock dividends are distributed from a corporation's own authorized but unissued shares. Sometimes, however, stock dividends are distributed from shares in the stock of other firms that the corporation owns. Courts have had difficulty determining who should receive shares obtained as a result of a stock dividend.

As a first step in examining this question, we need first to note the distinction that courts draw between increases in the market value of stocks and cash dividends. Suppose that a testator devises 100 shares of General Electric stock to A and the residue of her estate to B. At the time of execution, the shares were worth $5,000. Suppose further that General Electric had issued cash dividends to the testator totaling $1,000 between the time the testator executed the will and died and, at the time of the testator's death, the market value of the shares increased to $7,500. Under well-established principles, if the devise to A is treated as specific, A is entitled to the benefit of the increase in the capital value of the stock but not to the cash dividends, even if they can be traced. The law of devises regards increases in the capital value of stock as part of the asset, but views a cash dividend as a property interest distinct from the underlying asset. Any remaining cash from the dividend will pass to B, the residuary devisee.

The more troublesome question concerns stock dividends. Again, the choice will usually be between the devisee of the stock or the residuary devisee. The UPC treats stock dividends the same as stock splits, giving the benefit to the stock devisee. UPC § 2-605(a)(1). This approach maintains the devisee's percentage of ownership in the issuing firm. The majority of the decisions, however, appear to treat stock dividends the same as cash dividends, denying the benefit of the stock dividend accession to the stock devisee. See Note, 36 Alb. L. Rev. 182, 188-92 (1971); Annot., Change in Stock or Corporate

Structure, or Split or Substitution of Stock of Corporation, as Affecting Bequest of Stock, 46 A.L.R.3d 7 (1972). Contra, Edmundson v. Morton, 420 S.E.2d 106 (N.C. 1992) (announcing a presumption that accretions of stock through splits or dividends pass to the devisee of the originally devised stock). The usual rationale for the majority view is that stock dividends are like cash dividends because they are both paid out of the firm's earned surplus (sometimes called "retained earnings"). Thus both represent income on the asset, and are not part of the asset itself.

How accessions of stock occurring through splits or dividends should be sorted out depends on what we assume to be the thinking of testators who devise stock. It would seem to be most likely that a testator considers all stock received (other than shares obtained by a post-execution purchase) to be part of the devise. By providing that all stock received by way of stock split or dividend pass to the devisee of the stock, § 2-605 of the UPC establishes a rule that reflects probable intent.

3. *Will Substitutes.* No cases or statutes were found addressing the question of accessions and accretions regarding will substitutes. Should the law's treatment of accessions and accretions for specific devises be extended to the treatment of gifts found in will substitutes? See infra Chapter 8, Part B. Should a payable-on-death savings account be treated the same as a revocable lifetime trust for purposes of accessions and accretions?

3. *Abatement*

Statutory References: *UPC §§ 3-902, -916*

Suppose a will leaves "my antique desk to A, $10,000 to B, $5,000 to C, and the residue of my estate to D." The testator dies owning the antique desk and net assets of $20,000, consisting of stocks and bonds. Because all the provisions of the will can be satisfied leaving a residue of $5,000 for D, there is no problem of funding the specific and general devises.

But if the net assets apart from the antique desk are worth only $10,000, a question arises about how to distribute the decedent's estate. The different systems of reducing the devises, referred to as "abatement" systems, are the subject of this Section. In the absence of a will provision providing for an order of abatement, the default rule of abatement statutes and judge-made law control. As with the doctrine of ademption, the common-law doctrine of abatement turns on classification of the gifts. Under the usual common-law rules, the residuary devisee will take nothing and there will be a pro rata reduction of the general devises to B and C. The devise of the antique desk is specific and abates last, so that A will get the desk unless its sale is necessary to pay debts or expenses of administration. If the will also contained a demonstrative devise, this would be treated as specific for purposes of abatement. See Atkinson on Wills § 136.

Land. The estate included no land in the above example. Abatement may become more complicated when land is involved. At common law, title to personal property passed on the testator's death to the personal representative, but title to land went directly to the devisee. Unless the will provided otherwise, land could not be reached to satisfy the decedent's debts, unless the creditor had a claim secured by a lien on the land. The common-law rules concerning passage of title have persisted to this day, but land is now subject to the decedent's debts. In some states, however, all the personal property abates before any land. In some others, personal property devised in the residuary abates before land devised in the residuary and specifically devised personal property abates before specifically devised land. The UPC eliminates any distinction between real and personal property. See UPC §§ 1-201(10), (39), 3-902.

Devisees. Many states have statutes covering some or all of the problems of abatement, but they vary considerably in their treatment of the problem. See Lewis M. Simes & Paul E. Basye, Model Probate Code 353 (1946) (providing statutory analysis). Some, for example, give priority to specific devises to certain relatives over specific devises to others. See, e.g., 20 Pa. Cons. Stat. Ann. § 3541.

Estate Taxes. Under the federal estate tax, the taxable estate may include nonprobate property. Examples include life insurance and property the decedent gratuitously transferred reserving a life estate. See infra Chapter 7. The position usually taken in the earlier cases followed the "burden on the residue" rule, under which the burden of the estate taxes on nonprobate property was borne by the probate assets.[8] In recent years, a significant number of courts have held that there should be an "equitable apportionment," placing a proportionate part of the estate tax burden on nonprobate assets. That is to say, assets not forming a part of the decedent's probate estate but nevertheless includable in his or her taxable estate abate proportionally to pay the federal estate tax liability owed by

---

8. See, e.g., Ericson v. Childs, 198 A. 176, 115 A.L.R. 907 (Conn. 1938); Bemis v. Converse, 140 N.E. 686 (Mass. 1923); Austin Fleming, Apportionment of Federal Estate Taxes, 43 Ill. L. Rev. 153, 159 (1948); William P. Sutter, Apportionment of Federal Estate Tax in the Absence of Statute or an Expression of Intention, 51 Mich. L. Rev. 53 (1952).

the estate.[9] Legislation providing for a similar apportionment was enacted in 1930 in New York, and is now in force in about one-half of the states.

The typical provision in the apportionment statutes is similar to that contained in the Uniform Estate Tax Apportionment Act (UETAA), which is incorporated in UPC § 3-916. The UETAA apportions the burden among all recipients of property, whether probate or nonprobate, included in the taxable estate. The UETAA provides for an apportionment among those who take probate assets, instead of placing the whole burden on the residuary estate where the decedent dies testate. This goes beyond the decisions favoring an equitable apportionment among nonprobate assets. Do you think treating probate and nonprobate assets alike for purposes of discharging the estate tax liability is likely to coincide with most testators' intent? The Restatement 3d of Property § 1.1, comment g, takes the position that, unless the decedent's will provides otherwise, liability for estate taxes is "equitably apportioned" among nonprobate assets that are includible in the taxable estate, but within the probate estate, the full burden falls on the taxable portion of the residue. The Uniform Law Commission has appointed a committee to revise the UETAA.

Should nonprobate assets also be available to pay debts of the estate other than estate tax liability? Generally, the law requires the probate assets first to bear the burden of the estate's debts. Unsecured estate creditors are allowed to reach some types of nonprobate assets, but typically they can do so only if the probate assets are insufficient. Creditors' rights to nonprobate assets are considered infra Chapter 8.

4. Ademption By Satisfaction

Statutory References: *UPC § 2-609*

Restatement 3d of Property

§ *5.4 Ademption by Satisfaction*

An inter vivos gift made by a testator to a devisee or to a member of the devisee's family adeems the devise by satisfaction, in whole or in part, if the

9. See, e.g., Estate of Gowling, 411 N.E.2d 266 (Ill. 1980) (testate estate); Roe v. Farrell, 372 N.E.2d 662 (Ill. 1978) (intestate estate); Kintzinger v. Millin, 117 N.W.2d 68 (Iowa 1962); Sebree v. Rosen, 349 S.W.2d 865, 884 (Mo. 1961); Beatty v. Cake, 387 P.2d 355 (Or. 1963), rehearing denied 390 P.2d 176 (Or. 1964); Industrial Trust Co. v. Budlong, 76 A.2d 600 (R.I. 1950). Other cases are cited in Douglas A. Kahn, The Federal Estate Tax Burden Borne by a Dissenting Widow, 64 Mich. L. Rev. 1499, 1506 (1966). See also John H. Minan, The Allocation of Estate Taxes by Judicial Rule: A Case for Reform, 38 Ohio St. L.J. 539 (1977); Joan M. Sherwin, Note, 1979 U. Ill. L. F. 703.

testator indicated in a contemporaneous writing, or if the devisee acknowledged in a writing, that the gift was so to operate.

———

If a testator makes a lifetime gift to a devisee, that gift might be treated as satisfying the devise, in whole or in part. The doctrine of satisfaction essentially provides for the situation in which the testator decides to change the timing of a gift to permit the beneficiary to enjoy the gift before the testator's death. It is analogous to the doctrine of advancements that applies to lifetime gifts made by decedents who die intestate. See supra Chapter 2, Part D.

When the doctrine of satisfaction is applied, the distribution of the property owned at death is not made in accordance with the literal terms of the will. However, if we consider the subject of the gift *as if* it were a part of the distributable estate, then the will can be said to be enforced as written. It is *as if* part of the decedent's estate had been distributed pursuant to the terms of the will in advance of the testator's death. The words "as if" need to be emphasized, because the property given is not treated as part of the estate for other purposes. For example, it is not subject to the claims of creditors of the estate.

Writing. In contrast to advancements, the satisfaction doctrine was not the subject of widespread statutory enactment. In the nineteenth century, a handful of states adopted a writing requirement to prove a satisfaction. Over twenty states presently impose a writing requirement. A writing requirement avoids difficult factual inquiries about whether the testator intended a lifetime gift to be taken into account in distributing the estate. The writing requirement may be satisfied by a provision in the will expressly providing for lifetime advances. An attorney should raise this issue with the client and provide expressly whether lifetime gifts should or should not be taken into account for purposes of distributing the estate. Any other document written by the testator contemporaneously with the gift also qualifies. A satisfaction can also be proven by a writing in which the devisee acknowledges that the gift is in whole or in part satisfaction of a devise.

The UPC statutory provision concerning satisfaction allows the testator to make a gift in satisfaction of a devise to a person other than the devisee. The statutory change is a recognition that testators may want to reduce or eliminate a devise when they make gifts to family members of a devisee. See UPC § 2-609, comment.

Specific Devise. A lifetime gift can satisfy a specific devise. If the testator makes a lifetime gift of the devised property, the doctrine of ademption applies and no writing is necessary. If the testator makes a lifetime gift of different property, the application of the satisfaction doctrine under the UPC depends upon whether the gift was accompanied by a writing. Other than the writing requirement, this is not a change from the common law. The common law recognized that the doctrine could apply even if the nature of the lifetime gift differed significantly from the nature of the devise. In some jurisdictions, however, a substantial difference between the subject matter of the lifetime gift and the devise raises a presumption that the testator did not intend to make a satisfaction. See, e.g., Dugan v. Hollins, 4 Md. Ch. 139 (1853); Scholze v. Scholze, 2 Tenn. App. 80 (1925).

Land. Although the UPC and non-UPC statutes eliminate any distinction under the satisfaction doctrine between devises of real and personal property, that was not the early rule. Historically, satisfaction has not been applied to devises of land. If the testator's will devised Blackacre to A and thereafter the testator conveyed the land to B, the courts treated the transfer as a revocation of the devise. They did this even though it could have been regarded as an ademption by extinction. If the testator retained Blackacre, but gave other property to A, intending this as a satisfaction of the devise, this transfer also was regarded as an attempted revocation. When the second situation came before the English courts after the passage of the Statute of Frauds of 1677, which prescribed the methods of revocation, the English courts held that this was not a permitted method and hence was ineffective.[10] See Davys v. Boucher, 2 Y. & C. Ex. 397, 160 Eng. Rep. 757 (Ex. 1839). Older American cases took the same view: The question was decided, that is, by putting the transaction into the category of an attempted revocation of the devise, instead of an attempted satisfaction of the devise. See, e.g., Burnham v. Comfort, 15 N.E. 710, 2 Am. St. Rep. 462 (N.Y. 1888). Whether these older cases would still be followed today is uncertain.

Partial Satisfaction. At an early time, a gift of an amount less than the amount of a devise was presumed to have been intended to satisfy the whole devise. The theory was that the testator viewed the gift as a substitute for the devise. This rule is no longer followed. In the absence of evidence that the

---

10. One curious aspect of the matter is that after the Statute of Frauds, the court continued to treat an inter vivos conveyance of devised land as a revocation. Brydges v. Chandos, 2 Ves. Jr. 417, 30 Eng. Rep. 702 (Ch. 1794). In most instances, theory made no difference, because regardless of theory, the will could not operate to dispose of land not owned by the testator at his or her death. In some situations, however, theory became important. For example, where the testator conveyed the devised land and later reacquired it so that it was a part of the estate at death, a revocation theory means the will fails to dispose of the land. The holdings that the devise was ineffective in such circumstances could have been put on the ground that a will could not dispose of after-acquired land, so long as that doctrine prevailed. In fact, they were put on the ground of revocation. See, e.g., Grant v. Bridges, L.R. 3 Eq. 347 (1866). With the disappearance of the after-acquired property doctrine, it is vital today in the case of reacquisition to know whether the early rule of revocation by alienation remains good law. Most decisions have rejected it and have held that the reacquired land passes under the devise, but occasional cases still on the books adhere to the older law. See, e.g., Phillippe v. Clevenger, 87 N.E. 858 (Ill. 1909); Note, 34 Mich. L. Rev. 1272 (1936).

testator intended a satisfaction in whole, courts now hold that a gift of a part of a devise is a pro tanto satisfaction only.

UPC § 2-609 explicitly address the question of partial satisfaction. Both expressly refer to partial satisfactions when establishing the writing requirement and both provide that for purposes of a partial satisfaction, the lifetime gift of property should be valued when the devisee obtains possession or when the testator dies, whichever occurs first.

PART B. POST-EXECUTION DEATHS—LAPSE AND ANTILAPSE

Statutory References: *UPC §§ 2-601, -603 to -604, -702*

What happens to a devise if the devisee predeceases the testator? The short answer is that the devise "lapses" (fails). This is because a will transfers property when the testator dies, not when the will was executed, and because property can only be transferred to a living person. All devises, then, are automatically and by law conditioned on survival of the testator.

120-Hour Requirement of Survival. Although at common law, survival by only an instant prevents lapse, UPC § 2-702 extends the 120-hour requirement of survival to all "governing instruments" (as defined in § 1-201).

In Estate of Kerlee, 557 P.2d 599, 88 A.L.R.3d 1331 (Idaho 1976), the court held that the applicable statute (Former UPC § 2-601) did not apply to a will that devised property to the testator's sister and provided that "if [she] does not survive me" the property was to go to the North Idaho Children's Home. The testator's sister survived him by 74 hours. The court held that the devise in favor of the testator's sister did not lapse because the statute states that its 120-hour requirement of survival is nullified by language in the will "requiring that the devisee survive the testator." See also Estate of Acord v. Commissioner, 946 F.2d 1473 (9th Cir. 1991) (the 120-hour rule was nullified by a provision dealing with simultaneous deaths, resulting in the devisee's estate incurring an additional $150,000 in estate taxes). Though unnecessary because of the law-imposed requirement of survival, will forms commonly attach boilerplate language of survival to devises. How would *Kerlee* be decided under UPC § 2-702?

Devolution of a Lapsed Devise. If a devise lapses, what happens to it? In the absence of an applicable antilapse statute and in the absence of an expressly designated alternative taker, lapsed devises devolve in accordance with the following rules.

Lapse of a nonresiduary devise. Where lapse occurs in some part of the will other than the residuary clause, the judicial rule is uniform that lapsed devises of personal property pass to the decedent's residuary devisees. Under early common law, this rule was not followed for land. The view that a will could not dispose of after-acquired land was thought to prevent the residuary clause from passing lapsed nonresiduary devises of land. Thus, they bypassed the residuary clause and passed to the decedent's heirs by intestacy. Many states have enacted legislation that usually causes real as well as personal property to pass under the residuary clause. A few statutes, however, preserve the common-law rule for land.

Lapse in the residuary. When the residuary devisee predeceases the testator, the residue becomes intestate property. If the residuary clause is in favor of more than one person, and if that clause does not create a class gift,[11] the conventional view is that the death of one or more, but not all, of the residuary devisees before the death of the testator causes the share intended for the deceased devisee to pass by intestacy. This is known as the *no-residue-of-a-residue* rule. As the judges follow the rule, they sometimes express dissatisfaction with it. For example, in In re Dunster, [1909] 1 Ch. 103, the court said: "I think the effect of [the rule] is to defeat the testator's intention in almost every case in which it is applied."

A number of decisions have departed from the conventional view and have held that the lapsed share goes to the other residuary devisees, if there are others who survive. See, e.g., Estate of Jackson, 471 P.2d 278 (Ariz. 1970); Corbett v. Skaggs, 207 P. 819 (Kan. 1922); Niemann v. Zacharias, 176 N.W.2d 671 (Neb. 1970); Frolich Estate, 295 A.2d 448 (N.H. 1972); Commerce Nat'l Bank v. Browning, 107 N.E.2d 120 (Ohio 1952); Slack Trust, 220 A.2d 472 (Vt. 1966). Other courts, however, have held to the conventional view. See, e.g., Estate of Levy, 415 P.2d 1006 (Okla. 1966); Swearingen v. Giles, 565 S.W.2d 574 (Tex. Civ. App. 1978); Estate of Mory, 139 N.W.2d 623 (Wis. 1966).

The UPC and the Restatement 3d of Property are aligned with the trend away from the conventional view. See UPC § 2-604(b); Restatement 3d of Property § 5.5 comment o.

Estate of Griffen

543 P.2d 245 (Wash. 1975)

ROSELLINI, A.J. The will of Kizzie Belle Griffen declared that she was a widow having no child or issue, included one specific bequest to her friend, Mary Hoppe, "provided she survives me," named her stepdaughter, Willa Baughman, as executrix of her estate, and named her attorney alternate executor in the event Willa Baughman should predecease her or be unable or unwilling to serve.

---

11. The different treatment of class gifts is discussed infra p. 385.

The residue of her estate was disposed of in the following paragraph:

> I do give, devise and bequeath all of the rest, residue and remainder of my estate, wheresoever situated, possessed or owned by me at the time of my death, with all the remainder and remainders, reversion and reversions, together with the appurtenances thereunto belonging, unto my step-daughter, WILLA BAUGHMAN, of Bridgeport, Washington, to have to hold the same unto herself and her heirs forever.

The will made no mention of any of the testatrix' heirs at law, all of whom were collateral.

The stepdaughter predeceased the testatrix, leaving as her sole heir an adopted daughter. . . .

It is undoubtedly the general rule that the words "and his heirs" attached to a testamentary gift are words of limitation and not of purchase, and that such a devise or bequest lapses upon the death of the devisee or legatee in the lifetime of the testator, unless an intention on the part of the testator that such words shall effect a substitutionary gift appears from the will itself. See the cases cited in Annot., Devise or Bequest to One "Or His Heirs" or One "And His Heirs" as Affected by Death of Person Named Before Death of Testator, 128 A.L.R. 94 (1940). As the annotation explains, this doctrine had its origin in the technical rule requiring a mention of heirs to pass a fee simple to real property. That rule has long been abolished by statute in most jurisdictions.

Since words of inheritance are no longer needed to convey a fee simple title, it has been argued that where such words are used, they are used for a different purpose, namely, to express an intent that the heirs of the named beneficiary shall take in the event he predeceases the testator. However, the courts have generally rejected this theory, reasoning that lawyers continue to use these words for the purpose of describing the estate, even though it is no longer necessary to do so.

The presumption that the testator intended only to describe the estate and not to express an intent that the heirs of the named beneficiary should take the devise or bequest in the event of the beneficiary's predeceasing him, is not conclusive, however. Where it can be ascertained from the four corners of the will that it was intended that the gift go to the heirs of the named beneficiary under such circumstances, that intent will be given effect. Estate of Hoermann, 234 Wis. 130, 290 N.W. 608 (1940); Estate of Britt, 249 Wis. 30, 23 N.W.2d 498 (1946);[12] Estate of Newby, 146 Colo. 296, 361 P.2d 622 (1961) (recognizing the rule); 6 Bowe-Parker, Page on Wills § 50.8 at 75 (1962); G. Thompson,

12. Another Wisconsin decision reaching the same result is Estate of Mangel, 186 N.W.2d 276 (Wis. 1971). Eds.

Law of Wills § 493 (1947, Supp.1962); Annots., 128 A.L.R. supra at 95, 99; 78 A.L.R. supra at 994, 1004. . . .

We think the [correct construction is] that the testatrix was aware not only of the possibility that a legatee might predecease her, but specifically of the possibility that Willa Baughman might predecease her, for she provided that in that event an alternate executor should administer her estate; furthermore, . . . the specific bequest to Mary Hoppe was expressly contingent upon her surviving the testatrix, while the devise to Willa Baughman was not; finally, . . . the heirs of Willa Baughman were mentioned in the will, while the heirs of the testatrix were ignored.

No reasonable construction of this simple will could lead to the conclusion that the testatrix was unaware of the possibility that she might outlive the named residuary legatee or that she intended in any event to benefit her heirs at law. It is obvious that her affections were centered upon her stepdaughter, and that she desired her estate to go to the stepdaughter's heirs in the event she predeceased the testatrix, just as it would have gone to her natural grandchildren had Willa Baughman been her natural daughter. . . .

As the attorney who drafted the will is undoubtedly now aware, the better practice is to avoid such possible ambiguities as that which appears in the residuary clause by expressly providing that the heirs shall take the legacy in the event the named legatee should predecease the testator. We have no doubt that this is the general practice, since, insofar as we have been able to ascertain, the question has come to this court only twice in its history.

The judgment of the Court of Appeals is affirmed.

STAFFORD, C.J., and FINLEY, HUNTER, HAMILTON, WRIGHT, UTTER, BRACHTENBACH and HOROWITZ, JJ., concur.

Notes and Questions

1. *State of the Authorities*. The predominant view is contrary to *Griffen*. In Forester v. Marler, 228 S.E.2d 646 (N.C. Ct. App. 1976), the testator's will devised all of his property "unto my brother, Jack Freeman, absolutely and in fee simple forever." Jack predeceased the testator by four months. The court held that the testator's estate passed by intestacy, saying that the words "absolutely and in fee simple forever" are

> technical words which define the quantum and quality of the estate granted. They do not indicate an intention that the property affected should remain in the family of Jack Freeman in event he should predecease the testator.

Accord, e.g., Niemann v. Zacharias, 176 N.W.2d 671 (Neb. 1970).

2. *Uniform Probate Code*. How would the *Griffen* case have been resolved if it had been governed by UPC § 2-603?

3. *"Per Stirpes" as Creating an Alternative Devise*. In Richland Trust Co. v. Becvar, 339 N.E.2d 830 (Ohio 1975), the testatrix devised one-seventh of her residuary estate "to Louise Hummel, per stirpes." Louise predeceased the testatrix by some nine months, leaving no surviving husband, no parents, and no issue. Her heirs were four sisters and the son of a deceased brother. The court held:

> In its technical meaning, "per stirpes" generally relates to the mode of distribution. That is, it refers not to who shall take, but to the manner in which those who shall take come within the class entitled to take. Kraemer v. Hook (1958), 168 Ohio St. 221, 152 N.E.2d 430. However, in the present case, the manner of distribution is expressed, but the class to which that distribution is to be made is not expressed. Nonetheless, it is clear to this court that the testatrix intended a gift to secondary takers in the event that the primary taker, Louise Hummel, did not survive the testatrix. . . . In the absence of an express designation of the class of secondary takers, the class will be assumed to be the heirs at law of the named person, as determined by the statutes of descent and distribution.

See also Restatement 2d of Property § 25.1 comment i, illustration 14. In Estate of Walters, 519 N.E.2d 1270 (Ind. Ct. App. 1988), however, the court held that a residuary devise "to my beloved wife, Jessie E. Walters, per stirpes" lapsed when she predeceased the testator, causing the residue to pass by intestate succession to his children by a former marriage. The claim of her children by a former marriage that the phrase "per stirpes" created a substitutional devise to them was rejected, the court saying: "There is nothing in the will to indicate that the testator intended to disinherit his own children in favor of stepchildren."[13]

Antilapse Statutes. Almost all jurisdictions have antilapse statutes.[14] The "antilapse" label, however, is somewhat misleading. Strictly speaking, antilapse statutes (other than in Maryland and perhaps Iowa) do not reverse the common-law rule of lapse. They do not abrogate the law-imposed condition of survival so that devised property passes to the estates of predeceasing devisees. Antilapse statutes leave the law-imposed condition of survival intact, but modify the devolution of lapsed devises by providing a statutory substitute gift. The

13. See supra Chapter 2, Part B, for discussion of the per-stirpes representation system.

14. For a state-by-state compilation, see Restatement 3d of Property, Statutory Note to § 5.5.

statutory substitute gift is usually to the devisee's descendants who survive the testator.[15]

Antilapse statutes are remedial in nature, tending to preserve equality of treatment among different lines of succession. The statutes commonly provide that the substitute gift takes effect unless a contrary intention is demonstrated. See UPC § 2-601. What language suffices to make a jurisdiction's antilapse statute inapplicable has been the source of some controversy, as we will see in Detzel v. Nieberding, below.

The statutes were enacted in the belief that the statutory substitute gift for which they make provision is one the testator probably would have made had he or she thought about the matter. At the least, the substitute gifts are thought to produce a result closer to the testator's probable intention than the disposition that results under the common-law doctrine of lapse.

The antilapse statutes of most jurisdictions apply only to certain classes of devisees—relatives[16] or specified relatives of the testator. Very few statutes apply to any devisee who predeceases the testator leaving descendants who survive the testator. The UPC antilapse provision applies to devisees who are grandparents or descendants of grandparents of the testator. See UPC § 2-603(b). The UPC also extends its antilapse protection to the testator's step-children.

The UPC, like most antilapse statutes, does not apply to gifts to the testator's spouse. Antilapse statutes also typically exclude spouses of predeceased descendants as statutorily-substituted takers. What do you suppose are the reasons for these exclusions?

How should the devisee's descendants, as takers of a lapsed devise, be determined? As an example of the kinds of questions that can arise, should a child of unmarried parents participate as a substituted taker under an antilapse statute? Does the answer depend upon whether the nonmarital child would take under the jurisdiction's statute of intestacy, or whether the child would be presumptively included in class gifts under the rules of construction followed in the jurisdiction? See Murray v. Murray, 564 S.W.2d 5 (Ky. 1978); UPC § 1-201(9).

---

15. Under the UPC, the substituted descendants must survive the testator by 120 hours. See supra p. 374. Therefore, the UPC antilapse statutes apply even though the devisee survives the testator if the devisee fails to survive the testator by 120 hours.

16. The term "relative" is usually interpreted to mean blood relative. See, e.g., Estate of Bloomer, 620 S.W.2d 365 (Mo. 1981); Estate of Haese, 259 N.W.2d 54 (Wis. 1977).

Detzel v. Nieberding

219 N.E.2d 327 (Ohio P. Ct. 1966)

DAVIES, J. The evidence in this case discloses that Wilhelmina C. Guenther died testate on July 5, 1965. After making several specific bequests, she provided that the residue of her estate be converted into cash, that certain *contingent* monetary bequests be made to three brothers, a sister, Mary Detzel, a sister-in-law, a niece and a nephew, with a stipulation that the legatee "be living at the time of" the testatrix' death, and that the remainder of the residue be distributed in designated fractions to three named charitable institutions. The monetary bequest to Mary Detzel reads as follows:

> To my beloved sister, Mary Detzel, provided she be living at the time of my death, the sum of Five Thousand Dollars ($5,000.00).

Mary's daughter and sole issue, Helen Detzel, survived her aunt, the testatrix. Mary Detzel predeceased her sister, Wilhelmina.

Helen Detzel has instituted the present action for a declaratory judgment to declare her right as the sole issue of Mary Detzel to take the $5,000.00 bequest made by the testatrix to Mary Detzel under the provisions of Section 2107.52, Revised Code, commonly known as the antilapse statute. The court has been asked to determine, under the provisions of this action, if Helen Detzel will take the $5,000.00 bequest devised to her deceased mother, Mary Detzel; if the bequest will lapse because "a different disposition" of the devise has been made by the testatrix in stipulating in her will that $5,000.00 be given to Mary Detzel "provided she be living at the time of my death"; or if this section has no application to this case.

We have not found any Ohio cases involving the applicability of the Ohio antilapse statute to the exact facts of this case. We have found a number of cases in other jurisdictions in which courts have held that devises or bequests containing provisions similar to the "Detzel" bequest do lapse despite the existence of antilapse statutes in those jurisdictions. . . .

As a summation of the cases which hold that antilapse statutes do not apply to devises or legacies when words of survival are used in a will, we quote the following statement found in 92 A.L.R. 857, Section IXa:

> Where the testator uses words of survivorship, indicating an intention that the legatee shall take the gift only if he outlives the testator, it is clear that the statute against lapses has no application. In such a case the condition attached to the gift fails immediately upon the death of the legatee, and there is nothing upon which the statute can operate. This result is so obvious as not to require citation of authority.

Analyses of the . . . cases show that the courts categorically concluded that antilapse statutes do not apply to devises made to relatives when the indicated words of survival were used in connection with the devises, because in such events the testators have expressed intentions to nullify the provisions of the statutes. We, frankly, do not agree with the conclusions of the courts that the words of survivorship used by testators . . . leave "no possible room for legal construction to the contrary" or are "so obvious as not to require citation of authority." . . .

Section 2107.52, Revised Code, provides as follows:

> When a devise of real or personal estate is made to a relative of a testator and such relative was dead at the time the will was made, or dies thereafter, leaving issue surviving the testator, such issue shall take the estate devised as the devisee would have done if he had survived the testator. . . .

Antilapse statutes are remedial and should receive a liberal construction. . . . [T]o render statute inoperative contrary intent of testator must be plainly indicated. . . .

To prevent operation of the Ohio antilapse statute when a devise is made to a relative conditioned upon the survival of the testator by the relative, and the relative predeceases the testator leaving issue who survive the testator, it is necessary that the testator, in apt language, make an alternative provision in his will providing that in the event such relative predeceases or fails to survive the testator such devise shall be given to another specifically named or identifiable devisee or devisees.

Since the testatrix, Wilhelmina, made a devise to her sister, Mary, who predeceased the testatrix leaving issue, Helen, surviving the testatrix, and the testatrix did not make by apt language a different disposition of her property under such contingency to prevent the operation of Section 2107.52, Revised Code, Helen will take the $5,000 devised to her deceased mother by substitution under the provisions of said statute.

Judgment accordingly.

Notes and Questions

1. *Survival Language.* For a case holding (contrary to *Detzel*) that a bare expressly stated requirement of survival defeats the antilapse statute, see Estate of Stroble, 636 P.2d 236 (Kan. Ct. App. 1981). Subsequent Ohio cases have distinguished or rejected the approach taken in *Detzel.* E.g., Shalkhauser v. Beach, 233 N.E.2d 527 (Ohio Prob. Ct. 1968) (stating that *Detzel* is "clearly and completely erroneous"); Day v. Brooks, 224 N.E.2d 557 (Ohio Prob. Ct. 1967) (distinguishing *Detzel* on the ground that it involved a single devisee).

The question whether survival language alone should defeat the antilapse statute is discussed in Susan F. French, Antilapse Statutes Are Blunt Instruments: A Blueprint for Reform, 37 Hastings L.J. 335, 348-50, 369-70 (1985). Professor French generally approves of the result in *Detzel*, observing that "[c]ourts have tended to accord too much significance to survival requirements when deciding whether to apply antilapse statutes." In contrast, the *Detzel* case is discussed disapprovingly in Patricia J. Roberts, Lapse Statutes: Recurring Construction Problems, 37 Emory L.J. 323, 349-54 (1988). Professor Roberts argues that "express survivorship language should be given effect [to defeat antilapse statutes] unless there is clear and convincing evidence that to do so would be contrary to intent."

What do you think? Do you think that a client presented with an attorney-prepared draft will that devises property "to my surviving children" will understand that if one of her children predeceases her, the predeceased child's share will *not* go to the child's descendants, but if the draft had said "to my children" it *would* go to those descendants? The Restatement 3d of Property § 5.5 comments h and i provide:

> *h. Contrary intent; survival language.* An often litigated question is whether language requiring the devisee to survive the testator, without more, constitutes a sufficient expression of a contrary intent to defeat the antilapse statute. The majority view is that such language signifies a contrary intent. Because such a survival provision is often boiler-plate form-book language, the testator may not understand that such language could disinherit the line of descent headed by the deceased devisee. When the testator is older than the devisee and hence does not expect the devisee to die first, or if the devisee was childless when the will was executed, it seems especially unlikely that a provision requiring the devisee to survive the testator was intended to disinherit the devisee's descendants. . . .
>
> [T]he courts should be cautious in automatically concluding that survival language manifests a deliberate decision by the testator to disinherit the line of descent headed by a deceased devisee.
>
> *i. Contrary intent; clear, direct, unmistakable statement.* The clearest way of stating a contrary intent is to do so directly, in language that is understandable to the testator, language that leaves no doubt that the testator considered the possibility of the devisee failing to survive the testator and decided against substituting the devisee's descendants. Language such as "and not to [the devisee's] descendants if [the devisee] fails to survive me" is an unmistakable expression of a contrary intent. If the language occurs in a will drafted by an attorney, the client has the opportunity to approve or disapprove of the result. A blanket provision stating that if any devisee fails to survive the testator, the devised property is "not to pass to the devisee's descendants" is equally clear.

Capable lawyers do not and should not want the antilapse statute to apply to wills they draft. The Restatement suggests that clients would be better served if lawyers used words like "and not to [the devisee's] descendants if [the devisee] fails to survive me" to avoid the antilapse statute. Why do so many lawyers prefer to use survival language? Lawyers usually go to great lengths to spell out their clients' intention as explicitly and unmistakably as possible. Whose intent controls the meaning of wills and other donative documents, the client's intent or the lawyer's intent? Many lawyers profess that they deliberately use survival language to avoid the antilapse statute. If so, why do they use survival language indiscriminately, both with respect to devisees who are and devisees who are not protected by the antilapse statute, such as in the devise to the testator's friend, Mary Hoppe, in the *Griffen* case, supra p. 375?

2. *Uniform Probate Code.* The UPC addresses the survival-language question explicitly, by providing that survival language does not, in the absence of additional evidence, indicate a contrary intent. See UPC § 2-603(b)(3). Will UPC § 2-603 impose malpractice liability on a lawyer who uses survival language to avoid the antilapse statute? Compare Martin D. Begleiter, Article II of the Uniform Probate Code and the Malpractice Revolution, 59 Tenn. L. Rev. 101, 126-30 (1991), with Edward C. Halbach, Jr. & Lawrence W. Waggoner, The UPC's New Survivorship and Antilapse Provisions, 55 Alb. L. Rev. 1091, 1108 n.62 (1992).

UPC § 2-603 also establishes more elaborate rules for determining when the statute's substitute gift takes effect. The statute looks more complex than it really is.

The design of UPC § 2-603 is to follow the priorities established by the testator. *First priority* goes to the "primary" devisee. For example, suppose a devise of $10,000 "to son A if he survives me; if not, to daughter B if she survives me." If the primary devisee, A, survives the testator (*i.e.*, survives by 120 hours or more), A takes. It makes no difference whether B survived the testator or not. It also makes no difference whether A or B had descendants who survived the testator.

Second priority goes to the "secondary" devisee.[17] If A predeceases the testator (*i.e.*, fails to survive the testator by 120 hours) but B survives the testator, B takes. It makes no difference whether A or B had descendants who survived the testator.

Third priority goes to the descendants of either devisee if both predecease the testator but only one leaves descendants who survive the testator. If A and B predecease the testator, and only one of them leaves descendants who survive the testator, those descendants take by representation.

---

17. The term "secondary" devisee is not used in the statute. The statute treats A and B as "alternative" devisees.

Fourth priority goes to the descendants of the primary devisee if both predecease the testator and both leave descendants who survive the testator, except that if the secondary devisee is a descendant of the primary devisee, the priority goes to the descendants of the secondary devisee. If A and B predecease the testator, and both leave descendants who survive the testator, A's descendants take. If B had been a descendant of A, B's descendants would have taken.

External References. The scope and rationale of § 2-603 are explained in Edward C. Halbach, Jr. & Lawrence W. Waggoner, The UPC's New Survivorship and Antilapse Provisions, 55 Alb. L. Rev. 1091 (1992). The section is debated in Mark L. Ascher, The 1990 Uniform Probate Code: Older and Better, or More Like the Internal Revenue Code?, 77 Minn. L. Rev. 639 (1993) (sharply critical); Mary L. Fellows, Traveling the Road to Probate Reform: Finding the Way to Your Will (A Response to Professor Ascher), 77 Minn. L. Rev. 659 (1993).

Problems

With the design of UPC § 2-603 in mind, consider how the following problems would be resolved under the UPC. (The cases cited after a problem were decided under the former version of the UPC or a non-UPC antilapse statute. They are cited to demonstrate the split of authority that exists under conventional antilapse statutes with respect to most of the problems presented. The existence of the wide splits of authority was what led the framers of the UPC to develop the elaborate statutory provision.)

1. G's will devised "$10,000 to my sister, S" and "the residue of my estate to X-Charity." S predeceased G, leaving a child, N, who survived G by 120 hours.

2. G's will devised "$10,000 to my sister, S" and "the residue of my estate, including all failed and lapsed devises, to X-Charity." S predeceased G, leaving a child, N, who survived G by 120 hours.[18]

18. For a case holding that a conventional antilapse statute is counteracted (*i.e.*, X-Charity takes the $10,000 devise; N takes nothing) by this type of provision, see Estate of Salisbury, 143 Cal. Rptr. 81 (Ct. App. 1978); contra, Blevins v. Moran, 12 S.W.3d 698 (Ky. Ct. App. 2000). Cf. Larson v. Anderson, 167 N.W.2d 640 (Iowa 1969) (antilapse statute counteracted by clause stating that "if any [devisee] die[s] prior to [my death], such gifts shall lapse and become a part of the residue of my estate."); Starkey v. District of Columbia, 377 A.2d 382 (D.C. 1977) (antilapse statute counteracted by clause stating that if "any of the [devisees] do not survive me, then, in that event, his or her devise and bequest shall lapse.").

3. G's will devised "$10,000 to my surviving children." G had two children, A and B. A predeceased G, leaving a child, X, who survived G by 120 hours. B also survived G by 120 hours.[19]

4. G's will devised "$5,000 to my son, A, if he is living at my death; if not, to my daughter, B" and devised "$7,500 to my daughter, B, if she is living at my death; if not, to my son A." A and B predeceased G, both leaving descendants who survived G by 120 hours.

5. G's will devised "$5,000 to my child, A, if he is living at my death; if not, to A's children." A had two children, X and Y. A and X predeceased G. A's child, Y, and X's children, M and N, survived G by 120 hours.

6. The facts are the same as those in Problem 5, except that the alternative devise read: "if not, to A's children, X and Y."

Class Gifts.[20] A class gift is a gift of property to a group of persons identified by a group label, such as "children," "grandchildren," "issue," "descendants," "brothers," "sisters," "nieces," "nephews," or "first cousins." Not all gifts to a group of persons are class gifts, however. To be a class gift, the number of persons in the group must be able to increase or decrease. That is, the group must be described in a way that allows persons to be added to or dropped from the group as events (such as births, adoptions, or deaths) unfold in the future, so that the property is divided among the group as its membership is constituted at some future time. See Restatement of Property § 279. A gift to a static group is not a class gift; it is a series of separate gifts of a fractional share of the property to each member of the original group.

Generally speaking, the following rules of thumb determine whether a gift is or is not a class gift:

> *A gift is likely a class gift if the group members are only identified by a group label (such as "to my children").*

---

19. For cases holding that a conventional antilapse statute is counteracted (*i.e.*, B takes $10,000; X takes nothing), see Estate of Price, 454 P.2d 411 (Wash. 1969) (6-to-3 decision). Cf. Estate of Fitzpatrick, 406 N.W.2d 483 (Mich. Ct. App. 1987). For cases holding that a conventional antilapse statute is not counteracted (*i.e.*, X takes $5,000; B takes $5,000) if A was living when G's will was executed, see Henderson v. Parker, 728 S.W.2d 768 (Tex. 1987) (court said: "[W]e read the phrase 'surviving children of this marriage' to mean children 'surviving' at the time the will was executed."). Accord Restatement 2d of Property § 27.2 comment f, illustration 5. Cf. Id. § 27.1 comment e, illustration 6.

20. A more detailed exposition of class gifts and their operation can be found in Lawrence W. Waggoner, Estates in Land and Future Interests in a Nutshell § 15.1 (2d ed. 1993), from which the above textual discussion and examples are drawn. See also infra Chapter 18, Part B.

A gift is likely not a class gift, although the takers are identified by a group label, if the group members are also identified by name (such as "to my children, A, B, and C") or by number ("to my three children") or by both name and number ("to my three children, A, B, and C"). Gifts like these are gifts of a fixed fraction to each of the designated individuals—in this case, a gift of one-third to A, one-third to B, and one-third to C.

Although the law treats these rules as *presumptions* that can be rebutted by a contrary intent "found from additional language or circumstances,"[21] see Restatement of Property § 280, the case law shows that the presumptions are seldom rebutted. Because of the infrequency of actual rebuttal, the following examples assume that these presumptions are controlling.

The distinguishing feature of a class gift therefore is the ability of the group to fluctuate in number. Fluctuations in number can come about through an *increase* in the number of takers (caused by births or adoptions), and/or through a *decrease* in the number of takers (caused by deaths).

Increase in class membership. The ability of the takers to increase in number is unique to class gifts.

Example 6.1: G devised land "to my children." When the will was executed, G had two children (A and B). Subsequently, G had a third child (C). G was survived by A, B, and C. No children were in gestation at G's death.

Because G's will created a class gift, A, B, and C each take an undivided one-third interest in the devised land.

If, on the other hand, G's will had created individual gifts (suppose, for example, that the dispositive language had been "to my two children, A and B"), the result would have been different. The shares of A and B would not have been decreased to one-third each by C's birth and survival of G; the shares of A and B would have remained constant at one-half each. Not being a class gift, the devise would not have been subject to increase, and C would not have been entitled to share in the devised land.[22]

Decrease in class membership. The rule of lapse—that devisees must survive the testator to take—applies to class gifts as well as individual gifts. In the absence of an applicable antilapse statute, however, a class gift imports a built-in gift over to the other takers. There is no such gift over in the case of individual gifts.

---

21. Hence the word "likely" in the above formulations.

22. This analysis is based on the common law. Under UPC § 2-302, C would take an equal share in the devised land unless it is proved that G intentionally excluded C. Under statutory law in nearly all non-UPC states, C would take an intestate share unless it is proved that G intentionally excluded C; C's intestate share would ordinarily be paid out of G's residuary estate rather than out of the devised land.

Example 6.2: G devised land "to my children in equal shares." When the will was executed, G had three children (A, B and C). A predeceased G, but B and C survived her.

Because G's will created a class gift, B and C each take an undivided one-half interest in the devised land, probably as tenants in common.

If, on the other hand, G's will had created individual gifts of a one-third share to each of G's three children (suppose, for example, that the dispositive language had been "to my three children, A, B, and C"), the result would have been different. A's lost one-third share would not have been added to the shares of B and C; their shares would have remained constant. A's lost one-third share would have gone to G's residuary devisees or, in the unlikely event that there was no residuary clause, to G's heirs by intestate succession.

Because a class gift such as the one in the above example is an immediate testamentary gift of absolute ownership, it is subject to decrease between the time of execution of the will and the testator's death. Once the testator has died, the ability to decrease comes to an end. Thus if, after G's death, B dies survived by C, B's one-half interest would not be divested in favor of C.

Do antilapse statutes apply to class gifts? Some courts say no. Their reasoning is that the will makes a devise only to the members of the class who are living at the testator's death. The statute, therefore, has no application to a potential class member who predeceased the testator. In many decisions, however, the statutes have been construed to apply to class gifts and, the UPC and a growing number of non-UPC statutes explicitly apply to class gifts. The basis for applying antilapse statutes to class gifts is the idea that the remedial purpose of these statutes—to fill an unintended gap in the testator's dispositive plan—would be frustrated if the testator happened to use class gift language. See Hoverstad v. First National Bank & Trust Co., 74 N.W.2d 48 (S.D. 1955).

DIVISION TWO
PROBATE AND NONPROBATE TRANSFERS

Chapter 7

Taxation

UNTIL this point we have concentrated on probate transfers—property owned at death and passing by will or intestacy. Division Two brings nonprobate transfers into the discussion. Nonprobate transfers are of two general types: outright gifts and will substitutes. The first topic in Division Two is the federal tax system, primarily the federal transfer tax component of that system.

The Economic Growth and Tax Relief Reconciliation Act of 2001 [EGTRRA or Act] dramatically changes the federal transfer tax law and the income tax consequences of death. Effective in the year 2010, the Act repeals the estate tax (IRC § 2210(a)) and the generation-skipping transfer tax (IRC § 2664). It also repeals the income tax rule that permits persons acquiring property from a decedent to enjoy a basis in that property equal to its fair market value at the decedent's death (IRC § 1014(f)). Instead, in 2010, recipients of a decedent's property will take that decedent's basis in that property with some modifications. See IRC § 1022. The effect of these changes is to eliminate a tax on the transfer of property at death, but to impose a tax on any asset appreciation that occurred during a decedent's life at the time that a recipient of an asset of a decedent sells it. To protect against revenue loss from the transfer of property by gift to donees subject to income tax rates lower than those of their donors, the gift tax remains in effect. For further discussion of the modified carryover-basis rule, see infra p. 427. Up until 2010, the Act provides for lower transfer tax rates and higher exemptions. As of 2009, only estates in excess of $3.5 million will be subject to the estate tax. Experts estimate that "somewhere between 80 to 90 percent of all estates . . . subject to the tax" in

2001 will escape taxation in 2009. John Buckley, Estate and Gift Taxes: What Will Congress Do Next?, 91 Tax Notes 2069 (2001).

The nine-year delay in the implementation of the repeal creates considerable uncertainty for estate planners as to whether future Congresses will allow it to take effect. That uncertainty is further exacerbated, however, by § 901 of the Act that states that "[a]ll provisions of, and amendments made by, this Act shall not apply . . . after December 31, 2010." For estates of decedents dying after December 31, 2010, and for gifts made and generation-skipping transfers occurring after December 31, 2010, current law applies as if EGTRRA had never been enacted. The ultimate effect of the 2001 legislation then is to postpone the question of whether the federal government should impose a tax on the gratuitous transfer of property at death or during life.[1] The delay in the repeal of the estate and generation-skipping taxes, the uncertainty about whether the repeal will be permanent, and the continuing imposition of the gift tax mean that the need for family property lawyers to have some familiarity with the federal transfer tax law is unchanged. The goal of this chapter is to provide an overview of the federal transfer tax system so that students are better able to understand family property law and estate planning techniques. We emphasize that the presentation is merely an overview; it does not include the many details that would be discussed in a separate course in Federal Transfer Taxation.

Federal law subjects the gratuitous transfer of property—probate and nonprobate transfers—to an excise tax, which is usually imposed on the donor or the donor's estate. This excise tax can be derived from any of three taxes that make up the transfer tax component of the federal tax system: the federal gift tax, the federal estate tax, and the federal generation-skipping transfer tax. The two purposes for starting Division Two with the tax system are to show

---

1. Along side the federal tax system are various state tax systems. Many states have inheritance taxes, which tax the recipient of a gratuitous transfer, and estate and gift taxes, which tax the donor. Tax saving opportunities are available and state taxes need to be considered in the design of a client's estate plan. Unfortunately, these state taxes vary so greatly in detail that they can't be summarized in the brief presentation here.

Consideration of state taxes is also made difficult because of the EGTRRA. While the repeal of the federal estate tax may make it politically infeasible for states to continue to impose an inheritance tax, the loss of inheritance tax revenues places considerable strain on state budgets. The federal estate tax law had provided a credit for state death taxes paid, based on a formula, and many states based the taxes they assessed on that credit amount so that an estate's total tax liability would not be increased. The substantial reduction and ultimate repeal of the federal estate tax will, therefore, reduce state revenues. The effect on state revenues is even more severe than might first appear, because the EGTRRA reduces the state death tax credit between 2002 and 2004, repeals it as of January 1, 2005, and substitutes a deduction instead. See IRC §§ 2011(b)(2), 2058. How each state will respond to the changing political and economic climate is yet another uncertainty for individuals and estate planners. See Buckley, supra, at 2069-70; Kevin Sack, States Expecting to Lose Billions from Repeal of U.S. Estate Tax, N.Y. Times, June 21, 2001, at A1.

how that system integrates taxation of probate and nonprobate transfers and to set the stage for the subsequent chapters of this Division. Those chapters consider various aspects of family property law that are belatedly moving in the direction of an integrated treatment that is similar to that found in the federal transfer tax system. We will see that the transfer tax system has from its inception treated will substitutes, such as revocable trusts, life insurance, pension death benefits, and survivorship annuities, as the equivalent of probate transfers.

PART A. THE FEDERAL TRANSFER TAX SYSTEM

1. The Cumulative Estate and Gift Tax System

The federal estate and gift taxes use progressive rather than flat tax rates. Under a progressive system, the total taxes on gratuitous transfers of $2 million are supposed to be more than double the tax on gratuitous transfers of $1 million. To have integrity, a progressive transfer tax system must therefore be cumulative. That is to say, the tax on the latest round of taxable transfers, whether occurring at death or during life, must take account of all previous taxable transfers.

Until 1976, however, the progressivity of the system was compromised by the fact that the federal estate and gift taxes operated independently rather than cumulatively. The federal estate tax was enacted in 1916 to impose an excise tax on deathtime transfers of property, which as indicated above includes will substitutes as well as probate transfers under the heading of deathtime transfers. The federal gift tax was enacted in 1932 to impose an excise tax on lifetime gifts of property, which for the most part are outright gifts of property. Each tax had its own exemption and progressive rate schedule, but progressivity was compartmentalized. Although the gift tax was cumulative within itself, the estate tax rate applicable to a decedent's taxable estate was not based on the cumulative total of lifetime taxable gifts plus the taxable estate, but only on the taxable estate. A $1 million taxable estate incurred the same estate tax whether the decedent had made no lifetime taxable gifts or lifetime taxable gifts of, say, $5 million.

All this changed with the enactment of the Tax Reform Act of 1976. This act joined the estate and gift taxes into a unified transfer tax structure with a single exemption, in the form of a credit, and a single rate schedule under which the rate applicable to a decedent's taxable estate was based on the cumulative total of the decedent's lifetime taxable gifts and taxable estate. Under this unified system, deathtime transfers are treated as continuations of lifetime gift-giving.

The EGTRRA reintroduces bifurcation in the transfer tax system in two significant ways. First, over the next nine years the effective exemption amount in the form of a unified credit for estate taxes increases from $675,000 in 2001 to $1 million in 2002 and gradually increases to $3.5 million by the year 2009. See IRC § 2010. The effective exemption amount for gift taxes, however, increases to $1 million in 2002 and remains at that level. See IRC § 2505(a). Use of the credit during life means that it is not available at death to the extent it reduces a donor's gift tax liability and, therefore, referring to it as a unified credit continues to be accurate, even though, after the EGTRRA, it is no longer unified regarding the amount available during life and at death.

Second, in 2010, the Act repeals the estate tax, but leaves the gift tax in effect, continuing its $1 million exemption amount in the form of a credit and subjecting gifts to a maximum rate equal to the highest marginal rate imposed on individuals under the federal income tax law under the Act (35 percent). See IRC §§ 2210(a), 2502(a) (as revised effective after December 31, 2009). In 2011, however, the unified system first introduced in 1976 comes back into effect, unless Congress takes further action. Congressional concern for income tax avoidance by the assignment of income from property to donees who enjoy lower income tax rates than their donors accounts for both the lower exemption amount for lifetime transfers, as well as the retention of the gift tax after 2009. Another consequence of Congress having retained the gift tax, however, is that reintroduction of the estate tax is made more feasible. Without taxpayers having the opportunity to make tax-free gifts for the purpose of removing much of their wealth in anticipation of a reinstatement of an estate tax, an effective estate tax after 2010 remains possible. See Buckley, supra, at 2070.

Below is the unified rate schedule in effect in 2001 that will come back into effect in 2011 and thereafter absent further action by Congress.

Unified Rate Schedule from IRC § 2001(c)(1)

If the amount with respect to which the tentative tax to be computed is:	The tentative tax is:
Not over $10,000	18% of such amount.
Over $10,000 but not over $20,000	$1,800, plus 20% of the excess of such amount over $10,000.
Over $20,000 but not over $40,000	$3,800, plus 22% of the excess of such amount over $20,000.
Over $40,000 but not over $60,000	$8,200, plus 24% of the excess of such amount over $40,000.
Over $60,000 but not over $80,000	$13,000, plus 26% of the excess of such amount over $60,000.

If the amount with respect to which the tentative tax to be computed is:	The tentative tax is:
Over $80,000 but not over $100,000	$18,200, plus 28% of the excess of such amount over $80,000.
Over $100,000 but not over $150,000	$23,800, plus 30% of the excess of such amount over $100,000.
Over $150,000 but not over $250,000	$38,800, plus 32% of the excess of such amount over $150,000
Over $250,000 but not over $500,000	$70,800, plus 34% of the excess of such amount over $250,000.
Over $500,000 but not over $750,000	$155,800, plus 37% of the excess of such amount over $500,000.
Over $750,000 but not over $1,000,000	$248,300, plus 39% of the excess of such amount over $750,000.
Over $1,000,000 but not over $1,250,000	$345,800, plus 41% of the excess of such amount over $1,000,000.
Over $1,250,000 but not over $1,500,000	$448,300, plus 43% of the excess of such amount over $1,250,000.
Over $1,500,000 but not over $2,000,000	$555,800, plus 45% of the excess of such amount over $1,500,000.
Over $2,000,000 but not over $2,500,000	$780,800, plus 49% of the excess of such amount over $2,000,000.
Over $2,500,000 but not over $3,000,000	$1,025,800, plus 53% of the excess of such amount over $2,500,000.
Over $3,000,000	$1,290,800, plus 55% of the excess of such amount over $3,000,000.[2]

Under the EGTRRA, the rate schedule set forth above remains unchanged except that the Act in:

---

2. Under the estate tax law in effect in 2001, a 5 percent surtax is imposed on estates between $10,000,000 and $17,184,000. See IRC § 2001(c)(2). The effect of this surtax is to eliminate gradually the advantage of the low rate brackets on the first $3,000,000 for estates valued between $10,000,000 and $17,184,000 and to subject those estates to a top marginal rate of 60 percent. For all amounts in excess of $17,184,000, estates are subject to a flat rate of 55 percent.

The value of the low rate brackets is $359,200 ($1,650,000 ($3,000,000 x 55%) - $1,290,800). If an estate of $17,184,000 were taxed at a flat rate of 55 percent ($9,451,200), the tax liability would be $359,200 greater than if the estate used the table set forth in the text ($9,092,000) The surtax of 5 percent on the amount an estate of $17,184,000 exceeds $10,000,000 eliminates the benefit of the low rate brackets by increasing the tax liability of the estate by $359,200 (($17,184,000 - $10,000,000) x 5%).

The EGTRRA repeals the 5 percent surtax as of 2002, but it will come back into effect in 2011 unless Congress takes further action. See EGTRRA §§ 511(b), 901.

2002 repeals the rates in excess of 50 percent
2003 repeals the rates in excess of 49 percent
2004 repeals the rates in excess of 48 percent
2005 repeals the rates in excess of 47 percent
2006 repeals the rates in excess of 46 percent
2007, 2008, and 2009 repeals the rates in excess of 45 percent[3]

After 2009 when the estate tax is repealed, the gift tax is assessed according to the rate schedule set forth above, except that the maximum rate is set at 35 percent and applies to cumulative gifts in excess of $500,000. See IRC § 2502(a) (as revised effective after December 31, 2009).

The mechanics of the cumulative system for computing the estate tax are a bit complicated. They incorporate a number of steps in order to arrive at the final tax liability. The first of these steps is to compute the *tentative estate tax* by applying the unified rate schedule to the sum of the decedent's "taxable estate" (the decedent's gross estate less deductions) and "adjusted taxable gifts" (the aggregate amount of post-1976 lifetime taxable gifts that the decedent made and that are not otherwise included in the gross estate). See IRC § 2001(b)(1). The second step is to apply the gift tax offset, which is done by reducing the tentative estate tax by the aggregate amount of the gift tax that would have been payable with respect to the decedent's post-1976 gifts if the unified rate schedule (as in effect at the decedent's death) had been applicable at the time of the gifts (whether or not the gifts are includable in the gross estate) and taking into account the unified credit allowable on those gifts. See IRC § 2001(b)(2). The third step is to compute the *net estate tax* by subtracting the available credits from the tax determined under IRC § 2001. The principal credit is the *unified credit*, which is $345,800 (equivalent to an exemption of $1,000,000) in 2002.[4] See IRC §§ 2010. The other credits include a credit for state death taxes, a credit for federal gift taxes on pre-1977 gifts that are included in the decedent's gross estate, a credit for foreign death taxes, and a credit for federal estate taxes paid on certain prior transfers. The unified credit is the main means by which the federal transfer tax system restricts its effect to

---

3. The EGTRRA directs Treasury to adjust the brackets and amounts to the extent necessary to implement the lower maximum rate of taxes. See IRC § 2001(c)(2).

4. The unified credit for estate tax purposes increases as follows between 2002 and 2009 based on the rate schedule applicable during those years (See IRC § 2010 (c)):

Years 2002 and 2003: $345,800 (effective exemption amount of $1 million)
Years 2004 and 2005: $555,800 (effective exemption amount of $1.5 million)
Years 2006-08: $780,800 (effective exemption amount of $2 million)
Year 2009: $1,230,800 (effective exemption amount of $3.5 million)

the affluent and wealthy, leaving the vast majority of lifetime donors and decedents unaffected by the transfer tax system.

Example 7.1: G died with a taxable estate of $4.5 million in 2002. G made no post-1976 lifetime taxable gifts. The tax computed under IRC § 2001 is $2,025,800. If the only credit available to G is the unified credit, G's net estate tax is $1,680,000 ($2,025,800 - 345,800).

If, however, G had made a lifetime adjusted taxable gift of $1.5 million in 1997 when the unified credit amount available was $192,800 (effective exemption amount of $600,000), the tax computed under IRC § 2001 would be $2,412,800, a figure computed by determining the tentative tax on $6 million ($2,775,800) and subtracting $363,000, which is the gift tax payable on G's $1.5 million in lifetime taxable gifts. The gift tax payable of $363,000 is computed by subtracting the unified credit amount allowable in 1997 of $192,800 under IRC § 2505 from the tax computed in accordance with IRC § 2502 of $555,800 on $1.5 million. See IRC § 2001(b)(2). Again, if the only credit available to G is the unified credit, G's net estate tax would be $2,067,000 ($2,412,800 - 345,800).[5]

Before making the computations in this example, the values of G's taxable gifts and taxable estate must be determined. We turn now to these steps and a more detailed look at each of the transfer taxes, starting with the federal gift tax.

2. The Federal Gift Tax

The federal gift tax now in effect dates back to 1932, when it was enacted as an excise tax on lifetime gifts of property. The 1932 gift tax was not only intended to supplement the estate tax by exacting a cost for making inter vivos gifts that reduce the donor's taxable estate, but also to supplement the income tax by exacting a cost for making inter vivos gifts that reduce the donor's taxable income. The 1932 gift tax was preceded by a gift tax that was enacted in 1924 but repealed in 1926. Progressivity under the 1924 gift tax was largely undermined by the fact that the tax was computed on an annual basis, without regard to gifts made in prior years. Unlike its predecessor, the 1932 gift tax is computed on a cumulative basis. Although donors must report taxable gifts and pay gift taxes on an annual basis, the statute determines tax rates applicable to

---

5. While it might appear that there is a double allowance of the unified credit to the extent of the $192,800 taken once with regard to the 1997 gift and then again as part of the $345,800 credit taken with regard to the decedent's estate, in fact this is not the case. The reason is that the $1.5 million in taxable gifts increased the tentative estate tax computed in accordance with IRC § 2001(b)(1), and the $192,800 credit reduced the offset allowed for the gift tax payable on those gifts under IRC § 2001(b)(2). The reduction of the gift tax offset against the tentative estate tax eliminates any benefit from the apparent duplication of the use of the unified credit.

a gift by reference to the total amount of taxable lifetime gifts made by donors, rather than by reference only to taxable gifts made in a given year. See IRC § 2502(a). The cumulative aspect of the gift tax system works in a manner similar to the cumulative aspect of the transfer tax system as a whole, as described and illustrated above in Example 7.1.

> *Example 7.2:* In 1997, G made taxable gifts of $1 million. Using the unified rate schedule, the tentative gift tax on those gifts is $345,800, which is then reduced by the unified credit of $192,800; the gift tax due is $153,000. See IRC §§ 2502(a), 2505(a).
>
> In 2002, G made taxable gifts of $500,000. The gift tax on these gifts is determined by computing the tentative gift tax on $1.5 million ($555,800) and subtracting the tentative gift tax on $1 million ($345,800). See IRC § 2502(a). Having used $192,800 of the $345,800 credit amount available in 2002 when he made the gifts in 1997, G only has $153,000 of unified credit available to offset the gift tax liability computed under IRC § 2502(a) of $210,000 ($555,800 – 345,800). The gift tax due with respect to the $500,000 of gifts made in 2002 is $57,000 ($210,000 – 153,000). See IRC § 2505(a).

Until 1976, the gift tax rates were lower than the estate tax rates. This, combined with the fact that before 1976 the estate and gift taxes were not cumulative, encouraged lifetime gift-giving by the wealthy, for wealthy people can more easily afford to give away part of their property before death. As indicated above, the Tax Reform Act of 1976 adopted a unified rate schedule, which reduced, but as we will see below did not eliminate, the transfer tax savings of making lifetime gifts. With the enactment of the EGTRRA in 2001 and the scheduled reductions in transfer tax rates, the scheduled increases in the unified credit amount for estate tax purposes, and the repeal, albeit temporary, of the estate tax in 2010, estate planners are not likely to advise most of their clients to make lifetime gifts in excess of the unified credit exemption equivalent amount applicable to lifetime transfers. See Lee Sheppard, Debt in Contemplation of Death, 91 Tax Notes 1655, 1655 (2001).

Although the gift tax currently is designed to supplement the income tax and historically was designed to also supplement the estate tax, the sad fact is that the three taxes overlap to some extent, and the treatment accorded a given transaction in the application of the three taxes is not necessarily consistent. That is to say, for example, even though a donor might make a transfer of property that is subject to the gift tax, the donor may nevertheless be subject to the income tax on the income earned by the property or the property might be included in the donor's gross estate at death for estate tax purposes. Thus, when a gift is made, the donor must resolve three separate questions: (1) whether the transfer is one on which a gift tax is imposed; (2) whether the transferred property will be included in the donor's gross estate at the donor's death, notwithstanding the inter vivos transfer; and (3) whether the donor will continue to be taxed on the post-transfer income generated by the transferred property.[6]

Overview of the Gift Tax. The first step in the determination of a donor's gift tax consequences for a taxable period is to identify the donor's transactions during that period that constitute "gifts" for gift tax purposes and to value the donated property. Although a donor's transfer of cash without consideration to her son, B, on B's birthday will almost certainly constitute a gift, there are many less obvious circumstances in which gifts for gift tax purposes can arise. For example, a gift can include forgiving a loan to a family member, deliberately allowing the statute of limitations to run on the loan, or making the loan at a below-market rate of interest. See IRC § 7872.

The second step is to ascertain what amounts of the "gifts" made by the donor during the taxable period are "taxable gifts." IRC § 2503(b) excludes from taxation gifts made by a donor during a calendar year to the same donee up to the inflation-adjusted amount of $10,000.[7] This exclusion is frequently referred to as the *annual exclusion*. The annual exclusion, in general, is only available for gifts that do not constitute "future interests." Thus, G can make cash gifts of $10,000 each to all fifteen of his grandchildren this year, next year, and each year thereafter without incurring any gift taxation. Indeed, G won't even be required to file a gift tax return. A gift by G of a remainder interest in Blackacre, however, will not qualify for the annual exclusion because it is a gift of a future interest.

The third step is to subtract from the amount of gifts made during a taxable period (as reduced by the annual exclusion) any allowable deductions, such as the marital deduction or the charitable deduction, which are discussed infra pp. 417, 421. The difference between the total value of a donor's gifts and the allowed exclusions and deductions is the amount of taxable gifts of the donor. The rate schedule described supra at p. 394 is then applied to the taxable gifts.

Taxable Lifetime Transfers. If a donor reserves a power to revoke a transfer, the transfer is not subject to gift taxation. In gift tax terminology, the gift is called *incomplete* and the donor continues to be treated as owner of the transferred property for gift and income tax purposes. See IRC § 676; Treas. Reg. § 25.2511-2(c). If a donor transfers property, but retains certain nonbeneficial powers, the gift tax law (and perhaps the income tax laws under IRC § 674) continues to treat the gift as incomplete and the donor as owner. Although the donor relinquishes the right to enjoy personally the property or the

---

6. But see IRC § 2511(c), which, effective after December 31, 2009, coordinates the gift tax and income tax rules. See infra p. 400.

7. The annual exclusion amount is indexed for inflation occurring after 1997. In 2001, the inflation-adjusted exclusion amount remains at $10,000.

income it produces, the donor retains the power to decide who can enjoy the property or its income. Retaining the right to choose who will enjoy the property is sufficient under the gift tax law (and sometimes under the income tax law) to ignore the transfer. See Treas. Reg. § 25.2511-2(b), (c). For gifts made after 2009, however, the EGTRRA provides that "a transfer in trust shall be treated as a taxable gift . . . unless the trust is treated as wholly owned by the donor or the donor's spouse" for income tax purposes. IRC § 2511(c). This statutory provision serves to coordinate the income tax and gift tax rules to assure that a donor cannot escape taxation of income from property placed in trust without being subject to gift tax liability.

Powers of Appointment. IRC § 2514(b) provides that if a donee of a general power of appointment exercises or releases that power, a gift occurs. As defined in IRC § 2514(c), a general power of appointment is any power that the donee can exercise in favor of the donee, the donee's estate, the donee's creditors, or the creditors of the donee's estate. The definition excludes, however, a power to consume the property or to invade the trust property if that power is limited by an ascertainable standard relating to the "health, education, support, or maintenance of the donee." See IRC § 2514(c)(1). The definition also excludes a power that can be exercised only in conjunction with the donor of the power or an adverse party. See IRC § 2514(c)(3). See infra Chapter 16 for a further discussion of powers of appointment.

One exception to the rule that the release of a general power is a gift concerns a lapse of a general power of appointment with respect to an amount that does not exceed the greater of $5,000 or 5 percent of the aggregate value of the property subject to the power at the time of the lapse. See IRC § 2514(e). Trusts are often structured to take advantage of this so-called *5 and 5* exception.

> *Example 7.3:* G establishes a trust and gives A an income interest for life and a power to invade the corpus up to $5,000 or 5 percent, whichever is greater, of the aggregate value of the trust each year during A's life, and also gives B the right to the remaining trust corpus at A's death. Of course, if A invades the corpus up to the maximum amount allowed each year, no gift tax consequences occur except to the extent A subsequently makes a gift of the amount A received from the invasions. If A, however, does not invade the corpus but allows the power to lapse in any year, that lapse, but for IRC § 2514(e), would have resulted in a gift of the remainder interest to B.

The 5 and 5 power allows a donor to give a donee access to the trust corpus without putting the donee in a position of having to suffer gift taxation upon forgoing withdrawals.

Minimizing Income Tax Liability. Donors can reduce federal income taxes by making lifetime gifts. As for donees, the receipt of lifetime gifts of money or other property is not taxable to donees as income. See IRC § 102. The lifetime gift also has the income tax advantage of causing the post-transfer income from the property generally to be taxed at the donee's rate, which means that the donor can reduce the federal income tax liability of the family by transferring property to family members with lower marginal income tax rates.[8]

The one income tax disadvantage of making lifetime gifts is that, if the gift is of appreciated property or property that later appreciates, the donee will compute the gain from a sale or other disposition of the property received by using the donor's basis (which typically means the donor's cost of having acquired the property) with some adjustment for any gift taxes paid. See IRC § 1015. In contrast, until 2010 when the estate tax is repealed and a modified carryover-basis rule comes into effect for property acquired from a decedent, IRC § 1014 applies to property acquired from a decedent. It provides that a recipient of property included in a decedent's gross estate takes a stepped-up basis equal to the estate tax value of the property, which typically is the value of the property at the decedent's death. In other words, the benefits of having the post-transfer income from property taxed at a donee's lower tax rates must be weighed against the benefit of avoiding tax on any appreciation in the property that occurs between the time the donor acquires the property and the donor's death. Given the benefit of the step-up in basis rule of IRC § 1014 available until 2010, the scheduled reductions in transfer tax rates, the scheduled increases in the unified credit amount for estate tax purposes, and the repeal, albeit temporary, of the estate tax in 2010, the disadvantages of lifetime giving may outweigh its advantages in a number of situations.

Even after 2009 when the step-up in basis rule is no longer available, the modified carryover-basis rule enacted by Congress continues to provide more favorable basis treatment to deathtime transfers than lifetime transfers. See infra p. 427. The modified carryover-basis rule, however, has come under substantial criticism on both policy and feasibility grounds. If the criticisms continue to grow, even more uncertainty will arise about the future of the transfer taxes and how Congress will coordinate them with the income tax. See Sheppard, supra, at 1656 ("[T]he carryover basis provisions are so awful that they cause one to appreciate that the beauty of the estate tax is that it does not concern itself with the basis of assets.").

Minimizing Transfer Tax Liability. Although the EGTRRA creates considerable incentives for wealthy persons to retain their property until death, the advantages of having donative transfers taxed during life rather than at death

---

8. The one major limitation on the opportunity to shift income tax liability is the so-called "Kiddie Tax." See IRC § 1(g).

ought to be taken into account by estate planners as they develop strategies to assist their clients. Five features of the gift tax rules encourage lifetime giving.

Tax exclusive tax base. As indicated supra p. 393, the gift tax utilizes the same unified rate schedule as the estate tax and the decedent's estate tax rate is determined by taking into account both lifetime and deathtime transfers. In addition, to the extent the unified credit is used to reduce a decedent's gift tax liability, it is in effect unavailable to reduce the decedent's estate tax liability.[9] Although by making a lifetime gift of investment property, the donor can avoid a transfer tax on the investment return from that property, the donor also forgoes the investment return on the amount of any gift taxes paid. The loss of use of the money used to pay gift taxes offsets the benefits of avoiding gift tax on the return from the investment property.[10] Therefore, it would seem that the gift tax does not create incentives for making lifetime gifts on which gift taxes must actually be paid. But, because the donor, and not the donee, is liable to pay the gift tax, the gift tax itself is not included in the amount of the gift for gift tax purposes. In contrast, the decedent's estate is liable to pay the estate tax and, therefore, the estate tax is included in the amount of the estate for estate tax purposes. The difference in treatment of the two transfer taxes creates an incentive for making lifetime gifts. In other words, the incentive arises from the fact that the gift tax is *tax exclusive*, but the estate tax is *tax inclusive*. A comparison of Examples 7.4 and 7.5, below, demonstrates the tax savings available from making a lifetime gift.

Example 7.4 (lifetime transfer): G makes a gift to A of $100. The gift tax rate is 30 percent. G pays the government a gift tax of $30 and A receives the gift of $100.

Example 7.5 (deathtime transfer): G dies owning $130 that she devises to B. The estate tax rate is 30 percent. G's estate pays the government an estate tax of $39 and B receives the remaining $91 ($130 - 39).

These examples show that, to the extent a donor makes gifts exceeding the unified-credit-equivalent amount of $1,0000,000, every dollar of gift tax paid

---

9. See supra note 5 and accompanying text.

10. The observation that the benefit of avoiding a transfer tax on the investment return is offset by the cost of losing the investment return on the amount of gift taxes paid can be shown algebraically. If a grantor makes a lifetime gift of investment property **I**, pays a gift tax at rate **T** out of the investment property, and the donee invests the amount remaining after the grantor pays the gift taxes at interest rate **R**, then the donee will have the amount I(1 - T)(1 + R) one year later. If instead, the grantor does not make a lifetime gift of the investment property **I**, but instead invests it at interest rate **R** for one year and then dies paying an estate tax at rate **T**, then the donee will receive the amount I(1 + R)(1 - T) from the estate. The two amounts are equivalent because the commutative principle of multiplication makes the order of multiplication irrelevant.

is removed from the donor's taxable estate tax free. The tax exclusivity feature of the gift tax as compared to the tax inclusivity feature of the estate tax, of course, is of little consequence if the property would otherwise escape taxation completely at death either because of the higher unified credit amounts available under the estate tax up until 2009 but not available under the gift tax or because of the repeal of the estate tax for the year 2010.

Annual exclusion. The first $10,000 (indexed for inflation) of gifts made to each donee during the year is not included in the donor's taxable gifts. See IRC § 2503(b). Although the original purpose of the annual exclusion was to relieve taxpayers of the need to report and the government of the need to monitor holiday and birthday gifts, the introduction of an amount as high as $10,000 has made it a major tax-minimization tool. An annual gift plan to children, grandchildren, and possibly to their spouses or domestic partners can result in the tax-free removal of a significant amount of wealth from the donor's taxable estate.

The annual exclusion is only available with regard to gifts of present interests. If a donor transfers money or other property absolutely, the annual exclusion is, of course, available. It is also available if a donor gives a donee the right to the possession or enjoyment of or the income from the property for life or for a term of years as long as the right to possession or income begins immediately.

IRC § 2503(c) makes an exception to the present-interest rule for a gift to a minor. The donor can make a gift in trust giving a trustee the discretion to distribute or accumulate the income from the property as long as the property and any accumulated income is distributed when the minor attains 21. If the minor dies before attaining 21, IRC § 2503(c) requires the trust to provide that the property and any accumulated income be paid to the minor's estate or as the minor directs under a general power of appointment.

Estate planners may view the annual exclusion as a particularly attractive estate planning tool over the next decade while it remains unclear whether the estate tax repeal will, in fact, take effect. It allows clients to reduce their estates without gift tax liability in the event the repeal of the estate tax does not take effect in 2010. On the other hand, without the certainty of estate tax liability, some clients may prefer to retain ownership and control over their property, notwithstanding that a transfer qualifying for the annual exclusion would not lead either to use of the unified credit or gift tax liability.

Gift splitting. The benefits of the annual $10,000 exclusion are further enhanced by the fact that the Code gives the donor and the donor's spouse the right to elect to treat gifts as having been made one-half by the donor and one-half by the donor's spouse. See IRC § 2513. This gift-splitting rule allows a married couple to transfer $20,000 per year to a donee tax free.

Tuition-and-medical-expense exclusion. Yet another advantage of lifetime giving is found in IRC § 2503(e), which excludes from gift taxation any property or money that a donor pays directly to an educational organization for tuition on behalf of a donee or directly to any organization or individual who provides medical care to a donee. Before IRC § 2503(e) was enacted, payments for tuition and medical expenses might not have been taxable if the state law viewed them as discharging the donor's support obligation. See Kathleen C. Horan, Postmajority Support for College Education—A Legally Enforceable Obligation in Divorce Proceedings?, 20 Fam. L.Q. 589 (1987). IRC § 2503(e) goes far beyond support obligation payments, however, because it applies to tuition and medical payments made on behalf of any donee. The exclusion for tuition and medical expenses may also prove to be an attractive estate planning tool over the next decade while it remains unclear whether the estate tax repeal will, in fact, take effect. It too allows clients to reduce their estates without gift tax liability in the event the repeal of the estate tax does not take effect in 2010.

Valuation techniques. In general, property subject to a gift tax is valued at its fair market value at the time of the gift. See IRC § 2512(a). Fair market value is defined as "the price at which . . . [the] property would change hands between a willing buyer and a willing seller, neither being under any compulsion to buy or to sell, and both having reasonable knowledge of relevant facts." Treas. Reg. § 25.2512-1. Donors use this general valuation rule to reduce their total transfer taxes by dividing up property during life and making gifts of the fragmented interests through family limited partnerships or otherwise.

For example, if the sole stockholder of a closely held corporation makes a gift of 10 percent of the shares owned, they would have a fair market value of less than 10 percent of the value of the entire corporation because the donee is receiving a noncontrolling interest in the corporation. Under the valuation rules, a series of gifts of noncontrolling interests during life results in a stockholder paying less in taxes than the estate would pay if the entire corporate ownership had been transferred at death. Fragmentation results in the sum of the parts being less than the whole. Tax saving strategies relying on market-based discounts and premiums remain available.

In 1990, however, Congress enacted Chapter 14 (IRC §§ 2701-04) to limit the effectiveness of other fragmentation strategies frequently referred to as *estate freezes*. These strategies had the purpose of shifting predictable, but as of the time of the transfer only potential, appreciation to donees transfer tax free.

IRC § 2701 concerns preferred stock recapitalizations and similar techniques designed to transfer future appreciation to donees. IRC § 2702, in general, involves gifts of remainder interests in trust with donors retaining income interests in the underlying property. Both provisions apply for gift tax purposes and have only a limited effect on estate taxes. Their general approach is to tax the donor on the transfer of the entire value of the property even though the donor only transferred a partial interest in the property.

IRC § 2703 pertains to the use of buy-sell agreements that create rights in third parties to purchase a closely held business interest at a below market price or restrict the owner's ability to sell the interest at market value. Basically, IRC § 2703 provides that agreements, options, or other rights to acquire property for less than full and adequate consideration will be ignored for purposes of valuing property under the transfer tax laws. IRC § 2704 addresses the use of lapsing voting or liquidation rights in a closely held business. In general, the provision treats the lapses of certain rights in a closely held business as transfers for transfer tax purposes. Recent commentary suggests that estate planners may continue to use the fragmentation strategy to reduce the value of gifts even after the EGTRRA. See Sheppard, supra, at 1659.

Transfer tax disadvantages of lifetime gifts. In addition to the larger unified credit available under the estate tax, decedent's estates can enjoy other tax advantages that are not available to property that is transferred during life. IRC § 2032A allows, under certain circumstances, for real property, typically farmland, to be valued at an amount less than its fair market value. Another tax advantage of the estate tax is a deduction for qualified family-owned business interests if the value of the interest is more than 50 percent of the value of the decedent's estate, taking into account deductions for debt and expenses. It is coordinated with the unified credit. See IRC § 2057. The EGTRRA, however, provides that this provision is not available for estates of decedents dying after December 31, 2003. See IRC § 2057(j). IRC § 2031(c) allows an executor to exclude from the taxable estate 40 percent of the value of any land subject to a qualified conservation easement.[11] The exclusion amount cannot exceed $400,000 for decedents dying in 2001 and cannot exceed $500,000 for decedents dying in 2002 and thereafter. The EGTRRA expands the availability of qualified conservation easements by allowing it to be available to any land located anywhere in the United States and its possessions and clarifies the date for determining easement compliance.[12]

The Code also contains two other provisions to assist closely held business owners at death. IRC § 303 permits the redemption of stock of a closely held

---

11. The exclusion percentage of 40 is reduced by 2 percentage points for each percentage point by which the value of the qualified conservation easement is less than 30 percent of the value of the land. See IRC § 2031(c)(2).

12. Prior to 2001, the land had to be located with 25 miles of a metropolitan area or a national park or wilderness area, or within 10 miles of an Urban National Forest.

corporation for little or no gain (and if there is any gain, it will be a long-term capital gain) to the extent the stock represents a major asset of the estate and the amount received in the redemption does not exceed estate and inheritance taxes and funeral and administration expenses. In the absence of IRC § 303, all of the proceeds of such a redemption (not merely the amount in excess of the shareholder's basis) could be taxed to the shareholder as ordinary income. IRC § 6166 provides for deferral of the payment of estate taxes attributable to closely held businesses. A 2 percent interest rate applies to the estate tax attributable to the first $1,000,000 (adjusted for inflation after 1998 and resulting in an inflation-adjusted amount in 2001 of $1,060,000) of the value of the business. The interest rate applicable to the estate tax attributable to the value of the business in excess of the inflation-adjusted $1,000,000 amount is equal to only 45 percent of the rate applicable generally to underpayments of tax set forth in IRC § 6621. The portion of the estate tax attributable to the closely held business may remain entirely unpaid for five years during which only interest must be paid, after which the tax and interest may be paid over the next ten years. The EGTRRA generally expands the availability of the installment payment provisions by expanding the definition of a closely held business and otherwise clarifying qualification rules. Qualification for the deathtime tax advantages described above require attorneys and their clients to do a considerable level of estate planning during life.

Maximizing the Donor's Distributive Goals. To enjoy the remaining gift tax advantages after the EGTRRA, the donor must relinquish substantial interests and powers in the property. See IRC §§ 2035-38, 2040; infra pp. 409-13. Trusts, however, can be used to allow the donor to retain some degree of control over property and withhold from the donees complete and absolute control. The income and transfer tax laws allow donors to retain significant investment and management powers over property placed in trusts. They also allow donors to give trustees, other than designated family members or employees of donors, broad discretion to distribute income or corpus from trusts. If donors retain the right to remove trustees, however, the trustee powers will be attributed to the donors unless the donors cannot substitute themselves, designated family members, or their employees. See Treas. Reg. § 1.674(d)-2(a) (income tax); Rev. Rul. 95-58, 1995-2 C.B. 191 (estate tax).

Notwithstanding that the tax laws view independent trustees as beyond the donor's control, the donor's wishes are likely to influence such trustees because they have an economic incentive to please the donor in hopes of receiving other fiduciary appointments. In other words, practical considerations make it possible for donors to retain significant control over investment, management, and distribution of the transferred property. Furthermore, discretionary trusts allow donors to enjoy federal tax savings without having to be concerned that their children or grandchildren will receive the property at too young an age, or that their parents or grandparents will feel burdened by investment and management decisions.

Trusts not only facilitate tax planning by allowing donors indirectly to retain control, they also permit donors to transfer property while leaving the ultimate beneficiaries of the income and corpus undetermined. The advantage in this is that it allows the estate plan to take into account later changes in family and economic circumstances. Flexibility can be added by giving the trustee discretionary powers to distribute income and corpus among various beneficiaries at various times. It also can be accomplished by giving beneficiaries the power to appoint income or corpus among designated persons. It is unusual to give a general power to appoint in these circumstances unless the donor wants to qualify the gift for an annual exclusion, a marital deduction, or to avoid a generation-skipping transfer tax. By giving nongeneral powers, donors avoid having property taxed to their donees if they exercise the powers during life or die owning the powers.

Problems

1. G agrees to perform services for A for $1,000. G directs A to pay the $1,000 to B. What are the gift tax consequences, if any? See IRC §§ 2501(a)(1), 2503(b), 2511(a).

2. G deposits $1,000 in a joint bank account for herself and B. What are the gift tax consequences, if any? See IRC § 2511(a).

3. In 2002, G transfers $100,000 worth of securities in trust, directing the trustee to pay the income earned on the principal to G's domestic partner A for A's life and at A's death to distribute the trust principal to G's niece B.

a. What are the gift tax consequences if G retains the right to direct the trustee to accumulate the income on behalf of B? See IRC §§ 2503(b), 2511(a).

b. What are the gift tax consequences if G retains the right to invade the corpus on behalf of B? See IRC §§ 2503(b), 2511(a).

c. What are the gift tax consequences if G retains the right to invade the corpus on behalf of A? See IRC §§ 2503(b), 2511(a). Would it make a difference if the trust provided that G could only invade the corpus on behalf of A with the approval of B?

4. G transfers $100,000 worth of securities in trust, directing the trustee to pay the income earned on the principal to A until A attains the age of 35 and, upon A attaining the age of 35, to distribute the trust principal to A. What are the gift tax consequences if G retains the right to direct the trustee to accumulate the income and to distribute it at the time the trust terminates? See IRC §§ 2511(a), 2503(b).

3. The Federal Estate Tax

The federal estate tax was enacted in 1916 as an excise tax on the transfer of property at death. The tax is measured by the deathtime value of the property transferred. The core provision of the estate tax is IRC § 2033, which makes the decedent's probate estate subject to tax. From the beginning, however, Congress recognized that measures had to be taken to subject will substitutes to estate taxation; otherwise, will substitutes could be used as tax avoidance devices to achieve, in effect, tax free probate transfers. Most of the statutory provisions of the estate tax are devoted to the purpose of taxing will substitutes, such as life insurance, joint tenancies and joint accounts, pension death benefits, revocable trusts, and even irrevocable trusts with a retained life estate.

The architecture of the federal estate tax calls for a number of steps to be taken to calculate the *taxable estate*. The first step is to determine the property that is included in the decedent's *gross estate* and the valuation thereof. The second step is to determine the taxable estate by subtracting from the gross estate the deductions permitted the decedent's estate. We have already worked through the final three steps that determine the estate's tax liability. See supra p. 396.

Although the estate tax is scheduled for repeal in 2010, familiarity with the existing estate tax structure remains necessary because of the delay of the repeal and the continuing uncertainty about whether the repeal will be permanent. The discussion that follows is justified further by the fact that a number of the concepts found in the estate tax provisions have been incorporated into the modified carryover-basis rule. If the carryover-basis scheme comes into effect, precedent found in the estate tax law is likely, at least to some extent, to inform how it will be applied. See infra p. 430.

a. The Gross Estate

The decedent's gross estate includes the value of the decedent's probate estate, specified will substitutes, property over which the decedent held a general power of appointment, and certain transfers (QTIPs; discussed infra p. 418) for which a marital deduction was previously allowed.

Probate Property. Under IRC § 2033, the decedent's gross estate includes "the value of all property to the extent of the interest therein of the decedent at the time of his death." This statutory language describes the decedent's probate estate, the property that passes at the decedent's death by will or by intestacy. Examples would include the value of any real estate owned by the decedent in fee simple absolute and the value of any undivided portion of real estate owned as a tenant in common. The value of any transmissible remainder interest owned by the decedent at death would also be included.

Example 7.6: G's parent created a $1 million trust, directing the trustee to pay the income earned on the principal to G's other parent for life, and at the income beneficiary's death to distribute the trust's principal to G. G owns a devisable remainder interest. If G predeceases the income beneficiary, G's remainder interest is part of G's probate estate and is part of her gross estate for federal estate tax purposes under IRC § 2033. If the trust imposed a condition that G survive the income beneficiary and G predeceased the income beneficiary, then the remainder interest would have terminated and its value would not be included either in G's probate estate or her gross estate.[13]

An income interest that expires on the death of the income beneficiary is not included in the income beneficiary's probate or gross estates.

Example 7.7: G's parent created a $1 million trust, directing the trustee to pay the income earned on the principal to G for life, and at G's death to distribute the trust principal to G's descendants who survive G, by representation; if none, to X-charity. Because G's income interest expires on her death, nothing is included in her gross estate under IRC § 2033. Her estate would include, however, whatever income payments she received throughout her lifetime that she still had left and any income payments paid to her estate after her death representing income that had accrued at her death.

Lifetime Gifts Within Three Years of Death. The values of certain types of gifts are included in the decedent's gross estate simply because the decedent dies within the three-year period following the gift. The principal focus of this section is on gifts of life insurance policies within three years of death. Such a gift causes the full value of the proceeds to be included in the decedent's gross estate. See IRC § 2035(a)(2). This section also applies to transfers or relinquishments of retained interests or powers within three years of death. See IRC § 2035(a). An exception, however, is made for distributions from trusts that were revocable by the decedent. Instead, the distributions are treated as if the decedent had made the transfers directly. See IRC § 2035(e).

Another feature of the three-year rule is IRC § 2035(b), which provides that the decedent's gross estate includes the amount of any gift tax paid by the decedent on gifts made by the decedent (or the decedent's spouse) during the three-year period ending on the date of the decedent's death. This provision eliminates the tax exclusive advantage of making lifetime taxable gifts in those circumstances in which the decedent has enjoyed the property until shortly before death.

---

13. UPC § 2-707 adopts a rule of construction that imposes a condition of survivorship on the beneficiary of a future interest under the terms of a trust. Therefore, even if the trust does not explicitly impose a condition that G survive the income beneficiary, UPC § 2-707 would impose a survivorship condition unless the trust demonstrated a contrary intention.

Retained Property Interests. If a donor makes a lifetime gift of property but retains certain described interests in that property, the estate tax provides that the gross estate includes the value of that property. By not parting with complete ownership of the property, the donor is treated as owning the property at death for estate tax purposes.

Retention of an income interest. IRC § 2036(a)(1) provides that if a donor gratuitously transfers a remainder interest in property, in trust or otherwise, while retaining possession or enjoyment or the right to the income for life, then the value of the transferred property at the donor's death is included in the gross estate.[14] The donor is also treated as owner for income tax purposes, except that gains and losses incurred on the sale or exchange of the property usually will not be taxed to the donor. See IRC § 677. The transfer of the remainder interest is subject to the gift tax, but the estate tax computation is designed to treat the gift tax payment as the equivalent of a downpayment on the estate tax owed by the donor's estate. See IRC § 2001(b).

If the donor transfers the retained life estate in the property before death, IRC § 2036(a)(1) is no longer applicable. If, however, the donor transfers the retained life estate within three years of death, IRC § 2035(a) operates to include the property valued at the time of the donor's death, and IRC § 2035(b) operates to include the amount of any gift tax paid with regard to the transfer of the life estate.[15]

Retention of a reversionary interest. If a donor makes a gift of possession in or the income from property for the donee's life or a term of years, IRC § 2033 will include the value of the reversionary interest that the donor retained in the gross estate. Gifts of income interests with retained reversions are unusual since 1986 when Congress amended the income tax law to provide that the donor will be taxed on all income from trusts in which the donor retains a significant reversionary interest. See IRC § 673(a).

IRC § 2037 addresses transfers in which the donor retains a reversionary interest that terminates at the donor's death.

---

14. The period that possession or income must be retained for IRC § 2036(a)(1) to apply is "for . . . [the decedent's] life or for any period not ascertainable without reference to his death or for any period that does not in fact end before his death . . . ."

IRC § 2036(b)(1) treats a donor retaining "the right to vote (directly or indirectly) shares of stock of a controlled corporation" as having retained possession or enjoyment of the stock for purposes of IRC § 2036(a)(1). IRC § 2036(b)(2) defines controlled corporation.

15. IRC § 2035(a) applies regardless of whether the donor transfers the life estate by gift or sells it for full and adequate consideration. The exception of IRC § 2035(d), having to do with "bona fide sale[s]," is inapplicable. See United States v. Allen, 293 F.2d 916 (10th Cir.), cert. denied, 368 U.S. 944 (1961) (deciding under an earlier version of IRC § 2035 that full and adequate consideration for this purpose means an amount equal to the value of the entire property that would be includable under IRC § 2036(a)(1)).

Example 7.8: G establishes a trust and directs the trustee to pay the income earned on the principal to A for A's life and at A's death to distribute the trust's principal to G if G is alive or to B if G is dead.

For IRC § 2037 to apply, three requirements must be met: (1) the donor must have made a transfer of an interest in which possession or enjoyment of the property can, through ownership of the interest, be obtained only by surviving the donor; (2) the donor retained a reversionary interest in the property; and (3) the value of the reversionary interest immediately before the donor's death exceeds 5 percent of the value of the property.[16] Neither the income tax nor the transfer tax laws create incentives for a donor to establish trusts of this kind. Donors create irrevocable trusts reserving reversionary interests typically to meet family or business needs and not for the purpose of achieving tax savings. If the donor transfers the retained reversionary interest before death, IRC § 2037 does not apply. If the transfer occurs within three years of death, however, IRC § 2035(a) includes the transferred property in the donor's gross estate.

Retained Powers; Revocable Trusts. If a donor reserves a power to revoke a transfer, the donor is treated as owner of the transferred property for estate tax purposes. See IRC § 2038(a)(1). (The donor is also treated as owner for income tax, see IRC § 676(a), and gift tax purposes, see supra p. 399.) Typically donors establish revocable trusts retaining a right to possession or income from property along with a power to revoke. These trusts assist donors in asset management and they avoid probate and its potential costs, but they produce no tax savings. See infra Chapter 8.

If a donor transfers property but retains certain nonbeneficial powers, the estate tax law continues to treat the donor as owner.[17] Although the donor relinquishes the right to enjoy personally the property or the income it produces, the donor retains the power to decide who can enjoy the property or its income. Retaining the right to choose who will enjoy the property or its

---

16. The first federal estate tax statute contained a version of IRC § 2037. For transfers made before October 8, 1949, only reversionary interests that arise "out of the express terms of the instrument of transfer" are taken into account. See IRC § 2037(a)(2). For transfers made on or after October 8, 1949, IRC § 2037 applies even though the reversionary interest is not expressly retained and arises only by operation of law.

17. IRC § 2036(a)(2) applies to all transfers made on or after March 4, 1931. See IRC § 2036(c). IRC § 2038(a)(1) applies to all transfers made since the inception of the estate tax. Slightly different rules, however, apply to transfers made on or before June 22, 1936. See IRC § 2038(a)(2).

income is sufficient for the estate tax law to ignore the transfer.[18] See IRC §§ 2036(a)(2), 2038(a)(1); see also IRC § 674 (treating the donor who retains nonbeneficial powers as the owner for income tax purposes with some exceptions).

If the donor relinquishes the retained powers before death, IRC §§ 2036 and 2038 generally do not apply. If the transfer occurs within three years of death, however, IRC § 2035(a) includes the transferred property in the donor's gross estate. But see IRC § 2035(e), discussed supra p. 409, having to do with revocable trusts.

Powers of Appointment. The gross estate also may include property over which the decedent has a power of appointment created by another person. These are called *donee* powers, as distinguished from *reserved* powers, which are powers that the donor has retained in property that the donor has otherwise transferred by gift. IRC § 2041(a)(2) provides that if, at the death of decedents, they owned general powers of appointment, their gross estates include the value of property over which they owned the general powers.[19] A general power of appointment is defined in the same manner as it is defined in IRC § 2514(c) for gift tax purposes. See IRC § 2041(b)(1). Donors typically give general powers of appointment to their donees for the purpose of qualifying the gifts for the annual exclusion or the marital deduction or to avoid the generation-skipping transfer tax. See supra p. 400, infra pp. 419, 423.

Donees who receive nongeneral powers of appointment over property will not have that property included in their gross estates. For example, donees who die owning powers to consume property for health or education purposes will not have that property included in their gross estates. Similarly, donees who die owning powers to appoint property to their lineal descendants or even to anyone except themselves, their creditors, their estates, or the creditors of their estates

---

18. Sometimes a transfer is subject to the operation of both IRC §§ 2036 and 2038. In those cases, the Internal Revenue Service (IRS) will rely on IRC § 2036 because it results in the inclusion of the entire value of the property in the decedent's gross estate. In that way, the IRS avoids the limitation of IRC § 2038, which requires that the gross estate include only that portion of the property over which the decedent had retained a power to alter, amend, revoke, or terminate.

19. The Revenue Act of 1916, in which the modern estate tax originated, contained no provision specifically dealing with powers of appointment. United States v. Field, 255 U.S. 257 (1921), held that, under this original enactment, the gross estate did not include the value of property subject to an exercised general power of appointment. Congress had since enacted a specific provision in the Revenue Act of 1918 to tax property subject to an exercised general power of appointment.

Amendments in 1942 and 1951 provide that the value of property subject to general powers created after October 21, 1942, is includable in the decedent's gross estate regardless of whether the power is exercised.

will not have that property included in their gross estates. Although the benefits of these liberal rules regarding powers of appointment have been diminished by the introduction of the generation-skipping transfer tax, see infra p. 423, they continue to play important roles in estate planning as attorneys try to minimize taxes and achieve their clients' distribution schemes.

If the exercise or release of the power is of "such a nature that if it were a transfer of property owned by the [donee of the power] . . . , such property would be includible in the [donee's] . . . gross estate under IRC §§ 2035 to 2038, inclusive," then the property over which the power is exercised or released should be included in the donee's gross estate.

> *Example 7.9:* G establishes a trust and gives B an income interest for life as well as a general power to appoint the remainder interest. B subsequently appoints the remainder interest during life to C while retaining the income interest for life. IRC §§ 2041(a)(2) and 2036(a)(1) require that the entire value of the trust corpus be included in B's gross estate at B's death. If B wants to remove this property from his gross estate, he must make a lifetime gift of his income interest as well as make a lifetime appointment of the remainder interest.

One exception to the estate taxation rules concerns a lapse of a general power to appoint that does not exceed the greater of $5,000 or 5 percent of the aggregate value of the trust at the time of the lapse. See IRC § 2041(b)(2); supra p. 400 (discussing analogous gift tax rule). But for IRC § 2041(b)(2), § 2041(a)(2) and §§ 2035 through 2038 would operate to include in the donee's gross estate that portion of the trust corpus over which the donee had invasion rights. The 5 and 5 power is useful because it allows a donor to give a donee access to the trust corpus, but that access does not result in estate taxation to the donee.

Jointly Held Property. Jointly held property refers to property held in joint tenancy with right of survivorship, property held in tenancy by the entirety, joint bank and stock accounts, and jointly held U.S. Savings Bonds. A tenancy by the entirety can only be owned by persons who are legally married to each other. Joint ownership with the right of survivorship is popular, especially for people who have small estates, because it effectively avoids probate. The Economic Recovery Tax Act of 1981 greatly simplified the tax treatment of jointly held property for married couples and made this pattern of ownership even more desirable.

Unlike property owned in tenancy in common or community property, jointly owned property has a right of survivorship. The right of survivorship means that, when a decedent dies owning jointly held property, the decedent's interest in the property terminates and is therefore beyond the reach of IRC § 2033. IRC § 2040 establishes two rules for determining the amount includable in the decedent's gross estate: (1) a fractional-interest rule and (2) a percentage-of-consideration rule.

The fractional-interest rule applies in two situations. First, if the decedent received a jointly held interest as a gift or devise from a person who did not also become a joint tenant, then IRC § 2040(a) includes a fractional share of the property equal to the decedent's fractional cotenancy interest in the decedent's gross estate. Essentially, the survivorship rights are ignored and the decedent's interest is treated as if it were an interest held in a tenancy in common.

The second situation in which the fractional-interest rule applies is when a legally married couple owns jointly held property. IRC § 2040(b) includes one half of the value of the property in the estate of the first spouse to die regardless of how much the decedent spouse contributed to its purchase. The spouses' relative amounts of contribution to the purchase of the jointly held property are also irrelevant for gift tax purposes. See IRC § 2523, which provides that a gift of property between legal spouses made in a qualified manner is nontaxable and which is discussed further at p. 418. IRC § 2056(a), which provides that a decedent can deduct the value of property included in the gross estate that passes to the surviving spouse in a qualified manner, in combination with IRC § 2040(b), has the effect of excluding from taxation any portion of the jointly held property until the surviving spouse makes a lifetime gift or dies. See infra p. 417.

The percentage-of-consideration rule found in IRC § 2040(a) applies for all jointly held property owned by unmarried tenants who acquire the property by purchase. This rule plays an important role for domestic partners who own property jointly with right of survivorship and for others who, to avoid probate and to facilitate financial and personal living arrangements, take property in joint tenancy with right of survivorship. The percentage-of-consideration rule operates to withhold tax advantages from the donor who provided the consideration for the joint property. IRC § 2040(a) creates a presumption that the decedent provided all the consideration for the jointly held property. The decedent's estate has the burden of proving the amount of consideration, if any, that the surviving cotenant or cotenants provided. The amount of jointly held property included in the decedent's gross estate is determined by multiplying the property's value by the percentage of consideration the decedent is deemed to have provided.

Life Insurance. A life insurance contract on the life of the decedent and paid for by the decedent is a nonprobate transfer as long as the beneficiary of the insurance proceeds is someone other than the decedent's estate and the proceeds are not available to the creditors of the decedent's estate. IRC § 2042(2) provides that the insurance proceeds are included in the gross estate if at the decedent's death the decedent retained an "incident of ownership." Incidents of ownership are defined in Treas. Reg. § 20.2042-1(c)(2) to mean "the right of the insured or his estate to the economic benefits of the policy." It includes, among others, the power to change the beneficiary, to surrender or cancel the policy, to assign the policy, to revoke an assignment, to pledge the policy for a loan, or to obtain from the insurer a loan against the surrender value of the policy. Therefore, the only way that a decedent can keep insurance proceeds out of the gross estate is to make a lifetime gift of the policy, to relinquish all rights over the policy during life, and to assure that the proceeds are not paid to the estate or available to pay creditors of the estate. For further discussion of life insurance and trusts, see Chapter 8.

Annuities. If a decedent purchased an annuity contract that provided for periodic payments for life, the annuity contract would not be part of the decedent's probate or gross estate. This type of annuity, called a nonrefund-single-life annuity, does not lead to any gratuitous transfer but instead is fully exhausted at the decedent's death. (Of course, if the decedent owns any part of the payments at death, they will be included in the decedent's probate and gross estate.)

A second type of annuity contract is one where the decedent purchases a single-life annuity that pays a refund of a portion of the cost upon the decedent's premature death. If the refund is paid to the decedent's estate, it is included in the gross estate under IRC § 2033. If the refund is paid to a designated beneficiary, it is included in the gross estate under IRC § 2039.

A third type of annuity contract is one where the decedent purchases a joint-and-survivor annuity by which the insurance company obligates itself to make payments to the decedent and to the decedent's designated beneficiary during their joint lives and, upon the death of either, to make payments to the survivor for life. If the decedent dies first, IRC § 2039 includes the value of the survivor's right to future payments in the decedent's gross estate.

A fourth type of annuity contract is one where the decedent purchases a self-and-survivor annuity by which the insurance company obligates itself to make payments only to the decedent and to make payments to the designated beneficiary only after the decedent's death. If the decedent dies first, IRC § 2039 includes the value of the survivor's right to future payments in the decedent's gross estate. The purchase of either a joint-and-survivor annuity or a self-and-survivor annuity is a gift for gift tax purposes.

The last three types of annuity contracts do not become a part of the probate estate. The annuity payments, at least in part, are subject to the income tax. See IRC § 72.

IRC § 2039 is an important provision because it applies to benefits under employee retirement and pension plans and individual retirement accounts.[20] As a result of federal income tax policy encouraging savings through pension plans, for many middle- and upper middle-class clients, pension wealth is likely to be their largest asset. See John H. Langbein, The Twentieth-Century Revolution in Family Wealth Transmission, 86 Mich. L. Rev. 722, 740 (1988). Until 1984, qualified plans enjoyed an estate tax exemption. It was eliminated prospectively in 1984.

Problems

1. G made a gift of $800,000 to A in 2000, having never made a previous taxable gift. G died in 2002. What are the tax consequences of G having made the 2000 gift? See IRC §§ 2001, 2035, 2502(a), 2503(b), 2505(a).

2. What are the estate tax consequences at G's death in 2006, having established the trusts described in Problem 3, supra p. 407? See United States v. O'Malley, 383 U.S. 627 (1966); Lober v. United States, 346 U.S. 335 (1953); IRC §§ 2036(a)(2), 2038(a)(1).

3. G died survived by his domestic partner, A. G and A had purchased a home for $200,000 taking title in joint tenancy with right of survivorship. G provided the entire downpayment of $50,000 for the home, leaving an outstanding mortgage for which both G and A were jointly liable of $150,000. G and A equally contributed to the monthly mortgage payments. At G's death, the home was valued at $300,000 subject to an outstanding mortgage of $130,000. How much of the value of the home should be included in G's gross estate? See Bremer v. Luff, 7 F. Supp. 148 (N.D.N.Y. 1933); IRC §§ 2040(a), 2053(a)(4); Rev. Rul. 79-302, 1979-2 C.B. 328.

4. In 1995, G transferred $200,000 worth of securities in trust, directing the trustee to pay the income earned from the principal to A for A's life and at A's death to distribute the trust principal to B. A was also given the noncumulative right to withdraw 5 percent of the principal each year from the trust. At A's death in 2002, the trust principal had a value of $300,000. What are the estate tax consequences of A dying in 2002 having been a beneficiary of the trust? See IRC §§ 2033, 2041(a)(2), (b)(2).

---

20. IRC § 2039(b) provides that "any contribution by the decedent's employer or former employer to the purchase price of such contract . . . shall be considered to be contributed by the decedent if made by reason of his employment."

b. The Deductions for Expenses, Debts, and Losses

The various deductions the Code allows serve to reduce the gross estate to the taxable estate. The deductions are the marital deduction, the charitable deduction, the deduction for funeral and administration expenses, bona fide claims against the decedent's estate, and the deduction for certain losses during administration. There is no deduction for the estate tax payable to the federal government; hence the estate tax is tax inclusive.

Deductions for Debts, Expenses, and Losses. IRC § 2053 grants a deduction for the decedent's allowable funeral expenses and, subject to certain limitations, the expenses of administering property that was included in the decedent's gross estate. Some administration expenses also constitute allowable income tax deductions, and the executor must elect whether to deduct the expenses as either estate tax or income tax deductions.[21] IRC § 2053 also allows a deduction for outstanding bona fide debts of the decedent, but if a debt is based on a promise or agreement, the deduction is limited to the extent that the liability was undertaken for an adequate and full consideration in money or money's worth. Mortgage obligations of the decedent, which were incurred in a bona fide manner for adequate and full consideration in money or money's worth, are either deductible or constitute a reduction in the value of the property subject to the mortgage, depending upon whether the decedent was personally liable for the payment of the underlying debt.

IRC § 2054 permits the deduction of casualty and theft losses incurred during the administration of the estate, provided that the loss is not reflected in the valuation of the property where the alternate valuation date, which is allowed by IRC § 2032, was elected.

Marital and Charitable Deductions. Because the estate tax and gift tax allow similar deductions for marital and charitable devises or gifts, these deductions are considered together, below.

4. The Estate and Gift Tax Marital Deduction

The federal estate and gift taxes allow a married donor to transfer property to the donor's spouse without suffering taxation if the property is transferred in a qualified manner. In 2010, under the EGTRRA, transfers between spouses will remain nontaxable because the estate tax will have been repealed and the

---

21. See IRC § 642(g). Generally, the personal representative will make the election based on whether an income tax or estate tax deduction will result in the greatest tax savings. The Treasury Regulations make clear that "[i]t is not required that the total deductions, or the total amount of any deduction . . . be treated the same way. One deduction or portion of a deduction may be allowed for income tax purposes . . . while another deduction or portion is allowed for estate tax purposes." Treas. Reg. § 1.642(g)-2.

gift tax rules excluding qualified transfers between spouses will remain in effect. When Congress originally enacted the marital deduction in 1948, the rationale of the marital deduction was to grant married citizens of common-law states tax treatment similar to that enjoyed by married couples residing in community-property states. The estate tax deduction was limited to 50 percent of the decedent's adjusted gross estate and the gift tax deduction was limited to 50 percent of the value of the property transferred from one spouse to the other. In 1981, Congress removed all quantitative limitations on transfers between spouses and thereby abandoned the community-property model. Current law treats a married couple as the taxable unit for transfers between spouses. This means that transfers between spouses generally are ignored and that an estate or gift tax is assessed only when one or the other of the spouses transfers property to someone outside the marital unit.

The community-property model continues to play a role in the operation of the transfer tax marital deduction. The rules defining a qualified devise or gift, which were designed to mimic the kind of property a community-property spouse would own, remain applicable.[22] The removal of the quantitative limitations in 1981, however, was also accompanied by the introduction of another type of devise or gift that would qualify for the marital deduction—qualified terminable interest property (QTIP)—which does not require the surviving spouse to receive significant ownership rights. See IRC §§ 2056(b)(7), 2523(f). Estate planning tools, such as trusts and powers of appointment, are used frequently to meet the qualification requirements.

If donors transfer property to their spouses in absolute ownership form, the marital deduction is available. For example, if the married couple holds property in joint tenancy and one of the spouses dies, the one-half of the property's value included in the gross estate under IRC § 2040(b), see supra p. 413. That half qualifies for the marital deduction under IRC § 2056.

If a donor transfers, at death or during life, only an income interest to the donor's spouse that expires say in twenty years, however, IRC §§ 2056(b)(1) and 2523(b)(1) deny a marital deduction for the value of the term of years. Donors may, however, enjoy a marital deduction if they transfer copyrights or patents to their spouses, even though these property rights expire. The reason is that, unlike for the term of years, the donors have not retained or donatively transferred to third persons any interests in the copyrights or patents that would take effect upon the termination of the copyrights or patents. A terminable interest passing to the spouse is not deductible only if: (1) an interest in that

22. See Lily Kahng, Fiction in Tax, in Taxing America 25 (Karen B. Brown & Mary Louise Fellows eds., 1997), discussing the legislative history of the marital deduction. She describes the concerns of practitioners and academics about having to transfer control of the marital wealth to the surviving spouse (assumed to be the wife) to enjoy the benefits of the marital deduction.

same property was retained by the donor or donatively transferred to a third person and (2) the donor or the third person would take possession of the property after the interest transferred to the spouse terminated or failed.

Congress provides for several exceptions to the nondeductible-terminable-interest rule. The exceptions have one thing in common: the interests passing to the spouse will result in gift or estate taxation when that spouse transfers them during life or at death. By adopting qualification rules that assure transfer taxation will occur when the donee-spouse ultimately transfers the property during life or at death, the marital deduction operates only for the purpose of deferring property from transfer taxation until the death of the donee-spouse. The marital deduction does not exempt property from taxation; it just postpones taxation until the death of both spouses.

The two most popular of the terminable-interest exceptions have been the *life estate/general power of appointment* and the *QTIP*. See IRC §§ 2056(b)(5), (7), 2523(e), (f). Although, as explained below, the life estate/general power of appointment exception is not likely to be used any longer given the modified carryover-basis rule enacted under the EGTRRA. See infra p. 427. Both exceptions have particular and unique requirements. Planners typically find that the requirements can be met efficiently through the trust mechanism. Planners also find that they can infuse the disposition with the flexibility their clients want by using a trust, various types of powers of appointment, and fiduciary powers.

Life Estate/General Power of Appointment. IRC §§ 2056(b)(5) and 2523(e) provide that donors can enjoy the marital deduction if they give their spouses income interests for life along with powers to appoint the property alone to any person and in all events. IRC § 2033 assures that any unconsumed income will be subject to the estate tax. IRC § 2041 assures that the trust corpus will be subject to the estate tax. Similarly, if the spouse makes a gift of the life estate and makes a lifetime appointment of the remainder interest, then IRC §§ 2511 and 2514 will operate together to tax the fee.

For the income interest to qualify, the spouse must have an absolute right to be paid the current income at least annually. Regulations make clear that property placed in the trust must be property that produces a current income stream or, at least, that the spouse has the right to compel the trustee to convert any nonincome-producing property into property that will produce a fair current return. See Treas. Reg. §§ 20.2056(b)-5(f)(5), 25.2523(e)-1(f)(4).

For the power to qualify it must be unrestricted, except that IRC §§ 2056(b)(5) and 2523(c) provide that a general power only exercisable by will is sufficient. Although the trustee cannot have a power to appoint any part of the property to any person other than the surviving spouse, the trustee can be given additional fiduciary powers to distribute the trust principal to the spouse.

Nothing in the statutory requirements precludes a donor from supplementing the spouse's right to a lifetime income interest and general testamentary power with a lifetime power to appoint to a class of beneficiaries, such as the donor's lineal descendants. The exercise of this nongeneral power during life will result in a gift tax, because its exercise operates as a release of the general testamentary power. See IRC § 2514(b).

With the enactment of EGTRRA, estate planners are not likely to recommend anymore that their clients use the life estate/general power of appointment when making marital deduction gifts during life or at death. This type of transfer would continue to qualify for the marital deduction and would assure that the couple enjoy a unified credit effective exemption of up to $7 million ($3.5 million for the estates of each spouse) by the year 2009. In 2010, when the repeal of the estate tax takes effect and the modified carryover-basis rule begins to apply, however, the life estate/general power of appointment marital deduction trust leads to two unfavorable income tax results. First, IRC § 1022(c), which permits an additional basis increase for property acquired by a surviving spouse from the decedent of up to $3 million, only allows that basis increase for property acquired from the decedent outright or in the form of a QTIP trust. Consequently, estate planners are not likely to risk having surviving spouses of decedents who die in 2010 lose up to $3 million in step-up basis because they received the property in an unqualified manner. The second unfavorable income tax result is that, even if a decedent were to die before 2010 and the surviving spouse enjoys the full step-up in basis available under IRC § 1014 for the property held in the marital deduction trust, a transfer to a spouse in the form of a life estate/general power of appointment would not be eligible for the $1.3 million step-up in basis were that spouse to die in 2010. IRC § 1022(d)(1)(B)(iii) provides that a "decedent shall not be treated as owning any property by reason of holding a power of appointment with respect to such property" and, therefore, such property is not eligible for any step-up in basis. The prospect of losing the step-up in basis benefits either at the death of the decedent or at the death of the surviving spouse significantly diminishes the attractiveness of the life estate/general power of appointment marital deduction trust.[23]

QTIP. IRC §§ 2056(b)(7) and 2523(f) provide that a donor can obtain a marital deduction by transferring a life estate in property to the spouse. For the life estate to qualify for the marital deduction, the donor (for gift tax purposes) or the donor's executor (for estate tax purposes) must elect to have the life

---

23. Even before EGTRRA, the generation-skipping transfer tax encouraged use of the QTIP over an income interest/general power of appointment trust. The generation-skipping transfer tax makes it more feasible for both spouses to make maximum use of the generation-skipping transfer tax exemption through use of the QTIP. See IRC § 2652(a)(3); infra p. 424.

estate treated as a qualified terminable interest, and no person, not even the spouse, can have a power to appoint any part of the property to any person other than the surviving spouse during the spouse's life.

To assure that this property doesn't escape taxation in the donor's and the spouse's respective estates, Congress enacted IRC §§ 2044 and 2519. IRC § 2519 treats any disposition of any portion of the life estate as a transfer of the entire remainder interest and thereby assures that the remainder interest is subject to gift taxation. IRC § 2044 includes the value of the property at the spouse's death in the spouse's gross estate, unless IRC § 2519 applied previously. The effect of these two constructive transfer sections is to assure that property that enjoys a marital deduction in one spouse's estate is taxed in the other spouse's estate.

The life estate requirements parallel those found under IRC § 2056(b)(5), having to do with the life estate/general power of appointment exception. Just as under IRC § 2056(b)(5), the trustee can have a power to distribute principal to the spouse during the spouse's life. Unlike under IRC § 2056(b)(5), however, the spouse cannot have a lifetime power to appoint to anyone other than the spouse. In other words, donors can enjoy the marital deduction if they make a transfer of property in trust giving their spouses current income interests for life to be paid out annually and powers to appoint to the couple's lineal descendants by will and make the election as directed. Donors cannot enjoy the marital deduction, however, if the powers to appoint to lineal descendants are exercisable during the donee-spouses' lifetimes.

Estate Trust. Donors also may enjoy the marital deduction by placing property in trusts and giving the trustees discretion to distribute income or principal to their spouses. These trusts qualify for the marital deduction as long as a donor also provides that, at the spouse's death, any accumulated income and principal remaining must be distributed to the spouse's estate. The property placed in the trust is deductible under IRC §§ 2056 and 2523 because no person other than the spouse received an interest in the property from the donor. Before 1987, this so-called estate trust was attractive because it permitted the trustee to accumulate income at the then lower trust income tax rates. After the Tax Reform Act of 1986 and subsequent tax law changes, that advantage generally has been eliminated. Now an estate trust generally is only popular for donors who own assets that don't produce current income and who don't want to give the power to the trustee or to the spouse to convert the assets to income-producing property.

5. The Estate and Gift Tax Charitable Deduction

The federal tax system encourages charitable giving. For income tax purposes, a donor can deduct the value of property transferred to a qualifying charitable organization. See IRC § 170. Similarly, a donor can avoid estate and gift taxes for property transferred to a qualifying charitable organization. See IRC §§ 2055, 2522. The three statutes contain slight variations in their definitions of a qualifying charitable organization. Although the income tax deduction is limited to a percentage of adjusted gross income, the transfer tax law places no limitation on the amount deductible from the tax base.

Charitable deductions are available if the donor establishes a trust giving a charity either an income interest (a charitable lead trust) or a remainder interest (a charitable remainder trust). The deductibility of transfers to charities of income or remainder interests was significantly restricted by the Tax Reform Act of 1969. Before 1970, if donors transferred income interests to charities and remainder interests to noncharitable beneficiaries, they gave the trustees the power to follow investment policies that resulted in low current yields and high capital appreciation. If donors transferred remainder interests to charities and income interests to noncharitable beneficiaries, they gave the trustees the power to follow investment policies that resulted in high current yields and low capital appreciation. The effect of these strategies was to allow donors to enjoy charitable deductions in amounts that exceeded the economic value of the interests received by the charities because the deductions were computed on the assumption that the trust property would produce a reasonable investment yield. (Before 1970, the applicable rate was 3.5 percent per year.) The 1969 Act adopted rules to assure that the charities would receive interests that were reasonably related to the amount claimed as a deduction.

The additional requirements imposed by the 1969 Act apply to the estates of decedents dying after 1969. IRC § 2055(e)(3) provides that noncomplying trusts qualify for the deduction if the governing instrument is reformed by a state court to comply with the additional requirements imposed by the 1969 Act. See infra Chapter 12, Part C; Chapter 15, Part A.

IRC § 2056(b)(8), which was added by the Economic Recovery Tax Act of 1981, provides that a marital deduction is allowable for certain charitable remainder trusts as long as the trust has no noncharitable beneficiaries other than the surviving spouse. The full value of this type of trust is deductible by virtue of IRC §§ 2055 and 2056 by the decedent spouse's estate. The surviving spouse receives only an income interest and therefore no portion of the trust property is included in the surviving spouse's estate at death.

The estate tax charitable deduction will become less important over the next decade while the estate tax exemptions and lower rates are phased in and the prospect for ultimate repeal of the transfer tax continues. Whether these tax changes reduce philanthropic giving remains to be seen. See supra Chapter 1B.

6. The Federal Generation-Skipping Transfer Tax

The federal generation-skipping transfer tax was enacted in 1986 as an excise tax on gratuitous transfers that *skip* a generation. The tax was first introduced in 1976, but the 1976 version was retroactively repealed and replaced in 1986 by the current version. Congress believed that for a transfer tax to approach equity among families, it must apply to each family with approximately the same frequency. To this end, Congress designed the generation-skipping transfer tax to assure generally that a tax is paid whenever property skips a generation or passes through a generation in a form that would allow it to escape gift or estate taxation in the *skipped* generation. In the terminology of the generation-skipping transfer tax, a generation-skipping transfer occurs when property passes to a *skip person*. Along with the estate tax, the EGTRRA repeals the generation-skipping tax in 2010. See IRC § 2664.

Skip Person; Transferor; Interest. The generation-skipping transfer tax uses a special terminology. Key interlocking definitions are:

"Skip person"—either (1) a natural person assigned to a generation that is two or more generations below the generation assignment of the "transferor" or (2) a trust in which all "interests" are held by skip persons or in which no person holds an "interest" and at no time may a distribution, upon termination or otherwise, be made from the trust to a nonskip person. See IRC § 2613. The general rule for determining skip persons is subject to a predeceased-parent exception. See IRC § 2651(e). If an individual is a descendant of the transferor and that individual's parent who was also a descendant of the transferor is dead at the time a transfer subject to a gift or estate tax occurs, then that individual is assigned to one generation higher than that individual would otherwise be assigned. Collateral heirs are also eligible for the predeceased-parent exception, but only if, at the time of the transfer, the transferor does not have any living lineal descendants.

"Transferor"—the person who made the transfer insofar as the federal estate or gift tax is concerned, i.e., the decedent if the transfer was subject to the estate tax; the donor if the transfer was subject to the gift tax. See IRC § 2652(a).

"Interest"—A person has an "interest in property held in trust" if the person (1) has the right (other than a future right) to receive income or corpus from the trust, (2) is a permissible current recipient of income or corpus from the trust and is not a qualified charity, or (3) is a qualified charity and the trust is a qualified charitable remainder annuity or unitrust or a pooled income fund.[24] See IRC § 2652(c).

---

24. Charitable remainder annuity and unitrusts and pooled income funds are described infra Chapter 15, Part A.

The GST Exemption and Computation of the Tax. Like the federal estate and gift taxes, the generation-skipping transfer tax is targeted at the wealthy. IRC § 2631 provides each transferor a *GST exemption*. The exemption amount was $1 million in 1986. The Taxpayer Relief Act of 1997 provided that the exemption amount be adjusted for inflation so that in 2001 it was at $1,060,000 and is subject to an adjustment again in 2002 and 2003. After 2003, the EGTRRA provides that the exemption amount be the same as the unified credit effective exemption amount for estate taxes so that in 2004 the GST exemption will equal $1.5 million and increase to $3.5 million by 2009. IRC § 2631(c) (as revised effective after December 31, 2003); EGTRRA § 521(e)(3).

The EGTRRA includes a number of amendments to IRC §§ 2632 and 2642 that are designed to maximize the availability of the GST exemption and minimize the GST tax. The amendments modify the deemed allocation rules for the exemption, the rules pertaining to severance of trusts to which the exemption partially applies, and the valuation rules for purposes of allocating the exemption. The amendments also allow for retroactive allocation of the exemption, provide relief for late allocation elections, and introduce a substantial compliance rule for meeting the statutory and regulatory requirements for the allocation of the exemption.

The mechanism by which the GST exemption operates is through the use of an *inclusion ratio*, which gives the fraction of a transfer or a trust that is subject to the generation-skipping transfer tax. In the case of *direct skips* (defined below), the inclusion ratio is:

$$1 - \frac{\text{amount of GST exemption allocated to the skip}}{\text{value of the property transferred in the skip}}$$

In cases of *taxable terminations* and *taxable distributions* (defined below), the inclusion ratio is:

$$1 - \frac{\text{amount of GST exemption allocated to the trust}}{\text{value of the property transferred to the trust}}$$

The generation-skipping transfer tax is a flat-rate tax imposed at the maximum estate tax rate, which in 2002 is 50 percent and in 2009 will be 45 percent. See IRC § 2641(a)(1); supra p. 396. An inclusion ratio of 1 means that the entire amount of a taxable-event transfer (see below) is subject to the generation-skipping transfer tax, an inclusion ratio of 0 means that none of a taxable-event transfer is subject to the tax, and an inclusion ratio of something more than 0 but less than 1 means that that fraction of a taxable-event transfer is subject to the tax. The tax benefits of the GST exemption encourage wealthy donors to establish long-term trusts that last as long as perpetuity law permits. See infra Chapter 19.

Taxable Events. The generation-skipping transfer tax applies to three types of generation-skipping transfers: direct skips, taxable terminations, and taxable distributions. See IRC § 2611.

Direct skips. A direct skip is a transfer that is subject to either the gift or estate tax and is made to a skip person. See IRC § 2612(c). To the extent that a gift qualifies for the annual exclusion or the tuition-or-medical-expense exclusion, the gift is not subject to the generation-skipping transfer tax. See IRC §§ 2611(b)(1), 2642(c)(3). The generation-skipping transfer tax on a direct skip is computed on a tax-exclusive basis, but the transferor's payment of the tax is treated as a taxable gift. See IRC § 2515. Liability for payment of the tax is on the transferor or, if the direct skip came from a trust, on the trustee. See IRC § 2603(a)(2), (a)(3).

> *Example 7.10:* In 2002, G makes an outright taxable gift to her grandchild, X, bypassing her child, A (X's parent). The gift is a direct skip for which the inclusion ratio is 1. The gift is therefore subject to both the gift tax and the generation-skipping transfer tax, the latter based upon a rate of 50 percent of the value of the taxable gift. See IRC §§ 2601, 2612(c), 2641. In addition, G will pay a gift tax on the amount of generation-skipping transfer tax paid. See IRC § 2515. This provision has the effect of treating a transfer from G to X the same as a transfer from G to A, who in turn uses the transferred property to make a gift to X.[25]

Taxable terminations. A taxable termination is the termination (by death, lapse of time, release of power, or otherwise) of an interest in property held in a trust, unless immediately after such termination, a nonskip person has an interest in the property or unless at no time after the termination may a

---

25. The numerical example below explains the equivalency.

> G makes a gift of $100,000 to A who then uses the $100,000 to make a gift to X (grandchild) as well as pay the gift tax owed on that gift. Assume both G and A are subject to a 50 percent gift tax rate and that the annual exclusion and unified credit are unavailable. G pays a gift tax of $50,000 on her gift of $100,000 to A, thereby reducing her estate by a total of $150,000. A then makes a gift of $66,667 to X and pays a gift tax of $33,333. As a result of the two gifts, G and A pay a total gift tax of $83,333 ($50,000 + 33,333).
>
> The generation-skipping transfer tax obtains the same result if G makes the gift of $66,667 directly to X. On that gift, G owes a gift tax of $33,333. In addition, G owes a generation-skipping transfer tax of $33,333, as well as a gift tax on the amount of generation-skipping transfer tax paid of $16,667. G, X, and the government are left in the same position as they were when G made a gift to A and A made a gift to X: G's wealth is reduced by $150,000 ($66,667 + 33,333 + 33,333 + 16,667), X receives $66,667, and the government receives $83,333.

In Example 7.10, under the predeceased-parent exception, G's gift to X would not be a direct skip if A were dead when G made the gift. See IRC § 2652(e).

distribution (including a distribution upon termination) be made from the trust to a skip person. See IRC § 2612(a). The generation-skipping transfer tax on a taxable termination is computed on a tax inclusive basis. Liability for payment of the tax is on the trustee, and hence payable from the corpus of the trust. See IRC § 2603(a)(2).

Example 7.11: G transfers property to a trust directing the trustee to pay income annually to her child, A, for life and at A's death to distribute the corpus to A's descendants. The trust has an inclusion ratio of 1. G will incur a gift tax when she establishes the trust. A dies, survived by his child, X. Because immediately after the termination of A's income interest, the trust corpus passes to a skip person, the termination of A's interest is a taxable termination and the trust will be liable to pay a generation-skipping transfer tax based on the highest estate and gift tax rate in effect for the year the termination takes place on the value of the property, determined at the death of A, that is held in trust when A dies.[26]

Taxable distributions. A taxable distribution is any distribution from a trust to a skip person other than a taxable termination or a direct skip. See IRC § 2612(b). The generation-skipping transfer tax on a taxable distribution is computed on a tax-inclusive basis as a result of IRC § 2603(a)(1) placing tax liability for payment of the tax on the transferee.

Example 7.12: G transfers property to a trust, authorizing the trustee to distribute income and/or corpus to G's descendants. The trust has an inclusion ratio of 1. The trustee distributes $100,000 of the corpus to G's child, A, and $100,000 to G's grandchild, X. The distribution to A is not a taxable distribution because A is not a skip person. The distribution to X is a taxable distribution, taxed at the highest estate and gift tax rate in effect for the year that the distribution takes place. The transferee, X, is liable for the tax (IRC § 2603(a)(1)); if the trustee pays the tax out of the trust, the amount of the tax paid is itself a taxable distribution (IRC § 2621(b)).

The generation-skipping transfer tax is thought to be essential for the transfer tax system as a whole to apply in a progressive manner. As the examples show, it prevents the wealthier from avoiding taxation by giving a significant percentage of their wealth to very young or unborn beneficiaries rather than to older beneficiaries. The tax advantage that the generation-skipping transfer tax prevents is not that the older beneficiaries, were it not for the tax, would have been taxed sooner and the younger beneficiaries would have been taxed later. The generation-skipping transfer tax prevents the older beneficiaries from not having been taxed at all.

---

26. The predeceased-parent exception does not apply in this example because A was alive at the time G made the transfer into the trust that resulted in a taxable gift. See IRC § 2651(e).

While the estate and generation-skipping transfer tax remains in effect, estate planners will utilize trusts and powers of appointment to maximize flexibility of the plan while minimizing taxes. If Congress permanently repeals the estate and generation-skipping taxes, it remains to be seen whether donors and decedents continue to want to make use of multi-generational trusts (dynastic trusts) in order to exercise control over future generations and to protect family wealth from the claims of beneficiaries' creditors and spouses. For discussion of creditor and spousal claims, see infra Chapters 10A, 14A. To the extent that the multi-generational trusts were primarily motivated by the transfer tax law, they may become less popular.

7. The Modified Carryover-Basis Rule

Repeal of the estate and generation-skipping transfer taxes in 2010 is accompanied by a repeal of current law permitting a basis for property acquired from a decedent equal to its fair market value at the decedent's death. See IRC § 1014(f). Increasing the basis of property to its fair market value at a decedent's death has the effect of permanently excluding from income taxation the appreciation in value that occurred during the time a decedent held the property.[27] Without an estate tax, the income tax exclusion resulting from a step-up in basis rule becomes unsustainable politically and fiscally. Instead of a step-up in basis, the EGTRRA provides in IRC § 1022 for a carryover-basis rule, but one that allows for some increase in basis reflecting appreciation that occurred during the time the decedent owned the property. The design of the modified carryover-basis rule suggests that planners will continue to use trusts and powers of appointment to minimize income tax liability while furthering their clients' other estate planning goals.

---

27. Under the income tax, all property acquired by gift, devise, or inheritance is excluded from the income of the recipient. See IRC § 102. The extent of the exclusion under IRC § 102, however, depends on the treatment of noncash assets. A donee receives a carryover basis in property received from a donor under IRC § 1015 and, therefore, only the amount of the donor's basis in the property is ultimately excluded from the donee's income, because upon sale of the property the difference between the property's carryover basis and its fair market value will be included in the donee's income. In contrast, recipients of property acquired from a decedent have enjoyed an exclusion of the appreciation that occurred during the period that the decedent held the property under IRC § 1014, which allows a step-up in basis equal to the property's fair market value at the decedent's death. As the text indicates, IRC § 1022 contains provisions that allow for a step-up in basis, but it is not as broad a step-up as existed under IRC § 1014. Whether IRC § 1015 or § 1022 applies, the tax law remains the same regarding the issue of tax deferral. Recipients of donative transfers continue to be able to defer taxation on the appreciated property received, because the tax law does not treat a donative transfer as a taxable event resulting in a realization of gain.

IRC § 1022(a) provides that property acquired from a decedent in 2010 shall have a basis equal to the lesser of the adjusted basis of the decedent or the fair market value of the property at the date of the decedent's death.[28] To reduce the immediate impact of the carryover-basis rules, EGTRRA adopts two tax deferral provisions. The first has to do with funding of pecuniary bequests and the second has to do with property subject to debt.

In accordance with the general operation of the income tax law, a transfer of property to satisfy a claim is a taxable event. Congress wanted to avoid having estates or trusts recognize a gain for appreciation that occurred while the decedent held the property when personal representatives or trustees distribute appreciated assets to satisfy pecuniary devises or equivalent types of trust distributions. It wanted the gain deferred until the devisees or trust beneficiaries sold or exchanged the property. EGTRRA achieves this result by providing that an estate or trust has to recognize a gain only to the extent that the fair market value of the property on the date of the distribution exceeds the fair market value of that property on the date of decedent's death. See IRC § 1040(a), (b) (as revised effective after December 31, 2009, EGTRRA § 542(f)(1)). Persons acquiring property that satisfies a pecuniary devise or its trust equivalent take the carryover-basis in the property increased by the amount of the gain recognized by the estate or trust at the time of distribution. See IRC § 1040(c).

The second deferral provision concerns the treatment of property acquired from a decedent subject to debt in excess of the carryover basis. Whenever a taxpayer transfers mortgaged property by gift or otherwise, the amount of the debt is treated as an amount realized. To the extent that debt exceeds the taxpayer's basis in the property, the donor realizes gain. Congress wanted to avoid this result for mortgaged property acquired by reason of the death of the decedent from the decedent or from the decedent's estate. EGTRRA achieves this result by providing that liabilities in excess of basis shall be disregarded in determining whether gain is recognized upon the acquisition of property from a decedent or from a decedent's estate.[29] See IRC § 1022(g).

The carryover-basis rule means that some devisees are going to receive property subject to a tax liability representing unrealized gain. The import of that potential tax liability is particularly obvious for appreciated property that is subject to a debt in excess of the carryover basis.

---

28. Property acquired from a decedent is defined in IRC § 1022(e) generally to be property acquired by devise or inheritance, property acquired from or in a trust that the decedent had the power to revoke or amend, and property passing from the decedent by reason of the decedent's death to the extent it passed without consideration (e.g., joint tenancy property with right of survivorship).

29. To prevent permanent tax avoidance, IRC § 1022(g) provides that the liabilities are not disregarded if the property is acquired by a tax-exempt or foreign entity.

Example 7.13: G devises Blackacre to A. At G's death, Blackacre has a fair market value of $6 million and a carryover basis of $2.5 million. It is subject to a debt of $5 million. Although A seems to have received a devise worth $1 million ($6 million fair market value less the $5 million mortgage), the devise is in fact worth considerably less if A sells it for a $6 million. After A pays off the mortgage debt of $5 million, she will have $1 million remaining. The sale, however, results in a realized gain of $3.5 million ($6 million in cash received less the carryover basis of $2.5 million) A will have an income tax liability of at least $700,000 based on the lowest capital gains rate of 20 percent, leaving her with a devise worth only $300,000 after taxes. If the mortgage on the property had been $5.5 million, after A paid off the mortgage, she would be left with only $500,000, but her income tax liability would still be $700,000. In light of the income tax liability, the devise of Blackacre subject to the mortgage of $5.5 million turns out to be worth -$200,000.

In addition to ameliorating the income tax consequences of a carryover-basis regime by the two tax deferral provisions, EGTRRA contains two other provisions that ease the effects of a carryover-basis regime by permitting some step up in basis. Rather than merely deferring the tax on unrealized appreciation, these two provisions modify the carryover-basis rule by permanently excluding unrealized appreciation that occurred during the period that the decedent held the property. One provision permits the personal representative to increase the basis in certain eligible assets acquired from the decedent up to $1.3 million (an amount indexed for inflation) and by any unused capital losses, net operating losses, and other losses on investment assets. See IRC § 1022(b), (d)(4). The other provision allows for an additional basis increase of up to $3 million (an amount indexed for inflation) for property acquired from the decedent by the decedent's surviving spouse in a qualified manner. See IRC § 1022(c), (d)(4). These provisions are in addition to the exclusion of up to $250,000 of gain upon the sale of a principal residence of the decedent by the estate or heirs. See IRC § 121(d)(9).

Both the general step-up provision and the spousal step-up provision are subject to the following rules. The executor has the discretion to allocate the basis increases to eligible assets, but in no case can an asset's basis be increased above its fair market value determined at the date of the decedent's death. See IRC § 1022(d)(2), (3)(A). Assets acquired from the decedent but ineligible for basis increases include property owned by the decedent by reason of a power of appointment and rights to income in respect of a decedent (IRD) (having to do especially with annuities, individual retirement accounts (IRAs) and qualified retirement plan rights). See IRC § 1022 (d)(1)(B)(iii), (f). Also ineligible are stocks or securities of foreign personal holding companies, stocks of international sales corporations, stocks of foreign investment companies, and stocks of some passive foreign investment companies. IRC § 1022(d)(1)(D).

The exclusion of IRD rights is particularly troubling because it prevents employees who are likely to have the majority of their wealth in qualified pension plans and annuities from being able to take advantage of the step-up provisions.

IRC § 1022(d)(1)(B)(i) relies on the jointly held property rules of IRC § 2040 to determine what portion of jointly held property is eligible for a basis increase. For jointly held property owned by spouses, one-half of the jointly held property is eligible for a basis increase. The other half is not eligible for a basis increase. For jointly held property owned by the decedent and a person or persons other than the spouse, then either the fractional-interest rule or the percentage-of-consideration rule applies depending on how the asset was acquired. See supra pp. 413-14. The surviving spouse's share of community property is treated as owned by the decedent spouse and eligible for a basis increase. See IRC § 1022(d)(1)(B)(iv). Therefore, all of the couple's community property is eligible for a basis increase. The exclusion of the surviving spouse's share of jointly held property from eligibility and the inclusion of the surviving spouse's share of community property within the class of eligible assets mean that the modified carryover-basis rule favors community-property couples over couple living in common-law property states.

To discourage tax avoidance schemes designed to take advantage of the step-up provisions, IRC § 1022(d)(1)(C) treats property acquired by the decedent by gift within three years of the decedent's death as ineligible for any basis increase. Property acquired by the decedent by bequest within the three-year period and property acquired by the decedent by gift beyond the three-year period remain eligible for a basis increase. This provision is accompanied with a number of new reporting requirements all designed to prevent misuse and unwarranted use of the basis increase rules.[30]

The spousal step-up provision of up to $3 million is available only for transfers by decedents to their spouses of "qualified spousal property." IRC § 1022(c)(1), (3)-(5). It is available in addition to the $1.3 million step-up provision. Qualified spousal property is defined in a manner that mimics the terminable-interest rule and the QTIP requirements found in IRC §§ 2056 and 2523. Notwithstanding that IRC § 1022 incorporates the marital deduction requirements designed to assure only *deferral* of the estate and gift taxes, the increase in basis permitted upon qualification results in a *permanent exclusion*

30. The EGTRRA introduces a number of new reporting requirements with regard to gifts, noncash assets exceeding $1.3 million transferred at death, and appreciated property received by a decedent within three years of death. The Act also provides for penalties for failure to comply with the reporting requirements effective in 2010. See IRC §§ 6018, 6019(b), 6716. Congress introduced the reporting rules, along with a few other provisions, to address income tax avoidance concerns that arise as a result of the transfer tax law changes.

from income taxes of up to $3 million in unrealized gain that occurred during the period that the decedent held the property. Qualified spousal property acquired by the spouse outside of a QTIP trust can enjoy a further step-up in basis of up to $1.3 million upon the surviving spouse's death. Therefore, a total of up to $5.6 million of unrealized appreciation in marital property is eligible for permanent exclusion from income taxation and perhaps more depending on the appreciation of the personal residences of the spouses at their respective deaths, and the existence of unused capital losses, net operating losses, and other losses on investment assets.[31] See IRC §§ 121(d)(9), 1022(b)(2)(C). For an extensive critique of the modified carryover-basis rule, see Joseph M. Dodge, What's Wrong with Carryover Basis under H.R. 8, 91 Tax Notes 961 (2001).

Although the repeal of the estate tax and the introduction of a modified carryover-basis rule was part of the EGTRRA, which was generally intended to reduce the tax burden for U.S. taxpayers, lower tax liabilities may not occur in all situations.

> *Example 7.14:* G dies in 2009 leaving his entire estate to his lineal descendants. He made no lifetime gifts. G's taxable estate of $3.5 million (taking into account all available deductions) consists of $500,000 of cash in addition to three parcels of land, each with a carryover basis of $100,000 and a fair market value of $1,000,000. No estate tax is due because the unified credit equivalent exemption amount is $3.5 million in 2009. G's lineal descendants receive a basis in the parcels of land of $1,000,000 each in accordance with the step-up in basis rule of IRC § 1014, which remains in effect in 2009. If they were to sell the parcels at a later date, no part of the $2.7 million (($1,000,000 – 100,000) x 3 parcels) of unrealized appreciation will be subject to the income tax.
>
> If G were to have died in 2010 instead of 2009, again no estate tax liability would arise because the estate tax would have been repealed. G's lineal descendants, however, would incur an income tax upon sale of the parcels of the land on that amount of appreciation that occurred while G held the property that exceeds the $1.3 million of step-up permitted under IRC § 1022(b). G's lineal descendants will incur a tax on $1.4 million ($2.7 million – 1.3 million) of gain upon sale, which at the lowest capital gain rate of 20 percent would result in an income tax liability of $280,000.

Just as estate planners have developed strategies for maximizing use of the unified credit as between spouses, they will develop strategies for maximizing use of the basis increases. One obvious strategy is to advise clients to consider purchasing life insurance. IRC § 101(a) excludes the proceeds of life insurance

---

31. The $5.6 million includes both the $1.3 million and the $3 million step up available upon the death of the first spouse plus another $1.3 million step up available upon the death of the second spouse.

from the recipients income and does not tax the difference between the amount of proceeds and the amount of premiums paid. Therefore, it is the one asset that continues to enjoy a step-up in basis even after repeal of IRC § 1014. See Dodge, supra, at 968. Planners are likely to further advise clients how they may be able to further their planning objectives by placing the proceeds from life insurance into trusts. This is just one example of why we can expect that, although planners will use estate planning tools differently, trusts, powers of appointment, and fiduciary powers will continue to play important roles in achieving donative transfer goals.

EXTERNAL REFERENCES. AICPA Tax Division, Reform of the Estate and Gift Tax System, 91 Tax Notes 307 (2001); Joseph Bankman, What Can We Say About a Wealth Tax?, 53 Tax L. Rev. 477 (2000); Noel B. Cunningham, Observations on Retrospective Taxation, 53 Tax L. Rev. 489 (2000); Charles Davenport and Jay A. Soled, Enlivening the Death-Tax Death-Talk, 84 Tax Notes 591 (1999); Barbara H. Fried, Compared to What? Taxing Brute Luck and Other Second-Best Problems, 53 Tax L. Rev. 377 (2000); Glendall Jones, Jr., Repeal the Estate Tax? Bad Move: The Transfer Tax System Paradigm, 89 Tax Notes 793 (2000); Edward J. McCaffery, Grave Robbers: The Moral Case Against the Death Tax, 85 Tax Notes 1429 (1999); Eric Rakowski, Can Wealth Taxes Be Justified?, 53 Tax L. Rev. 263 (2000); Deborah H. Schenk, Saving the Income Tax with a Wealth Tax, 53 Tax L. Rev. 423 (2000); Daniel N. Shaviro, Inequality, Wealth, and Endowment, 53 Tax L. Rev. 397 (2000); Dennis J. Ventry, Jr., Straight Talk About the "Death" Tax: Politics, Economics, and Morality, 89 Tax Notes 1159 (2000).

PART B. FEDERAL TAXATION AND STATE LAW

Statutory Reference: *UTC § 416*

The assessment of federal income and transfer taxes depends upon the property owner's economic rights and obligations. Economic rights and obligations, with minor exceptions, such as U.S. Savings Bonds, patents, and copyrights, are created and protected by state law. Although state law's characterization or labeling of property interests is not controlling on the federal government's power to tax, state law's determination of a person's economic rights and obligations is controlling. Part B describes the role that state law plays in the federal tax law and how the federal authorities determine that state law.

If the tax dispute turns on state law and the taxpayer has not adjudicated the particular issue in state court, the Internal Revenue Service (IRS) and the federal courts determine state law in accordance with the *Erie* doctrine. The *Erie* doctrine provides that federal courts must apply state law as announced by state legislation or the state's highest court. See Erie Railroad Co. v. Tompkins, 304 U.S. 64 (1938). If the legislature or the highest court has failed to address the particular issue, then the federal authorities must apply what they find to be state law after giving proper regard to relevant rulings by a state's lower court decisions.

If the taxpayer has adjudicated the state law question in a state court before having had a final federal determination of the taxpayer's tax liability, is the state court's ruling regarding the taxpayer's economic interests and obligations a binding determination of the state law for purposes of determining federal tax liability? The Supreme Court's latest pronouncement on this question came in Commissioner v. Estate of Bosch, below.

Commissioner v. Estate of Bosch

387 U.S. 456 (1967)

CLARK, J. These two federal estate tax cases present a common issue for our determination: Whether a federal court or agency in a federal estate tax controversy is conclusively bound by a state trial court adjudication of property rights or characterization of property interests when the United States is not made a party to such proceeding.

In No. 673, Commissioner of Internal Revenue v. Estate of Bosch, 363 F. 2d 1009, the Court of Appeals for the Second Circuit held that since the state trial court had "authoritatively determined" the rights of the parties, it was not required to delve into the correctness of that state court decree. In No. 240, Second National Bank of New Haven, Executor v. United States, 351 F.2d 489, another panel of the same Circuit held that the "decrees of the Connecticut Probate Court . . . under no circumstances can be construed as binding" on a federal court in subsequent litigation involving federal revenue laws. Whether these cases conflict in principle or not, which is disputed here, there does exist a widespread conflict among the circuits over the question and we granted certiorari to resolve it. . . . We hold that where the federal estate tax liability turns upon the character of a property interest held and transferred by the decedent under state law, federal authorities are not bound by the determination made of such property interest by a state trial court. . . .

(a) No. 673, Commissioner v. Estate of Bosch. In 1930, decedent, a resident of New York, created a revocable trust which, as amended in 1931, provided that the income from the corpus was to be paid to his wife during her lifetime. The instrument also gave her a general [testamentary] power of appointment,

in default of which it provided that half of the corpus was to go to his heirs and the remaining half was to go to those of his wife. In 1951 the wife executed an instrument purporting to release the general power of appointment and convert it into a special power. Upon decedent's death in 1957, respondent, in paying federal estate taxes, claimed a marital deduction for the value of the widow's trust. The Commissioner determined, however, that the trust corpus did not qualify for the deduction under [IRC] § 2056(b)(5) . . . and levied a deficiency. Respondent then filed a petition for redetermination in the Tax Court. The ultimate outcome of the controversy hinged on whether the release executed by Mrs. Bosch in 1951 was invalid—as she claimed it to be—in which case she would have enjoyed a general power of appointment at her husband's death and the trust would therefore qualify for the marital deduction. While the Tax Court proceeding was pending, the respondent filed a petition in the Supreme Court of New York for settlement of the trustee's account; it also sought a determination as to the validity of the release under state law. The Tax Court, with the Commissioner's consent, abstained from making its decision pending the outcome of the state court action. The state court found the release to be a nullity; the Tax Court then accepted the state court judgment as being an "authoritative exposition of New York law and adjudication of the property rights involved," . . . and permitted the deduction. On appeal, a divided Court of Appeals affirmed. It held that "[t]he issue is . . . not whether the federal court is `bound by' the decision of the state tribunal, but whether or not a state tribunal has authoritatively determined the rights under state law of a party to the federal action." . . . The court concluded that the "New York judgment, rendered by a court which had jurisdiction over parties and subject matter, authoritatively settled the rights of the parties, not only for New York, but also for purposes of the application to those rights of the relevant provisions of federal tax law." . . . It declared that since the state court had held the wife to have a general power of appointment under its law, the corpus of the trust qualified for the marital deduction. We do not agree and reverse. . . .

The problem of what effect must be given a state trial court decree where the matter decided there is determinative of federal estate tax consequences has long burdened the Bar and the courts. This Court has not addressed itself to the problem for nearly a third of a century.[32] In Freuler v. Helvering, 291 U.S. 35 (1934), this Court, declining to find collusion between the parties on the record as presented there, held that a prior *in personam* judgment in the state court to which the United States was not made a party, "[o]bviously . . . had not the

32. It may be claimed that Blair v. Commissioner, 300 U.S. 5 (1937), dealt with the problem presently before us but that case involved the question of the effect of a property right determination by a state appellate court.

effect of *res judicata*, and could not furnish the basis for invocation of the full faith and credit clause . . . ." At 43. In *Freuler*'s wake, at least three positions have emerged among the circuits. The first of these holds that

> . . . if the question at issue is fairly presented to the state court for its independent decision and is so decided by the court the resulting judgment if binding upon the parties under the state law is conclusive as to their property rights in the federal tax case . . . . Gallagher v. Smith, 223 F. 2d 218, 225.

The opposite view is expressed in Faulkerson's Estate v. United States, 301 F.2d 231. This view seems to approach that of Erie R. Co. v. Tompkins, 304 U.S. 64 (1938), in that the federal court will consider itself bound by the state court decree only after independent examination of the state law as determined by the highest court of the State. The Government urges that an intermediate position be adopted; it suggests that a state trial court adjudication is binding in such cases only when the judgment is the result of an adversary proceeding in the state court. . . .

We look at the problem differently. First, the Commissioner was not made a party to either of the state proceedings here and neither had the effect of *res judicata* . . . ; nor did the principle of collateral estoppel apply. It can hardly be denied that both state proceedings were brought for the purpose of directly affecting federal estate tax liability. Next, it must be remembered that it was a federal taxing statute that the Congress enacted and upon which we are here passing. Therefore, in construing it, we must look to the legislative history surrounding it. We find that the report of the Senate Finance Committee recommending enactment of the marital deduction used very guarded language in referring to the very question involved here. It said that "proper regard," not finality, "should be given to interpretations of the will" by state courts and then only when entered by a court "in a bona fide adversary proceeding." . . . We cannot say that the authors of this directive intended that the decrees of state trial courts were to be conclusive and binding on the computation of the federal estate tax as levied by the Congress. If the Congress had intended state trial court determinations to have that effect on the federal actions, it certainly would have said so—which it did not do. On the contrary, we believe it intended the marital deduction to be strictly construed and applied. Not only did it indicate that only "proper regard" was to be accorded state decrees but it placed specific limitations on the allowance of the deduction as set out in [IRC] §§ 2056 (b), (c), and (d). These restrictive limitations clearly indicate the great care that Congress exercised in the drawing of the Act and indicate also a definite concern with the elimination of loopholes and escape hatches that might jeopardize the federal revenue. This also is in keeping with the long-established policy of the Congress, as expressed in the Rules of Decision Act, 28 U.S.C.

§ 1652. There it is provided that in the absence of federal requirements such as the Constitution or Acts of Congress, the "laws of the several states . . . shall be regarded as rules of decision in civil actions in the courts of the United States, in cases where they apply." This Court has held that judicial decisions are "laws of the . . . state" within the section. Moreover, even in diversity cases this Court has further held that while the decrees of "lower state courts" should be "attributed some weight . . . the decision [is] not controlling . . ." where the highest court of the State has not spoken on the point. And in West v. A.T.&T. Co., 311 U.S. 223 (1940), this Court further held that "an intermediate appellate state court . . . is a datum for ascertaining state law which is not to be disregarded by a federal court *unless it is convinced by other persuasive data that the highest court of the state would decide otherwise.*" . . . (Emphasis supplied.) Thus, under some conditions, federal authority may not be bound even by an intermediate state appellate court ruling. It follows here then, that when the application of a federal statute is involved, the decision of a state trial court as to an underlying issue of state law should *a fortiori* not be controlling. This is but an application of the rule of Erie R. Co. v. Tompkins, supra, where state law as announced by the highest court of the State is to be followed. This is not a diversity case but the same principle may be applied for the same reasons, *viz.*, the underlying substantive rule involved is based on state law and the State's highest court is the best authority on its own law. If there be no decision by that court then federal authorities must apply what they find to be the state law after giving "proper regard" to relevant rulings of other courts of the State. In this respect, it may be said to be, in effect, sitting as a state court.

We believe that this would avoid much of the uncertainty that would result from the "non-adversary" approach and at the same time would be fair to the taxpayer and protect the federal revenue as well.

The judgment in No. 240 is therefore affirmed while that in No. 673 is reversed and remanded for further proceedings not inconsistent with this opinion.

It is so ordered.

[The dissenting opinions of DOUGLAS, FORTAS, and HARLAN, JJ., are omitted.]

Notes and Questions

1. *The Aftermath of Bosch.* Did the *Bosch* court avoid the uncertainty that concerned it? Professor Verbit summarizes post-*Bosch* decisions as follows:

> [F]ederal courts have taken the following attitude towards state lower court decisions under the guise of following the rule of *Bosch*: (1) that lower state court

> rulings are entitled to no weight and are therefore not admissible in federal tax proceedings, (2) that lower state court decisions are relevant evidence even though the product of non-adversary proceedings, (3) that lower state court decisions are to be "followed" if they correctly applied state law, and (4) that the existence of the state court decision should be noted but the federal court will thereafter decide the case as if the state court decision did not exist.

Gilbert P. Verbit, State Court Decisions in Federal Transfer Tax Litigation: *Bosch* Revisited, 23 Real Prop. Prob. & Tr. J. 407, 444-45 (1988). See also F. Ladson Boyle, When It's Broke—Fix It: Reforming Irrevocable Trusts to Change Tax Consequences, 53 Tax Law. 821 (2000) (demonstrating that the tax consequences of reformation remain uncertain in some, but not all, areas of dispute that arise between taxpayers and the Service); Paul L. Caron, The Role of State Court Decisions in Federal Tax Litigation: *Bosch*, *Erie*, and Beyond, 71 Ore. L. Rev. 781, 784 (1992) (conducting a survey of post-*Bosch* cases and rulings that "reveals a quarter century of disarray caused by a misreading of the *Erie* underpinnings of the 'proper regard' standard").

2. *"Collusive" Decisions or Reformation of a Mistake?* Why is it wrong to accept the results of a collusive decision? Are there situations in which the federal government should be indifferent about whether a state decision determining property rights is collusive? If the issue is accomplishing the decedent's intent and if a state court determines what the decedent's intent was, why should a federal court disregard that holding?[33] Professors Langbein and Waggoner have argued:

> The Treasury occupies the position of an unintended beneficiary in these cases. . . . When the mistake arises in a lawyer-drafted instrument, as is usually the case, the Treasury's posture is particularly unattractive. The Treasury benefits through third-party negligence—a species of wrong-doing—at the expense of the innocent intended beneficiaries.

---

33. See Estate of Ellingson v. Commissioner, 964 F.2d 959 (9th Cir. 1992) (relying on an interpretative-aid savings clause contained in the trust that indicated the decedent's intent to have the trust qualify for the marital deduction in deciding which of two plausible readings of the trust agreement should be adopted); Kraus v. Commissioner, 59 T.C.M. (CCH) 1022 (1990) (finding that the interpretative-aid savings clause indicating the decedent's intent to have the trust qualify for the marital deduction was not controlling and that a state court's reformation of the trust to qualify it for the marital deduction was not binding, but ultimately holding that the trust was a product of mistake); Charles A. Redd, What Types of Savings Clauses Will Preserve the Marital Deduction?, 14 Est. Plan., Mar.-Apr. 1987, at 72 (analyzing the effectiveness and advocating for the use of an interpretative-aid savings clause to clarify a decedent's intent to take advantage of the marital deduction or other similar tax provisions).

John H. Langbein & Lawrence W. Waggoner, Reformation of Wills on the Ground of Mistake: Change of Direction in American Law?, 130 U. Pa. L. Rev. 521, 550 (1982).

Picking up on this point, Professor Verbit, in Verbit, supra, at 457-62, advocates an abandonment of the *Bosch* rule and the adoption of a rule in which all final decisions of state courts would be binding in federal tax cases. At the core of his argument is an acknowledgment that the courts are deciding cases for the purpose of carrying out the donor's intent:

> Adoption of such an approach would mean that federal courts must accept decisions from state court proceedings that might be characterized as pro forma, a "sham," a "stamp of approval," and similar characterizations. . . . [T]hese decisions allegedly result from the willingness of state court judges to distort the facts or misinterpret or misapply state law as a result of a de facto conspiracy among the court and the parties to do in the federal tax collector. . . .
>
> At the root of this concern about what state judges are doing is the question of why they are doing it. Are they "distorting" the facts or the law solely because they see the issue as one of the hometown crowd against Washington? Is it the case that they are amenable to the pleas and arguments of counsel and parties who are their friends, neighbors or even former colleagues? Are they, as Justice Harlan . . . suggested, simply too busy to devote much time and effort to the issues raised in the state proceeding and thus tend to approve whatever unopposed material is put before them? No reading of the cases yields a complete response to those questions. But it does reveal that many of the *Bosch*-type cases arise in the context of a mistake of law or a mistake in drafting by counsel for a decedent. . . .
>
> At least some of the state decisions that are criticized in federal tax proceedings are attempts to relieve the decedent's estate of the consequences of poor legal advice. Judges would, and frequently do, deny that it is the court's job to compensate for incompetent legal advice and, in particular, to remake the decedent's will. At the same time, however, state courts indicate that, in interpreting instruments, their primary task is to determine the grantor or testator's intent. As the courts are fond of noting, it is difficult to conceive of a testator whose goal is to benefit the Internal Revenue Service at the expense of the natural objects of his or her bounty.
>
> Instead of viewing the actions of state judges as participation in a "Great Treasury Raid," it is equally possible to view the situation as one in which state courts construe and reform instruments to effect the testator's intent while the IRS is attempting to capitalize on every drafting error, however slight. The case in which a taxpayer deliberately chooses to surrender a tax benefit for some non-tax reason, such as to disinherit a spouse, is rare indeed. Contemporary estate planning is often tax-driven. To the extent that is the case, a legitimate question should be considered: Why deny a tax benefit to a taxpayer who has omitted a phrase or used one word too many if the evidence is that the taxpayer intended to qualify for the tax benefit? This is particularly compelling if an error is of essentially a technical nature and the taxpayer is really the innocent victim of a

> drafter's error. This is not to say that the IRS should accept instruments that do not conform to the requirements of the Internal Revenue Code. But if a state court interprets an instrument to carry out the testator's intent, the IRS *ought* not to be in a position to brush aside such efforts.

The doctrine of reformation to correct mistakes in *unambiguous* documents, testamentary as well as nontestamentary, is becoming more widely accepted. See infra Chapter 12. In particular, courts have reformed instruments to correct drafting errors that would otherwise result in detrimental tax results. See, e.g., Walker v. Walker, 744 N.E.2d 60 (Mass. 2001); Putnam v. Putnam, 682 N.E.2d 1351 (Mass. 1997); see also Estate of Branigan, 609 A.2d 431 (N.J. 1992) (discussed infra Note 3). But see Kirchick v. Guerry, 706 N.E.2d 702, 703 (Mass. 1999) (refusing to rule on the question of when a testamentary power of appointment was created because the action was brought for "the sole reason" of using it "in the pending Federal tax case" and because the trustee could point "to no duty or issue which turns on the outcome of the present action *other* than estate tax liability under Federal tax law"). The effect for federal tax purposes of these state court decisions, even those made by a state's highest court, however, is in doubt.

The IRS takes the position that a state court order reforming a donative instrument does not have retroactive effect for tax purposes. See Rev. Rul. 93-79, 1993-2 C.B. 269; Tech. Adv. Mem. 83-46-008 (Aug. 4, 1983) (basing its holding on the statement in *Bosch* that a state decision must "determine property rights"); see also Rev. Rul. 73-142, 1973-1 C.B. 405 (holding that a lower state court decree will be controlling for federal estate tax purposes if the decree was issued before the taxing event, even if the proceeding was nonadversarial). But see Estate of Rapp v. Commissioner, 140 F.2d 1211 (9th Cir. 1998) (relying on *Bosch* to ignore a lower court ruling that bound the parties because it was contrary to state law and distinguishing Rev. Rul. 73-142, supra, and the line of cases that treat the taxable event for claiming a QTIP as the date of the QTIP election and not the date of the testator's death); Tech. Adv. Mem. 97-31-003 (May 31, 1997) (ignoring Rev. Rul. 73-142, supra, and holding gifts by a conservator approved by a lower state court were not supported by the law of Maryland and, therefore, the transferred property was includable in the decedent's estate under IRC § 2038).

Federal tax cases support the IRS' position. Van Den Wymelenberg v. United States, 397 F.2d 443 (7th Cir.), cert. denied, 393 U.S. 953 (1968), concerned a trust that, through inadvertence, did not qualify for federal gift tax annual exclusions under IRC § 2503(c). After the IRS disallowed the exclusion, the settlors executed a Corrected Trust Agreement to have the trust conform to the requirements of IRC § 2503(c) with the intention that it have retroactive effect.

The district court upheld the deficiencies assessed by the IRS and the Seventh Circuit affirmed, relying on concerns about collusion to support its decision.

> Taxpayers cite several Wisconsin state cases for the proposition that a written instrument which, through mistake, does not embody the intent of the parties may be reformed by the parties through voluntary execution of a corrected instrument. However, not even judicial reformation can operate to change the federal tax consequences of a completed transaction.
>
> As to the parties to the reformed instrument the reformation relates back to the date of the original instrument, but it does not affect the rights acquired by non-parties, including the Government. Were the law otherwise there would exist considerable opportunity for "collusive" state court actions having the sole purpose of reducing federal tax liabilities.

397 F.2d at 445. The claim that the government had nonparty rights is questionable. It neither changed its position in reliance on the prereformed instrument nor gave consideration for the taxes collected. The refusal to recognize the retroactive effect of a reformation based on the ground of collusive state court proceedings is also questionable. If the issue is distrust for state court decisions, the answer should not be that reformation has no retroactive effect. Rather the answer should be that the reformation issue be litigated or relitigated in the federal court applying state law with the IRS as a party. See Restatement 3d of Property § 12.1 reporter's note 11. For other cases supporting the view that reformation by state courts has no retroactive effect for tax purposes, see Estate of Bennett v. Commissioner, 100 T.C. 42 (1993); Estate of La Meres v. Commissioner, 98 T.C. 294 (1992); Estate of Nicholson v. Commissioner, 94 T.C. 666 (1990). But see Estate of Starkey v. United States, 223 F.3d 694 (7th Cir. 2000) (finding that an ambiguity in the documents was appropriately resolved by a state appellate court in nonadversarial litigation to construe a gift to charity after the Service had denied the estate a charitable deduction and holding that the charitable deduction was warranted); Flitcroft v. Commissioner, 328 F.2d 449 (9th Cir. 1964) (pre-*Bosch* case accepting as controlling for income tax purposes a state court decree reforming a lifetime trust to make it irrevocable; Rev. Rul 93-79, supra, indicates that it will not follow this case).

3. *Modification to Achieve Donor's Tax Objectives.* If between the time decedents execute their wills and their deaths the tax law changes, should courts be able to modify the wills so as to achieve tax savings? In Note 2 the argument for reformation was based on proof that a mistake occurred that resulted in the donative instrument failing to express decedent's original and particularized intent. If modification is appropriate in a situation of changed tax circumstances, it would have to be based on a determination of the donor's probable intention.

In Estate of Branigan, supra, the executors sought to modify decedent's will in two respects for the purpose of taking advantage of changes in the federal estate tax laws that occurred subsequent to the execution of the will and subsequent to the death of the testator. The first proposed modification was to divide the marital deduction trust into two trusts, which would permit the executor to take advantage of the "reverse QTIP" under IRC § 2652(a)(3) for the purpose of obtaining the $1 million generation-skipping tax exemption. The second proposed modification was to convert the sons' nongeneral testamentary powers of appointment into general testamentary powers of appointment. This modification would reduce taxes by having the sons taxed under the federal estate tax with its lower rates rather than under the federal generation-skipping transfer tax. The court granted the first proposed modification but not the second.

> The doctrine of probable intent as it has evolved is sufficiently broad to accommodate plaintiffs' request to alter the trust funds for purposes of minimizing GST taxes. Indeed, the doctrine has been applied in contextual settings in which the imputation of the presumed intent to minimize taxes was necessary to prevent the frustration of the testator's overall testamentary plans. Similarly, this case presents evidence material to the testator's intention with respect to the significance of federal taxes as a factor in his testamentary plan. Considerable evidence supports the finding that decedent had specifically attempted to minimize QTIP taxes generated under the existing will. . . .
>
> In addition to the extrinsic evidence supporting decedent's specific intent to minimize taxes, the doctrine of probable intent reasonably assumes, in its several possible applications, a widely-accepted intent on the part of most testators to save taxes. . . .
>
> Moreover, in this case the imputation of an intent on the part of the testator to incorporate in his will those technical provisions essential to achieve tax savings is not hampered by any possibly conflicting purpose relating to other aspects of his will. [E]ffectuating an intent to save taxes in the matter before us does not entail the alteration of a substantive provision of decedent's will. Plaintiffs can secure part of the tax savings they seek under the current federal tax laws by dividing the single QTIP trust into two QTIP trusts. That division does not affect or change any substantive disposition or bequest under decedent's will. The beneficiary, purposes, and powers of the trusts will remain intact. Moreover, the splitting of the trust does not entail modification of a material or significant administrative provision or structural feature of the will. Rather, the modification constitutes only a technical alteration relating to an aspect of estate administration that does not otherwise appear to have any material bearing on the decedent's testamentary plan. The change of that administrative provision is designed solely to conform the will to the existing federal tax scheme, an objective sought to be achieved by the testator.

> We therefore conclude that plaintiffs' request to reform decedent's will to modify the existing provisions of trust funds in order to derive maximum benefits under the federal estate tax laws is reasonable.
>
> . . . The reasoning that enables us to sanction a change in the will with respect to certain of its structural and administrative features but not the substantive terms of trust bequests prevents us from authorizing the reformation of the will to alter the testator's sons' limited powers of appointment. We understand that very substantial federal taxes could be saved by that change. Moreover, the executors argue that that modification will revitalize the original intent of the testator by making the donee of the power the deemed transferor and tax the skip property at the son's own rates. . . . The modification, however, certainly would alter the dispository provisions of the will. Under that proposed scheme, the interests of the grandchildren whose fathers were living at the time of decedent's death could be affected by making their father's power of appointment general with the possibility they could lose their inheritance. . . .
>
> We cannot conclude that plaintiffs' desire to evade taxes at the cost of the dispository scheme and the possible disinheritance of some of the heirs effectuates the testamentary intent of the testator.

609 A.2d at 436-38.[34]

The Restatement 3d of Property adopts a standard similar to the one found in *Branigan* for modifying donative documents to achieve the donor's tax objectives.

> § *12.2. Modifying Donative Documents to Achieve Donor's Tax Objectives.* A donative document may be modified, in a manner that does not violate the donor's probable intention, to achieve the donor's tax objectives.

UTC § 416 codifies Restatement 3d § 12.2. Whether the modifications will ultimately be successful in achieving tax savings in many situations, however, is in question. As indicated in Note 2, supra, the IRS and federal tax cases have taken the position that state court reformation proceedings do not have retroactive effect for tax purposes.

External References. Palmer on Restitution § 18.7(b); Richard B. Stephens, Guy B. Maxfield et al., Federal Estate and Gift Taxation (5th ed. 1983); F. Ladson Boyle, Letting the State Law Dog Wag the Tax Tail, 2 Prob. Prac. Rep., Feb. 1990, at 1; Paul L. Caron, The Federal Courts of Appeals' Use of State Court Decisions in Tax Cases: "Proper Regard" Means "No Regard," 46 Okla. L. Rev. 443 (1993); Paul L. Caron, The Role of State Court

---

34. EGTRRA makes severance of trusts for purposes of the generation-skipping transfer tax more easily available. See IRC § 2642(a)(3).

Decisions in Federal Tax Litigation: *Bosch*, *Erie*, and Beyond, 71 Or. L. Rev. 781 (1992); John H. Langbein & Lawrence W. Waggoner, Reformation of Wills on the Ground of Mistake: Change of Direction in American Law?, 130 U. Pa. L. Rev. 521, 550-54 (1982); Bernard Wolfman, *Bosch*, Its Implications and Aftermath: The Effect of State Court Adjudications on Federal Tax Litigation, 3 U. Miami Inst. Est. Plan. ch. 2 (1969).

Chapter 8

Revocable Trusts and Other Will Substitutes

As noted in Chapter 1, will substitutes are increasingly important in the deathtime transmission of wealth. The ideal will substitute allows the donor to retain lifetime enjoyment and control over the asset, while purporting to transfer to another person a property interest in (or a contract right to) future possession of that asset. Life insurance, pension accounts, joint accounts, and revocable trusts fit this mold and are widely used.

Joint tenancies also count as will substitutes, because they provide for a right of survivorship. The right to sever, however, doesn't operate like a power to revoke; it doesn't allow a joint tenant to regain the fractional portion represented by his or her monetary contribution toward the property's acquisition.[1] Instead, the right to sever allows a joint tenant, by unilateral act (such as conveying his or her interest to himself or herself), to convert the joint tenancy into an equal tenancy in common, destroying the right of survivorship.[2]

Although the above devices aren't wills, they are substitutes for wills. They function to pass property at death without being subject to the statutory

---

1. But see, e.g., Blanchette v. Blanchette, 287 N.E.2d 459 (Mass. 1972) (joint tenancy unscrambled because husband, who bought AT&T stock in joint tenancy with his then wife under an employee stock-purchase plan, established that he had not created the joint tenancy with donative intent).

2. See Powell on Real Property ¶ 618.

formalities required for executing wills. Also, although the affected property passes at death, it passes outside of probate. Will substitutes are sometimes aptly referred to as probate-avoidance devices, or as nonprobate wills. They do not, of course, eliminate the desirability of having a will. Will substitutes tend to be asset-specific, so a will remains necessary for the decedent's other property. Also, wills are helpful as a back-stop even for property affected by a will substitute, especially joint tenancy property, in case the decedent outlives the other joint tenants.

Because of their will-like characteristics, will substitutes have been exerting increasing pressure on the law of succession, which traditionally invokes somewhat different rules for testamentary and nontestamentary transfers. If will substitutes are not wills for purposes of the statutory formalities, are they wills for other purposes, such as the law of lapse or the revocation of wills by changed circumstances such as divorce? There is no necessary reason why they can't be treated as wills for some purposes but not for others. As we will see, the law of succession is tending in the direction of a unification of its testamentary and nontestamentary branches. In particular, the UPC and the Restatement 3d of Property include rules that extend the subsidiary law of wills to various will substitute arrangements.

PART A. VALIDITY OF WILL SUBSTITUTES—FORM OVER SUBSTANCE

Statutory References: *UPC §§ 6-101, -102*

Restatement 3d of Property

§ 7.1 Validity of Will Substitutes.

An arrangement established by the donor during the donor's life under which the right to possession or enjoyment of property or a contractual payment shifts outside of probate to the donee at the donor's death is a nonprobate transfer and need not be executed in compliance with the statutory formalities required for a will. The donor's retention of substantial rights for life, such as the right of dominion, control, possession, or enjoyment of the property or contract, does not transform the arrangement into a probate transfer.

1. Revocable Trusts—The Present-Transfer Test

Statutory References: *UTC §§ 406, 601-604*

Property law recognizes the validity of a revocable inter vivos trust, even one in which the settlor retains the right to income for life. It does so on the basis of the so-called "present-transfer" test: *Upon creation*, the trust transfers an equitable remainder interest in the trust corpus to the remainder beneficiary.

The fact that the remainder interest is subject to divestment does not jeopardize the validity of the trust. A *present* transfer of a remainder interest—even one that is subject to divestment by the settlor's exercise of the power to revoke—satisfies the present-transfer test and obviates the necessity of memorializing the trust in a document that is executed in accordance with the formalities for a valid will. The transfer is treated as inter vivos, not testamentary. See Restatement 3d of Property § 7.1, comment b.

The present-transfer test was critiqued in John H. Langbein, The Nonprobate Revolution and the Future of the Law of Succession, 97 Harv. L. Rev. 1108, 1128 (1984):

> The odor of legal fiction hangs heavily over the present-[transfer] test. We see courts straining to reach right results for wrong reasons and insisting that will-like transfers possess gift-like incidents. Courts have used such doctrinal ruses to validate not only the revocable inter vivos trust, but other will substitutes as well. . . . What is the difference between the revocable and ambulatory interest created by a will, and a vested but defeasible interest in life insurance or pension proceeds? None at all, except for the form of words.

Revocability of Inter Vivos Trusts. At common law, an inter vivos transfer in trust is treated like other inter vivos transfers of property: it is *irrevocable* unless the settlor expressly retains a power to revoke. This contrasts, of course, with wills, which are revocable without the necessity of an explicit reservation of a power to revoke or amend.

Statutes in a few states establish the opposite rule. They provide that transfers in trust are revocable unless expressly made irrevocable. See, e.g., Cal. Prob. Code § 15400; Okla. Stat. Ann. tit. 60 § 175.41; Tex. Prop. Code § 112.051.

UTC § 602(a) also reverses the common-law rule and provides: "Unless the terms of a trust expressly provide that the trust is irrevocable, the settlor may revoke or amend the trust." Section 602(a) provides that its new rule "does not apply to a trust created under an instrument executed before [the effective date of this [Code]]."

The Restatement 3d of Trusts § 63 provides that "[t]he settlor of an inter vivos trust has power to revoke and modify the trust to the extent the terms of the trust so provide." Comment b, however, provides that "[i]f the terms of the trust are otherwise expressed in writing but fail to provide whether or to what extent the settlor reserves the power to revoke or modify the trust, the writing is incomplete and its meaning is uncertain." Comment c amplifies this point further by providing:

> *c. Presumptions regarding revocability.* Where the settlor has failed expressly to provide whether a trust is subject to revocation or amendment, if the settlor has retained no beneficial interest in the trust . . . , it is rebuttably presumed that the

> settlor has no power to revoke or amend the trust. If, however, the settlor . . . has retained a beneficial interest in the trust . . . , the presumption is that the trust is revocable and amendable by the settlor.

Validity of Revocable, Self-Declared Trusts. A self-declared trust is a revocable inter vivos trust in which the *settlor* acts as trustee. The settlor declares himself or herself trustee for the benefit of himself or herself for life, remainder at the settlor's death to the settlor's chosen beneficiary. Because a self-declared trust involves no transfer of title to a third-party trustee, a self-declared trust might seem to present special difficulties under the present-transfer test. Not so. The clear weight of the authorities is in favor of validity as an inter vivos transaction. The transfer that satisfies the present-transfer test is the transfer of the equitable remainder interest to the beneficiary who is scheduled to take in possession or enjoyment at the settlor's death. See, e.g., Zuckerman v. Alter, 615 So.2d 661 (Fla. 1993); Estate of Brenner, 547 P.2d 938 (Colo. Ct. App. 1976); Ridge v. Bright, 93 S.E.2d 607 (N.C. 1956); Farkas v. Williams, 125 N.E.2d 600 (Ill. 1955); Restatement 2d of Trusts § 57 comment h. Contra, Mathias v. Fantine, 1990 WL 21466 (Ohio Ct. App. 1990). The Ohio legislature reacted quickly to reverse the *Mathias* decision, which surprisingly held that no trust was validly created where the grantor was both trustee and sole current beneficiary. See Ohio Rev. Code § 1335.01(C).

Mental Capacity Required for Creating a Trust. The Restatement 3d of Trusts § 11 (Capacity of Settlor to Create a Trust) provides:

> (1) A person has capacity to create a trust by will to the same extent that the person has capacity to devise or bequeath the property free of trust.
>
> (2) A person has capacity to create a revocable inter vivos trust by transfer to another or by declaration to the same extent that the person has capacity to create a trust by will.
>
> (3) A person has capacity to create an irrevocable inter vivos trust by transfer to another or by declaration to the same extent that the person has capacity to transfer the property inter vivos free of trust in similar circumstances.

Accord, UTC § 601; Restatement 3d of Property § 8.1.

Undue Influence, Duress, Fraud. A trust is void to the extent that its creation was induced by fraud, duress, or undue influence. See Restatement 3d of Trusts § 12; UTC § 406; Restatement 3d of Property § 8.3.

Marketing Revocable Trusts: Consumer Fraud and the Unauthorized Practice of Law. The revocable self-declared trust has become enormously popular in recent years. Part of the reason for its popularity is the way that it has been marketed. Beginning with the 1965 best-selling book by Norman Dacey, *How to Avoid Probate!*, non-attorneys have aggressively promoted the use of revocable trusts through a variety of media, including newspaper ads, telephone solicitations, and hotel "seminars." The promoters, sometimes called "trust mills," push standard-form inter vivos trust instruments (usually termed "living trusts") on targeted segments of the population, especially the elderly. These activities raise a number of potential legal problems, including consumer fraud and the unauthorized practice of law.

A growing number of consumer fraud cases have been filed against trust mills in recent years. State attorneys general in at least ten states have charged promoters with deceptive sales practices, such as telling customers that revocable trust are immune from creditor claims and income taxes. Another common practice is marketing standardized trust forms without informing customers that the terms may not meet their individual needs or interests. See, e.g., Press Release of Attorney General of Michigan, Feb. 5, 2001, available at www.ag.state.mi.us; Akron Bar Ass'n v. Miller, 684 N.E.2d 288 (Ohio 1997) (enjoining a trust mill from further activity in Ohio because the company marketed trust documents without concern for customers' particular circumstances). See also Jane Bryant Quinn, When Good Trusts Go Bad, Newsweek, October 5, 1992.

The problem of unauthorized practice occurs not only where the promoter is not an attorney, but also where there is limited attorney involvement in marketing the product. Three recent cases address the question of attorney/non-attorney collaboration in the preparation and selling of revocable trusts. In Committee on Professional Ethics v. Baker, 492 N.W.2d 695 (Iowa 1992), the court reprimanded an attorney for aiding in the unauthorized practice of law through various actions. The marketer, who was not an attorney, held seminars at the end of which he conferred with customers, supplying them with trust forms and a list of recommended attorneys. The reprimanded attorney, Baker, had provided the forms and had accepted many referrals from the list. He had also given the marketer advice on newsletters promoting living trusts and consulted with the marketer and its customers in three-way telephone conference calls.

In The Florida Bar Re Advisory Opinion, 613 So.2d 426 (Fla. 1992), the court issued an advisory opinion ruling that the gathering of information by a non-attorney does not itself constitute the unauthorized practice of law, but "[t]he assembling, drafting, execution, and funding of a living trust document [do] constitute the practice of law . . . [and] a lawyer must make the determination as to the client's need for a living trust and identify the type of living trust most appropriate for the client." Id. at 427-28.

In Trumbull County Bar Ass'n v. Hanna, 684 N.E.2d 329 (Ohio 1997), the court held that a non-attorney financial planner engaged in the unauthorized practice of law even though he worked in conjunction with an out-of-state lawyer. It was the planner who advised the clients about the suitability of living trusts, arranged for the preparation of the trust documents, and supervised the documents' execution. This, the court held, constituted the unauthorized rendering of legal services.

For a discussion of the problems raised by inter vivos trusts sold by non-lawyers, see Charles F. Gibbs, The Marketing of Living Trusts by Non-Attorney Promoters, 20 ACTEC Notes 193 (1994).

State legislatures are also cracking down on trust mills. For example, a Florida statute requires inter vivos trusts to be executed in accordance with the formalities of a will, and an Oregon statute prohibits, with very narrow exceptions, the preparation of a living trust by a non-lawyer. See Fla. Stat. Ann. § 737.111[3]; Or. Rev. Stat. § 128.001.

Rights of the Grantor's Creditors and Creditors of the Grantor's Estate. If a grantor transfers assets to a trust "in fraud of his or her creditors," the grantor's creditors can set the transfer aside to the extent necessary to satisfy the indebtedness, whether the indebtedness arose before or after the transfer. Restatement 2d of Property § 34.3; Unif. Fraudulent Transfer Act (1984) (in effect in about 40 states); Unif. Fraudulent Conveyance Act (1918) (in effect in about 5 states). A transfer "in fraud of creditors" is one made with actual intent to hinder, delay, or defraud a creditor or one that leaves the grantor's remaining assets insufficient to satisfy current debts or debts the grantor intended to incur. A transfer to a trust that is in fraud of creditors can be set aside under the "fraudulent-transfer" principle, whether the trust is revocable or irrevocable.

If the transfer to a *revocable* trust was *not* in fraud of creditors, can the grantor's creditors nevertheless satisfy an indebtedness out of the trust assets on the ground of the revocability of the trust? The traditional view is that the unexercised power to revoke is not property and therefore cannot be reached by the grantor's creditors. See Restatement 2d of Trusts § 330 comment o; Scott on Trusts § 330.12.

More recently, the UTC, UPC, Restatement 3d of Trusts, and several decisions have broken away from the traditional position and allow the grantor's creditors to reach assets in a revocable trust, even though the transfer to the trust was not in fraud of creditors. See UTC § 505 (applies to lifetime and estate creditors); UPC § 6-102 (only applies to estate creditors); Restatement 3d of

---

3. More specifically, the Florida statute provides that "[t]he testamentary aspects of a trust defined in § 731.201(33), are invalid unless the trust is executed with the formalities required for the execution of a will." The term "testamentary aspects" is defined as "those provisions of the trust that dispose of the trust property on or after the death of the settlor other than to the settlor's estate." The cited section excludes constructive trusts, pension trusts, land trusts, and trusts created by a deposit or account in any financial institution.

Trusts § 25 comment e (applies to lifetime and estate creditors); State Street Bank & Trust Co. v. Reiser, 389 N.E.2d 768 (Mass. Ct. App. 1979); Estate of Kovalyshyn, 343 A.2d 852 (Hudson Co., N.J., 1975); Johnson v. Commercial Bank, 588 P.2d 1096 (Or. 1978); see also Restatement 3d of Property § 7.2 comment b. The cases just cited all involved creditors' claims to the grantor's estate, but the holdings would seem to apply also to creditors' suits brought during the grantor's lifetime. In the *Johnson* case, the court reasoned that since the power to revoke is essentially the same as a general power of appointment, the rule allowing a donor's creditors to reach assets subject to a general power of appointment should be applied to a retained power to revoke as well.

Several states have enacted statutes that allow the grantor's estate and lifetime creditors to reach assets of a revocable trust. See, e.g., Cal. Prob. Code §§ 18200-18201; Mich. Comp. Laws Ann. § 556.128. Mo. Rev. Stat. § 461.071.[4]

The Bankruptcy Code, adopted in 1978,[5] is less clear than its predecessor on whether the grantor's bankruptcy trustee can reach a revocable trust. If the Bankruptcy Code addresses the question at all, it is by negative implication in the following provision:

> *Bankruptcy Code, 11 U.S.C. § 541. Property of the Estate*: . . . (b) Property of the estate does not include . . . any power that the debtor may exercise solely for the benefit of an entity other than the debtor. . .

No provision explicitly declares that "property of the estate" *includes* property over which the debtor retains a power exercisable for the debtor's own benefit, such as a power of revocation.

Rights of the Grantor's Surviving Spouse. In some jurisdictions, the grantor's surviving spouse may claim an elective share in the assets of a revocable trust. This subject is considered in Chapter 10.

Federal Taxation of Revocable Trusts: Substance Over Form. The federal system of income, estate, and gift taxation taxes revocable trusts according to their substance, not their form, as illustrated by the following example:

> *Example 8.1:* G transferred property to T, in trust, directing the trustee to pay the net income from the property to G for his lifetime and at his death to deliver the trust corpus to X. G retained a power to revoke the trust at any time and have the trust property returned to him.

---

4. See Committee Report, Rights of Creditors to Reach Assets of a Revocable Trust After the Death of the Grantor—The Missouri Approach, 20 Real Prop. Prob. & Tr. J. 1189 (1985).

5. A major reform of federal bankruptcy law is pending. As this casebook goes to press, the House of Representatives and the Senate have passed different versions of reform legislation, and a conference committee has been appointed to resolve the differences. For the latest developments, see the American Bankruptcy Institute's website, www.abiworld.org.

The tax consequences of G's transfer are as follows:

(1) Gift tax consequences: Because of his power to revoke, G's transfer of a remainder interest to X was not a taxable gift. See Treas. Reg. § 25.2511-2(c).

(2) Income tax consequences: G will continue until his death to be taxed on both the ordinary income generated by the property and also on capital gains (or losses) realized by the trust. See IRC §§ 676, 677(a)(1); Treas. Reg. § 1.671-3(b).

(3) Estate tax consequences: When G dies, the full value of the corpus of the trust will be included in G's gross estate under IRC § 2036(a)(1) or § 2038.

See supra Chapter 7.

2. *Other Will Substitutes—The Present-Transfer Test*

Statutory References: *UPC §§ 6-101, -203, -211 to -214*

The present-transfer test is widely used to validate many will substitutes, not only revocable trusts. Though wills in substance, transfers that can be characterized as having presently passed to a donee any *interest in property*, whether present or future, vested or contingent, are treated as inter vivos, not testamentary, and their validity does not depend upon compliance with the execution formalities required of wills. Likewise, transfers that can be characterized as presently conferring a *contract right* on another are exempted from the statutory formalities for wills, even though the time of performance of the contract is geared to the time of the transferor's death.

Life Insurance and Life-Insurance Trusts. Compliance with the statutory formalities for wills is not required of beneficiary designations of life-insurance policies. Although life-insurance contracts pay out at death, the beneficiary designation—when made—is treated as conferring a present contract right on the beneficiary. The will-like characteristics of life insurance can, therefore, be ignored, among which are the retained lifetime right of the owner of the policy (who typically is the person whose life is insured by the policy) to terminate the policy or to revoke the beneficiary designation and name a different beneficiary.

An additional will-like characteristic of life insurance is the requirement that the beneficiary must survive the insured to be entitled to the policy's proceeds. The requirement of survival is contained in the printed terms of all life insurance policies. Non-UPC antilapse statutes do not cover life-insurance beneficiary designations. The current UPC broke new ground by adopting an antilapse statute for life insurance (UPC § 2-706), but the life insurance industry, spearheaded by the American Council of Life Insurance (ACLI), the industry's trade association with paid lobbyists in every state, has mounted a well-funded lobbying effort to defeat the provision wherever it has been introduced. See infra Chapter 10, Part A.

In many states, due again to effective industry lobbying, the proceeds of life-insurance policies are wholly or partly exempt from the claims of the insured's creditors. The statutes vary, and may only apply if the proceeds are payable to specified members of the insured's family.

A popular estate-planning technique is to establish a life-insurance trust. Life-insurance trusts take different forms. One type of life-insurance trust is created by transferring the full ownership of the policy to the trustee. An arrangement in which the grantor irrevocably transfers the policy to the trustee and makes the trust itself irrevocable typically is tax motivated—that is, the arrangement is designed to avoid the inclusion of the value of the proceeds of the policy in the insured's gross estate under IRC § 2042. Trusts of this sort are sometimes "funded"—that is, other assets are irrevocably transferred to the trustee, in addition to the life-insurance policy, with directions to the trustee to pay the life-insurance premiums out of the income generated by the other assets. If the trust is not "funded," the grantor of the trust (the previous owner of the policy and the insured) usually continues to pay the premiums on the policy out of his or her own pocket.

A second type of life-insurance trust is created by naming the trustee as the beneficiary of the life-insurance policy, with directions to the trustee to collect the proceeds on the insured's death and carry out the terms of the trust. Trusts of this sort typically are revocable and hence are not tax motivated. Rather, the motive usually is the administrative convenience of having insurance proceeds added at death to an existing inter vivos trust. Not only is the trust itself revocable, but so is the designation of the trustee as the beneficiary of the policy. The insured, as owner of the policy, retains the right to renounce the beneficiary designation, to terminate the policy, to surrender the policy for its cash value, if any, and so on. Although the validity of this type of trust was at one time in doubt, it now seems settled that this type of arrangement creates a valid trust. As explained by the court in Gordon v. Portland Trust Bank, 271 P.2d 653 (Or. 1954):

> Our own view is that the ownership of the . . . policy is actually divided between the [trustee, as the] beneficiary [of the policy] and the insured. . . . [T]he loan and cash surrender values . . . are clearly the property of the insured. On the other hand, the [trustee as the] beneficiary [of the policy] is the owner of a promise to pay the proceeds at the death of insured, subject to insured's right of revocation.

Another decision, Gurnett v. Mutual Life Insurance Co., 191 N.E. 250 (Ill. 1934), said:

> The continuing [contract] right to receive the proceeds of an insurance policy is not impaired by the unexercised right or privilege of the insured to designate another beneficiary.

See also Allan F. Smith, Personal Life Insurance Trusts ch. 2 (1960).

Multiple-Party Accounts. Bank and other financial intermediary accounts frequently are registered in the names of more than one person. These multiple-party accounts generally take one of several forms: trust (so-called "Totten" trusts), joint, or payable on death (POD). These forms themselves are ambiguous concerning the depositor's substantive purpose. The depositor may or may not intend to confer on the other party beneficial lifetime rights or survivorship rights or both. For example, if *A* deposits funds in a savings account registered jointly in the names of "*A* or *B*," A may have used the joint form for any one of three different purposes: (1) to give A and B lifetime rights to withdraw funds for their personal benefit, with the survivor receiving funds remaining in the account upon the death of the first to die (a true joint tenancy); (2) to give B the legal power to draw from the account for A's benefit but not B's and no survivorship right (an agency account, in which B acts as A's agent); or (3) to give B the right to any funds remaining in the account at A's death, but no lifetime rights or powers (the equivalent of a payable-on-death account).

Totten trusts. The Totten trust is created when a person deposits his or her funds in a savings or bank account in his or her name "in trust for" another person. The depositor typically retains exclusive control of the account until death, when any remaining funds pass to the beneficiary. Totten trusts have been called the "poor person's will," but as Professor Friedman has observed, "It would be more accurate to call it a middle-class will." Lawrence M. Friedman, The Law of the Living, The Law of the Dead: Property, Succession, and Society, 1966 Wis. L. Rev. 340, 369 (1966). Totten trusts are usually created without legal advice, specifically for the purpose of bypassing probate. They are functionally equivalent to a will in every respect; only form distinguishes them from wills.

The Totten trust takes its name from the leading New York case, Matter of Totten, 71 N.E. 748 (N.Y. 1904). The court held that such a "trust" was a "tentative trust merely, revocable at will, until the depositor dies or completes the gift in his lifetime by some unequivocal act or declaration, such as delivery of the passbook or notice to the beneficiary."

The Totten trust has been accepted in a substantial number of states besides New York. See, e.g., Brucks v. Home Federal Saving & Loan Association, 228 P.2d 545 (Cal. 1951); Seymour v. Seymour, 85 So. 2d 726 (Fla. 1956); Estate of Petralia, 204 N.E.2d 1 (Ill. 1965); Estate of Morton, 769 P.2d 616 (Kan. 1987); Estate of McFetridge, 372 A.2d 823 (Pa. 1977); Reynolds v. Shambeau, 437 A.2d 1101 (Vt. 1981). Totten trusts have been validated by statute in several states. In some jurisdictions, however, the question is still open. The Restatement 3d of Trusts § 26 and the Restatement 3d of Property § 7.1

comment i recognize the validity of Totten trusts. One case upholds the trust but treats it as irrevocable. See Cazallis v. Ingraham, 110 A. 359 (Me. 1920).

Courts have held that creditors of the depositor can reach the deposit to satisfy their claims, both while the depositor is living, see Workmen's Compensation Board v. Furman, 106 N.Y.S.2d 404 (Sup. Ct. 1951), and after his or her death, see, e.g., Reich's Estate, 262 N.Y.S. 623 (Sur. Ct. 1933). Where the beneficiary dies before the depositor, it has been held that the trust "terminated ipso facto, and that the funds on deposit thereafter remained the sole property of the depositor, unimpressed by any trust." See In re United States Trust Co., 102 N.Y.S. 271 (App. Div. 1907).

There seems no reason to doubt that a Totten trust can be made irrevocable, but there has been very little discussion of what evidence of intent is needed for this purpose. The question was presented in Estate of Sulovich v. Commissioner, 587 F.2d 845 (6th Cir. 1978); Ingels' Estate, 92 A.2d 881 (Pa. 1952); and In re Farrell, 81 N.E.2d 51 (N.Y. 1948).

Joint accounts; POD accounts. Like Totten trust accounts, joint bank and other financial organization accounts contain a survivorship feature. The balance on hand in the account at the death of a depositor shifts to the surviving co-account holder without going through probate.

Except in a very few states, however, the funds in a joint account are not owned in joint tenancy (or tenancy by the entirety, if between spouses). That is to say, a deposit into such an account doesn't transfer an undivided interest therein to the other co-account holder. The fact that each account holder has a right to withdraw the whole of the account masks the true ownership of the funds in the account. The true ownership is that each account holder continues to own his or her own contribution to the balance on hand. If one co-account holder withdraws an amount in excess of his or her own contributions, the other co-account holder normally has a right to force that excess to be returned. This right is routinely waived by inaction, possibly triggering federal gift tax consequences when the statute of limitations expires. See Treas. Reg. § 25.2511-1(h)(4); Estate of Lang v. Commissioner, 613 F.2d 770 (9th Cir. 1980). Consequently, as between the co-account holders, a deposit into a joint bank account is revocable; no federal gift tax consequences are triggered because the tax law treats the deposit as an "incomplete" gift. See supra Chapter 7, Part A.

As with a revocable inter vivos trust, the validity of the survivorship feature depends upon satisfaction of the present-transfer test. Most courts have found the test to be satisfied on the same theory used to uphold life-insurance beneficiary designations, that is, upon deposit the non-depositing co-account holder acquires a present (though defeasible) contract right to the deposit, payable on the death of the depositor. Legislation in many states also validates or is treated as validating the survivorship feature of joint bank accounts. Finally, in seeming contradiction of the predominant view concerning the rights of each party during life, a group of cases validates the survivorship feature by utilizing a joint-tenancy analysis, especially when the deposit agreement, in tracking the language of a widely enacted bank-protection statute, describes the co-depositors as "joint tenants."

Payable on death (POD) accounts are created when a depositor registers the account in his or her name "payable on death" to another person. Unlike joint accounts, the form of POD accounts discloses the intention to transfer benefits only at the depositor's death. This difference in form has led most courts to treat joint and POD accounts differently. In the absence of validating legislation, POD accounts are generally held to be testamentary, invalidating the attempted transfer of ownership on the depositor's death. See, e.g., Compton v. Compton, 435 S.W.2d 76 (Ky. 1968); Matter of Collier, 381 So.2d 1338 (Miss. 1980); Blais v. Colebrook Guaranty Saving Bank, 220 A.2d 763 (N.H. 1966); Brown's Estate, 22 A.2d 821 (Pa. 1941); Methodist Church v. First Nat'l Bank, 211 A.2d 168 (Vt. 1965. Contra, e.g., Estate of Wright, 308 N.E.2d 319 (Ill. App. Ct. 1974). See generally William M. McGovern, Jr., The Payable on Death Account and Other Will Substitutes, 67 Nw. U.L. Rev. 7 (1972).

POD accounts have fared much better in the legislatures. Legislation in many states validates the survivorship feature of such accounts, without requiring compliance with the execution formalities required of wills. Restatement 3d of Property § 7.1 comment g recognizes the validity of POD accounts.

Multiple-party accounts under UPC. UPC Article VI deals with non-probate transfers. The original version separately identified and defined lifetime and survivorship rights in three types of multiple-party accounts: joint accounts, POD accounts, and trust accounts. Another group of provisions defined various protections for financial intermediaries in making payments according to the terms of account contracts.

Under this original version, lifetime ownership of co-account holders in joint accounts was presumptively proportionate to each party's contribution to the balance on deposit. A POD account was owned solely by the depositor and a trust account was owned solely by the trustee.

Concerning survivorship rights, § 6-104 of the original version presumptively created a survivorship feature in all accounts that were presently payable to two or more parties, regardless of whether the account form described them as joint tenants or referred in any way to a right of survivorship. The original version did recognize, however, that a multiple-party account need not contain a survivorship feature. Although a joint account was presumed to provide survivorship rights, this presumption was rebuttable by clear and convincing evidence of a contrary intent. Section 6-104 also established a presumptive death benefit for the named beneficiary of a trust account, but this presumption similarly was rebuttable by clear and convincing evidence. Finally, the section expressly provided a death benefit for the beneficiary of a POD account. Unlike the death benefits under joint or trust accounts, the death benefit for a POD account beneficiary was unqualified, rather than merely presumptive. Of course, evidence of incapacity, fraud, or undue influence affecting the creation of a POD account was admissible to defeat a beneficiary's claim.

For trust and POD accounts, the original version negated survivorship rights among multiple surviving beneficiaries. In contrast, survivorship continued for multiple joint account beneficiaries who survived the death of a third or other co-depositor. Moreover, § 6-104(e) of the original version explicitly negated any effort by an owner-party to use a will to alter the death benefit arising from the form of a deposit or the statute, thereby reversing a considerable body of case law involving Totten trusts. Finally, § 6-107 provided that, to the extent the decedent's probate estate proved insufficient, any right of a surviving party or account beneficiary was subject to claims of the decedent's creditors, the payment of estate administration expenses, and statutory allowances to the decedent's surviving family members.[6] This section also included procedures, subject to a two-year limitations period, for recovering sums necessary to satisfy the described charges from surviving account parties and beneficiaries.

The 1989 revision of Article VI's coverage of multiple-party accounts is basically consistent with the original version. The major changes include: (1) folding Totten trust accounts into the definition and coverage of POD accounts; (2) providing statutory forms for joint accounts with or without survivorship, transfer-on-death (TOD) accounts, and joint and single-name accounts designating an agent to act for the owner, (3) subjecting survivors' benefits in accounts covered by the legislation to an order (check) of any party who dies before the check is paid; and (4) providing that, when two persons named as parties to a survivorship joint account are married to each other and the account includes one or more additional parties, only the surviving spouse may receive additional ownership of account balances following the other spouse's death. In addition to these changes, the two-year statute of limitations is reduced to one year.

A major goal of the 1989 revision is to encourage financial institutions to use the statutory forms and abandon their practice of routinely offering joint accounts to customers who merely wish to add another person's name to an account for agency, death beneficiary, or multiple-owners-with-no-survivorship purposes. The new statutory forms and depository protection provisions extend

---

6. In Estate of Reed, 681 A.2d 460 (Me. 1996), the court held that IRA accounts were not "accounts" within the meaning of § 6-107 and, therefore, were not available to satisfy the claims of estate creditors.

greater and more explicit protection to financial institutions in connection with payments they make, pursuant to an agent's instructions, after a principal's death and payments they make to a surviving co-depositor after a party to a "non-survivorship" account has died.

Transfer on Death Deeds. POD and TOD beneficiary designations are not limited to personal property. Owners of real property in Ohio may execute deeds naming one or more TOD beneficiaries. See Ohio Rev. Code § 5302.22, effective August 29, 2000. Pursuant to this statute, any person who owns real property as sole owner or as a tenant in common may designate one or more primary and one or more contingent TOD beneficiaries, all of whom must be identified by name. (For the drawback of this last requirement, see the article by Jane Bryant Quinn, infra p. 490.) While the owner is alive, the beneficiaries have no interest in the property. At the owner's death, the property passes directly and outside of probate to the primary beneficiary or beneficiaries who survive the owner or, if none survive, to the contingent beneficiary or beneficiaries who survive the owner. The statute specifically provides that these transfers are not testamentary and, therefore, need not comply with the formalities for wills. If none of the named beneficiaries survives the owner, the property passes through the owner's probate estate.

Joint Tenancies; Tenancies by the Entirety. The validity of joint tenancy or tenancy by the entirety forms of ownership doesn't depend on compliance with the formalities of execution required of wills. This point is beyond argument, for the present-transfer test in these cases is well satisfied: Titling property in joint tenancy or in tenancy by the entirety—like titling property in tenancy in common—irrevocably creates a present undivided interest in the entire property in each co-tenant. Each co-tenant's undivided interest is an equal interest; if there are three joint tenants, for example, each tenant takes an undivided one-third interest in the property. Unless exempted by the marital deduction, an unequal contribution to the acquisition of property in joint tenancy triggers federal gift tax consequences for any joint tenant whose contribution exceeds his or her ownership interest. See Treas. Reg. § 25.2511-1(h)(5).

Unlike the interest of a tenant in common, the undivided interest of each joint tenant or tenant by the entirety includes the right of survivorship. Upon death, the interest of a joint tenant or a tenant by the entirety terminates—like a life estate. The property ownership shifts outside of probate to the surviving co-tenant. Since the tenancy-by-the-entirety form of ownership is restricted to spouses, the surviving spouse's interest becomes a fee simple absolute. In the case of a joint tenancy, the interest of a surviving joint tenant also becomes a fee simple absolute, unless there is more than one surviving joint tenant, in which case the surviving joint tenants continue to hold the property in joint tenancy as among themselves.

Unless a statute or case law makes joint tenancies indestructible, they are unilaterally severable by any joint tenant. To accomplish a severance, the severing tenant can convey by deed his or her interest to another. Or, if the severing tenant wants to retain ownership (albeit as a tenant in common), the severing tenant can convey his or her interest to a "straw person" who, in turn, conveys the interest back to the severing tenant. Alternatively, the severing tenant can execute a so-called severance deed. Not all states, however, permit the severance-deed method.

There is no requirement that a severing joint tenant notify the other joint tenant, although recordation of the severing instrument may be required to terminate the other joint tenant's right of survivorship. See Cal. Civ. Code § 683.2. Whatever method is used, it must be effected during the severing tenant's lifetime.

Since the interest of a joint tenant or a tenant by the entirety terminates upon a co-tenant's death, the creditors of the deceased co-tenant's estate have no claim against the property.

Testamentary Control of Joint Tenancy Property? Equitable Election. Because of the right of survivorship, joint tenants who predecease their co-tenants have no power to devise their interest in joint tenancy property. Suppose G, who owns Blackacre as joint tenant with A, leaves a will devising "$20,000 to A, and all my interest in Blackacre to B." Can the devise to B be given effect? Under the doctrine of equitable election, it can. Equitable election is a device of ancient origin by which testamentary power over owned property is extended to property owned by another. In effect, the court would be treating the devise to A as if it were a conditional devise, that is, as if it said "$20,000 to A *if* A transfers Blackacre to B." Is this characterization of the devise to A justified? See Neville Crago, Mistakes in Wills and Election in Equity, 106 L.Q. Rev. 487 (1990) (arguing that G never actually intended the devise to be conditional; rather, G's devise of the vacation home to B was merely the product of a mistake on G's part as to his testamentary power to devise it). In Williamson v. Williamson, 657 N.E.2d 651 (Ill. App. Ct. 1995), appeal den., 664 N.E.2d 640 (Ill. 1996), the court refused to apply the doctrine in the context of a devise of jointly-owned property, stating that the doctrine should be restricted to circumstances where it prevents injustice or where the testator has expressly put the devisee to an election.

Community-Property "Spouse's Election." A modern use of the doctrine of equitable election is the spouse's-election device in community-property states. Under community-property regimes, property acquired during the marriage, other than by gift, inheritance, or devise, becomes community property. Unlike joint tenancy or tenancy by the entirety, community property is a form of co-ownership that operates like a tenancy in common, in that each spouse owns an undivided one-half interest with no rights of survivorship in the other. When one spouse dies, that spouse has testamentary power over his or her half of the couple's community property, but not over the survivor's half.

The spouse's-election device seeks to extend the deceased spouse's testamentary power to the *entire* community. In effect, the decedent's will might say to the survivor: I devise my half of the community into a trust, income to you for life, remainder to our descendants, if you agree to contribute your half of the community into the same trust. The survivor is thus put to an election as to whether to (i) keep his or her half of the community outright and forfeit the income interest in the decedent's half or (ii) transfer his or her half into the same trust, thereby enjoying the right to the income from the whole.

TOD Registration of Securities. The amendments to Article VI of the Uniform Probate Code also added provisions authorizing a new form of ownership of investment securities, called Transfer on Death (TOD) registration. The new "TOD" provisions, §§ 6-301 to -310, are discussed in Richard V. Wellman, Transfer-On-Death Securities Registration: A New Title Form, 21 Ga. L. Rev. 789 (1987). See also Diane C. Amado, Note, Uniform Probate Code § 6-201: A Proposal to Include Stocks and Mutual Funds, 72 Cornell L. Rev. 397 (1987).

PART B. REVOKING OR AMENDING A WILL SUBSTITUTE

Statutory References: *UTC §§ 602-604*

Schmidt v. Sheet Metal Workers' National Pension Fund

128 F.3d 541 (7th Cir. 1997)

ILANA DIAMOND ROVNER, Circuit Judge. Richard A. Schmidt ("Richard") initiated this ERISA action against the Sheet Metal Workers' National Pension Fund ("NPF" or "Fund") and its Board of Trustees ("Trustees") to recover the portion of his father's death benefit that the Fund disbursed to Richard's sister. . . . After discovery, the district court granted summary judgment to defendants on each of Richard's claims. Richard now challenges that disposition here, and defendants cross-appeal from the denial of their request for an award of attorney's fees. We agree that defendants were entitled to summary judgment on each of Richard's claims under ERISA. We also do not believe that the district court abused its discretion in refusing to award attorney's fees. We therefore affirm the judgment below.

I. On March 4, 1994, Allen J. Schmidt ("Allen") was told by his doctors that he had pancreatic cancer and that he had but a few months to live. Allen was not married at the time, and he therefore wished to designate his son Richard as the sole beneficiary of the pension benefit that would be payable upon his death by the NPF, a multi-employer benefit trust fund maintained under ERISA. On March 10, Allen called the Fund's administrative office to inquire about the procedure for designating his son as the sole beneficiary of his death benefit. He spoke on that occasion to Eunjae Lee, an NPF benefit analyst. Allen explained to Lee that he was terminally ill and that he wished to designate his son as the sole beneficiary of his pension death benefit. Because Allen believed that Lee was not fully understanding his request, he asked Richard to attempt to explain it to her. Richard reiterated to Lee that Allen was terminally ill and that he wished to designate Richard as the sole beneficiary of his death benefit. Lee indicated to Richard that she understood and that she would send the proper paperwork. Several days later, the Schmidts received a "Pension or Vesting Application," which they promptly completed and returned to the Fund. On that application, Allen designated Richard as his primary beneficiary and his daughter, Ginger Riphahn, as the successor beneficiary. It turned out, however, that Lee had sent the Schmidts the incorrect form. The "Pension or Vesting Application" was exactly that—an application for pension benefits, and was not the proper mechanism for designating a beneficiary for a pension plan death benefit. A death benefit beneficiary was properly designated only once a plan participant submitted to the Fund the "benefit designation card" included in the front of the Fund's pension plan booklet (the "Booklet"). This Booklet had been mailed to all plan participants in 1990.

Allen died on April 16, 1994, and on August 29, 1994, Richard received a letter from Lee explaining that because his father had failed to name a beneficiary for his death benefit, the $22,693.13 benefit would be divided evenly between Allen's surviving children in accordance with section 7.01 of the pension plan. Lee included with this letter another copy of the Booklet, which sets out the death benefit eligibility rules and an individual's appeal rights. Upon receiving Lee's letter, Richard called the Fund's administrative office and this time spoke with Barry Sweger, an assistant benefits coordinator. Richard explained to Sweger that Lee had sent his father the wrong form after their March 10 telephone conversation, and Sweger indicated that Richard should write down exactly what had happened and note that his letter was to be considered an appeal to the Fund's Board of Trustees. Sweger explained that all information substantiating Richard's position should be included in the letter and that any supporting documentation should be appended. Sweger told Richard to mail the letter to him and that the Trustees then would consider Richard's appeal at their next meeting. Richard did as he was told, mailing his letter to Sweger on September 30, 1994. He received a letter in response which indicated that his appeal had been received and that it would be considered at the next meeting of the Fund's Trustees. By letter dated May 30, 1995, Richard was notified that the Appeals Committee of the Board of Trustees, consisting of two of the six trustees, had considered his appeal at their May 2 meeting and had determined to deny it. The letter provided the following explanation of the Appeals Committee's decision:

> As Mr. Schmidt died before he had become a Pensioner, and as he left no surviving spouse, a Death Benefit was payable under [section 7.01]. The designation of beneficiaries for such a benefit is to be made on the form established by the Fund Trustees, in accordance with Section 7.05. This form is a card, found in each Pension Booklet, designating beneficiaries to receive the Sheet Metal Workers National Pension Fund Death Benefit.
>
> Mr. Schmidt did not have such a designation on file at the time of his death. The designation of beneficiary section completed by Mr. Schmidt on the pension application received shortly before his death is not the form required by the Trustees to designate beneficiaries for a Death Benefit, but is a designation of beneficiary for pension benefits, in the event any such payments are payable after the death of the retiree.
>
> As is provided for in Section 7.01, as no Death Benefit beneficiary designation had been filed by Mr. Schmidt in accordance with Section 7.05, the Death Benefit is payable to Mr. Schmidt's surviving children. As Mr. Schmidt left two surviving children, you and Ginger Riphahn, each of you receives one-half of the Death Benefit.

(R. 32, Ex. J (emphasis in original).)

II. We review the district court's grant of summary judgment on Richard's ERISA claims de novo. We must affirm the judgment for defendants if the record reveals that there is no genuine issue of material fact and that they are entitled to judgment as a matter of law.

A. Richard does not dispute that the Trustees' decision to distribute his father's death benefit to him and his sister in equal shares is consistent with the explicit terms of the Plan and the Booklet describing it. The Plan provides that a participant's designation of a beneficiary for his death benefit must be made "in the form and manner required by the Trustees" (Plan § 7.05), and the Booklet explains that the only proper way to designate a death benefit beneficiary is by filing the attached beneficiary card with the participant's local union. (Plan Booklet at 13.) Both the Plan and Booklet note that if no card is on file, the death benefit will be paid first to the participant's surviving spouse, and if no spouse survives, to the participant's children. (Plan § 7.01; Plan Booklet at 13.) The Trustees determined that because Allen had no card on file at the time of his death, the benefit would be distributed to his two children in equal shares, as required by the Plan. Nor does Richard argue that defendants failed to notify his father of the requirement that he designate a beneficiary on the card provided in the Booklet. It is undisputed that the Booklet and Plan were mailed to all participants, including Allen Schmidt, in 1990. As a result, Richard does not assert that the Trustees' decision with respect to his father's death benefit was arbitrary and capricious. He argues instead that defendants should be estopped from adhering to the literal terms of the Plan because of the misrepresentation of its benefit analyst.

We agree with the district court, however, that defendants are not estopped from applying the literal terms of the Plan by any oral representation made by Lee in the course of the March 10, 1994 telephone conversation. As we have noted on many occasions, oral representations that conflict with the terms of a written plan will not be given effect, as the written instrument must control. . . . The oral representation upon which Richard's claim is based clearly conflicts with the designation method prescribed by the Plan Booklet, and the Plan itself requires all beneficiary designations to be in the proper form. That is presumably to avoid beneficiary disputes like this one, which only will arise upon a participant's death, when it is too late for his intent to be clarified. It is in precisely this situation, then, that we must refuse to apply estoppel principles to give effect to oral representations that contradict written Plan terms. For these reasons, we agree with the district court that Richard's estoppel claim must fail.

B. Richard also contends that the Trustees breached their fiduciary duties when Lee advised the Schmidts, erroneously it turned out, that the beneficiary designation could be made on the "Pension or Vesting Application." Lee's misstatement, according to Richard, breached the Trustees' duty to provide plan participants with complete and accurate material information regarding their status and options under an ERISA plan.

. . . . Richard contends that he and his father were affirmatively misled by Lee's directions for designating a death benefit beneficiary. The district court did not doubt that the Schmidts had been misled, but in granting summary judgment, the court focused on whether Lee's misstatement could be said to have breached the duties owed to plan participants by the Trustees themselves, as they were the only ERISA fiduciaries named as defendants in this case....

[T]he Trustees did not make the misstatement on which Richard's fiduciary duty claim is based—Lee did. Significantly, no evidence suggests that the Trustees either authorized, participated in, or had knowledge of Lee's misstatement, or that the Trustees deliberately withheld information from Lee about the proper means of making a beneficiary designation. Rather, this is a case in which the Trustees provided complete and correct information to participants both in the Plan itself and in the Plan Booklet only to have a ministerial employee make a negligent misrepresentation in response to a single question from a single participant. The district court concluded that absent evidence that the Trustees had participated in Lee's misstatement or had failed to exercise care in hiring her, the Trustees could not be said to have breached their fiduciary duties solely by virtue of Lee's misstatement. We believe that in general, the district court was correct, but we would add that the Trustees may also breach their fiduciary duties by failing to exercise care in training someone like Lee, or by retaining her in circumstances where they should know her performance to be inadequate. There is no evidence that the Trustees in this case were involved in any way with Lee's misstatement. Nor has Richard attempted to show that the Trustees failed to exercise due care either in hiring or retaining Lee, or in training her to respond to inquiries from plan participants. We therefore agree with the district court that Lee's misstatement would not in these circumstances support a breach of fiduciary duty claim against the Trustees. . . .

III. For the foregoing reasons, we agree with the district court that the NPF and its Board of Trustees were entitled to summary judgment on each of Richard Schmidt's claims. At the same time, however, we agree that Richard's litigation position was substantially justified and that defendants were therefore not entitled to an award of attorney's fees. No costs shall be awarded in this court.

AFFIRMED.

Notes and Questions

1. *Substantial Compliance under Federal Common Law.* In Phoenix Mut. Life Ins. Co. v. Adams, 30 F.3d 554 (4th Cir.1994), the Fourth Circuit held that ERISA preempted South Carolina law with regard to determining the validity of an attempted change in the designation of the beneficiary of an ERISA-covered life insurance policy, and recognized a federal common law of "substantial compliance." The Court defined the substantial compliance doctrine applicable under ERISA as follows:

> [A]n insured substantially complies with the change of beneficiary provisions of an ERISA life insurance policy when the insured: (1) evidences his or her intent to make the change and (2) attempts to effectuate the change by undertaking positive action which is for all practical purposes similar to the action required by the change of beneficiary provisions of the policy.

2. *Revoking or Amending a Revocable Trust.* The Restatement 3d of Trusts § 63, comments h and i, provides:

> *h. Form of exercise when no method is specified.* If the settlor reserves the power to revoke or modify the trust but does not specify the manner or form in which the power is to be exercised, the power can be exercised in any way that provides clear and convincing evidence of the settlor's intention to do so. Thus, the power can be exercised by a will or codicil that is executed after the creation of

> the trust and remains unrevoked at the settlor's death, and that refers expressly to the trust or the power or that otherwise clearly manifests the settlor-testator's intent to exercise the power.
>
> Similarly, a definitive manifestation by the settlor during life of his or her intention that the trust is thereby revoked is sufficient. . . .
>
> *i. Where method of revocation specified.* If the terms of the trust reserve to the settlor a power to revoke or amend the trust *exclusively* by a particular procedure, the settlor can exercise the power only by substantial compliance with the method prescribed. . . .
>
> Although the terms of the trust provide a method for the exercise of a power of revocation or amendment, if the terms do not make that method exclusive the power can be exercised either in the specified manner or by a method described in Comment *h*, above.

Section 602(c) of the UTC provides similar rules. See also Restatement 3d of Property § 7.2, comments d, e, and h.

In Trust Estate of Daoang, 953 P.2d 959 (Haw. Ct. App. 1998), the court considered the validity of an amendment to a self-declared trust that reserved to the settlor the power to amend the trust "in any respect, but only by another instrument signed by both the Settlor and the Trustee during the Settlor's lifetime." The court held that the trust was validly amended by a letter signed by the settlor confirming oral instructions previously given to his attorney concerning an amendment he wished to make. The settlor died about a year later. The court deemed it irrelevant that the settlor signed the letter only in his capacity as settlor, not as trustee, and that he may have contemplated that his attorney would subsequently prepare a formal trust amendment for him to sign.

In Estate and Trust of Pilafas, 836 P.2d 420 (Ariz. 1992), the court held that a revocable inter vivos trust that was in the settlor's possession but could not be found after his death was not revoked. The trust provided that "[t]he Settlor may at any time or times during the Settlor's lifetime by instrument in writing delivered to the Trustee amend or revoke this Agreement in whole or in part." The court held that the trust was not revoked because the settlor had not delivered to the trustee a writing that revoked the trust.

3. *Liability for Breach of Fiduciary Duties?* Suppose that the settlor-trustee of a self-declared revocable trust breached fiduciary duties in the administration of the trust. Would the settlor or the settlor's estate be liable, or would the breach of fiduciary duties be regarded as an implied exercise of the settlor's power of revocation? See UTC § 603(a).

In Breeze v. Breeze, 428 N.E.2d 286 (Ind. Ct. App. 1981), the settlor's widow, after the settlor's death, petitioned to have the court declare that the assets of a self-declared, revocable trust were part of the settlor's probate estate, to which she had a claim as heir, rather than passing to the settlor's nieces and nephews, whom the trust document designated as the trust beneficiaries after the settlor's death. The court rejected her claim, saying:

> [The widow] submitted evidence that [the settlor] failed to act in a fiduciary capacity. . . . [Her] evidence attempted to prove that [the settlor] treated the property as his own . . . . The essence of [her] argument is that the trust was revoked by [these actions] . . . . We cannot accept [her] argument . . . . [The settlor's failure] to fulfill his duties as trustee may have been grounds for his removal as trustee, but it was not grounds to find the trust was revoked.

Revoking or Amending a Revocable Trust by Later Will. Can the settlor of a revocable trust revoke the trust through an express provision in the settlor's later will? UTC § 602(c), Restatement 3d of Trusts § 63 comment i, and Restatement 3d of Property § 7.2 comment e all say yes.

If the trust instrument states that the revoking instrument must be delivered to the trustee, would the attempted revocation by will satisfy that requirement? In Estate of Lowry, 418 N.E.2d 10 (Ill. App. Ct. 1981), the court held that the testator had validly revoked her self-declared revocable trust, reasoning that since she had executed and retained the will, she had "delivered" it to herself as trustee. In Estate of Kovalyshyn, 343 A.2d 852 (Hudson Co., N.J., 1975), on the other hand, the court held that a decedent could not exercise the power to revoke a revocable trust in a will.

Revoking Other Will Substitutes by Will. If courts are divided over whether the settlor may revoke a revocable trust by will, may a transferor revoke other will substitutes by will?

Totten Trusts; Multiple-Party Accounts; POD Accounts. Some cases have held that a Totten trust may be revoked by appropriate provisions in the depositor's will. See Scanlon's Estate, 169 A. 106 (Pa. 1933). In Estate of Bol, 429 N.W.2d 467 (S.D. 1988), the court held that the testator's will effectively revoked her savings account trust and money-market certificates even though the will made no specific reference to any of the bank deposits. The surrounding circumstances, the court reasoned, indicated that the testator intended to revoke the bank account and money-market certificates. However, UPC § 6-213(b) provides that a will may *not* alter the survivorship right in any multiple-party account or POD designation.

See generally Scott on Trusts § 58.4 (Totten trusts), § 330.8 (revocable trusts); Annot., Exercise by Will of Trustor's Reserved Power to Revoke or Modify Inter Vivos Trust, 81 A.L.R.3d 959 (1977); Annot., Revocation of Tentative ("Totten") Trust of Savings Bank Account by Inter Vivos Declaration or Will, 46 A.L.R.3d 487 (1972); Annot., Rights in Survival Benefits under Public Pension or Retirement Plan as Between Designated Beneficiary and

Heirs, Legatees, or Personal Representatives of Deceased Employee, 5 A.L.R.3d 644 (1966).

Life Insurance. For a heartless example of an application of the rule that the insurance beneficiary of record, the insured's former spouse who divorced him when he contracted multiple sclerosis, prevails over the beneficiary named in the insured's will, the insured's father who supported and cared for him through his long illness, see McCarthy v. Aetna Life Ins. Co., 704 N.E.2d 557 (N.Y. 1998). For an equally heartless example of the application of the rule that account terms govern, defeating the effort of an ignorant insured to prefer by will his current wife and child over a former spouse who was the beneficiary of record on the account, see Cook v. Equitable Life As. Soc., 428 N.E.2d 110 (Ind. Ct. App. 1981). In Stone v. Stephens, 99 N.E.2d 766 (Ohio 1951), prior to their divorce in 1944, W was the beneficiary of a life-insurance policy on H's life. After the divorce, H executed a will that devised all his property, including insurance policies, to his grandmother "should I die unmarried."

The court held the will to be ineffective to change the beneficiary designation of his life-insurance policy, saying:

> To hold that a change in beneficiary may be made by testamentary disposition alone would open up a serious question as to payment of life insurance policies. It is in the public interest that an insurance company may pay a loss to the beneficiary designated in the policy as promptly after the death of insured as may reasonably be done. If there is uncertainty as to the beneficiary upon the death of insured, in all cases where the right to change the beneficiary had been reserved there would always be a question as to whom the proceeds of the insurance should be paid. If paid to the beneficiary, a will might later be probated designating a different disposition of the fund, and it would be a risk that few companies would be willing to take, unless some specified time had elapsed after the death of insured, or that there had been some court adjudication as to whom the proceeds should be paid. [quoting from Wannamaker v. Stroman, 166 S.E. 621, 623 (S.C. 1932).]
>
> It may also be observed that further delay in the payment of the proceeds of policies might be caused by a contest of such will or by a proceeding involving the construction of such will. The question of law involved herein is not affected by the interpleader of the insurers and their deposit of the disputed funds in court. There is substantial authority for the proposition that rights which become vested on the death of the insured and thus fixed by law can not thereafter be affected by such action of the insurer. 78 A.L.R. 981, and cases cited.

Most of the cases follow the view expressed in *Stone*, but a few courts have permitted testators to change a life-insurance beneficiary by will. See, e.g., Connecticut General Life Ins. Co. v. Peterson, 442 F. Supp. 533 (W.D. Mo. 1978); Burkett v. Mott, 733 P.2d 673 (Ariz. Ct. App. 1986). For a case reaching the same result as in *Stone* in the context of an ERISA-covered employee pension benefit plan on the basis of ERISA's preemption of state law, see MacLean v. Ford Motor Co., 831 F.2d 723 (7th Cir. 1987). ERISA is an acronym for the Employee Retirement Income Security Act, the federal law that controls qualified pension plans.

A Superwill? There has been discussion of permitting a so-called "superwill." The idea behind that term is that testamentary control should be expanded to allow testators to change the beneficiary designations of certain nonprobate transfers. In 1998, the superwill became a reality in the State of Washington, for certain will substitutes. Excluded, however, are real property joint tenancies, life insurance, and retirement plan beneficiary designations.

Revised Code of Washington

§ *11.11.020. Disposition of Nonprobate Assets Under Will.* (1) Subject to community property rights, upon the death of an owner the owner's interest in any nonprobate asset[7] specifically referred to in the owner's will belongs to the testamentary beneficiary named to receive the nonprobate asset, notwithstanding the rights of any beneficiary designated before the date of the will.

(2) A general residuary gift in an owner's will, or a will making general disposition of all of the owner's property, does not entitle the devisees or legatees to receive nonprobate assets of the owner.

(3) A disposition in a will of the owner's interest in "all nonprobate assets" or of all of a category of nonprobate asset under RCW 11.11.010(7), such as "all of my payable on death bank accounts" or similar language, is deemed to be a disposition of all the nonprobate assets the beneficiaries of which are designated before the date of the will.

(4) If the owner designates a beneficiary for a nonprobate asset after the date of the will, the will does not govern the disposition of that nonprobate asset. If the owner revokes the later beneficiary designation, the prior will does not govern the disposition of the nonprobate asset. A beneficiary designation with respect to an asset that renews without the signature of the owner is deemed to have been made on the date on which the account was first opened.

---

7. As defined in §§ 11.11.010(7)(a) and 11.02.005(15), the term "nonprobate assets" does not include: a payable-on-death provision of a life insurance policy, annuity, or other similar contract, or of an employee benefit plan; a right or interest if, before death, the person has irrevocably transferred the right or interest, the person has waived the power to transfer it or, in the case of contractual arrangement, the person has waived the unilateral right to rescind or modify the arrangement; a right or interest held by the person solely in a fiduciary capacity; a right or interest in real property passing under a joint tenancy with right of survivorship; a deed or conveyance for which possession has been postponed until the death of the owner; a right or interest passing under a community property agreement; and an individual retirement account or bond.

What are the advantages and disadvantages of superwills? For discussion, see Roberta R. Kwall & Anthony J. Aiello, The Superwill Debate: Opening the Pandora's Box?, 62 Temple L. Rev. 277 (1989); Cynthia J. Artura, Comment, Superwill to the Rescue? How Washington's Statute Falls Short of Being a Hero in the Field of Trust and Probate Law, 74 Wash. L. Rev. 799 (1999).

PART C. WILL SUBSTITUTES AND THE SUBSIDIARY LAW OF WILLS

Statutory References: *UTC § 112*

The question whether will substitutes should be treated as testamentary for purposes of the statutory formalities of execution implicates rules that are mandatory. Apart from a harmless-error rule, such as set forth in UPC § 2-503 or Restatement 3d of Property § 3.3, wills statute requirements apply regardless of the testator's intent. Indeed, as we have seen, the harmless-error rule was promulgated to prevent those requirements from defeating the testator's intent.

Other rules of the law of wills, including antilapse statutes and statutes providing for revocation upon changed circumstances, are different in character. These rules yield to the contrary intentions of testators. The question that we study in this Part is whether these intent-effectuating rules should apply to wills and will substitutes alike. Put differently, should will substitutes be treated as testamentary for purposes of the subsidiary law of wills even if they are not so treated for purposes of the mandatory requirements of will execution?

The Restatement 3d of Property provides:

> § *7.2 Application of Will Doctrines to Will Substitutes*
>
> Although a will substitute need not be executed in compliance with the statutory formalities required for a will, such an arrangement is, to the extent appropriate, subject to substantive restrictions on testation and to rules of construction and other rules applicable to testamentary dispositions.

1. Revocation Upon Divorce

Statutory References: *UPC §§ 2-508, 2-804*

Restatement 3d of Property

§ *4.1 [comment] p. Application to will substitutes.* The principles of Comment *o* [relating to revocation upon divorce] also apply to a donative transfer in the form of a will substitute, such as a revocable trust or a life insurance beneficiary designation. On the application of these principles to a revocable trust, see Restatement Third, Trusts § 25, Comment *c* and Illustration 11 (Tentative Draft No. 1, 1996). Any revocable provision in favor of the former spouse or relative of the former spouse in a will substitute is revoked upon dissolution of the marriage. The principles of Comment *o* also apply to a joint tenancy, effecting a severance of the joint tenancy and transforming the interests of the former spouses into an equal tenancy in common.

See also Restatement 3d of Property § 7.2, comment f.

Clymer v. Mayo. In the leading case of Clymer v. Mayo, 473 N.E.2d 1084 (Mass. 1985), the Supreme Judicial Court of Massachusetts held that a statute providing that "divorce . . . shall revoke any disposition . . . made by the [testator's pre-divorce] *will* to the [testator's] former spouse"[8] extended to an unfunded revocable inter vivos trust. The decedent, Clara Mayo, a professor of psychology at Boston University, executed her will in 1963, designating her husband, James, as the primary devisee. In 1964, she named James as the beneficiary of her group life insurance contract, and in 1964, named him beneficiary of her retirement account with TIAA-CREF. In 1973, she executed a new will and trust agreement, again naming James the primary beneficiary. The will made a pour-over devise of the residue of her estate into the revocable trust that she had created the same day. At the same time that she created the trust, Clara changed the beneficiary of her life insurance policy to the trustees of the inter vivos trust. She later also changed the beneficiary of her retirement plan to the trustees.

James and Clara divorced in 1978. Clara changed the life insurance beneficiary designation to her companion Marianne LaFrance, but not the retirement plan beneficiary designation. The divorce agreement provided that James waived any "right, title or interest" in Clara's "securities, savings accounts, savings certificates, and retirement fund" as well as in her "furniture, furnishings and art." James remarried a short while later and executed a new will in favor of his new wife. Clara died in 1981. Her heirs were her parents, the Weisses.

The court held that the divorce revoked James's interest in her inter vivos trust, saying:

> In the absence of an expressed contrary intent, [the] statute implies an intent on the part of a testator to revoke will provisions favoring a former spouse. It is incongruous then to ignore that same intent with regard to a trust funded in part through her will's pour-over at the decedent's death. . . .
>
> Restricting our holding to the particular facts of this case—specifically the existence of a revocable pour-over trust funded entirely at the time of the decedent's death—we conclude that [the statute], revokes [James]'s interest under [Clara's Trust].

---

8. (Emphasis added.) The Massachusetts statute is based on former UPC § 2-508. Eds.

Will Substitutes and Conventional Revocation-upon-Divorce Statutes. The Massachusetts revocation-upon-divorce statute is of a type widely enacted throughout the country and is nearly identical to former UPC § 2-508. These statutes expressly apply only to "wills."

Should the courts extend the application of these statutes beyond their express scope and apply them to "will substitutes," on the theory that will substitutes are substantively indistinguishable in function from wills?[9] Although the court in *Clymer* moved in this direction, other courts—faced with will substitutes such as life-insurance and pension death-benefit beneficiary designations, have not been willing to do so. See, e.g., Pepper v. Peacher, 742 P.2d 21 (Okla. 1987) (retirement plan); Estate of Adams, 288 A.2d 514 (Pa. 1972) (retirement plan); Equitable Life Assurance Society v. Stitzel, 1 Pa.Fiduc.2d 316, 19 D. & C. 3d 55 (Ct. C.P. 1981) (life insurance). Notice, too, that even the court in *Clymer* was reluctant to extend the Massachusetts statute to *all* revocable inter vivos trusts. The court took care to say that it was "restricting [its] holding to the particular facts of this case—specifically the existence of a revocable pour-over trust funded entirely at the time of the decedent's death."

In Vasconi v. Guardian Life Ins. Co., 590 A.2d 1161 (N.J. 1991), the New Jersey Supreme Court abandoned the traditional rule that if the revocation-upon-divorce statute does not apply to life insurance, the proceeds are presumptively payable to the divorced spouse who is the designated beneficiary, unless the property settlement expressly provides to the contrary. Observing that the rule is out of date, the court held that the presumption now is that the divorce property agreement revokes the designation of the ex-spouse as beneficiary. The ex-spouse is entitled to the proceeds only if the agreement expressly so provides.

Under the traditional revocation-upon-divorce statute, would the decedent's divorce attorney have any exposure to a claim for malpractice liability for failing to inquire about and take care of the decedent's life insurance, pension benefits, revocable trusts, and so on? See Smith v. Lewis, 530 P.2d 589 (Cal. 1975).

Piecemeal Legislation. A few states have enacted piecemeal legislation providing for revocation of certain will substitutes upon divorce. Ohio has a statute transforming spousal joint tenancies in land into tenancies in common upon the spouses' divorce. See Ohio Rev. Code Ann. § 5302.20(c)(5). Ohio and Oklahoma have enacted legislation effecting a revocation of certain provisions

---

9. In an influential article on statutory construction, Karl Llewellyn pointed out that "there are two opposing canons on almost every point." Among the opposing canons are the following: "A statute cannot go beyond its text." But "[t]o effect its purpose a statute may be implemented beyond its text." Karl N. Llewellyn, Remarks on the Theory of Appellate Decision and the Rules or Canons About How Statutes Are to be Construed, 3 Vand. L. Rev. 395, 401 (1950).

for the settlor's former spouse in revocable inter vivos trusts. See Ohio Rev. Code Ann. § 1339.62; Okla. Stat. Ann. tit. 60, § 175. Statutes in Ohio, Oklahoma, and Texas relate to the consequence of divorce on life-insurance and retirement-plan beneficiary designations. See Ohio Rev. Code § 1339.63; Okla. Stat. Ann. tit. 15, § 178; Tex. Fam. Code §§ 7.005, 9.302. See generally Alan S. Wilmit, Note, Applying the Doctrine of Revocation by Divorce to Life Insurance Policies, 73 Cornell L. Rev. 653 (1988).

Comprehensive Legislation—UPC. As noted supra Chapter 5, Part C, the current UPC significantly changes the former version of § 2-508. As revised and renumbered, § 2-804 expressly calls for the revocation, upon divorce or annulment, of any revocable disposition or appointment of property made by either divorced individual to his or her former spouse, in a deed, will, trust, beneficiary designation, power of attorney, transfer-on-death account, or donative instrument of any other type executed by the divorced individual before the divorce or annulment of his or her marriage to the former spouse. UPC § 2-804 not only revokes benefits to the former spouse, but also to the former spouse's relatives.

Retroactive Application. Under UPC § 8-101(b)(1), the provisions of the UPC apply to all decedents dying after the effective date of the Code's enactment by a state legislature, irrespective of when the decedent's will or will substitute is executed. Thus § 2-804, once enacted, operates to revoke on divorce beneficiary designations executed prior to the state's adoption of the UPC. The Joint Editorial Board of the UPC has issued a statement supporting the constitutionality of this approach. See Joint Editorial Board Statement Regarding the Constitutionality of Changes in Default Rules as Applied to Pre-Existing Documents, 17 ACTEC Notes 184 (1991). Several recent court decisions have agreed with the Board. See Dobert v. Dobert-Koesner, 963 P.2d 327 (Ariz. 1998); Mearns v. Scharbach, 12 P.3d 1048 (Wash. App. 2000); Estate of Becker, 2000 WL 1785278 (Colo. Ct. App. 2001).[10] However, there are other courts that have reached the opposite conclusion. See Whirlpool Corp. v. Ritter, 929 F.2d 1318 (8th Cir. 1991); Aetna Life Insurance Co. v. Schilling, 616 N.E.2d 893 (Ohio 1993); Parsonese v. Midland National Insurance Co., 706 A.2d 814 (Pa. 1994); Matter of Dewitt, 2000 WL 1785182 (Colo. Ct. App. 2000).

10. *Becker* and *DeWitt*, yielding opposite results, were decided by different panels of the Colorado Court of Appeals. As this casebook goes to press, petitions in both cases for certiorari in the state supreme court are pending.

Egelhoff v. Egelhoff

532 U.S. ___ (2001)

JUSTICE THOMAS delivered the opinion of the Court.

A Washington statute provides that the designation of a spouse as the beneficiary of a nonprobate asset is revoked automatically upon divorce. We are asked to decide whether the Employee Retirement Income Security Act of 1974 (ERISA), 88 Stat. 832, 29 U.S.C. § 1001 et seq., pre-empts that statute to the extent it applies to ERISA plans. We hold that it does.

I

Petitioner Donna Rae Egelhoff was married to David A. Egelhoff. Mr. Egelhoff was employed by the Boeing Company, which provided him with a life insurance policy and a pension plan. Both plans were governed by ERISA, and Mr. Egelhoff designated his wife as the beneficiary under both. In April 1994, the Egelhoffs divorced. Just over two months later, Mr. Egelhoff died intestate following an automobile accident. At that time, Mrs. Egelhoff remained the listed beneficiary under both the life insurance policy and the pension plan. The life insurance proceeds, totaling $46,000, were paid to her.

Respondents Samantha and David Egelhoff, Mr. Egelhoff's children by a previous marriage, are his statutory heirs under state law. They sued petitioner in Washington state court to recover the life insurance proceeds. Respondents relied on a Washington statute that provides:

> "If a marriage is dissolved or invalidated, a provision made prior to that event that relates to the payment or transfer at death of the decedent's interest in a nonprobate asset in favor of or granting an interest or power to the decedent's former spouse is revoked. A provision affected by this section must be interpreted, and the nonprobate asset affected passes, as if the former spouse failed to survive the decedent, having died at the time of entry of the decree of dissolution or declaration of invalidity." Wash. Rev.Code § 11.07.010(2)(a) (1994).

That statute applies to "all nonprobate assets, wherever situated, held at the time of entry by a superior court of this state of a decree of dissolution of marriage or a declaration of invalidity." § 11.07.010(1). It defines "nonprobate asset" to include "a life insurance policy, employee benefit plan, annuity or similar contract, or individual retirement account." § 11.07.010(5)(a).

Respondents argued that they were entitled to the life insurance proceeds because the Washington statute disqualified Mrs. Egelhoff as a beneficiary, and in the absence of a qualified named beneficiary, the proceeds would pass to them as Mr. Egelhoff's heirs. In a separate action, respondents also sued to recover the pension plan benefits. Respondents again argued that the

Washington statute disqualified Mrs. Egelhoff as a beneficiary and they were thus entitled to the benefits under the plan.

The trial courts, concluding that both the insurance policy and the pension plan "should be administered in accordance" with ERISA, granted summary judgment to petitioner in both cases. The Washington Court of Appeals consolidated the cases and reversed. It concluded that the Washington statute was not pre-empted by ERISA. Applying the statute, it held that respondents were entitled to the proceeds of both the insurance policy and the pension plan.

The Supreme Court of Washington affirmed. . . .

II

Petitioner argues that the Washington statute falls within the terms of ERISA's express pre-emption provision and that it is pre-empted by ERISA under traditional principles of conflict pre-emption. Because we conclude that the statute is expressly pre-empted by ERISA, we address only the first argument.

ERISA's pre-emption section, 29 U.S.C. § 1144(a), states that ERISA "shall supersede any and all State laws insofar as they may now or hereafter relate to any employee benefit plan" covered by ERISA. We have observed repeatedly that this broadly worded provision is "clearly expansive." New York State Conference of Blue Cross & Blue Shield Plans v. Travelers Ins. Co., 514 U.S. 645, 655 (1995); see, e.g., Morales v. Trans World Airlines, Inc., 504 U.S. 374, 384 (1992) (listing cases in which we have described ERISA pre-emption in broad terms). But at the same time, we have recognized that the term "relate to" cannot be taken "to extend to the furthest stretch of its indeterminacy," or else "for all practical purposes pre-emption would never run its course." Travelers, supra, at 655.

We have held that a state law relates to an ERISA plan "if it has a connection with or reference to such a plan." Shaw v. Delta Air Lines, Inc., 463 U.S. 85, 97 (1983). Petitioner focuses on the "connection with" part of this inquiry. Acknowledging that "connection with" is scarcely more restrictive than "relate to," we have cautioned against an "uncritical literalism" that would make preemption turn on "infinite connections." Travelers, supra, at 656. Instead, "to determine whether a state law has the forbidden connection, we look both to 'the objectives of the ERISA statute as a guide to the scope of the state law that Congress understood would survive,' as well as to the nature of the effect of the state law on ERISA plans." California Div. of Labor Standards Enforcement v. Dillingham Constr., N. A., Inc., 519 U.S. 316, 325 (1997), quoting Travelers, supra, at 656 (citation omitted).

Applying this framework, petitioner argues that the Washington statute has an impermissible connection with ERISA plans. We agree. The statute binds

ERISA plan administrators to a particular choice of rules for determining beneficiary status. The administrators must pay benefits to the beneficiaries chosen by state law, rather than to those identified in the plan documents. The statute thus implicates an area of core ERISA concern. In particular, it runs counter to ERISA's commands that a plan shall "specify the basis on which payments are made to and from the plan," § 1102(b)(4), and that the fiduciary shall administer the plan "in accordance with the documents and instruments governing the plan," § 1104(a)(1)(D), making payments to a "beneficiary" who is "designated by a participant, or by the terms of [the] plan." § 1002(8).[11] In other words, unlike generally applicable laws regulating "areas where ERISA has nothing to say," Dillingham, 519 U.S., at 330, which we have upheld notwithstanding their incidental effect on ERISA plans, see, e.g., ibid., this statute governs the payment of benefits, a central matter of plan administration.

The Washington statute also has a prohibited connection with ERISA plans because it interferes with nationally uniform plan administration. One of the principal goals of ERISA is to enable employers "to establish a uniform administrative scheme, which provides a set of standard procedures to guide processing of claims and disbursement of benefits." Fort Halifax Packing Co. v. Coyne, 482 U.S. 1, 9 (1987). Uniformity is impossible, however, if plans are subject to different legal obligations in different States.

The Washington statute at issue here poses precisely that threat. Plan administrators cannot make payments simply by identifying the beneficiary specified by the plan documents. Instead they must familiarize themselves with state statutes so that they can determine whether the named beneficiary's status has been "revoked" by operation of law. And in this context the burden is exacerbated by the choice-of-law problems that may confront an administrator when the employer is located in one State, the plan participant lives in another, and the participant's former spouse lives in a third. In such a situation, administrators might find that plan payments are subject to conflicting legal obligations.

---

11. One can of course escape the conflict between the plan documents (which require making payments to the named beneficiary) and the statute (which requires making payments to someone else) by calling the statute an "invalidation" of the designation of the named beneficiary, and by observing that the plan documents are silent on whether "invalidation" is to occur upon divorce. The dissent employs just such an approach. Reading a clear statement as an ambiguous metastatement enables one to avoid all kinds of conflicts between seemingly contradictory texts. Suppose, for example, that the statute required that all pension benefits be paid to the Governor of Washington. That seems inconsistent with the plan documents (and with ERISA), but the inconsistency disappears if one calls the statute an "invalidation" of the principal and alternate beneficiary designations. After all, neither the plan nor ERISA actually says that beneficiaries cannot be invalidated in favor of the Governor. This approach exploits the logical inability of any text to contain a complete set of instructions for its own interpretation. It has the vice—or perhaps the virtue, depending upon one's point of view—of draining all language of its meaning.

To be sure, the Washington statute protects administrators from liability for making payments to the named beneficiary unless they have "actual knowledge of the dissolution or other invalidation of marriage," Wash. Rev.Code § 11.07.010(3)(a) (1994), and it permits administrators to refuse to make payments until any dispute among putative beneficiaries is resolved, § 11.07.010(3)(b). But if administrators do pay benefits, they will face the risk that a court might later find that they had "actual knowledge" of a divorce. If they instead decide to await the results of litigation before paying benefits, they will simply transfer to the beneficiaries the costs of delay and uncertainty.[12] Requiring ERISA administrators to master the relevant laws of 50 States and to contend with litigation would undermine the congressional goal of "minimiz[ing] the administrative and financial burden[s]" on plan administrators—burdens ultimately borne by the beneficiaries. Ingersoll-Rand Co. v. McClendon, 498 U.S. 133, 142 (1990).

We recognize that all state laws create some potential for a lack of uniformity. But differing state regulations affecting an ERISA plan's "system for processing claims and paying benefits" impose "precisely the burden that ERISA pre-emption was intended to avoid." Fort Halifax, supra, at 10. And as we have noted, the statute at issue here directly conflicts with ERISA's requirements that plans be administered, and benefits be paid, in accordance with plan documents. We conclude that the Washington statute has a "connection with" ERISA plans and is therefore pre-empted.

III

Respondents suggest several reasons why ordinary ERISA pre-emption analysis should not apply here. First, they observe that the Washington statute allows employers to opt out. . . .

Second, respondents emphasize that the Washington statute involves both family law and probate law, areas of traditional state regulation. There is indeed a presumption against pre-emption in areas of traditional state regulation such as family law. But that presumption can be overcome where, as here, Congress has made clear its desire for pre-emption. Accordingly, we have not hesitated to find state family law pre-empted when it conflicts with ERISA or relates to ERISA plans. See, e.g., Boggs v. Boggs, 520 U.S. 833 (1997) (holding that ERISA pre-empts a state community property law permitting the testamentary transfer of an interest in a spouse's pension plan benefits).

---

12. The dissent observes that the Washington statute permits a plan administrator to avoid resolving the dispute himself and to let courts or parties settle the matter. This observation only presents an example of how the costs of delay and uncertainty can be passed on to beneficiaries, thereby thwarting ERISA's objective of efficient plan administration. Cf. Fort Halifax Packing Co. v. Coyne, 482 U.S. 1, 9 (1987).

Finally, respondents argue that if ERISA pre-empts this statute, then it also must pre-empt the various state statutes providing that a murdering heir is not entitled to receive property as a result of the killing. See, e.g., Cal. Prob.Code Ann. §§ 250-259 (West 1991 and Supp.2000); 755 Ill. Comp. Stat., ch. 755, § 5/2-6 (1999). In the ERISA context, these "slayer" statutes could revoke the beneficiary status of someone who murdered a plan participant. Those statutes are not before us, so we do not decide the issue. We note, however, that the principle underlying the statutes—which have been adopted by nearly every State—is well established in the law and has a long historical pedigree predating ERISA. See, e.g., Riggs v. Palmer, 115 N.Y. 506, 22 N.E. 188 (1889). And because the statutes are more or less uniform nationwide, their interference with the aims of ERISA is at least debatable.

* * *

The judgment of the Supreme Court of Washington is reversed, and the case is remanded for further proceedings not inconsistent with this opinion.

JUSTICE SCALIA, with whom JUSTICE GINSBURG joins, concurring.

I join the opinion of the Court, since I believe that the "relate to" pre-emptive provision of the Employee Retirement Income Security Act of 1974 (ERISA) is assuredly triggered by a state law that contradicts ERISA. . . . I remain unsure (as I think the lower courts and everyone else will be) as to what else triggers the "relate to" provision, which—if it is interpreted to be anything other than a reference to our established jurisprudence concerning conflict and field pre-emption—has no discernible content that would not pick up every ripple in the pond, producing a result "that no sensible person could have intended." California Div. of Labor Standards Enforcement v. Dillingham Constr., N. A., Inc., 519 U.S. 316, 336 (1997) (SCALIA, J., concurring). I persist in the view that we can bring some coherence to this area, and can give the statute both a plausible and precise content, only by interpreting the "relate to" clause as a reference to our ordinary pre-emption jurisprudence. See ibid.

JUSTICE BREYER, with whom JUSTICE STEVENS joins, dissenting.

Like JUSTICE SCALIA, I believe that we should apply normal conflict pre-emption and field pre-emption principles where, as here, a state statute covers ERISA and non-ERISA documents alike. Our more recent ERISA cases are consistent with this approach. See De Buono v. NYSA-ILA Medical and Clinical Services Fund, 520 U.S. 806, 812-813 (1997) (rejecting literal interpretation of ERISA's pre- emption clause); California Div. of Labor Standards Enforcement v. Dillingham Constr., N. A., Inc., 519 U.S. 316, 334 (1997) (narrowly interpreting the clause); New York State Conference of Blue Cross & Blue Shield Plans v. Travelers Ins. Co., 514 U.S. 645, 656 (1995) ("go[ing] beyond the unhelpful text [of the clause] and the frustrating difficulty of defining its key term, and look[ing] instead to the objectives of the ERISA statute as a guide"). See also Boggs v. Boggs, 520 U.S. 833, 841 (1997) (relying on conflict pre-emption principles instead of ERISA's pre-emption clause). . . .

I do not agree with JUSTICE SCALIA or with the majority, however, that there is any plausible pre-emption principle that leads to a conclusion that ERISA pre-empts the statute at issue here. No one could claim that ERISA pre-empts the entire field of state law governing inheritance—though such matters "relate to" ERISA broadly speaking. See Travelers, supra, at 655. Neither is there any direct conflict between the Washington statute and ERISA, for the one nowhere directly contradicts the other.

The Court correctly points out that ERISA requires a fiduciary to make payments to a beneficiary "in accordance with the documents and instruments governing the plan." 29 U.S.C. § 1104(a)(1)(D). But nothing in the Washington statute requires the contrary. Rather, the state statute simply sets forth a default rule for interpreting documentary silence. The statute specifies that a nonprobate asset will pass at A's death "as if" A's "former spouse" had died first—unless the "instrument governing disposition of the nonprobate asset expressly provides otherwise." Wash. Rev.Code § 11.07.010(2)(b)(i) (1994) (emphasis added). This state-law rule is a rule of interpretation, and it is designed to carry out, not to conflict with, the employee's likely intention as revealed in the plan documents.

There is no direct conflict or contradiction between the Washington statute and the terms of the plan documents here at issue. David Egelhoff's investment plan provides that when a "beneficiary designation" is "invalid," the "benefits will be paid" to a "surviving spouse," or "if there is no surviving spouse," to the "children in equal shares." The life insurance plan is silent about what occurs when a beneficiary designation is invalid. The Washington statute fills in these gaps, i.e., matters about which the documents themselves say nothing. Thus, the Washington statute specifies that a beneficiary designation—here "Donna R. Egelhoff wife" in the pension plan—is invalid where there is no longer any such person as Donna R. Egelhoff, wife. See Appendix, infra. And the statute adds that in such instance the funds would be paid to the children, who themselves are potential pension plan beneficiaries.

The Court's "direct conflict" conclusion rests upon its claim that "administrators must pay benefits to the beneficiaries chosen by state law, rather than to those identified in the plan documents." But the Court cannot mean "identified anywhere in the plan documents," for the Egelhoff children were "identified" as recipients in the pension plan documents should the initial designation to "Donna R. Egelhoff wife" become invalid. And whether that initial designation became invalid upon divorce is a matter about which the plan documents are silent.

To refer to state law to determine whether a given name makes a designation that is, or has become, invalid makes sense where background property or inheritance law is at issue, say, for example, where a written name is potentially ambiguous, where it is set forth near, but not in, the correct space, where it refers to a missing person perhaps presumed dead, where the name was written at a time the employee was incompetent, or where the name refers to an individual or entity disqualified by other law, say, the rule against perpetuities or rules prohibiting a murderer from benefiting from his crime. Why would Congress want the courts to create an ERISA-related federal property law to deal with such problems? Regardless, to refer to background state law in such circumstances does not directly conflict with any explicit ERISA provision, for no provision of ERISA forbids reading an instrument or document in light of state property law principles. In any event, in this case the plan documents explicitly foresee that a beneficiary designation may become "invalid," but they do not specify the invalidating circumstances. To refer to state property law to fill in that blank cannot possibly create any direct conflict with the plan documents.

The majority simply denies that there is any blank to fill in and suggests that the plan documents require the plan to pay the designated beneficiary under all circumstances. But there is nonetheless an open question, namely, whether a designation that (here explicitly) refers to a wife remains valid after divorce. . . . . The plan documents themselves do not answer the question any more than they describe what is to occur in a host of other special circumstances (e.g., mental incompetence, intoxication, ambiguous names, etc.). To determine whether ERISA permits state law to answer such questions requires a careful examination of the particular state law in light of ERISA's basic policies. We should not short-circuit that necessary inquiry simply by announcing a "direct conflict" where none exists.

The Court also complains that the Washington statute restricts the plan's choices to "two." But it is difficult to take this complaint seriously. After all, the two choices that Washington gives the plan are (1) to comply with Washington's rule or (2) not to comply with Washington's rule. What other choices could there be? A state statute that asks a plan to choose whether it intends to comply is not a statute that directly conflicts with a plan. Quite obviously, it is possible, not "'impossible,'" to comply with both the Washington statute and federal law. Geier v. American Honda Motor Co., 529 U.S. 861, 873 (2000).

The more serious pre-emption question is whether this state statute "'stands as an obstacle to the accomplishment and execution of the full purposes and objectives of Congress.'" Ibid. (quoting Hines v. Davidowitz, 312 U.S. 52, 67 (1941)). In answering that question, we must remember that petitioner has to overcome a strong presumption against pre-emption. That is because the Washington statute governs family property law—a "field of traditional state regulation," where courts will not find federal pre-emption unless such was the "'clear and manifest purpose of Congress,'" Travelers, 514 U.S., at 655 (quoting Rice v. Santa Fe Elevator Corp., 331 U.S. 218, 230 (1947)), or the state statute does "'major damage' to 'clear and substantial' federal interests," Hisquierdo v. Hisquierdo, 439 U.S. 572, 581 (1979) (quoting United States v. Yazell, 382 U.S. 341, 352 (1966)). No one can seriously argue that Congress has clearly resolved the question before us. And the only damage to federal interests that the Court identifies consists of the added administrative burden the state statute imposes upon ERISA plan administrators.

The Court claims that the Washington statute "interferes with nationally uniform plan administration" by requiring administrators to "familiarize themselves with state statutes." But administrators have to familiarize themselves with state law in any event when they answer such routine legal questions as whether amounts due are subject to garnishment, Mackey v. Lanier Collection Agency & Service, Inc., 486 U.S. 825, 838 (1988), who is a "spouse," who qualifies as a "child," or when an employee is legally dead. And were that "familiarizing burden" somehow overwhelming, the plan could easily avoid it by resolving the divorce revocation issue in the plan documents themselves, stating expressly that state law does not apply. The "burden" thus reduces to a one-time requirement that would fall primarily upon the few who draft model ERISA documents, not upon the many who administer them. So meager a burden cannot justify pre-empting a state law that enjoys a presumption against pre-emption.

The Court also fears that administrators would have to make difficult choice-of-law determinations when parties live in different States. Whether this problem is or is not "major" in practice, the Washington statute resolves it by expressly setting forth procedures whereby the parties or the courts, not the plan administrator, are responsible for resolving it. See §§ 11.07.010(3)(b)(i)-(ii) (stating that a plan may "without liability, refuse to pay or transfer a nonprobate asset" until "[a]ll beneficiaries and other interested persons claiming an interest have consented in writing to the payment or transfer" or "[t]he payment or transfer is authorized or directed by a court of proper jurisdiction"); § 11.07.010(3)(c) (plan may condition payment on provision of security by recipient to indemnify plan for costs); § 11.07.010(2)(b)(i) (plan may avoid default rule by expressing its intent in the plan documents).

The Court has previously made clear that the fact that state law "impose[s] some burde[n] on the administration of ERISA plans" does not necessarily require pre-emption. De Buono, 520 U.S., at 815; Mackey, supra, at 831 (upholding state garnishment law notwithstanding claim that "benefit plans subjected to garnishment will incur substantial administrative burdens"). Precisely, what is it about this statute's requirement that distinguishes it from the "'myriad state laws'" that impose some kind of burden on ERISA plans? De Buono, supra, at 815 (quoting Travelers, 514 U.S., at 668).

Indeed, if one looks beyond administrative burden, one finds that Washington's statute poses no obstacle, but furthers ERISA's ultimate objective—developing a fair system for protecting employee benefits. Cf. Pension Benefit Guaranty Corporation v. R.A. Gray & Co., 467 U.S. 717, 720 (1984). The Washington statute transfers an employee's pension assets at death to those individuals whom the worker would likely have wanted to receive them. As many jurisdictions have concluded, divorced workers more often prefer that a child, rather than a divorced spouse, receive those assets. Of course, an employee can secure this result by changing a beneficiary form; but doing so requires awareness, understanding, and time. That is why Washington and many other jurisdictions have created a statutory assumption that divorce works a revocation of a designation in favor of an ex-spouse. That assumption is embodied in the Uniform Probate Code; it is consistent with human experience; and those with expertise in the matter have concluded that it "more often" serves the cause of "[j]ustice." Langbein, The Nonprobate Revolution and the Future of the Law of Succession, 97 Harv. L.Rev. 1108, 1135 (1984).

In forbidding Washington to apply that assumption here, the Court permits a divorced wife, who already acquired, during the divorce proceeding, her fair share of the couple's community property, to receive in addition the benefits that the divorce court awarded to her former husband. To be more specific, Donna Egelhoff already received a business, an IRA account, and stock; David received, among other things, 100% of his pension benefits. David did not change the beneficiary designation in the pension plan or life insurance plan during the 6-month period between his divorce and his death. As a result, Donna will now receive a windfall of approximately $80,000 at the expense of David's children. The State of Washington enacted a statute to prevent precisely this kind of unfair result. But the Court, relying on an inconsequential administrative burden, concludes that Congress required it.

Finally, the logic of the Court's decision does not stop at divorce revocation laws. The Washington statute is virtually indistinguishable from other traditional state-law rules, for example, rules using presumptions to transfer assets in the case of simultaneous deaths, and rules that prohibit a husband who kills a wife from receiving benefits as a result of the wrongful death. It is particularly difficult to believe that Congress wanted to pre-empt the latter kind of statute. But how do these statutes differ from the one before us? Slayer statutes—like this statute—"gover[n] the payment of benefits, a central matter of plan administration." And contrary to the Court's suggestion, slayer statutes vary from State to State in their details just like divorce revocation statutes. Compare Ariz. Rev. Stat. Ann. § 14-2803(F) (1995) (requiring proof, in a civil proceeding, under preponderance of the evidence standard); Haw. Rev. Stat. § 560:2-803(g) (1999) (same), with Ga.Code Ann. § 53-1-5(d) (1997) (requiring proof under clear and convincing evidence standard); Me. Rev. Stat. Ann., Tit. 18-A, § 2-803(e) (1998) (same); and Ala.Code. § 43-8-253(e) (1991) (treating judgment of conviction as conclusive when it becomes final); Me. Rev. Stat. Ann., Tit 18-A, § 2-803(e) (1998) (same), with Ariz. Rev. Stat. Ann. § 14-2803(F) (1995) (treating judgment of conviction as conclusive only after "all right to appeal has been exhausted"); Haw. Rev. Stat. § 560:2-803(g) (1999) (same). Indeed, the "slayer" conflict would seem more serious, not less serious, than the conflict before us, for few, if any, slayer statutes permit plans to opt out of the state property law rule.

"ERISA pre-emption analysis," the Court has said, must "respect" the "separate spher[e]" of state "authority." Fort Halifax Packing Co. v. Coyne, 482 U.S. 1, 19, (1987) (quoting Alessi v. Raybestos—Manhattan, Inc., 451 U.S. 504, 522 (1981)) (internal quotation marks omitted). In so stating, the Court has recognized the practical importance of preserving local independence, at retail, i.e., by applying pre-emption analysis with care, statute by statute, line by line, in order to determine how best to reconcile a federal statute's language and purpose with federalism's need to preserve state autonomy. Indeed, in today's world, filled with legal complexity, the true test of federalist principle may lie, not in the occasional constitutional effort to trim Congress' commerce power at its edges, United States v. Morrison, 529 U.S. 598 (2000), or to protect a State's treasury from a private damages action, Board of Trustees of Univ. of Ala. v. Garrett, 531 U.S. ___ (2001), but rather in those many statutory cases where courts interpret the mass of technical detail that is the ordinary diet of the law, AT & T Corp. v. Iowa Utilities Bd., 525 U.S. 366, 427 (1999) (BREYER, J., concurring in part and dissenting in part).

In this case, "field pre-emption" is not at issue. There is no "direct" conflict between state and federal statutes. The state statute poses no significant obstacle to the accomplishment of any federal objective. Any effort to squeeze some additional pre-emptive force from ERISA's words (i.e., "relate to") is inconsistent with the Court's recent case law. And the state statute before us is one regarding family property—a "fiel[d] of traditional state regulation," where the interpretive presumption against pre-emption is particularly strong. Travelers, 514 U.S., at 655. For these reasons, I disagree with the Court's conclusion. And, consequently, I dissent.

APPENDIX TO OPINION OF BREYER, J.

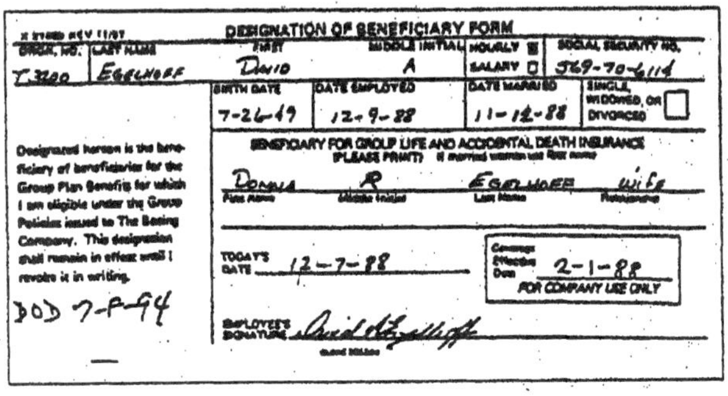

DESIGNATION OF BENEFICIARY FORM

LAST NAME	FIRST	MIDDLE INITIAL	HOURLY / SALARY	SOCIAL SECURITY NO.
T3200 EGELHOFF	DAVID	A	HOURLY	569-70-6114

BIRTH DATE	DATE EMPLOYED	DATE MARRIED	SINGLE, WIDOWED, OR DIVORCED
7-26-49	12-9-88	11-12-88	

Designated herein is the beneficiary of beneficiaries for the Group Plan Benefits for which I am eligible under the Group Policies issued to The Boeing Company. This designation shall remain in effect until I revoke it in writing.

DOD 7-8-94

BENEFICIARY FOR GROUP LIFE AND ACCIDENTAL DEATH INSURANCE (PLEASE PRINT)

Donna R Egelhoff wife

First Name · Middle Initial · Last Name · Relationship

TODAY'S DATE 12-7-88

Coverage Effective Date 2-1-88 FOR COMPANY USE ONLY

EMPLOYEE'S SIGNATURE David A. Egelhoff

Notes and Questions

1. *Remarriage*. Suppose that David Egelhoff had remarried after his divorce from Donna, and that David was survived by his second wife. What result under ERISA? See ERISA § 205(a), 29 U.S.C. § 1055(a).

2. *Federal Common Law*. In *Egelhoff*, the Court said:

> [The Washington statute revoking a beneficiary designation to the employee's former spouse] runs counter to ERISA's commands that a plan shall "specify the basis on which payments are made to and from the plan," § 1102(b)(4), and that the fiduciary shall administer the plan "in accordance with the documents and instruments governing the plan," § 1104(a)(1)(D), making payments to a "beneficiary" who is "designated by a participant, or by the terms of [the] plan." § 1002(8).

Does this mean that *any* state law that could invalidate a beneficiary designation is preempted because it is in conflict with ERISA's command that the fiduciary "shall" make payments to the beneficiary who is designated by the participant? Suppose that the employee's signature on the beneficiary designation form is forged, or that the employee lacked mental capacity[13] or was subject to undue influence when signing the beneficiary designation?

---

13. See Metropolitan Life Ins. Co. v. Hall, 9 F.Supp.2d 560 (D. Md. 1998), in which the court applied the following federal common law standard of mental capacity, which the court derived from Taylor v. United States, 113 F. Supp. 143 (W.D. Ark. 1953), aff'd, 211 F.2d 794 (8th Cir.1954):

> To be capable of effecting a valid change of beneficiary a person should have clearness of mind and memory sufficient to know the nature of the property for which he is about to name a beneficiary, the nature of the act which he is about to perform, the names and identities of those who are the natural objects of his bounty; his relationship towards them, and the consequences of his act, uninfluenced by any material delusions.

In Tinsley v. General Motors Corp., 227 F.3d 700 (6th Cir. 2000), Edward B. Williams, who died on December 18, 1996, had initially designated his niece, Willie Lee Tinsley, as the beneficiary of the life insurance plan that he maintained under the General Motors Life Insurance and Disability Program. Several days before his death, however, Williams executed a new "Designation of Beneficiary" form, naming his neighbor, Beulah Calloway, instead. Calloway had apparently cared for Williams while he was ill and resided with him for a period of time. Tinsley brought suit in federal district court, claiming that the beneficiary designation form naming Calloway as beneficiary was the product of undue influence. Reversing the decision of the district court, the Sixth Circuit said:

> Although the district court, like the parties, looked to Michigan state law in its discussion of Tinsley's claims, we believe that federal law governs this case, because it involves an employee welfare benefit plan that is governed by the Employee Retirement Income Security Act ("ERISA"), 29 U.S.C. § 1001 *et seq.* ERISA preempts any state law that relates to—that is, that "has a connection with or reference to"—an ERISA-covered plan. . . .
>
> . . . . We therefore conclude that the question whether Tinsley is entitled to the proceeds from Williams's life insurance plan due to the . . . alleged exercise of undue influence by Calloway is preempted by ERISA and governed by federal law.

The court went on to conclude that federal law is to be determined by "review[ing] the case law regarding undue influence in the various states that comprise this circuit" and "extract[ing] some shared general principles to guide our federal-common-law analysis of Tinsley's undue influence claim."

How is the administrative burden on plan administrators eased by forcing them to distill the possibly conflicting law of the various states in each circuit, as opposed to the law of one state? If federal common law is to be distilled from general state law, would the ALI Restatements of the Law be a more accessible source for determining such principles? The Restatement 3d of Property § 8.3, reproduced supra Chapter 4, sets forth general principles of undue influence applicable to all donative transfers, including the various will substitutes. See Restatement 3d of Property § 8.3, comment a.

3. *Revocation on Divorce as Federal Common Law?* If an ERISA beneficiary designation can be set aside on the ground of forgery, mental incapacity, or undue influence, and if these grounds are to be imported into federal common law on the basis of generally accepted state law (matters not yet decided by the Supreme Court), why is revocation by divorce not a matter of federal common law? The Restatement 3d of Property, as well as UPC § 2-804, provides that a revocable beneficiary designation of the former spouse in a will substitute is set aside by divorce. Restatement 3d of Property § 4.1, comment p.

4. *Codified Constructive Trust.* UPC § 2-804 provides that, in the event that federal courts decide that ERISA preempts § 2-804, subsection (h)(2) imposes an offsetting personal liability on the recipient of the proceeds in the amount of any payment received as a result of preemption. Does ERISA preempt subsection (h)(2)?

EXTERNAL REFERENCES. There is a considerable literature on ERISA preemption. Among the recent articles are Stephen F. Befort & Christopher J. Kopka, The Sounds of Silence: The Libertarian Ethos of ERISA Preemption, 52 Fla. L. Rev. 1 (2000); Edward A. Zelinsky, Travelers, Reasoned Textualism, and the New Jurisprudence of ERISA Preemption, 21 Cardozo L. Rev. 807 (1999); Catherine L. Fisk, The Last Article About the Language of ERISA Preemption?: A Case Study of the Failure of Textualism, 33 Harv. J. on Legis. 35 (1996).

2. Antilapse Statutes

Statutory References: *UPC §§ 2-702, -706, -707*

Antilapse statutes apply by their terms only to "wills." This is true of the antilapse statute contained in the former UPC and of almost all the antilapse statutes in non-UPC states.

Suppose the beneficiary of a revocable inter vivos trust predeceases the settlor, or the beneficiary of a life-insurance policy predeceases the insured, or the beneficiary of a death benefit under a retirement plan predeceases the participant. Should antilapse statutes be extended to these situations?

Estate of Button

490 P.2d 731 (Wash. 1971)

ROSELLINI, J. This action was instituted by the Old National Bank of Washington, asking the Superior Court for Whitman County to determine its obligations under two sets of trust instruments and the applicable Washington law.

The evidence presented at the hearing of the matter showed that in 1940, Robert H. Button executed a revocable trust, covering certain real property located in Whitman County, retaining a life estate, and naming the Old National Bank of Washington as trustee. The trust provided that it could be revoked or modified upon execution of an instrument in writing, duly signed by the trustor and delivered to the trustee, and, in case the trustee's duties were altered, upon its approval of the change. The trust contained the following provision:

> Upon the death of the Trustor without having withdrawn the entire fund, the balance of investments and cash remaining in the trust fund shall be delivered to the Trustor's mother, Audrey A. Burg, and her receipt for the residue of said trust fund shall thereupon release the Trustee from any further responsibility therefor.

There was no provision for the disposition of the trust property in the event the trustor's mother should predecease him.

In February 1964, Button, then living in California, executed and mailed to his Spokane attorney instruments revoking the 1940 trust, setting up a new trust agreement, and conveying the property described in the 1940 trust to the Old National Bank as trustee. This new trust made the trustor's niece, Stefanie Button, a minor, beneficiary of a life estate upon the trustor's death. It also provided that payments should be made to the trustor's wife in the event she should be in want and unmarried. The remainder of the estate was to be paid to Washington State University following the death of Stefanie Button and the trustor's wife.

At the same time that Button mailed these instruments to his attorney, he wrote a letter to the bank, advising it that he had sent the new trust instruments to his attorney and stating: "I think I would really only like that trust to take effect in the event of Mother's death prior to mine."

In his covering letter to his attorney, he said:

> I am enclosing as you see a copy of a letter sent to Luther [Luther Fendler, a trust officer of the Old National Bank] as well as the trust documents. I've wondered if the trust documents should be held in abeyance if my death is apt to precede that of Mothers? As it is now set up she is the sole heir, the only real effect would be that it now deletes Dorothy's name. As you know I have mixed emotions about Dorothy, although all is well between us as of this moment, but she is off the wagon again and that has always led to Trouble.

The evidence showed that Button and his wife had been having marital difficulties when these instruments were drawn and that Button was in very precarious health. It also showed that Stefanie Button was the only living issue of any of the children of Audrey A. Burg.

According to the testimony of Button's Spokane attorney, Button advised him by telephone to "hang onto" the trust documents until "further word from him." He received no further oral or written instructions concerning the trust. In the latter part of 1964, a mortgage was executed by the bank, covering the property then held in trust under the 1940 instruments, and the mortgage instrument, as well as a direction to the bank to execute the mortgage, signed by Button, and an assignment of the trust to secure the mortgage, all referred to the 1940 instrument.

On November 15, 1966, Audrey A. Burg died intestate, and on November 28, 1966, the trustor, Button, died, leaving a will which disposed of his California property but made no mention of his Washington property. Shortly thereafter, the Spokane attorney delivered the 1964 trust instruments to the Old National Bank and this action was instituted. Although she was given notice of the proceedings, the widow of Button did not appear and was not represented at the hearing. The adversaries before the court were the guardian ad litem of Stefanie Button and the heirs of Audrey A. Burg, namely her two sons, Kerry Burg and Fredric E. Button (father of Stefanie).

The trial court found that Button had never manifested an intent to revoke or modify the 1940 trust. It held that the 1940 trust remained in full force and effect, that the gift of the residue to the mother of the trustor lapsed upon her death, and there being no other provision for the disposition of the residue, that it reverted to the estate of the trustor. The court further held that the California will did not dispose of the Washington property of Button, and that consequently it should pass by the rules of intestate succession of the state of Washington.

The heirs of Audrey A. Burg and the guardian ad litem of Stefanie Button appealed to the Court of Appeals, which held that the gift to Audrey A. Burg had not lapsed, but further held that the trustor had manifested an intent to give "operative effect" to the 1964 trust, at least insofar as it benefited Stefanie Button and Washington State University,[14] while at the same time holding that the 1964 trust was not effective to revoke the 1940 trust.

The heirs of Audrey A. Burg petitioned for review and their petition was granted.

The first question presented is whether the trustor, during his lifetime, manifested an intent to revoke the trust which he had created in 1940 and to substitute a new and different trust. It has not been suggested that the instruments which he executed in 1964 conformed to the requirements of RCW 11.12.020 or could otherwise be given effect as a testamentary disposition.

The rule is that the settlor of a trust has the power to revoke the trust if and to the extent that, by the terms of the trust, he reserved such a power. Restatement (Second) of Trusts § 330 (1959); A. Scott, The Law of Trusts § 330, at 2595 (3d ed. 1967). Where the trust instrument specifies the method of revocation, only that method can be used. Restatement (Second) of Trusts § 330, comment j at 139 (1959); A. Scott, The Law of Trusts § 331, at 2618 (3d ed. 1967).

---

14. Apparently the court was of the opinion that, since the widow did not appear in the action to defend her interest under the trust, she forfeited that interest. Under the view which we take of the applicable law, it is unnecessary to consider the correctness of that opinion.

The 1940 trust instrument specified that it could be revoked or modified by an instrument in writing, signed by the trustor and delivered to the trustee. Button signed such instruments but they were never delivered to the trustee. Nor would the record support a finding that he instructed his attorney to deliver those instruments at any time prior to his death. On the contrary, his instructions were to hold the 1964 instruments until the attorney should receive further instructions from him. According to that attorney's testimony, no further instructions were ever received.

As far as the record discloses, Button never gave the matter further thought after he told his attorney to hold the documents. He communicated with the attorney a number of times before his death in 1966 but never again mentioned the trust instruments. The fact that he signed mortgage papers in the interim which showed that the 1940 trust was still in effect is further evidence that he had not intended to order delivery of the trust instruments to the trustee at the time he mailed them to his attorney.

We are compelled to hold that the Court of Appeals was in error when it found that Button had manifested an intent that the provisions of the 1964 instruments should have operative effect. On the contrary, the 1940 trust was never revoked and consequently it remained in full force and effect until the death of the trustor. . . .

We are thus brought to the question of the proper disposition of the trust property, the only named beneficiary of the 1940 trust (other than the trustor himself) having died prior to the death of the trustor.

It was the rule at common law that a gift in trust lapsed upon the death of the beneficiary prior to the death of the trustor. Restatement (Second) of Trusts § 112, comment f at 245 (1959); A. Scott, The Law of Trusts § 112.3 (3d ed. 1967). And in this state, if the named legatee in a will is not a relative by consanguinity, the common law rule that the gift lapses is still in effect. *In re Estate of Smith*, 49 Wn.2d 229, 299 P.2d 550, 63 A.L.R.2d 299 (1956) (where the testator's gift of the residue of his estate to his wife was held to have lapsed upon her death prior to the testator's), and *In re Estate of Sims*, 39 Wn.2d 288, 235 P.2d 204 (1951) (where a wife's bequest to her husband was held to have lapsed when he failed to survive the testatrix).

However, by the terms of RCW 11.12.110, when an estate is devised or bequeathed to any child, grandchild, or other relative of the testator, and the devisee or legatee dies before the testator, leaving lineal descendants, such descendants shall take the estate.

The act declares that under the provisions of that section a spouse is not a relative. It does not, however, exclude a parent from the definition of "relative."

Of course, the gift to Audrey A. Burg was not made by will, but by inter vivos trust. If it were made by testamentary trust, we do not think that it could be seriously suggested that this statute was not meant to affect it, and the only difference between such a gift and that involved here is that the inter vivos trust disposes of property upon the death of the settlor without the necessity of complying with the statute of wills. Similar statutes do indeed apply to trusts. Restatement (Second) of Trusts § 112, comment f (1959); A. Scott, The Law of Trusts § 112.3, n.3 (3d ed. 1967). Courts in other jurisdictions which have considered the question also have held that similar statutes apply to beneficiaries of testamentary trusts. See Annot., Statute to prevent lapse in event of death of devisee or legatee before testator as applicable to interest of beneficiary under trust who dies before testator, 118 A.L.R. 559 (1939).

A gift to be enjoyed only upon or after the death of the donor is in practical effect a legacy, whether it is created in an inter vivos instrument or in a will. RCW 11.12.110 declares the policy of the law of this state, and that policy is against the lapsing of gifts to relatives of the deceased. This does not mean that a testator or trustor cannot provide for a different disposition. If he does, of course, the statute has no application.

Where a statute (RCW 11.12.180) applied by its terms to devises of real estate, we held that it declared the policy of the state applicable to a trust covering personal property as well. *Abbott v. Everett Trust & Savings Bank*, 50 Wn.2d 398, 312 P.2d 203 (1957). By the same principle, there being no conflicting statutory provision, a statute covering gifts by will which would lapse in the absence of the statute, applies to gifts provided in a trust.

We conclude that the gift to Audrey A. Burg did not lapse, and that the trustee holds the residue for her descendants.

The Court of Appeals reached the same result on this question, but based its conclusion upon a rationale that the gift to Audrey A. Burg had vested. We do not examine the propriety of the conclusion that her interest had vested, since we are of the opinion that that conclusion does not answer the question whether that interest was intended to pass to her heirs upon her death. The case cited in support of the rationale was *Seattle-First Nat'l Bank v. Crosby*, 42 Wn.2d 234, 254 P.2d 732 (1953). There the trust instrument provided that if the principal beneficiary should die before attaining the age of 35, the trustee should distribute his share to his heirs at law. Since the trustor expressly provided for the disposition of the named beneficiary's share in the event of his death, no question of lapse was involved in the case.

Whether or not the interest of Audrey A. Burg had vested prior to the death of the trustor, it was subject to be divested if she died before the trustor died, under the rule as it existed prior to the enactment of RCW 11.12.110. That statute alone, interpreted to apply to trusts as well as to wills, saves her interest for her heirs.

The judgment of the Court of Appeals is reversed in part and the cause is remanded to the Superior Court for Whitman County with directions to enter an order in conformity with the views expressed herein.

Notes

State of the Authorities. The *Button* case represents a minority but growing view. The weight of authority favors the view that a future interest in a revocable trust is not conditioned on survival of the settlor unless the trust document expressly so provides. See, e.g., First National Bank of Bar Harbor v. Anthony, 557 A.2d 957 (Me. 1989); Estate of Capocy, 430 N.E.2d 1131 (Ill. App. Ct. 1981); Hinds v. McNair, 413 N.E.2d 586 (Ind. Ct. App. 1980); Detroit Bank & Trust Co. v. Grout, 289 N.W.2d 898 (Mich. Ct. App. 1980).

The Restatement 3d of Property sides with the *Button* case. Comment p to § 5.5 states that antilapse statutes should "apply by analogy to revocable trusts and other will substitutes." Accord Restatement 3d of Trusts § 25 comment e.

The Comment to § 2-603, the antilapse provision contained in the UPC, states that § 2-603 applies only to wills. However, § 2-707, which we consider in Chapter 18, establishes a similar rule with respect to revocable and irrevocable trusts.

Jane Bryant Quinn, Beneficiaries Who Don't Benefit

Washington Post, January 23, 2000, at H02

Say you're a young couple, writing a will. Would you leave your money only to the children you have, leaving future children out? Probably not.

Say you're a grandparent, whose will leaves everything equally to your adult children. If one of those children died before you did, would you reallocate his or her share to your other children? Probably not. That would cut out your grandchildren—the children of your child who died.

Yet the very thing you wouldn't do—cutting out grandchildren or future children—your insurance company or retirement plan is probably doing for you. Some of your descendants may wind up poorer than you meant them to be.

Here's what's going on and what you might be able to do about it.

When you buy life insurance or a tax-deferred annuity, or start a retirement plan such as an IRA or 401(k), you're given standard forms to sign. The forms ask whom you want as beneficiaries.

Typically, you put down your spouse's name or the names of your current children. That means no other people can be paid. Say you name your two adult children, Jim and Joe, as beneficiaries, and Jim dies before you do. Joe will get everything. Jim's share cannot pass to his children—your grandchildren—because they weren't named.

Or say you name your daughter Betty as the inheritor of your small retirement plan. Later, Sue is born—but you've forgotten about that beneficiary form. Years pass, the plan grows large, then you die. Betty gets all the money. Sue always wonders why you cut her out.

Beneficiaries in this position often ask the retirement plan or insurance company to divide the money as you probably would have wanted. No way. They'll pay by the book. The children who received the money could share voluntarily with the child left out. Check with your lawyer about how much can be given tax-free.

On the other hand, maybe they don't want to give any money away. Greed and obligation clash. You'll have sowed anger in your family, when you meant to treat everyone the same.

You might think you can solve this problem by writing a will. Wills typically cover children not yet born. In most cases, they also pass money down each family line. If your adult son is dead, his children will inherit his share.

But wills don't cover any asset that has a named beneficiary, including joint property, life insurance, annuities and retirement plans. Each of these assets will go only to the specific people named.

When inheritances are misdirected, insurers and retirement plans blame you. "We advise that you look at your finances, including your insurance policy, yearly," Jack Dolan of the American Council of Life Insurers in Washington, D.C, told my associate, Dori Perrucci.

He thinks that, if your adult son dies, you should instantly change your beneficiary designations, so that your son's children inherit his share. If you die before doing so, you're the one who cut your grandchildren out.

Lawrence Waggoner, professor of law at the University of Michigan in Ann Arbor, has a different take. He says that insurers and retirement plans are to blame.

If they wanted, they could give you some options on the beneficiary form. You could choose whether or not to include children born in the future, or whether your grandchildren could inherit your dead child's share.

The Life Office Management Association in Atlanta, an insurance trade association, even offers a standard form that insurers could use to include their grandchildren. Northwestern Mutual allows you to include future-born children and grandchildren. So do some retirement plans.

But most plans and insurers don't. "It's for their administrative convenience," Waggoner says. "They don't want to have to investigate who the grandchildren are."

How can you rectify this, so your own estate won't accidentally go astray?

You usually have to get a lawyer to amend the beneficiary form. Seymour Goldberg of Goldberg & Goldberg in Garden City, N.Y., says he amends as many as 400 forms a year, at $350 each.

But many insurance companies and retirement plans won't accept amended forms. "In that case, go to another company," advises attorney Natalie Choate of Bingham Dana in Boston.

Don't let a stubborn insurer or retirement plan leave your family in a potential mess.

Once you have amended the form, get a receipt from the company, acknowledging the specific change. Keep the amendment and receipt with your will. If the company loses the amendment, your family will need proof.

Note

Predeceasing Beneficiaries of Life Insurance, Retirement Plan Death Benefits, and POD Accounts. Although no cases have yet arisen seeking to extend antilapse statutes to other types of will substitutes such as life-insurance beneficiary designations, retirement-plan death benefits, and POD accounts, the case for doing so is much stronger than it is in the case of revocable inter vivos trusts. The reason is that beneficiaries of these types of contractual arrangements *do* lose their interests by virtue of predeceasing the decedent because, like wills, the arrangements impose a survival requirement on the beneficiaries.

In direct response to this problem, the UPC contains a new provision, § 2-706, which applies language similar to that of § 2-603 to "beneficiary designations" in favor of the decedent's grandparents, descendants of the decedent's grandparents, and the decedent's stepchildren. As defined in § 1-201, the term "beneficiary designation" refers to "a governing instrument naming a beneficiary of an insurance or annuity policy, of an account with POD designation, of a security registered in beneficiary form (TOD), or of a pension, profit-sharing, retirement, or similar benefit plan."

Would this section be controlling in the case of an employee benefit plan covered by ERISA? See Egelhoff v. Egelhoff, supra p. 473.

Simultaneous or Near Simultaneous Deaths; Uniform Simultaneous Death Act. Section 5 of the Uniform Simultaneous Death Act (1953) provides that, when the person whose life is insured under a life-insurance policy and the person who is the beneficiary of the policy die under circumstances in which there is "no sufficient evidence" that they died otherwise than simultaneously, the proceeds of the policy are to be distributed as if the beneficiary predeceased the insured.

Janus v. Tarasewicz

482 N.E.2d 418 (Ill. App. Ct. 1985)

[Stanley and Theresa Janus, having just returned from their honeymoon, gathered on September 29, 1982, with other family members to mourn the death of Stanley's brother, who had died earlier that day from ingesting what turned out to be cyanide-laced Tylenol capsules.[15] In the stress of the moment, Stanley and Theresa took some of the Tylenol capsules, not knowing these were poisoned. Within a short while, Stanley fell to the floor. While a neighbor, who was a registered nurse, applied emergency CPR on Stanley, Theresa began having seizures and within a few minutes she fell unconscious. Paramedics testified that Stanley's vital signs disappeared while he and Theresa were in the ambulance en route to the hospital. He was pronounced dead an hour and a half after arriving at the emergency room. Theresa required an artificial respirator in order to breathe by the time she was in the ambulance, but when she arrived at the hospital she did have a palpable pulse and blood pressure. She maintained a "measurable, though unsatisfactory" blood pressure later while she was in the emergency room. The next day, after receiving several tests to assess her brain function, Theresa was diagnosed as having sustained total brain death. Her life support systems were terminated, and she was pronounced dead on October 1, 1982. The death certificates listed Stanley's date of death as September 29, and Theresa's as October 1.

Theresa was the primary beneficiary of Stanley's life-insurance policy. The Metropolitan Life Insurance Company paid the proceeds to the administrator of Theresa's estate. Stanley's mother, Alojza Janus, as the contingent beneficiary of Stanley's policy, brought an action to recover the proceeds, claiming that there was insufficient evidence that Theresa survived Stanley. The trial court found that sufficient evidence that Theresa survived Stanley did exist. On appeal, Alojza's main argument was that there was insufficient evidence to prove that both victims did not suffer brain death before arriving at the hospital on September 29.]

O'CONNOR, J. . . . Dual standards for determining when legal death occurs in Illinois were set forth in the case of In Re Haymer (1983), 115 Ill.App.3d 349, 71 Ill.Dec. 252, 450 N.E.2d 940. There, the court determined that a comatose child attached to a mechanical life support system was legally dead on the date he was medically determined to have sustained total brain death, rather

15. Stanley and Theresa Janus and Stanley's brother were among seven people in the Chicago area murdered in 1982 by ingesting cyanide-laced Tylenol capsules. More than ten years later, these murders were still not solved. The killings led to new federal regulations requiring protective seals to be placed on nonprescription drugs. See Tylenol Deaths Leave Legacy of Fear, Detroit Free Press, Sept. 30, 1992, p. 2A.

than on the date that his heart stopped functioning. The court stated that in most instances death could be determined in accordance with the common law standard which is based upon the irreversible cessation of circulatory and respiratory functions. If these functions are artificially maintained, a brain death standard of death could be used if a person has sustained irreversible cessation of total brain function. . . .

Even though *Haymer* was decided after the deaths of Stanley and Theresa, we find that the trial court properly applied the *Haymer* standards under the general rule that a civil case is governed by the law as it exists when judgment is rendered, not when the facts underlying the case occur. . . .

Regardless of which standard of death is applied, survivorship is a fact which must be proven by a preponderance of the evidence by the party whose claim depends on survivorship. The operative provisions of the Illinois version of the Uniform Simultaneous Death Act provides in pertinent part:

> If the title to property or its devolution depends upon the priority of death and there is no sufficient evidence that the persons have died otherwise than simultaneously and there is no other provision in the will, trust agreement, deed, contract of insurance or other governing instrument for distribution of the property different from the provisions of this Section:
>
> (a) The property of each person shall be disposed of as if he had survived. . . .
>
> (d) If the insured and the beneficiary of a policy of life or accident insurance have so died, the proceeds of the policy shall be distributed as if the insured had survived the beneficiary.

Ill.Rev.Stat.1981, ch. 1101/2, par. 3-1.

In cases where the question of survivorship is determined by the testimony of lay witnesses, the burden of sufficient evidence may be met by evidence of a positive sign of life in one body and the absence of any such sign in the other. In cases such as the instant case where the death process is monitored by medical professionals, their testimony as to "the usual and customary standards of medical practice" will be highly relevant when considering what constitutes a positive sign of life and what constitutes a criteria for determining death. Although the use of sophisticated medical technology can also make it difficult to determine when death occurs, the context of this case does not require a determination as to the exact moment at which the decedents died. Rather, the trial court's task was to determine whether or not there was sufficient evidence that Theresa Janus survived her husband. Our task on review of this factually disputed case is to determine whether the trial court's finding was against the manifest weight of the evidence. . . . We hold that it was not.

In the case at bar, both victims arrived at the hospital with artificial respirators and no obvious vital signs. There is no dispute among the treating physicians and expert witnesses that Stanley Janus died in both a cardiopulmonary sense and a brain death sense when his vital signs disappeared en route to the hospital and were never reestablished. He was pronounced dead at 8:15 p.m. on September 29, 1982, only after intensive procedures such as electro-shock, medication, and the insertion of a pacemaker failed to resuscitate him.

In contrast, these intensive procedures were not necessary with Theresa Janus because hospital personnel were able to reestablish a spontaneous blood pressure and pulse which did not have to be artificially maintained by a pacemaker or medication. Once spontaneous circulation was restored in the emergency room, Theresa was put on a mechanical respirator and transferred to the intensive care unit. Clearly, efforts to preserve Theresa Janus' life continued after more intensive efforts on Stanley's behalf had failed.

It is argued that the significance of Theresa Janus' cardiopulmonary functions, as a sign of life, was rendered ambiguous by the use of artificial respiration. In particular, reliance is placed upon expert testimony that a person can be brain dead and still have a spontaneous pulse and blood pressure which is indirectly maintained by artificial respiration. The fact remains, however, that Dr. Kim, an intensive care specialist who treated Theresa, testified that her condition in the emergency room did not warrant a diagnosis of brain death. In his opinion, Theresa Janus did not suffer irreversible brain death until much later, when extensive treatment failed to preserve her brain function and vital signs. This diagnosis was confirmed by a consulting neurologist after a battery of tests were performed to assess her brain function. Dr. Kim denied that these examinations were made merely to see if brain death had already occurred. At trial, only Dr. Vatz disagreed with their finding, but even he admitted that the diagnosis and tests performed on Theresa Janus were in keeping with the usual and customary standards of medical practice.

There was also other evidence presented at trial which indicated that Theresa Janus was not brain dead on September 29, 1982. Theresa's EEG, taken on September 30, 1982, was not flat but rather it showed some delta waves of extremely low amplitude. Dr. Hanley concluded that Theresa's EEG taken on September 30 exhibited brain activity. Dr. Vatz disagreed. Since the trier of fact determines the credibility of expert witnesses and the weight to be given to their testimony . . . , the trial court in this case could have reasonably given greater weight to Dr. Hanley's opinion than to Dr. Vatz'. In addition, there is evidence that Theresa's pupil reacted to light on one occasion. It is argued that this evidence merely represents the subjective impression of a hospital staff member which is not corroborated by any other instance where Theresa's pupils reacted to light. However, this argument goes to the weight of this evidence and not to its admissibility. While these additional pieces of neurological data were by no means conclusive, they were competent evidence which tended to support the trial court's finding, and which also tended to disprove the contention that these tests merely verified that brain death had already taken place.

In support of the contention that Theresa Janus did not survive Stanley Janus, evidence was presented which showed that only Theresa Janus suffered seizures and exhibited a decerebrate posture shortly after ingesting the poisoned Tylenol. However, evidence that persons with these symptoms tend to die very quickly does not prove that Theresa Janus did not in fact survive Stanley Janus. Moreover, the evidence introduced is similar in nature to medical presumptions of survivorship based on decedents' health or physical condition which are considered too speculative to prove or disprove survivorship. Similarly, we find no support for the allegation that the hospital kept Theresa Janus on a mechanical respirator because her family requested that termination of her life support systems be delayed until the arrival of her brother, particularly since members of Theresa's family denied making such a request.

In conclusion, we believe that the record clearly established that the treating physicians' diagnoses of death with respect to Stanley and Theresa Janus were made in accordance with "the usual and customary standards of medical practice." [The physicians'] conclusion that Theresa Janus did not die until October 1, 1982, was based on various factors including the restoration of certain of her vital signs as well as other neurological evidence. The trial court found that these facts and circumstances constituted sufficient evidence that Theresa Janus survived her husband. It was not necessary to determine the exact moment at which Theresa died or by how long she survived him, and the trial court properly declined to do so. Viewing the record in its entirety, we cannot say that the trial court's finding of sufficient evidence of Theresa's survivorship was against the manifest weight of the evidence.

Because of our disposition of this case, we need not and do not consider whether the date of death listed on the victims' death certificates should be considered "facts" which constitute prima facie evidence of the date of their deaths. See Ill.Rev.Stat.1981, ch. 111 ½, par. 73-25; People v. Fiddler (1970), 45 Ill.2d 181, 184-86, 258 N.E.2d 359.

Accordingly, there being sufficient evidence that Theresa Janus survived Stanley Janus, the judgment of the circuit court of Cook County is affirmed.

AFFIRMED.

Notes

1. *Definition of Death; Uniform Determination of Death Act.* The definition of death used by the Illinois court in *Janus* is similar to that employed in the Uniform Determination of Death Act (1980), set forth supra Chapter 2, Part A. As noted, the Uniform Determination of Death Act was incorporated into § 1-107 of the UPC in 1991.

2. *Uniform Probate Code*. As noted supra Chapter 6, Part B, former UPC § 2-601 imposed a 120-hour requirement of survival upon the devisees of a decedent's will. No cases have sought to extend this will provision to all donative provisions, such as beneficiary designations in life-insurance polices. One reason, of course, is that the widely enacted Uniform Simultaneous Death Act (USDA) is inconsistent with a 120-hour requirement of survival. Insofar as the *Janus* case is concerned, another reason why Stanley's mother didn't have the option of making such an argument is that Illinois law hasn't adopted the UPC or any similar statutory provision even for devisees under wills.

Had *Janus* been governed by the current UPC, the outcome of the case would not only have been different, but the case itself need not have been litigated. Section 2-702 provides that, for purposes of a donative provision of a "governing instrument," a term defined in § 1-201 as including an insurance policy, an individual who is not established by clear and convincing evidence to have survived the death of another individual by 120 hours is deemed to have predeceased that other individual. Theresa's administrator would have had no hope of establishing by clear and convincing evidence that Theresa survived Stanley by 120 hours. The proceeds of Stanley's policy would have gone to Stanley's mother, Alojza, rather than to Theresa's estate and then to her relatives.

Note not only the extension of the 120-hour requirement of survival to all donative provisions of a governing instrument, but also the imposition of a clear-and-convincing standard of proof. Contrast this with the preponderance-of-the-evidence standard of proof under the USDA, as applied in *Janus*. The purposes of § 2-702 are to give a USDA-type result in cases of near-simultaneous as well as simultaneous deaths, to reduce litigation, and to resolve doubtful cases in favor of non-survival.

3. *Joint Tenancies and Multiple-Party Accounts Under the UPC.* Section 2-702 of the UPC also extends the 120-hour requirement of survival to joint tenancies, tenancies by the entirety, and multiple-party accounts.

4. *Revised Uniform Simultaneous Death Act.* In 1991, a revised version of the USDA adopting the provisions of UPC § 2-702 was approved by the Uniform Law Commissioners.

3. Ademption by Extinction

Wasserman v. Cohen

606 N.E.2d 901 (Mass. 1993)

LYNCH, J. This appeal raises the question whether the doctrine of ademption by extinction applies to a specific gift of real estate contained in a revocable inter vivos trust. The plaintiff, Elaine Wasserman, brought an action for declaratory judgment in the Middlesex Division of the Probate and Family Court against the defendant, David E. Cohen (trustee), as he is the surviving trustee of a trust established by Frieda M. Drapkin (Drapkin). In her complaint the plaintiff requested that the trustee be ordered to pay her the proceeds of the sale of an apartment building which, under the trust, would have been conveyed to the plaintiff had it not been sold by Drapkin prior to her death. Pursuant to the trustee's motion to dismiss under Mass. R. Civ. P. 12 (b) (6), 365 Mass. 754 (1974), the probate judge dismissed the action. The plaintiff appealed. We granted the plaintiff's application for direct appellate review and now affirm.

1. We summarize the relevant facts. Frieda Drapkin created the Joseph and Frieda Drapkin Memorial Trust (trust) in December, 1982, naming herself both settlor and trustee. She funded the trust with "certain property" delivered on the date of execution, and retained the right to add property by inter vivos transfer and by will. Drapkin also reserved the right to receive and to direct the payment of income or principal during her lifetime, to amend or to revoke the trust, and to withdraw property from the trust. On her death, the trustee was directed to distribute the property as set out in the trust. The trustee was ordered to convey to the plaintiff "12-14 Newton Street, Waltham, Massachusetts, Apartment Building, (consisting of approximately 11,296 square feet)."

When she executed the trust, Drapkin held record title to the property at 12-14 Newton Street in Waltham, as trustee of Z.P.Q. Realty Trust. However, she sold the property on September 29, 1988, for $575,000, and had never conveyed her interest in the property to the trust.[16]

Drapkin died on March 28, 1989. Her will, dated December 26, 1982, devised all property in her residuary estate to the trust to be disposed of in accordance with the trust's provisions.

2. The plaintiff first contends that the probate judge erred in failing to consider Drapkin's intent in regard to the gift when she sold the property. We disagree.

We have long adhered to the rule that, when a testator disposes, during his lifetime, of the subject of a specific legacy or devise in his will, that legacy or devise is held to be adeemed, "whatever may have been the intent or motive of the testator in doing so." Walsh v. Gillespie, 338 Mass. 278, 280 (1959), quoting Richards v. Humphreys, 15 Pick. 133, 135 (1833). The focus is on the actual existence or nonexistence of the bequeathed property, and not on the intent of the testator with respect to it. To be effective, a specific legacy or devise must be in existence and owned by the testator at the time of his death.

---

16. Drapkin amended the trust by instruments dated December 16, 1982, and February 8, 1989. The amendments did not reference the gift to the plaintiff.

The plaintiff asks us to abandon the doctrine of ademption. She contends that, because the doctrine ignores the testator's intent, it produces harsh and inequitable results and thus fosters litigation that the rule was intended to preclude. See Note, Ademption and the Testator's Intent, 74 Harv. L. Rev. 741 (1961). This rule has been followed in this Commonwealth for nearly 160 years. See Richards v. Humphreys, supra. Whatever else may be said about it, it is easily understood and applied by draftsmen, testators, and fiduciaries. The doctrine seeks to give effect to a testator's probable intent by presuming he intended to extinguish a specific gift of property when he disposed of that property prior to his death. As with any rule, exceptions have emerged.[17] These limited exceptions do not lead us to the abandonment of the rule. Its so-called harsh results can be easily avoided by careful draftsmanship and its existence must be recognized by any competent practitioner. When we consider the myriad of instruments drafted in reliance on its application, we conclude that stability in the field of trusts and estates requires that we continue the doctrine.

. . .

4. We have held that a trust, particularly when executed as part of a comprehensive estate plan, should be construed according to the same rules traditionally applied to wills. See Second Bank-State St. Trust Co. v. Pinion, 341 Mass. 366, 371 (1960) (doctrine of independent legal significance applied to pour-over trusts); Clymer v. Mayo, 393 Mass. 754 (1985) (G. L. c. 191, § 9, which revokes dispositions made in will to former spouses on divorce or annulment, applied to trust executed along with will as part of comprehensive estate plan). In Clymer v. Mayo, supra at 766, we reasoned that "[t]reating the components of the decedent's estate plan separately, and not as parts of an interrelated whole, brings about inconsistent results." We also quoted one commentator who wrote, "The subsidiary rules [of wills] are the product of centuries of legal experience in attempting to discern transferors' wishes and suppress litigation. These rules should be treated presumptively correct for will substitutes as well as for wills." Id. at 768, quoting Langbein, The Nonprobate Revolution and the Future of the Law of Succession, 97 Harv. L. Rev. 1108, 1136-1137 (1984). We agree with this reasoning. As discussed above, the

---

17. This court has created two exceptions to the "identity" theory. In Walsh v. Gillespie, 338 Mass. 278 (1959), a conservator appointed for the testatrix five years after her will was executed sold shares of stock that were the subject of a specific legacy. The court held that the sale did not operate as an ademption as to the unexpended balance remaining in the hands of the conservator at the death of the testatrix. Id. at 284. In Bostwick v. Hurstel, 364 Mass. 282 (1973), a conservator had sold, then repurchased, stock that was the subject of a specific legacy and that had been split twice, before the death of the testatrix. The court held that the bequest of stock was not adeemed but emphasized, "we do not violate our rule that 'identity' and not 'intent' governs ademption cases." Id. at 296. See BayBank Harvard Trust Co. v. Grant, 23 Mass. App. Ct. 653, 655 (1987).

doctrine of ademption has a "long established recognition" in Massachusetts. Furthermore, Drapkin created the trust along with her will as part of a comprehensive estate plan. Under the residuary clause of her will, Drapkin gave the majority of her estate to the trustee, who was then to dispose of the property on her death according to the terms of the trust. We see no reason to apply a different rule because she conveyed the property under the terms of the trust, rather than her will. Thus, we conclude that the doctrine of ademption, as traditionally applied to wills, should also apply to the trust in the instant case.

5. Conclusion. Since the plaintiff does not contest that the devise of 12-14 Newton Street was a specific devise,[18] it follows that the devise was adeemed by the act of Drapkin.

So ordered.

Note and Questions

1. *Questions*. Assuming that you share Professor Langbein's view that what he calls the "subsidiary rules of wills" are presumptively as correct for will substitutes as they are for wills, was the court correct in extending the identity theory of ademption, studied in Chapter 6, Part A, to the situation in *Wasserman*?

Suppose that the revocable trust that Frieda Drapkin created had not been part of a pour-over arrangement but was freestanding. Would the court have applied the identity theory in that situation? Should it?

2. *Restatement 3d of Property*. The Restatement 3d of Property § 5.2 comment i provides that its principle of ademption by extinction, which adopts the intent theory and rejects the identity theory, applies to a will substitute, such as a revocable trust, that contains the equivalent of a specific devise.

PART D. COORDINATING THE PARTS INTO A COHERENT WHOLE

Inter vivos trusts, particularly revocable trusts, are staples of the estate planner's inventory. Inter vivos trusts can be used to achieve a variety of financial objectives, including tax savings and coordinating life-insurance proceeds with other assets, and to anticipate a variety of contingencies, such as

18. "A specific legacy is one which separates and distinguishes the property bequeathed from the other property of the testator, so that it can be identified. It can only be satisfied by the thing bequeathed; if that has no existence, when the bequest would otherwise become operative, the legacy has no effect." Moffatt v. Heon, 242 Mass. 201, 203 (1922), quoting Tomlinson v. Bury, 145 Mass. 346, 347 (1887).

the possibility that the settlor will lapse into mental or physical incapacity in later life.

Other legal devices are also useful in contingency estate planning. In particular, so-called durable powers of attorney have proven to be helpful for persons acting on behalf of incapacitated property owners, enabling these agents to respond flexibly to changing circumstances. Durable powers may be used alone, but are better used in conjunction with inter vivos trusts. In this part, we examine these and other techniques of coordinating the various parts of the plan into a coherent whole.

1. Pour-Over Devises

Statutory References: *UPC § 2-511*

Restatement 3d of Property

§ *3.8 Pour-Over Devises*

(a) A "pour-over" devise is a provision in a will that (i) adds property to an inter vivos trust or (ii) funds a trust that was not funded during the testator's lifetime but whose terms are in a trust instrument that was executed during the testator's lifetime.

(b) A pour-over devise may be validated by statute, by incorporation by reference, or by independent significance.[19]

Supplemental Funding of Inter Vivos Trusts. After initially funding an inter vivos trust, the settlor may later want to supplement the trust with additional assets. Supplemental fundings fulfill various objectives. One is tax planning. Settlors who are wealthy enough to worry about federal transfer taxes frequently take maximum advantage of the gift tax annual exclusion by annually contributing to an irrevocable inter vivos trust.

Another motive behind supplemental funding of inter vivos trusts is to coordinate trust assets with other assets, including the settlor's probate estate at death and insurance proceeds. These assets can all be merged into a single trust entity through an arrangement known as the pour-over. To create this arrangement, the settlor creates an inter vivos trust and then executes a will devising part or all of the estate to the trustee of the receptacle trust. The settlor may also arrange to have life-insurance proceeds added to the receptacle trust by naming the trustee as the insurance beneficiary. Flexibility is maximized if the receptacle trust is revocable, but this comes at the sacrifice of tax savings.

19. See also Restatement 3d of Trusts § 19.

The Common-Law Background of Pour-Over Devises. Prior to statutory authorization of pour-over devises, there was substantial uncertainty about the validity of an attempted pour-over into a revocable trust. Little difficulty was encountered under common-law doctrines when the devise poured over into an irrevocable inter vivos trust that was established before execution of the will. Most courts seemed willing to accept either the theory that the will incorporated the terms of the trust by reference or the theory that the terms of the trust were facts of independent significance.

More difficulty existed if the trust was revocable or amendable. The likelihood that the court would invalidate the pour-over was greatest where the settlor amended the trust after executing the will.[20] Two issues existed in this situation: whether the amendment was effective as to property passing under the pour-over devise and, if not, whether the pour-over was effective at all. Insofar as the pour-over devise is concerned, the amendment could not be given effect under the doctrine of incorporation by reference because it failed the "in-existence" requirement. Eventually, a few courts held that the amendment was effective under the doctrine of facts of independent significance. See, e.g., Canal Nat'l Bank v. Chapman, 171 A.2d 919 (Me. 1961); Second Bank-State Street Trust Co. v. Pinion, 170 N.E.2d 350 (Mass. 1960). Concerning the second issue, it should have been possible to sustain the testamentary pour-over on the unamended terms of the trust, but at least one court held that the amendment caused the entire pour-over to fail. See President and Directors of Manhattan Co. v. Janowitz, 21 N.Y.S.2d 232 (App. Div. 1940). The court's theory was that the attempted devise to the trustee had to fail because it would frustrate the testator's intent to allow the testamentary assets to be administered under the unamended terms of the trust.

Uniform Testamentary Additions to Trusts Act (1960). Acting to facilitate pour-over devises, legislatures began to enact statutes that authorized testamentary additions to revocable or amendable trusts. The Uniform Testamentary Additions to Trusts Act (UTATA) was approved by the Uniform Law Commissioners in 1960, was incorporated into the former version of the UPC as § 2-511. The UTATA permits wills to pour probate assets into revocable or irrevocable inter vivos trusts. Under UTATA, pour-over devises are valid even if the trust is amended after execution of the will. The act requires the testator to identify the trust in his or her will and to state the terms of the trust in a writing (other than the will) executed before or concurrently

---

20. Some courts had even struck down pour-over devises to revocable trusts when the settlor had not exercised the power to revoke. See, e.g., Atwood v. Rhode Island Trust Co., 275 F. 513 (1st Cir. 1921). The court's objection was that the power to revoke or amend the trust itself was impermissible as an attempted power to dispose of probate assets without complying with the wills statute formalities.

with execution of his or her final will or the valid final will of another person who predeceased the testator.

UPC § 2-511. Section 2-511 of the current UPC makes several substantive changes to the former UPC version.

The first concerns pour-overs to unfunded inter vivos trusts. Suppose that a trust instrument is signed by the settlor, but the "trust" is not funded with any property at all—not even a penny. Assuming that the trust instrument was executed before or concurrently with the execution of the testator's will, can the testator's will validly devise property into the "trust," under the UTATA? The court in Clymer v. Mayo, 473 N.E.2d 1084 (Mass. 1985) (supra p. 470) said that it can. Accord, Trosch v. Maryland Nat'l Bank, 359 A.2d 564 (Md. Ct. Spec. App. 1976). But see Estate of Daniels, 665 P.2d 594 (Colo. 1983) (pour-over devise failed; before signing the trust instrument, the testator was advised by counsel that the "mere signing of the trust agreement would not activate it and that, before the trust could come into being, [the testator] would have to fund it"; testator then signed the trust agreement and returned it to counsel "to wait for further directions on it"; no further action was taken by the testator prior to death; the testator's will devised the residue of her estate to the trustee of the trust, but added that the residue should go elsewhere "if the trust created by said agreement is not in effect at my death.")

Current § 2-511 makes it clear that the inter vivos trust receptacle need not have been funded during the testator's lifetime, but can be funded with a trust res by the pour-over devise itself. The UPC also now allows the terms of the trust to be stated in a writing executed after as well as before or concurrently with the execution of the testator's will. It further allows the testator's will to provide that the pour-over devise is not to lapse even if the trust terminates or is revoked before the testator's death.

Upon the recommendation of the UPC Drafting Committee, comparable revisions of the UTATA were adopted by the Uniform Law Commissioners in 1991.

2. *Durable Powers of Attorney*

Statutory References: *UPC §§ 5-501 to -505*

A power of attorney creates an agency relationship between the maker of the power (the principal) and the attorney-in-fact (the agent). Under the traditional law of agency, the authority of the attorney-in-fact is automatically terminated upon the principal's death or incapacity. See Restatement 2d of Agency §§ 120, 122 (1958).

The former UPC brought forth a much-desired change in power-of-attorney law by authorizing durable powers of attorney. As opposed to an ordinary power of attorney, a durable power of attorney continues to be valid after the principal has become mentally incapacitated. In addition, the UPC provided that death of the principal does not automatically terminate the agent's authority. Under the UPC, written powers of attorney, durable or otherwise, continue to be valid after the principal's death; actions taken by the attorney-in-fact in good faith under the power are authorized until the attorney-in-fact gains actual knowledge of the principal's death.

In 1979, the UPC provisions were adopted, with slight modification, as a free-standing Uniform Durable Powers of Attorney Act, which was in turn incorporated into the UPC, as Part 5 of Article V (§§ 5-501 through 5-505). All fifty states and the District of Columbia now have legislation authorizing the creation of durable powers of attorney. For a state-by-state compilation, see Carolyn L. Dessin, Acting as Agent Under a Financial Durable Power of Attorney: An Unscripted Role, 75 Neb. L. Rev. 574, 580 n.28 (1996).

The next advance in power-of-attorney law was the promulgation of the freestanding Uniform Statutory Form Power of Attorney Act (USFPAA) (1988). The USFPAA authorizes the execution of a fill-in-the-blank durable power of attorney that grants the agent the authority to act for the principal in one or more or all of thirteen broad categories, by a check-off procedure, under which the principal checks off those categories in which he or she wants the agent to have power to act. The statute itself supplies the details concerning the exact actions that are authorized within each category checked off.

Durable powers of attorney, including statutory form durable powers, often authorize supplemental fundings of inter vivos trusts. Trusts, usually revocable trusts with discretionary provisions, provide a better tool for the management of the property of an incapacitated person than a formal guardianship or conservatorship. Moreover, trusts are more likely to be honored by transfer agents and other third parties than powers of attorney.[21] A technique now catching hold is for a settlor, while fully competent, to create a so-called standby trust, a trust funded with nominal assets such as $100 or $1000. In conjunction with the trust's creation, the settlor executes a durable power of attorney authorizing the attorney-in-fact (who might be the trustee of the trust) to transfer all or a specified portion of the settlor's assets into the trust, if the settlor later loses physical or mental capacity. This technique allows the settlor to retain control of his or her assets while the settlor is still able to manage

---

21. None of the various uniform acts on property powers of attorney provides any mechanism that forces financial institutions or any other entity or individual to honor the power of attorney. In response to this problem, the California Law Revision Commission recommended that the agent be authorized to bring an action to compel third persons to honor the agent's authority. 20 Cal. L. Rev. Comm'n Report 2629 (1990). This recommendation became law in 1994. See Cal. Prob. Code § 4406.

them, but also to have an arrangement in place by which the assets can be responsibly managed on the settlor's behalf should that become necessary.

External References. Carolyn L. Dessin, Acting as Agent Under a Financial Durable Power of Attorney: An Unscripted Role, 75 Neb. L. Rev. 574 (1996); Francis J. Collin, Jr., John J. Lombard, Albert L. Moses & Harley L. Spitler, Drafting the Durable Power of Attorney: A Systems Approach (1987); John J. Lombard, Planning for Disability: Durable Powers, Standby Trusts and Preserving Eligibility for Governmental Benefits, 20 Inst. on Est. Plan. Ch. 17 (1986); Shale D. Stiller & Sandra P. Gohn, Durable Powers of Attorney: ACTEC Study No. 17, in ACTEC Studies (American College of Trust and Estate Counsel, 1986).

3. Custodial Trusts

Statutory Reference: *Uniform Custodial Trust Act*

In 1987, the Uniform Law Commissioners took another step to facilitate the management of property on behalf of adult beneficiaries, whether incapacitated or not. The Uniform Custodial Trust Act (UCTA), enacted so far in fifteen states, establishes a statutory trust that can be invoked by transferring property to another person "as custodial trustee for (name of beneficiary, who can be the transferor) under the [enacting state] Uniform Custodial Trust Act." The UCTA is designed to provide a statutory standby trust similar to the custodial arrangement for minors established by the Uniform Transfers to Minors Act. The terms of the custodial trust, set forth in the statute itself, provide among other things that if the beneficiary is incapacitated the custodial trustee shall expend so much or all of the custodial trust property as the custodial trustee considers advisable for the use and benefit of the beneficiary. The statute also facilitates a pour-over into a trust designed to coordinate management and distribution of other assets by providing, in § 17(a)(3)(i), that the assets remaining in a custodial trust at the beneficiary's death are to be transferred "as last directed in a writing signed by the deceased beneficiary while not incapacitated and received by the custodial trustee during the life of the deceased beneficiary. . . ."

PART E. HOMICIDE AS AFFECTING SUCCESSION TO PROPERTY—THE SLAYER RULE

Statutory Reference: *UPC § 2-803*

Can a killer succeed to his or her victim's property? In cases of homicide, how does the state protect the right of the victim, now dead, to decide that his or her killer is no longer a preferred beneficiary? As indicated earlier, supra Chapter 3, Part A, some state statutes provide that spouses and parents forfeit their intestate succession shares if they commit certain statutorily proscribed acts, such as abandonment, nonsupport, or bigamy. In some respects, homicide is just another in the list of reprehensible acts that result in forfeiture because denying an heir the right to take accords with the community's sense of justice and likely reflects the decedent's dispositive preference.

Homicide is different from other wrongful conduct, however, because of the nexus between the killing and the transfer of the victim's property by operation of an intestacy statute, will, or property or contractual arrangement. After all, succession rights are determined by the order of the victim's and killer's deaths. The nexus between the act and property transfers, along with the moral imperative of preventing a killer from succeeding to the victim's property, has led many courts, in the absence of a statutory directive, to deny killers succession rights to their victims' property, and has led many legislatures to enact statutes denying killers succession rights.

The Restatement 3d of Property formulates the slayer rule as follows:

> *§ 8.4 Slayer Rule*
>
> (a) A slayer is denied any right to benefit from the wrong. For purposes of this section, a slayer is a person who, without legal excuse or justification, is responsible for the felonious and intentional killing of another.
>
> (b) Whether or not a person is a slayer is determined in a civil proceeding under the preponderance of the evidence standard rather than beyond a reasonable doubt. For purposes of the civil proceeding, however, a final judgment of conviction in a criminal proceeding conclusively establishes the convicted person as the decedent's slayer when the conviction is for the felonious and intentional killing of the decedent.

Neiman v. Hurff, involving realty held in tenancy by the entirety and corporate stock held in joint tenancy, suggests the difficulties in trying to determine what types of property the law should prevent the killer from taking.

Neiman v. Hurff

93 A.2d 345 (N.J. 1952)

VANDERBILT, C.J. On July 31, 1950 the defendant killed his wife and thereafter pleaded *non vult* to an indictment for second degree murder for which he is now confined in prison. During her lifetime the decedent and the defendant owned a residence in Collingswood, New Jersey, as tenants by the entirety, and certain shares of corporate stock as joint tenants. In her will the decedent named as her sole beneficiary the Damon Runyon Memorial Fund for Cancer Research, Inc.

The plaintiff Alberta A. Neiman as executrix of the decedent sought, first, the direction of the court in regard to the rights of the Cancer Fund and of the defendant respectively in the corporate stock owned jointly by the decedent and the defendant during her lifetime . . . . The Cancer Fund sought an adjudication that the real property held by the entirety and the jointly owned corporate stock be held in trust for it by the defendant and that he be ordered to convey them to it.

The defendant contended that the title to both the realty and the corporate stock vested in him on his wife's death. . . .

The trial court ruled that the decedent having met her death at the hands of the defendant, the title to the realty was vested in him as trustee for himself individually and for the Cancer Fund; that its value at the time of her death was $14,000; that the value of the Cancer Fund's interest was $11,597.98 (this sum representing the difference between $14,000 and "the commuted value as of the date of decedent's death of the net income of one-half of said property for the number of years of defendant's expectancy of life as determined according to the mortality tables used by this Court"); that $11,597.98 was imposed as a lien on the real property in favor of the Cancer Fund; that the defendant pay the Cancer Fund $11,597.98 within 45 days of service of the judgment or that the Cancer Fund have execution issue. The trial court further ruled that the title to the shares of stock likewise be held by the defendant as trustee for himself and the Cancer Fund; that the value of the stock at the time of the wife's death was $2,495.63; that the value of the interest of the Cancer Fund as the sole beneficiary under the decedent's will was $2,062.61 (representing the difference between $2,495.63 and "the commuted value as of the date of the decedent's death of the net income of one-half of the said shares of stock for the number of years of defendant's expectancy of life as determined according to the mortality tables used by this Court"); that $2,062.61 was imposed as a lien in favor of the Cancer Fund and that the defendant pay said sum within 45 days after service of the judgment or that execution issue. . . .

From this judgment the defendant appealed. . . . The question here presented is whether or not a murderer can acquire by right of survivorship and keep property the title to which he had held jointly with his victim. This question has never been before a court of last resort in this State. . . . Some states have held that the legal title passes to the murderer despite his crime and that he may retain it . . . . Some other states have held that the legal title will not pass to the murderer at all . . . . A third group of states has held that legal title passes to the murderer but that equity will treat him as a constructive trustee because of his unconscionable acquisition of the property and compel him to convey it to those to whom it has been devised or bequeathed by the will of his victim, or in the absence of a will to the heirs or next of kin of the decedent exclusive of the murderer. . . .

To permit the murderer to retain title to the property acquired by his crime as permitted in some states is abhorrent to even the most rudimentary sense of justice. It violates the policy of the common law that no one shall be allowed to profit by his own wrong . . . . On the other hand, to divest the surviving murderer of all legal title violates or does violence to the doctrine of vested rights and would conflict with N.J.S. 2A:152-2, N.J.S.A.:

> No conviction or judgment for any offense against this state, shall make or work corruption of blood, disinherison of heirs, loss of dower, or forfeiture of estate.

But to follow the principle enunciated in the [third group of states discussed above] does not interfere with vested legal rights, yet by applying the equitable doctrine of a constructive trust force is given to the sound principle of equity that a murderer or other wrongdoer shall not enrich himself by his inequity at the expense of an innocent person. To quote from "Can a Murderer Acquire Title by His Crime and Keep It?" in Ames, Lectures on Legal History (1913), 310, at 321:

> The results reached in these cases must commend themselves to everyone's sense of justice. But all will admit that these results could not be accomplished by common-law principles alone. The common law would make the criminal remainderman in the one case, and the criminal joint tenant in the other case, the absolute owner of the land. Equity alone, by acting *in personam*, can compel the criminal to surrender what, in spite of his crime, the common law has suffered him to acquire.

This doctrine is so consistent with the equitable principles that have obtained here for centuries that we have no hesitancy in applying it, and we find no merit at all in the defendant's argument that the decision below works a corruption of blood or a forfeiture of estate. It would be a strange system of jurisprudence that would be able to grant relief against many kinds of accidents, mistake and fraud, by compelling a defendant to act as a constructive trustee with respect to property vouchsafed him by the common law, and yet be unable similarly to touch the legal rights of a defendant who sought to profit by a heinous crime.

A more difficult question is involved in determining how much, if any, of the realty and of the shares of stock shall be held in constructive trust by the defendant for the benefit of the Cancer Fund. In the ordinary course of events the estate by the entirety in the real property would vest in the survivor absolutely and so would the ownership of the corporate stock, but it is now impossible here to determine whether husband or wife would have survived in the ordinary course of events and thus which would have become the sole owner of the property in question. Inasmuch as the husband by his wrongful act has prevented the determination in the natural course of events of whether he or his wife would survive, it is not inequitable to presume that the decedent would have survived the wrongdoer. In this situation there is no justification for determining survivorship according to the mathematical life expectancies of the decedent and her murderer. The wrongdoer, having prevented the natural ascertainment of the answer to the question of survivorship, should not be permitted to avail himself of mortality tables which may have no applicability as between him and the decedent in respect to their respective individual possibilities of survivorship. Equity therefore conclusively presumes for the purpose of working out justice that the decedent would have survived the wrongdoer. In no other way can complete justice be done and the criminal prevented from profiting through his crime.

This view inevitably leads us to the conclusion that both as to the realty and the corporate stock the Cancer Fund is entitled in equity to an absolute one-half interest and a remainder interest in the other half, subject only to the value of the life estate of the defendant in such half. Thus the defendant will hold the realty in trust for the Cancer Fund subject to a lien thereon for the commuted value at the time of the decedent's death of the net income of one-half of the real property for the number of years of his expectancy of life as determined according to the mortality tables used in our courts, i.e., $2,402.02. Likewise the defendant will hold the shares of stock in trust for the Cancer Fund subject to the commuted value at the date of the decedent's death of the net income of one-half of the shares of stock for the number of years of defendant's expectancy of life as determined according to the mortality tables, or $433.02. . . .

The judgment below is modified in accordance with this opinion but without costs to either party and the cause is remanded for such further proceedings as may be necessary.

Notes

1. *The Remedy in Neiman v. Hurff.* The judgment entered in *Neiman* uses the conventional language of constructive trust, which tends to conceal the nature of the actual decree and thereby causes unnecessary confusion. Literally, the judgment reads as though the husband, who is in prison at the time of judgment, will continue to hold legal title to the property, but as trustee for the wife's estate to the extent indicated. This would make no sense nor would it conform to the role played by a constructive trust, and one may be sure that this is not what the court had in mind. The actual decree in *Neiman* will (or at least should) order the husband to transfer legal title to the property to the wife's estate, upon payment by the latter of the amounts found to be the commuted value of the husband's beneficial interest in the property. (The only reason for finding commuted value was in order to effect such a transfer.) An example of such a decree appears in McCreary v. Shields, 52 N.W.2d 853, 856, 857 (Mich. 1952), where the decree also provided that if the defendant failed to deliver a deed "this decree may be recorded in the office of the register of deeds of the county with like effects as though such deed had been executed and delivered."

2. *Severance of Joint Tenancies and Tenancies by the Entirety.* State laws conflict over the treatment of joint tenancies with the right of survivorship.[22] Some states adopt the rule found in *Neiman* that the killer should retain only a one-half share in the property for life. The majority of state statutes and the UPC § 2-803, as well as more recent cases, adopt the rule that the killer should retain a one-half share in fee.

In allowing the killer to retain the present value of only a one-half share in the property for life, the *Neiman* rule may seem more appropriate for tenancies by the entirety than for joint tenancies. In a tenancy by the entirety, neither tenant has a unilateral right to sever. Nevertheless, the courts and statutes that allow a killer to take one-half the property in fee when the killer and victim owned property in joint tenancy extend that result to property owned by the entirety.[23]

---

22. A few states go so far as to deny the killer all rights to the jointly-held property. See, e.g., Estate of Castiglioni, 47 Cal.Rptr.2d 288 (Ct. App. 1995), petition for review denied (Feb. 15, 1996); Ohio Rev. Code Ann. § 2105.19(A); Oleff v. Holdapp, 195 N.E. 838 (Ohio 1935); Estate of Fiore, 476 N.E.2d 1093 (Ohio Ct. App. 1984). The *Castiglioni* decision, which was rendered under a statute patterned after the former UPC provision, is criticized in Charlotte K. Goldberg, Estate of Castiglioni: Spousal Murder and the Clash of Joint Tenancy and Equity in California Community Property Law, 33 Idaho L. Rev. 513 (1997).

23. See, e.g., National City Bank v. Bledsoe, 144 N.E.2d 710 (Ind. 1957); UPC § 2-803(b)(2). But see, e.g., 20 Pa. Cons. Stat. Ann. §§ 8805, 8806 (providing different rules for joint tenancies and tenancies by the entirety).

After *Neiman* was decided, the New Jersey legislature substantially enacted the former version of UPC § 2-803(b).

Subsequently, a case similar to *Neiman* arose, Estate of Karas, 485 A.2d 1083 (N.J. App. Div. 1984). Walter Karas murdered his wife, Krystina Karas. The couple had two infant children. Krystina died intestate. Walter and Krystina owned two improved parcels of land as tenants by the entirety (one being their residence).

The trial judge held that, under the New Jersey counterpart of former UPC § 2-803(b), the murder caused a severance of the tenancy-by-the-entirety property. One half passed to Krystina's estate, where it devolved to her two children (Walter being treated as having predeceased her for the purposes of intestate succession). Ownership of the other half went to Walter.

But the court went on to hold that Walter was not entitled to keep his half. The court explained:

> Does the killer take the remaining one-half not only legally but free and clear of the power of equity to impose a constructive trust. Clearly he may not. There is nothing in the Probate Reform Act of 1978 to indicate an intent to invert the strong public policy expressed in Neiman v. Hurff. There was no statement accompanying the legislation to indicate such intent; no commentators have suggested that conclusion. Under those circumstances it is presumed that the legislature did not intend to change the pre-existing common law. Before such intent may be found it must appear clearly and plainly from the legislation.
>
> An exception to that principle of statutory construction is sometimes found where the new statute is part of a complete system of laws covering all aspects of the subject with which it deals so that it may be said that it supersedes all prior law on that subject—whether statutory law or common law. The adoption of the Probate Reform Act of 1978 falls into that category. However, there is nothing in N.J.S.A.3B:7-2 which grants the killer a clear and unequivocal right to *use* his one-half interest.

The Appellate Division affirmed, holding further that the constructive trust on Walter's remainder interest was to be imposed in favor of Krystina's heirs—the couple's two children.

What is your reaction to the court's analysis? Is *Karas* a reliable precedent for interpreting former UPC § 2-803(b)?

Felonious and Intentional Killing. States generally provide for forfeiture only if the killing is felonious and intentional. The Restatement 3d of Property § 8.4 comment f provides that "[t]he term 'felonious' refers to criminal offenses that are felonies"[24] and that "[t]he term 'intentional' is not confined to consequences that are desired, . . . but includes consequences that the actor believes are substantially certain to result from his or her act."

The fact that the killing wasn't motivated by greed is appropriately treated as irrelevant to whether the state requires a forfeiture of succession rights, because, regardless of the reason for the intentional killing, the victim lost enjoyment of the property, the opportunity to change the distribution, and the possibility of surviving the killer.

A person who acts in self-defense isn't treated as a felonious and intentional killer. See, e.g., State Farm Life Insurance Co. v. Smith, 363 N.E.2d 785 (Ill. 1977); Restatement 3d of Property § 8.4 comment h. The majority of states don't deny succession rights to a killer who was insane at the time of the killing. See, e.g., Ford v. Ford, 512 A.2d 389 (Md. 1986); Restatement 3d of Property § 8.4 comment h. But see, e.g., Ind. Code § 29-1-2-12.1.

A minority of states require the killing to constitute murder before denying the killer the right to succeed to the victim's property. Other states require a person to be convicted of murder or an intentional homicide. Whether a state requires the killing to constitute murder, or whether it requires the killer to be convicted of an intentional homicide, can vary depending on the type of property transfer involved.[25]

In a jurisdiction that doesn't require a criminal conviction, a civil proceeding is necessary to determine whether a person claiming the decedent's property feloniously and intentionally killed the victim. Most jurisdictions require that the issue of whether a person feloniously and intentionally killed the decedent be decided by a preponderance of the evidence standard. The UPC and the Restatement 3d of Property take this position. A few states impose a clear and convincing standard of proof. See, e.g., Estate of Safran, 306 N.W.2d 27 (Wis. 1981); Me. Rev. Stat. Ann. tit. 18-A, § 2-803(e). Most of the statutes provide

---

24. The Model Penal Code § 1.04(2) provides that "[a] crime is a felony if it is so designated in this Code or if persons convicted thereof may be sentenced [to death or] to imprisonment for a term which, apart from an extended term, is in excess of one year."

25. For example, in Seipel v. State Employees' Retirement System, 289 N.E.2d 288 (Ill. App. Ct. 1972), a widow convicted of voluntary manslaughter of her husband was barred from receiving death benefits under her husband's state pension by the common-law principle that one may not profit by his own wrong; the pension benefits were ordered paid to the husband's estate. But, in Estate of Seipel, 329 N.E.2d 419 (Ill. App. Ct. 1975), the same widow was not barred from succeeding to her husband's estate as his sole heir because, as to the right of inheritance, the state statute barring inheritance in cases of "murder" superseded the common law. But see Life Insurance Co. of North America v. Wollett, 766 P.2d 893 (Nev. 1988) (statutory provision requiring conviction for murder to deny a killer an inheritance preempted the common law and, therefore, killer who entered a plea of voluntary manslaughter received insurance proceeds as beneficiary of a policy on the victim's life).

that a conviction for a felonious and intentional killing conclusively denies the killer succession rights. No jurisdiction, however, treats an acquittal as conclusive evidence of the innocence of the accused or the lawfulness of the killing. This is because of the higher standard of proof necessary to obtain a conviction in a criminal trial. See Restatement 2d of Judgments § 85(2)(a).

Suppose that X, who is the sole devisee under D's will, intentionally murders D but is able to prove by clear and convincing evidence that he did so for the purpose of relieving D's suffering from pain associated with a lethal illness. Should X be entitled to inherit under D's will? For an argument that he should, see Jeffrey G. Sherman, Mercy Killing and the Right to Inherit, 61 U. Cin. L. Rev. 803 (1993).

Property Owned by the Victim. All but a handful of states have statutes that deny the killer the right to receive property from the victim's estate by will or by intestacy and provide that the estate or the failed interest should be distributed in accordance with the fiction that the killer predeceased the victim. In the states without statutes expressly providing for forfeiture, the courts have reached the same result. See, e.g., Wright v. Wright, 449 S.W.2d 952 (Ark. 1970) (intestacy); Welch v. Welch, 252 A.2d 131 (Del. Ch. 1969) (will). Under UPC § 2-803(b), if the decedent died intestate, the estate passes as if the killer disclaimed his or her intestate interest. Under the UPC's disclaimer provision, § 2-801(d), this means that the killer is treated as having predeceased the decedent for purposes of allowing the killer's interest to pass to his or her surviving descendants, if any, but not for purposes of changing the shares.

Will Substitutes. Section 2-803 of the current UPC, while retaining the major thrust of the former version, is more comprehensive. Subsection (c) covers property arrangements that weren't expressly treated by the former UPC. For example, subsection (c)(1) provides that the felonious and intentional killing of the decedent revokes any revocable disposition made by the decedent to the killer. This includes life-insurance beneficiary designations and interests in revocable trusts.

General Principle. For situations not expressly covered, § 2-803(f) provides that they are controlled by the principle that a killer cannot profit from his or her wrong. See also Restatement 3d of Property § 8.4 comment q. In Estate of Macaro, 699 N.Y.S.2d 634 (Sur. Ct. 1999), the court held that the slayer was not entitled to take an intestate share from the decedent's estate. The slayer did not kill the intestate decedent. Rather, the slayer killed his father and aunt, who as the intestate-decedent's brother and sister would have been the intestate-decedent's heirs if they had survived the intestate-decedent.

Property Not Within the Victim's Control. Even if the victim doesn't have the power to control the disposition of the property, the killer still may forfeit property interests that are conditioned on survival of the victim.

Problems

1. G makes an irrevocable transfer in trust directing the trustee to pay income to A for life, and at A's death, to distribute the corpus of the trust to B. B kills A. Should A's estate be able to obtain an amount equal to the present value of the income interest based on A's life expectancy? See Restatement 3d of Property § 8.4 comment n illus. 8; cf. *Neiman*.

2. Same facts as in Problem 1, except the trust directs that if B fails to survive A, the corpus should be distributed to C. Should A's estate be able to obtain an amount equal to the present value of the income interest based on A's life expectancy or should C receive the entire corpus? See Restatement 3d of Property § 8.4 comment n illus. 9.

3. Same facts as in Problem 2, except that A kills B. Should A be able to retain her income interest? Should B or C receive the remainder interest? See Restatement 3d of Property § 8.4 comment p illus. 11.

4. G purchases an insurance policy on her own life and irrevocably names X as primary beneficiary of the proceeds. X feloniously and intentionally kills G. Should X be able to enjoy the proceeds? Should the result be different if the policy doesn't require X to survive G? See Restatement 3d of Property § 8.4 comment k illus. 4.

5. W's pension plan, which is an employee benefit plan covered by the Employee Retirement Income Security Act (ERISA), provides that a surviving spouse shall be entitled to an annuity. H kills W. Should H receive the annuity payments? Should the answer depend on state or federal law? See Restatement 3d of Property § 8.4 comment k illus. 5; Egelhoff v. Egelhoff, supra p. 473; Mendez-Bellido v. Board of Trustees, 709 F. Supp. 329 (E.D. N.Y. 1989).

Property Owned by the Killer. The general, and seemingly appropriate, rule is that the killer shouldn't forfeit any property he or she owns. See, e.g., Luecke v. Mercantile Bank of Jonesboro, 691 S.W.2d 843 (Ark. 1985); Meyer's Estate, 94 N.Y.S.2d 620 (App. Div. 1950); Restatement 3d of Property § 8.4 comment p. But see *Neiman* (allowing the killer to take only one-half of the jointly-owned corporate stock for life rather than in fee). Nevertheless, issues can arise that suggest that some exceptions to that rule are warranted. For example, if H feloniously and intentionally killed W and then committed suicide, should W's estate be able to claim an elective share against H's estate? See, e.g., Luecke v. Mercantile Bank of Jonesboro, 691 S.W.2d 843 (Ark. 1985); Debus v. Cook, 154 N.E. 484 (Ind. 1926); Parker v. Potter, 157 S.E. 68 (N.C. 1931). Could W's executor sue H's estate for wrongful death? See Fowler V. Harper, Fleming James, Jr. & Oscar S. Gray, Law of Torts §§ 8.10, 24.5 (2d ed. 1986).

Another troubling case concerns life-insurance policies on the life of the victim where the killer is the owner and primary beneficiary. Should the killer be able to receive the life-insurance proceeds? See, e.g., New York Mutual Ins. Co. v. Armstrong, 117 U.S. 591 (1886). Should the killer be able to obtain the cash surrender value, if any, on the policy? See, e.g., Manufacturers Life Ins. Co. v. Moore, 116 F. Supp. 171 (S.D. Cal. 1953); Restatement 3d of Property § 8.4 comment p illus. 11. If the killer named Y to take in the event the killer failed to survive the insured, should Y be able to take? Compare, e.g., First Kentucky Trust Co. v. United States, 737 F.2d 557 (6th Cir. 1984) with, e.g., Manufacturers Life Ins. Co. v. Moore, 116 F. Supp. 171 (S.D. Cal. 1953). See also Seidlitz v. Eames, 753 P.2d 775 (Colo. Ct. App. 1987) (children of the killer received proceeds as named successor-owners and contingent beneficiaries of a policy owned by the killer). Should the insured's estate be able to take? See, e.g., First Kentucky Trust Co. v. United States, supra. Should the insurance company be relieved of all liability? See, e.g., Travelers Ins. Co. v. Thompson, 163 N.W.2d 289 (Minn. 1968), appeal dismissed, 395 U.S. 161 (1969).

External References. Palmer on Restitution §§ 20.8-.17; Mary Louise Fellows, The Slayer Rule: Not Solely a Matter of Equity, 71 Iowa L. Rev. 489 (1986); Linda J. Maki & Alan M. Kaplan, Elmer's Case Revisited: The Problem of the Murdering Heir, 41 Ohio St. L.J. 905 (1980); William M. McGovern, Jr., Homicide and Succession to Property, 68 Mich. L. Rev. 65 (1969).

Chapter 9

Elder Law: Estate Planning for the Aged and the Disabled

ONE of the fastest growing areas of legal practice in recent years has been Elder Law. The term "Elder Law" itself is relatively new. It refers to a broad range of legal problems facing older persons and their families and friends. These include housing and employment discrimination on the basis of age; financial aspects of medical care, such as eligibility for Medicare and Medicaid; Social Security; and pension and other employee benefits. In this Chapter, we limit coverage to two aspects of Elder Law that most directly concern the estate planner: (1) health-care decisionmaking and (2) preservation and management of assets. We will also look at the problems of planning for disabled persons, including children.

The reasons for the rapid growth of Elder Law as a field of legal specialization are readily apparent. The number and percentage of elderly individuals in the United States have rapidly grown. Increasing age raises more concerns about health and how health care is paid for. These concerns require planning for both property and personal care. Older Americans are wealthier than ever, but the cost of medical care has also increased dramatically within the past several decades. Elderly persons today are faced with greater questions about how they will dispose of their accumulated wealth in their remaining years. They and their families are also faced with even more difficult and painful decisions about how much health care should be provided for them and who should be given the authority to make those decisions. These matters pose special challenges to the estate planner who represents an elderly client.

INTERNET REFERENCES. The Kansas Elder Law Network at www.keln.org is one of the most comprehensive web sites in the area of Elder Law. Also useful are the sites maintained by the National Senior Citizens Law Center at www.nsclc.org, AARP (formerly known as the American Association of Retired Persons) at www.aarp.org, and the National Academy of Elder Law Attorneys at www.naela.org. For relevant governmental sites, the best starting point is the federal Administration on Aging at www.aoa.gov.

PART A. DEMOGRAPHIC AND SOCIAL BACKGROUND

There is little doubt that the elderly population is rapidly increasing in this country. Some demographic figures tell the story. In 1950, the percentage of Americans 65 and older was 8.1 percent;[1] that number is projected to be 20.0 percent by 2050.[2] Similarly, in 1950, the percentage of Americans 80 and older was 1.1 percent;[3] by 2050, the percentage of Americans *85 and older* is projected to be 4.6 percent.[4] Contrary to popular belief, the age cohort with the largest percentage increase between 1980 and 1990 was not the "baby-boom" generation but persons aged 85 years and older.[5]

The economic status of the elderly has improved noticeably in recent decades. In 1960, with 20 percent of their population classified as poor, the elderly were the poorest age group in American society.[6] Yet by 1998, the poverty rate for persons 65 and older was only 10.5 percent, the same as the rate for nonelderly adults (ages 18-64).[7]

While the economic status of elderly has risen, so has the demand for, and the cost of, health care. Americans are not the healthiest people on the planet, as a recent report issued by the World Health Organization makes clear. According to the report, Americans can expect to enjoy, on average, only 70 healthy years, lower than the figures for Japan, Canada, Australia, Israel, and virtually every country in Europe. See Barbara Crossette, Americans Enjoy 70 Healthy Years, Behind Europe, U.N. Says, N.Y. Times, June 5, 2000, at A10.

---

1. Richard A. Posner, Aging and Old Age 35, tbl. 2.1 (1995).

2. Jacob Siegel, Aging Into the 21st Century, tbl. 1 (May 31, 1996) (report prepared for the Administration on Aging and available at www.aoa.gov/stats/aging21).

3. Posner, Aging and Old Age, supra note 1, at 35, tbl. 2.2.

4. Siegel, Aging Into the 21st Century, supra note 2, at tbl. 1.

5. See Lawrence Frolik & Richard L. Kaplan, Elder Law in a Nutshell 1 (2d ed. 1998).

6. Thomas S. Ulen, The Law and Economics of the Elderly, 4 Elder L.J. 99, 109 (1996).

7. Administration on Aging, Profile of Older Americans: 1999 (available at www.aoa.dhhs.gov/aoa/stats/profile).

Americans' rising longevity and comparative susceptibility to disease and disability increase the need for health care in this country, particularly custodial and long-term forms of care. These are especially expensive forms of health care, explaining why the elderly in the U.S. account for approximately one-third of all of the nation's health care expenditures even though they constitute only 12 percent of the population.[8] The upshot of these developments is growing anxiety over what has been called the "graying of America." Judge Richard A. Posner succinctly articulated this concern:

> Although as yet there appears to be no correlation, after other causes are corrected for, between the average age of a nation's population and the nation's per capita expenditures on health care, the combination of increasing medical costs due primarily to advances in medical technology with a rapid increase in the number of elderly people portends a significant increase in aggregate medical expenditures unless the demands for health care of younger people are to be scanted. Already persons age 65 and older, although less than 13 percent of the population, account for more than a third of all expenditures on health care in the United States. And this ignores the cost, as yet largely nonmonetary because borne by family members in the form of personal services rather than cash outlays, of the home care that many elderly people require. [T]his cost is real—is not just a matter of children's bounteous and unstinting desire to care for their aged parents.[9]

The costs of the most common forms of custodial care, home care and nursing-home care, are not covered by Medicare. These costs must be paid by the elderly themselves or their families. (Medicaid does cover part of cost of nursing-home care for the indigent.) Home health care can cost as much as $30,000 per year, and nursing homes commonly charge between $30,000 and $80,000 per year. Long-term custodial care insurance policies are available for these expenses, but they, too, are usually expensive.

A new and increasingly popular form of custodial care for the elderly are "assisted-living" facilities. These are residential complexes that provide help for elderly residents with ordinary tasks like dining and housecleaning as well as offering organized social activities. Staff attend to the residents' practical nursing needs, and medical personnel are available for emergency care. Generally, they are less costly and offer residents more independence and privacy than nursing homes. Most assisted living is privately financed with little or no Medicare or Medicaid contributions. The growing popularity of this alternative to nursing homes is indicated by the fact that the number of beds in assisted-care complexes will double between 1994 and 2000. See John J.

---

8. Peter J. Strauss and Nancy M. Lederman, The Elder Law Handbook xv (1996).

9. Posner, Aging and Old Age, supra note 1, at 36.

Hogan, The Senior Housing Industry: Market Characteristics and Market Data, Appraisal J., April 1, 1999, at 199.

PART B. LONG-TERM CARE PLANNING

1. Planning for the Elderly

Traditionally, individuals have had to pay for long-term care out of their own assets or those of their families. As the cost of such care has risen in recent years, the elderly and their families have looked for various alternative means of financing long-term residential care. In this Part, we look at some of the main devices currently used to help defray these costs and the estate planning implications of these financing options.

a. Qualifying for Medicare or Medicaid

Medicare and Medicaid are the two major federal programs that provide health-care benefits to the elderly. Medicare is a health insurance program for qualified elderly and disabled persons. Medicaid is a joint federal-state program intended to provide benefits to specific categories of poor people, including the elderly. Both programs offer assistance in paying for long-term care but only in limited circumstances.

Medicare. Medicare coverage is limited to persons over age 65 who qualify for Social Security benefits on the basis of their lifetime earnings record. There are two parts to the Medicare program. Part A, known as Hospital Insurance, covers inpatient hospital care; skilled nursing care in a medical institution, nursing facility, or private home; and hospice care. Part B, known as Supplemental Medical Insurance, primarily covers expenses for physician care. Unlike Part A, it is optional, and it requires payment of premiums and larger deductibles.

Medicare covers long-term care but only in exceptional circumstances and only to a limited extent. It provides full coverage for skilled nursing care in a skilled nursing care facility during a period of illness but only up to a limited period of time, after which the patient must pay increasingly large per diem deductibles. It also pays for skilled nursing services, as well as physical and speech therapy, provided in the patient's own home, but only if the patient is homebound and the services are provided under a plan of treatment prescribed by a physician. The term "skilled nursing care" refers to services ordered by a physician and provided by professional personnel such as registered nurses and licensed practical nurses. It does not include long-term custodial care, such as dressing, bathing, or administering medications; services like Meals-on-Wheels; or adult day care. Courts have demonstrated a reluctance to characterize services as "skilled," rather "custodial." In Friedman v. Secretary of the Department of Health and Human Services, 819 F.2d 42 (2d Cir. 1987), for example, the court affirmed the government's denial of Medicare benefits to a hospital patient who was admitted to the intensive care unit for treatment of head injuries and who also suffered from Parkinson's disease and inflammation of the veins. After treating him, his doctors concluded that he no longer required skilled medical care, but his family decided that it was best for him to stay in the hospital longer rather than being transferred to a custodial care facility. The government denied Medicare payments for the time after the first custodial care option became available, despite the fact that the patient received medical treatment for his Parkinson's condition and inflammation of the veins while he remained in the hospital. The safe course of action is to assume that most long-term care will not be covered by Medicare.

Medicaid. The primary federal program for assistance for nursing home care is Medicaid. Medicaid differs from Medicare in two important respects. First, while Medicare is exclusively a federal program, Medicaid funding and administration are jointly state and federal. Wide variations exist in state benefits and eligibility requirements. Second, unlike Medicare, which covers certain medical needs regardless of the beneficiary's financial status, Medicaid is strictly limited to low-income persons with few assets.

The income and asset limitations rules are quite complex. In general, however, states follow four principles.[10] First, the applicant must apply for all sources of income for which he or she is eligible, including pension and retirement benefits, annuities, and the like. Second, the individual must assign to the state any third-party payment or other medical support to which he or she is entitled. Third, the income and assets of family members other than the spouse are not taken into account. Fourth, family members other than the spouse are not held responsible for reimbursing the state for the costs of medical care provided to a Medicaid beneficiary. For married couples, the rules governing the non-applicant spouse's income and assets are varied and complex. With respect to income, only the applicant's income is generally considered where the applicant is institutionalized and the spouse is not. With respect to assets, only some of the non-institutionalized spouse's assets are exempt; others are taken into consideration.

Individuals who want to qualify for Medicaid to pay for long-term care do not have to deprive themselves of all assets. Only so-called "non-exempt" assets are counted under state eligibility rules.[11] Significant exempt assets that the

---

10. See John J. Regan, Entitlements (ACTEC Foundation, 1994).

11. One device by which individuals seeking to qualify for Medicaid may avoid excessive "spending down" is to use an annuity to shelter non-exempt assets. See James D. Palmer, New Planning Approaches to Cope with Stricter Medicaid Rules, 23 Medicaid Planning 76, 77-78

applicant may retain, or even use non-exempt assets to acquire, typically include the principal residence[12]; household goods and personal items up to a stated maximum (such as $2,000); a wedding ring; a vehicle; burial plots; and a stated amount of money to be used for funeral expenses. These exemption rules create opportunities for careful estate planning that maintain assets for Medicaid-qualifying clients. Where the principal residence is an exempt asset, for example, a person planning to finance long-term care through Medicaid can invest in buying a home or pay off an existing mortgage on the residence. Such planning must be done very carefully, however, because otherwise exempt assets may lose their exempt status under certain conditions. New York law, for example, provides that the personal residence loses its exempt status when the owner moves permanently into a nursing home and no spouse or dependent relative remains there. In Cacchillo v. Perales, 576 N.Y.S.2d 916 (App. Div. 1991), the petitioner's mother gratuitously transferred her home to her children in anticipation of moving into a nursing home after she was hospitalized for a stroke. The Department of Social Services included the value of her home in her assets, causing her to be ineligible for Medicaid benefits, a decision the court affirmed.

Until recently, two techniques were especially common in Medicaid-planning for the elderly: transfers of assets to the children and others, and Medicaid trusts. The availability of both of these techniques was considerably limited by the federal Omnibus Budget Reconciliation Act of 1993 (known as OBRA 93).

Asset Transfers. In recent years, it has become increasingly common, especially among the middle class, for elderly persons to transfer assets to their relatives to qualify for Medicaid without becoming destitute. Not atypically, the donor and donee have reached a tacit agreement that the donee will use some or all of the transferred assets to care for the donor. See Esther Fein, Elderly Transfer Assets to Qualify for Medicaid, N.Y. Times, Sept. 25, 1994, at A15.

Federal law imposes several restrictions on asset transfers as a means of qualifying for Medicaid. It creates a period of ineligibility for persons who transfer non-exempt assets or their personal residence[13] to anyone other than their spouse for less than fair market value within a certain period prior to applying for Medicaid for institutionalized care. For transfers made on or

---

(1996).

12. Exemption of the principal residence for a person who is institutionalized depends upon demonstrating an "intention to return" once the period of institutionalization has ended. A written and signed statement by owner is usually effective for this purpose. Rental of the residence during the period of institutionalization has several disadvantages for Medicaid purposes.

13. Transfer of the principal residence to a spouse continues to be exempt from penalty under the new Medicaid rules.

before August 10, 1993, generally transfers must be made at least 30 months prior to application. The period of ineligibility depends upon the uncompensated value of the transferred asset but cannot exceed 30 months from the date of transfer. OBRA 93, seeking to curb abuses of what some critics have called "middle-class welfare," made it more difficult to make Medicaid-qualifying asset transfers by extending both the look-back period and the ineligibility period. For transfers made after August 10, 1993, the look-back period is 36 months, and there is no outer limit on the length of ineligibility. The precise ineligibility period for any such transfer is determined according to a stated formula. Exempt assets other than a house can be transferred at any time.

The federal Health Insurance Portability and Accountability Act of 1996, which took effect January 1, 1997, further stiffened the rules against certain Medicaid-qualifying asset transfers. It made it a crime to "knowingly and willfully dispose[] of assets (including any transfer in trust) in order for an individual to become eligible for medical assistance under a State [Medicaid] plan . . . , if disposing of the assets results in the imposition of a period of ineligibility for such assistance under section 1917(c)."[14] Violators were subject to fines of up to $25,000 or imprisonment for up to five years, or both.

The harshness of this criminal penalty provoked many organizations to label it the "Granny Goes to Jail Act" and to call for its repeal. But rather than repeal the law altogether, Congress enacted § 4734 of the Balanced Budget Act of 1997.[15] Under this section, it was no longer a crime to dispose of certain assets in order to qualify for Medicaid; instead, it was a crime to *counsel or assist* anyone in disposing of certain assets in order to qualify for Medicaid. Now it was Granny's lawyer who was in danger of going to jail.

New York State Bar Association v. Reno

999 F.Supp. 710 (N.D.N.Y. 1998)

McAvoy, Chief Judge. Plaintiff, the New York State Bar Association ("NYSBA"), seeks to enjoin the Attorney General of the United States from enforcing section 4734 of the Balanced Budget Act of 1997, which was incorporated into section 217 of the Health Insurance Portability and Accountability Act of 1996, 42 U.S.C. § 1320a-7b(a). Plaintiff asserts that section 4734 violates the First and Fifth Amendments to the United States Constitution.

---

14. P.L. 104-191, § 217, amending 42 U.S.C. § 1320a-7b(a).

15. P.L. 105-33, § 4734, amending 42 U.S.C. § 1320a-7(b).

I. BACKGROUND

A. Statutory Background

Before Congress enacted section 217 of the Health Insurance Portability and Accountability Act of 1996, certain transfers of assets up to 36 months prior to an application for Medicaid benefits and certain transfers to trusts up to 60 months prior to application, could result in a period of ineligibility for Medicaid benefits. 42 U.S.C. § 1396p(c). In enacting section 217, Congress left the ineligibility period intact, but added certain criminal penalties. Essentially, section 217 made it a crime to dispose of assets in order to become eligible for Medicaid benefits if the disposition of assets "resulted in the imposition of a period of ineligibility." § 1320a-7b(a)(6) (sometimes referred to as the "Granny Goes to Jail Act"). Violators were subject to fines of up to $25,000 or imprisonment for up to 5 years, or both. Id.

A number of organizations lobbied for the repeal of section 217, including the NYSBA. Rather than repeal the Granny Goes to Jail Act, Congress amended section 217 by enacting section 4734 of the Balanced Budget Act of 1997. Section 4734, which became effective August 5, 1997, struck the former language and added a provision making it illegal to counsel or assist an individual to dispose of certain assets to qualify for Medicaid:

> Criminal penalties for acts involving Federal health care programs
> (a) Making or causing to be made false statements or representations
> Whoever—
>
> . . . .
>
> (6) for a fee knowingly and willfully counsels or assists an individual to dispose of assets (including by any transfer in trust) in order for the individual to become eligible for medical assistance under a State plan under subchapter XIX of this chapter, if disposing of the assets results in the imposition of a period of ineligibility for such assistance under section 1396p(c) of this title, shall ... (ii) in the case of such a statement, representation, concealment, failure, conversion, or provision of counsel or assistance by any other person, be guilty of a misdemeanor and upon conviction thereof fined not more than $10,000 or imprisoned for not more than one year, or both.

42 U.S.C. § 1320a-7b(a).

While section 4734 was in conference, the Congressional Research Service ("CRS") prepared a memorandum, dated July 11, 1997, analyzing the legal and constitutional issues raised by the proposed language of section 4734. CRS expressed concern that the language would infringe the First Amendment, noting: "To the extent that the provision would prohibit counseling about legal activities, a court would seem likely to declare it unconstitutional."

Congress nevertheless passed the provision without modification, and the President signed section 4734 into law.

B. Procedural Background

Plaintiff filed the instant motion for a preliminary injunction on January 27, 1998. After a number of extensions and adjournments, Defendant now states that it will neither defend the constitutionality of 42 U.S.C. § 1320a-7b(a)(6) nor enforce its criminal provisions. On March 11, 1998, Attorney General Janet Reno notified the United States House of Representatives and the United States Senate that the Department of Justice would not enforce the aforementioned criminal provisions. Not surprisingly, Defendant now argues that a preliminary injunction is no longer needed.

In response, NYSBA filed opposition arguing that its members' free speech rights are still being chilled. Essentially, NYSBA argues that section 4734 is unconstitutional for the following reasons: (1) it violates the First Amendment because it unconstitutionally restricts free speech; (2) it violates the First Amendment because it is overly broad; and (3) it violates the Fifth Amendment because it is vague.

II. DISCUSSION

A. Standing

[The court concluded that the NYSBA did have standing to bring this action.]

B. Preliminary Injunction

In this circuit the standard for obtaining a preliminary injunction is well established. In order to obtain a preliminary injunction the movant must make an affirmative showing of: (1) irreparable harm; and either (2) likelihood of success on the merits; or (3) sufficiently serious questions going to the merits to make them a fair ground for litigation and a balance of hardships tipping decidedly in favor of the movant. See, e.g., Covino v. Patrissi, 967 F.2d 73, 77 (2d Cir. 1992); Resolution Trust Corp. v. Elman, 949 F.2d 624, 626 (2d Cir. 1991); Jackson Dairy, Inc. v. H.P. Hood & Sons, Inc., 596 F.2d 70, 72 (2d Cir. 1979). However, "where the moving party seeks to stay governmental action taken in the public interest pursuant to a statutory or regulatory scheme, the district court ... should not grant the injunction unless the moving party establishes, along with irreparable injury, a likelihood that he will succeed on the merits of his claim." Plaza Health Laboratories, Inc. v. Perales, 878 F.2d 577, 580 (2d Cir. 1989); see also Union Carbide Agricultural Products Co. v. Costle, 632 F.2d 1014, 1018 (2d Cir. 1980).

i. Irreparable Harm

As this Court recently noted, "[c]ourts in this circuit have repeatedly stated that '[p]erhaps the single most important prerequisite for the issuance of a preliminary injunction is a demonstration that if it is not granted the applicant is likely to suffer irreparable harm before a decision on the merits can be rendered.'" Nakatomi Investments v. City of Schenectady, 949 F. Supp. 988, 990 (N.D.N.Y. 1997) (quoting Borey v. National Union Fire Ins. Co., 934

F.2d 30, 34 (2d Cir. 1991)). Irreparable injury, moreover, means injury for which a monetary award cannot be adequate compensation. Jackson Dairy, 596 F.2d at 72 (citing Studebaker Corp. v. Gittlin, 360 F.2d 692, 698 (2d Cir. 1966), Foundry Srvs. Inc., v. Beneflux Corp., 206 F.2d 214, 216 (2d Cir. 1948)).

Turning to the first prong of this test, if the government's enforcement of section 4734 will deprive Plaintiff of its First Amendment rights, this constitutes per se irreparable injury to Plaintiff. Elrod v. Burns, 427 U.S. 347, 49 L. Ed. 2d 547, 96 S. Ct. 2673 (1976). In *Elrod v. Burns*, the Supreme Court instructed that "[t]he loss of First Amendment freedoms, for even minimal periods of time, unquestionably constitutes irreparable injury." 427 U.S. at 373; see also Paulsen v. County of Nassau, 925 F.2d 65, 68 (2d Cir. 1991) (stating that even a temporary abridgment of the First Amendment right to free expression constitutes irreparable injury).

Here, the Attorney General states that the Department of Justice will not enforce section 1320a-7b(a)(6)'s criminal provisions. The Attorney General argues that NYSBA members face no threat of criminal sanction. As a result, Plaintiff will not suffer any irreparable harm, thus obviating Plaintiff's need for injunctive relief. Defendant's argument, however, misses the point. . . .

Here, the parties have staked out starkly opposing positions on the issue of whether a threat of enforcement presently exists. The Attorney General assures the Court that she will not enforce section 4734. Plaintiff responds that the Attorney General's statements do not eliminate the threat of future enforcement, and, in fact, may not represent the position of the President of the United States–who has been silent regarding his intentions concerning enforcement.

Fortunately, the Court need not resolve this issue definitively because the Court finds that Plaintiff will suffer injury irrespective of the imminent enforcement of section 4734.

Governmental infringement of the First Amendment does not exist merely in the imposition of criminal sanctions. As the Supreme Court noted in *Elrod*, the First Amendment is implicated whenever free speech is "either threatened or in fact being impaired at the time the relief [is] sought." Elrod, 96 S. Ct. At 2689. . . .

The irreparable harm that exists here is the potential for self censorship among NYSBA members. NYSBA members have an ethical obligation as attorneys to respect and uphold the law. In fact, Plaintiff's affidavits state that section 4734 actually has resulted in NYSBA members refraining from providing certain counsel and assistance to clients. Furthermore, Defendant provides no assurance that NYSBA members will not be prosecuted on some future date or that state Medicaid fraud units will also not enforce section 4734.

Accordingly, inasmuch as section 4734 remains part of the laws of the United States, which NYSBA members are ethically bound to uphold, the limitation on free speech found in section 4734 constitutes irreparable injury to Plaintiff. Thus, Plaintiff has satisfied the first of the two elements required for a preliminary injunction.

ii. Likelihood of Success

The second element requires the Court to determine whether Plaintiff is likely to succeed on the merits of its constitutional challenge. As this Court stated in *Nakatomi Investments*, "it has long been axiomatic that once a party shows that a regulation deprives them of a protected First Amendment interest, the burden shifts to the Government to justify the infringement." 949 F. Supp. At 990 (citing Members of City Council v. Taxpayers for Vincent, 466 U.S. 789, 803 n.22, 80 L. Ed. 2d 772, 104 S. Ct. 2118 (1984), City of Los Angeles v. Preferred Communications, Inc., 476 U.S. 488, 496, 90 L. Ed. 2d 480, 106 S. Ct. 2034 (1986)).

At this time, however, it does not appear that the government contests the unconstitutionality of section 4734. Therefore, the Court must find that Plaintiff will likely succeed on the merits of its claims.

III. CONCLUSION

For the foregoing reasons, Plaintiff's Motion for a Preliminary Injunction is GRANTED. It is hereby ORDERED that pending final judgment, the United States, its agents, servants, employees, attorneys, and all persons in active concert and participation with Defendant are enjoined from commencing, maintaining, or otherwise taking action to enforce 42 U.S.C. § 1320a-7b(a)(6).

IT IS SO ORDERED.

Medicaid Trusts. The Medicaid-qualifying device that was Congress's biggest target in enacting OBRA 93 is the so-called "Medicaid qualifying trust" (MQT). These are irrevocable inter vivos trusts created by a Medicaid applicant or beneficiary (or spouse) giving the trustee the power to apply income and/or principal for the benefit of the grantor or spouse. Prior to enactment of the federal Medicaid Qualifying Trusts rules of 1986, these self-settled trusts did qualify for Medicaid because under conventional trust law the discretionary character of the trust made the beneficiary's interest immune from creditor claims. Under the 1986 MQT law (which is actually a misnomer since it *dis*qualifies such trusts), the income and principal of this type of trust are considered available to the settlor-beneficiary to the full extent that the trustee *could* pay them to the beneficiary. Trusts created by a third party for the applicant (or spouse) are treated more favorably. Only the income and/or principal actually paid to the applicant (or spouse) counts as available to the beneficiary.

Seeking further to tighten perceived abuses of Medicaid, Congress repealed the 1986 MQT rules and substituted a highly complex and somewhat ambiguous set of rules. OBRA 93, which applies only to trusts created after August 10, 1993, tightens the rules for MQTs in two important ways. First, it expands the definition of "trusts" to include any arrangement that is "similar to a trust."[16] Second, the statute defines a self-settled trust, whose assets will be deemed to be available to the applicant, as any inter vivos trust created by the applicant, his or her spouse, a person (including a court) with legal authority to act on behalf of the applicant (or spouse), or a person acting at the applicant's (or spouse's) direction or request, where the trusts assets were provided by the applicant (or spouse). This expansive definition includes trusts created by a guardian, conservator, or attorney-in-fact acting under a power of attorney. If the trust is revocable by the applicant, its principal is considered an available asset and income paid to the applicant is considered available to the applicant. For irrevocable trusts, income and principal will be deemed available to the applicant to the extent that it *may* be paid to or applied for the benefit of the applicant. This means that the assets and income of a self-settled discretionary trust in which the trustee has complete discretion to pay principal and income to the applicant will count fully as available to the Medicaid applicant. Actual use of income and/or principal from the trust for any other purpose triggers the asset-transfer rules outlined above.[17]

There are three major exceptions to these rules. First, a trust for a disabled person under age 65 which contains that person's assets and is created by that person's parent, grandparent, legal guardian, or a court, will be exempt if the state will receive all the property remaining in the trust, up to the amount paid as Medicaid assistance, when the disabled person dies. Second, a trust for a disabled person (regardless of age) will be exempt if it meets several conditions. It must be created by a non-profit organization that maintains a separate account for each beneficiary, and the beneficiary's account must be established solely

---

16. 42 U.S.C. § 1396p(d)(6). The Health Care Financing Administration, which is the federal agency overseeing the Medicaid program, has defined "similar to a trust" to include "escrow accounts, investment accounts, pension funds, and other similar devices managed by an individual or entity with fiduciary obligations." HCFA State Medicaid Manual § 3259.1(A)(2).

17. OBRA 93 left open several interpretative issues. One of these concerned the status of income-only trusts, that is, irrevocable self-settled trusts from which only income can be paid to the applicant. On December 23, 1993, the HCFA issued a statement clarifying the law on this point. According to the HCFA, if no portion of the corpus can be distributed to the applicant, then no portion of the corpus will be deemed available to the applicant. For discussion, see Ira Stewart Wiesner, OBRA '93 and Medicaid: Asset Transfer, Trust Availability, and Estate Recovery Statutory Analysis in Context, 47 Soc. Sec. Rep. Ser. 757, 774-775 (1995).

for his or her benefit by his or her parent, grandparent, guardian, or a court. Remaining assets at the beneficiary's death must be paid to the state up to the amount paid as Medicaid benefits. Third, trusts created by the applicant's benefit are exempt where they are composed only of his or her pension, Social Security, or other income, if at the beneficiary's death the state will be reimbursed for the amount of Medicaid assistance.

Trusts created by a third person for the applicant's benefit are treated differently. Income and principal from such trusts are considered available to the applicant when they are "actually available" and when the applicant has "a legal interest in a liquidated sum and has the legal ability to make such sum available for support and maintenance." 45 C.F.R. § 233.20(a)(3)(ii)(D). Under this language, there is a crucial distinction between a discretionary trust, on the one hand, and a mandatory or support trust, on the other. Only the latter pose problems for Medicaid eligibility.

b. Other Financing Strategies

For the vast majority of elderly persons, Medicare and Medicaid are inadequate solutions to the problem of financing custodial and long-term skilled care. As already noted, Medicare does not cover long-term custodial care, nor does it cover skilled care in a skilled nursing facility beyond a limited time (currently 100 days). With respect to the services that it does cover, it has a substantial copayment element for participants. Medicaid *is* available to pay the costs of long-term custodial care but only for the indigent. Most elderly persons, then, need other means to finance such care. We will look briefly at the primary financing devices available to the middle-class elderly person who can rely neither on personal wealth nor government benefits to defray all or even most of the costs of long-term care.

Insurance. Perhaps the most obvious available means of financing the high cost of health care is private insurance. Two types of insurance should be mentioned, so-called "Medigap" insurance and long-term care insurance. A third arrangement involving insurance, also discussed below, is an accelerated benefit settlement.

Medigap insurance. Medigap insurance is only a limited financing device that does not answer the problem for those who need or will need long-term care. As its name suggests, it is designed instead to cover the gaps created by Medicare's deductibles and copayment obligations. Since 1992, federal law has standardized Medigap insurance policies, so that now persons may choose one of ten different packages with varying degrees of coverage. Even at their most comprehensive level, however, Medigap insurance does not fill all the gaps in Medicare's coverage. By far, the most important of these remaining gaps are custodial care and long-term institutionalized skilled care.

Long-Term Care Insurance. For elderly persons who do not qualify for Medicaid, most of the costs of long-term care are paid through a second form of private insurance, long-term care insurance. The market for such insurance has increased dramatically in recent years. Between 1983 and 1988, the number of companies selling long-term care insurance rose from 16 to more than 80.[18] Today, in the State of Florida alone, more than 470 companies are licensed to sell long-term care insurance.[19] Unlike Medigap insurance, long-term care insurance policies are not standardized, and there are considerable differences among the policies that various insurers offer. Policies usually cover skilled care in a skilled nursing facility and intermediate care. Most elderly residents of nursing homes require custodial care rather than skilled medical care. It is important to be clear, then, whether a policy covers institutionalized custodial care. For some elderly persons, however, custodial care need not require that they be institutionalized. Home health care services, such as visits by nurses, physical therapists, or home health aides, are not always covered by long-term care insurance, so, again, it is important to clarify whether the policy includes this form of custodial care.

There are several problems with long-term care insurance. First, nearly all policies have financial limitations. Long-term care insurance does not pay all costs but only up to a fixed daily amount. The duration of coverage is also fixed, and longer periods of coverage carry with them higher premiums. Second, policies exclude preexisting conditions and conditions that appear within the first six months of coverage. Third, and most important, long-term care insurance is very expensive. The older the insured person is, the higher the cost. People in their 60s and 70s can expect to pay thousands of dollars per year in premiums. Thus, despite the fact that long-term care insurance is growing, it is not a complete answer to the problem of financing care for the elderly.

Accelerated Life Insurance Benefits. A third method of using insurance to finance health care is through accelerated benefits on existing life insurance policies. Under an accelerated benefits rider, the insurer pays the policyowner a percentage of the death benefit before the insured's death. The typical rider states that payments will be made only to persons expected to die within six months to a year. Consequently, this arrangement is less a means of paying for long-term care than it is for the terminally ill, such as AIDS or cancer victims, to liquidate their existing life insurance policies.

---

18. Diane Belinkie, Piercing Together Health Care Protection: Medicare v. Medicaid v. Medigap, Fam. Advoc., Summer 1993, at 42, 44-45.

19. Glenn Singer, The Storm to Come: Have You Planned for Long-Term Care?, Ft. Lauderdale Sun-Sentinel, Feb. 14, 2000, at 16.

An advantageous feature of accelerated death benefits is that they are not included as taxable income for federal income tax purposes if three requirements are met. First, the payment can only be made to a person who is terminally ill. Second, the amount paid must equal the amount deducted from the policy's final death benefit minus a discount which can be no greater than the interest rate the insurer charges on policy loans. Third, the cash surrender value remaining after payment must be proportional to the amount of the remaining death benefit.

Insurance companies began to offer accelerated death benefits only in 1990, largely in response to the growing interest in viatical settlements. Under a viatical settlement (so called because of the ancient Roman practice of *viaticum*, in which officials received money and supplies before departing on risky journeys to the far-flung corners of the Roman empire) a financial intermediary purchases an existing life insurance policy from a terminally ill person and pays a portion of the policy's face amount in return for being named the beneficiary. A viatical settlement is necessary where the policy itself does not contain an accelerated benefits rider. Because their discount rate usually is greater than that allowed under federal tax law, viatical settlements may not receive the favorable tax treatment given to most accelerated death benefits. On the other hand, not many life insurance policies include accelerated benefits riders.

Home Equity Conversion. Many elderly persons lack sufficient liquid assets either to fund a trust for medical and custodial care or to buy long-term care insurance. They may well find themselves in the position of being "cash poor and house rich." For older Americans who are home owners, the house is typically their most valuable asset. They have likely paid off the mortgage, and the house's market value may have significantly appreciated since the owner first bought it. Home equity conversion allows an elderly homeowner in this position to use home equity as an income-producing asset without selling the house. If the person requires custodial care but is medically able to continue living at home, home equity conversion may be an effective means of financing long-term care.

Perhaps the most popular form of home equity conversion is the reverse mortgage. The reverse mortgage is a lending arrangement in which the borrower receives either a line of credit or periodic payments in exchange for a security interest on his or her house. The amount of the loan increases over time as more payments are made and interest is added to the principal loan amount. The amount of the loan is calculated on the basis of the house's appraised value, its expected appreciation, and the owner-borrower's life expectancy. The borrower does not have to repay the loan until he or she dies or sells the house, and the proceeds from sale are usually used to repay the loan. The mortgage is called "reverse" because, unlike the conventional "forward" mortgage, the principal amount is highest at the end, not the beginning, and interest is backloaded.

The terms and costs of reverse mortgage vary considerably depending upon the program under which the mortgage is offered, the duration of the loan, the borrower's age, and other factors. Eligibility requirements usually restrict borrowers to persons 62 and older owning a single-family dwelling or FHA-approved condominium. There are, however, no minimum or maximum income or asset limits. See generally Celeste M. Hammond, Reverse Mortgages: A Financial Planning Device for the Elderly, 1 Elder L.J. 75 (1993).

In 1996, the Federal National Mortgage Association ("Fannie Mae"), the nation's largest supplier of home mortgage capital, began to offer its own version of reverse mortgaging. This will no doubt spur competition among reverse mortgage lenders. See Jay Romano, For Reverse Mortgages, A Fannie Mae Imprimatur, N.Y. Times, June 23, 1996, sec. 3, at 9.

2. Planning for the Disabled

Parents and other relatives who have disabled children face a similar planning dilemma to that confronting the elderly. They want to provide for the needs of such children without impairing the child's eligibility for public assistance benefits. Trusts for disabled children are a common strategy that parents use for this purpose. To what extent will a disabled child's income and/or principal interest in a trust affect public assistance eligibility, and to what extent are trusts for disabled children liable for claims by the state? The *Myers* case which follows illustrates the standard judicial analysis of these questions. To provide some background for the problem, we first include the following excerpt.

Randall D. Van Dolson, Medicaid Eligibility Rules and Trusts for Disabled Children

133 Tr. & Est. 51, 51-52, 55 (1994)

A significant planning goal of a parent with a disabled child is to provide for the supplemental needs of the child following the parent's death without affecting the child's eligibility for need-based governmental support programs such as Supplemental Security Income ("SSI") and Medicaid. For many parents of moderate wealth, such programs are an important financial resource without which the family's other resources, during the lifetime of the parents or following their deaths, would be rapidly depleted. Since such programs provide support for persons who are, in effect, destitute, assets owned by or available to a disabled child must be spent-down to pay the cost of care and services which otherwise would be provided by the government. Only after the assets have been depleted will the child be eligible for government assistance.

. . . Since such programs provide little more than bare necessities, many parents view the child's best interest to be served by a strategy which supplements, but does not supplant, available government assistance.

Such a strategy should not be viewed as contrary to public policy or interest. Supplemental assistance enables a disabled child to enjoy a quality of life not available within the constraints of government support programs. Unless able to provide for the child's supplemental needs, many parents would not provide for the child at all. Government assistance would continue to provide basic support, but the child's quality of life would not be enhanced. . . .

The Medicaid program, administered by the states and jointly financed by federal and state funds, provides medical assistance, including institutionalization, to certain disabled persons whose available income and resources are limited. In those states where Medicaid will pay the cost of independent housing, the benefits over the lifetime of a disabled child who lives in a community setting are substantial. Resources affect Medicaid eligibility if actually available or to the extent an individual has the ability to make them available. . . .

Before June 1, 1986, an individual could transfer assets to an irrevocable trust which authorized the trustee to distribute income and principal to the individual. Because the trust funds could be distributed to or used for the benefit of the individual only in the discretion of the trustee, the trust was not considered an available resource for Medicaid eligibility purposes and upon expiration of the appropriate transfer penalty period the individual could qualify for Medicaid benefits. Often the transfer was to a friendly trustee, an arrangement which, in effect, might not significantly curtail the individual's control of and benefit from the transferred property.

The Medicaid Qualifying Trust ("MQT") rules, effective June 1, 1986, were enacted to curb the perceived abuse associated with such self-created trusts. Under the MQT rules the assets of an irrevocable trust established other than by Will by an individual or an individual's spouse were considered available to the full extent of the trustee's authority to make distributions of income and/or principal to the individual. If discretion were limited to income, the principal of the trust was disregarded as a resource in determining eligibility.

The MQT rules did not affect discretionary trusts established by a parent for a disabled child and funded with the parent's, not the child's, assets. . . .

Section 13611 of OBRA-93 [42 U.S.C.§ 1396p] . . . repeals the Medicaid Qualifying Trust provisions. . . . While the [OBRA 93] rules affect self-created trusts traditionally used to qualify persons who are disabled by the aging process for Medicaid benefits, they should not affect the eligibility of an adult disabled child who is a beneficiary of a discretionary spendthrift trust created by a parent and funded with the parent's assets.

Myers v. Department of Social and Rehabilitation Services

866 P.2d 1052 (Kan. 1994)

HOLMES, C.J. The Kansas Department of Social and Rehabilitation Services (SRS) appeals from a judgment of the district court holding Darrell E. Myers, Jr., was the beneficiary of a discretionary trust and that the assets of the trust could not be considered as resources available to Myers in determining whether he was eligible for medical assistance. The Court of Appeals affirmed the judgment of the district court in an unpublished decision decided May 28, 1993. We granted the petition for review of SRS and now affirm the Court of Appeals and the district court.

The facts are not in dispute. In 1981, Caroline H. Myers executed her will, which provided for a trust for the care, support, and maintenance of her son, Darrell E. Myers, Jr. She bequeathed the sum of $110,000 to the trust. Upon her son's death, the principal and any undistributed income were to be distributed to Caroline's daughter and granddaughter, or the survivor thereof. Caroline H. Myers died in 1989. The trust was funded on November 20, 1989.

Darrell E. Myers, Jr., had been receiving public medical assistance from the State prior to the death of Mrs. Myers and the funding of the trust in 1989. Myers had apparently suffered from severe mental and physical disabilities for several years although the record does not indicate when he began receiving public assistance. In July of 1990, SRS terminated Myers' medical assistance when he failed to return an annual eligibility review form. Myers reapplied for assistance in November of 1990, but SRS denied the application, claiming Myers had resources which exceeded the eligibility level established by SRS regulations. The denial notice stated that assets held in trust for Myers were considered available to meet his medical needs.

After several reapplications and denials, Myers appealed the SRS decision of October 25, 1991, denying him medical assistance. The decision of SRS was affirmed by the administrative hearing officer on January 6, 1992, and his decision was affirmed by the State Appeals Committee on March 24, 1992.

In April of 1992, Myers filed a petition for judicial review. The district court, after reviewing the record and hearing arguments of counsel, issued its judgment finding the trust established in Caroline H. Myers' will to be a discretionary trust. Because neither the principal nor income were available to Myers, SRS could not consider the trust assets in determining Myers eligibility for public medical assistance. SRS timely appealed the district court's decision, which was affirmed by the Court of Appeals.

The issue before us on review is whether the district court and Court of Appeals erred in determining that the Myers trust is a discretionary trust in which the assets are considered unavailable to Myers for the purpose of determining his eligibility for public medical assistance. The question on appeal is the meaning and intent of the trust language set forth in Caroline H. Myers' will. Our decision will control whether SRS may consider the trust principal and income "available" for purposes of determining Myers' eligibility for public medical assistance.

The will of Caroline H. Myers provides in pertinent part:

> In the event my husband does not survive me then all the rest, residue remainder of my property, of which I shall die seized or possessed, shall be divided and set apart by my Executors into the following shares:
>
> 1) The sum of one hundred and ten thousand ($110,000.00) dollars in trust to my trustee hereinafter named on the terms and conditions hereinafter stated *for the lifetime use and benefit of my son, Darrell E. Meyers [sic], Jr.* . . .
>
> A) In the event my son predeceases me I direct my Executor to divide his bequest equally and distribute it to my daughter and granddaughter or the survivors of them. In the event my granddaughter predeceases me, I direct my Executor to distribute her bequest to my daughter. In the event my daughter predeceases me, I direct my Executor to distribute her share to my granddaughter.
>
> B) *During my son's lifetime, my trustee shall hold, manage, invest and reinvest, collect the income there from* [sic] *any* [sic] *pay over so much or all the net income and principal to my son as my trustee deems advisable for his care, support, maintenance, emergencies and welfare.* At my son's death I direct this trust for his benefit be terminated and the principal and any undistributed net income be distributed in accordance with paragraph A above.
>
> *FIRST*: I hereby name and appoint the Overland Park State Bank and Trust Company of Overland Park, Kansas as my trustee.
>
> *SECOND*: The principal of the trust hereinabove created and the interest resulting herefore [*sic*] while in the hands of the Trustee shall not be subject to any conveyance, transfer or assignment, or be pledged as security for any debt by the beneficiary, and the same shall not be subject to any claim by and [*sic*] creditor of the beneficiary through legal process or otherwise. (Emphasis added.)

K.S.A. 1992 Supp. 39-708c (b) grants the Secretary of SRS the power and duty to determine general policies and to adopt rules and regulations relating to the forms of social welfare administered by SRS. K.S.A. 1992 Supp. 39-709(e) provides that medical assistance shall be granted to residents whose income and resources do not exceed the levels prescribed by the Secretary. K.A.R. 30-6-106 sets forth the general rules for consideration of resources and reads in relevant part:

> (c)(1) Resources shall be considered available both when actually available and when the applicant or recipient has the legal ability to make them available.[20] A

20. This language is similar to that used in the federal Medicaid regulation (45 C.F.R. § 233.20(a)(3)(ii)(D)). Eds.

> resource shall be considered unavailable when there is a legal impediment that precludes the disposal of the resource. The applicant or recipient shall pursue reasonable steps to overcome the legal impediment unless it is determined that the cost of pursuing legal action would be more than the applicant or recipient would gain, or the likelihood of succeeding in the legal action would be unfavorable to the applicant or recipient.

Pursuant to K.A.R. 30-6-107, an individual having non-exempt resources in excess of $2,000 is not eligible for public medical assistance.

The sole issue before this court is the interpretation, as a matter of law, of the meaning and intent of the language used by Caroline H. Myers in the trust provisions of her will. Both parties confine their arguments primarily to the language which reads:

> During my son's lifetime, my trustee shall hold, manage, invest and reinvest, collect the income there from [*sic*] any [*sic*] pay over so much or all the net income and principal to my son as my trustee deems advisable for his care, support, maintenance, emergencies and welfare.

. . . . SRS contends that the Myers trust is a support trust which requires the trustee to inquire into the basic support needs of the beneficiary and provide for those needs. As such, SRS argues the trust is an available resource within the meaning of K.A.R. 30-6-106(c)(1).

Myers, on the other hand, argues that the language of the trust is unambiguous in its creation of a discretionary trust. Thus, the trust language gives the trustee full discretion to decide whether payments from the trust income or principal are advisable. Because the trustee has complete authority to withhold all trust assets, the trust is not an available resource for Myers. Additionally, the trustee of the Myers trust, although not a party to this action, maintains that pursuant to the terms of the trust, the trustee has a responsibility to the remaindermen as well as to Myers.

The Court of Appeals, in affirming the district court's ruling that the Myers trust was discretionary and not an available resource of the beneficiary, relied primarily on this Court's recent decision in *State ex rel. Secretary of SRS v. Jackson*, 249 Kan. 635, 822 P.2d 1033 (1991) (*Jackson II*).

Both parties cite *Jackson II* as authority for their respective positions. In *Jackson II*, this court was similarly called upon to decide whether trust funds were an available resource for purposes of determining eligibility for public medical assistance. Carrie Jackson was the beneficiary of a trust fund created by her grandfather. During the period she was receiving nominal support from the trust, Jackson was also receiving public assistance benefits. The State contended that the trust fund providing support for Jackson was an available resource to her and was seeking reimbursement from Jackson, pursuant to

K.S.A. 39-719b, for public assistance benefits paid to her in an amount in excess of $35,000.

In *State ex rel. Secretary of SRS v. Jackson*, 15 Kan. App. 2d 126, 803 P.2d 1045 (1990) (*Jackson I*), the Court of Appeals determined that the trust was purely discretionary in nature, and thus the trust assets were not an available resource to Jackson. However, in *Jackson II*, this court modified the Court of Appeals' ruling, concluding that the language in the trust instrument treated the trust income differently from the trust principal. The Jackson trust read in relevant part:

> (A) During the lifetime of Carrie Conner Jackson, the Trustees, in their uncontrolled discretion, shall pay to Carrie Conner Jackson the net income of the Trust. In addition, the Trustees may pay to Carrie Conner Jackson, from the principal of the Trust from time to time, such amount or amounts as the Trustees in their uncontrolled discretion, may determine is necessary for the purposes of her health, education, support and maintenance. 249 Kan. at 641.

In construing the language of the trust instrument, this Court reasoned:

> Stripped down, the provision states the Trustees shall pay the net income and, in addition, may pay from the principal. The payment of the net income is not tied to any determination of need as are payments from the principal. . . .
>
> True, the term "in their uncontrolled discretion" is used in the provisions relating to the payment of income and principal, but its usage in payment of income provisions is inconsistent with the "shall pay" language except perhaps as to the form of the payment. . . . "Shall pay" so interpreted results in the payment of income not being a discretionary trust provision. 249 Kan. at 641-42.

The court concluded that the income of the trust was a resource available to Jackson but that the principal was not.

Although in *Jackson II* this court relied primarily upon the usage and meaning of the two terms "shall" and may," the court also raised legitimate social policy concerns in stating that "public assistance funds are ever in short supply, and public policy demands they be restricted to those without resources of their own." 249 Kan. at 644. While reliance on such public policy is appropriate in an applicable case, nothing in *Jackson II* indicates or implies that such policy overrides the intent of a testator or settlor if a discretionary trust is established.

SRS maintains that *Jackson II* is controlling of this case. Specifically, SRS argues that the phrase "as my trustee deems advisable" in the Myers trust is inconsistent with the language of "shall pay." SRS contends that under the holding in *Jackson II*, the "shall pay" language should control, limiting the trustee's discretion to how and when payments are to be made. SRS maintains that the language in the Myers will creates a support trust, requiring the trustee to inquire into and provide for the basic support needs of the beneficiary.

In reaching its conclusions, SRS reads the questioned language of the will as if the words "shall" and "pay" must be read together without consideration of the subsequent language "as my trustee deems advisable." We are not convinced such conclusion is justified when all the language is read and considered together.

Myers' reliance on *Jackson II* is based upon obvious differences in not only the language of the Jackson and Myers trusts but also the manner in which similar language in the two documents was used. Both trusts use discretionary language, "as my trustee deems advisable" here, and as the trustee "may determine is necessary' in the Jackson trust. Also, both trusts use the nondiscretionary term "shall" and in addition the Jackson trust used the word "may" in referring to payments from principal. Unfortunately, here the similarities end. Unlike the Jackson trust, the Myers language regarding income and principal is contained in the same sentence. Also, the nondiscretionary language, "shall", and the discretionary language "as my trustee deems advisable", occur in the same sentence. Thus, unlike the Jackson trust, the payment of both income and principal is tied to a determination of need and to the discretionary language "as my trustee deems advisable." . . . .

We now turn again to the specific language and intent of the Myers trust. In examining the language in the will of Caroline H. Myers it appears that she established the trust primarily for the care and support of her son. Specifically, the instrument states, "my trustee shall hold, manage, invest and reinvest, collect the income there from [*sic*] any [*sic*] pay over so much or all the net income and principal to my son as my trustee deems advisable for his care, support, maintenance, emergencies and welfare."

SRS contends that the word "shall" applies equally to the management of the trust, and the direction to pay, as well as to the language establishing the purposes for which the trust funds are to be paid. However, as Myers maintains, it is arguable that the word "shall" only applies to holding, managing, investing and reinvesting, and the collection of income; and that the balance of the sentence gives the trustee complete discretion to determine whether funds are to be paid out for Myers' support and maintenance.

The trial court in determining that the Myers will established a discretionary trust concluded:

> The trust created pursuant to the Will of Caroline H. Myers, in which Darrell E. Myers, Jr. is the beneficiary, is a discretionary trust. The trust provides that the trustee "shall . . . pay over so much or all the net income and principal as (it) deems advisable" for the care, support, maintenance, emergencies and welfare of Mr. Myers. It is clear that the trustee has discretion as to what, if any, of the trust funds are to be paid to or for the benefit of Mr. Myers. The Court is not persuaded by the argument of Respondent that the word "shall" mandates the trustee to make

> payments to Mr. Myers. Once the trustee decides, in its discretion, to release funds to Mr. Myers, it is at that point that it "shall" make the payment; until such discretionary determination is made, however, the trustee is under no duty to pay any portion of the net income or principal to Mr. Myers. The trustee is given the discretion to pay over "so much or all" of the trust funds to Mr. Myers, which clearly indicates that the trustee is under no duty to pay a specific sum or any sum at all. It is therefore the conclusion of the Court that the trust established by Caroline H. Myers is a discretionary trust and not an "available resource" that can be used to determine eligibility for state assistance, until such trust funds are actually paid to and received by Darrell E. Myers, Jr.

We agree with the trial court's reasoning. The Myers trust directs the trustee to pay out so much of the income and principal as, in the trustees' discretion, it deems advisable for Myers' support. We conclude this language creates a discretionary trust. The nondiscretionary language of "shall"pertains primarily to the management functions of the trust and does not control or override the discretionary language of "as my trustee deems advisable,"which pertains to whether payment of net income or principal will be made at all and, if so, the amount and purpose of any such payment. Neither the beneficiary nor any creditor can compel the trustee to pay any trust income or principal to the beneficiary, and SRS may not consider the trust assets to be resources available to Myers in determining whether Myers qualifies for medical assistance.

Our determination would appear to be consistent with the intent of Caroline H. Myers. In her will she directs the trustee at the death of her son to distribute "the principal and any undistributed net income" to the remaindermen. This language indicates that Caroline H. Myers did not presume that the trust principal would necessarily be exhausted. The record reveals that Myers was receiving public assistance prior to the death of his mother and she undoubtedly was aware of such assistance. At the time of this action, Myers was a resident of Johnson County Residential Care Facility. The record indicates that in 1991, the daily charge for Myers' care was $75 and there was additional monthly expense of approximately $600 for prescription medications. At that rate of expense, the trust fund would be exhausted in less than three and one-half years. We do not believe that exhausting the trust funds in this manner would be consistent with the purpose of the Myers trust.

At the time of Caroline H. Myers' death, her son was 50 years of age. The Myers trust was established to assist in the care and support of Myers during his "lifetime." This purpose cannot be met by a complete exhaustion of the trust assets in a short period of time or if complete discretionary authority was not placed in the trustee. Because the Myers trust is discretionary in nature, the trustee is allowed complete and uncontrolled discretion to allocate trust funds if and when it deems advisable. Only if it can be demonstrated that the trustee is abusing its discretion by acting arbitrarily, dishonestly, or improperly may the trustee be required to distribute funds. See *Jennings v. Murdock*, 220 Kan. 182, 201, 553 P.2d 846 (1976).

The judgment of the Court of Appeals affirming the judgment of the district court is affirmed. The judgment of the district court is affirmed.

Notes

1. *Liability of Trusts to State Agencies Providing Care to the Disabled.* There has been considerable litigation in recent years concerning an issue closely related to the Medicaid eligibility question posed by *Myers*: the right of a state to reimbursement from a trust for the care of an institutionalized beneficiary. In the case of self-settled trusts, courts have generally applied the conventional trust law rules governing creditors rights in self-settled trusts and allowed the state to reach as much of the trust estate as could have been paid to the settlor. The revocable or irrevocable character of the trust is irrelevant. See State v. Hawes, 564 N.Y.S.2d 637 (App. Div. 1991).

Where, as is usually the case, the trust is created by a third person, the standard analysis has been the same as that used in *Myers*: the trust's liability depends on whether the trust is a discretionary trust or a support trust. If it is a discretionary trust, then the state's claim is denied on the ground that the beneficiary lacks an ascertainable interest in income or principal that is subject to creditor claims. See, e.g., Miller v. Department of Mental Health, 442 N.W.2d 617 (Mich. 1989); First Nat'l Bank v. Dep't of Health & Mental Hygiene, 399 A.2d 891 (Md. 1979). These cases follow the general principles of creditor rights that we will study in greater detail infra Chapter 14, Part A.

Most of the trust instruments involved in these cases combine trustee discretion with a support purpose, creating what has been called a "discretionary support trust." The results of the cases in which the courts have analyzed whether such trusts are support or discretionary trusts have been rather unpredictable. The hybrid character of these trusts has led some courts to focus instead on whether the settlor intended the trust to support the institutionalized beneficiary or merely to supplement other sources of support, including government assistance. If the court finds that the settlor intended to create a supplemental needs trust, then the state's claim is usually denied. See, e.g., Lang v. Dept. of Public Welfare, 528 A.2d 1335 (Pa. 1987); In re Estate of Escher, 407 N.Y.S.2d 106 (Surr. Ct. 1978), *aff'd*, 426 N.Y.S.2d 1008 (App. Div. 1980), *aff'd sub nom.* In re Gross, 420 N.E.2d 91 (N.Y. 1981). *Question:* How would the trust instrument in the *Myers* case have fared under this approach?

The differences in the approaches that courts have taken to this question should lead the practitioner who is planning for a disabled person to be especially cautious in drafting the trust instrument. For guidance, see Clifton B.

Kruse, Jr., Discretionary Trusts: Insulating Discretionary Trust Assets for Elders and Incapacitated Persons from Consideration by Medicaid and Other Public Support Providers, 17 ACTEC Notes 26 (1991); Mayer Y. Silber, The Effect of a Trust on the Eligibility or Liability of the Trust Beneficiary for Public Assistance, 26 Real Prop., Prob. & Tr. J. 133 (1991).

2. *Statutory Approval of Supplemental Needs Trusts.* In some states, recent statutes expressly authorize the use of supplemental needs trusts for persons with disabilities. These statutes, however, carefully define the terms and scope of permissible trusts. The New York statute, for example, defines such trusts as discretionary trusts created by someone other than the beneficiary or the beneficiary's spouse, where the beneficiary is a chronically and severely disabled person. The statute shelters the income and principal of such trusts from providers of government health-care benefits where the trust instrument "clearly evidences the creator's intent to supplement, not supplant, impair or diminish, government benefits or assistance for which the beneficiary may otherwise be eligible or which the beneficiary may be receiving . . . ." Upon the beneficiary's death, the state is entitled to full reimbursement from the trust principal for the total amount of medical benefits provided to the trust beneficiary. N.Y. EPTL § 7-1.12.

A recent Minnesota statute takes a somewhat different approach. It declares void as against public policy trust provisions that purport to convert the beneficiary's income or principal interest from an available to a non-available resource if the beneficiary is found eligible for or receives public assistance for medical care. It then declares valid under public policy a "supplemental needs trust," defined as a trust intended "to provide for the reasonable living expenses and other basic needs of a person with a disability when benefits from publicly funded benefit programs are not sufficient to provide adequately for those needs." Minn. Stat. Ann. § 501B.89(2)(d).

3. *Statutory Prohibition of Supplemental Needs Trusts.* In other states, statutes have taken the opposite direction, declaring trusts that exclude liability for state-supported health-care benefits to be void as a matter of public policy. See, e.g., N.J. Stat. Ann. § 30:4D-6(f).

4. *Statutory Discretionary-Support Trusts Under Uniforms Acts.* Under § 9(b) of the Uniform Custodial Trust Act, the custodial trustee for an incapacitated beneficiary is authorized to make expenditures for support "without regard to other support, income, or property of the beneficiary." Note that, in providing a statutory discretionary-support trust for an incapacitated surviving spouse on whose behalf an elective share is taken, the Uniform Probate Code incorporates the Uniform Custodial Trust Act. In doing so, however, the UPC makes certain adjustments to the Custodial Trust Act, including an adjustment to § 9(b). Under UPC § 2-212(c)(2), the custodial trustee is *required* to take "other support,

income, and property of the [incapacitated surviving spouse]" into account in making expenditures for support; enacting states, however, are given a choice as to whether the items to be taken into account include or do not include "benefits of medical or other forms of assistance from any state or federal government or governmental agency for which the [incapacitated surviving spouse] must qualify on the basis of need."

PART C. MAKING HEALTH-CARE DECISIONS

1. Advance Health-Care Directives

Advance health-care directives are written instructions concerning the level of medical care to be given a person in the event of incapacity. The two most important types of such directives are "living wills" and durable powers of attorney. Use of both of these instruments has grown dramatically in recent years, as the rising cost of medical care and growing sophistication of medical technology are leading more Americans to try prevent what they regard as the excessive prolonging of life. The two instruments are often confused with each other, and it is important to understand the difference between them.

Living Wills. Probably the better known of the two types of health-care directives, the living will is a legal document by which an individual gives treatment instructions in the event that he or she becomes either terminally ill or is in a persistent vegetative state. It details what forms of medical care the patient wants and under what circumstances he or she wants life-sustaining treatment either administered or, more commonly, terminated.

Nearly all states now recognize living wills by statute. The statutes vary considerably in their details, but they have two factors in common. First, the statutes provide that a living will is effective only in circumstances of the individual's incapacity. Second, the statutes permit the living will to be used to terminate life-sustaining treatment in the event of the declarant's terminal illness or persistent vegetative state. Living wills are not designed to be total health-care decisional instruments. If an individual has a chance of recovery, the living will is not effective. Virtually no statute permits a living will to authorize termination of life-sustaining treatment where the patient is neither terminally ill nor in a persistent vegetative state. Some statutes define the meaning of the terms "terminal" and "persistent vegetative state" clearly, while others leave them undefined.

The statutory formalities required for execution of a living will also vary. Most statutes require a living will to be witnessed; a few also require notarization. Witnesses are usually required to be disinterested, and in some states hospital personnel are forbidden from serving as witnesses. Many states have statutory model forms, and a few states require the use of such forms.

Living will instructions are effective only if they are communicated to medical care providers, and hospitals now almost routinely provide living wills or other advance health-care directives to their patients. Under the federal Patient Self-Determination Act of 1990 (P.L. No. 101-508, § 4751, 104 Stat. 1388), hospitals and nursing homes are required to advise patients upon their admission of their rights under state law to refuse medical treatment.

While state law in nearly all states provides legal immunity to medical care providers who follow living will instructions, only a few states provide penalties for failure to obey them. See William Prip & Anna Moretti, Compliance: The Missing Component in Patient Autonomy Laws, Experience 4 (Spring 1996). A major 1995 study reported in the *Journal of the American Medical Association* (*JAMA*) found that many doctors ignore living will directions. Forty-nine percent of the patients who had stated that they did not want cardiopulmonary resuscitation did not receive the do-not-resuscitate (DNR) orders that they had requested. Those who did not receive such instructions had to wait a long time, in some cases more than two months, before receiving them. See Susan Gilbert, Doctors Often Fail to Heed Wishes of the Dying Patient, N.Y. Times, November 22, 1995, at A1. Earlier empirical studies found that physicians are not well-informed about living wills,[21] but the *JAMA* study indicated that this was not the case. The patients' wishes were not being honored, despite the fact that they had been communicated to the doctors. Another study found physicians evenly divided over their willingness to defer to a living will whose directives were expressed in general wording.[22] These findings cast doubt on the efficacy of living wills as an advance health-care directive. For recent evidence that living wills are still honored more in the breach than in the observancc, see Denise Grady, At Life's End, Many Patients Are Denied Peaceful Passing, N.Y. Times, May 29, 2000, at A1.

Sample Living Will[23]

I, __________, declare that if I become unable to make my own health care decisions, as determined by my attending physician, such decisions, including

21. See Marion Danis et al., A Prospective Study of Advance Directives for Life-Sustaining Care, 324 New Eng. J. Med. 882 (1991); Joel N. Zinberg, Decisions for the Dying: An Empirical Study of Physicians' Responses to Advance Directives, 13 Vt. L. Rev. 445 (1989).

22. Philip G. Peters, Jr., et al., Physician Willingness to Withhold Tube Feeding After *Cruzan*: An Empirical Study, 57 Mo. L. Rev. 831 (1992).

23. This form is reprinted from U.S. Trust Company, Practical Drafting—Trust and Will Provisions. This form is described by the publisher as a "common law" document and as having been prepared on the assumption that applicable state law recognizes its validity and imposes no requirements on its use; should such restrictions or requirements exist, the form must be modified.

those to accept or refuse any treatment, service or procedure used to diagnose, treat or care for me, and to withhold or withdraw life-sustaining measures, shall be made in accordance with my wishes which follow.

I do not want my life prolonged by life-sustaining measures, but want to be allowed to die naturally and to be given all care necessary to make me comfortable and to relieve pain:

1. If I am diagnosed as having an incurable and irreversible terminal condition; or
2. If I am diagnosed as being permanently unconscious or in a persistent vegetative state; or
3. If I am diagnosed as having an incurable and irreversible condition which is not terminal but which causes me to experience severe and progressive physical or mental deterioration and loss of capacities I value, so that the burdens of continued life (with treatment) are greater than the benefits I experience.

In the circumstances described, (a) artificially provided fluids and nutrition, such as by feeding tube or intravenous infusion, should be withheld or withdrawn, (b) if I should suffer cardiac or respiratory arrest, cardiopulmonary resuscitation should not be provided and (c) any other medicine or medical procedures that may be available to prolong my life should not be used.

Any invalid or unenforceable direction shall not affect my other directions.

This document shall not limit the powers given to any existing or future health care agent designated by me.

I understand the purpose and effect of this document and sign it after careful deliberation, this ___ day of _________, 19__.

________________________(L.S.)

Residing at: ______________________________

Each of the undersigned declares that the person who signed this document did so in his or her presence; that said person is personally known to him or her and appears to be of sound mind and acting willingly and free from duress or undue influence; and that he or she is 18 years of age or older and is not designated as the persons's health care proxy.

_________________________ residing at ___________________________

_________________________ residing at ___________________________

—

Can living wills be made more effective? One solution might be to increase the information they contain. A lengthy form, published in the Journal of the American Medical Association, presents four scenarios ranging from irreversible coma to incapacity of unknown duration. See Linda L. Emanuel and Ezekiel J. Emanuel, The Medical Directive: A New Comprehensive Advance

Care Document, 261 JAMA 3288, 3290 (1989). For each scenario, the patient's wishes are recorded in a grid (reprinted here with permission):[24]

	I Want	I Do Not Want	I Am Undecided	I Want a Trial: If No Clear Improvement, Stop Treatment
1. Cardiopulmonary Resuscitation - if on the point of dying the use of drugs and electric shock to start the heart beating, and artificial breathing.				
2. Mechanical Breathing - breathing by a machine.				
3. Artificial Nutrition and Hydration - nutrition and fluid given through a tube in the veins, nose, or stomach.				
4. Major Surgery - such as removing the gall bladder or part of the intestines.				
5. Kidney Dialysis - cleaning the blood by machine or by fluid passed through the belly.				
6. Chemotherapy - drugs to fight cancer.				
7. Minor Surgery - such as removing some tissue from an infected toe.				
8. Invasive Diagnostic Tests - such as using a flexible tube to look into the stomach.				

24. Copyright 1990 by Linda L. Emanuel and Ezekiel J. Emanuel. The authors of this form advise that it should be completed pursuant to a discussion between the principal and his or her physician, so that the principal can be adequately informed of any pertinent medical information, and so that the physician can be appraised of the intentions of the principal and the existence of such a document which may be a part of the principal's medical records. This form was originally published as part of an article by Linda L. Emanuel and Ezekiel J. Emanuel, "The Medical Directive: A New Comprehensive Advance Care Document," in Journal of the American Medical Association, June 9, 1989; 261 at 3290. It does not reflect the official policy of the American Medical Association. Copies of this form may be obtained from the Harvard Medical School Health Publications Group, P.O. Box 380, Boston, Massachusetts 02117, or on the web at www.medicaldirective.org.

9. Blood or Blood Products –				
10. Antibiotics – drugs to fight infections.				
11. Simple Diagnostic Tests – such as blood tests or x-rays.				
12. Pain Medications, Even If They Dull Consciousness And Indirectly Shorten My Life –				

Durable Health-Care Powers of Attorney. The other main type of advance health-care directive is the durable health-care power of attorney, sometimes called a "health-care proxy." Unlike a living will, the durable power names a surrogate decisionmaker who has authority to act in the event the principal becomes incapacitated. All fifty states, and the District of Columbia, now have statutes authorizing durable health-care powers.

Durable health-care powers have several advantages over living wills. Durable powers can be general or detailed, depending on what the principal wants. By using a third party, they enhance the flexibility needed to cover a wide variety of circumstances. The agent can be given powers as broad or narrow as the principal wants. Some state statutes limit the powers that can be delegated to a surrogate, so it is important in drafting a durable power to check whether the statute permits all the powers that the principal wants the agent to have. Where the agent is given broad powers, he or she can act in circumstances in which the principal's wishes are not specifically known.

As with living wills, the statutes permitting durable health-care powers vary widely in their details. Most of them, however, provide fewer formalities of execution than those usually required for living wills. While most do require witnessing, for example, only a few require notarization. Still, the recommended practice is to have a durable power both witnessed and notarized.

In 1993, the Uniform Law Commissioners approved the Uniform Health-Care Decisions Act (UHCDA). While only enacted in a few states thus far, the Act is likely to be a catalyst in many states for enacting or reforming laws that permit use of surrogates for health-care decisions. The Act authorizes use of durable health-care powers and living wills. It also allows an individual (an adult or emancipated minor) to designate a surrogate for health-care decisions by oral communication with the health-care provider. Designation of an agent, however, must be done in writing. (What do you suppose is the reason for this distinction?) If a patient fails to designate a surrogate, the statute identifies family members who may serve as surrogates if they are reasonably available. The powers that the statute allows to be delegated are extensive, including the power to prevent initiation of life-sustaining treatment by artificial nutrition and hydration. Finally, the Act provides for statutory damages against health-care providers who intentionally violate the Act.

The limitations of health-care decisional instruments are discussed in T.P. Gallanis, Write and Wrong: Rethinking the Way We Communicate Health-Care Decisions, 31 Conn. L. Rev. 1015 (1999); David Orentlicher, The Limitations of Legislation, 53 Md. L. Rev. 1255 (1994); Patricia D. White, Appointing a Proxy Under the Best of Circumstances, 1992 Utah L. Rev. 849 (1992).

Sample Durable Health Care Power of Attorney[25]

If my attending physician determines that I am unable to make my own health care decisions, I, ___________, appoint _______________, residing at__________, __________________, as my agent to make all health care decisions for me *except as otherwise provided in this document,* including decisions to accept or to refuse any treatment, service or procedure used to diagnose, treat or care for me, and to withhold or withdraw life-sustaining measures and to direct that artificially provided fluids and nutrition, such as by feeding tube or intravenous infusion, be withheld or withdrawn. This document shall be construed in the broadest possible manner and my agent may act or fail to act to the same extent as I could if I were able to make my own health care decisions, provided that my agent shall do so in accordance with my wishes and instructions as known to my agent or, in their absence, in accordance with my best interests.

If my attending physician shall determine that my agent is unable, unwilling or unavailable to act, I appoint ___________________, residing at ________ _____ __________________, as my health care agent.

Unless revoked, this proxy shall remain in effect indefinitely, even though a guardian or other representative shall be appointed to act on my behalf.

Any invalid or unenforceable power or provision shall not affect the other powers and provisions or the appointment of my health care agent.

I understand the purpose and effect of this document and sign it after careful deliberation, this ___ day of ____________, 19___.

_________________________(L.S.)

Residing at: ______________________________

Each of the undersigned declares that the person who signed this document did so in his or her presence; that said person is personally known to him or her and appears to be of sound mind and acting willingly and free from duress or

25. This form is reprinted from U.S. Trust Company, Practical Drafting—Trust and Will Provisions. This form is described by the publisher as a "common law" document and as having been prepared on the assumption that applicable state law recognizes its validity and imposes no requirements on its use; should such restrictions or requirements exist, the form must be modified.

undue influence; and that he or she is 18 years of age or older and is not designated as the persons's health care proxy.

__________________________ residing at ______________________________

__________________________ residing at ______________________________

EXTERNAL REFERENCES. Francis J. Collin, John J. Lombard, Albert L. Moses & Harley J. Spitler, Drafting the Durable Power of Attorney: A Systems Approach (1987); George J. Alexander, Writing a Living Will: Using a Durable Power of Attorney (1987); Dale L. Moore, The Durable Power of Attorney as an Alternative to the Improper Use of Conservatorship for Health Care Decisionmaking, 60 St. John's L. Rev. 631 (1986).

Recent empirical studies have indicated that the use of living wills and durable health-care powers has increased in the wake of the United States Supreme Court's decision in the *Cruzan* case that follows.

Cruzan v. Director, Missouri Department of Health

497 U.S. 261 (1990)

REHNQUIST, C.J. Petitioner Nancy Beth Cruzan was rendered incompetent as a result of severe injuries sustained during an automobile accident. Copetitioners Lester and Joyce Cruzan, Nancy's parents and coguardians, sought a court order directing the withdrawal of their daughter's artificial feeding and hydration equipment after it became apparent that she had virtually no chance of recovering her cognitive faculties. The Supreme Court of Missouri held that because there was no clear and convincing evidence of Nancy's desire to have life sustaining treatment withdrawn under such circumstances, her parents lacked authority to effectuate such a request. We granted certiorari, and now affirm.

On the night of January 11, 1983, Nancy Cruzan lost control of her car as she traveled down Elm Road in Jasper County, Missouri. The vehicle overturned, and Cruzan was discovered lying face down in a ditch without detectable respiratory or cardiac function. Paramedics were able to restore her breathing and heartbeat at the accident site, and she was transported to a hospital in an unconscious state. An attending neurosurgeon diagnosed her as having sustained probable cerebral contusions compounded by significant anoxia (lack of oxygen). The Missouri trial court in this case found that permanent brain damage generally results after 6 minutes in an anoxic state; it was estimated that Cruzan was deprived of oxygen from 12 to 14 minutes. She remained in a coma for approximately three weeks and then progressed to an unconscious state in which she was able to orally ingest some nutrition. In order to ease feeding and further the recovery, surgeons implanted a gastrostomy feeding and hydration tube in Cruzan with the consent of her then husband. Subsequent rehabilitative efforts proved unavailing. She now lies in a Missouri state hospital in what is commonly referred to as a persistent vegetative state: generally, a condition in which a person exhibits motor reflexes but evinces no indications of significant cognitive function. The State of Missouri is bearing the cost of her care.

After it had become apparent that Nancy Cruzan had virtually no chance of regaining her mental faculties, her parents asked hospital employees to terminate the artificial nutrition and hydration procedures. All agree that such a removal would cause her death. The employees refused to honor the request without court approval. The parents then sought and received authorization from the state trial court for termination. The court found that a person in Nancy's condition had a fundamental right under the State and Federal Constitutions to refuse or direct the withdrawal of "death prolonging procedures." The court also found that Nancy's "expressed thoughts at age twenty-five in somewhat serious conversation with a housemate friend that if sick or injured she would not wish to continue her life unless she could live at least halfway normally suggests that given her present condition she would not wish to continue on with her nutrition and hydration."

The Supreme Court of Missouri reversed by a divided vote. The court recognized a right to refuse treatment embodied in the common-law doctrine of informed consent, but expressed skepticism about the application of that doctrine in the circumstances of this case. Cruzan v. Harmon, 760 S. W. 2d 408, 416-417 (1988) (en banc). The court also declined to read a broad right of privacy into the State Constitution which would "support the right of a person to refuse medical treatment in every circumstance," and expressed doubt as to whether such a right existed under the United States Constitution. Id., at 417-418. It then decided that the Missouri Living Will statute embodied a state policy strongly favoring the preservation of life. The court found that Cruzan's statements to her roommate regarding her desire to live or die under certain conditions were "unreliable for the purpose of determining her intent," id., at 424, "and thus insufficient to support the co-guardians['] claim to exercise substituted judgment on Nancy's behalf." Id., at 426. It rejected the argument that Cruzan's parents were entitled to order the termination of her medical treatment, concluding that "no person can assume that choice for an incompetent in the absence of the formalities required under Missouri's Living Will statutes or the clear and convincing, inherently reliable evidence absent here." Id., at 425. The court also expressed its view that "[b]road policy questions bearing on life and death are more properly addressed by representative assemblies" than judicial bodies. Id., at 426.

We granted certiorari to consider the question whether Cruzan has a right under the United States Constitution which would require the hospital to withdraw life-sustaining treatment from her under these circumstances. . . .

As [various state] cases demonstrate, the common-law doctrine of informed consent is viewed as generally encompassing the right of a competent individual to refuse medical treatment. . . . State courts have available to them for decision a number of sources—state constitutions, statutes, and common law—which are not available to us. In this Court, the question is simply and starkly whether the United States Constitution prohibits Missouri from choosing the rule of decision which it did. This is the first case in which we have been squarely presented with the issue whether the United States Constitution grants what is in common parlance referred to as a "right to die." . . .

The Fourteenth Amendment provides that no State shall "deprive any person of life, liberty, or property, without due process of law." The principle that a competent person has a constitutionally protected liberty interest in refusing unwanted medical treatment may be inferred from our prior decisions. . . . But determining that a person has a "liberty interest" under the Due Process Clause does not end the inquiry;[26] "whether respondent's constitutional rights have been violated must be determined by balancing his liberty interests against the relevant state interests." Youngberg v. Romeo, 457 U.S. 307, 321 (1982). . . .

Petitioners insist that under the general holdings of our cases, the forced administration of life-sustaining medical treatment, and even of artificially delivered food and water essential to life, would implicate a competent person's liberty interest. Although we think the logic of the cases discussed above would embrace such a liberty interest, the dramatic consequences involved in refusal of such treatment would inform the inquiry as to whether the deprivation of that interest is constitutionally permissible. But for purposes of this case, we assume that the United States Constitution would grant a competent person a constitutionally protected right to refuse lifesaving hydration and nutrition.

Petitioners go on to assert that an incompetent person should possess the same right in this respect as is possessed by a competent person. . . . The difficulty with petitioners' claim is that in a sense it begs the question: An incompetent person is not able to make an informed and voluntary choice to exercise a hypothetical right to refuse treatment or any other right. Such a "right" must be exercised for her, if at all, by some sort of surrogate. Here, Missouri has in effect recognized that under certain circumstances a surrogate may act for the patient in electing to have hydration and nutrition withdrawn in such a way as

---

26. Although many state courts have held that a right to refuse treatment is encompassed by a generalized constitutional right of privacy, we have never so held. We believe this issue is more properly analyzed in terms of a Fourteenth Amendment liberty interest. See Bowers v. Hardwick, 478 U.S. 186, 194-195 (1986).

to cause death, but it has established a procedural safeguard to assure that the action of the surrogate conforms as best it may to the wishes expressed by the patient while competent. Missouri requires that evidence of the incompetent's wishes as to the withdrawal of treatment be proved by clear and convincing evidence. The question, then, is whether the United States Constitution forbids the establishment of this procedural requirement by the State. We hold that it does not.

Whether or not Missouri's clear and convincing evidence requirement comports with the United States Constitution depends in part on what interests the State may properly seek to protect in this situation. Missouri relies on its interest in the protection and preservation of human life, and there can be no gainsaying this interest. As a general matter, the States—indeed, all civilized nations—demonstrate their commitment to life by treating homicide as a serious crime. Moreover, the majority of States in this country have laws imposing criminal penalties on one who assists another to commit suicide. We do not think a State is required to remain neutral in the face of an informed and voluntary decision by a physically able adult to starve to death.

But in the context presented here, a State has more particular interests at stake. The choice between life and death is a deeply personal decision of obvious and overwhelming finality. We believe Missouri may legitimately seek to safeguard the personal element of this choice through the imposition of heightened evidentiary requirements. It cannot be disputed that the Due Process Clause protects an interest in life as well as an interest in refusing life-sustaining medical treatment. Not all incompetent patients will have loved ones available to serve as surrogate decisionmakers. And even where family members are present, "[t]here will, of course, be some unfortunate situations in which family members will not act to protect a patient." In re Jobes, 108 N.J. 394, 419, 529 A.2d 434, 447 (1987). A State is entitled to guard against potential abuses in such situations. Similarly, a State is entitled to consider that a judicial proceeding to make a determination regarding an incompetent's wishes may very well not be an adversarial one, with the added guarantee of accurate fact finding that the adversary process brings with it. Finally, we think a State may properly decline to make judgments about the "quality" of life that a particular individual may enjoy, and simply assert an unqualified interest in the preservation of human life to be weighed against the constitutionally protected interests of the individual.

In our view, Missouri has permissibly sought to advance these interests through the adoption of a "clear and convincing" standard of proof to govern such proceedings. . . . The more stringent the burden of proof a party must bear, the more that party bears the risk of an erroneous decision. We believe that Missouri may permissibly place an increased risk of an erroneous decision on those seeking to terminate an incompetent individual's life-sustaining treatment. An erroneous decision not to terminate results in a maintenance of the status quo; the possibility of subsequent developments such as advancements in medical science, the discovery of new evidence regarding the patient's intent, changes in the law, or simply the unexpected death of the patient despite the administration of life-sustaining treatment at least create the potential that a wrong decision will eventually be corrected or its impact mitigated. An erroneous decision to withdraw life-sustaining treatment, however, is not susceptible of correction. . . .

The Supreme Court of Missouri held that in this case the testimony adduced at trial did not amount to clear and convincing proof of the patient's desire to have hydration and nutrition withdrawn. . . . The testimony adduced at trial consisted primarily of Nancy Cruzan's statements made to a housemate about a year before her accident that she would not want to live should she face life as a "vegetable," and other observations to the same effect. The observations did not deal in terms with withdrawal of medical treatment or of hydration and nutrition. We cannot say that the Supreme Court of Missouri committed constitutional error in reaching the conclusion that it did.

Petitioners alternatively contend that Missouri must accept the "substituted judgment" of close family members even in the absence of substantial proof that their views reflect the views of the patient. . . . But we do not think the Due Process Clause requires the State to repose judgment on these matters with anyone but the patient herself. Close family members may have a strong feeling —a feeling not at all ignoble or unworthy, but not entirely disinterested, either —that they do not wish to witness the continuation of the life of a loved one which they regard as hopeless, meaningless, and even degrading. But there is no automatic assurance that the view of close family members will necessarily be the same as the patient's would have been had she been confronted with the prospect of her situation while competent. All of the reasons previously discussed for allowing Missouri to require clear and convincing evidence of the patient's wishes lead us to conclude that the State may choose to defer only to those wishes, rather than confide the decision to close family members.

The judgment of the Supreme Court of Missouri is affirmed.

SCALIA, J., concurring. [W]hile I agree with the Court's analysis today, and therefore join in its opinion, I would have preferred that we announce, clearly and promptly, that the federal courts have no business in this field; that American law has always accorded the State the power to prevent, by force if necessary, suicide—including suicide by refusing to take appropriate measures necessary to preserve one's life; that the point at which life becomes "worthless," and the point at which the means necessary to preserve it become "extraordinary" or "inappropriate," are neither set forth in the Constitution nor known to the nine Justices of this Court any better than they are known to nine people picked at random from the Kansas City telephone directory; and hence, that even when it is demonstrated by clear and convincing evidence that a patient no longer wishes certain measures to be taken to preserve his or her life, it is up to the citizens of Missouri to decide, through their elected representatives, whether that wish will be honored. It is quite impossible (because the Constitution says nothing about the matter) that those citizens will decide upon a line less lawful than the one we would choose; and it is unlikely (because we know no more about "life and death" than they do) that they will decide upon a line less reasonable. . . .

BRENNAN, J., with whom MARSHALL, J., and BLACKMUN, J., join, dissenting. [B]ecause I believe that Nancy Cruzan has a fundamental right to be free of unwanted artificial nutrition and hydration, which right is not outweighed by any interests of the State, and because I find that the improperly biased procedural obstacles imposed by the Missouri Supreme Court impermissibly burden that right, I respectfully dissent. Nancy Cruzan is entitled to choose to die with dignity. . .

The right to be free from medical attention without consent, to determine what shall be done with one's own body, is deeply rooted in this Nation's traditions, as the majority acknowledges. This right has long been "firmly entrenched in American tort law" and is securely grounded in the earliest common law. Ante, at 269. See also Mills v. Rogers, 457 U.S. 291, 294, n.4 (1982) ("[T]he right to refuse any medical treatment emerged from the doctrines of trespass and battery, which were applied to unauthorized touchings by a physician"). "Anglo-American law starts with the premise of thorough-going self determination. It follows that each man is considered to be master of his own body, and he may, if he be of sound mind, expressly prohibit the performance of lifesaving surgery, or other medical treatment." Natanson v. Kline, 186 Kan. 393, 406-407, 350 P.2d 1093, 1104 (1960). "The inviolability of the person" has been held as "sacred" and "carefully guarded" as any common-law right. Union Pacific R. Co. v. Botsford, 141 U.S. 250, 251-252 (1891). Thus, freedom from unwanted medical attention is unquestionably among those principles "so rooted in the traditions and conscience of our people as to be ranked as fundamental." Snyder v. Massachusetts, 291 U.S. 97, 105 (1934). . . .

Although the right to be free of unwanted medical intervention, like other constitutionally protected interests, may not be absolute, no state interest could outweigh the rights of an individual in Nancy Cruzan's position. Whatever a State's possible interests in mandating life-support treatment under other circumstances, there is no good to be obtained here by Missouri's insistence that Nancy Cruzan remain on life-support systems if it is indeed her wish not to do so. Missouri does not claim, nor could it, that society as a whole will be benefited by Nancy's receiving medical treatment. . . . The only state interest asserted here is a general interest in the preservation of life. But the State has no legitimate general interest in someone's life, completely abstracted from the interest of the person living that life, that could outweigh the person's choice to avoid medical treatment. . . . Thus, the State's general interest in life must accede to Nancy Cruzan's particularized and intense interest in self-determination in her choice of medical treatment. There is simply nothing legitimately within the State's purview to be gained by superseding her decision. . . .

This is not to say that the State has no legitimate interests to assert here. As the majority recognizes, . . . Missouri has a parens patriae interest in providing Nancy Cruzan, now incompetent, with as accurate as possible a determination of how she would exercise her rights under these circumstances. Second, if and when it is determined that Nancy Cruzan would want to continue treatment, the State may legitimately assert an interest in providing that treatment. But until Nancy's wishes have been determined, the only state interest that may be asserted is an interest in safeguarding the accuracy of that determination.

Accuracy, therefore, must be our touchstone. Missouri may constitutionally impose only those procedural requirements that serve to enhance the accuracy of a determination of Nancy Cruzan's wishes or are at least consistent with an accurate determination. The Missouri "safeguard" that the Court upholds today does not meet that standard. The determination needed in this context is whether the incompetent person would choose to live in a persistent vegetative state on life support or to avoid this medical treatment. Missouri's rule of decision imposes a markedly asymmetrical evidentiary burden. Only evidence of specific statements of treatment choice made by the patient when competent is admissible to support a finding that the patient, now in a persistent vegetative state, would wish to avoid further medical treatment. Moreover, this evidence must be clear and convincing. No proof is required to support a finding that the incompetent person would wish to continue treatment.

. . . . An erroneous decision to terminate life support is irrevocable, says the majority, while an erroneous decision not to terminate "results in a maintenance of the status quo." But, from the point of view of the patient, an erroneous decision in either direction is irrevocable. An erroneous decision to terminate artificial nutrition and hydration, to be sure, will lead to failure of that last remnant of physiological life, the brain stem, and result in complete brain death. An erroneous decision not to terminate life support, however, robs a patient of the very qualities protected by the right to avoid unwanted medical treatment. His own degraded existence is perpetuated; his family's suffering is protracted; the memory he leaves behind becomes more and more distorted.

Even a later decision to grant him his wish cannot undo the intervening harm. But a later decision is unlikely in any event. "[T]he discovery of new evidence," to which the majority refers, is more hypothetical than plausible. The majority also misconceives the relevance of the possibility of "advancements in medical science," by treating it as a reason to force someone to continue medical treatment against his will. The possibility of a medical miracle is indeed part of the calculus, but it is a part of the patient's calculus. If current research suggests that some hope for cure or even moderate improvement is possible within the lifespan projected, this is a factor that should be and would be accorded significant weight in assessing what the patient himself would choose.

Even more than its heightened evidentiary standard, the Missouri court's categorical exclusion of relevant evidence dispenses with any semblance of accurate fact finding. The court adverted to no evidence supporting its decision, but held that no clear and convincing, inherently reliable evidence had been presented to show that Nancy would want to avoid further treatment. In doing so, the court failed to consider statements Nancy had made to family members and a close friend. The court also failed to consider testimony from Nancy's mother and sister that they were certain that Nancy would want to discontinue artificial nutrition and hydration, even after the court found that Nancy's family was loving and without malignant motive. The court also failed to consider the conclusions of the guardian ad litem, appointed by the trial court, that there was clear and convincing evidence that Nancy would want to discontinue medical treatment and that this was in her best interests. The court did not specifically define what kind of evidence it would consider clear and convincing, but its general discussion suggests that only a living will or equivalently formal directive from the patient when competent would meet this standard.

Too few people execute living wills or equivalently formal directives for such an evidentiary rule to ensure adequately that the wishes of incompetent persons will be honored. While it might be a wise social policy to encourage people to furnish such instructions, no general conclusion about a patient's choice can be drawn from the absence of formalities. The probability of becoming irreversibly vegetative is so low that many people may not feel an urgency to marshal formal evidence of their preferences. Some may not wish to dwell on their own physical deterioration and mortality. Even someone with a resolute determination to avoid life support under circumstances such as Nancy's would still need to know that such things as living wills exist and how to execute one. Often legal help would be necessary, especially given the majority's apparent willingness to permit States to insist that a person's wishes are not truly known unless the particular medical treatment is specified.

As a California appellate court observed: "The lack of generalized public awareness of the statutory scheme and the typically human characteristics of procrastination and reluctance to contemplate the need for such arrangements however makes this a tool which will all too often go unused by those who might desire it." Barber v. Superior Court, 147 Cal. App. 3d 1006, 1015, 195 Cal. Rptr. 484, 489 (1983). When a person tells family or close friends that she does not want her life sustained artificially, she is "express[ing] her wishes in the only terms familiar to her, and . . . as clearly as a lay person should be asked to express them. To require more is unrealistic, and for all practical purposes, it precludes the right of patients to forego life-sustaining treatment." In re O'Connor, 72 N.Y.2d 517, 551, 531 N.E.2d 607, 626 (1988) (Simons, J., dissenting). When Missouri enacted a living will statute, it specifically provided that the absence of a living will does not warrant a presumption that a patient wishes continued medical treatment. Thus, apparently not even Missouri's own legislature believes that a person who does not execute a living will fails to do so because he wishes continuous medical treatment under all circumstances.

The testimony of close friends and family members, on the other hand, may often be the best evidence available of what the patient's choice would be. It is they with whom the patient most likely will have discussed such questions and they who know the patient best. "Family members have a unique knowledge of the patient which is vital to any decision on his or her behalf." Newman, Treatment Refusals for the Critically and Terminally Ill: Proposed Rules for the Family, the Physician, and the State, 3 N.Y.L.S. Human Rights Annual 35, 46 (1985). The Missouri court's decision to ignore this whole category of testimony is also at odds with the practices of other States.

The Missouri court's disdain for Nancy's statements in serious conversations not long before her accident, for the opinions of Nancy's family and friends as to her values, beliefs and certain choice, and even for the opinion of an outside objective factfinder appointed by the State evinces a disdain for Nancy Cruzan's own right to choose. The rules by which an incompetent person's wishes are determined must represent every effort to determine those wishes. The rule that the Missouri court adopted and that this Court upholds, however, skews the result away from a determination that as accurately as possible reflects the individual's own preferences and beliefs. It is a rule that transforms human beings into passive subjects of medical technology. . . .

I respectfully dissent.

MARSHALL, J., and BLACKMUN, J., concur.

[The concurring opinion of Justice O'Connor and the dissenting opinion of Justice Stevens are omitted.]

Notes and Questions

1. *Sequel to the Cruzan Case.* Nancy Cruzan, the auto-crash victim who was the subject of the *Cruzan* case, died at age 33 on December 26, 1990, twelve days after her feeding tube was removed by order of a Missouri probate court. She had been in a vegetative state for eight years. Although Nancy Cruzan hadn't signed a living will or a durable health-care power of attorney, the probate court found that there was clear and convincing evidence she would have wanted to die; the finding was based on testimony of former co-workers as to conversations in which she stated that she would never want to live "like a vegetable."

On August 17, 1996, at age 62, Nancy Cruzan's father, Lester ("Joe") Cruzan, apparently committed suicide by hanging himself. According to the New York Times, he had "expressed uncertainty about whether the right action had been taken" regarding his daughter. See N.Y. Times, Aug. 19, 1996, at C10.

2. One of the arguments made in support of the clear-and-convincing evidentiary standard is that it is easily satisfied by executing a living will or durable health-care power. In view of the finding of the study reported in the *Journal of the American Medical Association* that many doctors ignore their patients' wishes expressed in living wills, is this a persuasive argument?

3. Would it be better as a matter of public policy for states to reverse the current presumption that the patient would want life-sustaining treatment and adopt a default rule of death? Consider the following excerpt.

James Lindgren, Death By Default

56 Law & Contemp. Problems 185, 227-230 (1993)

[T]he states of New York and Missouri [which have adopted a clear-and-convincing evidence requirement] have put the rights of the state above the rights of the individual. Other states and much of the medical profession also start with a default rule of life in desperate end-of-life situations. Under the usual standards for default rules in law and economics, life as the default rule here makes no sense. Usually, a default rule is the one that the party would have chosen if she could speak. In end-of-life situations it usually isn't. Or a default rule promotes efficiency in the form of wealth maximization. Most assuredly, it doesn't here. Or it promotes efficiency in the form of happiness, welfare, or general utility. Either welfare analysis is theoretically impossible here or, if it isn't, a rough utilitarian approach would lead to a default rule of death (at least where the family agrees). Under all three ways of analyzing default rules, the current default rule in *Cruzan* and *O'Connor* fails. . . .

The default rule should switch wherever patient preferences switch. Thus, one must determine when most would prefer to have at least some treatments withdrawn. According to national public opinion polls, it appears that there are at least eight such overlapping situations:

(1) patients on life support who have no hope of recovery;

(2) patients in a coma with no brain activity being kept alive by a feeding tube;

(3) patients who are terminally ill or in irreversible coma, supported by life support systems, including food and water;

(4) patients with an illness that makes them totally dependent on a family member or other person for all their care (a situation in which they would not want their doctors "to do everything possible to save" life);

(5) patients with a disease with no hope of improvement suffering a great deal of physical pain;

(6) patients in a coma with no hope of recovery but no pain;

(7) hopelessly ill or comatose patients on life support if their families request the withdrawal of support; and

(8) permanently unconscious patients receiving food and water.

The study of medical directives and further polling of doctors, nursing home residents, the elderly, and retirees reveals more situations in which at least some treatments should be withheld:

(9) patients with a terminal illness which has progressed and caused their heart to stop beating;

(10) mentally incompetent patients with a terminal illness which has progressed and caused their heart to stop beating;

(11) permanently unconscious patients in a persistent vegetative state unable to eat normally, needing artificial feedings;

(12) nursing home patients, no matter what the level of cognitive functioning at the time of treatment, needing resuscitation, amputation, or tube feeding (either temporary or permanent);

(13) nursing home residents about to die of natural causes needing drugs, fluids, food by tubes, breathing machines, or heart massage; and

(14) terminally ill retirees needing CPR, a resuscitator, a nasogastric feeding tube, or intravenous fluids.

. . . . Medical care is supposed to be based on the informed consent of the patient. Unconsented treatment is supposed to be a battery. Yet under the influence of the *O'Connor* and *Cruzan* decisions, unconsented treatment has been made legally acceptable in a few jurisdictions. Some courts seem to be confused about what they're doing. They're willing to follow a patient's wishes when they're "clear and convincing," but ignore them if they aren't. Perhaps that would make sense if the default rule were set to reflect most people's wishes toward withdrawing life-sustaining treatment in desperate end-of-life situations. Then we would be saying: Unless we have proof that this terminally ill patient is different from other terminally ill patients, we will treat this patient as others would like to be treated and withdraw life support. But with life as the default rule, we are frustrating the intent of most patients subject to that rule.

Health-Care Decisionmaking in the Absence of a Formal Advance Directive. The *Cruzan* decision is a narrow, though important one. All that the Court held there was that a state may constitutionally impose a clear-and-convincing standard of proof of the patient's wishes. This leaves states free to adopt less stringent approaches to health-care decisionmaking, including deferring to informal directives from a patient or to the recommendation of a surrogate where the patient has not expressed his or her preferences.

Courts have followed several different approaches. Where the patient failed to leave written instructions but had made prior oral statements about life-sustaining treatment, several courts follow what has been called the "limited-objective" standard. In an important case applying this approach, In re Conroy, 486 A.2d 1209 (N.J. 1985), the court said that life-sustaining treatment could be withheld even though the patient had made no clear statement regarding her desires, so long as there was some trustworthy evidence that she would have refused treatment. Under the Missouri statute that the Court in *Cruzan* validated, such evidence would be insufficient. Similarly, the New York Court of Appeals in In re Westchester County Medical Center, 534 N.Y.S.2d 886 (N.Y. 1988), applied a clear-and-convincing evidence standard in holding that the patient's prior statements that "if she became ill and was unable to care for herself she would not want her life to be sustained artificially" were insufficient to support the family's request not to insert a feeding tube.

Where the patient had made no prior statements, or had made only ambiguous statements, or was incompetent, most courts have allowed a third party, such as a guardian or the patient's family, to authorize termination of life-sustaining treatment. These courts have followed either of two approaches: the substituted-judgment approach or the best-interests approach. Under the substituted-judgment approach, a court-appointed guardian, family member, or other proxy is supposed to stand in the patient's shoes and determine what the patient would have wanted under the circumstances. See, e.g., Superintendent of Belchertown State School v. Saikewicz, 370 N.E.2d 417 (Mass. 1977). Under the best-interests approach, the proxy is supposed to take into account the patient's condition and likelihood that the recommended treatment will succeed. On the implementation of this approach, see Norman L. Cantor, Discarding Substituted Judgment and Best Interests: Toward a Constructive Preference Standard for Dying, Previously Competent Patients Without Advance Instructions, 48 Rutgers L. Rev. 1193, 1221-1241 (1996).

Promulgated in 1993, the Uniform Health-Care Decisions Act enables surrogates or guardians to make medical decisions for patients lacking health-care directives. These decisions must be made in accordance with the patient's wishes, if known, or else in accordance with the patient's best interests. The UHCDA does not require clear and convincing evidence. See UHCDA §§ 5, 6. It is worth noting, however, the California Supreme Court held that, under a statute based upon the UHCDA, a guardian (appointed by the court, not by the patient, and thus not necessarily having special knowledge of the patient's wishes) would have to support with clear and convincing evidence a decision to remove artificial nutrition and hydration from a patient in the limited case where the patient, although incapacitated, was not comatose, terminally ill, or in a persistent vegetative state. See Wendland v. Wendland, __ P.3d ___ (Cal. 2001).

Moving the focus away from the patient, some recent commentators have suggested that the best approach would be to follow the wishes of the patient's family. These commentators argue that family members have interests distinct from the patient's and that these interests often are among the most important factors in situations where a decision must be made whether to terminate life-sustaining treatment. See Leslie Pickering Francis, The Roles of the Family in Making Health Care Decisions for Incompetent Patients, 1992 Utah L. Rev. 861 (1992); Nancy K. Rhoden, Litigating Life and Death, 102 Harv. L. Rev. 375 (1988).

For a thoughtful discussion of the legal standards used to decide when a court-appointed surrogate should intervene in making decisions for an elderly person, see Jan Ellen Rein, Preserving Dignity and Self-Determination of the Elderly in the Face of Competing Interests and Grim Alternatives: A Proposal for Statutory Refocus and Reform, 60 Geo. Wash. L. Rev. 1818 (1992).

2. *Physician-Assisted Suicide*

One of the most difficult and contentious policy issues of the past several years has been whether physicians should be legally permitted to assist their patients commit suicide. Physician-assisted suicide is a form of what medical ethicists term "voluntary euthanasia." It is also a form of "active" euthanasia, which is legally distinguished from acts of "passive" euthanasia such as terminating life-sustaining treatment. While passive euthanasia is legally permitted, active euthanasia, whether voluntary (that is, with the patient's consent) or involuntary, was illegal in all states until quite recently. In 1994, the Oregon legislature enacted the Oregon Death With Dignity Act, permitting qualified competent patients suffering from a terminal illness to request medication that would end their lives in a humane manner. After an unsuccessful court challenge, the Oregon statute went into effect in late 1997.

In response to the Oregon law, the federal government enacted the Assisted Suicide Funding Restriction Act, which prohibits the use of federal funds "for the purpose of assisting in causing the death of any individual, such as by assisted suicide, euthanasia, or mercy killing." 42 U.S.C. § 14402(a)(1).

In 1998, the first full year of the Oregon statute's operation, 16 patients used the law to end their lives. In 1999 and 2000, 27 patients each year used the law. See Assistance with Suicide is Increasing, Oregon Says, N.Y. Times, Feb. 24, 2000, at A16; 27 Dying Patients Used Suicide Law in Oregon, N.Y. Times, Feb. 22, 2001, at A18. Data on the patients who used the statute in 1999 are presented in Amy D. Sullivan et al., Legalized Physician-Assisted Suicide in Oregon: The Second Year, 342 New Eng. J. Med. 598 (2000). For a perceptive analysis of physicians' experiences with assisted suicide in Oregon, see Linda Ganzini et al., Physicians' Experiences with the Oregon Death With Dignity Act, 342 New Eng. J. Med. 557 (2000).

Other states have acted in the opposite direction. Responding to the heavily-reported cases involving Dr. Jack Kevorkian, dubbed "Dr. Death" in the press, the Michigan legislature in 1993 enacted a statute making assisted suicide a felony. Many other states have similar statutes.

The legal validity of statutes making assisted suicide a felony was largely unquestioned until two 1996 federal court decisions. In Compassion in Dying v. State of Washington, 79 F.3d 790 (9th Cir. 1996), the Court of Appeals for the Ninth Circuit, en banc, struck down the Washington state statute on Fourteenth Amendment due process grounds. Relying on the Supreme Court's abortion decisions and on its decision in the *Cruzan* case, the court reasoned that there is "a liberty interest in choosing the time and manner of one's death" and that this individual interest outweighs the state's interest in prohibiting assisted suicide. In Quill v. Vacco, 80 F.3d 716 (2d Cir. 1996), the Second Circuit rejected the due process argument but nevertheless struck down the New York statute on equal protection grounds. The court stated that in view of the fact that the state recognizes the right of the terminally ill to forego unwanted medical treatment, there is no rational basis for refusing to allow terminally ill individuals to have others assist their suicide.

Washington v. Glucksberg
521 U.S. 702 (1997)

CHIEF JUSTICE REHNQUIST delivered the opinion of the Court.

The question presented in this case is whether Washington's prohibition against "caus[ing]" or "aid[ing]" a suicide offends the Fourteenth Amendment to the United States Constitution. We hold that it does not.

It has always been a crime to assist a suicide in the State of Washington....

The plaintiffs asserted "the existence of a liberty interest protected by the Fourteenth Amendment which extends to a personal choice by a mentally competent, terminally ill adult to commit physician-assisted suicide." Relying primarily on Planned Parenthood v. Casey, 505 U.S. 833 (1992), and Cruzan v. Director, Missouri Dept. of Health, 497 U.S. 261 (1990), the District Court agreed, and concluded that Washington's assisted-suicide ban is unconstitutional because it "places an undue burden on the exercise of [that] constitutionally protected liberty interest." . . .

. . . . The Ninth Circuit [heard] the case en banc, reversed the panel's decision, and affirmed the District Court. Compassion in Dying v. Washington, 79 F.3d 790, 798 (1996). . . . The court . . . concluded that "the Constitution encompasses a due process liberty interest in controlling the time and manner of one's death—that there is, in short, a constitutionally-recognized 'right to die.'" After "[w]eighing and then balancing" this interest against Washington's various interests, the court held that the State's assisted-suicide ban was unconstitutional "as applied to terminally ill competent adults who wish to hasten their deaths with medication prescribed by their physicians.". . . We granted certiorari, and now reverse.

We begin, as we do in all due-process cases, by examining our Nation's history, legal traditions, and practices. In almost every State—indeed, in almost every western democracy—it is a crime to assist a suicide.[27] The States' assisted-suicide bans are not innovations. Rather, they are longstanding expressions of the States' commitment to the protection and preservation of all human life. Indeed, opposition to and condemnation of suicide—and, therefore, of assisting suicide—are consistent and enduring themes of our philosophical, legal, and cultural heritages. . . .

---

27. See Compassion in Dying v. Washington, 79 F.3d 790, 847, and nn. 10-13 (CA9 1996) (Beezer, J., dissenting) ("In total, forty-four states, the District of Columbia and two territories prohibit or condemn assisted suicide") (citing statutes and cases) . . . Since the Ninth Circuit's decision, Louisiana, Rhode Island, and Iowa have enacted statutory assisted-suicide bans. La. Rev. Stat. Ann. §14:32.12 (Supp.1997); R.I. Gen. Laws §§ 11-60-1, 11-60-3 (Supp.1996); Iowa Code Ann. §§ 707A.2, 707A.3 (Supp.1997). . . .

Though deeply rooted, the States' assisted-suicide bans have in recent years been reexamined and, generally, reaffirmed. Because of advances in medicine and technology, Americans today are increasingly likely to die in institutions, from chronic illnesses. Public concern and democratic action are therefore sharply focused on how best to protect dignity and independence at the end of life, with the result that there have been many significant changes in state laws and in the attitudes these laws reflect. Many States, for example, now permit "living wills," surrogate health-care decisionmaking, and the withdrawal or refusal of life-sustaining medical treatment. At the same time, however, voters and legislators continue for the most part to reaffirm their States' prohibitions on assisting suicide . . . .

The Due Process Clause guarantees more than fair process, and the "liberty" it protects includes more than the absence of physical restraint. The Clause also provides heightened protection against government interference with certain fundamental rights and liberty interests. In a long line of cases, we have held that, in addition to the specific freedoms protected by the Bill of Rights, the "liberty" specially protected by the Due Process Clause includes the rights to marry, to have children, to direct the education and upbringing of one's children, to marital privacy, to use contraception, to bodily integrity, and to abortion. We have also assumed, and strongly suggested, that the Due Process Clause protects the traditional right to refuse unwanted lifesaving medical treatment. *Cruzan*, 497 U.S., at 278-279.

But we "ha[ve] always been reluctant to expand the concept of substantive due process because guideposts for responsible decisionmaking in this unchartered area are scarce and open-ended." By extending constitutional protection to an asserted right or liberty interest, we, to a great extent, place the matter outside the arena of public debate and legislative action. We must therefore "exercise the utmost care whenever we are asked to break new ground in this field," lest the liberty protected by the Due Process Clause be subtly transformed into the policy preferences of the members of this Court.

Our established method of substantive-due-process analysis has two primary features: First, we have regularly observed that the Due Process Clause specially protects those fundamental rights and liberties which are, objectively, "deeply rooted in this Nation's history and tradition,"and "implicit in the concept of ordered liberty," such that "neither liberty nor justice would exist if they were sacrificed." Second, we have required in substantive-due-process cases a "careful description" of the asserted fundamental liberty interest. Our Nation's history, legal traditions, and practices thus provide the crucial "guideposts for responsible decisionmaking," that direct and restrain our exposition of the Due Process Clause. . . .

. . . . The Washington statute at issue in this case prohibits "aid[ing] another person to attempt suicide," Wash. Rev. Code § 9A.36.060(1) (1994), and, thus, the question before us is whether the "liberty" specially protected by the Due Process Clause includes a right to commit suicide which itself includes a right to assistance in doing so.

We now inquire whether this asserted right has any place in our Nation's traditions. Here, as discussed above, we are confronted with a consistent and almost universal tradition that has long rejected the asserted right, and continues explicitly to reject it today, even for terminally ill, mentally competent adults. To hold for respondents, we would have to reverse centuries of legal doctrine and practice, and strike down the considered policy choice of almost every State.

Respondents contend, however, that the liberty interest they assert is consistent with this Court's substantive-due-process line of cases, if not with this Nation's history and practice. Pointing to *Casey* and *Cruzan*, respondents read our jurisprudence in this area as reflecting a general tradition of "self-sovereignty," Brief of Respondents 12, and as teaching that the "liberty" protected by the Due Process Clause includes "basic and intimate exercises of personal autonomy," id., at 10. According to respondents, our liberty jurisprudence, and the broad, individualistic principles it reflects, protects the "liberty of competent, terminally ill adults to make end-of-life decisions free of undue government interference." Brief for Respondents 10. The question presented in this case, however, is whether the protections of the Due Process Clause include a right to commit suicide with another's assistance. With this "careful description" of respondents' claim in mind, we turn to *Casey* and *Cruzan*.

In *Cruzan*, we considered whether Nancy Beth Cruzan, who had been severely injured in an automobile accident and was in a persistive vegetative state, "ha[d] a right under the United States Constitution which would require the hospital to withdraw life-sustaining treatment" at her parents' request. . . . After reviewing a long line of relevant state cases, we concluded that "the common-law doctrine of informed consent is viewed as generally encompassing the right of a competent individual to refuse medical treatment." Next, we reviewed our own cases on the subject, and stated that "[t]he principle that a competent person has a constitutionally protected liberty interest in refusing unwanted medical treatment may be inferred from our prior decisions." Therefore, "for purposes of [that] case, we assume[d] that the United States Constitution would grant a competent person a constitutionally protected right to refuse lifesaving hydration and nutrition." We concluded that, notwithstanding this right, the Constitution permitted Missouri to require clear and convincing evidence of an incompetent patient's wishes concerning the withdrawal of life-sustaining treatment. . . .

The right assumed in *Cruzan* . . . was not simply deduced from abstract concepts of personal autonomy. Given the common-law rule that forced medication was a battery, and the long legal tradition protecting the decision to refuse unwanted medical treatment, our assumption was entirely consistent with this Nation's history and constitutional traditions. The decision to commit suicide with the assistance of another may be just as personal and profound as the decision to refuse unwanted medical treatment, but it has never enjoyed similar legal protection. Indeed, the two acts are widely and reasonably regarded as quite distinct. . . .

Respondents also rely on *Casey*. There, the Court's opinion concluded that "the essential holding of Roe v. Wade should be retained and once again reaffirmed." We held, first, that a woman has a right, before her fetus is viable, to an abortion "without undue interference from the State"; second, that States may restrict post-viability abortions, so long as exceptions are made to protect a woman's life and health; and third, that the State has legitimate interests throughout a pregnancy in protecting the health of the woman and the life of the unborn child. In reaching this conclusion, the opinion discussed in some detail this Court's substantive-due-process tradition of interpreting the Due Process Clause to protect certain fundamental rights and "personal decisions relating to marriage, procreation, contraception, family relationships, child rearing, and education," and noted that many of those rights and liberties "involv[e] the most intimate and personal choices a person may make in a lifetime."

The Court of Appeals, like the District Court, found *Casey* "'highly instructive'" and "'almost prescriptive'" for determining "'what liberty interest may inhere in a terminally ill person's choice to commit suicide'": "Like the decision of whether or not to have an abortion, the decision how and when to die is one of 'the most intimate and personal choices a person may make in a lifetime,' a choice 'central to personal dignity and autonomy.'" 79 F.3d, at 813-814. Similarly, respondents emphasize the statement in *Casey* that: "At the heart of liberty is the right to define one's own concept of existence, of meaning, of the universe, and of the mystery of human life. Beliefs about these matters could not define the attributes of personhood were they formed under compulsion of the State." *Casey*, 505 U.S., at 851. Brief for Respondents 12. By choosing this language, the Court's opinion in *Casey* described, in a general way and in light of our prior cases, those personal activities and decisions that this Court has identified as so deeply rooted in our history and traditions, or so fundamental to our concept of constitutionally ordered liberty, that they are protected by the Fourteenth Amendment. The opinion moved from the recognition that liberty necessarily includes freedom of conscience and belief about ultimate considerations to the observation that "though the abortion decision may originate within the zone of conscience and belief, it is more than a philosophic exercise." *Casey*, 505 U.S., at 852 (emphasis added). That many of the rights and liberties protected by the Due Process Clause sound in personal autonomy does not warrant the sweeping conclusion that any and all important, intimate, and personal decisions are so protected, . . . and *Casey* did not suggest otherwise.

The history of the law's treatment of assisted suicide in this country has been and continues to be one of the rejection of nearly all efforts to permit it. That being the case, our decisions lead us to conclude that the asserted "right" to assistance in committing suicide is not a fundamental liberty interest protected by the Due Process Clause. The Constitution also requires, however, that Washington's assisted-suicide ban be rationally related to legitimate government interests. This requirement is unquestionably met here. . . . Washington's assisted-suicide ban implicates a number of state interests.

First, Washington has an "unqualified interest in the preservation of human life." The State's prohibition on assisted suicide, like all homicide laws, both reflects and advances its commitment to this interest. . . .

Respondents admit that "[t]he State has a real interest in preserving the lives of those who can still contribute to society and enjoy life." Brief for Respondents 35, n.23. The Court of Appeals also recognized Washington's interest in protecting life, but held that the "weight" of this interest depends on the "medical condition and the wishes of the person whose life is at stake." Washington, however, has rejected this sliding-scale approach and, through its assisted-suicide ban, insists that all persons' lives, from beginning to end, regardless of physical or mental condition, are under the full protection of the law. As we have previously affirmed, the States "may properly decline to make judgments about the 'quality' of life that a particular individual may enjoy." This remains true, as *Cruzan* makes clear, even for those who are near death.

Relatedly, all admit that suicide is a serious public-health problem, especially among persons in otherwise vulnerable groups.

Those who attempt suicide—terminally ill or not—often suffer from depression or other mental disorders. Research indicates, however, that many people who request physician-assisted suicide withdraw that request if their depression and pain are treated. Thus, legal physician-assisted suicide could make it more difficult for the State to protect depressed or mentally ill persons, or those who are suffering from untreated pain, from suicidal impulses.

The State also has an interest in protecting the integrity and ethics of the medical profession. In contrast to the Court of Appeals' conclusion that "the integrity of the medical profession would [not] be threatened in any way by [physician-assisted suicide]," the American Medical Association, like many other medical and physicians' groups, has concluded that "[p]hysician-assisted suicide is fundamentally incompatible with the physician's role as healer." American Medical Association, Code of Ethics §2.211 (1994).

Next, the State has an interest in protecting vulnerable groups—including the poor, the elderly, and disabled persons—from abuse, neglect, and mistakes. The Court of Appeals dismissed the State's concern that disadvantaged persons might be pressured into physician-assisted suicide as "ludicrous on its face." We have recognized, however, the real risk of subtle coercion and undue influence in end-of-life situations. . . . If physician-assisted suicide were permitted, many might resort to it to spare their families the substantial financial burden of end-of-life health-care costs.

The State's interest here goes beyond protecting the vulnerable from coercion; it extends to protecting disabled and terminally ill people from prejudice, negative and inaccurate stereotypes, and "societal indifference." The State's assisted-suicide ban reflects and reinforces its policy that the lives of terminally ill, disabled, and elderly people must be no less valued than the lives of the young and healthy, and that a seriously disabled person's suicidal impulses should be interpreted and treated the same way as anyone else's.

Finally, the State may fear that permitting assisted suicide will start it down the path to voluntary and perhaps even involuntary euthanasia. The Court of Appeals struck down Washington's assisted-suicide ban only "as applied to competent, terminally ill adults who wish to hasten their deaths by obtaining medication prescribed by their doctors." Washington insists, however, that the impact of the court's decision will not and cannot be so limited. Brief for Petitioners 44-47. If suicide is protected as a matter of constitutional right, it is argued, "every man and woman in the United States must enjoy it." The Court of Appeals' decision, and its expansive reasoning, provide ample support for the State's concerns. The court noted, for example, that the "decision of a duly appointed surrogate decision maker is for all legal purposes the decision of the patient himself," 79 F.3d, at 832, n. 120; that "in some instances, the patient may be unable to self-administer the drugs and . . . administration by the physician . . . may be the only way the patient may be able to receive them," id., at 831; and that not only physicians, but also family members and loved ones, will inevitably participate in assisting suicide. Id., at 838, n.140. Thus, it turns out that what is couched as a limited right to "physician-assisted suicide" is likely, in effect, a much broader license, which could prove extremely difficult to police and contain. Washington's ban on assisting suicide prevents such erosion.

This concern is further supported by evidence about the practice of euthanasia in the Netherlands. The Dutch government's own study revealed that in 1990, there were 2,300 cases of voluntary euthanasia (defined as "the deliberate termination of another's life at his request"), 400 cases of assisted suicide, and more than 1,000 cases of euthanasia without an explicit request. In addition to these latter 1,000 cases, the study found an additional 4,941 cases where physicians administered lethal morphine overdoses without the patients' explicit consent. Physician-Assisted Suicide and Euthanasia in the Netherlands: A Report of Chairman Charles T. Canady, at 12-13 (citing Dutch study). This study suggests that, despite the existence of various reporting procedures, euthanasia in the Netherlands has not been limited to competent, terminally ill adults who are enduring physical suffering, and that regulation of the practice may not have prevented abuses in cases involving vulnerable persons, including severely disabled neonates and elderly persons suffering from dementia. . . . Washington, like most other States, reasonably ensures against this risk by banning, rather than regulating, assisting suicide.

We need not weigh exactingly the relative strengths of these various interests. They are unquestionably important and legitimate, and Washington's ban on assisted suicide is at least reasonably related to their promotion and protection. We therefore hold that Wash. Rev.Code §9A.36.060(1) (1994) does not violate the Fourteenth Amendment, either on its face or "as applied to competent, terminally ill adults who wish to hasten their deaths by obtaining medication prescribed by their doctors." 79 F.3d, at 838.

Throughout the Nation, Americans are engaged in an earnest and profound debate about the morality, legality, and practicality of physician-assisted suicide. Our holding permits this debate to continue, as it should in a democratic society. The decision of the en banc Court of Appeals is reversed, and the case is remanded for further proceedings consistent with this opinion.

It is so ordered.

[The concurring opinions of O'CONNOR, STEVENS, SOUTER, GINSBURG, and BREYER, J.J., are omitted. Eds.]

Notes

1. *Vacco v. Quill.* In Vacco v. Quill, 521 U.S. 793 (1997), the Supreme Court held that New York's prohibition on assisting suicide does not violate the Equal Protection Clause of the Fourteenth Amendment. The opinion of the Court, delivered by Chief Justice Rehnquist, stated:

> The Equal Protection Clause commands that no State shall "deny to any person within its jurisdiction the equal protection of the laws." This provision creates no substantive rights. Instead, it embodies a general rule that States must treat like cases alike but may treat unlike cases accordingly. If a legislative classification or distinction "neither burdens a fundamental right nor targets a suspect class, we will uphold [it] so long as it bears a rational relation to some legitimate end."

New York's statutes outlawing assisting suicide affect and address matters of profound significance to all New Yorkers alike. They neither infringe fundamental rights nor involve suspect classifications. These laws are therefore entitled to a "strong presumption of validity."

On their faces, neither New York's ban on assisting suicide nor its statutes permitting patients to refuse medical treatment treat anyone differently than anyone else or draw any distinctions between persons. Everyone, regardless of physical condition, is entitled, if competent, to refuse unwanted lifesaving medical treatment; no one is permitted to assist a suicide. Generally speaking, laws that apply evenhandedly to all "unquestionably comply" with the Equal Protection Clause.

The Court of Appeals, however, concluded that some terminally ill people—those who are on life-support systems—are treated differently than those who are not, in that the former may "hasten death" by ending treatment, but the latter may not "hasten death" through physician-assisted suicide. 80 F.3d, at 729. This conclusion depends on the submission that ending or refusing lifesaving medical treatment "is nothing more nor less than assisted suicide." Ibid. Unlike the Court of Appeals, we think the distinction between assisting suicide and withdrawing life-sustaining treatment, a distinction widely recognized and endorsed in the medical profession and in our legal traditions, is both important and logical; it is certainly rational.

The distinction comports with fundamental legal principles of causation and intent. First, when a patient refuses life-sustaining medical treatment, he dies from an underlying fatal disease or pathology; but if a patient ingests lethal medication prescribed by a physician, he is killed by that medication.

Furthermore, a physician who withdraws, or honors a patient's refusal to begin, life-sustaining medical treatment purposefully intends, or may so intend, only to respect his patient's wishes and "to cease doing useless and futile or degrading things to the patient when [the patient] no longer stands to benefit from them." Assisted Suicide in the United States, Hearing before the Subcommittee on the Constitution of the House Committee on the Judiciary, 104th Cong., 2d Sess., 368 (1996) (testimony of Dr. Leon R. Kass). The same is true when a doctor provides aggressive palliative care; in some cases, painkilling drugs may hasten a patient's death, but the physician's purpose and intent is, or may be, only to ease his patient's pain. A doctor who assists a suicide, however, "must, necessarily and indubitably, intend primarily that the patient be made dead." Id., at 367. Similarly, a patient who commits suicide with a doctor's aid necessarily has the specific intent to end his or her own life, while a patient who refuses or discontinues treatment might not.

The law has long used actors' intent or purpose to distinguish between two acts that may have the same result. Put differently, the law distinguishes actions taken "because of" a given end from actions taken "in spite of" their unintended but foreseen consequences.

Given these general principles, it is not surprising that many courts, including New York courts, have carefully distinguished refusing life- sustaining treatment from suicide. . . .

Similarly, the overwhelming majority of state legislatures have drawn a clear line between assisting suicide and withdrawing or permitting the refusal of unwanted lifesaving medical treatment by prohibiting the former and permitting the latter. . . . Thus, even as the States move to protect and promote patients' dignity at the end of life, they remain opposed to physician-assisted suicide. . . .

This Court has also recognized, at least implicitly, the distinction between letting a patient die and making that patient die. In Cruzan v. Director, Mo. Dept. of Health, 497 U.S. 261, 278 (1990), we concluded that "[t]he principle that a competent person has a constitutionally protected liberty interest in refusing unwanted medical treatment may be inferred from our prior decisions," and we assumed the existence of such a right for purposes of that case, id., at 279. But our assumption of a right to refuse treatment was grounded not, as the Court of Appeals supposed, on the proposition that patients have a general and abstract "right to hasten death," 80 F.3d, at 727-728, but on well established, traditional rights to bodily integrity and freedom from unwanted touching. In fact, we observed that "the majority of States in this country have laws imposing criminal penalties on one who assists another to commit suicide." *Cruzan* therefore provides no support for the notion that refusing life-sustaining medical treatment is "nothing more nor less than suicide."

For all these reasons, we disagree with respondents' claim that the distinction between refusing lifesaving medical treatment and assisted suicide is "arbitrary" and "irrational." Granted, in some cases, the line between the two may not be clear, but certainty is not required, even were it possible. Logic and contemporary practice support New York's judgment that the two acts are different, and New York may therefore, consistent with the Constitution, treat them differently. By permitting everyone to refuse unwanted medical treatment while prohibiting anyone from assisting a suicide, New York law follows a longstanding and rational distinction.

2. *Krischer v. McIver.* In a five-to-one decision, the Florida Supreme Court held that a privacy provision in the state constitution did not render unconstitutional a 129-year-old state statute barring physician-assisted suicide. The lone dissenter, KOGAN, C.J., stated:

When [the plaintiff's] pain becomes unbearable, which one of us on this Court will be at his bedside telling him to be brave and bear it? . . . . What possible interest does society have in saving life when there is nothing of life to save but a final convulsion of agony? . . . Terminal illness is not a portrait in blacks and whites, but unending shades of gray, involving the most profound of personal, moral, and religious questions. Many people can and do disagree over these questions, but the fact remains that it is the dying person who must resolve them in the particular case. And while we certainly cannot ignore the slippery-slope problem, we previously have established fully adequate standards to police the exercise of privacy rights in this context to ensure against abuse.

Krischer v. McIver, 697 So.2d 97, 111 (1997).

3. *Survey of Seriously Ill Patients*. In a comprehensive study, 3,262 seriously ill patients in five hospitals from various regions responded to a survey that asked "Would you be very willing, somewhat willing, somewhat unwilling, very unwilling, or would you rather die than put up with living in a nursing home all the time?" The answers broke down as follows:

Very Willing	7%
Somewhat Willing	19%
Somewhat Unwilling	11%
Very Unwilling	26%
Rather Die than Put up with Living in a Nursing Home All the Time	30%
Don't Know	6%

The study also found a serious mismatch between what the patients say and what their families and doctors thought they would say, with the families matching the patients' choices only 35 percent of the time and the doctors matching only 18 percent of the time. See Dr. Thomas J. Mattimore et al., Surrogate and Physical Understanding of Patients' Preferences for Living Permanently in a Nursing Home, 45 J. Am. Geriatrics Soc'y 818 (July 1997).

4. *External References*. Law at the End of Life: The Supreme Court and Assisted Suicide (Carl E. Schneider ed. 2000); Cass R. Sunstein, The Right to Die, 106 Yale L.J. 1123 (1997).

Gina Kolata, "Passive Euthanasia" Is the Norm In Today's Hospitals, Doctors Say

New York Times, June 28, 1997, at 10

When the Supreme Court ruled on Thursday that states may continue to ban doctor-assisted suicide, it addressed the kind of death in which doctors actively help patients kill themselves. What was not considered in that decision is the fact that nowadays many, if not most, American die because someone—doctors, family members or they themselves—has decided that it is time for them to go.

What might be called managed deaths, as distinct from suicides, are now the norm in the United States, doctors say. The American Hospital Association says that about 70 percent of the deaths in hospitals happen after a decision has been made to withhold treatment. Other patients die when the medication they are taking to ease their pain depresses, then stops, their breathing.

There is less information on the deaths that occur in nursing homes and in private homes. But doctors say they often discharge patients from a hospital with the implicit understanding that they are sending them home to die, with a morphine drip for pain or without the ministrations of what they would call over-zealous doctors at a hospital who might start antibiotics to quell a fever or drugs to stabilize a fluttering heart.

"It's called passive euthanasia," said Dr. Norman Fost, director of the Program in Medical Ethics at the University of Wisconsin. "You can ask who's involved and is it really consensual, but there is no question that these are planned deaths. We know who is dying. Patients aren't just found dead in their beds."

Doctors, Dr. Fost said, decide not to provide antibiotics to treat an infection, or they withdraw drugs that maintain a patient's blood pressure, or they remove a patient from a ventilator.

Dr. Maurie Markman, a gynecological cancer specialist at the Cleveland Clinic, said a typical case might involve a woman with ovarian cancer who at first responded to chemotherapy but whose cancer now seemed imperious to the powerful drugs, and had developed bowel obstructions.

He could operate to try to remove the obstructions, but the chances are that it would do no good. Or, Dr. Markman said, "you can put a tube in to drain her stomach so she doesn't throw up." But then, he added, "you have to ask the woman, "Is that what you really want?" She would have to live with that tube for the rest of her life.

Dr. Markman, who said he sees such patients "at least once a week" tells the woman that he wants to focus on her symptoms rather than on her underlying disease. He sends her home with pain medications if she is in pain and anti-nausea drugs if she is nauseated, but the woman will never eat or drink again because of her obstructions. She will not return to the hospital for any sort of aggressive treatment.

Dr. Markman said he never bluntly tells the woman that there is no hope and she is going to die, but he, and probably she, know what is going to happen—and soon.

Is that assisted suicide or assisted death, or is it relief of suffering? For Dr. Markman, the answer is clear, "My intent always is to relieve suffering. If that's my goal, I can look myself in the eye. I can go to sleep at night."

Dr. Joanne Lynn, director of the Center to Improve Care of the Dying at George Washington University School of Medicine, said her typical case might be an old man, fragile and with multiple medical problems. She will finally discharge him from the hospital and send him home to his family, knowing that the decision to send him home is a decision to let death come soon. If he develops a fever, there is no reason even to take his temperature, she said. "The agreement is that he will not come back into the hospital for almost anything."

Dr. Lynn added: "Many of the decisions may be ambiguously articulated. They may be as much as a nod, something brought up in conversation, 'How do you feel about staying here?' " But underneath the nods and significant glances, she said, is a conclusion that it is time for the patient to die.

Yet, Dr. Margaret P. Battin, an ethicist at the University of Utah, asks, how much do the patients and family members really understand? She said patients and family members might not grasp the hidden message in their doctor's words. "When a patient is asked, 'Do you want to go home and be with your family? It would be easy to misinterpret that," Dr. Battin said.

Or she said, if a doctor says, "I can see you're in pain, let's start a morphine drip," a patient may not realize that the pain medication will shorten his life. "I can imagine a great many patients who would say, 'I don't want this pain, but if the medication is shortening my life, I can live with the pain,'" she said.

"That lack of candor about how the patient's death will occur and under what conditions is the thing that's particularly troubling," Dr. Battin added. "The patient is being invited to make a choice without understanding what the stakes are."

It is even worse, she said, when family members make these choices for patients. Dr. Battin said she spoke about the issue to an ethicist when she visited the Netherlands, where doctors who help patients kill themselves are typically not prosecuted.

"You Americans talk so much about the slippery slope," she recalled the ethicist saying, "But we perceive you as being much farther along the slippery slope than we are." Dr. Battin said she agreed.

But that analysis is glib, some doctors say, and they tell heart-wrenching stories to support their view.

Dr. Beth Y. Karlin, director of Gilda Radner Ovarian Cancer Program at Cedars Sinai Medical Center in Los Angeles, said she had a 40 year old patient with ovarian cancer. The cancer had spread to her liver and she was jaundiced and in such agonizing pain that she could not sit up. "She did not want to die," Dr. Karlin said, but death was near and living as she was was agony.

Dr. Karlin sent her home with a morphine drip, which soothed her pain, sedated her—and hastened her death. The woman's death was peaceful.

But Dr. Karlin said she had never specifically asked the woman whether she wanted to die more quickly, and tranquilly, with morphine. "It is the ultimate caring to allow patients to have some dignity," she said.

Dr. Karlin and other doctors recoil from the idea of bluntly telling patients they are going home to die.

"You take away hope when you say that nothing can be done," Dr. Markman said, adding that he does not even tell a patient that he wants to relieve suffering.

"Suffering has a horrible connotation," he said. "I say, 'Let's focus on another aspect of your cancer—symptom management."

Dr. Daniel Brock, director of the Center for Bioethics at Brown University School of Medicine, said Americans debating death and dying have assumed that the decision to allow doctor-assisted suicides is "the big leap where bad things are likely to happen."

"That seems to me clearly wrong," Dr. Brock said, adding that his concern is with the covert managing of death. At least with doctor-assisted suicide, he said, the patients ask to die and take the lethal medicine themselves. But many doctors oppose the notion of routinely prescribing lethal drugs for dying patients, and deny that by managing death they are breaching moral boundaries.

Dr. Fost said: "Every civilization throughout history has had strict rules against killing, but almost none have prohibitions against letting people die. Many people feel that there is a kind of brutalization when doctors kill people, a dulling of sensibilities, a feeling of dirty hands.

Dr. Lynn said: "It's one of these things where the spin is the message. If the question is, 'Is there some decision made that affects the time and manner of dying? The answer is, "Yes, and of course there should be."

But that is not the same as actively killing, she said, adding: "When a patient is ready to die, I can stop nutrition and hydration. I can stop insulin and ventilation. I can sedate them. I can creatively collaborate with the forces of nature. But if they really want the control of being dead tomorrow morning at 10, I cannot promise that.

Dr. Lynn said that some people "find it startling or worrisome or a little bit scandalous to think that there may be some discretion over how they die." Others, she added, would say, "But of course."

That is not to dismiss the anguishing questions about how far doctors should go in managing death, Dr. Lynn said. "Almost all who have multiple grounds from which they find their morals find this a terribly troubling issue," she added. "If you don't find it troubling, you aren't thinking hard enough."

The Dutch Experience. Voluntary euthanasia has been officially permitted in the Netherlands since 1993, although it has been practiced openly since the 1970s.[27] Dutch rules limit physician-assisted suicide to circumstances in which

27. See G.K. Kimsma and E. van Leeuvan, Dutch Euthanasia: Background, Practice, and Present Justifications, 2 Cambridge Quarterly of Healthcare Ethics 19 (1993

the request comes from a mentally competent patient who is terminally ill and is in unbearable physical or mental suffering. The doctor administering the lethal medication must first consult with another experienced physician and must then report the death and its circumstances to the city coroner. Case studies of euthanasia in the Netherlands suggest that Dutch doctors have not abused their power and that the practice of euthanasia has not increased the suicide rate in the Netherlands, as some feared it would. What appears to have happened is a substitution of euthanasia for conventional suicide. See Posner, Aging and Old Age, at 252-53. This does not mean, however, that the Dutch experience has been free from trouble. A recent study indicates that clinical problems–such as difficulty in administering the lethal medication, failure to induce a comatose state, or a longer-than-anticipated time between administration of the medication and death–arise in approximately 16 percent of the cases of euthanasia and assisted suicide in the Netherlands. See Johanna H. Groenewoud et al., Clinical Problems with the Performance of Euthanasia and Physician-Assisted Suicide in the Netherlands, 342 New Eng. J. Med. 551, 554 (2000). Does the Dutch experience suggest that American laws criminalizing physician-assisted suicide should be repealed?

The Effect of Health-Care Payment Systems on Physician-Assisted Suicide. One of the most important trends in American health care in the past several years has been the remarkable rise of health-maintenance organizations (HMOs) and other forms of managed health care. The growth of managed care institutions represents a shift in the dominant system of paying for health care. The traditional, and still prevailing, payment system used in the United States is fee-for-services. In HMOs and many other managed-care institutions, however, doctors become employees, paid on a salary basis rather than on the basis of fees for services rendered. Might this change affect doctors' incentives if physician-assisted suicide were permitted? Some people think so. Consider the following argument:

> Physician-assisted suicide may be a lethal weapon in the managed care revolution. There have long been incentives for unscrupulous doctors to put private gain ahead of patient welfare. Under the old regime of fee-for-service medicine, the more medical services doctors and hospitals provided, the more money they made. But under managed care, doctors and hospitals may find that they make more money by providing less care. . . .
>
> A recent study has suggested that withholding high-technology life support will not significantly lower the overall expense of caring for the terminally ill. If every person diagnosed with a terminal illness is seen as a potential candidate for assisted suicide, a fatal overdose prescribed by a doctor could well become the most powerful cost-control tool available to managed care.

M. Cathleen Kaveny and John P. Langan, The Doctor's Call, N.Y. Times, July 15, 1996, at A13. Judge Posner, who otherwise finds the case for assisted suicide to be strong, agrees with this analysis. He states, "If doctors are paid for services rendered . . . the incentive is to give patients too much rather than too little treatment. . . . [Under a managed-care regime, however,] the financial incentive is to avoid expensive end-of-life treatments, for which euthanasia might be a cheap alternative." Posner, Aging and Old Age, at 242. See also Yale Kamisar, The Reasons So Many People Support Physician-Assisted Suicide—And Why These Reasons Are Not Convincing, 12 Issues in Law & Medicine 113 (1996); Yale Kamisar, The "Right to Die": On Drawing (and Erasing) Lines, 35 Duq. L. Rev. 481 (1996).

INTERNET REFERENCES. Public interest in assisted suicide appears to be growing. One sign of this is the success of Derek Humphrey's book Final Exit (Hemlock Society/Carol, 1991), a how-to manual on suicide. A more recent sign is the appearance of sites on the Internet where individuals can access information about assisted suicide and communicate with others about the right to die. Three popular sites are: DeathNET, www.rights.org/~deathnet; the Euthanasia World Directory Web Page, www.bart.efn.org/finalexit, and Choice in Dying, www.choices.org.

3. *Organ Donations*

Henry Hansmann, The Economics and Ethics of Markets for Human Organs

14 J. of Health Politics, Policy & Law 57, 58-59 (1989)

Historically, the common law did not provide anyone with a clear property right in a human corpse, and thus did not give anyone the authority to transfer a cadaver or any of its parts for any purpose by gift or sale . . . .[28] Thus when transplants first became feasible, there was no mechanism whereby individuals could designate that their organs could be used for transplants upon death. To rectify this situation, the Uniform Anatomical Gift Act (UAGA) was promulgated in 1968 and adopted in some form in every state by 1973[29] . . . . The UAGA explicitly gives individuals the right to designate prior to death whether their bodies or organs are to be donated for transplants. In cases where

28. This does not mean that sales or gifts were illegal, but only contracts for sale or deeds of gift were not enforceable at law.

29. A revised version of the Uniform Anatomical Gift Act was promulgated in 1987. The revised act simplifies the process of organ donations by eliminating the witnessing requirement. Eds.

a decedent's wishes are not known, the act gives the next of kin the right to designate whether or not organs are to be donated.

The UAGA deals expressly only with donations of organs; it is silent on the subject of sales. According to the chairman of the committee that drafted the UAGA, it was intended neither to encourage nor to discourage remuneration: ". . . it is possible, of course, that abuses may occur if payment could customarily be demanded, but every payment is not necessarily unethical. . . . Until the matter of payment becomes a problem of some dimensions, the matter should be left to the decency of intelligent human beings." . . .

In the 1960s (prior to the adoption of the UAGA) some states adopted statutes explicitly prohibiting the sale of human bodies and organs. Most of these states repealed such statutes when they adopted the UAGA. It is unclear whether these repeals were simply the result of a program of repealing all relevant statutes predating the UAGA or whether they reflected a judgment that the prohibitions on sales were either overridden by the UAGA or, conversely, made redundant by it. In any event, Delaware evidently did not hold the latter view, since it added an explicit prohibition on sales to its version of the UAGA.

The status of the sale of organs for transplantation therefore remained uncertain until Congress adopted the National Organ Transplant ACT (NOTA) in 1984. NOTA was essentially an effort to enhance the system of voluntary provision of transplantable organs contemplated by the UAGA. Its principal provisions established federal financial support for local nonprofit organ procurement organizations and for a national organ procurement and transplantation network to assist in matching organ donors and recipients. However, NOTA also effectively outlawed commercial markets in transplantable organs by making it a federal crime "for any person to knowingly acquire, receive, or otherwise transfer any human organ for valuable consideration for use in human transplantation if the transfer affects interstate commerce."[30] Several states have subsequently supplemented this act with separate statutes of their own outlawing the sale or purchase of human organs. As a consequence, any effort to establish a market for organs today would require the repeal or amendment of legislation at both the federal and state levels.

Neither the federal nor the state legislation outlawing markets for organs were accompanied by careful policy analysis justifying the ban. NOTA did, however, establish the federal Task Force on Organ Procurement and Transplantation to inquire further into the policy issues raised by transplants. But when the task force submitted its report in 1986 it affirmed NOTA's ban on commercialization

30. 42 U.S. C. § 274(e) (1982). The act specifies that its prohibition does not extend to payments made to cover costs incurred in the process of transplanting the organ.

of organ transplantation without further analysis, simply offering the conclusory observation that "society's moral values militate against regarding the body as a commodity" and suggesting that such a ban is appropriate to "encourage altruism" . . . . The task force also proceeded to encourage individual states to adopt their own prohibitions on the commercial sale of organs because NOTA, limited as it is to sales affecting interstate commerce, might not be entirely effective in suppressing such sales.

Further Steps to Increase Organ Donations. The federal Task Force on Organ Procurement and Transplantation took two other steps to increase the supply of organs for transplantation. First, its report urged states to adopt statutes requiring hospitals to request the families of prospective organ donors to grant permission to remove organs for transplantation. It recommended a federal regulation, since promulgated, that makes it a condition for Medicare eligibility that hospitals make "routine request[s]" of families to consent to organ donations. See U.S. Dept. of Health & Human Services, Report of Task Force on Organ Procurement and Transplantation (April 1986).

A Legal Market for Human Organs? Despite these steps, there remains a wide gap between the demand and the supply of human organs available for transplantation. In March 2000, the number of people on the United Network for Organ Sharing waiting list for organ transplants was over 68,000.[31] It is likely that the actual number of people who would benefit from organ transplants is much higher. Yet the number of transplants performed is only a small fraction of the demand. In 1998, only 21,197 transplants were performed.[32]

One problem is the lack of public awareness of the process of making organ donations. Lawyers bear some of the responsibility for this. Few lawyers are knowledgeable about the law of organ transfers. Most lawyers do not raise the issue with their clients. Oversight and ignorance, then, may account for most people's failure to leave directions regarding donation of their organs, rather than the intention not to donate.

However, it seems unlikely that education alone will close the gap between the supply and demand for human organs. The prohibition against compensating donors or their families is also an important cause of the problem. The United Network for Organ Sharing and the National Kidney Foundation have recently urged Congress to amend NOTA to permit payments for the donor's burial expenses, but Congress thus far has failed to act.

---

31. Data obtained from the website of the United Network for Organ Sharing, www.unos.org.

32. Id.

Several scholars have urged that the ban on selling human organs be lifted for the purpose of permitting more transplants. Some organs, such as kidneys, can be obtained from living donors, and it would be relatively simple to structure a compensation system for them. Indeed, the provision in NOTA permitting payments for service connected with the collection of organs donated for transplantation has opened up a gray market for organs already. A large transplant support industry has emerged, and private organ procurement firms have charged as much as $22,000 for a single harvesting. See Michael Finkel, Complications, N.Y. Times Magazine, May 27, 2001, at 26; Peter S. Young, Moving to Compensate Families in Human-Organ Market, N.Y. Times, July 8, 1994, at B10. With respect to cadaveric organs, the market might be structured as a futures market. The donor would receive a current payment in exchange for the buyer's right to harvest the organ if the donor dies under circumstances in which a transplant is feasible.

Several different objections have been raised to the idea of allowing human organs to be bought and sold in an open market. One is that compensation would drive out voluntarism; that is, individuals who otherwise would be willing to donate organs out of a sense of altruism would be less willing to do so if they could be compensated. If this effect were widespread, then compensation would not significantly increase the supply of human organs for transplantation. This issue has been most fully discussed in the context of blood donations.[33] The available empirical data on the effect of compensation on the supply of blood are ambiguous.[34]

Another objection, one that relates only to markets for organs from living donors, is that organ-selling would exploit the poor and the ill-informed for the benefit of the rich. The poor, it is argued, are likely to be the main group of sellers, and the sale of an organ such as a kidney increases the risk of death. One possible response is that the existence of a market for kidneys would especially benefit the poor, as purchasers, since they are disproportionately represented among those who suffer from kidney failure. Another, more general response is that prohibiting the poor from selling their kidneys or other organs in order to protect them represents a perverse form of paternalism. The legitimate concern with improvident sales, the argument continues, can easily be met through regulation rather than through total prohibition.

A third objection frequently raised in discussions about sales of human organs comes under the aegis of commodification. The commercial sale of human organs, it is argued, should be prohibited because it would commodify them.

---

33. See, e.g., Richard Titmuss, The Gift Relationship (1971); Kenneth Arrow, Gifts and Exchanges, in Altruism, Morality, and Economic Theory, E. Phelps ed. (1975).

34. See Hansmann, Markets for Human Organs, supra, at 68, 68 n.23.

Why commodification is objectionable is not always made clear, but one reason sometimes given is that commodifying certain goods is morally objectionable because it would injure human dignity. Certain goods are special in the sense that they are inextricably connected with human dignity and personality. Allowing these goods to be freely bought and sold would transform their character in ways that undermine their moral function. Which goods count in this special class is, of course, a highly contentious question, but some scholars have argued that human organs are among those goods. On the question of commodification generally, see Margaret Jane Radin, Market-Inalienability, 100 Harv. L. Rev. 1849 (1987).

External References. Henry Hansmann, The Economics and Ethics of Markets for Human Organs, 14 J. of Health Politics, Policy & Law 57 (1989); Lori B. Andrews, My Body, My Property, 16 Hastings Center Rep. 28 (1986); Arthur Caplan, Ethical and Policy Issues in the Procurement of Cadaver Organs for Transplantation, 314 New Eng. J. Med. 981 (1984).

Chapter 10

Protection of the Family: Limitations on the Freedom of Disposition

FREEDOM of disposition is the hallmark of the American law of succession. In the United States, testamentary freedom is abridged only in limited circumstances and only in a limited way. In contrast, in the western European nations, a decedent cannot totally disinherit his or her children and sometimes cannot totally disinherit other blood relatives. In England and the principal commonwealth jurisdictions (the Australian states, most of the Canadian provinces, New Zealand), the statutory scheme known as Testator's Family Maintenance (TFM) is in place, by which the chancery judge is empowered to revise the dispositive provisions of a testator's will (including intestate shares, in an intestate estate) for the benefit of the decedent's relatives and other dependents.[1]

1. See, e.g., Inheritance (Provision for Family and Dependents) Act 1975, c. 63 (U.K.). Most commentators have argued that the TFM approach, because of its highly discretionary character, should not be adopted in the United States. See Mary Ann Glendon, Fixed Rules and Discretion in Contemporary Family Law and Succession Law, 60 Tul. L. Rev. 1165, 1186-91 (1986); John

In American law, the decedent's spouse is the only relative favored by a protection against intentional disinheritance. The decedent's children and possibly more remote descendants are granted protection only against unintentional disinheritance.

PART A. THE SPOUSE'S ELECTIVE SHARE

Statutory References: *UPC §§ 2-201 to -214*

1. The Partnership Theory of Marriage

Disinheritance of a surviving spouse brings into question the fundamental nature of the economic rights of parties to a marital relationship, and of how the institution of marriage is viewed in society. The contemporary view of marriage is that it is an economic partnership.[2] The partnership theory of

---

H. Langbein & Lawrence W. Waggoner, Redesigning the Spouse's Forced Share, 22 Real Prop. Prob. & Tr. J. 303, 314 (1987). See generally Rosalind F. Atherton, Family Provision Legislation in Common Law Jurisdictions, in International Academy of Estate and Trust Law: Selected Papers 1997-1999, at 681 (Rosalind F. Atherton ed. 2001).

2. One of the earliest American expressions of the partnership theory of marriage appears in the 1963 Report of the Committee on Civil and Political Rights to the President's Commission on the Status of Women. As quoted in the Prefatory Note to the Uniform Marital Property Act, the Report states:

> Marriage is a partnership to which each spouse makes a different but equally important contribution. This fact has become increasingly recognized in the realities of American family living. While the laws of other countries have reflected this trend, family laws in the United States have lagged behind.

The strength of the attribution to marriage of an economic partnership is evidenced by the New Jersey case of Carr v. Carr, 576 A.2d 872 (N.J. 1990). In that case, a husband, after having left his wife of seventeen years, died during the pendency of a divorce proceeding initiated by the wife. The husband's will devised his entire estate to his children by a former marriage. The court held that the husband's death terminated the divorce proceeding under which the wife would have been entitled to a share determined under New Jersey's equitable-distribution statute. The wife also had no recourse under New Jersey's elective-share statute because that statute withheld an elective share from a surviving spouse if the decedent and spouse were not living together at the time of the decedent's death. Despite the wife's inability to recover under either the divorce or elective-share statute, the court held:

> We conclude . . . that the principle that animates both [the equitable-distribution and elective-share] statutes is that a spouse may acquire an interest in marital property by virtue of the mutuality of efforts during marriage that contribute to the creation, acquisition, and preservation of such property. This principle, primarily equitable in nature, is derived from notions of fairness, common decency, and good faith. Further, we are convinced that these laws do not reflect a legislative intent to extinguish the property entitlements of a spouse who finds himself or herself beyond the reach of either statute because the marriage has realistically but not legally ended at the time of the other's death.
>
> In the exercise of their common-law jurisdiction, courts should seek to effectuate sound public policy and mold the law to embody the societal values that are exemplified by such public policy. . . .
>
> The constructive trust, we believe, is an appropriate equitable remedy in this type of case . . . [that]

marriage, sometimes also called the marital-sharing theory, is stated and supported in various ways. Sometimes it is portrayed "as an expression of the presumed intent of husbands and wives to pool their fortunes on an equal basis, share and share alike." Mary Ann Glendon, The Transformation of Family Law 131 (1989). Under this approach, the economic rights of each spouse are seen as deriving from an unspoken or imputed marital bargain under which the partners agree that each is to enjoy a half interest in the fruits of the marriage, that is, in the property nominally acquired by and titled in the sole name of either partner during the marriage (other than in property acquired by gift or inheritance). A decedent who disinherits his or her surviving spouse is seen as having reneged on the bargain. Sometimes the theory is visualized in restitutionary terms, a return-of-contribution notion. Under this approach, the law grants each spouse an entitlement to compensation for non-monetary contributions to the marital enterprise, as "a recognition of the activity of one spouse in the home and to compensate not only for this activity but for opportunities lost." Id. Sometimes the theory is stated in aspirational and behavior-shaping terms:

> [T]he ideal to which marriage aspires [is] that of equal partnerships between spouses who share resources, responsibilities, and risks. . . .
>
> From a policy standpoint, this partnership framework is desirable both because it encourages cooperative commitments between spouses and because it serves broader egalitarian and caretaking objectives. In effect, sharing principles hold promise for bridging traditional public/private divisions between family and market. A partnership model can cushion the impact of persistent gender biases in couples' private allocation of homemaking tasks and in the public allocation of salaries and benefits. By sharing their total resources, families can spread the risks and benefits of sex-linked roles, the remnants of a socioeconomic system that makes it difficult for any one individual to accommodate a full work and family life. . . .
>
> Not only do partnership principles promote gender equality; they also support caretaking commitments toward children and elderly dependents.

Deborah L. Rhode & Martha Minow, Reforming the Questions, Questioning the Reforms, in Divorce Reform at the Crossroads 191, 198-99 (Stephen D. Sugarman & Herma Hill Kay eds. 1990).

It is often said that of the two marital-property systems prevailing in the United States—community property and common-law, or separate property—the community property system implements the partnership theory while the

---

should be invoked and imposed on the marital property under the control of the executor of [the husband's] estate . . . to avoid the unjust enrichment that would occur if the marital property devolving to [the husband's] estate included the share beneficially belonging to [the wife].

common-law (title-based) system does not. This view is only partly accurate. To understand the differences and similarities between the community and separate property regimes, we need first to trace the development of the two systems.

a. Community Property and Marital-Property Systems

Separate Property and Community Property. The separate-property (title-based) system derives from English common law, while community property developed in continental Europe and was transplanted to the new world by French and Spanish settlers. The basic distinction between the two systems is this: Under the common law's system of separate property, the husband and wife are separate owners of the assets that each acquires after marriage (except for items that they have agreed to hold jointly). Under the community-property system, husband and wife own all assets acquired by either of them during marriage in equal undivided shares. The particular community-property model followed in the community-property states is derived from the *community of acquests* concept of the Spanish legal system, under which each spouse owns a half interest in the earnings of the other acquired during the marriage, in effect as a tenant in common; property acquired prior to the marriage and property acquired during the marriage by gift, bequest, or inheritance are not counted in the community, and so remain separate property. The other community--property model, called universal community, has not appeared in this country. In universal-community systems, each spouse owns a half interest in all the property of the other, regardless of the property's source or time of acquisition.[3]

Historical Background. The distinction between separate and community marital property ideas dates to the thirteenth century. The reasons for the divergence between the systems in England and continental nations remain somewhat obscure. One plausible explanation is that, while England had all of the other ingredients that led to community property in France, it lacked any strong tradition of community within the family, at least one that extended beyond the nuclear family. Professor Donahue has argued: "Without any strong tradition of community, the English lawyers could not group these same

---

3. Because both spouses own community property, problems arise concerning management of community assets. Community-property states have statutes prescribing who has power to manage and deal with the assets. These statutes vary considerably in their details, but some generalizations are possible. In Texas, the wife has sole management power over her earnings that are kept separate, and the husband has sole management power over his. In California and several other community-property states either spouse has power, acting alone, to manage community assets. Both spouses, however, ordinarily are required to join in transfers or mortgages of community real property. If one spouse makes a gift of community property to a third party, the non-donor spouse may set it aside entirely or in excess of a stated amount. See generally J. Thomas Oldham, Management of the Community Estate During an Intact Marriage, 56 L. & Contemp. Prob. 99 (1993).

[French] elements together and call it community. They lacked at an early stage the social practice around which the legal concept could crystallize and at a slightly later stage the legal concept around which the social practice could crystallize." Charles Donahue, Jr., What Causes Fundamental Legal Ideas? Marital Property in England and France in the Thirteenth Century, 78 Mich. L. Rev. 59, 86-87 (1979).

Although only nine states (Arizona, California, Idaho, Louisiana, Nevada, New Mexico, Texas, Washington, and Wisconsin[4]) can be called community-property states, interest in the community-property system over the years has not been limited to these states. During the 1930s and 40s, before Congress enacted legislation allowing the joint income-tax return for married persons, several separate-property (title-based) states converted their marital-property regimes to community property in order to grant their residents the tax benefits of community property's income-splitting effect. When the income-splitting joint return was adopted in 1948, these states converted back to the separate-property regime, which had the effect of conserving traditional gender roles and power relationships within the marriage. See Carolyn C. Jones, Split-Income and Separate Spheres: Tax Law and Gender Roles in the 1940s, 6 Law & Hist. Rev. 259 (1988).

The Uniform Marital Property Act. More recently, interest in community property has been rekindled by a growing conviction in favor of economic equalization between husbands and wives. The idea that both marital partners should share equally acquests from the economic activity of either led to the promulgation in 1983 of the Uniform Marital Property Act (UMPA). The UMPA adopts a version of the community of acquests, although the terminology used in the UMPA is different—community property is called "marital property," separate property is called "individual property."[5] Under the UMPA, as under community property, the property interest that each spouse acquires in all the assets acquired by the economic activities of either during the marriage is a present, vested ownership right that does not depend on survival

---

4. Wisconsin's enactment of the Uniform Marital Property Act made it a community property state. The Wisconsin legislature, however, modified the UMPA in several respects. See Howard S. Erlanger & June M. Weisberger, From Common Law Property to Community Property: Wisconsin's Marital Property Act Four Years Later, 1990 Wis. L. Rev. 769 (1990).

Alaska recently became an optional community property state. Under the Alaska Community Property Act, effective May 23, 1998, married persons resident in Alaska may, if they choose, classify some or all of their assets as community property. For discussion, see Jonathan G. Blattmachr, Howard M. Zaritsky & Mark L. Ascher, Tax Planning with Consensual Community Property: Alaska's New Community Property Law, 33 Real Prop., Prob. & Tr. J. 615 (1999).

5. With respect to income earned on individual property, the UMPA follows the minority view and provides in § 4(d) that "income earned or accrued by a spouse or attributable to property of a spouse during marriage . . . is marital property."

of the other spouse. Wisconsin adopted the UMPA in 1986 (Wis. Stat. Ann. §§ 766.001-766.97), and is now properly counted as the ninth community-property state.[6]

Elective Share Thought Unnecessary Under Community Property. A unique feature of community-property regimes is that the surviving spouse is not seen as needing "protection" against disinheritance by means of a so-called "elective" share in the estate of the deceased spouse. The survivor already owns a half interest in the fruits of the marriage. No elective share is provided with respect to the separate or individual property of the other spouse because that property was not attributable to the fruits of the marriage. Contribution having been rewarded, decedents can be allowed unfettered power of disposition over their separate property and their portion of the community property. In practice, however, decedents often want their community property to pass to their surviving spouses, and it is for this reason that the California legislature recently enacted a statute enabling spouses to create "community property with right of survivorship." Community property titled in this form passes automatically to the survivor as if it were held in joint tenancy. See Cal. Civ. Code § 682.1 (effective July 1, 2001).

Classification. Under community-property systems and the UMPA, the couple's property must be classified upon the first spouse's death and this in turn sometimes requires tracing the property to its source. To help resolve disputes, these systems recognize a presumption that all property is community or marital property. The spouse alleging that an item is separate or individual property must be able to prove it, and this can be a difficult task as assets over time in a marriage are commingled, invested, reinvested, exchanged, and consumed.

To resolve classification problems, courts have developed subsidiary rules applicable to certain types of transactions. We can give here only a few examples of this highly complex body of law:

Acquisitions where the consideration is partly community, partly separate. Suppose that H purchases a boat under an installment contract executed prior to his marriage to W, and H pays some of the consideration after his marriage. Is the boat separate or community property? Three inconsistent legal theories for classifying ownership are available in this situation: inception-of-title, time-of-vesting, and pro-rata. W would have rights in the boat under the third theory but probably not under the second (depending on whether title transfers at the inception of the transaction or, more likely, when the last payment is made) and

---

6. See Rev. Rul. 87-13, 1987-1 C.B. 20. For tax purposes, the implication of this ruling is that the basis in *both* halves of marital property is stepped up to its value at the date of the decedent's death under IRC § 1014(b)(6). If marital property had been treated for tax purposes as tenancy-in-common property, only the decedent's half would have received a step-up in basis.

certainly not under the first. Compare, e.g., McCurdy v. McCurdy, 372 S.W.2d 381 (Tex. Civ. App. 1963) (applying the inception-of-title theory to a life-insurance policy purchased before the owner/beneficiary's marriage and holding that the proceeds are entirely his separate property) with Cosey v. Cosey, 364 So.2d 186 (La. Ct. App. 1978), aff'd, 376 So.2d 486 (La. 1979) (applying the time-of-vesting (or receipt) theory to a premarital land sales contract as to which H paid all of the consideration prior to his marriage but did not receive title until after the marriage and holding the land was not part of the community). No state uses a single theory consistently for all types of acquisitions over time.

Acquisitions on credit. Suppose that W, while married to H, borrows money from a lender, who takes no security interest, and that W still has the borrowed funds on hand when she dies. Are the funds separate or community property? Courts have taken several different approaches to resolving classification questions concerning credit acquisitions by one spouse during marriage. In Texas, for example, all credit acquisitions are community property unless there is "clear and satisfactory evidence that the creditor agreed to look solely to the separate estate or the contracting spouse for satisfaction." Mortenson v. Trammell, 604 S.W.2d 269 (Tex. Civ. App. 1980). In other states, proceeds from unsecured loans given on personal credit of either spouse are presumed community property. In some of these states, the presumption is rebutted by showing that the lender's state of mind was such that it made the loan primarily because the borrower's separate property made repayment likely. See, e.g., Shovlain v. Shovlain, 305 P.2d 737 (Idaho 1956); Finley v. Finley, 287 P.2d 475 (Wash. 1955). Louisiana follows yet a different test: Loan proceeds are community property unless there is evidence that the borrower intended to repay with separate funds and had the wealth to do so. See, e.g., Succession of Milton, 278 So.2d 159 (La. Ct. App. 1973).

Improvements of separate property with community funds (and vice versa). Suppose that W uses community funds to improve H's separate assets or uses her separate property to improve community assets. Is she entitled to any reimbursement? The answer is not always clear. The California Supreme Court, for example, had presumed that the improving spouse intends to make a gift when she uses separate funds to improve community property. See, e.g., Marriage of Lucas, 614 P.2d 285 (Cal. 1980), but the California legislature subsequently reversed this presumption by statute. See Cal. Fam. Code § 2640.

As these examples indicate, classification issues are highly complex and subject to a bewildering variety of rules. For a discussion of the details of these matters, see William A. Reppy, Jr. & Cynthia A. Samuel, Community Property in the United States 51-164 (2d ed. 1982).

Classification rules are default rules: Couples in community-property states generally may contract out from under them. By agreement, they may change community property into separate property, separate property into community property, community property into joint tenancy or tenancy in common property, and so on. Such changes in classification are called "transmutation." For further discussion, see id. at 23-49.

Migratory Couples and Quasi-Community Property. If a couple moves from a separate-property state to a community-property state, the surviving spouse may effectively lose protection against disinheritance. The law of the state where the couple was domiciled at the time assets were acquired controls ownership of these assets. Thus, assets that either spouse earned during marriage in a separate-property state remain separate property. If one spouse was the sole wage earner and most or all of the couple's assets were registered in his or her name, the surviving spouse who is a non-wage earner may be left with little protection against disinheritance, at least as to those assets. The law of the state of domicile controls the disposition of property of death. If the couple had remained domiciled in a separate-property state at the time of the decedent's death, the surviving spouse would have been protected by that state's elective share statute.

Three of the community-property states, California, Idaho, and Washington, address the problem of migratory couples through the recognition of "quasi-community property." Quasi-community property is property, other than real property located in other states, that would have been community property, but for the fact that it was acquired by the decedent when the couple was domiciled in another state. In California and Washington, the surviving spouse of the acquiring decedent has an automatic half interest in the decedent's quasi-community property. See Cal. Prob. Code §§ 66, 101; Wash. Rev. Code §§ 26.16.220-.250. During the marriage, quasi-community property is regarded for most purposes as separate property of the acquiring spouse.[7] Since this right arises only upon the death of the acquiring spouse, quasi-community property might appropriately be called deferred community property. It is analogous to an elective share in that portion of the decedent's property that was acquired from earnings while the couple was domiciled in a separate property state.

A similar idea, called deferred marital property, is adopted in §§ 17 (divorce) and 18 (death) of the UMPA. Idaho, a UPC state, takes a different approach to the survivor's rights in quasi-community property. Rather than granting the survivor an automatic half interest, Idaho applies the UPC's

---

7. Two other states, Arizona and Texas, apply the quasi-community property concept to division of property upon divorce, but do not apply it to division at death. See Ariz. Rev. Stat. § 25-318; Tex. Fam. Code § 7.002.

augmented-estate elective-share system to quasi-community property. See Idaho Code §§ 15-2-101, -102. See also Wis. Stat. Ann. § 861.02.

For migrating couples going the other way—*from* a community-property state *to* a common-law or separate-property state—the change in domicile does not change the couple's pre-existing rights, at least not in theory. Community property theoretically retains its character when it is moved to a separate-property state. In practice, however, lawyers and courts in separate-property states, who frequently are unfamiliar with community property, treat community property as analogous to a tenancy in common or, if title is in one spouse's sole name, as separate property subject to a constructive trust for the other spouse.

If spouses moving from a community-property to a separate-property state wish to retain the community character of their assets, they should take special care to do so. Mingling community property with separate property may make tracing impracticable. Furthermore, proceeds from the sale of community assets should be taken in the names of the husband and wife as community property. Alternatively, title may be taken in one spouse's name, while the spouses execute a contemporaneous agreement indicating their intention to retain the new assets as community property.

The Uniform Disposition of Community Property Rights at Death Act (1971), enacted in fourteen states (Alaska, Arkansas, Colorado, Connecticut, Florida, Hawaii, Kentucky, Michigan, Montana, New York, North Carolina, Oregon, Virginia and Wyoming), clarifies the rights of a surviving spouse of a couple who move from a community-property to a separate-property state. It creates a rebuttable presumption that property acquired during marriage by either spouse while the couple was domiciled in a community-property state was acquired as and remains property that is subject to the Act. Upon the death of the first to die one-half of the property subject to the Act is the property of the surviving spouse and is not subject to the decedent's testamentary control or distributable as his or her intestate estate. Moreover, the one-half which is the decedent's property is not subject to the surviving spouse's elective share. See Stanley M. Johanson, The Migrating Client: Estate Planning for the Couple from a Community Property State, 9 Inst. on Est. Plan. Ch. 8 (1975); Note, Community Property in a Common Law Jurisdiction: A Seriously Neglected Area of the Law, 16 Washburn L.J. 77 (1976).

b. Equitable Distribution Upon Divorce

The community-property system, by granting each spouse a one-half interest in the earnings of the other immediately upon acquisition, directly treats a couple's enterprise as collaborative. However, all of the separate property states[8] also give effect, or purport to give effect, to the partnership theory at dissolution of a marriage upon divorce.[9] Under so-called equitable distribution upon divorce statutes, courts have broad discretion "to assign to either spouse property acquired during the marriage, irrespective of title, taking into account the circumstances of the particular case and recognizing the value of the contributions of a nonworking spouse or homemaker to the acquisition of that property. Simply stated, the system of equitable distribution views marriage as essentially a shared enterprise or joint undertaking in the nature of a partnership to which both spouses contribute directly and indirectly, financially and nonfinancially—the fruits of which are distributable at divorce." John D. Gregory, The Law of Equitable Distribution § 1.03 at 1-6 (1989).

The equitable distribution scheme was first introduced by the Uniform Marriage and Divorce Act (UMDA). As originally promulgated in 1970, the UMDA required that "marital" property be distinguished from "nonmarital" or "separate" property. Only the former was subject to distribution at divorce. This distinction, which was drawn from community-property law and generally corresponds to community and separate property, has created various characterization problems. For example, are increases in value of admittedly nonmarital property during marriage marital or nonmarital? The statute's approach to

---

8. Writing in 1989, Professor Oldham stated that "Mississippi is the only state that has not clearly accepted [the equitable apportionment] system. J. Thomas Oldham, Tracing, Commingling, and Transmutation, 23 Fam. L. Q. 219, 219 n.1 (1989) (citing Jones v. Jones, 532 So.2d 574 (Miss. 1988)). This state of affairs changed in 1994, when the Mississippi Supreme Court definitively adopted equitable apportionment in divorce. See Ferguson v. Ferguson, 639 So.2d 921, 925 (Miss. 1994).

For a fascinating account of how this system swept the country, see Mary Ann Glendon, Property Rights Upon Dissolution of Marriages and Informal Unions, in The Cambridge Lectures 245 (Nancy E. Eastham & Boris Krivy eds. 1981).

9. In Rothman v. Rothman, 320 A.2d 496 (N.J. 1974), a landmark case interpreting New Jersey's equitable-distribution statute, the New Jersey Supreme Court stated:

> The statute we are considering authorizes the courts, upon divorce, to divide marital assets equitably between the spouses. . . . [T]he enactment seeks to right what many have felt to be a grave wrong. It gives recognition to the essential supportive role played by the wife in the home, acknowledging that as homemaker, wife and mother she should clearly be entitled to a share of family assets accumulated during the marriage. Thus the division of property upon divorce is responsive to the concept that marriage is a shared enterprise, a joint undertaking, that in many ways it is akin to a partnership. Only if it is clearly understood that far more than economic factors are involved, will the resulting distribution be equitable within the true intent and meaning of the statute. . . . The widely pervasive effect this remedial legislation will almost certainly have throughout our society betokens its great significance.

Id. at 501-02. Although in this early equitable-distribution case, the court refused to establish a presumptive division of marital assets on a 50/50 basis, see id. at 503 n.6, many courts today do indulge in such a presumption of equal division, and many of the more recently enacted statutes explicitly do so also. See John D. Gregory, The Law of Equitable Distribution § 8.03 (1989).

characterization was similar to that in a community of acquests regime: a presumption that all assets acquired by either spouse during marriage are marital. Several exceptions to this presumption existed: (1) assets that either spouse brought to the marriage, including assets that can be traced back to such assets; (2) assets that either spouse acquired during marriage other than from earnings; and (3) assets that both spouses have agreed to exclude from distribution upon dissolution of their marriage.

In response to characterization problems that the marital/nonmarital assets dichotomy created, the UMDA was subsequently amended to abolish that distinction. Section 307 now describes as the property subject to distribution "property and assets belonging to either [spouse] or both however and whenever acquired. . . ." This provision creates what is called a "hotchpot" property scheme. This change eliminates the characterization problem, but it makes the question of how the property should be distributed more difficult. See Robert J. Levy, An Introduction to Divorce-Property Issues, 23 Fam. L.Q. 147, 151-56, 159-61 (1989).

Among the states that have not adopted the UMDA, there are considerable differences in the statutes concerning what property is subject to division.[10] Once the court has determined what property is divisible, however, it has power to order the title-holding spouse to transfer all or a part of divisible assets to the other spouse. The statutes differ as to the criteria by which courts are to make distributive decisions. Some statutes include among these criteria the relative spousal contributions to the property's acquisition. In situations where one spouse is a wage-earner and the other is a homemaker, some courts have read such statutes as favoring the wage-earning spouse over the homemaker spouse. A few legislatures have responded to this interpretation by adding to the statute a "homemaker" provision, which directs the court to consider the "non-monetary contributions" of homemakers to the "acquisition, preservation and maintenance, or increase in value of marital property." E.g., W.Va. Code § 48-2-32. Courts have discretion to ignore this factor like any other factor, and some have done so. See, e.g., Axtell v. Axtell, 482 A.2d 1261, 1264 (Me. 1984). Other courts, however, have interpreted such homemaker provisions as establishing an irrebuttable presumption that both spousal contributed equally to the property's acquisition. See, e.g., Ferguson v. Ferguson, 357 N.W.2d 104 (Minn. App. 1984).

In general, equitable distribution is characterized by a considerable degree of judicial discretion. This feature is an important difference between the

10. The various schemes are canvassed, state-by-state, in John D. Gregory, supra; J. Thomas Oldham, Divorce, Separation and the Distribution of Property (1989); and Lawrence J. Golden, Equitable Distribution of Property (1983).

equitable-distribution and community-property regimes. Despite this difference, however, equitable distribution approximates community property at divorce by implementing the partnership theory. See Comment, The Development of Sharing Principles in Common Law Marital Property States, 28 UCLA L. Rev. 1269 (1981).

The widespread adoption of equitable-distribution statutes is a source of pressure on separate-property states to implement the partnership theory in the other circumstances in which spousal property rights loom large—dissolution of marriage at death.

External References. For a collection of excellent essays on divorce-reform laws, see Divorce Reform at the Crossroads (Stephen D. Sugarman & Herma Hill Kay eds. 1990).

c. Conventional Elective-Share Law

All but one of the separate-property states[11] have decided that disinheritance of the surviving spouse at death is one of the few instances in which the decedent's testamentary freedom with respect to his or her title-based ownership interests must be curtailed. No matter what the decedent's intent, the separate-property states recognize that the surviving spouse does have some claim to a portion of the decedent's estate. These statutes, which in all but a few states have replaced the common-law estates of dower and curtesy,[12] provide the spouse a so-called "forced" share. Because the forced share is expressed as an option that the survivor can elect or let lapse during the administration of the decedent's estate, and not as a retitling of the decedent's property that automatically occurs at death, the UPC uses the more descriptive term "elective" share.

Elective-share law in the separate-property states has not caught up to the partnership theory of marriage. Under the traditional American elective-share

---

11. Georgia is the only separate-property state lacking an elective-share statute. For a discussion of the reasons for Georgia's position, including its unusual "year's support" practice, and an argument that elective-share statutes are generally unnecessary, see Verner F. Chaffin, A Reappraisal of the Wealth Transmission Process: The Surviving Spouse, Year's Support and Intestate Succession, 10 Ga. L. Rev. 447 (1976). For an opposing view, see Note, Preventing Spousal Disinheritance in Georgia, 19 Ga. L. Rev. 427 (1985).

12. The Restatement 2d of Property, Statutory Note to § 34.1, lists five jurisdictions as providing the surviving spouse a dower or dower-like interest in the decedent's real property—Arkansas, District of Columbia, Kentucky, Ohio, and West Virginia. West Virginia should be dropped from this list; dower and curtesy were abolished there in 1992. See W. Va. Code § 43-1-1. North Carolina, which statutorily provides a dower right for both spouses, should be added to the list. See N.C. Stat. § 29-30.

statute, including the elective share provided by the former version of the UPC promulgated in 1969, a surviving spouse is granted a personal non-transferable right to claim a one-third share of the decedent's estate, not a transmissible right to claim the fifty percent share of the couple's combined assets that the partnership theory would imply. Indeed, in a few states the elective share is not even a right to a fee interest but, like common-law dower, only a life interest in one-third or one-half.[13]

To illustrate the discrepancy between the partnership theory and conventional elective-share law, consider first a long-term marriage, in which the couple's combined assets were accumulated mostly during the course of the marriage. The elective-share fraction of one-third of the decedent's estate plainly does not implement a partnership principle. The actual result is governed by which spouse happens to die first and by how the property accumulated during the marriage was nominally titled.

Consider Harry and Wilma. Assume that Harry and Wilma were married in their twenties or early thirties. They never divorced, and Harry died somewhat prematurely, say at age 62, survived by Wilma. For whatever reason, Harry left a will entirely disinheriting Wilma. Throughout their long life together, the couple managed to accumulate assets worth $600,000, marking them as a somewhat affluent but hardly wealthy couple.

Under conventional elective-share law, Wilma's ultimate entitlement is governed by the manner in which these $600,000 in assets were titled. Wilma could end up much poorer or much richer than a 50/50 principle would suggest. The reason is that under conventional elective-share law, Wilma has a claim to one-third of Harry's *"estate."*

When the marital assets have been disproportionately titled in the decedent's name, conventional elective-share law often entitles the survivor to less than an equal share. Thus, if Harry "owned" all $600,000 of the marital assets, Wilma's claim against Harry's estate would only be for $200,000—well below Wilma's $300,000 entitlement produced by the partnership/marital-sharing principle. And, if Harry "owned" $500,000 of the marital assets, Wilma's claim against Harry's estate would only be for $166,500 (1/3 of $500,000), which

13. See, e.g., Conn. Gen. Stat. § 45a-436; Mass. Ann. Laws c.191, § 15.

Until recently, the New York statute allowed the decedent to satisfy the elective share by giving the surviving spouse $10,000 plus a life income interest in a trust. Criticized for leaving surviving spouses—particularly women, who are more likely to be the survivor— with a lack of control, the statute was amended. As of 1992, the survivor is entitled to an outright one-third share or $50,000, whichever is greater. N.Y. EPTL § 5-1.1-A(a)(4)-(5). The current South Carolina statute is similar to the former New York statute, allowing the decedent to satisfy the elective share by transferring one-third of the estate into a trust that qualifies for the federal estate tax marital deduction. S.C. Code Ann. § 62-2-207. As we saw in Chapter 7, under the QTIP rules, the surviving spouse may be given only a life income interest.

when combined with Wilma's "own" $100,000 yields a less-than-equal share of $266,500 for Wilma—still below the $300,000 figure produced by the partnership/marital-sharing principle.

When, on the other hand, the marital assets have already been more or less equally divided, conventional elective-share law grants the survivor a right to take a disproportionately large share. If Harry and Wilma each owned $300,000, Wilma is still granted a claim against Harry's estate for an additional $100,000.

Finally, when the marital assets have been disproportionately titled in the survivor's name, conventional elective-share law entitles the survivor to magnify the disproportion. If only $200,000 were titled in Harry's name, Wilma would still have a claim against Harry's estate for $66,667 (1/3 of $200,000), even though Wilma was *already* overcompensated as measured by the partnership/marital-sharing theory.

Let us now turn our attention to a very different sort of marriage—a short-term marriage, particularly the short-term marriage later in life, in which each spouse typically comes into the marriage with assets derived from a former marriage. In these marriages, the one-third fraction of the decedent's estate far exceeds a fifty/fifty division of assets acquired during the marriage.

To illustrate this sort of marriage, let us turn to the case of Wilma and Sam. Suppose that a few years after Harry's death, Wilma married Sam. Suppose that both Wilma and Sam were in their mid-to-late sixties when they were married. Then suppose that after a few years of marriage—five, let us say—Wilma died survived by Sam. Assume further that both Wilma and Sam have adult children and a few grandchildren by their prior marriages, and that each would prefer to leave most or all of his or her property to those children.

The value of the couple's combined assets is $600,000, $300,000 of which is titled in Wilma's name (the decedent) and $300,000 of which is titled in Sam's name (the survivor).

Under conventional elective-share law, Sam would have a claim to one-third of Wilma's estate, or $100,000. Keep in mind that when this short-term, late-in-life marriage terminated by Wilma's death, Wilma's assets were $300,000 and Sam's assets were $300,000. For reasons that aren't immediately apparent, conventional elective-share law gives the survivor, Sam, a right to shrink Wilma's estate (and hence the share to Wilma's children by her prior marriage to Harry) by $100,000 (reducing it to $200,000) while supplementing Sam's assets (which will likely go to Sam's children by his prior marriage) by $100,000 (increasing their value to $400,000).

Conventional elective-share law, in other words, basically rewards the children of the remarried spouse who manages to outlive the other, arranging for those children a windfall share of one-third of the "loser's" estate. The "winning" spouse—the one who chanced to survive—gains a windfall, for this "winner" is unlikely to have made a contribution, monetary or otherwise, to the "loser's" wealth remotely worth one-third.

How prevalent are marriages like that between Wilma and Sam—the remarriage later in life ending in the death of one of the partners a few years later? Plainly, such marriages do not affect a high proportion of the widowed and divorced population. Nevertheless, government data suggest that the incidence of such marriages may not be insignificant.[14] Equally to the point, when such marriages occur, conventional elective-share law renders results that are dramatically inconsistent with the partnership theory of marriage. That these results are seen as unjust by the children of the decedent's former marriage is both unsurprising and well documented in the elective-share case law.[15] In a case like that of Wilma and Sam—the short-term, late-in-life marriage, which produces no children—a decedent who disinherits or largely disinherits the surviving spouse may not be acting so much from malice or spite toward the surviving spouse, but from an obligation to the children of his or her former, long-term marriage.

d. The Uniform Probate Code's Elective Share

The 1990 revisions of the UPC made sweeping changes in the elective share. The purpose is to grant the surviving spouse a right of election that implements the partnership theory for the division of marital property at death. As we have already seen, elective-share law in separate-property states has not caught up with the partnership theory. Under both the traditional type and the augmented-

---

14. Data published by the federal government in 1989 reveal that about 21% of widowed men and about 8% of widowed women remarry. For divorced men and divorced women, the figures are 83% and 78% respectively. U.S. Dep't of Health & Human Services, Pub. No. 89-1923, Remarriages and Subsequent Divorces–United States 12 (1989). The median ages at the time of remarriage of widowed men and women have increased noticeably over the past two decades; in 1990, the most recent year for which such statistics are available, the ages were 61.1 for men and 53.4 for women. The median ages at remarriage of divorced men and women have also been increasing, but the ages are, of course, much lower. In 1990, the median ages were 39.0 for divorced men and 35.6 for divorced women. National Center for Health Statistics, Monthly Vital Statistics Report, July 15, 1995, tbl. 9.

15. See William D. Macdonald, Fraud on the Widow's Share 156-57 (1960). Of the elective-share cases in the law reports up to the time of writing and in which the author could identify the relationships, more than half pitted children of a former marriage against a later spouse.

According to federal government statistics published in 1989, "on average, women ending first marriages had 1.06 children under 18 years, those ending second marriages had 0.64 children, and those ending third marriages had 0.36 children. These differences are due at least in part to the fact that most children are born into first marriages and may not be mentioned on divorce records of subsequent marriages unless custody becomes an issue." U.S. Dep't of Health & Human Services, supra note 14, at 3.

estate type of elective-share statute, a surviving spouse's share is less than the fifty percent share of the couple's combined assets that the sharing theory would imply. The redesigned elective share is intended to change this by bringing elective-share law into line with the partnership theory.

Accrual-Type Elective Share. The redesigned elective-share system can be called an accrual-type elective share.[16] It has three essential features. The first, implemented by § 2-202(a), establishes a schedule under which the elective share adjusts to the length of the marriage. The longer the marriage, the larger the "elective-share percentage." The elective-share percentage starts by giving the survivor, during the first year of marriage, a right to elect the "supplemental elective-share amount" only.[17] After one year of marriage, the surviving spouse's elective-share percentage is three percent. It increases with each additional year of marriage until, after fifteen years of marriage, it reaches the full share, which has been increased to fifty percent.

The second feature of the redesigned system is that the elective-share percentage is applied to the value of the augmented estate, which, as defined in §§ 2-203 to 2-208, includes the couple's *combined* assets. Specifically, the augmented estate consists of the sum of the values of four components: On the decedent's side are (1) the decedent's net probate estate and (2) the decedent's nonprobate transfers to others.[18] Straddling between the decedent's side and the surviving spouse's side are (3) the decedent's nonprobate transfers to the surviving spouse.[19] On the surviving spouse's side are (4) property owned by the surviving spouse and amounts that would have been included in the surviving spouse's nonprobate transfers to others had the spouse been the decedent. The purpose behind combining the couple's assets is to implement the marital-sharing theory by denying significance to the possibly fortuitous factor of how the spouses happen to have taken title to particular assets.

The third feature, implemented by § 2-209, is that the surviving spouse's own assets are counted first (or a portion of them in under-fifteen-year marriages) in making up the spouse's ultimate entitlement, so that the decedent's assets are liable only if there is a deficiency.

---

16. For a proposal that divorce law utilize an accrual-type system for division of assets, see Stephen D. Sugarman, Dividing Financial Interests on Divorce, in Divorce Reform at the Crossroads 130, 159-60 (Stephen D. Sugarman & Herma Hill Kay eds. 1990).

17. The supplemental elective-share amount is discussed infra p. 597.

18. The content of the decedent's nonprobate-transfers-to-others component and its role in preventing "fraud on the spouse's share" are discussed infra p. 609.

19. This component covers items such as the decedent's fractional interest in property held by the decedent and surviving spouse in joint tenancy and life insurance on the decedent's life payable to the surviving spouse.

To illustrate these three features, let us return to Wilma and Sam. Recall that the value of the couple's combined assets was $600,000, of which $300,000 was titled in Wilma's name (the decedent) and $300,000 in Sam's name (the survivor). Their marriage having lasted five years, the elective-share percentage prescribed in the statute is fifteen percent. See UPC § 2-202(a). Sam's elective-share entitlement is $90,000, but this does not mean that he has a $90,000 claim against Wilma's estate. Thirty percent of Sam's own $300,000 in assets (double the elective-share percentage) count in fulfilling Sam's elective-share amount. Since thirty percent of Sam's assets is $90,000, there is no deficiency and hence no claim to any of Wilma's assets.

The redesigned UPC elective-share system differs from the community-property regime in two ways. The rights accorded a spouse under the UPC are conditioned on surviving the decedent. In contrast, under a community-property regime each spouse has a right to control one-half of the marital estate regardless of the order of deaths. The second difference is that the UPC adds together and then splits all of the couple's assets, including assets acquired before marriage to each other and assets acquired by gift or inheritance, rather than only acquisitions from earnings during marriage to each other. The reason for this more inclusive approach is to make the system more administratively convenient by avoiding the tracing problems that arise under the community-property system. In practice, the gap between the two systems is unlikely to be great. It is unusual for either spouse to bring substantial separate property to a long-duration first marriage. In cases of short-duration marriages, the accrual mechanism abates some of the consequences of an expanded forced share by reducing the vested portion of the survivor's entitlement. Finally, where there is substantial disparity in the wealth of the parties, they can contract out of the elective-share law through a premarital agreement.

Implementation of a Support Theory; Supplemental Elective-Share Amount. The partnership/marital-sharing theory is not the only driving force behind elective-share law. Another theoretical basis for elective-share law is that the spouses' mutual duties of support during their joint lifetimes should be continued in some form after death in favor of the survivor, as a claim on the decedent's estate. Conventional elective-share law implements this theory poorly. The fixed fraction, whether it is the typical one-third or some other fraction, disregards the survivor's actual needs. A one-third share may be inadequate to the surviving spouse's needs, especially in a modest estate. On the other hand, in a very large estate, a one-third share may go far beyond the survivor's needs. In either a modest or a large estate, the survivor may or may not have ample independent means, and this factor, too, is disregarded in conventional elective-share law.

The UPC's redesigned elective-share system seeks to implement the support theory by granting the survivor a supplemental elective-share amount related to the survivor's actual needs. In implementing a support rationale, the length of the marriage is quite irrelevant. Because the duty of support is founded upon status, it arises at the time of the marriage.

Section 2-202(b) of the UPC implements the support theory by providing a supplemental elective-share amount of $50,000. Counted first in making up this $50,000 amount are the surviving spouse's own title-based ownership interests, including amounts shifting to the survivor at the decedent's death and amounts owing to the survivor from the decedent's estate under the accrual-type elective-share discussed above, but excluding amounts going to the survivor under the Code's probate exemptions and allowances and the survivor's Social Security and other governmental benefits. Under § 2-209(b) and (c), if the survivor's assets are less than the $50,000 minimum, then the survivor is entitled to whatever additional portion of the decedent's estate is necessary to bring the survivor's assets up to that minimum level.

Gender Inequality and the Elective Share. Some commentators have criticized the partnership theory generally and the UPC elective share specifically on the ground that they fail adequately to take into account the disparity in the economic circumstances of married men and women. They argue that the partnership theory is fundamentally flawed because wives are much less likely to be self-sufficient than husbands are. In general, men earn more than women do, and men have more assets titled in their names than do women. These circumstances have led to criticism of the partnership theory as applied to divorce law on the ground that it sometimes leaves many divorced women without an adequate means of support. This is especially so with respect to divorced women who have children and invested more time in raising their children than they did in their jobs. See, e.g., Lenore J. Weitzman, The Divorce Revolution: The Unexpected Social and Economic Consequences for Women and Children in America Ch. 7 (1985); Deborah L. Rhode & Martha Minow, Reforming the Questions, Questioning the Reforms, in Divorce Reform at the Crossroads 191, 201-04 (Stephen D. Sugarman & Herma Hill Kay eds. 1990); Bea A. Smith, The Partnership Theory of Marriage: A Borrowed Solution Fails, 68 Texas L. Rev. 689 (1990). For criticism of the Weitzman study, see Stephen D. Sugarman, Dividing Financial Interests on Divorce, in Divorce Reform at the Crossroads 130 (Stephen D. Sugarman & Herma Hill Kay eds. 1990).

The same criticism has been extended to elective share law. Because women's average life expectancy is seven years longer than men's, the surviving spouse is more likely to be a woman. The economic disparity between men and women increases as they age. Among men and women age 65 and older, for example, women are nearly twice as likely as men to be poor. See Administration on Aging, Profile of Older Americans: 1999, available at www.aoa.gov/aoa/stats/profile. Under these circumstances, some have argued, the UPC's supplemental elective-share amount is too small adequately to protect substantial numbers of women, especially those who gave up a career to be homemakers and whose husbands die within ten years of marriage. See Margaret V. Turano, UPC Section 2-201 [renumbered 2-202]: Equal Treatment of Spouses?, 55 Alb. L. Rev. 983, 1003-1006 (1992).

Criticizing the UPC elective share from another direction, it has been argued that while the statute makes a nod to the contribution theory, its actual rationale is support or need. See Mary Moers Wenig, The Marital Property Law of Connecticut: Past, Present, and Future, 1990 Wis. L. Rev. 807, 877. See also Charles H. Whitebread, The Uniform Probate Code's Nod to the Partnership Theory of Marriage, 11 Prob. L.J. 125 (1992).

The Partnership Theory and the Problem of Nonmarital Property. Yet another criticism concerns the UPC's use of a fifteen-year phase-in period to deal with the problem of nonmarital property. It has been argued that this approach is arbitrary and may often result in the elective-share amount not being consistent with the objective of one-half the marital, and only the marital, property. For example, it is possible even after a fifteen-year marriage that most of the assets of both spouses are separate property, if the marriage occurred late in life. Conversely, property owned by both spouses after a five year marriage in some cases may be entirely marital property. To deal with this problem of over- and under-inclusiveness, it has been suggested that the accrual approach be replaced with a flat elective-share percentage of 50% coupled with an exception for separate property to the extent that either the decedent's estate or the surviving spouse can prove it. To ameliorate proof problems, there would be a strong rebuttable presumption that all property is marital property. See Susan N. Gary, Marital Partnership Theory and the Elective Share: Federal Estate Tax Law Provides a Solution, 49 U. Miami L. Rev. 567 (1995).

Problems

To evaluate the redesigned system, compare the results that would be reached under that system in the following cases with the results under (i) the former UPC elective share (supra p. 592) and (ii) a community-property or UMPA regime. For shorthand purposes, the term "D's estate" is used to mean the assets on the decedent's side that are included in the augmented estate under § 2-204 and the term "S's assets" is used to mean the assets on the surviving spouse's side that are included in the augmented estate under § 2-207. Assume that D died with a will completely disinheriting S and that D made no nonprobate transfers that are included in the augmented estate under either § 2-205 or § 2-206.

1. Married in their twenties, D and S lived a long life together. D died at age 75, survived by S.

(a) D's estate is valued at $500,000; S's assets are valued at $100,000.

(b) D's estate is valued at $100,000; S's assets are valued at $500,000.

2. D and S got married late in life, after having previously been married; each had children by the prior marriage. Five years after their marriage to each other, D died, survived by S.

(a) D's estate is valued at $500,000 and S's assets are valued at $100,000.

(b) D's estate is valued at $100,000; S's assets are valued at $500,000.

(c) D's estate is valued at $90,000; S's assets are valued at $10,000.

External References. John W. Fisher II & Scott A. Curnutte, Reforming the Law of Intestate Succession and Elective Shares: New Solutions to Age-Old Problems, 93 W. Va. L. Rev. 61 (1990); Lawrence W. Waggoner, Spousal Rights in our Multiple-Marriage Society: The Revised Uniform Probate Code, 26 Real Prop. Prob. & Tr. J. 683 (1992).

2. Protection Against Will Substitutes

One of the most troublesome issues regarding elective-share law is the extent to which the surviving spouse's rights extend to will substitutes. An elective share may be of little value to a surviving spouse if it applies only to a fraction of the decedent's probate estate. The decedent could use one or more will substitutes to implement an estate plan that effectively disinherits his or her spouse. Many courts, using different approaches, have worked to preserve the effectiveness of the statutory elective share. While legislation has changed elective-share statutes in many states to respond to deficiencies in traditional-type statutes, these judicial doctrines remain important in those states that have not amended their statutes. In these states, the judicial response is the surviving spouse's only protection against disinheritance by will substitutes. We shall first examine these judicial approaches and then address the different legislative approaches to will substitutes.

a. Common-Law Theories

The courts have adopted one or the other of two approaches: the *fraudulent-intent* test or the *illusory-transfer* test. The illusory-transfer test is the predominant view. The leading case adopting this test is Newman v. Dore, 9 N.E.2d 966 (N.Y. 1937). In that case, Ferdinand Straus, an 80-year-old testator, executed trust agreements by which he transferred all his real and personal property to his trustees. The trust agreements were executed three days before his death and when cross actions for dissolution of his marriage were pending. The terms of the trusts reserved to Straus the right to the income for life, the power to revoke the trusts, and the power to control the trustees in all aspects of the trusts' administration; needless to say, Straus's wife of four years, a woman in her thirties, received no beneficial interest in these trusts. She challenged the validity of the transfers to the trustees. The trial court found that Straus's motive in creating the trusts was to evade New York's elective-share statute, and held that the transfers weren't valid. In holding that the trusts were illusory, and therefore part of Straus's estate for purposes of his widow's rights, the New York Court of Appeals held:

> In this case the decedent . . . retained not only the income for life and power to revoke the trust, but also the right to control the trustees. We need not now determine whether such a trust is, for any purpose, a valid present trust. . . .
>
> Judged by the substance, not by the form, the testator's conveyance is illusory, intended only as a mask for the effective retention by the settlor of the property which in form he had conveyed.

Although promising in theory, the illusory-transfer doctrine of Newman v. Dore has, for the most part, given the surviving spouse very limited protection against will substitutes. Among the courts accepting the doctrine, one of the most common will substitutes of all, the revocable trust with a retained life estate, has been held not to be illusory.[20]

More recently, however, there has been a shift in attitude with respect to the elective share and revocable trusts. A leading case here is Sullivan v. Burkin, 460 N.E.2d 572 (Mass. 1984). Ernest Sullivan created a revocable trust while he was married to, but separated from, his wife Mary. Upon Ernest's death, Mary claimed an elective-share right against the assets in the trust, relying upon the following statutory language: "The surviving husband or wife of a deceased

---

20. See, e.g., Johnson v. LaGrange State Bank, 383 N.E.2d 185 (Ill. 1978) (see also Ill. Rev. Stat. ch. 110 ½ § 601); Kerwin v. Donaghy, 59 N.E.2d 299 (Mass. 1945) (prospectively overruled in Sullivan v. Burkin, 460 N.E.2d 572 (Mass. 1984)); Beirne v. Continental-Equitable Trust Co., 161 A. 721 (Pa. 1932); see Johnson v. Farmers & Merchants Bank, 379 S.E.2d 752 (W. Va. 1989) (West Virginia subsequently enacted the UPC augmented-estate system); Restatement 2d of Trusts § 57 comment c. In a 1944 Ohio decision, such a trust was held ineffective against the claim of a surviving spouse (Bolles v. Toledo Trust Co., 58 N.E.2d 381 (Ohio 1944)), but the decision was later overruled (Smyth v. Cleveland Trust Co., 179 N.E.2d 60 (Ohio 1961)). There has also been some doubt about whether a Totten trust would be illusory under the illusory-transfer test. Compare Matter of Halpern, 100 N.E.2d 120 (N.Y. 1951) and Jeruzal's Estate v. Jeruzal, 130 N.W.2d 473 (Minn. 1964), with Montgomery v. Michaels, 301 N.E.2d 465 (Ill. 1973).

person . . . [may claim a] portion of the estate of the deceased." Mass. Gen. Laws ch. 191, § 15. The Supreme Judicial Court of Massachusetts held that the revocable trust was valid and thus, under the earlier Massachusetts case of Kerwin v. Donaghy, not part of Ernest's "estate" and not subject to the elective share. However, the court declared that it would apply a different rule in the future:

> We announce for the future that, as to any inter vivos trust created or amended after the date of this opinion, we shall no longer follow the rule announced in Kerwin v. Donaghy. There have been significant changes since 1945 in public policy considerations bearing on the right of one spouse to treat his or her property as he or she wishes during marriage. The interests of one spouse in the property of the other have been substantially increased upon the dissolution of a marriage by divorce. We believe that, when a marriage is terminated by the death of one spouse, the rights of the surviving spouse should not be so restricted as they are by the rule in Kerwin v. Donaghy. It is neither equitable nor logical to extend to a divorced spouse greater rights in the assets of an inter vivos trust created and controlled by the other spouse than are extended to a spouse who remains married until the death of his or her spouse.
>
> The rule we now favor would treat as part of "the estate of the deceased" for the purposes of G.L. c. 191, § 15, assets of an inter vivos trust created during the marriage by the deceased spouse over which he or she alone had a general power of appointment, exercisable by deed or by will. This objective test would involve no consideration of the motive or intention of the spouse in creating the trust. We would not need to engage in a determination of "whether the [spouse] has in good faith divested himself [or herself] of ownership of his [or her] property or has made an illusory transfer" (Newman v. Dore, 275 N.Y. 371, 379, 9 N.E.2d 966 [1937]) or with the factual question whether the spouse "intended to surrender complete dominion over the property" (Staples v. King, 433 A.2d 407, 411 [Me. 1981]). Nor would we have to participate in the rather unsatisfactory process of determining whether the inter vivos trust was, on some standard, "colorable," "fraudulent," or "illusory."
>
> What we have announced as a rule for the future hardly resolves all the problems that may arise. There may be a different rule if some or all of the trust assets were conveyed to such a trust by a third person. Cf. Theodore v. Theodore, 356 Mass. 297, 249 N.E.2d 3 (1969). We have not, of course, dealt with a case in which the power of appointment is held jointly with another person. If the surviving spouse assented to the creation of the inter vivos trust, perhaps the rule we announce would not apply. We have not discussed which assets should be used to satisfy a surviving spouse's claim. We have not discussed the question whether a surviving spouse's interest in the intestate estate of a deceased spouse should reflect the value of assets held in an inter vivos trust created by the intestate spouse over which he or she had a general power of appointment. That situation and the one before us, however, do not seem readily distinguishable. A general power of appointment over assets in a trust created by a third person is said to present a

different situation. Restatement (Second) of Property, Supplement to Tent. Draft No. 5, reporter's note to § 13.7 at 29 (1982). Nor have we dealt with other assets not passing by will, such as a trust created before the marriage or insurance policies over which a deceased spouse had control. Id. at 30, 38.

The question of the rights of a surviving spouse in the estate of a deceased spouse, using the word "estate" in its broad sense, is one that can best be handled by legislation. See [Original] Uniform Probate Code, §§ 2-201, 2-202. See also Uniform Marital Property Act, § 18 (Nat'l Conference of Comm'rs on Uniform State Laws, July, 1983), which adopts the concept of community property as to "marital property." But, until it is, the answers to these problems will "be determined in the usual way through the decisional process." Tucker v. Badoian, 376 Mass. 907, 918-919, 384 N.E.2d 1195 (1978) (Kaplan, J., concurring).

Similarly, the Supreme Court of Maine seemed to indicate that a revocable trust with a retained life estate might be "illusory" under the illusory-transfer doctrine. See Staples v. King, 433 A.2d 407 (Me. 1981) (Maine subsequently enacted the augmented-estate system of the former UPC). See also Knell v. Price, 569 A.2d 636 (Md. 1990) (holding that any transfer in which the decedent retained "dominion and control" over the property during life is subject to the spouse's forced share).

The Restatement 3d of Property provides:

Restatement 3d of Property § *9.1(c)*. In a state whose statute subjects the decedent's "estate" to the elective share, the elective share is applied to the value of the decedent's estate which, for purposes of calculating the elective share, includes (i) the value of the decedent's probate estate, (ii) the value of property owned or owned in substance by the decedent immediately before death that passed outside of probate at the decedent's death to donees other than the surviving spouse, and (iii) the value of irrevocable gifts to donees other than the surviving spouse made by the decedent in anticipation of imminent death.

Seifert v. Southern National Bank of South Carolina

409 S.E.2d 337 (S.C. 1991)

TOAL, J. Widow (Agnes T. Seifert, appellant) instituted this declaratory judgment action alleging that a revocable inter-vivos trust, established by Husband (Harry E. Seifert) in favor of respondents Barbara S. Meyers and Charlotte S. Knaub, should be included in Husband's estate. We agree and reverse the Master's finding to the contrary.

Facts. Widow and Husband were married approximately ten (10) years. On August 5, 1987, Husband created a revocable inter-vivos trust in favor of respondents, Husband's daughters from a former marriage, to which he transferred the better part of his estate. At his death, the value of the trust was approximately $800,000.

Under the terms of the trust, upon Husband's death, a separate trust containing $150,000, known as the Agnes T. Seifert Trust, was carved from respondents' trust. Widow received a life interest in the income of the Agnes T. Seifert Trust and could invade the principal for medical purposes only. Under Husband's will, Widow received a one-half life interest in the marital home, half of which she already owned. The will also provided that the residue of the estate be transferred to respondents' trust.

Widow made a timely request for her elective share pursuant to S.C. Code Ann. § 62-2-201 (1990 Supp.); however, Husband's will was designed so that there were no other assets in the estate, other than the life interest in the house, his personal property, and what was contained in the residue.

Widow challenged Husband's dispositions by filing a complaint in Anderson County probate court. The matter was removed to circuit court. From there it was transferred to the Master-in-Equity with direct appeal to this Court.

The Master found that the revocable, inter-vivos trust should not be included in the probate estate. Widow then instituted this appeal.

Law/Analysis. Widow contends that Husband's revocable inter-vivos trust is void because it is illusory, since he used it to reduce her elective share, and that the trust assets should be included in Husband's estate for purposes of valuing her elective share. This is a question of first impression in this Court. Other jurisdictions have held that a trust was invalid where the settlor retained powers over the trust assets so extensive that he had until his death the same rights in the assets of the trust after creating it that he had before its creation. See, e.g., Moore v. Jones, 44 N.C. App. 578, 261 S.E.2d 289 (1980); Newman v. Dore, 275 N.Y. 371, 9 N.E.2d 966 (1937).

Husband's trust was completely revocable. The role of the trustee was described in the trust agreement and in a subsequent amendment as "custodial." Article XIV of the trust agreement granted settlor extensive powers. Furthermore, the trustee was expressly forbidden from exercising any powers of sale, investment or reinvestment during Husband's lifetime unless by (1) written notice of Husband or (2) certification of Husband's incompetence. In light of the evidence of Husband's extensive control over the trust, we find that the trust is illusory and, thus, invalid.

Respondents point to S.C. Code Ann. §§ 62-2-201 and 202 (1990 Supp.) as specifically barring inclusion of the trust in the estate. Section 62-2-201 (1986) originally provided in pertinent part: "(a) If a married person domiciled in this state dies, the surviving spouse has a right of election to take an elective share of one-third of the decedent's estate, as computed under § 62-2-202." In 1987, § 62-2-201 was amended by the legislature to insert the adjective "probate" between the words "decedent's" and "estate."

Section 62-2-201 originally defined "estate" as the "estate reduced by funeral and administration expenses and enforceable claims." In 1987, § 62-2-201 was revised. It now provides: "For purposes of this Part, probate estate means the decedent's property passing under the decedent's will plus the decedent's property passing by intestacy, reduced by funeral and administration expenses and enforceable claims."

Respondents argue that the legislature's addition of the word "probate" in the 1987 amendment to § 62-2-201 and the revision of § 62-2-202 indicate the legislature's intention to keep trusts like the one at issue out of the estate because the "decedent's probate estate" only includes property passing under the will and by intestacy and does not include property in trusts.

We disagree with respondents' interpretation of the §§ 62-2-201 and -202 because those sections do not specifically preclude the proceeds of the trust from being included in decedent's estate. We see very little difference between this situation and one in which an otherwise valid trust fails. The proceeds of the failed trust would revert back to the settlor's estate and become part of the residue. The trust property would then be part of the estate for elective share purposes. Similarly, nothing in the Probate Code prohibits a trust, declared invalid as illusory, from reverting to the probate estate and being included in it for elective share purposes.

Respondents also point to the legislature's purported rejection of the Uniform Probate Code's "augmented estate," as evidenced by the reporter's comment to § 62-2-202. The augmented estate, however, is an elaborate system of incorporating various non-probate assets into the estate. See [Former] Uniform Probate Code, § 2-202, 8 U.L.A. 75 (1983). Rejection of it does not prohibit invalidation of husband's inter-vivos trust in this situation.

Furthermore, contrary to respondents' contentions, we note that S.C. Code Ann. § 62-2-204 (1986) protects the spouse's elective share by requiring that any waiver be made in writing. Thus, the legislature has indicated that the right to receive the elective share is a substantial one. Surely, then, it was not the legislature's intent to allow this substantial right to be circumvented as respondents urge. Thus, we hold that, where a spouse seeks to avoid payment of the elective share by creating a trust over which he or she exercises substantial control,[21] the trust may be declared invalid as illusory, and the trust assets will be included in the decedent's estate for calculation of the elective share.

21. Substantial control means that a settlor has retained such extensive powers over the assets of the trust that he has until death the same rights in the assets after creation of the trust that he had before its creation.

Since nothing in §§ 62-2-201 and 62-2-202 prohibits the proceeds of a trust, once declared invalid or illusory from being included in the probate estate, we hold that the proceeds of the trust should be included in Husband's estate for the purpose of calculating Widow's elective share. Due to our disposition of this issue, we need not reach Widow's remaining exception. We remand the matter for determination of Widow's elective share.

REVERSED AND REMANDED.

Notes and Questions

1. *Judicial Interpretation of the South Carolina Statute.* As the court in *Seifert* noted, the South Carolina legislature rejected the UPC's augmented estate concept. The Reporter's Comment to S.C. Code Ann. § 62-2-2-202 stated:

> This section rejects the "augmented estate" concept promulgated by the drafters of the Uniform Probate Code as unnecessarily complex. The spouse's protection relates to all real and personal assets owned by the decedent at death but does not take into account the use of various will substitutes which permit an owner to transfer ownership at death without use of a will.

In view of this comment, can the court's interpretation of the statute be sustained?[22]

2. The South Carolina legislature subsequently enacted a statute providing that a judicial decision finding that a trust is illusory shall only have the effect of treating the trust assets as part of the probate estate for purposes of the elective share. S.C. Code Ann. § 62-7-112. Does this confirm or repudiate the court's decision in *Seifert*? The same approach—making the assets of a revocable trust available for purposes of the statutory election without entirely invalidating the trust—was taken by the court in Taliaferro v. Taliaferro, 843 P.2d 240 (Kan. 1992). The Kansas legislature subsequently enacted the current version of the UPC augmented estate.

3. *Computation; Contribution.* For purposes of computing the amount of the elective share, the value of a will substitute that is subject to the elective share is added to the value of the decedent's probate estate. In satisfying the elective-share amount, however, is the probate estate used first, so that the beneficiaries of the will substitutes are liable for contribution only to the extent the probate estate is insufficient to satisfy the elective-share amount? Or are the beneficiaries of will substitutes liable to contribution of a proportional part of their gifts in making up the spouse's elective share? UPC § 2-209 establishes the

---

22. For a critical discussion of *Seifert* by one who participated in the drafting of the legislation, see S. Alan Medlin, Result-Oriented Interpretations of the South Carolina Code Create Estate of Confusion, 44 S.C.L. Rev. 287 (1993).

latter rule. The Restatement 3d of Property § 9.1 comment *l* suggests that the court should try to retain the decedent's dispositive plan to the extent possible.

5. *Will Substitutes and Intestate Estates*. Note that the elective-share provisions of the UPC apply to intestate as well as to testate estates.

EXTERNAL REFERENCES. The comprehensive work in the field is William D. Macdonald, Fraud on the Widow's Share (1960). See also Sidney Kwestel & Rena C. Seplowitz, Testamentary Substitutes—A Time for Statutory Clarification, 23 Real Prop., Prob. & Tr. J. 467 (1988); Daniel M. Schuyler, Revocable Trusts—Spouses, Creditors and Other Predators, 1974 Inst. on Est. Plan. ¶ 74.1300.

Protection of Spousal Rights in Pension Benefits Under ERISA. The rights of a spouse in an employee spouse's ERISA-covered pension are protected under the Retirement Equity Act of 1984 (REAct). With respect to marriages ending at death, REAct creates new spousal interests in the form of survivorship rights. These rights exist only if the nonemployee spouse survives the employee spouse. If the employee spouse survives to retirement age, the pension must be paid as a "qualified joint and survivor annuity" (QJSA), unless the nonemployee spouse consents to some other form of payment. If the employee spouse dies before retirement age and his or her pension is vested, the surviving spouse is entitled to a "qualified preretirement survivor annuity" (QPSA). These two types of REAct annuities are discussed in John H. Langbein & Bruce A. Wolk, Pension and Employee Benefit Law 577-87 (3d ed. 2000).

For marriages ending on divorce, REAct basically authorizes deference to state law. It prescribes certain conditions for enforcing state-court decrees that divide or transfer pension property, referred to as "qualified domestic-relations orders" (QDROs). In effect, this represents an exception to both ERISA's anti-alienation and preemption rules, which would otherwise have immunized pension wealth from domestic relations judgments.

In Boggs v. Boggs, 520 U.S. 833 (1997), the Supreme Court held that ERISA preempts state property law. The employee's first wife of 30 years predeceased him. Her will devised part of her community share of his then-undistributed pension plan benefits to their three children. He remarried within a year after her death, retired five years later, and died four years after retirement, survived by his second wife. Upon retirement, the employee received certain shares of stock, a cash payment, and an annuity for his life and afterwards for his surviving second wife.

After the employee's death, his second wife began collecting the annuity payments. His children filed a suit in state court against their stepmother and their father's estate, seeking an accounting for the portion of his pension benefits devised to them under their predeceased mother's will. The employee's surviving second wife then filed a complaint in federal district court, seeking a declaratory judgment that ERISA preempts the application of the state's community property and succession laws to the extent they recognize the children's claim to an interest in the disputed pension benefits. The district court held for the children. The Fifth Circuit affirmed, holding that the first wife's ownership interest and devise were valid and not preempted by ERISA. The Supreme Court reversed, holding that ERISA preempts state community property law to the extent it allowed the employee's first wife to devise her community share of his pension benefits. Writing for the majority, JUSTICE KENNEDY stated:

> The principal object of [ERISA] is to protect plan participants and beneficiaries. . . .
>
> . . . . ERISA's silence with respect to the right of a nonparticipant spouse to control pension plan benefits by testamentary transfer provides powerful support for the conclusion that the right does not exist. . . .
>
> We conclude the [children] have no claim under ERISA to a share of the retirement benefits. To begin with, the [children] are neither participants nor beneficiaries. . . .
>
> . . . . Reading ERISA to permit nonbeneficiary interests, even if not enforced against the plan, would result in troubling anomalies. . . .
>
> . . . . [R]etirees could find their retirement benefits reduced by substantial sums because they have been diverted to testamentary recipients. Retirement benefits and the income stream provided for by ERISA-regulated plans would be disrupted in the name of protecting a nonparticipant spouse's successors over plan participants and beneficiaries . . . .
>
> . . . . If state law is not pre-empted, the diversion of retirement benefits will occur regardless of whether the interest in the pension plan is enforced against the plan or the recipient of the pension benefit. . . .
>
> . . . . It does not matter that the [children] have sought to enforce their rights only after the retirement benefits have been distributed since their asserted rights are based on the theory that they had an interest in the undistributed pension plan benefits. Their state-law claims are pre-empted.

JUSTICE BREYER filed a dissenting opinion, in which JUSTICE O'CONNOR joined, and in which CHIEF JUSTICE REHNQUIST and JUSTICE GINSBERG joined in part, saying in part:

> [I] can find no basis for pre-emption. . . .
>
> The state law in question concerns the ownership of benefits. . . . [I] cannot say that the state law at issue here concerns a subject that Congress wished to place outside the State's legal reach.

My reason in part lies in the fact that the state law in question involves family, property, and probate—all areas of traditional, and important, state concern. . . .

. . . . This case does not involve a lawsuit against a [pension] fund. [ERISA] would likely pre-empt state law that permitted such a suit. . . .

The lawsuit before us concerns benefits that the [pension] fund has already distributed; it asks not the fund, but others, for a subsequent accounting. [T]his lawsuit will not interfere with the payment of a survivor annuity to [the surviving spouse]. Under these circumstances, I do not see how allowing the respondents' suit to go forward could interfere with the administration of the [company] pension plan according to ERISA's requirements. Whether or not the children are allowed to seek an accounting, the plan fiduciaries will continue to owe a duty only to plan participants and beneficiaries. . . . Moreover, the children here are seeking an accounting only after the plan participant has died. But even were that not so, any threat the children's lawsuit could pose to plan administration is far less than that posed by the division of plan assets upon separation or divorce, which is allowed under §1056(d).

b. The Decedent's Nonprobate-Transfers-to-Others Component of the Uniform Probate Code's Augmented-Estate System

Statutory References: *UPC §§ 2-205, 2-207*

We saw earlier that, under the UPC, the surviving spouse's elective-share percentage is applied to the augmented estate. The augmented estate serves two basic functions. By *combining* the couple's assets, it plays a crucial part in implementing the UPC's marital-sharing theory. The other function is to provide a means of dealing with "fraud on the spouse's share." To these ends, the augmented estate consists of the sum of the values of four components: (1) the decedent's net probate estate; (2) the decedent's nonprobate transfers to others; (3) the decedent's nonprobate transfers to the surviving spouse; and (4) property owned by the surviving spouse and amounts that would have been included in the surviving spouse's nonprobate transfers to others had the spouse been the decedent.

We are concerned here with the second of the two functions—preventing "fraud on the spouse's share." This function is performed by the decedent's nonprobate-transfers-to-others component of the augmented estate. Section 2-205 gives a detailed list of will substitutes that are included in this component. Examine § 2-205 itself for a complete rundown of the specific types of will substitutes included. You should notice that the listed items are, in general, quite similar to the will substitutes included in a decedent's gross estate for federal estate tax purposes. See supra Chapter 7.

The concept of providing in the statute itself a list of will substitutes to be subjected to the surviving spouse's elective share was pioneered by legislation in New York and Pennsylvania and adopted by the former version of the UPC.

This approach resolves the problem that arises under conventional elective-share statutes, illustrated by Newman v. Dore, of shifting to the courts the burden of deciding whether and under what circumstances will substitutes are subject to the elective share.

The 1990 revisions to the UPC sought to strengthen the decedent's nonprobate-transfers-to-others component. The former version contained several loopholes. The most important of these was life insurance that the decedent purchased, naming someone other than his or her spouse as the beneficiary. Under the current version, proceeds of these policies are included.

The other important feature of the current version is that the decedent's nonprobate transfers to others now include property that is subject to a presently exercisable general power of appointment (including a power to revoke) held solely by the decedent. Such powers are viewed as substantively indistinguishable from outright ownership. It is immaterial whether the power was created by the decedent or another and whether the power was created during the marriage. The decedent need only have held the power immediately before his or her death or have exercised or released the power in favor of someone other than the decedent, the decedent's estate, or the decedent's spouse while married to the spouse and during the two-year period immediately preceding the decedent's death.

Problem

Hector died on May 7, 1996, survived by his wife, Wanda. He was also survived (i) by his father, Fred; and (ii) by his three children from his prior marriage to Martha that ended in divorce, Alice, Betty, and Carl.

Hector and Wanda were first married to each other on April 7, 1984. They got divorced on May 7, 1985, but became remarried to each other on May 6, 1987. Neither signed a waiver of rights in the estate of the other. Hector's will, executed on April 15, 1993, devised $100,000 to Wanda and the residue of his estate to his children in equal shares. Hector's net probate estate, after payment of expenses and enforceable claims (excluding estate and inheritance taxes) and after payment of probate exemptions and allowances, was worth $2.5 million.

On December 23, 1975, Hector signed a written declaration of trust of certain financial assets; the trust was to pay the income to his father for life, remainder in corpus to his children in equal shares; Hector retained no property interest in the trust, but did retain the power of revocation until his death. At the time of his death, the value of the trust corpus was $200,000. On September 1, 1984, Hector transferred his summer house and lot, title to which had been solely in his name, to Alice, retaining the right to use and possess the property until his death. The value of the summer house and lot at the time of Hector's death was $110,000. On July 21, 1985, Hector deposited $60,000 in a savings account registered in the names of "Hector, in trust for Betty"; at the time of his death, the account had a balance of $100,000. On October 5, 1986, Hector purchased a $90,000 life-insurance policy naming Carl as the beneficiary. All of these transactions were gratuitous.

On May 20, 1987, Hector purchased a $200,000 life-insurance policy naming Wanda as the beneficiary.

When Hector died, Wanda's property was valued at $800,000, not counting the $200,000 in life-insurance proceeds she collected by reason of Hector's death or the $100,000 devised to her by Hector's will.

Wanda believes that Hector shortchanged her, and has decided to explore the possibility of obtaining a larger share of Hector's assets.

Under the UPC, what are Wanda's rights and what impact on the distribution of Hector's estate would occur if Wanda chooses to exercise those rights?

Jane Bryant Quinn, Insurance Ploy Can Leave Spouse Penniless[23]

The Washington Post Writers Group
For release Nov. 16, 1995
Published in Over 200 U.S. Newspapers

NEW YORK—The life insurance industry loves to show pictures of good-looking men buying life insurance to save their grateful wives from the poorhouse.

Guess what? In most states, those good-looking men can also use life insurance to disinherit their wives (and wives can disinherit their husbands). You just dump your savings into a cash-value policy and leave that policy to someone else.

A number of states are considering laws to prevent this from happening. But the powerful insurance lobby is obstructing change. Only three states have blocked disinheritance-by-insurance (Kansas, Minnesota and South Dakota). Other states have rolled over when the lobbyists came to call.

In an attack on the laws, Jerry O'Leary, former senior counsel of the American Council on Life Insurance (ACLI) and now retired, wrote the following last year: "I believe we can all agree that the surviving spouse should be protected, but many question whether the surviving spouse should be 'canonized' and protected to the detriment of the insurance policy beneficiary. . . ."

At issue is a change proposed in probate law. It's part of the Uniform Probate Code (UPC), developed by a committee of lawyers to improve and simplify the

---

23. Each newspaper writes its own headline. The above came from the Chicago Tribune, Nov. 19, 1995, § 5, at 3.

process of leaving property to heirs. States decide individually what to accept from the UPC.

Probate assures that, when you die, the property you've left by will goes to the people you designate. But state law makes one exception. You're not allowed to disinherit a spouse unless the spouse consents.

In the nine states (Arizona, California, Idaho, Louisiana, Nevada, New Mexico, Texas, Washington, Wisconsin) with community property laws, spouses own one-half of the marital property. In most of the other states, they get at least one-third or one-half of their spouse's property at death.

If you write a will that leaves your spouse too small a share, he or she can demand the full portion owed by law. Spouses, however, can give up their share voluntarily, by signing an agreement to do so.

Spousal-support laws have a valid public purpose. No monied spouse should be allowed to leave a penniless mate, who might have to go on welfare.

You're pretty well protected in a community property state, where half of the marital property is yours by law, says Los Angeles attorney Charles Collier. In most of the states, however, huge loopholes exist, which can be used to cut a spouse out.

That's because the spousal share applies only to the property that's left by will. Billions of dollars in assets pass outside the will: through joint ownership and the named beneficiaries of living trusts, annuities, Individual Retirement Accounts or life insurance policies. In non-community property states, you can generally leave this property to anyone you want—even if your spouse winds up without a dime.

The new UPC would stop all that. It says that, when a married person dies, all the assets of both spouses must be added up, including life-insurance proceeds. The surviving spouse gets a share of the entire pot but no less than $50,000 (unless the spouse has formally waived his or her rights). Spouses in long marriages get a larger share than spouses in short ones.

Seven states have adopted this idea so far. But life insurance has been excluded in four of them (Colorado, Montana, North Dakota and West Virginia), as well as New York, which reformed along different lines from the UPC. There, a spouse can still be shortchanged, says Professor Lawrence Waggoner of The University of Michigan Law School.

Insurers think that the person who buys the coverage should decide where it goes, says Michael Bartholomew, managing counsel for the ACLI. Bartholomew also claimed that, if a spouse could challenge the contract, insurers would have to go to court to figure out who to pay.

That's not true, however. The UPC says that insurers can pay the policy's named beneficiary, if the spouse hasn't entered a contrary claim. If the spouse makes a claim, the payment goes to a court with no proceedings necessary for the insurance company. In both cases, the insurer has no further liability.

Bartholomew backpedaled in a second interview. He knows of no state that requires a court proceeding. I mention this incident because some of the information used by the insurance lobby to defeat the UPC is similarly misleading.

Bartholomew says that there's no proof that life insurance is used to disinherit a spouse. He's right that no data exist. But Denver attorney James Wade is sure that it's done. "It's a strategy discussed in estate-planning programs," he says.

If the UPC ends other ways of disinheriting spouses, why should life insurance be exempt?

Note

Position of American Council of Life Insurance. After the Quinn column was published, the Joint Editorial Board for the Uniform Probate Code (Board) sent a letter to the Chief Executive Officer of several leading life insurance companies, questioning whether the position of the American Council of Life Insurance (ACLI) was backed by its larger constituent members. A few CEOs responded, some saying that the company did support ACLI's position and some saying that the company was studying the matter. The President and CEO of ACLI itself also responded to the Board's letter, although the Board did not send a copy of the letter to him. That response follows.

American Council of Life Insurance

Carroll A. Campbell, Jr.
President & Chief Executive Officer
1011 Pennsylvania Avenue, N.W.
Washington, D.C. 20004-2599

February 29, 1996

Mr. Lawrence W. Waggoner
Director of Research
Joint Editorial Board for Uniform Probate Code
University of Michigan Law School
625 S. State Street
Ann Arbor, MI 48109-1215

Dear Mr. Waggoner:

Thank you for your letter raising certain questions about the industry's position on state legislation seeking to implement the 1990 proposed changes to the Uniform Probate Code.

The ACLI opposes enactment of the 1990 amendment regarding life insurance in the states because it completely reverses the Code's original philosophy of the relationship between non-testamentary devises and the augmented estate. More specifically, this proposed change fails to recognize the crucial role life insurance plays in helping individuals address fundamental estate planning concerns that the insured is best suited to evaluate.

For many, life insurance products provide a much-needed, unique estate planning tool to address individual life situations. Life insurance products are sold every day in order to provide for these specific scenarios that only the insured can anticipate. For example:

- an insured might purchase a policy to provide funds for his or her children's education, housing or welfare—a particular concern for children from previous marriages;
- an insured might purchase a policy to secure payment for the ongoing, long-term care of his or her aging parents or a handicapped child;
- an insured might also purchase insurance to provide for immediate needs at the time of death, such as probate costs, estate taxes, etc. This keeps dependents from having to sell assets at an inopportune time, such as when real estate values are low, or in situations where the family does not want to sell family property (i.e., family farms).

These examples are just a few of the many circumstances an insured would need to consider when planning his or her estate. Including life insurance in the augmented estate would abrogate an individual's ability to address these unique needs. A person's desire to provide this financial protection for his or her family and loved ones should not be overridden by a court's application of a uniform distribution of part of those proceeds.

In our view, the flexibility and protection that life insurance historically has provided should not be compromised. The ACLI believes that preserving life insurance as a legitimate form of nonprobate transfers best serves the public interest.

Sincerely,
/s/Carroll A. Campbell, Jr.

Notes and Questions

1. *About the ACLI and Carroll A. Campbell, Jr.* The ACLI is a trade association representing 552 legal reserve life insurance companies. Located in Washington, D.C., it has a budget of $39 million and a staff of 204. Its members meet annually in November at various locations. It publishes a biweekly newsletter called the ACLI Digest and an annual booklet called the Life Insurance Fact Book. See 1 Encyclopedia of Associations 204 (Christine Maurer & Tara E. Sheets eds. 33d ed. 1998). According to the ACLI's home page on the world wide web (www.acli.com), the association "advocates the interests of life insurers and their millions of policyholders."

Carroll A. Campbell, Jr., is a career politician, not a career insurance executive. A Republican, he served two terms as governor of South Carolina (1986-95) and, before that, served four terms as a member of congress representing the Fourth Congressional District in South Carolina. He was widely regarded as a finalist for the vice-presidential nomination in Senator Robert Dole's 1996 campaign for president. See, e.g., Katharine Q. Seelye, Dole "Very Near" Decision on a Running Mate, N.Y. Times, August 8, 1996, at A12; Richard L. Berke, Dole Develops a Short List, Dominated by Governors, N.Y. Times, July 23, 1996, at A8. After the Republican convention, Mr. Campbell became the Dole campaign's chief representative in negotiating the terms of the presidential debates. See Neil A. Lewis, Two Clinton-Dole Debates Set, With One Meeting for Gore and Kemp, N.Y. Times, Sept. 22, 1996, § 1, at 10. In the run-up to the November 2000 election, Mr. Campbell was mentioned as a possible Secretary of Commerce in a George W. Bush administration. See William Safire, The Great Mentioning, N.Y. Times, Oct. 26, 2000, at A35.

2. *ACLI's Case.* Does Mr. Campbell's letter make a persuasive case on the merits? His letter is undoubtedly correct in stating that there are many benign estate-planning uses of life insurance by a married person that might not involve naming his or her spouse as beneficiary. Does the UPC require every life insurance policy to benefit the surviving spouse? Does including life insurance in the augmented estate "abrogate an individual's ability to address [his or her] unique needs"? Could Mr. Campbell's claim about benign uses of life insurance not also be made about the other will substitutes? About wills themselves? Indeed, consider how Mr. Campbell's letter would read if you substituted "revocable trust" or "will" for "life insurance." What is "unique" about life insurance?

In listing benign uses of life insurance, Mr. Campbell's letter cites the case of an insured purchasing life insurance "to provide for immediate needs at the time of death, such as probate costs, estate taxes, etc." The standard way of using life insurance for this purpose is to name one's own estate as beneficiary of the policy. Insurance proceeds payable to a decedent's estate become part of the decedent's probate estate. *All* elective share statutes subject the decedent's probate estate to the elective share.

3. *About Life Insurance*. Life insurance is one of the most important forms of wealth transmission in the United States. Indeed, a prominent writer on life insurance has described the life insurance beneficiary designation as "the principal 'last will and testament' of our legal system." Spencer Kimball, The Functions of Designations of Beneficiaries in Modern Life Insurance: U.S.A., in Life Insurance Law in International Perspective 74, 76 (J. Hellner & G. Nord eds. 1969).

According to the ACLI, there was over $14.47 trillion in life insurance coverage in the United States in 1998, up from about $8 trillion a decade earlier. In 1998, the average amount of coverage per household was $141,100, and the average amount of coverage per insured household was $178,600. During 1998, life insurance companies took in $119.9 billion in premiums and paid out $40.1 billion to beneficiaries of policyholders who died. *See* ACLI, 1999 LIFE INSURANCE FACT BOOK 1, 3, 25, 88, 101.

4. *Restatement 3d of Property*. The Restatement 3d of Property § 9.1(c) provides that

> (c) In a state whose statute subjects the decedent's "estate" to the elective share, the elective share is applied to the value of the decedent's estate which, for purposes of calculating the elective share, includes . . . the value of property owned or owned in substance by the decedent immediately before death that passed outside of probate at the decedent's death to donees other than the surviving spouse . . . .

5. *Purchasing Life Insurance over the Internet*. Purchasing a life insurance policy can be done in a matter of minutes on the Internet. By typing in some personal information and the type of policy you want, you can get competitive bids from a number of insurance companies and purchase the policy you choose. See Joseph B. Treaster, Insurance Shortcuts, On Line, N.Y. Times, Nov. 15, 1998, § 3 at 9; Joseph B. Treaster, When the Agent of Change is a Click of The Mouse, N.Y. Times, Sept. 6, 1996, at C1. Some of the websites are www.insweb. com, www.quickquote.com, and www.quotesmith.com.

Matter of Scheiner

535 N.Y.S.2d 920 (Sur. Ct. 1988)

BLOOM, S. All objections filed by the surviving spouse in this contested accounting proceeding, except those relating to her right to elect against certain United States Treasury bills, were withdrawn after conference with the court.

All issues pertaining to the validity of the spouse's right to elect against the Treasury bills, purchased by the decedent in the joint names of himself and his sister prior to his marriage to the electing spouse, were submitted to the court for determination.

Based upon the facts and the circumstances herein, the court determines that these United States Treasury bills cannot be considered testamentary substitutes against which a surviving spouse can elect for the following reasons:

(1) All inter vivos transactions against which a spouse can elect as testamentary substitutes pursuant to EPTL 5-1.1 (b)[24] are exempt from that right where the transaction occurred prior to the marriage (EPTL 5-1.1 [b] [1]). Even if these Treasury bills were usually considered as testamentary substitutes pursuant to the EPTL, which they are not for the reasons set forth later in the decision, the spouse's right to elect against them would be nullified by the fact that they were purchased prior to the marriage even though they rolled over during the course of the marriage.

(2) Certain money transactions, under EPTL 5-1.1 (b) (2), are never deemed to be testamentary substitutes against which a spouse can elect. Included in this exempt category are "any United States savings bonds payable to a designated person" (EPTL 5-1.1 [b] [2] [C]). The Practice Commentary to EPTL 5-1.1 (Rohan, McKinney's Cons Laws of NY, Book 17B, at 18) gives a reason for their omission as testamentary substitutes the fact that their inclusion would conflict with existing Federal regulations and present serious constitutional questions.

---

24. EPTL § 5-1.1(b) provides in relevant part as follows:

> (b) Inter vivos dispositions treated as testamentary substitutes for the purpose of election by surviving spouse.
>
> (1) Where a person dies after August thirty-first, nineteen hundred sixty-six and is survived by a spouse who exercises a right of election under paragraph (c), the following transactions effected by such decedent at any time after the date of the marriage and after August thirty-first, nineteen hundred sixty-six, whether benefitting the surviving spouse or any other person, shall be treated as testamentary substitutes and the capital value thereof, as of the decedent's death, included in the net estate subject to the surviving spouse's elective right:. . . .
>
> (D) Any disposition of property made by the decedent after August thirty-first, nineteen hundred sixty-six whereby property is held, at the date of his death, by the decedent and another person as joint tenants with a right of survivorship or as tenants by the entirety. . . .
>
> (2) Nothing in this paragraph shall affect, impair or defeat the right of any person entitled to receive . . . (C) payment of any United States savings bond payable to a designated person, and such transactions are not testamentary substitutes within the meaning of this paragraph.

The United States Department of the Treasury adopted regulations on July 1, 1986 that are found in 31 CFR part 357 and are known as Treasury Direct. One of the purposes for the enactment of Treasury Direct was to override any inconsistent State law concerning Treasury bills so that they would be treated in the exact manner as United States savings bonds. Evidence of the Government's intent to treat both United States savings bonds and Treasury bills in the same manner thereby enabling them to pass as registered free of the spouse's right of election is clearly set forth in Appendix A (Discussion of Final Rule) to the Federal regulations (31 CFR part 357). It states:

> *Forms of Registration*. The proposed rule provides the investor with a variety of registration options. They are essentially similar to those provided for registered, definitive marketable treasury securities. Investors should be particularly aware that, where the security is held in the names of two individuals, the registration chosen may establish rights of survivorship.
>
> The reason for establishing the rights of ownership for securities held in Treasury Direct is that it will give investors the assurance that the forms of registration they select will establish conclusively the rights to their book-entry securities. It will also serve to eliminate some of the uncertainties, as well as possible conflicts, between the varying laws of the several States.
>
> A Federal rule of ownership is being adopted by the Treasury for Treasury Direct securities. This regulatory approach is consistent with the one previously taken in the case of United States Savings Bonds. It will have the effect of overriding inconsistent State laws. See, Free v. Bland, 369 U.S. 663 (1962).

Accordingly, the Treasury bills in dispute are not testamentary substitutes against which a spouse can elect. The Federal regulations known as Treasury Direct preempted any existing inconsistent State law by mandating that these securities should pass as registered. In order to be consistent with the regulations in Treasury Direct, EPTL 5-1.1 (b) (2) (C) must be construed to include United States Treasury bills within the term United States savings bonds.

All remaining objections are dismissed.

Notes and Questions

1. *Federal Preemption of State Elective-Share Law*. The decision in *Scheiner* interpreting the Treasury Direct Book-Entry regulations as preempting state law creates an opportunity for individuals to evade the surviving spouse's elective share through United States Treasury bills purchased through the book-entry account system of the Federal Reserve Banks. In reaching its decision, the court relied on Free v. Bland, 369 U.S. 663 (1962). In *Free*, the husband, who was the manager of the couple's community property under Texas law, purchased United States savings bonds in the names of "Mr. or Mrs." Free. The Treasury

Department's savings bonds regulations provided that "the survivor will be recognized as the sole and absolute owner" and that "no judicial impairment will be recognized which would . . . impair the rights of survivorship conferred." 31 C.F.R. §§ 315.20, 315.61.

The wife died first, and her son, Bland, as the devisee under her will, claimed that one-half of the savings bonds were part of her estate as community property. The Texas court held that, although Free had full title by virtue of the federal regulations, Bland was entitled to be reimbursed for his mother's one-half interest. The Supreme Court reversed, holding that under the Supremacy Clause of the Constitution the savings bonds registration allowed by federal regulations must prevail over Texas's community property law. The Court, however, found that there was an implicit exception in the savings bond regulations in cases of fraud. The Court stated: "The regulations are not intended to be a shield for fraud, and relief would be available in a case where the circumstances manifest fraud or a breach of trust tantamount thereto on the part of the husband while acting in his capacity as manager of the general community property." 369 U.S. at 670. Although *Free* involved savings bond regulations rather than Treasury Direct regulations governing treasury bills, the latter regulations are a clone of the savings bond regulation insofar as they provide that "[r]egistration of a security conclusively establishes ownership. . . ." 31 C.F.R. § 357.21(a)(1).

The opinion in *Scheiner* doesn't mention another federal preemption case decided two years after *Free*. In Yiatchos v. Yiatchos, 376 U.S. 306 (1964), the Supreme Court developed the "fraud or breach of trust" exception that it had recognized in dictum in *Free*. In *Yiatchos*, the decedent husband, manager of the community property under Washington law, used community funds to purchase United States savings bonds in his name, payable on his death to his brother. The Court held that, unless the wife had consented to the POD registration or would receive her full half of the community property without the bonds, she was entitled to her one-half community property interest in the bonds. Applying the "fraud or breach of trust" exception, the Court stated: "[W]e shall be guided by state law insofar as the property interests of the widow created by state law are concerned. It would seem obvious that the bonds may not be used as a device to deprive the widow of property rights she enjoys under [state] law and which would not be transferable by her husband but for the survivorship provisions of the federal bonds." 376 U.S. at 309.

Was *Yiatchos* relevant to the problem in *Scheiner*? Unlike a spouse's community-property interest, the elective share is technically not a property interest. Should this fact preclude application of the "fraud or breach of trust" exception to the preemption doctrine? See Charles F. Gibbs & Marilyn G.

Ordover, Right of Election by Surviving Spouse, N.Y. L.J., Sept. 13, 1989, 3, col. 4.

Note that § 2-210(b) of the UPC attempts to handle the preemption problem by imposing a personal liability on the recipient of any item of property or payment made to the recipient resulting from federal preemption.

2. *Joint Editorial Board's Request for Reconsideration of the Treasury Regulations.* The Treasury regulations at issue in *Scheiner* were issued by the Bureau of the Public Debt. On February 23, 1996, the Joint Editorial Board wrote to the head of that agency requesting a reconsideration of the regulation insofar as state elective-share law is concerned. The agency never responded to the Board's request. In the hope of eliciting a response, the Board sent a follow-up letter on October 2, 1996. The original letter noted:

> Treasury's original concern [appears to have been] centered on state *court* decisions invalidating POD designations because they were not signed and witnessed as required by state statutory law for wills. This concern might explain why the savings bond regulations singled out "*judicial* impairment" for preemption. The Uniform Probate Code has long since reversed this judicial rule and made POD designations valid. It does not seem likely that the Treasury Department's original intent was to preempt state *forced share* law, even though that appears to be the effect of the regulations today. When these regulations were originally promulgated, state forced share law generally protected spouses from disinheritance by will, but not by will substitute, and so state forced share law is unlikely to have been Treasury's original concern.

Letter from Lawrence W. Waggoner, Director of Research, Joint Editorial Board for the Uniform Probate Code, to Richard Gregg, Commissioner, Bureau of the Public Debt (Feb. 23, 1996). The agency never responded to the Board's follow-up letter.

Hidden Assets. Suppose that the decedent spouse or the surviving spouse is suspected of hiding assets. As the following article shows, there are private investigators who specialize in finding them.

Steve Lohr, A New Breed of Sam Spade Trails Crook's Hidden Assets

New York Times, February 20, 1992, at A1

HOUSTON—Ed Pankau is a private investigator who seems to have walked off the pages of a pulp novel. A former Green Beret and the son of a bootlegger, the 46-year-old private eye has had his share of cases involving murder, mayhem and colorful characters. . . .

Despite his hard-boiled manner, Mr. Pankau is one of the new breed of financial sleuths who track down the assets hidden by white-collar crooks. And it is a booming field, thanks to the savings and loan debacle, bank failures, corporate bankruptcies and financial scandals like the collapse of the Bank of Credit and Commerce International. When successful, these asset hunters can save taxpayers and lenders million of dollars.

"We're in an age of high-tech crime, so the people with the skills to handle those investigations are in demand," said Joseph Wells, chairman of the National Association of Certified Fraud Examiners, a 5,000-member organization that trains investigators.

Today, financial investigation has become a flourishing business, embracing several hundred practitioners with a variety of skills, including so-called forensic accountants at major accounting firms like Price Waterhouse and Arthur Andersen.

But the new-breed private investigators are on the front lines. Some are lone wolves; others work for large firms like Kroll Associates Inc. of New York, which tracked Saddam Hussein's assets for Kuwait, or medium-size firms like Mr. Pankau's Intertect Inc. in Houston, which has pursued the assets of many failed savings and loans and helped the Panamanian Government search for the assets of Gen. Manuel Noriega, its deposed leader. . . .

Unlike the Sam Spades of the past, who relied on a .38, a hip flask and a hunch, today's private eyes use computers and data bases. They tend to be accountants or former agents of the Federal Bureau of Investigation or, like Mr. Pankau, of the Internal Revenue Service. . . .

By most accounts, Mr. Pankau is a leader in applying computer-age technology to the cottage industry of private investigation.

"He's established the standards in this industry," said Charles Peck, vice president of marketing for Prentice Hall Legal and Financial Services, a unit of Paramount Communications, Inc. that markets data bases of business and government records. "Once you get beyond Ed Pankau's rough-hewn promotional style, there is a lot of substance."

[Prentice Hall Legal and Financial Services, a unit of Paramount Communications Inc. that markets data bases of business and government records,] looked for a partner with expertise in finding hidden assets. After interviewing major accounting firms and several financial investigation firms, it chose Mr. Pankau to help develop methods so that Prentice Hall's extensive data bases of corporate and public records could be used more efficiently for asset searches. . . .

Recognizing the potential for automation, Mr. Pankau bought 10 computers in 1983 in a bankruptcy sale. That move was prescient. In the last five years or so, the amount of information on people and companies available to anyone with a computer and a telephone has grown enormously. There are now thousands of data bases listing motor vehicle registrations, property held, assumed names, utility bills and owners of race horses and private aircraft.

Saving Time. While the computer does not solve cases, it cuts the time spent on asset searches from days to hours. Mr. Pankau's contribution to the craft has been devising the methodology for searches, starting with personal information, by feeding Social Security numbers and dates of birth into a computer, then moving to business records, litigation history and other clues. . . .

3. The Incapacitated Surviving Spouse

As longevity increases, so does the incidence of mental deficiency, often due to Alzheimer's disease.[25] Should the elective share be available to a mentally incapacitated surviving spouse? If so, who should have the power to make the election and by what standard should that power be exercised? Clarkson v. First National Bank, below, raises these issues.

Clarkson v. First National Bank

226 N.W.2d 334 (Neb. 1975)

SPENCER, J. This is an action under section 30-108(2), R.R.S.1943. It involves an election on behalf of an incompetent surviving spouse to either take under or against her husband's will. The District Court vacated an order of the county court electing on behalf of the widow to take the provision made for her in her husband's will. The executor prosecutes this appeal. We affirm.

Joseph D. Clarkson, deceased, married Evelyn Bell Clarkson April 16, 1953. Mr. Clarkson had two daughters from a prior marriage. Mrs. Clarkson had a son and a daughter by a prior marriage. No children were born of the second marriage. Mrs. Clarkson, who is 80 years of age, has been mentally incompetent since June 1965. The record indicates that her chances of recovery were and are nil. The will in question was executed November 18, 1969. The inventory filed in the estate indicates the value of the estate to be $1,229,263.56. The report of the guardian ad litem indicates the net value of the estate is $1,372,224. Only $62,000 is real estate, a Missouri farm valued at $40,000 and the residence property valued at $22,000.

The will makes the following provision for the incompetent:

---

25. Alzheimer's disease, a form of dementia that progressively impairs intellectual abilities, has become a major problem among the over-65 portion of the American population. A recent report issued by the Surgeon General estimates that the disease affects 8 to 15 percent of people over age 65. See Robert Pear, Mental Disorders Common, U.S. Says; Many Not Treated, N.Y. Times, Dec. 13, 1999, at A1. As American society ages, it is likely that the percentage of the population afflicted with the disease, the incidence of which increases sharply with age, will grow yet higher.

> If my wife, Evelyn Bell Clarkson, survives me, I give, devise and bequeath to the FIRST NATIONAL BANK OF OMAHA, as TRUSTEE for my said wife, an amount equal to one-fourth (1/4) of the value of my net estate as finally determined for Federal Estate Tax purposes, unreduced by any taxes.

The will directs the trustee to pay all income therefrom to Mrs. Clarkson and in addition provides for such amounts of principal to be paid to her from time to time as the trustee deems necessary or desirable to provide for her proper support and maintenance. The will further provides that upon Mrs. Clarkson's death the trust estate shall terminate and the assets remaining in the trust shall then be distributed and disposed of to such persons in such manner as Mrs. Clarkson by her last will and testament shall direct and appoint. If Mrs. Clarkson fails to exercise the general testamentary power of appointment upon her death, the will provides that the remaining assets shall be distributed as follows:

> Twenty-five Thousand Dollars ($25,000) thereof shall be paid to each of my wife's children, JERRY W. MENCK and PEGGY LOU McVEA, with the children of either of them who may be then deceased to take equally the share which the parent would have taken if then living; and the balance of said assets remaining shall be distributed to my daughters, HELEN E. CLARKSON and RUTH C. BOLLINGER, share and share alike.

The will was made at a time when Mrs. Clarkson was incompetent. There is no possibility of her exercising the power of appointment granted in the will because her condition cannot improve.

Pursuant to the provisions of section 30-108(2), R.R.S. 1943, the Douglas county court appointed Jack W. Marer as guardian ad litem to make such investigation as he deemed necessary and to report his recommendation to the court as to whether the court should elect on behalf of Mrs. Clarkson to take the provisions made for her under the last will and testament of Joseph D. Clarkson or to take by descent and distribution as provided by law. The guardian ad litem, after investigation, filed a report recommending that the court renounce the provision made for Evelyn Clarkson under the last will and testament of Joseph D. Clarkson and elect to take by descent and distribution as provided by law. The county judge declined to accept the recommendation. He determined her interests were not better served by renouncing the will but that the equities of the matter dictated that the testamentary plan of Joseph D. Clarkson should be adhered to.

The special guardian of the incompetent prosecuted an appeal to the District Court for Douglas County. The District Judge disagreed with the opinion of the county judge and followed the recommendation made by the guardian ad litem. He found an estate in fee title would be of greater value than a beneficial interest in a trust. He specifically determined that the best interests of the surviving spouse would require renouncing the provisions of the will and taking the estate in fee . . . notwithstanding that title would vest in her guardian who would have fiduciary limitations on its disposal.

The incompetent, as the second wife of deceased, would receive one-fourth of the estate if she takes under the statute rather than the will. The parties are in agreement that there is no dollar difference between what Mr. Clarkson left his wife in trust and what she would take by an election. The difference comes about in that a fee title is of much greater value than a beneficial interest in the trust.

While this is a case of first impression in Nebraska, the question has arisen in many other jurisdictions. . . . [T]here is an irreconcilable conflict in the decisions. This conflict arises because of various theories used by the courts in interpreting and defining the meaning of the words "best interests" or similar words which are found in the several statutes under consideration. . . .

In the so-called minority view, all the decisions in one way or another indicate that the best interests of the incompetent will be served by electing the method which is the most valuable to the surviving spouse. This usually means the one having the greater pecuniary value is the one selected.

The language of the various statutes may differ but essentially most of them will provide that the election should be made which is to the best interests, advantage, welfare, or the like of the incompetent person. Our statute provides that the court should make such election as it deems *the* best interests of the surviving wife or husband shall require. This seems to narrow the range of consideration.[26]

The majority view, as stated in Kinnett v. Hood (1962), 25 Ill.2d 600, 185 N.E.2d 888, 3 A.L.R.3d 1, is that all the surrounding facts and circumstances should be taken into consideration by the court in order to make the election to take under the will or against it. . . .

The majority rule emphasizes other considerations than monetary. It characterizes the minority cases as placing the election purely on monetary standards or what would result in the larger pecuniary value, to the detriment of other considerations. We concede that in some instances there may be other considerations than monetary which may promote the best interests of the incompetent. What, however, are those other considerations? It is impractical to delineate factors which could apply in every case or to specify the relative weight which should be given to such other possible considerations. If we

---

26. Nebraska repealed this statute, incident to enactment of the former version of the UPC in 1974. However, Neb. Rev. Stat. § 30-2315, the Nebraska counterpart of the former UPC's § 2-203, substitutes "in the best interests of" for the UPC's "necessary to provide adequate support for," thereby continuing the authority of *Clarkson*. Eds.

follow our statutes, the best interests of an incompetent in most instances will require the election which will result in the larger pecuniary value. We cannot agree that the preservation of the decedent's estate plan is a major consideration as found by the county judge and as it appears to be in many cases espousing the majority view. Under our law the testator's testamentary desires have little or no importance in relation to the best interests of the surviving spouse. . . .

Many of the majority view cases criticize the minority cases, suggesting that they tend to sanction: (1) The interests of the heirs of the incompetent as a consideration; and (2) give too much weight to what the surviving spouse would have done had she made her own election as a consideration. We are in full accord with the view that the interests of possible heirs of the incompetent should play no part in the decision. We would not, however, entirely ignore what the surviving spouse might have done had she made her own election. . . .

It seems a little inconsistent under our law to say, as do some of the majority cases, that the election by the court to renounce the will should be made only if necessary to provide for the widow's needs. This would write a restriction into our statute. The statute requires the court to make the election which it deems is in the best interests of the incompetent spouse. This must be made without reference to whether she may be provided for otherwise. We observe that neither section 30-107 nor section 30-108, which create the right of election and provide the necessary procedural steps, make any mention of or suggest any restrictions under which an election might be made. While a competent surviving spouse may elect to take against the will, even if it would seem obviously against her best interests to do so, a court in making the choice for an incompetent does not have that privilege. It must consider only the best interests of the incompetent.

On the record we find no considerations other than the monetary value of the estate. We find that an estate in fee is of much greater value than a beneficial interest in a trust. We agree with the District Judge that the best interests of the surviving spouse require taking the estate in fee with full incidents of ownership notwithstanding the title would vest in her guardian who would have fiduciary limitations on its disposal.

The judgment is affirmed.

[The dissenting opinion of McCown, J., in which Newton and Clinton, JJ., joined, is omitted.]

Notes

1. *"Best Interests."* Whose "best interests" were served by the decision in *Clarkson*?

2. *Current Costs of Long Term Care.* The cost of long term care for an incapacitated person varies considerably from state to state. According to a 1999 Kiplinger survey, long term care costs in Nebraska average $142 per day. The costliest state is Alaska at $414 per day; the least costly state is Louisiana at $90 per day. The daily cost in New York is $178 per day; in California it is $156 per day; and in Michigan it is $127 per day. A link to the survey can be found at www.efmoody.com. See also supra Chapter 9, Part A.

The average daily cost in Nebraska in 1975, when *Clarkson* was decided, was of course much lower.

3. *Uniform Probate Code.* UPC § 2-212 includes several innovations. The most important of these is that, under subsection (b), an election made on behalf of a surviving spouse who is an "incapacitated person" under § 5-103(7) requires that the portion of the elective share and supplemental elective-share amounts that are payable from the decedent's probate estate and nonprobate transfers to others under § 2-209(b) and (c) goes into a custodial trust created under the Uniform Custodial Trust Act. The purpose of this provision is to assure that the portion of the elective-share amount that represents involuntary transfers from the decedent is used to benefit the surviving spouse personally rather than the spouse's heirs or devisees. Upon the surviving spouse's death, the remaining custodial trust property passes to the predeceased spouse's residuary devisees or heirs.

4. *Timing of the Election.* The statutory right of election is personal and does not survive the surviving spouse's death. See, e.g., Estate of Anderson, 394 So.2d 1146 (Fla. Dist. Ct. App. 1981), where the court explained that the elective share "is a substitute for dower and curtesy, which were abolished [by statute]. The purpose of dower and curtesy was to insure provision for the surviving spouse's needs [and not for the spouse's heirs or devisees]. When the surviving spouse dies, no like purpose remains."[27]

5. *Incapacitated Spouse's Elective Share and Medicaid Eligibility.* In Estate of Cross, 664 N.E.2d 905 (Ohio 1996), the surviving spouse, who had been declared incompetent, was dependent on Medicaid benefits to pay her nursing

---

27. In Will of Sayre, 415 S.E.2d 263 (W.Va. 1992), the testator's wife was unable to make the election because she had previously suffered a mentally debilitating stroke. She was not declared incompetent until shortly after her husband's death. Three weeks after the declaration of incompetency, her committee filed her elective share claim. She died while the claim was being processed but before it was finally allowed. The court held that because the spouse's committee had timely commenced the election, the elective share right survived her death.

home expenses. Her husband had devised his entire estate to his child from an earlier marriage. The court held that the probate court, acting on behalf of the incompetent spouse, had properly decided to elect her statutory share. Under Ohio law, the spouse's statutory share is a "potential resource" for purposes of Medicaid eligibility, and the nonutilization of it would disqualify her for Medicaid. In order to maintain her eligibility, the probate judge was required to elect to take against the will.

4. Premarital and Marital Agreements

Statutory References: *UPC § 2-213*
Uniform Premarital Agreement Act

The right to an elective share (and other death benefits, such as homestead and family allowances) may be waived by premarital or marital agreement.[28] In the absence of statute, the validity of these agreements depends upon general principles of contract law. However, because of the confidential relationship between the parties, the law has moved largely to the view that the agreement will be closely scrutinized for any overreaching by either party.

This was not always the standard. In an early Massachusetts decision, the court in Wellington v. Rugg, 136 N.E. 831 (Mass. 1922), held that mere failure to disclose a party's true financial situation was not a sufficient ground for setting aside a premarital agreement; it took a showing of actual fraud to avoid enforcement. The rule of the *Wellington* case was prospectively overruled, however, in Rosenberg v. Lipnick, 389 N.E.2d 385 (Mass. 1979). In place of the *Wellington* rule, the *Rosenberg* decision announced the following position, believed to reflect the prevailing position today, in the absence of statute:

> [I]n future cases . . . we shall feel free to hold that the parties by definition occupy a confidential relationship and that the burden of disclosure rests upon both of them.
>
> In judging the validity of such an antenuptial agreement, other relevant factors which we may consider are whether (1) it contains a fair and reasonable provision as measured at the time of its execution for the party contesting the agreement; (2) the contesting party was fully informed of the other party's worth prior to the agreement's execution, or had, or should have had, independent knowledge of the other party's worth; and (3) a waiver by the contesting party is set forth. It is clear

---

28. At one time, agreements governing property rights on *divorce* were held to encourage divorce, and hence unenforceable as against public policy. Today, the prevailing view is that such agreements are enforceable if fair and reasonable. Posner v. Posner, 233 So.2d 381 (Fla. 1970), was the leading decision breaking new ground on the question. One of the most recent states to come over to the *Posner* view is Kentucky. See Edwardson v. Edwardson, 798 S.W.2d 941 (Ky. 1990).

> that the reasonableness of any monetary provision in an antenuptial contract cannot ultimately be judged in isolation. Rather, reference may appropriately be made to such factors as the parties' respective worth, the parties' respective ages, the parties' respective intelligence, literacy, and business acumen, and prior family ties or commitments. . . .
>
> The right to make antenuptial agreements settling property rights in advance of marriage is a valuable personal right which courts should not regulate destructively. Neither should the exercise of that right be looked upon with disfavor. Thus, we recognize that antenuptial agreements must be so construed as to give full effect to the parties' intentions, but we are concerned that such agreements be executed fairly and understandingly and be free from fraud, imposition, deception, or over-reaching.[29]

For other decisions adopting a similar set of standards, see Martin v. Farber, 510 A.2d 608 (Md. Ct. Spec. App.1986); Estate of Benker, 331 N.W.2d 193 (Mich. 1982); Juhasz v. Juhasz, 16 N.E.2d 328 (Ohio 1938); Estate of Crawford, 730 P.2d 675 (Wash. 1986). A decision of the Supreme Court of Pennsylvania, Estate of Geyer, 533 A.2d 423 (Pa. 1987), also adopted a similar set of standards, but that decision has been reexamined in the *Simeone* decision, below.

Simeone v. Simeone

581 A.2d 162 (Pa. 1990)

FLAHERTY J. At issue in this appeal is the validity of a prenuptial agreement executed between the appellant, Catherine E. Walsh Simeone, and the appellee, Frederick A. Simeone. At the time of their marriage, in 1975, appellant was a twenty-three year old nurse and appellee was a thirty-nine year old neurosurgeon. Appellee had an income of approximately $90,000 per year, and appellant was unemployed. Appellee also had assets worth approximately $300,000. On the eve of the parties' wedding, appellee's attorney presented appellant with a prenuptial agreement to be signed. Appellant, without the benefit of counsel, signed the agreement. Appellee's attorney had not advised appellant regarding any legal rights that the agreement surrendered. The parties are in disagreement as to whether appellant knew in advance of that date that such an agreement would be presented for signature. Appellant denies having had such knowledge and claims to have signed under adverse circumstances, which, she contends, provide a basis for declaring it void.

29. The Massachusetts court subsequently extended the *Rosenberg* rules to the validity of a premarital contract relating to divorce as well as death. See Osborne v. Osborne, 428 N.E.2d 810 (Mass. 1981).

The agreement limited appellant to support payments of $200 per week in the event of separation or divorce, subject to a maximum total payment of $25,000. The parties separated in 1982, and, in 1984, divorce proceedings were commenced. Between 1982 and 1984 appellee made payments which satisfied the $25,000 limit. In 1985, appellant filed a claim for alimony pendente lite. A master's report upheld the validity of the prenuptial agreement and denied this claim. Exceptions to the master's report were dismissed by the Court of Common Pleas of Philadelphia County. The Superior Court affirmed. . . .

[T]here is need for a reexamination of the foundations upon which . . . and a need for clarification of the standards by which the validity of prenuptial agreements will be judged. There is no longer validity in the implicit presumption that . . . spouses are of unequal status and that women are not knowledgeable enough to understand the nature of contracts that they enter. Society has advanced . . . to the point where women are no longer regarded as the "weaker" party in marriage, or in society generally. Indeed, the stereotype that women serve as homemakers while men work as breadwinners is no longer viable. Quite often today both spouses are income earners. Nor is there viability in the presumption that women are uninformed, uneducated, and readily subjected to unfair advantage in marital agreements. Indeed, women nowadays quite often have substantial education, financial awareness, income, and assets.

Accordingly, the law has advanced to recognize the equal status of men and women in our society. . . . Paternalistic presumptions and protections that arose to shelter women from the inferiorities and incapacities which they were perceived as having in earlier times have, appropriately, been discarded. . . .

Further, [prior law] embodied substantial departures from traditional rules of contract law, to the extent that they allowed consideration of the knowledge of the contracting parties and reasonableness of their bargain as factors governing whether to uphold an agreement. Traditional principles of contract law provide perfectly adequate remedies where contracts are procured through fraud, misrepresentation, or duress. Consideration of other factors, such as the knowledge of the parties and the reasonableness of their bargain, is inappropriate. Prenuptial agreements are contracts, and, as such, should be evaluated under the same criteria as are applicable to other types of contracts. Absent fraud, misrepresentation, or duress, spouses should be bound by the terms of their agreements.

Contracting parties are normally bound by their agreements, without regard to whether the terms thereof were read and fully understood and irrespective of whether the agreements embodied reasonable or good bargains. . . .

Accordingly, we find no merit in a contention raised by appellant that the agreement should be declared void on the ground that she did not consult with independent legal counsel. To impose a per se requirement that parties entering a prenuptial agreement must obtain independent legal counsel would be contrary to traditional principles of contract law, and would constitute a paternalistic and unwarranted interference with the parties' freedom to enter contracts.

Further, the reasonableness of a prenuptial bargain is not a proper subject for judicial review. . . . [E]arlier decisions required that, at least where there had been an inadequate disclosure made by the parties, the bargain must have been reasonable at its inception. Some have even suggested that prenuptial agreements should be examined with regard to whether their terms remain reasonable at the time of dissolution of the parties' marriage.

By invoking inquiries into reasonableness, however, the functioning and reliability of prenuptial agreements is severely undermined. Parties would not have entered such agreements, and, indeed, might not have entered their marriages, if they did not expect their agreements to be strictly enforced. If parties viewed an agreement as reasonable at the time of its inception, as evidenced by their having signed the agreement, they should be foreclosed from later trying to evade its terms by asserting that it was not in fact reasonable. Pertinently, the present agreement contained a clause reciting that "each of the parties considers this agreement fair, just and reasonable. . . ."

Further, everyone who enters a long-term agreement knows that circumstances can change during its term, so that what initially appeared desirable might prove to be an unfavorable bargain. Such are the risks that contracting parties routinely assume. Certainly, the possibilities of illness, birth of children, reliance upon a spouse, career change, financial gain or loss, and numerous other events that can occur in the course of a marriage cannot be regarded as unforeseeable. If parties choose not to address such matters in their prenuptial agreements, they must be regarded as having contracted to bear the risk of events that alter the value of their bargains.

We are reluctant to interfere with the power of persons contemplating marriage to agree upon, and to act in reliance upon, what they regard as an acceptable distribution scheme for their property. A court should not ignore the parties' expressed intent by proceeding to determine whether a prenuptial agreement was, in the court's view, reasonable at the time of its inception or the time of divorce. These are exactly the sorts of judicial determinations that such agreements are designed to avoid. Rare indeed is the agreement that is beyond possible challenge when reasonableness is placed at issue. Parties can routinely assert some lack of fairness relating to the inception of the agreement, thereby placing the validity of the agreement at risk. And if reasonableness at the time of divorce were to be taken into account an additional problem would arise. Virtually nonexistent is the marriage in which there has been absolutely no change in the circumstances of either spouse during the course of the marriage.

Every change in circumstance, foreseeable or not, and substantial or not, might be asserted as a basis for finding that an agreement is no longer reasonable.

In discarding the [prior] approach . . . that permitted examination of the reasonableness of prenuptial agreements and allowed inquiries into whether parties had attained informed understandings of the rights they were surrendering, we do not depart from the longstanding principle that a full and fair disclosure of the financial positions of the parties is required. Absent this disclosure, a material misrepresentation in the inducement for entering a prenuptial agreement may be asserted. Parties to these agreements do not quite deal at arm's length, but rather at the time the contract is entered into stand in a relation of mutual confidence and trust that calls for disclosure of their financial resources. It is well settled that this disclosure need not be exact, so long as it is "full and fair." Kaufmann Estate, 404 Pa. 131, 136 n. 8, 171 A.2d 48, 51 n. 8 (1961). In essence therefore, the duty of disclosure under these circumstances is consistent with traditional principles of contract law.

If an agreement provides that full disclosure has been made, a presumption of full disclosure arises. If a spouse attempts to rebut this presumption through an assertion of fraud or misrepresentation then this presumption can be rebutted if it is proven by clear and convincing evidence.

The present agreement recited that full disclosure had been made, and included a list of appellee's assets totaling approximately $300,000. Appellant contends that this list understated by roughly $183,000 the value of a classic car collection which appellee had included at a value of $200,000. The master, reviewing the parties' conflicting testimony regarding the value of the car collection, found that appellant failed to prove by clear and convincing evidence that the value of the collection had been understated. The courts below affirmed that finding. We have examined the record and find ample basis for concluding that the value of the car collection was fully disclosed. Appellee offered expert witnesses who testified to a value of approximately $200,000. Further, appellee's disclosure included numerous cars that appellee did not even own but which he merely hoped to inherit from his mother at some time in the future. Appellant's contention is plainly without merit.

Appellant's final contention is that the agreement was executed under conditions of duress in that it was presented to her at 5 p.m. on the eve of her wedding, a time when she could not seek counsel without the trauma, expense, and embarrassment of postponing the wedding. The master found this claim not credible. The courts below affirmed that finding, upon an ample evidentiary basis.

Although appellant testified that she did not discover until the eve of her wedding that there was going to be a prenuptial agreement, testimony from a number of other witnesses was to the contrary. Appellee testified that, although the final version of the agreement was indeed presented to appellant on the eve of the wedding, he had engaged in several discussions with appellant regarding the contents of the agreement during the six month period preceding that date. Another witness testified that appellant mentioned, approximately two or three weeks before the wedding, that she was going to enter a prenuptial agreement. Yet another witness confirmed that, during the months preceding the wedding, appellant participated in several discussions of prenuptial agreements. And the legal counsel who prepared the agreement for appellee testified that, prior to the eve of the wedding, changes were made in the agreement to increase the sums payable to appellant in the event of separation or divorce. He also stated that he was present when the agreement was signed and that appellant expressed absolutely no reluctance about signing. It should be noted, too, that during the months when the agreement was being discussed appellant had more than sufficient time to consult with independent legal counsel if she had so desired. Under these circumstances, there was plainly no error in finding that appellant failed to prove duress.

Hence, the courts below properly held that the present agreement is valid and enforceable. Appellant is barred, therefore, from receiving alimony pendente lite.

Order affirmed.

PAPADAKOS, J., Concurring. Although I continue to adhere to the [prior] principles . . . I concur in the result because the facts fully support the existence of a valid and enforceable agreement between the parties and any suggestion of duress is totally negated by the facts. The full and fair disclosure, as well as the lack of unfairness and inequity, . . . are supported by the facts in this case so that I can concur in the result.

However, I cannot join the opinion authored by Mr. Justice Flaherty, because, it must be clear to all readers, it contains a number of unnecessary and unwarranted declarations regarding the "equality" of women. Mr. Justice Flaherty believes that, with the hard-fought victory of the Equal Rights Amendment in Pennsylvania, all vestiges of inequality between the sexes have been erased and women are now treated equally under the law. I fear my colleague does not live in the real world. If I did not know him better I would think that his statements smack of male chauvinism, an attitude that "you women asked for it, now live with it." If you want to know about equality of women, just ask them about comparable wages for comparable work. Just ask them about sexual harassment in the workplace. Just ask them about the sexual discrimination in the Executive Suites of big business. And the list of discrimination based on sex goes on and on.

I view prenuptial agreements as being in the nature of contracts of adhesion with one party generally having greater authority than the other who deals in a subservient role. I believe the law protects the subservient party, regardless of that party's sex, to insure equal protection and treatment under the law.

The present case does not involve the broader issues to which the gratuitous declarations in question are addressed, and it is injudicious to offer declarations in a case which does not involve those issues. Especially when those declarations are inconsistent with reality.

[The dissenting opinion of MCDERMOTT, J.,in which LARSEN, J., joined, is omitted.]

Notes and Questions

1. *Equal Bargaining Power?* Their genders aside, do you think an unemployed twenty-three year old nurse and a thirty-nine year old practicing neurosurgeon have equal bargaining power regarding a premarital agreement drafted by the neurosurgeon's attorney?

Gender *not* aside, consider how the following conclusions bear on the bargaining power of a woman with respect to a premarital agreement presented to her by the man's attorney on the eve of the wedding:

> Despite more than twenty-five years of experience with federal and state laws prohibiting discrimination in employment based on sex, . . . in most cases, marriage is still the most promising opportunity open to women who want to raise their standard of living. If the marriage terminates in divorce, . . . remarriage is the most efficient path to an immediate return to a higher standard of living. Marriage, it seems, is both a long-term cause and a short-term cure of female poverty.

Herma Hill Kay, Beyond No Fault, in Divorce Reform at the Crossroads 6, 30 (Stephen D. Sugarman & Herma Hill Kay eds. 1990).

2. *Is Separate Counsel Required?* The court in *Simone* rejected the argument that agreements should be declared void if one party did not have independent counsel. This is the prevailing view. See Marriage of Bonds, 5 P.3d 815 (Cal. 2000) (describing the absence of separate counsel as only one of several factors to be considered in evaluating whether a divorcing spouse had executed a premarital agreement "voluntarily" under the California version of the Uniform Premarital Agreement Act); In re Matson, 730 P.2d 668 (Wash. 1986) (rejecting a requirement of separate counsel but nonetheless stating: "We still strongly urge both parties to seek advice from independent counsel before signing a premarital agreement. This would provide the best opportunity for both sides to receive objective and independent information regarding the legal consequences of the agreement.")

Restatement 3d of Property

§ 9.4 Premarital or Marital Agreement

(a) The elective share and other statutory rights accruing to a surviving spouse may be waived, wholly or partially, or otherwise altered, before or during marriage, by a written agreement that was signed by both parties. An agreement that was entered into before marriage is a premarital agreement. An agreement that was entered into during marriage is a marital agreement. Consideration is not necessary to the enforcement of a premarital or a marital agreement.

(b) For a premarital or a marital agreement to be enforceable against the surviving spouse, the enforcing party must show that the agreement was not unconscionable when executed and that the surviving spouse's consent was informed and was not obtained by undue influence or duress.

(c) A rebuttable presumption arises that the requirements of subsection (b) are satisfied, shifting the burden of proof to the surviving spouse to show that the agreement was unconscionable when executed or that his or her consent was not informed or was obtained by undue influence or duress, if the enforcing party shows that:

(1) before the agreement's execution, (i) the surviving spouse knew, at least approximately, the decedent's assets and asset values, income, and liabilities; or (ii) the decedent or his or her representative provided in timely fashion to the surviving spouse a written statement accurately disclosing the decedent's significant assets and asset values, income, and liabilities; and either

(2) the surviving spouse was represented by independent legal counsel; or

(3) if the surviving spouse was not represented by independent legal counsel, (i) the decedent or the decedent's representative advised the surviving spouse, in timely fashion, to obtain independent legal counsel, and if the surviving spouse was needy, offered to pay for the costs of the surviving spouse's representation; and (ii) the agreement stated, in language easily understandable by an adult of ordinary intelligence with no legal training, the nature of any rights or claims otherwise arising at death that were altered by the agreement, and the nature of that alteration.

Notes

1. The Restatement applies to premarital and marital agreements dealing with the elective share and other spousal statutory rights arising on death. The American Law Institutes's position on the enforceability of premarital and marital agreements dealing with dissolution of marriage during life is set forth in similar terms in Chapter 7 of The Principles of the Law of Family Dissolution.

2. *Uniform Premarital Agreement Act*. Under the Uniform Premarital Agreement Act (1983) (UPAA),[30] agreements pertaining to property rights on divorce or death are enforceable unless the party against whom enforcement is sought proves (a) that he or she did not execute the agreement voluntarily; or (b) that the agreement was unconscionable[31] when made *and* that, before execution of the agreements, he or she (1) was *not* provided a fair and reasonable disclosure of the property or financial obligations of the other party, (2) did *not* voluntarily and expressly waive, in writing, any right to disclosure of the property or financial obligations of the other party beyond the disclosure provided, *and* (3) did *not* have, or reasonably could not have had, an adequate knowledge of the property and financial obligations of the other party. See also UPC § 2-213.

3. *Premarital Waiver of Spousal Rights Under ERISA*. As noted earlier, ERISA was amended in 1984 by the Retirement Equity Act (REAct) to require each employee benefit plan subject to its provisions to provide the surviving spouse with the right to an annuity. The spouse may, however, elect to waive that right, but the waiver is invalid unless:

> (i) the spouse of the participant consents in writing to such election, (ii) such election designates a beneficiary (or a form of benefits) which may not be changed without spousal consent (or the consent of the spouse expressly permits designations by the participant without any requirement of further consent by the spouse), and (iii) the spouse's consent acknowledges the effect of such election and is witnessed by a plan representative or a notary public.

See 29 U.S.C. § 1055(c)(2)(A); IRC § 417(a)(2)(A).

In Hurwitz v. Sher, 982 F.2d 778 (2d Cir. 1992), the court held that a premarital agreement was not an effective waiver of a wife's rights under an ERISA-covered profit sharing plan in which the deceased husband was the sole participant. The premarital agreement provided, in part, that "each party hereby waives and releases to the other party and to the other party's heirs, executor, administrators and assigns any and all rights and causes of action which may arise by reason of the marriage between the parties . . . with respect to any property, real or personal, tangible or intangible . . . now owned or hereafter

30. The UPAA has been enacted in 24 states (Arizona, Arkansas, California, Connecticut, Delaware, Hawaii, Idaho, Illinois, Indiana, Kansas, Maine, Montana, Nebraska, Nevada, New Jersey, New Mexico, North Carolina, North Dakota, Oregon, Rhode Island, South Dakota, Texas, Utah and Virginia) and the District of Columbia.

31. The term "unconscionable," derived from § 306 of the Uniform Marriage and Divorce Act, is explained in a Commissioner's Note to § 306 as encompassing overreaching, concealment of assets, or sharp dealings inconsistent with the obligations of marital partners to deal fairly with each other.

acquired by the other party, as fully as though the parties had never married . . . ." The court held that the premarital agreement was not an effective waiver because it "did not designate a beneficiary and did not acknowledge the effect of the waiver as required by ERISA." 982 F.2d at 781. Although the district court had held that the premarital agreement was also ineffective because the wife was not married to the participant when she signed the agreement, the Second Circuit "reserve[d] judgment on whether the [premarital] agreement might have operated as an effective waiver if its only deficiency were that it had been entered into before marriage." Id. at 781 n.3. The court did, however, quote Treas. Reg. § 1.401(a)-20, which specifically states that "an agreement entered into prior to marriage does not satisfy the applicable consent requirements . . . ." Id. at 782. Other cases involving the validity of premarital agreements on ERISA-covered pension benefits include Pedro Enterprises v. Perdue, 998 F.2d 491 (7th Cir. 1993); Zinn v. Donaldson Co., Inc., 799 F. Supp. 69 (D. Minn. 1992); Estate of Hopkins, 574 N.E.2d 230 (Ill. App. Ct. 1991); see also Howard v. Branham & Baker Coal Co., 1992 U.S.App. LEXIS 16247 (6th Cir. 1992). See Lynn Wintriss, Waiver of REA Rights in Premarital Agreements, Probate & Property 16 (May/June 1993); Michael D. Rose, Why Antenuptial Agreements Cannot Relinquish Survivor Benefits, 43 Fla. L. Rev. 723 (1991).

External References. Alexander Lindey, Separation Agreements and Ante-Nuptial Contracts (1961 & Supp.); Jo Ann T. Harllee, Using Premarital Agreements in the Estate Planning Practice, 25 ACTEC Notes 145 (1999); Martha M. Ertman, Commercializing Marriage: A Proposal for Valuing Women's Work Through Premarital Security Agreements, 77 Tex. L. Rev. 17 (1998); Clare H. Springs & Jackson M. Bruce, Jr., Marital Agreements: Uses, Techniques, and Tax Ramifications in the Estate Planning Context, 21 Inst. on Est. Plan. ch. 7 (1987); Homer H. Clark, Jr., Antenuptial Contracts, 50 U. Colo. L. Rev. 141 (1979); Annot., 27 A.L.R.2d 883 (1953).

5. Tax Implications of an Election

In an age in which married partners often have children from prior marriages, an aspect of elective-share law that makes election attractive is that, by electing, the spouse receives absolute ownership of all (or part of[32]) his or her entitlement. Absolute ownership means that the spouse has power to give the property to his or her children during life or at death.

---

32. To repeat a point made earlier, UPC § 2-209(a)(1) provides that the elective share is funded first with property interests passing to the surviving spouse that may or may not be absolute ownership interests.

To the extent that an elective share confers an absolute-ownership interest on the surviving spouse, it qualifies for the federal estate tax marital deduction. Under the UPC scheme, that part of the elective share made up of augmented-estate property that passes or has passed to the surviving spouse might also qualify for the federal estate tax marital deduction, depending on the terms of the disposition.

As noted in Chapter 7, the Economic Recovery Tax Act of 1981 amended the federal estate tax by allowing a marital deduction for qualified terminable interest property—"QTIPs" in estate-planning parlance. See IRC § 2056(b)(7). The great attraction of QTIPs is that they allow the decedent spouse to create a deductible trust in which the surviving spouse receives only a lifetime income interest in the property. QTIPs are now in widespread use, and may in fact be the predominant method of gaining the marital deduction in estate-planning practice. In a QTIP, of course, the surviving spouse does not have testamentary control over the devolution of the trust property after his or her death.[33]

Consider a surviving spouse who has not been disinherited in any strict sense, but rather has been provided for by means of a QTIP trust. The elective-share provisions, as they are currently constituted in non-UPC states, where the forced share entitles the survivor to an absolute-ownership interest, provide this surviving spouse with an incentive to elect the statutory share if he or she has children by a former marriage. To the extent that the electing spouse can take an absolute-ownership interest, as opposed to an interest that expires on his or her death (such as a life estate), the elective share is attractive because it gives the survivor the power to benefit those children upon his or her death.

In an estate large enough to incur federal estate tax, a more subtle problem pertains to the calculation of the elective share. (The same problem exists, incidentally, in the calculation of the spouse's intestate share in an intestate estate.) The problem is whether the elective-share fraction (or intestate-share fraction) is applied to the estate before or after the federal estate tax has been subtracted. The elective or intestate share will be greater, perhaps substantially greater, under the before-tax approach than under the after-tax approach; also, under the before-tax approach, the federal estate tax itself will be lower, to the extent that the amount of the elective or intestate share qualifies for the marital deduction and reduces the amount subject to estate taxation.

The UPC incorporates as § 3-916 the Uniform Estate Tax Apportionment Act. UPC § 3-916(e)(2) provides that any "deduction allowed by reason of the relationship of any person to the decedent . . . inures to the benefit of the person

---

33. Prior to the 1981 tax-law changes, the only methods available for qualifying for the marital deduction required the surviving spouse to be given testamentary control over the property, either through outright ownership of that property or under a general power of appointment. See IRC § 2056(b)(5), discussed supra in Chapter 7, Part A.

bearing such relationship. . . ." Because transfers that qualify for the marital deduction are not taxable transfers under the federal estate tax, the import of this provision is that the estate tax should be apportioned only among the recipients of taxable transfers. Consequently, almost all courts have held, under the Uniform Act or similar tax-apportionment legislation, that the amount of the spouse's elective share (and the amount of the spouse's intestate share in an intestate estate) is calculated on the basis of the estate *before* estate taxes have been subtracted.[34] Wolf's Estate, 121 N.E.2d 224 (N.Y. 1954); Rosenfeld's Estate, 101 A.2d 684 (Pa. 1954); Third Nat'l Bank v. Cotten, 536 S.W.2d 330 (Tenn. 1976); Alexandria Nat'l Bank v. Thomas, 194 S.E.2d 723 (Va. 1973). Contra, Weinberg v. Safe Deposit & Trust Co., 85 A.2d 50 (Md. 1951).

Unfortunately, some non-UPC states do not have tax-apportionment legislation. In the absence of such legislation, the decisions on the question are divided. Spurrier v. First Nat'l Bank, 485 P.2d 209 (Kan. 1971), a leading decision for the view that the spouse's elective or intestate share is calculated on a before-tax basis, reasoned:

> When K.S.A. 59-502 providing that all interests by intestate succession are subject to "homestead rights, the allowances . . . , and the payment of reasonable funeral expenses, expenses of last sickness and costs of administration, taxes and debts" was enacted in 1939, the tax advantage of the marital deduction did not exist. . . . We cannot attribute legislative inactivity in this instance as an indication that taxpayers of this state were intended to be deprived of the benefits of the marital deduction.

This is the position adopted in the Restatement 3d of Property § 9.3.

A pair of leading decisions for the contrary view, that the spouse's elective share and intestate share are calculated on an after-tax basis,[35] are Del Mar v. United States, 390 F.2d 466 (D.C. Cir. 1968) (elective share); Herson v. Mills, 221 F. Supp. 714 (D.D.C. 1963) (intestate share). In *Del Mar*, the court said:

> Other jurisdictions have permitted the result for which appellants contend, either by specific statute or judicial adoption of general equitable apportionment of estate

---

34. With respect to the elective share, the former and current versions of the UPC do not rely solely on § 3-916(e)(2). Section 2-204 of the current UPC provides that the fraction (or percentage) applies to an amount "reduced by funeral and administration expenses, homestead allowance, family allowances, exempt property, and enforceable claims." The definition of the word "claims" in § 1-201 carefully states that the "term does not include estate or inheritance taxes. . . ." See Former UPC § 1-202(4); Current UPC § 1-201(6).

35. This approach makes the amount of the forced or intestate share dependent on the amount of the estate tax, which in turn is dependent on the amount of the forced or intestate share! The calculations must be done algebraically. See, e.g., Jacob Mertens, The Law of Federal Gift and Estate Taxation § 30.12 et seq. (1959 & current supp.).

> taxes. However, we are not inclined to modify our settled course of decisions—either to upset the general law of decedents' estates in the District of Columbia merely to allow a dissenting widow a larger portion of the estate at the expense of the remaining legatees and the Government, or to carve out a narrow exception for the widow's intestate share, a course which other states have taken only through actions of their legislatures.
>
> If the marital deduction provision of the tax law reflects a policy that Congress considers applicable to govern local law in the District of Columbia, Congress can easily provide a remedy. If Congress has been sluggish as a local legislature in making available to the District of Columbia benefits it has enabled the various legislatures to provide to the citizens of the states and commonwealths, petitions for relief from this anomaly are properly addressed to Congress.

Subsequently, in 1987, the District of Columbia enacted an apportionment statute reversing the rule of *Del Mar* and *Herson*. D.C. Code § 47-3714.

PART B. PROBATE EXEMPTIONS AND ALLOWANCES

Statutory References: *UPC §§ 2-401 to -405*

The elective share in the common-law states and the community interest in the community-property states are not the only protections against disinheritance afforded the surviving spouse. Additional layers of protection routinely run in favor of the decedent's surviving spouse (and often also in favor of the decedent's children, sometimes limited to minor or dependent children). These are the right of homestead, the exempt property allowance, and the family allowance.

Although the statutes vary in considerable detail, the UPC provisions are fairly representative of the type of legislation likely to be found even in non-UPC states, but with one exception: The UPC's homestead allowance is unique, in that it provides for a lump-sum amount rather than a right to occupy the spouses' dwelling house as long as the surviving spouse or minor children wish to do so.

In the 1990 revisions to the UPC, each dollar figure reflects a tripling of the original figures. This was done to align them with the increases in the cost of living that occurred in the twenty or so years between 1969, when the UPC was first promulgated, and 1990, when the UPC was revised.

Effect of the Probate Exemptions and Allowances In Small Estates. Under the UPC, the probate exemptions and allowances—homestead, exempt property, and family allowance (up to the maximum that can be made without special court order)—can be distributed to the surviving spouse without delay, other than as may be necessary for the personal representative to locate, liquidate, and distribute the necessary estate funds or assets in kind. Estates worth as much as $43,000 (in excess of liens) can be closed by distribution of these probate exemptions and allowances, once a personal representative has been appointed. The decedent's will is rendered irrelevant in such cases. However, with the exception of multiple-party accounts in financial institutions (such as checking or savings accounts or certificates) with a right of survivorship or a POD designation,[36] the restraint on testation represented by the probate exemptions and allowances is inapplicable to will substitutes.

Probate Exemptions and Allowances Are Neither Charged Against the Elective Share Nor Against Devises Unless the Decedent's Will So Directs. The UPC clarifies a matter on which many non-UPC statutes are silent, which is whether the exemptions and allowances are in addition to or are charged against devises to the persons entitled to the exemptions and allowances. The UPC does not charge the exemptions and allowances against devises unless the decedent's will directs otherwise. Nor are they charged against the elective share.

Homestead. The homestead allowance provided for by UPC § 2-402 is derived, in name at least, from a uniquely American contribution to laws giving a decedent's dependent survivors limited protection in the family home.[37] English law is the source of a different idea. Under Magna Carta, the widow had a right, called the widow's quarantine, to "tarry in the chief house of her husband for forty days,"[38] and there are early American decisions recognizing this as a part of the common law. Some American legislation has extended this

---

36. UPC § 6-215(a) provides:

> (a) A transfer resulting from a right of survivorship or POD designation under this part is not effective against an estate of a deceased party to transfer sums needed to pay debts, taxes, and expenses of administration, including statutory allowances to the surviving spouse, minor children, and dependent children, if other assets of the estate are insufficient.

Note that § 6-212(a) gives a further right to a surviving spouse in multiple-party accounts by providing:

> (a) Except as otherwise provided in this section, on death of a party sums on deposit in a multiple-party account belong to the surviving party or parties as against the estate of the decedent. If two or more parties survive and one is the surviving spouse of the decedent, the amount to which the decedent, immediately before death, was beneficially entitled under Section 6-211 belongs to the surviving spouse. If two or more parties survive and none is the surviving spouse of the decedent, the amount to which the decedent, immediately before death, was beneficially entitled under Section 6-211 belongs to the surviving parties in equal shares, and augments that proportion to which each survivor, immediately before the decedent's death, was beneficially entitled under Section 6-211, and the right of survivorship continues between the surviving parties.

37. The laws are said to have originated in 1839 in the Republic of Texas.

38. The quotation is from 4 James Kent, Commentaries 61 (1st ed. 1830). See generally, "Widow's Right of Quarantine," 126 A.L.R. 796 (1940).

right for a year, as in Ohio.[39] By contrast, more prevalent American homestead legislation, though framed primarily in terms of exempting the homestead from the claims of the owner's creditors during his or her lifetime, commonly grants a decedent's spouse or minor children a right of occupancy in certain real estate of the decedent that may continue for much longer periods. (A title in fee simple passes to homestead beneficiaries in Wyoming.) These homestead statutes vary markedly in the amount and scope of protection given to family survivors.

The UPC homestead allowance shifts the exemption from a right of occupancy of realty to a money substitute. In doing so, the UPC protects all surviving spouses and minor children, including those of renters, owners of mobile homes not classified as real estate, and decedents who owned no interest in a residence of any sort. The fact that the UPC's homestead allowance doesn't grant a right of occupancy does not mean that a surviving spouse has no prospect of remaining in possession of realty in the name of the deceased spouse. With the cooperation of the personal representative, a spouse's right to money from an estate can readily be converted into a title to real estate—as a distribution in kind to the spouse, as a sale of land to the spouse, or as some combination of the two. In this connection, it may be noted that under the UPC, the surviving spouse has priority either to serve as the personal representative or to choose who serves, unless a probated will nominates someone else who qualifies and accepts the appointment.

External Reference. On homestead legislation generally, see Restatement 3d of Property § 1.1, comment j, and Statutory Note.

PART C. PROTECTION AGAINST UNINTENTIONAL DISINHERITANCE

In this Part, we consider two measures that protect the family against unintentional disinheritance: pretermitted heir statutes and omitted spouse statutes. The former protect children; the latter protect surviving spouses.

1. Pretermitted Heir Statutes

Statutory Reference: *UPC § 2-302*

Putting aside the probate exemptions and allowances considered in Part B, children may be *intentionally* disinherited in every American state except Louisi-

39. Ohio Rev. Code § 2106.15: "A surviving spouse may remain in the mansion house free of charge for one year. . . ."

ana.[40] The power to disinherit one's children is a major difference between American succession law and the system that exists in all civil-law nations. The civil law recognizes the *legitime*, a device that guarantees that close family members will inherit a fixed share of a decedent owner's estate.[41] Although the legitime is frequently said to have originated in Roman law, Professor Dawson determined that it owes to classical Roman law not much more than the name. The origins of forced heirship lie elsewhere, he wrote:

> The antecedents of these ideas [guaranteed share for the forced heir] lie far back in the forms of social organization among the races of Germanic origin that came to occupy Europe, including Gaul, as Roman power declined. They had notions of family solidarity and of subordination of individuals to decisions of family groups that were no part of the heritage from Rome.

John P. Dawson, Gifts and Promises 29 (1980).

What advantages might be attributed to this system in modern society? Professor James Buchanan, a Nobel laureate in economics, has suggested that fixed shares would reduce waste of economic resources on the part of hopeful beneficiaries attempting to induce gifts and devises to them.[42] Other commentators have argued that the increasing incidence of multiple marriages increases the need to protect dependent children from intentional disinheritance by noncustodial parents. See Deborah A. Batts, I Didn't Ask to Be Born: The

---

40. The Louisiana constitution was amended in 1995 to limit forced heirship to children who are 23 years of age or younger or are incapable of taking care of their persons or administering their estates because of mental incapacity or physical infirmity. See La. Const. of 1974 art. XII, § 5, as amended in 1995. If the testator leaves one forced heir, the forced heir is entitled to one-fourth of the testator's estate. If the testator leaves more than one forced heir, the forced heirs are entitled to one-half of the testator's estate. See La. Civ. Code art. 1495. For discussion, see Max Nathan, Jr., Forced Heirship: The Unheralded "New" Disherison Rules, 74 Tul. L. Rev. 1027 (2000).

41. Early English law also recognized restrictions on an owner's power to disinherit his heirs. The treatise that we know as Glanvill states that an owner could give away to the exclusion of his heirs only a "reasonable" part of his land. See 2 Frederick Pollock & Frederic W. Maitland, The History of English Law 308 (2d ed. 1898, reprinted 1968). Reference to these restraints disappeared around 1200, probably because they couldn't be well-enforced in the king's courts. See Stroud F. C. Milsom, The Legal Framework of English Feudalism 122 (1976).

42. James M. Buchanan, Rent-Seeking, Noncompensated Transfers, and the Laws of Succession, 26 J.L. & Econ. 71 (1983). Similarly, in criticizing a previous amendment to Louisiana's forced heirship law, Professor Cynthia Samuel has stated: "Greed, prejudice, jealousy, meanness and fear will henceforth have a much freer hand in influencing a parent's testamentary plan." Moreover, she contends that the traditional legitime device serves the modern function of "guaranteeing that kids don't get divorced from their inheritance when their parents get divorced from each other." N.Y. Times, Dec. 1, 1989, at B7.

American Law of Disinheritance and a Proposal for Change to a System of Protected Disinheritance, 41 Hastings L.J. 1197 (1990).

Unintentional disinheritance is another matter: Nearly all states have statutes, called "pretermitted heir" statutes, that grant children a measure of protection from being unintentionally disinherited. Some statutes bear considerable resemblance to § 2-302 of the former UPC. Others make no mention of the testator's intention, and provide simply that a child (occasionally, any "issue") not named or provided for in the testator's will takes his or her intestate share.[43] Most statutes protect only children born (or adopted) *after* the execution of the will; a few protect any omitted child. The UPC appears to have broken new ground by providing that nonprobate transfers to a child can defeat that child's statutory protection.[44]

The current UPC substantially amends § 2-302. Two basic changes were made. First, if the testator had no child alive when he or she executed the will, an omitted after-born or after-adopted child takes no portion of the estate if the testator devised all or substantially all of the estate to the other parent of the omitted child and the other parent survives the testator and is entitled to take the property. This extends the rule of the former version of § 2-302, namely that an omitted child does not receive an intestate share if at the time of execution the testator had one or more children and the testator devised substantially all of his or her estate to the other parent of the omitted child. Whether or not a testator has children at the time of execution, a devise of the bulk of the estate to the other parent of the omitted child usually indicates that the testator trusts the surviving parent to use the property to benefit an after-born or after-adopted child.

The other major change concerns situations in which the testator had one or more children alive when the will was executed and devised property to at least one of the then-living children. An omitted after-born or after-adopted child does not take a full intestate share in this situation but only a pro rata share of the property devised to the then-living children.

On pretermitted heir statutes generally, see Restatement 3d of Property § 9.6.

---

43. The constitutionality of this type of a statute was upheld in Holland v. Willis, 739 S.W.2d 529 (Ark. 1987).

44. For a collection of cases dealing with what constitutes a sufficient indication of a contrary intent, see Annot., Pretermitted Heir Statutes: What Constitutes Sufficient Testamentary Reference To, or Evidence of Contemplation Of, Heir to Render Statute Inapplicable, 83 A.L.R.4th 779 (1991).

Azcunce v. Estate of Azcunce

586 So. 2d 1216 (Fla. Ct. App. 1991)

HUBBART, J. The central issue presented by this appeal is whether a child who is born after the execution of her father's will but before the execution of a codicil to the said will is entitled to take a statutory share of her father's estate under Florida's pretermitted child statute—when the will and codicils fail to provide for such child and all the other statutory requirements for pretermitted-child status are otherwise satisfied. We hold that where inter alia the subject codicil expressly republishes the original will, as here, the testator's child who is living at the time the codicil is executed is not a pretermitted child within the meaning of the statute. We, accordingly, affirm the final order under review which denies the child herein a statutory share of her father's estate as a pretermitted child.

I. The facts of this case are entirely undisputed. On May 4, 1983, the testator Rene R. Azcunce executed a will which established a trust for the benefit of his surviving spouse and his then-born children: Lisette, Natalie, and Gabriel; the will contained no provision for after-born children. On August 8, 1983, and June 25, 1986, the testator executed two codicils which did not alter in any way this testamentary disposition and also made no provision for after-born children.

On March 14, 1984, the testator's daughter Patricia Azcunce was born—after the first codicil was executed, but before the second codicil was executed. The first codicil expressly republished all the terms of the original will; the second codicil expressly republished all the terms of the original will and first codicil.

On December 30, 1986, the testator, who was thirty-eight (38) years old, unexpectedly died of a heart attack—four months after executing the second codicil. After the will and codicils were admitted to probate, Patricia filed a petition seeking a statutory share of her father's estate as a pretermitted child; the trial court denied this petition. Patricia appeals.

II. The statute on which Patricia relies for a share of her father's estate provides:

> When a testator omits to provide in his will for any of his children *born or adopted after making the will* and the child has not received a part of the testator's property equivalent to a child's part by way of advancement, the child shall receive a share of the estate equal in value to that he would have received if the testator had died intestate, unless:
>
> (1) It appears from the will that the omission was intentional; or
>
> (2) The testator had one or more children when the will was executed and devised substantially all his estate to the other parent of the pretermitted child.

Section 732.302, Florida Statutes (1985) (emphasis added). Without dispute, Patricia was a pretermitted child both at the time the testator's will and the first codicil thereto were executed, as, in each instance, the testator "omitted to provide in his will [or codicil] for [Patricia who was] born . . . after . . . the will [or codicil was executed]"; moreover, Patricia at no time received a part of the testator's property by way of advancement, the will and first codicil do not expressly disinherit Patricia, and the testator did not substantially devise all of his estate to Patricia's mother. The question in this case is whether the testator's execution of the *second* codicil to the will *after* Patricia had been born destroyed her prior statutory status as a pretermitted child.

It is well settled in Florida that, as a general rule, the execution of a codicil to a will has the effect of republishing the prior will as of the date of the codicil. Although this is not an inflexible rule and must at times give way to a contrary intent of the testator, it always applies where, as here, the codicil expressly adopts the terms of the prior will; this is so for the obvious reason that such a result comports with the express intent of the testator.

III. Turning to the instant case, it is clear that the testator's second codicil republished the original will and first codicil because the second codicil expressly so states. This being so, Patricia's prior status as a pretermitted child was destroyed inasmuch as Patricia was alive when the second codicil was executed and was not, as required by Florida's pretermitted child statute, born after such codicil was made. Presumably, if the testator had wished to provide for Patricia, he would have done so in the second codicil as she had been born by that time; because he did not, Patricia was, in effect, disinherited which the testator clearly had the power to do. Indeed, the result we reach herein is in full accord with the results reached by courts throughout the country based on identical circumstances.

To avoid this inevitable result, Patricia argues that the will and two codicils are somehow ambiguous and that, accordingly, the court should have accepted the parol evidence adduced below that the testator intended to provide for Patricia; Patricia also urges that the will should have been voided because the draftsman made a "mistake" in failing to provide for Patricia in the second codicil. These arguments are unavailing. First, there is utterly no ambiguity in the subject will and codicils which would authorize the taking of parol evidence herein, and the trial court was entirely correct in rejecting same. Second, the mistake of which Patricia complains amounts, at best, to the draftsman's alleged professional negligence in failing to apprise the testator of the need to expressly provide for Patricia in the second codicil; this is not the type of mistake which voids a will under Section 732.5165, Florida Statutes (1987).

For the above-stated reasons, the final order under review is, in all respects,

AFFIRMED.

LEVY, J. (specially concurring). I write separately only to express my frustration with the apparent inability of the justice system of this State to be in a position to provide relief to someone who is clearly entitled to it, to-wit: Patricia Azcunce, the appellant herein who was the daughter of Rene R. Azcunce. . . .

On June 25, 1986, decedent executed a second codicil which removed a certain person as a Trustee in order to qualify for a marital deduction under the federal and state tax laws. Testimony from the attorney who prepared the second codicil revealed that the decedent had contacted him and mentioned that he (the decedent) and his wife had another child. At the request of the decedent, the attorney prepared a new will which included that child, Patricia, as a beneficiary. A copy of the new will was mailed to the decedent on April 4, 1986, for the decedent to review. The new will, however, was not executed due to a disagreement that the attorney had with the decedent over the worth of decedent's assets. The disagreement between the decedent and the attorney, which caused the decedent not to sign the new will, was totally unrelated to the provision in the new will relating to Patricia. Based upon decedent's concern that a change in the marital trust, contained in the original will, had to be effected expeditiously, the second codicil was prepared by the attorney, and signed by decedent, so that the marital trust change could be effectuated immediately, rather than waiting for the preparation of another draft of a new will. The second codicil contained language that specifically republished the terms of the original will and the first codicil. Not long thereafter, decedent died.

The lower court held there was no ambiguity between the will and the first and second codicils as to the definition of issue or children and, thus, there was no ambiguity as to the testator's intent. Because the second codicil made no reference to Patricia, but did specifically republish the original will, her status as a pretermitted child was destroyed, pursuant to Section 732.02, Florida Statutes (1985), and she was no longer able to share in her father's estate.

What makes this case so troubling is that, beyond the fact that she is being denied the opportunity to share in her deceased father's assets, the record in this case . . . clearly reflects that it is virtually uncontroverted that Rene R. Azcunce intended that his daughter, the appellant herein, share in his assets after his death. Based upon the evidence presented before the trial court, it is clear that her apparent inability to receive that which her father clearly wanted her to have is the result of the current state of the case law in the State of Florida.

Lest there be any misunderstanding, I hasten to add that I understand that the majority opinion has correctly interpreted and applied the current law of this State that relates to the facts of this case. The majority opinion reflects that the current posture of the law in this area is designed to give effect to the testator's wishes and to deny any relief to false or fraudulent claimants. However, the fear of false or fraudulent claims should never be allowed to be used as the reason to bar claimants from filing their claims with the courts of this State. Rather, the courthouse doors must always remain open in the hope that the justice system will do what it is supposed to do—render justice. In furtherance of that end, hopefully, valid claims will prevail and false claims will fail. If, however, courthouse doors are barred to any type of claimant, then we all, as members of a supposedly free and just society, suffer from such a denial of access to the courts.

As I indicated above, the unrefuted evidence in this case reflects that Patricia's father, the decedent herein, intended Patricia to receive her fair share. It is only through an unfortunate series of circumstances, and the legal implications springing therefrom, that Patricia is being denied what her father wanted her to receive.

The next to last paragraph of the majority opinion seems to suggest the possibility that Patricia might find relief in a professional malpractice action against the professional draftsman who prepared the second codicil knowing, according to the undisputed evidence, that Patricia's father wanted Patricia to receive her fair share of his estate, but still allowed Patricia's father to sign it (thereby extinguishing Patricia's right to receive her share as a "pretermitted child") without either advising her father of the legal consequences of signing the second codicil (to-wit: that Patricia would lose her status as a pretermitted child) or providing for her in the second codicil, or some other such document, so as to give life and vitality to her father's (the testator's) wishes. However, this flicker of light of possible relief, that might appear to offer hope to Patricia, is soon doused as one reads the majority opinion of this Court in *Espinosa v. Sparber Shevin, et al.*, which is the appeal growing out of the trial court's dismissal of the professional malpractice case filed, on behalf of Patricia, against the draftsman of the codicil. For the reasons stated in my concurring opinion in the case of *Espinosa v. Sparber Shevin, et. al.*, and the cases that I refer to therein, it would appear that the case law of this State has "missed the boat" in its efforts to make sure that there is "a remedy for every wrong."

Notes and Questions

1. *Aftermath: The Malpractice Action.* As Judge Levy's opinion indicates, Patricia Azcunce received no relief in the malpractice action brought against the law firm that drafted Rene Azcunce's will and codicils. In Espinosa v. Sparber, Shevin, Shapo, Rosen & Heilbronner, 612 So.2d 1378 (Fla. 1993), the Florida Supreme Court held that the action could not be brought on behalf of Patricia because she was not in privity of estate with the attorney. An action by the estate, however, could be brought.

2. *Restatement 3d of Property.* The Restatement 3d of Property § 3.4, comment b states:

> *b. Intent-effecting doctrine.* The doctrine of republication by codicil is to be applied unless the effect would be inconsistent with the testator's intent. That a codicil contains a provision expressly republishing the prior will does not require the doctrine to be applied. The doctrine is still inapplicable if the effect of applying it would be inconsistent with the testator's intent.

See also Restatement 3d of Property § 9.6, comment e.

2. Omitted Spouse Statutes

Statutory Reference: *UPC § 2-301*

Although pretermitted-heir statutes are common, protection for the decedent's surviving spouse in that form is rare—apart from the UPC states. The earlier approach to the problem took the form of the common-law doctrines revoking a person's will if he or she later married. As elective-share statutes came to replace dower and curtesy, the elective share was thought to provide sufficient protection in the situation of a premarital will. The UPC embarks on a different course by providing, in § 2-301, an omitted spouse provision in addition to the apparatus of the elective share. The purpose is not only to reduce the frequency of elections under the elective share, but also to provide a share for the surviving spouse more related to the amount the decedent would probably have wanted to give, had he or she gotten around to revising the premarital will. As revealed by the following problems, however, there is a marked difference in detail between the former and current versions of UPC § 2-301.

Problems

In the following problems, the term "net estate" refers to the estate after the deduction of debts, expenses, and allowances, but not after deduction of estate or inheritance taxes.

1. A, a widower, executed a will devising $50,000 to his friend, B, $100,000 to his sister, S, and the residue of his estate to the children of his former marriage, X and Y. Subsequently, A and B married each other. A later died, leaving a net estate worth $500,000. A was survived by B, S, X, and Y. Under the former version of UPC § 2-301, would B be entitled to the $50,000 devise plus the share of A's estate she would have taken if A had left no will? Compare Estate of Ganier, 418 So.2d 256 (Fla. 1982), with Estate of Christensen, 655 P.2d 646 (Utah 1982). The Restatement 3d of Property § 9.5, comment e, provides:

> *e. Premarital will must "fail to provide" for the surviving spouse. . . .* This Restatement adopts the interpretation [of the former version of UPC § 2-301] that the surviving spouse is entitled to an omitted-spouse's share unless the premarital

> will containing a devise to the later-to-be spouse was executed in contemplation of the marriage. The burden of proving that the will was executed in contemplation of the marriage is on the party opposing the spouse's entitlement.[45]

How would this problem be handled under the current version of UPC § 2-301?

2. H and W enjoyed a long happy marriage to each other, which produced two children, A and B, and three grandchildren, X, Y, and Z. W died at age 70, survived by H, age 68. W's will devised her entire estate to H if he survived her; if not, to A and B in equal shares. H's will, executed at the same time, devised his entire estate to W if she survived him; if not, to A and B in equal shares.

Some few years after W's death, H remarried. He never thought to change his will after the marriage; he assumed that W having predeceased him, his property would be divided equally between A and B. (His new wife, W-2, was financially well off.)

A few months after his second marriage, his son B, age 48, was killed in an airplane crash. B was survived by his wife and by his 19-year-old child, Z. Upon learning of B's tragic death, H suffered a heart attack and died. H was survived (by 120 hours) by his second wife, W-2, and by A, X, Y, and Z.

H's net estate was valued at $150,000. How would H's estate be distributed under the former version of UPC § 2-301? Under the current version of UPC § 2-301? (W-2's assets at H's death are valued at $500,000.)

External Reference. Restatement 3d of Property § 9.5; Lawrence W. Waggoner, Spousal Rights in Our Multiple-Marriage Society: The Revised Uniform Probate Code, 26 Real Prop., Prob. & Tr. J. 683 (1992).

---

45. Comment d provides that "[i]n order to be executed in contemplation of the marriage, the will must be executed when the testator and the prospective spouse had marriage plans. Merely being romantically involved is not sufficient to establish that the will was executed in contemplation of the marriage."

Chapter 11

Will Contracts

TRANSFERS by will are normally perceived as *donative*, not obligatory. Obligatory transfers by will are also possible, however. A promise, supported by consideration, to leave property by will to the promisee or to third-party beneficiaries can be enforceable as a contract. Such contracts are called *will contracts*, and they take various forms. They may involve a promise to make a will, not to make a will, to revoke a will already made, or not to revoke a will already made. The two most common types of will contracts, however, are (1) contracts not to revoke mutual or joint and mutual wills in favor of third-party beneficiaries and (2) contracts to make a will in favor of the promisee in return for services rendered to the decedent.

PART A. CONTRACTS NOT TO REVOKE

Statutory Reference: *UPC § 2-514*

Mutual and Joint Wills. Litigation over the existence of a contract not to revoke typically occurs in the context of mutual or joint wills executed by a married couple. Mutual wills are separate wills, executed by each of two persons; they contain similar or reciprocal provisions. Mutual wills are frequently executed by married couples as part of an overall estate plan for the disposition of their property. A *joint will* is a single instrument, executed by two persons, that they intend to operate as the will of each. Typically, joint wills are executed by a husband and wife. Because it acts twice, as the will for each party, a joint will must be probated twice, upon the death of each testator. Joint wills that contain reciprocal provisions, as they commonly do, are sometimes called *joint and mutual*. Because they tend to invite litigation over the existence of a will contract, joint wills are not favored by estate planners.

Where a couple has executed mutual wills or a joint will and the survivor subsequently changes his or her will, the existence of a common scheme expressed by mutual wills or a joint will may lead disappointed beneficiaries later to claim that the original will was executed pursuant to a will contract. The initial question is what evidence is required to prove that a contract not to revoke was made.

Junot v. Estate of Gilliam

759 S.W.2d 654 (Tenn. 1988)

HARBISON, C.J. Appellants brought this action to set aside the probate of a will executed on January 28, 1985, by decedent, Emma Jean Gilliam. The theory of the suit was that Mrs. Gilliam and her deceased husband, Thaddeaus Evans Gilliam, had executed mutual and reciprocal wills in 1974 and that upon the death of Mr. Gilliam in January, 1985, the 1974 will of Mrs. Gilliam had become irrevocable.

Appellants also filed a claim against the estate of Mrs. Gilliam for the portion of the estate which they claim under her 1974 will. Appellee filed a response, alleging that there was no contract between the parties and that the 1985 will of Mrs. Gilliam, already admitted to probate, should stand and be carried out according to its terms. . . .

After a full trial, the judge held that appellants had not carried their burden of proof to establish a contract between Mr. and Mrs. Gilliam that would make her 1974 will irrevocable. The Court of Appeals affirmed. After careful consideration of all of the issues, we also affirm. . . .

The 1974 Wills. Mr. and Mrs. Gilliam were married in 1967. This was the second marriage for each. Mr. Gilliam had three children by his former marriage, and Mrs. Gilliam had two. No children were born to this second marriage.

Prior to February 22, 1974, Mr. and Mrs. Gilliam had discussed making their wills. Mr. Gilliam is shown to have had a separate estate, the amount of which does not appear in the record. It is shown that he owned several pieces of real estate. Whether Mrs. Gilliam had a separate estate does not appear.

On or about February 1, 1974, Mr. and Mrs. Gilliam made an appointment with Mr. Thomas McKinney, Jr., an attorney who had practiced in Kingsport, Tennessee, for several years. He had never met either of the Gilliams previously. He testified that he discussed with them a number of possible dispositions which they might make of their property, including life estates with remainder. There was a general discussion of the subject of wills, the revocation thereof and contracts to make wills irrevocable. Inter vivos gifts were also discussed, but no conclusions were reached during the first meeting.

About three weeks later, on February 22, 1974, Mr. and Mrs. Gilliam returned to the attorney's office and instructed him to write the wills which are in question. They also instructed him to write a warranty deed from Mr. Gilliam to himself and his wife so as to create a tenancy by the entirety in the property on which their residence was situated. This warranty deed was duly executed and was recorded. It is in the record, and there is no issue between the parties concerning it.

The parties executed separate wills on February 22, 1974, which were mutual and reciprocal. In his will, Mr. Gilliam directed payment of debts and funeral expenses. He then left all of his property outright to his wife, Mrs. Gilliam, "except as otherwise directed in Item III hereof. . . ."

In Item III the will provided that if Mrs. Gilliam did not survive the testator, or if she died within 90 days after his death as a result of a common disaster, then all of Mr. Gilliam's estate was to be divided equally among the five children of the parties; that is, Mr. Gilliam's three children and the two children of Mrs. Gilliam.

The will of Mrs. Gilliam was written in exactly the same language, leaving everything to Mr. Gilliam but to the five children of the parties in the event he did not survive her. The same persons witnessed both wills.

Mr. Gilliam died on January 21, 1985. Mrs. Gilliam did survive, and the parties were not involved in "a common accident." She survived for more than 90 days, although she did die a little less than 7 months later, on August 11, 1985.

In the meanwhile, shortly after the death of her husband, Mrs. Gilliam wrote another will, executed on January 28, 1985, leaving the entire estate to her children by her first marriage. They are the executors of her estate and are the appellees herein. There is no evidence of fraud, undue influence or lack of mental capacity, and no claim of such. Mr. McKinney, who also wrote the second will, did state that Mrs. Gilliam appeared to be very emotional and upset after the death of her husband. Her statements to him seem to indicate a feeling of insecurity as to whether Mr. Gilliam's children by his first marriage might be able to take the estate from her and leave her with very few assets. There is no testimony in the record, however, concerning any actual controversy between Mrs. Gilliam and the children of Mr. Gilliam's first marriage, who are the appellants here.

Under the terms of Mr. Gilliam's 1974 will, the entire estate vested in Mrs. Gilliam upon his death, unconditionally and without any kind of restraint or restriction. Unless a contract between the parties could be proved, so as to make her will of the same date irrevocable, she was free to dispose of the estate as she saw fit.

There was very little evidence concerning any such contract. Mr. Gilliam's brother and other witnesses testified that in the eleven years between the execution of the 1974 wills and the death of Mr. Gilliam in January, 1985, Mr. and Mrs. Gilliam made reference that they had "traded wills." Counsel for appellants insist that this is clear evidence that the wills were intended by Mr. and Mrs. Gilliam to be irrevocable after the death of the first of them and resulted from a contract between the parties to that effect.

We respectfully disagree. It is well settled that in order to establish a contract to make or not to revoke a will, where the contract is not otherwise documented, evidence of such a contract must be clear and convincing. The mere fact that parties have executed mutual and reciprocal wills on the same date is not, in and of itself, sufficient to establish the existence of such a contract. That fact, together with other evidence concerning the circumstances of the parties, may be sufficient to establish such a contract. The issue, however, in every case is one of fact, not law, to be determined in light of all of the surrounding circumstances. . . .

In the present case, there is a concurrent finding of fact by the trial court and the Court of Appeals that no such agreement was established by the evidence. That conclusion . . . is binding here if supported by material evidence.

The evidence to establish a contract not to revoke a will must be clear and convincing. The evidence offered by the appellants to show such a contract in the present case was not sufficiently clear or precise to establish a binding contract between Mr. and Mrs. Gilliam that the survivor would not revoke his or her 1974 will. The wills accomplished what each of the spouses apparently desired—that is, each left everything to the survivor provided they were not involved in a common accident with the survivor expiring within 90 days thereafter. Alternate dispositions in each will were identical, but it is clear that the children of the parties were no more than just that—alternate beneficiaries. Legally the entire estate vested in the survivor, and there is nothing in the text of the wills themselves nor in the brief and informal remarks of Mr. and Mrs. Gilliam shown in evidence to establish a firm and binding agreement that the survivor was restricted in any way in his or her subsequent disposition of the property covered by these wills. The residence of the parties, which was the subject of a simultaneous deed, of course, passed to the survivor under the tenancy by the entirety which was created, without restraint, condition or restriction.

Wholly apart from the testimony of the scrivener of the will, Mr. McKinney, the trier of fact was not compelled in this case to conclude that such a contract as contended for by appellants in fact existed. When the testimony of Mr. McKinney is considered, however, it clearly affords material evidence to support the conclusions of the trial court that no such contract was ever made.

Appellants contend that the testimony of Mr. McKinney as to the intention of Mr. and Mrs. Gilliam is inadmissible. In support of that proposition they cite Fisher v. Malmo, 650 S.W.2d 43, 45-46 (Tenn. App. 1983) and Nichols v. Todd, 20 Tenn. App. 564, 101 S.W.2d 486 (1936). Both of these cases hold that the draftsman of a will cannot express an opinion as to the intention of the testator with respect to the interpretation of legal terms such as "heirs."

Even if Mr. McKinney's testimony in the present case may have partly offended that rule, the bulk of it did not. Most of his testimony consisted of his general discussion of the law of wills and several possible dispositions with the parties on February 1, 1974, and his testimony that they expressly disclaimed to him any contractual restrictions upon the survivor when they executed their wills on February 22 which contain no such restrictions.

The judgments of the courts below that the surviving spouse received the estate free of any contractual restrictions are affirmed.

The 1977-78 Statutes. The Court has been furnished excellent briefs by the parties in this case and has been greatly assisted by the able oral argument presented on both sides. The briefs of the parties refer to the numerous cases in Tennessee on the subject of joint wills and of mutual and reciprocal wills.

Probably because of the large body of case law in this state dealing with the subject, the General Assembly has enacted statutes rather rigidly prescribing the requirements of a contract to make a will, not to revoke a will or to die intestate. The first of the statutes was 1977 Tenn. Public Acts, chapter 88, which provided that contracts of this nature might be established in certain ways. This statute was replaced by 1978 Tenn. Public Acts, chapter 745, now codified as T.C.A. § 32-3-107, providing that such contracts can be established only by:

> (1) Provisions of a will stating material provisions of the contract;
>
> (2) An express reference in a will to a contract and extrinsic evidence proving the terms of the contract; or
>
> (3) A writing signed by the decedent evidencing the contract.
>
> (b) The execution of a joint will or mutual wills does not create a presumption of a contract to make a will, or to refrain from revoking a will.

The latter statute . . . is patterned after a model which has been enacted in a number of states. Unlike the provisions in most states, however, this statute contains no provision limiting its effect to wills executed on or after its effective date.

For this reason, counsel for appellees has insisted that the statute should be deemed retroactive and should apply to contracts to make wills entered into before its effective date. It is clear that the 1978 statute is more restrictive than that which was first enacted in 1977. If the 1978 provisions should be applicable to any alleged contract between Mr. and Mrs. Gilliam made in 1974, it is obvious that no contract meeting its requirements has been established.

While the omission from the Tennessee statutes of a provision contained in a model code could have some significance, in our opinion, the 1978 statute, which is the only one remaining in effect, should not be construed as applying retroactively. It prescribes exclusive methods by which a contract to make a will, to revoke a will or to die intestate may be established. There is some authority in other states that such statutes can be given retroactive effect without offending constitutional prohibitions against the impairment of contracts.

Appellees particularly cite and rely upon the case of Floerchinger v. Williams, 260 Iowa 53, 148 N.W.2d 410 (1967).

The provisions of the Iowa statute are not the same as those of the Tennessee statute under consideration. Regardless of whether any constitutional limitations may be involved, it is our opinion that the General Assembly did not intend for the 1978 statute to be retroactive. The Legislature replaced a 1977 statute which was merely directory or permissive, prescribing certain ways in which such contracts "may be established." These provisions were replaced by the more stringent terms of the 1978 statute quoted above, to the effect that such contracts "can be established only" in certain prescribed ways.

The 1977 statute did not purport to be exclusive in its terms. The provisions of the 1978 statute were exclusive and mandatory. In our opinion, the rights of parties, contingent or otherwise, which might have come into existence prior to the adoption of the 1978 statute should not be deemed to be affected thereby, and we decline to give retroactive effect to that statute as requested by counsel for appellees.

The judgments of the courts below are affirmed at the cost of appellants. The cause will be remanded to the trial court for collection of costs accrued there and for any other proceedings which may be necessary.

FONES, COOPER, DROWOTA and O'BRIEN, JJ., concur.

Notes and Questions

1. *Proving a Contract Not to Revoke*. Exactly what did the court in *Junot* require the plaintiff to prove in order to establish that a mutual will is subject to a contract not to revoke? Compare the following statement from Wiemers v. Wiemers, 663 S.W.2d 25, 29-30 (Tex. Ct. App. 1983):

> In order to prevail the party asserting a binding contract must prove more than a mere agreement to make reciprocal wills. . . . The agreement must involve the assumption of an obligation to dispose of the property as therein provided, or not to revoke such will, which is to remain in force at the death of the testators.

The majority of decisions hold that contracts not to revoke must be proven by clear and convincing evidence and that the existence of mutual wills does not create a presumption of a contract.

Why are courts typically reluctant to find that mutual wills are subject to contracts not to revoke? Consider the following statement:

> The clear weight of authority, and certainly the sounder view, is that the mere presence of either joint or mutual wills does not raise any presumption that they were executed in pursuance of a contract. Nor is this rule altered by evidence that the parties had "agreed" to the making of such wills. Of course they had so agreed. The mere presence of such wills reveals that the parties must have talked

> the matter over and must have arrived at an understanding or agreement concerning their testamentary dispositions. Such discussions and such understandings between persons of close affinities, especially between husbands and wives, are not unusual and the fact that they have taken place is no indication that there has been any thought of a binding contract. . . .
>
> It is quite apparent that [the] cases which are contrary to the general rule stated above result from a confusion of evidence of an understanding or a common plan with evidence of a contract. This confusion has resulted in the finding of some contracts on extremely slender evidence and in the occasional suggestion that the presence of reciprocal provisions is sufficient without more to prove the contractual relationship.

Bertal M. Sparks, Contracts to Make Wills 27-28, 30 (1956).

2. *Presumptions*. Courts have disagreed on whether a *joint* will with reciprocal provisions is sufficient evidence of a contract. In a few decisions, joint and mutual wills have been *conclusively* presumed contractual. E.g., Estate of Knight v. Knight, 533 N.E.2d 949 (Ill. App. Ct. 1989) ("The provisions of a valid joint and mutual will become irrevocable upon the death of one of the testators and the survivor may not dispose of the property other than as contemplated in the will."); Rauch v. Rauch, 445 N.E.2d 77 (Ill. App. Ct. 1983) ("A joint and mutual will must be executed pursuant to a contract between the testators."); Fiew v. Qualtrough, 624 S.W.2d 335 (Tex. Ct. App. 1981) (court applied the established Texas rule that a joint and mutual will is binding on the testators); Estate of Chayka, 162 N.W.2d 632 (Wis. 1968) (joint and mutual wills are conclusively presumed contractual, in order that "the legal consequences of executing [such wills] remain clear, fixed and predictable.").[1]

That a joint will with reciprocal provisions is *rebuttably* presumed contractual is the rule adopted by some courts (see, e.g., Glass v. Battista, 374 N.E.2d 116 (N.Y. 1978)), while other courts reject that idea.

A few cases have extended the inference of a contract to *mutual* wills that are not joint. See, e.g., Hoff v. Armbruster, 242 P.2d 604 (Colo. 1952) (overridden by Colo. Rev. Stat. § 153-5-41).

3. *Revocable Trusts*. Do the will-contract principles followed in a jurisdiction, particularly the presumptions, if any, arising from joint or mutual wills, apply to revocable and amendable trusts containing reciprocal provisions? Compare Reznik v. McKee, 534 P.2d 243 (Kan. 1975) (holding that they do), with Northern Trust Co. v. Tarre, 427 N.E.2d 1217 (Ill. 1981) (holding that they do

---

1. As to non-joint wills, Wisconsin legislation provides:

> *Wis. Stat. Ann. § 238.19.* No will shall be construed as contractual unless such fact affirmatively appears in express language on the face of the instrument. This section shall not apply to joint wills which exist as a single document.

not).

4. *Statutory Requirements*. The 1978 Tennessee statute held inapplicable in *Junot* is virtually identical to UPC § 2-514.[2] Its purpose is to reduce the likelihood of litigation in circumstances like that in *Junot* by requiring that all will contracts be reduced to writing. Notice that section 2-514 applies only to contracts executed after the statute's enactment. In Fryxell v. Clark, 856 S.W.2d 892 (Ky. 1993), the testator and her husband executed a joint will in 1951, devising their respective estates to the other and upon the death of the survivor, to be divided among their children from prior marriages. Apparently, there was no reference in the will to a contract not to revoke. After the husband's death, the wife executed a new will, revoking the joint will and devising her estate to her children only. The court held that the Kentucky statute, which was substantially the same as section 2-514, could not be given retroactive effect and did not apply to the joint will. As a consequence, the court upheld the joint will, relying apparently on the common law presumption that execution of a joint will indicates intent to create a contract not to revoke.

In the absence of a statute specifically directed at will contracts, most courts have held that the general provision of the Statute of Frauds requiring a writing for contracts for the sale of land applies to contracts to devise *land*. They have further held that the same statutory provision extends to contracts to devise both land and personal property on the theory that these contracts are indivisible. (The provision of the Statute of Frauds relating to contracts not to be performed within one year is held inapplicable to will contracts.)

When the Statute of Frauds does apply and is raised as a defense to the enforcement of an oral will contract, the defense is often unsuccessful *in cases involving joint or mutual wills*.[3] The familiar judicial techniques for avoiding the Statute of Frauds in other contexts may also be available in will-contract litigation. The most important of these theories for taking the case out of the Statute of Frauds are part performance and estoppel. See, e.g., Redke v. Silvertrust, 490 P.2d 805 (Cal. 1971); Notten v. Mensing, 45 P.2d 198, 200-01 (Cal. 1935).

Could a court justifiably adopt either theory to avoid UPC § 2-514? In Juran v. Epstein, 28 Cal. Rptr. 2d 588 (Cal. Ct. App. 1994), the court held that Cal. Probate Code § 150, which is identical to UPC § 2-514, did not abolish the doctrine of equitable estoppel as a basis for enforcing an oral will contract when the surviving promisor is still alive and able to testify.

---

2. Section 2-514 appeared without substantial amendment in the former UPC as § 2-701.

3. As we shall see in Green v. Richmond, infra p. 670, the Statute of Frauds is a more formidable obstacle in cases of attempted enforcement of an oral promise by the decedent to devise part or all of his or her property in exchange for services rendered to the decedent during life.

Shimp v. Huff

556 A.2d 252 (Md. 1989)

MURPHY, C. J. . . . In the present case, the issue is whether Lester Shimp's second wife, upon his death, is entitled to receive an elective share and a family allowance under Maryland Code (1974, 1988 Cum.Supp.) § 3-203 and § 3-201 of the Estates and Trusts Article when Lester had previously contracted, by virtue of a joint will with his first wife, to will his entire estate to others.

Section 3-203 . . . provides that "[i]nstead of property left to him by will, the surviving spouse may elect to take a one-third share of the net estate if there is also a surviving issue, or a one-half share of the net estate if there is no surviving issue." As to the family allowance, § 3-201 provides in part, that a surviving spouse is entitled to "an allowance of $2000 for his personal use."

Lester Shimp married his first wife, Clara, in 1941. At the time of their marriage, neither Lester nor Clara possessed any property of consequence. Subsequently, in 1954, they acquired a farm which they sold in 1973; thereafter they bought a home. Lester and Clara took title to both the farm and the home as tenants by the entireties.

On May 8, 1974, in Washington County, the couple executed an instrument titled "Last Will and Testament of Clara V. Shimp and Lester Shimp." It stated in relevant part:

> WE, CLARA V. SHIMP AND LESTER SHIMP, of Washington County, Maryland, being of sound and disposing mind, memory and understanding, and capable of making a valid deed and contract, do make, publish and declare this to be our Last Will and Testament, hereby revoking all other Wills and Codicils by each of us made.
>
> After the payment of all just debts and funeral expenses, we dispose of our estate and property as follows:
>
> ITEM I. A. MUTUAL BEQUEST—We mutually give to whichever of us shall be the survivor the entire estate of which we may respectfully own at our death.
>
> B. SURVIVOR'S BEQUEST—The survivor of us gives the entire estate of his or her property which he or she may own at death as follows:
>
> 1) Unto James Shimp, if he is living at the death of the survivor of us, the sum of One Thousand ($1,000.00) Dollars.
>
> 2) Unto Emma Plotner, if living at the death of the survivor of us, the sum of One Thousand ($1,000.00) Dollars.
>
> 3) Unto Mary Virginia Huff and Betty Jane Moats all household goods and machinery to do with as they desire. This bequest is made unto them due to the care that they have given us.
>
> 4) All of the rest and residue of the estate of the survivor is hereby devised unto Mary Virginia Huff, Betty Jane Moats, Paul R. Mijanovich and Ruth C. Thomas to be divided equally among them. In the event of the death of any of said persons, their children shall inherit the share to which the parent would have been entitled,

> if living. . . .
>
> ITEM III. We, the Testators, do hereby declare that it is our purpose to dispose of our property in accordance with a common plan. The reciprocal and other gifts made herein are in fulfillment of this purpose and in consideration of each of us waiving the right, during our joint lives, to alter, amend or revoke this Will in whole or in part, by Codicil or otherwise, without notice to the other, or under any circumstances after the death of the first of us to die. Unless mutually agreed upon, this Last Will and Testament is an irrevocable act and may not be changed.

Clara died in 1975 in Washington County. At the time of her death she did not own property solely in her name and possessed no probate estate. Lester did not offer the will for probate following his wife's death. He did, however, file a petition in the Circuit Court for Washington County seeking declaratory relief and requesting the right to execute a new last will and testament. The court found that the will was revocable, but that the contract under which the will was executed might be specifically enforced in equity or damages recovered upon it at law. Lester appealed to the Court of Special Appeals, and ultimately, by writ of certiorari, the case came before us.

In [Shimp v. Shimp, 412 A.2d 228 (Md. 1980)], we found that the Shimps had executed their joint will pursuant to and in accordance with a valid, binding contract. We held that Lester was "entitled to a declaratory decree stating that he may revoke his will but that an enforceable contract was entered into between him and his wife. . . . [and that] [a]t his death it may be specifically enforced in equity or damages may be recovered upon it at law." Thereafter, Lester did not execute another will or otherwise disturb the testamentary plan set forth in the joint will.

On April 4, 1985, in Washington County, Lester married Lisa Mae; they remained married until his death on January 11, 1986. Lester was not survived by any children.

Following Lester's death, Clara and Lester's joint will was admitted to probate in Washington County. Mary Virginia Huff and Wallace R. Huff were appointed Personal Representatives of the Estate on January 30, 1986. Lisa Mae and Lester had not entered into any marital agreement waiving Lisa Mae's marital rights, and she sought payment of a family allowance and filed an election for her statutory share of Lester's estate. On June 4, 1986, the Personal Representatives declined to pay Lisa Mae either her family allowance or her elective share. On July 10, 1986, Lisa Mae filed suit for a declaratory judgment in the Circuit Court for Washington County, requesting that the court pass an order that she was entitled to both a family allowance and an elective share of Lester's estate.

The court (Corderman, J.) . . . found that because Lester, before his marriage to Lisa Mae, had entered into a binding contract to devise all of his estate, he was not seized of an estate of inheritance at the time of his second marriage, but rather was merely a trustee of that estate. Because a widow is entitled to no part of her husband's estate except that of which he dies seized or possessed, the court concluded that since Lester was merely a trustee for the property, there was no estate from which Lisa Mae could take an elective share. Similarly, the court found that Lisa Mae could not claim a family allowance because there were no estate assets from which the allowance could be paid. Lisa Mae appealed to the Court of Special Appeals; we granted certiorari prior to a decision by that court to resolve the important issues raised in the case. . . .

While we have not previously addressed the issue of a surviving spouse's right to take an elective share in conflict with claims under a contract to convey by will, courts in other jurisdictions have examined the issue under varying factual situations.

In a number of these cases one spouse, after entering into a divorce or separation agreement which requires that spouse to leave part or all of the estate to the first spouse, remarries and then dies. In other cases, the decedent has contracted to make a will leaving property to children or other relatives. Still other cases have arisen where the decedent had remarried after entering into an agreement to will property in exchange for services, or for forbearance from legal action, or to facilitate an adoption. In some cases, the decedent has executed a will conforming to the contract, while in others he has breached the contract by executing a nonconforming will or by dying intestate.

The majority of these cases arise from the decedent having breached a contract to devise property by executing a nonconforming will or by dying intestate. In these cases, the claimants under the contract generally proceed on a theory of specific performance. While the rights of beneficiaries of a contract vest after the contract is made, nevertheless, where suit is brought for specific performance of the contract, "the after acquired rights of third parties are equitable considerations to be regarded in adjudicating the questions." Owens [v. McNally, 113 Cal. 444, 45 P. 710 (1896)]. In determining whether to award specific performance to contract beneficiaries, courts have considered several different factors, including whether the surviving spouse had notice of the contract prior to the marriage, the length of the marriage and the natural affection shared between the decedent and the surviving spouse, whether the surviving spouse would be deprived of the entire estate by enforcement of the contract, and the public policy concerning the marriage relationship and the rights of surviving spouses. In a great many cases consideration of these factors has led the court to determine that the superior equities were with the surviving spouse, while in other cases it has not.

In those cases where the decedent has executed a will conforming to the contract, the claimants cannot seek specific performance, and courts, therefore, do not use equitable powers in resolving these cases. Instead, courts have analyzed the conflicting claims by characterizing the competing claimants as either creditors or legatees and evaluating their claims under the applicable priority rules. In a number of cases involving divorce settlements, the courts have found that where the decedent executes a will, which conforms to the terms of a contract, the beneficiaries take as legatees under the will and not as contract creditors. Consequently, because the applicable statutes give a higher priority to a surviving spouse's elective share than to testamentary bequests, the courts upheld the surviving spouse's claim over the claims of the contract beneficiaries. As the court explained in In Re Hoyt's Estate[, 174 Misc. 512, 21 N.Y.S.2d 107 (Sur. Ct. 1940)]

> . . . [we] hold that the claimants are not creditors under paragraph seventh of the separation agreement, but that the agreement merely created an enforceable obligation to make a testamentary provision for the benefit of the first wife of the testator and his children after her death. The testator performed that agreement. He undertook to do no more. The status of the claimants is therefore that of legatees or beneficiaries under the will. As such legatees or beneficiaries they take subject to the operation of the statutes relating to testamentary dispositions, including the right of the surviving widow to take her intestate share under Section 18 of the Decedent Estate Law. Their rights are also subordinate to all true creditors of the estate. The widow of the testator is therefore entitled to a one-third share of the net estate. The respective interests of the claimants as legatees or beneficiaries must be satisfied out of the balance. 21 N.Y.S.2d at 111.

At least one court, however, has suggested that analyzing the competing claims under the applicable priority statutes should be limited to cases involving divorce settlement agreements. In Rubenstein [v. Mueller, 225 N.E.2d 540 (N.Y. 967)], which involved an ordinary contract to devise property rather than a separation agreement, the court distinguished those cases involving marital separation agreements, under which husbands covenanted to make a will, noting that different equitable considerations control in the two situations. The court explained:

> Separation agreements are usually attended by a present division of any jointly held property, and any provision for a future legacy is usually but an incident to the over-all settlement to be made with respect to the husband's individual property and his obligation of support. In the case of the joint will, however, this instrument typically represents the sole attempt by the signatories to effect a distribution of their collective property in a fashion agreeable to both. Most importantly, in those separation agreements there was no irrevocable obligation concerning the collective property. The husband did not . . . become sole owner of jointly owned property by virtue of surviving the former wife. As the divorced husband's property after the agreement remains his own individual property, to which he holds beneficial

as well as legal title, his widow's right of election may be asserted against such assets. 225 N.E.2d at 544, 278 N.Y.S.2d at 850.

Thus, the court suggests that in these cases whether the surviving spouse's claim is given priority does not depend upon whether the contract beneficiaries are characterized as contract creditors or legatees. Instead the court reasoned that this priority is based upon the decedent having held both the legal and beneficial title to the property completely independent of the first spouse as a result of the property division effectuated by the separation agreement—a division which does not occur when one spouse acquires rights in the property pursuant to a joint will.

Courts have cited other reasons for rejecting the practice of categorizing contract beneficiaries as legatees where the decedent has executed a conforming will. These courts acknowledge that technically the contract beneficiary becomes a creditor of the estate only after the decedent breaches the contract by dying intestate or executing a nonconforming will; and that where the decedent executes a conforming will the contract beneficiaries take as legatees under the will. Nevertheless, they note that this analysis leads to the anomalous result that the contract beneficiaries are in a better position where the decedent breaches the contract than where the decedent fully and properly performs in accordance with it. See In Re Erstein's Estate, supra, 129 N.Y.S.2d at 321 ("[i]t would be anomalous if the rights of the promisees would be substantially greater in the case of intestacy than they would be had the testator left a will which carried out his promise").

Other courts have suggested that the resolution of the conflict between the surviving spouse's rights and the rights of contract beneficiaries may be based upon public policy underlying wills statutes. Some courts have held that the right of election is personal to the surviving spouse and cannot be waived or otherwise defeated by the acts of the deceased spouse. . . .

Other courts have upheld the surviving spouse's right to claim an elective share over the claims of contract beneficiaries by relying upon the general principle that the right to will property is not absolute, but instead is a privilege afforded the decedent by the State. Under these cases, the State may impose limitations on that privilege, including the condition that all bequests are subject to the surviving spouse's right to claim an elective share. . . .

Other courts have relied upon the public policy surrounding the marriage relationship as the basis for upholding the surviving spouse's claim to an elective share over the claims of contract beneficiaries. . . . They characterize contracts which require a decedent to devise his entire estate to a third party as being contracts which might restrain or discourage marriage. Therefore, to prevent having these contracts declared void as against public policy, courts have construed the contract to imply that when entering into the agreement the parties contemplated that the testator might remarry. . . .

This case does not present a claim for specific performance because Lester performed his obligation under the contract and died leaving a will which conformed to the contract. Thus, we need not consider whether the superior equities lie with the Personal Representatives or with Lisa Mae.

Because Lester died leaving a will which conformed to the contract, we might consider drawing an analogy between the present case and the divorce cases, wherein courts found that where the decedent died leaving a conforming will, the contract beneficiaries were more properly characterized as legatees rather than contract creditors. Under this approach, we would find the respondents to be legatees under Lester's will whose interest in the estate, like the interest of any other legatee under any will, is subject to the abatement procedure outlined in § 3-208 of the Estates and Trusts Article.[4] Under this procedure Lisa Mae's elective share would have priority over the respondents' claims and their share of the estate would be abated. Nevertheless, we acknowledge . . . that this method of resolving the issue of priority leads to the anomalous result that the contract beneficiaries' rights would be greater where the contract is breached than where the testator performs in accordance with its terms. Consequently, we decline to adopt this theory as the controlling law in this case.

Instead, we find the question of priorities between a surviving spouse and beneficiaries under a contract to make a will should be resolved based upon the public policy which surrounds the marriage relationship and which underlies the elective share statute. . . . The Legislature on several occasions has limited [the right to make a will] by enacting restrictions such as those contained in § 3-203, which grants a surviving spouse the right to receive an elective share of a decedent's estate, regardless of the provisions contained in the decedent's will. In addition, § 3-204 suggests that the right to receive the elective share is a personal right, which cannot be waived by the unilateral acts of others, including the actions of the deceased spouse. These statutes and principles of law suggest that there is a strong public policy in favor of protecting the surviving spouse's right to receive an elective share. This Court on other occasions has recognized the strong public policy interest in protecting the surviving spouse's elective share from the unilateral acts of a deceased spouse. For example, in a number of cases this Court has declared transfers in fraud of marital rights to be void. We have indicated that this doctrine also applies to transfers made prior to the marriage.

In addition to the public policy underlying these statutes, the public policy surrounding the marriage relationship also suggests that the surviving spouse's

---

4. Section 3-208(b) provides in relevant part that "[i]f there is an election to take an intestate share, contribution to the payment of it shall be prorated among all legatees."

claim to an elective share should be afforded priority over the claims of beneficiaries of a contract to make a will. Like the majority of other courts, we have recognized the well settled principle that contracts which discourage or restrain the right to marry are void as against public policy. In executing a will, a testator is presumed to know that a spouse might renounce the will, thus extinguishing or reducing legacies contained in the will, and if the testator does not provide for this contingency then the beneficiaries under the will might lose the property left them. Thus, we find that the respondents' rights under the contract were limited by the possibility that the survivor might remarry and that the subsequent spouse might elect against the will. Consequently, we conclude that their claims under the contract are subordinate to Lisa Mae's superior right to receive her elective share.

Finally, we address the issue of whether Lisa Mae is entitled to a $2000 family allowance under § 3-201. . . .

The respondents' claim upon the estate of Lester Shimp must be characterized as being either that of a general creditor or of a legatee under the will. Under § 8-105, the family allowance receives priority over the claims of both contract creditors and legatees. Therefore, while the respondents' claim is more properly characterized as being that of a legatee, rather than that of a creditor, regardless of which characterization is used, Lisa Mae's claim for a family allowance takes precedence over the respondents' claim. Therefore, Lisa Mae is entitled to receive the family allowance provided for in § 3-201. . . .

JUDGMENT VACATED; CASE REMANDED TO THE CIRCUIT COURT FOR WASHINGTON COUNTY FOR ENTRY OF A DECLARATORY JUDGMENT CONSISTENT WITH THIS OPINION. COSTS TO BE PAID BY THE APPELLEES.

Notes and Questions

1. *Uniform Probate Code*. How would *Shimp* be resolved if it were governed by the UPC? Had Lester's will not been contractual, what elective-share rights would Lisa Mae have under § 2-201? Would Lisa Mae have any rights to an intestate share under § 2-301? Would Lester's will be found contractual under § 2-514? If so, how would the contractual nature of the will affect Lisa Mae's rights under §§ 2-201 and 2-301?

2. *Theories Supporting the Contract Beneficiaries*. Quite a number of courts have held for the contract beneficiaries rather than for the surviving spouse in cases like *Shimp*. In Rubenstein v. Mueller, for example, cited in *Shimp*, the New York Court of Appeals held that the decedent's second spouse had no right to an elective share in the decedent's assets covered by a will contract entered into with his prior, deceased spouse. The reason given was that the will contract transformed the ownership interest in those assets into a life estate in the decedent and a remainder interest in the contract beneficiaries. Other courts

have held for the contract beneficiaries on the similar theory that the surviving spouse's statutory rights attach only to assets equitably as well as legally owned by the decedent and that equitably owned assets do not include assets that the decedent received under a will executed pursuant to a will contract, since a court will impress those assets with a constructive trust for the contract beneficiaries. See, e.g., Estate of Stewart, 444 P.2d 337 (Cal. 1968); Bever v. Bever, 364 S.E.2d 34 (W. Va. 1987). Another theory is that breach of the will contract places the contract beneficiary in the position of a creditor and that creditors' rights are superior to the surviving spouse's elective-share right. See, e.g., Estate of Beeruk, 241 A.2d 755 (Pa. 1968).

3. *Enforcement of Contractual Wills and Remedies for Breach.* Apart from competing claims of a surviving spouse, most cases brought to enforce a will contract arise because the survivor has breached the contract by making a new will revoking the contractual will. Courts sometimes say that the contractual will became irrevocable. The logical implication of this is that the contractual will is entitled to probate despite the decedent's later attempt to revoke it. Occasionally this is what courts have done. See, e.g., Walker v. Yarbrough, 76 So. 390 (Ala. 1917); Helms v. Darmstatter, 215 N.E.2d 245 (Ill. 1966) (joint will). But this result conflicts with the long-accepted view that a will is always revocable. In most cases, then, the contract is enforced not by probating the contractual will, but rather through a subsequent proceeding for breach of contract. See, e.g., Estate of Chapman, 239 N.W.2d 869 (Iowa 1976).

This two-step process for enforcing will contracts, probate of the subsequent will followed by a proceeding on the contract, indicates the separate relationship between the contract and the will. The breach-of-contract proceeding may be one at law for damages or in equity for specific performance or a constructive trust. The usual remedy is a constructive trust upon the property passing in violation of the contract.

4. *Survivor's Rights to Consume or Make Gifts.* To what extent is the survivor free to consume or give away during his or her lifetime property that is subject to a will contract? To prevent the survivor from breaching an obligation under a will contract, courts have held that inter vivos gifts by the survivor of substantial portions of the property can be set aside. See, e.g., Lawrence v. Ashba, 59 N.E.2d 568 (Ind. Ct. App. 1945); Schwartz v. Horn, 290 N.E.2d 816 (N.Y. 1972); Estate of Chayka, 176 N.W.2d 561 (Wis. 1970). Some courts have analyzed the question under a reasonableness requirement. Under this approach, the survivor is free to make "reasonable gifts"; the question is said to be "one of degree, and depends upon the proportion that the value of the gift bears to the amount of the donor's estate." Dickinson v. Seaman, 85 N.E. 818 (N.Y. 1908). Other courts have held that, since the will contract converts the survivor's estate to a life estate, a deed purporting to convey a fee effectively

transfers only a life estate for the survivor's life. See, e.g., First United Presbyterian Church v. Christenson, 356 N.E.2d 532 (Ill. 1976). It has also been held that the survivor may set aside gifts made by the first to die that are in breach of the will contract. See, e.g., Conitz v. Walker, 541 P.2d 1028 (Mont. 1975). Is the survivor protected against testamentary gifts contrary to the contract? See Duhme v. Duhme, 260 N.W.2d 415 (Iowa 1977); Irving J. Kornfield, Note, 48 Calif. L. Rev. 858, 862-63 (1960).

An analogous problem arose in Blackmon v. Battcock, 587 N.E.2d 280 (N.Y. 1991). In that case, the testator, Elizabeth Battcock, had entered into a settlement contract with her late husband's estate, according to which in exchange for receiving a portion of his estate, she agreed to drop her elective share claim and further agreed not to revoke her existing will. The will devised the bulk of her estate to her two children. Several years later, after the death of one of her children, Battcock opened several savings account trusts, naming various charities as beneficiaries. Her surviving child brought an action seeking a declaration that the Totten trusts were in breach of the contract not to revoke. The Court of Appeals held, by a 4-3 vote, that a promise not to create Totten trusts could not be implied into the contract not to revoke a will. The court stated that the cases limiting freedom to make inter vivos gifts that would undermine the purpose of joint or mutual wills that are subject to a will contract were inapposite: "Inconsistent testamentary dispositions or inter vivos gifts would defeat the very purpose of particularized promises, expectations, and mutuality of benefits involved with joint and mutual wills. That is not this case." Do you agree?

5. *What Property Is Covered by a Will Contract?* Questions frequently arise concerning whether a will contract covers property that the survivor acquired after the death of the first to die. Suppose that H died in 1950, survived by W. The value of H's estate, which passed to W pursuant to a contractual will, was $5,000. After H's death, W inherited real estate from a deceased friend, and acquired other property. W left a will devising $5,000 to the beneficiaries of the will contract, but left the remaining portion of her property to others. The terms of the will contract, however, bound the survivor as to "all the property . . . that the survivor may die seized and possessed of." Under these circumstances, courts have held that this language covered the after-acquired property. See, e.g., Wallace v. Turriff, 531 S.W.2d 692 (Tex. Civ. App. 1975); Estate of Jud, 710 P.2d 1241 (Kan. 1985).

A similar problem concerns post-death appreciation. Suppose, for example, that when H died in 1948, the value of the combined estates of H and W was approximately $60,000 and that at the time of W's death in 1969, it had grown to over $200,000. Courts have interpreted the contract as covering the entire estate as it existed at W's death. See, e.g., Matter of Wiggins, 360 N.Y.S.2d

129 (App. Div. 1974), aff'd per curiam, 350 N.E.2d 618 (N.Y. 1976).

Suppose that a will contract refers to the decedent's "property." Does this include non-probate assets? In Bergheger v. Boyle, 629 N.E.2d 1168 (Ill. App. Ct. 1994), the court held that a premarital contract to devise the "residue of the estate" referred only to the husband's probate estate and consequently did not include annuities.

6. *Lapse*. Suppose that a contract beneficiary predeceases the surviving contracting party. How should the survivor's estate be distributed? Most courts have held that the contract beneficiary's rights vest upon the death of first of the contracting parties to die. The property covered by the will contract passes through the beneficiary's estate rather than under the otherwise applicable antilapse statute. See, e.g., Rauch v. Rauch, 445 N.E.2d 77 (Ill. App. Ct. 1983); Estate of Maloney v. Carsten, 381 N.E.2d 1263 (Ind. Ct. App. 1978); Estate of Duncan, 638 P.2d 992 (Kan. Ct. App. 1982); Jones v. Jones, 692 S.W.2d 406 (Mo. Ct. App. 1985); Fiew v. Qualtrough, 624 S.W.2d 335 (Tex. Ct. App. 1981). Contra, e.g., Estate of Arends, 311 N.W.2d 686 (Iowa Ct. App. 1981). What theory or theories support the majority view? In this connection, consider the effect of the various approaches to the question of the surviving spouse's elective share. Professor Roberts argues that the majority view that "a beneficiary need not survive when there is a contract not to revoke [can be] intent-defeating." "[T]he lapse rule," she argues, "should still apply [, invoking the antilapse statute,] if applicable. To the extent that [anti]lapse statutes effectuate intent, they would do so in this context as well." Patricia J. Roberts, Lapse Statutes: Recurring Construction Problems, 37 Emory L.J. 323, 384-93 (1988).

7. *Tax Consequences*. Married couples who have children by prior marriages may want special assurance that their property will be split between the two families when the survivor dies. The desirability of using contractual wills for this purpose may be greatly affected by tax consequences. The cost of using a contract not to revoke may be the loss of the estate-tax marital deduction.[5]

An alternative device, at least for assuring the decedent's control over the

5. E.g., Estate of Opal v. Commissioner, 450 F.2d 1085 (2d Cir. 1971); Estate of Krampf v. Commissioner, 56 T.C. 293 (1972); Estate of Siegel v. Commissioner, 67 T.C. 662 (1977). The disallowance of the marital deduction applies only to property passing under the decedent's will. Property passing outside of probate—for example, joint tenancy property and life insurance proceeds—can qualify for the estate tax marital deduction even though the surviving spouse is under a contractual obligation as to how this property is to be disposed of on the surviving spouse's death. Rev. Rul. 71-51, 1971-1 Cum. Bull. 274. See also Tech. Adv. Mem. 91-01-002. The tax consequences are discussed in Joel C. Dobris, Do Contractual Will Arrangements Qualify for Qualified Terminable Interest Treatment Under ERTA, 19 Real Prop. Prob. & Tr. J. 625 (1984); Amy M. Hess, The Federal Transfer Tax Consequences of Joint and Mutual Wills, 24 Real Prop. Prob. & Tr. J. 469 (1990).

disposition of his or her property on the survivor's death, is to devise a life estate (or, more likely, an income interest for life in a trust) to the surviving spouse, coupled with a remainder interest in favor of beneficiaries selected by the decedent. Until the early 1980s, this device suffered the same tax disadvantage—the loss of the estate tax marital deduction. The Economic Recovery Tax Act of 1981, however, amended the Internal Revenue Code so that the life estate/remainder combination, called a "QTIP," can now qualify for the estate tax marital deduction, provided that certain technical requirements are satisfied. See supra Chapter 7. The allowance of a favorable tax consequence for the life estate/remainder combination has made it a more attractive device for controlling the disposition of the decedent's property on the surviving spouse's death than the contract not to revoke. This device, however, does not control after-acquired property.

8. *Planning and Drafting*. Couples who use joint or mutual wills should insert in their wills language clearly indicating whether or not they have contractually bound themselves not to revoke. If the parties *do* want to be contractually bound not to revoke, the contract should be reduced to writing and should spell out what property is covered and the survivor's powers with respect to making gifts.

In preparing this contract, can one lawyer ethically represent both parties, or must each party engage a lawyer? See ABA Model Rules of Professional Conduct, Rules 1.7, 2.1 (1983); Report, Developments Regarding the Professional Responsibility of the Estate Planning Lawyer: The Effect of the Model Rules of Professional Conduct, 22 Real Prop. Prob. & Tr. J. 1, 10-23 (1987). Cf. Whitney v. Seattle-First Nat'l Bank, 560 P.2d 360 (Wash. Ct. App. 1977); Bank of New York v. United States, 526 F.2d 1012 (3d Cir. 1975).

External Reference: Annot., Surviving Spouse's Right to Marital Share as Affected by Valid Contract to Convey by Will, 85 A.L.R.4th 418 (1991).

PART B. CONTRACTS TO DEVISE

Claims that a decedent promise to devise property in return for certain services arise in a variety of contexts. In many states the Statute of Frauds prevents enforcement of oral promises to devise either in an action at law for breach of contract damages or in equity for specific performance. Despite non-enforceability of an oral contract to devise, though, the disappointed promisee may bring an action in quantum meruit to recover from the promisor's estate the value of any benefit for services rendered to the promisor.

Green v. Richmond

337 N.E.2d 691 (Mass. 1975)

HENNESSEY, J. This is an appeal by the defendant from a judgment rendered against him as the personal representative of the estate of Maxwell Evans Richmond (the decedent). The action was in the nature of quantum meruit and sought recovery for services rendered by the plaintiff in reliance on the decedent's oral promise to leave a will bequeathing his entire estate to her.

A jury trial in the Superior Court resulted in a verdict for the plaintiff in the amount of $1,350,000. . . .

The facts are as follows: The plaintiff testified that she met the decedent in November, 1962, and shortly thereafter accepted his proposal of marriage. She was thirty-six years of age at the time, divorced, and had a fifteen-year old son; she was then employed as a secretary. The decedent was a wealthy, forty-nine year old bachelor whose holdings included licenses to operate three radio stations. Later the plaintiff became a stockbroker, earning about $20,000 a year.

About a year after they met, in October, 1963, the decedent stated that he had a "mental hangup" about marriage and asked to be released from the engagement; he said, however, that if the plaintiff would agree to "stay" with him, he would bequeath his entire estate to her at his death. The plaintiff agreed. There was other evidence directly corroborating the agreement. During the eight-year period between October, 1963, when bargain was made, and October, 1971, when the decedent died, there was evidence that the decedent, on several occasions, made statements to the plaintiff and other persons which could be found to be an acknowledgment by him of the original agreement. The last such occasion was on July 26, 1971, about three months before his death.

There was also evidence from which it could be found that the plaintiff kept her part of the agreement in reliance on the decedent's promise. There was detailed evidence of many services, of a social and domestic as well as of a business nature, performed by the plaintiff for the decedent over the eight-year period. There was evidence of many instances of sexual intercourse between the plaintiff and the decedent. The decedent died in October, 1971. The inventory value of his estate, which the judge permitted to be shown in evidence, was approximately $7,232,000.

It is clear that the oral agreement involved a promise to make a will, and as such was not binding. G.L. c. 259, § 5. Nevertheless, if the oral agreement were legal and not contrary to public policy, the plaintiff could recover the fair value of her services.

We consider first the defendant's argument that a verdict should have been directed in his favor on the ground that the contract was illegal. The argument offered is that as matter of law the agreement included sexual intercourse or cohabitation as part of the consideration, and that such a contract will not be enforced as against public policy. Further, the argument is that even if the agreement did not expressly include illicit terms, the unlawful performance of the bargain precludes recovery. We conclude that there was no error in the denial of a directed verdict because these issues were properly submitted to the jury under appropriate instructions, and the jury obviously reached conclusions favorable to the plaintiff.[6]

The defendant . . . argues that sexual intercourse was within the scope of the agreement and that the plaintiff therefore can recover nothing for her services; that additionally, or in the alternative, the plaintiff's performance in an illegal manner, by indulging in sexual intercourse, entitles her to no compensation, since her illegal performance was serious and not merely incidental to the agreement; that the illegality of the agreement and the illegality of the performance thereof were established as matter of law by the plaintiff's admissions on the witness stand at the trial, which the defendant argues were binding on her since there was no other evidence more favorable to her as to these issues; and that a directed verdict for the defendant was therefore required. . . .

The judge, in denying the defendant's motion for a directed verdict, submitted to the jury the issue of illegality, both as to the content of the agreement and the nature of the plaintiff's performance. There was no error. . . . Where the evidence is disputed as to the terms or performance of an oral agreement, or the meaning of words used by the parties, the matter should be left to the jury. In this case there was disputed evidence, some of which was sufficiently favorable to the plaintiff to warrant submission of the issues to the jury.

Thus, the plaintiff's testimony as to the terms of the contract contained no reference to sexual intercourse as follows, viz.;

> He said he couldn't lose me, either, and then he said, "I have been thinking about something, and I want you to listen to me." He said: "I have been looking for you all my life. You're the perfect woman for me." He said: "If you will agree to stay with me without marriage, you will be happy. I will see that your life will be happy. There's only one thing you won't have. You won't have the emotional security a woman has when she knows she is married, but I will make it up to you. I am going to make my will out right away. Everything I have when I die will be yours. I owe nothing to anyone else."

The defendant contends, however, that other evidence particularly admissions by the plaintiff, required a conclusion that the contract included an agreement

---

6. It could persuasively be argued that only naive persons would conclude that sexual intercourse was not central to the arrangement between the parties. Nevertheless that reasoning is not relevant, since the evidence as summarized, infra, warranted the submission of the issues to the jury.

for sexual intercourse. The plaintiff had testified of many instances of sexual relations with the decedent. However, on this issue as well as on the related issue of illegality of performance, there was other evidence, including other testimony from the plaintiff, which was more favorable to the plaintiff. Therefore the issue was for the jury's consideration. From the totality of the evidence the jury were warranted in inferring that the illicit relations were no part of the contract, and were no more than an incidental part of the plaintiff's performance.

Thus, inferences favorable to the plaintiff were supported by the evidence. For example, the plaintiff testified that, throughout their relationship, she maintained her own apartment and paid all her own household bills; that the decedent bought her no expensive gifts, furs, cars, jewelry or diamonds and made no contribution to her son's tuition at college; that she did not even accompany him on his annual vacations, customarily taken at Christmastime, until 1966 or 1967, because she felt that she owed it to her son to be home with him during his Christmas vacations from school; and that the decedent, with the plaintiff's knowledge, took another woman with him when the plaintiff could not accompany him on his annual vacation.

Further, the witness Norman Solomon, who shared the decedent's apartment, testified that he never saw the plaintiff or any trace of her at the former residences of the decedent and that the decedent slept in his own apartment every night. The witness recalled only one time when he saw the plaintiff at the decedent's last residence. Solomon further testified that the decedent "traveled a lot with . . . (a certain woman)," both before and after 1962, and "they made many trips together." Solomon quoted the plaintiff as saying, on one occasion, that both she and the decedent were free to "see" whomever of the opposite sex they might want to see.

A female witness, the "certain woman" referred to, supra, called by the defendant, testified that she took trips with the decedent each year between 1954 and 1958, inclusive. During the summer of 1963, she stayed at the defendant's apartment for about ten days. In 1964, she went on a trip to Jamaica with the decedent. In 1965, she went to St. Thomas and Puerto Rico with him. In 1967, she spent a week in Bermuda with him and then spent the entire summer at his apartment in Boston. Over the 1968 New Year's holiday, she went on a thirteen-day cruise with the decedent and, later in that year, went to St. Thomas with him. In 1969, she spent about a week with him at his summer residence in Marblehead and, in November of that year, the two of them went together to Florida for a week.

From all of this evidence the jury were justified in concluding that the sexual aspect of the relationship between the plaintiff and the decedent was no part of the bargain between the two, and no more than incidental to their relationship.

The defendant also argues that if the inventory of the probate estate had been excluded from evidence, as the defendant contends that it should have been, there would have been no evidence before the jury as to the value of the plaintiff's services. For this additional reason, the defendant says, there should have been a directed verdict for the defendant. There is no merit to this contention. Of the many and varied services as to which the plaintiff presented evidence, at least some of them were of such a routine and ordinary nature as to make their fair value a matter of common knowledge for the jury's consideration.

It follows from all that we have said that there was no error in the judge's denial of the defendant's motion for a directed verdict.

2. We turn now to the second issue argued by the defendant, viz.: that it was error to admit in evidence, over the objection and exception of the defendant, the Probate Court inventory showing the value of the estate. Actually there are two related questions raised here: (1) whether evidence as to the value of the estate is admissible and (2) if such evidence is admissible whether the probate inventory is an appropriate form of proof.

We consider first the question of the admissibility of the value of the estate. There is a divergence of opinion in other jurisdictions on the issue whether evidence of the contract terms, including value bargained for, shall be admitted as evidence of the value of the services sought by an action in quantum meruit. This divergence also exists with respect to the narrower question before us, i.e., whether the value of the decedent's estate was properly admitted as evidence of the value of the services rendered by the plaintiff on the basis that the value of the estate is the "price" put on the services by one of the contracting parties. There is precedent in somewhat similar Massachusetts cases for the admission of such evidence and the judge here undoubtedly relied on those decisions in making his rulings. We conclude that those decisions are controlling in the instant case and that the value of the estate was admissible in evidence.

There is substantial authority both judicial and scholarly which favors admissibility. Professor Corbin is emphatic as to the admissibility of this evidence:

> No one doubts, however, that the contract price or rate agreed upon by the parties is admissible in evidence to show what is the reasonable value of the performance that the defendant has received.

Corbin, Contracts, § 1113 (1964). The annotation in 21 A.L.R.3d 9, 18 (1968) is further supportive of admissibility, noting that there is "considerable authority" for admitting the contract price terms as evidence of the value of the services, under the theory that it is an admission against interest and is evidence of the general making and performance of the contract. The annotation further cites authority for admitting the contract price terms although the contract is not enforceable as violative of the statute of frauds, in cases where the promise, as here, is to transfer an estate in consideration of services, and concludes that many courts have admitted the value of the estate in these cases. . . .

We conclude that in the instant case appropriate proof of the value of the decedent's estate was admissible in evidence, and should be admitted at any subsequent retrial of the case.[7] Much of the reasoning advanced in favor of a directed verdict should receive consideration by the judge as substance for cautionary instructions to the jury against misuse of the evidence.

3. We turn now to a consideration of whether the probate inventory was an appropriate form of proof of the value of the estate, and whether, if it was not, it was error to admit the inventory in evidence in this case. We conclude that it was error.

The asset value was shown on the inventory as approximately $7,232,000. We have no way of knowing whether this amount accurately, or even remotely, represents the net value of the estate. We take notice that taxes, debts and other appropriate charges will substantially reduce this gross value. We assume that the inventory amount shown had some basis in fact, but the value of an estate is not shown by a list of its assets alone. . . . [I]n the special circumstances of this case we conclude that a preliminary showing of reliability was required before the amount of the inventory, which may or may not have been reflective of the value of the estate, was disclosed to the jury. . . .

We conclude, therefore, that the judgment should be reversed and the case remanded to the Superior Court for a new trial limited to the issue of damages.

So ordered.

Notes and Questions

1. *Enforceability of the Contract.* If Maxwell Evans had made his promise to leave his entire estate to Bernyce Green in a signed letter to her, would she have been able to recover damages for breach of contract from his estate? Consider the following observations:

> Where there is a contract to devise or bequeath and the promisee fully performs on his part, if the promisor dies without fulfilling his obligation an ordinary action at law for breach of contract will lie. The action is for breach of contract by the deceased and should be brought against the personal representative in the same way as any other contract claim against the estate. The claim is assignable and may

---

7. An interesting issue has been suggested: As of what date should the value of the estate be shown? Is it the date of the agreement or the date of the death? In the instant case the issue is not pressed, presumably because there was evidence that the decedent renewed his promise just a few months before his death.

> be enforced in the name of the assignee. Ordinarily the measure of damages will be the value of the thing promised by the promisor. Where the thing promised is a specific sum of money or a specific item of property the amount of damages is easily determined. If the promise is to give the entire estate or a fractional part thereof an action at law is hardly the appropriate remedy, but if that remedy is entertained the value of the thing promised is still the measure of damages. The difficulty here is with the remedy itself. Before the amount of damages can be fixed the net value of the estate must be ascertained. Since a jury is not a satisfactory body to supervise an estate accounting the law court should decline jurisdiction and transfer the case to equity where the parties will find a forum more adapted to their needs. . . .
>
> Recovery in quantum meruit such as is described above should not be confused with an action for damages for breach of the contract where an entirely different measure of damages is demanded. However, recovery in quantum meruit cannot be had unless the contract, even though oral, is proved.

Bertel M. Sparks, Contracts to Make Wills 136-40 (1956).

2. *Quantum Meruit Recovery by Unmarried Cohabitors.* Even without an explicit oral promise to devise all or part of the estate in return for services, a surviving cohabitor may have a claim in quantum meruit against the other's estate for the value of services rendered the decedent in the expectation of compensation. See, e.g., Estate of Zent, 459 N.W.2d 795 (N.D. 1990); Suggs v. Norris, 364 S.E.2d 159 (N.C. Ct. App. 1988). See the discussion of unmarried cohabitors' recovery in quantum meruit, supra Chapter 3, Part A.

3. One of the more spectacular lawsuits concerning alleged oral promises to make a devise involved the estate of Doris Duke, the late billionaire heir of James B. Duke, the founder of American Tobacco Co. In 1988, Ms. Duke, who had no children biologically, adopted Chandi Gail Heffner, a Hare Krishna follower with whom Duke shared interests in dance, animals, and Eastern philosophy. The two later had a falling-out, and Heffner was not named in Duke's last will (a will that was contested on other grounds). Heffner sued the Duke estate for breach of an alleged oral promise to provide for her in the style to which she had become accustomed. The suit was settled, and Heffner received more than $65 million from the Duke estate. See George James, Duke Estate Gives Daughter $65 Million, N.Y. Times, Dec. 30, 1995, at A20.

Chapter 12

Mistakes in Donative Documents

Restatement 3d of Property

§ *10.1 Donor's Intention Determines the Meaning of a Donative Document and Is Given Effect to the Maximum Extent Allowed by Law*

The controlling consideration in determining the meaning of a donative document is the donor's intention. The donor's intention is given effect to the maximum extent allowed by law.

NEARLY every authority would agree with the Restatement's general proposition that the controlling consideration in determining the meaning of a donative document is the donor's intention, and that the donor's intention should be given effect to the maximum extent allowed by law. This chapter, however, is about instances in which there is evidence suggesting that the written terms of a donative document, usually a will, vary from actual intention. This type of evidence is inherently suspect, especially when the heart of it consists, as it often does, of testimony regarding predeath statements of intention allegedly made by the testator—so-called direct declarations of intent. After death, the testator can't corroborate or deny the truthfulness of such evidence. The main protection against fabricated or mistaken evidence is the will itself. After all, the will is a document that is executed in accordance with statutory formalities that have as their underlying purposes the protection of the testator against fraud and undue influence (the so-called protective function), the providing of reliable written evidence of intent (the evidentiary function), the protection of the testator against effectuation of casual or unconsidered declarations of intent (the cautionary function), and the assurance that documents executed in accordance with the prescribed formalities will control the devolution of the property on death (the channeling function).

And yet, evidence offered against a will's literal meaning is sometimes correct. Mistake in translating intention into legally effective language is a frequent occurrence. Clerical error and lawyer incompetence make mistakes a phenomenon that's not limited to self-drawn wills.

The dilemma of how the law should respond to allegations of mistake (and uncertainty about the meaning of language) is the subject of the materials in this chapter. Most of the cases deal with wills. A few, however, deal with nonprobate transfers, such as lifetime trusts. The first case we present involving a pour-over devise, in fact, concerns the question of whether a particular trust arrangement was nontestamentary or testamentary.[1] The question was decisive to the outcome of *Brinker v. Wobaco Trust Ltd.*, because, as the opinion makes clear, the conventional view is that, upon a proper showing of mistake, donative lifetime instruments can be reformed, but that wills cannot be. For nontestamentary instruments, courts have used their equity powers to prevent unjust enrichment by correcting well-proven mistakes—clear and convincing evidence is the standard used. If the mistake were not corrected, the mistaken beneficiary would be unjustly enriched at the expense of the intended beneficiary. Why won't courts reform wills?

EXTERNAL REFERENCES. Joseph W. deFuria, Jr., Mistakes in Wills Resulting from Scriveners' Errors: The Argument for Reformation, 40 Cath. U.L. Rev. 1 (1990); Mary Louise Fellows, In Search of Donative Intent, 73 Iowa L. Rev. 611 (1988); Clifton B. Kruse, Jr., Reformation of Wills: The Implication of Restatement (Third) of Property (Donative Transfers) on Flawed but Unambiguous Testaments, 25 ACTEC Notes 299 (2000); John H. Langbein & Lawrence W. Waggoner, Reformation of Wills on the Ground of Mistake: Change of Direction in American Law?, 130 U. Pa. L. Rev. 521 (1982).

PART A. REFORMING DONATIVE DOCUMENTS OTHER THAN WILLS

Brinker v. Wobaco Trust Ltd.

610 S.W.2d 160 (Tex. Civ. App. 1980)

[Norman and Maureen Brinker, husband and wife, had two children, Cynthia and Brenda. Before Maureen's death in 1969, Maureen and Norman established an inter vivos trust, called the "Norman E. Brinker Family Trusts." The trust instrument named Norman as the "settlor" and named Maureen and a bank,

1. For discussion of pour-over devises, see supra Chapter 8, Part C.

collectively, as the "trustee." The trust was to be principally funded by the proceeds of life insurance on Norman's life, but since Norman was still living at the time of the lawsuit no proceeds had yet become payable. Maureen's will, however, appointed Norman as trustee of her residuary estate and directed that after a certain period it should pour over into the inter-vivos trust, where it should "be held or disposed of in accordance with the provisions of Article IV" thereof. Article IV of the trust provided that income and ultimately principal be paid to "the issue of settlor." In 1970, after Maureen's death, Norman created two other separate trusts for the benefit of Cynthia and Brenda. These trusts named Norman as "settlor," and provided that if the principal beneficiary dies without issue, the trust assets are to be paid to the "settlor's issue then living."

In 1971, Norman married Magrit; this marriage produced two children, Christina and Mark. In 1973, Norman conferred with his attorney and decided on a plan to bestow some of Maureen's residuary estate upon the children of this second marriage; to that end he transferred assets of Maureen's residuary estate to another trust he had set up through a banking corporation in the Bahamas. After his second marriage ended in divorce in 1977, Norman had second thoughts and told Cynthia and Brenda what he had done.

Cynthia and Brenda then brought suit to impose a constructive trust on the assets removed from Maureen's estate and to construe or reform the Norman E. Brinker Family Trusts and the two 1970 trusts. The suit asked that Christina and Mark, the children born of their father's second marriage, be excluded as beneficiaries of these trusts. In a bench trial, the court refused to admit evidence seeking to establish Norman's and Maureen's intention in creating the trusts or to show that in the drafting of the trust instruments a mistake had been made that would warrant reformation of the instruments to reflect the true intention.]

CORNELIUS, C.J. . . . On a bill of exceptions, appellants [Cynthia and Brenda] produced evidence that Maureen and Norman Brinker intended for the trusts to benefit only the issue born of their marriage to each other, and that if the term "issue of settlor" as used in the trust indentures meant the issue of Norman Brinker by any other union, a mistake had been made in the drafting of the trust indentures which warranted reformation of the instruments.

The evidence consisted of the testimony of Norman Brinker and Mr. Robert Taylor, a tax lawyer who prepared both the trust indentures and Maureen's will. The evidence may be generally summarized as follows: Mr. Brinker testified that he and Maureen primarily wanted to be certain that whatever assets went into the trust would go for the benefit of their two children at that time, i.e., Cynthia and Brenda. He said they knew Maureen could not have any other children and that they intended for the trust to be just for Cynthia and Brenda. He further testified that neither he nor Maureen was familiar with trusts or wills or legal terminology, and that they depended entirely on their lawyer to correctly put into the trust instruments what they wanted done; that neither he nor Maureen chose to use the word "settlor" or even knew what it meant; that the word was never mentioned or discussed with their lawyer or the bank; and that although they read the trust instruments before executing them they did not understand them, and in effect told their lawyer, "You are the lawyer; we don't understand this, did you do what we asked you to do?", and upon the lawyer's assurance that he had, they completed the transaction.

Mr. Taylor testified in detail. He testified that the Brinkers instructed him to prepare the family trust; in the discussion it was mentioned that Maureen could not have any more children; he understood that they wanted only Cynthia and Brenda to share in that trust; and that was the way he intended to draw the instruments and thought he had done so. When asked if either Norman or Maureen said anything about wanting to include children who might be born of other marriages, he answered "No, just the opposite", although he admitted that they did not specifically tell him to cut out all afterborn children. He further testified that if the trust indentures were written so as to include other children as beneficiaries, he had made a mistake in drafting the trust instruments.

Upon being questioned about Norman alone being named settlor, Mr. Taylor stated that he considered Maureen to be a co-settlor, and had intended to designate her as such in the same manner as he had designated her and the bank as co-trustee, and that was the reason he had her execute the trust indenture along with Norman. He also recalled that Maureen discussed with him the possible remarriage of her husband and that she shared "the normal concern of a wife that her husband, if something happened to her, might remarry and reiterated that she wanted her property to go to Cindy and Brenda." On cross-examination appellees brought out concessions from Mr. Taylor that the trusts did benefit Cynthia and Brenda, which literally complied with the directions he received from Norman and Maureen, and that the Brinker Family Trust indenture did not contain typographical errors, but contained the actual words he dictated. On the suggestion that many corrections would be necessary to change the trust indenture to designate Maureen as co-settlor, Mr. Taylor disagreed and said he intended to so designate her and then use the singular of the word "settlor" to refer to both Maureen and Norman as he had done with the singular word "trustee" to refer to Maureen and the bank. Other features of the drafting and signing of the trust indentures were pointed out which could be construed to impeach Mr. Taylor's testimony that a mistake in the drafting had been made.

The foregoing summary demonstrates that a fact issue was made on the question of mistake in the drafting of the trust indenture to correctly express the parties' intention. The evidence raising such issue should have been admitted on appellants' plea for reformation.

If, by mistake, an instrument as written fails to express the true intention or agreement of the parties, equity will grant reformation of the instrument so as to make it correctly express the agreement actually made. The rule applies to express inter vivos trusts as well as to other written instruments. The mistake may be shown by parol evidence. And although a mutual mistake of the parties is required in most instances, if a settlor of a trust receives no consideration for the creation of the trust, a unilateral mistake on his part is sufficient. It is immaterial whether the mistake be one of fact or law. Any mistake of the scrivener which could defeat the true intention may be corrected in equity by reformation, whether the mistake is one of fact or law. The fact that the written instrument is couched in unambiguous language, or that the parties knew what words were used and were aware of their ordinary meaning, or that they were negligent in failing to discover the mistake before signing the instrument, will not preclude relief by reformation. . . .

Appellees contend, however, that because the residuary trust in Mrs. Brinker's will eventually will pour over into the Brinker Family Trust, and Mrs. Brinker's will has now been probated, the Brinker Family Trust, so far as the pour over assets are concerned, has become testamentary and consequently it cannot be reformed. We disagree.

It is true that a testamentary disposition is not subject to reformation. But we hold that the Brinker Family Trust did not become testamentary by reason of Mrs. Brinker's residuary trust pour over.

Prior to the drafting of the Uniform Testamentary Additions to Trusts Act [supra Chapter 8, Part C], there were two legal doctrines concerning the validity and nature of testamentary additions to inter vivos trusts. One was the doctrine of incorporation by reference, which held that the terms of the inter vivos trust became incorporated into the will by reference and became a part of it, thus rendering the trust testamentary insofar as the gift was concerned. . . . The other was the doctrine of independent significance, which held that the trust did not become a part of the will, but that the testamentary bequest or devise simply was added to and augmented the trust corpus to be administered as a part of the trust according to its provisions. Under that doctrine the trust provisions concerning disposition of the gift did not become testamentary. . . . The Uniform Testamentary Additions to Trusts Act was designed to validate testamentary additions to trusts even though such trusts were amendable, and to prevent the trust provisions affecting such gift from becoming testamentary. The Act provides in part as follows:

> . . . the property so devised or bequeathed (a) *shall not be deemed to be held under a testamentary trust of the testator but shall become a part of the trust to which it is given and (b) shall be administered and disposed of in accordance with*

> *the provisions of the instrument* . . . setting forth the terms of the trust, ... (Emphasis supplied.)

Texas adopted the Uniform Act in 1961. . . . Although the Texas version does not specifically provide that such a gift will not be deemed to be held under a testamentary trust, in other respects it is essentially the same as the Uniform Act, and it specifically provides that the gift ". . . shall be added to the corpus of such trust to be administered as a part thereof and shall thereafter be governed by the terms and provisions of the instrument establishing such trust. . . ." We hold that the intention of the Texas Act was that the trust provisions would not become testamentary by reason of such a gift, but that the gift would simply augment the corpus of the trust and become a part of it.

Appellees assert that a reformation of the Family Trust would violate that portion of [the Texas version of the Uniform Act] which provides that a gift to a trust will be governed by the trust instrument *and any written amendments or modifications made before the death of the testator*. It is argued that to reform the Family Trust would be the equivalent of amending or modifying it after the death of Maureen Brinker. We cannot agree.

To amend or modify an agreement means to change it. . . . Reformation does not change the agreement; it enforces the agreement. It orders a change in the drafted instrument so that it will correctly express what has been the real agreement from its inception.

The excluded evidence on the issue of reformation is before us in the bill of exceptions, but as indicated in our summary of that evidence it is not so conclusive that it determines the issue as a matter of law and allows us to render a judgment. There is positive evidence of mistake; yet there are circumstances which bear upon the credibility and accuracy of the testimony which might lead reasonable minds to reject it. A fact issue has been created which requires resolution by a trier of fact. The judgment will therefore be reversed and remanded for a new trial.

Notes

1. *Meaning of the Term "issue."* The court in *Brinker* thought that the only way to restrict the term "issue of settlor" to the settlor's issue by his first marriage was to reform the trust. According to the Restatement 2d of Property, however, the term only presumptively means all of the settlor's issue, a presumption that is rebuttable if the language or circumstances indicate a contrary intent. See Restatement 2d of Property § 25.9 and comment d. The Restatement 3d of Property has not yet addressed this topic.

2. *Reformation of Will Substitutes*. In Estate of Robinson v. Robinson, 720 So.2d 540 (Fla. Dist. Ct. App. 1998), the court confronted an argument that a

revocable inter vivos trust could not be reformed because it was in substance a will. The court rejected the argument, saying that "we hold that a trust with testamentary aspects may be reformed after the death of the settlor for a unilateral drafting mistake so long as the reformation is not contrary to the interest of the settlor." Id. at 543.

Mahoney v. Grainger

186 N.E. 86 (Mass. 1933)

RUGG, C.J. This is an appeal from a decree of a probate court denying a petition for distribution of a legacy under the will of Helen A. Sullivan among her first cousins who are contended to be her heirs at law. The residuary clause was as follows:

> All the rest and residue of my estate, both real and personal property, I give, demise [sic] and bequeath to my heirs at law living at the time of my decease, absolutely; to be divided among them equally, share and share alike; provided, however, that the real property which I own at my decease shall not be sold or disposed of until five (5) years after my decease, unless there is not sufficient personal property at the time of my decease to pay my specific legatees; in which case said real property may be sold. The income from said real property during said five (5) years is to be distributed among my heirs at law as I have directed.

The trial judge made a report of the material facts in substance as follows: The sole heir at law of the testatrix at the time of her death was her maternal aunt, Frances Hawkes Greene, who is still living and who was named in the petition for probate of her will. The will was duly proved and allowed on October 8, 1931, and letters testamentary issued accordingly. The testatrix was a single woman about sixty-four years of age, and had been a school teacher. She always maintained her own home but her relations with her aunt who was her sole heir and with several first cousins were cordial and friendly. In her will she gave general legacies in considerable sums to two of her first cousins. About ten days before her death the testatrix sent for an attorney who found her sick but intelligent about the subjects of their conversation. She told the attorney she wanted to make a will. She gave him instructions as to general pecuniary legacies. In response to the questions "Whom do you want to leave the rest of your property to? Who are your nearest relations?" she replied "I've got about twenty-five first cousins . . . let them share it equally." The attorney then drafted the will and read it to the testatrix and it was executed by her.

The trial judge ruled that statements of the testatrix

> were admissible only in so far as they tended to give evidence of the material circumstances surrounding the testatrix at the time of the execution of the will; that the words heirs at law were words in common use, susceptible of application to

> one or many; that when applied to the special circumstances of this case that the testatrix had but one heir, notwithstanding the added words "to be divided among them equally, share and share alike," there was no latent ambiguity or equivocation in the will itself which would permit the introduction of the statements of the testatrix to prove her testamentary intention.

Certain first cousins have appealed from the decree dismissing the petition for distribution to them.

There is no doubt as to the meaning of the words "heirs at law living at the time of my decease" as used in the will. Confessedly they refer alone to the aunt of the testatrix and do not include her cousins.

A will duly executed and allowed by the court must under the statute of wills be accepted as the final expression of the intent of the person executing it. The fact that it was not in conformity to the instructions given to the draftsman who prepared it or that he made a mistake does not authorize a court to reform or alter it or remold it by amendments. The will must be construed as it came from the hands of the testatrix. Mistakes in the drafting of the will may be of significance in some circumstances in a trial as to the due execution and allowance of the alleged testamentary instrument. Proof that the legatee actually designated was not the particular person intended by the one executing the will cannot be received to aid in the interpretation of a will. When the instrument has been proved and allowed as a will oral testimony as to the meaning and purpose of a testator in using language must be rigidly excluded.

It is only where testamentary language is not clear in its application to facts that evidence may be introduced as to the circumstances under which the testator used that language in order to throw light upon its meaning. Where no doubt exists as to the property bequeathed or the identity of the beneficiary there is no room for extrinsic evidence; the will must stand as written.

In the case at bar there is no doubt as to the heirs at law of the testatrix. The aunt alone falls within that description. The cousins are excluded. The circumstance that the plural word "heirs" was used does not prevent one individual from taking the entire gift.

Decree affirmed.

Notes

1. *Plain-Meaning Rule*. The rule applied in *Mahoney* is sometimes known as the "plain-meaning" rule. When the meaning of words of the will is "plain," no deviation can be permitted. Accord Gustafson v. Svenson, 366 N.E.2d 761 (Mass. 1977) (holding that devises to testators' brother or "his heirs per stirpes" found in the wills of two sisters is unambiguous and rejecting extrinsic evidence of attorney that testators did not intend that their brother's wife should share in

their estate). The following passage is a familiar statement of the plain-meaning rule:

> Where there is nothing in the context of a will from which it is apparent that a testator has used the words in which he has expressed himself in any other than their strict and primary sense, and where his words so interpreted are sensible with reference to extrinsic circumstances, it is an inflexible rule of construction, that the words of the will shall be interpreted in their strict and primary sense, and in no other, although they may be capable of some popular or secondary interpretation, and although the most conclusive evidence of intention to use them in such popular or secondary sense be tendered.

James Wigram, An Examination of the Rules of Law, Respecting the Admission of Extrinsic Evidence in Aid of the Interpretation of Wills 18 (5th ed. 1914).

Closely linked to the plain-meaning rule is another rule—the no-extrinsic-evidence rule. If equity will not entertain suits to reform wills, no purpose would be served by allowing the introduction of extrinsic evidence to contradict clear and unambiguous terms in a will.

2. *Continental Legal Tradition.* The Anglo-American approach to construction questions is in sharp contrast to the continental legal tradition. As explained by Erich Schanze:

> Broadly stated, the Anglo-American tradition emphasises objective, literal interpretation of statutory texts and private declarations of intention. Extrinsic or subjective factors are admissible only in a limited number of exceptions. In contrast, Continental legal systems tend to be generous in ascertaining purposes and intentions of legislative and private texts. The radically different styles of construction are associated with a different philosophy of legislating and drafting. The scrutiny of legal definitions and the length of documents in the Anglo-American context are still a source of amazement for many civil lawyers. Likewise, the brevity of similar texts on the Continent must appear cryptic for a common lawyer. The diverging position is most notable in the interpretation of testaments . . . .

Erich Schanze, Interpretation of Wills—An Essay Critical and Comparative, in Comparative and Historical Essays in Scots Law 104 (D. L. Carey Miller and D. W. Meyers eds. 1992).

PART B. RESOLVING AMBIGUITIES IN WILLS AND OTHER DONATIVE DOCUMENTS

Although courts won't "reform" wills, they will resolve ambiguities in wills in accordance with the testator's intention as proved by extrinsic evidence. An "ambiguity" is defined in the Restatement as "an uncertainty in meaning that is revealed by the text or by extrinsic evidence other than direct evidence of intention contradicting the plain meaning of the text." Restatement 3d of Property § 11.1. The Restatement declares that an ambiguity "is resolved by construing the text of the donative document in accordance with the donor's intention, to the extent that the donor's intention is established by a preponderance of the evidence." Id. § 11.2.

The Restatement provides that "all relevant evidence, whether direct or circumstantial, may be considered. Thus, the text of the donative document and relevant extrinsic evidence may both be considered" for purposes of determining a donor's intent. Id. § 10.2. The Restatement includes a list of some types of ambiguities that should be resolved by determining donor's intent through use of extrinsic evidence. That list includes: (1) the text or extrinsic evidence (other than direct evidence contradicting the plain meaning of the text) reveals a mistaken description of persons or property; (2) the text reveals an apparent mistaken inclusion or omission; or (3) extrinsic evidence (other than direct evidence contradicting the plain meaning of the text) reveals that the donor's personal usage differs from the ordinary meaning of a term used in the text. Id. § 11.2. The material that follows examines these types of ambiguities and the remedies the courts have provided to cure defective expressions of donative intent.

1. Ambiguous Descriptions of Persons or Property

Arnheiter v. Arnheiter

125 A.2d 914 (N.J. Ch. 1956)

SULLIVAN, J.S.C. Burnette K. Guterl died on December 31, 1953, leaving a last will and testament which has been admitted to probate by the Surrogate of Essex County. By paragraph 2 of said will her executrix was directed "to sell my undivided one-half interest of premises known as No. 304 Harrison Avenue, Harrison, New Jersey," and use the proceeds of sale to establish trusts for each of decedent's two nieces.

This suit comes about because the decedent did not own or have any interest in 304 Harrison Avenue either at her death or at the time her will was executed. At the hearing it was established that the decedent, at the time her will was executed and also at the time of her death, owned an undivided one-half interest in 317 Harrison Avenue, Harrison, New Jersey, and that this was the only property on Harrison Avenue that she had any interest in.

Plaintiff-executrix has applied to this court to correct an obvious mistake and to change the street number in paragraph "2" of the will to read "No. 317 Harrison Avenue" instead of "No. 304 Harrison Avenue." Relief cannot be granted to the plaintiff in the precise manner sought. It matters not that an obvious mistake in the form of a misdescription is proved. A court has no power to correct or reform a will or change any of the language therein by substituting or adding words. The will of a decedent executed pursuant to statute is what it is and no court can add to it.

Plaintiff, however, is not without recourse. In the construction of wills and other instruments there is a principle "*falsa demonstratio non nocet*" (mere erroneous description does not vitiate), which applies directly to the difficulty at hand.

> Where a description of a thing or person consists of several particulars and all of them do not fit any one person or thing, less essential particulars may be rejected provided the remainder of the description clearly fits. This is known as the doctrine of falsa demonstratio non nocet. [Clapp, 5 N.J. Practice, section 114, page 274.]

A leading case involving the application of the above maxim to facts similar to our own is Patch v. White, 117 U.S. 210 (1886). There, the testator bequeathed to his brother land which he described as belonging to himself and as containing improvements, the lot being "numbered six, in square four hundred and three." He did not own the lot so numbered but did own lot number 3, in square 406, which was improved. The lot numbered 6 in square 403 had no improvements. The court applied the principle of *falsa demonstratio non nocet,* and by disregarding or rejecting the words "six" and "three" in the description, concluded that the lot owned by the decedent passed to his brother under this provision of the will.

Turning to the problem at hand and to the description of the property as set forth in paragraph 2 of the will, we find the street number "304" to be erroneous because decedent did not own that property. If we disregard or reject that item of description, the will then directs the executrix "to sell my undivided one-half interest of premises known as Harrison Avenue, Harrison, New Jersey." Since it has been established that the decedent, at the time of her death and also when she executed her will, had an interest in only one piece of property on Harrison Avenue, Harrison, New Jersey; that her interest was an undivided one-half interest; that the property in question is 317 Harrison Avenue; and that decedent made no other specific provision in her will relating to 317 Harrison Avenue, we are led inevitably to the conclusion that even without a street number, the rest of the description in paragraph 2 of the will is sufficient to identify the property passing thereunder as 317 Harrison Avenue.

Judgment will be entered construing decedent's will as aforesaid.

Notes, Questions, and Problems

1. *Remedying Ambiguities. Arnheiter* not only illustrates the admissibility of extrinsic evidence in cases of ambiguity but also introduces one of the remedial techniques employed in such cases—the deletion of the erroneous parts of a mistaken description, so that what is left accurately describes the testator's intention. As the court noted, the leading case for this approach is Patch v. White, 117 U.S. 210, but the decision in that case was not reached without a struggle. Four justices dissented. They asserted that the action of the court "is not construing the will of the testator; it is making a will for him." Id. at 227.

This statement from the dissenting opinion raises a challenging question: If courts have no power to reform wills by substituting or adding words to them, by what authority do they have the power to delete words from them?

More recently, the opposite question has been raised: If courts have the power to delete words from wills, why don't they have the power to substitute or add words to them? The Restatement 3d of Property § 11.2, comment c rejects the view that the only technique for resolving an ambiguity is deleting the erroneous portions of the description. The Restatement declares that the remedy should forthrightly correct the misdescription:

> Once an ambiguity is revealed, it is well accepted that extrinsic evidence may be considered in resolving the ambiguity. When the donor's intention is then proved by a preponderance of the evidence, the final step, correcting the mistaken expression, should follow as a matter of remedy, and should not be unnecessarily hindered by an artificial line between deleting and adding.

2. *Problems on Ambiguity*. Applying the conventional distinction between ambiguous and unambiguous descriptions of persons or property, would extrinsic evidence be admissible in the following cases? Could the misdescriptions be remedied by the technique employed in *Arnheiter* and *Patch*?

(a) Nathaniel Tucker knew about the work of the American Seaman's Friend Society in New York City and intended to devise a part of his estate to this society. The scrivener who prepared his will only knew about one association for the benefit of seamen, the Seaman's Aid Society of Boston. Nathaniel knew nothing of this society, but the scrivener persuaded him that the society he had in mind went by the name "Seaman's Aid Society of Boston," and this is the way the will was written. See Tucker v. Seaman's Aid Soc'y, 48 Mass. (7 Metc.) 188 (1843). For other cases raising a similar question, see In re Girard Trust Corn Exchange Bank, 208 A.2d 857 (Pa. 1965) (inter vivos deed of trust); Vadman v. American Cancer Soc'y, 615 P.2d 500 (Wash. Ct. App. 1980); National Soc'y for the Prevention of Cruelty to Children v. Scottish Nat'l Soc'y for the Prevention of Cruelty to Children, [1915] App. Cas. 207 (H.L.). See also Estate of Hillyer, 664 So. 2d 361 (Fla. Dist. Ct. App. 1995) (reversing the lower court for admitting any extrinsic evidence regarding the testator's contrary intent because the disposition of the property was unambiguous).

Many charities have sound-alike names. See Chapter 15, infra.

(b) The testator's will devised certain property "to my well-beloved nephews John and William Willard." The testator had two sets of relatives by the names of John and William Willard—grandnephews and grandsons. Evidence was sought to be introduced that the grandnephews were strangers to the testator, never visited him, and never resided near him. The grandsons, however, lived near the testator. The testator was very intimate and friendly with them and repeatedly declared that he had bought the devised property for his grandsons. The lawyer who drew the will sought to testify that the testator directed that the property in question should be given to the grandsons, but by mistake the lawyer wrote "nephews" instead. See Willard v. Darrah, 68 S.W. 1023 (Mo. 1902). For another case raising a similar question, see Siegley v. Simpson, 131 P. 479 (Wash. 1913) in which the testator made a devise to "my friend Richard H. Simpson." Extrinsic evidence showed that Hamilton Ross Simpson, whom the testator called "Bill" or "Rotary Bill," was the testator's "friend" and that Richard H. Simpson was merely a remote acquaintance.

3. *Significance of Language of Ownership*. Of what significance was it that the devise in *Arnheiter* contained explicit language of ownership: "*my* undivided one-half interest of premises known as No. 304 Harrison Avenue"? (The devise in *Patch* also said that the devised property "belongs to me.") Is it reasonable to infer, in the absence of express language of ownership, that the will refers to property owned by the testator? In Lynch's Estate, 75 P. 1086 (Cal. 1904), Lynch devised to his nephew Dennis "that certain lot . . . in Tulare County, State of California, and described as follows, to wit: the S. ½ of the N.W. 1/4 of Sec. 1, T. 21, R. 27 E." Lynch never owned this tract but he did own the west half of the southwest quarter of the same section. The court held that the intended devise was ineffective. The court was willing to disregard the "false description," leaving the will as though it read "the ½ of the 1/4 of Sec. 1" etc., but in its opinion this left the description too uncertain to be given effect:

> There are four quarter sections within the section, each of which can be divided into halves in four different ways, so that there are sixteen descriptions of land to which this language could apply with equal certainty.

Compare *Lynch* with Whitehouse v. Whitehouse, 113 N.W. 759 (Iowa 1907). The will devised "the north half of the northwest quarter of section 29, township 80, range 25, Polk County, Iowa." The testator owned only the north half of the northeast quarter of the same section. The court held that extrinsic evidence was admissible to show to which of the north quarters the description should be applied after omitting the word "west." "[T]he presumption should prevail," the court stated, "that the testator is undertaking in his will, without saying so in express terms, to dispose of property which he believed belonged to him, rather than to belong to another." Accord Restatement 3d of Property § 12.2, comment i, illus. 5.

Patent and Latent Ambiguities. According to the Restatement 3d of Property, a *patent ambiguity* "is an ambiguity that is apparent from the text of the donative document." A *latent ambiguity* "is an ambiguity that is not apparent merely from reading the text of the donative document but becomes apparent from extrinsic evidence. . . . [D]irect evidence of intention contradicting the plain meaning of the text does not establish a latent ambiguity." Restatement 3d of Property § 11.1, comments b, c. *Arnheiter* and *Patch* present examples of latent ambiguities.

A common statement found in court opinions and other legal authority is that extrinsic evidence can be used to resolve a *latent* ambiguity but not a *patent* ambiguity. The distinction between latent and patent ambiguities was given currency by Sir Francis Bacon in his Maxims of the Law, in which he said that a patent ambiguity "is never holpen by averrement . . . because the law will not couple and mingle matter of specialty, which is of the higher account, with matter of averrement, which is of inferiour account." Francis Bacon, Elements of Common Law 82 (1639), reprinted in Francis Bacon, Law Tracts 99 (1737), and 7 Francis Bacon's Works 385 (1870).

American scholars of evidence law long ago repudiated Bacon's distinction. In his great Preliminary Treatise on Evidence 424 (1898), James Bradley Thayer described Bacon's distinction as an "unprofitable subtlety," and Dean Wigmore likewise condemned the distinction as resting on a "play upon words." 9 John H. Wigmore, Evidence 226, 239 (3d ed. 1940).[2] That the distinction has any important influence on decisions today is doubtful, but it can't be wholly ignored if for no other reason than that courts occasionally still talk in such terms. See, e.g., Estate of Schultheis, 747 A.2d 918 (Pa. Super. Ct. 2000). The Restatement 3d of Property provides that "no legal consequences attach to the distinction" between latent and patent ambiguities. Restatement 3d of Property § 11.1, comment a. In Estate of Florio, 697 N.Y.S.2d 908 (Sur. Ct. 1999), the court admitted extrinsic evidence of a scrivener's error upon finding

---

2. Wigmore had in mind the argument, repeated by the United States Supreme Court in Patch v. White, 117 U.S. 210, 217 (1886), that "as a latent ambiguity is only disclosed by extrinsic evidence, it may be removed by extrinsic evidence."

that will contained two irreconcilable sentences and held that one of the sentences should be excised.

Admissibility of Evidence of Direct Declarations of Intent. In general, then, extrinsic evidence is available as an aid to construction and to resolve an ambiguity whether latent or patent. See, e.g., First Union Nat'l Bank of Florida v. Frumkin, 659 So. 2d 463 (Fla. Dist. Ct. App. 1995) (involving the patent ambiguity of an inconsistency between two testamentary trust provisions regarding the trustee's discretionary power to invade principal on behalf of a beneficiary); Maurice F. Jones Trust v. Barnett Banks Trust Co., 637 N.E.2d 1301 (Ind. Ct. App. 1994) (concerning the latent ambiguity of whether the phrase "which I am legally obligated to pay" applied to that portion of the federal estate taxes resulting from inclusion of a QTIP trust created by the testator's husband). But there is one general prohibition on the type of evidence that may be used. Traditionally, testimony about the testator's statements as to what language in the will was intended to mean is not admissible—testimony as to "declarations of intention," as Wigmore called it. 9 Wigmore, supra, at 229.

According to Wigmore, this limitation rests upon the "rule which prohibits setting up any extrinsic utterance to compete with and overthrow the words of a document." He recognized that such declarations could be used not for this purpose but rather for that of interpreting the words of the document, yet concluded: "There being two conceivable purposes for which it could be used, the one proper, the [other] improper, it is excluded because of the risk that the latter would dominate and that the temptation to abuse would be too strong." Id. at 229-30.

Equivocations. Despite the traditional inadmissibility of the testator's direct declarations of intent, there is one instance where it is well established that such evidence will be received, that is, where there is an *equivocation*. An equivocation exists when the words of the will apply equally to two persons or things.

The Commonwealth courts have been somewhat more insistent than the American courts that the words fit the two persons or things more or less equally. In addition, they have tended to limit the equivocation exception to a situation in which the words are a fairly exact description of the two persons or things. An example of this narrow reading of the exception comes from an Ontario case, In re Gray, [1934] Ont. W.N. 17. The testator had one brother whose full name was "John Gray" and another whose full name was "Norman Farquharson Gray." His will left a part of the residue of his estate in equal shares to his brothers and sisters, with a proviso that the share of his brother "John Norman Gray" was to be placed in trust so that he was to have only a life estate instead of an absolute interest. The court rejected evidence of statements by the testator that this special provision was to apply to Norman. "In this case," the court said, "the name 'John Norman' cannot be said to be equally applicable in all its parts to each of the brothers . . . although the name so used in the will is in part correctly applicable to each of these brothers." Lacking competent evidence of which of the two brothers was meant, the court held that this part of the will was void because of uncertainty.

For a time it was suggested that the equivocation exception was limited to latent ambiguities. Older cases should have put this artificial distinction to rest. See, e.g., Doe d. George Gord v. Needs, 2 Mees. & W. 129, 150 Eng. Rep. 698 (Ex. 1836) (resolving patent ambiguity by testator's declarations of intention). The distinction, however, keeps reappearing in cases. See, e.g., Virginia Nat'l Bank v. United States, 443 F.2d 1030, 1034 (4th Cir. 1971) (treating an equivocation as a patent ambiguity and not allowing into evidence the testator's direct declaration of intent but allowing into evidence advice given to the testator pertaining to the testator's overall tax objectives); Breckner v. Prestwood, 600 S.W.2d 52, 56 (Mo. Ct. App. 1980) (admitting direct declarations of intent for latent but not patent ambiguities); see also Lehr v. Collier, 909 S.W.2d 717 (Mo. Ct. App. 1995) (allowing reformation of lifetime trust but holding that patent ambiguity precluded admission of direct declarations of intent).

Other cases have abandoned restrictions on the admissibility of a testator's direct declarations. For example, consider the case of Estate of Smith, 580 P.2d 754 (Ariz. Ct. App. 1978). In that case, Hazel Smith's will devised "my money and coin collection to Todd Fehlhaber and Sue Fehlhaber in equal shares, or to the survivor thereof." Included in Smith's estate were a collection of thirty-six coins and six two-dollar bills found in her safe deposit box and appraised at $49, and various bank accounts and certificates of deposit valued at close to $107,000. The residuary devisees sought to introduce an affidavit of the attorney who drew the will that related the testator's directions to the attorney. The affidavit indicated that the testator wanted the collection of coins and bills to go to Todd and Sue and that she wanted the rest of her assets, including the certificates of deposit and savings accounts, to go to the named residuary devisees. The lower court admitted this affidavit into evidence. The court of appeals affirmed, saying:

> We agree there was an ambiguity in the instant will and it was a patent one. The term "money" when used in wills is essentially ambiguous. . . . The word may have any meaning which the testamentary intent, as manifested by the will read in the light of proper evidence, imparts to it. . . . Once having established an ambiguity, parol evidence is admissible for the purpose of explaining it. . . . The language used here admits of two constructions. . . . It was therefore proper to resort to extrinsic proof, including the statement of the attorney who drew up the will.

The Restatement of Property considerably broadened the definition of equivocation to be a description "indifferently applicable to two or more persons or objects." Restatement of Property § 242, comment j. This definition would seem to apply to nearly all ambiguous descriptions of persons or property, either latent or patent. The Restatement 3d of Property abandons the restriction completely and provides that evidence of the testator's direct declarations of intent may be considered in resolving ambiguities of any type, latent or patent. See Restatement 3d of Property § 10.2, comment f; § 11.2, comment d.

Potential Evidentiary Bars to the Admissibility of the Testator's Statements. In addition to the traditional rule against admitting direct declarations of intent, other evidentiary rules may bar admission of the testator's statements. The Restatement 3d of Property § 10.2, comment h provides that "[t]o the extent appropriate, the rules of evidence should be construed to allow direct evidence of the donor's intention, whether that evidence concerns utterances or events occurring before or after execution of the donative document."

Dead Man's Acts. In Estate of Thomas, 327 A.2d 31 (Pa. 1974), the court disposed of the so-called Dead Man's Act as an obstacle to the admission of the testator's statements, saying:

> Appellant contends finally that the Orphans' Court committed a clear violation of the Dean Man's Statute . . . in permitting the appellee and his wife to testify as to appellee's conversations with the decedent with reference to the shares of stock and the savings account mentioned in Paragraph Eighth and to decedent's intent to benefit him.[3] This contention is without merit. Where opposing parties in a controversy involving merely the testamentary distribution of property present their claims under the will, either party is competent under language of the Statute to testify as to prior conversations with the testator regardless of any individual interest possessed by them in the testator's property.

But see Estate of Malnar, 243 N.W.2d 435 (Wis. 1976) (applying Dead Man's Statute); Estate of Christen, 239 N.W.2d 528 (Wis. 1976) (holding that incom-

---

3. The Dead Man's Statute provides in pertinent part:

> Nor, where any party to a thing or contract in action is dead, or has been adjudged a lunatic and his right thereto or therein has passed, either by his own act or by the act of the law, to a party on the record who represents his interest in the subject in controversy, shall any surviving or remaining party to such thing or contract, or any other person whose interest shall be adverse to the said right to such deceased or lunatic party, be a competent witness to any matter occurring before the death of said party or the adjudication of his lunacy . . . unless the issue or inquiry be devisavit vel non, or be any other issue or inquiry respecting the property of a deceased owner, and the controversy be between parties respectively claiming such property by devolution on the death of such owner, in which case all persons shall be fully competent witnesses.

[Footnote by the court. Eds.]

petency of legatee under prior will to testify as to conversations with the decedent does not extend to the spouse of the legatee). See generally Report, Dead Man Statutes: Their Purposes, Effect and Future, 7 Real Prop. Prob. & Trust J. 343 (1972). Rule 601 of the Uniform Rules of Evidence (1974, amended 1988) provides that "[e]very person is competent to be a witness except as otherwise provided in these rules." The Official Comment to Rule 601 states that "[t]his repeals the 'deadman's statute.'"

Hearsay Rule. The hearsay rule is not an obstacle to the admission of a testator's statements made before the will was executed. Such statements come within the exception to the rule for declarations showing a state of mind. As to postexecution statements, however, there is a split of authority, some courts holding their admission barred by the hearsay rule, others holding their admission not barred by that rule. 6 Wigmore, supra, §§ 1734-40. Rule 803(3) of the Uniform Rules of Evidence (1974, amended 1988) provides that the testator's statements relating to "the execution, revocation, identification, or terms of the declarant's will" are not barred by the hearsay rule.

Attorney-client privilege. The following analysis of the attorney-client privilege appears in Stevens v. Thurston, 289 A.2d 398 (N.H. 1972):

> Defendants as contestants moved to discover the contents of the file of the attorney who drafted the will . . . The Trial Court denied [the] motion and reserved and transferred defendants' exceptions.
>
> It appears from the reserved case that the denial of the motion for discovery was based solely on the attorney-client privilege. We recognize and enforce the common-law rule that confidential communications between a client and attorney are privileged and protected from inquiry in the absence of a waiver by the client. . . . We have also held that the privilege continues after the death of the client in actions against the estate and may be waived by the representatives of the decedent. . . .
>
> This appeal from the probate of the will, however, . . . is not an adverse proceeding against the estate . . . , but a contest between parties claiming through the testator. If the defendants are successful, they, rather than the plaintiff, will be the representatives of the testator. Here the privilege is being asserted not for the protection of the testator or his estate but for the protection of a claimant to his estate. The authorities uniformly hold that in this situation all reason for assertion of the privilege disappears and that the protection of the testator lies in the admission of all relevant evidence that will aid in the determination of his true will. . . . Defendants' exception to the denial of their motion for discovery is sustained.

The distinction drawn by *Stevens* is well accepted. See, e.g., Fletcher v. Alameda County Superior Court, 52 Cal. Rptr. 2d 65 (Ct. App. 1996). It is embodied in Rule 502 of the Uniform Rules of Evidence (1974, amended 1988) ("[t]here is no [lawyer-client] privilege . . . [a]s to a communication relevant to an issue between parties who claim through the same deceased client, regardless of whether the claims are by testate or intestate succession or by transaction inter vivos"), in § 81 of the Restatement (Third) of the Law Governing Lawyers ("The attorney-client privilege does not apply to a communication from or to a decedent relevant to an issue between parties who claim an interest through the same deceased client, either by testate or intestate succession or by an inter vivos transaction."), and in § 10.2 comment f of the Restatement 3d of Property.

Admissibility of Evidence in Tax Cases. The resolution of an ambiguity found in a will may determine tax consequences to an estate. An ancillary question in these cases is whether the federal court must decide whether to apply state law precedents on the issues of whether to admit extrinsic evidence and what type of evidence to admit. The decisions are in conflict as to whether state law is controlling.

In Estate of Trunk v. Commissioner, 550 F.2d 81, 84-85 (2d Cir. 1977), for example, the court said:

> It would seem that the most compelling evidence of a testator's intent would be his own statements concerning it. . . . Although some state courts continue to reject testimony of this nature where the ambiguity is patent, . . . we see little justification, in a proceeding before the Tax Court, for applying different evidentiary rules to latent and patent ambiguities. Proceedings before that Court are equitable in nature; and, because the Court is concerned with substance and realities rather than form, its search for the truth is not rigidly restricted to the contents of writings. . . .
>
> Whether declarations would be admitted in state court probate proceedings in order to resolve patent ambiguities is not determinative of the issue before us. The Tax Court does not apply state rules of evidence. Where, as here, the language of the will may be interpreted in several equally reasonable ways and the declarations of the testator neither add to, alter or compete with his written words, his declarations of intent should be admitted by the Tax Court in carrying out its equitable obligation to search out the truth.

On remand, the Tax Court received testimony from the attorney who drew the will concerning the testator's statements to him and on this basis allowed the estate a federal estate tax marital deduction. 37 T.C.M. (CCH) 497 (1978).

A different conclusion was reached in Estate of Craft v. Commissioner, 68 T.C. 249, 263 (1977), aff'd per curiam, 608 F.2d 240 (5th Cir. 1979). In this case, the Tax Court said:

> [We hold] that in those instances where we are called upon to make a state law determination as to the existence and extent of legal rights and interests created by a written instrument, we must look to that state's parol evidence rule in deciding

> whether or not to exclude extrinsic evidence that bears on the disputed rights and interests under the instrument.
>
> To hold otherwise could conceivably lead to an anomalous situation in which, because we had admitted and found convincing parol evidence that would have been excluded by a state court, we might determine and cause to be taxed certain interests and rights that a state court applying state law would find to be nonexistent. Such a result would do violence to that fundamental principle of tax law that state law creates legal rights and property interests while the Federal law determines what, and to what extent, interests or rights, so created, shall be taxed.

See also Priv. Ltr. Rul. 9725031 (Mar. 24, 1997) (looking to state law to determine admissibility of extrinsic evidence to resolve latent ambiguity); Priv. Ltr. Rul. 9623043 (June 7, 1996) (looking to state law to determine whether parol evidence was admissible to resolve patent ambiguity).

INTERNAL REFERENCE. See the discussion in Chapter 7, Part B addressing the question of whether a state court's ruling regarding the relevant parties' economic interests and obligations has a binding effect on federal authorities for purposes of determining federal tax liability.

Moseley v. Goodman

195 S.W. 590 (Tenn. 1917)

NEIL, C.J. E.J. Halley died on October 19, 1910, leaving the following will:

> I, E.J. Halley, of a sound mind, will make this my last will and testament. I bequeath to the following people mound set of the names, E.O. Kolley, $500.00, Mr. R.G. Ramsey, $500.00, Miss Elizabeth Berry $500.00. I give to A. Goodman and Armstrong $10,000 a piece, Ed. Hurlburt $5000. Jack Brennan $5000. George Becktall $20,000, Mrs. Moseley $20,000. Mrs. Moseley's housekeeper $20,000, W.M. Palmer $20,000. Mrs. Mergle, Sr., $20,000, Ed. Mergle, $20,000, Theadore Mergle $10,000, the balance of my real estate I give to the St. Peter's Orphan Asylum.

The controversy arises over the legacy: "Mrs. Moseley $20,000, Mrs. Moseley's housekeeper $20,000." That is to say, while the legacy to Mrs. Moseley is the only one directly involved here, it is necessary to consider the legacy to the housekeeper in connection with it, so far as the word "housekeeper" is descriptive of the Mrs. Moseley, intended, as the one who had a housekeeper. . . .

The facts disclosed by the record, by the overwhelming weight of the evidence, are as follows:

The testator was for many years engaged with his mother in business on Main street, in the city of Memphis, in the sale of liquors, tobacco, and cigars. He and his mother bought, through a series of years, cigars from Mr. F.S.

Trimble, the husband of Mrs. Lillian E. Trimble. Mr. Trimble was the city salesman for one R.L. Moseley, and, as such, for several years, sold cigars to testator and his mother. Testator generally addressed him as "Moseley," it seems, because he sold the Moseley cigars, and the Moseley sign was very prominently displayed at the front of the building where Trimble worked. It does not appear that testator dealt personally with R. L. Moseley himself at all. Mrs. Trimble, during the same period, bought goods about once a month from testator and his mother, and the testator called her "Mrs. Moseley," and admired her character very greatly. He spoke of her to others as a fine woman. The mother of testator died about January, 1910, and he then fell into the habit of drinking, and became quite dissipated. He made a foreign tour with one Harper, he himself paying all the expenses. His mother had left him about $230,000. He claimed, when he came back, that he had spent $6,000 on this trip. He drank a great deal while he was traveling, and came back in a bad state of health. After his mother died, and before he started on the foreign tour, he engaged a room at an apartment house known as "The Monarch," which was owned, or leased, by Mr. Trimble. Mrs. Trimble had charge of it as manager. When testator started on his foreign tour he gave up his room, but immediately on his return he secured the same or another room at "The Monarch," Mrs. Trimble being still the manager. He still drank heavily and was ill. He stayed at "The Monarch" two or three weeks, and was then removed to the hospital, and died within a day or two thereafter, having made the will Monday night and died Wednesday morning.

Mrs. Trimble, at the time testator returned to "The Monarch," had, as her housekeeper for that institution, Mrs. Anna Lang. Both Mrs. Trimble and Mrs. Lang gave the testator very devoted attention, such attention as a sick man needs, serving night and day. Mrs. Trimble brought him milk and soup and other delicacies. Mrs. Lang ministered to him very assiduously and with great kindness in the way of sponging him and doing other things for his comfort. He appeared to be very grateful for these attentions. He generally called Mrs. Trimble Mrs. Moseley, though occasionally he called her Mrs. Trimble. There is evidence to the effect that he always called her Mrs. Moseley. The witness Rothschild deposed to this fact. He testified that on one occasion, when he was in the room of testator, the latter was talking about Mrs. Moseley quite a good deal, and he asked him who he was referring to, and he said: "Mrs. Trimble; I always call her Mrs. Moseley." He always spoke of Mrs. Lang as "housekeeper," or "the good woman."

It does not appear that he knew Mrs. Lenoir Moseley. It does appear that he knew her husband, R.L. Moseley. Mrs. Moseley herself testified that she did not know Mr. Halley at all. She endeavors to connect herself with the legacy not only by the fact that her name was Mrs. Moseley, but by the further fact that her sister, Miss Jessie Dunlap, was her housekeeper at her private home. It is in proof that the testator incidentally met Miss Dunlap on one occasion at "The Monarch." . . . [T]here is no real evidence that Halley knew that Miss Dunlap was housekeeper to the complainant. However, in our further treatment of the case we shall assume that he did have such information.

If the testimony was competent to the effect that the testator always or generally spoke of Mrs. Trimble as Mrs. Moseley, or generally called her Mrs. Moseley, there was ample evidence to sustain the verdict [in favor of Mrs. Trimble], and that point is not questioned. However, it is said that the evidence was not competent; that when it was proven that there was in existence a Mrs. Moseley, whose legal name was such, this satisfied the language of the will, and the testimony above referred to concerning Mrs. Trimble's being called Mrs. Moseley by the testator could not be used to raise a latent ambiguity. We are of the opinion that this view is erroneous.

The general principle is well stated in Ayres v. Weed, 16 Conn. 290, as follows:

> If a person is commonly called and known by a name which does not properly belong to him, but which properly belongs to another, it cannot with propriety be said that that name, although a false one, is not in fact descriptive of the former, unless we go so far as to say that a person is not described by the name by which he is known. That would clearly be a case where two different persons would be described by the same name, and where, therefore, parol evidence might be introduced to remove the doubt as to which of them was intended. That the name given to a person is a nickname does not render it the less a description of him, although, indeed, a less correct one, that if his true name were used; and it is well settled that if a legacy is given, or a devise made, to a person by his nickname, parol evidence is admissible to show that the testator usually called him by that name, in order to show that he was intended; much more would it be admissible to show that he was generally known in the community by that name.

Now, there is no evidence in this record that Mrs. Trimble was generally known by the name of Mrs. Moseley; but it was sufficient to indicate the meaning of the testator if it be shown, as it is shown here, that he was accustomed to call her by that name. . . .

[A] devise to a person by any name, however different the name used in the will from the true name of the person, is good, provided it is shown that the name used was one by which the testator was accustomed to designate the person, and such showing may be made by parol proof. . . .

Counsel for the complainant insist that if the court should hold that Mrs. Trimble was the person intended, and so should affirm the judgment of the chancellor and the Court of Civil Appeals decreeing the legacy to her, that would be nothing short of striking the name of Mrs. Moseley from the will, and inserting in its place that of Mrs. Trimble, and so writing a new will for the testator. This argument is clearly fallacious. We look to the evidence merely to ascertain what individual the testator had in mind when he wrote the term "Mrs. Moseley." The evidence recited, if competent, must convince any one, as it did the jury, that he meant Mrs. Trimble, because "Mrs. Moseley" was the name by which he called her, and because of his long acquaintanceship with her, the esteem in which he had long held her, and the kindnesses on account of which he was indebted to her, and because of his associating with her the person whom he always called "the housekeeper," Mrs. Anna Lang. . . .

Judgment will therefore be entered here affirming the judgment of the Court of Civil Appeals, with costs.

Note and Questions

1. *The Personal-Usage Doctrine. Moseley* illustrates an established exception to the no-extrinsic-evidence rule, the "personal usage" doctrine. See Estate of Fabian, 483 S.E.2d 474 (S.C. Ct. App. 1997) (admitting extrinsic evidence to determine meaning of "brother"); Martin v. Palmer, 1 S.W.2d 875 (Tex. App. 1999) (admitting extrinsic evidence to determine meaning of "my nieces and nephews"); Restatement 3d of Property § 11.2(b)(3), comments r to u; Restatement of Property § 242, comment d. The language in the *Moseley* will was not manifestly ambiguous, yet the court admitted extrinsic evidence regarding the testator's intent. What is the reason for this exception? Was the extrinsic evidence in *Moseley* demonstrably more reliable than that rejected by the court in Mahoney v. Grainger? See also In re Nelson, 906 S.W.2d 707 (Mo. Ct. App. 1996) (refusing to admit extrinsic evidence to show that the testator intended the term "bank accounts" to refer to insurance annuity contracts as well as bank accounts, holding that the term was neither patently nor latently ambiguous and that it should be given its "plain and ordinary meaning"). But see Sammons v. Elder, 940 S.W.2d 276 (Tex. App. 1997) (finding "savings account and/or savings certificate" is ambiguous).

2. *Questions.* Could the personal-usage doctrine have been used in Mahoney v. Granger, supra p. 683, or in Tucker v. Seaman's Aid Soc'y, supra p. 688?

2. Mistakes in the Inducement

Statutory Reference: *UPC § 2-302*

Gifford v. Dyer

2 R.I. 99 (1852)

This was an appeal from a decree of the Court of Probate of Little Compton, proving and approving the last will and testament of Abigail Irish. The will was dated December 4, 1850, and the testatrix died December 6, 1850. After several bequests of small sums to the children of Robin Gifford and to others, she gives and bequeaths the rest and residue of her property, one half to John Dyer, who was her brother-in-law, and the other half to her two nephews, Jesse and Alexander Dyer. Robin Gifford, the only child of the testatrix, was not mentioned in the will. It appeared in evidence, that at the date of the will, Robin Gifford had been absent from home, leaving a family, for a period of ten years, unheard from; that all the neighbors considered him dead, and that his estate had been administered upon as of a person deceased. The scrivener who drew the will, testified as follows:

> After I had read the will to her, she asked if it would make any difference if she did not mention her son. I asked if she considered him living. She said she supposed he had been dead for years; she said, if it would make any difference she would put his name in, for they will break the will if they can. I think that was the expression she used. I think she said what she had given her grandchildren was in lieu of what he would have, but am not positive. I think her son left in 1841, and was not heard of to my knowledge. She was speaking of a home at Mr. Dyer's and said, what she had given him would pay him well. She said her grandchildren had not been to see her while she was sick.

It appeared that the testatrix had resided with John Dyer for some time previous to her death. . . .

GREENE, C.J. delivered the opinion of the court. It is very apparent in the present case, that the testatrix would have made the same will, had she known her son was living. She did not intend to give him anything, if living.

But if this were not apparent and she had made the will under a mistake as to the supposed death of her son, this could not be shown *dehors* the will. The mistake must appear on the face of the will, and it must also appear what would have been the will of the testatrix but for the mistake. Thus, where the testator revokes a legacy, upon the mistaken supposition that the legatee is dead, and this appears on the face of the instrument of revocation, such revocation was held void. Campbell v. French, 3 Vesey, 321.

Notes

1. *State of the Authorities.* Most of the decisions follow the view reflected in *Gifford*. See, e.g., Clapp v. Fullerton, 34 N.Y. 190 (1866); Arnold's Estate, 107 N.Y.S.2d 356 (Sur. Ct. 1951), aff'd, 122 N.Y.S.2d 804 (App. Div.), appeal denied, 124 N.Y.S.2d 343 (App. Div. 1953); Bowerman v. Burris, 197 S.W. 490 (Tenn. 1917); Carpenter v. Tinney, 420 S.W.2d 241 (Tex. Civ. App. 1967).

In line with the principle announced in *Gifford*, courts have given effect to a will that omitted or gave a nominal amount to a natural object of the testator's bounty even though the will itself recited a reason for the action that was in fact false. See, e.g., Le Flore v. Handlin, 240 S.W. 712 (Ark. 1922); Riley v. Casey, 170 N.W. 742 (Iowa 1919); Woelk's Estate, 296 P. 359 (Kan. 1931); Shumway's Will, 246 N.Y.S. 178 (Sur. Ct. 1930); Bedlow's Will, 22 N.Y.S. 290 (Sup. Ct. 1893).

2. *Children Omitted Because Thought Dead; Uniform Probate Code.* UPC § 2-302(c) creates one exception to the general rule that mistakes in the inducement can't be corrected. If a testator fails to provide for a child living at the time a testator executes a will solely because the testator mistakenly believes the child to be dead, the child receives a share of the testator's estate as if the child were an omitted afterborn child. See supra Chapter 10, Part C.

Children can be omitted from a parent's will because thought dead in a variety of settings. According to the National Center for Missing and Exploited Children, nearly 90 percent of persons reported missing are young children and youths. Although incidences of reports of missing persons declining in 1998 and 1999 after fifteen years of steady increases, the percentage of missing adults is increasing. See National Center for Missing and Exploited Children, 1999 Missing Child Statistics (News Release, Feb. 3, 2000). For both youths and adults, only about one percent are never found. See Deborah Sharp, More Cases of Missing Children Now Adults, USA Today, Mar. 24, 1999, at 1A. In war time, children in the armed forces can be listed as missing or killed in action who later are found alive. See Joseph L. Galloway, Detective Work; Identifying the Missing, U.S. News & World Rep., Jan. 17, 1994, at 50.

3. *Relief for Fraud in the Inducement.* As we noted in Chapter 4, Part C, supra, courts ordinarily will not relieve a mistake that induced the testator to make a devise. They will provide, however, a remedy for fraud in the inducement. An appropriate remedy may include invalidating all or part of the will or imposing a constructive trust remedy to prevent unjust enrichment. A constructive trust is imposed even on innocent devisees or heirs to assure that those persons who the testator would have intended to share in the estate had the fraud not occurred receive their intended shares.

3. Mistaken Omissions

The Restatement 3d of Property provides that a donative document is ambiguous if "the text reveals an apparent mistaken . . . omission." Restatement 3d of Property § 11.2(b)(2). The Restatement 3d also provides that "extrinsic evidence may be considered to establish the content of the mistakenly . . . omitted language," and that if the content of a mistaken omission is established by extrinsic evidence, the omitted language may be inserted into the document. See Restatement 3d of Property § 11.2(b)(2), comments n to q.

Burnett v. First Commercial Trust Co.
939 S.W.2d 827 (Ark. 1997)

ARNOLD, C. J. This is a case involving a testamentary trust. The issue is whether the will containing the trust is ambiguous in its disposition of the testatrix's property. We hold that the will is not ambiguous, and that the chancellor erred in receiving parol evidence on the question of the testatrix's intent. We therefore reverse and remand.

The testatrix, Lois E. Burnett, died on June 10, 1994. At the time of her death, her family consisted of her brother, James Burnett, her nephew, William Spencer, Jr., and Spencer's six children. Mrs. Burnett's will provided for her funeral expenses and made several small, specific bequests. The will then disposed of the remainder of her estate as follows:

> I give, devise, and bequeath all the rest and residue of my estate, whether real, personal, or mixed, and of whatever kind or nature, wheresoever located and whenever acquired to Arkansas Bank and Trust [now First Commercial Trust Company] in Trust for my friend, Flournoy Adkins, during his lifetime.
>
> The terms of said trust being as follows:
>
> 1. Flournoy Adkins is to receive my automobile at the time of my death for his use and benefit.
> 2. Flournoy Adkins has the right and use of my home located as follows: [description of the property].
>
> Upon the death of Flournoy Adkins, the Trustee shall distribute the above described land as follows: one-half interest to my nephew, William Spencer, Jr., and one-half interest to his six children . . . in equal shares, share and share alike.

As can be seen, the will instructs the trustee that the realty contained in the trust corpus is to be distributed upon the death of Flournoy Adkins. However, it makes no provision for the distribution of the *personalty* contained in the trust corpus. The distinction is important. At the time of Mrs. Burnett's death, the real property in the trust was valued at $25,000.00; the personal property was valued at $194,702.14.

On May 3, 1995, First Commercial brought an action for declaratory judgment seeking instructions on how to distribute the personalty in the trust upon Flournoy Adkins's death. First Commercial claimed that the trust's failure to expressly provide for such distribution was the result of a clerical error. The complaint asked that the personalty be distributed in the same manner as the realty: one-half to William Spencer, Jr., and one-half to the Spencer children. James Burnett, who had received no bequest in the will, answered the complaint. He contended that any part of the trust corpus lacking specific directions for distribution should pass through the laws of intestate succession. The chancellor found that the silence of the will regarding the distribution of the personalty created an ambiguity. He thus allowed the use of parol evidence to explain the omission.

Bruce Garrett, the attorney who prepared Mrs. Burnett's will, testified that Mrs. Burnett came to him in 1992 to change her will. Garrett testified that the will's failure to provide for the disposition of the trust's personal property was the result of a clerical error. The provision which read, "upon the death of Flournoy Adkins, the Trustee shall distribute the above described *land* "should have read,"shall distribute the above described *land and personalty*." Garrett further testified that Mrs. Burnett had decided to cut James out of the will and to provide for her friend, Flournoy Adkins. The previous will, which Mrs. Burnett executed in 1990, had bequeathed the bulk of her estate to James Burnett and William Spencer, Jr. A copy of Mrs. Burnett's old will reflecting the deletions, additions, and handwritten notes of Garrett and his secretary, was introduced into evidence. The exhibit shows that the provisions which were made for James Burnett in 1990 were marked through. A witness who was experienced in the use of shorthand testified that some of the secretary's notes on the will could be translated as directing the personal property to be distributed to the residual beneficiaries upon Adkins's death.

The chancellor, after hearing the evidence, found that the testatrix intended to bequeath all trust property, including personal property, to William Spencer, Jr., and his six children, upon the death of Flournoy Adkins. Jeanne Burnett, as special administratrix of her late husband's estate, brings this appeal.

Ordinarily, the intention of the testator is to be gathered from the four corners of the instrument itself. Extrinsic evidence may be received on the issue of the testator's intent, but only where the terms of the will are ambiguous. The language of Mrs. Burnett's will unequivocally expresses the intention that, upon the death of Flournoy Adkins, the land contained in the trust shall be distributed. No mention is made of her substantial personal estate. The question we must answer is whether Mrs. Burnett's failure to dispose of her entire estate creates an ambiguity. An ambiguity has been defined as an indistinctness or uncertainty of meaning of an expression used in a written instrument. Such a definition contemplates the need for interpretation of terms actually used in the will. As such, it does not encompass the situation in which a testatrix does not dispose of a portion of her estate. We have recognized that oral evidence should not be used to supply terms in a writing which are wholly absent.

In a similar case from Texas, *In re Estate of Hunt*, 908 S.W.2d 483 (Tex. App. 1995), a testatrix failed to completely dispose of a remainder interest in a trust. The court said the following:

> It is true that Marguerite Hunt failed to completely dispose of her estate in the Will. It is also true that upon reading the entire will it is reasonable to presume that it was Marguerite Hunt's intention to award the remainder interest in the Delph Trust to the Salvation Army. But she did not say so. And we are prohibited from speculating as to what Marguerite Hunt would have done had she completed her will. A court may not rewrite a will or add provisions under the guise of construction of the language of the will in order to reflect some presumed intention of the testatrix. Even though there is a strong presumption against intestacy, the presumption does not arise when the testatrix fails, through design or otherwise, to make a complete disposition of her property. (Citations omitted).

Our own case law has espoused much the same philosophy—that the paramount objective in interpreting a will is the intention of the testator as expressed in the language of the will, and that it is presumed that a testatrix knows the contents of the will she executes. *Chlanda v. Estate of Fuller*, 326 Ark. 551, 932 S.W.2d 760 (1996); *Heirs of Mills v. Wylie*, 250 Ark. 703, 466 S.W.2d 937 (1971). The *Heirs of Mills* case is particularly enlightening. There, Mr. Mills's will contained a number of contingency provisions, including a provision that bequeathed most of his estate to a nephew and a sister-in-law, should Mills and his wife die in a "common disaster". However, the will failed to provide for the situation in which Mrs. Mills might predecease her husband. In fact, she did predecease him. Mr. Mills's heirs (who were not provided for in his will) filed suit, contending that, since the will made no bequest in the event Mrs. Mills predeceased her husband, Mr. Mills's estate should pass through the laws of intestate succession. In holding that the will contained no ambiguity, we said the following:

> actually our holding in this case may not be in accord with the actual intention of the testator—existing in his mind—but certainly it is in accord with long established law that the court's finding shall be based on the intention of the testator—*as expressed by the language of the will.*

Id. at 704, 466 S.W.2d at 938.

First Commercial argues that our acceptance of the appellant's argument will result in a partial intestacy. In response to a similar contention, we said the following in Chlanda v. Estate of Fuller, supra:

> It is correct to state that there is a presumption in the rules of construction that 'a person who takes the time and effort to make a will does not desire partial intestacy'. *Kidd v. Sparks*, 276 Ark. 85, 633 S.W.2d 13 (1982). However, a probate court should not resort to the rules of construction unless the intent of the testator, as shown by his express words, is in doubt.

326 Ark. at 555, 932 S.W.2d at 763.

The express language of Mrs. Burnett's testamentary disposition reflects the unambiguous intention that, upon the death of Flournoy Adkins, the land, and no other property contained in the trust corpus, shall pass under the will. We must therefore reverse and remand this case with instructions to enter orders consistent with this opinion.

REVERSED AND REMANDED.

GLAZE and THORNTON, JJ., dissent.

THORNTON, J., dissenting. . . . I would affirm the order of the Chancellor.

While there are numerous granting clauses in the will, all of the internally inconsistent provisions are contained in Section III of the will. Section III B reads as follows:

> B. Provided, however, in the event my friend, Flournoy Adkins, should predecease me, co-decease with me, or in the event that we should die at the same time or as a result of a common accident or catastrophe, then and in that event, I give, devise, and bequeath all the rest and residue of my estate as follows: one-half (½) to my nephew, William Spencer, Jr., and one-half (½) to my nephew's six children, Billy Spencer, Jasen Spencer, Adam Spencer, Mary Fagan, Ann Griffen, and Elizabeth Forbes, in equal shares, share and share alike.

In the event Flournoy Adkins survives Ms. Burnett's death, Section III A. establishes a trust for his benefit during his lifetime, with the following provision:

> A. I give, devise, and bequeath all the rest and residue of my estate, whether real, personal, or mixed, and of whatever kind or nature, wheresoever located and whenever acquired to Arkansas Bank and Trust as Trustee in Trust for my friend, Flournoy Adkins, during his lifetime.

Within these two provisions, there is no ambiguity. Ms. Burnett's estate goes to her nephew and his children if Mr. Adkins does not survive her, but if he does survive her, he is to have a life interest in all the property placed into trust. However, the instrument contains an ambiguity in directing the trustee's distribution of the estate following Mr. Adkins's death. From the four corners of the instrument, it is apparent that Ms. Burnett intended for all of her property to be distributed in accordance with her will, and that following her death and the death of her friend, Flournoy Adkins, the property was to be distributed to her nephew and his children. Unfortunately, ambiguity arises because the instructions to the trustee fail to clearly specify that "personal" property should be distributed to *anyone* upon Mr. Adkins's death, providing only that upon the termination of the trust for the benefit of Mr. Adkins, the "land" shall be distributed to the nephew and his children.

Chancellor Switzer correctly finds that placing all the property in the trust, without addressing the distribution of personal property, creates an ambiguity. He states that "there is a conflict and repugnance between the provisions such as to require judicial interpretation."

As we consider whether a potential flaw in the establishment of the trust gives rise to an ambiguity requiring judicial interpretation, we should be reminded of these principles:

1) The testatrix did not want to die intestate, but intended all property to pass under her will. Whenever possible, wills should be interpreted so as to give effect to the intent of the testator and avoid a partial intestacy.

2) Here, it is not necessary to look beyond the four corners of Section III to determine that an ambiguity exists requiring interpretation. We should remember that we are addressing an ambiguity in a trust provision established by the will, which also provides in the same section for the distribution of all the estate to her nephew and his children upon Mr. Adkins's death, if that occurs before the death of the testatrix. If the ambiguity is not resolved, the trust will fail. We are not called upon to reform the will, but to interpret ambiguous instructions to trustees managing a trust clearly established by the will in order to resolve the conflict and repugnance between provisions of section III of the instrument itself.

In the circumstances of this case, it was appropriate for the Chancellor to consider evidence to resolve the ambiguity and to determine what interpretation effectuates the testatrix's intent in the establishment of the trust. . . .

Appellant relies upon our decision in *Mills' Heirs v. Wylie*, 250 Ark. 703, 466 S.W.2d 937 (1971), in which we cited *Smith v. Smith*, 229 Ark. 579, 317 S.W.2d 275 (1958), as follows:

> It is well settled law in this state, so well settled as to require no citation of authority, that where there is no ambiguity, or no conflict or repugnance between the provisions of the will, judicial interpretation or construction is not required.

Id. at 707, 466 S.W.2d at 940. In *Mills' Heirs*, we also state the rule that "where the meaning of the language is *not ambiguous*, testimony as to the testator's intention is 'inadmissible' . . ." and then concluded: "Since we find that there was no ambiguity, there is no necessity to discuss the testimony." *Id.* at 708, 466 S.W.2d at 940 (emphasis added).

Unlike the will in *Mills' Heirs*, which had no internal inconsistencies, here we have an internally inconsistent testamentary trust, the ambiguous language of which would devise and bequeath the testatrix's property to her nephew and his children if her friend predecease her, but provided no instruction to the trustee as to the disposition of her personal property after her friend's death, should he survive her. This internal ambiguity requires that evidence of the testatrix's intent be admitted to resolve the conflict between provisions of the instrument.

I believe that the instrument must be looked at as a whole; that from the four corners of the instrument, it is apparent that an ambiguity exists; that evidence of the testatrix's intent was required to resolve the ambiguity; and that the Chancellor's rulings and order should be sustained. I would affirm the decision.

GLAZE, J., joins in this dissent.

Notes and Question

1. *Inserting Omitted Language into Wills by Construction.* Seemingly in conflict with the no-reformation rule are cases in which courts have inserted language mistakenly omitted from wills. Where courts have added the missing language, they have explained their decisions on the theory that they are engaging in a process called "construction." The term "construction" in these cases is being used in the specialized sense of constructing the omitted language by implication from the language that is contained in the will rather than supplying it from extrinsic evidence. The construction theory has produced some curious results. In a pair of cases decided by the same court on the same day, for example, missing language was inserted in one but not the other.

In Dorson's Estate, 196 N.Y.S.2d 344 (Sur. Ct. 1959), the testator's will divided the residue of his estate into two trusts, Funds A and B. The testator's widow was the initial income beneficiary of both funds; when her interest terminated, each fund was to be divided into three parts, one part for each of the testator's three children. His daughter Marjorie was the beneficiary of Part 2 of both Fund A and B. Part 2 of Fund A provided for the income to be paid to Marjorie until she reached 35, at which time she was to receive one-third of the corpus; the income from the remaining two-thirds of corpus was to be paid to her until she reached 40, at which time one-half of the remaining corpus was to be paid to her until she reached 45, whereupon she was to receive the entire remaining corpus. Part 2 of Fund B contained identical language, except that the language directing that one-half of the remaining corpus be paid to Marjorie at age 40 was omitted. The court inserted that language into Fund B, saying that "[t]he testator's general dispositive scheme is clearly discernible from a reading of the will. . . ." See also In re Bieley, 695 N.E.2d 1119 (N.Y. 1998) (using doctrine of gift by implication thereby avoiding question of whether court should admit evidence of scrivener's error); McCauley v. Alexander, 543 S.W.2d 699 (Tex. Civ. App. 1976) (inserting the word "estate," which appeared in the third paragraph of the will into a devise in the second paragraph of the will, which named the devisee but failed to state what property was devised).

In Estate of Calabi, 196 N.Y.S.2d 443 (Sur. Ct. 1959), the testator's will, drafted by counsel, divided the residue of his estate into four trusts. Trusts C and D were to receive one-twelfth each of the residue. For Trusts A and B, the will spelled out the trust terms and identified the beneficiaries but the will omitted the terms and beneficiaries for Trusts C and D. The one-sixth of the residue not expressly disposed of was held to pass by intestacy to the testator's heirs, notwithstanding an allegation that Trusts C and D were intended to be for the benefit of the testator's grandchildren until each reached the age of 24. The court noted that no supporting evidence of this allegation was submitted, but it went on to say that "if such supporting evidence were available it would not be admissible." See also Farmers & Merchants Bank v. Farmers & Merchants Bank, 216 S.E.2d 769 (W. Va. 1975) (holding inadmissible the lawyer's testimony that the intended amount was $35,000 and that it was inadvertently omitted by the lawyer's typist with regard to a devise that named the devisee but failed to state the amount of the devise).

Would extrinsic evidence supporting the allegation, if offered in *Calabi*, have been inherently less reliable a basis for correcting the mistake than the basis for relief that the court used in *Dorson*?

2. *Inserting Omitted Language into Inter Vivos Trusts.* In contrast with the attitude toward reformation reflected in *Burnett* and *Calabi*, courts have openly reformed revocable trusts on the basis of extrinsic evidence of mistakenly omitted language, even after the settlor's death. A striking example of this incongruity between the law of wills and the law of trusts is Berman v. Sandler, 399 N.E.2d 17 (Mass. 1980). Ellen Sandler created a revocable and amendable inter vivos trust. Later, her attorney found that the first paragraph of section 1 of Article Third of the trust jeopardized the qualification of the trust for the federal estate tax marital deduction. The attorney drafted a document amending the trust. The amending document, which Sandler signed, directed that section 1 of Article Third be deleted and that certain new language be substituted for it. After Sandler's death, it was discovered that the amendment deleted section 1 in its entirety rather than the first paragraph thereof, as intended. In a suit for reformation brought by the trustee the court ordered the insertion into the amending document of the mistakenly omitted phrase "the first paragraph of." The court stated:

> It is settled that a written instrument, including a trust, will be reformed on grounds of mistake upon "full, clear, and decisive proof" of the mistake. . . . Since a settlor usually receives no consideration for the creation of a trust, a unilateral mistake on the part of the settlor is ordinarily sufficient to warrant reformation. . . . The additional fact that the settlor in the case at bar has died should not foreclose relief, . . . so long as the evidence of mistake meets the requisite standard of proof. . . . The overwhelming weight of the evidence . . . clearly and decisively points to a scrivener's error as the source of the mistake. . . . Accordingly, judgment shall enter in the court below reforming the trust amendment so as to delete only the first paragraph of the first section of Article Third and to retain the remainder of section 1 as it appears in the original trust agreement.

For a recent post-death application of the reformation doctrine to correct a mistaken omission of a trustee power to invade the corpus of an inter vivos trust for the benefit of the income beneficiary, see Estate of Tuthill, 754 A.2d 272 (D.C. 2000). The result in *Tuthill* is to be contrasted with the earlier refusal by the same court in Knupp v. District of Columbia, 578 A.2d 702 (D.C. 1990), to correct a mistaken omission of the residuary clause in a will.

4. *Mistaken Inclusions*

The Restatement 3d of Property provides that a donative document is ambiguous if "the text reveals an apparent mistaken inclusion . . . ." Restatement 3d of Property § 11.2(b)(2). The Restatement 3d also provides that "extrinsic evidence may be considered to establish the content of the mistakenly included . . . language," and that if the content of a mistaken inclusion is established by extrinsic evidence, the included language may be removed from the document. See Restatement 3d of Property § 11.2(b)(2), comments n to q.

Connecticut Junior Republic v. Sharon Hospital
448 A.2d 190 (Conn. 1982)

HEALEY, J. The sole issue presented in this case is whether extrinsic evidence of a mistake by a scrivener of a testamentary instrument is admissible in a proceeding to determine the validity of the testamentary instrument. On October 3, 1979, Richards Haskell Emerson, a resident of Lakeville, died at the age of seventy-nine. He had never married and left several cousins as his closest heirs at law. Emerson left a will dated May 19, 1960, and two codicils dated December 4, 1969 (first codicil) and October 24, 1975 (second codicil), all of which were offered for probate by the named executor, the Third National Bank of Hampden County, Springfield, Massachusetts.

The Probate Court for the district of Salisbury admitted the will and codicils on February 19, 1980, after a hearing on the application for probate. This appeal rises out of the court's decision to admit portions of the second codicil which the plaintiffs contend were inserted by mistake of the scrivener and therefore do not embody the dispositions intended by the testator.

Contained in the decedent's will are three articles which set up trusts for the distribution of part of the decedent's estate and designate, as remaindermen, seven named charitable organizations (1960 charities), the defendants in this case. In the first codicil to his will, the decedent deleted the seven 1960 charities and substituted another group of eleven charitable organizations (1969 charities) as remaindermen, which are the plaintiffs in this case. There was only one charity named in both the will and the first codicil.

Subsequently, in 1975, the decedent instructed the trust officer of the Third National Bank of Hampden County to make changes in his will, as amended by the first codicil, so as to qualify the trusts as charitable annuity trusts under the Tax Reform Act of 1969, so that the charitable remainder interests would be allowable as federal estate tax deductions. The trust officer, thereafter, similarly instructed the decedent's attorney. The attorney, however, in drafting the second codicil, not only made the requested changes but also mistakenly reinstated the 1960 charities, which had originally been named in the will, as beneficiaries under two of the three articles of the will which are relevant to this case.[4] The decedent, who had never requested or authorized this change, signed the second codicil apparently without realizing the change in beneficiaries.

At the hearing on the application for the admission of the will and the two codicils, the Probate Court heard evidence on the matter and ruled that Connecticut law does not permit the introduction of extrinsic evidence on the issue of mistake, and found that in the absence of such evidence the presumption of the validity of a testamentary instrument mandated the admission of the entire second codicil to probate.[5] On appeal to the Superior Court, the defendants moved to strike the plaintiffs' reasons of appeal. Practice Book § 194. The Superior Court granted the defendants' motion and held that extrinsic

---

4. The remaining article relevant to this case continued to provide for the eleven 1969 charities.

5. The Probate Court made this holding in spite of finding the following:

> Substantial and convincing evidence was offered to establish that the testator had directed that the second codicil to his will be prepared only for the purpose of qualifying the charitable bequests under Paragraphs Seventh and Eighth of the will and first codicil as charitable remainder annuity trusts eligible for an estate tax charitable deduction in the decedent's estate; and that by scrivener's error the "1960 charities" were substituted for the "1969 charities" in the 1975 codicil; and that the proposed 1975 codicil was presented to the testator in a context of innocent misrepresentation of its contents resulting in mistake in the instrument as executed with respect as to which charitable beneficiaries the testator intended to benefit.

evidence is not admissible to prove that the second codicil, which uses unambiguous language, contained a mistake due to a scrivener's error and, therefore, should not be admitted to probate. The defendants next joined in the executor's motion for summary judgment which was granted by agreement of the parties. From this judgment, the plaintiffs have appealed to this court.

The plaintiffs claim that the lower court erred (1) in failing to find a distinction between a "will construction" proceeding and a proceeding to "admit a will to probate"; (2) in failing to hold that Connecticut cases support the admissibility of extrinsic evidence to prove that material has been mistakenly inserted into a testamentary instrument. . . .

I. The plaintiffs' first argument states that since the issue in this case is the validity of the second codicil and not its meaning, extrinsic evidence should be admissible to prove the scrivener's error. Specifically, they claim that courts which have considered the question have made a distinction between proceedings to admit a will to probate and will construction proceedings, holding or recognizing that extrinsic evidence showing a scrivener's error is admissible in the former but not in the latter proceeding, absent an ambiguity. See Annot., 90 A.L.R.2d 924, 931. Because of the scrivener's error, the plaintiffs claim that the mistake in reinstating the 1960 charities into the second codicil should have been allowed to have been proven by extrinsic evidence and should not have been admitted to probate. The lower court rejected this argument. . . .

In Connecticut, our cases have not, to this point, distinguished between the two types of proceedings. See *Stearns v. Stearns*, 103 Conn. 213, 130 A. 112 (1925) (will construction proceeding); *Comstock v. Hadlyme Ecclesiastical Society*, 8 Conn. 254 (1830) (proceeding to establish a will); *Avery v. Chappel*, 6 Conn. 270 (1826) (proceeding to establish a will). Neither the plaintiffs nor the defendants have presented us with any Connecticut authority which recognizes any distinction between the rules of evidence applicable to either of these two forms of proceedings.[6] While it is obvious that the purpose behind each type of proceeding may be different, we are not inclined to establish a rule which would effectuate such a distinction. It would be unwise to maintain a separate rule regarding the admission of extrinsic evidence for each of these two proceedings. This is because a litigant, knowing that more favorable evidentiary rules await those with claims of mistake due to scrivener's error, will always strive to phrase his argument in a way so to state such a claim.

This result would elevate the form over the substance of the argument and transform probate proceedings into mere semantic exercises. As an example, we

---

6. We do not deem it necessary to undertake any discussion of the matter that jurisdictions outside Connecticut permit extrinsic evidence to prove a mistake in a testamentary instrument.

point to the situation where a beneficiary under an unambiguous will, which also contains a scrivener's error, or words which effectuate a different result than that allegedly intended, knows that the extrinsic evidence demonstrating the mistake or a different intention than that expressed in the will is inadmissible in a will construction proceeding. To avoid this substantive barrier, he can merely rephrase his argument to allege that the scrivener did not follow instructions and, therefore, the will, even though otherwise validly executed, should not be admitted to probate since it does not represent the testator's true intention. Such a situation would expose many wills to litigation merely because a disappointed beneficiary did not receive exactly what he thought the testator would leave him. If a testator, during his lifetime, represented to a beneficiary that he would receive a certain bequest and, later, the testator changed the bequest in his will but neglected to inform the beneficiary, the beneficiary, knowing that extrinsic evidence is admissible in one but not the other proceeding, could certainly at least allege a scrivener's error and challenge the will's admission to probate on the basis that the testamentary document did not represent the true intent of the testator. This would tend to produce needless litigation by transforming a simple will construction proceeding into an admission to probate problem where no problem may have actually existed.

In order to avoid this, we believe that the better course is to recognize that the same evidentiary rules apply to both types of proceedings.

II. We now turn to the major issue presented by this case. The trial court held that "parol evidence may not be admitted in the instant case to show that the scrivener erred in drafting the codicil or that the testator mistakenly signed it. Connecticut law does not allow extrinsic evidence of a testator's intent to be admitted in cases dealing with either will construction or cases challenging the probate of an instrument. While there is an exception to this rule when there is ambiguity on the face of the will or codicil itself, this exception is not applicable in the instant case." We agree with the trial court. . . .

[The plaintiffs] seek to introduce evidence that the testator's true intent was not to divide his estate among the combined eighteen charitable institutions as appears on the face of the will and codicils, but that his true intent, which was allegedly communicated to the scrivener, was to replace the eleven charitable institutions named in the first codicil with the seven charitable institutions originally named in his will. It is clear that whether this is a "will construction" proceeding or a proceeding to "admit a will to probate," where the claimants seek to introduce extrinsic evidence of a scrivener's error resulting in a disposition of property allegedly contrary to the testator's intention, as expressed to the scrivener, such evidence, absent an ambiguity, is not admissible because "'if such testimony is to be admitted, we do away [with] part at least of the beneficial effect of the statute of frauds, and leave every will exposed to litigation, on a claim of a different intent.'" *Stearns v. Stearns*, supra, 103 Conn. 224-25, 130 A. 112. See *Comstock v. Hadlyme Ecclesiastical Society*, 8 Conn. 254, 265-66 (1830);[7] *Rapp v. Reehling*, 124 Ind. 36, 23 N.E. 777 (1889). "Claimed errors in the drafting of a will, either by the testator or his scrivener, do not permit the introduction of extrinsic evidence." *McFarland v. Chase Manhattan Bank, N.A.*, 32 Conn.Sup. 20, 37, 337 A.2d 1 (1973), aff'd, 168 Conn. 411, 362 A.2d 834 (1975). We find that this is the relevant public policy as expressed through our cases; therefore, we will not additionally discuss the plaintiffs' fourth claim of error set out above.

We would, however, properly make these observations. It is beyond cavil that "[p]rinciples of law which serve one generation well may, by reason of changing conditions, disserve a later one. . . ." *Herald Publishing Co. v. Bill*, 142 Conn. 53, 62, 111 A.2d 4 (1955). "Experience can and often does demonstrate that a rule, once believed sound, needs modification to serve justice better. . . ." *Herald Publishing Co. v. Bill*, supra. The principle of law, which we reiterate today, has been viable for many years and we have not been given nor do we glean any persuasive reason that justice, experience or logic requires it be changed. . . .

There is no error.

In this opinion ARMENTANO and SPONZO, JJ., concurred.

PETERS, A.J., dissenting. In order to bring into focus my disagreement with the majority opinion, I want first to note where I am in total accord with that opinion. Like the majority, I note that the only issue is whether extrinsic evidence of a mistake by a scrivener is admissible in a proceeding to determine the validity of a testamentary instrument. I would add, however, that the issue

---

7. Our holding today is limited to the case where a mistake due to a scrivener's error with no resulting ambiguity is alleged. It is clear that there are certain types of "mistakes" which would merit the introduction of extrinsic evidence as proof thereof. *In re Gluckman's Will*, 87 N.J.Eq. 638, 641, 101 A. 295 (1917), the court stated:

> Where a testator, in addition to complete testamentary mental capacity, is in full enjoyment of average physical and educational faculties, it would seem that in the absence of fraud or of undue influence, a mistake, in order to defeat probate of his entire will, must in substance or effect really amount to one of identity of the instrument executed; as, for instance, where two sisters, in one case, or a husband and wife, in another, prepared their respective wills for simultaneous execution, and through pure error one executed the other's, and vice versa. *Anon.*, 14 Jur. 402 [1850]; *Re Hunt*, L.R. 3 P. & D. 250 [1875]; *Nelson v. McDonald*, 61 Hun. 406, 16 N.Y.Supp. 273 [1891]. Short of this, however, or of something amounting in effect to the same thing, it is against sound public policy to permit a pure mistake to defeat the duly solemnized and completely competent testamentary act. It is more important that the probate of the wills of dead people be effectively shielded from the attacks of a multitude of fictitious mistakes than that it be purged of wills containing a few real ones. The latter a testator may, by due care, avoid in his lifetime. Against the former he would be helpless. . . .

[For a similar argument, see Richard W. Power, Wills: A Primer of Interpretation and Construction, 51 Iowa L. Rev. 75, 103-06 (1965). Eds.]

is even narrower than stated by the majority since the present aim of the proponents of the evidence of mistake is only to delete provisions from, rather than add provisions to, the disputed testamentary disposition. Like the majority, I note that the issue comes to us in the procedural context of a motion to strike, so that we must accept as accurate, for the purposes of this appeal, the allegations that the attorney who drafted the testator's second codicil erroneously included therein a change of beneficiaries that the decedent had neither requested nor authorized. Furthermore, I would add that the Probate Court expressly found that substantial and convincing evidence had been offered in support of the proposition that innocent misrepresentation of the contents of the will had resulted in a mistake in the instrument as executed. Like the majority, I too would find insufficient evidence of ambiguity in the will itself to warrant recourse to extrinsic evidence that would not otherwise be admissible.

We are left, then, with the question which I would answer differently than does the majority. Must the true intent of the testator be thwarted when, because of the mistake of a scrivener, he has formally subscribed to a written bequest that substantially misstates his testamentary intention? For all practical purposes, this is a question of first impression in this state, certainly in this state in this century. I would permit extrinsic evidence of a scrivener's error to be introduced in litigation concerned with the admissibility of a disputed will to probate.

I take as a point of departure the established proposition that a will cannot validly be probated if it was executed by a testator in reliance on erroneous beliefs induced by fraud, duress, or undue influence. . . . [T]he testamentary process is distorted by the interference of a third person who misleads the testator into making a testamentary disposition that would not otherwise have occurred. There is similar distortion when a will is executed in reliance on erroneous beliefs induced by the innocent error, by the innocent misrepresentation, of the scrivener of a will. I can see no reason of logic or of policy to treat the mistake case differently from the fraud or undue influence case. In each instance, extrinsic evidence is required to demonstrate that a will, despite its formally proper execution, substantially misrepresents the true intent of the testator.

The majority would disallow extrinsic evidence of a scrivener's error for two principal reasons: the existing Connecticut case law, and the risk of subverting the policy of the Statute of Wills. I find neither reason persuasive.

The existing case law is, as the majority opinion acknowledges, of ancient vintage. I agree that antiquity does not automatically disqualify common law precedents that continue to serve modern needs. But I find our case law less persuasive than does the majority.

The principal case is *Comstock v. Hadlyme Ecclesiastical Society*, 8 Conn. 254 (1830), because it, like this case, deals with the question of admission of a will to probate. *Comstock* seems to me to be distinguishable because there the proponents of extrinsic evidence of mistake were seeking to reform the will by *adding* new provisions to its contents. The case before us would result, if the extrinsic evidence were considered, in the *deletion* of unintended testamentary bequests, surely a less problematical confrontation with the policy of the Statute of Wills. . . .

That brings us to considerations arising out of the policy of the Statute of Wills. General Statutes § 45-161. The risk of subversion of the intent of a testator, who cannot personally defend his testamentary bequest, is without doubt a serious concern. Balanced against that concern is the risk of blindly enforcing a testamentary disposition that substantially misstates the testator's true intent. We have long ago resolved this balance in favor of admitting extrinsic evidence when the testator's intent is undermined by fraud, undue influence or incapacity. Had the decedent's lawyer deliberately and fraudulently altered the second codicil, the relevant extrinsic evidence would unquestionably have been admitted. Under the modern law of misrepresentation, innocent misrepresentation is treated as generally equivalent to fraud in terms of its legal consequences. To allow the admissibility of extrinsic evidence to turn on the scrivener's fraudulent intent or lack thereof is to distort the purpose of a Probate Court. Its proper business is to determine what instrument, if any, the decedent properly executed as his will. Gray, "Striking Words Out of a Will," 26 Harv.L.Rev. 212, 217 (1913). The guilt or negligence of third parties is only incidentally relevant to such a determination, since the effect on the testator's mind of either fraud or mistake is subjectively the same. The Statute of Wills does not compel enforcement of testamentary dispositions that a testator never intended to make.

Objection to the admission of extrinsic evidence in this case must therefore find support outside the direct commandments of the Statute of Wills. Two such objections have been advanced. One objection relies on the effect of the will's formal execution as a validation by the testator of the contested provision. The second points to the juridical risk of spurious will contests.

The first objection, raised by the defendants at oral argument and in their brief, states that whatever error the scrivener may have made was validated and ratified by the testator's act in signing his will. Neither American law in general, nor the case law of this state, has ever assigned so conclusive an effect to the reading and subsequent execution of a will. While signing the will creates a strong presumption that the will accurately represents the intentions of the testator, that presumption is a rebuttable one.

The second objection is a fear that allowing extrinsic evidence of mistake will give rise to a proliferation of groundless will contests. There is no doubt that our increasingly fact-based jurisprudence serves to expose many apparently final dispositions to the juridical risk of unjustified judicial intervention. In the law of contracts, where the parol evidence rule has undergone considerable erosion, this risk has not been found to be unmanageable. In the law of wills, the risk is limited by the narrowness of the exception that this case would warrant. I would today do no more than permit the opponent of a will to introduce extrinsic evidence of the error of a scrivener, and would require proof of such an extrinsic error to be established by clear and convincing evidence.

In sum, I see no greater risk of juridical error in the case of a scrivener's error than in the case of fraud or undue influence. I find it difficult to draw a clear line of demarcation between a scrivener's mistake and an innocent misrepresentation. I believe that the true interests of a testator are better protected by admitting rather than suppressing evidence of substantial third party interference with the formulation of a testamentary disposition. Wills that do not reflect the true intent of the testator should be refused probate.

In this opinion SHEA, J., concurred.

Notes and Question

1. *Justice Peters's Dissent Becomes Law*. In Erickson v. Erickson, 716 A.2d 92 (Conn. 1998), the Supreme Court of Connecticut concluded "the reasons given by the dissent in [*Connecticut Junior Republic*] are persuasive" and overruled *Connecticut Junior Republic*. *Erickson*, which is discussed in Chapter 5, Part C, involved a statute that revoked a will upon marriage unless the will provided for the contingency of marriage. The court held that

> If a scrivener's error has misled the testator into executing a will on the belief that it will be valid notwithstanding the testator's subsequent marriage, extrinsic evidence of that error is admissible to establish the intent of the testator that his or her will be valid notwithstanding the subsequent marriage. Furthermore, if those two facts, namely, the scrivener's error and its effect on the testator's intent, are established by clear and convincing evidence, they will be sufficient to establish that 'provision has been made in such will for such contingency,' within the meaning of § 45a-257(a) [the statute resulting in revocation of the will upon marriage].

2. *English Practice: Partial Denial of Probate*. Under some circumstances, English practice goes so far as to deny probate of particular words of a will that were included by mistake. E.g., Re Reynette-James, [1975] 3 All E.R. 1037; Re Phelan, [1972] Fam. 33; Re Morris, [1971] P. 62; Goods of Boehm, L.R. 16 Prob. 247 (1891).

3. *Ratification of the Mistake by Signing the Will?* In *Connecticut Junior Republic*, part of the argument advanced by the proponents of the second codicil was that "whatever error the scrivener may have made was validated and ratified by the testator's act in signing his will." Does Justice Peters in her dissent provide an adequate response to this argument? See Estate of Smelser, 818 P.2d 822 (Kan. Ct. App. 1991) (refusing to probate a part of a codicil that mistakenly revoked a devise based in part on fact that there was no "affirmative evidence" that the testator actually knew the codicil revoked the devise when she executed it). Accord Restatement 3d of Property § 12.1, comment l.

4. *Malpractice Action Against Drafting Attorney*. After losing the case in the Connecticut Supreme Court, the disappointed charitable remainder beneficiaries brought a malpractice action in a Massachusetts court against the Massachusetts drafting attorney, Paul S. Doherty. Although the trial court in the malpractice case found that the drafting attorney had "inadvertently substituted the original charities for the first codicil charities," the trial court found that the testator, Richards Haskell Emerson, had ratified the reversion to the original charitable beneficiaries. The court's finding was not based merely on the fact that the testator had signed the second codicil, but on additional evidence. The additional evidence consisted of:

(1) evidence that Emerson was "an avid reader and an intelligent and meticulous man who paid careful attention to his personal and financial affairs,"

(2) evidence that Emerson had a forty-five minute meeting with Sagar McDonald, a senior vice-president of the trust company, before executing the second codicil, during which McDonald read aloud the second codicil, while Emerson followed a copy, that Emerson's questions "focused on the effects of the new trust arrangements on the life interests he had created," and that "Emerson made no comment about the names of the charitable remaindermen," and

(3) a deposition of Harvey Moses, a long-time friend of Emerson who died before the trial, in which Moses said that Emerson had told him that he, Emerson, had "reverted or returned or gone back to his original list of charities."

The trial court's judgment in favor of the drafting attorney was affirmed in Connecticut Junior Republic v. Doherty, 478 N.E.2d 735 (Mass. App. Ct. 1985).

PART C. A REFORMATION DOCTRINE FOR WILLS?

Statutory References: *UTC §§ 414, 415*

1. General Reformation Doctrine

Restatement 3d of Property

§ *12.1. Reforming Donative Documents to Correct Mistakes*

A donative document, though unambiguous, may be reformed to conform the text to the donor's intention if the following are established by clear and convincing evidence:

(1) that a mistake of fact or law, whether in expression or inducement, affected specific terms of the document; and

(2) what the donor's intention was.

Direct evidence of intention contradicting the plain meaning of the text as well as other evidence of intention may be considered in determining whether elements (1) and (2) have been established by clear and convincing evidence.[8]

In this Part, we examine several mistake cases and the Restatement 3d of Property supporting a reformation doctrine for wills similar to the one long in place for instruments pertaining to lifetime donative transfers. The cases do not purport to adopt a general reformation doctrine, but—apart from the step backward taken by the majority opinion in Flannery v. McNamara—they substantially depart in effect and attitude from most of the decisions we have been reading up to now.

The no-reformation-of-wills and no-extrinsic-evidence rules have not been universally acclaimed or followed. For example, Dean Wigmore objected to the no-extrinsic-evidence rule.[9] He contended that "[t]he ordinary standard, or

---

8. UTC § 414, which is based on the Restatement, authorizes reformation of the terms of either testamentary or inter vivos trusts "if there is clear and convincing evidence both of the settlor's intent and that the terms of the trust were affected by a mistake of fact or law . . . ." The Restatement (Third) of Restitution and Unjust Enrichment § 11, comment a (Discussion Draft March 31, 2000) also adopts the same approach for correcting mistakes found in the Restatement 3d of Property.

9. The role of the plain-meaning rule is an issue in statutory interpretation. See Antonin Scalia, A Matter of Interpretation: Federal Courts and the Law (1997); Cass R. Sunstein, Formalism and Statutory Interpretation, 66 U. Chi. L. Rev. 636 (1999). The process of interpreting statutes is distinguishable from the process of interpreting donative documents. First, determining the intent of a single donor by looking to the written document as well as extrinsic evidence is quite different from determining the intent of legislators based on the statutory language and legislative history. Second, unlike legislators who have the power to amend or clarify statutes if they disagree with a court's interpretation, the donors, who in many instances are dead, cannot amend or clarify their

'plain meaning,' is simply the meaning of the people who did *not* write the document." He further stated, "The fallacy [of the conventional view] consists in assuming that there is or ever can be *some one real* or absolute meaning. In truth, there can be only *some person's* meaning; and that person, whose meaning the law is seeking, is the writer of the document. . . ." 9 John H. Wigmore, Evidence 190-92 (3d ed. 1940). See also Restatement of Property § 242, comment c (largely rejecting plain-meaning rule); James B. Thayer, A Preliminary Treatise on Evidence at the Common Law 423-25, 471-73 (1898) (critiquing the plain-meaning rule).

Courts have occasionally departed from the conventional rules. In Estate of Gibbs, 111 N.W.2d 413 (Wis. 1961), for example, the court openly substituted a correct term for a mistaken term despite finding no ambiguity. Gibbs's will devised one percent of his estate "to Robert J. Krause, now of 4708 North 46th Street, Milwaukee, Wisconsin." At Gibbs's death, and presumably when the will was executed, there was a Robert J. Krause who lived at the 46th Street address. For this reason, the court said, "there is no ambiguity." Nevertheless, the court held that extrinsic evidence could be introduced to the effect that Gibbs never knew Robert *J.* Krause of 46th Street, but that he did know and intended to benefit one Robert *W.* Krause, an employee and friend of Gibbs's for some thirty years. The court explained:

> [D]etails of identification, particularly such matters as middle initials, street addresses, and the like, which are highly susceptible to mistake, particularly in metropolitan areas, should not be accorded such sanctity as to frustrate an otherwise clearly demonstrable intent. Where such details of identification are involved, courts should receive evidence tending to show that a mistake has been made and should disregard the details when the proof establishes to the highest degree of certainty that a mistake was, in fact, made.

See also Wilson v. First Florida Bank, 498 So. 2d 1289 (Fla. Dist. Ct. App. 1986) (after holding the will to be ambiguous and admitting the attorney's testimony, along with other corroborating extrinsic evidence, court found that the testator intended the devise to the university to be of the residue of his estate under a will in which the testator made a series of devises of tangible personal property and specified amounts of money, and then stated "To the University of Georgia, Financial Aid Department . . . in trust . . . to establish a Scholarship Fund. . . ."); Estate of Ikuta, 639 P.2d 400, 405-06 (Haw. 1981) (court

---

instruments if their intent is inadequately or mistakenly expressed. Therefore, the implications regarding the plain-meaning rule are not the same when the rule is applied to interpretation of donative documents as when it is applied to statutory interpretation. The two situations are usefully treated as distinct from each other. See Restatement 3d of Property § 12.1, Reporter's Note 4.

replaced the word "old[e]st" with the word "youngest,"saying, "[t]he purpose of the policy against reformation of a will is to prevent distortion of the testator's intent"); Estate of Lohr, 497 N.W.2d 730 (Wis. Ct. App. 1993) (after finding of an ambiguity in the will language and proof of a drafting error, court inserted under the rubric of construction, "[i]n the event my spouse shall not predecease me and shall be living THIRTY (30) Days after the date of my death" in place of "[i]n the event my spouse shall predecease me or shall not be living THIRTY (30) Days after the date of my death").

Flannery v. McNamara

738 N.E.2d 739 (Mass. 2000)

IRELAND, J. The plaintiffs, Helen M. Flannery and Margaret M. Moran (Flannerys), filed a complaint against the defendants, Paul J. McNamara, administrator of the estate of William H. White, Jr. (decedent), and the decedent's heirs, the Daleys and the Whites (heirs), seeking declaratory relief and reformation of the decedent's will. The Flannerys alleged that they, and not the decedent's heirs, are the rightful beneficiaries under the will. The heirs filed motions to dismiss the complaint, pursuant to Mass.R.Civ.P. 12(b)(6), 365 Mass. 754 (1974), for failure to state a claim on which relief can be granted. By agreement of the parties, the judge subsequently treated the rule 12(b)(6) motions as motions for summary judgment, under Mass.R.Civ.P. 56(e), 365 Mass. 824 (1974).

The judge granted the heirs' motions for summary judgment, ruling that, because the will was unambiguous on its face, extrinsic evidence of the decedent's alleged intent was inadmissible. Moreover, she held that, because the will did not provide for disposition of the decedent's property in the event his wife predeceased him, his property passed to the heirs by way of intestacy.

Subsequently, the Flannerys appealed from the Probate Court's grant of summary judgment for the heirs. We granted their application for direct appellate review. The Flannerys argue that the Probate Court judge erred by holding inadmissible extrinsic evidence that might persuade the court to (1) construe; or (2) reform a poorly drawn will, albeit unambiguous on its face, to reflect the decedent's intent, thereby avoiding unjust enrichment.

This appeal presents the question whether we should overrule (1) the so-called "plain meaning" rule, that prohibits the admission of extrinsic evidence to construe unambiguous wills; and (2) the rule prohibiting the reformation of wills. We decline to do so, and thus, affirm the Probate Court's decision.

1. *Statement of Facts*. On September 30, 1995, the decedent died in Arlington. The decedent's will, dated January 20, 1973, left his entire estate to his wife, Katherine M. White (Katherine). The relevant part of the will provides that:

> I give, devise, and bequeath all of the property of which I die possessed real, personal, and mixed of nature and wheresoever located to my beloved wife, Katherine M. White.

The decedent's will failed to name a contingent beneficiary and it did not contain a residuary clause.

Katherine died October 14, 1993, survived by the decedent and her two sisters, the Flannerys. The couple had no children. McNamara, the decedent's attorney, repeatedly advised the decedent to let him review the will, but the decedent never showed the will to McNamara. The decedent died survived by his intestate heirs who were discovered through a genealogical search. The heirs are the decedent's first cousins, once removed.

The Flannerys make the following allegations. For almost five decades, they had a close relationship with the decedent. Moreover, after Katherine's death, the decedent relied heavily on the Flannerys for advice and assistance with daily matters. After the decedent died, he was buried in the Flannerys' family plot. On several occasions, the decedent told members of the Flannerys' family that his Arlington residence and its contents "will be [theirs] some day." Additionally, the decedent informed McNamara that he understood that, if Katherine were to predecease him, his will provided for his property to go to the Flannerys. In contrast, the decedent did not have a close relationship with the heirs.

After the decedent died in 1995, McNamara was appointed administrator of the decedent's estate. He received the decedent's will for probate and was preparing to distribute the estate to the heirs by way of intestate succession, when the Flannerys filed for declaratory relief and reformation of the will on November 25, 1997.

2. *Discussion*. The Flannerys claim that, although the decedent's will made no mention of them, he intended to pass his estate to them in the event that Katherine predeceased him. Specifically, the Flannerys contend that the portion of the will that reads, "all . . . to my beloved wife, Katherine M. White," should be either construed or reformed to read, "all . . . to my beloved wife, Katherine M. White, if she survives me, but if not, then to her sisters who survive me," namely, the Flannerys. We disagree.

a. *Construction*. "The fundamental object in the construction of a will is to ascertain the testator's intention from the whole instrument, attributing due weight to all its language, considered in light of the circumstances known to the testator at the time of its execution, and to give effect to that intent unless some positive rule of law forbids." Putnam v. Putnam, 366 Mass. 261, 266, 316 N.E.2d 729 (1974).

Here, the Flannerys assert that the decedent intended to name them as the beneficiaries of his estate in the event that his wife predeceased him. To prove this, the Flannerys seek to introduce extrinsic evidence of their relationship with the decedent and the decedent's statements concerning his intent.

Under current Massachusetts law, however, "[i]f a will is not ambiguous, extrinsic evidence to explain its terms is inadmissible . . . even where the language involved has a legal consequence either not likely to have been understood by the testator . . . or contrary to his intention expressed orally" (citations omitted). Putnam v. Putnam, supra. See Gustafson v. Svenson, 373 Mass. 273, 275, 366 N.E.2d 761 (1977) (extrinsic evidence of testatrices' alleged intent inadmissible where will, in particular the phrase "his heirs per stirpes," unambiguous). Thus, extrinsic evidence of the decedent's alleged intent is only admissible if his will is ambiguous. See Mahoney v. Grainger, 283 Mass. 189, 192, 186 N.E. 86 (1933) ("It is only where the testamentary language is not clear in its application to the facts that evidence may be introduced as to the circumstances under which the testator used that language in order to throw light upon its meaning") . . . . The will before us is not ambiguous.

First, the decedent's will contains no patent ambiguities. A patent ambiguity is one created by obvious conflicts in the language of the will itself. The decedent's will unequivocally states "all . . . to my beloved wife, Katherine M. White." No conflict or inconsistency arises from such clear and plain language.

Second, the will contains no latent ambiguities. A latent ambiguity emerges when the words of a will appear to be unambiguous on their face, but certain extrinsic facts render their meaning uncertain. There are two types of latent ambiguities. "The first type occurs when a will clearly describes a person or thing, and two or more persons or things exactly fit that description. The second type of latent ambiguity exists when no person or thing exactly fits the description, but two or more persons or things partially fit." Phipps v. Barbera, [498 N.E.2d 411 (Mass. Ct. App. 1986)]. Neither type of ambiguity exists here. Indeed, there is only one person fitting the description of "my beloved wife, Katherine M. White," namely, the decedent's wife, Katherine. Moreover, Katherine alone fit that description exactly. Neither the fact that she predeceased the decedent, nor the absence of a residuary clause or a contingent beneficiary provision makes the will ambiguous. Long before the decedent's execution of his will in 1973, it was settled law that, when a beneficiary predeceases the testator, the legacy lapses and falls into residue if there is one; otherwise it must pass as intestate property. As such, the will contains no latent ambiguity.

The Flannerys, however, argue that extrinsic evidence is admissible to create a latent ambiguity. The Flannerys seek to show, through extrinsic evidence, that the decedent had a "personal usage" of the will's language that differed from its plain, commonly accepted usage, and that the will should be construed consistently with this usage. They specifically want to demonstrate that the plain language of the will, "to my beloved wife," was actually intended and understood by the decedent to mean, "to my wife if she survives me, but if not, then to her sisters who survive me."

Generally, we have flatly rejected the idea that extrinsic evidence may be used to create an ambiguity where the language of the will is otherwise plain and unambiguous. Indeed, "[i]t is not an aid to interpretation to resort to testimony as to what may have been in the testator's mind in order to create an ambiguity not evident from the language of the will." Pagliarulo v. National Shawmut Bank, [233 N.E.2d 213 (Mass. 1968)]. Furthermore, we have traditionally rejected this type of "personal usage" argument proffered by the Flannerys. See Gustafson v. Svenson, supra (extrinsic evidence inadmissible when offered to prove testatrices intended the term "heirs," as used in their wills, not to include specific individual who qualified legally as heir).

Nonetheless, in support of their position, the Flannerys rely on Dansereau v. Dansereau, 318 Mass. 363, 61 N.E.2d 661 (1945); Sullivan v. Sullivan, 26 Mass.App.Ct. 502, 529 N.E.2d 890 (1988); and Restatement (Third) of Property (Donative Transfers) § 11.2(b)(3) (Tent. Draft No. 1, 1995) (Restatement). However, each of these authorities is distinguishable.

In Dansereau v. Dansereau, supra, the admissibility of extrinsic evidence was not at issue. There was, however, a legitimate question as to how properly to construe the will. Id. at 364, 61 N.E.2d 661. "Uncertainty as to its construction" arose when the testator was predeceased by the intended life beneficiary of the testator's estate. Id. Due to poor draftsmanship and "[confused] grammatical construction," it was unclear whether the estate would pass by intestacy or to the individuals named as remainderpersons. Id. at 365, 61 N.E.2d 661. This court applied the so-called presumption against intestacy,[10] and using what is referred to as a "settled" rule of construction—"a transposition of clauses . . . where upon the whole will that appears to accord

10. In further support of their claim, the Flannerys rely on this presumption, under which "a construction of a will resulting in intestacy is not to be adopted unless plainly required; and it is to be presumed that when a will is made the testator intended a disposition of all his property and did not intend to leave an intestate estate." Lyman v. Sohier, 266 Mass. 4, 8, 164 N.E. 460 (1929). However, as a rule of construction, the presumption only applies when the court can ascertain from the face of the will how the testator intended that his or her property be distributed. Notwithstanding the presumption, it is well settled that a testator's estate passes by intestacy when the plain language of the will requires such a result. For example, when the testator has failed to anticipate an event that has transpired (such as the named beneficiary predeceasing the testator), and the face of the document does not indicate how the testator would have distributed the property had he or she foreseen that event, the presumption would not apply. . . .

with the intention of the testator"—construed the will as leaving the estate to the remainderpersons. Id. at 365, 61 N.E.2d 661.

The *Dansereau* case did not involve the use of extrinsic evidence either to create or resolve any ambiguity; and, contrary to the Flannerys' assertion here, it did not involve a will that was "plain on its face." Although the court did not expressly describe the document as ambiguous, it treated it as such, employing transposition to make the will "complete, natural and comparatively plain." Id. Moreover, the court could discern the testatrix's intent from the face of the will, and did not have to look beyond the four corners of the document, as the Flannerys would have us do. The court then effected that intent by applying a settled principle of construction, namely, transposition. Id. Finally, the court did nothing more than apply the presumption against intestacy as it was meant to be applied.

In Sullivan v. Sullivan, 26 Mass.App.Ct. 502, 504-505, 529 N.E.2d 890 (1988), the Appeals Court expressly concluded that the will was ambiguous, and therefore that the extrinsic evidence proffered by the plaintiffs should have been admitted. Contrary to the Flannerys' contention that the *Sullivan* will was "plain on its face," the Appeals Court expressly characterized the will as "not clear on its face." Id. at 505, 529 N.E.2d 890. Consequently, *Sullivan* lends no support for what the Flannerys seek to do—use extrinsic evidence to create an ambiguity in an unambiguous document. Indeed, the Appeals Court noted in passing that if, as here, "the meaning of the will had been clear on its face, the judge could not have considered extrinsic evidence to vary its effect." Id. at 505-506, 529 N.E.2d 890. That precise principle governs the instant case.

Finally, the Flannerys rely on the Restatement.[11] The Flannerys correctly claim that the language of the Restatement would liberalize the use of extrinsic evidence in will cases. It would still not, however, expand the admissibility of extrinsic evidence so far as to permit the evidence at issue in the present appeal. Section 11.1 states:

> An ambiguity in a donative document is an uncertainty in meaning that is revealed by the text or by extrinsic evidence other than direct evidence of intention contradicting the plain meaning of the text.

---

11. This draft was submitted to the members of the American Law Institute for discussion at its seventy-second annual meeting in May, 1995. The discussion is reported in Proceeding of the American Law Institute, May, 1995, at 45-65 (1996). The members voted to approve the draft "subject to the customary consideration [by the Reporters] of the comments on the floor and to the usual editorial leeway." Id. at 65. The final version of this portion of the Restatement has not been drafted. However, we have cited this draft of the Restatement with approval in at least two recent decisions. See BankBoston v. Marlow, 428 Mass. 283, 285-286, 701 N.E.2d 304 (1998) (reformation of trust); Putnam v. Putnam, 425 Mass. 770, 772-773, 682 N.E.2d 1351 (1997) (same)).

Restatement, supra at 27. Because it is arguable that most of the Flannerys' extrinsic evidence in this case would be "direct evidence of intention contradicting the plain meaning of the text," and as such, inadmissible to establish an ambiguity under § 11.1, the Flannerys turn to § 11.2(b)(3), which states:

> Ambiguities to which no rule of construction or constructional preference applies include those arising when . . . (3) extrinsic evidence (other than direct evidence contradicting the plain meaning of the text) reveals that the donor's personal usage differs from the ordinary meaning of a term used in the text.

Restatement, supra at 31. The Flannerys claim that § 11.2(b)(3) supports the admission of extrinsic evidence to establish the decedent's "personal usage" of the phrase "to my beloved wife" actually meant "to my beloved wife if she survives me, but if not then to her sisters who survive me." This argument seriously distorts what is meant by evidence of "personal usage" in the Restatement. The Restatement expressly provides:

> [t]he donor's personal usage is the donor's habitual use of a term in an idiosyncratic manner . . . [such as] the donor's profession, business, religion, or academic discipline. . . . Personal usage does not, however, embrace *direct extrinsic evidence of intention contradicting the plain meaning of the text*" (emphasis in original).

Id. at § 11.2 commentor at 56.

Additionally, all of the relevant illustrations of this principle set forth in the Restatement make it clear that "personal usage" evidence is permitted only where the testator habitually referred to someone or something in an idiosyncratic manner during his lifetime, and then used that idiosyncratic terminology in his will.[12] Id. at § 11.2 comments t and u, illustrations 21-24, at 59-62. The Restatement's "personal usage" doctrine obviously does not apply in this case, because the Flannerys do not claim, and it would be essentially inconceivable, that the decedent habitually used the term "my wife" to mean "my wife or her sisters if she predeceases me."[13]

---

12. Additional proof that the plaintiffs have misinterpreted the Restatement's "personal usage" doctrine comes from remarks at the annual meeting at which this draft of the Restatement was discussed. The Reporter clearly states that nothing less than "habitual reference in common speech" constitutes "personal usage." Proceedings of the American Law Institute, supra at 57, 60.

13. Comment t to § 11.2 of the Restatement (Third) of Property (Donative Transfers) (Tent. Draft No. 1, 1995), poses an additional hurdle for the Flannerys in this case: "A complicating factor that can affect some personal-usage cases arises if the term in question is a legal term appearing in a document drafted by a legal professional. Despite the donor's personal usage, the

Consequently, the authorities offered by the Flannerys do not support the admission of extrinsic evidence to construe the will in these circumstances. As such, we find that the probate judge did not err in her ruling.

b. *Reformation*. Reformation of wills is presently prohibited in Massachusetts. The traditional rule with respect to reformation has been stated as follows:

> Courts have no power to reform wills. Hypothetical or imaginary mistakes of testators cannot be corrected. Omissions cannot be supplied. Language cannot be modified to meet unforeseen changes in conditions. The only means for ascertaining the intent of the testator are the words written and the acts done by him.

Sanderson v. Norcross, 242 Mass. 43, 46, 136 N.E. 170 (1922). Moreover, "[t]he fact that [the will] was not in conformity to the instructions given to the draftsman who prepared it or that he made a mistake does not authorize a court to reform or alter it or remould it by amendments." Mahoney v. Grainger, 283 Mass. 189, 191, 186 N.E. 86 (1933).

Nevertheless, the Flannerys urge us to reject this basic tenet. Specifically, they point to Putnam v. Putnam, where in the dictum of a footnote we noted that "[t]he case may be hard to make . . . for denying reformation of a will where in substantively similar circumstances, we would allow reformation of a trust instrument. . . . Evidence of intention may be relevant and admissible on the issue of mistake, that is, to support the reformation of the instrument." The Flannerys use this statement to argue that we should join, what the Restatement terms, "the minority but growing view," under which mistaken wills can be reformed. Restatement, supra at § 12.1 Reporter's Note at 134.

Section 12.1 of the Restatement provides for the reformation of an unambiguous donative document in order to conform the text to the donor's intention. Such reformation is permitted where the party seeking reformation can establish (1) a mistake of fact or law in the document; and (2) the donor's intention by clear and convincing evidence. Restatement, supra at 113.

However, the reformation of a will, which would dispose of estate property based on unattested testamentary language, would violate the Statute of Wills.

---

appearing in a document drafted by a legal professional. Despite the donor's personal usage, the use of a legal term by a legal professional constitutes circumstantial evidence that the term was intended to be defined in accordance with its legal meaning. . . . Because the professional-use evidence tends to offset the personal-usage evidence, the legal term would ordinarily be construed in accordance with its legal meaning. If there is other evidence on the question, however, that evidence is considered in seeking to determine the donor's intention." Id. at 60. Thus, in this case, if an attorney drafted the decedent's will (a fact which is not clear in the record, but which the Flannerys seem to be assuming), the use of the phrase "to my beloved wife," which carries plain legal consequences that do not include Katherine's sisters if the she predeceases the decedent, would not easily be modified by personal usage evidence.

G.L. c. 191, § 1. Strong policy reasons also militate against the requested reformation. To allow for reformation in this case would open the floodgates of litigation and lead to untold confusion in the probate of wills. It would essentially invite disgruntled individuals excluded from a will to demonstrate extrinsic evidence of the decedent's "intent" to include them. The number of groundless will contests could soar. We disagree that employing "full, clear and decisive proof" as the standard for reformation of wills would suffice to remedy such problems. Cf. Putnam v. Putnam, 425 Mass. 770, 772-773, 682 N.E.2d 1351 (1997), quoting Berman v. Sandler, 379 Mass. 506, 509, 399 N.E.2d 17 (1980), and citing Restatement, supra at § 12.1. Judicial resources are simply too scarce to squander on such consequences. Finally, we are not persuaded by the decisions of other jurisdictions.[14] Therefore, we decline to join the minority and decline to follow the Restatement.

Additionally, the Flannerys urge us to apply the holdings of Putnam v. Putnam, 366 Mass. 261, 316 N.E.2d 729 (1974), and Shawmut Bank, N.A. v. Buckley, 422 Mass. 706, 665 N.E.2d 29 (1996), that allowed for the reformation of wills to achieve the testators' intent with respect to tax objectives.[15] In Putnam v. Putnam, we construed a will to resolve a conflict, as

---

14. The Flannerys cite Erickson v. Erickson, 246 Conn. 359, 716 A.2d 92 (1998), in support of reformation. That case held that extrinsic evidence of a scrivener's mistake in a testamentary document was admissible in a proceeding to determine the validity of that document. Id. at 371, 716 A.2d 92. Although the case did discuss several of our objections to reformation, it did not involve a will reformation. Id. at 361, 716 A.2d 92. Moreover, even assuming, arguendo, that it did apply, we would nonetheless expressly disagree with the *Erickson* court's response to our objections, and decline to adopt it in lieu of well-established Massachusetts precedent.

Additionally, the Restatement, supra at Reporter's Note at 135, cites Matter of Snide, 52 N.Y.2d 193, 199-197, 437 N.Y.S.2d 63, 418 N.E.2d 656 (1981), which permitted reformation of a will to correct a mistake, where the decedent and his wife, both intending to execute mutual wills, each accidentally executed the will intended for the other. The court allowed for reformation solely, on "these very narrow facts," id . at 197, 437 N.Y.S.2d 63, 418 N.E.2d 656, noting that it was a "very unusual case." Id. at 196, 437 N.Y.S.2d 63, 418 N.E.2d 656. Given the narrow holding, it does not support reformation as a general doctrine. The Restatement notes that other jurisdictions have implicitly allowed for the reformation of wills by ordering a remedy "that is reformation, whether so described or not." Restatement, supra at Reporter's Note at 134. See Wilson v. First Fla. Bank, 498 So.2d 1289 (Fla.Dist.Ct.App.1986); Estate of Ikuta, 64 Haw. 236, 639 P.2d 400 (1981); McCauley v. Alexander, 543 S.W.2d 699 (Tex.Civ.App.1976); Estate of Lohr, 174 Wis.2d 468, 497 N.W.2d 730 (Ct.App.1993). However, each of these cases involves an ambiguous will, making them inapplicable to the case at bar.

15. The Flannerys note that this court has allowed for the reformation of inter vivos trusts where the results of the trust were clearly inconsistent with the settlors' tax objectives. See DiCarlo v. Mazzarella, 430 Mass. 248, 717 N.E.2d 257 (1999); Fleet Bank, N.A. v. Fleet Bank, N.A., 429 Mass. 1003, 706 N.E.2d 627 (1999); BankBoston v. Marlow, 428 Mass. 283, 701 N.E.2d 304 (1998); Pond v. Pond, 424 Mass. 894, 678 N.E.2d 1321 (1997); Simches v. Simches, 423 Mass. 683, 671 N.E.2d 1226 (1996); Loeser v. Talbot, 412 Mass. 361, 589 N.E.2d 301 (1992); Berman v. Sandler, 379 Mass. 506, 399 N.E.2d 17 (1980). However, inter vivos trusts

we would an ambiguity, to conform to the decedent's intentions to take advantage of the maximum marital deduction permitted under the Federal estate tax law. The Flannerys interpret this case to mean that we implicitly ordered reformation.[16] In Shawmut Bank, N.A. v. Buckley, we eliminated a clause from a will to effectuate the testator's intention to minimize the Federal estate taxation of her testamentary trust.

Both cases are distinguishable from the present claim for reformation. First, the decisions permitted reformation in very limited circumstances: namely, achieving favorable Federal estate tax treatment with respect to testamentary trusts. In Massachusetts, "[w]e have allowed the reformation of trust instruments which produced tax results that were clearly inconsistent with the settlor's tax objectives." BankBoston v. Marlow, 428 Mass. 283, 285, 701 N.E.2d 304 (1998). However, given the absence of any tax issues here, it certainly does not fall within the ambit of that very narrow exception.[17]

Second, neither the *Putnam* nor the *Buckley* case admitted extrinsic evidence to ascertain the testators' intent, as the Flannerys urge us to do. On the contrary, the *Putnam* court looked only at the document's face to find that its language, "standing alone shows that [the testator] intended to have his estate utilize the maximum permissible marital deduction in computing the Federal estate tax payable on his death."[18] Putnam v. Putnam, supra at 267, 316 N.E.2d 729. Likewise, the *Buckley* court looked only at the will to determine that it was "obviously written with tax considerations in mind and was a standard instrument in many ways for accomplishing estate tax minimization." Shawmut Bank, N.A. v. Buckley, supra at 711, 665 N.E.2d 29.

---

are not testamentary documents, and therefore need not meet the formalities required for the execution of a will under G.L. c. 191, § 1.

16. The Flannerys contend that when we ordered the trial court, in Putnam v. Putnam, 366 Mass. 261, 272, 316 N.E.2d 729 (1974), to enter a decree declaring that all inheritance taxes ever imposed on future interests in the marital trust be paid from the companion nonmarital trust, we implicitly reformed the will.

17. Moreover, both cases noted that unless otherwise stated, "[i]nherent in the provisions of [a] will is the intent that no general provision should be applied to produce a Federal estate . . . tax result that would solely benefit" the taxing authorities. Shawmut Bank, N.A. v. Buckley, 422 Mass. 706, 711, 665 N.E.2d 29 (1996). See Putnam v. Putnam, supra at 271, 316 N.E.2d 729. It cannot be said that an intent to benefit the decedent's sisters-in-law if his wife predeceased him is similarly inherent in the provisions of his will.

18. Putnam v. Putnam, 366 Mass. 261, 267-269, 316 N.E.2d 729 (1974), did advert to extrinsic evidence, but only to resolve the ambiguous language in the will, not to ascertain the testator's intent.

Third, in both cases, none of the parties to the proceedings objected to the construction or reformation of the wills. To be sure, in this case, there is no such consensus among the parties.

Accordingly, neither case supports the admission of extrinsic evidence of the decedent's alleged intent in order to reform the will.

3. *Conclusion.* For the reasons stated, the decedent's will can neither be construed nor reformed to read, "all . . . to my beloved wife, Katherine M. White, if she survives me, but if not, then to her sisters who survive me," in lieu of what the will plainly states on its face: "all . . . to my beloved wife, Katherine M. White." The order of the Probate Court granting the defendants' motions for summary judgment is affirmed, and a declaratory judgment shall issue.

So ordered.

GREANEY, J. (concurring in the result, with whom ABRAMS, J., joins). I agree with the conclusion that summary judgment was properly entered for the defendants. I write separately because I disagree with the court's reasoning on the reformation issue.

There is, as the court has discussed, no ambiguity in the will. As to reformation, the court concludes that our rule prohibiting the reformation of a will applies and precludes consideration of the remedy. In reaching this conclusion, the court effectively shuts the door on consideration, in an appropriate case, of reformation of a will to correct a mistake which negates the testator's intent.

In writing for the court in Putnam v. Putnam, Chief Justice Wilkins stated: "For reasons that may no longer be meaningful, we have been less willing to recognize the possibility of proof of mistake in the drafting of a will (as opposed to an inter vivos trust) that is unambiguous on its face. The case may be hard to make, however, for denying reformation of a will where, in substantively similar circumstances, we would allow reformation of a trust instrument. See Restatement of Property (Donative Transfers) § 12.1 comment c (Tent. Draft No. 1 1995)." Section 12.1 of the Restatement states principles that would permit an unambiguous will to be reformed to conform the text of the will to the testator's intent when clear and convincing evidence establishes "(1) that a mistake of fact or law, whether in expression or inducement, affected specific terms of the document; and (2) what the donor's intention was." As the Restatement points out, and cases demonstrate, there are instances where mistakes in a will, of the nature described above, caused by scrivener's error, incorrect legal advice, misrepresentations, and the like, may call for reformation of an unambiguous text. See Restatement, supra at comment i [illustrations] 4 and 6, at 121-122. See also Erickson v. Erickson, 246 Conn.

359, 716 A.2d 92 (1998); and cases collected in the Reporter's Note to comment e of the Restatement, supra at 134-137.

In addition to the discussion in the Restatement, supra, the analysis in Erickson v. Erickson, supra at 373-375, 716 A.2d 92, persuasively dispels the usual arguments for not permitting extrinsic evidence, in an appropriate case, to reform an unambiguous will so the will's provisions accurately express the testator's intent. The most common argument against reformation is the one adopted by the court that allowance of the remedy would open the floodgates to "invite disgruntled individuals excluded from a will to demonstrate extrinsic evidence of the decedent's 'intent' to include them." Ante at 674, 738 N.E.2d at 746. There is a short and complete answer that discloses the speciousness of this statement. That answer, given by the Restatement, supra, is that reformation is not available, as matter of law, to an individual claiming that he is the true object of the testator's bounty, because the will states the testator's intent accurately, and the testator's mistake, if one occurred at all, was his own subsequent failure to execute a codicil or new will to carry out his new intent. See Restatement, supra at comment h illustration 2, at 120.

I suspect that, in an appropriate case, the court will conclude that an unambiguous will should be reformed because of a proven mistake in expression or inducement. When that case arrives, the court will either have to reject or revise what is said about reformation in this opinion or struggle to create an ambiguity, where none exists, in order to permit reformation. On the reformation issue, I would frame the analysis in these terms:

(a) in an appropriate case, consistent with what was said by the unanimous court in Putnam v. Putnam, supra, we are open to consider reformation of an unambiguous will to correct a mistake;

(b) the plaintiffs are not entitled to reformation here, because, even accepting the principles expressed in the Restatement, supra, a case for reformation is not present. There is no mistake in expression or inducement. The will states the decedent's intent accurately, and the mistake was his own for failing to execute a codicil or a new will.[19]

---

19. Even though this general principle governs the case, it is worth noting that the plaintiffs' complaint states their belief that the defendant Paul J. McNamara, the administrator of the estate with the will annexed and a lawyer, "recommended to [the decedent] on numerous occasions that [the decedent] arrange for . . . McNamara to review [the decedent's] will," but the decedent never did so because "he . . . understood that his [w]ill provided for property to go to [p]laintiffs if [his wife] were to predecease him." The decedent's mistake, if he made one at all, was grounded in his own failure to obtain review of his will by a lawyer.

Engle v. Siegel

377 A.2d 892 (N.J. 1977)

MOUNTAIN, J. The facts in this will construction case are not in dispute. In September, 1973, Albert and Judith Siegel, together with their two children, lost their lives as the result of a tragic hotel fire in Copenhagen, Denmark. All died within thirty days of one another. Albert's will was dated April 2, 1964 and Judith's was dated September 29, 1964. The instruments were admitted to probate October 3, 1973 and Louis Engle, Judith's father, qualified as executor of both. A common disaster clause appears in each will. The provision in Albert's will reads as follows:

> In the event my wife JUDITH and my children predecease me, or (this is the event which occurred) if we all die as a result of a common accident, or within thirty (30) days from the date of my death, then in that event, I give, devise and bequeath all the rest, residue and remainder of my estate and property of every kind and nature unto my mother, ROSE SIEGEL, and my mother-in-law, IDA ENGLE, to be divided between them share and share alike.

The corresponding clause in Judith's will was identical except for appropriate alterations as to names and relationships. Rose Siegel, Albert's mother, predeceased her son and daughter-in-law, having died in or about 1967. Judith's mother, Ida Engle, survived and is a party to this action.

The contest has arisen due to the fact that Rose Siegel, named in each will as a residuary legatee, predeceased her son and daughter-in-law. Ida Engle, the other residuary legatee, takes the position that under these circumstances our statute, N.J.S.A. 3A:3-14, becomes operative to cause the entire residuary estate of each decedent to pass to her. This statute reads as follows:

> When a residuary devise or bequest shall be made to 2 or more persons by the will of any testator dying after July 3, 1947, unless a contrary intention shall appear by the will, the share of any such residuary devisees or legatees dying before the testator and not saved from lapse by section 3A:3-13 of this title, or not capable of taking effect because of any other circumstance or cause, shall go to and be vested in the remaining residuary devisee or legatee, if any there be, and if more than 1, then to the remaining residuary devisees or legatees in proportion to their respective shares in said residue. [N.J.S.A. 3A:3-14]

Appellants, Leo H. Siegel and Judith Siegel Baron, are brother and sister of the decedent, Albert Siegel. All three, of course, are also children of the decedent, Rose. It is these appellants' position that the foregoing statute has no relevance here because, by a proper application of the rule of probable intent,[20] the share of each residuary estate set apart for their mother, should now pass to them in equal shares. The trial court found in favor of Ida Engle and the Appellate Division affirmed. Both opinions are unpublished. We granted certification, 71 N.J. 527, 366 A.2d 682 (1976), and now reverse.

Traditionally, and perhaps rather monotonously, courts have repeated, as we do here again, that in construing the terms of a will, a court's task is always to determine the intent of the testator. But these words may be given different meanings and the quest for intent can be undertaken and pursued in various ways. The generally accepted method of determining testamentary intent was once described by this Court in these words,

> It is elementary principle in the construction of wills that the controlling consideration is the effect of the words as actually written rather than the actual intention of the testator independently of the written words. The question is not what the testator actually intended, or what he was minded to say, but rather the meaning of the terms chosen to state the testamentary purpose . . . [In re Armour, 11 N.J. 257, 271, 94 A.2d 286, 292 (1953)]

This statement can no longer be said accurately to express the law of our State. In Fidelity Union Trust Co. v. Robert, 36 N.J. 561, 178 A.2d 185 (1962) this Court, speaking through Justice Jacobs, announced what has come to be known as the doctrine of probable intent. The rule has been stated thus,

> While a court may not, of course, conjure up an interpretation or derive a missing testamentary provision out of the whole cloth, it may, on the basis of the entire will, competent extrinsic evidence and common human impulses strive reasonably to ascertain and carry out what the testator probably intended should be the disposition if the present situation developed. [In re Estate of Burke, 48 N.J. 50, 64, 222 A.2d 273, 280 (1966)]

It must be clear that the quest for intent projected by this definition is something quite different from the more traditional approach set forth in *Armour*. In applying the new rule a court not only examines "the entire will" but also studies "competent extrinsic evidence"; it attributes to the testator "common human impulses" and seeks to find what he would subjectively have

20. [New Jersey's doctrine of probable intent is codified in N.J. Stat. Ann. § 3B:3-33, which provides in relevant part:

> *3B:3-33. . . . [T[estator's intention* . . . The intention of a testator as expressed in his will controls the legal effect of his dispositions, ... unless the probable intention of the testator, as indicated by the will and relevant circumstances, is contrary.

Eds.]

desired had he in fact actually addressed the contingency which has arisen. We are no longer limited simply to searching out the probable meaning intended by the words and phrases in the will. Relevant circumstances, including the testator's own expressions of intent, Wilson v. Flowers, 58 N.J. 250, 262-63, 277 A.2d 199 (1971), must also be studied, and their significance assayed. Within prescribed limits, guided primarily by the terms of the will, but also giving due weight to the other factors mentioned above, a court should strive to construe a testamentary instrument to achieve the result most consonant with the testator's "probable intent." . . .

A search for probable intent was greatly facilitated by this Court's decision in Wilson v. Flowers, supra, 58 N.J. 250, 277 A.2d 199, (1971). There we held that direct statements made by the testator were admissible to show such intent. As Justice Proctor observed,

> If our task is to ascertain and follow the testator's probable intent, we cannot fairly exclude evidence of that intent. [58 N.J. at 262, 277 A.2d at 206] . . . In considering *Flowers* it is also important to perceive the breadth of the ruling as to the admissibility of extrinsic testimony.
>
> We do not, of course, mean to imply that [extrinsic] evidence can be used to vary the terms of the will, but rather that *it should be admitted first to show if there is an ambiguity and second, if one exists, to shed light on the testator's actual intent*. [58 N.J. at 263, 277 A.2d at 207; emphasis added] . . .

Respondents rely heavily upon N.J.S.A. 3A:3-14. It is important to consider the nature and purpose of this enactment. It is designed to avoid partial intestacy in those instances where one of several residuary legatees or devisees predeceases the testator and the will contains no limitation over in the event of such contingency. The statute rests upon the legislative judgment that under such circumstances a testator would normally prefer that the presumptive share of the beneficiary so dying should pass to other residuary legatees rather than devolve by intestate succession. It is important to realize fully that the act is in no way intended to pre-empt a testamentary plan that can be discerned by a search for probable intent. . . . Not until a quest for probable intent has proven fruitless, will there be any occasion to resort to the statute.

With these considerations in mind, we turn to the facts of this case.

We are satisfied that the death of Rose Siegel, prior to the tragic deaths of the testators, was a contingency not treated specifically in the wills and not actually foreseen or anticipated by the testators. That inference can be readily drawn from an examination of the wills in their entirety, noting especially the numerous provisions therein for gifts or bequests over to named legatees upon death or failure to survive, indicating clearly enough that the testators were mindful of contingencies of this sort and did anticipate dispositions to be made where this occurred. The failure to make a similar provision in the event of the premature death of either mother, where to do so would be completely logical and in keeping with the tenor of the wills, must be ascribed to inadvertence. It is not to be inferred that that omission was purposeful or that, by implication, and intestacy was intended, or that a gift over by operation of the statute was desired. We thus have no hesitancy in concluding that one element justifying the quest for probable intent has been established in this case, namely, that there has indeed occurred a contingency not foreseen or anticipated when the wills were drafted.

We next turn to the relevant and competent extrinsic evidence which bears upon the probable intention of the testators with respect to this unforeseen situation. The attorney who drafted the will, Samuel J. Zucker, Esq., testified as to his conference with Albert and Judith Siegel preceding the drafting of the will. He testified from memory, aided by notes he had made at the conference. The question as to what disposition should be made of their assets in the event of a common disaster was squarely raised. After conferring together, Albert, speaking for his wife and himself, declared that in that event they would like all of their property to be divided equally between their two families. As Albert put it, "split it down the middle so they (the respective families) each get half . . . ." Mr. Zucker pointed out that the word "family" was inappropriate as being "a broad term." The problem so posed by the attorney was obviously perceived as one of form or draftsmanship. Certainly, the attorney did not suggest that the Siegels should not provide for the persons constituting their "family." Nor can his advice to his clients be interpreted to mean that the Siegels were being told to designate an individual legatee rather than one standing in a representative capacity or an identifiable group or class of persons. The sense of this exchange between Mr. Zucker and the Siegels is that, if it was their intention to benefit the class of persons constituting their respective families, that designation would have to be accomplished with more definite and precise language.

The Siegels, after again conferring together, suggested that, in the event then being considered, their property be equally divided between their respective mothers, Rose Siegel and Ida Engle. The will was, of course, drawn to reflect this decision.

We have no difficulty in reaching the conclusion that the primary wish of each decedent, given the contingency that occurred, would have been to divide the property included in their residuary estates between the Siegel family and the Engle family. The designation of their respective mothers resulted solely from the scrivener's rejection of the word "family" as a term to describe the recipient of a testamentary benefaction. Each mother was obviously thought of as an appropriate representative of a "family."

To give the assets of both estates entirely to Mrs. Engle would seem to fly directly in the face of all the evidence bearing upon probable intent. It is perhaps pertinent to note at this point that the assets constituting the estates of both Albert and Judith were derived almost entirely from Albert's earnings. Judith had no money that had come from her own family.

On the other hand, to divide one-half of each residuary estate equally between Leo H. Siegel and Judith Siegel Baron, now obviously the persons constituting the Siegel "family," would seem completely to carry out probable intent. It may be added that Rose Siegel's will, although never probated because she had no assets, was received in evidence. It left everything to her three children in equal shares. Hence, had the order of the deaths of Rose and her son Albert been reversed, presumably Leo Siegel and Judith Baron would have inherited directly from their mother, the shares of their brother's and sister-in-law's estates set aside for the Siegel "family."

We do not adopt the suggestion that the "Siegel" share of the two estates should be deemed to pass through Rose's estate. Having predeceased her son and daughter-in-law she could hardly qualify as a recipient under their wills. We think rather, as stated above, that one-half of the residuary estate of Albert and one-half the residuary estate of Judith should be divided equally between Leo H. Siegel and Judith Siegel Baron. The other shares of each estate will of course pass to Ida Engle.

The judgment of the Appellate Division is reversed and Louis Engle, as executor of each of the two wills, is directed, as soon as may be appropriate, to effect distribution of the assets of both estates pursuant to what we have said above.

CLIFFORD, J. dissenting. Even with the decent burial given by the Court to In re Armour, 11 N.J. 257, 271, 94 A.2d 286 (1953), I think I would not consign to the decisional graveyard the following from that case:

> The question is not what the testator actually intended, or what he was minded to say, but rather the meaning of the terms chosen to state the testamentary purpose. . . . [Id. at 292].

While this statement no longer carries the dogmatic weight it once did, it retains value as a rule of construction. In the construing of a will the basic statutory policy (N.J.S.A. 3A:3-1 et seq.) of allowing the instrument to speak for the testator as of the date of death must be accorded great respect. I understand the court's function to be to determine the testator's intent from the language employed in the will; only if an ambiguity is shown does the doctrine of probable intent as developed in Fidelity Union v. Robert, 36 N.J. 561, 178 A.2d 185 (1962), and its progeny allow extrinsic evidence to be utilized to construe the document.

Mindful of the difficulties which are often present in determining what is or what is not an ambiguity in any instrument, I nevertheless approach this case with the conviction that the doctrine of probable intent should not be used to create an ambiguity in a will which the doctrine will then be called upon to resolve. I am afraid that is exactly what is happening here.

As I understand the operation of the doctrine of probable intent, an ambiguity in the instrument is the condition which triggers the doctrine's application to change the result which would attend a literal application of the language of the will. Wilson v. Flowers, 58 N.J. 250, 263, 277 A.2d 199 (1971). An ambiguity is a "condition of admitting of two or more meanings, of being understood in more than one way, or of referring to two or more things at the same time. . . ." Webster's Third International Dictionary (1961); cf. Allen v. Metropolitan Life Ins. Co., 83 N.J.Super. 223, 237-38, 199 A.2d 254, (App.Div.1964).

I am unable to discern, anymore than could the trial judge, (as he put it) "any uncertainties of expression [or] latent ambiguities of expression within the testamentary writing . . . which would authorize departure from the result prescribed by N.J.S.A. 3A:3-14." The problem as I see it is simply that the instrument omits the necessary language which would save from lapse a bequest to a predeceased legatee. . . . [T]he "contrary intention" required by the statute is likewise absent.

It seems to me that this is the classic situation the legislature had in mind when it enacted N.J.S.A. 3A:3-14 and we should heed its direction rather than rewrite the testator's will. Having survived his mother by about 6 years, he had the opportunity to undertake that rewriting himself. The testator not having done so, I see no reason why this Court should gratuitously second guess him and perform that service.

Notes and Questions

1. *Cases Giving New Meaning to the Use of Extrinsic Evidence to Establish "Ambiguity." Engle* is a case in which the court engaged in reformation in all but name. The "probable intent" doctrine hid what was actually going on. While that doctrine is peculiar to New Jersey, courts in other states have reached similar results under different rationales. One rationale, of course, is construction.

In Estate of Taff, 133 Cal. Rptr. 737 (Ct. App. 1976), the court used the rubric of construction to reform a mistaken description in a will. Pearl Taff devised the residue of her estate

> to my heirs in accordance with the laws of intestate succession, in effect at my death in the State of California, or in effect in such other state or such other place as I may be a resident at the time of my death.

The residue of Taff's estate consisted of community property which she had owned with her previously-deceased husband. Under the California intestacy statute, the community character of the property and the fact that Pearl died without any surviving issue or spouse meant that one half of the property should go to Pearl's blood relatives and the other half should go to the blood relatives of her deceased husband.

The trial court, however, permitted the attorney who drew Pearl's will to testify that Pearl had instructed him that she wanted the residue "to go to her family, her own blood relatives" and that "she felt she was making adequate provision for Harry's (her predeceased husband's) family in the two specific gifts to Harry's sister which she was providing in her will and she felt no obligation to the other members of Harry's blood relations and was making no gifts to them." In view of this testimony, the trial court held that Harry's blood relatives had no right to any portion of the residuary estate. Affirming this judgment, the appellate court said:

> [I]n Estate of Russell (1968) 69 Cal.2d 200, 70 Cal.Rptr. 561, 444 P.2d 353, our Supreme Court substantially abrogated the "plain meaning" rule. . . .
>
> Under *Russell*, supra, extrinsic evidence is admissible both to show that a latent ambiguity exists and to resolve the latent ambiguity. . . .
>
> In the present case the declarations of the decedent to her attorney and her sister exposed a latent ambiguity, i.e., that when the testatrix used the term "my heirs" in her will, she intended to exclude the relatives of her predeceased husband, Harry. Under *Russell*, supra, the extrinsic evidence was properly received both to create the ambiguity in the word "heirs" and to resolve the ambiguity. . . .
>
> Because the extrinsic evidence is not in conflict as to the decedent's intention to exclude the relatives of Harry C. Taff from taking any part of the residuary estate, and because the term "my heirs" as used in the will is reasonably susceptible to mean that decedent's heirs other than the relatives of Harry Taff, the trial court properly decided as a matter of law that appellants have no right to any portion of the residuary estate.

Professors Langbein and Waggoner have made the following observations about *Taff*:

> In the key passage, the court in *Taff* says that "the extrinsic evidence was properly received both to create the ambiguity in the word 'heirs' and to resolve the ambiguity." But this way of stating the matter obliterates the fundamental distinction between ambiguity and mistake. The disputed term in *Taff* that had been mistakenly employed was quite unambiguous. The effect of the decision in *Taff* was to substitute a phrase such as "my natural heirs" for the inapt phrase that the

> will had employed ("my heirs in accordance with the laws of intestate succession, in effect at my death in the State of California"), in order to carry out what the court conceived to be the actual or subjective intent of the testatrix. . . . *Taff* reformed the will without admitting, hence without justifying, this departure from traditional law.

John H. Langbein & Lawrence W. Waggoner, Reformation of Wills on the Ground of Mistake: Change of Direction in American Law?, 130 U. Pa. L. Rev. 521, 557-58 (1982).

Can *Taff* be distinguished from Mahoney v. Grainger, in which the court refused to admit extrinsic evidence of a mistaken description?

Essentially the same approach adopted in *Taff* was taken by the Michigan court in Estate of Kremlick, 331 N.W.2d 228 (Mich. 1983). In that case, John Kremlick's will devised half the residue of his estate "to the Michigan Cancer Society. . . ." Competing claims to the devise were made by the Michigan Cancer Society (an affiliate of the Michigan Cancer Foundation) and by the American Cancer Society, Michigan Division. The probate court held that the term "Michigan Cancer Society" was unambiguous and refused to hear extrinsic evidence that the American Cancer Society, Michigan Division, was actually the intended devisee. The Supreme Court of Michigan reversed, holding:

> [N]ot only may extrinsic evidence be used to clarify the meaning of a latent ambiguity, but it may be used to demonstrate that an ambiguity exists in the first place and to establish intent.
>
> In this case, appellants [the American Cancer Society, Michigan Division] produced an affidavit from the executrix of Mr. Kremlick's estate in which she asserted that the intended beneficiary was the American Cancer Society, Michigan Division, instead of the Michigan Cancer Society, an affiliate of the Michigan Cancer Foundation. The executrix stated that she had discussed the provisions of Mr. Kremlick's will with him on many occasions, and that he frequently had mentioned that the American Cancer Society was to be a beneficiary. Appellants also sought to establish that Mr. Kremlick previously had made substantial direct contributions to the American Cancer Society, that the society had helped his wife when she was dying of cancer, and that at the time of her death he requested memorials to the American Cancer Society.
>
> This is the very kind of information that may be used both to establish an ambiguity and to help resolve it. Appellants should have been given the opportunity to do that.

2. *Explicit Reformation.* Apart from *Flannery*, the cases studied in this part have been instances of reformation in disguise. In re Snide, 418 N.E.2d 656 (N.Y. 1981), is a case in which the court openly reformed a mistaken will. The decision, however, expressly limited the extent to which it allowed departure from the traditional rules. In *Snide*, an attorney prepared mutual wills for

Harvey and Rose Snide, husband and wife. At the execution ceremony, the wills were presented to Harvey and Rose in envelopes, with the envelope marked for each containing the will intended for the other. The attorney, the attesting witnesses, Harvey, and Rose all proceeded with the ceremony without anyone taking care to read the front pages or even the attestation clauses of the wills, either of which would have indicated the error.

After Harvey died, Rose sought to probate the will signed by Harvey (but intended as her will). The Surrogate decreed that it could be admitted to probate, and that it could be reformed to substitute the name "Harvey" wherever the name "Rose" appeared, and the name "Rose" wherever the name "Harvey" appeared. The Surrogate reached this result on general equitable principles, apparently without having understood that reformation had traditionally been refused even for a mistake so obvious. The Appellate Division reversed in a memorandum opinion limited to pointing out that the Surrogate ignored contrary New York authority dating back into the 1800s.

The New York Court of Appeals reversed the Appellate Division and sustained the power of the Surrogate to reform the will. The Court of Appeals said:

> Under such facts it would indeed be ironic if not perverse to state that because what has occurred is so obvious, and what was intended so clear, we must act to nullify rather than sustain this testamentary scheme. . . .
>
> In reaching this conclusion we do not disregard settled principles, nor are we unmindful of the evils which the formalities of will execution are designed to avoid; namely, fraud and mistake. To be sure, full illumination of the nature of Harvey's testamentary scheme is dependent in part on proof outside of the will itself. However, this is a very unusual case, and the nature of the additional proof should not be ignored. Not only did the two instruments constitute reciprocal elements of a unified testamentary plan, they both were executed with statutory formality, including the same attesting witnesses, at a contemporaneous execution ceremony. There is absolutely no danger of fraud, and the refusal to read these wills together would serve merely to unnecessarily expand formalism, without any corresponding benefit. On these narrow facts we decline this unjust course.
>
> Nor can we share the fears of the dissent that our holding will be the first step in the exercise of judicial imagination relating to the reformation of wills. Again, we are dealing here solely with identical mutual wills both simultaneously executed with statutory formality.

In Matter of Provenzano, N.Y.L.J., Dec. 13, 1982, at 17 (Sur. Ct.), Joseph Provenzano's will devised all of his property "to my beloved husband, Joseph Provenzano." His widow, Josephine Provenzano, contended that she was the intended devisee of his estate. Her argument was that "the literal form of [the will] is the result of an obvious typographical error, due in part to the similarity of [her] name, Josephine, and the decedent's name, Joseph."

Surrogate Signorelli interpreted the *Snide* decision as holding that "the Surrogate's Court [now has] full equitable power to correct obvious mistakes or drafting errors," and proceeded to exercise the newly conferred power, saying:

> Upon a reading of the will in its entirety and upon all the evidence submitted, the court is satisfied that the testator intended to name his spouse as the sole beneficiary of his estate and that the present form of paragraph "First" of the will propounded exists solely as a result of a typographical error. The circumstances existing in Matter of Snide, supra, were likewise the result of an obvious error, although the facts in the instant case do otherwise differ. Notwithstanding, I believe that Matter of Snide, supra, is controlling here. . . . Accordingly, the court does hereby reform paragraph "First" of decedent's will by substituting the words "wife, Josephine Provenzano" for "my beloved husband Joseph Provenzano."

For similar cases in which the surrogate court exercised its equitable powers to reform pursuant to *Snide*, see Estate of McCormick, N.Y.L.J., Aug. 13, 1998, at 27 (Sur. Ct.); In re Barnett, N.Y.L.J., Nov. 9, 1994, at 26 (Sur. Ct.); Estate of Porat, N.Y.L.J., Feb. 18, 1986, at 18 (Sur. Ct.). See also Estate of Tolin, 622 So. 2d 988 (Fla. 1993), which is described in Chapter 5, Part B. But see Estate of Lowney, N.Y.L.J., June 25, 1998, at 37 (denying reformation of residuary provision to add two granddaughters even though court was satisfied by the extrinsic evidence that an error of omission had been made).

3. *Reformation in Other Limited Circumstances.* It is widely recognized that courts have general equity power to reform charitable trusts, whether created by will or otherwise, if the specific charitable purpose becomes impracticable. See infra Chapter 15, Part B.

Legislation and judicial authority exists in a number of states authorizing courts to reform dispositive provisions created by will or otherwise that violate the Rule Against Perpetuities. See infra Chapter 19, Part D.

4. *Commonwealth Reformation Legislation.* One path for changing the traditional common-law rule against reformation of wills is legislation that authorizes the court to correct mistakes in wills. In the United Kingdom, § 20 of the Administration of Justice Act of 1982 provides that "[i]f a court is satisfied that a will is so expressed that it fails to carry out the testator's intentions, in consequence (a) of a clerical error; or (b) of a failure to understand his instructions, it may order that the will shall be rectified so as to carry out his intentions. . . ."

The New South Wales Wills, Probate and Administration (Amendment) Act of 1989 in § 29A(1) adopts a broader authorization for courts to reform wills. The statute provides that "[i]f the court is satisfied that a will is so expressed that it fails to carry out the testator's intentions, it may order that the will be rectified so as to carry out the testator's intentions." A similar statute is found in the South Australia Wills Act 1936, § 25AA (adopted in 1994). The

Tasmania Wills Act 1992, § 47 also gives the courts broad authorization to reform wills if "the Court is satisfied that there can be no reasonable doubt" that the testator made an error in expressing testamentary intention.

The Australian Capital Territory Wills (Amendment) Act No. 67, 1991 § 12A goes one step further. It authorizes reformation

> [i]f the court is satisfied that circumstances or events existed or occurred before, at or after the execution by a testator of his or her last will, being circumstances of events—
>
> (a) that were not known to, or anticipated by, the testator;
>
> (b) the effects of which were not fully appreciated by the testator; or
>
> (c) that occurred at or after the death of the testator,
>
> in consequence of which the provisions of the will applied according to their tenor would fail to accord with the probable intention of the testator had he or she known of, anticipated or fully appreciated the effects of those circumstances or events . . . .

5. *Questions.* In many of the cases studied in previous chapters, the testator's intent was apparently frustrated. Examples include Estate of Spencer, supra Chapter 5, Part C, and Crosby v. Alton Ochsner Medical Foundation, supra Chapter 5, Part E. Would the adoption of a general reformation doctrine for wills, as endorsed by the Restatement 3d of Property, provide an avenue for remedying the mistakes that occurred in these cases? What about under § 20 of the U.K. Administration of Justice Act of 1982, supra?

2. *Reformation or Modification to Achieve Tax Objectives*

Restatement 3d of Property

§ *12.2. Modifying Donative Documents to Achieve Donor's Tax Objectives*

A donative document may be modified, in a manner that does not violate the donor's probable intention, to achieve the donor's tax objectives.[21]

Courts have been willing to reform wills when the reformation is necessary to achieve certain tax benefits. Despite the general acceptance of the no-reformation rule for wills, state courts are inclined to reform split-interest charitable trusts, created by will or otherwise, to conform them to the federal tax requirements for an estate or gift tax charitable deduction. See, e.g., Estate of Burdon-Miller, 456 A.2d 1266 (Me. 1983). IRC § 2055(e)(3) provides that

---

21. UTC § 415, which is based on the Restatement, authorizes modification of the terms of a trust to achieve the settlor's tax objectives.

a charitable deduction shall be allowed for the charitable interest in a split-interest trust "in respect of any qualified reformation." "Qualified reformation" is defined as "a change of a governing instrument by reformation, amendment, construction, or otherwise which changes a reformable interest into a qualified interest but only if . . . such change is effective as of the date of the decedent's death." For rulings in which the Internal Revenue Service found that reformation entitled an estate to a charitable deduction, see, e.g., Priv. Ltr. Rul. 200027014 (July 7, 2000); Priv. Ltr. Rul. 9844008 (July 30, 1998). Many states have enacted statutes that authorize modification of split-interest charitable trusts, either by the trustee or by the court, to qualify them for a federal tax deduction. See Restatement 3d of Property § 12.2 statutory note.

Courts have also reformed a will to give a better federal tax result by splitting a single QTIP trust into three separate QTIP trusts, one of which would be a GST exempt trust with an "inclusion ratio" of 0. See supra Chapter 7, Part A. See also Treas. Reg. § 26.2654-1(b) (recognizing a division of a single trust into separate trusts for purposes of the generation-skipping tax if certain conditions are met). In Will of Choate, 533 N.Y.S.2d 272, 275 (Sur. Ct. 1988), the court emphasized that "[a]ll interested persons under the present single QTIP trust would remain entitled to precisely the same interests as he or she would have if the will were not construed as proposed," and noted further that "[t]his court has the power to construe and reform testator's will if the will, as written, does not carry out his intention, provided such reformation does not attempt to alter tax consequences retroactively or to change in any respect the dispositive provisions of his will." Accord First Agricultural Bank v. Coxe, 550 N.E.2d 875 (Mass. 1990); see also Shawmut Bank v. Buckley, 665 N.E.2d 29 (Mass. 1996) (authorizing excision of certain terms to prevent potential adverse tax consequences to surviving spouse regarding the nonmarital deduction trust created by the decedent).

Another type of reformation that courts frequently have used to achieve the decedent's tax objectives is to divide a QTIP marital deduction trust into two trusts in order to allow the decedent's executor to make the so-called *reverse QTIP* election under IRC § 2652(a)(3). See, e.g., Estate of Branigan, 609 A.2d 431 (N.J. 1992) (discussed supra Chapter 7, Part B); see also In re Quigan, N.Y.L.J., Nov. 17, 1994, at 34 (in reforming the will to assure the effectiveness of a credit shelter trust, the court said that, "[h]aving discerned the intent of the testatrix, the court may reform the will by modifying, adding, or deleting language to give effect to decedent's testamentary plan and to avoid any inadvertent, adverse tax consequences of the language actually used").

Courts have reformed wills to achieve tax objectives either to correct drafting errors or to achieve tax savings resulting from tax law changes that occurred between execution of a will and death. But see Estate of Dunlop, 617 N.Y.S.2d

119 (Sur. Ct. 1994). In *Dunlop* the executor petitioned the court to reform the testator's will to create five separate trusts so that, through the use of certain elections, the GST exemption could be utilized in both the decedent and the surviving spouse's estates. The court refused to reform the will because the adverse tax consequences did not result from unforeseen changes in the tax law, but because the testator and the attorney-drafter were not aware of applicable law.

> This court finds that there is no presumption that the Will of the decedent, which never mentions or even alludes to the generation-skipping tax, sets forth an intent to minimize such tax in the estate of his surviving spouse.
>
> The result reached by this Court may seem harsh. Perhaps it is. . . . It is inappropriate, however, for this Court to be the mechanism to create a new estate plan for the testator and his widow. If such were the duty of this Court, what would be the limit to its functions in that regard? Would the Court always be bound to reform each and every Will of every testator so as to achieve maximum tax benefits, no matter what the Will stated? If that were the case, the courts would be overwhelmed with such requests for reformation, and the rule of law respecting testamentary dispositions would be undermined.
>
> It is one thing to seek reformation where an important tax law, or other statute, has been changed to adversely affect a carefully drawn estate plan. To permit such reformation, in every case, because the testator or his draftsman was uninformed or overlooked something, is beyond the power of the Court and is unwarranted.

A Washington statute provides that "[if a governing instrument contains a marital deduction gift, the governing instrument shall be construed to comply with the marital deduction provisions of the Internal Revenue Code in every respect." Wash. Rev. Code § 11.108.020(1). For further discussion of reformation for tax purposes, see Steve R. Akers, Reformation Proceedings in Post-Mortem Tax Planning, 17 Am. Col. Tr. & Est. Couns. Notes 254 (1992); Carlyn S. McCaffrey & Alan H. Hirschfeld, Restructuring Wills and Trusts to Reduce Generation-Skipping Taxes, 131 Tr. & Est., Mar. 1992, at 8.

The Restatement 3d of Property § 12.2, which authorizes modification of donative instruments, including wills, to achieve the donor's tax objectives, only permits modification if it is in done in "a manner that does not violate the donor's probable intent." In Estate of Burkett, N.Y.L.J., Nov. 7, 1997, at 27 (Sur. Ct.), the court refused to modify a trust agreement because it would not effectuate the testator's intent.

PART D. ATTORNEY LIABILITY FOR MISTAKE

Would liability for malpractice or for breach of a third-party beneficiary contract be better solutions to the problem of attorney mistake than the adoption of a reformation doctrine? If a reformation remedy were to become available, would there still be room for liability even in cases where the reformation remedy was successfully invoked? Consider the following discussion of these questions in Langbein & Waggoner, supra, at 588-90:

> Because the error in many mistake cases is sufficiently egregious that a victim might be able to invoke the malpractice liability of the lawyer-draftsman if relief of mistake were denied, the argument can be made the malpractice remedy makes relief for mistake unnecessary. The intended beneficiary whose devise has been frustrated by the lawyer's mistake can be remitted to his malpractice remedy against the offending draftsman. We think that there are a variety of responses to this contention.
>
> Initially, we note that there is a range of mistake cases that fall outside the scope of malpractice relief, including homedrawn wills and those lawyer-drafted wills where for whatever reason the mistake does not rise to the level of malpractice. Furthermore, in a considerable fraction of lawyer malpractice cases, the draftsman may be wholly or partially judgment-proof, as when he is long since deceased,[22] or when he is uninsured or underinsured. In one region of the country for which a specialist insurance broker has supplied recent data on malpractice coverage to the American Bar Association's Standing Committee on Lawyers' Professional Liability, 51% of the policies in force have $100,000/$300,000 limits, well below the value of significant numbers of testate estates. For devises of unique property, for example, Blackacre or the family bible, relief in damages would not be an adequate substitute.
>
> The malpractice solution is also objectionable because it would channel mistake cases into the tort system. When translated into a tort claim and discounted for the litigation expenses and counsel fees, and for the unpredictability and delay incident to the jury-dominated tort system, a devise frustrated by mistake would be worth but a fraction of the value in the testator's estate.
>
> More fundamentally, the change in theory from devise to tort raises a serious problem of unjust enrichment. Whereas most forms of malpractice inflict deadweight loss that can only be put right by compensation, in these testamentary mistake cases a benefit is being transferred from the intended beneficiary to a mistaken devisee. That devisee is a volunteer lacking any claim of entitlement or justified reliance. The malpractice solution would leave the benefit where it fortuitously fell, thereby creating a needless loss to be charged against the draftsman (or his insurer). So long as the draftsman's error was innocent (which is what distinguishes mistake from fraud), there is no reason to exaggerate his liability in this way. If, on the other hand, the lawyer were charged with the malpractice but subrogated to the tort plaintiff's mistake claim, the mistake doctrine would simply be recognized in a circular and more litigious fashion.
>
> We do not mean to say that negligent draftsmen will be immune from malpractice liability in testamentary mistake cases. When the malpractice causes

22. A malpractice claim against an attorney may survive the attorney's death. McStowe v. Borenstein, 377 Mass. 804, 388 N.E.2d 674 (1979).

true loss, that loss should be compensable. One such item of compensable loss may be the reasonable litigation expenses of the parties to the reformation (or other) proceeding occasioned by the mistake. We can also imagine circumstances in which a mistake might come to light after distribution and dissipation of the mistakenly devised property; here the change of position of the mistaken devisee would constitute justified reliance and require that the intended beneficiary be remitted to his malpractice remedy.

Finally, we point once more to the experience under the many existing doctrines that provide partial relief in the field of testamentary mistake. There has been no suggestion in the "mere construction" and other cases [set forth supra Part B] that malpractice should be regarded as an alternative to direct relief.

Professors Langbein and Waggoner argue that a reformation remedy is a better means of promoting justice than a malpractice remedy. In the malpractice case that follows, consider whether judicial reformation or malpractice liability is the better means of remedying the lawyer's mistake.

Ogle v. Fuiten

466 N.E.2d 224 (Ill. 1984)

GOLDENHERSH, J. Plaintiffs, James Elvin Ogle and Leland W. Ogle, initiated this action in the circuit court of Sangamon County against defendants, Lorraine Fuiten, as executrix of the estate of William F. Fuiten, and Robert G. Heckenkamp, who, under the name of Heckenkamp and Fuiten, had been associated with William F. Fuiten in the practice of law. In a two-count complaint plaintiffs alleged that William F. Fuiten had negligently drafted wills for Oscar H. Smith and Alma I. Smith, respectively an uncle and aunt of plaintiffs, and alternatively, that Fuiten failed to properly perform his contract with the Smiths to fulfill their testamentary intentions, and in so doing, failed to benefit the plaintiffs. Defendants moved to dismiss for failure to state a cause of action. The circuit court allowed the motion, and plaintiffs appealed. The appellate court reversed and remanded, and we allowed defendants' petition for leave to appeal.

The appellate court summarized the allegations contained in the complaint as follows:

> Count I essentially alleges: (1) Testators employed defendant Fuiten and the law firm of Heckenkamp and Fuiten to prepare wills in accordance with the testators' intentions; (2) the wills were prepared; (3) neither testator intended their property to devolve by the law of intestate succession; (4) it was their intention that their property be left to plaintiffs if neither testator survived the other by 30 days; (5) this contingency occurred; (6) Fuiten owed plaintiffs the duty of ascertaining the testators' intentions in all foreseeable events and to draft wills which would effec-

> tuate these intentions; (7) Fuiten breached this duty and negligently drafted the subject wills; and (8) plaintiffs suffered damage as a direct result of this breach.
>
> Count II essentially alleges the first five allegations noted above and additionally alleges: (6) the purpose of the employment of Fuiten and the firm was to draft wills not only for the benefit of testators, but for the benefit of these plaintiffs; (7) Fuiten and the firm were paid the agreed consideration under the employment agreement; (8) Fuiten and the firm knew plaintiffs were intended beneficiaries of the wills and the employment agreement; (9) Fuiten and the firm had agreed to draft wills leaving the property to plaintiffs in the event neither testator survived the other by 30 days; (10) Fuiten breached this agreement in that the wills failed to fulfill the testators' intentions; and (11) plaintiffs suffered foreseeable, direct damage as a consequence of this breach.

The wills of Oscar H. Smith and Alma I. Smith contained the following provisions:

> SECOND: I give, devise and bequeath all of my estate, real, personal and mixed wheresoever situated to my wife, ALMA I. SMITH, if she [my husband, OSCAR H. SMITH, if he] shall survive me within thirty (30) days from the date of my death.
>
> THIRD: I direct that if my wife, ALMA I. SMITH, [my husband, OSCAR H. SMITH] and I die in or from a common disaster that my estate be equally divided between my nephews, JAMES ELVIN OGLE, and LELAND OGLE, share and share alike.

These wills were construed in In re Estate of Smith (1979), 68 Ill.App.3d 30, 24 Ill.Dec. 451, 385 N.E.2d 363, and it was held that because Oscar Smith died suddenly of a stroke on April 10, 1977, and his wife, Alma, died 15 days later from a lingering cancer illness, and neither will contained any other dispositive provisions, their estates passed by intestacy to persons other than plaintiffs.

Because the judgment appealed from was entered upon allowance of defendants' motion to dismiss, all facts properly pleaded in the complaint must be taken as true. A cause of action should not be dismissed on the pleadings unless it clearly appears that no set of facts can be proved which will entitle plaintiffs to recover.

Conceding that under Pelham v. Griesheimer (1982), 92 Ill.2d 13, 64 Ill.Dec. 544, 440 N.E.2d 96, privity is not a prerequisite to an action by a nonclient against an attorney, defendants argue that the complaint fails to allege a duty owed plaintiffs. They argue that the only duty owed by defendants was to provide each testator "with a valid testamentary instrument that disposes of the testators' property at his death in the manner expressly stated in his will." They argue that to permit persons unnamed in the will, or persons named with a precondition which fails to occur, to bring an action against the attorney "creates an unlimited and unknown class of potential plaintiffs." They contend, too, that in order to recover from an attorney, a nonclient must allege and prove "that the primary purpose and intent of the attorney-client relationship itself was to benefit or influence the third party." Defendants argue that under this "intent to directly benefit" test, plaintiffs' cause fails because the testators' intent, as defined in the will-construction action, shows that plaintiffs were to benefit only under certain circumstances which did not occur. Thus, defendants contend, the intent of the testators to benefit plaintiffs is not, as required by *Pelham*, "clearly evident."

Also citing *Pelham*, plaintiffs contend that they have alleged facts which show that the testators, in obtaining the services of the defendants in the preparations of the wills, intended to "directly benefit" plaintiffs and that, as held by the appellate court, they have stated a cause of action in both counts of the complaint. . . .

Defendants argue that to state a cause of action plaintiffs should be required to show, from the express terms of the will, that the plaintiff was an intended beneficiary of the relationship between the defendant attorney and the testator. They argue that this would protect against a flood of litigation. Defendants have cited no authority which has applied the rule which they espouse, and we find no basis in the cases which we have examined for imposing such a requirement.

We agree with the appellate court that "the allegations of count I sufficiently state the traditional elements of negligence in tort and count II sufficiently states the traditional elements of a third-party beneficiary/breach of contract theory." We note parenthetically that, unlike *Pelham*, the defendants' representation of the testators here was of a nonadversarial nature and consisted only of the drafting of the wills which plaintiffs alleged were for their benefit as intended beneficiaries. See Pelham v. Griesheimer (1982), 92 Ill.2d 13, 22, 64 Ill.Dec. 544, 440 N.E.2d 96.

Defendants contend that this action is an impermissible collateral attack upon the judicial determination of the validity of the testators' wills. Defendants' argument appears to be that because the wills were held valid, the question of the testators' intent has been settled, and plaintiffs may not now state a cause of action based on the allegation that the wills do not reflect the true intent of the testators.

In support of their position defendants cite Robinson v. First State Bank (1983), 97 Ill.2d 174, 73 Ill.Dec. 428, 454 N.E.2d 288, and attempt to analogize the claim in Robinson that the testator's attorney, through tortious interference, had prevented the plaintiffs from receiving their inheritance to the allegations here that the testators' attorney, because of negligence or breach of contract, had prevented plaintiffs from receiving the testators' estates. In *Robinson*, holding that the action, in effect, was a tardy will contest, this court affirmed the circuit court's dismissal of the action for tortious interference.

Defendants argue that the present action necessarily assumes that the wills are invalid, without having been contested by plaintiffs on that ground within the statutory time.

We find *Robinson* distinguishable in that the basis for the plaintiffs' complaint was that the testator had been subject to the undue influence of her attorney. Claims of undue influence are properly raised in a will-contest action. In the present case, however, the basis for the plaintiffs' complaint is that, because of the attorney's negligence, the testators' true intent is not reflected in the wills. Thus, while the plaintiffs in *Robinson* had the opportunity to pursue their claims in a will-contest action, plaintiffs here had no similar opportunity to do so.

We note further that if plaintiffs here are successful in their action, the orderly disposition of the testators' property is not disrupted, and the provisions of the wills, and the probate administration, remain unaffected. On these facts, the present action is not a collateral attack on the wills. . . .

For the foregoing reasons, the judgment of the appellate court is affirmed.

Notes

1. *The Privity Problem. Ogle* illustrates the modern trend to abrogate the privity requirement and allow malpractice actions in tort, contract, or both by the intended beneficiaries for mistakes in wills. See Restatement (Third) of the Law Governing Lawyers § 51, comment f, illustrations 2, 3. A small number of jurisdictions, however, continue to dismiss cases for lack of privity. See, e.g., Noble v. Bruce, 709 A.2d 1264 (Md. 1998); Barcelo v. Elliott, 923 S.W.2d 575 (Tex. 1996).

Other courts have adopted an intermediate position regarding the privity question, holding that a cause of action is available only to plaintiffs who can show that they were intended third-party beneficiaries of the contract between the lawyer and the testator. See, e.g., Hale v. Groce, 744 P.2d 1289 (Or. 1987); Guy v. Liederbach, 459 A.2d 744 (Pa. 1983).

Yet another group of cases has limited malpractice claims to those beneficiaries identified in the will. See, e.g., Glover v. Southard, 894 P.2d 21 (Colo. Ct. App. 1994); Mieras v. DeBona, 550 N.W.2d 202 (Mich. 1996). These cases reflect the courts' traditional hesitation to find testamentary intent beyond the four corners of the will. Rather than relying on the doctrine of privity, § 51 of the Restatement of the Law Governing Lawyers responds to this concern by requiring the plaintiff to prove testator's intent by clear and convincing evidence. See comment f, illustration 3; accord Pivnick v. Beck, 762 A.2d 653 (N.J. 2000).

2. *Collateral Estoppel.* Courts have generally rejected the defendant's argument in *Ogle* that a malpractice action is an impermissible collateral attack upon the probate court's ruling on the validity of the testator's will. The courts

have recognized that a consequence of the no-reformation-of-wills rule is that will construction proceedings do not necessarily lead to determination of a testator's intent. For example, consider Simpson v. Calivas, 650 A.2d 318, 323-24 (N.H. 1994), in which an alleged intended beneficiary sued the drafting attorney after the probate court had found that the will should be construed to exclude the plaintiff.

> The principal task of the probate court is to determine the testator's intent . . . . In this effort, the probate court is always permitted to consider the "surrounding circumstances" of the testator, and where the terms of a will are ambiguous, as here, extrinsic evidence may be admitted to the extent that it does not contradict the express terms of the will. Direct declarations of a testator's intent, however, are generally inadmissible in all probate proceedings. The defendant argues that even though his notes of his meeting with the decedent recorded the decedent's direct declarations of intent, they could have been admissible as an exception to the general rule had there been a proper proffer. We need not reach the issue of whether the defendant's notes fall within an exception to the general rule because even assuming admissibility and therefore an identity of evidence, there remain distinct issues. Quite simply the task of the probate court is a limited one: to determine the intent of the testator as expressed in the language of the will. Obviously, the hope is that the application of rules of construction and consideration of extrinsic evidence (where authorized) will produce a finding of expressed intent that corresponds to actual intent. Further, the likelihood of such convergence presumably increases as the probate court considers more extrinsic evidence; however, even with access to all extrinsic evidence, there is no requirement or guarantee that the testator's intent as construed will match the testator's actual intent. . . .
>
> Inasmuch as the mandate of the probate court is simply to determine and give effect to the intent of the testator as expressed in the language of the will, a finding of actual intent is not necessary to that judgment. Accordingly, even an explicit finding of actual intent by a probate court cannot be the basis for collateral estoppel.

But see Pivnick v. Beck, supra, in which the court held that collateral estoppel barred the plaintiff in a situation where extrinsic evidence was admissible in earlier probate proceeding to show that the trust did not reflect the settlor/testator's intent and the plaintiff had failed to meet the required clear and convincing evidentiary standard of proof.

EXTERNAL REFERENCES. Martin D. Begleiter, First Let's Sue All the Lawyers—What Will We Get: Damages for Estate Planning Malpractice, 51 Hastings L.J. 325 (2000); Martin D. Begleiter, Article II of the Uniform Probate Code and the Malpractice Revolution, 59 Tenn. L. Rev. 101 (1991); Martin D. Begleiter, Attorney Malpractice in Estate Planning—You've Got to

Know When to Hold Up, Know When to Fold Up, 38 U. Kan. L. Rev. 193 (1990); Helen B. Jenkins, Privity—A Texas-Size Barrier to Third Parties for Negligent Will Drafting—An Assessment and Proposal, 42 Baylor L. Rev. 687 (1990); Gerald P. Johnston, Legal Malpractice in Estate Planning—Perilous Times Ahead for the Practitioner, 67 Iowa L. Rev. 629 (1982); Matthew R. Bogart, Note, Legal Malpractice for the Negligent Drafting of a Testamentary Instrument: Schreiner v. Scoville, 73 Iowa L. Rev. 1231 (1988); Michael P. Moorley, Note, Privity as a Bar to Recovery in Negligent Will-Preparation Cases: A Rule Without a Reason, 57 U. Cin. L. Rev. 1123 (1989); Kerry J. Shepherd, Note, *Hale v. Groce*: Lawyer Liability to Intended Beneficiaries of Negligently Drafted Wills—Last Stand of the Immutable Privity Doctrine, 24 Willamette L. Rev. 843 (1988).

Chapter 13

Trusts: Formation and Formality

PART A. INTRODUCTION

Restatement 3d of Trusts

§ 2. *Definition of Trust*. A trust, as the term is used in this Restatement when not qualified by the word "resulting" or "constructive," is a fiduciary relationship with respect to property, arising as a result of a manifestation of an intention to create that relationship and subjecting the person who holds title to the property to duties to deal with it for the benefit of charity or for one or more persons, at least one of whom is not the sole trustee.

BACON said that the use (or trust) "grew to strength and credit by degrees."[1] In 1911, Sir Frederic Maitland looked back on the development of the trust idea and declared it to be "the greatest and most distinctive achievement performed by Englishmen in the field of

1. Quoted in Scott on Trusts § 1.2.

jurisprudence."[2] Today, without doubt, private trusts and, to a lesser extent, charitable trusts (see Chapter 15) sit at the core of modern estate-planning practice. In 1994, the Federal Reserve Board reported that federally insured commercial and savings banks held 971,000 personal trust accounts averaging about $693,000 each in value, for an aggregate value of $672.6 billion.[3] Not counted in these figures are the vast numbers of personal trusts held by private trustees.

For a definition of an express trust (sometimes called an intentional trust), we turn first to the Restatement 3d of Trusts:

> § 2. *Definition of Trust.* A trust [other than a "resulting" or a "constructive" trust] is a fiduciary relationship with respect to property, arising as a result of a manifestation of an intention to create that relationship and subjecting the person who holds title to the property to duties to deal with it for the benefit of a charity or for one or more persons, at least one of whom is not the sole trustee.[4]

1. Historical Development of Trusts

The modern trust described in the Restatement grew out of the *feoffment to uses*. In the thirteenth century, shortly after the Norman Conquest, people (nearly always men) from time to time enfeoffed land to another "to the use" of a third.[5] The maker of the enfeoffment was called the feoffor. In the modern trust, that person is called the *settlor* (or the grantor, trustor, founder, donor,

---

2. Frederic W. Maitland, The Unincorporated Body, in 3 Frederic W. Maitland, Collected Papers 271, 272 (1911). This is not to suggest, however, that concepts similar to the trust have not been developed by other legal systems. A statutory adoption of the common-law trust is in place in Louisiana. La. Rev. Stat. Ann. §§ 9:1731-9:2252; Kathryn V. Lorio, Louisiana Trusts: The Experience of a Civil Law Jurisdiction With the Trust, 42 La. L. Rev. 1721 (1982). And, several civil-law countries have adopted concepts serving similar purposes, such as the German *Treuhand.* See Stefan Grundmann, Trust and Treuhand at the End of the 20th Century: Key Problems and Shift of Interests, 47 Am. J. Comp. L. 401 (1999). Also, the Islamic legal system judicially developed a concept similar to a charitable trust, called the *waghf*, which has been extended by statute in some Islamic states to permit a use similar to the private express trust. E.g., Iranian Civ. Code ch. 2. For insightful comparisons between the *waghf* and the trust, see David Powers, The Islamic Family Endowment (*Waqf*), 32 Vand. J. Transnat'l L. 1167 (1999); Jeffrey A. Schoenblum, The Role of Legal Doctrine in the Decline of the Islamic *Waqf*: A Comparison with the Trust, id. at 1191.

3. Board of Governors of the Federal Reserve System, Trust Assets of Financial Institutions—1994, at 9 (Table A-2) (1995).

4. This definition expressly exempts resulting and constructive trusts, which are trusts that arise by operation of law, rather than expressly by a grantor or testator.

5. In these early times, the use arrangement was often made for the benefit of the Franciscan friars, whose poverty vows made it impossible for them to own property but who still had to have shelter and land to cultivate.

or creator). The one to whom the land was enfeoffed was called the feoffee to uses. Today, we call that person the *trustee*. The third person, the one for whose benefit the land was held, was called the cestui que uses. We know that person today as the *beneficiary* or, less commonly, the cestui que trust. Back then, the evidence suggests that the nearly invariable subject of a use was land.[6] Today, the subject of a trust can still be land, but more commonly it is personal property in the form of investment securities. Whether real or personal property, the subject of the trust is also variously identified as the trust property, the corpus, the principal, or the *res*.

Normally, there is more than one beneficiary, such as when G transfers property to T, in trust, with a direction to pay income to A for life, then at A's death to transfer the corpus to B. Such a trust gives A an "equitable life estate" and B an "equitable remainder." T's interest usually is a "legal" estate, typically a fee simple.[7]

The settlor can create a trust during his or her lifetime (an inter vivos or living trust) or by will (a testamentary trust). An inter vivos trust can be either irrevocable or, as we know from Chapter 8, revocable. The settlor of an inter vivos trust can name himself or herself as trustee (a self-declared trust) or name a third-party as trustee. The settlor can also reserve for himself or herself a beneficial interest in the trust; chapter 8 taught us that this often happens in the case of a revocable inter vivos trust, where the arrangement is essentially a probate-avoidance device, with the settlor commonly being the beneficiary of the income interest.

Nature of the Beneficiary's Interest. It was once thought that the beneficiary's interest is nothing more than a right in personam, enforceable in equity against the trustee.[8] But today a trust is seen as a property arrangement under which ownership of the property is divided: The trust property's *legal* title goes to the trustee[9] and its *equitable* (or beneficial) title goes to the

---

6. E.g., Frederic W. Maitland, The Unincorporated Body, in 3 Frederic W. Maitland, Collected Papers 271, 273 (1911). But see Willard T. Barbour, Some Aspects of Fifteenth-Century Chancery, 31 Harv. L. Rev. 834, 850 (1918).

7. This statement requires some qualification. As the Restatement 3d of Trusts points out, while the trust beneficiaries' interest is always equitable in nature, the trustee's interest may be legal or equitable: "Although it is usually true (and is, unfortunately, often stated without qualification in cases and texts) that the trustee has legal title, in some instances the trustee will hold only an equitable title." Restatement 3d of Trusts § 2 comment d.

8. Frederic W. Maitland, Equity 29, 107 (2d ed. 1936); James B. Ames, Lectures on Legal History 76, 262 (1913); Harlan F. Stone, The Nature of the Rights of the Cestui Que Trust, 17 Colum. L. Rev. 467 (1917). One of the modern-era writers on trusts who espouses this view is Richard R. Powell, Law of Real Property ¶515 (rev. ed. 1990).

9. Subject to the qualification noted supra Note 7.

beneficiary or, more usually, is divided along temporal lines between income beneficiaries and beneficiaries of future interests in corpus.

To say that the trustee holds "legal" title signifies that the law courts recognized the feoffee to uses (the trustee) as the sole owner of the trust property, with the chancery or equity courts recognizing and enforcing the rights of the cestui que uses (the beneficiary). Despite the general merging of law and equity, we still speak of "legal" and "equitable" obligations, though in most states today they are enforced by the same court. To be sure, also, this division-of-ownership idea embraces within it an allocation of rights and duties. Holding legal but not beneficial title carries with it fiduciary duties with respect to the property; holding equitable title confers rights in personam to enforce those duties. But it is now generally agreed that the beneficiary also has rights in rem, an equitable property interest in the assets held in trust.[10] See Restatement 3d of Trusts Introductory Note to Part 4; Restatement 2d of Trusts § 130. Of decisive influence in this regard is the application of the Rule Against Perpetuities to beneficial interests in trust. The Rule Against Perpetuities is strictly a rule of property law. Most perpetuity cases are concerned with the validity of a beneficial interest in trust.

Enforcement. Despite the earlier question about the nature of the beneficiary's interest, one point has long been clear: The trustee's fiduciary duties run in favor of the beneficiary. Unless the settlor is also a beneficiary, the settlor has no standing to enforce the trust.

In the beginning stages, the feoffor could do little more than trust to the honor of the feoffee to uses. When that trust was misplaced, the law courts gave no remedy.[11] In such circumstances, it was to be expected that appeals would be made to the Chancellor for relief, and in the first half of the fifteenth century, at the suit of the cestui que use (beneficiary), the Chancellor began to force the feoffee (trustee) to perform his undertakings.[12]

---

10. Bogert on Trusts § 183; Charles A. Huston, The Enforcement of Decrees in Equity 136-48 (1915); Scott on Trusts §§ 1, 130; Edgar N. Durfee, Equity in Rem, 14 Mich. L. Rev. 219 (1916); Austin W. Scott, The Nature of the Rights of the Cestui Que Trust, 17 Colum. L. Rev. 269 (1917).

11. Pollock and Maitland suggested that some of the earlier uses "may have been enforced by the ecclesiastical courts." Frederick Pollock & Frederic W. Maitland, History of English Law 232 (2d ed. 1911). Historical evidence has since been uncovered suggesting that Pollock and Maitland were right about this. Professor Helmholz has established that, from the last quarter of the 14th century through the middle of the 15th century, some ecclesiastical courts regularly enforced feoffments to uses. Richard H. Helmholz, The Early Enforcement of Uses, 79 Colum. L. Rev. 1503 (1979).

12. James B. Ames, Lectures on Legal History 237 (1913).

In the same century, the law courts developed the action of assumpsit and thus began the enforcement of simple contracts. It could have happened that assumpsit would be used to enforce the obligations of the trustee, but it did not happen. The idea of privity would have stood in the way of enforcement at the suit of a third-party beneficiary, and for that matter it would today in English law since, on a contract analysis, this would be a contract for the benefit of a third person. A remedy in favor of the feoffor (settlor) would have been within the modes of thought of the law judges, especially since many of the early uses were for the benefit of the feoffor, but this was not the path that was taken. Maitland's explanation is that by the time assumpsit developed "the Chancellor was already in possession, was already enforcing uses by means of a procedure far more efficient and flexible than any which the old courts could have employed."[13] The law court's judgment presumably would have been for money, a judgment that would then have needed to be executed. The Chancellor, however, gave specific relief by directly ordering the feoffee to perform his obligations and by enforcing obedience to that order, if necessary, through contempt. The remedy was given to the cestui que use; if the feoffee was to hold to the use of the feoffor, the latter's suit apparently was in his right as cestui que use, not as creator of the arrangement.

Today, the action against a trustee for breach of duties is not in contract or at law. Except in very limited circumstances, the jurisdiction of equity has remained exclusive.[14] Moreover, the remedy against the trustee remains in the beneficiary. Although the point is not much discussed, it still seems to be taken for granted that the creator of the trust, the settlor, has neither a remedy for the trustee's breach, nor otherwise has standing to enforce the trust.[15]

While the law traditionally has not treated trusts as contracts, leading legal scholars like Austin Wakeman Scott have long acknowledged that there is a contractual aspect to trusts. The Restatement 3d of Trusts points out, however, that "[t]his 'contractual approach' . . . was certainly a limited one . . . ."[16] More recently, Professor Langbein has extended this approach, arguing that "[t]rusts *are* contracts." See John H. Langbein, The Contractarian Basis of

---

13. Frederic W. Maitland, Equity 28 (2d ed. 1936).

14. A legal remedy is available to the beneficiary where the trustee is under an immediate and unconditioned obligation to pay the beneficiary money. Scott on Trusts § 198.1.

15. Note, 62 Harv. L. Rev. 1370 (1949). But see John T. Gaubatz, Grantor Enforcement of Trusts: Standing in One Private Law Setting, 62 N.C. L. Rev. 905 (1984), concluding that "if the grantor has an economic, expectation, or representational interest in the trust, such that he can be trusted to fully and fairly litigate the validity of the transactions that he challenges, and his interest was foreseeable at the time the trust was created, he can maintain the action."

16. Restatement 3d of Trusts, Reporter's Notes on § 2, at 38.

Trusts, 105 Yale L.J. 625, 625 (1995) (emphasis added). The Langbein contractarian thesis is refuted, however, in Henry Hansmann & Ugo Mattei, The Functions of Trust Law: A Comparative Legal and Economic Analysis, 73 N.Y.U. L. Rev. 434 (1998), who argue (at 469-72):

> [I]t is precisely the property-like aspects of the trust that are the principal contributions of trust law. . . . In effect, trust law provides for the creation of an entity—the trust—that is separate from the three principal parties. . . . [T]he essential purpose served by trust law . . . is to facilitate an accompanying reorganization of rights and responsibilities between the three principal parties and third parties, such as creditors, with whom the principal parties deal. That reorganization of the rights of third parties—which is the property-like aspect of the trust relationship—is difficult to accomplish without the law of trusts.

Uses and Abuses. Professor Scott points out that there was "a darker side to the picture." Scott on Trusts § 1. Uses provided a means of defrauding creditors and purchasers. To the annoyance of the overlords and the Crown, they also provided a means of escaping the consequences of many rules of law that landowners had come to regard as burdensome. Through the device of a use, an individual could in effect dispose of land at death at a time when wills of land were not recognized. This was done by conveying land to another to hold to the use of the feoffor and then to the use of such persons as the feoffor should designate in his will. In this way, land could be passed to younger sons or daughters, or even strangers, to the exclusion and chagrin of the eldest son and heir. Furthermore, the burden of feudal obligations could be escaped or lessened by depriving the lord of feudal rights that arose when his tenant died and the land passed to the tenant's heir. In the eyes of the law, legal title to the land was in the feoffee to uses; thus nothing passed on the death of the cestui que use. Of course, the feudal rights attached on inheritance from the feoffee, but inheritance here could be avoided for a long period by placing the title in a large group as joint tenants.[17]

Statute of Uses (1536). The King finally became fed up. Henry VIII, in need of more revenue, insisted that something be done about the situation. Various measures were proposed to Parliament, but they met with opposition.[18] Finally, compromise was reached. In 1536, Parliament enacted the Statute of Uses to eliminate "subtile practiced feoffementes, . . . abuses and errours . . . to the subversion of the good and anncyent laws of the [realm]." The statute itself provided:

---

17. Frederic W. Maitland, Equity 26-27 (2d ed. 1936).

18. The story is told in J. H. Baker, An Introduction to English Legal History 210-19 (1979). See also E. W. Ives, The Genesis of the Statute of Uses, 82 Eng. Hist. Rev. 673 (1967).

> *Statute of Uses, 27 Henry 8, ch. 10.* That where any person or persons stand or be seized . . . of . . . lands . . . to the use, confidence or trust of any person or persons, or of any body politick, . . . in every such case, all and every such person and persons, shall henceforth stand and be seized . . . of . . . the same . . . lands . . . in such like estates as they had or shall have in use, trust or confidence.

Although the statute sought to abolish existing uses, the mechanism used to achieve that objective was not to deprive the cestui que use of his beneficial interest; rather, the statute converted that beneficial interest into a legal interest. In the words of the statute, the cestui shall "henceforth stand and be seized" of the land "in such like estates as they had . . . in use." Converting the cestui's beneficial interest into a legal one brought it under the jurisdiction of the courts of common law rather than the Court of Chancery. For our purposes, conversion rather than abolition was a crucial development, for it meant that, in one form or another, the use was allowed to persist. In addition, the Statute of Wills of 1540 restored the right to devise land by will. As for the Statute of Uses, the common-law judges were inclined to a narrow interpretation.

The modern trust, in fact, arises out of those situations in which the courts held that the statute didn't apply. Principally this was in the case of the *active* use. Within a few years after the statute, it was held that it didn't apply to an active use. If land was conveyed by G to T to the use of B with B to "take the profits," the statute applied; but if T was to "take the profits and deliver them" to B, it didn't apply. Brooke's New Cases, March's Translation 94 (1651). The common use before the statute was "passive," a form of dummy ownership, with the cestui que use in possession of the land and the feoffee holding the bare legal title; this was held to be the only use to which the statute was meant to apply.[19] Hence the modern trust, placing active duties on the trustee, is unaffected by the Statute of Uses so long as the trust remains active.

Remarkably, the statute was also held inapplicable to a use on a use. If G conveyed to X to the use of T to the use of B, the statute executed the first use, so that T got legal title, but didn't execute the second use, even though both uses were passive. Sambach v. Dalston, Tothill 188 (1634).[20] Lord Chancellor Hardwicke, in a later case, remarked that this doctrine reduced the statute's effect to "add[ing] at most three words to a conveyance." Hopkins v. Hopkins, 1 Atk. 581, 26 Eng. Rep. 365, 372 (Ch. 1738).

---

19. Note, 17 Mich. L. Rev. 87 (1918).

20. See also James B. Ames, Lectures on Legal History 243-47 (1913).

Finally, it was clear from the language of the statute that it didn't apply to personal property, but only to a case in which the feoffee was "seized" of land.[21]

Current American law recognizes the three exemptions from the Statute of Uses, especially the exemptions for active trusts and for trusts of personal property. See Restatement 3d of Trusts § 6, comment b.

Trusts for Commercial Purposes. While we are primarily concerned in this book with trusts as a mechanism for transmitting and managing family wealth, we note that the trust device is also widely used for commercial purposes. As Professor Langbein has recently noted, "[M]ost of the wealth that is held in trust in the United States is placed there incident to business deals, and not in connection with gratuitous transfers." John H. Langbein, The Secret Life of the Trust: The Trust as an Instrument of Commerce, 107 Yale L.J. 165, 166 (1997). These commercial purposes range from investment trusts to trusts established to comply with regulatory requirements, such as foreign insurer trusts.

EXTERNAL REFERENCES. Scott on Trusts § 1; Thurman Arnold, The Restatement of the Law of Trusts, 31 Colum. L. Rev. 800, 1266 (1931); Austin W. Scott, The Trust as an Instrument of Law Reform, 31 Yale L.J. 457 (1922).

2. Estate-Planning Uses of Trusts

We began this part by noting that express trusts are at the core of modern estate-planning practice. This is so, basically, because trusts are responsive to so many financial and estate-planning needs. The variety of reasons why settlors create trusts, or are led by their lawyers to create trusts, include probate avoidance, property management, tax reasons, and control through successive generations. Ultimately, all trusts serve donative purposes, but different types of trusts satisfy one or more additional purposes.

As we saw in Chapters 7 and 8, revocable inter vivos trusts carry no tax advantages, but do avoid probate. They may also provide independent property management, but not if self-declared. A self-declared, revocable inter vivos trust allows the settlor to retain lifetime management control of his or her own property. A standby trust with an independent trustee, to be more fully funded through the exercise of a durable power of attorney in case of the settlor's incompetence, is a superior alternative to a guardianship or conservatorship.

Whether self-declared or not, a revocable inter vivos trust acts as a will substitute. On the settlor's death, it may provide for outright distributions, in the manner of outright specific, general, or residuary devises; or, it may provide

---

21. Scott on Trusts § 1.6.

for the property or a portion of it to continue in trust, in which case it serves the same purposes as a testamentary trust. It may, in fact, receive additional property from the settlor's estate as the result of a pour-over devise.

Irrevocable inter vivos trusts satisfy entirely different purposes. Chapter 7 surveyed how they can be structured to offer significant tax advantages, by freezing the value of the assets at the date of conveyance and by providing for the receipt of supplemental fundings that qualify for the annual gift-tax exclusion. Pour-over devises from the settlor's estate can also provide additional funding of irrevocable inter vivos trusts.

In the case of a married testator, testamentary trusts are typically structured to qualify for the estate-tax marital deduction; the continuation after the settlor's death of a revocable inter vivos trust can also serve this purpose. See the Sample Trust Instrument, set forth below. After the surviving spouse's death, marital-deduction trusts can continue for a further time, for the benefit of successive generations of descendants or down collateral lines. By-pass trusts also can continue for successive generations. The Rule Against Perpetuities in effect places an outer limit on the duration of such trusts. Successive-generation trusts can provide considerable transfer-tax savings, to the extent they come within the protection of the GST exemption from the federal generation-skipping tax. Where the corpus of a trust consists of intangible personal property, such as corporate securities, a trust preserves the integrity of such a fund in a manner not possible in the case of a succession of legal interests not in trust.

Trusts Compared to Other Types of Management Arrangements. There are other kinds of arrangements under which property is managed for persons other than the owners. There are also property arrangements that in the circumstances may leave the nature of the transaction in some doubt.

Section 5 of the Restatement 3d of Trusts distinguishes "trusts" from a series of arrangements, some of which also create fiduciary relationships. The distinction between a trustee and the *personal representative* (executor or administrator) of a decedent's estate is more practical than theoretical. Some but not all of the duties of a trustee are imposed upon a personal representative. The latter must be appointed by a court, and his or her duties are limited to winding up the estate of a decedent and so are implicitly temporary in duration. For different reasons, an *officer* or *director* of a corporation is a fiduciary, but not a trustee. So also with a guardian or with a receiver of the property of an insolvent person or corporation. In several of these instances, the fiduciary doesn't take title to the property involved, whereas a trustee is regarded as taking the legal title to the trust estate.

A *bailee* of personal property owes certain duties to the bailor, but takes only possession of the property, not legal title, and is not a trustee. Similarly, an *agent* is not a trustee; but the distinction between an agent who is authorized to transfer title to property and a trustee is sometimes not easy to draw.

A conveyance of property upon a *condition subsequent* or subject to a *lien* or an *equitable charge* does not create a trust. The most difficult problem to resolve in a variety of circumstances involves the distinction between trust law and certain aspects of the law of contract, specifically the distinction between a trust and a *debt* or between a trust and a *third-party-beneficiary* contract.

Sample Revocable Inter Vivos Trust

The following trust instrument is reproduced here to give you some idea of what a modern trust instrument looks like. The instrument suggests especially (a) how a trust can be used to make provision for successive generations, (b) the possibility of giving some flexibility to the dispositions through the use of powers, and (c) the amount of detail commonly found in the administrative provisions of a trust instrument.

This trust agreement is made this _____ day of _____, 19_, between JOHN DOE, the Grantor, and OLD FAITHFUL TRUST COMPANY OF ____, as Trustee.

The Grantor hereby transfers to the trustee the property described in the attached schedule. Such property, and any other property that may be received by the trustee, shall be held and disposed of upon the following trusts:

ARTICLE I

The Grantor may by signed instruments delivered to the trustee revoke the trusts hereunder in whole or in part or amend this agreement from time to time in any manner. No amendment changing the powers or duties of the trustee shall be effective unless approved in writing by the trustee.

ARTICLE II

The trustee shall pay all the net income of the trust estate, and such portions of the principal as the Grantor from time to time directs in writing, to the Grantor, or otherwise as he directs in writing, during his life. In addition, the trustee may in its discretion pay to the Grantor, or use for his benefit, such portions or all of the principal of the trust estate as the trustee determines to be required for the Grantor's support and comfort, or for any other purpose which the trustee determines to be to his best interests.

ARTICLE III

After the Grantor's death the trustee shall hold and dispose of the trust estate as follows:

1. (a) The trustee shall pay all the net income of the trust estate to MARY DOE, wife of the Grantor, during her life, beginning as of the date of the Grantor's death and payable at least as often as quarter-annually. Unproductive property shall not be held as

an asset of the trust estate for more than a reasonable time during the life of the Grantor's said wife without her consent.

(b) Whenever the trustee determines that the income of the Grantor's said wife from all sources known to the trustee is not sufficient for her reasonable support and comfort, the trustee shall pay to her, or use for her benefit, so much of the principal of the trust estate as the trustee determines to be required for those purposes.

2. Upon the death of the Grantor's said wife the trustee shall distribute the trust estate to such person or persons, or the estate of the Grantor's said wife, upon such conditions and estates, in trust or otherwise, in such manner and at such time or times as she appoints and directs by will specifically referring to this power of appointment.

3. In default of appointment by the Grantor's wife as aforesaid the trustee shall upon her death, or if she does not survive the Grantor the trustee shall upon the Grantor's death, divide the trust estate into equal funds, one for each child of the Grantor then living and one for the then-living descendants of each child of the Grantor then deceased. Each such fund shall be held and administered as a separate trust and shall be held and disposed of as follows:

(a) While any child of the Grantor is under the age of twenty-one years, the trustee shall use so much of the income of his or her fund for his or her reasonable support, comfort and education as the trustee determines to be required for those purposes. After he or she attains that age, the trustee shall pay all the current net income of his or her fund to him or her.

(b) Whenever the trustee determines that the income of any child of the Grantor from all sources known to the trustee is not sufficient for his or her reasonable support, comfort and education, the trustee shall pay to him or her, or use for his or her benefit, so much of the principal of his or her fund as the trustee determines to be required for those purposes.

(c) When any child of the Grantor shall have attained the age of twenty-five years, the trustee shall distribute to him or her one-third of the principal of his or her fund as constituted at the time of distribution. When he or she shall have attained the age of thirty years, the trustee shall further distribute to him or her one-half of the remaining principal of his or her fund as constituted at the time of distribution. When he or she shall have attained the age of thirty-five years, the trustee shall further distribute to him or her the balance of his or her fund.

(d) Upon the death of any child of the Grantor before he or she becomes entitled to receive the entire principal of his or her fund, the trustee shall distribute his or her fund, or any remaining portion of it, to, or in trust for the benefit of, such person or persons among the Grantor's descendants and their spouses, including such child's own spouse, upon such conditions and estates, in such manner and at such time or times as he or she appoints and directs by will specifically referring to this power of appointment, and in default of such appointment, to his or her descendants then living, by representation, or if there is no descendant of his or her then living, to the Grantor's descendants then living, by representation; provided that if the trustee is then holding another fund or portion hereunder for the primary benefit of any such descendant, his or her share shall be added to and commingled with such other fund or portion and held, or partly held and partly distributed, as if it had been an original part thereof.

(e) The trustee shall distribute each fund set aside for the descendants of a deceased child of the Grantor to such descendants, by representation.

4. Notwithstanding anything in this instrument to the contrary, if any descendant of a deceased child of the Grantor is under the age of twenty-one years when the trustee is directed in the foregoing provisions of this instrument to distribute to him or her any portion of the principal of the trust property, his or her portion shall immediately vest in interest in him or her indefeasibly, but the trustee may in its discretion withhold possession of it and hold it in trust for his or her benefit until he or she attains that age. In the meantime, the trustee shall use so much of the income and principal for his or her reasonable support, comfort, and education as the trustee determines to be required for those purposes.

ARTICLE IV

1. If at any time any person to whom the trustee is directed in this instrument to pay any income is under legal disability or is in the opinion of the trustee incapable of properly managing his or her affairs, the trustee may use so much of such income for his or her support and comfort as the trustee determines to be required for the purposes.

2. The trustee either may expend directly any income or principal that it is authorized in this instrument to use for the benefit of any person, or may pay it over to him or her or for his or her use to his or her parent or guardian, or to any person with whom he or she is residing, without responsibility for its expenditure. The trustee shall withhold any such income not so used, and at its discretion add it to principal; provided that during the life of the Grantor's wife the trustee shall in any event pay all the net income of the trust estate to her or use it for her benefit.

3. No interest of any beneficiary in the income or principal of this trust shall be assignable in anticipation of payment or be liable in any way for the beneficiary's debts or obligations and shall not be subject to attachment.

4. Upon the death of my wife, any income accrued or undistributed shall be paid to her estate; upon the death of any other beneficiary, any income accrued or undistributed shall be held and accounted for, or distributed, in the same manner as if it had been income accrued and received after such beneficiary's death.

5. Notwithstanding anything herein to the contrary, the trusts hereunder shall terminate not later than twenty-one years after the death of the last survivor of the Grantor's wife and his descendants living at the Grantor's death, at the end of which period the trustee shall distribute each remaining portion of the trust property to the beneficiaries, at that time, of the income thereof, and in the proportions in which they are beneficiaries of such income.

ARTICLE V

1. The trustee shall have the following powers with respect to each trust hereunder, to be exercised as the trustee in its discretion determines to be to the best interests of the beneficiaries:

(a) Subject to Article III, paragraph 1(a), to retain any property transferred, devised, or bequeathed to the trustee, or any undivided interest therein, regardless of any lack of diversification, risk, or non-productivity;

(b) To invest and reinvest the trust estate in any property or undivided interests therein, wherever located, including bonds, notes (secured or unsecured), stocks of corporations, real estate, or any interest therein, and interests in trusts including common trust funds, without being limited by any statute or rule of law concerning investments by trustees;

(c) To sell any trust property, for cash or on credit, at public or private sale; to exchange any trust property for other property; to grant options to purchase or acquire any trust property; and to determine the prices and terms of sales, exchanges, and options;

(d) To execute leases and sub-leases for terms as long as two hundred years, even though such terms may extend beyond the termination of the trust; to subdivide or improve real estate and tear down or alter improvements; to grant easements, give consents, and make contracts relating to real estate or its use; and to release or dedicate any interest in real estate;

(e) To borrow money and to mortgage or pledge any trust property;

(f) To take any action with respect to conserving or realizing upon the value of any trust property, and with respect to foreclosures, reorganizations, or other changes affecting the trust property; to collect, pay, contest, compromise, or abandon demands of or against the trust estate, wherever situated; and to execute contracts, notes, conveyances, and other instruments containing covenants and warranties binding upon and creating a charge against the trust estate, and containing provisions excluding personal liability;

(g) To keep any property in the name of a nominee with or without disclosure of any fiduciary relationship;

(h) To employ agents, attorneys, auditors, depositaries, and proxies, with or without discretionary powers;

(i) To determine the manner of ascertainment of income and principal, and the apportionment between income and principal of all receipts and disbursements, and to select an annual accounting period;

(j) To receive additional property from any source and add it to and commingle it with the trust estate;

(k) To enter into any transaction authorized by this Article with trustees or legal representatives of any other trust or estate in which any beneficiary hereunder has any beneficial interest, even though any such trustee or legal representative is also trustee hereunder;

(l) To make any distribution or division of the trust property in cash or in kind or both, and to allot different kinds or disproportionate shares of property or undivided interests in property among the beneficiaries or portions, and to determine the value of any such property; and to continue to exercise any powers and discretion herein given for a reasonable period after the termination of the trust, but only for so long as no rule of law relating to perpetuities would be violated.

2. To the extent that any such requirements can legally be waived, no trustee shall ever be required to give any bond as trustee or qualify before, be appointed by, or in the absence of breach of trust account to any court, or obtain the order or approval of any court in the exercise of any power or discretion herein given. No person paying

money or delivering any property to any trustee shall be required to see to its application.

3. Any trustee shall be entitled to reasonable compensation for services in administering and distributing the trust property, and to reimbursement for expenses.

ARTICLE VI

1. Any trustee may resign at any time by giving written notice, specifying the effective date of such resignation, to the beneficiaries, at the time of giving notice, of the current income of the trust property.

2. If any trustee at any time resigns or is unable to act, another corporation authorized under the law of any State or of the United States to administer trusts may be appointed as successor trustee, by an instrument delivered to such successor and signed by the beneficiaries, at the time of such appointment, of at least two-thirds of the current income of the trust property, and such beneficiaries may direct the successor trustee to accept the accounts of any former trustee, in which event the successor trustee shall have no responsibility thereof.

3. Every successor trustee shall have all the title, powers, and discretion herein given the trustee, without any act of conveyance or transfer.

4. The guardian or conservator of the estate of a beneficiary under legal disability, or the parents or surviving parent of a minor beneficiary for whose estate no guardian has been appointed, may act for such beneficiary in making any appointment and giving any direction under this Article.

5. If another corporation succeeds to the trust business of any corporate trustee hereunder, such successor shall become trustee hereunder.

ARTICLE VII

After the Grantor's death, the trustee may in its discretion make loans, with or without security, to the executor or administrator of the Grantor's estate, purchase from such executor or administrator, at such value as may be determined by the trustee, any property constituting part or all of the Grantor's estate, and, subject to Article III, paragraph 1(a), retain all or any part of such property regardless of risk, unproductivity, or lack of diversification.

IN WITNESS WHEREOF, the parties hereto have signed and sealed this instrument on the date first above written.

____________________(Seal)
Grantor

OLD FAITHFUL TRUST
COMPANY OF ________

By ________________
President

Attest________________
Trust Officer

Constructive Trusts/Resulting Trusts. When we speak of the estate-planning uses of trusts, we are referring to express trusts. Express trusts are intentionally created for the ongoing management of the trust property, whether for private or charitable beneficiaries or for a combination of the two. Express trusts persist over some period of time; in some cases, they persist over a substantial period of time.

We have already mentioned two other trust categories—the constructive trust and the resulting trust. Neither type is truly a "trust," in the sense of requiring ongoing management of trust property. The conventional classification of trusts that emerged in the late nineteenth century identified these as trusts that arise by operation of law rather than by private intention. Some legal scholars, though, who wanted to avoid associating either trust type with collective interference with private intention, attacked this classification scheme. Costigan argued that resulting trusts were "implied in fact," while constructive trusts were "fraud-rectifying." See George P. Costigan, Jr., The Classification of Trusts as Express, Resulting, and Constructive, 27 Harv. L. Rev. 437 (1914).

Constructive trusts. The constructive trust is not a trust at all, but a remedy. It is closely associated with quasi contract, which likewise is not a contract but a remedy. In fact, quasi contract is the law's principal answer to unjust enrichment; constructive trust is equity's principal answer. George Palmer gives the following sketch of this story, at the beginning of his great treatise on restitution (Palmer on Restitution):

> § *1.1. The Scope of Restitution*. It has been traditional to regard tort and contract as the two principal sources of civil liability at common law, although liability arising out of a fiduciary relationship has developed largely outside these two great categories. There is another category that must be separated from all of these; this is liability based in unjust enrichment. In particularized form this has been a part of our law from an early time, but it has been slow to emerge as a general theory. In present American law, however, the idea of unjust enrichment has been generally accepted and widely applied.
>
> Restitution based upon unjust enrichment cuts across many branches of the law, including contract, tort, and fiduciary relationship, but it also occupies much territory that is its sole preserve . . . .
>
> For a long time restitution developed more or less independently at law and in equity. If the defendant stole the plaintiff's goods and sold them, the plaintiff was given a money judgment in the amount of the proceeds in an action at law. This has come to be known as "quasi contract," although the broader term "restitution" is gaining general acceptance. The action developed out of the common-law action of assumpsit, which was used initially to recover for breach of an express contract. There was of course no express contract by which the thief agreed to pay the proceeds to the plaintiff, but the court treated the situation as though there were for the purpose of making available the writ of assumpsit. If the thief used the proceeds to buy land, courts exercising equity power in this country will order him

> or her to transfer title to the land to the plaintiff through a remedy almost universally known as constructive trust, though it also can be called specific restitution. The court treats the defendant as though he were a trustee of the land for the benefit of the plaintiff when in fact there was no express trust, any more than there was an express contract in the first action.
>
> The link that connects these two judgments is the idea of unjust enrichment, just as it is the connecting link in an unending variety of cases in which relief is given. Today, anything like a whole view of the law of restitution must take into account both law and equity . . . .
>
> The term "restitution" . . . is not wholly apt since it suggests restoration to the successful party of some benefit obtained from him or her. Usually this will be the case where relief is given, but by no means always. There are cases in which the successful party obtains restitution of something he did not have before, for example a benefit received by the defendant from a third person which justly should go to the plaintiff.

Resulting trusts. At several points in the succeeding materials, we will also encounter one kind of resulting trust, that is, the kind of "trust" that arises when an express trust fails or doesn't completely dispose of the trust property. Like the constructive trust, the resulting trust is no trust at all in the sense of prescribing ongoing management of the property. It is, rather, a property interest analogous to the reversion retained by a grantor who conveys one or more legal interests in property for life or for years without creating a remainder thereafter. In other words, a reversion is a legal interest, but the beneficial interest under a resulting trust is equitable, since a resulting trust arises from a conveyance of the legal title in fee simple, but without disposing of the complete beneficial interest.

Another kind of resulting trust is the so-called "purchase-money" resulting trust. The "purchase-money" resulting trust further demonstrates the versatility of the "trust" idea or label, but it is not part of this course. The basic principle is that where property is transferred to one person and the purchase price is paid by another person, a resulting trust presumptively arises in favor of the person who pays the purchase price. For further elaboration of the purchase-money resulting trust, see Restatement 3d of Trusts § 9; Scott on Trusts §§ 440-60.

External References. Gregory S. Alexander, The Transformation of Trusts as a Legal Category, 1800-1914, 5 Law & Hist. Rev. 303 (1987); A.I. Ogus, The Trust As a Governance Structure, 36 U. Toronto L.J. 186 (1986).

PART B. FORMATION OF A TRUST

Statutory References: *UTC §§ 401-404*

Modern legal theory defines the trust form in terms of discrete "elements." It is commonly said that in order for any trust to exist there must be a specific trust res (property), a trustee, identifiable beneficiaries, and specific trust intent. Together, these elements constitute the formal model of the trust. Although aspects of these elements certainly were evident in pre-nineteenth century Equity practice, it wasn't until the nineteenth century that English and American legal thought abstracted them into constituents of a formal model. As we will see, challenges to this trust model have been made in recent years. These challenges have sought to make the distinction between the trust and other legal forms for disposing of property, such as gift, promise, and agency, less important.

1. The Trust As A Property Arrangement

Trust law requires that there be an identifiable trust property (sometimes called the trust *res*). See Restatement 3d of Trusts § 2, comment f; §§ 3, 10, 40. The requirement of trust property is sometimes codified, as in the Uniform Trust Code and in the recent California and Texas codifications of trust law. See UTC § 401; Cal. Prob. Code § 15202; Tex. Prop. Code § 112.005. Any legally recognized property interest that is transferable can be the subject of a trust. See Restatement 3d of Trusts § 40. In most trusts, the requirement of a trust *res* presents no difficulties, but occasionally it does, as the *Brainard* case, below, illustrates. Relevant to *Brainard* is § 41 of the Restatement 3d of Trusts, which provides:

> § *41. Expectancies; Nonexistent Property Interests.* An expectation or hope of receiving property in the future, or an interest that has not come into existence or has ceased to exist, cannot be held in trust.

Brainard v. Commissioner

91 F.2d 880 (7th Cir. 1937)

SPARKS, J. This petition for review involves income taxes for the year 1928. The question presented is whether under the circumstances set forth in the findings of the Board of Tax Appeals, the taxpayer created a valid trust, the income of which was taxable to the beneficiaries under section 162 of the Revenue Act of 1928.[22]

---

22. § 162. The net income of the estate or trust shall be computed in the same manner and on the same basis as in the case of an individual, except that— . . .

The facts as found by the Board of Tax Appeals are substantially as follows: In December, 1927, the taxpayer, having decided that conditions were favorable, contemplated trading in the stock market during 1928. He consulted a lawyer and was advised that it was possible for him to trade in trust for his children and other members of his family. Taxpayer thereupon discussed the matter with his wife and mother, and stated to them that he declared a trust of his stock trading during 1928 for the benefit of his family upon certain terms and conditions. Taxpayer agreed to assume personally any losses resulting from the venture, and to distribute the profits, if any, in equal shares to his wife, mother, and two minor children after deducting a reasonable compensation for his services. During 1928 taxpayer carried on the trading operations contemplated and at the end of the year determined his compensation at slightly less than $10,000, which he reported in his income tax return for that year. The profits remaining were then divided in approximately equal shares among the members of his family, and the amounts were reported in their respective tax returns for 1928. The amounts allocated to the beneficiaries were credited to them on taxpayer's books, but they did not receive the cash, except taxpayer's mother, to a small extent.

In addition to these findings the record discloses that taxpayer's two children were one and three years of age. Upon these facts the Board held that the income in controversy was taxable to the petitioner as a part of his gross income for 1928, and decided that there was a deficiency. It is here sought to review that decision.

In the determination of the questions here raised it is necessary to consider the nature of the trust, if any, that is said to have been created by the circumstances hereinbefore recited. It is clear that the taxpayer, at the time of his declaration, had no property interest in "profits in stock trading in 1928, if any," because there were none in existence at that time. Indeed it is not disclosed that the declarer at that time owned any stock.[23] It is obvious,

---

(b) There shall be allowed as an additional deduction in computing the net income of the estate or trust the amount of the income of the estate or trust for its taxable year which is to be distributed currently by the fiduciary to the beneficiaries, and the amount of the income collected by a guardian of an infant which is to be held or distributed as the court may direct, but the amount so allowed as a deduction shall be included in computing the net income of the beneficiaries whether distributed to them or not.

[Section 162, as amended in certain particulars, now appears as IRC § 661. Eds.]

23. If the "declarer" had owned stock in December, 1927, and had then declared himself trustee of that stock, a trust of that stock would clearly have arisen and any profits realized in trading that stock during 1928 would clearly have been part of the corpus of that trust. Even so, the Internal Revenue Code now contains provisions not part of the Code in the 1920's that would likely make the trust income (probably including realized capital gains) taxable to the transferor or at the transferor's rate. See IRC §§ 644, 671-77. Eds.

therefore, that the taxpayer based his declaration of trust upon an interest which at that time had not come into existence and in which no one had a present interest. In the Restatement of the Law of Trusts, vol. 1, § 75, it is said that an interest which has not come into existence or which has ceased to exist can not be held in trust. It is there further said:

> A person can, it is true, make a contract binding himself to create a trust of an interest if he should thereafter acquire it; but such an agreement is not binding as a contract unless the requirements of the law of Contracts are complied with . . .
>
> Thus, if a person gratuitously declares himself trustee of such shares as he may thereafter acquire in a corporation not yet organized, no trust is created. The result is the same where instead of declaring himself trustee, he purports to transfer to another as trustee such shares as he may thereafter acquire in a corporation not yet organized. In such a case there is at most a gratuitous undertaking to create a trust in the future, and such an undertaking is not binding as a contract for lack of consideration . . .
>
> If a person purports to declare himself trustee of an interest not in existence, or if he purports to transfer such an interest to another in trust, he is liable as upon a contract to create a trust if, but only if, the requirements of the law of Contracts are complied with.

See, also, Restatement, § 30b; Bogert, Trusts and Trustees, vol. 1, § 112. In 42 Harvard Law Review 561, it is said:

> With logical consistency, the courts have uniformly held that an expectancy cannot be the subject matter of a trust and that an attempted creation, being merely a promise to transfer property in the future, is invalid unless supported by consideration.

Citing Lehigh Valley R. R. Co. v. Woodring, 116 Pa. 513, 9 A. 58. Hence, it is obvious under the facts here presented that taxpayer's declaration amounted to nothing more than a promise to create a trust in the future, and its binding force must be determined by the requirements of the law of contracts.

It is elementary that an executory contract, in order to be enforceable, must be based upon a valuable consideration. Here there was none. The declaration was gratuitous. If we assume that it was based on love and affection that would add nothing to its enforceability, for love and affection, though a sufficient consideration for an executed conveyance, is not a sufficient consideration for a promise.

What has been said, however, does not mean that the taxpayer had no right to carry out his declaration after the subject matter had come into existence, even though there were no consideration. This he did and the trust thereby became effective, after which it was enforceable by the beneficiaries.

The questions with which we are concerned are at what times did the respective earnings which constitute the trust fund come into existence, and at what times did the trust attach to them. It is obvious that the respective profits came into existence when and if such stocks were sold at a profit in 1928. Did they come into existence impressed with the trust, or was there any period of time intervening between the time they came into existence and the time the trust attached? If there were such intervening time, then during that time the taxpayer must be considered as the sole owner of the profits and they were properly taxed to him as a part of his income.

It is said in the Restatement of the Law of Trusts, § 75c:

> If a person purports to declare himself trustee of an interest not in existence or if he purports to transfer such an interest to another in trust, no trust arises even when the interest comes into existence in the absence of a manifestation of intention at that time.

This we think is especially applicable where, as here, there was no consideration for the declaration. It is further stated, however, in the Restatement, § 26k:

> If a person manifests an intention to become trustee at a subsequent time, his conduct at that subsequent time considered in connection with his original manifestation may be a sufficient manifestation of intention at that subsequent time to create a trust . . . the act of acquiring the property coupled with the earlier declaration of trust *may be* a sufficient manifestation of an intention to create a trust at the time of the acquisition of the property. (Our italics, here and hereafter.)

In subsection 1 it is said " . . . Mere silence, however, ordinarily will not be such a manifestation. Whether silence is or is not such a manifestation is a question of interpretation." In such interpretation, subsection m is quite pertinent and controlling:

> A promise to create a trust in the future is *enforceable*, if . . . the requirements for an enforceable contract are complied with. Whether a promise to transfer property in trust or to become trustee creates in the promisee a right to recover damages for breach of the promise, and whether such a promise is specifically enforceable, are determined by the law governing contracts. Thus, if the owner of property transfers the property in trust and agrees to pay a sum of money to the trustee to be held upon the same trust, he is not liable for failing to pay the money if the promise was made gratuitously . . . but if the promise was made for consideration . . . the promisor is liable thereon. So also, a promise to create a trust of property if thereafter acquired by the promisor imposes no liability upon the promisor if the promise was gratuitous . . . .

These matters are discussed by Mr. Bogert in his work on Trusts and Trustees, vol. 1, § 112, and we think there is no contrariety of opinion between his conclusions and those of the Restatement. In speaking of the attitudes of courts of law and equity, he says:

> Courts of *law* treat transactions which purport to be present transfers, . . . or trusts of interests in future things as not amounting to *contracts* and as void, with some rare exceptions (referring to potential possession) . . . *Equity* has taken a different attitude toward present efforts to create property interests in future things. It has reasoned that such a transaction could not have been intended to operate as a present transfer because of the inherent impossibility of such an effect. The parties must therefore have expected the only other possible operative result, namely, that there should arise a *contract* to create property interests in the future, by way of absolute transfer, mortgage, trust, or what not . . . Viewed as a *contract* to create property interests in the future, when the things involved are acquired, equity found that in the older common law there was no remedy at all. The law did not recognize the existence of such a *contract*. There was more than inadequacy of remedy; there was total absence of remedy at law. Equity therefore took the position that it would give specific performance or its equivalent. When the things came into existence and into the hands of the intended transferor, they would at once be deemed transferred by way of absolute deed, mortgage, or trust. In other words . . . equity would treat the trust as immediately taking effect and an equitable interest as then passing to the cestui.

For instance, he says:

> The employee under an existing contract has no present interest in wages to be earned. Such right to receive wages when later earned is a future chose in action. An attempted present conveyance or trust of it can only operate as a *contract* to transfer it when and if acquired, which equity will turn into a perfected transfer when the wages are due.

It is obvious that the author's conclusions presuppose . . . the existence of a valid and enforceable contract between the declarer and the beneficiary. Otherwise the law of contracts would be violated, and equity would be in the attitude of establishing a trust upon an invalid and unenforceable contract, or rather upon no contract at all. The authorities cited by the author in support of his last quoted statement involve valid and enforceable contracts which were based on valuable considerations . . . .

From what has been said we are convinced that appellant's profits in question were not impressed with a trust when they first came into existence. The Board was obviously of the impression that the trust first attached when appellant credited them to the beneficiaries on his books of account. This act, it seems to us, constituted his first subsequent expression of intention to become a trustee of the fund referred to in his original and gratuitous declaration. Prior to that time we think it is clear that the declaration could not have been enforced against him, and that his mere silence with respect thereto should not be considered as an expression of his intention to establish a trust at a time earlier than the credits. . . .

The order of the Board is affirmed.

Notes and Questions

1. Did the taxpayer's December 1927 declaration legally obligate him to restate his intent to transfer his 1928 stock market profits into the trust?

2. *When Is an Inter Vivos Trust Created?* The Restatement 3d of Trusts provides that "[an inter vivos] trust may be created by an owner's inter vivos *transfer* of property to another person as trustee . . . ." Restatement 3d of Trusts § 10, comment d (emphasis added). Comment e, however, provides that "[i]f the owner of property declares himself or herself trustee . . . , a trust is created, even though there is no transfer of the title to the trust property to another . . . ." Comment e then provides:

> *e. Declaration of trust.* . . . In this Restatement, the declaration of trust is generally considered to be an additional means of creating a trust inter vivos, and is thus an exception to or substitute for the usual requirement that there be a transfer of the trust property to the trustee. Conceptually, however, it is not inappropriate for the declaration of trust to be viewed as a form of "transfer" from the property owner individually to the property owner in a representative capacity. Accordingly, regardless of which of these views may be preferred in a particular jurisdiction, an owner of property may create a trust by executing an instrument worded as a transfer of the property to himself or herself as trustee. . . .
>
> In addition, except as precluded by statute, a trust may be established by the settlor's signing of an instrument that begins, essentially, "I hereby declare myself trustee of the property listed in Schedule A attached hereto" or "O, as settlor, hereby transfers to O, as trustee, the property listed in the attached Schedule A," even though in either case the document is not supported at the time of execution, or by the time of the settlor's death or incompetency, by other acts or other documents of transfer or title.

See also UTC § 401; Estate of Heggstad, 20 Cal. Rptr. 2d 443 (Cal. Ct. App. 1993); Taliaferro v. Taliaferro, 921 P.2d 803 (Kan. 1996).

In Bibby v. Comm'r, 44 T.C. 638 (1965), C.O. Bibby and his wife, residents of Texas, executed a trust instrument on September 3, 1957, naming themselves as trustees and granting his father the right to the income for a term of "ten years and one day from the date of execution hereof . . . ." Upon termination, the corpus was to be returned to the settlor. Sometime after the date of execution, C.O. Bibby executed a warranty deed conveying a farm to the trustees of the trust. The deed was recorded on August 20, 1958. There being no indication in the record that the deed was delivered to the trustees before its recordation, the court held that the trust was created on August 20, 1958. The court said:

> It is an elementary principle of trust law that in order for a trust to exist, it must have a res. In the instant case no res was put into the trust at the time the trust agreement was signed.[24]

Similarly, a New York statute requires "recordation of the deed" or "completion of registration of the asset in the name of the trust or trustee" for self-declared trusts of assets that are "capable of registration." N.Y. Est. Powers & Trust Law § 7-1.18 (b).

3. *Assignment of Future Earnings*. Under existing law, a person can validly assign future earnings from an existing contract. Suppose the taxpayer in *Brainard* had introduced evidence that at the time of his declaration he owned sufficient capital to engage in stock trading. Would (or should) the result change? If so, then, did Brainard lose because of a failure of proof? Assuming that Brainard owned sufficient capital, how could his lawyer have met the trust *res* requirement?

4. *Expectancies*. That mere expectancies cannot be the subject of a trusts is well-settled. See Restatement 3d of Trusts § 41. The question is, what *is* an "expectancy"?

The interests of presumptive heirs or devisees of a living person traditionally have been characterized as "expectancies" and not as property. See Simes & Smith on Future Interests § 391. Nevertheless, historically, Equity courts enforced expectancy assignments but only if "value" was given, by which the courts meant that they retained the power to review the fairness of the exchange. Consideration sufficient to support a contract was not by itself sufficient. Quite commonly, the consideration that expectant heirs received for their birthright was insubstantial, the equivalent of the pottage of lentils for which Esau sold his birthright to his brother Jacob, according to Genesis (Genesis 25: 29-34).

Dawson gives the following explanation of Chancery decisions during the formative period:

---

24. Under IRC § 673 as it then existed (the provision has since been repealed), the grantor of a trust in which the grantor retained a reversionary interest was taxed on the income if the reversionary interest was to take effect in possession or enjoyment within 10 years of its creation. Consequently, since the Bibby trust was to terminate 10 years and 1 day after the trust *instrument* was executed, the duration of the trust itself was less than 10 years. As a result the income of the trust was taxed to C.O. Bibby, even though it was paid to his father.

> The need for special protection arose from prevailing standards of fashionable conduct, which dictated a high level of conspicuous expenditure. It was honorable to maintain a gentlemanly extravagance, even where current income did not suffice; all blame was reserved for those hangers-on of polite society who pandered to extravagance by supplying it with the necessary means. Their special prey was the expectant heir or reversioner, in urgent need of ready cash but precluded from borrowing at moderate rates of interest by the uncertainty of his prospects. The Chancellors of the late seventeenth and eighteenth centuries imposed a firm control on traffic with such persons. In the Chancery reports they published their determination to prevent dispersal of family estates through improvident sales by their prospective owners. The motive was clear—to preserve for a dominant class the economic resources on which its prestige and power depended.

John P. Dawson, Economic Duress—An Essay in Perspective, 45 Mich. L. Rev. 253, 268 (1947).

Quite apart from the protection given the expectant heir or devisee against selling an expectancy for a "mess of pottage," equity did not then give specific performance of a contract under seal (putting aside the special case of an option to purchase). See Jefferys v. Jefferys, Cr. & Ph. 138, 41 Eng. Rep. 443 (Ch. 1841).

Courts have held that the expectancy of an heir can be *released* voluntarily for valuable consideration, with the result that the heir is excluded from participation as heir in the ancestor's intestate estate. See Martin v. Smith, 404 So.2d 341 (Ala. 1981).

5. *Debts as Trust Property*. Any legally recognized property interest or contract right that is transferrable can be the subject of a trust. If A has a legally enforceable claim against B, A can create a trust of that debt, either by declaration of a trust or by transfer. However, if B declares that he or she holds the debt he or she owes to A in trust for A, no trust is created. B is a debtor, and a debtor cannot be a trustee of his or her own debt. Why might it matter whether B is treated as a debtor or a trustee? See Scott on Trusts § 12.

6. *Uncashed Checks as Trust Property*. Suppose that prior to her death, Susan delivered to her daughter, Emily, a check for $20,000, designating on the check that it was to be held in trust for Emily's minor child. Before Emily was able to cash the check, Susan died. Was a trust created? Is there a legally recognized property interest that can serve as the subject matter of the trust? Compare Estate of Bolton, 444 N.W.2d 482 (Iowa 1989) (holding that an uncashed check is not a completed gift) with Sinclair v. Fleischman, 773 P.2d 101 (Wash. Ct. App. 1989) (holding that an uncashed check constituted a completed gift because it was legally delivered by the donor and accepted by the donee prior to the donor's death).

In Hieber v. Uptown Nat'l Bank of Chicago, 557 N.E.2d 408 (Ill. App. Ct. 1990), the decedent had executed an inter vivos trust instrument naming Hieber as trustee and beneficiary. To fund the trust decedent also executed bank instruments enabling Hieber, who held decedent's power of attorney, to withdraw funds from decedent's bank account. Shortly thereafter, decedent died, and Hieber presented the bank instruments to the bank later the same day. The bank refused the instrument because of the decedent's death. The court held that no trust was created because there was no trust property. The bank instruments did not survive the decedent's death. Neither did the power of attorney since it was coupled with the trust.

Whether gifts by check are complete when the donor dies before the check is cashed has been a problem for federal estate tax purposes. The federal courts, relying on applicable state law, have held that the gift is not complete and therefore that the cash represented by the check is includable in the decedent-donor's gross estate under IRC § 2033. Rosano v. U.S., 245 F.3d 212 (2d Cir. 2001); Estate of Owen v. Commissioner, 104 T.C. 498 (1995); Estate of Dillingham v. Commissioner, 90-1 USTC ¶60,021 (10th Cir. 1990); Estate of Gagliardi v. Commissioner, 89 T.C. 1207 (1987). But see Metzger v. Comm'r, 38 F.3d 118 (4th Cir. 1994) (holding that relation-back doctrine applies where no uncertainty of donor's intent exists and, since donor was still alive, there is no danger of estate tax avoidance). In Estate of Newman, 99-2 USTC ¶60,358 (D.C. Cir. 1999), the Tax Court distinguished *Metzger* on the ground that in the instant case the donor was dead at the time the check, which her attorney-in-fact had drawn on her account, was presented and paid by the bank.

Where the check was to a charity, the Tax Court has held that the gift became complete upon the delivery of the check. See Estate of Belcher v. Commissioner, 83 T.C. 227 (1984). Under state law, charitable pledges if relied upon by the charity are enforceable even though not supported by consideration. See, e.g., King v. Trustees of Boston University, 647 N.E.2d 1196 (Mass. 1995).

7. *Relaxation of the Trust Res Requirement?* Should the trust property requirement be eliminated or at least be weakened where there is clear evidence of donative intent? Suppose that a person declares that she holds "a checking/savings account" in a specified bank trust and that in fact she has four separate accounts in the named bank. Should a trust be found to exist in any or all or the accounts? In Wilkerson v. McClary, 647 S.W.2d 79 (Tex. Ct. App. 1983), the court held that no trust existed because the trust *res* was insufficiently identified. For a criticism of the decision, see Jane B. Baron, The Trust Res and Donative Intent, 61 Tul. L. Rev. 45 (1986).

2. *Trust Purposes*

Statutory Reference: *UTC §§ 105(b)(3), 404*

Restatement 3d of Trusts

§ *27. Purposes for Which a Trust Can Be Created*

(1) Subject to the rules of §§ 28 and 29, a trust may be created for charitable purposes . . . or for private purposes, or for a combination of charitable and private purposes.

(2) Subject to the special rules in §§ 46 and 47 [dealing with indefinite beneficiaries and trusts for noncharitable purposes], a private trust, its terms, and its administration must be for the benefit of its beneficiaries, who must be identified or ascertainable as provided in § 44.

§ *28. General Rule Concerning Unlawful Purposes.* An intended trust or a trust provision is invalid if its purpose or performance is unlawful.

§ *29. Perpetuities and Provisions Against Public Policy.* Even though the performance of a trust or trust provision does not involve the commission of a criminal or tortious act by the trustee (§ 28), a provision in the terms of a trust is invalid if implementation of the provision would be (a) a violation of rules relating to perpetuities or (b) otherwise contrary to public policy.

3. *Intent to Create a Trust*

Restatement 3d of Trusts

§ *13. Intention to Create Trust.* A trust is created only if the settlor properly manifests an intention to create a trust relationship.

§ *14. Notice and Acceptance Not Required to Create Trust.* A trust can be created without notice to or acceptance by any beneficiary or trustee.[25]

A trust is a *property* arrangement, requiring a *res* as its subject. Normally, the property forming the trust res is owned outright by the settlor. The trust is created when the ownership of that property is divided into its legal and

25. UTC § 813(b), however, provides that a trustee "within 60 days after accepting a trusteeship, shall notify the qualified beneficiaries of the acceptance and of the trustee's name, address, and telephone number" and "within 60 days after the date the trustee acquires knowledge of the creation of an irrevocable trust, or the date the trustee acquires knowledge that a formerly revocable trust has become irrevocable, whether by the death of the settlor or otherwise, shall notify the qualified beneficiaries of the trust's existence, of the identity of the settlor or settlors, of the right to request a copy of the trust instrument, and of the right to a trustee's report . . . ." Eds.

equitable portions, with the legal-title portion being transferred to the trustee (or, in the case of a self-declared trust, being retained by the settlor as trustee) and the equitable-title portion being transferred to (and being further subdivided among) the beneficiaries.

The transfer of the equitable title to the beneficiaries via a self-declared trust doesn't require the same formalities as would be required for making an outright gift, such as physical, constructive, or symbolic delivery of the subject matter[26] or delivery of a document of transfer or some manifestation that the document is to be presently effective.[27] See UTC §§ 401(2), 402(a)(2). As the court said in Matter of Brown, 169 N.E. 612 (N.Y. 1930):

> [D]elivery is not necessary to constitute a valid trust. While a transfer of the property to a trustee for the purposes of the settlement may be the surest way to create a trust, yet the same result will be accomplished if the owner declares that he himself holds the property in trust for the person designated, and this trust may be created either in writing or, if relating to personal property, by parol. The declaration need not be made to the beneficiary, nor the writing given to him; in fact, his ignorance of the trust is immaterial. There must be proof of a declaration of trust in writing to pass real property, but the declaration varies with the circumstances of each case; it may be contained in a letter, or as here by formal witnessed statement. A declaration implies an announcement of an act performed, not a mere intention, and in most instances to another party. However, a writing formally creating a trust, kept by the donor without delivery to any one, under such circumstances and conditions as to show that a trust was declared, created and intended, will be given effect as such by the courts.

The near absence of formality required to confer upon (transfer to) others the equitable interest in property, making them trust beneficiaries, has led to pressure to treat transactions that would otherwise fail, such as imperfect gifts, as self-declared trusts. This was the argument made, but not accepted, in the next case, Farmers' Loan & Trust Co. v. Winthrop. As background to understanding the *Winthrop* case, remember that, unless modified by statute,[28] an agent's authority under a power of attorney is terminated by the death of the

26. See Restatement 3d of Property § 6.2.

27. See Restatement 3d of Property § 6.2, comment yy, stating that "this Restatement adopts the position that a gift of personal property can be perfected on the basis of donative intent alone if the donor's intent to make a gift is established by clear and convincing evidence."

28. UPC § 5-504(a) provides: "The death of a principal who has executed a written power of attorney, durable or otherwise, does not revoke or terminate the agency as to the attorney in fact or other person, who, without actual knowledge of the death of the principal, acts in good faith under the power. Any action so taken, unless otherwise invalid or unenforceable, binds successors in interest of the principal."

principal. See supra Chapter 8, Part C. Also note that an equitable interest, including the interest of a beneficiary of a trust, can itself be made the subject of a trust. Kekewich v. Manning, 1 DeG. M. & G. 176, 42 Eng. Rep. 519 (Ch. 1851); Merchants' Loan & Trust Co. v. Patterson, 139 N.E. 912 (Ill. 1923).

Farmers' Loan & Trust Co. v. Winthrop

144 N.E. 686 (N.Y. 1924)

CARDOZO, J. On February 3, 1920, Helen C. Bostwick executed her deed of trust to the Farmers' Loan & Trust Company as trustee. It is described as the 1920 deed, to distinguish it from an earlier one made in 1918, which is the subject of another action. By the later of the two deeds she gave to her trustee $5,000, "the said sum, and all other property hereafter delivered to said trustee as hereinafter provided," to be held upon the trusts and limitations therein set forth. The income was to be paid to her own use during life, and the principal on her death was to be divided into two parts—one for the benefit of the children of a deceased son, Albert; the other for the benefit of a daughter, Fannie, and the children of said daughter. The donor reserved "the right, at any time and from time to time during the continuance of the trusts, . . . to deliver to said trustee additional property to be held by it" thereunder. She reserved also a power of revocation.

At the date of the execution of this deed, a proceeding was pending in the Surrogate's Court for the settlement of the accounts of the United States Trust Company as trustee of a trust under the will of [Helen's late husband,] Jabez A. Bostwick. The effect of the decree, when entered, would be to transfer to Mrs. Bostwick money, shares of stock, and other property of the value of upwards of $2,300,000. The plan was that this property, when ready to be transferred, should be delivered to the trustee, and held subject to the trust. On February 3, 1920, simultaneously with the execution of the trust deed, three other documents, intended to effectuate this plan, were signed by the donor. One is a power of attorney whereby she authorized the Farmers' Loan & Trust Company as her attorney "to collect and receive any and all cash, shares of stock and other property" to which she might "be entitled under any decree or order made or entered" in the proceeding above mentioned. A second is a power of attorney authorizing the Farmers' Loan & Trust Company to sell and transfer any and all shares of stock then or thereafter standing in her name. A third is a letter, addressed to the Farmers' Loan & Trust Company, in which she states that she hands to the company the powers of attorney just described, and in which she gives instructions in respect of the action to be taken thereunder:

> My desire is and I hereby authorize you to receive from the United States Trust Company of New York all securities and property coming to me under the decree or order on the settlement of its account and to transfer such securities and property to yourself as trustee under agreement of trust bearing even date herewith executed by me to you.

The decree in the accounting proceeding was entered March 16, 1920. It established the right of Helen C. Bostwick to the payment or transfer of shares of stock and other property of the market value (then or shortly thereafter) of $2,327,353.70. On April 27, 1920, a representative of the Farmers' Loan & Trust Company presented the power of attorney to the United States Trust Company and stated that he was authorized to receive such securities as were ready for delivery. Shares of stock having a market value of $856,880 were handed to him then and there. No question is made that these became subject to the provisions of the deed of trust. The controversy arises in respect of the rest of the securities, $1,470,473.70 in value, which were retained in the custody of the United States Trust Company, apparently for the reason that they were not yet ready for delivery. During the night of April 27, 1920, Helen C. Bostwick died. She left a will, appointing the Farmers' Loan & Trust Company executor, and disposing of an estate of the value of over $20,000,000. The securities retained, as we have seen, in the custody of the United States Trust Company, were delivered on or about July 13, 1920, to the executor under the will. Conflicting claims of ownership are made by the legatees under the will and the remaindermen under the deed.

We think, with the majority of the Appellate Division, that the gift remained inchoate at the death of the donor. There is no occasion to deny that in the setting of other circumstances a power of attorney, authorizing a donee to reduce to possession the subject of a gift, may be significant as evidence of a symbolical delivery. We assume, without deciding, that such effect will be allowed if, apart from the power, there is established an intention that the title of the donor shall be presently divested and presently transferred . . . . [T]here is here no expression of a purpose to effectuate a present gift. The power of attorney, standing by itself, results, as all concede, in the creation of a revocable agency.

If something more was intended, if what was meant was a gift that was to be operative at once, the expression of the meaning will have to be found elsewhere, in the deed of trust or in the letter. Neither in the one, however, nor in the other, can such a purpose be discerned. Deed and letter alike are framed on the assumption that the gift is executory and future, and this though the addition of a few words would have established it beyond cavil as executed and present. In the deed there is a present transfer of $5,000 and no more. This wrought, there is merely the reservation of a privilege to augment the subject-matter of the trust by deliveries thereafter. The absence of words of present assignment is emphasized when we consider with what simplicity an assignment could have been stated. All that was needed was to expand the description by a phrase:

> The right, title, and interest of the grantor in the securities and other property due or to become due from the United States Trust Company as trustee under the will.

The deed and the other documents, we must remember, were not separated in time. They were parts of a single plan, and were executed together. In these circumstances, a present transfer, if intended, would naturally have found its place in the description of the deed itself. If omitted for some reason there, the least we should expect would be to find it in the letter. Again words of present transfer are conspicuously absent. What we have instead is a request, or at best a mandate, incompetent without more to divest title, or transfer it, serving no other purpose than a memorandum of instructions from principal to agent as a guide to future action. Deed and documents were prepared by counsel learned in the law. With industrious iteration, they rejected the familiar formulas that would have given unmistakable expression to the transfer of a present title. With like iteration, they chose the words and methods appropriate to a gift that was conceived of as executory and future. We must take the transaction as they made it. The very facility with which they could have made it something else is a warning that we are not at liberty, under the guise of construction, to make it other than it is. They were willing to leave open what they might readily have closed. Death overtook the signer before the gap was filled.

Viewed thus as a gift, the transaction was inchoate. An intention may be assumed, and indeed is not disputed, that what was incomplete at the moment should be completed in the future. The difficulty is that the intention was never carried out. Mrs. Bostwick remained free (apart from any power of revocation reserved in the deed of trust) to revoke the executory mandate, and keep the property as her own. Very likely different forms and instrumentalities would have been utilized, if he or she counsel had supposed that death was to come so swiftly. We might say as much if she had left in her desk a letter or memorandum expressing her resolutions for the morrow. With appropriate forms and instrumentalities available, she chose what the course of events has proved to be the wrong one. The court is without power to substitute another.

The transaction, failing as a gift, because inchoate or incomplete, is not to be sustained as the declaration of a trust. The donor had no intention of becoming a trustee herself. The donee never got title, and so could not hold it for another.

There was no equitable assignment. Equity does not enforce a voluntary promise to make a gift thereafter . . . .

One other question is in the case. It concerns the right of the executor to charge a proportionate part of the estate and inheritance taxes upon the interest of the remaindermen under the 1920 deed of trust. For the reasons stated in another action between the same parties involving the 1918 deed, the federal taxes are to be borne by the residuary estate.

The judgment of the Appellate Division should be modified, so as to affirm the judgment entered on the report of the referee in respect of the payment of the federal estate taxes, and, as so modified, affirmed, with a separate bill of costs to each party or set of parties appearing by separate attorney and to the several guardians ad litem, all payable out of the estate.

Notes

1. *A Constructive Trust Approach.* Without changing the basic rule that no express transfer trust is created unless the owner completes an intended transfer to the trustee, Restatement 3d of Trusts § 16 adopts a different approach that would have changed the outcome in *Winthrop*. It provides that the trust intent of someone who dies or becomes incompetent before the transfer is completed "may be given effect by a constructive trust in order to prevent unjust enrichment of the property owner's successor's in interest." See id. comment c, illustration 8. See also Restatement 3d of Property § 6.1, comment o; Restatement 3d of Restitution and Unjust Enrichment § 11.

2. *Origins of the* Winthrop *Principle.* That an imperfect gift won't be salvaged by attributing to the would-be donor a fictitious intent to create a self-declared trust has pretty well been settled since Richards v. Delbridge, L.R. 18 Eq. 11 (1874). The principle is adopted in Restatement 3d of Trusts § 16(2) and is codified by statute in some states. E.g., Cal. Prob. Code §§ 15200, 15201; Tex. Prop. Code §§ 112.001, 112.002.

In *Richards*, John Delbridge, shortly before his death, executed a deed of gift assigning his leasehold in a mill to his grandson, Edward Bennetto Richards. Because Edward was a minor, John delivered the deed to Edwards's mother on Edward's behalf. The gift was ineffective under the law of the time (8 & 9 Vict. c. 106, § 3) because the deed wasn't under seal.

Sir George Jessell, M.R., held that the gift couldn't be saved by labeling the deed a declaration of trust:

> The principal is a very simple one. A man may transfer his property, without valuable consideration, in one of two ways: he may either do such acts as amount in law to a conveyance or assignment of the property, and thus completely divest himself of the legal ownership, in which case the person who by those acts acquires the property takes it beneficially, or on trust, as the case may be; or the legal owner of the property may, by one or other of the modes recognised as amounting to a valid declaration of trust, constitute himself a trustee, and, without

> an actual transfer of the legal title, may so deal with the property as to deprive himself of its beneficial ownership, and declare that he will hold it from that time forward on trust for the other person. It is true he need not use the words, "I declare myself a trustee," but he must do something which is equivalent to it, and use the expressions which have that meaning; for, however anxious the Court may be to carry out the man's intention, it is not at liberty to construe words otherwise than according to their proper meaning . . . .
>
> The true distinction appears to me to be plain, and beyond dispute: for a man to make himself a trustee there must be an expression of intention to become a trustee, whereas words of present gift shew an intention to give over property to another, and not retain it in the donor's own hands for any purpose, fiduciary or otherwise.

Prior to *Richards*, there were cases on both sides of the equation. The earliest and most famous of the cases using the self-declared trust label to salvage an imperfect gift was Ex parte Pye, 18 Ves. 140, 34 Eng. Rep. 271 (Ch. 1811). In *Pye*, one William Mowbray, a married English gentleman, wrote a letter to his agent in Paris, Christopher Dubost, instructing Christopher to purchase an annuity of £100 for the benefit of Marie Genevieve Garos for her life, and, to pay for the purchase, to draw £1500 upon William's account. It appears that Marie, though not William's wife, was the mother of three children by him.

Christopher purchased the annuity as instructed, but violated his instructions to put the annuity in Marie's name; he put it in William's name instead, because Marie was then married to another man and also was deranged. Learning of what Christopher had done, William dispatched to Christopher a power of attorney that authorized Christopher to transfer the annuity to Marie. After William's death (in England), but in ignorance thereof, Christopher, in exercise of the power, executed a deed of gift of the annuity to Marie, Marie's husband having died in the meantime, and she having regained mental competency.

In a dispute between William's estate and Marie concerning the ownership of the annuity, Marie argued that under French law, the exercise of the power of attorney in these circumstances was valid, for under French law, a power continues until the agent has knowledge of the principal's death. (Under English law, the exercise of the power wouldn't have been valid because William's death revoked the power.[29])

---

29. For American law on this point, see Chapter 8, Part C.

The Chancellor, Lord Eldon,[30] sustained Marie's claim on a different ground. Apart from the proper construction of French law as to when a power of attorney is revoked, Lord Eldon treated William's power of attorney as a declaration of trust, *i.e.*, that William held this part of his estate in trust for Marie.

Although Lord Eldon's approach of salvaging an imperfect gift has not endured, another aspect of his decision theretofore in doubt has persisted. Lord Eldon took it for granted that no consideration was necessary to support the self-declared trust for Marie. Although English courts resisted this conclusion for a time after that decision, the point is today well settled. Restatement 3d of Trusts § 15; Bogert on Trusts §§ 201, 202; Scott on Trusts § 28. The point is stated explicitly in the recent California and Texas codifications of the law of trusts. Cal. Prob. Code § 15208; Tex. Prop. Code § 112.003. The California statute states:

> § *15208. Consideration.* Consideration is not required to create a trust, but a promise to create a trust in the future is enforceable only if the requirements for an enforceable contract are satisfied.

Precatory Language. The next case, Colton v. Colton, explores another aspect of an intent to create a trust—whether, in a given case, "precatory" language in a will or other governing instrument is properly interpreted as creating a trust. The Restatement 3d of Trusts § 13, comment d provides:

> *d. Precatory language.* Unless a testator or other transferor manifests an intention to impose enforceable duties on the transferee, the intention to create a trust is lacking and no trust is created.

The distinction, therefore, is between imposing legally enforceable duties on the devisee and merely seeking to impose a moral obligation on the devisee. If

---

30. The Chancellorship of Lord Eldon (nee John Scott, 1751-1838), which lasted from 1801 to 1838, is widely considered to have exemplified the interventionist approach to trusts that prevailed in England before notions of economic liberalism began to influence Equity doctrine. *Pye* may be said to illustrate this outlook.

Eldon's notorious dilatoriness is thought by some to have contributed to the backlog in Chancery practice that Dickens immortalized in the opening scene of his novel Bleak House: "Never can there come fog too thick, never can there come mind and mire too deep, to assort with the groping and floundering condition which this High Court of Chancery, most pestilent of hoary sinners, holds, this day, in the sight of heaven and earth." Charles Dickens, Bleak House 1 (Riverside ed. 1956; 1st pub. 1852-53). For a suggestion that Eldon's "legendary lack of expedition on the bench" owed more to "excessive zeal to get things right than to simple tardiness," see Simon Gardiner, An Introduction to the Law of Trusts 194 n.44 (1990).

the court finds that the imposition of legally enforceable duties was intended, the trust is sometimes called a "precatory trust."

In determining whether the transferor intended to impose enforceable legal duties rather than a moral obligation, the Restatement 3d of Trusts § 13, comment d lists the following factors to be considered:

> (1) the specific terms and overall tenor of the words used; (2) the definiteness or indefiniteness of the property involved; (3) the ease or difficulty of ascertaining possible beneficiaries and their interests; (4) the interests or motives and the nature and degree of concerns that may reasonably be supposed to have influenced the transferor; (5) the financial situation, dependencies, and expectations of the parties; (6) the transferor's prior conduct, statements, and relationships with respect to possible trust beneficiaries; (7) the personal and any fiduciary relationships between the transferor and transferee; (8) other dispositions the transferor is making or has made of his or her wealth; and (9) whether the result of construing the disposition as involving a trust or not would be such as a person in the situation of the transferor would be likely to desire.

In the *Colton* case below, what result would these factors have produced?

Colton v. Colton

127 U.S. 300 (1888)

These are two bills in equity, one filed by Martha Colton and the other by Abigail R. Colton, each of whom is a citizen of the state of New York, against Ellen M. Colton, a citizen of California.

Martha Colton alleges in her bill that she was a sister of David D. Colton, who died in San Francisco, Cal., on October 9, 1878, and that the defendant, Ellen M. Colton, is his widow; that on October 8, 1878, the said David D. Colton made and executed in due form his last will and testament, a copy of which is made a part of the bill, and is set out as follows:

> I, David D. Colton, of San Francisco, make this my last will and testament. I declare that all of the estate of which I shall die possessed is community property, and was acquired since my marriage with my wife. I give and bequeath to my said wife, Ellen M. Colton, all of the estate, real and personal, of which I shall die seized or possessed or entitled to. I recommend to her the care and protection of my mother and sister, and request her to make such gift and provision for them as in her judgment will be best. . . .

The bill then alleges that the estate of David D. Colton thus distributed to the defendant was of the value of about $1,000,000, and that the defendant, though often demanded, has failed, neglected, and refused to make to the plaintiff any gift or provision whatever from the estate of said David D. Colton . . . .

[The bill filed by Abigail, mother of the testator, was much the same as Martha Colton's bill, except that it also alleged that the petitioner was 75 years old and in poor health, that her only income was the interest on a sum of $15,000, and that she was in "very straitened circumstances." A demurrer was sustained to each bill. The trial judge concluded that the "precatory words" of the will did not create a trust. 21 F. 594 (1884).]

MATTHEWS J. These appeals bring before us the will of David D. Colton for construction. The question is whether his widow, Ellen M. Colton, by its provisions, takes the whole estate of which he died seized and possessed absolutely in her own right, or whether she takes it charged with a trust enforceable in equity in favor of the complainants, and, if so, to what extent . . . . No technical language . . . is necessary to the creation of a trust, either by deed or by will. It is not necessary to use the words "upon trust" or "trustee," if the creation of a trust is otherwise sufficiently evident. If it appear to be the intention of the parties from the whole instrument creating it that the property conveyed is to be held or dealt with for the benefit of another, a court of equity will affix to it the character of a trust, and impose corresponding duties upon the party receiving the title, if it be capable of lawful enforcement . . . .

The situation of the testator at the time he framed these provisions is to be considered. He made his will October 8, 1878; he died the next day. It may be assumed that it was made in view of impending dissolution, in the very shadow of approaching death. There is room enough for the supposition that by this necessity the contents of his will were required to be brief; the conception of the general idea to give everything to his wife was simple and easily expressed, and capable of covering all other intended dispositions. The time and the circumstances perhaps disabled him from specifying satisfactory details concerning a provision for his mother and his sister, but he did not forget that he owed them care and protection. That care and protection, therefore, he recommended to his wife as his legatee; but he was not satisfied with that; he wished that care and protection to be embodied in a gift and provision for them out of the estate which he was to leave to her. He therefore requested her to make it, and that request he addressed to his legatee and principal beneficiary as expressive of his will that a gift and provision for his mother and sister should come out of it. . . .

It is an error to suppose that the word "request" necessarily imports an option to refuse, and excludes the idea of obedience as corresponding duty. If a testator requests his executor to pay a given sum to a particular person, the legacy would be complete and recoverable. According to its context and manifest use, an expression of desire or wish will often be equivalent to a positive direction, where that is the evident purpose and meaning of the testator; as where a testator desired that all of his just debts, and those of a firm for which he was not liable, should be paid as soon as convenient after his decease, it was construed to operate as a legacy in favor of the creditors of the latter. Burt v. Herron, 66 Pa. St. 400. And in such a case as the present, it would be but natural for the testator to suppose that a request, which, in its terms, implied no alternative, addressed to his widow and principal legatee, would be understood and obeyed as strictly as though it were couched in the language of direction and command . . . .

On the whole, therefore, our conclusion is that each of the complainants in these bills is entitled to take a beneficial interest under the will of David D. Colton, to the extent, out of the estate given by him to his wife, of a permanent provision for them during their respective lives, suitable and sufficient for their care and protection, having regard to their condition and necessities, and the amount and value of the fund from which it must come. It will be the duty of the court to ascertain after proper inquiry, and thereupon to determine and declare, what provision will be suitable and best under the circumstances, and all particulars and details for securing and paying it. The decrees of the circuit court are accordingly reversed, and the causes remanded, with directions to overrule the demurrers to the several bills, and to take with this opinion; and it is so ordered.

4. Parties To A Trust

a. The Trustee

Statutory References: *UTC §§ 701, 703-705*

Restatement 3d of Trusts

§ *31. Trust Does Not Fail for Lack of Trustee.* A trust does not fail because no trustee is designated or because the designated trustee declines, is unable, or ceases to act, unless its creation or continuation depends on a specific person serving as trustee; a proper court will appoint a trustee as necessary and appropriate (see § 34).

As explained earlier, an owner of property can create a trust either by declaring himself or herself trustee for designated beneficiaries or by selecting another person as trustee and transferring title to the property to that other person. Once established, the principal relation with respect to the property is between the trustee and the beneficiary, although the settlor may of course retain interests not only as beneficiary but also through retention of various sorts of powers, the commonest being a power to amend or a power to revoke or both. In the remainder of this part, the subjects of study will be the trustee and the beneficiaries, with emphasis on whether either is necessary to establish a trust.

Adams v. Adams

88 U.S. (21 Wall.) 185 (1874)

Appeal from the Supreme Court of the District of Columbia. The case was thus: Adams, a government clerk, in Washington, owning a house and lot there, on the 13th of August, 1861, executed, with his wife, a deed of the premises to one Appleton, in fee, as trustee for the wife. The deed by appropriate words *in praesenti* conveyed, so far as its terms were concerned, the property for the sole and separate use of the wife for life, with power to lease and to take the rents for her own use, as if she was a *feme sole*; the trustee having power, on request of the wife, to sell and convey the premises in fee and pay the proceeds to her or as she might direct; and after her death (no sale having been made), the trust being that the trustee should hold the property for the children of the marriage as tenants in common, and in default of issue living at the death of the wife, then for Adams, the husband, his heirs and assigns.

The deed was signed by the grantors, and the husband acknowledged it before two justices "to be his act and deed." The wife did the same; being separately examined. The instrument purported to be "signed, sealed, and delivered" in the presence of the same justices, and they signed it as attesting witnesses. The husband put it himself on record in the registry of deeds for the county of Washington, D.C., which was the appropriate place of record for it.

Subsequent to this, that is to say in September, 1870, the husband and wife were divorced by judicial decree.

And subsequently to this again, that is to say, in December, 1871—the husband being in possession of the deed, and denying that any trust was ever created and executed, and Appleton, [declining] the wife's request . . . to assert the trust, or to act as trustee, Mrs. Adams filed a bill in the court below against them both, to establish the deed as a settlement made upon her by her husband, to compel a delivery of it to her; to remove Appleton, the trustee named in it, and to have some suitable person appointed trustee in his place . . . .

The bill further alleged the dissolution of the marriage by law, and that the complainant, relying upon the provisions of the deed referred to, neither sought nor obtained alimony in that suit; and further, that she has accepted, and still accepted the benefits of the trust; that Appleton declined to act as trustee, to allow the use of his name, or in any way to aid her in the matter; that her husband, the defendant, was in possession receiving the rents and profits, and declined to acknowledge her rights in the premises . . . .

Appleton also answered, alleging that if any such deed as described was executed, it was executed without his knowledge or consent; that no such deed was ever delivered to him, and that he never accepted any trust imposed by it; that he was never informed of the existence of the deed till 1870, when he was informed of it by the complainant, and that he then declined to act as trustee . . . .

The court below declared the trust valid and effective in equity as between the parties; appointed a new trustee; required the husband to deliver up the deed to the wife or to the new trustee; and to deliver also to him possession of the premises described in the deed of trust, and to account before the master for the rents and profits of it which had accrued since the filing of the bill, receiving credit for any payment made to the complainant in the meantime, and to pay the complainant's costs of the suit.

From a decree accordingly, the husband appealed.

HUNT J. . . . Upon the evidence before us we have no doubt that the deed was executed, acknowledged, and recorded by the defendant with the intent to make provision for his wife and children; that he took the deed into his own possession with the understanding, and upon the belief on his part, that he had accomplished that purpose by acknowledging and procuring the record of the deed, by showing the same to his wife, informing her of its contents, and placing the same in the house therein conveyed in a place equally accessible to her and to himself.

The defendant now seeks to repudiate what he then intended, and to overthrow what he then asserted and believed he had then accomplished.

It may be conceded, as a general rule, that delivery is essential, both in law and in equity, to the validity of a gift, whether of real or personal estate. What constitutes a delivery is a subject of great difference of opinion, some cases holding that a parting with a deed, even for the purpose of recording, is in itself a delivery.

It may be conceded also to have been held many times that courts of equity will not enforce a merely gratuitous gift of mere moral obligation.

These concessions do not, however, dispose of the present case. . . .

We are of opinion that the refusal of Appleton, in 1870, to accept the deed, or to act as trustee, is not a controlling circumstance.

Although a trustee may never have heard of the deed, the title vests in him, subject to a disclaimer on his part. Such disclaimer will not, however, defeat the conveyance as a transfer of the equitable interest to a third person. A trust cannot fail for want of a trustee, or by the refusal of all the trustees to accept the trust. The court of chancery will appoint new trustees. . . .

The defense rests upon the alleged non-delivery by Mr. Adams of the deed of August 13th, 1861, to Mrs. Adams, or for her benefit. We have referred at length to the authorities which show that as matter of law the deed was sufficiently delivered, and that it is the duty of the court to establish the trust.

We think that the decree of the court below was well made, and that it should be

AFFIRMED.

Notes

1. *Resignation Distinguished from Disclaimer.* In *Adams*, the trustee, Appleton, disclaimed the trust. A trustee can always disclaim (refuse to accept) a trust (see UTC § 701), but once accepted, the trustee can resign only with the permission of the appropriate court, or in accordance with the terms of the trust, or with the consent of the beneficiaries if they are competent to give such consent. UTC § 705; Restatement 3d of Trusts § 36; Scott on Trusts § 106. See also Tex. Prop. Code § 113.081; Cal. Prob. Code § 15640. Trust instruments often provide that the trustee may resign, as in Article VI of the John Doe trust reproduced supra p. 760.

2. *Devolution of a Trustee's Title Upon Death.* At common law, a sole trustee's title to the trust property passed to his or her heirs on the trustee's death intestate and could also be disposed of by will. Restatement 2d of Trusts §§ 104, 105. In some states, this has been changed by statute; New York, for example, provides that title "vests in the supreme court or the surrogate's court, as the case may be, and the trust shall be executed by a person appointed by the court . . . ." N.Y. Est. Powers & Trust Law § 7-2.3. Trust documents commonly take control of this question by expressly designating a successor trustee.

Co-trustees hold title as joint tenants so that, on the death of one, legal title to the trust property is in the survivor. Reichert v. Missouri & Illinois Coal Co., 83 N.E. 166 (Ill. 1907); UTC §704(b); Restatement 3d of Trusts § 34, comment d; Scott on Trusts § 103.

3. *Multiple Trustees; Exercise of Powers.* Traditionally, co-trustees of a private trust must all join in the exercise of their powers as trustees, unless the terms of the trust or of a statute provide otherwise. This rule did not apply, however, to charitable trusts, where action could be taken by a majority of the trustees if there are three or more. Restatement 3d of Trusts § 39 and the UTC § 703, however, break new ground by extending the majority-rule principle to private trusts having three or more trustees. Some states have statutes reaffirming the traditional rule. E.g., Cal. Prob. Code § 15620.

4. *Lack of a Trustee.* Suppose that G dies leaving a will that devises his or her entire estate in trust to named beneficiaries. Or, suppose that the will names a trustee but the designated trustee dies prior to G's death. Is there a valid trust? In these circumstances, courts will appoint a trustee to carry out the term of the

will, relying on the old saw that a trust will not fail for lack of a trustee. See, e.g., Restatement 3d of Trusts §14, comment b; § 31; UTC § 704; Estate of McCray, 268 P. 647 (Cal. 1928); Woodruff v. Woodruff, 16 A. 4 (N.J. Ch. 1888); Perfect Union Lodge No. 10 v. Interfirst Bank, 748 S.W.2d 218 (Tex. 1988).

b. The Beneficiaries

Statutory Reference: *UTC § 402*

(1) Unborn and Unascertained Beneficiaries

Restatement 3d of Trusts

§ *44. Definite Beneficiary Requirement.* A trust is not created, or if created will not continue, unless the terms of the trust provide a beneficiary who is ascertainable at the time or who may later become ascertainable within the period and terms of the rule against perpetuities.

§ *48. Incidental Benefits.* A person is a beneficiary of a trust if the settlor manifests an intention to give the person a beneficial interest; a person who merely benefits incidentally from the performance of the trust is not a beneficiary.

There is no doubt that a valid trust can be created that includes unborn and unascertained persons among its beneficiaries. Suppose, for example, a parent transfers property to a trustee, directing that the income from the property be paid to the parent for life, corpus at the parent's death to be equally divided among his or her children. The trust would be valid without question, and later born children would be included in the class, also without question. See Restatement 3d of Trusts § 44 comment c.

Can a trust be validly created if *all* of its beneficiaries are unborn, unascertained, or both?

Morsman v. Commissioner

90 F.2d 18, 113 A.L.R. 441 (8th Cir. 1937)

[On January 28, 1929, Robert P. Morsman, president of the United States Trust Company, signed a document declaring himself trustee of certain publicly traded securities; the United States Trust Company was named successor trustee. The securities had substantially appreciated in value during Morsman's ownership. Morsman, being in a high income-tax bracket, hoped that putting the securities into the self-declared trust would cause the ordinary income and any capital gain realized on sale to be taxed to the lower-bracket trust.

The trust document provided that the trust income was to be accumulated and added to principal until January 1, 1934. Thereafter, income was to be paid to Morsman himself for life. On termination of the trust, the principal was to go to his issue, or to his widow if there were no issue, or to his legal heirs if he had neither issue nor a widow then living.

Throughout the period in question, Mr. Morsman was unmarried and had no issue. Apparently his closest blood relative was a brother, who was Morsman's heir apparent.

Shortly after signing the trust document, Morsman sold the securities at a profit. Then, on May 3, 1929, he turned the trust property over to the United States Trust Company as successor trustee. The gains realized on these sales were reported as income of the trust. The Commissioner of Internal Revenue determined that the gains should have been reported as income on Morsman's personal return.]

THOMAS, J. . . . The question for consideration is whether or not the arrangement so devised resulted in the creation of an express trust covering the period and the transactions between January 28 and May 3, 1929. No claim is made that a charitable trust is involved. [Morsman] contends that a private express trust did exist during the period in question and that the profits realized from the sale of the securities should be taxed as income to the trust and not as income to himself individually . . . .

First. With respect to the position of Morsman, it is settled that a trust cannot exist where the same person possesses both the legal and equitable titles to the trust fund at the same time. In such a case the two titles are said to merge . . . . This principle is not denied. The result, of course, is different where one person conveys property to another who agrees to hold in trust for the grantor, as in the case of Doctor v. Hughes, 225 N.Y. 305, 122 N.E. 221. In such a case there is an immediate severance of the legal and equitable titles, and a trust arises at once. In the instant case that provision of the agreement by which [Morsman] undertook to hold for himself, standing alone, therefore, contributes nothing toward the creation of a trust . . . .

Second. With respect to the possibility of issue, it . . . is true that . . . it has been held in several cases that a present trust may be created where the beneficiary of an express trust is an unborn child. [E.g.,] Folk v. Hughes, 100 S.C. 220, 84 S.E. 713. The rationale of these cases, however, is not believed to rest on the theory that an unborn child can be the express cestui of an immediate trust. To so hold would violate fundamental principles of trusts which require a present conveyance of the beneficial interest and the existence of present enforceable duties and it would permit the suspension of the beneficial ownership, a notion repugnant to the requirements of a trust. The rationale of such a case is that the instrument has the effect of creating an immediate resulting trust for the settlor (which will cease if the expected child is born) "with an express trust for the child springing up when and if such child ever materializes." Bogert, Trusts and Trustees, § 163 . . . . So if A, a bachelor, transfers property to B in trust to accumulate the rents and profits and to convey the same to A's eldest son on reaching its majority (Trusts, Restatement, § 112, Illustration 6), a trust will arise at once—B now holding as a resulting trustee for A with the express trust arising if and when the eldest son comes into existence—the resulting trust then to cease. But in that view if A, a bachelor, or any person without issue, declares himself trustee of property for his own eldest son on identical or similar terms, no trust will presently arise. The express trust for the child cannot arise until the child comes into existence, and A cannot hold as a resulting trustee for himself during his lifetime because of the necessary merger in such a case of the legal and equitable interests in the same person. If A should die without issue under these circumstances, the property constituting the so-called trust fund is as much a part of his estate as if he had never made the purported declaration. The distinction thus noted between the case where A declares himself trustee for his unborn issue and where he conveys to B to hold in trust for such issue is vital; and this is the point at which Morsman failed in his attempt to create a present trust . . . .

To hold that a *present* trust arises where the owner of property declares that he holds it in trust for himself and other persons who are as yet nonexistent not only lacks a logical explanation but is incapable of practical application. To a creditor seeking to subject the property to the satisfaction of a debt [Morsman] would say that it was no longer his, but belonged, in equity, to others who were not yet in existence. But if he sought to dissipate the property, there is no person in being who has such an interest that he may go into a court of equity and prevent the dissipation. To say that [Morsman] in this case has an interest in enforcing such an obligation against himself or that the community at large is interested in preserving the rights of issue as yet not conceived is, to say the least, an unwarranted assumption. For the court to regard possible unborn issue as present beneficiaries is to permit the substance and realities of the transaction to be obscured by words and phrases . . . .

Third. With respect to the "heirs" as present beneficiaries and to the possible suggestion that [Morsman's] brother now living may take a present equitable interest under paragraph (8) of the trust agreement, it is observed that one of the elementary rules of law is that "A living person has no heirs". . . . Only on death do heirs come into existence, "for the ancestor during his life beareth in his body (in judgment of law) all his heirs, and therefore, it is truly said that haeres est pars antecessoris." Co. Litt. 22b. Quoted in Doctor v. Hughes, 225 N.Y. 305, 122 N.E. 221, 222. What has been said with reference to the rights of unborn children applies with equal force to the rights of heirs, two classes equally nonexistent. "Heirs," therefore, have no present beneficial interest, and cannot be considered beneficiaries . . . .

Finally, with respect to the status of a widow as a beneficiary, what has been said in reference to the nonexistence of issue and heirs is applicable here. The record, as pointed out above, does not show the existence of a wife. A widow is, therefore, a mere potentiality without existence and with no one to represent her. As a fiction, she belongs to no class. In case of an hypothetical breach of duty of the trustee, no woman in all the world, upon the record here, has a present right to come forward and enforce any rights under the trust agreement, and no existing person is authorized to enforce her imaginary rights.

The trust agreement, therefore, failed to effect the creation of a trust on January 28, 1929. This results from the fact that no existing beneficiaries were named therein and, consequently, there was no present severance of the legal and equitable titles to the property. The question here determined is whether there was a valid declaration of trust operating in praesenti between January 28 and May 3, 1929. That question must necessarily be answered in the negative since there was at that time no person in being who could claim any beneficial interest in the property other than the holder of the legal title. It is true, of course, that in equity a trust may not fail for want of a trustee, nevertheless the courts cannot supply a private express beneficiary . . . .

AFFIRMED.

GARDNER, J. dissenting. Authority is not wanting to the effect that a trust may be created even though the cestui que trust at the time of its creation is not in existence. For instance, the case of Folk v. Hughes, 100 S.C. 220, 84 S.E. 713, 714, cited in the majority opinion, specifically so holds . . . . But if it be assumed that there must have been in existence at the time of the creation of the trust a cestui que capable of taking, yet a prospective or potential heir, who under the terms of the trust may, under certain contingencies, be a beneficiary, fulfills this requirement.

Note and Questions

Trusts With Unborn Beneficiaries. Compare with *Morsman*, Folk v. Hughes, 84 S.E. 713 (S.C. 1915), cited in both the majority and dissenting opinions in *Morsman*. In *Folk,* a father transferred real property to his son under a deed that provided:

> To have and to hold the said described tract of land with all privileges and appurtenances thereof to [my son] for his uses and benefits, and for the maintenance and support of [my son's] children during the term of [my son's] natural life. And I . . . for and in consideration of the love and affection I have for the lawful children of [my son], do hereby grant, release and convey unto the lawful children of [my son] all the above described tract of land. To have and to

hold the same immediately after the death of [my son]. Together with all the rights and appurtenances thereto belonging. To have and to hold all and singular the said premises unto the children of [my son], their heirs and assigns forever.

At the time of the transfer, the son was married but childless. A child was born to the son later, however, and the court held that a valid trust had been created for that child at the time of the original transfer. As a consequence, the son was unable by reconveying the property to his father to destroy the contingent remainder in his unborn children. The court said, in part:

> It is not necessary to the creation of a trust estate that the cestui que trust should be in existence at the time of its creation. In [Ashurst v. Given, 5 Watts & S. (Pa.) 329], a devise to a father in trust for his children at the time of his death was held to be good, although the father had no children at the time of the vesting of the estate in him as trustee.
>
> A trustee will not be allowed by his own act to defeat or destroy his trust, and those who deal with him in respect of the trust estate, with knowledge of the trust, are bound by the terms of the trust, and if they purchase the trust estate, they take it incumbered with the trust.

Are *Folk* and *Morsman* distinguishable, as the *Morsman* majority thought, or was the dissenting judge right that they are inconsistent? Should it matter that in *Folk* the trust was created by transfer of legal title, while the *Morsman* trust was self-declared?[31]

(2) *Merger: Beneficiary as Trustee*

One Person as Both Trustee and Sole Beneficiary. The Restatement 3d of Trusts provides that "[t]he settlor or the trustee, or both, may be beneficiaries [of a trust]; but a sole trustee may not be the sole beneficiary." Restatement 3d of Trusts § 3, comment d; see also id. § 10. Accord, UTC § 402(a)(5). A transfer of legal title to a person to hold in trust for himself or herself, as sole beneficiary, doesn't create a trust. This is commonly explained, as it was in the *Morsman* opinion, by saying that there is a merger of the legal and equitable titles. But in truth, no separation of legal and equitable title ever occurred so as to bring about a merger—in short, the transfer didn't create a trust.

31. The Restatement 3d of Trusts § 44 gives an illustration based on facts like those in *Folk* (declaring such a trust valid) but does not give an illustration based on facts like those in *Morsman*. The Reporter's Notes to § 44, comment c, however, state the Reporter's view that "the dissent [in *Morsman*] seems correct, and the majority's generally criticized view seems strained in order to block tax avoidance plan." Reporter's Notes state the Reporter's view; they are not an official part of the Restatement.

The problem of merger may arise, however, either *after* the inception of an admittedly valid trust or *at* the inception of an intended trust. If title is transferred to A to hold on active trust for B, there is of course a trust at the inception of the arrangement. Should A thereafter die intestate, leaving B as his or her sole heir, in a state in which title to trust property passes to an intestate trustee's heirs, legal and equitable title will have become vested in one person, and there will often be a merger, which will normally put an end to the trust. See Restatement 3d of Trusts § 69, which provides that "[i]f the legal title to the trust property and the entire beneficial interest become united in one person, the trust terminates." It's commonly said that equity will prevent a merger in order to effectuate the settlor's intent, and while the maxim is stated more frequently than it's applied there seems little reason to doubt that it will sometimes be applied. In the case just put, for example, if the subject matter of the trust were land, the trust instrument provided that the land wasn't to be sold for ten years, and the period hadn't elapsed when A died, the court would probably hold there was no merger and would appoint another trustee in order to effectuate the settlor's wishes.

Much the same issue could arise at the inception of the intended trust. If the trust were testamentary and the named trustee predeceased the testator, the legal title to the trust property might pass to the sole beneficiary as heir or residuary devisee of the settlor. Again, the issue would be whether equity will prevent a merger. If it does, this will have the effect of saving the trust at its inception.

Some statutes specifically recognize certain limited exceptions to the doctrine of merger. See, e.g., Tex. Prop. Code § 112.034; Cal. Prob. Code § 15209.

Multiple Parties, Overlapping Interests as Trustee and Beneficiary. The problems are more complicated once we get beyond the situation of one person as sole trustee and sole beneficiary. Three situations are most troublesome:

> *Category (1)*: G transfers to A and B in trust for A and B, where the beneficial interests are concurrent.
>
> *Category (2)*: G transfers to A in trust for A and B, where the beneficial interests are concurrent—for example, the beneficiaries are given equal shares in income and principal.
>
> *Category (3)*: G transfers to A in trust for A and B, where the beneficial interests are successive—for example, income is to be paid to A for life, with principal then to be transferred to B.

A valid trust would be created in all these situations according to Restatement 3d of Trusts § 69, comment c. In Category (1), a technical argument favoring validity is that the trustees hold the legal title as joint tenants, while the beneficiaries hold as tenants in common. A purposeful argument is that applying the merger doctrine would defeat the expressed intent of the settlor, which public policy does not require inasmuch as a beneficiary exists who can enforce the trust against a trustee other than himself or herself. Most of the cases that have dealt with the above categories have avoided the merger of interests, and this is certainly the trend. A case in Alabama dealing with Category (1) sustained the trust and overruled a prior case to the contrary. See First Alabama Bank v. Webb, 373 So.2d 631 (Ala. 1979). The court said that merger should operate only where one person is both trustee and beneficiary.

A point applicable only to Category (3) is that, at the very least, it should be clear that A holds the remainder interest in trust for B. The only real question should be whether A's equitable life estate, which A holds as beneficiary, merges with the legal life estate, which A holds as trustee, so that A holds the life estate free of trust. The better authority holds that A does not hold the life estate free of trust. The ground, again, is that merger defeats the intention of the settlor for no good reason. Thus the trustee holds the entire legal title in trust, as intended by the settlor; a court should not reduce that legal title to separate undivided interests.

A number of New York cases, however, have held that A does hold the life estate free of trust. Indeed, they have gone even further and held that no trust is created at all: that B holds the remainder interest free of trust. In these cases, the ground offered is not merger but the extent of the trustee's legal title. In New York, the trustee is said to take the legal title only for life, making the trustee the sole beneficiary of the trust. Reed v. Browne, 66 N.E.2d 47 (N.Y. 1946).

(3) Indefinite Beneficiaries

Restatement 3d of Trusts

§ *46. Members of an Indefinite Class as Beneficiaries*

(1) Except as stated in (2), where the owner of property transfers it upon intended trust for the members of an indefinite class of persons, no trust is created.

(2) If the transferee is directed to distribute the property to such members of the indefinite class as the transferee shall select, the transferee holds the property in trust with power but no duty to distribute the property to such class members as the transferee may select; to whatever extent the power (presumptively personal) is not exercised, the transferee will then hold for reversionary beneficiaries implied by law.

In connection with the above provision of the Restatement, UTC § 402(c), Clark v. Campbell, and the succeeding materials, consider whether a trust is created where G's will purports to create a trust on the following alternative terms:

1. "Income to A for life, remainder in corpus to my (G's) friends"; or
2. "Income to A for life, remainder in corpus to such of my (G's) friends as the trustee shall select"; or
3. "Income to A for life, remainder in corpus to such of my (G's) friends as A shall select."

Because the word "friends" is considered to constitute an indefinite class, the remainder interest given to G's "friends" in Problem 1 is generally considered to be invalid.

The power given to A in Problem 3 is called a *discretionary* power of appointment.[32] Discretionary powers are almost always valid because the test for their validity is so easily satisfied. Discretionary powers are valid unless the group of permissible appointees (G's "friends" in Problem 3) is so indefinite that "it is impossible to identify any person who the donor intended should be [permissible appointees] of the power." Restatement 2d of Property § 12.1 comment h & illustration 18; Restatement of Property § 323 comment h.

The power given to the trustee in Problem 2 is called a *mandatory* power of appointment. Despite § 46(2) of the Restatement 3d of Trusts, supra (as well as § 402(c) of the UTC), which attempts to treat mandatory and discretionary powers alike, Clark v. Campbell shows that the traditional test for validity of a mandatory power is much more stringent than the one for a discretionary power.

Clark v. Campbell

133 A. 166 (N.H. 1926)

Petition for instructions, by the trustees under the will of Charles H. Cummings. Questions, which appear in the opinion, were reserved without ruling by Sawyer, J.

SNOW, J. The ninth clause of the will of deceased reads:

> My estate will comprise so many and such a variety of articles of personal property such as books, photographic albums, pictures, statuary, bronzes, bric-a-brac, hunting and fishing equipment, antiques, rugs, scrap books, canes and masonic jewels, that probably I shall not distribute all, and perhaps no great part thereof during my life by gift among my friends. Each of my trustees is competent by reason of familiarity with the property, my wishes and friendships, to wisely

---

32. This chapter does not deal comprehensively with discretionary powers. Discretionary powers are considered later in Chapter 16.

> distribute some portion at least of said property. I therefore give and bequeath to my trustees all my property embraced within the classification aforesaid in trust to make disposal by the way of a memento from myself, of such articles to such of my friends as they, my trustees, shall select. All of said property, not so disposed of by them, my trustees are directed to sell and the proceeds of such sale or sales to become and be disposed of as a part of the residue of my estate.

. . . . By the common law there cannot be a valid bequest to an indefinite person. There must be a beneficiary or a class of beneficiaries indicated in the will capable of coming into court and claiming the benefit of the bequest. This principle applies to private but not to public trusts and charities. Morice v. Bishop of Durham, 9 Vest. 399, 10 Ves. 521.

The basis assigned for this distinction is the difference in the enforceability of the two classes of trusts. In the former, there being no definite *cestui que trust* to assert his right, there is no one who can compel performance, with the consequent unjust enrichment of the trustee; while, in the case of the latter, performance is considered to be sufficiently secured by the authority of the Attorney General to invoke the power of the courts. The soundness of this distinction and the grounds upon which it rests, as applied to cases where the trustee is willing to act, has been questioned by distinguished authorities (5 Harvard Law Review, 390, 394, 395; 65 University of Pennsylvania Law Review, 538, 540; 37 Harvard Law Review, 687, 688) and has been supported by other authorities of equal note (15 Harvard Law Review, 510, 513-515, 530).[33] It is, however, conceded by the former that, since the doctrine was first stated in Morice v. Bishop of Durham, supra, more than a century ago, it has remained unchallenged, and has been followed by the courts in a practically unbroken line of decisions. Although it be conceded that the doctrine is not a legal necessity, the fact that it has never been impeached affords strong evidence that in its practical application it has been generally found just and reasonable. This is a sufficient ground for continued adherence to the rule . . .

"A gift to trustees to dispose of the same as they think fit is too uncertain to be carried out by the court." Theobald on Wills, 7th ed., 495 . . . .

That the foregoing is the established doctrine seems to be conceded, but it is contended in argument that it was not the intention of the testator by the ninth clause to create a trust, at least as respects the selected articles, but to make an absolute gift thereof to the trustees individually. It is suggested that the recital of the qualifications of the trustees may be considered as investing them with

---

33. The distinguished authorities referred to are James B. Ames, The Failure of the"Tilden Trust," 5 Harv. L. Rev. 389 (1892); John C. Gray, Gifts for a Non-Charitable Purpose, 15 Harv. L. Rev. 509 (1902); and Austin W. Scott, Control of Property by the Dead, 65 U. Pa. L. Rev. 527 (1917), Conveyances Upon Trusts Not Property Declared, 37 Harv. L. Rev. 653 (1924). Eds.

personal and nonofficial character, and that the word "trustees" is merely descriptive of the persons who had been earlier named as trustees, and was not intended to limit the capacity in which they were to act here . . . . If is a sufficient answer to this contention that the language of the ninth clause does not warrant the assumed construction. The assertion of the competency of the trustees to wisely distribute the articles in question by reason of their familiarity with the testator's property, wishes and friendships seem quite as consistent with a design to clothe them with a trusteeship as with an intention to impose upon them a moral obligation only. Blunt v. Taylor, 230 Mass. 303, 305, 119 N.E. 954. If, however, the recited qualifications had the significance ascribed to them the language of the bequest is too plain to admit of the assumed construction. When the clause is ended of unnecessary verbiage the testator is made to say: "I give to my trustee my property (of the described class) in trust to make disposal of to such of my friends as they shall select." It is difficult to conceive of language more clearly disclosing an intention to create a trust. However, if the trust idea introduced by the words "trustees" and in "trust" were not controlling, all the evidence within the will confirms such idea. In the first clause of the will the testator nominates three trustees, and an alternate in case of vacancy. Throughout the will these nominees are repeatedly and invariably referred as "my trustees," whenever the testator is dealing with their trust duties. Whenever rights are conferred upon them individually, as happens in the fifth, sixth, and eighth clauses, they are as invariably severally referred to solely by their individual names. The clause under consideration (ninth) expressly provides for the disposal of only a portion of the classified articles, and imposes upon the trustees the duty of selling the balance thereof and adding the proceeds to the residue which they are to continue to hold, and administer in their capacity as trustees. The proceeds thus accruing under this clause are expressly referred to in the eleventh clause in enumeration of the ultimate funds to be distributed by them as trustees "in and among such charitable . . . institutions" as they shall select and designate. The conclusion is inescapable that there was no intention to bestow any part of the property enumerated is the ninth clause upon the trustees for their own benefit. This necessarily follows, since the direction to make disposal is clearly as broad as the gift.

It is further sought to sustain the bequest as a power. The distinction apparently relied upon is that a power, unlike a trust, is not imperative and leaves the act to be done at the will of the donee of the power. But the ninth clause by its terms imposes upon the trustees the imperative duty to dispose of the selected articles among the testator's friends. If, therefore, the authority bestowed by the testator by the use of a loose terminology may be called a power, it is not an optional power, but a power coupled with a trust, to which the principles incident to a trust so far as here involved, clearly apply.

We must therefore conclude that this clause presents the case of an attempt to create a private trust, and clearly falls within the principle of well-considered authorities. Nichols v. Allen, 130 Mass. 211, 212, 39 Am.Rep. 445; Blunt v. Taylor, 230 Mass. 303, 305, 119 N.E. 954. In so far as the cases cited by the petitioners upon this phase of the case are not readily distinguishable from the case at bar, they are in conflict with the great weight of authority.

The question presented, therefore, is whether or not the ninth clause provides for definite and ascertainable beneficiaries, so that the bequest therein can be sustained as a private trust. In this state the identity of a beneficiary is a question of fact to be found from the language of the will, construed in the light of all the competent evidence rather than by the application of arbitrary rules of law. It is believed that in no other jurisdiction is there greater liberality shown in seeking the intention of the testator in this, as in other particulars. We find, however, no case in which our courts have sustained a gift where the testator has attempted to delegate to a trustee the arbitrary selection of the beneficiaries of his bounty through means of a private trust.

Like the direct legatees in a will, the beneficiaries under a trust may be designated by class. But in such case the class must be capable of delimitation, as "brothers and sisters," "children," issue," "nephews and nieces." A bequest giving the executor authority to distribute his property "among his relatives and for benevolent objects is such sums as in their judgment shall be for the best" was sustained upon evidence within the will that by "relatives" the testator intended such of his relatives within the statute of distributions as were needy, and thus brought the bequest within the line of charitable gifts, and excluded all other as individuals. Goodale v. Mooney, 60 N.H. 528, 526, 49 Am. Rep. 334. Where a testator bequeathed his stocks to be apportioned to his "relations" according to the discretion of the trustee, to be enjoyed by them after his decease, it was held to be a power to appoint amongst his relations who were next of kin under the statute of distribution. Varrell v. Wendell, 20 N.H. 431, 436. Likewise where a devise over after a particular estate was to the testator's "next of kin" simpliciter. Pinkham v. Blair, 57 N.H. 226, 243. Unless the will discloses a plain purpose to the contrary, the words "relatives" or "relations," to prevent gifts from being void for uncertainty, are commonly construed to mean those who would take under statutes of distribution or descent.

In the case now under consideration the cestuis que trust are designated as the "friends" of the testator. The word "friends," unlike "relations," has no accepted statutory or other controlling limitations, and in fact has no precise sense at all. Friendship is a word of broad and varied application. It is commonly used to describe the undefinable relationships which exists, not only between those connected by ties of kinship or marriage, but as well between strangers in blood, and which vary in degree from the greatest intimacy to an acquaintance more or less casual. "Friend" is sometimes used in contradistinction to "enemy." "A friendless man is an outlaw." Cowell, Bouvier. Although the word was formerly sometimes used a synonymous with relatives, there is no evidence that it was so used here. The inference is to the contrary. The testator in the will refers to eight different persons, some of them already deceased, by the title of "friends." He never uses the appellation concurrently with "nephew" or "niece," which words occur several times in describing legatees. Nor is there anything to indicate that the word "friends" in the ninth clause was intended to apply only to those who had been thus referred to in the will. There is no express evidence that the word is used in any restricted sense . . . .

It was the evident purpose of the testator to invest his trustees with the power after his death to make disposition of the enumerated articles among an undefined class with practically the same freedom and irresponsibility that he himself would have exercised if living; that is, to substitute for the will of the testator the will and discretion of the trustees. Such a purpose is in contravention of the policy of the statute which provides that

> No will shall be effectual to pass any real or personal estate . . . unless made by a person . . . in writing, signed by the testator or by some one in his presence and by his direction, and attested and subscribed in his presence by three or more credible witnesses.

Where a gift is impressed with a trust, ineffectively declared, and incapable of taking effect because of the indefiniteness of the cestui que trust, the donee will hold the property in trust for the next taker under the will or for the next of kin by way of a resulting trust. . . . The trustees therefore hold title to the property enumerated in the paragraph under consideration to be disposed of as a part of the residue, and the trustees are so advised. This conclusion makes it unnecessary to answer the question reserved, and it has not been considered. . .

Case discharged.

Notes and Questions

1. *Requirement of a Definite Class*. What reasoning explains the rule, applied in *Clark*, that where a fiduciary is under a duty to select the beneficiaries of a trust from amongst a class, the entire membership of the class must be definite and ascertainable? The court in *Clark* pointed to the policy of the statute of wills as a basis for the rule. But a moment's reflection should tell you that this can't be so.

In Nichols v. Allen, 130 Mass. 211, 221 (1881), the leading American case on the problem, the court said:

> The conclusion of the whole matter is, that, the testatrix having given the residue of her property to her executors in trust and not having defined the trust sufficiently to enable the court to execute it, the plaintiff, being her next of kin, is entitled to the residue by way of resulting trust.

Compare this statement with the explanation for the rule put forward by the court in *Clark*.

The first and leading case on the problem was Morice v. The Bishop of Durham, 10 Ves. 522, 32 Eng. Rep. 947 (Ch. 1805), in which property was given by will to the Bishop of Durham upon trust, after the payment of the testatrix's debts and legacies, "to dispose of the ultimate residue to such objects of benevolence and liberality as the Bishop of Durham in his own discretion shall most approve of." The Chancellor, Lord Eldon (whom we met in connection with Ex parte Pye), held that there was no intent that the Bishop take beneficially, and that the Bishop's discretion was not limited to purposes that were charitable, and that, therefore, the trust must fail because it was "for purposes not sufficiently defined to be controlled and managed by this Court." A decree in favor of the next of kin of the testatrix was affirmed.

Prior to this case, English Equity judges had been more willing to exercise control over trustees' powers to select beneficiaries. The *Bishop of Durham's* case sharpened the distinction between trust powers and "bare" powers. As a result, Equity embarked on a course that violated donors' intentions in a much wider range of cases.

2. *Discretionary vs. Mandatory Powers of Appointment*. Because the tests for validity of discretionary and mandatory powers are so different, the process of identifying which type of power is created in a particular case can be crucial to the outcome. The distinction between mandatory and discretionary powers, however, is not always easy to draw. In Gibbs v. Rumsey, 2 Ves. & B. 294, 35 Eng. Rep. 331 (Ch. 1813), for example, a will devised the testator's estate to "my said trustees and executors [naming them] to be disposed of unto such person and persons and in such manner and form and in such sum and sums of money as they in their discretion shall think proper and expedient." In upholding the devise, the Master of the Rolls concluded that the will authorized appointment to anyone, including the fiduciaries, and so created "a purely arbitrary power of disposition." In District of Columbia v. Adams, 57 F. Supp. 946 (D.D.C. 1944), however, the court concluded that the following language created a mandatory power rather than a discretionary power in the executor: "I order that my executor shall collect all monies and property of any description due and belonging to me from any bank or insurance company, or from any other source, and dispose of all of the same according to his best judgment." The court held that the trust failed because no general power was intended and "those to whom the property is to be distributed are uncertain."

More recently, in Leach v. Hyatt, 423 S.E.2d 165 (Va. 1992), the court treated a power in "executors" as a discretionary power, and seemed to be ignorant of the law on indefinite beneficiaries of a mandatory power.

3. *Reforming the Traditional Rules*. Restatement 3d of Trusts § 46(2), supra, and UTC § 402(c) attempt to change the traditional trust rules concerning indefinite beneficiaries. Both treat a power in a trustee to select a beneficiary from an indefinite class as a discretionary power, i.e., as a power that can but need not be exercised. This was essentially the view adopted in Restatement 2d of Trusts § 122. In the United Kingdom, however, the House of Lords has held that a provision in a trust deed directing trustees, in their absolute discretion, to distribute property to a named company's past or present employees or their relatives created a trust rather a mere power but that the test for the validity for both should be the same. McPhail v. Doulton, [1971] App. Cas. 424 (H.L. 1970); George E. Palmer, Private Trusts for Indefinite Beneficiaries, 71 Mich. L. Rev. 359 (1972).

4. *"Friends" As an Indefinite Class*. Why does the word "friends" create a class too indefinite to sustain a trust? Recall what the court in Clark v. Campbell said about the point:

> The word "friends," unlike "relations," has no accepted statutory or other controlling limitations, and in fact has no precise sense at all. Friendship is a word of broad and varied application. It is commonly used to describe the undefinable relationships which exist, not only between those connected by ties of kinship or marriage, but as well between strangers in blood, and which vary in degree from the greatest intimacy to an acquaintance more or less casual.

In her book *Necessary Losses*, the author Judith Viorst identifies several categories of friendship:

> 1. *Convenience friends*. These are the neighbor or office mate or members of our car pool whose lives routinely intersect with ours. These are the people with whom we exchange small favors. They lend us their cups and silverware for a party. They drive our children to soccer when we are sick. They keep our cat for a week when we go on vacation. And, when we need a lift, they give us a ride to the garage to pick up the Honda. And we do for them.
>
> But we don't with convenience friends, ever come too close or tell too much: We maintain our public face and emotional distance. . . .
>
> 2. *Special-interest friends*. These friendships depend on the sharing of some activity or concern. These are sports friends, work friends, yoga friends, nuclear-freeze friends. We meet to participate jointly in knocking a ball across a net, or saving the world. . . .
>
> 3. *Historical friends*. With luck we also have a friend who knew us . . . way back when. . . .

> The years have gone by, [we] have gone separate ways, [we] have little in common now, but [we] still are an intimate part of each other's past. . . .
>
> 4. *Crossroads friends.* Like historical friends, our crossroads friends are important for what was—for the friendship we shared at a crucial, now past, time of life: a time, perhaps, when we roomed in college together; or served a stint in the U.S. Air Force together; or worked as eager young singles in Manhattan together; or went through pregnancy, birth and those first difficult years of motherhood together.
>
> With historical friends and crossroads friends we forge links strong enough to endure with not much more contact than once-a-year letters at Christmas, maintaining a special intimacy—dormant but always ready to be revived—on those rare but tender occasions when we meet.
>
> 5. *Cross-generational friends.* Another tender intimacy—tender but unequal—exists in the friendships that form across generations, the friendships that one woman calls her daughter-mother and her mother-daughter relationships. Across the generations the younger enlivens the older, the older instructs the younger. Each role, as mentor or quester, as adult or child, offers gratifications of its own. And because we are unconnected by blood, our words of advice are accepted as wise, not intrusive, our childish lapses don't summon up warnings and groans. Without the risks, and without the ferocious investment, which are always a part of a real parent-child connection, we enjoy the rich disparities to be found among our cross-generational friends.
>
> 6. *Close friends.* Emotionally and physically (by seeing each other, by mail, by talks on the phone) we maintain some ongoing friendships of deep intimacy. And although we may not expose as much—or the same kinds of things—to each of our closest friends, close friendships involve revealing aspects of our private self—of our private feelings and thoughts, of our private wishes and fears and fantasies and dreams.

Judith Viorst, Necessary Losses 197-99 (1986). To which of the above types of "friends" did Charles Cummings' will refer in Clark v. Campbell?

The Restatement 3d of Trusts gives a somewhat different rationale for the indefiniteness of the word "friends":

> § *46 comment a*. A class of persons is indefinite . . . if the identity of the individuals comprising its membership cannot be ascertained. Although it is possible to determine that certain persons fall within a class and that others do not, it may be impossible to determine *all* the persons who fall within it. This is the case, for example, of a class consisting of all of the "friends" of the settlor or of another person.

Note also the Canadian case of Re Connor, 10 D.L.R.3d 5 (App. Div., Alberta, Canada 1970). The testator's residuary clause provided: "I direct that the residue be divided among my close friends in such a way and at such time as my trustee in her discretion should determine." The trial judge held the trust valid, but on appeal his decision was reversed. McDermid, J.A., construed the residuary clause as requiring that the residue "must be divided amongst all of the close friends," and so the trust failed. He continued:

> Obviously the trustee was not able to designate all of the close friends of the testatrix for the Court ordered that an advertisement be run in the newspaper in six different localities asking any close friend to file an affidavit with the Clerk of the Court setting out the facts on which such person claimed to be a close friend. If a close friend missed reading or hearing about the advertisement owing to absence from the locality or not being a person who habitually read legal notices, such person could be excluded from the gift to which she is entitled. Where advertisements are considered necessary in order to ascertain the members of the class, it indicates the difficulty of ascertaining the class. This is not a case where the members of a class have been ascertained and the advertisements are for the purpose of discovering their whereabouts. Each case, of course, must be decided on its own facts and it is primarily a question of fact to say whether the object of a gift is capable of ascertainment: see Re H. J. Ogden [1933] 1 Ch. 678. Here, as I have said, the mere fact that advertising has to be resorted to in hopes of ascertaining the persons who make up the class demonstrates to my mind the uncertainty.

One judge dissented; he concluded that, since the testator lived in a small town for over forty-two years, "it should be possible without too great difficulty to ascertain who her close friends were."

5. *Meaning of "Relatives."* In Binns v. Vick, 538 S.W.2d 283 (Ark. 1976), a testator's residuary clause provided:

> All the rest and residue of my estate . . . I give, devise and bequeath [to] Kenneth Binns [a nephew of the testator and also the testator's executor] to distribute among my relatives as he sees fit.

The trial court held that a trust was intended, but failed for want of definite beneficiaries. The decision was affirmed. The court said that if "relatives" meant legal heirs, the appellant Binns' claim to the property beneficially must be denied because the testator's sole heir was a sister; and that if "relatives" meant all persons related to the testator, the bequest failed for uncertainty.

Compare Restatement 3d of Trusts, which provides:

> § *45 comment d.* A trust for the benefit of "relatives" of the settlor or other designated person does not fail if the trustee has the power to select who among the relatives shall take and in what proportions.

See also UPC § 2-711 (donative disposition of a present or a future interest to an individual's "relatives" or "family" is presumptively a disposition to the individual's heirs); Cal. Prob. Code § 6151 (devise to an individual's "relatives" or "family" is a devise "to those who would be the . . . person's heirs . . . .").

EXTERNAL REFERENCES. George E. Palmer, Private Trusts for Indefinite Beneficiaries, 71 Mich. L. Rev. 359, 366-67 (1972); John Hopkins, Certain Uncertainties of Trusts and Powers, 29 Camb. L.J. 68 (1971).

Estate of Searight

95 N.E.2d 779 (Ohio Ct. App. 1950)

HUNSICKER, J. George P. Searight, a resident of Wayne county, Ohio, died testate on November 27, 1948. Item "third" of his will provided:

> I give and bequeath my dog, Trixie, to Florence Hand of Wooster, Ohio, and I direct my executor to deposit in the Peoples Federal Savings and Loan Association, Wooster, Ohio, the sum of $1000.00 to be used by him to pay Florence Hand at the rate of 75 cents per day for the keep and care of my dog as long as it shall live. If my dog shall die before the said $1000.00 and the interest accruing therefrom shall have been used up, I give and bequeath whatever remains of said $1000.00 to be divided equally among those of the following persons who are living at that time, to wit: Bessie Immler, Florence Hand, Reed Searight, Fern Olson and Willis Horn.

At the time of his death, all of the persons, and his dog, Trixie, named in such item third, were living.

Florence Hand accepted the bequest of Trixie, and the executor paid to her from the $1000 fund, 75 cents a day for the keep and care of the dog. The value of Trixie was agreed to be $5. . . .

We do not have, in the instant case, the question of a trust established for the care of dogs in general or of an indefinite number of dogs, but we are here considering the validity of a testamentary bequest for the benefit of a specific dog. This is not a charitable trust, nor is it a gift of money to the Ohio Humane Society or a county humane society, which societies are vested with broad statutory authority, Section 10062, General Code, for the care of animals.

Text writers on the subject of trusts and many law professors designate a bequest for the care of a specific animal as an "honorary trust"; that is, one binding the conscience of the trustee, since there is no beneficiary capable of enforcing the trust.

The rule in Ohio, that the absence of a beneficiary having a legal standing in court and capable of demanding an accounting of the trustee is fatal and the trust fails, was first announced in Mannix, Assignee, v. Purcell, 46 Ohio St. 102, 19 N.E. 572, 2 L.R.A. 753 . . . .

In 1 Scott on the Law of Trusts, Section 124, the author says:

> There are certain classes of cases similar to those discussed in the preceding section in that there is no one who as beneficiary can enforce the purpose of the testator, but different in one respect, namely, that the purpose is definite. Such, for example, are bequests for the erection or maintenance of tombstones or monuments or for the care of graves, and bequests for the support of specific animals. It has been held in a number of cases that such bequests as these do not necessarily fail. It is true that the legatee cannot be compelled to carry out the intended purpose, since there is no one to whom he owes a duty to carry out the purpose.
>
> Even though the legatee cannot be compelled to apply the property to the designated purpose, the courts have very generally held that he can properly do so, and that no resulting trust arises so long as he is ready and willing to carry it out. The legatee will not, however, be permitted to retain the property for his own benefit; and if he refuses or neglects to carry out the purpose, a resulting trust will arise in favor of the testator's residuary legatee or next of kin.

. . . . To call this bequest for the care of the dog, Trixie, a trust in the accepted sense in which that term is defined is, we know, an unjustified conclusion. The modern authorities, as shown by the cases cited earlier in this discussion, however, uphold the validity of a gift for the purpose designated in the instant case, where the person to whom the power is given is willing to carry out the testator's wishes. Whether called an "honorary trust" or whatever terminology is used, we conclude that the bequest for the care of the dog, Trixie, is not in and of itself unlawful. . . .

[As to the common-law Rule Against Perpetuities,] it is to be noted, in every situation where the so-called "honorary trust" is established for specific animals, that, unless the instrument creating such trust limits the duration of the trust—that is, the time during which the power is to be exercised—to human lives, we will have "honorary trusts" established for animals of great longevity, such as crocodiles, elephants and sea turtles. . . .

If we then examine item third of testator's will, we discover that, although the bequest for his dog is for "as long as it shall live," the money given for this purpose is $1000 payable at the rate of 75¢ a day. By simple mathematical computation, this sum of money, expended at the rate determined by the testator, will be fully exhausted in three years and 238-1/3 days. If we assume that this $1000 is deposited in a bank so that interest at the high rate of 6% per annum were earned thereon, the time needed to consume both principal and interest thereon (based on semi-annual computation of such interest on the average unused balance during such six month period) would be four years, 57 ½ days.

It is thus very apparent that the testator provided a time limit for the exercise of the power given his executor, and that such time limit is much less than the maximum period allowed under the rule against perpetuities. . . .

We therefore conclude that the bequest in the instant case for the care of the dog, Trixie, does not, by the terms of the creating instrument, violate the rule against perpetuities. . . .

The judgment of the Probate Court is affirmed.

Notes

1. *The Tax Question in Searight*. Believe it or not, *Searight* was a state inheritance tax case. The Ohio Department of Taxation claimed that an inheritance tax was due on the amount devised to Trixie for Trixie's care and on the value of the devise of Trixie to Florence Hand. The Ohio statute imposed an inheritance tax on property passing "to or for the use of a person, institution or corporation." The court held that Trixie herself, a fox-terrier, was not any of these and no inheritance tax was due on the amount devised to Trixie for Trixie's care. An inheritance tax was, however, imposed on the devise of Trixie to Florence Hand. Trixie's value? $5.00.

2. *Trusts for Animals*. UPC § 2-907(b) authorizes trusts for the care of a designated domestic or pet animal, authorizes the court to reduce extravagant amounts devised to such trusts, provides a mechanism for their enforcement, and limits the duration to the life of the animal. Similarly, UTC § 408 provides that "[a] trust may be created to provide for the care of an animal alive during the settlor's lifetime" and directs that the trust terminate upon the animal's death.

3. *Honorary Trusts (Noncharitable Purpose Trusts)*. Trusts have been upheld that provided for the saying of masses, for the erection of a tombstone, and the upkeep of a burial plot. Scott on Trusts § 124. One of the few cases going beyond the limited purposes just described is In re Thompson, [1934] Ch. 342, upholding a testamentary trust for the "promotion and furthering of fox-hunting." The court was of the opinion that "the object of the gift has been defined with sufficient clearness and is of a nature to which effect can be given." The devisee was willing to carry out the stated purposes and the court decided that he should be permitted to do so. If he should thereafter misapply the fund, "the residuary legatees are to be at liberty to apply," presumably for an order that the fund be paid over to them on the theory of resulting trust.

Under the common-law Rule Against Perpetuities, a contingent future interest is invalid unless it is certain to vest, if at all, within a life in being plus 21 years from the creation of the interest. See infra Chapter 19. It is now generally recognized that this period applies to honorary trusts and that the trust is invalid if it may last longer than the perpetuities period. Foshee v. Republic Nat'l Bank, 617 S.W.2d 675 (Tex. 1981) (perpetual trust to maintain family burial space in mausoleum). Neither courts nor writers have been in complete agreement on whether such a trust violates the rule against remoteness of vesting itself or only some associated rule. In Bryant Smith, Honorary Trusts and the Rule Against Perpetuities, 30 Colum. L. Rev. 60 (1930), the author suggested that the Rule Against Perpetuities was violated, on the theory that the trustee of the honorary trust has a special (nongeneral) power of appointment, and that under perpetuities doctrine such a power is void if it is exercisable beyond a life in being plus 21 years. This position is embraced by other writers on perpetuities. See, e.g., John C. Gray, The Rule Against Perpetuities § 909.1 (4th ed. 1942); Scott on Trusts § 124.1.

UPC § 2-907(a) authorizes trusts for a specific lawful noncharitable purpose, authorizes the court to reduce extravagant amounts devised to such trusts, provides a mechanism for their enforcement, and limits the duration to 21 years. Similarly, UTC § 409 provides that "[a] trust may be created for a noncharitable purpose without a definite or definitely ascertainable beneficiary or for a noncharitable but otherwise valid purpose to be selected by the trustee." The duration of such trusts is limited to 21 years.

The Restatement 3d of Trusts takes a somewhat different approach to the problem of noncharitable purpose trusts. Applying its "adapted trust" technique, it provides that a transferee of property for indefinite or general purposes, not limited to charitable purposes, holds the property "as trustee with the power but not the duty to distribute or apply the property . . . ." Id. § 47(1). Similarly, § 47(2) provides:

> § *47(2). Trusts for Non-charitable Purposes.* If the owner of property transfers it in trust for a specific noncharitable purpose and no definite or ascertainable beneficiary is designated, unless the purpose is capricious, the transferee holds the property as trustee with power exercisable for a reasonable period of time, normally not to exceed 21 years, to apply the property to the designated purpose; if and to the extent the power is personal and not exercised, or the property exceeds what reasonably may be needed for the purpose, the trustee holds the property or the excess for reversionary beneficiaries implied by law.

Comment d goes on to explain that the 21-year period "is neither sacred nor necessarily suitable to all cases of adapted trust powers." Thus, for example, a trust power to maintain a grave "should be allowed for the lifetime of the decedent's spouse and children, or of other concerned individuals designated in the will . . . ."

External References. Richard R. Powell, Law of Real Property ¶¶ 588-89 (rev. 1990); Roger B. M. Cotterrell, Some Sociological Aspects of the Controversy Around the Legal Validity of Private Purpose Trusts, in Equity and Contemporary Legal Developments 302 (Stephen Goldstein ed. 1992).

PART C. FORMALITIES IN THE CREATION OF A TRUST

Statutory Reference: *UTC § 407*

Apart from the substantive requirements just discussed—specific trust property, trust intent, trustee, and at least one definite beneficiary—trust law imposes no formal requirements for creating a trust. A declaration of trust of personal property may be entirely oral.[34] See Restatement 3d of Trusts § 20; UTC § 407 (requires proof of an oral trust by clear and convincing evidence). However, as the old maxim states, "Equity follows the law." There are two situations in which certain statutory formalities have created problems in proving either trust intent or the substantive terms of the trust. One situation is where the subject matter of the trust is land. If the trust is intended to become effective during the settlor's lifetime, the Statute of Frauds imposes requirements of a signed writing. The other situation involves trusts created at the settlor's death through a will. Testamentary trusts are subject to the requirements of the Statute of Wills.

Both the Statute of Frauds and Statute of Wills impose formalities for evidentiary purposes. In some situations, however, the question arises whether the restitutionary principle of avoiding unjust enrichment should override these evidentiary concerns. In this Part, we examine the problems created by the tension between the unjust enrichment principle and statutory formalities in the creation and enforcement of trusts.

1. Inter Vivos Trusts of Land: Statute of Frauds

Most states have statutes that require trusts of real property to be evidenced by a signed writing. See Restatement 3d of Trusts §§ 22-24. The statutes vary in their language. Some explicitly provide that trusts of land must be "created or declared" by a writing,[35] while others require that trusts of real property be proved by a writing of the transferor or transferee.[36] Statutes of the latter type are based on § 7 of the English Statute of Frauds of 1677. The conceptual

34. Only a few states have statutes that impose a writing requirement for inter vivos trusts of personalty. E.g., Ind. Code § 30-4-2-1(a); W. Va. Code § 36-1-6 (applicable only to declarations of trust). The UTC and California require clear and convincing evidence. UTC § 407; Cal. Prob. Code § 15207.

35. E.g., Ga. Code Ann. § 53-12-23; Mass. Gen. Laws ch. 203, § 1; Me. Rev. Stat. Ann. tit. 33, § 851.

36. E.g., Fla. Stat. Ann. § 689.05; Mo. Stat. Ann. 456.010; N.J. Stat. Ann. 25: 1-3; Pa. Stat. Ann. tit. 33, § 2.

distinction between a writing requirement necessary to effect a transfer and one required only to prove the transfer, however, appears to have had little, if any, influence on the substantive development of the law. It's generally thought that the writing requirement affects the trust's enforcement and not its existence.

Typically, the writing requirement is met by a formal written instrument that is signed by both the settlor and the trustee or, in the case of a self-declared trust, by the settlor alone. In general, in the case of a trust created by transfer, the instrument must be signed either by the settlor before or contemporaneously with the transfer or by the trustee prior to, contemporaneously with, or even subsequent to the transfer (so long as the trustee has not transferred the interest to a third party). See Restatement 3d of Trusts § 23; Stephenson v. Stephenson, 171 S.W.2d 565 (Mo. 1943).

It should be mentioned that in a few states, there is no statutory requirement that a trust of land be evidenced by a writing. E.g., Ellis v. Vespoint, 403 S.E.2d 542 (N.C. Ct. App. 1991); Burns v. Equitable Assoc., 265 S.E.2d 737 (Va. 1980). See Bogert on Trusts § 64; Scott on Trusts § 40.1. In these states, the problem becomes one under the parol-evidence rule: May it be shown under a deed absolute in form that the grantee was to hold the land in trust for the grantor or a third person? As Wigmore saw it, the question is "whether the parties, under all the circumstances, appear to have intended the document to cover merely the kind of estate transferred, or to cover all possible aspects of the transfer. . . ." 9 John C. Wigmore, Evidence § 2437 (James H. Chadbourn rev. 3d ed. 1981). Usually, the former construction is adopted and the extrinsic evidence is received (e.g., Boggs v. Yates, 132 S.E. 876 (W. Va. 1926)); however, a few states do not permit proof of the oral trust where the grantor himself or herself was the intended beneficiary. Scott on Trusts § 38; Bogert on Trusts § 64. The Restatement 3d of Trusts § 21 provides that where a writing purporting to transfer the property does exist but doesn't affirmatively declare "that the transferee is to take the property for the transferee's own benefit or that the transferee is to hold it upon a particular trust . . . ," extrinsic evidence is admissible to show that the transferor intended that the transferee hold the property in trust, either for the transferor or a third person. UTC § 407 provides that "[e]xcept as required by a statute other than this [Code], a trust need not be evidenced by a trust instrument, but the creation of an oral trust and its terms may be established only by clear and convincing evidence."

Finally, as indicated earlier, even if the statute states that an oral trust is void, courts have treated such trusts as voidable only. If the trustee doesn't raise the bar of the Statute of Frauds, the trust is enforceable. In consequence, creditors of an oral trustee can't defeat the trust if the trustee chooses to recognize it. Courts have held, for example, that where an oral trustee conveys title of land that is the subject matter of the oral trust to the intended beneficiary, the trustee's creditors may not defeat the conveyance as being fraudulent. Hays v. Reger, 1 N.E. 386 (Ind. 1885); Berenato v. Gazzara, 31 A.2d 81 (Pa. 1943). This result is codified by statute in some states. See, e.g., Tex. Prop. Code § 101.002.[37]

Person v. Pagnotta

541 P.2d 483 (Or. 1975)

O'CONNELL, C.J. This is a suit brought by Nellie Person through her conservator to require defendant Michael Pagnotta to reconvey real property previously conveyed to him by Nellie Person on the ground that he holds the property upon a resulting trust. Plaintiff appeals from a decree in favor of defendants.

Plaintiff, an elderly woman, and defendants had a very close relationship over a long period of time. The trial court assessed the evidence as being "strong that the parties treated each other as blood relations." While plaintiff was seriously ill in a convalescent home she executed and delivered to defendant Michael Pagnotta a deed naming him as grantee but reserving to herself a life estate. Michael Pagnotta testified that plaintiff said that she wanted the property to go to the Pagnottas' daughter after plaintiff's death, which she deemed to be imminent. . . .

The trial court held that plaintiff effectively made a gift to defendants' daughter of the remainder interest in the real property. In effect, this recognized that Michael Pagnotta held the remainder interest as trustee for his daughter. Plaintiff contends that this constituted error for the reason that the trust was oral and thus violated the Statute of Frauds. (ORS 93.020).

It will be noted that subsection (2) of [the Oregon Statute of Frauds] makes it clear that the section does not "prevent a trust from arising. . . . by implication or operation of law." A constructive trust is one kind of trust which arises by "operation of law," and is therefore not prevented from arising simply because the evidence necessary to prove it is an oral agreement to hold the property in trust. The question in the present case is, then, whether a constructive trust arose out of Michael Pagnotta's oral agreement to convey to his daughter the real property conveyed to him by plaintiff. The applicable principle is found in Restatement of Restitution § 183, pp. 737-38 (1937):

> Where the owner of an interest in land transfers it inter vivos to another upon an oral trust in favor of a third person or upon an oral agreement to convey the

---

37. Under the federal Bankruptcy Code of 1978, however, if a bankrupt who is the trustee of an oral trust to which the statute of frauds applies under local law attempts to recognize the trust after bankruptcy, the bankruptcy trustee may reach the trust property. 11 U.S.C. § 541(e).

land to a third person, and the trust or agreement is unenforceable because of the Statute of Frauds, and the transferee refuses to perform the trust or agreement, he holds the interest upon a constructive trust for the third person, if, but only if,

[(a) the transferee by fraud, duress or undue influence induced the transferor not to create an enforceable interest in the third person, or]

(b) the transferee at the time of the transfer was in a confidential relation to the transferor, or,

(c) the transfer was made by the transferor in contemplation of death.[38]

The evidence in the case before us clearly establishes that the transferee, Michael Pagnotta, was in a confidential relation to the transferor.[39] As we have already observed, the trial judge found that "the parties treated each other as blood relations." We reach the same conclusion on the basis of the record.

There is also evidence that the transfer was made by the transferor in contemplation of death, thus falling within subsection (c) of Section 183.[40] There was testimony that plaintiff made the conveyance in the manner that she did because she "didn't want any probate" and that she "wanted the property to go to . . . (the) daughter after . . . (plaintiff's) death." There was also evidence that plaintiff had previously executed a will in which she devised the property to the daughter.

Since a constructive trust arose in favor of the daughter, this case does not fall within the principle found in Restatement (Second) of Trusts, § 411, p. 333 (1959), relied upon by plaintiff, which states that

---

38. See also, Restatement (Second) of Trusts § 44 (1959), and Hanscom v. Irwin, 186 Or. 541, 208 P.2d 330 (1949); Harrington v. Harrington, 252 Or. 39, 448 P.2d 364 (1968).

39. Comment c of Section 182, Restatement of Restitution, pp. 734-35 (1937), defines confidential relation as follows:

> A confidential relation exists not only where there is a fiduciary relation such as that between attorney and client, trustee and beneficiary, guardian and ward, partner and partner, and the like, but also where, because of family relationship or otherwise, the transferor is in fact accustomed to be guided by the judgment or advice of the transferee or is justified in placing confidence in the belief that the transferee will act in the interest of the transferor. It might seem, indeed, that wherever the transferee orally agrees to hold the property transferred to him in trust for the transferor or agrees to retransfer it, there is in this very fact a sufficient relation of confidence thereby created to justify imposing a constructive trust upon him if he breaks his promise; but some courts require additional evidence of confidence in the relation between them before imposing a constructive trust (see the Caveat).

40. Comment f of § 183, Restatement of Restitution, p. 742 (1937), explains:

> at the time of the transfer that he will hold the land in trust for or convey it to a third person, and the transfer was made by the transferor in contemplation of death and intended by him as a substitute for a testamentary disposition of his property, the transferee holds the property upon a constructive trust for the third person (see Restatement of Trusts, § 45, Comment d). This situation is treated as analogous to the situation where a testator devises or bequeaths property to a person in reliance upon his agreement to hold the property in trust for or to convey it to another (see § 186).

> Where the owner of property gratuitously transfers it and properly manifests an intention that the transferee should hold the property in trust but the trust fails, the transferee holds the trust estate upon a resulting trust for the transferor or his estate, unless the transferor properly manifested an intention that no resulting trust should arise or the intended trust fails for illegality.

As we have demonstrated, this is not a case where the "trust fails"; a valid trust in favor of the daughter arose by operation of law. . . .

We hold that the evidence does not support a resulting trust and therefore the decree of the trial court is affirmed.

Notes and Questions

1. *Constructive Trust.* That wrongdoing on the part of the grantee (promisor) provides a ground for the imposition of a constructive trust is well recognized in the cases. The wrongdoing includes that of committing fraud, duress, or undue influence, or of abusing a confidential relationship or the fact that the transferor made the transfer in contemplation of death.

If the grantee orally promised to hold the land in trust for the settlor, the constructive trust is imposed in favor of the settlor. Restatement of Restitution § 182 (1937); Restatement 3d of Trusts § 24(2). If the grantee orally promised to hold the land in trust for a third person, as in Person v. Pagnotta, the third person can regularly obtain constructive trust relief in his or her own favor. Restatement of Restitution § 183 (1937); Restatement 3d of Trusts § 24(2); Kester v. Crilly, 91 N.E.2d 419 (Ill. 1950). Some text-writers have been inclined to disapprove of the latter result, arguing that restitution should be given to the settlor rather than to the intended beneficiary (Bogert on Trusts § 496; Scott on Trusts § 45.2), but their views seem to have had no influence on the courts. See Palmer on Restitution § 19.3(f)-(g).

Person v. Pagnotta raises an interesting variation of the typical case. The suit wasn't brought by the intended beneficiary, Michael Pagnotta's daughter. Neither she nor her natural guardian had reason to do so. Why not? The court purported to apply § 183 of the Restatement of Restitution, but neglected to note the absence of a necessary element. What element was absent? Could the court have reached the same result on a different basis? See Palmer on Restitution § 19.3(g) at 127-28 and n.5 (Supp.).

2. *Confidential Relationship.* Although abuse of a confidential relationship is ground for the imposition of a constructive trust, the term "confidential relationship" hasn't proved easy to define. The Restatement 3d of Trusts § 24 comment f provides:

> A confidential relationship exists not only when there is a fiduciary relationship, such as that between attorney and client, trustee and beneficiary, agent and

> principal, or conservator and conservatee, but also where there is a confidential relationship as a matter of applicable law or on the basis of the particular facts involved. Illustrative of the latter are situations in which, because of family relationship or otherwise, the transferor is in fact accustomed to relying on the guidance or judgment of the transferee or is otherwise specially justified in assuming that the transferee will act in the interest of the transferor. . . . More is required for this purpose, however, than the trust and confidence implicit in the transferor's reliance on the transferee's oral promise in making the transfer to him or her as an intended trustee.

Some attempts at definition seem to be wholly circular, such as the Illinois court's statement that "the relation exists in all cases where there has been a special confidence reposed in one who is bound to act in good faith and with due regard to the interests of the one reposing the confidence." Dick v. Albers, 236, 90 N.E. 683, 685 (Ill. 1910). From one point of view, the concept is so broad as to subsume *all* of the oral trust cases. As the authors of a recent text point out, "[a]rguably, such a [confidential] relationship exists whenever a transferor intended to create a trust, for trust and confidence are synonyms." William F. McGovern, Jr. & Sheldon F. Kurtz, Wills, Trusts and Estates 263 (2d ed. 2001). This understanding of what constitutes a confidential relationship could lead, in effect, to an abandonment of the requirement altogether, and this is what occurred in California. In Orella v. Johnson, 242 P.2d 5 (Cal. 1952), the California Supreme Court based constructive trust relief on the oral promise alone.

Most courts, however, haven't been prepared to go that far, so that the search continues for some means of giving content to the idea of a confidential relationship. Since most cases involve conveyances from one family member to another, a recurring problem is whether the family connection alone is enough. Although results are largely unpredictable, it does appear that the number of cases may be increasing in which relief is given where nothing more appears than a close family relationship. Note the further step taken in Person v. Pagnotta, where the court found a confidential relationship between Nellie Person and Michael Pagnotta because they "treated each other as blood relations."

Yet the attitude expressed by the Massachusetts court must be taken into account on the other side. In refusing to find a confidential relationship in a conveyance by father to son on oral trust for the grantor, the court cited numerous Massachusetts cases in which relief had been denied where the conveyances were between members of a family, and concluded: "To adopt the plaintiff's contention would require us to overrule these cases, a course that we are not disposed to follow." Ranicar v. Goodwin, 96 N.E.2d 853 (Mass. 1951).

3. *Fraud.* Fraud is another basis for imposition of a constructive trust. Fraud requires establishing that the grantee never intended to keep the oral promise. The grantee's refusal to perform the promise is not usually sufficient, but it may be where the refusal occurred shortly after the promise was made. Lipp v. Lipp, 148 A. 531 (Md. 1930).

4. *Value Restitution for Simple Breach?* In the absence of a wrong on the grantee/promisor's part, the case is generally viewed as one of simple breach of an oral and unenforceable promise; no relief is granted if the grantee/promisor raises the Statute of Frauds as a defense. Examples are Funk v. Engel, 209 N.W. 160 (Mich. 1926); Horsley v. Hrenchir, 73 P.2d 1010 (Kan. 1937).

Most decisions reaching this result make no attempt to relate it to the general law of restitution for breach of an unenforceable agreement. Yet, under the general law of restitution, one who confers a benefit in the performance of an unenforceable agreement will be given restitution of the value of the benefit if the other party repudiates or refuses to perform the agreement. Thus, in a quasi-contract action, a person who has paid money under an oral agreement to purchase land will be permitted to recover the amount paid if the vendor repudiates or refuses to perform. E.g., Ford v. Stroud, 64 S.E. 1 (N.C. 1909).

In view of the large number of oral-trust cases that have refused constructive trust relief (specific restitution), it is therefore surprising that there are so few in which the grantor has sought to recover the value of the land (value restitution). This may reflect the widespread professional ignorance of the law of restitution. In Massachusetts, restitution of the value of the land has been allowed, while at the same time the constructive trust remedy has been denied. Kemp v. Kemp, 142 N.E. 779 (Mass. 1924); Cromwell v. Norton, 79 N.E. 433 (Mass. 1906).

External Reference. Palmer on Restitution § 19.3.

5. *Improvident Gifts.* There is no doctrine in the law that allows the donor or the donor's conservator to set aside improvident gifts. The closest that the law comes is that in the law of mental capacity, the donor of an irrevocable gift must not only have capacity to make a will but also "must be capable of understanding the effect that the gift may have on the future financial security of the donor and of anyone who may be dependent on the donor." Restatement 3d of Property § 8.1(c).

6. *Necessity of a Promise?* In Person v. Pagnotta, Michael Pagnotta expressly promised Nellie Person that he would convey the property to his daughter upon Nellie's death. Is an express promise on the part of the grantee necessary to the imposition of a constructive trust? The next case, Sharp v. Kosmalski, shows that a promise is sometimes implied in fact.

Sharp v. Kosmalski

351 N.E.2d 721 (N.Y. 1976)

GABRIELLI, J. Plaintiff [J. Rodney Sharp] commenced this action to impose a constructive trust upon property transferred to defendant [Jean C. Kosmalski], on the ground that the retention of the property and the subsequent ejection of the plaintiff therefrom was in violation of a relationship of trust and confidence and constituted unjust enrichment. The Trial Judge dismissed plaintiff's complaint and his decision was affirmed without opinion by the Appellate Division.

Upon the death of his wife of 32 years, plaintiff, a 56-year old dairy farmer whose education did not go beyond the eighth grade, developed a very close relationship with defendant, a school teacher and a woman 16 years his junior. Defendant assisted plaintiff in disposing of his wife's belongings, performed certain domestic tasks for him such as ironing his shirts and was a frequent companion of the plaintiff. Plaintiff came to depend upon defendant's companionship and, eventually, declared his love for her, proposing marriage to her. Notwithstanding her refusal of his proposal of marriage, defendant continued her association with plaintiff and permitted him to shower her with many gifts, fanning his hope that he could induce defendant to alter her decision concerning his marriage proposal. Defendant was given access to plaintiff's bank account, from which it is not denied that she withdrew substantial amounts of money. Eventually, plaintiff made a will naming defendant as his sole beneficiary and executed a deed naming her a joint owner of his farm. The record reveals that numerous alterations in the way of modernization were made to plaintiff's farmhouse in alleged furtherance of "domestic plans" made by plaintiff and defendant.

In September, 1971, while the renovations were still in progress, plaintiff transferred his remaining joint interest to defendant. At the time of the conveyance, a farm liability policy was issued to plaintiff naming defendant and her daughter as additional insureds. Furthermore, the insurance agent was requested by plaintiff, in the presence of defendant, to change the policy to read "J. Rodney Sharp, life tenant. Jean C. Kosmalski, owner." In February, 1973, the liaison between the parties was abruptly severed as defendant ordered plaintiff to move out of his home and vacate the farm. Defendant took possession of the home, the farm and all the equipment thereon, leaving plaintiff with assets of $300.

Generally, a constructive trust may be imposed "[w]hen property has been acquired in such circumstances that the holder of the legal title may not in good conscience retain the beneficial interest." (Beatty v. Guggenheim Exploration Co., 225 N.Y. 380, 386, 122 N.E. 378, 380; 1 Scott, Trusts [3d ed], § 44.2 . . .). In the development of the doctrine of constructive trust as a remedy available to courts of equity, the following four requirements were posited: (1) a confidential or fiduciary relation, (2) a promise, (3) a transfer in reliance thereon and (4) unjust enrichment.

Most frequently, it is the existence of a confidential relationship which triggers the equitable considerations leading to the imposition of a constructive trust. Although no marital or other family relationship is present in this case, such is not essential for the existence of a confidential relation. The record in this case clearly indicates that a relationship of trust and confidence did exist between the parties and, hence, the defendant must be charged with an obligation not to abuse the trust and confidence placed in her by the plaintiff. The disparity in education between the plaintiff and defendant highlights the degree of dependence of the plaintiff upon the trust and honor of the defendant.

Unquestionably, there is a transfer of property here, but the Trial Judge found that the transfer was made "without a promise or understanding of any kind." Even without an express promise, however, courts of equity have imposed a constructive trust upon property transferred in reliance upon a confidential relationship. In such a situation, a promise may be implied or inferred from the very transaction itself. As Judge Cardozo so eloquently observed: "Though a promise in words was lacking, the whole transaction, it might be found, was 'instinct with an obligation' imperfectly expressed." (Sinclair v. Purdy, 235 N.Y. 245, 254, 139 N.E. 255, 258). In deciding that a formal writing or express promise was not essential to the application of the doctrine of constructive trust, Judge Cardozo further observed in language that is most fitting in the instant case:

> Here was a man transferring to his sister the only property he had in the world. . . . He was doing this, as she admits, in reliance upon her honor. Even if we were to accept her statement that there was no distinct promise to hold for his benefit, the exaction of such a promise, in view of the relation, might well have seemed to be superfluous (Sinclair v. Purdy, supra, p 254).

. . . . Indeed, in the case before us, it is inconceivable that plaintiff would convey all of his interest in property which was not only his abode but the very means of his livelihood without at least tacit consent upon the part of the defendant that she would permit him to continue to live on and operate the farm. . . .

The salutary purpose of the constructive trust remedy is to prevent unjust enrichment. . . . A person may be deemed to be unjustly enriched if he (or she) has received a benefit, the retention of which would be unjust (Restatement, Restitution, § 1, Comment a). A conclusion that one has been unjustly enriched is essentially a legal inference drawn from the circumstances surrounding the transfer of property and the relationship of the parties. It is a conclusion reached through the application of principles of equity. Having determined that the relationship between plaintiff and defendant in this case is of such a nature as to invoke consideration of the equitable remedy of constructive trust, it remains to be determined whether defendant's conduct following the transfer of plaintiff's farm was in violation of that relationship and, consequently, resulted in the unjust enrichment of the defendant. This must be determined from the circumstances of the transfer since there is no express promise concerning plaintiff's continued use of the land. Therefore, the case should be remitted to the Appellate Division for a review of the facts. In so doing I would emphasize that the conveyance herein should be interpreted "not literally or irrespective of its setting, but sensibly and broadly with all its human implications" (Sinclair v Purdy, 235 N.Y. 245, 254, 139 N.E. 255, 258, supra). This case seems to present the classic example of a situation where equity should intervene to scrutinize a transaction pregnant with opportunity for abuse and unfairness. It was for just this type of case that there evolved equitable principles and remedies to prevent injustices. Equity still lives. . . .

Accordingly, the order of the Appellate Division should be reversed and the case remitted to that court for a review of the facts, or, if it be so advised, in its discretion, to order a new trial in the interest of justice.[41]

2. *Testamentary Trusts: Statute Of Wills*

Suppose a testator's will devises property to a devisee outright. After the testator's death, a plaintiff alleges that the devisee had promised the testator that the devisee would hold the property for the benefit of the plaintiff. Or, suppose a testator's will expressly indicates that a devisee is to hold the devised property in trust, but neglects to state the substantive terms of the trust, including the intended beneficiary. The two situations involve so-called "secret" and "partially secret" trusts, respectively. Both situations involve issues concerning compliance with the Statute of Wills, analogous to the Statute of Frauds problem in cases of oral inter vivos trusts of land.

"Secret" Testamentary Trusts. If the plaintiff, who claims to be the intended beneficiary, proves that the devisee promised to hold the property in trust for the plaintiff, whether the promise was made before or after the will was executed, most jurisdictions impose a constructive trust on the devisee in favor of the plaintiff. See Restatement 3d of Trusts § 18. In the leading case of Trustees of Amherst College v. Ritch, 45 N.E. 876 (N.Y. 1897), the court gave this explanation for the result:

---

41. The decision in this case is cited with apparent approval in Kopelman v. Kopelman, 710 F. Supp. 99 (S.D.N.Y. 1989) (applying New York law); Bankers Security Life Ins. Soc'y v. Shakerdge, 406 N.E.2d 440 (N.Y. 1980).

> If the testator is induced either to make a will or not to change one after it is made, by a promise, express or implied, on the part of a legatee that he will devote his legacy to a certain lawful purpose, a secret trust is created, and equity will compel him to apply property thus obtained in accordance with his promise. . . . The trust springs from the intention of the testator and the promise of the legatee. The same rule applies to heirs and next of kin who induce their ancestor or relative not to make a will by promising, in case his property falls to them through intestacy, to dispose of it, or a part of it, in the manner indicated by him. . . . The rule is founded on the principle that the legacy would not have been given, or intestacy allowed to ensue, unless the promise had been made; and hence the person promising is bound, in equity, to keep it, as to violate it would be fraud. While a promise is essential, it need not be expressly made, for active co-operation or silent acquiescence may have the same effect as an express promise. If a legatee knows what the testator expects of him, and having an opportunity to speak, says nothing, it may be equivalent to a promise, provided the testator acts upon it. Whenever it appears that the testator was prevented from action by the action or silence of a legatee, who knew the facts in time to act or speak, he will not be permitted to apply the legacy to his own use when that would defeat the expectations of the testator. . . .
>
> The trust does not act directly upon the will by modifying the gift, for the law requires wills to be wholly in writing, but it acts upon the gift itself as it reaches the possession of the legatee, or as soon as he is entitled to receive it. The theory is that the will has full effect, by passing an absolute legacy to the legatee, and that then equity, in order to defeat fraud, raises a trust in favor of those intended to be benefited by the testator, and compels the legatee, as a trustee ex maleficio, to turn over the gift to them. The law, not the will, fastens the trust upon the fund, by requiring the legatee to act in accordance with the instructions of the testator and his own promise. Neither the statute of frauds nor the statute of wills applies, because the will takes effect as written and proved; but, to promote justice and prevent wrong, the courts compel the legatee to dispose of his gift in accordance with equity and good conscience.

The Restatement 3d of Trusts § 18, comment h, states that "the existence of the agreement to hold the property in trust must be shown by clear and convincing evidence." The rationale is that the proof must overcome "what appears on the face of the will to be an outright bequest or devise . . . ." Accord, Restatement 3d of Property § 12.1, comment b.

Although there is little dissent in the cases from the proposition of the *Ritch* case,[42] the result has been criticized. Professor Scott argued that the decisions giving relief in favor of the intended beneficiary are in conflict with the Statute of Wills.[43] In other words, the unjust enrichment should be remedied by

42. Cases are collected in Annots., 66 A.L.R. 156 (1930); 155 A.L.R. 106 (1955).

43. Scott on Trusts § 55.1.

imposing the constructive trust in favor of those who would be entitled to the property had the devise not been made. See, however, the following for discussions approving the results of the cases: Restatement 3d of Trusts § 18; Palmer on Restitution § 20.6(e); John H. Langbein & Lawrence W. Waggoner, Reformation of Wills on the Ground of Mistake: Change of Direction in American Law?, 130 U. Pa. L. Rev. 521, 574-76 (1982). Compare with the results in these cases the treatment of the partially secret trust involved in Olliffe v. Wells, which follows.

Olliffe v. Wells

130 Mass. 221 (1881)

[Ellen Donovan died in 1877. Her will devised the residue of her estate "to the Rev. Eleazer M.P. Wells . . . to distribute the same in such manner as in his discretion shall appear best calculated to carry out wishes which I have expressed to him or may express to him." Her will also nominated the Reverend Wells to be the executor. Donovan's heirs sued, claiming that the residue should be distributed to them. The Reverend Wells claimed the right to carry out Donovan's wishes, which she had expressed to him and to which he had assented before she executed her will. According to Rev. Wells, her intention was that the residue be used to provide for persons who were under the care of the St. Stephen's Mission of Boston.[44] The heirs treated Rev. Wells' allegation as true.]

GRAY, C.J. Upon the face of this will the residuary bequest to the defendant gives him no beneficial interest. It expressly requires him to distribute all the property bequeathed to him, giving him no discretion upon the question whether he shall or shall not distribute it, or shall or shall not carry out the intentions of the testatrix, but allowing him a discretionary authority as to the manner only in which the property shall be distributed according to her intentions. The will declares a trust too indefinite to be carried out, and the next of kin of the testatrix must take by way of a resulting trust, unless the facts agreed show such a trust for the benefit of others as the court can execute. Nichols v. Allen, [130 Mass.] 211. No other written instrument was signed by the testatrix, and made part of the will by reference. . . .

It has been held in England and in other States, although the question has never arisen in this Commonwealth, that, if a person procures an absolute

44. The St. Stephen's Mission was destroyed in the great Boston fire of 1872. Rev. Wells worked to restore the mission, but to no avail. Rev. Wells died in 1878 at age 95. In reading the court's opinion, consider whether these facts might have influenced the result. (We owe information about the St. Stephen's Mission to Jesse Dukeminier & Stanley M. Johanson, Wills, Trusts, and Estates 485-86 n.32 (4th ed. 1990)). Eds.

devise or bequest to himself by orally promising the testator that he will convey the property to or hold it for the benefit of third persons, and afterwards refuses to perform his promise, a trust arises out of the confidence reposed in him by the testator and of his own fraud, which a court of equity, upon clear and satisfactory proof of the facts, will enforce against him at the suit of such third persons. . . .

Upon like grounds, it has been held in England that, if a testator devises or bequeaths property to his executors upon trusts not defined in the will, but which, as he states in the will, he has communicated to them before its execution, such trusts, if for lawful purposes, may be proved by the admission of the executors, or by oral evidence, and enforced against them. . . . And in two or three comparatively recent cases it has been held that such trusts may be enforced against the heirs or next of kin of the testator, as well as against the devisee. . . . But these cases appear to us to have overlooked or disregarded a fundamental distinction.

Where a trust not declared in the will is established by a court of chancery against the devisee, it is by reason of the obligation resting upon the conscience of the devisee, and not as a valid testamentary disposition by the deceased. . . . Where the bequest is outright upon its face, the setting up of a trust, while it diminishes the right of the devisee, does not impair any right of the heirs or next of kin, in any aspect of the case; for if the trust were not set up, the whole property would go to the devisee by force of the devise; if the trust set up is a lawful one, it enures to the benefit of the *cestuis que trust*; and if the trust set up is unlawful, the heirs or next of kin take by way of resulting trust. . . .

[In the present case, w]here the bequest is declared upon its face to be upon such trusts as the testator has otherwise signified to the devisee, it is equally clear that the devisee takes no beneficial interest; and, as between him and the beneficiaries intended, there is as much ground for establishing the trust as if the bequest to him were absolute on its face. But as between the devisee and the heirs or next of kin, the case stands differently. They are not excluded by the will itself. The will upon its face showing that the devisee takes the legal title only and not the beneficial interest, and the trust not being sufficiently defined by the will to take effect, the equitable interest goes, by way of resulting trust, to the heirs or next of kin, as property of the deceased, not disposed of by his will. Sears v. Hardy, 120 Mass. 524, 541, 542. They cannot be deprived of that equitable interest, which accrues to them directly from the deceased, by any conduct of the devisee; nor by any intention of the deceased, unless signified in those forms which the law makes essential to every testamentary disposition. A trust not sufficiently declared on the face of the will cannot therefore be set up by extrinsic evidence to defeat the rights of the heirs at law or next of kin. . . .

Decree for the plaintiffs.

Notes and Questions

1. *Contrary Authority*. As the court's opinion in *Olliffe* indicated, the English courts do not differentiate between partially secret and secret testamentary trusts; they uphold both types. The principal decision is Blackwell v. Blackwell, [1929] App. Cas. 318 (H.L.). In that case, Blackwell's will devised £12,000 to five named persons "upon trust . . . for the purposes indicated by me to them." Blackwell communicated to some of the trustees his intention that the fund be used to care for a "woman who was not his wife" and their sixteen-year-old son,[45] and these trustees accepted the trust. The court held that no distinction should be drawn between a case in which the devise was on its face absolute and a case in which the will disclosed that the devisee was to hold the devise in trust. In each case, Lord Warrington said:

> The solution is to be found by bearing in mind that what is enforced is not a trust imposed by the will, but one arising from the acceptance by the legatee of a trust, communicated to him by the testator, on the faith of which the will was made or left unrevoked.

This result is the same as that reached by English courts in cases of secret inter vivos trusts of land. In both the testamentary and inter vivos contexts, that is, the result has been to effectuate the trust.

The Restatement of Trusts adopted the English view in 1935 and has adhered to it in the most recent revision. See Restatement 3d of Trusts § 18(1) comment c. A number of American decisions have followed the Restatement, rejecting *Olliffe*. See Curdy v. Berton, 21 P. 858 (Cal. 1889); Linney v. Cleveland Trust Co., 165 N.E. 101 (Ohio Ct. App. 1928); Hartman's Estate (No. 2), 182 A. 232 (Pa. 1936). In Estate of Brandenburg, 108 N.W.2d 374 (Wis. 1961), the Wisconsin court held that constructive relief is available to the intended beneficiaries, but the court ignored this decision in a case decided the same year in which it held that the heirs took on resulting trust. Estate of Liginger, 111 N.W.2d 407, 3 A.L.R.3d 1372 (Wis. 1961).

2. *Statute of Frauds Compared*. Very few cases have arisen concerning partially secret trusts contained in deeds of land. One such case is Muhm v. Davis, 580 S.W.2d 98 (Tex. Civ. App. 1979). Perry McNeill conveyed by deed his undivided one-half interest in 300 acres of land to "Cleveland Davis,

---

45. Historically, secret and partially secret trusts were sometimes created by wealthy men who wished to provide for their mistresses and/or non-marital children. See Simon Gardner, An Introduction to the Law of Trusts 85-87 (1990). Disclosing the terms of the trust in the will was undesirable because a probated will is a public document. Nowadays, of course, there are other, more effective ways to keep confidential the terms of one's dispositions (including a pour-over will, as we saw in Chapter 8, Part C, or a multiple-party bank account), but these techniques weren't available until modern times.

Trustee." The conveyance was made pursuant to a prior oral agreement under which Davis, McNeill's attorney, agreed to hold the land in trust until McNeill's youngest grandchild reached the age of eighteen, at which time Davis was to convey the land in equal shares to McNeill's two children and three grandchildren. Subsequently, McNeill's youngest grandchild reached eighteen, and Davis carried out his promise.

After McNeill's death, his principal devisee, one of his children, brought an action to set aside the conveyance from McNeill to Davis and the conveyance from Davis to McNeill's children and grandchildren. The trial court granted a motion for summary judgment in favor of the defendants. Affirming, the Texas Court of Civil Appeals said:

> The rule is thoroughly settled "that a trust in land declared by parol only, although wholly unenforceable against the trustee, has yet enough of vitality, so that, if voluntarily executed by the trustee at any time, it will become validated as of the date of the original oral agreement. . . ." Blaha v. Borgman, 142 Wis. 43, 46, 124 N.W. 1047, 1048 (1910).
>
> The seventh section of the English Statute of Frauds which was enacted in many American states commonly provides that trusts of land shall be "void and of no effect", unless manifested or proved by a writing. In these states the word "void" has been held to mean "unenforceable against the objection of the trustee." In Bogert, Trusts and Trustees 2d ed., § 69, the author says that the trustee in an oral trust is not forbidden to carry out his trust. He has a moral obligation to carry out his trust duties, and the performance of the oral trust is a legal and commendable act.
>
> This approach to the problem has been adopted in the Restatement of the Law of Trusts, where the Rule is stated in these words:
>
> > Where an oral trust of an interest in land is created inter vivos, the trustee can properly perform the trust if he has not transferred the interest, although he cannot be compelled to do so.
>
> Restatement (Second) of Trusts, § 43 at 112.
>
> The summary judgment evidence presents no issues of material fact and establishes as a matter of law an executed parol express trust. The trial court did not err in granting summary judgment.

See also Restatement 3d of Trusts § 24 comments b and i.

3. *Questions*. Are the Statute of Frauds and Statute of Wills problems in cases of partially secret trusts strictly comparable? That is, should courts treat partially secret testamentary trusts the same way as they do partially secret inter vivos trusts of land? Is the distinction that the *Olliffe* court drew between partially secret and secret testamentary trusts sound, or is it evidence that, as one writer has stated, this is "an area of law rife with anomalous distinctions

and irreconcilable precedents"? Robi Blumenstein, Secret Trusts, 36 U. Toronto Fac. of L. Rev. 108 (1978).

External Reference. Palmer on Restitution § 20.7.

Chapter 14

Spendthrift, Discretionary, and Support Trusts

Now that the basic requirements necessary to form a trust have been introduced, we turn to a fundamental question of policy. Once a trust has been properly formed, should the law ensure that it will endure? Or, should the law enable the beneficiaries to undo the trust against the wishes of the settlor? The question is one of distributing power between successive property owners, past and present. Where the preferences of present beneficiaries conflict with those expressed by the donor, the law can't simultaneously respect the autonomy of both, and must choose between them.

The conflict between the donor's wishes and the preferences of current trust beneficiaries arises primarily in the context of three types of trusts: spendthrift, discretionary, and support. Most trusts created today fall into one or more of these categories. The principal features of each are briefly summarized as follows:

> *Spendthrift Trusts*. A spendthrift trust is a trust that contains a provision imposing a disabling restraint on the alienation of the beneficiaries' equitable interests. A disabling restraint on alienation is one that purports to nullify any attempted assignment by a beneficiary of his or her equitable interest and any attempted attachment of a beneficiary's interest by the beneficiary's creditors.

> *Discretionary Trusts.* A discretionary trust is a trust that contains a provision giving the trustee discretion to pay to or apply for the benefit of the beneficiary only so much of the income and principal or either as the trustee sees fit.
>
> *Support Trusts.* A support trust is a trust that contains a provision directing the trustee to pay to or apply for the benefit of the beneficiary so much of the income and principal or either as is necessary for the beneficiary's education and support.

See Restatement 3d of Trusts §§ 58, 60.

To illustrate these types of trusts and the general problem that they pose, consider Example 14.1.

> *Example 14.1:* G has just died at age 75, survived by her 55-year-old daughter, A, and A's 21-year-old son, X. During the last few years of her life, G had been thinking about how to divide her $1 million estate between A and X. G decided to make a will giving most of the benefit of the million-dollar estate, say 80 percent of it, to A. In exploring how to formulate her will with A and X, a choice discussed was simply to devise $800,000 outright to A and $200,000 outright to X. A and X respectfully expressed preference for that form, although A wasn't so sure that X should be devised such an amount in a lump sum.
>
> Although G didn't mention her feelings to A or X, G secretly had reservations about devising lump-sum amounts to either one. G's concern wasn't about A's lack of maturity or ability to handle money, but she was worried that A's husband, H, who she often referred to as that "no-account bum," might somehow get his hands on the money and squander it on some risky business venture. So, after consulting her lawyer (one of your former classmates), G decided to follow a different path. To the surprise and chagrin of A, H, and X, G's will devised the full $1 million into a trust, the terms of which are that A is to receive the income for life, with the corpus at A's death going to X.

Suppose that, using the actuarial tables currently in use for tax purposes (see IRC § 7520), the present value of A's right to the income from $1 million for life is $800,000 and the present value of X's right to $1 million at A's death is $200,000.

With all due respect for G and her wishes, A and X still prefer the cash. Accompanied by H, they consult you as their lawyer and ask a straightforward question: Can they somehow exchange their trust interests for cash? Well, you tell them, there are two potential sources—the trust and outsiders. A and X could try to find a buyer or buyers for their interests (or find a lender or lenders who would loan them the cash, accepting the beneficial interests as security). Or, A and X could try to terminate the trust and have the $1 million corpus distributed to them on an 80/20 basis.

Putting aside the impracticability of the first option,[1] your examination of G's will reveals that the trust is a spendthrift trust, *i.e.*, it contains a disabling restraint on alienation. Under prevailing American law, disabling restraints on alienation of equitable interests in trust are valid. Moreover, a spendthrift trust is indestructible, *i.e.*, the beneficiaries can't compel the trustee prematurely to terminate such a trust. See Restatement 2d of Trusts §§ 152, 153, 330 & comment l.

These rules of American trust law represent a shift away from the English law of trusts. Under English law, disabling restraints on the alienation of equitable interests in trust are invalid. This was established by the Chancellor, Lord Eldon, in Brandon v. Robinson, 18 Ves. 429, 34 Eng. Rep. 379 (Ch. 1811). And, English law allows the beneficiaries of any type of trust, irrespective of the settlor's wishes, to undo the trust by demanding the trust property outright and free of trust. This rule was adopted in Saunders v. Vautier, 4 Beav. 115, 49 Eng. Rep. 282 (Ch. 1841), aff'd, Cr. & Ph. 240, 41 Eng. Rep. 482 (Ch. 1841), and solidified in Wharton v. Masterman, [1895] App. Cas. 186 (H.L.). English law, then, empowers trust beneficiaries to control their interests and thereby limits the donor's control. American trust doctrine reverses this allocation of control.

The American shift away from the English rules occurred in the latter part of the nineteenth century. A pair of 1880s decisions of the Supreme Judicial Court of Massachusetts are mainly credited with having engineered these departures from prior law: Broadway National Bank v. Adams (1882) and Claflin v. Claflin (1889). We will study both of these cases shortly.

External References. Gregory S. Alexander, The Dead Hand and the Law of Trusts in the Nineteenth Century, 37 Stan. L. Rev. 1189 (1985); Lawrence M. Friedman, The Dynastic Trust, 73 Yale L.J. 547 (1964).

---

1. A and X would have difficulty finding buyers for their interests, let alone buyers who would pay full actuarial value. Compare Estate of Vought, infra p. 841. A different situation exists in England, where it has been reported that an organized auction is held once a month at the London Auction Mart for the sale of future interests in property, either vested or contingent. See "Speculation," Newsweek, Jan. 25, 1971, at 66; "Some Britishers Sell Birthrights for More Than Mess of Pottage," Wall St. J., May 10, 1971. In America, no such auction market exists.

PART A. RESTRAINING ALIENABILITY OF BENEFICIAL INTERESTS/SHIELDING BENEFICIAL INTERESTS FROM CREDITORS

1. Spendthrift Trusts

Statutory References: *UTC §§ 501-502*

In the absence of a valid restraint on alienation, a beneficiary of a trust can transfer his or her beneficial interest and the beneficiary's creditors can subject such interest to the satisfaction of their claims to the same extent as a corresponding legal interest. See Restatement 3d of Trusts §§ 51, 56.

We begin out study of spendthrift trusts with Broadway National Bank v. Adams. Although *Broadway Bank* wasn't the first American decision to depart from the English rule by upholding spendthrift trusts, it—along with Justice Miller's dictum in Nichols v. Eaton, 91 U.S. 716 (1875), expressing approval of such trusts—is usually credited with having turned the tide of American law.

To put *Broadway Bank* into perspective, the subject of restraints on alienation of *legal* interests must be briefly examined. (When you read the *Broadway Bank* opinion, note that this is what the court is referring to when it mentions "the rule of the common law.") For our purposes, two types of restraints on alienation are relevant—disabling restraints and forfeiture restraints. The terms are defined and their validity is addressed in the Restatement 2d of Property as follows:

> § *3.1 Disabling Restraint.* Terms of a donative transfer of an interest in property which seek to invalidate a later transfer of that interest, in whole or in part, constitute a disabling restraint on alienation (hereinafter referred to as a disabling restraint).
>
> § *4.1 Validity of Disabling Restraint.* (1) A disabling restraint imposed in a donative transfer on an interest in property is invalid if the restraint, if effective, would make it impossible for any period of time from the date of the donative transfer to transfer such interest. . . .
>
> § *3.2 Forfeiture Restraint.* Terms of a donative transfer of an interest in property which seek to terminate, or to subject to termination, that interest, in whole or in part, in the event of a later transfer constitute a forfeiture restraint on alienation (hereinafter referred to as a forfeiture restraint). A forfeiture restraint may apply to any attempted later transfer or only to some types of such transfers and may be limited or unlimited in duration. But the person that is to take in the event of a forfeiture must have a valid interest under the rule against perpetuities.
>
> § *4.2 Validity of Forfeiture Restraint.* (1) A forfeiture restraint imposed in a donative transfer on a life interest in property, or on an interest for a term of years

> that will terminate at the end of a life (or reasonable number of lives) in being at the time of the transfer, is valid. . . .

In *Broadway Bank*, the beneficiary, Charles Adams, was given an *equitable* life estate, with the statement that it was not to be subject (a) to voluntary alienation by him or (b) to the claims of his creditors. The second provision is often described as a restraint on involuntary alienation, since if a creditor *is* permitted to reach an asset of the debtor the consequence will sometimes be a forced sale of the debtor's interest. The typical spendthrift trust restrains both voluntary and involuntary alienation.[2]

Had Charles Adams been given a *legal* life estate, the restraint would have been void. As the above provisions of the Restatement demonstrate, the general position of the common law is that such "disabling" restraints on legal interests in property are void.

One of Lord Eldon's goals as Chancellor was to move the English rules of equity into greater alignment with those of the common law. This may account for his holding in Brandon v. Robinson voiding disabling restraints on equitable life estates. It may also explain his statement that the equitable interest of the beneficiary could validly have been subjected to a forfeiture restraint, which he expressed in terms of approval of a grant of an equitable interest to a beneficiary "until he shall become bankrupt."

Broadway National Bank v. Adams

133 Mass. 170 (1882)

MORTON, C.J. The object of this bill in equity is to reach and apply in payment of the plaintiff's debt due from the defendant Adams the income of a trust fund created for his benefit by the will of his brother. The eleventh article of the will is as follows:

> I give the sum of seventy-five thousand dollars to my said executors and the survivors or survivor of them, in trust to invest the same in such manner as to them may seem prudent, and to pay the net income thereof, semiannually, to my said brother Charles W. Adams, during his natural life, such payments to be made to him personally when convenient, otherwise, upon his order or receipt in writing; in either case free from the interference or control of his creditors, my intention being that the use of said income shall not be anticipated by assignment. . . .

---

2. See, for example, the sample clause set forth infra p. 840. Restatement 3d of Trusts § 58, comment b states that for policy reasons a spendthrift clause that restrains involuntary alienation but permits voluntary alienation is invalid. *Accord* UTC § 502(a). Massachusetts takes the contrary view. See Bank of New England v. Strandlund, 529 N.E.2d 394 (Mass. 1988).

There is no room for doubt as to the intention of the testator. It is clear if the trustee was to pay the income to the plaintiff under an order of the court, it would be in direct violation of the intention of the testator and of the provisions of his will. The court will not compel the trustee thus to do what the will forbids him to do, unless the provisions and intention of the testator are unlawful. . . .

It is true that the rule of the common law is, that a man cannot attach to a grant or transfer of property, otherwise absolute, the condition that it shall not be alienated; such condition being repugnant to the nature of the estate granted. Co.Lit. 223 a. Blackstone Bank v. Davis, 21 Pick. 42.

Lord Coke gives as the reason of the rule, that "it is absurd and repugnant to reason that he, that hath no possibility to have the land revert to him, should restrain his feoffee in fee simple of all his power to alien," and that this is "against the height and puritie of a fee simple." By such a condition, the grantor undertakes to deprive the property in the hands of the grantee of one of its legal incidents and attributes, namely its alienability, which is deemed to be against public policy. But the reasons for the rule do not apply in the case of a transfer of property in trust. By the creation of a trust like the one before us, the trust property passes to the trustee with all its incidents and attributes unimpaired. He takes the whole legal title to the property, with the power of alienation; the *cestui que trust* takes the whole legal title to the accrued income at the moment it is paid over to him. Neither the principal nor the income is at any time inalienable.

The question whether the rule of the common law should be applied to equitable life estates created by will or deed, has been the subject of conflicting adjudications by different courts. . . . [F]rom the time of Lord Eldon the rule has prevailed in the English Court of Chancery, to the extent of holding that when the income of a trust estate is given to any person (other than a married woman) for life, the equitable estate for life is alienable by, and liable in equity to the debts of, the *cestui que trust*, and that this quality is so inseparable from the estate that no provision, however express, which does not operate as a cesser or limitation of the estate itself, can protect it from his debts. Brandon v. Robinson, 18 Ves. 429. The English rule has been adopted in several of the courts of this country. Other courts have rejected it. . . .

The founder of this trust was the absolute owner of his property. He had the entire right to dispose of it, either by any absolute gift to his brother, or by a gift with such restrictions or limitations, not repugnant to law, as he saw fit to impose. His clear intention, as shown in his will, was not to give his brother an absolute right to the income which might hereafter accrue upon the trust fund, with the power of alienating it in advance, but only the right to receive semiannually the income of the fund, which upon its payment to him, and not before, was to become his absolute property. His intentions ought to be carried out, unless they are against public policy. There is nothing in the nature or tenure of the estate given to the *cestui que trust* which should prevent this. The power of alienating in advance is not a necessary attribute or incident of such an estate or interest, so that the restraint of such alienation would introduce repugnant or inconsistent elements.

We are not able to see that it would violate any principles of sound public policy to permit a testator to give to the object of his bounty such a qualified interest in the income of a trust fund, and thus provide against the improvidence or misfortune of the beneficiary. The only ground upon which it can be held to be against public policy is, that it defrauds the creditors of the beneficiary.

It is argued that investing a man with apparent value tends to mislead creditors, and to induce them to give him credit. The answer is, that creditors have no right to rely upon property thus held, and to give him credit upon the basis of an estate which, by the instrument creating it, is declared to be inalienable by him, and not liable for his debts. By the exercise of proper diligence they can ascertain the nature and extent of his estate, especially in this Commonwealth, where all wills and most deeds are spread upon the public record. There is the same danger of their being misled by false appearances, and induced to give credit to the equitable life tenant when the will or deed of trust provides for a cesser or limitation over, in case of an attempted alienation, or of bankruptcy or attachment, and the argument would lead to the conclusion that the English rule is equally in violation of public policy. . . .

The rule of public policy which subjects a debtor's property to the payment of his debts, does not subject the property of a donor to the debts of his beneficiary, and does not give the creditor a right to complain that, in the exercise of his absolute right of disposition, the donor has not seen fit to give the property to the creditor, but has left it out of his reach. . . .

It follows that, under the provisions of the will which we are considering, the income of the trust fund created for the benefit of the defendant Adams cannot be reached by attachment, either at law or in equity, before it is paid to him.

Bill dismissed.

The Dead Hand Dilemma: Whose Freedom of Disposition Do or Should We Protect? Spendthrift trusts raise what Professor Alexander has called the "dead hand dilemma,"[3] which is that the general idea of freedom of disposition can be invoked on either side—for or against the validity of spendthrift trusts. Several writers have opposed the validity of spendthrift trusts, focusing on the infringe-

3. Gregory S. Alexander, The Dead Hand and the Law of Trusts in the Nineteenth Century, 37 Stan. L. Rev. 1189, 1193 (1985).

ment of the donee's freedom of disposition. The most outspoken critic of the time was John Chipman Gray, who was prompted by Nichols v. Eaton to write a short book titled Restraints on the Alienation of Property (1883), arguing:

> The fallacy [of validating spendthrift trusts is in the notion] that the only objection to such inalienable life estates is that they defraud the creditors of the life tenant; and the courts labor, with more or less success, to show that these creditors are not defrauded. . . . But, with submission, this is not the ground why equitable life estates cannot be made inalienable and free from debts. The true ground is the same on which the whole law of property, legal and equitable, is based;—that inalienable rights of property are opposed to the fundamental principles of the common law; that it is against public policy that a man "should have an estate to live on, but not an estate to pay his debts with"; Tillinghast v. Bradford, 5 R.I. 205, 212; that a man should have the benefits of wealth without the responsibilities. The common law has recognized certain classes of persons who may be kept in pupilage, viz. infants, lunatics, married women; but it has held that sane grown men must look out for themselves,—that it is not the function of the law to join in the futile effort to save the foolish and the vicious from the consequences of their own vice and folly. It is wholesome doctrine, fit to produce a manly race, based on sound morality and wise philosophy. . . .
>
> That grown men should be kept all their lives in pupilage, that men not paying their debts should live in luxury on inherited wealth, are doctrines as undemocratic as can well be conceived. . . . The general introduction of spendthrift trusts would be to form a privileged class, who could indulge in every speculation, could practice every fraud, and, provided they kept on the safe side of the criminal law, could yet roll in wealth. They would be an aristocracy, though certainly the most contemptible aristocracy with which a country was ever cursed.

Id. at 169-70, 173-74. Gray's opposition to spendthrift trusts was to little avail. In the preface to the second edition of his book, published in 1895, Gray lamented:

> State after State has given in its adhesion to the new doctrine. Were it not for an occasional dissenting opinion I should be *vox clamantis in deserto*.
>
> And yet I cannot recant. Doubtless I may exaggerate the importance of the matter; but, so far as it goes, I still believe, as I said in the first edition, that the old doctrine was a wholesome one, fit to produce a manly race, based on sound morality and wise philosophy; and that the new doctrine is contrary thereto.[4]

To the judges (and legislators) of the time (and since), the donor's freedom of disposition has apparently seemed more worthy of protection. This is vividly expressed in the *Broadway Bank* case, where the court said:

---

4. John C. Gray, Restraints on the Alienation of Property iv-v (2d ed. 1895).

> The founder of this trust was the absolute owner of his property. . . . His clear intention . . . was not to give his brother an absolute right to the income . . . with power of alienating it in advance, but only the right to receive semiannually the income. . . . His intentions ought to be carried out, unless they are against public policy. . . . We are not able to see that it would violate any principles of sound public policy to permit a testator to give to the object of his bounty such a qualified interest in the income . . . and thus provide against the improvidence or misfortune of the beneficiary.

See also Steib v. Whitehead, 111 Ill. 247, 250-52 (1884).

An important but perhaps less obvious role of trusts is structuring and regulating relations within families, especially among wealthier social classes.

The term spendthrift trust is a somewhat of a misnomer, since judicial recognition has not limited such trusts to spendthrifts or to persons who may be in need of special protection. Apart from statute, any person can be the beneficiary of a spendthrift trust in a state recognizing such trusts, without regard to the beneficiary's ability to look after himself or herself and his or her business affairs. Nor has the case law placed any limitation on the amount of income that can be validly protected from the claims of the beneficiary's creditors. In an Illinois case, Congress Hotel Co. v. Martin, 143 N.E. 838 (Ill. 1924), the beneficiary was entitled to income of over $171,000 for the year 1921. In that year, she ran up a hotel bill of some $6,700 and the hotel sought to reach income in the hands of the trustee by garnishment. The court denied relief because the will creating the trust included a spendthrift provision.

The Minority View. Only a small number of jurisdictions refuses recognition of spendthrift trusts. One such jurisdiction is New Hampshire. In Brahmey v. Rollins, 179 A. 186, 191-94 (N.H. 1935), the New Hampshire court held that, despite a spendthrift clause, a creditor could reach an income interest of his debtor under a trust, saying:

> The view that the right to seize property is in any way an essential attribute of it which the owner may destroy is considered erroneous. It is an exposure to loss of ownership, and not any part of the makeup of title. It is an instrument of attack upon title, and does not enter into it as a constituent. It is a right, not of the owner, but of the creditor. It is not a quality of property, but is wholly external thereto. It is a burden of incidence, and not of inherence. It is a consequence, and not an element of ownership. It is a public regulation of property beyond private control. . . .
>
> If the restraint against alienation is valid, it is because the right to alienate is an inherent element of ownership which the donor may withhold in a gift of the property. . . . If he may bar seizure, why may he not as well bar taxability? . . .
>
> The policy to attach so great weight to the enjoyment of ownership as to permit the owner to prescribe, in a gift of the property owned, special terms which conflict with the general laws of ownership, has no forceful appeal. By the gift the

> owner parts with all benefit from the property which he may personally enjoy. Why should he have the right to free the property from a burden resting on it while he owns it, during the term the donee in equity may have it, and thereby give or create rights which he himself does not possess? Besides the conflict with general law, there is also the conflict with the general policy that only those needing protective relief should have it.

Other cases and statutes adopting the minority view, mainly from Kentucky and Rhode Island,[5] are collected in Scott on Trusts § 152.1 n.3. Ohio had been another hold-out, but the Ohio Supreme Court recently recognized spendthrift trusts in Scott v. Bank One Trust Co., 577 N.E.2d 1077 (Ohio 1991).

For recent policy discussions of the spendthrift trust doctrine, see Adam J. Hirsch, Spendthrift Trusts and Public Policy: Economic and Cognitive Perspectives, 73 Wash. U.L.Q. 1 (1995); Anne S. Emanuel, Spendthrift Trusts: It's Time to Codify the Compromise, 72 Neb. L. Rev. 179 (1993).

Spendthrift-Trust Legislation. Spendthrift trusts are recognized by statute in many states, but the statutes take a variety of forms. No attempt at exhaustive classification is made here; for a state-by-state compilation, see Scott on Trusts § 152.1.

As is true of the common-law decisions, most statutes place no limit on the amount that can be protected by or on who can be the beneficiary of a spendthrift trust, by reference either to need, competency, or relationship to the settlor. In Nevada[6] and Texas,[7] for example, the statute authorizes the creation of spendthrift trusts in terms about as broad as could be devised. Both income and principal may be placed beyond the reach of creditors without regard to the amount of wealth involved. The Nevada statute states explicitly that the validity of such a trust "does not depend on the character, capacity, incapacity, competency or incompetency of the beneficiary." In Alabama,[8] however, the statute limits spendthrift protection to beneficiaries who are the settlor's "child, grandchild, or other relation by blood or marriage."

---

5. In 1988, Rhode Island enacted a statute declaring:

> *R.I. Gen. Laws § 18-9.1-1.* Establishment of spendthrift trust.—Any person creating an express trust for the benefit of any other person or persons may by the terms thereof establish valid restraints on the voluntary and/or involuntary transfer of interests therein by the beneficiaries thereof, whether by way of anticipation or acceleration, assignment, hypothecation or by virtue of legal process in judgement, execution, attachment, garnishment, bankruptcy or otherwise.

6. Nev. Rev. Stat. §§ 166.010-166.160. But see Ambrose v. First Nat'l Bank, 482 P.2d 828 (Nev. 1971), which construed the statute as limiting spendthrift trusts to trusts for support.

7. Tex. Prop. Code § 112.035.

8. Ala. Code § 19-3-1.

The New York statute deserves mention because it has been copied in a number of states, in whole or in part. By legislation that had its beginnings in 1828, well before the *Broadway Bank* case was decided, virtually all trusts are automatically made spendthrift trusts by statute, without the need of any provision to that effect in the trust instrument. The central provision in the present New York statute reads:

> *N.Y. Est. Powers & Trusts Law § 7-1.5. When trust interest inalienable; exception.* (a) . . . (1) The right of a beneficiary of an express trust to receive the income from property and apply it to the use of or pay it to any person may not be transferred by assignment or otherwise unless a power to transfer such right, or any part thereof, is conferred upon such beneficiary by the instrument creating or declaring the trust. . . .

Unlike the judge-approved spendthrift trust, however, the New York statute allows voluntary transfer of any amount of income in excess of $10,000 per year, provided the transfer is made to specified relatives, is gratuitous, and is not expressly prohibited by the trust instrument. N.Y. Est. Powers & Trusts Law § 7-1.5(b). The New York statute also places a limit on the amount of income that can be shielded from the claims of creditors: Creditors can reach income "in excess of the sum necessary for the education and support of the beneficiary." N.Y. Est. Powers & Trusts Law § 7-3.4. This limitation in New York has been substantially vitiated, however, by construing needs to relate to the beneficiary's "station in life."[9] In Kilroy v. Wood, 42 Hun. 636 (N.Y. 1886), for example, creditors were unsuccessful in trying to reach surplus income of a spendthrift trust because they failed to show that the income was more than sufficient for the beneficiary's support. The court said:

> [The beneficiary is] a gentleman of high social standing, whose associations are chiefly with men of leisure, and is connected with a number of clubs, with the usages and customs of which he seems to be in harmony both in practice and expenditure, and it is insisted on his behalf that his income is not more than sufficient to maintain his position according to his education, habits and associations.

Id. at 638. See also Erwin N. Griswold, Spendthrift Trusts § 379 (2d ed. 1947); Richard R. Powell, The Rule Against Perpetuities and Spendthrift Trusts in New York: Comments and Suggestions, 71 Colum. L. Rev. 688, 699 (1971) [hereinafter Powell, Spendthrift Trusts].

---

9. More recently, provisions of the N.Y. Civil Practice Law and Rules have removed some of the protection previously afforded by this station-in-life test. See Gregory S. Alexander, Spendthrift Trusts and Their Functional Substitutes, in Debtor-Creditor Law ¶22A.03[A] (Theodore Eisenberg ed. 1986).

The California statute is a variation of the New York scheme. Unlike the New York statute, the restraint on alienation is imposed only if the settlor so provides. Cal. Prob. Code § 15300. But once this has occurred, judgment creditors (as under the New York scheme) can reach any amount "in excess of the amount that is or will be necessary for education and support of the beneficiary"; unlike New York, however, there is apparently an additional cap preventing judgment creditors from reaching more than 25 percent of the amounts otherwise payable. Cal. Prob. Code §§ 15306.5, 15307.

In interpreting the education-and-support limit, the California courts also apply a station-in-life test. But the extremes of the New York cases have arguably been avoided, as the following passage from Canfield v. Security-First Nat'l Bank, 87 P.2d 830, 840-41 (Cal. 1939), suggests:

> No set sum can be fixed to apply to all cases. The amount varies according to the station in life of the beneficiary. This does not mean, however, that the needs of the beneficiary are to be measured by his extravagance or his ability to spend. It does not mean that an allowance is to be made for extravagant entertaining, and for unbridled luxuries. The manner of living of the beneficiary in the past, if such living was unreasonably extravagant and profuse, is no criterion of the reasonable amount necessary for support and maintenance. Evidence as to cost of living, wages of servants, medical expense and reasonable entertainment, and other reasonably necessary expenses, fixes the amount. . . .
>
> The cost of living, cost of housing, medical cost, the manner in which the beneficiary has been reared, the number and health of his dependents, his own health, his entire background—all these and perhaps others should be considered. But cost of lavish entertaining, cost of betting on race horses and cost of obvious luxuries, etc.—these are all false factors.

The station-in-life test, even as administered by the California courts, shields from creditors' claims income sufficient to support a fairly luxurious style of living, if this is the style of living to which the beneficiary is accustomed. Dean Griswold and Professor Powell bridled at the station-in-life test and argued for a different approach. In Powell, Spendthrift Trusts, supra, at 704-05, the author argued:

> It would not be wise to prohibit *all* spendthrift trusts. There are occasions when a possessor of substantial wealth has, close to his heart, a relative who lacks the business experience to protect himself from the ever-present vultures. A modest sum, so set up as to protect such a person from dissipating his substance and unreachable by creditors generally, constitutes no threat to social welfare. The trouble arises when the amount entrusted becomes large and the immunities of the beneficiary cease to be reasonable.

Earlier, Dean Griswold had drafted a model spendthrift-trust statute, which provided that all income "in excess of $5000 per annum shall be subject to attachment by a creditor of the beneficiary [of a spendthrift trust] and shall be freely alienable by the beneficiary." Griswold, supra, at 648. Griswold wrote this in 1947; in today's dollars, the $5000 figure would translate roughly to $30-35,000 per year.

Griswold's model statute was enacted in Louisiana and Oklahoma. In Louisiana, the $5,000 figure was raised to $10,000 in 1985; in 1987, the limit was repealed altogether.[10] In Oklahoma, the figure is $25,000 per year.[11] In Virginia, the statute provides that $600,000 of trust principal can be made the subject of a spendthrift trust.[12]

In 1979, North Carolina repealed its original statute on spendthrift trusts and replaced it with a statute that provides that the interest of a beneficiary shall be alienable, voluntarily or involuntarily, except where the trust is a discretionary trust, a support trust, or a protective trust.[13] A protective trust is defined as one wherein it is provided that the interest of the beneficiary shall cease if the beneficiary alienates or attempts to alienate the interest, if any creditor attempts to reach the interest, or if the beneficiary becomes insolvent or bankrupt. This is a retreat from the full-scale American spendthrift trust and, although the terminology isn't entirely the same, amounts substantially to an acceptance of the English law.

Life-Insurance Proceeds. More than half the states have statutes that either automatically shield from the beneficiary's creditors life-insurance proceeds payable under an installment method, or permit the insured to do so by provision in the policy.

ERISA Pension Trusts. Pension plans regulated by the Employee Retirement Income Security Act (ERISA) are required to include a spendthrift clause: "Each pension plan shall provide that benefits provided under the plan may not be assigned or alienated." ERISA § 206(d)(1), 29 U.S.C. § 1056(d)(1). Note that this is a mandatory rule, not a default rule. The policy basis for ERISA's mandatory antialienation rule is the employee's retirement security interest overrides the interest of creditors. See Guidry v. Sheet Metal Workers Nat'l Pension Fund, 493 U.S. 365 (1990).

---

10. La. Rev. Stat. § 9:2004.

11. Okla. Stat. Ann. tit. 60 § 175.25.

12. Va. Code § 55-19. The statute provides that an estate, "not exceeding $500,000 in actual value, may be holden or possessed in trust upon condition that the corpus thereof and income therefrom, or either of them, shall be applied by the trustee to the support and maintenance of the beneficiaries without being subject to their liabilities or to alienation by them. . . ."

13. N.C. Gen. Stat. § 36A-115.

ERISA applies to pension plans of employers who engage in or affect interstate or foreign commerce. See also IRC § 401(a)(13). State law also often provides that pension benefits are unassignable and exempt from execution. See generally Jeffrey G. Sherman, Spendthrift Trusts and Employee Pensions: The Problem of Creditors' Rights, 55 Ind. L.J. 247 (1980). Various pension plans for federal employees include restraints on alienation. See Scott on Trusts § 157.1 at 200-01.

Federal Bankruptcy. To the extent that a spendthrift restraint is valid under or automatically imposed by state law or federal law, it is also effective in bankruptcy. The Bankruptcy Code, 11 U.S.C. § 541(c)(2),[14] specifically provides that "a restriction on the transfer of a beneficial interest of the debtor in a trust that is enforceable under applicable nonbankruptcy law is enforceable in a case under this title." Courts have consistently construed this provision to exclude from a bankrupt debtor's estate any beneficial trust interest that is subject to a valid spendthrift restraint. E.g., Bass v. Denney (*in re* Bass), 171 F.3d 1016 (3d Cir. 1999). In Patterson v. Shumate, 504 U.S. 753 (1992), the Supreme Court held that the phrase "applicable nonbankruptcy law" included the antialienation provision of ERISA. Consequently, interests in ERISA pensions are excluded from the bankrupt's estate.

Boiler-Plate Use of Spendthrift Clauses. In practice, nearly every private trust drafted by a lawyer contains a spendthrift clause. A spendthrift clause is routinely included in law-office and published form-book trust forms. Here is the clause contained in the sample revocable inter vivos trust from Chapter 13, Part A:

> No interest of any beneficiary in the income or principal of this trust shall be assignable in anticipation of payment or be liable in any way for the beneficiary's debts or obligations and shall not be subject to attachment.

The location of the spendthrift clause may also be significant. It's not unusual for a modern trust instrument to be fairly lengthy, consisting of thirty or more typewritten pages. Unlike the testator's will in the *Broadway Bank* case, where the spendthrift restraint was part of the same sentence granting Charles Adams the right to the income, the modern trust forms bury the spendthrift clause in a separate Article toward the end of the document, near the perpetuity saving clause (see infra Chapter 19, Part C). We doubt that very many clients are told the significance of the clause, except where the client expresses concern about

---

14. A major reform of federal bankruptcy law is pending. As this casebook goes to press, the House of Representatives and the Senate have passed different versions of reform legislation, and a conference committee has been appointed to resolve the differences. For the latest developments, see the American Bankruptcy Institute's website, www.abiworld.org.

one or more of the beneficiaries (such as G did in Example 14.1, supra). Nor do we think that very many clients notice the clause on their own and inquire about its significance; and, of those that do, we doubt they get much of an explanation of its significance beyond the standard "Oh, that's a technical-legal clause that we put in all the trusts we draft." To the extent that this is an accurate picture of current legal practice, what risk does this practice create for settlors, beneficiaries, or society in general?

Notice that the sample spendthrift clause, supra, applies not only to the interest of the income beneficiary (A, in Example 14.1, supra), but also to the interest of the remainder beneficiary in principal (X, in that Example). Are spendthrift restraints on future interests in principal valid?

Estate of Vought

250 N.E.2d 343 (N.Y. 1969)

[Chance M. Vought, Sr.,[15] died in 1930, survived by his wife, Edna, and his two sons, Peter Vought and Chance M. Vought, Jr. The will of Chance, Sr., created a trust, the income to be paid to Edna for life, remainder in corpus in equal shares to the two sons. Edna died at age 67 in 1965, survived by Peter. Although Chance, Jr., predeceased his mother by about a year and a half, his remainder interest in half of the corpus (valued at about $1 million) was not conditioned on survivorship to the time of possession or enjoyment and so passed through his estate to his successors in interest, presumably his widow and surviving children.

The trust expressly prohibited alienation of the sons' remainder interests in principal. Nevertheless, Chance, Jr., during his lifetime, purported to assign his remainder interest in the corpus in a series of transactions as follows: (a) on October 27, 1959, he sold to Inheritance Estates Ltd. a right to $450,000, for which he allegedly received $78,750; (b) on October 27, 1959, he sold to the Allied Investment & Discount Corporation a right to $150,000, subject to the prior assignment, for which he allegedly received $15,000; (c) on January 8, 1960, he sold to Lex Company Inc. a right to $500,000, subject to the two prior assignments; and (d) on August 11, 1960, he sold to Leonard P. Levy, all his interest in the principal, subject to the three prior assignments. Chance, Jr.,

---

15. Chance M. Vought, Sr., was one of the pioneers of the American aviation industry. As chief engineer for the Wright brothers' firm, he designed several of the aircraft used in the First World War. After the War, he began his own aviation company, which later merged with Pratt & Whitney Aircraft Company and the Boeing Airplane Company. This merger produced a substantial fortune for him by the time of his death in 1930.

allegedly received $12,000 for these last two assignments.[16] There was evidence that these amounts allegedly received by Chance, Jr. were substantially below the actuarial values of the interests purportedly assigned by him.[17] There was also evidence that Chance, Jr., was, at the time of these transactions "an alcoholic suffering from chronic relapsing pancreatitis and diabetes and was addicted to the use of drugs as a result of the suffering caused by this condition [and] in the words of one witness [he was also] in `desperate financial straights'. . . . "[18] The Surrogate's Court held that the clause restraining alienation of Chance, Jr.'s remainder interest in the trust principal was valid and, therefore, that his assignments were void. The Appellate Division affirmed, and the assignees appealed to the Court of Appeals.]

BREITEL, J. . . . The precise question of whether a settlor has the power to make inalienable a principal remainder limited on an entrusted life estate is one of first impression. In this State, although there are many precedents which offer close analogies, they yield no conclusive or authoritative holding or doctrine. It is evident, however, that the prevailing weight of decisional authority in the Nation, based more or less on common-law principles, would sustain the restraint of alienation of a remainder limited on an equitable life interest, if so provided by the creator of the trust. Moreover, in policy, there are no persuasive modern reasons, and aside from conceptual and historical grounds, for nullifying attempts at restraining alienation on transfers in fee absolute, no compelling legal ground why the creator's wishes must be ignored during the measured period involved. Consequently, it is concluded that the determinations of the Surrogate and the Appellate Division should be affirmed. . . .

In the instant case, the issue is whether generally a creator may postpone for a limited period the beneficiary's control of material wealth until a time when the beneficiary is believed to be more able to manage it more wisely. Such a desire is not unnatural in a creator of trusts, nor does it work an undue hardship on those who extend aid to the beneficiary, provided they extend aid with the knowledge that they will not be reimbursed out of the principal against the creator's wishes.

The weight of authority, where not controlled by statute, supports the power to impose inalienability of principal as well as of life interests (see 2 Scott, Law of Trusts [3d ed.], § 153, p. 1170; see, also, 2 Bogert, Law of Trusts and

---

16. The details of the transactions are reported in Estate of Vought, 334 N.Y.S.2d 720, 723 (Sur. Ct. 1972).

17. Estate of Vought, 351 N.Y.S.2d 816, 821 (Sur. Ct. 1973).

18. Id. at 757, 351 N.Y.S.2d at 820-21.

Trustees [2d. ed.], § 222, p. 639, at n. 2). Scott has noted: "The courts seem to feel that the protection of the beneficiary of a trust should extend not merely to his right to receive income but to his right to receive principal in the future, whether in the meantime he or another person is entitled to receive the income" (op. cit., at pp. 1170-1171). As a reflection of a trend in favor of allowing principal inalienability, the Restatement, 2d Trusts, reversing the position of the first Restatement, now allows for inalienability of the principal (compare Restatement, 2d Trusts, § 153, with Restatement, Trusts, § 153). . . .

Given the history of the rules and the statutes expressing the rules, giving only limited value to the ideal of consistency of patterns in the law, and according substantial weight to modern policy considerations and the purpose of permitting owners enlarged freedom to dispose of their property as they will unless there is injury to the public, the law of this State should conform to the prevailing weight of authority. In this way, the intended beneficiaries of the remainders of principal will be protected as the settlors intend, and the assignees suffer no loss greater than that for which they bargained on the face of the instruments with which they were dealing. Interests in property are not restrained of alienation or transfer for any greater time than the permissible life interests and the legal title of the particular assets . . . is always capable of being transferred [under the trustee's power of sale.]

In the absence of any strong statutory direction or any developed body of precedent restricting provisions making principal inalienable, the will of the testator should be given effect, and the interest of the assignor be deemed unassignable during the life of the trust.

The assignees argue, however, that even if the interest in principal be deemed unassignable, the assignees should be entitled to that interest now that the trust has ended and the principal is now to be paid out. They argue it would be inequitable to have allowed the assignor to renounce the assignment, and urge that his estate be charged with his obligation to facilitate a transfer.

Such a result, however, would render meaningless any provision providing for inalienability of the principal for, indeed, the beneficial owner has no present interest to be protected but the right to receive the principal at a later date. If by an assignment during the life of the trust he is deemed to have transferred this sole right of later possession he has transferred virtually all his interest. Moreover, the creator's wishes would be completely frustrated, the beneficiary not only getting the funds the creator had intended be delayed, but the beneficiary receiving a fraction, after discount, of what was eventually intended.

Thus the courts below correctly determined that the assignees were not entitled to the principal of the trust.

Accordingly, the order of the Appellate Division should be affirmed, with costs to all parties filing briefs payable out of the estate.

FULD, C.J., dissenting. I would reverse on the ground that the estate created in the will for the testator's son constituted both a legal and equitable vested remainder in fee, the alienability of which, under long-established principles, may not be proscribed. (EPTL, 7-1.5 [replacing former Personal Property Law, § 15].) Moreover, the policy considerations in favor of permitting a restraint upon the alienability of property until such time as the beneficiary is believed to be equipped to manage it wisely do not operate where a remainderman is given an absolute and unqualified right to dispose of the property as he chooses, subject only to the prior life estate of another.

Notes and Questions

1. *State of Authorities*. Prior to *Vought*, most of the cases upholding spendthrift restraints on remainder interests in principal were cases of postponement-of-enjoyment trusts. Unlike *Vought*, which is a successive-beneficiary trust (income to A for life, remainder in corpus to B), these cases were of the income-to-A-until-A-reaches-30,-then-principal-to-A type. See, e.g., Erickson v. Erickson, 266 N.W. 161, reh'g denied, 267 N.W. 426 (Minn. 1936). The original Restatement of Trusts § 153 (1935) restricted the validity of spendthrift restraints on remainder interests to this type of trust, i.e., where the remainder beneficiary "is entitled to the income from the trust property."

As the New York court pointed out in *Vought*, the position of the original Restatement of Trusts (1935) was reversed in the Restatement 2d of Trusts § 153. According to Scott on Trusts § 153, the "weight of authority today [is that a spendthrift restraint on remainder interests in principal] is valid whether or not the beneficiary is entitled to the income in the meantime." The Restatement 3d of Trusts § 58 comment a continues to treat spendthrift restraints on remainder interests as valid. The UTC and the recent California and Texas codifications of trust law also adopt this position. See UTC § 502; Cal. Prob. Code § 15301(a); Tex. Prop. Code § 112.035.

2. *Effect of Restraint After Principal/Income Due*. If a spendthrift provision is valid regarding principal, does it continue to be effective once the time has arrived for but prior to actual distribution? Although the decisions are divided on the question (Scott on Trusts § 153), the Restatement 3d of Trusts § 58, comment d states that "property that has become distributable to the beneficiary but is retained by the trustee beyond a time reasonably necessary to make distribution to a beneficiary, and thus to which the beneficiary has a right to demand immediate distribution, is then subject to attachment by creditors of the beneficiary." This rule is codified in some states. See, e.g., Cal. Prob. Code § 15301. UTC § 506 similarly provides that "[w]hether or not a trust contains a

spendthrift provision, a creditor or assignee of a beneficiary may reach a mandatory distribution of income or principal, including a distribution upon termination of the trust, if the trustee has not made the distribution to the beneficiary within a reasonable time after the required distribution date."

3. *Enforceability of a Contract to Pay Over the Amount of a Spendthrift Trust Payment.* All authorities agree that both income and principal are transferable and attachable once received by the beneficiary. Does it follow that a spendthrift-trust beneficiary who, for value, agrees or purports to transfer his or her interest to another is liable for breach of contract? Substantial authority states that the beneficiary is liable.

In Moffat v. Lynch, 642 S.W.2d 624 (Mo. 1982), James D. Moffat III and his two sisters were the equal income beneficiaries of a testamentary trust that provided that upon the death of any one of the income beneficiaries, his or her portion of the income was to be distributed equally among the survivors of them. The trust contained a spendthrift clause. Several years after creation of the trust, James and his sisters entered into an agreement that upon the death of any one of them, the survivors would pay over to the children of the deceased beneficiary the proportion of the income to which the deceased beneficiary had been entitled while living. After James died, his sisters refused to honor the agreement. James's son sought to enforce the agreement against them. The court held that the agreement was enforceable, reasoning that recovery on the contract by the promisee or contract beneficiary comes out of the general property of the trust beneficiary rather than the beneficiary's interest in the trust. The contract beneficiary, the court said, is reaching no more than any general creditor of the beneficiary could reach. Accord, Restatement 2d of Trusts § 152 comment k; Kelly v. Kelly, 79 P.2d 1059 (Cal. 1938); Minot v. Minot, 66 N.E.2d 5 (Mass. 1946).

Compare Estate of Vought, 351 N.Y.S.2d 816 (Sur. Ct. 1973), holding that Chance Vought, Jr.'s estate was neither liable on the contract nor for restitution. The transactions (see supra p. 841), the court found, were unconscionable, usurious, and void; also, the assignees knew of the spendthrift restraint and assumed the risk as to its validity.

2. Discretionary, Support, and Discretionary-Support Trusts

Statutory References: *UTC § 504*

Traditional Trust Law Classification. Conventional trust law doctrine draws a categorical distinction between discretionary trusts and support trusts. Restatement 2d of Trusts § 154, for example, defined a support trust as one in which "by the terms of the trust the amount to be paid or applied for the beneficiary is limited to so much of the income or principal as in fact is necessary for his education or support." By contrast, § 155 of the 2d Restatement defined a discretionary trust as one in which the terms of the trust provide that "the trustee may in his absolute discretion refuse to make any payment to the beneficiary or to apply any of the trust property for his benefit." Comment c. These definitions led the Restatement—and many courts, following the Restatement's lead—to resolve important disputes about the nature of the beneficiary's interest, the extent of the trustee's duties to the beneficiary, and the ability of a trust beneficiary's creditors to reach the beneficiary's interest by determining into which of the two categories, discretionary or support, the instant trust should be placed. If the trust was classified as a discretionary trust, for example, the beneficiary's interest was considered to be inalienable because of the nature of the interest. As one court recently stated, "Because discretionary trusts give the trustee complete discretion to distribute all, some, or none of the trust assets, the beneficiary has a 'mere expectancy' in the non-distributed income and principal until the trustee elects to make a payment." United States v. O'Shaughnessy, 517 N.W.2d 574, 577 (Minn. 1994) (holding that the IRS could not enforce a tax levy against a discretionary trust beneficiary's interest). The same reasoning has led courts to hold that creditors of the beneficiary of a discretionary trust cannot reach the beneficiary's interest, whether or not the interest is subject to a valid spendthrift restriction. On the other hand, if the trust is deemed to be a support trust rather than a discretionary trust, then the beneficiary and creditors can compel payment by the trustee but only to the extent of the restricted support purpose of the trust. Restatement 2d of Trusts § 154, Comment c.

The effect of these rules has been substantial confusion in case law. This confusion is especially evident in cases involving the question whether a trust beneficiary's interest should be taken into account in determining whether the beneficiary qualifies for Medicaid or other forms of public assistance, a topic addressed in Chapter 9. As we saw there, many courts have reasoned that the beneficiary's interest should be taken into account if the trust is a support trust but not if it is a discretionary trust. Different outcomes have turned on the slightest differences in the language used in the trust instruments.

A New Approach. Recognizing these difficulties, both the Restatement 3d of Trusts and the Uniform Trust Code have abandoned the traditional distinction between discretionary trusts and support trusts in favor of a single standard. As the Reporter's Notes on § 60 explain, §§ 50 and 60 "depart[] significantly from prior Restatements, and from some lines of cases that were largely influenced by the prior Restatement positions . . . in that this Restatement Third does not attempt to draw a bright line between 'discretionary' interests . . . and 'support' interests . . . . The so-called 'support trust' is viewed here as a discretionary trust with a support standard. This in turn requires asking and examining all of the questions that follow from that view, such as how a particular standard, in context, is to be interpreted and whether a beneficiary's other resources are to be taken into account in making a fiduciary judgment about appropriate distributions to the beneficiary. . . . The fact of the matter is that there is a continuum of discretionary trusts, with the terms of distributive powers ranging from the most objective . . . of standards (pure "support") to the most open ended (e.g., "happiness") or vague ("benefit") of standards, or even with no standards manifested at all (for which a court will probably apply "a general standard of reasonableness"). And these trusts use an unlimited variety of combinations of such terms or standards, with any standard or combination about as likely as another to be accompanied by language of extended discretion (such as "absolute" or "sole and uncontrolled") . . . ." UTC § 504 similarly provides a single rule for all discretionary trusts. The statutory trust set forth in the Uniform Custodial Trust Act is a discretionary trust when it is for an incapacitated beneficiary. Unif. Custodial Trust Act § 9(b) (1987). The materials that follow discuss some of the implications of this new approach.

a. Range of the Trustee's Discretion

By conferring discretion, a settlor manifests an intention to trust the trustee's judgment. Restatement 3d of Trusts § 50 provides that a discretionary power of a trustee to determine the benefits of a beneficiary is subject to judicial control only to prevent misinterpretation or abuse of discretion. This, of course, leaves open the question what constitutes an abuse of discretion. On this question, consider the following discussion.

Restatement 3d of Trusts

§ *50(2)*. [W]hat may constitute an abuse of discretion by the trustee . . . depend[s] on the terms of the discretion , including the proper construction of any accompanying standards, and on the settlor's purposes in granting the discretionary power and in creating the trust. . . .

[Comment] b. Judicial review and control of trustee's discretion. . . . Court intervention may be obtained to rectify abuses resulting from bad faith or improper motive, and to correct errors resulting from mistakes of interpretation. Absent language of extended (e.g., "absolute" or "uncontrolled") discretion (Comment *c*), a court will also intervene if it finds that the payments made, or not made, to be unreasonable as a means of carrying out the trust provisions. For example, a beneficiary may be entitled to amounts sufficient to provide support, or to meet some other standard, and the amounts being paid by the trustee may be clearly excessive or inadequate for the purpose. It is not necessary, however, that the terms of the trust provide specific standards in

order for a trustee's good faith decision to be found unreasonable and thus to constitute an abuse of discretion. . . .

[Comment] c. Effect of extended discretion. Although the discretionary character of a power of distribution does not ordinarily authorize the trustee to act beyond the bounds of reasonable judgment (Comment *b*), a settlor may manifest an intention to grant the trustee greater than ordinary latitude in exercising discretionary judgment. How does such an intention affect the duty of the trustee and the role of the court?

It is contrary to sound policy, and a contradiction in terms, to permit the settlor to relieve a "trustee" of all accountability. . . . Once it is determined that the authority over trust distributions is held in the role of trustee . . . , words such as "absolute" or "unlimited" or "sole and uncontrolled" are not interpreted literally. Even under the broadest grant of fiduciary discretion, a trustee must act honestly and in a state of mind contemplated by the settlor. Thus, the court will not permit the trustee to act in bad faith or for some purpose or motive other than to accomplish the purposes of the discretionary power. Except as the power is for the trustee's personal benefit, the court will also prevent the trustee from *failing* to act, either arbitrarily or from a misunderstanding of the trustee's duty or authority.

Within these limits, it is a matter of interpretation to ascertain the *degree* to which the settlor's language of extended (e.g., "absolute") discretion manifests an intention to relieve the trustee of normal judicial supervision and control in the exercise of a discretionary power over trust distributions. . . .

[Comment] e. Significance of beneficiary's other resources. It is important to ascertain whether a trustee, in determining the distributions to be made to a beneficiary under an objective standard (such as a support standard, (i) is *required* to take account of the beneficiary's other resources, (ii) is *prohibited* from doing so, or (iii) is to consider the other resources but *has some discretion* in the matter. If the trust provisions do not address the question, the general rule of construction presumes the last of these. . . .

One qualification is that, if the discretionary power is one to invade principal for (or to distribute additional income to) a beneficiary who is entitled to all or a specific part of the trust income . . ., the trustee must take the mandatory distributions into account before making additional payments under the discretionary power. Where the beneficiary is entitled to payments from another trust created by the same settlor . . . or as part of coordinated estate planning with another (such as the settlor's spouse), required distributions from the other trust–and the purposes of both trusts–are to be taken into account by the trustee in deciding whether, in what amounts, and from which trust(s) discretionary payments are to be made.

Another qualification is that, to the extent and for as long as the discretionary interest is intended to provide for the support, education, or health care of a beneficiary . . . for periods during which a beneficiary was probably not expected to be self-supporting, the usual inference is that the trustee is *not* to deny or reduce payments for these purposes because of a beneficiary's personal resources. (But contrast the effect of *another's* duty to support the beneficiary . . . .)

Problem

Wilma Brown is a 50-year-old state supreme court justice. Wilma's spouse, Harry, age 47, is a self-employed cello teacher. Wilma and Harry have two children, Sonny and Cher, both of whom are over 18 and are undergraduates at Snootymore University. All members of the family are in good health.

Major assets, liabilities, and annual income and expenses of the family are roughly as follows:

MAJOR ASSETS		MAJOR LIABILITY	
House and Furnishings	$300,000	Mortgage	$50,000
Automobiles	$25,000		
Investments	$200,000		
Total	$525,000	*Net Worth*	$475,000
ANNUAL INCOME		ANNUAL EXPENSES	
Wilma's Salary	$95,000	Automobile Loan Payments	$5,000
Harry's Income	$10,000	Mortgage Payments	$12,000
Interest	$15,000	College Expenses for Cher and Sonny	$40,000
		Taxes (Income and Real Estate)	$45,000

		Other expenses (Food, clothing, donations, travel, medical, entertainment, etc.)	$50,000
Total Income	$120,000	Total Expenses	$152,000

1. Justice Brown's mother, Gertrude, died last year. Her will, executed five years earlier, devised $5 million in trust. You, as trustee, are directed to pay so much of the income, principal, or both as you, in your absolute and uncontrolled discretion, determine is necessary for Wilma's support and maintenance; unexpended income is to be accumulated and added to principal; upon Wilma's death, the principal (including accumulated income) is to go to Sonny and Cher.

You have invested the $5 million in such a way that it produces income at the rate of about $165,000 per year. In light of the Third Restatement's new approach, what amount would you decide to distribute to Wilma this year?

2. Same facts as Problem 1, except that Gertrude is Harry's mother, not Wilma's mother, and the beneficiary of the trust is Harry, not Wilma.

3. Same facts as Problem 1, except that the amount Gertrude devised in trust was $1,300,000, producing income at the rate of about $44,000 per year. See Tidrow v. Director, Missouri State Division of Family Services, 688 S.W.2d 9, 12 (Mo. Ct. App. 1985) (suggesting that the amount of the principal is a factor in deciding whether the beneficiary's other assets or sources of income can or must be taken into account by the trustee).

4. Same facts as Problem 1, except for the additional information that Wilma had been appointed by the governor to fill a vacancy on the state supreme court only two years ago. Prior to that time, Wilma had been a partner in and head of the trusts, estates, and personal financial counseling department of a large law firm, earning about $325,000 per year. The cut in pay Wilma took to become a judge considerably curtailed the style of living to which the family had previously been accustomed.

5. From your perspective as trustee, how could the drafting of Gertrude's trust have been improved?

External References. Scott on Trusts §§ 187, 128.3; Bogert on Trusts § 560; Evelyn G. Abravanel, Discretionary Support Trusts, 68 Iowa L. Rev. 273 (1983).

b. Alienability

As we have seen, according to the traditional approach the interest of the beneficiary of a pure discretionary trust, as where the trust instrument gives the trustee discretion, or "uncontrolled" or "absolute" discretion to pay or not to pay income or principal to the beneficiary, is viewed as a "mere expectancy." As such, it is inalienable, even in the absence of a spendthrift restraint. The beneficiary can't compel the trustee to pay, nor can an assignee or creditor of the beneficiary compel the trustee to pay, any part of the income or principal to him or her. See Restatement 3d of Trusts § 60, comment e; UTC § 504(b). This view of the status of the discretionary trust beneficiary is somewhat misleading, however. As the Restatement Comment states, "[i]t is rare . . . that the beneficiary's circumstances, the terms of the discretionary power, and the purposes of the trust leave the beneficiary so powerless. The exercise or non-exercise of fiduciary discretion is always subject to judicial review to prevent abuse. What might constitute an abuse, however, is not only affected by the extent of trustee's discretion, standards applicable to its exercise, and purposes of the trust, but also by the beneficiary's circumstances and the effect discretionary decisions will have on the discretionary beneficiary and on others in relation to the fulfillment of trust purposes."

The Third Restatement adopts a different approach. Section 60 provides: "Subject to the rules . . . (on spendthrift trusts), it the terms of a trust provide for a beneficiary to receive distributions in the trustee's discretion, a transferee or creditor of the beneficiary is entitled to receive or attach any distributions the trustee makes or is required to make in the exercise of that discretion after the trustee has knowledge of the transfer or attachment. The amounts a creditor can reach may be limited to provide for the beneficiary's needs . . ., or the amounts may be increased as where the beneficiary either is the settlor . . . or holds the discretionary power to determine his or her own distributions . . . ."

Trustee Liability After Notice of an Assignment. Creditors cannot judicially compel a trustee of a discretionary trust to pay them rather than the beneficiary. One might suppose, therefore, that the trustee may pay the beneficiary without incurring liability to the creditor. According to Restatement 3d of Trusts § 60, comment c, however, if there is no spendthrift restraint and if the trustee has knowledge that the beneficiary has assigned his or her interest or if the beneficiary's creditors have served the trustee with process in a proceeding to reach that interest, the trustee is liable to the assignee or the creditor if the trustee first pays the beneficiary.

This principle was established in New York by Hamilton v. Drogo, 150 N.E. 496 (N.Y. 1926). In that case, the dowager Duchess of Manchester devised a large sum in trust, giving the trustees "sole and uncontrolled discretion" to pay the income for the benefit of all or any among her son (the ninth Duke of

Manchester, who, incidentally, was a genuine spendthrift extraordinaire[19]), his wife, or his descendants. A judgment creditor of the Duke, after an execution was issued and returned unsatisfied, applied for an order that an execution issue against the trust income in the amount of ten percent thereof pursuant to N.Y. Civil Practice Law § 684.[20] The court ordered that the execution be granted, relying on this reasoning:

> In the present case no income may ever become due to the judgment debtor. We may not interfere with the discretion which the testatrix has vested in the trustee. . . . But at least annually this judgment must be exercised. And if it is exercised in favor of the duke, then there is due him the whole or such part of the income as the trustee may allot to him. After such allotment, he may compel its payment. At least for some appreciable time, however brief, the award must precede the delivery of the income he is to receive, and during that time the lien of the execution attaches.[21]

California courts later adopted the rule of Hamilton v. Drogo. See, e.g., Canfield v. Security-First Nat'l Bank, 87 P.2d 830 (Cal. 1939). The rule is now codified and its scope expanded in the California Probate Code § 15303, which provides that the trustee is liable to the beneficiary's transferee or creditor "to the extent that the payment to or for the benefit of the beneficiary impairs the right of the transferee or creditor." The statute further provides that it applies even if the trust wasn't a "pure" discretionary trust, i.e., the trust instrument provides a standard for the exercise of the trustee's discretion.[22]

Protective Trusts. A variation on discretionary trusts, the "protective trust," was developed by English lawyers to achieve much the same purpose as a spendthrift restriction despite English law's non-recognition of spendthrift

---

19. See Time, June 17, 1935, at 19. According to Time, the Duke (née William Angus Drogo Montagu) once owed $5,000 for tennis balls alone.

20. N.Y. Civ. Prac. Law § 684 then provided that "where any . . . income from trust funds . . . are due and owing to the judgment debtor or shall thereafter become due and owing to him," upon application of the creditor the justice must grant "an order directing that execution issue against the . . . income from trust funds of said judgment debtor, and on presentation of such execution . . . to the person . . . from whom such . . . income from trust funds . . . are due and owing or may thereafter become due and owing to the judgment debtor, said execution shall become a lien and a continuing levy upon the . . . income from trust funds . . . due or to become due to said judgment debtor" for "ten percent thereof."

21. This reasoning had been used in an earlier English case involving an assignment by the beneficiary of his interest under a discretionary trust. In re Neil, 62 L.T.R. 649 (1890).

22. An Oklahoma statute also embraces the substance of the Restatement's position, but the statute itself is based upon § 5 of a proposed statute found in Erwin N. Griswold, Spendthrift Trusts, app. A (2d ed. 1947). See Okla. Stat. Ann. tit. 60 § 175.25E; First Nat'l Bank v. Clark, 402 P.2d 248 (Okla. 1965).

trusts.[23] At creation, a protective trust typically gives the beneficiary a *right* to the income, but provides that, upon an attempted alienation, voluntary or involuntary, the beneficiary's right is forfeited and the trust becomes a discretionary trust. The protective-trust device takes advantage of the English rule that forfeiture restraints on equitable life estates are valid.

Protective trusts are commonly used as a substitute for a spendthrift trust in the few remaining American jurisdictions that don't recognize spendthrift trusts. See, e.g., Industrial Nat'l Bank v. Budlong, 264 A.2d 18 (R.I. 1970); Restatement 3d of Trusts § 57, comment a.[24]

Discretionary Trust Interests as Non-Marital Property. Patricia Jones was the beneficiary of a trust created by her grandfather's will. The trust instrument provided that the trustees had absolute discretion to pay so much income and principal to Patricia as the trustees determined was necessary for her health, support, maintenance, and education. When originally funded, the value of the trust corpus was $118,379. At the time of Patricia's subsequent divorce from her husband David, the value had appreciated to $160,519. In In re Marriage of Jones, 812 P.2d 1152 (Colo. 1991), the court held that the amount of capital appreciation of the trust was not marital property, subject to equitable division

---

23. In re Bullock, 60 L.J. Ch. 341 (1891). In 1925, England enacted legislation under which a settlor may create a protective trust of income merely by providing that the income is to be held on a "protective trust" for a person for "his life or for any less period." Trustee Act, 1925, 15 Geo. 5, ch. 19, § 33(1).

24. There are limits, however, to the enforceability of protective trusts. As we will learn later, governmental claims for past due income taxes are treated as special even in jurisdictions that do recognize spendthrift trusts. In United States v. Riggs Nat'l Bank, 636 F. Supp. 172 (D.D.C. 1986), a testamentary trust created by the will of Isabel G. Zantzinger provided for payment of a third of the income to her son, William, subject to a spendthrift restraint and a forfeiture provision providing that if William attempts to assign his interest or if his creditors attempt to subject his interest to a levy of execution, writ of attachment, or garnishment, the trustee should have discretion to apply income for the support of William or accumulate it and add it to corpus. A federal district court held that the protective-trust device was ineffective as against the federal tax lien. The court stated:

> [W]hile [protective] trust clauses create a legitimate property right under state law which can shield the beneficiary from ordinary creditors, such trusts cannot be effective against a federal tax lien, as a matter of federal law. . . . It would be offensive and disruptive to federal tax law for a beneficiary to receive an income stream for years without paying taxes on it, only to have the income stream disappear once the IRS discovers the misfeasance and moves against it.

The trust's beneficiary, William Devereaux Zantzinger, was the subject of an early song by Bob Dylan, "The Lonesome Death of Hattie Carroll." According to the song's lyrics, "William Zantzinger killed poor Hattie Carroll/With a cane that he twirled around his diamond ring finger/At a Baltimore hotel society gath'rin'." See Bob Dylan, *The Times They Are A-Changin'* (1964). We are grateful to Kevin FitzPatrick, Esq., of Detroit, Michigan, for providing us with this information. Eds.

upon divorce. Because of the trust's discretionary nature, the wife's beneficial interest was not separate property, the appreciation of which during marriage is marital property, but only an "expectancy." The fact that the trustee's discretion was limited by a support standard, the court stated, did not change its character as "completely discretionary."

Tax Classification of Discretionary Trusts. Trusts requiring the trustee to pay the income to a specified beneficiary or divide it equally among a specified group of beneficiaries are sometimes called "straight-income trusts." Another term sometimes used is "successive-beneficiary trusts." In income-tax parlance, the term "simple trust" is somewhat comparable; a simple trust is defined as one in which income is required to be distributed currently, no amounts can be devoted to charitable purposes, and no distribution of corpus is made in the taxable year. Treas. Reg. § 1.651(a)-1. Simple trusts are subject to Subpart B (§§ 651-52) of Subchapter J of the IRC. Generally speaking, this means that for income-tax purposes the ordinary income is taxed to the beneficiary receiving it (or entitled to receive it) rather than to the trust; realized capital gains or losses, however, are taxed to the trust.

By these definitions, the spendthrift trust created by G in Example 14.1, supra, is a straight-income, successive-beneficiary, simple trust. Note, too, that to qualify for the federal gift-tax or estate-tax marital deduction under IRC § 2523(e) or (f) or IRC § 2056(b)(5) or (b)(7), the spouse must be entitled for life to all the income from the entire interest, or all the income from a specific portion thereof, payable annually or at more frequent intervals. In practical effect, such trusts are quite rigid.

To add flexibility and opportunity for post-creation tax planning, trust documents often confer discretionary powers on the trustee. The extent of the trustee's discretionary power varies with the situation. It may relate to income, principal, or both. For example, in Example 14.1, supra, G might have created a so-called *spray* (or *sprinkle*) trust: Although the trustee would be required to distribute all the income, the trustee would be given a discretionary power to allocate that income all to G's daughter, A; all to A's son, X; or part to A and the remaining part to X. Thus, as time goes along, the trustee would be enabled to adjust the allocation of income to take account of matters such as the different income-tax brackets of A and X and the different needs of A and X. Such a trust, incidentally, would be a "discretionary trust" in trust-law parlance, but would still be a simple trust in income-tax parlance (Treas. Reg. § 1.651(a)-2(b)); it would become a "complex trust," however, if the trustee were authorized to accumulate some or all of the income rather than pay it out.

Even in the case of a marital-deduction trust, where the spouse must be entitled to all the income for life, the trustee often is given a discretionary power exercisable in favor of the spouse to invade the corpus of the trust. Such a power doesn't disqualify the trust for the marital deduction. E.g., Treas. Reg. § 20.2056(b)-5(i).

Marital-Deduction/By-Pass Trusts. To select one example of many that could be given of the sophisticated use of discretionary powers, consider the standard marital-deduction/by-pass trust combination, illustrated by the following example. Suppose H died, leaving a net estate of $4 million. H's will split his estate into two equal parts, $2 million going into a standard QTIP marital-deduction trust and the remaining $2 million into a standard by-pass trust. The marital-deduction trust provides that W is to receive the entire income for life, and both trusts provide that the remainder in corpus at her death goes to their then-surviving descendants by representation. In this form, the marital-deduction trust isn't taxed in H's estate (IRC § 2056) but will be taxed in W's estate when she dies (IRC § 2044); and the by-pass trust is taxed in H's estate (IRC § 2033) but won't be taxed in W's estate when she dies (IRC §§ 2033; 2041).

It was anticipated that the marital-deduction trust would initially produce about $100,000 income annually and that the by-pass trust would initially produce about the same amount. Considering the style of living to which W was accustomed, pre-tax income of roughly $200,000 a year was just about sufficient for her to squeeze by on.

Suppose, however, that H's lawyer, having taken a course from your trusts and estates teacher in law school, knew of the following trick. Instead of requiring the trustee of the by-pass trust to pay out its income to W for life, she drafted the by-pass trust so that the trustee was given a discretionary power to accumulate the income or pay it out to W (or to any one or more of their descendants). And, she drafted the marital-deduction trust so that the trustee was given a discretionary power to invade the corpus for W.

The plan still called for W to receive about $200,000 a year. But, instead of that sum being made up of all the income from the marital-deduction trust and all the income from the by-pass trust, it would be made up of all the income from the marital-deduction trust and, by virtue of an annual exercise of the trustee's discretionary power, an amount of principal from the marital-deduction trust sufficient, after taxes, to give W a yearly pre-tax income of the required $200,000. The trustee was also expected to utilize the discretionary power to accumulate the income from the by-pass trust and add it to corpus. Over time, as the corpus of the marital-deduction trust (which will be taxed in W's estate) dwindles, the corpus of the by-pass trust (which won't be taxed in W's estate) swells.

Both the marital-deduction and the by-pass trust are "discretionary trusts." In income-tax parlance, the marital-deduction trust is a "complex trust" in its termination year and in any prior year in which corpus is paid out to W; the by-pass trust is a "complex trust" throughout its existence, regardless of whether the trustee accumulates the income or pays it out. See Treas. Reg. § 1.661(a)-1. Complex trusts are subject to Subparts C and D of Subchapter J (IRC §§ 661-67). Generally speaking, this means that for income-tax purposes income but not principal distributions are taxed to the beneficiary receiving them; income accumulated is taxed to the trust, subject to a later application of the so-called throwback rules upon actual distribution.

Ronald Kessler, The Season: Inside Palm Beach And America's Richest Society 49-51 (1999)

Controlling much of the money [for many members of Palm Beach society[25]] are trust department officers . . . .

Trust-fund babies try to outsmart trust officers . . . . That's their job, living off inherited wealth. They wake up late, go to their clubs, have a few drinks, and urge [their trust officers] to give them money.

One heir to an industrial fortune has homes in Palm Beach, New York, France, and Italy. He has a yellow Rolls-Royce Corniche convertible but wanted a red Ferrari as well. The trust department of his bank kept turning him down, considering the purchase frivolous. Finally, he bought the Ferrari using his American Express platinum card. The trust department automatically paid the charge. . . .

. . . . At Palm Beach, I learned, people are judged not by their accomplishments—most do nothing but cash checks from trust departments—but by the quality of their balloon decorations [at the parties they give]. . . .

3. Preferred Creditors

Statutory Reference: *UTC § 503*

Hurley v. Hurley

309 N.W.2d 225 (Mich. Ct. App. 1981)

ALLEN, J. On March 31, 1980, Ingham County Circuit Court ordered garnishee-defendant, Michigan National Bank, to pay accrued and future income of a spendthrift trust to the court in satisfaction of an outstanding judgment for past due child support taken against defendant, James Hurley, former husband of plaintiff, Phyllis Hurley. Garnishee-defendant's motion for rehearing was denied on April 14, 1980. Garnishee-defendant appeals as of right.

---

25. See Kessler, supra chapter 1.

The facts before this Court are undisputed. On September 26, 1966, Maybelle Hurley, defendant's mother and a resident of Missouri, executed a will in Missouri. The will devised [approximately one-half of her estate] in a spendthrift trust for James. He was to receive all income from the trust during his lifetime with the principal passing upon James' death into [trusts] for James' two daughters, Linda Kay and Cherri Ann, the decedent's granddaughters. . . .

Plaintiff and defendant were divorced in Missouri approximately six years before the decedent executed her will in September 1966. The decedent did not provide for plaintiff in her will. In 1970, decedent moved from Missouri to Michigan where she remained until her death in 1978. Defendant, James Hurley, moved from Missouri and presently resides in California. He failed to maintain his child support payments. In 1977, plaintiff filed suit in Missouri for past due child support, and in 1979 obtained a Missouri judgment of $19,630 principal plus $5,728 interest. In 1978, Maybelle Hurley died in Michigan, and her will was admitted into probate in Ingham County, Michigan. Garnishee-defendant, Michigan National Bank, was appointed trustee under the will.

In 1979, plaintiff filed a complaint in the Ingham County Circuit Court against defendant and garnishee-defendant, seeking full faith and credit of the Missouri child support judgment. Plaintiff then moved to require the garnishee-defendant, as trustee, to pay plaintiff the past due and future income from defendant's trust to satisfy the outstanding Missouri child support judgment. Garnishee-defendant answered, claiming that the income from the spendthrift trust was not subject to process by the court. On March 31, 1980, the trial court granted plaintiff's motion and ordered garnishee-defendant to pay due and future income into the court to satisfy plaintiff's outstanding judgment. Only garnishee-defendant appeals as of right.

The sole issue before the Court is whether plaintiff, as defendant's former wife, can reach by judicial process the income from a spendthrift trust created in favor of defendant, her former husband, to obtain satisfaction of plaintiff's judgment against defendant for past due child support. The trust established under the terms of Maybelle Hurley's will meets the definition of a spendthrift trust. . . .

Although the issue is one of first impression in Michigan,[26] it has been ruled upon in several other jurisdictions. The majority rule is that, in the absence of a specific state statute, the income of a spendthrift trust of which a former husband is the current income beneficiary may be reached to satisfy his former

---

26. Gilkey v. Gilkey, 162 Mich. 664, 127 N.W. 715 (1910), cited by garnishee-defendant, is not applicable to the present facts. Gilkey involved a discretionary trust, not a spendthrift trust. . . .

wife's claim for alimony, separate maintenance, or child support. Restatement, Trusts 2d, § 157, p. 328 provides:

> Although a trust is a spendthrift trust or a trust for support, the interest of the beneficiary can be reached in satisfaction of an enforceable claim against the beneficiary,
>
> (a) by the wife or child of the beneficiary for support, or by the wife for alimony;[27]
>
> [(b) for necessary services rendered to the beneficiary or necessary supplies furnished to him;
>
> (c) for services rendered and materials furnished which preserve or benefit the interest of the beneficiary;
>
> (d) by the United States or a State to satisfy a claim against the beneficiary.]

See also II Scott on Trusts, 3d ed., § 157.1, pp. 1206-1216.

Several reasons have been advanced in support of the rule. Some courts adhere to the rationale by finding an intention on behalf of the settlor of the trust to allow a wife to enforce a claim for alimony, maintenance, or child support. In Keller v. Keller, 284 Ill. App. 198, 1 N.E.2d 773 (1936), it was held that such an intention will be found unless the trust instrument discloses an intention that such a claim may not be enforced. Other courts have held that child support is not a "debt" contemplated by the spendthrift provision of a trust. . . .Still other courts have held that it would be against public policy to hold that a wife may not enforce child support claims against a recalcitrant husband. . . . In accord with holding a spendthrift provision contrary to public policy is Shelley v. Shelley, 354 P.2d 282 (Or. 1960), which opines that if the beneficiary's interest cannot be reached to satisfy claims for alimony or child support, the state may be called upon to support the wife and children. Further, O'Connor v. O'Connor, 3 Ohio Op.2d 186, 141 N.E.2d 691, 75 Ohio Law Abst. 420 (Oh.Com.Pl., 1957), holds that the husband has a legal duty to support his wife, that a father has a legal duty to support his minor children, and that these elements of public policy outweigh the public policy that an owner of property, such as the settlor of a trust, may dispose of it as he pleases and may impose spendthrift restraints on the disposition of income.

---

27. The special Comment on § 157(a) of the Restatement, Trusts 2d, is as follows:

> Although a trust is a spendthrift trust or a trust for support, the interest of the beneficiary can be reached in satisfaction of an enforceable claim against him for support by his wife or children. In some cases a spendthrift clause is construed as not intended to exclude the beneficiary's dependents. Even if the clause is construed as applicable to claims of his dependents for support, it is against public policy to give full effect to the provision. The beneficiary should not be permitted to have the enjoyment of his interest under the trust while neglecting to support his dependents.

We find all of the above reasons persuasive and affirm, particularly in light of the existing law in Missouri at the time of the execution of the decedent's will and the creation of the present trusts. Missouri law provides, Mo.Rev.Stat. § 456.080:

> All restraints . . . in the form of a spendthrift trust, or otherwise [are] of no effect, as against the claims of any wife, child or children, of [the beneficiary] for support and maintenance, or, as against the claim of any said wife for alimony.

This law was in effect at the time of the creation of the present trusts. Therefore, the trusts as created, even though of a spendthrift nature, could not bar the recovery of the income from the trust for child support. We do not find that the settlor of these trusts intended to exclude such claims but rather intended the trusts to be administered in accordance with the laws of the state in which the trusts were created thereby allowing such claims.

The lower court order . . . was proper and is sustained.

AFFIRMED.[28]

Notes and Questions

1. *Alimony and Child Support Claims to Spendthrift Trusts.* The view taken in *Hurley*—that a spendthrift clause doesn't protect a trust beneficiary's interest from claims for child support—represents the prevailing view. Though alimony awards are less common today than they once were, the same view prevails regarding the right of a recipient of an alimony award to reached the obligor's interest in a trust despite a spendthrift restraint on that interest. See, e.g., Shelley v. Shelley, 354 P.2d 282 (Or. 1960); Restatement 3d of Trusts § 59(a). Several courts, however, have refused to permit a former spouse or children to reach a spendthrift trust to satisfy alimony or child support judgments. An example is Erickson v. Erickson, 266 N.W. 161, reh'g denied, 267 N.W. 426 (Minn. 1936). In that case, the court rejected the theory, mentioned in *Hurley*, that the exceptions in favor of alimony and child support claimants are justified, in part, on the basis of the settlor's imputed intent. The court stated: "If alimony or support money is to be an exception to the protection offered by spendthrift provisions it must be by some justifiable interpretation of the donor's language by which such implied exception may be fairly construed into the instrument of the trust."

---

28. In Miller v. Department of Mental Health, 442 N.W.2d 617, 619 (Mich. 1989), the Michigan Supreme Court noted in dictum that "the interest of a beneficiary of [a spendthrift or a support trust] can be reached to enforce claims by the beneficiary's wife or child for alimony or support. . . ." Eds.

From the perspective of the settlor's probable intent, should courts distinguish between the claims of the beneficiary's former spouse and those of the beneficiary's children?[29] As the opinion in *Hurley* indicates, of course, the settlor's imputed intention isn't the only rationale for the exceptions in favor of alimony or support claimants.

2. *Alimony and Child Support Claims to Pension Benefits.* Although ERISA requires pension plans to prohibit assignment and alienation of plan benefits (29 U.S.C. § 1056(d)(1)), it also requires such plans to "provide for the payment of benefits in accordance with the applicable requirements of any qualified domestic relations order" for "child support, alimony payments, or marital property rights." 29 U.S.C. § 1056(d)(3).

Sligh v. First National Bank, Trustee

704 So.2d 1020 (Miss. 1997)

MILLS, J., for the Court: This case comes on appeal from the Chancery Court of Holmes County, where Will and Lucy Sligh sought to garnish Gene Lorance's beneficial interest in two spendthrift trusts in order to partially satisfy a tort judgment for damages resulting from injuries sustained by Will Sligh in an automobile accident with Gene Lorance. On December 15, 1995, the chancellor dismissed the Slighs' complaint, ruling that the assets of spendthrift trusts may not be garnished to satisfy the claims of tort judgment creditors. Aggrieved, the Slighs appeal to this Court . . . .

Facts. On January 30, 1993, William B. Sligh was involved in an automobile accident with Gene A. Lorance, an uninsured motorist who was operating a vehicle while intoxicated. As a result, Will Sligh suffered a broken spine and resulting paralysis, including loss of the use of both legs, loss of all sexual functions and loss of the ability to control bowel and urinary functions. Lorance was convicted of the felony of driving under the influence and causing bodily injury to another, for which he was sentenced to serve ten years, with six years suspended, in the custody of the Mississippi Department of Corrections.

On April 2, 1993, Will and his wife, Lucy M. Sligh, filed in the Circuit Court of Holmes County an action against Lorance alleging gross negligence resulting in personal injury, property damage and loss of consortium, for which they sought compensatory and punitive damages. Lorance failed to respond, and after entry of default and a hearing on the Slighs' Motion for Writ of Inquiry

---

29. Interestingly, a recent article advocating the routine use of spendthrift trusts recommends a clause that specifically states that the interest of any beneficiary "shall be free from the control or interference . . . of any spouse of a married beneficiary," but doesn't mention claims of children for child support. Nancy S. Roush & Robert K. Kirkland, Spendthrift Trusts Are Not Limited to Protection of Immature Dependents, 18 Est. Plan. 16, 18 (Jan.-Feb. 1991).

on January 25, 1994, the circuit court entered default judgment against Lorance for $5,000,000 in compensatory and punitive damages.

Lorance has no assets other than his interest as beneficiary of two spendthrift trusts established by his mother in 1984 and 1988, respectively, before she died in 1993. Both trusts, whose trustee is First National Bank of Holmes County ("First National Bank"), provide as follows:

> 1. My said Trustee shall have full and complete authority to expend all or any part of the income or corpus of said trust property for the benefit of myself and my said son, Gene Lorance, and shall have the right to make payments directly to me and to my said son or to anyone for myself or my said son.
> 2. The Trustee shall have the right to invest, re-invest, manage and care for said property in the same manner as though said property was the individual property of said Trustee, and my said Trustee shall not be required to give bond, or account to Court, and shall have all the powers conferred by the Uniform Trustees' Powers Act as the same is now in force in the State of Mississippi and the power to sell, lease or encumber real property. My said Trustee shall exercise the powers herein granted for what may be, in the discretion of my said Trustee, in the best interest of myself and said Gene Lorance, and shall pay to me or the said Gene Lorance such sums and at such times as my said Trustee thinks in my or his best interest. *No part of this trust, either principal or income, shall be liable for the debts of the said Gene Lorance, nor shall the same be subject to seizure by any creditor of his* and he shall not have the right to sell, assign, transfer, encumber or in any manner anticipate or dispose of his interest in said property, or any part of same, or the income produced from said trust or any part thereof.

(emphasis added). Lorance is the lifetime beneficiary of the two trusts, which each have two remaindermen, Virginia Tate and William C. Bardin.

On June 29, 1994, Will and Lucy Sligh filed in the Circuit Court of Holmes County a Suggestion for Writ of Garnishment as to First National Bank, either in its corporate capacity or in its capacity as trustee of the two trusts. A Writ of Garnishment was issued and served upon First National Bank, who, in its answer filed on June 30, 1994, admitted that it was indebted to Lorance in the amount of $313,677.48, but asserted that such sum was held in trust for Lorance and was not subject to seizure. After the Slighs filed a motion for judgment on the answer and First National Bank filed its response, First National Bank moved for a dismissal or, in the alternative, for a transferal of the garnishment proceeding to chancery court. On October 5, 1994, the circuit court transferred the proceeding to the Chancery Court of Holmes County.

On October 25, 1994, the Slighs filed in that court their complaint naming as defendants First National Bank, Gene Lorance, Viginia Tate and William Bardin. The Slighs alleged, in addition to the aforementioned facts, that Lorance's mother, Edith Lorance, had actual knowledge of the following facts: her son was an habitual drunkard who had been unsuccessfully treated for alcoholism; he was mentally deficient and had been previously committed to mental institutions; he had impaired facilities due to his alcoholism and mental disorders; he regularly operated motor vehicles while intoxicated; he was a reckless driver who had been involved in numerous automobile accidents; and he had been arrested and convicted on numerous occasions for driving under the influence. The complaint alleged that despite her actual knowledge of these facts, Mrs. Lorance established the two trusts as part of her intentional plan and design to enable her son to continue to lead his intemperate, debauched, wanton and depraved lifestyle while at the same time shielding his beneficial interest in the trusts from the claims of his involuntary tort creditors. The Slighs alleged that it was a violation of public policy to enforce and give priority to spendthrift trust provisions over involuntary tort judgments against the beneficiary, and they urged the court to recognize and enforce a public policy exception to the spendthrift trust doctrine in favor of involuntary tort creditors by subjecting Lorance's beneficial interests to the payment of their tort judgment in one or more of several equitable ways suggested in their complaint.

After the defendants filed their respective answers, First National Bank filed a Motion for Dismissal on October 27, 1995. On December 15, 1995, the chancellor granted the motion, ruling that the Slighs failed to state a claim upon which relief can be granted. The chancellor ruled that "a tort judgment creditor may not garnish the trustee of a spendthrift trust in which the tort judgment defendant is a mere lifetime discretionary income beneficiary, nor are the assets of such trust subject to the claims of the tort judgment creditor."

Discussion . . . .The spendthrift trust doctrine is codified by statute in some states and is a judicially created doctrine in others. . . .

Legal scholars for years have called for the recognition of a public policy exception to the spendthrift trust doctrine in favor of tort judgment creditors.[30] However, there is little case law on the matter. In Thackara v. Mintzer, 100 Pa. 151, 154-55 (1882), the Pennsylvania Supreme Court, in upholding the validity of a spendthrift trust, declared in dicta that "whether the judgment be for a breach of contract or for a tort, matters not." In Kirk v. Kirk, 254 Ore. 44, 456 P.2d 1009 (1969), the Oregon Supreme Court held that the interest of a spendthrift trust created by the United States for the Klamath Tribe of American Indians was unreachable by the Indian beneficiary's tort judgment creditor.

---

30. See Laurene M. Brooks, Comment, A Tort-Creditor Exception to the Spendthrift Trust Doctrine: A Call to the Wisconsin Legislature, 73 Marq. L. Rev. 109 (1989); Frank A. Gregory, Note, Trusts: Tort Claims as an Exception to the Spendthrift Trust Doctrine, 17 Okla. L. Rev. 235 (1964); Antonis, Spendthrift Trusts, Attachability of a Beneficiary's Interests in Satisfaction of a Tort Claim, 28 Notre Dame L. Rev. 509 (1952); Costigan, Those Protective Trusts Which Are Miscalled "Spendthrift Trusts" Reexamined, 22 Cal. L. Rev. 471 (1934); Griswold, Reaching the Interest of a Spendthrift Trust, *43 Harv. L. Rev. 63 (1929)*.

However, at least one state, Louisiana, has recognized an exception to the spendthrift trust doctrine in favor of tort judgment creditors, which doctrine and exception were codified by the Louisiana Legislature.[31] . . .

. . . . [O]ne can identify three public policy considerations . . . when enforcing spendthrift trust provisions: (1) the right of donors to dispose of their property as they wish; (2) the public interest in protecting spendthrift individuals from personal pauperism, so that they do not become public burdens; and (3) the responsibility of creditors to make themselves aware of their debtors' spendthrift trust protections. Upon consideration of these public policy concerns in the present context, we find that they do not weigh in favor of enforcing spendthrift trust provisions as against the claims of tort creditors or those found liable for gross negligence.

Regarding the responsibility of creditors when entering into transactions with spendthrift trust beneficiaries, Austin W. Scott stated in The Law of Trusts:

> In many of the cases in which it has been held that by the terms of the trust the interest of a beneficiary may be put beyond the reach of his creditors, the courts have laid some stress on the fact that the creditors had only themselves to blame for extending credit to a person whose interest under the trust had been put beyond their reach. The courts have said that before extending credit they could have ascertained the extent and character of the debtor's resources. Certainly, the situation of a tort creditor is quite different from that of a contract creditor. A man who is about to be knocked down by an automobile has no opportunity to investigate the credit of the driver of the automobile and has no opportunity to avoid being injured no matter what the resources of the driver may be.

Scott, supra. Likewise, George T. Bogert reasoned in Trusts and Trustees:

> It is true that a tort creditor has had no chance to choose his debtor and cannot be said to have assumed the risk of the collectibility of his claim. The argument for the validity of spendthrift trusts based on notice to the business world of the limited interest of the beneficiary does not apply. It may be argued that the beneficiary should not be permitted to circumvent the case and statute law as to liability for wrongs by taking advantage of the spendthrift clause.

George T. Bogert, Trusts and Trustees § 224 (2d ed. Rev. 1992). As these scholars point out, it is plain to see that one of the main reasons for enforcing spendthrift trust provisions—the responsibility of creditors to be aware of the

---

31. The Louisiana Trust Code provides that the beneficiary's interest in a spendthrift trust may be seized to satisfy a judgment for "an offense or quasi-offense committed by the beneficiary or by a person for whose acts the beneficiary is individually responsible." La. Rev. Stat. Ann. § 9:2005 (West 1991).

law and of the substance of such provisions—simply does not apply in the case of tort judgment creditors.

As for the public interest in protecting spendthrift individuals from personal pauperism, we believe that this interest is not as strong in the case of tort judgment creditors, where the inability to collect on their claims may well result in their own personal pauperism. While it is true that most contract creditors do not risk becoming insolvent if they do not collect on a particular claim, such is often not the case with tort judgment creditors, particularly those who have suffered such devastating and expensive injuries as did the Slighs. The public interest against individuals becoming public burdens would not be served by protecting a spendthrift tortfeasor from personal pauperism where such protection would result merely in the pauperism of his victim. If one must choose whom to reduce to personal pauperism in such a case, the spendthrift tortfeasor or the innocent tort judgment creditor, we are inclined to choose the party at fault, especially where that fault rises to the level of gross negligence or intentional conduct.

This limitation on the public interest in protecting individuals from personal pauperism is reflected in our federal bankruptcy laws, whose very purpose is to protect debtors from pauperism. Under the Federal Bankruptcy Act, debtors may not discharge their debts to tort victim creditors whose claims are based on "willful and malicious" injuries. 11 U.S.C.A. § 523(a)(6) (West 1993). Thus, it has been recognized that the rights of intentional tort creditors are greater than the public interest in protecting debtors from personal pauperism.

Perhaps the most important policy consideration in favor of enforcing spendthrift trust provisions is the right of donors to dispose of their property as they wish. On this subject, Austin W. Scott stated in The Law of Trusts:

> It may be argued that the settlor can properly impose such restrictions as he chooses on the property that he gives. But surely he cannot impose restrictions that are against public policy. It is true that the tortfeasor may have no other property than that which is given him under the trust, and that the victim of the tort is no worse off where the tortfeasor has property that cannot be reached than he would if the tortfeasor had no property at all. Nevertheless, there seems to be something rather shocking in the notion that a man should be allowed to continue in the enjoyment of property without satisfying the claims of persons whom he has injured. It may well be held that it is against public policy to permit the beneficiary of a spendthrift trust to enjoy an income under the trust without discharging his tort liabilities to others.

Scott, supra.

Clearly, the right of donors to place restrictions on the disposition of their property is not absolute, for . . . there are several generally recognized exceptions to the spendthrift trust doctrine. Rather, a donor may dispose of his property as he sees fit so long as such disposition does not violate the law or public policy. We find that it is indeed against public policy to dispose of property in such a way that the beneficiary may enjoy the income from such property without fear that his interest may be attached to satisfy the claims of his gross negligence or intentional torts.

Our tort doctrine has evolved into two types of torts, ordinary torts and intentional torts. Public policy deems it so important to deter the commission of intentional torts or acts of gross negligence, that we allow victims of gross negligence or intentional torts to recover damages above and beyond what is necessary to compensate them for their injuries, i.e., punitive damages. However, the intended deterrent effect would be completely lost upon individuals whose interests are immune from the satisfaction of such claims.

The Slighs have alleged facts to the effect that Lorance's mother intended that her son should be able to commit acts of gross negligence or intentional torts without fear that his beneficial interests would be attached as a result thereof. However, in cases such as this where the donor has died, such facts may often be difficult, if not impossible, to prove. We hold that plaintiffs need not prove such facts but that such intent shall be presumed where a party has obtained a judgment based upon facts evidencing gross negligence or an intentional tort against the beneficiary of a spendthrift trust. Furthermore, we state the natural corollary that when assessing punitive damages against a tortfeasor found to have committed gross negligence or an intentional tort who is a spendthrift trust beneficiary, the beneficiary's interest should be taken into account as a factor in determining his monetary worth. However, in order to uphold spendthrift trust provisions so much as is reasonably possible, we hold that the beneficiary's interest in a spendthrift trust should not be attached in satisfaction of a claim until all of his other available assets have first been exhausted. . . .

The parties agree that the trusts' two remaindermen, Virginia Tate and William Bardin, have vested remainders. The trusts provide that First National Bank "shall have full and complete authority to expend *all or any part* of the income or corpus of said trust property for the benefit of myself and my said son." (emphasis added). Therefore, the interests of Ms. Tate and Mr. Bardin are vested remainders subject to complete defeasance in the event that all of the trust assets are expended to satisfy the interest of Lorance. Put another way, Lorance has a beneficial interest in all of the trust assets. Accordingly, we hold that all of the trust assets should be subject to the Slighs' claim, thereby defeating the interests of the two remaindermen.

In Deposit Guaranty Nat'l Bank v. Walter E. Heller & Co., 204 So. 2d 856 (Miss. 1967), the settlor of the trust created a lifetime beneficial interest in himself with a single remainderman. As a matter of public policy, we held the trust's spendthrift provisions invalid as against the claim of the donor/beneficiary's creditor, ruling that the remainderman would take subject to the claim of the creditor. Deposit Guaranty Nat'l Bank, 204 So. 2d at 862-63. Likewise, the Slighs' claim shall take priority over the interests of the two remaindermen.

Conclusion. We find, as a matter of public policy, that a beneficiary's interest in spendthrift trust assets is not immune from attachment to satisfy the claims of the beneficiary's intentional or gross negligence tort creditors, and that such claims take priority over any remainder interests in such assets. Accordingly, we reverse and render.

REVERSED AND RENDERED.

DAN LEE, C.J., SULLIVAN, P.J., and PITTMAN, BANKS, MCRAE AND JAMES L. ROBERTS, JR., JJ., concur.

PRATHER, P.J., dissents with separate written opinion joined by SMITH, J.

PRATHER, Presiding Justice, dissenting: I must respectfully dissent to the limitations placed by the majority on the exempt status of spendthrift trust benefits. The majority acknowledges that Louisiana is the only other State to place such limitations on spendthrift trust benefits for tort creditors, and said limitations were implemented by the Louisiana legislature rather than the courts of said state. This Court is thus, apparently, the first to so limit the exempt status of spendthrift trust benefits. I am aware of the public policy considerations which motivated the majority's decision, but, in my view, the general rule favoring the exempt status of spendthrift trusts benefits is a sound one which is in no need of revision.

Spendthrift trusts provide a means for a parent or other concerned party to provide for the basic needs of a beneficiary, and the largely exempt status of the trust benefits has given comfort and support to countless settlors and beneficiaries. The facts of the present case are tragic, but this Court should, in my view, avoid changing longstanding precedent based on the fact pattern of a particular case. Creditors in this state have at their disposal a number of means of collecting judgments, and I fear that the majority opinion signals the start of a gradual decline of the spendthrift trust in this state. I would affirm the ruling of the trial court, and I must accordingly dissent.

SMITH, J., joins this opinion.

Note

1. *Questions.* Wasn't the trust in *Sligh* a discretionary trust? If so, should preferred-creditor status have applied?

2. *Aftermath in Mississippi.* After *Sligh* was decided, the Mississippi legislature enacted the Family Trust Preservation Act of 1998, which provides that a beneficiary's interest that is protected by a spendthrift clause "may not be transferred and is not subject to the enforcement of a money judgment until paid

to the beneficiary." Miss. Code Ann. § 91-9-503. This legislation was supported and drafted by the estate planning bar. Does this legislation also eliminate preferred-creditor status for spouses for alimony and children for child support?

3. *Contrasting Views of the* Sligh *Decision.* Citing Charles D. Fox, IV, & Roschi Murphy, Are Spendthrift Trusts Vulnerable to a Beneficiary's Tort Creditors?, 136 Trusts and Estates 57 (Feb. 1998), a prominent Michigan estate planning practitioner wrote: "The Mississippi Supreme Court abused basic trust, property and contract law by creating a common law exception to the spendthrift doctrine for a beneficiary who engages in gross negligence and intentional torts." Allan J. Claypool, Asset Protection Overview (Techniques in the United States and Offshore), 24 ACTEC Notes 302, 312 (1999). Edward C. Halbach, Jr., the reporter for the Restatement 3d of Trusts, however, described the *Sligh* decision as "widely acclaimed." Edward C. Halbach, Jr., The 1999 Joseph Trachtman Lecture—Uniform Acts, Restatements and Other Trends in American Trust Law at Century's End, 25 ACTEC Notes 101, 108 (1999).

4. *Uniform Trust Code.* The drafting committee for the Uniform Trust Code debated whether to include tort creditors in the category of preferred creditors, and ultimately decided not to do so. See UTC § 503.

5. *Claimants Who Provided Necessities/Government Claimants.* The Restatement specifically includes claimants who provided the beneficiary with necessary services or supplies, such as medical personnel, as having special claims on spendthrift trusts. Restatement 3d of Trusts § 59(b). Comment *a* states that "[i]t is implicit in the rule of this section, as a statement of the common law, that governmental claimants, and other claimants as well, may reach the interest of a beneficiary of a spendthrift trust to the extent provided by federal law or an applicable state statute." This certainly includes federal tax claims. UTC § 503 adopts the same position.

4. Self-Settled Spendthrift, Discretionary, and Support Trusts

Statutory Reference: *UTC § 505*

Common law Prohibition of Self-Settled Spendthrift and Discretionary Trusts. In nearly all states, except as to pension trusts, a settlor may not create a spendthrift or discretionary trust for his or her own benefit.[32] Such a "self-settled" trust isn't void, but the settlor's interest in a spendthrift trust is alienable and can be reached by creditors and the maximum amount that the trustee can pay the settlor or apply for his or her benefit in a discretionary trust is alienable and can be reached by creditors.[33] See Restatement 3d of Trusts § 58(2); § 60, comment f.

The application of the rules against self-settled spendthrift trusts isn't dependent upon the fraudulent-transfer principle. The right of the settlor's creditors to satisfy their claims from the settlor's beneficial interest doesn't depend upon the trust having been created in fraud of creditors.

Conceding the rules, certain problems remain. Sometimes a trust is only partially for the benefit of the settlor, as where the settlor retains only an income interest or confers a discretionary power over income only. In such cases, only the income interest is affected by the above rules. In some circumstances, such as reciprocal trusts or trusts created or continued as the result of a failure to exercise a general power of appointment, the true identity of the settlor may not be obvious. See, e.g., McColgan v. Walter Magee, Inc., 155 P. 995 (Cal. 1916); American Security & Trust Co. v. Utley, 382 F.2d 451 (D.C. Cir. 1967). Finally, if a trust has multiple settlors, there may be a problem in determining the extent to which the trust is self-settled regarding one of the settlors. See, e.g., In re Shurley, 171 B.R. 769 (Bankr. W.D. Tex. 1994); David B. Young, The *Pro Tanto* Invalidity of Protective Trusts: Partial Self-Settlement and Beneficiary Control, 78 Marq. L. Rev. 807 (1995).

Offshore Asset Protection Trusts. The use of self-settled spendthrift trusts as a means of sheltering assets from potential creditors has taken a new twist in recent years through an estate-planning arrangement known as an offshore asset protection trust ("OAPT"). OAPTs are trusts created under the law of a foreign jurisdiction in which the settlor typically retains a beneficial interest and some measure of control.[34] While the trust is irrevocable, the settlor retains control

---

32. In Missouri, a settlor may create a self-settled spendthrift trust under limited circumstances: (1) the trust transfer must not constitute a fraudulent conveyance; (2) the settlor may not be the sole income or principal beneficiary and may not have the power to revoke the trust; and (3) and, if the settlor was a member of a class of beneficiaries, he or she may not have retained a right to receive a specific portion of income or principal determinable solely from the terms of the trust instrument. See Mo. Rev. Stat. § 456.080(3).

33. As described in Chapter 9, Part B, Congress has enacted a complicated set of rules designed to prevent a settlor from using a self-settled inter vivos trust to qualify himself or herself or his or her spouse for Medicaid.

34. *International Trusts and the Hague Convention on Trusts.* Offshore asset protection trusts are only one example of the expanding market of international trusts. The growth of international trusts results from the general globalization of wealth management. This development has

either by serving as a member of a "committee of advisors" or as the designated "trust protector." It is estimated that as much as $1 *trillion* dollars worth of assets are held in OAPTs.[35] They have become especially popular with American professionals, such as physicians and lawyers, who wish to shield assets from potential malpractice liability judgments. Most of the favored situses of these foreign trusts are nations that are members of the British Commonwealth, including the Bahamas, the Cayman Islands, Bermuda, and the Cook Islands. All of them have enacted legislation that directly facilitates the use of self-settled trusts for asset protection. The Cayman Islands recently went one step further and enacted a statute that allows an individual to shield his or her assets in a trust *after* a suit is filed against him or her.[36] For a good overview of OAPTs, see Elena Marty-Nelson, Offshore Asset Protection Trusts: Having Your Cake and Eating It Too, 47 Rutgers L. Rev. 11 (1994).

FTC v. Affordable Media, LLC

179 F.3d 1228 (9th Cir. 1999)

WIGGINS, Circuit Judge. A husband and wife, Denyse and Michael Anderson, were involved in a telemarketing venture that offered investors the chance to participate in a project that sold such modern marvels as talking pet tags and water-filled barbells by means of late-night television. Although the promoters promised that an investment in the project would return 50 per cent in a mere 60 to 90 days, the venture in fact was a Ponzi scheme, which eventually unraveled and left thousands of investors with tremendous losses. When the Federal Trade Commission brought a complaint against the telemarketing duo, they claimed that they were simply innocent dupes rather than a modern day telephonic Bonnie and Clyde.

While the investors' money was lost in the fraudulent scheme, the Andersons' profits from their commissions remained safely tucked away across the sea in a Cook Islands trust. When the Commission brought a civil action to recover as

---

heightened the need for legislation that clarifies the status of trusts in other countries, especially in civil-law jurisdictions, whose legal systems do not recognize the trust. The most serious effort to date at responding to this need is the Hague Convention on the Law Applicable to Trusts, first signed in 1985. Unfortunately, the Hague Convention has had only limited success in answering questions about the effect of trusts in civil-law countries. It has been signed only by a handful of nations, and has gone into force in only one major civil-law country, Italy. Lawyers who work in the field of offshore trusts have criticized many of its provisions on important topics. For a perceptive critique, see Jeffrey A. Schoenblum, The Hague Convention on Trusts: Much Ado About Very Little, 3 J. Int'l Trust & Corp. Planning 5 (1994).

35. See William J. Zink, Assets of Foreign Grantor Trust Not Includible in Grantor's U.S. Gross Estate, Tax Advisor, Feb. 1994, at 84, 84.

36. See Gene Epstein, Pocket Protector, Barron's, Aug. 7, 1995, at 37.

much money as possible for the defrauded investors, the Andersons advanced two incredible propositions. First, they claimed that they should retain the 45 percent commissions they received for their role in the fraud, even though they acknowledged that the investors were defrauded. They claimed this entitlement because they merely sold the toxic investments that fueled the scheme and propped up the duplicitous house of cards. Second, the Andersons claimed that they were unable to repatriate the assets in the Cook Islands trust because they had willingly relinquished all control over the millions of dollars of commissions in order to place this money overseas in the benevolent hands of unaccountable overseers, just on the off chance that a law suit might result from their business activities. The learned district court was skeptical of both arguments and choose to grant the Commission its requested preliminary relief.

An old adage warns that a fool and his money are easily parted. This case shows that the same is not true of a district court judge and his common sense. After the Andersons refused to comply with the preliminary injunction by refusing to return their illicit proceeds, the district court found the Andersons in civil contempt of court. The Andersons appealed. We have jurisdiction under 28 U.S.C. § 1292(a)(1) and we affirm.

I. Sometime after April 1997, Denyse and Michael Anderson became involved with The Sterling Group ("Sterling"). Sterling sold such imaginative products as the "Aquabell," a water-filled dumbbell, the "Talking Pet Tag," and a plastic wrap dispenser known as "KenKut" by means of late-night television commercials broadcast between the hours of 11:00 p.m. and 4:00 a.m. The Andersons formed Financial Growth Consultants, LLC ("Financial") to serve as the primary telemarketer of media units, an investment that afforded purchasers the opportunity to receive a portion of the profits generated from the sales of Sterling's outlandish products. Financial's telemarketers thereupon set about locating prospective investors in the media unit scheme.

The media units sold for $5,000. Each media unit entitled the investor to participate in the sale of Sterling's products from 201 of the late-night commercials. Each product sold for $20.00. The investor would receive $7.50 for each product sold during his 201 commercials, up to a maximum of five products per commercial. According to Financial's telemarketers, the investors would likely receive $37.50 per commercial (from five products sold during each commercial) for a total of $7,537.50—an astronomical fifty percent return in sixty to ninety days. Financial, for its part, would receive forty-five percent of the investor's $5,000.00 investment, an amount that the Andersons assert is the industry standard.

It appears that Financial's telemarketers were especially skilled at marketing the media units. Financial may have raised at least $13,000,000 from investors in the media-unit scheme, retaining an estimated $6,300,000 in commissions for itself. Perhaps unsurprisingly to those not involved in the media-unit project, it turned out that Sterling could not sell enough Talking Pet Tags and Aquabells to return the promised yields to the media-unit investors. Instead, it appears that Sterling used later investors' investments to pay the promised yields to earlier investors—a classic Ponzi scheme.

On April 23, 1998, the Federal Trade Commission (the "Commission") filed a complaint in the United States District Court for the District of Nevada, charging the Andersons, Financial, and others with violations of the Federal Trade Commission Act (the "Act") and the Telemarketing Sales Rule for their participation in a scheme to telemarket fraudulent investments to consumers. Upon motion by the Commission, the district court issued an ex parte temporary restraining order against the defendants. After hearings on April 30 and May 8, 1998, the district court entered a preliminary injunction against the defendants, which incorporated the provisions of the temporary restraining order. Both the temporary restraining order and the preliminary injunction required the Andersons to repatriate any assets held for their benefit outside of the United States.

In July, 1995, the Andersons had created an irrevocable trust under the law of the Cook Islands. The Andersons were named as co-trustees of the trust, together with AsiaCiti Trust Limited ("AsiaCiti"), a company licensed to conduct trustee services under Cook Islands law. Apparently, the Andersons created the trust in an effort to protect their assets from business risks and liabilities by placing the assets beyond the jurisdiction of the United States courts. As discussed more fully below, the provisions of the trust were intended to frustrate the operation of domestic courts, by removing the Andersons as trustees and preventing AsiaCiti from repatriating any of the trust assets to the United States if a so-called "event of duress" occurred.

In response to the preliminary injunction, the Andersons faxed a letter to AsiaCiti on May 12, 1998, instructing AsiaCiti to provide an accounting of the assets held in the trust and to repatriate the assets to the United States to be held under the control of the district court. AsiaCiti thereupon notified the Andersons that the temporary restraining order was an event of duress under the trust, removed the Andersons as co-trustees under the trust because of the event of duress, and refused to provide an accounting or repatriation of the assets. The trust assets were therefore not repatriated to the United States and the Andersons have provided only limited information to the district court and the Commission regarding the trust assets.

On May 7, 1998, the Commission moved the district court to find the Andersons in civil contempt for their failure to comply with the temporary restraining order's requirements that they submit an accounting of their foreign assets to the Commission and to repatriate all assets located abroad. At a hearing on June 4, 1998, the district court found the Andersons in civil contempt of court for failing to repatriate the trust assets to the United States and failing to provide an accounting of the trust's assets. The district court, however, continued the hearing until June 9, then until June 11, and finally until June 17, in an effort to allow the Andersons to purge themselves of their contempt. In attempting to purge themselves of their contempt, the Andersons attempted to appoint their children as trustees of the trust, but AsiaCiti removed them from acting as trustees because the event of duress was continuing. At the June 17 hearing, the district court indicated that it believed that the Andersons remained in control of the trust and rejected their assertion that compliance with the repatriation provisions of the trust was impossible. At the close of the June 17 hearing, the district judge ordered the Andersons taken into custody because they had not purged themselves of their contempt. The Andersons timely appealed the district court's issuance of the preliminary injunction and finding them in contempt. We affirm the district court.

II. The first issue in the Anderson's appeal concerns the district court's issuance of the preliminary injunction. . . . [W]e conclude that the district court did not abuse its discretion in issuing the preliminary injunction, based on the factual record available at such a preliminary stage of the proceeding.

III. The next issue on appeal is the district court's finding the Andersons in contempt for refusing to repatriate the assets in their Cook Islands trust. We review a district court's civil contempt order for an abuse of discretion. Hilao v. Estate of Marcos, 103 F.3d 762, 764 (9th Cir.1996). We review the district court's findings of fact in connection with the civil contempt adjudication for clear error. Reliance Ins. Co. v. Mast Constr. Co., 84 F.3d 372, 375 (10th Cir.1996). We review a district court's findings in connection with rejecting an impossibility defense for clear error. See Fortin v. Commissioner of Mass. Dep't of Pub. Welfare, 692 F.2d 790, 797 (1st Cir.1982) (affirming contempt order when district court's finding that compliance was not impossible was not clearly erroneous). Based on the record before us, we find that the district court did not abuse its discretion in holding the Andersons in contempt.

The standard for finding a party in civil contempt is well settled:

> The moving party has the burden of showing by clear and convincing evidence that the contemnors violated a specific and definite order of the court. The burden then shifts to the contemnors to demonstrate why they were unable to comply.

Stone v. City and County of San Francisco, 968 F.2d 850, 856 n. 9 (9th Cir.1992) (citations omitted).

The temporary restraining order required the Andersons, in relevant part, to "transfer to the territory of the United States all funds, documents and assets in foreign countries held either: (1) by them; (2) for their benefit; or (3) under their direct or indirect control, jointly or singly." Temporary Restraining Order, entered and served April 23, 1998, at 8. These provisions were continued in the preliminary injunction. See Preliminary Injunction, entered and served May 22, 1998, at 9. It is undisputed that the Andersons are beneficiaries of an irrevocable trust established under the laws of the Cook Islands. The Andersons do not dispute that the trust assets have not been repatriated to the United States. Instead, the Andersons claim that compliance with the temporary restraining order is impossible because the trustee, in accordance with the terms of the trust, will not repatriate the trust assets to the United States.

A party's inability to comply with a judicial order constitutes a defense to a charge of civil contempt. The Andersons claim that the refusal of the foreign trustee to repatriate the trust assets to the United States, which apparently was the goal of the trust, makes their compliance with the preliminary injunction impossible.

Although the Andersons assert that their "inability to comply with a judicial decree is a complete defense to a charge of civil contempt, regardless of whether the inability to comply is self-induced," Appellants' Reply Brief at 12 (emphasis added), we are not certain that the Andersons' inability to comply in this case would be a defense to a finding of contempt. It is readily apparent that the Andersons' inability to comply with the district court's repatriation order is the intended result of their own conduct-their inability to comply and the foreign trustee's refusal to comply appears to be the precise goal of the Andersons' trust.[37] The Andersons claim that they created their trust as part of an "asset protection plan." See Appellant's Opening Brief at 36. These "[s]o-called asset protection trusts are designed to shield wealth by moving it to a foreign

---

37. The Andersons' trust created the circumstances in which a foreign trustee would refuse to repatriate assets to the United States by means of so-called duress provisions. Under the trust agreement, an event of duress includes "[t]he issuance of any order, decree or judgment of any court or tribunal in any part of the world which in the opinion of the protector will or may directly or indirectly, expropriate, sequester, levy, lien or in any way control, restrict or prevent the free disposal by a trustee of any monies, investments or property which may from time to time be included in or form part of this trust and any distributions therefrom." Trust Agreement at 3. Upon the happening of an event of duress, the trust agreement provides that the Andersons would be terminated as co-trustees, so that control over the trust assets would appear to be exclusively in the hands of a foreign trustee, beyond the jurisdiction of a United States court:

> Notwithstanding any other provision contained in this deed any trustee hereof shall automatically cease to be a trustee upon the happening of an event of duress within the territory where such trustee is ... resident (in the case of an individual) and upon ceasing to be a trustee pursuant to this clause such trustee shall be divested of title to the property of this trust which shall automatically vest in the remaining or continuing trustee (if any) located in a territory not having an event of duress and the form for administration of this trust shall notwithstanding any other provision in this deed be deemed to be the place of residence or incorporation (if a corporation) of such continuing trustee.

Trust Agreement at 17 (emphasis added).

jurisdiction that does not recognize U.S. judgments or other legal processes, such as asset freezes." Debra Baker, Island Castaway, ABA Journal, October 1998, at 55. The "asset protection" aspect of these foreign trusts arises from the ability of people, such as the Andersons, to frustrate and impede the United States courts by moving their assets beyond those courts' jurisdictions:

> Perhaps most importantly, situs courts typically ignore United States courts' demands to repatriate trust assets to the United States. A situs court will not enforce a United States order from a state court compelling the turnover of trust assets to a creditor that was defrauded under United States law, or assets that were placed into a self-settled spendthrift trust.

James T. Lorenzetti, The Offshore Trust: A Contemporary Asset Protection Scheme, 102 Com. L.J. 138, 143-144 (1997).

Because these asset protection trusts move the trust assets beyond the jurisdiction of domestic courts, often times all that remains within the jurisdiction is the physical person of the defendant. Because the physical person of the defendant remains subject to domestic courts' jurisdictions, courts could normally utilize their contempt powers to force a defendant to return the assets to their jurisdictions. Recognizing this risk, asset protection trusts typically are designed so that a defendant can assert that compliance with a court's order to repatriate the trust assets is impossible:

> Another common issue is whether the client may someday be in the awkward position of either having to repatriate assets or else be held in contempt of court. A well-drafted [asset protection trust] would, under such a circumstance, make it impossible for the client to repatriate assets held by the trust. Impossibility of performance is a complete defense to a civil contempt charge.

Barry S. Engel, Using Foreign Situs Trusts For Asset Protection Planning, 20 Est. Plan. 212, 218 (1993).

Given that these offshore trusts operate by means of frustrating domestic courts' jurisdiction, we are unsure that we would find that the Andersons' inability to comply with the district court's order is a defense to a civil contempt charge. We leave for another day the resolution of this more difficult question because we find that the Andersons have not satisfied their burden of proving that compliance with the district court's repatriation order was impossible. It is well established that a party petitioning for an adjudication that another party is in civil contempt does not have the burden of showing that the other party has the capacity to comply with the court's order. See NLRB v. Trans Ocean Export Packing, Inc., 473 F.2d 612, 616 (9th Cir.1973). Instead, the party asserting the impossibility defense must show "categorically and in detail" why he is unable to comply. Id.

In the asset protection trust context, moreover, the burden on the party asserting an impossibility defense will be particularly high because of the likelihood that any attempted compliance with the court's orders will be merely a charade rather than a good faith effort to comply. Foreign trusts are often designed to assist the settlor in avoiding being held in contempt of a domestic court while only feigning compliance with the court's orders:

> Finally, the settlor should be aware that, although his trust will probably prove unassailable by domestic creditors, he may face minor hassles while defending his trust in court. In particular, if a creditor attacks an offshore trust in United States court, the settlor may face contempt of court orders during the proceedings. . . . [T]here is a possibility that the court will . . . order the settlor to collect his assets from the trust and turn them over to the court. If the settlor does not comply with these orders, a court may hold him in contempt. However, there are ways around such a conflict. . . . [T]he settlor could comply with the court order and 'order' his trustee to turn over the funds, knowing full well that the trustee will not comply with his request. Thereby, the settlor would technically comply with the court's orders, escape contempt of court charges, and still rest assured that his assets will remain protected.

James T. Lorenzetti, The Offshore Trust: A Contemporary Asset Protection Scheme, 102 Com. L.J. 138, 158 (1997). With foreign laws designed to frustrate the operation of domestic courts and foreign trustees acting in concert with domestic persons to thwart the United States courts, the domestic courts will have to be especially chary of accepting a defendant's assertions that repatriation or other compliance with a court's order concerning a foreign trust is impossible. Consequently, the burden on the defendant of proving impossibility as a defense to a contempt charge will be especially high.

Given these considerations, we cannot find that the district court clearly erred in finding that the Andersons' compliance with the repatriation order was not impossible because the Andersons remain in control of their Cook Islands trust. In finding the Andersons in civil contempt, the district court rejected the Andersons' impossibility defense, specifically finding that the Andersons "in the judgment of the Court [and] from the evidence that I've heard are in control of this trust." Transcript of June 17, 1998 Hearing Regarding Plaintiff's Motion for Civil Contempt, p. 30. Because we only review a district court's findings in connection with rejecting an impossibility defense for clear error, we will treat the district court's finding that the Andersons were in control of their trust as a finding of fact, subject only to the clearly erroneous standard of review. Based upon the record before us, we find that the district court's finding that compliance with the repatriation order was possible because the Andersons remain in control of their trust was not clearly erroneous.

The Andersons claim that they have "demonstrated to the district court 'categorically and in detail' that they can not comply with the repatriation section of the preliminary injunction." Appellants' Reply Brief at 13. The district court was not convinced and neither are we. While it is possible that a rational person would send millions of dollars overseas and retain absolutely no control over the assets, we share the district court's skepticism. The district court found, notwithstanding the Andersons' protestations, that

> As I look at the totality of the scheme of what I see before me at this time, I have no doubt that the Andersons can if they wish to correct this problem and provide the means of putting these funds in a position that they can be accountable if the final determination of the Court is that the funds should be returned to those who made these payments.

Transcript of June 9, 1998 Hearing Regarding Plaintiff's Motion for Civil Contempt, p. 18.

We cannot say that this finding was clearly erroneous. The Andersons had previously been able to obtain in excess of $1 million from the trust in order to pay their taxes. Given their ability to obtain, with ease, such large sums from the trust, we share the district court's skepticism regarding the Andersons' claim that they cannot make the trust assets subject to the court's jurisdiction.

Moreover, beyond this general skepticism concerning the Andersons' lack of control over their trust, the specifics of the Andersons' trust indicate that they retained control over the trust assets. These offshore trusts allow settlors, such as the Andersons, significant control over the trust assets by allowing the settlor to act as a cotrustee or "protector" of the trust. See Debra Baker, Island Castaway, ABA Journal, October 1998, at 56 ("Further, an offshore trust, may allow settlors to maintain significant control over their assets. Trusts can include cotrustees in the United States to watch over the actions of the foreign trustees, and settlors can name anyone, including themselves, as 'protectors' to oversee the trustees and veto their actions if necessary."). When the settlors retain this type of control, however, they can jeopardize the asset protection scheme because they will be subject to a U.S. court's personal jurisdiction and be forced to exercise their control to repatriate the assets. See id. ("If litigation is threatened, the protector and the co-trustee can resign so that no one within the personal jurisdiction of a federal or state court has control over the assets of the trust.").

The district court's finding that the Andersons were in control of their trust is well supported by the record given that the Andersons were the protectors of their trust. A protector has significant powers to control an offshore trust. See Gideon Rothschild, "Establishing and Drafting Offshore Asset Protection Trusts," 23 Est. Plan. 65, 70 (1996) ("The use of a trust protector or advisor is common among foreign trusts. This person . . . has the power to replace trustees and veto certain actions by the trustees."). A protector can be compelled to exercise control over a trust to repatriate assets if the protector's powers are not drafted solely as the negative powers to veto trustee decisions or if the protector's powers are not subject to the anti-duress provisions of the trust. See id. ("The protector's powers should generally be drafted as negative powers and subject to the anti-duress provisions to protect against an order compelling the protector to exercise control over the trust."). The Andersons' trust gives them affirmative powers to appoint new trustees and makes the anti-duress provisions subject to the protectors' powers,[38] therefore, they can force the foreign trustee to repatriate the trust assets to the United States.

Perhaps the most telling evidence of the Andersons' control over the trust was their conduct after the district court issued its temporary restraining order ordering the repatriation of the trust funds. The Andersons sent a notice to the foreign trustee, ordering it to repatriate the trust assets because the district court had issued a temporary restraining order. The foreign trustee removed the Andersons from their positions as co- trustees and refused to comply with the repatriation order. After the Andersons claimed that compliance with the repatriation provisions of the temporary restraining order was impossible, the Commission revealed to the court that the Andersons were the protectors of the trust. The Andersons immediately attempted to resign as protectors of the trust. This attempted resignation indicates that the Andersons knew that, as the protectors of the trust, they remained in control of the trust and could force the foreign trustee to repatriate the assets.[39]

The Andersons contend that even though they are the protectors of the trust, it is impossible for them to repatriate the trust assets. The Andersons' argument, that "[t]here is a misstep in the FTC's logic," Appellants' Reply Brief at 17, ignores the fact that they bear the burden of proving impossibility, not the Commission. Their pointing to a few provisions of the trust, alone, is

---

38. For example, the trust provides the protectors with discretion to conclusively determine that an event of duress has not occurred: "For the purpose of determining whether an Event of Duress has occurred pursuant to paragraph (c) and paragraph (d) of this clause (1)(a)(vi) of this Deed, the written certificate of the Protector to that effect shall be conclusive." Trust Agreement at 3 (emphasis added).

39. Although we have concentrated on the Andersons' capacity as protectors of the trust to support the district court's finding that the Andersons remain in control of the trust, we have not considered whether other facts might support the Andersons' continuing control over the trust, regardless of who is the protector of the trust. The Andersons attempted to resign their position as protectors and that attempt appears to have failed. If the Andersons have in fact resigned their position as protectors, they may still remain in control of the trust. We have not resolved this issue at this time because the Andersons have conceded that they are the protectors of the trust.

insufficient to carry their burden or to establish that the district court's finding that they remain in control of their trust was clearly erroneous.[40]

Because we see no clear error in the district court's finding that the Andersons remain in control of their trust and could repatriate the trust assets, the district court did not abuse its discretion in holding them in contempt. We, therefore, affirm the district court's finding the Andersons in contempt. Given the nature of the Andersons' so-called "asset protection" trust, which was designed to frustrate the power of United States' courts to enforce judgments, there may be little else that a district court judge can do besides exercise its contempt powers to coerce people like the Andersons into removing the obstacles they placed in the way of a court. Given that the Andersons' trust is operating precisely as they intended, we are not overly sympathetic to their claims and would be hesitant to overly-restrict the district court's discretion, and thus legitimize what the Andersons have done.

AFFIRMED.

Notes and Questions

1. *Efficacy of the Civil Contempt Sanction*. Is the civil contempt sanction used in *Affordable Media* likely to be a complete solution to the problems associated with offshore asset protection trusts? In their Cook Islands trust, the Andersons had retained extensive powers over the trust funds as trust protectors, and the court pointed to these powers as evidence that the settlors possessed the legal power to repatriate the trust assets. What if, as is frequently the case, an offshore trust does not provide the settlor with such extensive powers? In Goldberg v. Lawrence (*In re* Lawrence), 238 B.R. 498 (Bankr. S.D. Fla. 1999), a federal bankruptcy court followed *Affordable Media* despite the fact that the settlor of an offshore trust whose stated situs was Mauritius had fewer

40. The provisions of the trust also make clear that the Andersons' position as protectors gives them control over the trust. In provisions of the trust agreement that the Andersons conveniently fail to reference, the trust agreement makes clear that the Andersons, as protectors, have the power to determine whether or not an event of duress has occurred: "For the purpose of determining whether an Event of Duress has occurred pursuant to paragraph (c) and paragraph (d) of this clause (1)(a)(vi) of this Deed, the written certificate of the Protector to that effect shall be conclusive." Trust Agreement at 3 (emphasis added). Moreover, the very definition of an event of duress that the Andersons assert has occurred makes clear that whether or not an event of duress has occurred depends upon the opinion of the protector: "The issuance of any order, decree or judgement of any court or tribunal in any part of the world which in the opinion of the Protector will or may directly or indirectly, expropriate. . . ." Trust Agreement at 3 (emphasis added). Therefore, notwithstanding the provisions of the trust agreement that the Andersons point to, it is clear that the Andersons could have ordered the trust assets repatriated simply by certifying to the foreign trustee that in their opinion, as protectors, no event of duress had occurred.

powers than the Andersons had retained. The court stated that its conclusion that the settlor had the power to repatriate the trust assets was not based on the presence of any particular provision. Instead the court relied on its own "common sense":

> it defies reason–it tortures reason–to accept and believe that this Debtor transferred over $7,000,000 in 1991, an amount then constituting over ninety percent of his liquid net worth, to a trust in a faraway place administered by a stranger–pursuant to an Alleged Trust which purports to allow the trustee . . . total discretion over the administration and distribution of the trust res.

Id. at 500-01. Are there any other reasons why civil contempt might be a sanction of limited efficacy? For a discussion of these matters, see Stewart E. Sterk, Asset Protection Trusts: Trust Law's Race to the Bottom?, 85 Cornell L. Rev. 1035, 1100-1104 (2000).

2. *Denial of Bankruptcy Discharge.* Another check on the ability of debtors to use offshore asset protection trusts as a means of avoiding liability is the power of bankruptcy courts to deny a debtor-settlor discharge. Recent bankruptcy cases illustrate how bankruptcy courts have successfully used this power. In Marine Midland Bank v. Portnoy (*In re* Portnoy), 201 B.R. 685 (Bankr. S.D.N.Y. 1996), a settlor created an asset protection trust in the Jersey Channel Islands. The trust included a choice-of-law clause stating that Jersey law governed all legal issues involving the trust. The bankruptcy court refused to enforce the choice-of-law clause and denied the settlor's petition for discharge of his debts. Citing the settlor's power to remove the trustee for any reason, the bankruptcy court stated that the debtor-settlor "may not unilaterally remove the characterization of property as his simply by incorporating a favorable choice of law provision into a self-settled trust of which he is the primary beneficiary." Id. at 701. The court applied bankruptcy law's "continuous concealment" doctrine as the basis for denying discharge despite the fact that the initial transfer of trust assets had occurred more than a year before the debtor-settlor's petition for discharge.

Following the *Portnoy* court's lead, the bankruptcy court in Sattin v. Brooks (*In re* Brooks), 217 B.R. 98 (Bankr. D. Conn. 1998), held that assets in a debtor's Jersey and Bermuda self-settled trusts should be included in his bankruptcy estate despite the presence of a choice-of-law clause directing the application of foreign law. The court concluded that Connecticut law applied, and under Connecticut law self-settled spendthrift provisions are unenforceable.

3. *Domestic Asset Protection Trusts—the New Frontier.* Wealthy Americans no longer need to move their assets offshore to put them beyond the reach of their creditors. You can add Alaska to the list of havens for asset-protection trusts. The new Alaska Trust Act, Alaska Stat. § 34.40.110, enacted in 1997 is

carefully crafted to allow a client to protect owned assets from creditors and claims of all types (including his or her child support obligations and, perhaps, his or her spouse in a divorce proceeding) by transferring those assets into an irrevocable discretionary trust (with a friendly trustee?). Another provision of the Act seeks to exempt discretionary trusts from the Rule Against Perpetuities (see infra Ch. 19), making it possible to create perpetual asset-protection trusts.

The Alaska Trust Act was developed and principally authored by Jonathan Blattmachr, a New York lawyer, in partnership with Donald Blattmachr, his brother and the CEO of an Anchorage Trust Company, and Robert Manley, an Anchorage attorney. In publicizing their achievement in an article published in the National Law Journal, the authors stated:

> The new Alaska Trust Act offers a new tool in accomplishing the dual goals of asset protection and tax reduction. . . . [T]he general rule that has prevailed throughout the United States, *at least until the enactment of the Alaska Trust Act*, has been that the assets in the trust may be claimed by the creditors of the grantor to the extent the grantor is entitled or eligible to receive assets from the trust . . . .
>
> [To have the Alaska Trust Act apply,] some of the trust assets must be deposited in [Alaska] and be administered by a qualified person. . . [,] the Alaskan trustee's duties must include an obligation to maintain records for the trust . . . and the obligation to prepare or arrange for the preparation of income tax returns . . . [, and] part of the administration must occur in [Alaska].

Jonathan Blattmachr et al., Alaska's Revision of its Trust Act, Which Sets out to Permit Trusts to Preserve Assets and Reduce Taxes, May Have Implications for Trust Planning Nationwide, Nat'l L. J. B5, B6-B7 (June 16, 1997) (emphasis added).

Competition for perpetual asset-protection trust business is heating up. Delaware, which previously abolished the Rule Against Perpetuities for trusts of personal property (see Ch. 19, p. 1162), has now substantially copied the asset-protection provisions of the Alaska Trust Act, calling it the Qualified Dispositions in Trust Act. The Act applies to "qualified dispositions" made on or after July 1, 1997. See Del. Code Ann. tit. 12, §§ 3570-3576. According to the legislative synopsis, "[t]he act . . . is intended to maintain Delaware's role as the most favored domestic jurisdiction for the establishment of trusts." Nevada and Rhode Island have now made it possible to settle asset protection trusts in their respective jurisdictions. Spendthrift Trust Act, Nev. Rev. Stat. § 166.015; Qualified Dispositions in Trust Act, R.I. Gen. Laws § 18-9.2-1.

The following article, written by a prominent estate planning attorney, gives a practitioner's perspective on the growing desire for asset-protection trusts.

Allan J. Claypool, Asset Protection Overview (Techniques in the United States and Offshore)

24 ACTEC Notes 302 (1999)

A. What is "Asset Protection"? The term "asset protection" means planning to protect a client's assets from potential creditor claims. . . .

Asset protection methods should be considered in all estate plans. Although it may be relatively immaterial and secondary in most estate plans, an attorney may be acting unethically or with risk of malpractice for failing to discuss appropriate asset protection strategies to certain clients; e.g., high net worth clients, professional and business persons with lawsuit risk. . . .

While advising a client of laws relevant to minimizing risk of loss to future potential creditors, the attorney must be sensitive to the fact that inappropriate advice could result in aiding and abetting criminal activity or subjecting the attorney to civil liability and loss of the licensce to practice law.

B. Why an Interest in Asset Protection?

• *Concern About the American Legal System.* The plaintiffs' bar has been able to persuade courts to adopt unique new theories of liability in many areas of the law. Some plaintiff's attorneys have contributed huge sums of money to support particular judicial candidates. The lack of confidence in an independent jhudiciary is reflecrted in the oft-heard references to certain judges as "plaintiff's judges."

Many people distrust the U.S. jury system. They believe that contingency fee arrangements encourage frivolous claims, as contrasted to certain foreignjurisdictions where the loser pays all the legal fees.

• *Regulatory Restrictions.* Wealthy persons who accumulated their wealth through industry and enterprise are often frustrated and increasingly encumbered by regulatory restrictions. Well intended legislation such as the Americans with Disabilities Act, and the Family Medical Leave Act, create new causes of action and add to the cost of doing business.

Global competition requires one to be increasingly concerned about protecting and conserving assets in order to survive in the world marketplace.

• *Lack of Confidence in the Direction of American Government.* Confidence in the American government is los in many quarters where individuals perceive thge government's redistribution of wealth as invading individual freedoms. These factors often result in the movement of assets offshore, the outright expatriation by individuals, and foreign investment by American business—all to protect wealth, or to help businesses survive competition.

C. Asset Protection Transfers Should Not Be Made to Avoid Legitimate Creditors or to Conceal Assets.

• *Consideration of the Laws of Fraudulent Transfers and Bankruptcy Preferences Is a Prerequisite to All Asset Protection Planning.* Most of the states have fraudulent transfer laws based upon either the Uniform Fraudulent Conveyance Act (UFCA) or the Uniform Fraudulent Transfer Act (UFTA). Approximately 11 states, the District of Columbia, and Puerto Rico have not adopted either or these acts. These 11 states (except, of course, Louisiana) base their laws on the English common law. Patricia Donlevy-Rosen, [Asset Protection: Planning, RIA Tax Advisors Planning Series, July 1996] ¶ 4.01, at 17.

Nevertheless, the law universally provides that every conveyance is fraudulent as to both present and future creditors if it is made with actual intent, as distinguished from intent presumed in law, to hinder, delay, or defraud either present or future creditors. UFCA § 7; UFTA § 4(a)(1); 11 USC § 545, 548; Mich. Comp. Laws § 566.17. Present creditors include those with contingent and unmatured claims where the cause of action arose prior to the transfer, as well as creditors with explicit claims of fixed accounts. A bank holding a personal guarantee is generally a present creditor of the guarantor for fraudulent conveyance purposes even though there is no default of the underlying obligation.

• *State Law Deems Certain Transfers to Be Fraudulent.* A debtor is deemed to have made a fraudulent transfer if made with no or inadequate consideration, or if it renders the transferor insolvent, or if the transferor was already insolvent at the time of the transfer. Mich. Comp. Laws §§ 566.11-[.]23. Transfers by persons in business without fair or adequate consideration are deemed fraudulent. A transfer made when the transferor will not be able to pay his debts as they currently mature is deemed to be fraudulent.

• *Attorneys Wishing to Avoid Civil and Criminal Liability, as Well as Professional Misconduct Charges, Will Decline to Undertake Asset Protection Planning for Insolvent Clients.* An attorney establishing an asset protection trust could be committing a crime if the attorney is conspiring to defraud a future creditor. This and other criminal implications arise from various penal codes relating to fraudulent conduct, or to a variety of federal statutes. For example, RICO, 18 USC § 1962 applies to the investment of funds derived from a pattern of criminal activity in a business affecting interstate commerce. Criminal mail and wire fraud, 18 USC §§ 1341 and 1343, include perpetuating or attempting to perpetuate a fraudulent scheme by mail, wire, radio, telephone and television. Transferring assets with the intent to evade tax collection is a tax crime. § 7206(4). Professionals who perform otherwise lawful actions designed to impede the administration of the tax may be committing a crime under § 7212(a). U.S. v. Hanson, 2 F.3d 942 (9th Cir. 1993). Criminal Money Laundering, 18 USC §§ 1956 and 1957, makes it a crime to use the proceeds of specified illegal activity including all sorts of fraudulent financial offenses in addition to traditional crimes such as dealing in illegal drugs. There are also bankruptcy crimes, 18 USC §§ 152 and 157; and crimes relating to conspiracy against the government and various government agencies.

It is possible that an attorney could be held liable for damages to the client's creditors. McElhanan Jr. v. Hing, 151 Ariz. 386, 728 P.2d 256 (Ariz. Ct. App. 1985), aff'd in part and vacated in part, 151 Ariz. 403, 728 P.2d 273 (Ariz. 1986), cert. denied, 481 U.S. 1030 (S.Ct. 1987).

It is also possible that an attorney involved in a conspiracy to make a fraudulent conveyance could be suspended from the practice of law. Townsend v. State Bar, 32 Cal. 2d 592, 197 P.2d 326 (Cal. 1948) (a three year suspension for violation of ethical rules). Rule 1.2(d) of the Model Rule[s] provides that an attorney "shall not counsel a client to engage, or assist a client, in conduct that the lawyer knows or reasonably should know is criminal or fraudulent . . ."

The attorney's file may be the best evidence of what has transpired, what he said and was told, and the attorney's due diligence. An attorney may want a written representation that the financial data provided the attorney is accurate. Many asset protection attorneys typically require clients to provide an affidavit of solvency. It may be appropriate to review tax returns and financial statements as well as communicate with other professionals advising the client.

The trust and estate attorney needs to remember that the attorney-client privilege does not apply when the attorney is a participant, or alleged to be a participant, in a criminal fraud.

External Reference. Henry J. Lischer, Jr., Domestic Asset Protection Trusts: Pallbearers to Liability?, 35 Real. Prop. Prob. & Tr. J. 479 (2000); Stewart E. Sterk, Asset Protection Trusts: Trust Law's Race to the Bottom? 85 Cornell L. Rev. 1035 (2000).

PART B. TERMINATION (OR MODIFICATION) BY THE BENEFICIARIES

Statutory References: *UTC §§ 301-305; 410-411, 414*

As we stated at the beginning of this chapter, a fundamental policy question that courts frequently face when the preferences of the settlor and the trust beneficiaries conflict is which side the law should empower. In this part, we consider another aspect of this question: Once a trust has been properly formed, should the law ensure that it will endure? Or should the law enable the beneficiaries to undo or alter the trust against the previously stated or implied wishes of the settlor?

Consider, again, Example 14.1, where A and X—both of whom are competent adults—prefer cash to their income and remainder interests in the spendthrift trust created by A's mother, G. Recall that under English law, A and

X could fulfill their wish by either finding a buyer or buyers for their interests (disabling restraints on alienation being invalid in England) or terminating the trust.

In the United States, however, spendthrift restraints, as we have seen, are valid in the vast majority of states. A and X can neither sell their interests nor borrow against them. In their quest for cash, of course, the inalienability of their interests wouldn't be of much concern if they could terminate the trust. Practically speaking, third-party purchasers are like the "good man" in the song—they're hard to find. The trust itself is a far more promising source of cash.[41]

Under English law, as noted, A and X could compel the termination of the trust. In Saunders v. Vautier, 4 Beav. 115, 49 Eng. Rep. 282 (Ch. 1841), the testator, Richard Wright, died in 1832, devising all his East India stock (worth £2,000) to trustees, in trust, directing them to accumulate the interest and dividends accruing thereon until his great-nephew, Daniel Wright Vautier, became 25; when Daniel became 25, the trustees were to transfer the East India stock, together with the accumulated interest and dividends, to Daniel, absolutely.

Daniel had grander ideas. Promptly upon becoming 21, in March, 1841, Daniel petitioned the court for the fund's immediate transfer to him. Lord Langdale, the Master of the Rolls, upheld Daniel's claim, saying:

> I think that principle has been repeatedly acted upon; and where a legacy is directed to accumulate for a certain period, or where the payment is postponed, the legatee, if he has an absolute indefeasible interest in the legacy, is not bound to wait until the expiration of that period, but may require payment the moment he is competent to give a valid discharge.

On appeal, Lord Langdale's decision was affirmed by the Chancellor, Lord Cottenham. Saunders v. Vautier, Cr. & Ph. 240, 41 Eng. Rep. 482 (Ch. 1841).

In his article, The Dead Hand and the Law of Trusts in the Nineteenth Century, 37 Stan. L. Rev. 1189, 1201 (1985), Professor Alexander gives this account of the developments following *Saunders*:

---

41. Actually, on termination, the trust assets would probably be distributed in kind; see, e.g., Restatement 2d of Trusts §§ 344-47; Cal. Prob. Code § 15410. Generally speaking, for federal income-tax purposes, the beneficiaries' basis in trust assets distributed to them in kind is the adjusted basis of the property in the hands of the trustee; the trustee can elect, however, to recognize gain or loss on the distribution, in which case the beneficiaries' basis is the fair market value of the property on the date of distribution. IRC § 643(e).

Although the doctrine of *Saunders* was not accepted by the House of Lords until some fifty years later,[42] it was quickly and widely followed in equity practice. In Curtis v. Luken, decided in 1842,[43] the Master of the Rolls explained the *Saunders* doctrine:

> [The beneficiary] has the legal power of disposing of it, he may sell, charge, or assign it, for he has an absolute, indefeasible interest in a thing defined and certain; the Court, therefore, has thought fit . . . to say, that since the legatee has such the legal right and power over the property, and can deal with it as he pleases, it will not subject him to the disadvantage of raising money by selling or charging his interest, when the thing is his own, at this very moment.[44]

The court here explicitly connected the question of a beneficiary's power to compel termination in anticipation of the time prescribed by the trustor with the question of the beneficiary's power to alienate his equitable interest. Since no valid restraint could be imposed upon an equitable fee, a provision postponing possession of the trust estate could not be given effect, since it would be inconsistent with the property given to him. The *Saunders* doctrine thereafter was understood to require premature termination when all parties having an equitable interest in the trust and having legal capacity to consent petitioned for termination and distribution of the trust estate.

The English doctrine was generally followed by American courts prior to 1889.[45] Since American courts had followed the English position on the validity of restraints on alienation of equitable interests, including equitable fees and more limited interests such as life estates in income, it was to be expected that they would not enforce provisions postponing possession of trust property by legally competent beneficiaries who, individually or collectively, held the entire equitable interest.

Claflin v. Claflin

20 N.E. 454 (Mass. 1889)

FIELD, J. By the eleventh article of his will, as modified by a codicil, Wilbur F. Claflin gave all the residue of his personal estate to trustees,

> to sell and dispose of the same, and to pay to my wife, Mary A. Claflin, one-third part of the proceeds thereof, and to pay to my son Clarence A. Claflin, one-third

---

42. Wharton v. Masterman, 1895 App. Cas. 186 (H.L.).

43. 5 Beav. 147, 49 Eng. Rep. 533 (Ch. 1842).

44. Id. at 156, 49 Eng. Rep. at 536.

45. E.g., Sanford v. Lackland, 21 Fed. Cas. 358 (C.C.D. Mo. 1871) (No. 12,312); Gray v. Obear, 54 Ga. 231 (1875); Thompson v. Ballard, 70 Md. 10, 16 A. 378 (1889); Philadelphia v. Girard, 45 Pa. 9, 27 (1863).

> part of the proceeds thereof, and to pay the remaining one-third thereof to my son Adelbert E. Claflin, in the manner following, viz.: Ten thousand dollars when he is of the age of twenty-one years, ten thousand dollars when he is of the age of twenty-five years, and the balance when he is of the age of thirty years.

Apparently, Adelbert E. Claflin was not quite 21 years old when his father died, but he some time ago reached that age, and received $10,000 from the trust. He has not yet reached the age of 25 years, and he brings this bill to compel the trustees to pay to him the remainder of the trust fund. His contention is, in effect, that the provisions of the will postponing the payment of the money beyond the time when he is 21 years are void. There is no doubt that his interest in the trust fund is vested and absolute, and that no other person has any interest in it; and the authority is undisputed that the provisions postponing payment to him until some time after he reaches the age of 21 years would be treated as void by those courts which hold that restrictions against the alienation of absolute interests in the income of trust property are void. There has indeed, been no decision of this question in England by the House of Lords, and but one by a Lord Chancellor, but there are several decisions to this effect by Masters of the Rolls, and by Vice-Chancellors.

These decisions do not proceed on the ground that it was the intention of the testator that the property should be conveyed to the beneficiary on his reaching the age of 21 years, because in each case it was clear that such was not his intention, but on the ground that the direction to withhold the possession of the property from the beneficiary after he reached his majority was inconsistent with the absolute rights of property given him by the will.

This court has ordered trust property conveyed by the trustee to the beneficiary when there was a dry trust, or when the purposes of the trust had been accomplished, or when no good reason was shown why the trust should continue, and all the persons interested in it were *sui juris*, and desired that it be terminated; but we have found no expression of any opinion in our reports that provisions requiring a trustee to hold and manage the trust property until the beneficiary reached an age beyond that of 21 years are void if the interest of the beneficiary is vested and absolute. This is not a dry trust, nor have the purposes of the trust been accomplished, if the intention of the testator is to be carried out. . . .

In the case at bar nothing has happened which the testator did not anticipate, and for which he has not made provision. It is plainly his will that neither the income nor any part of the principal should now be paid to the plaintiff. It is true that the plaintiff's interest is alienable by him, and can be taken by his creditors to pay his debts, but it does not follow because the testator has not imposed all possible restrictions that the restrictions which he has imposed should not be carried into effect.

The decision in Broadway National Bank v. Adams, 133 Mass. 170, rests upon the doctrine that a testator has a right to dispose of his own property with such restrictions and limitations, not repugnant to law, as he sees fit, and that his intentions ought to be carried out, unless they contravene some positive rule of law, or are against public policy. The rule contended for by the plaintiff in that case was founded upon the same considerations as that contended for by the plaintiff in this, and the grounds on which this court declined to follow the English rule in that case are applicable to this; and for the reasons there given we are unable to see that the directions of the testator to the trustees to pay the money to the plaintiff when he reaches the ages of 25 and 30 years are against public policy, or are so far inconsistent with the rights of property given to the plaintiff that they should not be carried into effect. It cannot be said that these restrictions upon the plaintiff's possession and control of the property are altogether useless, for there is not the same danger that he will spend the property while it is in the hands of the trustees as there would be if it were in his own. . . .

Decree affirmed.

Notes

1. *State of the Authorities.* The *Claflin* doctrine is widely followed in this country. See Scott on Trusts § 337. The American rule, as expressed in Restatement 2d of Trusts § 337, is that the beneficiaries of a trust cannot compel the trust's premature termination (or modification) unless: (i) all beneficiaries consent (and are competent to do so) and (ii) premature termination (or modification) will not defeat a "material purpose" of the trust. The Uniform Trust Code adheres to the *Claflin* doctrine as to irrevocable trusts. See UTC § 411(b). (As to revocable trusts, see UTC § 602.)

2. *Consent of the Settlor.* Although a trust contains a "material purpose," it is widely (though not universally) held that the beneficiaries can compel its termination (or modification) if they obtain the settlor's consent. See UTC § 411(a); Restatement 3d of Trusts § 65; Restatement 2d of Trusts § 338.

3. *Premature Termination of Uneconomical Trusts.* Both the Uniform Trust Code and a recent Alaska statute permit the trustee, upon notice to beneficiaries, to terminate a trust whose value is less than $50,000. UTC § 414(a); Alaska Stat. § 13.36.365 (a). The Alaska statute but not the UTC allows the trust instrument to provide otherwise.

1. Material Purpose

Current Case Law. Trusts that contain a "material purpose," precluding their premature termination or modification, are sometimes called indestructible trusts. Under current case law, postponement-of-enjoyment, spendthrift, support, and discretionary trusts are usually deemed to contain a material purpose, making them indestructible.

1. *Postponement-of-Enjoyment Trusts*. In the case of a postponement-of-enjoyment trust, such as in *Claflin* (and *Saunders*), the settlor wants the beneficiary to have the trust property and its income, but not until the beneficiary reaches a specified age, a certain period of time has elapsed, or a certain date. Obviously, the settlor's purpose ("material" purpose) would be defeated if the beneficiary were permitted to obtain the trust property earlier.

A postponement-of-enjoyment trust sometimes has only one beneficiary. A key factor in classifying the trusts in *Claflin* and *Saunders* as single-beneficiary trusts was the fact that the beneficiary's interest was indefeasibly vested, giving the beneficiary an equitable fee. This is not a necessary element of a postponement-of-enjoyment trust, however; the beneficiary's interest can be and often is conditioned on surviving the specified age (or on surviving the specified period of time or date certain), with a gift over to another on the beneficiary's failure to survive. Thus the following trust is considered a postponement-of-enjoyment trust:

> *Example 14.2:* G died, devising property in trust, to pay the income to A until A reaches 35 and to pay the principal to A when A reaches that age; but if A dies before reaching 35, to pay the principal to B upon A's death.
>
> Even though A (age 28) and B desire to terminate the trust, they cannot do so.

Typically, a spendthrift clause is included in postponement-of-enjoyment trusts. Judged by estate-planning practices of today, the trust in *Claflin* is unusual for its absence of a spendthrift restraint. The absence of such a restraint in a similar case, Moxley v. Title Insurance & Trust Co., 165 P.2d 15 (Cal. 1946), led Justice Traynor (in dissent) to launch an assault upon the *Claflin* doctrine. Peggy Ann Moxley was the principal beneficiary of a testamentary trust created by her mother, Mabelle E. Kent. By its terms, the trust was to continue until Peggy Ann was 35 years old. Peggy Ann sought termination at age 26, alleging that she was "happily married and living with her husband, capable of managing the estate left in trust by her mother, and is desirous of purchasing a home."

The court refused to order termination of the trust. Dissenting, Justice Traynor argued that a "court will better serve the intentions of the settlor by weighing the actual interests of the beneficiary of a trust in its termination against the benefits intended by its continuance." In other words, since in the absence of a spendthrift restriction the settlor's dominant intention is to benefit the beneficiary, the court should permit premature termination where there is no spendthrift, support, or other more specific motive for the trust. The effect of the decision in *Moxley* was to prevent a beneficiary from using the trust funds for urgent needs or highly desirable purposes. To Justice Traynor, such an effect was incongruous since it wouldn't prevent the beneficiary from selling her equitable interest in the trust. Since a purchaser of that interest couldn't obtain the trust property before the end of the period specified in the trust instrument, it is unlikely, Traynor argued, that the purchaser would pay a price commensurate with the present value of the interest.

Identifying this incongruity is not a very telling revelation, however. One answer to it is that although theoretically marketable, beneficial interests in indestructible trusts are practically unmarketable. The beneficiary often is unaware of the power to sell, and few willing buyers for such interests exist. See Edward W. Cleary, Indestructible Testamentary Trusts, 43 Yale L.J. 393, 400 (1934).

Of course, the practical inalienability of beneficial interests such as those held by Adelbert Claflin in the *Claflin* case and Peggy Ann Moxley in the *Moxley* case might largely disappear if the beneficiary's assignee could compel termination of the trust. A supply of willing buyers likely would emerge. Deals could be structured in a variety of ways to ensure assignees a profit, after expenses (including legal fees) and other risks. Consequently, the *Claflin* rule—to have any force—requires that the beneficiary's assignee also be precluded from compelling the termination of the trust. Thus, Comment k to § 337 of the Restatement 2d of Trusts states that provisions postponing termination of the trust are effective against all assignees as well as the original beneficiary. The cases support the Restatement's position on this point, although such cases are not numerous. See, e.g., Stier v. Nashville Trust Co., 158 F. 601 (6th Cir. 1908); Will of Hamburger, 201 N.W. 267 (Wis. 1924). But see, e.g., Sanford v. Lackland, 2 Dill. 6, F. Cas. (C.C.D. Mo. 1871) (No. 12,312).

Apart from the practical inalienability of beneficial interests, most indestructible trusts create beneficial interests that are legally inalienable, also.

2. *Spendthrift Trusts*. According to the Restatement 2d of Trusts and substantial case authority, spendthrift trusts are indestructible. See Restatement 2d of Trusts § 337 comment l; Scott on Trusts § 337.2.

The California codification of trust law adheres to the traditional view, stating that "the court does not have discretion to permit termination of a trust" on petition of the beneficiaries if the trust "is subject to a valid restraint on transfer of the beneficiary's interest." Cal. Prob. Code § 15403(b). The Texas codification, however, breaks with tradition by stating that "the court shall consider spendthrift provisions as a factor in making its decision whether to modify or terminate, but the court is not precluded from exercising its discretion to modify or terminate solely because the trust is a spendthrift trust." Tex. Prop. Code § 112.054(b).

3. *Discretionary Trusts*. According to the Restatement 2d of Trusts and substantial case authority, all forms of discretionary trusts are indestructible. See Restatement 2d of Trusts § 337 comments m & n; cases cited in Scott on Trusts § 337.4.

4. *Successive-Beneficiary (Straight-Income) Trusts Without Spendthrift Provisions*. Are there any trusts that *can* be terminated (or modified) by the beneficiaries, trusts that aren't indestructible? In a position continued in the Restatement 3d of Trusts § 65 comment d, the Restatement 2d of Trusts § 337 comment f presumptively treats successive-beneficiary trusts as destructible, for example, income to A for life, remainder in principal at A's death to B. The reason given in the Restatement 3d is that the creation of a successive-beneficiary trust "is not itself sufficient to indicate, for example, that the settlor had a material purpose of depriving the beneficiaries of the property management or otherwise of protecting them from the risks of their own judgment. In the absence of additional circumstances indicating a further purpose, the inference is that the trust was intended merely to allow one or more persons to enjoy the benefits of the property during the period of the trust and to allow the other beneficiary or beneficiaries to receive the property thereafter."

Relaxation of the Claflin Doctrine? The Restatement 3d of Trusts § 65, while basically adhering to the *Claflin* doctrine's "material purpose" requirement, substantially relaxes that requirement by providing that the court may authorize termination "if it determines that the reason for termination outweighs the material purpose."[46]

---

46. An Alaska statute, enacted in 2000, provides a similar rule. See Alaska Stat. § 13.36.360(a). Two other recent statutes may, if construed literally, abolish the *Claflin* doctrine. The Virginia statute, enacted in 1991, provides that a "trustee, personal representative or beneficiary" may petition the court for amendment of the trust "including . . . terminating the trust and ordering distribution of the trust property regardless of any spendthrift or similar protective provision." Va. Code Ann. § 55-19.4. The only requirement is that the petitioners show "good cause." The Missouri statute, enacted in 1983, provides that "[w]hen all the adult beneficiaries who are not disabled consent, the court may, upon finding that such variation will benefit the disabled, minor, unborn and unascertained beneficiaries, vary the terms of a private trust so as to reduce or eliminate the interest of some beneficiaries and increase those of others, to change the times or amounts of payment and distributions to beneficiaries, or to provide for termination of the trust at a time earlier or later than that specified by the terms." Mo. Ann. Stat. § 456.590.2.

The two statutes have been construed differently by Virginia and Missouri courts. In Herndon v. Chesapeake Nat'l Bank, 33 Va. Cir. 152 (Lancaster Co. 1994), a county court rejected a literal construction, concluding that the statute was intended to allow reformation or termination of a trust only when unforeseen changes in circumstances, notably changes in tax laws, adversely affect a trust. In Hamerstrom v. Commerce Bank of Kansas City, 808 S.W.2d 434 (Mo. Ct. App. 1991), the court construed the statute to modify the *Claflin* doctrine: where all adult beneficiaries who are not disabled consent, they may compel termination of a trust without consideration of the

Furthermore, the Restatement 3d of Trusts § 65 comment d provides that "[m]aterial purposes are not readily to be inferred. A finding of such a purpose generally requires some showing of a particular concern or objective on the part of the settlor, such as concern with regard to a beneficiary's management skills, judgment, or level of maturity."

1. *Spendthrift Trusts.* The Restatement 3d of Trusts provides that "[s]pendthrift restrictions are not sufficient in and of themselves to establish, or to create a presumption of, a material purpose that would prevent termination by consent of all of the beneficiaries." Restatement 3d of Trusts § 65 comment e. The Uniform Trust Code provides that "[a] spendthrift provision in the terms of the trust is not presumed to constitute a material purpose of the trust." UTC § 411(c).[47]

2. *Discretionary Trusts.* The Restatement 3d of Trusts provides that "[discretionary provisions] are not sufficient in and of themselves to establish, or to create a presumption of, a material purpose that would prevent termination by consent of all of the beneficiaries." Restatement 3d of Trusts § 65 comment e.

3. *Question.* Can trust drafters foil the proposed relaxation of the *Claflin* rules by adding boilerplate language to spendthrift clauses asserting concern for the management skills of the beneficiaries? For example, suppose the following modified version of the spendthrift clause reproduced supra p. 840 becomes standard:

> Because I have concern about the management skills of the beneficiaries of this trust, I direct that no interest of any beneficiary in the income or principal of this trust shall be assignable in anticipation of payment or be liable in any way for the beneficiary's debts or obligations and shall not be subject to attachment.

Permissible Duration of Indestructible Trusts. Apart from statute (and an occasional judicial aberration), there is no direct legal limit on the duration of a trust. There probably is, however, a limit on the time during which a trust may be made indestructible. As yet, the cases are far from conclusive as to just what time limit will be imposed, but the writers have usually assumed that it will be the period of the Rule Against Perpetuities, that is, lives in being plus 21 years or a reasonable approximation thereof as established in the Uniform Statutory Rule Against Perpetuities (Uniform Rule). See Restatement 2d of

---

settlor's purpose. See Jessica L. Lacey, Note, The Dead Hand Loses Its Grip in Virginia: A New Rule for Trust Amendment and Termination?, 29 U. Rich. L. Rev. 1235 (1995).

47. The Alaska statute is to the same effect. See Alaska Stat. § 13.36.360(a).

Trusts § 62 comment o; Restatement 2d of Property § 2.1; Uniform Rule § 1 comment.

A trust meant to be indestructible for a longer period is valid, but subject to termination at suit of the beneficiaries, either from the inception of the trust (as some writers assert) or, more probably, and as set forth in the Restatements and the Comment to the Uniform Rule, at the expiration of the permissible period. In 1959, California enacted a statute stating that "a provision, express or implied, in the instrument creating the trust that the trust may not be terminated is ineffective insofar as it purports to be applicable beyond" the permissible perpetuity period. Cal. Civ. Code § 716.5.

Modification Distinguished from Termination. Do the same considerations apply to a proposed modification as apply to a proposed termination of a trust? The Restatement 3d of Trusts § 65 comment f provides:

> *f. Material purpose and modification.* Although a trust may have a material purpose that would preclude complete or even partial termination of the trust, a particular modification agreed to by the beneficiaries might not be inconsistent with any material purpose of the trust. In such a case all of the beneficiaries could join together to modify the terms of the trust to that extent. Thus, where modification is involved, . . . the material purpose inquiry focuses on the particular amendment sought by the beneficiaries.
>
> For example, a proposed modification might change the trustee or create a simple, inexpensive procedure for appointing successor trustees, or it might create or change procedures for removing and replacing trustees. Modifications of these types may well improve the administration of a trust and be more satisfactory to the beneficiaries without interfering with a material purpose of the trust. On the other hand, a particular change of trustee or repeated modifications to change trustees, or an amendment of provisions relating to the trusteeship, might materially undermine the contemplated qualities or independence of trustees. A given change might even have the effect of shifting effective control of the trust in such a way as to be inconsistent with a protective management purpose or other material purpose of the trust. Thus, changes of trustees or in trustee provisions are to be particularly scrutinized for possible conflict with a material trust purpose.

2. *Beneficiaries' Consent*

Premature termination of a trust requires the consent of all of the beneficiaries. This is the sole requirement under English law. Under prevailing American law, it is a requirement additional to the no-material-purpose rule.

Problems

1. G, a widow, died, survived by her 55-year-old daughter, A; her 52-year-old son, B; A's 25-year-old child, X; and B's 22-year-old child, Y. G's will

devised the residue of her estate in trust, without a spendthrift restraint. At common law (see Note 3, infra), whose consent is necessary to terminate G's trust, if the dispositive terms of the trust provided:

(a) Income to A for life, remainder in principal to X?

(b) Income to A for life, remainder in principal to X if X survives A?

(c) Income to A for life, remainder in principal to A's children?

Compare Bassett's Estate, 190 A.2d 415, 417 (N.H. 1963) ("This state rejects the 'notion' there is a conclusive presumption that a man or woman is always capable of bearing children regardless of age, physical condition and medical opinion to the contrary."); Restatement 2d of Trusts § 340 comment e[48] ("If the unascertained beneficiaries are the children of a designated woman, and the woman is beyond the age of child bearing or otherwise physically incapable of bearing children, the court may terminate the trust."); and Cal. Prob. Code §§ 15406, 6152, with Clark v. Citizens & Southern Nat'l Bank, 257 S.E.2d 244, 246 (Ga. 1979) ("There is a conclusive presumption of Georgia law that the possibility of issue is not extinct in a female until death. . . . Even if this were not the law in Georgia, the class would be subject to reopening upon the adoption of a child or children by the daughter Elizabeth."). See Mark V. Sauer et al., A Preliminary Report on Oocyte Donation Extending Reproductive Potential to Women Over 40, 323 N. Eng. J. Med. 1157 (1990) (reporting that a post-menopausal woman can still become pregnant by implantation of an embryo produced by an egg donated by a younger woman and fertilized by sperm from a man, typically the older woman's husband); Lawrence W. Waggoner, Perpetuity Reform, 81 Mich. L. Rev. 1718, 1728-34 (1983) (reporting on the possibility of an older woman (or man) adopting a child). For further information on reproductive technology, see the web site of the American Society for Reproductive Medicine, www.asrm.org.

(d) Income to B for life, remainder in principal to B's children?

(e) Income to A for life, remainder in principal to A's descendants who survive A, by representation; if none, to A's heirs?

2. Would you reach a different answer in any of the cases in Problem 1 if G's trust were an irrevocable inter vivos trust and if G were alive and gave her consent to the trust's termination?

3. *Effect of UPC § 2-707.* By creating a substitute gift to descendants of remainder beneficiaries who predecease the distribution date, UPC § 2-707 would change the identity of the beneficiaries whose consent is necessary to terminate a trust. Professor Dukeminier argued that this "makes it more difficult to terminate trusts." Jesse Dukeminier, The Uniform Probate Code Upends the Law of Remainders, 94 Mich. L. Rev. 148, 195 (1995). Professor Waggoner

---

48. The Restatement 3d of Trusts § 65 does not address the issue.

responded by pointing out that "*very* few trusts can be terminated before the distribution date" because they contain a boilerplate spendthrift provision or because they grant discretionary powers or discretionary-support powers to the trustee. In addition, most trusts create future interests in classes that are still subject to open. In any event, "an easy solution to the trust termination problem . . . is to add a section resembling [Cal. Prob. Code § 15405] that permits a guardian ad litem to consent to termination or modification on behalf of 'a beneficiary who lacks legal capacity, including a minor, or who is an unascertained or unborn person.'" Lawrence W. Waggoner, The Uniform Probate Code Extends Antilapse-type Protection to Poorly Drafted Trusts, 94 Mich. L. Rev. 2309, 2346-47 (1996).

4. G created a trust, directing the trustee to divide the income equally between A and B for 10 years and to divide the principal equally between A and B at the expiration of the 10-year period. A wants to try to get the trust terminated, but B refuses to consent. Can A compel termination of half the trust? The Restatement 3d of Trusts provides that even though some of the beneficiaries do not consent to termination or are incapable of giving consent, "a court may order a partial termination of the trust (or other arrangement that might involve bonding, insurance or impounding of some trust property) in a manner that will not prejudice the interests of non-consenting beneficiaries" if "the court is satisfied that the best interests of the beneficiaries as a whole would be served by a proposed termination or modification and if continuation of the trust is not required." See Restatement 3d of Trusts § 65, comment c.

5. G created a trust, directing the trustee to divide the income equally between A and B during their joint lives, and on A's death to pay half the principal to X and on B's death to pay the other half of the principal to Y. A and X want to terminate the trust, but B and Y refuse to consent. Can A and X compel termination of half the trust? See Shaller v. Mississippi Valley Trust Co., 3 S.W.2d 726 (Mo. 1928).

Settlor's Right as Sole Beneficiary to Terminate. In Phillips v. Lowe, 639 S.W.2d 782 (Ky. 1982), the court held that the settlor, who was the sole beneficiary of a trust, could terminate the trust, even though the trust instrument expressly declared that the trust was irrevocable. Accord, e.g., Woodruff v. Trust Co. of Georgia, 210 S.E.2d 321 (Ga. 1974); Johnson v. First Nat'l Bank, 386 So.2d 1112 (Miss. 1980); Restatement 2d of Trusts § 339. See also Restatement 3d of Trusts § 65, which is consistent with but less explicit on this position.

It should go without saying that if the settlor is not the sole beneficiary, the settlor cannot unilaterally revoke, terminate, or modify an irrevocable trust. Note, however, that the mistake doctrine allows for such a trust to be rescinded or reformed to incorporate a power to revoke if it can be shown that the trust was created as the result of a "material mistake" or that the power was omitted by mistake. See Restatement 3d of Trusts §§ 62, 63 comment d; Restatement 3d of Property § 12.1 comment i, illustration 7; Palmer on Restitution § 18.7(a); Berger v. United States, 487 F.Supp. 49 (W.D. Pa. 1980).

Consent on Behalf of Minors, Incapacitated Persons, and Unborn or Unascertained Persons. Section 340(1) of the Restatement 2d of Trusts states that if one or more of the beneficiaries is under an incapacity, "the *others* cannot compel the termination of the trust." Thus, for example, in Problem 1(a), supra, where the income from G's non-spendthrift trust was to be paid to A for life, remainder in principal to X, A could not compel the termination of the trust if X was a minor or incapacitated in some other way. Is it possible, however, for the court or X's conservator or guardian to join with A in consenting to the trust's termination? The Restatement 3d of Trusts § 65 comment b and some courts have held that consent can be given on the beneficiary's behalf by the guardian of the incapacitated beneficiary's property or the incapacitated beneficiary's conservator. See, e.g., Randall v. Randall, 60 F. Supp. 308 (S.D. Fla. 1944); Riedlin's Guardian v. Cobb, 1 S.W.2d 1071 (Ky. 1928); Flexner's Trust, 288 N.Y.S.2d 494, aff'd mem., 294 N.Y.S.2d 669 (App. Div. 1968) (the New York court expressed approval of a guardian of the property having authority to consent on behalf of his ward, and deferred to the order of a California court, which had held that the guardian had such authority, because California had more significant contacts with the trust). See also UPC §§ 5-407, 5-423. Contra, e.g., Application of Michael, 333 N.Y.S.2d 301 (Sup. Ct. 1972).

To be contrasted with the problem of gaining consent on behalf of minors, incapacitated persons, or persons under a disability is the problem of unborn or unascertained beneficiaries. Can anyone consent on their behalf? In Hatch v. Riggs Nat'l Bank, 361 F.2d 559 (D.C. Cir. 1966), the court held:

> It is hornbook law that any trust, no matter how "irrevocable" by its terms, may be revoked with the consent of the settlor and all beneficiaries.
>
> The beneficiaries of the trust created by appellant are herself, as life tenant, and her heirs, as remaindermen. Her heirs, if determined as of the present time, are her two sisters. There is no assurance that they will in fact be the heirs who take the remainder under the trust; appellant might survive one or both. Yet their consent is necessary, we think, to revocation, since they are at least the persons who would be beneficiaries if the settlor died today.[49]

---

49. One of the sisters is not *sui juris*. In referring to her consent, we do not mean to exclude consent by her guardian ad litem.

In addition, it is necessary to protect the interests of those additional persons, both living and unborn, who may, depending on circumstances, be members of the class of heirs at the time the corpus is distributed. We think that upon an adequate showing, by the party petitioning to revoke or modify the trust, that those who are, so to speak, the heirs as of the present time consent to the modification, and that there is a reasonable possibility that the modification that has been proposed adequately protects the interests of those other persons who might be heirs at the time the corpus is to be distributed, the District Court may appoint a guardian ad litem to represent the interests of those additional persons.

Although the question has not been previously discussed by this court we think basic principles of trust law are in accord with appointment of a guardian ad litem to represent interests of unborn or unascertained beneficiaries, for purposes of consent to modification or revocation of a trust. This use of a guardian ad litem is not uncommon in other jurisdictions. In a number of states authority for such appointments is provided by statute. These statutes reflect a broad sentiment of the approaches that are consistent with the Anglo-American system of law and adopted to promote the objective of justice. Where it is at least debatable whether rulings must await express legislative authorization, this court must take into account the fact that the legislature for the District of Columbia is primarily concerned with awesome questions of national policy, and we should be more ready to accept our obligation as a court to refine and adapt the corpus of law without waiting for a legislative go-ahead. Here we are certainly in a field where it is not inappropriate for courts to act without statutory foundation. . . . "Courts of justice as an incident of their jurisdiction have inherent power to appoint guardians ad litem." [Mabry v. Scott, 124 P.2d 659 (Cal. Ct. App. 1942).] The efficacy of a guardian ad litem appointed to protect the interests of unborn persons is no different whether he be appointed pursuant to statute or the court's inherent power. Given such protection, the equitable doctrine of representation embraces the flexibility, born of convenience and necessity, to act upon the interests of unborn contingent remaindermen to the same effect as if they had been *sui juris* and parties.

The use of guardians ad litem to represent interests of unborn and/or otherwise unascertainable beneficiaries of a trust seems to us wholly appropriate. Though the persons whose interests the guardian ad litem represents would be unascertainable as individuals, they are identifiable as a class and their interest, as such, recognizable.

The settlor seeking to revoke or modify the trust may supplement his appeal to equity with a quid pro quo offered to the heirs for their consent. In many cases it may well be consistent with or even in furtherance of the interest of the heirs to grant such consent. The case at bar provides a good example. Here the interest of all heirs is contingent, since appellant can defeat their remainder by exercising her testamentary power of appointment. If the modification agreed upon not only increased the annual income of the life tenant but also transferred assets in trust for the benefit of the heirs, without any power of alteration in the settlor, the heirs' remainder interest would be secure, and accordingly more valuable than it is now. The pattern of such a modification is clearly available where the remaindermen of a trust are specific named persons, and, we think, should also be available where the remaindermen are recognizable as a class even though the members of the class are not now individually ascertainable.

Notes

1. *Revoking Irrevocable Trusts.* Not infrequently, settlors of irrevocable inter vivos trusts share a common plight with that of the settlor in the *Hatch* case. Sometimes, the worthier-title doctrine has been successfully invoked. See, e.g., Stewart v. Merchants Nat'l Bank, 278 N.E.2d 10 (Ill. App. Ct. 1972). This works, however, only if the worthier-title doctrine is followed in the jurisdiction and is applicable to the particular case, i.e., if the beneficial interest is in the "heirs" of the settlor. Otherwise, despite the fact that the inter vivos trust has proved to be improvident, an order to meet pressing needs of the settlor is often denied because of the impossibility of gaining the consent of unborn or unascertained beneficiaries. Improvidence of the trust is not usually held to provide a ground for rescission. See Palmer on Restitution § 18.7(a). Only occasionally has a decision ordered cancellation. See, e.g., Reuther v. Fidelity Union Trust Co., 172 A. 386 (N.J. 1934).

The UTC deals with the problem in a way that is somewhat similar to the approach taken in *Hatch*. See UTC § 305. The recent Alaska statute tracks the language of this provision. See Alaska Stat. § 13.36.360(c).

Legislation in a few states also alleviates the problem, but in a variety of ways. In North Carolina, for example, the settlor is empowered to revoke provisions in favor of persons "not in esse or not determined until the happening of a future event," if the revocation is effected before "the happening of the contingency vesting the future estates" and if the trust instrument does not expressly provide otherwise. N.C. Gen. Stat. § 39-6.

New York authorizes the settlor to revoke a trust with the consent of "all the persons beneficially interested. . . ." N.Y. Est. Powers & Trusts Law § 7-1.9. The phrase "persons beneficially interested" has been interpreted as excluding possible unborn beneficiaries. See, e.g., Smith v. Title Guarantee & Trust Co., 41 N.E.2d 72 (N.Y. 1942). Section 7-1.9 further provides that, for purposes of trust termination, a disposition in favor of a class of persons described only as heirs, next of kin, or distributees of the creator of the trust does not create a beneficial interest in such persons.

2. *Consent on Behalf of Unborn or Unascertained Beneficiaries.* The court in *Hatch* found a still different and quite novel solution to the settlor's plight. Many states, to be sure, have statutes authorizing the *appointment* of guardians ad litem to represent certain classes of persons (unborn, unascertained, incapacitated, or protected persons, minors, or persons whose identities or addresses are unknown). See, e.g., UPC § 1-403. But these statutes only authorize the appointment of a guardian ad litem to represent such persons *in*

litigation.[50] These statutes address a compelling need, for some machinery is necessary to bind such parties by judgments; otherwise, many cases involving certain kinds of disputes or to establish title to property would be impossible to resolve conclusively. Many statutes, such as UPC § 1-403, apply to any formal proceeding or judicially supervised settlement, while other statutes specify the kinds of judicial proceedings in which the guardian ad litem is authorized to act, such as probate, quiet title, partition, trust accounting, or title registration. The statutes either expressly provide, or seem clearly to imply, that the result of such representation of unborn parties is to make the result of the litigation binding upon any person so represented who later comes into being.

Another doctrine under which unborn or unascertained persons are bound by litigation is that of *virtual representation.* Under this doctrine, which is generally held to be available to courts without legislation, unborn or unascertained persons are held to have been represented by living parties to a suit if the latter have the same or similar interests as those of the later-born or later-ascertained beneficiaries, and if the respective classes of interests are not otherwise adverse to one another. See generally UPC § 1-403; Petition of Wolcott, infra p. 901.

In suggesting the appointment of a guardian ad litem "for the purposes of consent to modification or revocation of a trust," the court in *Hatch* went beyond these traditional limits. Unfortunately, the court didn't seem to notice the novelty of its approach. Instead, the discussion concentrated on the power of a court to *appoint* a guardian ad litem without statutory authority, not on the *authority* of a guardian ad litem once appointed. The same narrow focus of discussion occurred in a subsequent decision of the District Court in *Hatch.* Following up on the Court of Appeals's suggestion, a guardian ad litem was appointed and a modification agreement was reached. In reaching this agreement, the guardian ad litem acted for the unborn and unascertained beneficiaries; the court didn't note whether the guardian ad litem also acted for the settlor's sister who wasn't *sui juris*. The trustee objected to the guardian ad litem's authority, claiming that the Circuit Court's discussion of this point was dictum. In Hatch v. Riggs Nat'l Bank, 284 F. Supp 396 (D.D.C. 1968), the District Court approved the appointment and the modification agreement. The court didn't disclose the terms of the modification agreement, but noted that it was satisfied that the agreed-upon modification "fully protect[s] the interests of any unborn heirs. . . ." See also Restatement 3d of Trusts § 65 comment b, which states that the consent of potential beneficiaries who cannot consent for themselves "may be provided by guardians ad litem, by court appointed or

---

50. Indeed, the term "guardian ad litem" means guardian for the purpose of the lawsuit.

other legally authorized representatives, or through representation by other beneficiaries under the doctrine of virtual representation."

3. *Enabling Legislation*. The UTC § 305 provides that the court may appoint a representative to give consent on behalf of a "minor, incapacitated, or unborn individual, or whose identity or location is unknown" and that, in making the decision whether or not to give consent, the representative "may consider general benefit accruing to the living members of the individual's family."[51]

EXTERNAL REFERENCE: Edward C. Halbach, Jr., Uniform Acts, Restatements, and Trends in American Trust Law at Century's End, 88 Calif. L. Rev. 1877, 1899-1900 (2000).

PART C. MODIFICATION (OR TERMINATION) BECAUSE OF UNANTICIPATED CIRCUMSTANCES

Statutory Reference: *UTC § 412*

If trust beneficiaries have a right to compel termination of the trust, they also have a right to compel modification of its provisions. But suppose modification on petition of the beneficiaries is impossible, for example, because there are unborn or unascertained beneficiaries or because one or more of the living beneficiaries refuses to consent. The court still might modify or terminate the trust on the basis of unforeseen circumstances. The Restatement 3d of Trusts § 66 and UTC § 412(a) provide that a court may modify the administrative or beneficial terms of a trust if "because of circumstances not anticipated by the settlor," modification will further the purposes of the trust.[52] Furthermore, the trustee may deviate from the trust terms without prior court approval if the trustee reasonably believes that there is an emergency and if the trustee has no opportunity to apply for court approval before deviating.

---

51. The UTC provision is based on the following, more explicit provision of the California Probate Code:

> *Cal. Prob. Code § 15405. Guardian ad litem.* For [the purposes of trust termination or modification], the consent of a beneficiary who lacks legal capacity, including a minor, or who is an unascertained or unborn person may be given in proceedings before the court by a guardian ad litem, if it would be appropriate to do so. In determining whether to give consent, the guardian ad litem may rely on general family benefit accruing to living members of the beneficiary's family as a basis for approving a modification or termination of the trust.

See also N.C. Gen. Stat. § 36A-125.5; Wis. Stat. § 701.12.

52. To the same effect is Alaska Stat. § 13.36.345 (a).

1. Distributive Deviations

A trust beneficiary in need may seek to accelerate or increase his or her right to income or principal beyond that which is granted by the terms of the trust. Such deviations have been permitted in cases of single-beneficiary, postponement-of-enjoyment trusts—trusts, for example, in which the beneficiary is given income and principal upon attaining a certain age or at the end of some other period. See, e.g., Post v. Grand Rapids Trust Co., 238 N.W. 206 (Mich. 1931); Bennett v. Nashville Trust Co., 153 S.W. 840 (Tenn. 1912). The deviation in such cases, of course, amounts to a judicially declared power to invade principal for support.[53]

Where, on the other hand, there are other beneficiaries who will be adversely affected by such a deviation, as where the corpus is given to one or more persons other than the income beneficiary, the deviation will usually be denied. See, e.g., Van Deusen's Estate, 182 P.2d 565 (Cal. 1947); Staley v. Ligon, 210 A.2d 384 (Md. 1965); Matter of Rotermund, 61 Misc. 2d 324, 305 N.Y.S.2d 413 (Sur. Ct. 1969). Arguing that support of the income beneficiary was the testator's or settlor's primary purpose in establishing the trust has usually been to no avail. Justice Traynor's statement in the *Van Deusen's Estate* case is representative of dominant judicial philosophy on this point:

> If the courts could increase the payments under testamentary trusts without the consent of all the beneficiaries merely because the income therefrom is not what it was at the time the will was executed and because at one time or another the testator expressed the desire to provide adequately for the beneficiaries, there would be no stability to any testamentary trust in this state.

More recently, however, trusts are lasting longer and longer, trust income has declined in current financial market conditions, and inflation has made some older trusts that provide for a specific sum to be paid to the income beneficiary badly out of date. Consequently, the UTC and the Restatement 3d of Trusts have responded to the need for courts to have the authority to adjust the distributive terms of a trust in cases of changed and unanticipated circumstances. The Restatement 3d of Trusts provides:

> *§ 66. Power of Court to Modify: Unanticipated Circumstances*
>
> (1) The court may modify an administrative or distributive provision of a trust, or direct or permit the trustee to deviate from an administrative or distributive

53. Contrast Pierowich v. Metropolitan Life Ins. Co., 275 N.W. 789 (Mich. 1937), where a mother, as guardian of the infant beneficiaries under a life-insurance contract, sought a decree for payment to them of sums from the insurance proceeds prior to the times specified in the insurance contract. In denying the petition, the court found that the arrangement created a contract, not a trust, and held that it was without power to modify the terms of a contract.

> provision, if because of circumstances not anticipated by the settlor the modification or deviation will further the purposes of the trust.
>
> (2) If a trustee knows or should know of circumstances that justify judicial action under Subsection (1), the trustee has a duty to petition the court for appropriate modification of or deviation from the terms of the trust.

UTC § 412(a) adoptes a similar approach. How would Petition of Wolcott, below, be decided under either the Restatement 3d's approach or that of the UTC?

Petition of Wolcott

56 A.2d 641 (N.H. 1948)

[Francis E. Getty died in 1944, leaving a will executed in 1932 that devised $2,500 to his widow, Ada C. Getty, $5,000 each to his two sons, and the residue of his estate in trust. The income from the trust was to be paid to Ada during her lifetime, and on her death the principal was to be paid to his then-living issue or, if none, to his heirs. The will conferred on the trustees broad discretionary powers concerning investment and management of trust assets, including the power to allocate receipts between income and principal and the power "generally to do all things in relation to the trust fund which the testator could have done if living."

The trustees sought authority to invade principal for Ms. Getty in an amount not to exceed $4,000 per year, on proof of her needs resulting from her advanced age and illness. The income amounted to about $2,300 per year and her needs were estimated at $5,800 per year; the trust principal was valued at $107,000. All living issue—the couple's two sons and an 18-year-old grandson, who was represented by a guardian ad litem—consented to the deviation.]

DUNCAN, J. . . . Despite broad discretionary powers conferred upon the trustees, the will contains no provision for the use of principal for the benefit of the widow. On the other hand, such use is not specifically forbidden. It may fairly be assumed that the beneficiary's need of the principal was not anticipated because of a failure to foresee changes which have occurred since the testator's death, including shrinkage in investment returns, decline in purchasing power, and the expense occasioned by the widow's extreme infirmity. The powers conferred upon the trustees as to investments and the allocation of receipts to income are indicative of a purpose to provide the widow with a liberal income, unrestricted by technical rules. No purpose to transmit any specific residuary amount to the sons or any other issue is disclosed. Fairly construed, the will evidences as its primary purpose "ample and certain provision" for the testator's wife.

What is sought by the petition is not construction of any particular provision of the will but rather authority to deviate from the provisions by which principal would be retained intact during the widow's lifetime. No reliance is placed by the trustees upon their general power "to do all things in relation to the trust which the testator could have done if living." The power is at best obscure in meaning, and if construed independently of other provisions, would have doubtful validity. Clark v. Campbell, 82 N.H. 281, 133 A. 166, 45 A.L.R. 1433. Because of the emergency confronting the life beneficiary, the trustees seek authority to do what the testator presumably would have authorized had he foreseen the emergency.

Where a remainder succeeding a life estate may ultimately vest in persons as yet undetermined and perhaps unborn, courts of equity have at times hesitated or refused to sanction an invasion of principal for the benefit of the life tenant. . . . In one view, permission is sought to appropriate to the use of one beneficiary the property of others without the consent of all. But this view, in our opinion, may be deemed applicable only to the extent the testator's disclosed intention affords it a foundation. Strictly speaking, it may prevent accomplishment of the testator's primary purpose. As is said in 2 Scott, Trusts, § 168, p. 855: "As a matter of strict logic it may be necessary to permit a child to suffer in order to protect the possible children which he may ultimately have, but it is difficult to believe that the settlor would ever desire such a result." Where the testator's desire may be gathered from the will, "strict logic" need not be controlling.

Traditionally, the courts of this jurisdiction have shown a signal regard for the intent of the testator . . . , at times at the expense of other recognized principles deemed less cogent in their application. Cf. Edgerly v. Barker, 66 N.H. 434, 31 A. 900, 28 L.R.A. 328. In order to prevent impairment of a testator's primary purpose, authority to deviate from the express terms of a gift has been granted in cases of emergency unforeseen by him, even though contingent remainder interests were incidentally affected. . . .

In the will before us, the testator's purpose to furnish reasonable support for his wife is not expressed in words, but is nevertheless implicit in the disposition made of his estate. His direction that his wife should have the income was a means of executing his purpose, and is "properly to be read as subordinate to (his) paramount intention." In re Walker, [1901] 1 Ch. 879, 885. His intent to provide reasonable support to the widow being evident from the will, those whose interests are secondary to hers take subject to the execution of that intent. The remaindermen are deprived of no rights so long as rights which the life tenant was intended to have are not exceeded.

Because of circumstances not provided for by the will and obviously not anticipated by the testator, an emergency threatens accomplishment of his purpose by the means which he provided. Those whose interests are most immediate consent to the authorization sought by the trustees, and there is no objection by the guardian ad litem. If the consent or acquiescence of the parties is not binding upon unborn contingent remaindermen, still they are sufficiently represented by those having like interests to be bound by a decree. . . . In this situation a court of equity need not hesitate to exercise its undoubted power to permit a deviation from the literal provisions of the will. A means of accomplishing the testator's purpose is thereby furnished, which it may reasonably be inferred that he himself would have provided, had he been able to foresee the exigency. . . .

The trustees are advised that principal not in excess of $4,000 a year may be used to supplement the income of the trust, for the purpose of providing the widow with reasonable support, if the trial court shall find in accordance with the uncontroverted allegations of the petition, and it shall appear that the widow has no other income. In view of the discretion vested in the trustees by the testator, there is no reason why they may not safely be left to determine the amount of principal necessary within the limit specified, due regard being given to considerations of what is prudent and reasonable, and best calculated to accomplish the testator's purposes as a whole.

If the requisite findings are made, a decree in accordance with this opinion may be entered by the Superior Court.

Case discharged.

All concurred.

Notes and Questions

1. *Questions.* In what way was the testator's purpose to furnish reasonable support for his widow "implicit in the disposition made of his estate"?

Suppose the testator had directed his personal representative to determine the actuarial value of an income interest for life in favor of a person of his widow's age in a fund the value of his estate (minus the $12,500 pecuniary devises to his wife and sons), directing his executor to use that amount to purchase a straight-life annuity for her. Suppose further that his will had then devised the remaining part of his estate in a separate trust in which the income was to be accumulated during her lifetime and added to corpus, the corpus and accumulated income to be paid over to his then-living descendants at his wife's death or, if none, to his heirs. If the annuity payments later proved insufficient to meet his widow's needs, would the court have ordered an invasion of the principal of the residuary trust to be invaded for her benefit?

2. *Legislation.* A few statutes authorize expansion of a beneficiary's benefits on a showing of need. In Wisconsin, for example, a statute provides:

Wis. Stat. Ann. § 701.13. Modification and termination of trusts by court action.

(1) Anticipation of directed accumulation of income. When an accumulation of income is directed for the benefit of a beneficiary without other sufficient means to support or educate himself, the court on the application of such person or his guardian may direct that a suitable sum from the income accumulated or to be accumulated be applied for the support or education of such person.

(2) Application of principal to income beneficiary. Unless the creating instrument provides to the contrary, if a beneficiary is entitled to income or to have it applied for his benefit, the court may make an allowance from principal to or for the benefit of such beneficiary if his support or education is not sufficiently provided for, taking into account all other resources available to the beneficiary.

Note that subsection (1) of the Wisconsin statute is within traditional limits, but that subsection (2) goes beyond those limits in much the same way as the *Wolcott* decision. For similar statutes authorizing limited invasions of principal, see N.Y. Est. Powers & Trusts Law § 7-1.6; Pa. Stat. Ann. tit. 20, § 301.2. See also Cal. Prob. Code § 15409; Fla. Stat. Ann. § 738.12(1)(a); Tex. Prop. Code § 112.054.

In In re Tutino, 550 N.Y.S.2d 21, appeal denied, 559 N.E.2d 1287 (N.Y. 1990), the court held that an income beneficiary was required to demand invasion of the trust principal under the New York statute in order to qualify for Medicaid. The statute provides that, unless the trust instrument expressly prohibits, a court may invade the principal for an income beneficiary whether or not the income beneficiary is entitled to do so.

In England, the Variation of Trusts Act, 1958, 6 & 7 Eliz. 2, ch. 53, authorizes a court to approve an arrangement varying or revoking a trust, or enlarging the powers of a trustee in administering any of the trust property, on behalf of any beneficiary who is an infant or otherwise incompetent, an unborn or unascertained person, or a person having a discretionary interest under a protective trust.

External References. Lawrence A. Frolik, Adjustment for Inflation for Fixed-Income Trust Beneficiaries, 54 Notre Dame Law. 661 (1979); Paul G. Haskell, Justifying the Principle of Distributive Deviation in the Law of Trusts, 18 Hastings L.J. 267 (1967); Committee Report, Modification of Terms Regarding Amount or Time of Payments to Income Beneficiaries, 4 Real Prop. Prob. & Tr. J. 359 (1969).

2. *Administrative Deviations*

Requests for deviations from the administrative provisions of a trust are handled differently from requests for distributive deviations. The most common examples of administrative deviations that courts usually permit involve the power of trustees to sell or invest trust assets. These cases involve changes in circumstances which the settlor didn't anticipate, and which would defeat or substantially impair the accomplishment of the purposes of the trust. Courts often say that the changed circumstances must produce an exigency or emergency, and it's not enough that a deviation would be beneficial to the beneficiaries. Obviously, this standard is one of degree, making prediction and generalization difficult, as the following materials indicate.

Matter of Pulitzer

249 N.Y.S. 87 (Sur. Ct. 1931), aff'd mem.,
260 N.Y.S. 975 (App. Div. 1932)

FOLEY, S. This is a proceeding for . . . instruction and determination of the court as to the propriety, price, manner, and time of sale of a substantial portion of the assets of the Press Publishing Company, the stock of which constitutes a material part of the assets of the trust here involved. . . . A serious and imperative emergency is claimed to exist, whereby, if such a sale is not made, a valuable asset of the trust estate may be in great part or wholly lost to the trust, the life tenants, and remaindermen. . . .

Joseph Pulitzer[54] died in the year 1911. He left a will and four codicils which were admitted to probate by this court on November 29, 1911. The provisions directly pertinent to the issues here are contained in the first codicil, which is dated March 23, 1909. By its terms he gave the shares of the capital stock of the Press Publishing Company, which were owned by him, and his shares of the Pulitzer Publishing Company, of St. Louis, in trust for the life of each of the two youngest of his sons, Joseph Pulitzer, Jr., and Herbert Pulitzer. . . . There

---

54. A German immigrant to this country, Joseph Pulitzer became one of its wealthiest and most influential journalists. Almost overnight, he converted the New York World, the first modern daily newspaper, from a moribund sheet into the most widely-read daily newspaper in the world. The World's success owed to several innovations that other sensationalist newspapers would later borrow, including multi-columned headlines, pictures and illustrations, and a daily sports page. Using resources generated by its huge circulation, the World mounted stunts that seemed larger than life, including sending Nellie Bly around the world in 72 days to best the fictional record that Jules Verne conceived for Phineas Fogg. The World's editorial page regularly railed against the moneyed elites, although Pulitzer's other newspaper, the St. Louis Post Dispatch was a very different kind of paper, preaching solid middle-class values rather than Mugwump reformism. The World's fascinating story is told in George Juergens, Joseph Pulitzer and the New York World (1966).

Pulitzer himself was profoundly influenced by the Horatio Alger story of American life and greatly coveted wealth. His estate was a comparatively modest $18,525,116, much less than the thirty to eighty million dollar figure that many had guessed. See W. A. Swanberg, Pulitzer 413 (1967). The estate would have been larger but for the family's luxurious lifestyle. Eds.

were directions to pay the income in certain fractional shares to his three sons[55] and to certain other persons. . . .

To distinguish it from the residuary trust, the particular trust here has been called the "Newspaper Trust." Its trustees are the testator's three sons, Ralph Pulitzer, Herbert Pulitzer, and Joseph Pulitzer, Jr. The Pulitzer Publishing Company publishes the St. Louis Post Dispatch. The Press Publishing Company publishes the New York World, the Sunday World, and the Evening World. The trustees of the so-called "Newspaper Trust" hold within the trust a very large majority of shares of the Press Publishing Company. The remaining shares are owned by the trustees individually. The paragraph particularly sought to be construed here, which deals with the powers of the trustees and the limitations thereon, is contained in article seventh of the codicil of March 23, 1909, and reads as follows:

> I further authorize and empower my Executors and Trustees to whom I have hereinbefore bequeathed my stock in the Pulitzer Publishing Company of St. Louis, at any time, and from time to time, to sell and dispose of said stock, or any part thereof, at public or private sale, at such prices and on such terms as they may think best, and to hold the proceeds of any stock sold in trust for the beneficiaries for whom such shares were held in lieu thereof, and upon the same trusts. This power is not to be construed as in any respect mandatory, but purely discretionary. This power of sale, however, is limited to the said stock of the Pulitzer Publishing Company of St. Louis, and shall not be taken to authorize or empower the sale or disposition under any circumstances whatever, by the Trustees of any stock of the Press Publishing Company, publisher of "The World" newspaper (to the maintenance and upbuilding of which I have sacrificed my health and strength) in the same spirit which I have striven to create and conduct it as a public institution, from motives higher than mere gain, it having been my desire that it should be at all times conducted in a spirit of independence and with a view to inculcating high standards and public spirit among the people and their official representatives, and

55. In fact, the distribution plan made a flurry of newspaper headlines. Herbert, the youngest child, was given a six-tenths interest in the trust income, three times the size of his eldest brother Ralph's share, while Joseph, Jr., was given only a one-tenth interest. Pulitzer's partiality for Herbert was revealed also by the terms for appointment of trustees. Initially, four independent trustees were appointed, and two of which were to be replaced by Herbert when he reached 21 and by Joseph, Jr., when he reached 30. Ralph, who was 32 at the time of his father's death and had already made his mark in the newspaper business, was the only one of the brothers not given a trusteeship, a fact that led him to make a public statement indicating that the omission might mistakenly suggest "a lack of confidence in me on my father's part." In fact, in an unexecuted will prepared for him in 1911, Pulitzer did name Ralph as a trustee. It is also notable that neither of Pulitzer's two daughters were made trustees or received any interest in the newspaper trust, although they were given income interests in a $1.5 million trust. See Swanberg, supra note 54, at 414. Eds.

> it is my earnest wish that said newspaper shall hereafter be conducted upon the same principles.

There are fifteen remaindermen in existence. One of them is an adult; the other fourteen are infants. Because of a possible adversity of interest they are represented here by two separate special guardians. The adult life tenants and remaindermen join in requesting the relief sought by the trustees.

Counsel for the trustees contend that the express denial of a power of sale contained in the paragraph was modified and cut down, as a matter of testamentary intent, by Mr. Pulitzer in subsequent language. . . . There is some support to be found in the provisions of the will for these contentions. Indication of an intent to authorize a sale in certain emergencies is thus found in article 6 of the codicil dated May 11, 1910.

But I prefer to place my determination here upon broader grounds and upon the power of a court of equity, in emergencies, to protect the beneficiaries of a trust from serious loss, or a total destruction of a substantial asset of the corpus. The law, in the case of necessity, reads into the will an implied power of sale. . . .

The same rule applies to emergencies in trusts not only where there is an absence of power of sale in a will, but also where there is a prohibition against sale. It has been satisfactorily established by the evidence before me that the continuance of the publication of the newspapers, which are the principal assets of the Press Publishing Company, will in all probability lead to a serious impairment or the destruction of a large part of the trust estate. The dominant purpose of Mr. Pulitzer must have been the maintenance of a fair income for his children and the ultimate reception of the unimpaired corpus by the remaindermen. Permanence of the trust and ultimate enjoyment by his grandchildren were intended. A man of his sagacity and business ability could not have intended that from mere vanity, the publication of the newspapers, with which his name and efforts had been associated, should be persisted in until the entire trust asset was destroyed or wrecked by bankruptcy or dissolution. His expectation was that his New York newspapers would flourish. Despite his optimism, he must have contemplated that they might become entirely unprofitable and their disposal would be required to avert a complete loss of the trust assets. The power of a court of equity, with its jurisdiction over trusts, to save the beneficiaries in such a situation has been repeatedly sustained in New York and other jurisdictions. . . .

The trustees here find themselves in a crisis where there is no self-help available to them. A judicial declaration is necessary, not only as to their general authority, but as to the effect of the words of Mr. Pulitzer contained in his will. The widest equity powers exist in the Surrogate's Court of this state by the grant of the legislative authority contained in section 40 of the Surrogate's

Court Act. Matter of Raymond v. Davis' Estate, 248 N.Y. 67, 71, 161 N.E. 421.

I accordingly hold, in this phase of the decision, that the terms of the will and codicils do not prohibit the trustees from disposing of any assets of the Press Publishing Company, that the trustees have general power and authority to act in the conveyance of the assets proposed to be sold, and that this court, in the exercise of its equitable jurisdiction, should authorize them by an appropriate direction in the decree to exercise such general authority. . . .

Notes and Question

1. *Sequel.* The decline in profitability of the *World* newspapers, which led the court to order their sale despite the express provision to the contrary in the will, postdated Joseph Pulitzer's death. After assuming control of the *World* newspapers, Pulitzer's sons changed the papers's style in an effort to appeal to a more educated readership. Circulation and advertising plummeted and, by 1928, all three newspapers were operating with deep deficits. In 1931, the papers were sold to the Scripps-Howard organization for $5 million. The story is told in W. A. Swanberg, Pulitzer 411-18 (1967).

2. *Legislation on the Trustee's Administrative Powers.* The Uniform Trust Code provides that the court may modify the administrative provisions of a trust "if continuation of the trust on its existing terms would be impracticable or wasteful or impair the trust's administration." UTC § 412(b).[56] How would *Pulitzer* have be resolved under this provision?

The Restatement 3d of Trusts and the UTC introduce a new and rather vague principle into trust law, which is that a trust "must be for the benefit of its beneficiaries." Restatement 3d of Trusts § 27; UTC § 404. Was Joseph Pulitzer's "Newspaper Trust" established for the benefit of its beneficiaries or for the perpetuation of the *The World* newspaper?

3. *Permissible Investments.* In Stanton v. Wells Fargo Bank & Union Trust Co., 310 P.2d 1010 (Cal. Dist. Ct. App. 1957), the income of a testamentary trust was given to named persons for life, with a general power in each to appoint the remainder, and in default of appointment the share of the income beneficiary was given to his or her issue, or for want of issue, to surviving life beneficiaries. The will provided that trust investments were to be made only in bonds of the United States or state governments or such other bonds as were rated "AA" by Moody Investor's Service.

---

56. A recent Alaska statute provides substantially the same approach. See Alaska Stat. § 13.36.345 (enacted June 1, 2000).

In 1951, twenty years after the testator's death, all living beneficiaries sued for modification of the trust to permit investment in securities permitted by the Civil Code, which would include corporate stocks. In favor of the deviation, evidence was offered showing an inflationary trend that had reduced the purchasing power of the dollar, and evidence showing the relative return on stocks and bonds.

In reversing a judgment allowing the deviation, the court said:

> The distributable annual income was $88,890.66 in 1938, and by 1954 this had increased to $109,942.84. There is no evidence that any beneficiary is in want or that the distributable net income is not sufficient to supply the reasonable needs of all beneficiaries. No emergency exists. . . . [W]hile the settlor might not have been omniscient [about future economic conditions such as inflationary trends], neither are the beneficiaries nor the courts, omniscient. No one can forecast, with any certainty, future events. Certainly, it is true that misguided restrictions imposed by a settlor should not be permitted to defeat his fundamental trust purpose, but it is equally true that the court should not try to guess what economic conditions may be in a few years by permitting deviations when no real emergency exists or is threatened.

Compare with *Stanton* the decision in Trusteeship With Mayo, 105 N.W.2d 900 (Minn. 1960). In that case, Dr. Charles H. Mayo[57] created two revocable trusts, one in 1917, the other in 1919. Dr. Mayo died in 1939 without having revoked either trust. One trust, by its terms, was to continue until 21 years after the death of the petitioner, a beneficiary; the other was partially to terminate when each child of the petitioner attained the age of 30.

The trusts directed the trustees to invest in "real estate mortgages, municipal bonds or any other form of income bearing property (but not real estate nor corporate stock)." The petitioner sought a deviation from this restriction so as to permit investment in corporate stock. She alleged that, after the settlor's death, inflation had reduced the real value of the trust assets by more than 50 percent, but that the market value of common stock had almost doubled since 1939.

In opposition, the trustees alleged that the testator had witnessed post-World War I inflation, the stock market crash of 1929, and the subsequent depression, and hadn't amended the trust to permit investment in corporate stock, which indicated that he was satisfied with the terms as written.

The decree below denying the petition was reversed, the court saying:

---

57. Dr. Charles H. Mayo and his brother, Dr. William J. Mayo, founded the Mayo Clinic in 1915 in Rochester, Minnesota. In 1919, the Mayo brothers dissolved their partnership and turned over the Mayo Clinic's name and assets to the Mayo Foundation. The Mayo brothers died within nine months of each other in 1939.

It appears without substantial dispute that if deviation is not permitted the accomplishment of the purposes of the trusts will be substantially impaired because of changed conditions due to inflation since the trusts were created; that unless deviation is allowed the assets of the trusts, within the next 20 years, will, in all likelihood, be worth less than one-fourth of the value they had at the time of the donor's death. To avoid this we conclude that in equity the trustees should have the right and be authorized to deviate from the restrictive provisions of the trusts by permitting them, when and as they deem advisable, to invest a reasonable amount of the trust assets in corporate stocks of good, sound investment issues. Through an investment in bonds and mortgages of the type designated by the donor, plus corporate stocks of good, sound investment issues, in our opinion, the trusts will, so far as possible, be fortified against inflation, recession, depression, or decline in prices.

PART D. COMPROMISE OF CONTROVERSIES

Statutory References: *UTC § 111*
UPC §§ 1-403, 3-1101, -1102

Adams v. Link

145 A.2d 753 (Conn. 1958)

KING, J. The defendants Link and the United States Trust Company of New York are the executors and trustees under the will and codicil of Mildred A. Kingsmill, late of Darien. Mrs. Kingsmill left, as her sole heirs at law, two brothers, Orson Adams, Jr., and Alvin P. Adams, and a sister, Ethel A. Martin. This action grows out of, although it is distinct from, an appeal by Orson Adams, Jr., and Alvin P. Adams, two of the three heirs at law, from the admission of the will and codicil to probate.

In the view which we take of the case, only the right to terminate the trust created in paragraph sixth of the will need be considered. This paragraph disposed of the residue by a trust. It provided for the payment of the net income for life, in monthly or quarterly installments at their written election, to Joan K. Pringle and Mayes M. Foeppel, neither of whom was an heir at law. At the death of the survivor, the trust was to terminate and distribution of the corpus was to be made to the New York Association for the Blind. In fact, Joan K. Pringle predeceased the testatrix, leaving Mayes M. Foeppel as the sole income beneficiary and entitled, under the terms of the trust, to the entire net income for life.

During the pendency of the appeal from probate, a so-called compromise agreement was entered into between Mayes M. Foeppel, party of the first part, the New York Association for the Blind, party of the second part, and the three heirs at law of the testatrix, parties of the third part. The agreement in effect provided that (1) the appeal from the admission of the will and codicil to probate would be withdrawn; (2) 15 per cent of the residuary estate, i.e. the trust corpus, would be paid outright to the three heirs at law in equal shares; (3) 37 per cent would be paid outright to the New York Association for the Blind; and (4) 48 per cent would be paid outright to Mayes M. Foeppel less a deduction of $15,000 which would be used to establish a new trust, the precise terms of which are not material. Basically, it was for the education of a son of Alvin P. Adams, and upon completion of his education the trust would terminate and any unused corpus and interest would be returned to Mayes M. Foeppel. The compromise agreement was by its express terms made subject to the approval of the Superior Court. The defendant executors and trustees refused to participate in the agreement or to carry it out. The present action, the plaintiffs in which include all parties to the agreement except the New York Association for the Blind, which was made a party defendant, seeks in effect (a) the approval of the agreement by the Superior Court, and (b) a decree compelling the defendant executors and trustees to carry it out. Since the provision for the New York Association for the Blind was a charitable gift, the attorney general was made a defendant to represent the public interest, under the provisions of § 212 of the General Statutes. The court refused to approve the agreement, and from this action the plaintiffs took this appeal. . . .

The fundamental effect of the compromise agreement, if approved by the court, would be to abolish the trust. . . .

Conditions precedent which should concur in order to warrant termination of a testamentary trust by judicial decree are (1) that all the parties in interest unite in seeking the termination, (2) that every reasonable ultimate purpose of the trust's creation and existence has been accomplished, and (3) that no fair and lawful restriction imposed by the testator will be nullified or disturbed by such a result. . . .

The underlying rationale of our rule is the protection, if reasonably possible, of any reasonable, properly expressed, testamentary desire of a decedent. 3 Scott, Trusts (2d Ed.) § 337.

It appears that all the interested beneficiaries have joined in the agreement under consideration. For the purposes of this case only, we will assume, without in any way deciding, that the plaintiffs are correct in their claim that the defendant executors and trustees have no standing to attack the compromise. This assumption is permissible because the compromise was in terms made contingent upon court approval, and this approval could not be compelled by any agreement of the trust beneficiaries among themselves. Thus we may assume, without deciding, that the first condition precedent under our rule is satisfied. The second and third conditions precedent have not, however, been satisfied. The obvious objectives of the testatrix were to provide (a) an assured income for life for Mayes M. Foeppel, and (b) at her death an intact corpus for the New York Association for the Blind. In carrying out these objectives, the testatrix took two important steps. In the first place, the management of the trust corpus was committed to trustees selected by her and in whose financial judgment she is presumed to have had confidence. Secondly, expenditure of any principal by the life beneficiary was precluded. Taken together, these two steps would tend to achieve, and in all reasonable probability would achieve, the testatrix' two basic objectives. To abolish the trust and turn over a fraction of the corpus outright to the life beneficiary would be to enable her in a moment to lose the protection of the practically assured life income provided by the testatrix. The two basic objectives of the trust's creation and existence were reasonable and commendable and cannot be fully accomplished prior to the death of the life beneficiary. Obviously, had the testatrix intended to entrust the life beneficiary with the handling of any part of the corpus, she would have so provided by a simple, outright gift.

The plaintiffs attempt to avoid the impact of our rule by two main claims. The first is that since the protection accorded the life beneficiary could be lost by her voluntary alienation of the income or by its involuntary alienation through attachment or seizure under an order in equity, the testatrix could not have intended to protect the beneficiary. This amounts in effect to a claim that only a spendthrift trust is protected from termination by agreement of all interested beneficiaries. The case against termination under our rule is of course even stronger where a spendthrift trust is involved. But the operation of our rule is not restricted to such trusts. The mere fact that the testatrix failed to provide the maximum possible protection for the life beneficiary by creating a spendthrift trust . . . does not warrant a conclusion that she intended no protection at all, so that we can consider that the trust no longer has any purpose.

The plaintiffs also claim that whatever the rule may be in cases involving no will contest, a more liberal rule applies where, as here, the termination of the trust is a part of the settlement of such a contest. Some support for this position may be found in cases cited in 3 Scott, Trusts (2d Ed.) § 337.6. The rationale of our rule as to the power to set aside or terminate a trust is not, however, such that its applicability would be affected by the mere fact that the motivation of a trust termination agreement is the compromise of a will contest. It is true that such contests are not infrequently compromised by agreements involving the transfer of legacies or devises, in whole or in part, by beneficiaries under the will. Where such gifts are alienable this is permissible, since no violence is done to the provisions of the will. But that is not this case. Here the provisions of the will itself are being drastically changed so as to abolish a trust contrary to our rule. This cannot be done. It follows that the court below was not in error in denying approval of the agreement. Indeed, it was the only decision which could properly have been made. This conclusion makes unnecessary the consideration of the other grounds of appeal.

There is no error.

In this opinion the other judges concurred.

Notes

1. *State of the Authorities.* The Restatement and most authority tend in the direction of Adams v. Link. See, e.g., Restatement 2d of Trusts § 337 comment o; Heritage Bank-North v. Hunterdon Medical Center, 395 A.2d 552 (N.J. Super. Ct. App. Div. 1978). There is some authority to the contrary, however. In Budin v. Levy, 180 N.E.2d 74 (Mass. 1962), for example, the court, in approving a compromise agreement that prematurely terminated a trust, stated that the agreement's validity did not depend on finding that it did not defeat a material purpose of the trust.

On the tax implications, see Jackson M. Bruce, Jr., *Bosch* and Other Dilemmas: Binding the Parties and the Tax Consequences in Trust Dispute Resolution, 18 Inst. on Est. Plan. Ch. 9 (1984).

2. *Uniform Probate Code.* Section 3-1101 of the UPC provides that a compromise of any controversy as to the admission of an instrument offered to formal probate as the testator's will is binding even though it may affect a trust or inalienable interest. Section 3-1102 details the procedure for securing court approval of a compromise agreement. Section 1-403 states that unborn or unascertained beneficiaries who are not otherwise represented in a proceeding are bound by court orders that bind other parties to the extent that their interests are adequately represented by other parties who have a "substantially identical interest" in the proceeding.

Chapter 15

Charitable Trusts

CHARITIES, an old maxim goes, are a favorite of the law. If this is the case today, it wasn't always so. As Professor Friedman has observed, "In the early 19th century, charity was associated with privilege, with the dead hand, with established churches, with massive wealth in perpetuity. None of these were particularly popular." Lawrence M. Friedman, A History of American Law 254 (2d ed. 1985).

Today, the hostile attitude toward charities has largely dissipated. In fact, charitable trusts enjoy some legal privileges. Some of the rules restricting private trusts are suspended for charitable trusts. Not all the restrictive rules are suspended, of course. Like a private trust, a charitable trust is a fiduciary relationship with respect to property, requiring a trust res, an intent to create a trust, compliance with the Statute of Frauds or the Statute of Wills, as appropriate, and so on. But the requirement of definite beneficiaries doesn't apply to charitable trusts, nor does the Rule Against Perpetuities (if the trust includes only charitable interests) or associated rules relating to accumulations of income.[1] In addition, charitable trusts enjoy certain tax benefits not accorded private trusts.

Validity of Charitable Trusts. Although the validity of charitable trusts is now universally recognized in the United States, the question was in doubt in the early part of our history. Since charitable trusts are created to accomplish charitable purposes, not to benefit definite beneficiaries, special machinery had to be developed for their enforcement. Such procedure was provided in England by the Statute of Charitable Uses, 43 Eliz. ch. 4 (1601). Some early American courts assumed that authority to enforce charitable trusts originated with and

---

1. Many charitable trusts are in fact designed to last without time limit, through providing that only the income shall be used for the charitable purpose. A perpetual charitable trust facilitated by a warrant from William Penn in 1706 presumably continues today. See Trustees of New Castle Common v. Gordy, 93 A.2d 509 (Del. Ch. 1952).

depended upon the English statute. Trustees of Philadelphia Baptist Ass'n v. Hart's Ex'rs, 17 U.S. (4 Wheat.) 1 (1819), held that if that statute wasn't imported into the state as part of the common law, state legislation was needed for charitable trusts to be created in the jurisdiction. More rigorous historical work showed, however, that the English Court of Chancery had enforced charitable trusts long before the Statute of Charitable Uses, and continued to do so after the enforcement procedure provided by that statute had been repealed. See Vidal v. Girard's Ex'rs, 43 U.S. (2 How.) 127 (1844). On this basis, charitable trusts came to be fully recognized—with or without supporting legislation—as legitimate vehicles for devoting wealth to charitable purposes.

Enforcement of Charitable Trusts. One of the central features of a charitable trust is that it need not have definite beneficiaries. The beneficiaries of a private trust, as we know, are the ones who have standing for its enforcement. Normally lacking definite beneficiaries, however, a charitable trust is principally enforceable by the state Attorney General. The Restatement 2d of Trusts provides:

> § *391. Who Can Enforce a Charitable Trust.* A suit can be maintained for the enforcement of a charitable trust by the Attorney General or other public officer, or by a co-trustee, or by a person who has a special interest in the enforcement of the charitable trust, but not by persons who have no special interest or by the settlor or his heirs, personal representatives or next of kin.

See also Uniform Supervision of Trustees for Charitable Purposes Act (1954).

The reference in the Restatement to "a person who has a special interest" is intended to cover situations in which an individual derives a benefit from the trust that is not available to the public at large or has a unique stake in the proper enforcement of the trust. Trustees of charitable corporation and charitable trusts, for example, have been allowed to sue their co-trustees for breaches of trust. See, e.g., Holt v. College of Osteopathic Physicians & Surgeons, 394 P.2d 932 (Cal. 1964). The cases are conflicting over whether students may sue the trustees of their colleges or universities. Compare Jones v. Grant, 344 So. 2d 1210 (Ala. 1977) (granting standing) with Miller v. Alderhold, 184 S.E.2d 172 (Ga. 1971) (denying standing). The UTC breaks new ground by providing in § 405(c) that the settlor of a charitable trust also may enforce the terms of the trust. See infra Part C.

Charitable Organizations. A newly created charitable organization can be formed in a variety of ways, including that of a charitable trust or that of a charitable corporation. Existing charitable organizations, including the well-known public charities such as the American Cancer Society and the major charitable foundations such as the Ford Foundation, are usually (but not always) formed as corporations. Generally speaking, the rules and principles applicable to charitable trusts are usually applicable to charitable corporations or other organizations, including the cy pres doctrine and the imposition of fiduciary duties on the corporation's Board of Directors and the method of enforcing these duties. See Restatement 2d of Trusts § 348, comment f; § 386, comment b; § 399, comment o. See, e.g., St. Joseph's Hosp. v. Bennett, 22 N.E.2d 305 (N.Y. 1939) (cy-pres doctrine); Stern v. Lucy Webb Hayes Nat'l Training School, 381 F. Supp. 1003 (D.D.C. 1974) (fiduciary duties).

Charitable organizations and trusts hold an enormous amount of the nation's wealth and the amount is growing rapidly. As of 2000, a total of 10,492 charitable foundations held nearly $360 billion in assets. *The Foundation Directory* ix (2000 ed.). Private foundations provided more than $15.1 billion in contributions, gifts, and grants in 1996, an 18-percent increase over 1995. Statistics of Income Bulletin, Department of the Treasury, Internal Revenue Service (Fall 1999).

Sound-Alike Names. There are over 650 thousand charities in the United States, some of which have similar names. For example, there is the Make-A-Wish Foundation, the Grant-A-Wish Foundation, the Children's Wish Foundation International, the Wishing Well Foundation, the Fulfill A Wish Foundation (now Kids Wish Network), and the Grant-A-Wish Network. And then there is the Guide Dogs for the Blind and the Guide Dog Foundation for the Blind, not to mention the American Heart Association and the American Heart Disease Prevention Foundation. See Reed Ableson, Some Charities Cash In by Playing the Name Game, N.Y. Times, Dec. 30, 1999, at A1.

Ratings of Charities. You can find out how a charity is rated, including what proportion of its contributions actually go to the charitable purpose, by checking with the Better Business Bureau (www.bbb.org) the National Charities Information Bureau (www.give.org), or the American Institute of Philanthropy (www. charitywatch.org).

Tax-Exempt Status. The income of charitable trusts and charitable corporations is generally exempt from federal income tax. See IRC § 501.

Contributions to Existing Charitable Organizations. A gift or devise to an existing charitable organization is often treated as having created a separate charitable trust with respect to that contribution, with the organization as the trustee. The idea that a charitable trust has been created is more likely if the donor imposed one or more restrictions on the gift or devise. A restriction can take a variety of forms. The donor may restrict the use of the property to one of the purposes for which the charitable organization has been formed; for example, the donor may restrict a donation to an educational institution to the school's scholarship fund. The donor may specify that only the income is to be used, not the principal. Whether or not the transaction is characterized as a trust, the rules and principles applicable to charitable trusts are usually applicable to charitable organizations. See Restatement 2d of Trusts § 348, comment f; Scott on Trusts § 348.1.

PART A. CHARITABLE PURPOSES

In this Part, we present cases in which trusts have been challenged on the ground that they are not charitable trusts because their purposes are not "charitable." In the leading English case of Commissioners of Internal Revenue v. Pemsel, [1891] App. Cas. 531, 583 (H.L.), Lord Macnaghten expressed the following understanding of charitable trusts:

> "Charity" in its legal sense comprises four principal divisions: trusts for the relief of poverty; trusts for the advancement of education; trusts for the advancement of religion; and trusts for other purposes beneficial to the community, not falling under any of the preceding heads. The trusts last referred to are not the less charitable in the eye of the law, because incidentally they benefit the rich as well as the poor, as indeed, every charity that deserves the name must do either directly or indirectly.

In this country, the Restatement 3d of Trusts § 28 defines charitable purposes as including the relief of poverty; the advancement of education; the advancement of religion; the promotion of health; governmental or municipal purposes; and other purposes that are beneficial to the community. See also UTC § 405(a). As you read the cases in this Part, consider why the trust would be invalid as a private trust if it fails to meet the charitable-trust definition.

Tax Deductibility. For qualified gifts to charity, the Internal Revenue Code allows a limited deduction from income taxation and an unlimited deduction from gift taxation; and for qualified devises to charity, the Code allows an unlimited deduction from estate taxation. See IRC §§ 170, 642(c), 2055, 2522. The estate-tax provision, set forth below, is nearly identical to the income and gift tax provisions:

> § *2055. Transfers for public, charitable, and religious uses.*
>
> (a) In general.—For purposes of the tax imposed by section 2001, the value of the taxable estate shall be determined by deducting from the value of the gross estate the amount of all bequests, legacies, devises, or transfers—
>
> (1) to or for the use of the United States, any State, any political subdivision thereof, or the District of Columbia, for exclusively public purposes;
>
> (2) to or for the use of any corporation organized and operated exclusively for religious, charitable, scientific, literary, or educational purposes, including the encouragement of art, or to foster national or international amateur sports competition (but only if no part of its activities involve the provision of athletic facilities or equipment), and the prevention of cruelty to children or animals, no part of the net earnings of which inures to the benefit of any private stockholder

or individual, which is not disqualified for tax exemption under § 501(c)(3) by reason of attempting to influence legislation, and which does not participate in, or intervene in (including the publishing or distributing of statements), any political campaign on behalf of (or in opposition to) any candidate for public office;

(3) to a trustee or trustees, or a fraternal society, order, or association operating under the lodge system, but only if such contributions or gifts are to be used by such trustee or trustees, or by such fraternal society, order, or association, exclusively for religious, charitable, scientific, literary, or educational purposes, or for the prevention of cruelty to children or animals, such trust, fraternal society, order, or association would not be disqualified for tax exemption under § 501(c)(3) by reason of attempting to influence legislation, and such trustee or trustees, or such fraternal society, order, or association, does not participate in, or intervene in (including the publishing or distributing of statements), any political campaign on behalf of (or in opposition to) any candidate for public office; or

(4) to or for the use of any veterans' organization incorporated by Act of Congress, or of its departments or local chapters or posts, no part of the net earnings of which inures to the benefit of any private shareholder or individual. . . .

Are the trust-law and tax-law definitions of charitable purposes identical? Rev. Rul. 71-447, 1971-2 C.B. 230, states:

> Both the courts and the Internal Revenue Service have long recognized that the statutory requirements [of IRC section 501(c)(3)] of being "organized and operated exclusively for religious, charitable, . . . or educational purposes" was intended to express the basic common law concept.

See also Rev. Rul. 67-325, 1967-2 C.B. 113, declaring that the phrase "charitable purposes" in IRC §§ 170, 2055, and 2522 is used "in the generally accepted legal sense."

Foreign Beneficiaries. The fact that a charitable trust is for the benefit of a community outside the United States doesn't prevent the trust from being upheld as a charitable trust or disqualify it for the federal estate or gift tax charitable deduction. Restatement 2d of Trusts § 374, comment i; Scott on Trusts § 374.8; Rev. Rul. 74-523, 1974-2 C.B. 304. For federal income-tax purposes, a contribution or gift *by a corporation* to a trust, chest, fund, or foundation is deductible "only if it is to be used within the United States or any of its possessions . . . ." IRC § 170(c).

1. General Gifts to Charity

Suppose a testator devises property in trust "for such charitable purposes as my trustee shall select" or "to apply the income therefrom, in perpetuity, for the promotion of religion." According to Restatement 3d of Trusts § 28, comment a, and most authority, both dispositions create charitable trusts. In Estate of

Small, 58 N.W.2d 477 (Iowa 1953), the court upheld a trust created by the will of Dr. W.B. Small. To Dr. Small, divine guidance, though necessary, was not sufficient. His will retained a post-death veto power:

> I direct that my said trustees or their successors shall distribute . . . income . . . for such purposes as they may feel is directed by God the Father, Jesus Christ the Son, and Holy Spirit, *and* as they believe would be acceptable to *me* and meet *my* approval were *I* able to give it . . . . (Emphasis added.)

A charitable trust is also created if the testator simply devises property "to charity" or "to the poor." See Jordan's Estate, 197 A. 150 (Pa. 1938) (devise "to charity" upheld as a charitable trust); Restatement 3d of Trusts § 28, comment a; Scott on Trusts § 397. In these cases, of course, the court must select a trustee or frame a scheme for the application of the devise to the intended purpose.

Does a trust authorizing distribution of income "to such charitable organizations as the trustee shall select" qualify for a federal estate or gift tax deduction? See, e.g., Beggs v. United States, 27 F. Supp. 599 (Ct. Cl. 1939) (deduction allowed because court did "not find in the will involved any grant of discretionary authority to the executor to distribute any part of the net proceeds of the estate to other than charities."); Rev. Rul. 71-200, 1971-1 C.B. 272 (deduction denied because there were "no applicable decisions of the courts of the state in which the will was probated that construe similar clauses as limiting the trustees [*sic*] choice of organizations to those qualifying under IRC § 2055 . . . ."); Rev. Rul. 69-285, 1969-1 C.B. 222 (deduction allowed on theory that Massachusetts decisions define "charitable" in a way that is "at least as restrictive as the Federal definition of that term under § 2055."); 5 Boris I. Bittker, Federal Taxation of Income, Estates and Gifts ¶130.2 (1984); Richard B. Stephens et al., Federal Estate and Gift Taxation ¶5.05[1] (5th ed. 1983).

Devises for purposes not restricted to charitable purposes have generated considerable litigation. Recall the leading case of Morice v. Bishop of Durham, 10 Ves. 522, 32 Eng. Rep. 947 (Ch. 1805), supra Chapter 13, Part B. In that case, Lord Chancellor Eldon held that a devise in trust "to dispose of the ultimate residue to such objects of benevolence and liberality as the Bishop of Durham in his own discretion shall most approve of" failed to create a charitable trust because the purposes were not limited to charity and failed to create a valid private trust because the beneficiaries were indefinite. Some century and a half later, in Chichester Diocesan Fund v. Simpson, [1944] App. Cas. 341 (H.L.), the House of Lords applied the idea that "benevolence" is not restricted to "charity," in the case of a devise to the testator's executors to apply it "for such charitable institution or institutions or other charitable or benevolent object or objects in England as my acting executors or executor may in their or his absolute discretion select."

In this country, most courts have generally agreed with the English view that "benevolence," standing alone, potentially encompasses purposes broader than those that are "charitable." Thus, most American courts have held that a devise "to be used for such benevolent purposes as the trustees shall select" does not create a charitable trust. See, e.g., Estate of Kradwell, 170 N.W.2d 773 (Wis. 1969); Adye v. Smith, 44 Conn. 60 (1876). Contra, e.g., Goodale v. Mooney, 60 N.H. 528 (1881). See Restatement 3d of Trusts § 28 comment a; Scott on Trusts § 398.1 n.11.

Can you think of a "benevolent" use of property or income that wouldn't come within the definition of "charity"? Of a "charitable" use that wouldn't come within the definition of "benevolent"? Which of these questions is more important for our purposes? Do you think the distinction between "benevolent" and "charitable" is widely understood by the lay public? By the average lawyer?

Problems

1. G's will devised property in trust, directing her trustee to apply the income therefrom, in perpetuity:

(a) for such "charitable and benevolent purposes" as my trustee shall select.

(b) for such "charitable or benevolent purposes" as my trustee shall select.

(c) for such "charitable or benevolent purpose" as my trustee shall select.

Which version presents the strongest case for validity as a charitable trust? See Restatement 3d of Trusts § 28 comment a; Scott on Trusts § 398.1.

2. Would the case for validity in the above cases be strengthened if G's trust had been an inter vivos trust and if, during G's lifetime, the trustee had administered the trust for purposes clearly "charitable"? Would it matter whether the inter vivos trust was revocable or irrevocable? In Hight v. United States, 256 F.2d 795 (2d Cir. 1958), the court held that the word "benevolent" has "no fixed meaning which is self-defining." Relying in part on extrinsic evidence concerning the type of institution the testator had selected during life for her benefactions, the court upheld as charitable a devise for "such charitable, benevolent, religious or educational institutions as my executors hereinafter named may determine."

Wilson v. Flowers

277 A.2d 199 (N.J. 1971)

PROCTOR, J. This is a will construction case. Plaintiffs, trustees under the will of Joseph L.K. Snyder, filed a complaint in the Chancery Division seeking instructions regarding the validity of Article Sixth (C)(12) of the testator's residuary trust of his will which directs them, *inter alia*, to contribute 20% of the residue "to such *philanthropic* causes as my Trustees may select" (emphasis added).

Defendants are the next-of-kin of the testator,[2] and the Attorney General of New Jersey. The latter did not participate in the litigation.

After a hearing, Judge Mintz held that the plaintiffs had established the testator's probable intent that the gifts to "philanthropic causes" be solely charitable in nature. Thus, the gifts were not void and did not pass by intestate succession. Judgment directed 1) that the plaintiffs "shall contribute solely to charitable purposes the income to be disposed under Article Sixth (C)(12) of" the will, 2) that "the dispositions . . . do not violate the rule against perpetuities," and 3) that plaintiffs-trustees "in making contributions to philanthropic causes pursuant to Article Sixth (C)(12) of said will are restricted solely to charities which qualify as charities under [the federal estate tax and the state inheritance tax]." . . .

The primary issue on this appeal is whether the testator, in using the term "philanthropic causes," intended to limit his bounty to charitable causes or whether he intended the term to have a broader meaning. If the trust is not limited to charitable purposes, it is void either for uncertainty or for a violation of the rule against perpetuities. Defendants contend that the trust is void and that it should pass to them by intestate succession.

On February 28, 1965, Joseph L.K. Snyder died leaving a Will dated September 30, 1960 and a Codicil thereto dated December 18, 1964. . . . The great bulk of his estate was disposed of by Article Sixth, which deals with the residuary. By this provision he bequeathed his residuary estate in trust, with directions to pay the income therefrom to three individuals for life (no beneficiary to receive income exceeding an average of $25,000 per year over a period of five consecutive years). Under Subsections (1) to (12) of Section (C) of Article Sixth the decedent directed that the balance of principal and accumulated income of the residuary estate be continued "in perpetual trust" and that the net income be distributed to the beneficiaries in the following proportions: [Here were listed gifts in specified proportions to eleven charitable organizations.] Defendants do not challenge the qualification of the above beneficiaries as charities. Their attack is limited to the language of Subsection (12) by which the remainder of the residue is disposed. That subsection reads in pertinent part:

---

2. The next-of-kin are Sara Louise Flowers, a daughter of Nevin Snyder, a brother who predeceased testator, and Anna Douds Snyder, executrix under the Will of Jacob Marchand Snyder, a brother who survived testator by six months.

> (12) To contribute the remaining twenty per cent (20%) thereof, together with income on hand by reason of the defection of any bequest under Subsections (1) through (11) of Section (C) of this Article Sixth, to such philanthropic causes as my Trustees may select, special consideration, however, to be given to charitable, educational and scientific fields, including universities, research laboratories, foundations or organizations formed for the purpose of the combating of and research on degenerative diseases.

It is estimated that the residuary estate will amount to $2,000,000.

Defendants contend that the word "philanthropic" is broader than the word "charitable" both in terms of the testator's intent so far as that intent can be gleaned from the four corners of the will and in terms of its generally accepted meaning.

Turning to the second point first, we have been cited to no New Jersey case construing the word "philanthropic." However, there are many cases construing the word "benevolent" which defendants contend is more restrictive than "philanthropic." The cases follow the English rule that "benevolent" is broader than "charitable" and that a trust for such purposes is therefore void.

Defendants urge that since New Jersey courts follow the English cases that hold "benevolent" is broader than "charitable," they must, a fortiori, follow the English cases that hold that "philanthropic" is broader than "charitable." We cannot accept this argument. It is no longer clear that "philanthropic" by legal connotation is broader than "charitable" in its legal connotation. Bogert has stated:

> At the present time it would seem that the intent of a donor who leaves property to be distributed for "benevolent" or "philanthropic" purposes is in most cases charitable. If the duration of the trust is indefinite or perpetual a trust to show mere liberality will be void and in addition it will be subject to heavy tax burdens. Few trustors will desire these results. Common usage has made these words synonyms for charity. . . .

The word "philanthropic" would seem, in its liberal sense, to include all acts of friendliness to mankind, whether conducive to improvement of society or merely to enrichment and enjoyment. In some English cases the word has been construed in this sense, and the result has been that a trust for "philanthropic purposes" has been held non-charitable because it would permit the trustee to perform acts of mere friendliness and generosity, having no connection with the need of the recipients of the benefits and no regard for the effect of the bounty upon the "beneficiaries." This is, however, perhaps a rather bookish meaning of the word. Probably in common use it is taken to mean charity, and some tendency to give it that effect is observable, especially where it is linked with the word "charitable" or with admittedly charitable objects. Bogert, Trusts & Trustees, § 370, p. 69, 70 (2d ed. 1964).

There are a number of cases which have rejected the English cases and have treated "philanthropic" as synonymous with "charitable." E.g., MacKinnon v. MacKinnon (1909) Sess. Cas. 1041 ("charitable or philanthropic" institutions are charitable institutions); Rotch v. Emerson, 105 Mass. 431 (1870) ("for the promotion of agricultural or horticultural improvements, or other philosophical or philanthropic purposes" are charitable purposes); Thorp v. Lund, 227 Mass. 474, 116 N.E. 946 (1917) ("national and philanthropic purposes" are charitable purposes); Brewer v. McCauley (Matter of Loggie), (1954) S.C.R. 645 ("for such charitable, religious, educational or philanthropic purposes as the trustees shall appoint" are charitable purposes) (noted in 33 Can.B.Rev. 334 (1955); Moore v. Sellers, 201 S.W.2d 248 (Tex.Civ.App. 1947) ("charitable, philanthropic, religious and/or educational institutions, societies, organizations or undertakings" are charitable purposes).

But defendants contend that even if philanthropic and charitable have come to mean the same thing, the manner in which the word "philanthropic" is used in the present case indicates a contrary intent. Testator's will directs that 20% of the residue of the estate be given, in trust, "to such philanthropic causes as my Trustees may select, special consideration, however, to be given to charitable, educational and scientific fields." Defendants argue that the "special consideration" clause evidences an intent that charitable, educational and scientific uses must merely be some of the philanthropic uses to which the funds may be given. Thus, they contend "philanthropic" is broader than "charitable" as the testator used it.

It is our duty to follow what we find to be the testator's probable intention. The commonly accepted meaning of words and their context is a strong indication of intent, but that is not the end of the matter. There are frequently other manifestations of intent. In the present case, if we were to accept defendants' argument, we would be left with the conclusion that the testator intended to die intestate. Yet as we noted in Fidelity Union Trust Co. v. Robert, 36 N.J. 561, 572, 178 A.2d 185, 191 (1962), there is a strong presumption that testators do not intend to die intestate, particularly where, as here, the gift is made out of the residuary estate. . . . This presumption is reinforced by the testator's mandate that his trust be perpetual. A perpetual trust for noncharitable purposes would be void, and it is unlikely that the testator intended that result.

There is another factor which indicates the testator intended "philanthropic" to be synonymous with "charitable." The other parts of his will demonstrate an interest in charitable causes. In sections (C)(1) through (C)(11), the testator disposed of 80% of the residuary to eleven specific admittedly charitable causes. Only (C)(12), the remaining section of his residuary trust, is challenged here.

An overall feeling of charity pervades section (C) and that the testator should link 11 specific charitable causes with the term "philanthropic causes" is an indication that he intended his entire residuary estate to be devoted to charitable causes. See Bogert, supra at § 370, p. 69, 70.

Of course, these general indications of intent do not answer defendants' argument that the juxtaposition of the language employed shows the testator intended "philanthropic" to be broader than "charitable." But there is direct evidence which answers the argument. . . .

[The Court considered testimony by the scrivener of the will that he had used the word "philanthropic" synonymously with "charitable," and two memoranda by the testator containing expressions of charitable purposes in the making of his will.] . . .

[I]t is apparent that the trial court properly admitted the testator's memoranda and the scrivener's testimony regarding the testator's statements to him and the origin of the disputed word "philanthropic." While "philanthropic" may be technically broader than "charitable," we think that it has come to mean the same thing in modern usage. However, even if it has not, it is ambiguous enough to be construed as such. Most words are susceptible of more than one meaning. . . . Whether the use of a word which admits of more than one meaning is a patent ambiguity in the technical sense is not important; rather, the significant point is that there is an ambiguity at all. And in deciding whether there is an ambiguity, a court should always admit extrinsic evidence including direct statements of intent since experience teaches that language is so poor an instrument for communication or expression that ordinarily all such evidence must be examined before a court can be satisfied of whether an ambiguity exists. We do not, of course, mean to imply that such evidence can be used to vary the terms of the will, but rather that it should be admitted first to show if there is an ambiguity and second, if one exists, to shed light on the testator's actual intent.

In light of the above, it appears clear to us that the testator intended "philanthropic" to have the legal equivalence of "charitable." And if there were any doubt, well established rules of construction would lead us to lean in favor of a construction which upheld the gift as charitable. . . .

The judgment of the Chancery Division is affirmed.

Notes

1. *Curative Legislation.* In 1891, the New York Court of Appeals struck down for indefiniteness a charitable trust that Governor Tilden[3] had attempted to create by his will. The will provided for the establishment of a public library in the city of New York, but granted the trustees broad authority to apply the trust fund to "such charitable educational purposes" as in their judgment would be "most widely and substantially beneficial to mankind." Tilden v. Green, 28 N.E. 880 (N.Y. 1891), reh. den., 29 N.E. 1033 (N.Y. 1891). Two years later, the "Tilden Act" was adopted.

The current version of the New York statute provides that "[n]o disposition of property for religious, charitable, educational or benevolent uses . . . is invalid by reason of the indefiniteness or uncertainty of the persons designated as the beneficiaries." N.Y. Est. Powers & Trust Law § 8-1.1(a). Similar statutes appear in about ten other states. See, e.g., Mich. Comp. Laws Ann. § 554.351. Statutory citations are listed in Scott on Trusts § 398.1 n.20. The story is told in Stanley N. Katz et al., Legal Change and Legal Autonomy: Charitable Trusts in New York, 1777-1893, 3 Law & Hist. Rev. 51 (1985).

2. *Mixed-Purposes Trusts; Separability.* There is nothing unusual about trusts partly for private and partly for charitable purposes. For tax reasons (see below), charitable-remainder trusts and charitable-lead trusts are staples in the modern estate-planner's inventory. A charitable-remainder trust provides for certain payments to a private beneficiary or beneficiaries for life, remainder in principal to a specified charity or for charitable purposes. A charitable-lead trust provides for income to be paid to a specified charity or for charitable purposes for a period of years, remainder in principal to a private beneficiary or beneficiaries.

The fact that such "split-interest" trusts have both charitable and private beneficiaries does not cause them to fail. The charitable portion is separable and upheld. The private portion is also upheld if the private beneficiaries are definite and ascertainable, as they almost always are in such cases. A split-interest trust, however, might fail in part if the remainder interest violates the Rule Against Perpetuities. A charitable remainder preceded by non-charitable interests is not

3. Samuel J. Tilden, elected governor of New York in 1874, was the unsuccessful Democratic candidate for President in the infamous 1876 election, narrowly (and perhaps fraudulently) losing to Rutherford B. Hayes. Tilden actually polled more popular votes than Hayes. There were disputed electoral votes in several states, however, and a congressional committee of eight Republicans and seven Democrats, voting along strict party lines, awarded the disputed states to Hayes, making him the winner by a single electoral vote. A reform candidate, Tilden gained his reputation fighting the famed Boss Tweed ring in New York politics. The story of the 1876 Presidential election is interestingly told in Gore Vidal's historical novel, 1876 (1976).

exempt from the Rule Against Perpetuities. But that matter is deferred until Chapter 19.

3. *Tax Deductibility of Split-Interest Trusts.* For federal income, gift, and estate tax purposes, a devise to a *corporation* is deductible only if the corporation was organized and is operated exclusively for charitable purposes. A devise in *trust*, however, is not disqualified merely because the trust has private as well as charitable purposes. Such trusts, called split-interest trusts, either confer current benefits on a private beneficiary for life, and the remainder interest on a charity (charitable-remainder trusts); or confer current benefits on a charity for a term, and the remainder interest on a private beneficiary (charitable-lead trusts). In either case, of course, the deduction is limited to the value of the actual charitable benefit.

If a transfer is made for both charitable and private purposes, the value of the charitable interest is deductible only to the extent that the interest is ascertainable and thus severable from the noncharitable interest. Treas. Reg. § 20.2055-2(a). Prior to 1969, this was the main requirement. The Tax Reform Act of 1969, however, imposed additional requirements. The concern that promoted their imposition was stated by the Treasury Department in its Studies and Proposals and in similar terms by the committee reports accompanying the 1969 Act. See U.S. Treasury Department, 91st Cong., 1st Sess., Tax Reform Studies and Proposals (pt. 3) at 366-367, 381-382 (Committee Print 1969); S. Rep. No. 552, 91st Cong., 1st Sess. 86-93 (1969), in 1969-3 C.B. 423, 479-83; H.R. Rep. No. 413, 91st Cong., 1st Sess. (pt. 1) (1969), in 1969-3 C.B. 200, 237-240. The following is an excerpt from the Treasury Studies:

> [Pre-1969] rules provide[d] that, in the case of split interest transfers, the income beneficiary's interest [was] to be valued on the assumption that the property [would] be invested to yield 3.5 percent interest per year. Obviously, the actual investment experience . . . rarely correspond[ed] to the 3.5 percent assumption. Abuses [arose] because of this fact. For example, assume a charity [was] the income beneficiary for a specified term, the property then to go to the transferor's grandchildren. The transfer [was] exempt for gift tax purposes to the extent of the value of the charity's interest, which [was] based on an assumed 3.5 percent return. But if the property [was] invested to maximize growth for the benefit of the transferor's grandchildren, then the charity . . . in fact [got] less than assumed. The result [was] that the transferor . . . paid less gift tax than he should have. If the charity [got] the remainder and an individual [had] the income interest, then the abuse possibility [was] the reverse, i.e., the property [could] be invested to maximize the income yield, even at the risk of the principal. Again, a deduction for the charitable transfer [was] permitted in a greater amount than in fact [went] to charity.

Charitable-Remainder Trusts. Under IRC § 2055(e)(2)(A), as amended, where a transfer of a remainder interest is made to a qualified charity and where a beneficiary of all or part of the income interest in the transferred property is someone other than a qualified charity, an estate-tax charitable deduction is granted for the actuarial value of the charity's remainder interest only if one of the following conditions is satisfied:

(1) The transferred property is either a personal residence or a farm; or

(2) The transferred property is realty in which a remainder interest is granted to certain charities (generally, publicly supported charities) for conservation purposes; or

(3) The transfer is made to a "charitable-remainder annuity trust," a "charitable-remainder unitrust," or a "pooled-income fund."

A *charitable-remainder annuity trust* is a trust from which a sum certain (which must be no less than an amount equal to 5 percent of the initial fair market value of all the property transferred to the trust)[4] is payable at least annually to beneficiaries, at least one of whom is not a charitable organization, for a term of years (not to exceed 20 years) or for the life or lives of such individual beneficiaries; and upon the termination of those payments, the trust assets must be transferred to, or for the use of, a qualified charitable organization. No payments may be made to noncharitable beneficiaries other than the annuity payments described in the preceding sentence. IRC § 664(d)(1).

A *charitable-remainder unitrust* is a trust from which a fixed percentage (which must not be less than 5 percent)[5] of the net fair market value of the trust's assets (valued annually) is payable at least annually to beneficiaries, at least one of whom is not a charitable organization, for a term of years (not to exceed 20 years) or for the life or lives of such individual beneficiaries; and upon termination of those payments, the trust assets must be transferred to, or

---

4. The requirement of a payout of *at least 5%* was explained by the Senate committee report as follows:

> [R]equiring a charitable remainder trust to distribute currently at least the amount of its income (other than long-term capital gains), if this is less than 5 percent payout and the requirement that the charitable remainder interest be valued by assuming at least a 5 percent payout to the income beneficiary will prevent a charitable remainder trust from being used to circumvent the current income distribution requirement imposed on private foundations. In the absence of these rules, a charitable remainder trust could be established which provided for a minimal payout to the noncharitable income beneficiary (substantially less than the amount of the trust income). Since the trust generally is exempt from income taxes this would allow it to accumulate trust income in excess of the payout requirement of the unitrust or annuity trust without tax for the future benefit of charity.

S. Rep. No. 552, 91st Cong., 1st Sess. 90 (1969), in 1969-3 C.B. 423, 482. Note also that § 201(b) of the 1969 Act also amended IRC § 642(c)(2) to preclude a charitable deduction for income permanently set aside for future distribution to a charity.

5. See supra note 4.

for the use of, a qualified charitable organization. In lieu of a percentage payment, the trust instrument may provide for the distribution of trust income to the income beneficiaries in any year in which the trust income is a smaller amount than the percentage payment. It may also provide for the distribution to the income beneficiaries of a year's trust income that is in excess of the percentage payment, but only to the extent that the aggregate trust distributions to the income beneficiaries in prior years was less than the percentage payments would have been. Treas. Reg. § 1.664-3(b). No other amounts may be distributed to them. IRC §§ 664(d)(2), 664(d)(3).

A *pooled-income fund* is a trust, usually run by universities or large charities, to which any number of donors can contribute property. The income from the proportionate part of the fund represented by each donor's contribution is payable to the donor and/or the donor's designated beneficiary or beneficiaries during their lives. At each beneficiary's death, the charity that manages the fund withdraws assets proportionate to the share from which the beneficiary had been receiving income. IRC § 642(c)(5).

Under the 1969 amendment, a deduction is allowable for a charitable remainder subject to a condition only if the likelihood that the charity will not take the property is so remote as to be negligible (Treas. Reg. § 20.2055-2(e)) and if there is no power (other than a power to pay the required annual amount) to invade principal for a noncharitable purpose or beneficiary.

The Internal Revenue Service has promulgated illustrative sample provisions that are *required* to be included in governing instruments creating charitable-remainder annuity trusts or charitable-remainder unitrusts.[6] The Service has also promulgated sample inter vivos declarations of trust that meet the requirements of IRC § 664(d)(1) for a charitable remainder annuity trust,[7] of IRC § 664(d)(2) for a charitable remainder unitrust,[8] and of IRC §§ 644(d)(2) and (3) for a charitable remainder unitrust.[9] Finally, the Service has promulgated sample provisions for the creation of and transfers to pooled-income funds.[10]

Charitable-Lead Trusts. Under IRC § 2055(e)(2)(B), the charitable interest in a charitable-lead trust is deductible only if it is "in the form of a guaranteed

6. See Rev. Rul. 72-395, 1972-2 C.B. 340, modified by Rev. Rul. 80-123, 1980-1 C.B. 205, clarified by Rev. Rul. 82-165, 1982-2 C.B. 117, and modified by Rev. Rul. 88-81, 1988-2 C.B. 127.

7. Rev. Proc. 89-21, 1989-1 C.B. 842, amplified by Rev. Proc. 90-32, 1990-1 C.B. 546.

8. Rev. Proc. 89-20, 1989-1 C.B. 841, amplified by Rev. Proc. 90-30, 1990-1 C.B. 534.

9. Proc. 90-31, 1990-1 C.B. 53.

10. Rev. Rul. 82-38, 1982-1 C.B. 96, amplified in Rev. Rul. 90-103, 1990-51 Int. Rev. Bull. 14.

annuity or is a fixed percentage distributed yearly of the fair market value of the property (to be determined yearly)."

Reformation of Defective Instruments. Under IRC § 2055(e)(3), as amended in 1984, a permanent reformation rule is provided for defective split-interest trusts. Under this rule, if certain split-interest trusts that fail to qualify for the charitable deduction are judicially reformed so as to make them qualify, the reformation, subject to the qualifications and limitations set forth in IRC § 2055(e)(3), is recognized for purposes of the estate-tax charitable deduction under federal law. See 5 Boris I. Bittker, Federal Taxation of Income, Estates and Gifts ¶130.5.7 (Cum. Supp. No. 4, 1990). For state legislation authorizing reformation of split-interest trusts in certain circumstances and in certain respects, see, e.g., Tex. Prop. Code §§ 112.055, 112.056. See also Estate of Burdon-Miller, 456 A.2d 1266 (Me. 1983).

Combined Marital and Charitable Deductions. The Economic Recovery Tax Act of 1981 added subsection (b)(8) to IRC § 2056. IRC § 2056(b)(8) provides that a marital deduction is allowable for the actuarial value of a surviving spouse's interest in a qualified charitable remainder unitrust or annuity trust so long as the trust has no noncharitable beneficiaries other than the surviving spouse. In such cases, the full value of the trust is deductible—the remainder interest as a charitable deduction under IRC § 2055, the unitrust or annuity interest as a marital deduction under IRC § 2056.

4. *Accumulation of Income.* In the case of private trusts, accumulations of income beyond the perpetuity period are strictly forbidden. See infra Chapter 19. Charitable trusts fall under a different rule, a rule of reasonableness. See Restatement 2d of Property § 2.2. The standard by which reasonableness is to be determined was explored in James' Estate, 199 A.2d 275 (Pa. 1964). Frank James died in 1960, devising the residue of his estate (amounting to around $40,000) in trust, with elaborate provisions directing that a portion of the income be accumulated for 400 years, at which time the principal and accumulated income was to be paid over absolutely for the use of the Masonic Homes at Elizabethtown, Pennsylvania. The court held the direction for accumulation to be invalid, saying:

> The will of Frank James supplies no indication of purpose for the 400 year accumulation provision, nor does it, either by express language or by implication, reveal any particular plan or need for retaining accumulations over such an extended period of time. . . .
>
> No case has been cited to us, nor have we been able to locate any authority, which appears to recognize the validity of a proposed gift whose enjoyment is delayed for a period of four centuries without apparent reason.
>
> We hold, therefore, that the provisions for accumulation of income are unreasonable and void as being unnecessary, charitably purposeless and contrary to public policy. . . .

Under the *James' Estate* analysis, would the following trust be valid?

> G devised $ 1 million in trust, to accumulate the income until the principal and accumulated income reach the amount of the national debt, at which time the fund is to be paid to the federal government to pay off the country's creditors.

See Girard Trust Co. v. Russell, 179 F. 446 (3d Cir. 1910). Compare Trusts of Holdeen, 403 A.2d 978 (Pa. 1979) (invalidating accumulation provisions in five inter vivos trusts of modest initial sums under which income was to be accumulated for periods ranging from 500 to 1000 years, after which time the funds were to be paid to the Commonwealth of Pennsylvania), with Frazier v. Merchants Nat'l Bank, 5 N.E.2d 550 (Mass. 1936) (upholding a testamentary trust of about $117,000, under which the trustee was directed to accumulate the income until the principal and accumulated income reached $1,000,000, whereupon income was to be paid perpetually to the Salem Hospital). See also Estate of Orphanos v. Commissioner, 67 T.C. 780 (1977) (allowing a federal estate-tax charitable deduction for a testamentary trust that directed the trustee to accumulate the income until it and the original property reached a "sufficient amount . . . to erect a hospitol [*sic*] in Kerasitsa, Greece. . . ."); cf. Matter of Booker, 682 P.2d 320 (Wash. Ct. App. 1984).

When a provision for accumulation is found invalid, as in *James' Estate,* how is the trust fund to be administered? On this point, Restatement 2d of Trusts § 401, comment k, states that if the court decides that under all the circumstances the period of accumulation is unreasonably long, it will direct that the property "be applied to the designated charitable purpose either immediately or at a time to be fixed by the court, and, if necessary, will apply the doctrine of cy pres in order to carry out the settlor's general charitable intention." In *James' Estate,* the court noted that the testator "did not point to capital improvements or to any other needs of the charitable institution which ordinarily could not be met by drawing on current funds," and ordered the income to be distributed to the charitable institution currently. See generally Scott on Trusts § 401.9. On tax penalties imposed on private non-operating charitable foundations for accumulating income, see IRC § 4942; Richard B. Stephens et al., Federal Estate and Gift Taxation ¶5.05[5][a] (5th ed. 1983).

5. *Mortmain Legislation.* One aspect of the struggle between church and state in England following the Norman Conquest concerned land holdings by religious organizations. The feudal benefits to the king or other overlord, which were dependent upon the heir's succession to land on death of the tenant, disappeared when the land was held by an ecclesiastical corporation, which did not die. Such lands were "in dead hands," and the results must have been particularly objectionable to the Crown where this was to continue in perpetuity. Beginning in the thirteenth century, "mortmain" (dead hand) statutes were

passed with the central purpose of prohibiting the acquisition or holding of land by religious bodies. It became possible, however, to avoid these statutes through the device of a use. One of the purposes of the Statute of Uses was to eliminate such practices.

In this country, there is some legislation limiting the amount of land that may be held by a religious organization. Until recently, there was a more important type of mortmain statute that either (or both) (a) limited the proportion of a decedent's estate that could be devised to charity or (b) provided that a devise to charity was valid only if the will was executed a certain period of time before death. These statutes have now all been repealed, and the Restatement 3d of Property § 9.7 provides that "[a]ny rule that a charitable devise is invalid if it exceeds a certain proportion of the testator's estate or if it is contained in a will that was executed within a certain time before the testator's death is abolished." See supra Chapter 10, Part C.

2. *Specified Purposes*

Whether or not any particular trust has a charitable purpose depends on "whether at the time when the question arises and in the state in which it arises the purpose is one that might reasonably be held to be of community or social interest." Restatement 3d of Trusts § 28 comment *l*. The community is automatically interested in the enforcement of charitable trusts for the benefit of charity in general, for the benefit of the community at large, or for governmental purposes. When a trust is for the benefit of a specified segment of the community, however, the community-interest requirement is met only if the trust purposes relate to the relief of poverty, the advancement of education or of religion, or the promotion of health. Thus, comment a to § 375 explicitly states that when a trust is for any of the latter purposes, "the class of persons who are to benefit directly by the performance of the trust need not be as large as it must be where the trust is simply for the general benefit of the class. . . ."

Shenandoah Valley National Bank v. Taylor

63 S.E.2d 786 (Va. 1951)

MILLER, J. Charles B. Henry, a resident of Winchester, Virginia, died testate on the 23rd day of April, 1949. His will dated April 21, 1949, was duly admitted to probate and the Shenandoah Valley National Bank of Winchester, the designated executor and trustee, qualified thereunder. Subject to two inconsequential provisions not material to this litigation, the testator's entire estate valued at $86,000, was left as follows:

> Second: All the rest, residue and remainder of my estate, real, personal, intangible and mixed, of whatsoever kind and wherever situate, . . . , I give,

> bequeath and devise to the Shenandoah Valley National Bank of Winchester, Virginia, in trust, to be known as the "Charles B. Henry and Fannie Belle Henry Fund", for the following uses and purposes:
>
> (a) My Trustee shall invest and reinvest my trust estate, shall collect the income therefrom and shall pay the net income as follows:
>
> (1) On the last school day of each calendar year before Easter my Trustee shall divide the net income into as many equal parts as there are children in the first, second and third grades of the John Kerr School of the City of Winchester, and shall pay one of such equal parts to each child in such grades, to be used by such child in the furtherance of his or her obtainment of an education.
>
> (2) On the last school day of each calendar year before Christmas my trustee shall divide the net income into as many equal parts as there are children in the first, second and third grades of the John Kerr School of the City of Winchester, and shall pay one of such equal parts to each child in such grades, to be used by such child in the furtherance of his or her obtainment of an education.

By paragraphs (3) and (4) it is provided that the names of the children in the three grades shall be determined each year from the school records, and payment of the income to them "shall be as nearly equal in amounts as it is practicable" to arrange. Paragraph (5) provides that if the John Kerr School is ever discontinued for any reason the payments shall be made to the children of the same grades of the school or schools that take its place, and the School Board of Winchester is to determine what school or schools are substituted for it. . . .

The John Kerr School is a public school used by the local school board for primary grades and had an enrollment of 458 boys and girls so there will be that number of pupils or thereabouts who would share in the distribution of the income.

The testator left no children or near relatives. Those who would be his heirs and distributees in case of intestacy were first cousins and others more remotely related. One of these next of kin filed a suit against the executor and trustee, and others challenging the validity of the provisions of the will which undertook to create a charitable trust. . . .

The sole question presented is: does the will create a valid charitable trust?

Construction of the challenged provisions is required and in this undertaking the testator's intent as disclosed by the words used in the will must be ascertained. If his dominant intent as expressed was charitable, the trust should be accorded efficacy and sustained. But on the other hand, if the testator's intent as expressed is merely benevolent, though the disposition of his property be meritorious and evince traits of generosity, the trust must nevertheless be declared invalid because it violates the rule against perpetuities. . . .

Authoritative definitions of charitable trusts may be found in 4 Pomeroy's Equity Jurisprudence, 5th Ed., sec. 1020, and Restatement of the Law of

Trusts, sec. 368, p. 1140. The latter gives a comprehensive classification definition. It is:

> Charitable purposes include:
> (a) the relief of poverty;
> (b) the advancement of education;
> (c) the advancement of religion;
> (d) the promotion of health;
> (e) governmental or municipal purposes; and
> (f) other purposes the accomplishment of which is beneficial to the community. . . .

We now turn to the language of the will for from its context the testator's intent is to be derived. . . . In mandatory language the duty and the duty alone to make cash payments to each individual child just before Easter and Christmas is enjoined upon the trustee by the certain and explicit words that it "shall divide the net income . . . and shall pay one of such equal shares to each child in such grades."

Without more, that language and the occasions specified for payment of the funds to the children being when their minds and interests would be far removed from studies or other school activities definitely indicate that no educational purpose was in the testator's mind. It is manifest that there was no intent or belief that the funds would be put to any use other than such as youthful impulse and desire might dictate. But in each instance immediately following the above-quoted language the sentence concludes with the words or phrase "to be used by such child in the furtherance of his or her obtainment of an education." It is significant that by this latter phrase the trustee is given no power, control or discretion over the funds so received by the child. Full and complete execution of the mandate and trust imposed upon the trustee accomplishes no educational purpose. Nothing toward the advancement of education is attained by the ultimate performance by the trustee of its full duty. It merely places the income irretrievably and forever beyond the range of the trust. . . .

In our opinion, the words of the will import an intent to have the trustee pay to each child his allotted share. If that be true,—and it is directed to be done in no uncertain language—we know that the admonition to the children would be wholly impotent and of no avail. . . .

If it be determined that the will fails to create a charitable trust for *educational purposes* (and our conclusion is that it is inoperative to create such a trust), it is earnestly insisted that the trust provided for is nevertheless charitable and valid. In this respect it is claimed that the two yearly payments to be made to the children just before Christmas and Easter produce "a desirable social effect" and are "promotive of public convenience and needs, and happiness and contentment" and thus the fund set up in the will constitutes a charitable trust. 2 Bogert on Trusts, sec. 361, p. 1090, and 3 Scott on Trusts, sec. 368, p. 1972. . . .

Numerous cases that deal with and construe specific provisions of wills or other instruments are cited by appellant to uphold the contention that the provisions of this will, without reference to and deleting the phrase "to be used by such child in the furtherance of his or her obtainment of an education" meet the requirements of a charitable trust. . . . Upon examination of these decisions, it will be found that where a gift results in mere financial enrichment, a trust was sustained only when the court found and concluded from the entire context of the will that the ultimate intended recipients were poor or in necessitous circumstances.

A trust from which the income is to be paid at stated intervals to each member of a designated segment of the public, without regard to whether or not the recipients are poor or in need, is not for the relief of poverty, nor is it a social benefit to the community. It is a mere benevolence—a private trust—and may not be upheld as a charitable trust. . . . Upon examination of these decisions, it will be found that where a gift results in mere financial enrichment, a trust was sustained only when the court found and concluded from the entire context of the will that the ultimate intended recipients were poor or in necessitous circumstances. . . . Payment to the children of their cash bequests on the two occasions specified would bring to them pleasure and happiness and no doubt cause them to remember or think of their benefactor with gratitude and thanksgiving. That was, we think, Charles B. Henry's intent. Laudable, generous and praiseworthy though it may be, it is not for the relief of the poor or needy, nor does it otherwise so benefit or advance the social interest of the community as to justify its continuance in perpetuity as a charitable trust. . . .

No error is found in the decrees appealed from and they are affirmed.

Notes, Questions, and Problems

1. *Duration of Trusts for Noncharitable Purposes.* Under the court's construction, the trust in *Taylor* was a so-called honorary trust, that is, a non-charitable specific purpose trust. Some commentators have worried about the duration of such trusts under the Uniform Statutory Rule Against Perpetuities Act, which effectively permits private trusts to last up to 90 years. The Uniform Trust Code and the Uniform Probate Code avoid the problem, however, by providing that the duration of an honorary trust is limited to 21 years. See UTC § 409; UPC § 2-907.[11]

---

11. Section 2-907 is not officially part of the Uniform Act, but its enactment is recommended in conjunction with the Act.

2. *Scholarships and Awards.* The fact that only one or a small number of persons are to receive the benefits of a trust does not disqualify it from being a valid charitable trust, as long as the class of persons from whom the recipients are to be selected is sufficiently large. Thus, trusts awarding scholarships or awards are generally held to be charitable, even though there may be only one recipient. See, e.g., Estate of Carlson, 358 P.2d 669 (Kan. 1961) (upholding a devise in trust to the city of Sylvia, Kansas, to provide funds for the medical education of a young man from Sylvia Township, "upon his promise that he will return to the City of Sylvia, and remain there for the purpose of practicing his profession."); but see, e.g., Estate of Huebner, 15 P.2d 758 (Cal. Ct. App. 1932) (testamentary trust providing that the income be used "to help defray the expense of some girl or boy in music or art" held not to be charitable.) See generally Scott on Trusts § 375.1.

Trusts to provide education for one's own relatives are non-charitable, but courts have sustained trusts to provide scholarships for needy students in which the settlor expresses a preference for his or her relatives. See, e.g., Estate of Sells v. Commissioner, 10 T.C. 692 (1948) (trust "to provide scholarship first to relatives or other boys or girls" qualified for the federal estate-tax charitable deduction.); but see, e.g., Griffen v. United States, 400 F.2d 612 (6th Cir. 1968) (Trust stated that income was "to be used for the education of my grandchildren and for the education of deserving boys and girls . . . to obtain [a] college education in a Protestant Christian College. . . . It is my intention and desire to make my grandchildren the primary beneficiaries of this trust, and if at any time any grandchild of mine desires to avail himself or herself of the benefits of this trust, he or she shall be entitled to such benefits [not to exceed $750.00 in any one school year] even to the exclusion of all other persons." A state court held that the trust was charitable, but the federal court held that it did not qualify for the estate-tax charitable deduction.) On qualification as a charitable trust under state law, see Restatement 3d of Trusts § 28, Reporter's Note on comment h; Scott on Trusts § 375.3; Ralph H. Dawn, Charities for Definite Persons, 82 U. Pa. L. Rev. 12 (1933). On qualification for a charitable deduction under the federal tax laws, see Crellin v. Commissioner, 46 B.T.A. 1152 (1944) (deduction denied where principal as well as income was available to relatives, who were sufficient in number to exhaust fund, leaving nothing for educational expenses of non-relatives); Priv. Ltr. Rul. 79-23-001.

3. *Changing Law/Political Purposes/Illegal Purposes.* The Restatement 3d of Trusts § 28 comment *l* states that

> [a] trust may be charitable although the accomplishment of the purpose for which the trust is created involves a change in existing law. . . . [A] trust to improve the structure and methods of government is charitable. . . .

The same comment provides, however, that trusts to promote the success of particular political parties are not charitable. Finally, concerning trusts for unpopular causes, comment *a-2* states that "[i]f the general purposes for which a trust is created are such as may be reasonably thought to promote the social interest of the community, the mere fact that a majority of the people or of the members of the court believe that the particular purpose of the settlor is unwise or not well adapted to its social objective, does not prevent the trust from being charitable." Of course, trusts that induce or tend to induce the commission of a crime are invalid. See Restatement 3d of Trusts § 28 comment *l*.

Jackson v. Phillips, 96 Mass. (14 Allen) 539 (1867), is a well-known Massachusetts case contrary to the Restatement position concerning change in existing law. In that case, a testamentary trust was established to be used "to secure the passage of laws granting women, whether married or unmarried, the right to vote" as well as "all other civil rights enjoyed by men." The Massachusetts court struck the trust down as not having been created for a valid charitable purpose:

> This bequest differs from the others in aiming directly and exclusively to change the laws; and its object cannot be accomplished without changing the Constitution also. Whether such an alteration of the existing laws and frame of government would be wise and desirable is a question upon which we cannot, sitting in a judicial capacity, properly express any opinion. Our duty is limited to expounding the laws as they stand. And those laws do not recognize the purpose of overthrowing or changing them, in whole or in part, as a charitable use.

The court adhered to this view as late as 1922, in a case involving a trust for the promotion of women's rights established by the son of Francis Jackson, the testator in Jackson v. Phillips. Bowditch v. Attorney General, 134 N.E. 796 (Mass. 1922). This view has found no favor elsewhere. See, e.g., Collier v. Lindley, 266 P. 526 (Cal. 1928); Register of Wills v. Cook, 216 A.2d 542 (Md. 1966). In Massachusetts today, legislation defines charitable trusts in terms of trusts having tax-exempt status under the federal tax laws (see supra p. 827). Mass. Gen. Laws Ann. ch. 68A.

The distinctions reflected in the Restatement, while generally followed in the cases, make for many close questions. To start with a straightforward example, however, it should be clear that a trust to support the Socialist Party (or the Democrat Party, the Republican Party, or the Libertarian Party) and its candidates is not charitable. But what about a trust providing for payments "to persons, entities and causes advancing the principles of socialism and those causes related to socialism? This shall include, but not be limited to, subsidizing publications, establishing and conducting reading rooms, supporting radio, television and the newspaper media and candidates for public office." See Estate of Breeden, 208 Cal. App. 3d 981, 256 Cal. Rptr. 813 (1989). Or, a trust "to provide a place where the doctrines of socialism could be taught by example as well as by precept"? See Peth v. Spear, 115 P. 164 (Wash. 1911). In George v. Braddock, 18 A. 881 (N.J. 1889), the court held that a valid charitable trust had been created where the testator devised property in trust for the purpose of "'spreading the light' on social and political liberty and justice in these United States" by way of distributing the publications of Henry George, whose teachings included the doctrine "that no private, absolute ownership in land can rightfully exist." Is such a trust deductible for federal estate-tax purposes? Leubuscher v. Commissioner, 54 F.2d 998 (2d Cir. 1932), held that it was.

What about a trust to provide for support and education "of such minor Negro child or children, whose father or mother, or both, have been . . . imprisoned . . . as a result of the conviction of a crime or misdemeanor of a political nature"? The will gave examples of the types of crimes the testator had in mind, such as contempt convictions in connection with appearances before the House Un-American Activities Committee. See Estate of Robbins, 57 Cal.2d 718, 21 Cal. Rptr. 797, 371 P.2d 573 (1962).

What about a trust to oppose candidates for public office who favor decriminalization of the use of marijuana? Cf. People *ex rel.* Hartigan v. National Anti-Drug Coalition, 464 N.E.2d 690 (Ill. App. Ct. 1984).

4. *Influencing Legislation/Political Campaigns/Tax Aspects.* Having a purpose to influence legislation or to support or oppose candidates for public office may jeopardize the tax-exempt status of a charitable organization and jeopardize the deductibility of contributions thereto. Under IRC § 501(c)(3), tax-exempt status is denied to certain charitable organizations if attempting to influence legislation constitutes a "substantial part of the [organization's] activities"[12] or if the organization participates in or intervenes in "any political campaign on behalf of (or in opposition to) any candidate for public office."

Gifts and devises to an organization or a trust are deductible for income, estate, and gift tax purposes only if the recipient "is not disqualified for tax exemption under IRC § 501(c)(3) by reason of attempting to influence

---

12. IRC § 501(h) permits certain organizations to elect to replace the "substantial part of the activities" test of IRC § 501(c)(3) with limits defined in terms of expenditures for influencing legislation. Under IRC § 4911, the basic permitted level of such expenditures (the "lobbying nontaxable amount") for a year is 20% of the first $500,000 of the organization's exempt purpose expenditures for the year, plus 15% of the second $500,000, plus 10% of the third $500,000, plus 5% of any additional expenditures. In no event, however, can this permitted level exceed $1,000,000 for any one year. Within these limits, a separate limitation is placed on "grass roots lobbying" (attempting to influence the general public on legislative matters); the "grass roots nontaxable amount" is one fourth of the "lobbying nontaxable amount." An electing organization that exceeds either the "lobbying nontaxable amount" or the "grass roots nontaxable amount" in a taxable year is subject to an excise tax but does not necessarily lose its tax-exempt status. Loss of tax-exempt status occurs only if the organization "normally" makes expenditures of 150% of either limitation.

legislation, and . . . does not participate in, or intervene in (including the publishing or distributing of statements), any political campaign on behalf of (or in opposition to) any candidate for public office." IRC §§ 170(c)(2)(D), 2055(a)(2), (a)(3), 2522(a)(2).

Does a bar association that rates candidates for both appointive and elective judgeships at the municipal, state, and federal level as either "approved," "not approved," or "approved as highly qualified" and that communicates its ratings to the public in the form of press releases and publishes them in a regular publication of the association that is sent out to the association's members and approximately 120 other subscribers, including libraries and law schools, qualify for tax-exempt status under IRC § 501(c)(3)? Does it matter that the association evaluates judicial candidates on a nonpartisan basis? That the rating of judicial candidates is not a substantial part of its activities? See Association of the Bar of the City of New York v. Commissioner, 858 F.2d 876 (2d Cir. 1988).

5. *Unpopular Purposes.* According to Professor Scott, "a trust is not a valid charitable trust if [it is for the dissemination of beliefs or doctrines that] are so irrational that it cannot be said that their dissemination can be of any benefit to the community." Scott on Trusts § 370.4. In addition, a trust for the accomplishment of a purpose that is against public policy is one for an illegal purpose and invalid. Restatement 3d of Trusts § 29. On the other hand, a trust is not invalid merely because the beliefs or doctrines to be disseminated are unpopular or accepted by a minority of the population.

How does a court go about applying the distinction between views that are merely unpopular and those that are so irrational or absurd that their dissemination is of no benefit to the community whatsoever? Some cases are not so difficult. Trusts for the promotion of agnosticism have been held to create valid charitable trusts. See Estate of Connolly, 48 Cal. App. 3d 129, 121 Cal. Rptr. 325 (1975) (promotion of agnosticism serves an educational purpose; court did "not imply that the viewpoint of agnosticism is correct or incorrect," but noted that "the sense of today is all too frequently the nonsense of tomorrow."). Trusts for the promotion of atheism have also been upheld as serving an educational function. See Scott on Trusts § 377. A trust for the promotion of racism would certainly not be upheld.

In Estate of Kidd, 479 P.2d 697 (Ariz. 1971), James Kidd's holographic will devised his entire estate, amounting to $175,000, "to go in a reserach (sic) or some scientific proof of a soul of a human body which leaves at death. I think in time their (*sic*) can be a Photograph of soul leaving the human at death."

The court held that a charitable trust had been created, and that where as here only a charitable purpose is stated, "the court will either appoint a trustee to carry out the purpose or will approve a scheme to carry it out," citing

Restatement 2d of Trusts § 397 comment e. The devise was claimed by 102 claimants and the trial court awarded the funds to the Barrow Neurological Institute. On appeal by six other claimants, the award was rejected on the ground that the Institute wasn't engaged in any research of the kind sought by the testator. The court directed the trial court to select from among two persons and two organizations which of them "is most suitable to carry out the trust expressed in Kidd's will." Since the court was concerned only about who was qualified to carry on the research specified, the decision seems to require, not that a trustee would be appointed to administer the fund, but that the fund would be given directly to a qualified claimant who would be obligated to use it for the specified purpose. On remand, the trial court awarded the fund to the American Society for Psychical Research, which some several years later reported that it had spent the money without having succeeded in photographing the human soul.

EXTERNAL REFERENCE. Mary Kay Lundwall, Inconsistency and Uncertainty in the Charitable Purposes Doctrine, 41 Wayne L. Rev. 1341 (1995).

PART B. THE CY-PRES DOCTRINE

1. General Principles

The cy-pres doctrine, unique to charitable trusts, is described in the Restatement 3d of Trusts § 67 in this way:

> § *67. Failure of Designated Charitable Purpose: The Doctrine of Cy Pres.* Unless the terms of the trust provide otherwise, where property is placed in trust to be applied to a designated charitable purpose and it is or becomes unlawful, impossible or impracticable to carry out that purpose, or to the extent it is or becomes wasteful to apply all of the property to the designated purpose, the charitable trust will not fail but the court will direct application of the property or appropriate portion thereof to a charitable purpose that reasonably approximates the designated purpose.

See also UTC § 413(a). This description departs from the traditional description of the cy-pres doctrine in two important respects. First, both the Restatement 3d and the UTC, unlike the traditional law, *presume* a general charitable intent, which is a precondition for application of the cy-pres doctrine.[13] Because the

---

13. UTC § 413(b) also departs from traditional law by providing that an express gift over to a noncharitable beneficiary prevails over the power of the court to apply cy pres only if it would cause the trust property to revert to a living settlor or if fewer than 21 years have elapsed since

traditional law did not provide such a presumption, courts had to determine whether the settlor had a general charitable purpose or only the specified charitable purpose.

Second, both the new Restatement and the UTC add the term "wasteful" to the list or circumstances under which a charitable trust may be judicially modified. The traditional statement of the doctrine, expressed in the Restatement 2d of Trusts § 399, limits the doctrine's applicable conditions to when it becomes "impossible or impracticable or illegal to carry out [the trust's] particular purpose . . . ." What, if any, difference does the addition of "wasteful" to the UTC's description make? Consider this question in connection with the Buck Trust, discussed infra.

Is judicial modification of the terms of a charitable trust under the cy-pres doctrine incompatible with the principle of donative freedom? Consider Judge Posner's explanation:

> A policy of rigid adherence to the letter of the donative instrument is likely to frustrate both the donor's purposes and the efficient use of resources. . . .
>
> Where the continued enforcement of conditions in a charitable gift is no longer economically feasible, because of illegality . . . or opportunity costs . . . the court, rather than declaring the gift void and transferring the property to the residuary legatees (if any can be identified), will authorize the administrators of the charitable trust to apply the assets of the trust to a related (*cy pres*) purpose within the general scope of the donor's intent.

Richard A. Posner, Economic Analysis of Law 556-57 (5th ed. 1998).

Note how Judge Posner's rationale gains strength under the Restatement 3d's and UTC's presumption of a general charitable intent. Without that presumption (or a judicial finding of a general charitable intent), the impossibility, impracticability, or illegality of the trust's specified purposes requires that the trust fail entirely, with a resulting trust back to the settlor or the settlor's successors in interest.

In the absence of a presumption of a general charitable intent, how is a general charitable intent to be found in a given case? What is the court to look for? On these questions, consider the following excerpt from Howard Savings Institution v. Peep, 170 A.2d 39 (N.J. 1961):

> First, the term "general charitable intent" ordinarily used by courts articulating the [cy-pres] doctrine does not require an intention to benefit charity generally. It requires only a charitable purpose which is broader than the particular purpose the effectuation of which is impossible, impracticable or illegal. . . . Second, the inquiry "did the settlor manifest a general charitable intent" is just another way of

---

the date of the trust's creation.

> asking "would he have wanted the trust funds devoted to a like charitable purpose, or would he have wanted them withdrawn from charitable channels." . . . So stated, it can be seen that *cy pres* is an intent-enforcing doctrine. But it is well to keep in mind that it is a surmise rather than an actual intent which the courts enforce through application of the doctrine. Rarely does a settlor contemplate the possible nonfulfillment of his precise purpose. Therefore, the court must make an educated guess based on the trust instrument and relevant extrinsic evidence as to what he would have intended had he been aware of the contingency which has frustrated the exact effectuation of his expressed intent. . . .

On occasion, the terms of the trust make it appear that the settlor *has* contemplated the failure of the trust's purposes. A specific provision that the trust should terminate in the event of a failure of its purpose is given effect. Cy pres is usually then denied, for the provision for termination tends strongly to negate the idea that the settlor had a more general charitable intent than the articulated charitable purpose. Restatement 3d of Trusts § 67 comment b.

Preliminary to the general-charitable-intent inquiry, of course, is a finding, under the traditional standard, that the trust's articulated purpose is or has become impossible, impracticable, or illegal. Failing this finding, cy pres will be denied regardless of a broader charitable intent. In thinking about how the court should go about deciding whether the trust has become impracticable, consider the next case, which has attracted considerable attention in California and elsewhere in recent years.

Estate of Buck

Superior Court of Marin County, California, 1986
[Opinion reprinted from 21 U.S.F.L. Rev. 691 (1987)]

[In 1975, Beryl Buck, a resident of Marin County, California,[14] died a childless widow. Her will devised the residue of her estate to the San Francisco Foundation, a community trust administering charitable funds throughout the five-county San Francisco Bay Area. This devise became known as the "Buck Trust." The will directed that the residue

> shall always be held and used for exclusively non-profit charitable, religious or educational purposes in providing care for the needy in Marin County, California, and for other non-profit charitable, religious, or educational purposes in that county.

---

14. Marin County is located north of San Francisco, immediately across the Golden Gate Bridge. It has one of the highest per-capita incomes in the country. Known for its trend-setting ways, it is sometimes called the "hot-tub capital of the world."

Ms. Buck's residuary estate consisted primarily of a block of shares in Belridge Oil Company stock. Belridge, which Buck's father-in-law had founded, was a privately-held company with substantial oil reserves in Southern California. The value of Ms. Buck's interest in the Belridge stock at the time she executed her will was $7 million, and it had not changed significantly by the time she died in 1975. In 1979, however, the value of the Belridge stock in the Buck Trust had shot up to $260 million as a result of a bidding war when Shell Oil bought Belridge. By 1984, when the trial began, the value of the stock had increased to over $400 million, and the trust was generating an annual income of $30 million.

In 1984, the Foundation, having concluded that it was "impractical and inexpedient to continue to expend all of the income from the Buck Trust solely within Marin County," sought judicial authorization to spend some portion of Buck Trust income in the other four counties of the Bay Area. Its petition for cy-pres rested upon the theory that the dramatic increase in the trust fund's value was a posthumous "surprise," a change in circumstances raising doubt whether Ms. Buck, had she anticipated its occurrence, would have limited the scope of her charitable objective to Marin County. The Foundation relied on the proposed testimony of Yale law professor John Simon. Professor Simon contended that charitable behavior by "major American philanthropists" is characterized by breadth of purpose, a desire to serve "a community that is broadly defined in terms of population size and socioeconomic class." His theory was that Ms. Buck should be viewed as a major American philanthropist and in the absence of any evidence explaining her departure from this "philanthropic standard," it is reasonable to assume that she would have wanted some of her money spent elsewhere in the Bay Area.[15] The trial court ruled that Simon's proposed testimony was inadmissible as evidence of the testator's intent.

Near the close of the respondent's case, the Foundation, strongly criticized by the Marin County authorities, the press, and the state Attorney General, offered to resign as trustee. All the parties except the Objector-Beneficiaries agreed to a settlement, with the trust to be administered by a new Marin-based community foundation. The Objector-Beneficiaries, forty-six individuals and charitable organizations in the other four Bay Area counties, refused to join in the settlement on the ground that it was a "sell-out" of the needy in the Bay Area. On July 31, 1986, the Foundation was permitted to resign, and the court

15. Professor Simon's theory is set out in John G. Simon, American Philanthropy and the Buck Trust, 21 U.S.F. L. Rev. 641 (1987).

dismissed its cy-pres petition. On August 15, 1986, the trial court issued a judgment against the Objector-Beneficiaries.][16]

THOMPSON, J. . . .

A. *CY PRES* APPLIES ONLY WHERE THE PURPOSE OF A TRUST HAS BECOME ILLEGAL, IMPOSSIBLE OR PERMANENTLY IMPRACTICABLE OF PERFORMANCE. The purpose of the cy pres doctrine "is to prevent the failure of valid charitable trust gifts." Estate of Zahn (1971) 16 Cal.App.3d 106, 114, cert. denied sub nom. Zahn v. Security Pacific Nat. Bank, 404 U.S. 938. As explained by Professor Scott:

> Where property is given in trust for a particular charitable purpose, the trust will not ordinarily fail even though it is impossible to carry out the particular purpose. In such a case the court will ordinarily direct that the property be applied to a similar charitable purpose. 4 Scott on Trusts (3d ed. 1967), Charitable Trusts, § 399 at 3084.

The words "cy pres" means "as near." The full phrase in Norman French was "cy pres comme possible," meaning "as near as possible." Bogert, Trusts and Trustees (2d ed. 1964) § 431 at 490. Thus, cy pres is a rule "of construction, the object of which is 'to permit the main purpose of the donor of a charitable trust to be carried out as nearly as may be where it cannot be done to the letter.'" Society of California Pioneers v. McElroy (1944) 63 Cal. App.2d 332, 337.

The Restatement (Second) of Trusts, section 399 at 297, describes the cy pres doctrine as follows:

> If property is given in trust to be applied to a particular charitable purpose and *it is or becomes impossible or impracticable or illegal to carry out the particular purpose,* and if the settlor manifested a more general intention to devote the property to charitable purposes, the trust will not fail but the court will direct the application of the property to some charitable purpose which falls within the general charitable intention of the settlor. (Emphasis added).

These eminent authorities, followed by statutory and/or case law in many states, provide that where a purpose of a charitable trust becomes illegal, impossible or impracticable of fulfillment, and the testator manifested a general charitable

16. This statement of facts is based on Ronald Hayes Malone et al., The Buck Trust Trial—A Litigator's Perspective, 21 U.S.F.L. Rev. 585 (1987).

intention, the court may direct that the property be applied to a similar charitable purpose.[17]

Courts in California, as in other states, exercise extreme caution before they will vary the terms of a charitable trust:

> Basically, "charitable contributions must be used only for the purposes for which they were received in trust." (Holt v. College of Osteopathic Physicians & Surgeons (1964) 61 Cal.2d 750, 754 [40 Cal. Rptr. 244, 394 P.2d 932]). "The policy of the law in favor of charitable gifts requires a court to carry out the dominant purpose of the donor to make a charitable gift for the purposes expressed in the articles of the original corporate donee." (In re Los Angeles County Pioneer Soc. (1953) 40 Cal.2d 852, 865-66). Only when compliance with these foregoing rules becomes impossible does the application of *cy pres* come into play.

California courts have often quoted the language of the Restatement of Trusts setting forth the cy pres standard of illegality, impossibility, or impracticability. The impossibility or impracticability prerequisite, however, has been interpreted in California to require a "permanency of the impossibility or impracticability of carrying out the specific charitable purpose or purposes of the creator of the trust." Estate of Mabury (1976) 54 Cal.App.3d 969, 985 (emphasis in original).

. . .

In practice, cy pres has most often been applied in California in such cases—where the charitable trust purpose is or has become literally impossible to fulfill (it "cannot be accomplished")—or in cases where it has become "reasonably impossible of performance." E.g., Society of California Pioneers v. McElroy, supra, 63 Cal.App.2d 332, 334-35 ("no longer reasonably possible to carry out the testator's intention"), O'Hara v. Grand Lodge of I.O.G.T. (1931) 213 Cal. 131, 140 (method of carrying out the general charitable purpose "has become reasonably impossible of performance").

B. NEITHER INEFFICIENCY NOR INEFFECTIVE PHILANTHROPY CONSTITUTES IMPRACTICABILITY. "Impracticability" has been defined as "impossible" as early as 1850 in Dr. Johnson's famous dictionary (A Dictionary of the English Language (Henry G. Bohn: London, 1850), p. 616). Other prestigious

---

17. Bogert includes "inexpedient" as a possible prerequisite for the application of cy pres. He describes the doctrine as follows:

> Roughly speaking, it is the doctrine that equity will, when a charity is originally or later becomes impossible, inexpedient, or impracticable of fulfillment, substitute another charitable object which is believed to approach the original purpose as closely as possible. Bogert, Trusts and Trustees, supra, § 431 at 490.

Although a few California courts have quoted Bogert in dicta, no California court has ever applied cy pres upon finding "inexpediency," or ever applied an "inexpediency" standard for cy pres.

dictionaries have defined impracticability in the same sense, e.g., "incapable of being done or carried out," "a practical impossibility" (Oxford English Dictionary Vol. V. (Oxford University Press: England, 1933), p. 106); "incapable of accomplishment" (The Century Dictionary (The Century Co.: New York, 1897), p. 3014); "incapable of being performed or carried out" (Webster's Third International Dictionary (G.& C. Merriam Co.: Springfield, Massachusetts, 1967), p. 1136); "practically impossible" (The Dictionary of Hard Words (Dodd Mead: New York, 1910), p. 275).

California courts have never adopted a broad interpretation of the term "impracticable" in charitable trust cases. . . .

Like California courts, courts from other states often describe the standard for cy pres as one of "illegality, impossibility or impracticability." In many of those jurisdictions, however, "impracticability" is equated with "impossibility." Dunbar v. Board of Trustees (1969) 170 Colo. 327, 461 P.2d 28, 32 (dicta).

The Restatement (Second) of Trusts, (1959) section 399, comment q at 306, does not require a literal impossibility. Rather, it defines "impracticability" as follows:

> The doctrine of cy pres is applicable even though it is possible to carry out the particular purpose of the settlor, if to carry it out would *fail to accomplish the general charitable intention* of the settlor. In such case it is "impracticable" to carry out the particular purpose. . . . (Emphasis added)..

Ineffective philanthropy, inefficiency and relative inefficiency, that is, inefficiency of trust expenditures in one location given greater relative needs or benefits elsewhere, do not constitute impracticability under either view. Such situation is not the equivalent of impossibility; nor is there any threat that the operation of the trust will fail to fulfill the general charitable intention of the settlor.[18] As stated by one court, "the court's power over the disposition of other

18. To the extent that concepts of effective philanthropy or efficiency relate to achieving the greatest benefit for the cost incurred they should not form the basis for modifying a donor's wishes. No law requires a testator to make a gift which the trustees deem efficient or to constitute effective philanthropy. Moreover, calculating "benefit" involves inherently subjective determinations; thus, what is "effective" or "efficient" will vary, depending on the interests and concerns of the person or persons making the determination. Cy pres does not authorize a court to vary the terms of a bequest merely because the variation will accommodate the desire of the trustee.

To the extent that the term efficiency embraces the concept of relative need, it is not an appropriate basis for modifying the terms of a testamentary trust. (The Foundation itself has acknowledged this, and indicated that such a concept "is neither what Mrs. Buck's will contemplates, nor a term which has an readily ascertainable meaning." (San Francisco Foundation's Statement Regarding Attorney General's Supplemental Response to Second Annual Report, judicially noticed on February 6, 1986.)) If it were otherwise, all charitable gifts, and the fundamental basis of philanthropy would be threatened, as there may always be more compelling

people's assets is limited to removing restrictions only if they are incompatible with the testator's dominant purpose." Estate of Wilson (1982) 451 N.Y.S.2d 891, 894 aff'd (1983) 465 N.Y.S.2d 900, 452 N.E.2d 1228. In Wilson, although the alternative scheme proposed a gender neutral educational trust, which would have been preferable on public policy grounds, the court stated that:

> there is another competing public policy consideration, namely, preserving the right of the testator to dispose of his property as he wishes. (Citation omitted). This rule becomes even more compelling when applied to the area of private charitable trusts, for one of the very reasons for the rule is to encourage bequests for charitable purposes. Id.

The foregoing policy considerations fully justify the dominant tendency of courts to require a situation of illegality, impossibility or strict impracticability before they will vary the terms of a charitable trust through an application of cy pres.

The present and well-tested law that cy pres will be invoked to save a charitable bequest that has become impossible or impracticable of fulfillment where the testator has a general charitable intent provides an intermediate concept "between the well established rules of construction that a will is to be construed so as to effectuate the intent of the testator, and that a gift to charity should be effectuated whenever possible." Estate of Klinkner, supra, 85 Cal.App.3d 942, 951. Where both the testator's intent and the charitable gift can, in fact, be effectuated, i.e., the specified trust purpose has not become impossible or impracticable of performance, there is no justification for cy pres.

The cy pres doctrine should not be so distorted by the adoption of subjective, relative, and nebulous standards such as "inefficiency" or "ineffective philanthropy" to the extent that it becomes a facile vehicle for charitable trustees to vary the terms of a trust simply because they believe that they can spend the trust income better or more wisely elsewhere, or as in this case, prefer to do so. There is no basis in law for the application of standards such as "efficiency" or "effectiveness" to modify a trust, nor is there any authority that would elevate these standards to the level of impracticability.

"needs" to fill than the gift chosen by the testator. Gifts to Harvard or Stanford University, for example, could fail simply because institutions elsewhere are more needy. Similarly, needs in the Bay Area cannot be equated with the grueling poverty of India or the soul-wrenching famine in Ethiopia. Moreover, a standard of relative need would interpose governmental regulation on philanthropy because courts would be required to consider questions of comparable equity, social utility, or benefit, perhaps even wisdom, and ultimately substitute their judgments or those of the trustees for those of the donors.

C. CY PRES MAY NOT BE INVOKED UPON THE BELIEF THAT THE MODIFIED SCHEME WOULD BE MORE DESIRABLE OR WOULD CONSTITUTE A BETTER USE OF THE INCOME. Where the income of a charitable trust can be used for the purpose specified by the testator, cy pres may not be invoked on the grounds that a different use of the income would be more useful or desirable. . . .

Courts have also held that terms of a charitable trust may not be modified on the grounds that a different use would be more beneficial to the community or advantageous to the charity. . . .

Thus, cy pres may not be invoked on the grounds that it would be more "fair," "equitable" or "efficient" to spend the Trust funds in a manner different from that specified by the testator.

D. CY PRES DOES NOT AUTHORIZE THE COURT TO VARY THE TERMS OF A TRUST MERELY BECAUSE THE VARIATION WILL MEET THE DESIRE AND SUIT THE CONVENIENCE OF THE TRUSTEE. Nor is cy pres warranted to alleviate the strain or burden a trust has placed on a trustee organization and as stated by Martin Paley [Director of the San Francisco Foundation], to "modify the nature of the Buck Trust to conform to and become compatible with the values and procedures of the Foundation as a whole."

> [T]he cy pres doctrine does not authorize or permit a court to vary the terms of a bequest and to that extent defeat the intention of the testator merely because the *variation will meet the desire and suit the convenience of the trustee.* Connecticut College v. United States (1960) 276 F.2d 491, 497. (Emphasis added).

Rather, "[e]ither impossibility or impracticability of literal compliance with the donor's plan is indispensably necessary if cy pres is applied." Id. . . .

The Foundation accepted the Buck Trust fully cognizant of the increased value of its assets and of the administrative burden such a large trust would impose on a relatively small community foundation. That, in fact, it has caused an administrative burden on the Foundation and is perceived to be a threat to the integrity of the Foundation as a whole does not warrant varying the terms of Mrs. Buck's bequest. . . .

Cy Pres may not be applied to modify the terms of the Buck Trust.

CONCLUSIONS

Based upon clear principles of trust law and the overwhelming factual record before the Court . . . the Court makes the following conclusions. . . .

16. The residents of Marin County have substantial unmet needs which are within the scope of the purposes of the Buck Trust. In addition, there are significant opportunities to spend Buck Trust funds on nonprofit charitable, religious or educational purposes in Marin County which could benefit Marin County, and, if appropriate, all of humankind. The entire income of the Buck

Trust is presently insufficient, and will remain insufficient in the future, to address all of these needs and opportunities.

17. A Judgment pursuant to this Statement of Decision should be entered denying the Petition for Modification.

Notes and Questions

1. *Aftermath.* The trial court's decision in *Buck* was not appealed. The trial court ordered the creation of the Marin Community Foundation to administer the Buck Trust. The court also appointed a special master to supervise the foundation. The court order required that the trustee expend twenty percent of the trust income annually on major projects "located in Marin County, the benefits from which will inure not only to Marin County but all of mankind." See Douglas J. Maloney, The Aftermath, 21 U.S.F.L. Rev. 681 (1987). The 2000 edition of *The Foundation Directory* reports that at the close the 1999 fiscal year, the Marin Community Foundation had in excess of $1.1 billion, making it the forty-first wealthiest foundation in the country.

2. *"Waste" as a Basis for Cy Pres?* Recall that UTC § 413 and Restatement 3d of Trusts § 67 provide that a court may apply cy pres modification to a charitable trust whose specific purpose has become "wasteful." Would the circumstances in the Buck Trust dispute have met that standard? Consider the following

3. *Cy Pres as to Excess Income.* If the articulated purposes of the trust have not become impossible, impracticable, or illegal, but the income or principal exceeds that which is necessary for their accomplishment, the cy-pres power may be applied as to the excess. In Thatcher v. City of St. Louis, 76 S.W.2d 677 (Mo. 1934), for example, a testamentary trust was established in 1851 by Judge Bryan Mullanphy, when St. Louis was the gateway to the West, for the articulated purpose of furnishing "relief to all poor immigrants and travelers coming to St. Louis on their way, bona fide, to settle in the West." Over time, other westward routes were opened up, and other historical events intervened to make St. Louis no longer the bottleneck for westward travel. Consequently, the trust's income became more than sufficient for the trust's articulated purposes. The court found that Judge Mullanphy's primary intent "was to alleviate a local condition in his home city of St. Louis, which grew out of the mass movement of a great population into the new western lands," rather than "to build up the West by aiding in its settlement." On the strength of this finding, the court applied its cy-pres power as to the excess income, directing that it be applied to "furnishing relief to poor immigrants and travelers generally in the City of St. Louis in need and distress, and found worthy of assistance." Would this decision have supported the use of cy pres in *Buck*?

4. *Gift Over as Blocking Cy-Pres Modification?* A familiar rule of charitable trust law is that upon failure of the initial charitable gift, the existence of a gift over precludes application of cy pres because the gift over shows a specific alternative intent inconsistent with the finding of general charitable intent. In practice, however, the rule operates only as a rule of construction; other factors may indicate that the donor did have a general charitable intent. See C. Ronald Chester, Cy Pres or Gift Over?: The Search for Coherence in Judicial Reform of Failed Charitable Trusts, 23 Suffolk L. Rev. 41 (1989).

5. *Expanded Use of Cy Pres?* Recent commentators have argued that courts should apply cy pres more readily to modify charitable trust provisions in view of changing community needs. See Alex M. Johnson & Ross D. Taylor, Revolutionizing Judicial Interpretation of Charitable Trusts: Applying Relational Contracts and Dynamic Interpretation to Cy Pres and America's Cup Litigation, 74 Iowa L. Rev. 545 (1989); C. Ronald Chester, Cy Pres: A Promise Unfulfilled, 54 Ind. L.J. 407 (1979); Joseph A. DiClerico, Jr., Cy Pres: A Proposal for Change, 47 B.U.L. Rev. 153 (1967). Other commentators have argued that the cy-pres doctrine should be used sparingly. See, e.g., Rob Atkinson, Reforming Cy Pres Reform, 44 Hastings L.J. 1112 (1993) (cy pres increases dead hand control); Jonathan R. Macey, Private Trusts for the Provision of Private Goods, 37 Emory L.J. 295 (1988) (cy pres entails high error and transaction costs)

6. *Devises to Non-Existent Charities.* Recently there has been a fair amount of litigation involving devises to charitable institutions that existed when the will was drafted but ceased to exist at the time of the testator's death. The first question facing courts in these cases is whether the devise lapses. In In re Estate of Lind, 734 N.E.2d 47 (Ill. App. 2000), the court held that a devise to "Northwestern University Dental School" did not lapse where, although a dental school existed at the time of execution, it was thereafter abolished. The court concluded that the devise should go to the university for the benefit of the dental school, thereby making it subject to cy pres. See also Crisp Area YMCA v. Nationsbank, 526 S.E.2d 23 (Ga. 2000)cy pres held not to apply).

7. *Cy Pres Under UMIFA.* In Yale University v. Blumenthal, 621 A.2d 1304 (Conn.1993), Yale sought to be released from a restriction in a devise made to its medical school. The testator's will specified that the money, a sum of $225,000, was to be used to build a wing to the medical school for the segregated treatment of the "sick poor." The university stated that it no longer maintained separate physical facilities for treatment of the "sick poor" as it did when the testator was a student at Yale and that the amount of money devised was insufficient to construct a separate wing. It sought to be released from the restriction under the Uniform Management of Institutional Funds Act (UMIFA), which Connecticut has adopted. Under UMIFA, if a donor's consent may not

be obtained, an institution may seek judicial release from a restriction imposed by a gift instrument on use of an "institutional fund" if the restriction is "obsolete, inappropriate or impracticable." Unlike the general doctrine of cy pres, the fund is not required to be used to approximate the donor's general intent, here, benefitting the "sick poor," but may be used for the institution's general purposes. The question in the case was whether the devise was an "institutional fund" within the meaning of UMIFA. The court held that it was, reasoning that a restriction placed on a gift to an institution does not violate the statutory requirements that the gift be for the institution's "exclusive use, benefit or purposes" and that only the institution may have an interest in the fund.

8. *Revising UMIFA?* A Study Committee of the National Conference of Commissioners on Uniform State Laws recently recommended several important changes to UMIFA. One of these changes involves UMIFA's "release of restrictions" provision (§ 7), which functions as a cy pres doctrine. The Committee recommended that the provision be revised to conform to the more liberalized versions of the cy pres doctrine adopted in the new Uniform Trust Code and Restatement 3d of Trusts.

Another change which also would bring UMIFA into line with UTC is to permit a settlor (donor) to enforce a charitable trust. Currently UMIFA does not allow donor enforcement, thereby enabling an institution to accept a gift that is subject to restrictions which the institution later disregards. See, e.g., Herzog Foundation v. University of Bridgeport, 699 A.2d 995 (Conn. 1997).

A third change would avoid litigation of the kind involved in the *Blumenthal* case, supra. The definitions of "institution" and "institutional fund" would be changed to clarify that UMIFA does apply to a large charitable trust.

2. Discriminatory Trusts

Over the years, trusts containing terms that discriminate on the basis of race, gender, religion, or other factors have generated considerable cy-pres litigation.

The Girard College Trust Litigation. One of the earliest series of racial discrimination cases in charitable trusts was generated by the will of Stephen Girard, one of the nation's first millionaires. Girard died a widower, without descendants, in 1831. His will devised $2 million out of the residue of his estate to "The Mayor, Alderman, and Citizens of Philadelphia" in trust to establish and maintain in Philadelphia a college

> to provide for such a number of poor white male orphans, as can be trained in one institution, a better education as well as a more comfortable maintenance than they usually receive from the application of public funds.

The will also provided that "no ecclesiastic, missionary, or minister of any sect whatever, shall ever hold or exercise any station or duty whatever in the said college" or be admitted for any purpose to the premises. In Vidal v. Girard's Ex'rs, 43 U.S. (2 How.) 127 (1844), the United States Supreme Court held that the trust was a valid and enforceable charitable trust under the law of Pennsylvania. The Court rejected the allegation that the trust was "hostile to the Christian religion" and against public policy.

In 1869, the Pennsylvania legislature provided for the appointment of a board, called "Directors of City Trusts," to administer the trusts under Girard's will as well as other trusts of which the city of Philadelphia had been made trustee. The legislation was upheld in Philadelphia v. Fox, 64 Pa. 169 (1870). In 1954, two persons were denied admission to Girard College because of their race. The Supreme Court of Pennsylvania held that this denial, required by the will of Stephen Girard, was not a violation of the equal protection clause of the Fourteenth Amendment. Girard Will Case, 127 A.2d 287 (Pa. 1956). The Supreme Court of the United States reversed. In the Court's opinion, the Board of Directors of City Trusts was an agency of the state; thus, the Board's exclusion of the applicants for admission on the ground of race was state action in violation of the Fourteenth Amendment. Pennsylvania v. Board of Directors of City Trusts of Philadelphia, 353 U.S. 230 (1956).

When the case was remanded to the Pennsylvania trial court, it entered an order removing the Board of Directors of City Trusts as the trustee under Girard's will, replaced the Board with thirteen private trustees who were sworn to uphold the letter of the will, and dismissed the petitions seeking admission to the College. This decree was affirmed in Girard College Trusteeship, 138 A.2d 844 (Pa. 1958), cert. denied, 357 U.S. 570 (1958).

Thereafter, the plaintiffs sued in federal district court, seeking an injunction against their exclusion from Girard College on the ground of race. The injunction was granted, and on appeal the judgment was affirmed. Pennsylvania v. Brown, 392 F.2d 120 (3d Cir. 1968). The Court of Appeals held that the change in trustees did not succeed in avoiding a violation of the equal protection clause of the Fourteenth Amendment. Under the authority of Evans v. Newton, 382 U.S. 296 (1966) (see infra p. 953) and Shelley v. Kraemer, 334 U.S. 1 (1948), state action was found in the trial court's substitution of private trustees in place of the Board of Directors of City Trusts. The Supreme Court denied certiorari. 391 U.S. 921 (1968).

As an aside, it may be noted that, starting with the original $2 million in 1831, the value of the Girard Trust had grown to $85 million by 1950 and over $90 million by 1959. By 1957, Girard College had the fifth largest endowment among privately endowed educational institutions in the country, exceeded only by Harvard, Yale, Columbia, and the University of Texas. Of Girard himself, Professor Elias Clark has written: "Stephen Girard deserves better than to be discredited by a provision which was seemingly only incidental to his overall design. His career marks him as a creative, generous and, by the standards of his time, tolerant man." Elias Clark, Charitable Trusts, the Fourteenth Amendment and the Will of Stephen Girard, 66 Yale L.J. 979, 984 (1957). And, the Third Circuit in Pennsylvania v. Brown, supra, noted: "Given everything we know of Mr. Girard, it is inconceivable that in this changed world he would not be quietly happy that his cherished project had raised its sights with the times and joyfully recognized that all human beings are created equal." 392 F.2d at 125.

The Baconsfield Litigation. Another celebrated series of discriminatory-charitable-trust cases arose from the will of Senator Augustus O. Bacon of Georgia, who died in 1914 devising land and an endowment fund to the City of Macon as trustee to hold the land in perpetuity as a park and pleasure ground, to be called Baconsfield, for "white women, white girls, white boys and white children of the City of Macon," with discretion in the trustees to admit "white men of the City of Macon, and white persons of other communities." Senator Bacon's will added:

> I am . . . without hesitation in the opinion that the two races should be forever separate and that they should not have pleasure or recreation grounds to be used or enjoyed, together and in common.

In 1963, several African-Americans sought admission to the park in reliance on Pennsylvania v. Board of Directors of City Trusts of Philadelphia, supra, and for a time African-Americans were admitted. Members of the Board of Managers objected and sought to prevent desegregation of the park by way of appointment by the probate court of new private trustees. The city resigned as trustee and new trustees were appointed. This action was affirmed by the Supreme Court of Georgia. The judgment, however, was reversed by the United States Supreme Court in Evans v. Newton, 382 U.S. 296 (1966). The court found that the park had for many years been an integral part of the city's activities, that it was maintained by the city as a park for white persons only, and enjoyed tax exemption. The mere change in trustees, the court said, could not be assumed to have transferred the park from the public to the private sector.

Thereafter, a Georgia trial court held that the accomplishment of the trust's purpose had become impossible, that the trust had failed and was terminated, and that the trust property reverted to Senator Bacon's heirs. The cy-pres doctrine was held inapplicable because of the finding that the racial restriction was so basic to Senator Bacon's purpose that he would have preferred termination to integration. On appeal, the Supreme Court of Georgia affirmed. In Evans v. Abney, 396 U.S. 435 (1970), the Supreme Court reviewed and affirmed the Georgia decision. The Court held:

> The Fourteenth Amendment is not violated where, as here, a state court operating in its judicial capacity fairly applies its normal principles of construction to determine the testator's true intent in establishing a charitable trust and then reaches a conclusion with regard to that intent which, because of the operation of neutral and nondiscriminatory state trust laws, effectively denies every one, whites as well as Negroes, the benefits of the trust.

Justices Douglas and Brennan dissented.

The import of Evans v. Newton and Evans v. Abney figures prominently in the *Trammell* and *Tinnin* cases that follow.

Trammell v. Elliott

199 S.E.2d 194 (Ga. 1973)

[Clem Boyd died in 1962, devising the residue of her estate in equal portions to the Trustees of Georgia Institute of Technology, Emory University, and Agnes Scott College. The articulated purpose of Clem Boyd's devise was to establish an educational scholarship fund in memory of her parents, to be known as the Boyd-McCord Memorial Scholarship. The scholarships were to be provided out of the income of the fund "for [the] benefit of deserving and qualified poor white boys and girls." The trial court determined that the racial restriction was invalid and applied the cy-pres doctrine to remove that restriction.]

HAWES, J. The appeal here is from an order of the Superior Court of Dekalb County entered on motion for summary judgment in a case brought by the executor of the estate of Miss Clem Boyd seeking construction of her will and direction from the court. . . .

Although two of the named universities to act as trustees of the funds are private institutions, the Attorney General representing the Board of Regents of the University System of Georgia has conceded the requisite state interest with regard to the trust administration on behalf of the Georgia Institute of Technology. We proceed, therefore, on the basis that there is sufficient state action involved to invoke the strictures of the Fourteenth Amendment of the United States Constitution and that the racial restrictions in the devise may not be enforced save in violation of equal protection of law. Evans v. Newton, 382 U.S. 296 (1966); Pennsylvania v. Board of Directors of City Trust, 353 U.S. 230 (1957). The single issue before the court with regard to the devise is whether the trial court erred in applying the doctrine of *cy pres* to exclude the offensive and discriminatory classification. . . .

The existence of a general charitable intent is inferred upon the establishment that the grant conforms in subject matter to any of the legitimate subjects of charity . . . . However, in deference to the intent of the testator, *cy pres* will not be applied where there is demonstrated an intention of the settlor contrary to the inference of general charitable intent that the property should be applied exclusively to the purpose which is or has become impracticable or illegal. Evans v. Abney, 224 Ga. 826, 165 S.E.2d 160 (1968). See, also, Restatement, Second, Trusts Vol. 2, § 399 Comment c, p. 299, and IV Scott, Trusts § 399.2 (3rd ed. 1967). In view of the public policy . . . favoring the effectuation of charitable grants promoting the public good and our own rule disfavoring forfeitures, such demonstration of a specific intent of the settlor as would result in a failure of the devise must be clear, definite, and unambiguous. In such event the trust will fail, and a resulting trust will be implied for the benefit of the testator or his heirs. . . .

The appellant has argued on the basis of Evans v. Abney . . . . This argument is not, we believe, of substance. . . . *Evans* . . . stood for the recognized exception in the use of cy pres whereby from the will the specific intent of the testator conclusively negated any general charitable intention.

The will in the present case did not contain language by which the testatrix intended that the charitable trusts be administered exclusively in the manner prescribed. Other evidence supportive of the establishment of a specific and exclusive intention was also absent from the will, for example, for a reverter clause or an alternative gift over in the event of a failure of the grant. On the other hand, in other parts of the will, the testatrix indicated strongly that she desired that no provision of the will should fail and the funds as set aside revert to her heirs. In Item IX, she noted in this regard that "Adults do not need my life's earnings, and the children who need a college education are the ones who interest me most."

We conclude from the foregoing that the evidence on summary judgment was conclusive of the trial court's finding of a general charitable intent on the part of the testatrix and that the doctrine of cy pres was correctly applied in excluding the illegal racial classification from the charitable grant. . . .

Judgment affirmed.

All the Justices concur except JORDAN, J., who dissents from . . . the judgment of affirmance.

Tinnin v. First United Bank

502 So.2d 659 (Miss. 1987)

[Allan R. Hobgood, a bachelor without descendants, died in 1968. His closest surviving relatives and heirs at law were "the Tinnins," a group comprised of Hobgood's aunt of the half-blood and four first cousins. They were omitted from Hobgood's holographic will and codicil, which were executed in 1962 and 1967, respectively, when his mother was still alive. Although Hobgood's will and codicil devised the bulk of his property in trust for the benefit of his mother for life, this part of the trust never took effect because she predeceased him by a month. The lapse of her income interest caused the acceleration of the remainder interest in the trust, which created an educational trust to be named after his parents, T.H. and Allie R. Hobgood. The trust specifically provided:

> [M]y trustees shall, in their discretion, make loans to students of a state college or university of and operated by the State of Mississippi, who are found worthy and who are of the Caucassion [*sic*] race and to none other.

In 1969, the trustee, First United Bank, applied on behalf of the trust to the Internal Revenue Service for tax-exempt status. In that application, the trustee declared its intention to make loans from the trust to eligible beneficiaries without regard to race, color, or creed. The Internal Revenue Service granted the trustee's application.

The trustee did not seek judicial approval of its decision to deviate from the terms of the trust, nor did it notify the probate court or Hobgood's heirs, the Tinnins, of its decision to deviate. The Tinnins did not learn of the trustee's action until the early 1980s, when the value of the trust assets was around $293,000. The Tinnins then brought an action in the Chancery Court, arguing that the trust must be terminated and its assets distributed to them. The Chancery Court dismissed the Tinnins' complaint, determining that "the unlawful racial restriction, being only incidental, not integral, to the primary objective of the testator, must be set aside to enable the testator's principal purpose to be carried out." The Tinnins appealed.]

ROBERTSON, J. This case tests our confidence in ourselves as a free pluralistic people. It also tests our fidelity to the rule of law.

On the one hand we are asked to decree that a charitable educational trust be administered in a racially nondiscriminatory manner, notwithstanding the testator's unmistakable language that the beneficiaries be "worthy" college students "who are of the caucassian [sic] race and . . . none other."

On the other hand, the testator's heirs at law ask that we employ the law generally applicable to void or lapsed bequests and give them the trust assets which amount to almost $300,000.00, as the federal constitution prohibits state judicial enforcement of such a racially restrictive provision.

We find the holographic will before us, properly understood, ambiguous. Because the court below proceeded without regard to extrinsic evidence, we cannot say with confidence that its decision striking the racially restrictive clause and otherwise upholding the trust accords the will its most just and reasonable reading consistent with the general plan divined from the will and our positive law. We reverse and remand. . . .

One of the great chapters in the evolution of the rights of man records the winning of the right of testation, the power by will to control from the grave what becomes of one's property. The power derives from legislative grant.

Miss.Code Ann. § 91-5-1 (1972). It is exercised by the competent adult as he sees fit, subject to few limitations, and where the testator has acted in conformity with our empowering statutory rules, his will is valid. It becomes in theory almost sacred and in practice judicially enforceable, notwithstanding the testator's death and public or private inconvenience.

A will is privately made law. Like all law, wills are inevitably open textured to one degree or another, notwithstanding the most skillful draftsmanship. Questions of meaning and effect abound. This is more often so with holographic wills. The ultimate authority for the construction of a will lies in the judicial department of the state. The exercise of that authority from time to time requires enforcement of directives not in so many words a part of an otherwise valid will, a task we perform according to certain familiar canons of construction. . . .

As important and central as we regard our duty to implement the testator's intent, even to the point of supplementation or modification in aid thereof, the coin has another side. The testator's right to make his will as he pleases is not unentailed. Our encounter with one of these entailments adds to the difficulty of today's case.

We have often said the testator's intention is given effect only so long as that intent "does not violate the law or public policy." Dealy v. Keatts, 157 Miss. 412, 418, 128 So. 268, 270 (1930); Matter of Griffin's Will, 411 So.2d 766, 767 (Miss.1982). For reasons of social policy, our law has come to provide that one may not wholly disinherit one's spouse, that one may not attempt purchase of a ticket to heaven by leaving his entire estate to the church, that one may not control ownership of property beyond [a] life in being plus twenty-one years. Whatever may once have been the attitudes of many, it is much too late to doubt that a major social policy of our society is that entitlement one is eligible to enjoy on one's merits shall not be denied by reason of one's race, color or creed. This policy is a part of our organic law by virtue of the Equal Protection Clause. There are limitations upon our authority to enforce racially discriminating testamentary trusts. . . .

Without doubt, the T.H. Hobgood and Allie R. Hobgood Educational Trust is a charitable trust . . . . [A]dvancement of education and relief of poverty have been noted as two favorite subjects of charitable trusts. . . .

None of this carries us far, for our question concerns, not the nature or type of testamentary trust before us, but whether the will of Allan Hobgood . . . should be held to have established a non-discriminatory educational trust or, failing that, to direct distribution of the residuum of Hobgood's estate to the Tinnins as his heirs at law.

The Tinnins argue that the racial exclusion was an integral part of the testator's creative scheme and, as it may not be judicially enforced, the trust must fail. The Bank, on the other hand, as trustee, argues that the Court should employ its equitable powers, cy pres variety or otherwise, and strike the racial exclusion from the trust, also for the reason that it may not be judicially enforced. Indeed, all parties conceded at oral argument that judicial enforcement of the racially discriminatory features of the trust is not an available option. It is helpful to consider briefly why and to what extent this is so.

The seminal case is Shelley v. Kraemer, 334 U.S. 1 (1948). There the Court found an equal protection violation in judicial enforcement of a private covenant that prohibited the sale of affected properties to black persons. More specifically, *Shelley* held the action of state courts ordering enforcement of such racially restrictive covenants was state action within the meaning and contemplation of the Fourteenth Amendment. 334 U.S. at 14-18. See also, Evans v. Newton, 382 U.S. 296 (1966).

By way of contrast, the United States Constitution erects no barrier against purely private conduct, however discriminating or offensive.[19] Evans v. Abney, 396 U.S. 435, 445-47 (1970); Shelley v. Kraemer, 334 U.S. at 13. Had the Bank sought to administer the trust adhering to the racial restrictions thereof, *sans* IRS exemption status, of course, and without reliance upon any arm of the state in aid of enforcement thereof, the Fourteenth Amendment may not have been offended.

Assuming nonenforceability of the racial exclusion, what law governs our choice between excision of the offensive restriction or, at the other extreme, declaring the charitable bequest void so that the property passes to those who would take under the statute of descent and distribution?

We find guidance in Evans v. Abney, supra. Evans refused to disturb Georgia's employment of its long-standing and racially neutral law of trusts to decree termination of a charitable trust in the context of the unenforceability of the testator's clearly expressed racially discriminatory enjoyment clause. Holding that the question is one of state law to which the Fourteenth Amendment does not speak, *Evans* expressly

---

19. Excellent summaries of the present state of the law regarding federal constitutional regulation of private educational trust burdened with racial and other discriminatory selection provisions may be found in Matter of Estate of Wilson, 59 N.Y.2d 461, 465 N.Y.S.2d 900, 452 N.E.2d 1228, 1235-37 (1983); and Shapiro v. Columbia Union National Bank and Trust Co., 576 S.W.2d 310, 316-21 (Mo.1978). These cases consider the point in detail unnecessary to today's decision in light of the parties' concession that judicial enforcement of the racial exclusion is not available. See also cases collected in Annotation, Validity and Effect Of Gift For Charitable Purposes Which Excludes Otherwise Qualified Beneficiaries Because Of Their Race or Religion, 25 A.L.R.3d 736 (1969 and Supp. 1986); Bogert, The Law of Trusts and Trustees § 378, pp. 191-92 (Rev.2d Ed.1977).

> reaffirms the traditional role of the States in determining whether or not to apply their cy pres doctrines to particular trusts. Nothing we have said here prevents a state court from applying its cy pres rule in a case where the Georgia court, for example, might not apply its rule.

396 U.S. at 447.

By reason of this state's racially neutral and long standing law of wills and trusts, we would give effect to a clause in a testamentary instrument which provided, for example, for a charitable, educational trust

> for worthy college students who are of the Caucasian race and none others; provided, however, that, if for any reason the aforesaid racial restriction is violated or held unenforceable, I direct that all assets then held by my trustee be delivered to my heirs at law.

This view is the consequence of the existence in our law of the power of testation. Such a testamentary directive would vest rights persons might claim and judicially enforce no matter how inconvenient and offensive to others. See In re Brown, 478 So.2d 1033, 1036-37 (Miss.1985).

We have no such will before us. It is thus incorrect to ask, in the context of today's case, whether Allan Hobgood might have prevented any of his money from going to black college students, if only he had expressed clearly his intent in that regard in his will. Of course, he could have done that. Our question is, given the options of administration of the trust on a non-discriminatory basis or dismantling the trust and delivery of its assets to the Tinnins, which would Hobgood have preferred? Our polestar consideration, as always, is the intent of the testator, the right our law has given each competent adult to direct from the grave the disposition of his worldly goods. . . .

Although today's question is one of first impression in this state, it has been decided often and variously elsewhere—in varying factual contexts, of course. Most famous is the Girard College case, the subject of much litigation, finally resolved in Pennsylvania v. Brown, 392 F.2d 120 (3d Cir. 1968). A will which provided for an educational institution for "poor male white orphan children" was modified through *cy pres* power to include all poor male orphans regardless of race. . . .

On the other hand, we are impressed by the force of Evans v. Newton, 221 Ga. 870, 148 S.E.2d 329 (1966), affirmed sub nom. Evans v. Abney, 396 U.S. 435 (1970), wherein the Georgia Supreme Court held that the trust which provided the for-whites-only Baconsfield Park in Macon must fail; the doctrine of cy pres, unquestionably a part of Georgia law, could not be applied so as to continue the trust by simply removing restrictive racial provisions. The Georgia Supreme Court made no attempt at second guessing the expressed racially exclusive intent of the testator, the late U.S. Senator Augustus O. Bacon, who designated that the "private" park established as his devise be restricted to whites only. . . .

In the end these cases boil down to a question of whether the court considered the unenforceable racial exclusion "incidental" or "integral" to the testator's purpose. This is the approach of the court below in today's case, its ultimate conclusion being that the racial restriction in Allan Hobgood's will was "only incidental, not integral" and thus "must be set aside." But labels so subjective are of little use, as the judicial eyesight varies widely. Our gaze is upon the choice between two options, each of which bears features we are confident Hobgood did not intend, in the context of which efforts at fitting the racially restrictive language of his will under labels such as "incidental" or "integral" seem vain.

The answer to today's dilemma must be found within the context of our general rules regarding will construction . . . .

We will never know what Allan Hobgood would have preferred to do with his money if he had known that no court would enforce his wish that his money be loaned exclusively to white students. The language he employed leaves no doubt that he did not want any of his money to be loaned to non-whites. Disingenuity attends the suggestion that the racially exclusive language of the will was [incidental] or an afterthought. Given the historical context of the writing of the will—the racial turbulence of the 1960's—it is difficult to hold the words "Caucassion [sic] race and to none other" idly inserted.

Recognition of the unmistakable meaning of this clause, however, leaves us far short of solution to today's construction riddle. The Tinnins' gaze has been so focused upon the tree they have found to their liking that they have given us little help in understanding the complex forest that is Allan Hobgood's reconstructed will. The Chancery Court recognized that the racially restrictive clause should not be viewed in isolation but its world also was too small. That Court looked at the racially restrictive clause and asked whether it was incidental or integral. The Court should have directed its attention to the alternative dispositions argued for and sought a just and reasonable disposition of Allan Hobgood's will as consistent as may be decreed by reference to the general plan reflected by his reconstructed will. More precisely, the alternatives below and here are (a) striking the racially restrictive clause and continuing the trust and (b) causing the trust to fail and the property to be distributed to the Tinnins, the testator's heirs at law. We know for a fact that Allan Hobgood did not wish either of these alternatives. The question is which is less offensive [to] the general plan of his reconstructed will.

The point takes on color in the context of the fact that Lucille Hamilton Hobgood Tinnin, Allan's aunt of the half blood, was not mentioned in his will. Indeed, when the will was made, Allan's mother appears to have been his sole heir at law, so that there is no reason for him to have thought of the possibility that Aunt Lucille would share in his estate, much less that her four children might take it all. While it is true that we construe wills favorably to those who would take under the laws of descent and distribution, unless the testator has manifest[ed] an intent to the contrary, we do so far more readily in favor of next of kin than remote kin. If we understand the facts correctly, Allan's mother was still alive on April 22, 1967, when he made his codicil, meaning that even then it was a near certainty that Allan was unaware that the Tinnins might wind up with his estate. Allan's mother died December 31, 1967, a bare month before her son's death on January 31, 1968. Nothing in the record tells us whether Allan, during January of 1968, was competent to revise his will in light of his mother's death. . . .

The question resolves itself to whether, given the unenforceability of the racially restrictive clause, Allan Hobgood's reconstructed will should be held to direct that the trust continue on a non-discriminatory basis or that all of its assets go to the Tinnins. The will as reconstructed in accordance with the principles . . . above is unclear in this regard. The record before us, which is wholly documentary, is inadequate to enable us to answer this question with confidence.

We hold Allan Hobgood's will, so reconstructed, ambiguous regarding the question before us. The Chancery Court erred when it construed the will wholly upon the documentary record. Resort to extrinsic evidence is desirable, if not essential, to the correct resolution of the weighty claims presented. For example, in deciding whether the Tinnins, as statutory residuary legatees, should prevail it would be helpful to know how close they were to Allan Hobgood, whether they were in fact objects of his affection. On the other hand, the Court should ascertain, if possible, the power and source of Allan Hobgood's interest in helping young people go to college and how important this was vis-a-vis his clearly expressed racially discriminatory intent.

We vacate the Judgment entered October 15, 1984, and remand this case to the active docket of the Chancery Court of Lauderdale County for further proceedings consistent with this opinion. At trial on the merits, and because the will is ambiguous, parol or extrinsic evidence shall be admissible in accordance with our familiar rules.

In the absence of extrinsic evidence which, when coupled with the wording of Allan Hobgood's will reconstructed according to Section III above, will provide a discernible answer to the choice presented by this case, there are certain further principles recognized in our law to which the Chancery Court may resort. Charitable trusts are favored and should be enforced where possible. Instruments . . . purportedly creating charitable trusts will be liberally construed in favor of the charity. Where there are two possible constructions of the instrument in question, one of which will render the charitable gift valid and the other of which will cause it to fail, we will adopt the construction which will sustain the charitable bequest, absent manifest countervailing considerations. Finally, there is a presumption, albeit a rebuttable one, that the testator preferred the charitable trust to survive so far as may be within the law.

REVERSED AND REMANDED.

WALKER, C.J., ROY NOBLE LEE and HAWKINS, P.JJ., and PRATHER, SULLIVAN, ANDERSON and GRIFFIN, JJ., concur. DAN M. LEE, J., concurs in result only.

Notes

1. *Canadian Authority*. In an apparent case of first impression in Canada, Leonard Foundation v. Ontario Human Rights Comm'n, [1990] Ont. J. No. 615 (C.A.), the court held that a trust that restricted scholarships to "white Protestants of British descent" violated public policy and exercised its cy- pres power to delete the discriminatory restrictions.

2. *Tax Deductibility of Discriminatory Trusts*. In Rev. Rul. 67-235, 1967-2 C.B. 79, the Internal Revenue Service disallowed a deduction for a gift to an organization that provided recreational facilities that were open to only a portion of an entire community, on a racial basis. See also Priv. Ltr. Rul. 79-23-001. A three-judge federal court enjoined the Service from allowing a deduction for gifts to fraternal organizations that exclude non-whites from membership. McGlotten v. Connally, 338 F. Supp. 448 (D.D.C. 1972), discussed in Boris I. Bittker & Kenneth M. Kaufman, Taxes and Civil Rights: "Constitutionalizing" the Internal Revenue Code, 82 Yale L.J. 51 (1972).

The tax laws appear to be quite tolerant of non-racial forms of discrimination. In private letter rulings, the Commissioner has determined that devises in trust to provide scholarships for deserving Jewish children of high academic ability or to provide scholarships for male Protestant graduates of a specified high school qualified for the charitable deduction. Priv. Ltr. Rul. 77-44-005; Priv. Ltr. Rul. 77-44-007. In these rulings, the Commissioner stated that religious and sexual restrictions are permissible in charitable devises.

3. *Tax-Exempt Status*. In Rev. Rul. 71-447, 1971-2 C.B. 230, the Internal Revenue Service, declaring that "racial discrimination in education is contrary to Federal public policy," concluded that "a school not having a racially nondiscriminatory policy as to students is not 'charitable' within the common law concepts reflected in §§ 170 and 501(c)(3) of the Code." The Service's position was upheld in Bob Jones University v. United States, 461 U.S. 574 (1983). See also Rev. Proc. 75-50, 1975-2 C.B. 581, which sets forth the following guidelines for determining whether private schools have racially

nondiscriminatory policies so as to qualify for tax-exempt status under IRC § 501(c)(3):

> § *3.02.* The Service considers discrimination on the basis of race to include discrimination on the basis of color and national or ethnic origin. A policy of a school that favors racial minority groups with respect to admissions, facilities and programs, and financial assistance will not constitute discrimination on the basis of race when the purpose and effect is to promote the establishment and maintenance of that school's racially nondiscriminatory policy as to students.
>
> § *3.03.* A school that selects students on the basis of membership in a religious denomination or unit thereof will not be deemed to have a discriminatory policy if membership in the denomination or unit is open to all on a racially nondiscriminatory basis.

In McCoy v. Shultz, 73-1 USTC ¶12,906 (D.D.C. 1973), the court dismissed a suit to force the Internal Revenue Service to withdraw tax-exempt status previously granted under IRC § 501(c)(3) to the Portland City Club Foundation, Inc., a private organization that excluded women from membership.

EXTERNAL REFERENCE. Martin D. Ginsburg, Sex Discrimination and the IRS: Public Policy and the Charitable Deduction, Tax Notes, Jan. 14, 1980, at 27.

4. *Gender and Religious Restrictions/Trust and Property Law.* Restatement 3d of Trusts § 28 comment f states:

> When a scholarship or other form of assistance or opportunity is to be awarded on a basis that . . . explicitly excludes potential beneficiaries on the basis of membership in a particular . . . religious group, the restriction is ordinarily invidious and therefore unenforceable. . . .
>
> This does not mean that a criterion such as gender, religion, or national origin may not be used in a charitable trust when it is a reasonable element of a settlor's charitable motivation.

Estate of Wilson

452 N.E.2d 1228 (N.Y. 1983)

[This case consolidated appeals from lower court judgments in two cases, Estate of Wilson and Estate of Johnson.

Clark W. Wilson devised the residue of his estate to the Key Bank in Central New York, in trust, to apply the income

> to defraying the education and other expenses of the first year at college of five (5) young men [from] Canastota High School, three (3) of whom who shall have attained the highest grades in science and two (2) of whom shall have attained the highest grades in chemistry, as may be certified by the Superintendent of Schools for the Canastota Central School District.

Edwin Irving Johnson devised the residue of his estate to the Board of Education of the Croton-Harmon Union Free School District, in trust, to apply the income

> for scholarships or grants for bright and deserving young men who have graduated from the High School of [the Croton-Harmon Union Free] School District, and whose parents are financially unable to send them to college, and who shall be selected by the Board of Education of such School District with the assistance of the Principal of such High School.

Complaints were filed in both cases with the Civil Rights Office of the United States Department of Education. The allegation was that participation in the selection process by the school districts would violate Title IX of the Education Amendments of 1972, 20 U.S.C. § 1681 et seq., which prohibits gender discrimination in federally financed education programs. The Department of Education notified each school district of its intent to conduct an investigation into the complaints. During the pendency of these investigations, the Canastota Central School District agreed to refrain from again providing names of students to the trustee of the Wilson Trust, and the executor of the Johnson will, the president of the Croton-Harmon Union Free board of education, and the state Attorney General agreed that the Johnson Trust would be administered on a sex-neutral basis, as if Johnson's Trust had used the word "persons" instead of "men."

In the *Wilson* case, the trustee brought an action in Surrogate's Court for a determination of the effect and validity of the above-quoted provision in the Wilson Trust. In *Johnson*, the state Attorney General brought an action in Surrogate's Court for construction of the above-quoted provision in the Johnson Trust.

The Surrogate in *Wilson* held that the school district's participation in the selection process was not unlawful, and ordered the trustee to continue administering the trust. On appeal, the Appellate Division held that the administration of the trust according to its literal terms was rendered impossible by the fact that the school district was under no legal obligation to supply the names of qualified male candidates. The Appellate Division therefore exercised its cy pres power by striking the clause requiring the district's certification; candidates were permitted to apply directly to the trustee.

The Surrogate in *Johnson* held that the administration of the trust according to its literal terms was rendered impossible by the school district's unwillingness to do so. Declining to reform the trust in accordance with the agreement reached among the parties, the Surrogate ordered the school district replaced as trustee with a private trustee who would give effect to the trust as written. On appeal, the Appellate Division held that the Surrogate's substitution of trustees constituted state action and a denial of equal protection of the laws in violation of the fourteenth amendment; the Appellate Division, in exercise of its cy pres power, ordered the gender restriction eliminated from the trust.

Appeals to the Court of Appeals followed in both cases.]

COOKE, C.J. These appeals present the question whether the equal protection clause of the Fourteenth Amendment is violated when a court permits the administration of private charitable trusts according to the testators' intent to finance the education of male and not female students. When a court applies trust law that neither encourages, nor affirmatively promotes, nor compels private discrimination but allows parties to engage in private selection in the devise or bequest of their property, that choice will not be attributable to the State and subjected to the Fourteenth Amendment's strictures.

I. The factual patterns in each of these matters are different, but the underlying legal issues are the same. In each there is imposed a decedent's intention to create a testamentary trust under which the class of beneficiaries are members of one sex. . . .

II. . . . There can be no question that these trusts, established for the promotion of education, are for a charitable purpose within the meaning of the law. . . . Charitable trusts are encouraged and favored by the law. . . . [U]nlike other trusts, a charitable trust will not necessarily fail when the settlor's specific charitable purpose or direction can no longer be accomplished. . . .

The court, of course, cannot invoke its cy pres power without first determining that the testator's specific charitable purpose is no longer capable of being performed by the trust. In establishing these trusts, the testators expressly and unequivocally intended that they provide for the educational expenses of male students. It cannot be said that the accomplishment of the testators' specific expression of charitable intent is "impossible or impracticable." So long as the subject high schools graduate boys with the requisite qualifications, the testators' specific charitable intent can be fulfilled.

Nor are the trusts' particular limitation of beneficiaries by gender invalid and incapable of being accomplished as violative of public policy. It is true that the eradication in this State of gender-based discrimination is an important public policy. Indeed, the Legislature has barred gender-based discrimination in education (see Education Law, § 3201-a), employment (see Labor Law, §§ 194, 197, 220-e; General Business Law, § 187), housing, credit, and many other areas (see Executive Law, § 296). . . . The restrictions in these trusts run contrary to this policy favoring equal opportunity and treatment of men and women. A provision in a charitable trust, however, that is central to the testator's or settlor's charitable purpose, and is not illegal, should not be invalidated on public policy grounds unless that provision, if given effect, would substantially mitigate the general charitable effect of the gift (see 4 Scott, Trusts [3d ed.], § 399.4).

Proscribing the enforcement of gender restrictions in private charitable trusts would operate with equal force towards trusts whose benefits are bestowed exclusively on women. "Reduction of the disparity in economic condition between men and women caused by the long history of discrimination against women has been recognized as . . . an important governmental objective" (Califano v. Webster, 430 U.S. 313, 317). There can be little doubt that important efforts in effecting this type of social change can be and are performed through private philanthropy (see, generally, Commission on Private Philanthropy and Public Needs, Giving in America: Toward a Stronger Voluntary Section [1975]). And, the private funding of programs for the advancement of women is substantial and growing (see Bernstein, Funding for Women's Higher Education: Looking Backward and Ahead, Grant Magazine, vol. 4, No. 4, pp. 225-229; Ford Foundation, Financial Support of Women's Programs in the 1970's [1979]; Yarrow, Feminist Philanthropy Comes Into Its Own, NY Times, May 21, 1983, p. 7, col. 2). Indeed, one compilation of financial assistance offered primarily or exclusively to women lists 854 sources of funding (see Schlacter, Directory of Financial Aids for Women [2d ed., 1981]; see, also, Note, Sex Restricted Scholarships and the Charitable Trust, 59 Iowa L. Rev. 1000, 1000-1001, & nn. 10, 11). Current thinking in private philanthropic institutions advocates that funding offered by such institutions and the opportunities within the institutions themselves be directly responsive to the needs of particular groups (see Ford Foundation, op. cit., at pp. 41- 44; Fleming, Foundations and Affirmative Action, 4 Foundation News No. 4, at pp. 14-17; Griffen, Funding for Women's Programs, 6 Grantsmanship Center News, No. 2, at pp. 34-45). It is evident, therefore, that the focusing of private philanthropy on certain classes within society may be consistent with public policy. Consequently, that the restrictions in the trusts before this court may run contrary to public efforts promoting equality of opportunity for women does not justify imposing a per se rule that gender restrictions in private charitable trusts violate public policy.

Finally, this is not an instance in which the restriction of the trusts serves to frustrate a paramount charitable purpose. In Howard Sav. Inst. v. Peep, 34 N.J. 494, 170 A.2d 39, for example, the testator made a charitable bequest to Amherst College to be placed in trust and to provide scholarships for "deserving American born, Protestant, Gentile boys of good moral repute, not given to gambling, smoking, drinking or similar acts." Due to the religious restrictions, the college declined to accept the bequest as contrary to its charter. The court found that the college was the principal beneficiary of the trust, so that removing the religious restriction and thereby allowing the college to accept the gift would permit administration of the trust in a manner most closely effectuating the testator's intent.

In contrast, the trusts subject to these appeals were not intended to directly benefit the school districts. Although the testators sought the school districts' participation, this was incidental to their primary intent of financing part of the college education of boys who attended the schools. Consequently, severance of the school districts' role in the trusts' administration will not frustrate any part of the testators' charitable purposes. Inasmuch as the specific charitable intent of the testators is not inherently "impossible or impracticable" of being achieved by the trusts, there is no occasion to exercise cy pres power.

Although not inherently so, these trusts are currently incapable of being administered as originally intended because of the school districts' unwillingness to co-operate. These impediments, however, may be remedied by an exercise of a court's general equitable power over all trusts to permit a deviation from the administrative terms of a trust and to appoint a successor trustee.

A testamentary trust will not fail for want of a trustee. . . . Accordingly, the proper means of continuing the Johnson Trust would be to replace the school district with someone able and willing to administer the trust according to its terms.

When an impasse is reached in the administration of a trust due to an incidental requirement of its terms, a court may effect, or permit the trustee to effect, a deviation from the trust's literal terms. This power differs from a court's cy pres power in that "[t]hrough exercise of its deviation power the court alters or amends administrative provisions in the trust instrument but does not alter the purpose of the charitable trust or change its dispositive provisions". The Wilson Trust provision that the school district certify a list of students is an incidental part of the trust's administrative requirements, which no longer can be satisfied in light of the district's refusal to co-operate. The same result intended by the testator may be accomplished by permitting the students to apply directly to the trustee. Therefore, a deviation from the Wilson Trust's administrative terms by eliminating the certification requirement would be the appropriate method of continuing that trust's administration. . . .

III. It is argued before this court that the judicial facilitation of the continued administration of gender-restrictive charitable trusts violates the equal protection clause of the Fourteenth Amendment (see U.S. Const., 14th Amdt., § 1). The strictures of the equal protection clause are invoked when the State engages in invidious discrimination. Indeed, the State itself cannot, consistent with the Fourteenth Amendment, award scholarships that are gender restrictive.

The Fourteenth Amendment, however, "erects no shield against merely private conduct, however discriminatory or wrongful." (Shelly v. Kraemer, 334 U.S. 1). Private discrimination may violate equal protection of the law when accompanied by State participation in, facilitation of, and, in some cases, acquiescence in the discrimination. Although there is no conclusive test to determine when State involvement in private discrimination will violate the Fourteenth Amendment, the general standard that has evolved is whether "the conduct allegedly causing the deprivation of a federal right [is] fairly attributable to the state" (Lugar v. Edmondson Oil Co., 457 U.S. 922, 937). Therefore, it is a question of "state responsibility" and "[o]nly by sifting facts and weighing circumstances can the . . . involvement of the State in private conduct be attributed its true significance" (Burton v. Wilmington Parking Auth., 365 U.S. 715, 722, supra). . . .

The State generally may not be held responsible for private discrimination solely on the basis that it permits the discrimination to occur. Nor is the State under an affirmative obligation to prevent purely private discrimination. Therefore, when the State regulates private dealings it may be responsible for private discrimination occurring in the regulated field only when enforcement of its regulation has the effect of compelling the private discrimination.

In Shelley v. Kraemer (supra), for example, the Supreme Court held that the equal protection clause was violated by judicial enforcement of a private covenant that prohibited the sale of affected properties to "people of Negro or Mongolian Race." When one of the properties was sold to a black family, the other property owners sought to enforce the covenant in State court and the family was ordered to move from the property. The Supreme Court noted "that the restrictive agreements standing alone cannot be regarded as violative of any rights guaranteed to petitioners by the Fourteenth Amendment. So long as the purposes of those agreements are effectuated by voluntary adherence to their terms, it would appear clear that there has been no action by the State and the provisions of the Amendment have not been violated" (334 U.S., at p. 13). The court held, however, that it did [not] have before it cases "in which the States have merely abstained from action leaving private individuals free to impose such discriminations as they see fit. Rather, these are cases in which the States have made available to such individuals the full coercive power of the government to deny petitioners, on the grounds of race or color, the enjoyment of property rights" (id., at p. 19). It was not the neutral regulation of contracts permitting parties to enter discriminatory agreements that caused the discrimination to be attributable to the State. Instead, it was that the State court's exercise of its judicial power directly effected a discriminatory act.

In Barrows v. Jackson, 346 U.S. 249, the court applied the same reasoning when it held that a court's awarding damages against a party who has breached a racially restrictive covenant also violates the equal protection clause. The court reiterated that "voluntary adherence [to the covenant] would constitute individual action only" (id., at p. 253). But, "[t]o compel respondent to respond in damages would be for the State to punish her for failure to perform her covenant to continue to discriminate against non-Caucasians in the use of her property . . . Thus, it becomes not respondent's voluntary choice but the State's choice that she observe her covenant or suffer damages" (id., at p. 254). . . .

A court's application of its equitable power to permit the continued administration of the trusts involved in these appeals falls outside the ambit of the Fourteenth Amendment. Although the field of trusts is regulated by the State, the Legislature's failure to forbid private discriminatory trusts does not cause such trusts, when they arise, to be attributable to the State. It naturally follows that, when a court applies this trust law and determines that it permits the continued existence of private discriminatory trusts, the Fourteenth Amendment is not implicated.

In the present appeals, the coercive power of the State has never been enlisted to enforce private discrimination. Upon finding that requisite formalities of creating a trust had been met, the courts below determined the testator's intent, and applied the relevant law permitting those intentions to be privately carried out. The court's power compelled no discrimination. That discrimination had been sealed in the private execution of the wills. Recourse to the courts was had here only for the purpose of facilitating the administration of the trusts, not for enforcement of their discriminatory dispositive provisions.

This is not to say that a court's exercise of its power over trusts can never invoke the scrutiny of the Fourteenth Amendment. This court holds only that a trust's discriminatory terms are not fairly attributable to the State when a court applies trust principles that permit private discrimination but do not encourage, affirmatively promote, or compel it.

The testators' intention to involve the State in the administration of these trusts does not alter this result, notwithstanding that the effect of the courts' action respecting the trusts was to eliminate this involvement. The courts' power to replace a trustee who is unwilling to act as in Johnson or to permit a deviation from an incidental administrative term in the trust as in Wilson is a part of the law permitting this private conduct and extends to all trusts regardless of their purposes. It compels no discrimination. Moreover, the minimal State participation in the trusts' administration prior to the time that they reached the courts for the constructions under review did not cause the trusts to take on an indelible public character.

In sum, the Fourteenth Amendment does not require the State to exercise the full extent of its power to eradicate private discrimination. It is only when the State itself discriminates, compels another to discriminate, or allows another to assume one of its functions and discriminate that such discrimination will implicate the amendment.

Accordingly, in Matter of Wilson, the order of the Appellate Division should be affirmed, with costs payable out of the estate to all parties appearing separately and filing separate briefs.

In Matter of Johnson, the order of the Appellate Division should be reversed, with costs payable out of the estate to all parties appearing separately and filing separate briefs and the decree of the Surrogate's Court, Westchester County, reinstated.

MEYER, Judge (concurring in Matter of Wilson and dissenting in Matter of Johnson). I would affirm in both cases. Although the Constitution does not proscribe private bias, it does proscribe affirmative State action in furtherance of bias.

In Matter of Wilson the trust is private and the only involvement of a public official (the superintendent of schools) is his certification of a student's class standing, information which is, in any event, available to any student applying to the trustee for a scholarship. There is, therefore, no State action.

In Matter of Johnson, however, the trustee is the board of education, a public body. The establishment of a public trust for a discriminatory purpose is constitutionally improper, as Presiding Justice Mollen has fully spelled out in his opinion. For the State to legitimize that impropriety by replacement of the trustee is unconstitutional State action. The only permissible corrective court action is, as the Appellate Division held, excision of the discriminatory limitation. . . .

Notes

1. *Compensatory Preferences*. In Trustees of University of Delaware v. Gebelein, 420 A.2d 1191 (Del. Ch. 1980), the court considered the validity of Harriott E. Higgins' devise of the residue of her estate to the Trustees of the University of Delaware, to pay the educational expenses of "a young, white, female student" enrolled in the Women's College of the University of Delaware who graduated from the Commodore MacDonough School, a public high school in St. Georges, Delaware. The scholarship recipient was to be selected by the president of the University of Delaware in collaboration with the teaching staff at Commodore MacDonough School, subject only to the restriction "that the young woman is not to be selected from a family with ample means. . . ."

In a prior proceeding, brought by the university trustees in 1979, the court exercised its cy-pres power to eliminate the racial restriction in the trust. In this proceeding, the Attorney General sought removal of the gender restriction; the university trustees opposed the petition. Denying the petition, the court first held that administration of the trust constituted state action. It then concluded that "the benign discrimination set forth in the Higgins' scholarship fund does not subvert equal opportunity, but rather promotes it by compensating for past acts of discrimination." Cf. Mississippi University for Women v. Hogan, 458 U.S. 718 (1982), holding unconstitutional the denial of admission of a male applicant, on the ground of gender, to the School of Nursing of the Mississippi University for Women, a state university.

In Crichfield Trust, 426 A.2d 88 (N.J. Super. Ct. Ch. Div. 1980), the court removed the gender restriction of Frieda Crichfield's devise to the Summit, New Jersey, Board of Education to provide a yearly college scholarship for "worthy boys of Summit High School." The court noted that "[h]ere, no party has defended the discrimination as compensatory for past discrimination." In deciding to apply the cy-pres power to remove the gender restriction, the court further noted that at the time the trust was created few female high school graduates sought scholarships for higher education.

Under guidelines adopted by the U.S. Department of Education, effective May 1994, colleges and universities may award scholarships to disadvantaged students even if the effect is that people of color receive a disproportionate number of such scholarships. However, the guidelines forbid awarding scholarships solely on the basis of race.

In Podberesky v. Kirwan, 38 F.3d 147 (4th Cir. 1994), cert. denied, 514 U.S. 1128 (1996), a white student challenged the constitutional validity of a University of Maryland scholarship program for which only African-American students were eligible. The court held that the university's poor reputation within the African-American community did not constitute present effects of past discrimination sufficient to justify the program. It further found that the program was not narrowly tailored to the university's asserted goals.

An important federal court decision involving the legality of university admissions practices have led some schools to rethink their scholarship programs. In Hopwood v. State of Texas, 78 F.3d 932 (5th Cir. 1996), cert. denied, 518 U.S. 1033 (1996), the court ruled that the University of Texas Law School's admissions preference for minority students violated the equal protection clause of the Fourteenth Amendment. Following that decision, the state of Texas announced that it was discontinuing its minority scholarship program. Sam Howe Verhovek, Texas Ending a Scholarship Limited to Minority Students, N.Y. Times, April 16, 1996, at C20.

2. *Other Approaches.* Howard Savings Institution v. Peep, 170 A.2d 39 (N.J. 1961), the court exercised its cy-pres power to excise discriminatory restrictions in the will of C. Edward McKinney, Jr., who devised the residue of his estate

> to Amherst College . . . to be held in trust to be used as a scholarship loan fund for deserving American born, Protestant, Gentile boys of good moral repute, not given to gambling, smoking, drinking or similar acts. (It being my thought that if a young man has enough funds to allow the waste of smoking, he certainly does not need help.)

Amherst refused to accept the devise unless the "Protestant, Gentile" restriction was removed, on the ground that the administration of such a gift would be contrary to its charter. The appellate court held that cy pres was appropriate because the terms of McKinney's will, including the absence of any gift over upon failure of the trust, indicated that "Mr. McKinney was more interested in benefiting Amherst and its needy students than he was in Protestantism." But cf. La Fond v. City of Detroit, 98 N.W.2d 530 (Mich. 1959) (1955 devise of about $25,000 "to the city of Detroit . . . for a playfield for white children"; city resolved to accept the devise "provided the court will . . . make the playfield available to all children without regard to race, color or creed"; held, cy pres denied because "the will does not indicate a general charitable intention to provide for a general charitable purpose rather than for a particular designated object.")

In Lockwood v. Killian, 375 A.2d 998 (Conn. 1977), 425 A.2d 909 (Conn. 1979), Frank Fuller devised the residue of his estate to the town of East Hartford, Connecticut, to establish a scholarship fund for boys from Hartford high schools "who are members of the Caucasian race and who have severally, specifically professed themselves to be of the Protestant Congregationalist faith . . . ." There was no gift over in case the trust failed. Given the racial, gender, religious, and geographical restrictions, the selection committee found it impossible to find a sufficient number of recipients to expend the annual income. They petitioned the court for instructions. The Connecticut Supreme Court found that Fuller was most concerned about the geographical and religious qualifications, and ordered the others removed. The court stated the selection committee would be unable to attract sufficient applicants for scholarships until the racial and gender restrictions are eliminated because no institution would publicize the availability of these racially and sexually biased scholarships. The court found that enforcement of the religious restriction did not involve state action.

3. *Construction*. Modern trust forms often contain a definitions article. It's not unusual to find in that definitions article a boilerplate clause such as the following:

> *Gender and Form*. The use of any gender herein shall be deemed to be or include the other gender and the use of the singular herein shall be deemed to be or include the plural, and *vice versa*, wherever appropriate.

Had such a clause been included in Clark Wilson's will, would a court have been justified in construing "men" to mean "men or women"? Could "female" in Harriott Higgins' will have been appropriately construed to mean "female or male"? What about construing "boys" in Frieda Crichfield's trust to mean "boys or girls"?

EXTERNAL REFERENCES. David Luria, Prying Loose the Dead Hand of the Past: How Courts Apply Cy Pres to Race, Gender, and Religiously Restricted Trusts, 21 U.S.F.L. Rev. 41 (1987); Steven R. Swanson, Discriminatory Charitable Trusts: Time for a Legislative Solution, 48 U. Pitt. L. Rev. 153 (1986); Stephen J. Leacock, Racial Preferences in Educational Trusts: An Overview of the United States Experience, 28 How. L.J. 515 (1985); Roy M. Adams, Racial and Religious Discrimination in Charitable Trusts, 25 Clev. St. L. Rev. 1 (1976);

PART C. SUPERVISION OF CHARITABLE TRUSTS

Richard A. Posner, Economic Analysis of Law

557-558 (5th ed. 1998)

Even where no unforeseen contingencies occur, perpetual charitable gifts raise an economic issue that echoes the concern with the separation of ownership and control in the modern business corporation. A charitable foundation that enjoys a substantial income, in perpetuity, from its original endowment is an institution that does not compete in any product market or in the capital markets and that has no stockholders. Its board of directors is self-perpetuating and is accountable to no one (except itself) for the performance of the enterprise. (Although state attorneys general have legal authority over the administration of charitable trusts, it is largely formal.) At the same time, neither the trustees nor the staff have the kind of property right in the foundation's assets or income that would generate a strong incentive for them to maximize value. Neither the carrot nor the stick is in play.

The incentives to efficient management of foundation assets could be strengthened by a rule requiring charitable foundations to distribute every gift received, principal and income, including the original endowment, within a specified period of years. The foundation would not be required to wind up its operations within the period; it could continue indefinitely. But it would have to receive new gifts from time to time in order to avoid exhausting all of its funds. Since donors are unlikely to give money to an enterprise known to be slack, the necessity of returning to the market for charitable donations would give trustees and managers of charitable foundations an incentive they now lack to conduct a tight operation. Foundations—mostly religious and educational—that market their services or depend on continuing charitable support, and are therefore already subject to some competitive constraints, could be exempt from the exhaustion rule.

The objections to the suggested rule are that it is unnecessary—donors are already free to limit the duration of their charitable bequests—and that it might therefore (why therefore?) reduce the incentives to make charitable gifts. A counterargument is that many perpetual foundations were established at a time when the foundation was a novel institution; a person creating one at that time simply could not have foreseen the problem of inefficient and unresponsive management that might plague a perpetual foundation as a result of the peculiar set of constraints (or lack of constraints) under which they operate.

Notes

1. *Supervision of Charitable Trusts and Foundations.* There is a substantial body of evidence to support Judge Posner's view that closer supervision of charitable trusts is needed. By general recognition, the state attorney general has common-law power to seek judicial enforcement of such trusts, but until recently the power was rarely exercised. The attorney general was usually unaware of the existence of such trusts, and of the possible need for remedial action. The problem isn't limited to the prevention of an unlawful diversion of trust funds. In many instances, charitable trusts, particularly the smaller ones, become dormant or nearly so—the fund isn't being put to use, although the trustee presumably is collecting fees. Dormancy may be the consequence of a variety of factors, including the obsolescence of a poorly conceived trust.

In 1954, the Uniform Supervision of Trustees for Charitable Purposes Act was promulgated by the National Conference of Commissioners on Uniform State Laws. The Uniform Act has been adopted in four states, California, Illinois, Michigan, and Oregon. A substantial number of other states, although still only a minority, have also enacted statutes designed to correct the misuse or non-use of charitable trust funds. Statutes are collected in Scott on Trusts § 391. The central features of the Uniform Act are that charitable trusts and charitable corporations are covered, with the exception of governments, governmental agencies or subdivisions, and charitable corporations organized and operated primarily for educational, religious, or hospital purposes; that the attorney general must maintain a register of charitable trusts; that trustees must file a copy of the trust and periodic reports with the attorney general; and that the attorney general is authorized to investigate the trust's activities and institute appropriate proceedings to secure compliance with the Act and proper administration of the trust.

2. *The Bishop Estate Trust.* A recent and particularly egregious example of the need for closer supervision of charitable trusts and foundation involves a charitable trust established under the will of Princess Bernice Pauahi Bishop, the last descendant of King Kamehameha I, the powerful Hawaiian king who united the islands. With assets worth $10 billion, including 8 percent of all the land in Hawaii, the Bishop Estate Trust is one of the richest private charities in the world. Under the terms of Princess Bishop's will, the trust has only one beneficiary, the Kamehameha Schools, a 3,200-student school for native

Hawaiian children. Of the trust's $200 million in annual income, the trustees have spent about $70 million on the schools. The rest has been added to corpus, after, that is, paying each of the five trustees more than $800,000 a year.

Princess Bishop's will directed that members of the state (then pre-state) supreme court select the trust's five trustees. Over time, the trustees were all well-connected with the Hawaiian political establishment. In 1997, when the scandal broke, the members were Henry Peters, then speaker of the state assembly, Richard Wong, former president of the state senate, Gerard Jervis, chair of the state judicial selection commission (which chose the list of approved candidates for positions on the state supreme court), Oswald Stender, former CEO of a large charitable institution, and Lokelani Lindsey, a key aide to the governor and a former district superintendent of education. Of the five, only Stender had any experience in managing a large charitable trust.

The scandal broke in 1997 when a major Honolulu newspaper published an article entitled "Broken Trust," a scathing indictment of the Bishop Trust's management practices and the trustees. The article's authors included Professor Randall Roth, a member of the University of Hawaii law faculty; a retired Roman Catholic priest who was a trustee of another royal Hawaiian trust; a retired state appeals court judge; and a former principal of the Kamehameha School for Girls. What triggered the article was a massive protest in downtown Honolulu by School alumni, teachers, and students. The protesters accused trustee Lokelani Lindsey of intermeddling in the day-to-day operations of the Schools, unilaterally countermanding decisions of the Schools' principals and the student president. When the students initially objected to the trustee's actions, she called the student president, Michael Chun, into her office and threatened him with telling officials at Princeton University, which had offered him a scholarship, that he was a "rabble-rouser." See N.Y. Times, October 14, 1997, at A1.

Once the scandal broke, the state attorney general and a court-appointed special master launched investigations into the trustees' management. The master's report disclosed repeated accounting and investment irregularities and the absence of any overall plan for spending the Trust's income. The report further found that the trustees had secretly and without any bookkeeping records moved $350 million of accumulated income to corpus and that the trustees had compromised their fiduciary duties by investing Trust assets in investments in which they had personal interests. The attorney general's report, which was consistent with the special master's, recommended that four of the five trustees be removed (the other trustee, Stender, had broken with the others when the scandal first emerged).

Then, incredibly, there was a sex scandal. One of the trustees was discovered having sex with an attorney for the Trust in the toilet cubicle of a hotel men's room. The attorney, who was a married woman, committed suicide the next day, and the trustee unsuccessfully attempted suicide.

Things didn't go smoothly for several of the other trustees either. Two of them were indicted for fraudulent use of Trust assets. The federal Internal Revenue Service, which had been investigating charges of self-dealing and other conflicts of interest, threatened to revoke the Trust's tax-exempt status unless all of the trustees were removed. In May 1999, trustee Stender resigned, and the probate court ordered the removal of the others. See N.Y. Times, May 15, 1999, at A1.

The Trust is now being restructured by the probate court. Four of the five state supreme court justices have announced that they will no longer participate in selecting trustees. The removed trustees face the prospect of millions of dollars in liability under both federal tax law and Hawaiian fiduciary law.

3. *Standing of Donors to Enforce Charitable Trusts and Gifts*. As we noted at the beginning of this chapter, the state attorney general and persons with a "special interest" in a charitable have standing to enforce the terms of the trust. Under traditional trust law, however, the settlor does not have standing. See Scott on Trusts § 200.1. The same is true of donors of charitable gifts, including charitable foundations. In Carl J. Herzog Foundation, Inc. v. University of Bridgeport, 699 A.2d 995 (Conn. 1997), the Herzog Foundation brought an action to enforce the terms of a completed gift that it had previously made to the University of Bridgeport to provide scholarships to students in the university's nursing program. After the gift was made, the university closed its nursing program, and the foundation sought an injunction forcing the university either to reestablish the fund according to the original terms or to transfer the gifted fund to another foundation that was prepared to use it for the original purpose. The court held that the Herzog Foundation lacked standing under the Connecticut Uniform Management of Institutional Funds Act. The court observed that "it would have been anomalous for the drafters of UMIFA to strive to assist charitable institutions by creating smoother procedural avenues for the release of restrictions [for purposes of assuring that their gifts qualify for the federal income tax charitable contributions deduction] while simultaneously establishing standing for a new class of litigants, donors, who would defeat this very purpose by virtue of the potential of lengthy and complicated litigation." Id. at 1002. In light of the dilemma described in the excerpt from Judge Posner's book, do you agree with this reasoning? The UTC reverses the common law rule followed in the *Herzog Foundation* case and authorizes the settlor of a charitable trust to initiate proceedings to enforce the terms of the trust. See UTC § 405(c).

External References. Evelyn Brody, The Limits of Charity Fiduciary Law, 57 Md. L. Rev. 1400 (1998); Evelyn Brody, Charitable Endowments and the Democratization of Dynasty, 39 Ariz. L. Rev. 873 (1997).

DIVISION THREE
POWERS OF APPOINTMENT AND FUTURE INTERESTS

Chapter 16

Powers Of Appointment

PART A. INTRODUCTION TO POWERS

POWERS of appointment are staples in modern estate-planning practice. They are routinely included in trusts for tax reasons and for reasons of adding flexibility to the arrangement.

Power Of Appointment Defined. A power of appointment is generally defined as the authority to designate recipients of beneficial interests in or powers of appointment over property. An owner has the authority with respect to his or her property to designate recipients of beneficial interests in or powers of appointment over property. By creating a power of appointment, the owner confers this authority on someone who is not the property's owner. See Restatement 2d of Property § 11.1.

The property or property interest subject to a power of appointment is called the *appointive property*. The property interest subject to appointment need not be an absolute-ownership interest. In fact, powers of appointment frequently authorize appointment of only a remainder interest in the appointive property, as in the following example.

> *Example 16.1:* G transferred property in trust, income to A for life, remainder in corpus to those of A's descendants as A shall by will appoint; in default of appointment, to X-Charity.
>
> A subsequently dies, leaving a will that exercises her power of appointment in favor of her adult child, B.

Parties. The parties connected to a power of appointment are identified by a special terminology. The *donor* is the person who created the power of appointment—G in the above example. The *donee* (powerholder) is the person upon whom the power of appointment was conferred—A in the above example.

The *objects* (permissible appointees) are the persons in whose favor the power can be exercised—A's descendants in the above example. The donor determines who the objects are by expressly designating them in the instrument creating the power. If the donor doesn't expressly designate objects, the donee is free in almost all states to appoint in favor of anyone in the world, including the donee, the donee's estate, the donee's creditors, or the creditors of the donee's estate.

The *appointee* is the person to whom an appointment has been made—B in the above example. The appointment makes the appointee the owner of the appointed property interest.

The *taker in default* is the person who takes the appointive property to the extent the power isn't effectively exercised—X-Charity in the above example. The taker in default has a property interest that is subject to the power of appointment. Upon A's death, X-Charity's property interest was divested in favor of the appointee, B.

In all cases, there is a donor, a donee, and someone in whose favor an appointment can be made. The other parties are not indispensable. The donee is under no duty to exercise a power of appointment[1] and, therefore, appointees might not always exist. Also, the donor need not expressly designate takers in default.

Powers of appointment are personal to the donee. If the donee dies without having exercised the power, the power expires. Upon the donee's death, an unexercised power is not and cannot be passed along to the donee's successors in interest.

---

1. The *nonmandatory* nature of a power of appointment is in that regard distinguishable from the *mandatory* type of power, studied supra Chapter 13, Part B.

1. Different Kinds Of Powers Of Appointment

Powers of appointment are differentiated in many ways. Two of the most important distinctions are between presently exercisable and testamentary powers; and between general and nongeneral powers. Both of these distinctions relate to the scope of the donee's authority. An extremely important, overarching principle, set forth in Restatement 2d of Property § 12.2, and followed in almost all states, is that the scope of the donee's authority is presumptively unlimited—that is, the donee's authority as to appointees and the time and manner of appointment is limited only to the extent the donor effectively manifests an intent to impose limits.

Presently Exercisable Powers/Testamentary Powers. When the donee can exercise a power only in the donee's will, the power is called *testamentary*. When the donee can exercise a power *either* in an inter vivos instrument or in the donee's will, the power is called *presently exercisable*.

Occasionally, the donee can exercise a power only in an inter vivos instrument. This type of power is sometimes described as a power exercisable by deed alone, although technically speaking the power can be exercised by any instrument or act that is formally sufficient under applicable law to accomplish an inter vivos transfer. Testamentary exercises of powers to appoint a remainder interest are rarely prohibited, but some powers, such as powers to revoke or amend a trust, or to invade the corpus of a trust, are generally thought to be inherently restricted to inter vivos exercises.

General Powers/Nongeneral Powers.[2] A *general* power is one that is exercisable in favor of the donee, the donee's estate, the donee's creditors, or the creditors of the donee's estate. See Restatement 2d of Property § 11.4; IRC §§ 2041(b), 2514(c). In accordance with the overarching presumption of unlimited authority, the *absence* of express language excluding the donee, the donee's creditors, the donee's estate, or the creditors of the donee's estate, indicates a general power.[3]

---

2. Under an older terminology, adopted by the Restatement of Property § 320, but abandoned by the Restatement 2d of Property, there were three types of powers. *General* powers were defined as powers exercisable wholly in favor of the donee or the donee's estate. *Special* (or limited) powers were defined as powers exercisable only in favor of persons, not including the donee, who constitute a group not unreasonably large. All other powers were called *hybrid* powers.

3. In at least one state, however, Maryland, the donee is authorized to appoint to the donee, the donee's estate, the donee's creditors, or the creditors of the donee's estate only if there is express language affirmatively authorizing such an appointment. See, e.g., Frank v. Frank, 253 A.2d 377 (Md. 1969).

A *nongeneral* power is one in which the donee, the donee's estate, the donee's creditors, or the creditors of the donee's estate are excluded as objects. See Restatement 2d of Property § 11.4 comment b.

The following examples illustrate the overarching presumption of unlimited authority:

> *Example 16.2:* G transferred real property "to A for life, remainder to such person or persons as A shall appoint; in default of appointment, remainder to B."
>
> A's power is a presently exercisable general power. It is presently exercisable because the donor, G, did not expressly restrict the exercise of the power either to a will or to an inter vivos instrument. The power is general because the donor did not forbid A from exercising the power in A's own favor.[4]

> *Example 16.3*: G transferred real property "to A for life, remainder to such of A's descendants as A shall by will appoint; in default of appointment, remainder to B."
>
> A's power is a nongeneral testamentary power. It is testamentary because of the donor's insertion of the phrase "by will." Thus any purported inter vivos exercise of this power by A would be invalid. A's power is nongeneral because A is authorized to appoint only among her own descendants, a group that doesn't include A.[5]

> *Example 16.4:* G transferred real property "to A for life, remainder to such person or persons except A, A's estate, A's creditors, or the creditors of A's estate, as A shall by will appoint; in default of appointment, remainder to B."
>
> In accordance with the Restatement 2d's categories, A's power is in the same category as A's power in the preceding example—a nongeneral testamentary power.[6]

2. Invalid Powers

Powers Appendant. Another way that powers of appointment are differentiated is on the basis of the donee's property interest, if any, in the appointive property. There are three categories: collateral powers, powers in gross, and powers appendant. Collateral powers and powers in gross are valid; powers appendant are widely thought to be invalid, *i.e.*, to have no separate existence.

---

4. In Maryland, however, the absence of such a restriction is not sufficient to authorize the donee to appoint to himself or herself; the language would have to say something like: "remainder to such person or persons, *including A or A's estate*, as A shall appoint." See supra note 3.

5. This power would be classified as a *special* power under the older nomenclature because the objects are reasonable in number.

6. The older nomenclature would classify this as a *hybrid* power, not a special power, because the donor didn't identify objects that are reasonable in number.

A power is a *collateral* power if the donee owns *no* property interest in the appointive property. A power is a *power in gross* if the donee has a property interest in the appointive property that can't be affected by the exercise of the power. A power of appointment over the remainder interest held by the life tenant or the life income-beneficiary of a trust is a power in gross.

A *power appendant* arises where the donee has a property interest in the appointive property that can be affected by the exercise of the power. In other words, the power of appointment purports to authorize the donee to divest the donee's own property interest and confer it on someone else through an exercise of the power. If the donee owns an equitable property interest that's subject to a spendthrift limitation, see supra Chapter 14, Part A, should the power be treated as a power appendant?

Powers appendant are commonly assumed to be invalid in the United States. The power merges into the property interest owned by the donee and ceases to have any separate existence with respect to that interest. See Restatement of Property § 325; Restatement 2d of Property § 12.3.

Example 16.5: G transferred real property "to such persons as A shall appoint, and until and in default of appointment, to A and her heirs."

Since the power appendant purportedly conferred on A is invalid, A owns a fee simple absolute interest in the property, not a power of appointment and a fee simple subject to divestment by the exercise of the power. If A executes an instrument purporting to exercise the "power," the instrument is construed as a transfer of A's owned interest. See Restatement 2d of Property § 12.3 comment f. If A executes and delivers a deed conveying the property or an interest therein to another, A thereafter has no power to divest the grantee's property interest by a purported exercise of A's "power."

Example 16.6: G transferred property in trust, income to A for life, remainder in corpus to B. A is empowered by the trust instrument to direct the trustee to transfer all or any part of the trust corpus to any one or more of A's descendants as A by deed or will directs.

A has a life income interest in the trust and a presently exercisable nongeneral power of appointment over the *remainder* interest. Despite the terms of the trust instrument, A has no "power of appointment" over A's own income interest. If A directs the trustee to pay out part or all of the trust corpus to an object of the nongeneral power, the transaction is treated as a transfer of A's remaining income interest in the assets and an exercise of A's nongeneral power over the remainder interest.[7]

---

7. The consequence of invalidating the power with respect to the income interest has important federal gift tax consequences. The exercise of the nongeneral power over the remainder is nontaxable, see IRC § 2514; but the transfer of the remaining portion of the income interest is a taxable gift.

A power can become a power appendant—and *then* become invalid—at some time after its creation, by the acquisition of the property interest subject to the power.

Example 16.7: G by will devises real property to A for life, remainder to such of A's descendants as A shall appoint; in default of appointment, to B. Subsequently, B dies devising all his estate to A.

Until B's death, A had a valid presently exercisable nongeneral power of appointment over the remainder interest. When B died, A acquired the remainder interest subject to the power, causing the extinguishment of the power. Since A's life estate and remainder interest merge, A owns a fee simple absolute interest in the property, but no power of appointment over it or any interest in it.

Powers that Violate the Rule Against Perpetuities. Powers of appointment (other than general powers presently exercisable) are subject to the Rule Against Perpetuities. A power that violates the Rule is invalid and cannot be validly exercised. The question of whether a power is invalid under the Rule is discussed in Chapter 19, Part E.

Powers Without Any Ascertainable Object. A power of appointment is invalid if it has no identifiable objects. A power of appointment has no identifiable objects, and hence the power is invalid, if the objects are described in a way that makes it impossible to identify any person who fits the donor's description of the objects. See Restatement 2d of Property § 12.1 comment h & illustration 18. So long as the donee can appoint to at least one person who fits the donor's description, the courts uphold the power. The fact that the description makes it impossible to know all the objects of the power is not relevant.[8]

3. Creation of a Power of Appointment

A donor creates a power of appointment "if the transferor manifests an intent that [the transfer] shall do so and if the transfer is otherwise effective." Restatement 2d of Property § 12.1. The intent can be manifested by the donor either expressly or by implication. No particular language is necessary; the words "power of appointment" or "appoint" need not be used.

Example 16.8: G transfers "to A for life, remainder, if A dies intestate, to B in fee." This might be construed as implying a general power in A to appoint by will. See Simes & Smith on Future Interests § 892.

8. This test for evaluating a donor's description of objects of a power of appointment is significantly less demanding than the traditional test for evaluating mandatory powers in the United States. See supra Chapter 13, Part B.

Different courts have construed recurring ambiguous dispositive patterns differently and have reached results that are difficult to reconcile. When, for example, property is devised to a devisee "to be disposed of in [the devisee's] discretion," or words of similar import, a court might adopt one of three interpretations. One is that the devisee takes an absolute-ownership interest on the theory that the added language is without legal effect. The language is treated as either precatory or surplusage—merely describing that which any owner of property has power to do as an incident of that ownership.[9] A second interpretation does not regard the language as mere surplusage, but as negating ownership and creating only a power of appointment in the devisee. Under this construction, a further question is whether the power is general or nongeneral. The answer has depended on the devisee's relationship to the testator and on whether the testator has indicated by some additional language that the property should be disposed of within a certain class of objects.[10] A third interpretation treats the language as creating a *mandatory* power that is invalid if the class of objects is not definite and ascertainable. See supra Chapter 13, Part B. This interpretation is likely only if the devisee is an independent fiduciary.[11]

---

9. *Example*: (1) G's will devises the residue of her estate "to A to dispose of as A sees fit."

(2) G's will states: "In case of my death, notify A to dispose of my belongings as A sees fit to."

Although Cases (1) and (2) differ in that in Case (2) there is no language of gift to A, decisions can be found that treat both cases alike. In Cameron v. Parish, 57 N.E. 547 (Ind. 1900) (like Case (1)), and Weiss v. Broadway Nat'l Bank, 322 S.W.2d 427 (Tenn. 1959) (like Case (2)), the courts held that A took an absolute-ownership interest. In Kuttler's Estate, 325 P.2d 624 (Cal. Ct. App. 1958) (like Case (2)), and Dormer's Estate, 35 A.2d 299 (Pa. 1944) (like Case (1), except that A was G's executor), thc courts held that A took a power of appointment. The differing views have obvious differences in result when A dies after G without attempting to dispose of the propcrty.

10. *Example*: (1) G's will devises the residue of his estate "to A, my wife, to dispose of among such of my children as she sees fit."

(2) G's will devises the residue of his estate "to A, my sister, with the request that she dispose of some of the property to my blood relatives."

In McClure's Will, 32 N.E. 758 (N.Y. 1892), a case like Case (1), where A was G's second wife and not the mother of his children, the court held that A took a life estate and a nongeneral power of appointment over the remainder interest. In Flynn v. Flynn, 469 S.W.2d 886 (Ky. 1971), a case like Case (2), the court held that A took an absolute-ownership interest and that the language requesting A (who was a blood relative of G's) to dispose of some of the property among G's blood relatives was merely precatory.

11. *Example*: G's will devises the residue of her estate "to my executor, E, to distribute among such of my friends as E shall select."

In the much-criticized case of Clark v. Campbell, supra Chapter 13, Part B, the court held that E's power was a *mandatory* power and invalid because the class of objects (G's "friends") was an indefinite class. UTC § 402(c), the Restatement 3d of Trusts § 46, and the Restatement 2d of Property § 12.1 comment e provide that this type of disposition confers on E a *nonmandatory-discretionary-power of appointment*. E's power would be valid under this construction.

Another recurring and perplexing dispositive pattern is the devise to someone for life, remainder to the life tenant's "executors and administrators" or some similar phrase, such as "executors, administrators, and assigns," "heirs, devisees, and legatees," or "estate." Courts have had great difficulty in deciding the import of this type of devise.[12] Some courts hold that the life tenant takes a general power of appointment. See, e.g., Keeter v. United States, 461 F.2d 714 (5th Cir. 1972); Estate of Rosecrans, 480 P.2d 296 (Cal. 1971); Powell's Estate, 207 A.2d 857 (Pa. 1965). Other courts hold that a life tenant takes a remainder interest. See, e.g., Newlin v. Girard Trust Co., 174 A. 479 (N.J. Ch. 1934). One court, Will of Grady, 235 S.E.2d 425 (N.C. Ct. App. 1977), held that a remainder in favor of the life tenant's "estate" created either (1) a general testamentary power of appointment in the life tenant, with a gift in default in favor of the life tenant's heirs or (2) a remainder in the life tenant's heirs with no power of appointment in the life tenant. It went on to hold that either way, the Rule in Shelley's Case (see infra Chapter 17, Part B) applied to give the life tenant the remainder interest, which then merged with the life estate to give the life tenant absolute ownership!

If the remainder to the life tenant's "executors and administrators" is conditioned on some event, such as "income to A for life, and if A dies with issue, to A's executors and administrators," other possible constructions arise. Bredin v. Wilmington Trust Co., 216 A.2d 685 (Del. Ch. 1965), held that an implied remainder interest in favor of A's issue was created. In re Clark, 274 A.D. 49, 80 N.Y.S.2d 1 (1948), held that the life tenant took a general power of appointment over the remainder interest. Another possibility would be to hold that A took a *nongeneral* power. Yet another would be that A received a legal remainder in fee (to go with her life estate) on condition that A leaves issue.

PART B. WHO REALLY OWNS THE APPOINTIVE PROPERTY?—FEDERAL TAXES, SPOUSES, CREDITORS

As a technical matter, there is no doubt that the donee of a power of appointment is not recognized as the owner of the appointive property. The conventional distinction between beneficial ownership and a power is stated in Restatement 2d of Property § 11.1 comment b:

12. A possibility that probably can be eliminated is that the life tenant's executors take a beneficial interest or a general power of appointment.

> The beneficial owner of an interest in property ordinarily has the power to transfer to others beneficial rights in the owned interest. This power is an incident of the owned interest and the transfer is directly from the owner to the beneficiary of the transfer. A power, however, is the authority to designate beneficial interests in property other than as an incident of the beneficial ownership of the property. When the power is exercised, it is the completion of the terms of a transfer that started with the creator of the power.

Upon exercise of a power of appointment, the notion is that the appointed interest passes directly from the donor to the appointee. This is called the *doctrine of "relation back"*: The donee's appointment is deemed to relate back to and become part of the *donor's* original instrument. The donee is viewed as the donor's agent, as it were; an appointment retroactively fills in the blanks in the original instrument.

> *Example 16.9:* G transferred property in trust, income to A for life, remainder to such of A's descendants as A shall appoint. A makes an inter vivos appointment to his child, C. Under the doctrine of relation back, A's appointment is viewed as changing G's original disposition to read: "income to A for life, remainder to C."

Technical ownership aside, when it comes to federal taxation and the rights of the donee's surviving spouse and creditors, the law doesn't always follow the relation-back doctrine. The likelihood that the donee will be treated as if he or she owned the appointive property is greater in the case of a reserved power, as distinguished from a power conferred on the donee by another.

1. Reserved Powers

a. Federal Tax Consequences

The application of the federal tax laws to the various kinds of powers of appointment is a complicated subject. See supra Chapter 7, Part A. For reserved powers, basically, the federal tax laws treat the transferor as still owning the appointive property, whether the reserved power is general or nongeneral.

Federal Estate Tax. If the decedent holds at the time of his or her death, or releases within three years of his or her death, a reserved power over income or corpus of property transferred inter vivos, the value of the property is taxed in the decedent's estate. See IRC §§ 2035, 2036(a)(2), 2038.

Federal Gift Tax. An inter vivos transfer is not subject to the federal gift tax, to the extent that the transferor reserves to himself or herself a power of appointment over the transferred property, whether the reserved power is a general power (such as a power to revoke the trust) or a nongeneral power (such as a power to amend the trust in any way except for the transferor's benefit). The theory is that the reserved power renders the gift incomplete because the transferor has not parted with sufficient dominion or control over the property. See Treas. Reg. § 25.2511-2.

Federal Income Tax. The transferor of an inter vivos transfer in which a general or, subject to certain statutory exceptions, a nongeneral power is reserved continues to be taxed on the income generated by the appointive property. The transferor may also be taxed on the income in cases where a power exercisable in his or her own favor, in favor of his or her spouse, or solely in favor of others, is conferred on a "nonadverse party" such as an independent trustee. See IRC §§ 674; 676; 677.

> *Example 16.10:* G transferred property to T, in trust, directing the trustee to pay the income to G for life, remainder in corpus to X. G retained the power to revoke the trust at any time and have the trust property returned to him.
>
> G's transfer of the remainder interest to X was not a taxable gift because of G's reserved general power over the entire trust corpus.
>
> G will continue until his death to be taxed on both the ordinary income generated by the property and also on capital gains (or losses) realized by the trust.
>
> When G dies, the full value of the trust corpus will be taxed in G's estate.

b. Rights of the Donor-Donee's Surviving Spouse

Statutory Reference: *UPC § 2-205*

We have already considered the rights of the donor-donee's surviving spouse in assets over which the donor-donee retained a power to revoke or another type of power of appointment. See supra Chapter 10; Restatement 3d of Property § 9.1, comment j.

Non-UPC legislation in a few states makes property subject to a reserved general power available to the elective share of the donor-donee's surviving spouse, but only if the donor-donee's will exercised the power or manifested an intent to do so. See, e.g., Mich. Comp. Laws § 556.116.

Uniform Probate Code. UPC § 2-205(1)(i) includes in the decedent's-nonprobate-transfers-to-others component of the augmented estate, to which the decedent's surviving spouse has a right to an elective share, "property over which the decedent alone, immediately before death, held a presently exercisable general power of appointment," regardless of when or by whom that power was created. Section 2-205(2)(ii) includes property subject to a power, "exercisable by the decedent alone or in conjunction with any other person, or exercisable by a nonadverse party, to or for the benefit of the decedent, creditors of the decedent, the decedent's estate, or creditors of the decedent's estate" but only if that power was created by the decedent during the decedent's marriage to the surviving spouse. See supra Chapter 10.

The above provisions replaced provisions of the former UPC under which the "augmented estate" merely included the value of property transferred by the decedent *during the marriage* "to the extent that the decedent retained at the time of his death a power, either alone or in conjunction with any other person, to revoke or to consume, invade or dispose of the principal for his own benefit."

c. Rights of the Donor-Donee's Creditors

Statutory Reference: *UPC § 6-102*

If a reserved power of appointment, even a nongeneral power, was created in a transfer that was in fraud of creditors, the appointive assets can be subjected to the payment of the donor-donee's debts.

Even if the transfer wasn't in fraud of creditors, the appointive assets are subject to the claims of the donor-donee's creditors if the reserved power is a general power. It makes no difference whether the debt was incurred by the donor-donee before or after the transfer. See Restatement 3d of Property § 7.2, comment b; Restatement 3d of Trusts § 25. comment e; UPC § 6-102.

> *Example 16.11:* G transfers property "to G for life, then to such person or persons, including G or G's estate, as G may appoint by deed or by will, and in default of appointment to A and her heirs." Creditors of G can subject not only G's owned life estate to the payment of their claims, but the remainder interest also. On G's death, the claims against G's estate can be satisfied out of the property to the same extent as if G owned the property at G's death and had devised the property to A by will.

Until recently, an anomaly existed with respect to a reserved power to revoke, such as that contained in a revocable inter vivos trust. The Restatement of Property § 318(2) and comment i excluded powers to revoke from the definition of the term power of appointment, making the rule that a reserved power of appointment subjects the appointive assets to the claims of the donor-donee's creditors inapplicable. Thus it was generally held that the trust assets of a revocable trust were exempt from the claims of the settlor's creditors. See, e.g., National Shawmut Bank v. Joy, 53 N.E.2d 113 (Mass. 1944); Restatement 2d of Trusts § 330 comment o; Scott on Trusts § 330.12. Several states now have statutes to the contrary, see, e.g., Mich. Comp. Laws § 556.128, and recent decisions have also held to the contrary. See, e.g., State Street Bank & Trust Co. v. Reiser, 389 N.E.2d 768 (Mass. App. Ct. 1979). See supra Chapter 8, Part A.

Another recent development is that the Restatement 2d of Property § 34.3(3) squarely holds that the settlor's creditors are entitled to have their claims satisfied out of property in a revocable trust. The path to the adoption of this rule was cleared by Restatement 2d of Property § 11.1 comment c, which specifically *includes* powers to revoke in the definition of the term "power of appointment." This change in nomenclature resolves the anomaly: It extends the rule of Restatement 2d of Property § 13.3—that the donor-donee's creditors can reach assets subject to a reserved general power of appointment—to powers to revoke in revocable trusts.[13]

2. Donee Powers

a. Federal Tax Consequences

Donee's Tax Consequences—General Powers. Even if the power isn't a reserved power, but a donee power (a power conferred on the donee by another), the federal tax laws still treat the donee of a general power of appointment as the owner of the appointive property. For certain purposes, however, a distinction is drawn by the federal estate and gift tax laws between powers created after October 21, 1942 (called "post-42 powers") and powers created on or before October 21, 1942 (called "pre-42 powers"). See supra Chapter 7, Part A.

For estate tax purposes, the value of property subject to a post-42 general power of appointment held by the donee at the donee's death, and conferred on the donee by another, is taxed in the donee's estate regardless of whether the power is exercised. As for pre-42 powers, the value of the appointive property is taxed in the donee's estate only if the power is exercised. See IRC § 2041.

For gift tax purposes, an inter vivos exercise of a general power of appointment, conferred on the donee by another, is subject to the federal gift tax regardless of when the power was created. A release of a post-42, but not a pre-42, general power of appointment, conferred on the donee by another, is subject to the federal gift tax. See IRC § 2514(a), (b).

For income tax purposes, the donee of a general power of appointment, conferred on the donee by another and presently exercisable by the donee alone, may be taxed on the income generated by the appointive property. See IRC § 678(a).

Donee's Tax Consequences—Nongeneral Powers. For federal income, estate, and gift tax purposes, the donee of a nongeneral power, conferred on the donee by another, isn't treated as the owner of the appointive property.

No federal gift tax consequences occur upon the inter vivos exercise (or release) of a nongeneral power. No federal estate tax consequences occur from holding a nongeneral power at death or from making a testamentary exercise of

---

13. The court in Sullivan v. Burkin, supra Chapter 10, Part A, an elective-share case, considered a power to revoke to be a power of appointment.

a nongeneral power. Being the donee of a nongeneral power doesn't cause the donee to be taxed on the income generated by the appointive property.

Nongeneral powers are implicated by the federal generation-skipping transfer tax. In general, that tax applies whenever property passes to a younger generation of family members without suffering estate or gift taxation in the next oldest generation.

> *Example 16.12:* G's will devises the residue of her estate into a trust, income to her daughter A for life, remainder in corpus to such of A's children as A by will appoints; in default of appointment, to A's children in equal shares. At A's death, her will appoints 50% of the corpus of the trust to one of her children, and the other 50% to be equally divided between her other two children.
>
> Under the federal estate tax, the property is taxed in G's estate and in the estates of A's appointees (G's grandchildren), if they still own the property when they die. The estate tax does not, however, tax the property in A's estate because A's power was a nongeneral power—the estate tax "skips" A's generation. Under the generation-skipping transfer tax, the trust property might no longer go untaxed when A dies.[14]

Donor's Tax Consequences—Why Create a General Power? Apart from the generation-skipping tax, which contains rather liberal exemptions, the considerations discussed so far seem to point in the direction of conferring only nongeneral powers on donees. And it's not only the tax considerations that seem to point in this direction. Conferring a nongeneral power on the donee virtually guarantees the appointive property's freedom from the claims of the donee's creditors and surviving spouse. See infra pp. 995, 996.

The reason why general powers are created is *not* that a general power confers such a greater benefit on the donee that the donor considers its creation to be worth the extra tax and other costs to the donee. At least, this is true if the choice is between conferring a general *testamentary* power or conferring a nongeneral power.[15] The donee of a nongeneral power can be given substantially the same degree of flexibility as the donee of a general testamentary power. The exclusion of the donee, the donee's estate, the donee's creditors,

---

14. The part of the property that is taxed is the fractional part, if any, that exceeded the transferor's GST exemption of up to $1 million when the trust was created. See IRC § 2631; supra Chapter 7, Part A.

15. General powers presently exercisable are seldom created anyway, except for powers granted to the income beneficiary of a trust to invade the corpus of the trust. Even powers to invade corpus are not considered general powers for estate or gift tax purposes if their exercise is explicitly governed by an ascertainable standard relating to the health, education, support, or maintenance of the donee or if they can be exercised only in conjunction with the donor of the power or a person having a substantial interest in the appointive property that is adverse to the power's exercise in favor of the donee.

and the creditors of the donee's estate from the list of permissible appointees is an insignificant reduction in the flexibility granted to the donee because donees seldom desire to appoint to their own estates. The scope of objects of a nongeneral power can be so broad as to include virtually every person to whom the donee would conceivably want to appoint.

In addition, in many circumstances, the donor may consider it highly desirable to limit the permissible appointees. The donor who confers a power of appointment on his or her surviving spouse may anticipate remarriage, or his or her surviving spouse may have children by a prior marriage. The donor may, therefore, limit the appointees to assure that the donor's property isn't diverted from his or her children or other family members.

Why, then, are general powers ever created? The main reason is that there are certain tax *benefits* to the *donor* that can be obtained by conferring on the donee a general power. The most important of these are to qualify the transfer for either the federal estate or gift tax marital deduction or the federal gift tax annual exclusion. See supra Chapter 7.

Federal Estate and Gift Tax Marital Deduction. A trust qualifies for the federal estate or gift tax marital deduction if the terms of the trust grant the transferor's spouse the right to all the income from the trust for life, payable annually or at more frequent intervals, and a power of appointment over the remainder interest, exercisable by the spouse alone and in all events and in favor of the spouse or the spouse's estate. IRC §§ 2056(b)(5); 2523(e). Until 1981, such a trust—called a power of appointment trust—was the most popular device for creating a trust that qualified for the marital deduction.

The Economic Recovery Tax Act of 1981 added a new subsection to the marital deduction sections that authorizes the use of a "qualified terminable interest property trust"—called a QTIP trust—under which the spouse is granted the right to the income from the trust for life, payable annually or at more frequent intervals; if properly elected, the trust can qualify even if the donor's spouse is given a nongeneral testamentary power of appointment over the remainder interest or no power of appointment at all.

QTIP trusts have now become a very popular marital deduction device, cutting down even further the incidence of the creation of general powers of appointment.

Federal Gift Tax Annual Exclusion. Under IRC § 2503(c), a trust for a minor qualifies for the federal gift tax annual exclusion if, among other requirements, the minor is given a general power of appointment over the remainder interest should the minor die before attaining the age of 21 years; a nongeneral power disqualifies the trust for the gift tax exclusion under this section. A "Crummey" power, named after the case of Crummey v. Commissioner, 397 F.2d 82 (9th Cir. 1968), is another device for qualifying for the annual gift tax exclusion; a Crummey power is a general power conferred on the donee by the donor of a trust that authorizes the donee to withdraw from the corpus all or a specified portion of subsequent contributions into the trust, usually made by the donor annually.

b. Rights of the Donee's Surviving Spouse

Statutory Reference: *UPC § 2-205*

Common Law. At common law, the surviving spouse of a donee receives less protection than the donee's creditors. As long as the power is not a reserved power, the donee's surviving spouse cannot ordinarily reach the appointive property (against the wishes of the donee), whether the power is general or nongeneral, presently exercisable or testamentary, exercised or unexercised. The explanation offered by the courts is that the surviving spouse's elective-share claim is against the donee's probate estate and the appointive assets are not a part of the probate estate because they are not owned beneficially by the donee.

A relevant consideration, perhaps, is the context that generates a surviving spouse's claim to an elective share in assets subject to a general power conferred on the donee by another. The major reason by far today for conferring a general power on another is to qualify a trust for the federal estate or gift tax marital deduction. In almost all other cases, the creation of a nongeneral power is preferable. The following example is therefore typical. The donee of a general power, conferred on the donee by another, is likely to be the remarried surviving spouse of the donor of the power (in which case the appointive property was originally owned by the donor) and the takers in default are likely to be either the children of the marriage between the donor and donee or the donor's children by a prior marriage.

Example 16.13: G's will devised the residue of his estate into a marital deduction trust, income "to W, my wife, for life, then to such person or persons, including W's estate, as W shall by will appoint; in default of appointment, remainder to my descendants who survive W, such descendants to take by representation, and if none of my descendants survives W, then in default of appointment, to the X charity." W subsequently remarries. At W's death, her will exercises her general testamentary power in favor of the children of her marriage to G. W is survived by her second husband, H-2. H-2 elects to renounce W's will and claim a statutory elective share in W's estate.

The appointive property is not included in the assets in W's estate to which H-2's elective share attaches. The same result has been reached even in cases where W's appointment was in a blending clause or where W's appointment was in favor of her own estate. See Kate's Estate, 128 A. 97 (Pa. 1925) (rule of this case codified in 20 Pa. Cons. Stat. § 2203, but restricted to general powers conferred on the donee by another); Restatement 2d of Property § 13.7 illus. 3; Restatement of Property § 332 comment b.

Uniform Probate Code. UPC § 2-205(1)(i) broke new ground by including in the decedent's-nonprobate-transfers-to-others component of the augmented estate "property over which the decedent alone, immediately before death, held a presently exercisable general power of appointment," regardless of when or by whom that power was created. Should the framers of the UPC have gone even further and included property subject to a testamentary general power of appointment? Is the donee's relationship to such property as close to ownership as it is to property subject to a presently exercisable general power? Would the inclusion of property subject to a general testamentary power further encourage the already wide-spread use of the QTIP trust for marital-deduction purposes? A QTIP trust is completely immune from an elective-share claim by the surviving spouse's surviving spouse because the surviving spouse either has no power of appointment or a nongeneral testamentary power over such a trust. (The former version of UPC § 2-205 (Former UPC § 2-202) did not include in the augmented estate property over which the decedent owned a general power created by another.)

Non-UPC Legislation. Legislation in a few other states makes property subject to a general power of appointment, conferred on the donee by another, available to the elective share of the donee's surviving spouse. Unlike the UPC, however, it is available only if the decedent's will exercised the power or manifested an intent to do so. See, e.g., Mich. Comp. Laws § 556.116.

c. *Rights of the Donee's Creditors*

Statutory Reference: *UPC § 6-102*

The majority view at common law is that the donee of a general power, conferred on the donee by another, is treated as the beneficial owner of the appointive property *only if the donee exercises the power*. No distinction is made between a general testamentary power and one that is presently exercisable. See Restatement 2d of Property § 13.2. Creditors of donees of special powers, on the other hand, cannot reach the appointive assets even if the power was effectively exercised. The theory is that the donor did not intend to benefit the donee. In a recent case, however, the children of the life beneficiary who also held a special inter vivos power to appoint the principal to his descendants were permitted to reach the principal to execute a support order. This was so even though the trust contained a spendthrift clause. In re Marriage of Chapman, 697 N.E.2d 365 (Ill. App. Ct. 1998).

Explaining the distinction between the exercise and non-exercise of a general power for purposes of creditor access, one court stated:

> When a donor gives to another the power of appointment over property, the donee of the power does not thereby become the owner of the property. Rather, the appointee [donee] of the power, in its exercise, acts as a "mere conduit or agent for the donor." The appointee [donee], having received from the owner of the property instructions as to how the power may be utilized, possesses nothing but the authority to do an act which the owner might lawfully perform.

University Nat'l Bank v. Rhoadarmer, 827 P.2d 561, 563 (Colo. Ct. App. 1991).

When the donee of a general power exercises the power *by will*, the view that the appointed property is treated as if it were owned by the donee means that the creditors of the donee's estate can reach the appointed property for the payment of their claims. See, e.g., Clapp v. Ingraham, 126 Mass. 200 (1879); Restatement 2d of Property § 13.4. The rule prevails even if this is contrary to the expressed wishes of the donor of the power. See, e.g., State Street Trust Co. v. Kissel, 19 N.E.2d 25 (Mass. 1939).

The exercise of the power by will does not confer actual beneficial ownership of the appointive assets on the donee for all purposes. The assets do not ordinarily become part of the donee's probate estate. Thus, in terms of priority, the donee's own estate assets are ordinarily used first to pay estate debts, so that the appointive assets are used only to the extent the donee's probate estate is insolvent. See supra Chapter 6 for further discussion of abatement rules.

In most jurisdictions, the donee's creditors can reach the appointive assets only to the extent the donee's exercise was an *effective* exercise. See Restatement 2d of Property § 13.2 comment b. A few states, however, follow the view that even an ineffective exercise entitles the donee's creditors to reach the appointive assets. See, e.g., Estate of Breault, 211 N.E.2d 424 (Ill. App. Ct. 1965). Moreover, even in states adhering to the majority view, an ineffective exercise frequently "captures" the appointive assets for the donee's estate, in which case the appointive assets become part of the donee's probate estate for all purposes, including creditors' rights. For an explanation of the "capture doctrine," see infra p. 1020.

When the donee of a general power is authorized to and makes an inter vivos appointment, treating the appointed assets as if they were owned by the donee does not automatically mean that the donee's creditors can subject the appointed assets to the payment of their claims. If the appointment is in favor of a *creditor*, the donee's other, unsatisfied creditors can reach the appointed assets only by having the appointment avoided as a "preference" in bankruptcy proceedings. Apart from bankruptcy, the donee can choose to pay one creditor rather than another with his or her owned assets, and the same is true with respect to appointive assets. If the appointment is in favor of a *volunteer* (*i.e.*, the appointment is gratuitous), the donee's creditors can reach the appointed assets only if the transfer is the equivalent of a fraudulent transfer under applicable state law.[16]

In a minority of jurisdictions, the donee of a general power, conferred on him or her by another, isn't treated as the owner of the appointive property even if the power is exercised. See, e.g., St. Matthews Bank v. DeCharette, 83 S.W.2d 471 (Ky. 1935). Of course, if the donee exercises the power in favor of himself or herself or his or her estate, the appointed property becomes owned in the technical sense, and creditors even in states adhering to the minority view would be able to subject the assets to the payment of their claims to the same extent as other property owned beneficially by the donee.

In at least one state, an exercise of a general power in a so-called blending clause (also called a blanket exercise clause) is treated as the equivalent of an appointment in favor of the donee's estate for this purpose. See Stannert's Estate, 15 A.2d 360 (Pa. 1940). A blending clause is one that combines owned and appointive assets together, such as:

> All the rest, residue, and remainder of my estate, *including property over which I have a power of appointment,* I give, devise, and bequeath to. . . .

A minority of states has enacted legislation that affects the rights of the donee's creditors. The legislation is not uniform. Some of the legislation expands the rights of the donee's creditors and some contracts them. The following is a nonexhaustive sampling of the legislation.

> *Michigan* legislation expands the rights of the creditors of the donee of an *unexercised* general power. During the donee's lifetime, the donee's creditors can subject the appointive property to the payment of their claims if the power is presently exercisable. (If the donee has actually made an inter vivos exercise of the power, the rules explained above with respect to inter vivos exercises presumably would be applied.) At the donee's death, the donee's creditors can subject the appointive property to the payment of their claims. In both instances, however, the appointive property is available only to the extent that the donee's owned property is insufficient to meet the debts. See Mich. Comp. Laws § 556.123.

16. In most states, the applicable state law on fraudulent transfers derives from the Uniform Fraudulent Conveyances Act (1918) (in force in about 10 states) or the newer Uniform Fraudulent Transfers Act (1984) (in force in about 26 states). Under § 4(a) of the Uniform Fraudulent Transfers Act, a transfer is in fraud of present or future creditors if it was made "with actual intent to hinder, delay, or defraud" or "without receiving a reasonably equivalent value in exchange for the transfer" and the transferor "(i) was engaged or was about to engage in a business or a transaction for which the remaining assets of the [transferor] were unreasonably small in relation to the business or transaction; or (ii) intended to incur . . . debts beyond his ability to pay as they became due."

Wisconsin legislation adopts the same rules as the Michigan legislation. In addition to general powers, however, powers that are exercisable in favor of anyone but the donee, his or her estate, his or her creditors, and the creditors of his or her estate are subjected to the same rules. See Wis. Stat. § 702.17.

New York legislation expands the rights of the donee's creditors in some particulars but restricts them in other particulars. The legislation adopts the same rules as the Michigan legislation, but limits their application to general powers that are presently exercisable. As to general testamentary powers, the donee's estate creditors can subject the appointive property to the payment of their claims only if the donee, as donor, reserved the power in himself or herself; as to general testamentary powers conferred on the donee by another, the donee's estate creditors can't reach the appointive property even when the donee's will *exercises* the power! See N.Y. Est. Powers & Trusts Law §§ 10-7.1 et seq.

UPC § 6-102, granting estate creditors a right to satisfaction out of nonprobate transfers, applies to donee powers whether or not exercised.

The federal bankruptcy code implies that a general power presently exercisable passes to the donee's trustee in bankruptcy. A nongeneral power and a general testamentary power clearly do not. See 11 U.S.C. § 541(b).

EXTERNAL REFERENCE. Lawrence Berger, The General Power of Appointment as an Interest in Property, 40 Neb. L. Rev. 104 (1960).

PART C. EXERCISING A POWER OF APPOINTMENT

Statutory References: *UPC §§ 2-608, -701, -703 to -704*

Capacity of the Donee. An effective appointment can only be made by a donee who has the requisite capacity. The capacity needed to make an effective appointment is the same capacity needed to make an effective transfer of the property if it were owned by the donee.

Compliance With Formalities. An appointment must satisfy the formal conveyancing requirements that would be applicable to a transfer of the property if it were owned by the donee. A testamentary appointment, for example, must be contained in a validly executed will.

Intent to Exercise. A donee must intend to exercise a power in order for the power to be exercised. The recommended method for exercising a power of appointment is by a direct-exercise clause:

> I hereby exercise the power of appointment conferred upon me by my mother's will of [date] as follows: I appoint [fill in details of appointment].

Unfortunately, the recommended method isn't always used. Often, a so-called blending (blanket-exercise) clause is used. A blanket-exercise clause typically blends the donee's own residuary estate with any property over which the donee has a power of appointment:

> All the rest, residue, and remainder of my estate, including any property over which I have a power of appointment, I give, devise, and bequeath as follows: [fill in details of devise].

Blending clauses, like direct-exercise clauses, clearly express the donee's intent to exercise a power of appointment. They are not recommended, however, because, among other things, they can raise a question about whether the exercise of the power complies with the formality of a specific reference commonly imposed by donors (see below) and because they may subject the appointive property to the claims of the donee's creditors.

In the absence of an express exercise of a power, an intent by the donee to exercise the power can be implied. In the leading case of Blagge v. Miles, 1 Story 426, 3 F. Cas. 559 (C.C. Mass. 1841) (No. 1479), the court described circumstances giving rise to an implied exercise:

> Three classes of cases have been held to be sufficient demonstrations of an intended execution of a power: (1) Where there has been some reference in the will, or other instrument, to the power; (2) or a reference to the property, which is the subject, on which it is to be executed; (3) or, where the provision in the will or other instrument, executed by the donee of the power, would otherwise be ineffectual, or a mere nullity; in other words, it would have no operation, except as an execution of the power.[17]

The majority view at common law is that a residuary clause or other clause referring generally to "my estate" or "my property" does not exercise a general or nongeneral power of appointment, unless other facts establish intent. See Restatement 2d of Property § 17.3.

A minority of jurisdictions follows the so-called *Massachusetts view*, that rebuttably presumes that a residuary clause was intended to exercise a general

---

17. The Restatement 2d of Property adopted the *Blagge* principles.

§ *17.4 comment a, illustration 1*: O, owner of Blackacre in fee simple, by will transfers Blackacre "to D for life, remainder to such one or more of D's children as D shall appoint by her will, and in default of appointment to D's children who survive her and their heirs as tenants in common." D dies and her will provides: "I devise Blackacre to my daughter Mary." D has manifested an intent to exercise her non-general power to appoint Blackacre by her will.

§ *17.5 comment b, illustration 3*: O by will transfers $500,000 to T in trust. T is directed "to pay the income to O's daughter D for life and on D's death to pay the trust property to such persons as D may appoint and in default of appointment to pay the same to O's other children who survive D." D executes a will containing $10,000 in pecuniary bequests to servants, $15,000 in pecuniary bequests to distant relatives and a residuary disposition in favor of her three children. At the time D executed her will her owned assets were worth $35,000 . . . . D has manifested an intent to exercise her power.

power of appointment even though the clause makes no reference to powers.[18] These states recognize the tendency of donees to view general powers as equivalent to ownership. See, e.g., Amory v. Meredith, 7 Allen (Mass.) 397 (1863). A number of jurisdictions have adopted the minority (Massachusetts) view by legislation, and occasionally that view has been extended to nongeneral powers in cases in which the residuary legatees were objects of the nongeneral power.

The UPC adopts a variation of the minority (Massachusetts) view. Under § 2-608, a general power is presumed exercised by a residuary clause, but only if the donor failed to create a gift in default of appointment. This rule recognizes the fact that most general powers are created in marital deduction trusts that include a well-thought-out gift-in-default clause, the terms of which usually represent the shared intent of both the donor and donee. The strict minority (Massachusetts) view defeats that gift-in-default clause, but the UPC view does not.

If there is no gift-in-default clause, the UPC presumes the residuary clause exercises the power. The alternative would be that the appointive property would return to the donor's estate and require that it be reopened if, as is likely, the donor predeceased the donee. The UPC view is codified in Mich. Comp. Laws § 556.114.

Conflict of Laws. The traditional view is that the law of the donor's domicile governs issues concerning the donee's intent to exercise a power. See, e.g., Beals v. State Street Bank & Trust Co., 326 N.E.2d 896 (Mass. 1975); Bank of New York v. Black, 139 A.2d 393 (N.J. 1958)); Matter of Estate of Rossi, 634 N.Y.S.2d 372 (Surr. Ct. 1995). But see, e.g., White v. United States, 680 F.2d 1156 (7th Cir. 1982) (law of donee's domicile governs). See also Restatement 2d Conflict of Laws § 275 (1971) ("Whether a power to appoint by will interests in movables is exercised by a general bequest not mentioning the power is determined by the law governing the construction of the donee's will (see § 264), unless the donor manifested a different intention."); UPC § 2-703 (1990).

EXTERNAL REFERENCES. See (as to movables) Scott on Trusts §§ 629-42 and (as to real property) Restatement 2d of Conflict of Laws §§ 281-82 (1971); Scott on Trusts §§ 661-63. See also Sheldon F. Kurtz, Powers of Appointment Under the 1990 Uniform Probate Code: What Was Done—What Remains to be Done, 55 Alb. L. Rev.1151, 1172-1182 (1992); Harrison F. Durand & Charles

---

18. In 1978, Massachusetts itself abrogated that view by adopting a statute similar to former UPC § 2-610, which codified the majority common-law view. See Mass. Gen. Laws ch. 191, § 1(A)(4).

L. Herterich, Conflict of Laws and the Exercise of Powers of Appointment, 42 Cornell L. Q. 185 (1957).

Specific-Reference Requirements. In creating powers of appointment, it has become common practice for donors to provide that the power can only be exercised by language that specifically refers to the power. Specific-reference clauses were a pre-1942 invention to prevent inadvertent exercises of general powers and thereby avoid federal transfer taxes that applied only if the general power was exercised. See supra p. 992.

Motes/Henes Trust v. Motes

761 S.W.2d 938 (Ark. 1988)

HAYS, J. The single issue presented by this appeal is whether a reference in the testator's will to a power of appointment was sufficient to exercise a power of appointment in a trust instrument.

Helen Fay Henes, deceased, executed a will in 1979 containing the following residuary clause:

> I give, devise and bequeath all of the remainder and residue of my estate together with *property to which I may have a power of appointment at the time of my death,* to the trustee hereinafter named, to be held in trust for the uses. . . . [Emphasis added.]

In 1982, the Motes/Henes trust was established for Helen Fay Henes and her sister, Elizabeth Henes Motes, in which was placed approximately $6,000,000 from interests the sisters had redeemed from their ownership in certain businesses. The trust contained the following provision:

> This trust shall terminate with respect to the separate trust share of each grantor [the two sisters] upon the death of said grantor. Upon such termination, the remaining assets of said separate trust shall be paid to such person or persons or trusts as grantor may, *by specific reference hereto, appoint in her Last Will and Testament.* [Emphasis added.]

Helen Fay Henes died in April 1983 and in February 1988 the trustee of the Motes/Henes trust petitioned for the consolidation of the probate and chancery proceedings and for construction of the power of appointment in the will. Consolidation was granted and following a hearing the trial court held that the language of the will was sufficient to exercise the power of appointment defined in the trust. The trustee and Elizabeth Henes Motes have appealed. Respondent-Appellees are the children of Elizabeth Henes Motes.

The question is: When a power of appointment requires a specific reference to it, as does the trust in this case, will a general reference in the will be sufficient to exercise the power requiring specific reference?

The general rule is defined in Restatement (Second) of Property, (1986):

> § 17.1 Significance of Donee's Intent to Appoint.
>
> In order for a donee to exercise a power effectively it must be established—
>
> (1) That the donee intended to exercise it; and
>
> (2) That the expression of the intention complies with the requirements of exercise imposed by the donor and by rules of law.

The problem here concerns the second requirement and the question we must decide is whether Ms. Henes' will provision, making reference to "property to which I may have a power of appointment at the time of my death," is sufficient to exercise the power of appointment in the trust, or does the law require that she must have made reference to the trust instrument itself.

Finding no cases of our own on this topic, we have turned to other sources for guidance. The Reporter's Note to section 17.1 of the Restatement is primarily devoted to the problem in our case. While the Restatement discusses cases it classifies as "supporting" the rule and those "contrary" to the rule, a closer examination of those cases reveals that the division would be more aptly placed between those cases that construe the "specific reference" requirement literally, and those that favor a flexible interpretation, focusing more on the intent of the donee. See also Annotation, 15 A.L.R. 4th 810 (1982), which distinguishes the cases between those that require specific reference and those that do not.

Our research does not produce a clear majority or trend on either side of the question. We prefer the approach focusing on the intent of the donor, however, as we regard it as the better reasoned view.[19] It is also in keeping with our general approach to the interpretation of wills, which has as its paramount principle that the intention of the testator will govern, as well as the rule that wills should be liberally construed. [I]n Moore v. Avery, 146 Ark. 193, 225 S.W. 599 (1920), in construing a will, we held that the phrase, "all my property," was sufficient to refer to and exercise a power of appointment. While Moore does not involve a "specific reference" requirement, it nevertheless reflects the more liberal approach. See generally, Annotation, Power of Appointment-Execution, 15 A.L.R.3d 346 (1967).

In Roberts v. Northern Trust Co., 550 F. Supp. 729 (N.D. Ill. 1982), the court was faced with the same issue and reviewed Illinois law to determine the correct approach. The court found that in a significant power of appointment case, the Illinois court had drawn on three basic principles of will construction:

---

19. Other cases favoring the "intent" approach include: Roberts v. Northern Trust Co., 550 F. Supp. 729 (N.D. Ill. 1982); Cross v. Cross, 559 S.W.2d 196 (Mo. App. 1977); First Union National Bank v. Moss, 32 N.C. App. 499, 233 S.E.2d 88 (1977); McKelvy v. Terry, 370 Mass. 328, 346 N.E.2d 912 (1976).

1) that the intent of the testator controls and courts should construe wills to give effect to that intention; 2) a devise or bequest should not be voided because of errors in describing the subject matter as long as enough remains to show the testator's intent; and 3) the court will use its equitable powers to correct technical defects in a will in order to effect the testator's intent. From those general rules the court fashioned the following test for the "specific reference" problem:

> Where the evidence of intent is powerful, the question of compliance should be examined in a light which favors fulfillment of both the donor's desire for assurance and the donee's intent. Where, however, evidence of the donee's intent is weak, a liberal construction of the condition of specific reference may well defeat the limitations of both donor and donee.

Following the approach in *Roberts*, supra, we find the evidence of intent in this case is very strong and therefore have no problem with a more liberal construction of the "specific reference" requirement. The evidence of Fay Henes's intent came from the testimony of John L. Johnson, who was the attorney for both sisters. He had drafted the wills for both, and had also drafted the trust agreement. He testified that at the time of drafting the will he had discussed with Ms. Henes how she wanted to dispose of her property and she told him she wanted her sister to be benefitted and the property to go to her nieces and nephews, her sister's children. The will was drafted to effectuate that intent, giving her sister a life estate through the trust, for her enjoyment during her lifetime, with the property ultimately going to the nieces and nephews.

When Johnson drafted the trust agreement he reviewed Ms. Henes' will and decided there was no need to make any changes in it. He noted that the provision in the will on the power of appointment would operate to exercise all powers of appointment that Ms. Henes would have, to pass the property under a trust arrangement that was set up under her will. Johnson stated that this was absolutely consistent with his view and understanding of Ms. Henes' intent.

Johnson further commented that in drafting the trust, which was irrevocable, he wanted to avoid placing Ms. Henes in the position of being unable to change the beneficiaries of her estate by naming them in the trust instrument. By not putting final testamentary disposition provisions in the trust, it retained for Ms. Henes the ability at any point to change her mind as to the disposition of her estate.

The trial court noted that another significant factor was the problem of estate taxes. If the power was not exercised by the will, double taxation would result, and the trial judge observed that people do not intend tax consequences of that nature. We agree.

Appellant urges that we must ascertain the intent of the testator at the time of the execution of the will, citing *Moore*, supra. That is true, but it does not mean that we eliminate after-acquired property from being disposed by way of a will executed previously. . . . This is also the rule specifically as it relates to powers of appointment. Restatement (Second) of Property, § 17.6 (1986).

In this case, Ms. Henes' will refers first to, "*all* of the remainder and residue of my estate," and then specifically refers to "property to which *I may have a power of appointment at the time of my death*." It seems clear that the testator's intent at the time of execution was to include any after-acquired property.

AFFIRMED.

Note and Questions

1. *Restatement 2d of Property*. In *Motes/Henes Trust*, the court referred the § 17.1 of the Restatement 2d of Property. The court did not refer to comment b, however, which provides:

> *b. Requirements imposed by the donor.* The donor may impose formal requirements on the effective exercise of the power. . . . The donor may want to make certain that the donee does not inadvertently exercise the power; and to avoid this possibility, specific reference to the power may be required in order for it to be effectively exercised. Failure by the donee to comply with the formal requirements imposed by the donor in regard to the exercise of a power may prevent an effective exercise of it even though the intention of the donee to exercise the power is otherwise clearly manifested. . . .
>
> Illustrations:
>
> 1. O by will transfers property to T in trust. T is directed to pay the income to W, O's wife, for life. On W's death "T shall pay the trust property to or hold the same for the benefit of such person or persons or the estate of W in such amounts and proportions and for such estates and interests and outright or upon such terms, trusts, conditions, and limitations as W shall appoint by a will executed after O's death referring specifically to the power herein given to W." O's will makes provision for the disposition of the trust property on W's death in default of her exercise of her general power to appoint by will. The residuary clause in W's will provides as follows: "All the rest and residue of my property, wheresoever the same is situated, including any property over which I may have any power of appointment, I hereby bequeath, devise and appoint as follows." The general language of W's residuary clause does not satisfy the requirement imposed by O that specific reference to the power must be made in any exercise of it. W has not effectively exercised her power to appoint, and the appointive property passes to the takers in default of appointment.

2. *Uniform Probate Code.* How would *Motes/Henes Trust* have been decided under UPC §§ 2-701 and 2-704? How would First National Bank v. Walker, below, have been decided?

First National Bank v. Walker

607 S.W.2d 469 (Tenn. 1980)

BROCK, C.J. Charles Miller died on March 17, 1975, leaving an estate of approximately $800,000.00 which by his last will and testament, dated October 4, 1972, was divided into two trusts, a "marital deduction" trust and a residuary trust. His wife, Allie Bess Walker Miller, was made the lifetime beneficiary of the marital deduction trust and was given a power of appointment over the corpus thereof. However, this power of appointment was limited by the following language:

> Such power of appointment shall be exercisable by my said wife exclusively and in all events but shall be exercisable only by specific reference to said power in her last will and testament.

At issue is the question whether Allie Bess effectively exercised the power of appointment thus granted by the language employed in her last will and testament, dated October 17, 1969. That language is as follows:

> I give, bequeath and devise all my property both real, personal and mixed to Charles C. Miller, my husband, but if he predeceases me, then I bequeath and devise my property, including all property over which I shall have any power of appointment at my death, to my nephew, William Bryan Walker, Jr., of Oneonta, Alabama, and to my husband's nephew, Harold Fred Miller, in equal parts. If either of said persons shall be deceased, then their share is to go to their next of kin.

The crucial question is whether Mrs. Miller's reference to ". . . all property over which I shall have any power of appointment . . ." is a sufficient compliance with the stipulation in her husband's will that her power of appointment ". . . shall be exercisable only by a specific reference to said power in her last will and testament."[20]

The Chancellor held that the power of appointment granted to Mrs. Miller had been effectively exercised; but, the Court of Appeals reached a contrary conclusion and reversed the decree of the Chancellor.

---

20. Inherent in this question is another: Will the courts recognize the validity of and require compliance with a donor's requirement that the donee of a power of appointment must, to effect an exercise thereof, make "specific reference" to the power.

The real parties in interest are Mr. Bryan Walker, Jr., of Oneonta, Alabama, and Mr. Harold Fred Miller of Athens, Tennessee. If the power of appointment granted to Mrs. Miller was effectively exercised, upon her death the corpus of the marital deduction trust vested equally in Mr. Walker and Mr. Harold Fred Miller under the will of Mrs. Miller; but, if the power is held to have been not properly exercised, the whole of the corpus would be distributed to Mr. Harold Fred Miller under the residuary trust created by the last will and testament of Mr. Charles Miller.

The material facts have been stated by the Court of Appeals in an opinion by Judge Goddard as follows:

> Harold Fred Miller is the nephew of Charles Miller, deceased. For many years Harold and Charles were very close, and were jointly engaged in various business enterprises. In October, 1973, Charles and Allie Bess Miller adopted Harold as their son. A few days later they deeded him their very substantial farm. William Bryan Walker is the nephew of Allie Bess, but is in no way related to Charles. He was on good terms with both of them and saw them once or twice a year. . . .
>
> The proof shows that Charles made several wills. The first will was executed in 1964 and was drafted by Attorney Thomas Boyd. It contained a marital deduction trust with the power of appointment which provided:
>
>> Upon the death of my said wife, the trustee shall pay and distribute the entire principal of trust A and any accrued, accumulated or unpaid net income thereof which would have been payable to my said wife had she lived, as she appoint by a provision of her will, specifically referring to this power of appointment (including the power in her to appoint all thereof to her estate and free of trust).
>
> After executing three codicils, Charles executed a new will in September, 1969, which revoked the 1964 will. The 1969 will contained, verbatim, the above quoted grant of a power of appointment. Then in October, 1969, Attorney Thomas Boyd drafted Allie Bess' last will and testament in which she devised and bequeathed "all property over which I shall [sic] any power of appointment at my death" equally to the appellant and the appellee. Allie Bess' 1969 will revoked a prior will which contained no reference to a power of appointment. Finally, sometime around 1970, Charles changed attorneys, employing William Biddle in place of Thomas Boyd. In October, 1972, Charles executed his final will containing the previously quoted grant of a general testamentary power of appointment to Allie Bess.
>
> At trial, attorney Boyd testified that when he drafted Allie Bess' last will and testament he had a copy of Charles' 1969 will in his file which contained the marital deduction trust, and that he was aware that it granted her a power of appointment. He testified that he had no personal knowledge of who instructed him to draw Allie Bess' last will, since the instructions came to him through his secretary. He further testified that any instructions to him were always as a result

of either a joint consultation with the Millers or a consultation with Charles alone. He was certain that the Millers were aware of the status of each other's will.

In addition to the above, Boyd testified that it was the intent of Allie Bess to make the appellant and the appellee equal beneficiaries of her estate, and that in writing the will it was his intention to exercise the power of appointment granted to Allie Bess and Charles' 1969 will, because that was what she had wanted.

Attorney William Biddle also testified at trial, which testimony will be summarized. Biddle had a special interest in estate planning to avoid federal and state death taxes. He drafted Charles' last will, at which time he was aware of Allie Bess' last will. Charles' major concerns were (1) to avoid as much tax as possible and (2) to provide for Allie Bess without giving her the estate outright. Biddle advised Charles that to qualify for the marital deduction he must give Allie Bess a general power of appointment over the marital deduction trust; but, that the power could be restricted by requiring a specific reference in her will to exercise it. If Allie Bess improperly exercised the power, Charles could designate the beneficiaries under his will to receive the corpus of the trust. Biddle specifically advised Charles that in his opinion the general reference in Allie Bess' will would not exercise the power granted in Charles' will since it required a specific reference.

Our first task, of course, is to ascertain, as best we can, the intent of the testator-donor of the power of appointment. Just what did Charles Miller mean by use of the words ". . . shall be exercisable only by specific reference to said power in her last will and testimony [sic]"? Did he mean a more specific reference than that employed by Allie Bess in her will by use of the words " . . . all property over which I shall have any power of appointment at my death . . . ."? We must determine that intent by making a fair assessment of the words used by the testator-donor in his will, considering the instrument as a whole, read in light of the circumstances known to the testator at the time the will was executed.

We have no reported decision in this state dealing with the particular problem presented. The reported decisions in other jurisdictions, as might be expected, are not unanimous. Some have held that a donor's requirement that the donee make "a specific reference" to the donated power in order to effect its exercise, was intended merely to prevent an inadvertent exercise of such power; whereas, other courts have held that the donor in making such a requirement truly intends to require that the donee refer specifically to the donated power in order to effect an exercise thereof, hoping that the donee will fail to comply with this requirement with the result that the property subject to the power will pass under the will of the donor to recipients of his own choosing rather than to beneficiaries who might be appointed by the donee. Holding that the donor's intent in requiring a specific reference to the power donated was merely to prevent an inadvertent exercise thereof, are Shine v. Monahan, 354 Mass. 680,

241 N.E.2d 854 (1968); McKelvy v. Terry, 370 Mass. 328, 346 N.E.2d 912 (1976); First Union Nat. Bank v. Moss, 32 N.C. App. 499, 233 S.E.2d 88 (1977); Cross v. Cross, Mo. App., 559 S.W.2d 196 (1977). See, also, Restatement of Property, § 347 (American Law Institute). Cases holding that the donor intended a strict and literal compliance with his requirement that the donee exercise the donated power by specific reference thereto are In Re Estate of Schede, 426 Pa. 93, 231 A.2d 135 (1967); Holzbach v. United Virginia Bank, 216 Va. 482, 219 S.E.2d 868 (1975).

The cited cases as well as the instant case may be better understood if we digress for a brief consideration of certain aspects of the federal estate tax laws. Powers of appointment play an important role under the marital deduction trust provisions of the Internal Revenue Code, § 2056. In order to qualify for the marital deduction, the code makes it clear that any property which passes to a spouse without taxation should end up in that spouse's estate and, therefore, cannot be a "terminable interest." Thus, under Internal Revenue Code, § 2056(b)(5), if marital deduction property is placed in trust with income for life to the spouse, that spouse must have a power of appointment which will include the trust corpus in the subsequent estate under Internal Revenue Code, § 2041, that is, some general power of appointment.

It has become a popular estate planning technique for an owner of property to grant to the spouse a life interest and a general power of appointment in order to qualify for the marital deduction, but, to limit the manner in which it can be exercised. Under existing federal law and regulations, such a restriction does not deprive the power of its general character and, thus, does not defeat the marital deduction. Treasury Regulation, § 20-2056(b)-5(g)(4). Under this arrangement, the residual beneficiary under the will of the original grantor will receive the trust corpus unless the spouse has exercised the power of appointment *exactly as directed*. Obviously, this technique was attempted in the case at bar. . . .

Considering Charles Miller's will as a whole and the facts surrounding its execution, we conclude that Charles intended to require of Allie Bess strict compliance with his requirement that in order to exercise her power of appointment she must make "a specific reference" to the power which he had granted her. We further conclude that the general reference contained in her last will and testament was not a compliance with Charles' requirement, although we are satisfied, as found by the Chancellor, that Allie Bess intended the language that she used to be effective to exercise the power that Charles had granted to her. . . .

We find of compelling force the evidence that Charles continued to require a "specific reference" after learning from an attorney schooled in estate planning and death taxes that the general reference to "any power of appointment" contained in Allie Bess' will dated 1969 probably was not an effective exercise of the power of appointment which he had granted to her.

Each case of this kind, of course, must be determined upon its own facts respecting the sometimes elusive intent of the testator. We believe our conclusion to be the correct one, but, it is limited to the peculiar facts of this case.

The decree of the Court of Appeals is affirmed. Costs are taxed against petitioner, William Bryan Walker, Jr., and surety.

FONES, COOPER and HARBISON, JJ., concur.

Notes and Questions

1. *Testator's Intent.* The court in the *Walker* case was concerned about carrying out the testator's intent. In cases such as this, however, there are two testators and their intents conflict. Why did the court prefer Mr. Miller's intent? Mr. Miller's intent was to deprive by all legal means the power of his wife to exercise her general power, an act on her part that he could not directly prohibit. Ms. Miller's intent was to exercise her general power, and she instructed her attorney to that effect. If a general reformation doctrine for wills were to be adopted, would *Walker* have been an appropriate case for reforming Ms. Miller's will—by inserting an appropriately specific reference to her husband's will? See supra Chapter 12, Part C.

2. *Restatement 2d of Property.* The *Walker* decision is supported by the Restatement 2d of Property § 17.1 comment b, illustration 1 (set forth supra p. 1005).

3. *Quality of Legal Services.* Consider the quality of legal services provided to both the donor and the donee in the *Walker* case. If you were the attorney for Ms. Miller, the donee, and if you knew—as attorney Boyd did—that Mr. Miller's 1969 will contained a specific-reference requirement, would you have drafted her will differently? If you were the attorney for Mr. Miller, and if you knew—as attorney Biddle did—that Ms. Miller's 1969 will was drafted as it was, would you have drafted Mr. Miller's 1972 will differently? See Restatement 2d of Property § 17.1 comment b, illustration 2; Treas. Reg. § 20.2056(b)-5(g)(4).

4. *Reference to Prior Revoked Will Creating a Power.* Suppose the donee of a power created by a second will that includes a specific-reference clause attempts to exercise the power but refers to an earlier revoked will that also created a power with a specific-reference clause. Is the exercise effective? In Estate of Hamilton, 593 N.Y.S.2d 372 (App. Div. 1993), the court held that since the exercise referred to the earlier revoked will, it did not comply with the second will's specific-reference requirement.

PART D. EFFECTIVENESS OF THE DONEE'S APPOINTMENT

Statutory Reference: *UPC § 2-603*

Deceased Appointee. An exercise of a power of appointment in favor of a deceased person is ineffective, except as saved by an antilapse statute. Restatement 3d of Property § 5.5 comment *l*.

Testamentary Appointments—Applicability of Antilapse Statutes. Antilapse statutes in non-UPC states are commonly silent as to their application to the exercise of a power of appointment. Nevertheless, these statutes usually are held to apply to the testamentary exercise of a *general* power in favor of a deceased appointee, as long as the deceased appointee is in the protected relationship to the donee of the power. As to a *nongeneral* power, the authority that exists suggests that the statute doesn't apply unless the deceased appointee is in the protected relationship to the donee of the power *and* the substituted takers specified in the antilapse statute were objects of the power.[21]

The UPC antilapse statute expressly applies to the exercise of a power of appointment, by defining the term "devisee" as including "an appointee under a power of appointment exercised by the testator's will" if the appointee is a "grandparent, a descendant of a grandparent, or a stepchild[22] of either the testator or the donor of the power." UPC § 2-603(a)(4), (b).

UPC § 2-603 and Restatement 3d of Property § 5.5 comment *l* provide that the substitute gift is not defeated merely because the substitute takers are not objects of the power. The UPC expressly states that "a surviving descendant of a deceased appointee of a power of appointment can be substituted for the appointee under this section, whether or not the descendant is an object of the power." UPC § 2-603(b)(5).

1. Permissible and Impermissible Appointments

Permissibility of Appointment Not Creating an Absolute-Ownership Interest—Appointment in Trust. The donee of a general power can validly create limited and future interests in his or her appointees, in trust or otherwise, just as if the donee were the owner of the appointive property. By the

---

21. An appointee need not accept an appointment. A disclaimer relates back and operates as a nonacceptance and, therefore, an appointee who disclaims is treated as if he or she predeceased the appointment and an antilapse statute may apply.

22. "Stepchild" is defined as a "child of the surviving, deceased, or former spouse of the testator or of the donor of a power of appointment, and not of the testator or donor." UPC § 2-603(a)(5).

apparently prevailing view, even an explicit prohibition of this type of an appointment in the language creating the power is ineffective, because it would be useless to try to enforce it. The donee merely could appoint to himself or herself or to his or her estate outright and then convey or devise the owned property as he or she chose. See Restatement 2d of Property § 19.1.

In Equitable Trust Co. v. James, 47 A.2d 303 (Del. Ch. 1946), the court stated, contrary to the prevailing view, that an explicit prohibition of less than an outright appointment would be enforced, but also held as a matter of construction that the language must clearly impose this type of prohibition. It held that no prohibition was manifested in the language conferring a power on the donee to appoint the property "in fee simple" to such person or persons as the donee shall by will appoint.

In the absence of a contrary intent manifested in the language creating the power, the prevailing view is that the donee of a nongeneral power can validly create limited and future interests in the objects of the power, in trust or otherwise. See, e.g., Loring v. Karri-Davies, 357 N.E.2d 11 (Mass. 1976) (overruling prospectively Hooper v. Hooper, 89 N.E. 161 (Mass. 1909)). A manifested prohibition of this type of an appointment, however, is effective. See Restatement 2d of Property § 19.3.

Permissibility of Appointment Creating a New Power. The donee of a general power can confer a new power of appointment on his or her appointee. See Restatement 2d of Property § 19.2.

With respect to a nongeneral power, the better view is that the donee of a nongeneral power can create a general power in an object. See Restatement 2d of Property § 19.4. The fact that the donee of the appointed general power can exercise it in favor of nonobjects of the original power is irrelevant because, had the donee of the original power appointed outright to the object, the object would be free to transfer the property, by gift or otherwise, to a nonobject of the original power. Conferring a general power on an object is the equivalent of appointing outright to the object.

A few courts have held to the contrary, however. These courts take the view that the ability of the donee of the appointed general power to exercise it in favor of nonobjects of the original power precludes the donee of the nongeneral power from conferring a general power on an object. See, e.g., Thayer v. Rivers, 60 N.E. 796 (Mass. 1901).

The donee of a nongeneral power can create a nongeneral power in an object so long as the objects of the appointed nongeneral power do not include anyone who is not an object of the first nongeneral power. See Restatement 2d of Property § 19.4.

Example 16.14: G's will devised real property to A for life, remainder to such of A's descendants as A shall appoint. At his death, A exercised his nongeneral

> power by appointing to his child B for life, remainder to such of B's descendants as B shall appoint. A and B were living at G's death.
>
> A's appointment is valid because all the objects of the nongeneral power conferred on B by A's appointment were objects of A's nongeneral power. If A had purported to confer on B a power exercisable in favor of B's spouse and descendants as B shall appoint, that part of A's appointment creating the power in B would have been ineffective.

So long as the donee of the appointed nongeneral power is an object, what is the justification for limiting who can be objects of the appointed nongeneral power? See Restatement 2d of Property § 19.4 comment a. Should a donee of a nongeneral power be able to appoint by giving a nonobject a power to appoint among objects of the first nongeneral power? Restatement 2d of Property § 19.4(2) and comment b say yes.

Estate of Kohler

344 A.2d 469 (Pa. 1975)

EAGEN, J. This is an appeal from a final decree entered by the Orphans' Court Division of the Court of Common Pleas of Montgomery County sustaining preliminary objections to a petition to reopen an adjudication.

The facts are not in dispute.

Martin Luther Kohler died August 20, 1916, leaving a will which created a trust. According to the terms of the will, income from the trust was to be paid to his two surviving daughters, Ruth K. Bates and Else K. Campbell, during their respective lifetimes. The will provided further:

> Upon the death of either of my said daughters then I direct the share of such daughter to be paid to her issue per stirpes as such issue shall arrive at the age of twenty-five years, or that the same be paid to such issue in such manner and in such sums as my said daughters shall by their respective wills direct.

Else K. Campbell died testate. Her will directed that the balance of the residue of her estate, including the power of appointment granted to her by the will of her father, Martin Luther Kohler, was to be divided into four equal shares. One share was bequeathed "to my son, Robert F. Campbell, if he survives me. Should my said son, Robert F. Campbell, predecease me, then his share shall fall into my residuary estate and shall thus increase the shares of the other residuary legatees."

Robert F. Campbell predeceased his mother, Else K. Campbell.

The Fidelity Bank, trustee of the Kohler trust, filed a final account and a petition for adjudication following the death of Else K. Campbell. No notice was given to the children of Robert F. Campbell, and the distribution suggested by the Fidelity Bank made no award to them. On December 6, 1973, the

Orphans' Court Division of the Court of Common Pleas of Montgomery County rendered an adjudication confirming the account of, and approving the distribution proposed by the Fidelity Bank.

The children of Robert F. Campbell filed a petition to reopen the adjudication naming as respondents the Fidelity Bank, and the six beneficiaries among whom distribution was awarded by the adjudication. Preliminary objections were filed by the Fidelity Bank. Dismissal of the petition was sought on the ground that the children of Robert F. Campbell lacked standing to file the petition since they were not parties in interest in the trust. The court sustained Fidelity's preliminary objections. The children of Robert F. Campbell then filed this appeal.

The issue presented on this appeal is whether the will of Martin Luther Kohler created an *exclusive* power of appointment in Else K. Campbell or, more specifically, did the will give Else K. Campbell the power to exclude her son's issue from participation in the trust. The appellants contend it did not and maintain that there is nothing in the will of Martin Luther Kohler giving Else K. Campbell "the right to distribute her share of the estate to `such of her issue' as she might by will appoint". . . .

[T]he appellants argue that the language of the Kohler will, properly interpreted, provides for a gift to Else K. Campbell's issue per stirpes with power in her merely to vary the time and method of distribution. This argument is premised solely upon an interpretation of the words "such issue". . . .

Specifically, appellants contend that the term "such issue" in the clause "or that the same be paid to such issue" has as its antecedent the phrase "issue per stirpes" as used previously in the clause "I direct the share of such daughter to be paid to her issue per stirpes". From this it follows, they assert, that the testator did not intend that either daughter have the power to exclude any of their respective issue from a distributive share of the trust.

Appellants would have us read the disputed language as presenting the following alternatives:

> Upon the death of either of my said daughters, then I direct the share of such daughter to be paid to her issue per stirpes (1) as such issue shall arrive at the age of twenty-five years, or (2) that the same be paid to such issue in such manner and in such sums as my said daughters shall by their respective wills direct.

Such an interpretation, we believe, would render superfluous the words "that the same be paid to such issue". If the power in the daughters to vary the time *for distribution* of the shares of payment were intended merely as an alternative to distribution at the age of twenty-five, there would be no apparent reason to have repeated the words "or the same be paid to such issue".

Given the structure of the language actually used, we feel a much more natural interpretation is the following:

> Upon the death of either of my said daughters then I direct (1) the share of such daughter to be paid to her issue per stirpes as such issue shall arrive at the age of twenty-five years, or (2) that the same be paid to such issue in such manner and such sums as my said daughters shall by their respective wills direct.

With this interpretation no words are superfluous, and the alternatives expressed as noun clauses with identical subjects are in parallel construction. Since wills are to be construed so as to give effect to every word employed by the testator, we deem the latter interpretation preferable.

In addition, appellants' interpretation would have us interpret the term "such issue" to mean "said issue". However, the fact that the testator in the introductory phrases of the contested sentence used the adjective "said" to refer back to his previously mentioned daughters indicates that if he did, in fact, intend to have the term "such issue" refer to an antecedent, he would more likely have used the term "said issue".

In view of the interpretation we adopt, there can be little doubt that the testator intended the power of appointment to be exclusive. A power to appoint to "such" of the class as the donee may select was long ago held to be an exclusive power, permitting the donee to select one or more of the class, to the exclusion of others. Cf. Pepper's Appeal, 120 Pa. 235, 13 A. 929 (1888);[23] Lewis's Estate, 269 Pa. 379, 112 A. 454 (1921).[24]

The appellants argue, nevertheless, that if a power of appointment is intended to be exclusive, it is necessary that the class of possible appointees be introduced by the words "such of". However, an illustration from the Restatement of Property serves to demonstrate the weakness of this contention. Illustration 1 of Section 360 states:

> A by will transfers a fund in trust to pay the income to B for life and then to pay the principal to the children of B as B shall by will appoint and in default of appointment to the children of B equally. B has an exclusive power.

In addition, we have already observed that no particular words are necessary to create a power of appointment.

Decree affirmed. Each side to pay own costs. . . .

---

23. Therein the language determined to have created an exclusive power of appointment was:

> And from and after his death, then to the use of such of his children and issue, and in such shares and for such estates, as he shall by last will appoint and in default of such appointment. . . .

24. Therein an exclusive power of appointment was held to have been intended by the following:

> To such person or persons, being my lineal descendants, as my said deceased daughter may have appointed by her will, in such shares and amounts as she may choose and direct by such will.

ROBERTS, J. (dissenting). I dissent. In my view the language of the will creating the testamentary trust here was intended only to empower the first life tenants to alter the timing and manner of distribution to their issue and not to confer the power entirely to exclude some of their issue from the class of beneficiaries. I would, therefore, vacate the decree and remand for the entry of a decree permitting distribution to appellants herein.

MANDERINO, J., joins in this dissent.

Notes

1. *Exclusive and Nonexclusive Powers Defined.* An *exclusive power* does not require the donee, if he or she exercises the power, to assure that each object receives a part of the appointive assets. One or more of the objects can be omitted or excluded. A *nonexclusive power* requires that, if the donee exercises the power, each object must receive a part of the appointive assets (either via the appointment or as a taker in default).

An example of clear language creating an *exclusive power* would be a power to appoint "to any one or more of the donee's children." An example of clear language creating a *nonexclusive power* would be a power to appoint "to all and every one of the donee's children."

2. *Construction of Ambiguous Language.* When the language is ambiguous, as it was in the *Kohler* case, some courts have adopted the constructional preference in favor of a nonexclusive power. See, e.g., Hopkins v. Dimock, 48 A.2d 204 (N.J. Ch. 1946). The Restatement of Property § 360, followed by the court in *Kohler*, adopts the contrary constructional preference.

3. *Doctrine of Illusory Appointments.* Under the *doctrine of illusory appointments,* each object of a nonexclusive power must receive a "substantial part" of the appointive assets, not merely a nominal part. See Restatement of Property § 361(1). The Restatement 2d of Property § 21.2 obviates the necessity of recognizing the doctrine by redefining nonexclusive powers as powers wherein the donor has specified the share of the appointive assets from which an object cannot be excluded.

Estate of duPont

379 A.2d 570 (Pa. 1977)

ROBERTS, J. Philip F. duPont died testate in 1928, leaving one-third of the residue of his estate to the Fidelity-Philadelphia Trust Company in trust for the benefit of his daughter, Mrs. Frances duPont Rust. In his will, Mr. duPont created in Mrs. Rust a special testamentary power of appointment over the one-third share of the residue. The will provides that Fidelity-Philadelphia is

> upon her death to transfer, assign, and pay over the principal of her share of (Mr. duPont's) residuary estate unto *such of her children and issue of deceased children,* and in such proportions as she may by her Last Will and Testament or any writing in the nature thereof direct, limit and appoint (emphasis added).

Mrs. Rust died in 1975. In her will, Mrs. Rust appointed a part of this share to appellants William Shore, Harry Devine, and Girard Trust Bank in trust for the benefit of her surviving daughter Carroll (Mr. duPont's granddaughter) for life and then for the benefit of the issue of Carroll (Mr. duPont's great grandchildren). Mrs. Rust gave appellants the discretion to make periodic payments from principal to Carroll's issue.

Upon Mrs. Rust's death, Fidelity-Philadelphia filed an account in the Orphans' Court Division of the Court of Common Pleas of Chester County. The auditing judge reviewed the objection to Mrs. Rust's exercise of her special power of appointment and concluded that Mrs. Rust exceeded the bounds of her special power by appointing part of the residue for the benefit of the issue of Mrs. Rust's surviving daughter Carroll. Objections to the adjudication of the auditing judge were dismissed by the orphans' court. In this appeal, appellants contend that Mr. duPont authorized Mrs. Rust to appoint to Carroll's issue while Carroll is still living. We do not agree. We agree with the holding of the orphans' court that Mrs. Rust exceeded her special power and therefore affirm.

The orphans' court interpreted "children and issue of deceased children" to include those persons who are either living "children" of Mrs. Rust or "issue of deceased children" of Mrs. Rust at the time of her death. The court concluded that the potential beneficiaries of the special power are confined to those persons within the precise class defined in Mr. duPont's will, and that Mrs. Rust could not alter or expand that group. Hence, the court held invalid the appointment in trust for the benefit of the issue of Mrs. Rust's surviving daughter Carroll because Carroll's issue were not "issue of deceased children" of Mrs. Rust at Mrs. Rust's death.

"The donee of a power is simply a trustee for the donor to carry into effect the authority conferred by the power. In exercising the power, he must observe strictly its provisions and limitations." Rogers' Estate, 218 Pa. 431, 433, 67 A. 762, 762 (1907); Schede Estate, 426 Pa. 93, 231 A.2d 135 (1967). For her exercise of the special power to be effective, Mrs. Rust had to exercise that power within the limits of her authority. Schede Estate, supra; Restatement of Property § 351 (1940); V American Law of Property § 23.52 (Casner ed. 1952).

To validate Mrs. Rust's appointment to Mr. duPont's great grandchildren while their mother Carroll is still living would be to ignore the express language of Mr. duPont's will. Mr. duPont's testamentary plan is explicit: the language "children and issue of deceased children" gives Mrs. Rust the power to benefit her living "children" (Mr. duPont's grandchildren). This language provides in the alternative that if any of those children predecease Mrs. Rust, and if those deceased children are survived by issue, those "issue of deceased children" (Mr. duPont's great grandchildren) should be eligible beneficiaries. Such a scheme is a reasonable method of avoiding the potentially harsh exclusion of the great grandchildren of Mr. duPont whose parent happened to predecease Mrs. Rust. By including "issue of deceased children" as permissible beneficiaries, Mr. duPont allowed Mrs. Rust to appoint to such issue in place of their parent who predeceased Mrs. Rust.

Mr. duPont, in granting Mrs. Rust the power, "upon her death," to benefit "(her) children and issue of (her) deceased children . . . in such proportions" as she should choose, decided that living children of Mrs. Rust are best qualified to see to the needs of their issue; only the issue of deceased children were to be provided for by Mrs. Rust directly. While Mr. duPont authorized Mrs. Rust to have the power to appoint "in such proportions" as she saw fit, he did not authorize the expansion or alteration of the class of permissible beneficiaries so as to encompass issue of living children. We find such an attempt to be in excess of the limits of Mrs. Rust's powers and therefore hold it invalid.

Mrs. Rust attempted to circumvent Mr. duPont's limitation to appoint only to "issue of *deceased* children" by delegating to appellants the authority to make appointments from principal to Carroll's issue after Carroll's death. Mrs. Rust authorized appellants to exercise at Carroll's death the discretion of Mr. duPont conferred exclusively upon Mrs. Rust to decide how the principal should be apportioned among members of the class of beneficiaries. However, Mr. duPont authorized Mrs. Rust to appoint "by her Last Will and Testament or any writing in the nature thereof." This language reflects an intent that Mrs. Rust exercise her appointment power at the time of her death. The testamentary nature of her special power is inconsistent with her attempt to postpone the choice of beneficiaries beyond the time of her death.

Appellants, at oral argument, contended that the decision of the orphans' court will burden Carroll's issue with harsh tax consequences. That concern does not relieve a court from the duty of discerning the testator's intent as it is expressed in the will and the overall testamentary plan.

> As to the obviation of taxes, it is incontestable that almost every settlor and testator desires to minimize his tax burden to the greatest extent possible. However, courts cannot be placed in the position of estate planners, charged with the task of reinterpreting deeds of trust and testamentary dispositions so as to generate the most favorable possible tax consequences for the estate. Rather courts are obliged to construe the settlor's or testator's intent as evidenced by the language of the

instrument itself, the overall scheme of distributions, and the surrounding circumstances.

Estate of Benson, 447 Pa. 62, 72, 285 A.2d 101, 106 (1971).

Decree affirmed. Each party to pay own costs.

POMEROY and NIX, JJ., concur in the result.

Notes

1. *Impermissibility of Direct or Indirect Appointments to Nonobjects.* A direct appointment in favor of a person who is not an object of a nongeneral power is obviously ineffective. See Restatement 2d of Property § 20.1. Even an appointment in favor of an object is ineffective—a so-called *fraud on the power*—if the donee's purpose was to benefit a nonobject. See Restatement 2d of Property § 20.2.

Example 16.15: G devised the residue of her estate in trust, income to her husband, H, for life, remainder in corpus "to such of G's children by a former marriage as H should by will appoint." On H's subsequent death, H appointed the trust corpus to A, who was one of G's children by her former marriage. Evidence showed, however, that A had agreed, in consideration of the appointment, to transfer half of the appointive assets to X, H's child of a former marriage.

H's appointment is invalid because his effort to benefit the nonobject, X, constitutes a fraud on his nongeneral power.

2. *Donee's "Estate" As the Object.* Suppose that a donor creates a power exercisable in favor of the donee's "estate" and the donee's will, making specific reference to the power, exercises the power by making direct devises of the appointive property. Is the exercise valid? In Matter of Estate of Rossi, 634 N.Y.S.2d 372 (Surr. Ct. 1995), the court held it was, reasoning that the donee of a general power "should be allowed to accomplish by the single act of unrestricted appointment what he could do by an appointment to himself and a later disposition of the assets so appointed . . . ." Id. at 374 (citing Restatement 2d of Property § 19.1 com. a).

3. *Effectiveness of Appointment to Takers in Default.* There is disagreement among the cases as to the effectiveness of an appointment to a taker in default. The rationale of the cases holding that an appointment to a taker in default is ineffective is that the taker in default holds an interest created by the donor that can be defeated or changed by the exercise of the power. A purported exercise of the power in conformity with the interest of the taker in default is a nullity, not an exercise of the power. See Restatement 2d of Property § 24.4.

The capacity in which the person takes, as appointee or taker in default, is of no great concern to the person taking, as long as he or she takes. The significance of whether the appointment is effective or not lies elsewhere. The question usually arises in cases of general powers and the claims of the donee's creditors, usually the donee's estate creditors. By the majority common-law view, an ineffective appointment of a general power does not allow creditors to reach the appointive assets. It takes an effective appointment to subject the appointive assets to the claims of the donee's creditors. See supra p. 997. The issue of whether an appointment to default takers is an exercise of a power may also have tax implications if the donee had a pre-1942 general power. See supra p. 992.

2. Failures to Appoint; Ineffective Appointments

General Powers—Failure to Exercise. If the donee of a general power of appointment fails to exercise the power, the appointive assets pass under the donor's gift-in-default clause. If there is no gift-in-default clause, the appointive assets revert to the donor (or the donor's successor in interest).

Recall that the most likely donee of a general power is the donor's surviving spouse, in which case the power will be a power to appoint the remainder interest in a marital deduction trust. If the donor's estate was well planned, there will be a gift-in-default clause. If the donee doesn't wish to disturb the gift-in-default clause, the donee should not only refrain from exercising the general power, but should affirmatively declare this intention in the donee's will by a clause such as:

> I hereby refrain from exercising the power of appointment conferred on me by my spouse's will of [date].

Ineffective Exercise of General Power—The "Capture Doctrine." If the donee of a general power of appointment makes an ineffective exercise, the appointive property ordinarily goes to the takers in default or, if none, reverts to the donor (or the donor's successor in interest). If, however, the donee's appointment manifests an intent to assume control of the property for all purposes and not merely for the limited purpose of giving effect to the expressed appointment, courts apply the "capture doctrine," which means that the appointive property goes to the donee's estate rather than to the takers in default or to the donor (or the donor's successor in interest). See Restatement 2d of Property § 23.2. Some courts have used the theory that the donee's ineffective appointment constitutes an implied appointment in favor of the donee's own estate.

The donee's intent to assume control of the property for all purposes is manifested by: (1) a blending clause, see, e.g., Fiduciary Trust Co. v. Mishou, 75 N.E.2d 3 (Mass. 1947); (2) a residuary clause that presumptively demonstrates an intent to exercise the power pursuant to a statute or rule of common law; (3) a residuary clause that demonstrates an intent to exercise the power because the donee's estate is insufficient to satisfy the donee's bequests; or (4) in the view of some but not all courts, an appointment in trust. Compare Talbot v. Riggs, 191 N.E. 360 (Mass. 1934) (capture doctrine applied because donee's ineffective appointment was in trust), with Northern Trust Co. v. Porter, 13 N.E.2d 487 (Ill. 1938) (capture doctrine not applied even though donee's ineffective appointment was in trust).

Donors often attempt to protect their gift-in-default clauses against the capture doctrine. A standard clause in frequent use introduces the gift-in-default clause with the phrase:

> To the extent the donee does not effectively exercise this power of appointment, ...

Since one of the theories used to justify an application of the capture doctrine is that, in the circumstances, the import of the donee's ineffective express appointment is an effective implied appointment in favor of his or her own estate, this type of clause may not give the donor the desired protection. Greater protection would be afforded by a slight rewording of the standard clause:

> To the extent the donee does not expressly exercise this power of appointment effectively, ...

Nongeneral Powers. If the donee fails to exercise a nongeneral power of appointment, or makes an ineffective exercise thereof, the property goes to the takers in default. If there are no takers in default, the appointive property will go to the objects of the power if the objects are a defined limited class and not revert to the donor or the donor's successor in interest.

Two different theories are employed to reach this result. Some courts take the view that the donee of a nongeneral power with a defined limited class of objects has a duty to exercise the power, *i.e.*, that the power is a power in trust (also called an imperative or mandatory power). The court will not permit the objects of the power to suffer by the negligence of the donee in failing to appoint or making an ineffective appointment, "but fastens upon the property a trust for their benefit." See, e.g., Daniel v. Brown, 159 S.E. 209 (Va. 1931).

Other courts imply a gift in default in favor of the objects of the nongeneral power. See, e.g., Loring v. Marshall, 484 N.E.2d 1315 (Mass. 1985); Polen v. Baird, 25 S.E.2d 767 (W. Va. 1943); Restatement 2d of Property § 24.2. See also Restatement 2d of Trusts § 120 comment e, § 121 comment a.

> *Example 16.16:* The objects of A's nongeneral power are A's children; there is no express gift in default.
>
> If A dies without exercising the power, or makes an ineffective appointment, the appointive assets will go to his children who survive A (and substituted takers for a deceased child, if an antilapse statute applies). Both the power-in-trust theory

and the implied-gift-in-default theory lead to this result. If, however, there are no objects to which the property can pass, the appointive assets revert back to the donor (or the donor's successor in interest).

> *Example 16.17:* The objects of A's nongeneral power are anyone in the world except A, A's estate, A's creditors, and the creditors of A's estate.
>
> If A dies without exercising the power, or makes an ineffective appointment, the appointive assets revert to the donor (or the donor's successor in interest). The power is not a power in trust and there is no implied gift in default because the objects of A's power are not a defined limited class.

3. Contracts to Appoint

Presently Exercisable Powers. A contract by the donee of a presently exercisable power of appointment to make a specified appointment in the future is enforceable if neither the contract nor the promised appointment confers a benefit on a nonobject. See Restatement 2d of Property § 16.1.

If the presently exercisable power is a general power, it follows that a contract to appoint is enforceable, regardless of on whom the benefits are conferred.

If the presently exercisable power is a nongeneral power, a contract to appoint is likely to confer a benefit on a nonobject. If so, the contract is unenforceable, but the promisee, if his or her conduct was not consciously wrongful, is entitled to restitution of the value of the consideration paid for the promise.

> *Example 16.18:* A was the donee of a nongeneral power to appoint among her nephews and nieces. In exchange for consideration of $10,000, A contracted with one of her nephews, X, to appoint all the property to X, to the exclusion of A's other nieces and nephews.
>
> Even though X is an object of the power, the contract is unenforceable because the contract benefitted A, the promisor-donee. A was not an object of the power.

If the donee doesn't breach the unenforceable contract, but instead abides by it, the donee's appointment may be ineffective on the ground that it constitutes a fraud on the nongeneral power.

Testamentary Powers. A contract to appoint a testamentary power, whether general or nongeneral, violates the donor's intent in limiting the exercise of the power to a testamentary exercise. Thus a contract to appoint a testamentary power is unenforceable. The promisee may, however, be entitled to restitution of the value of the consideration paid for the promise. See Restatement 2d of Property § 16.2.

If the donee doesn't breach the unenforceable contract, but instead abides by it, the donee's appointment is valid if the power was a general power. See, e.g.,

Rogers' Estate, 168 Misc. 633, 6 N.Y.S.2d 255 (Sur. Ct. 1938). If the power was a nongeneral power, if the promisee-appointee was an object of the power, and if the promisor-donee received consideration for the promise, it would seem that the appointment should be ineffective as a fraud on the power and that the promisee should then be able to obtain restitution from the promisor-donee (or his or her estate) of the value of the consideration paid for the promise. See, e.g., Pitman v. Pitman, 50 N.E.2d 69 (Mass. 1943). The Restatement 2d of Property § 16.2 comment c, however, suggests that the appointment is effective, but also suggests that, to prevent the nonobject-donee-promisor from receiving a benefit, the promisee-appointee should be entitled to receive restitution of the value of the consideration paid for the promise.

4. Releases of Powers

The Restatement 2d of Property §§ 14.1 and 14.2 declare that all powers of appointment, general and nongeneral, testamentary and presently exercisable, are releasable in whole or in part, unless the donor has effectively manifested an intent that the power not be releasable. Several states have enacted legislation that is basically or wholly in accord with this proposition.

If the donor of a *general* power expressly provides that the power cannot be released, the donor's intention may not be effective. Its validity still must be examined under the rules governing unreasonable restraints on alienation. See Restatement 2d of Property § 14.1 comment a.

An express provision prohibiting the release of a *nongeneral* power is probably valid. Apart from an express prohibition, the release of a nongeneral power is impliedly prohibited if the nongeneral power is a power in trust (also called an imperative or mandatory power). A nongeneral power is a power in trust if the objects are a defined limited class and if the donor has not provided for a disposition of the property in case the power is not exercised. See Restatement 2d of Property § 14.2 comment d.

The release of a power of appointment, when permissible, is effectively an exercise in favor of the takers in default, even in cases where an actual exercise in favor of the takers in default would be prohibited or ineffective. (An *actual* exercise in favor of the takers in default can be ineffective because the released power was a testamentary power, because one or more of the takers in default died prior to the release, or because the jurisdiction doesn't recognize an appointment in favor of the takers in default as an effective appointment.)

Example 16.19: G's will devised property in trust, income "to A for life, remainder in corpus to such of A's children as A by will appoints; in default of appointment, to A's children equally." G was survived by A and A's children, X and Y. X then died, leaving all his estate to his wife, W. Then A released her power of appointment.

At the time of the release, the gift in default in favor of A's children became indefeasibly vested. At A's death, the corpus of the trust will go to Y and X's successor in interest (W).

Chapter 17

Classification of Estates and Future Interests

HAVING studied the role of powers of appointment in the fashioning of trusts, we now turn to the subject of future interests. If powers of appointment are staples in modern estate-planning practice, future interests are nothing short of indispensable. Future interests are intrinsic to trusts: It's nearly impossible to create a trust without creating one or more future interests.

The study of future interests was at one time dominated by—some would say obsessed with—the study of classification. The goal was to teach students to be able to attach the proper label or labels to a possessory or future estate. The preoccupation with classification was appropriate, though tedious, as long as important legal consequences turned on classification. Today, few legal consequences turn on classification. Why, then, study classification at all? The reason is that classification is still important in solving some legal problems, such as the Rule Against Perpetuities. Additionally, you need to become familiar with the terms associated with classification to understand the legal literature and communicate to others in practice. This explains why we study classification in this Chapter, although the subject is presented in less detail than would have been offered in the past.[1]

PART A. CLASSIFICATION: THE HIERARCHY OF ESTATES

As indicated above, classification means fixing the proper label or labels to a possessory or future estate. The hierarchy of estates is a refined, artificial structure that took centuries to develop fully. If it had been designed in one fell swoop, the flexibility it provides estate planners and clients of today could surely be achieved with a system of much greater simplicity. A proposal for a simplified system is noted later.

The complexity and artificiality in the current system evolved, step by step over a fairly long period of time, from the struggles of competing interest groups. The owners of the great landed estates, assisted by ingenious lawyers, sought to avoid the estate taxes of the day and to safeguard their estates through the generations. As one loophole was plugged in favor of exacting the tax or promoting freer alienability and control for the recipients of the property, the ingenious lawyers found another. The result was that great distinctions were drawn on the basis of the words used in creating dispositions. Through classification, different ways of saying the same thing were accorded different legal consequences. Form controlled over substance. In classification, form still controls over substance. Form controls legal consequences less than before, however, because the legal consequences flowing from classification gradually have been reduced.

As we study the current system, bear in mind also that the system of classification, which was originally developed in feudal times mainly for legal

1. For greater detail, see Thomas F. Bergin & Paul C. Haskell, Preface to Estates in Land and Future Interests (2d ed. 1984); Lewis M. Simes, Handbook on the Law of Future Interests (2d ed. 1966); Lawrence W. Waggoner, Estates in Land and Future Interests in a Nutshell (2d ed. 1993).

interests in land, has been transposed today to the classification of the beneficial interests in the modern trust. See Olin L. Browder, Jr., Trusts and the Doctrine of Estates, 72 Mich. L. Rev. 1509 (1974).

Quantum of Estates. According to the hierarchy of estates, the possessory estates are ordered by "quantum." In descending order of quantum, the groupings are: (1) fee simple estate (all fee simple estates are of the same quantum); (2) fee tail; (3) life estate; (4) term of years; (5) estate from period to period; (6) estate at will; and (7) estate at sufferance.[2]

Particular Estate. The term *particular estate* is a term of art denoting any estate that is less than a fee simple—a fee tail, a life estate, a term of years, and so on.

1. The Possessory Estates

The Estates in Fee Simple. Although there are four fee simple estates, they can be divided into two general categories: fee simple absolute and fee simple defeasible.

The estate in *fee simple absolute* is an estate in land that isn't subject to termination; it is unlimited in duration. (The personal property counterpart of the fee simple absolute is called absolute or outright ownership.) A fee simple absolute is never followed by a future interest.

> *Example 17.1:* G conveyed real property "to A and his heirs." A has a fee simple absolute; no future interest follows it.
>
> The words "and his heirs" are "words of limitation," meaning words defining the estate granted to A, not "words of purchase," meaning words granting an interest in the property to A's heirs.

The *defeasible fee simple* estates are subject to termination upon the happening of an event specified in the grant. There are three defeasible fee simple estates: (1) the fee simple determinable; (2) the fee simple subject to a condition subsequent; and (3) the fee simple subject to an executory limitation. Distinguishing each of these estates from the others requires an understanding of the concept of defeasance.

Defeasance means loss of ownership—in other words, that the holder of the possessory interest will lose that interest upon the happening of an event that is

---

2. An estate at will is "an estate which is terminable at the will of the transferor and also at the will of the transferee and which has no other designated period of duration." Restatement of Property § 21. An estate at sufferance is "an interest in land which exists when a person who had a possessory interest in land by virtue of an effective conveyance, wrongfully continues in the possession of the land after the termination of such interest, but without asserting a claim to a superior title." Id. at § 22.

stipulated in the grant. A possessory interest that is subject to defeasance is either subject to a *condition subsequent* or a *limitation.*

Possessory interests that are subject to a limitation are said to terminate *naturally* or *by their own terms.* The language in the grant that signifies a limitation are words such as "during," "until," "while," "so long as," "for so long as," or simply "for [a designated period]," followed by words such as "at," "upon," or "then." The limitation is called a *special limitation* if it describes an event that is not certain to happen.

Possessory interests that are subject to a condition subsequent (also called divestment) are said to terminate by being *cut short* or *divested* upon the happening of the stipulated event. The language in the grant that signifies a condition subsequent are words such as "on condition that" or "provided that," followed by words such as "but if" or "and if." (In some grants, only the "but if" or "and if" language will appear.)

The *fee simple determinable* is a fee estate that is subject to a *special limitation,* which means that it automatically terminates if the specified event happens; the specified event is any event that is not certain to happen. The future interest following the estate in fee simple determinable is either reversionary or nonreversionary (for the meaning of these terms, see infra p. 1030). If this future interest is reversionary, it is called a possibility of reverter; if it is nonreversionary, it is called an executory interest.

Example 17.2: G conveyed real property "to A and her heirs *so long as* A does not allow liquor to be sold on the premises; upon A's allowing liquor to be sold on the premises, the property to revert to me."

Example 17.3: G conveyed real property "to A and her heirs *so long as* A does not allow liquor to be sold on the premises; and upon A's allowing liquor to be sold on the premises, the property to go to B."[3]

The *fee simple subject to a condition subsequent* is a fee estate that is subject to *divestment* in favor of a reversionary future interest called a right of entry (also called a power of termination). The happening of the specified event doesn't automatically divest the estate; rather, it empowers the grantor or the grantor's successor in interest to divest the estate by exercising the right of entry.

Example 17.4: G conveyed real property "to A and his heirs *on condition that* A not allow liquor to be sold on the premises, *and if* A allows liquor to be sold on

---

3. The limitation regarding selling liquor applies only to A and not to A's successors in interest. Therefore, the executory interest to B is valid under the Rule Against Perpetuities because it must vest or fail within A's lifetime.

the premises, then the grantor is to have the right to re-enter and take possession of the premises."

The *fee simple subject to an executory limitation* is a fee estate that is subject to *divestment* in favor of a nonreversionary future interest called an executory interest. The happening of the specified event divests the estate.

Example 17.5: G conveyed real property "to A and her heirs, *but if* A allows liquor to be sold on the premises, then to B."

Fee Tail. The fee tail estate is subject to termination if and when the line of the tenant in tail's issue fails. That is, the estate terminates upon the death of the tenant in tail's last living descendant.

The fee tail estate has an interesting history,[4] but its present is no longer very important and its future even less so. In almost all states, the fee tail estate is abolished. Language purporting to create it—"to A and the heirs of his body"—has different consequences in different states. The most predominant results are that it creates a fee simple absolute in A or that it creates a life estate in A, with a remainder in fee in A's issue.

Life Estates and Terms of Years. Life estates and terms of years are estates that are defeasible: As estates that are subject to a *limitation*,[5] they expire naturally (by their own terms) on the life tenant's death or the expiration of the term.

The phrases *equitable life estate* or *equitable term* are sometimes used to describe the interest of a trust beneficiary who has the right to the income from a trust for the beneficiary's lifetime or for a term. Equitable terms are most frequently encountered in charitable lead trusts, but they are also used in trusts that give the right to the income to a family member until that family member reaches a specified age.

Life estates and terms of years are by definition defeasible estates, as noted above. Both, however, can be made prematurely defeasible so that they end before the life tenant's death or the expiration of the term. This occurs when either a special limitation or a condition subsequent is added to the grant.

Example 17.6: G transferred real property "to A for life or until A remarries." A's estate is called a *life estate subject to a special limitation*. Another name for it is a *determinable life estate*.

---

4. See Restatement of Property Ch. 5; Bergin & Haskell, supra note 1, at 28-34.

5. "To A *for* life;" "to A *so long as* A lives;" "to A *until* A's death;" "to A *during* A's lifetime;" "to A *for* 10 years."

Example 17.7: (1) G transferred real property "to A for life, remainder to B; but if A remarries, to B immediately." A's estate is called a *life estate subject to an executory limitation.*

(2) G transferred real property "to A for life on condition that A not remarry; and if A remarries, G is to have the right to re-enter and take possession of the premises." A's estate is called a *life estate subject to a condition subsequent.*

The duration of a life estate need not be measured by the life of the one in possession, but instead it can be measured by the life of another. This type of estate is called a *life estate pur autre vie.*

Example 17.8: G transferred real property "to A for the life of B." A predeceases B. A's will devises her entire estate to X. A has a life estate *pur autre vie.* Unlike a life estate that terminates on the life tenant's death, A can devise the remaining portion of her life estate to X. After A's death, X has a life estate *pur autre vie*—for the life of B.

2. Future Interests: Basic Division Between Reversionary and Nonreversionary Interests

The first step in the process of classification of future interests is to decide whether the future interest is a reversionary interest or a nonreversionary interest. There are five future interests: (1) reversions; (2) possibilities of reverter; (3) rights of entry (also called powers of termination); (4) remainders; and (5) executory interests. Of these, the first three—reversions, possibilities of reverter, and rights of entry—are reversionary interests. Reversionary interests are interests retained by (or created in) the transferor *when the interest was created.* The other two future interests—remainders and executory interests—are nonreversionary interests. Nonreversionary interests are interests *created in* a transferee (someone other than the transferor).

Once made, a classification based on the reversionary/nonreversionary distinction is not altered by subsequent transfers of the interest from one person to another. So, a reversionary interest does not become a nonreversionary interest by virtue of a subsequent transfer of that interest from the transferor to a transferee. And, conversely, a nonreversionary interest does not become reversionary if it subsequently comes into the hands of the transferor. It makes no difference whether the subsequent transfer is inter vivos, testamentary, or the result of intestate succession.

Problems

Classify the future interests in the following problems:

1. G conveyed real property "to A for life."

(a) Later, G conveyed all her interest in that property to B.

(b) Instead of conveying her interest to B, G later died leaving a will that didn't mention the real property but contained a residuary clause devising and bequeathing all her property not otherwise disposed of to B. G was survived by A and B.

(c) In Problem 1(b), G died intestate. G was survived by A and by her sole heir, B.

2. G's will devised real property to A for life; the will contained no residuary clause, and so the residue of her estate passed by intestacy to her sole heir, B.

3. G's will devised real property "to A for life, and upon A's death, the property is to go to B."

4. G's will devised real property "to A for life." G's will contained a residuary clause devising "all my property not otherwise disposed of to B."

3. The Reversionary Future Interests: Reversions, Possibilities of Reverter, and Rights of Entry

If a future interest is reversionary, it's either a reversion, a possibility of reverter, or a right of entry.

a. Reversions

Reversions are future interests retained by the transferor (or the transferor's successors in interest) when the transferor conveys an estate or estates of *less* quantum than the transferor had originally. The most common example is that of an owner of property in fee simple absolute who transfers out a particular estate (a possessory interest other than a fee simple interest).

> *Example 17.9:* G conveyed real property "to A for life." G retained a reversionary interest, and that reversionary interest is called a reversion.

b. Possibilities of Reverter

Possibilities of reverter are future interests retained by the transferor (or the transferor's successors in interest) when the transferor transfers an estate or estates of the *same* quantum as the transferor had originally. The most common example is that of an owner of property in fee simple absolute who transfers out a fee simple determinable.

> *Example 17.10:* G conveyed real property "to A and his heirs so long as A does not allow liquor to be sold on the premises[, and upon A's allowing liquor to be

sold on the premises, the property is to revert to the grantor]." G retained a reversionary interest, and that reversionary interest is called a possibility of reverter.

The words contained in the brackets in the preceding example are not necessary to create a possibility of reverter. Possibilities of reverter need not be expressly stated because, like reversions, they constitute an undisposed-of interest remaining in the transferor. See Simes & Smith on Future Interests § 286. In practice, however, it is common expressly to state the possibility of reverter, and a small minority of decisions has held (erroneously) that, without the bracketed words, A takes a fee simple absolute. See, e.g., In re Copps Chapel Methodist Episcopal Church, 166 N.E. 218 (Ohio 1929).

c. Rights of Entry (Powers of Termination)

Rights of entry—also called powers of termination[6]—are future interests created in the transferor (or the transferor's successors in interest) when the transferor transfers an estate subject to a condition subsequent (i.e., subject to divestment). (Whether the quantum of the estate is the same as or lesser than that of the transferor's original estate is unimportant.) The most common example is that of an owner of property in fee simple absolute who transfers a fee simple subject to a condition subsequent and who expressly creates the right to re-enter and retake the premises if and when the condition is broken.

Example 17.11: G conveyed real property "to A and her heirs on condition that A not allow liquor to be sold on the premises, but if A allows liquor to be sold on the premises, the grantor is to have the right to re-enter and take possession of the premises." G retained (more accurately, created in himself) a reversionary interest, and that reversionary interest is called a right of entry.

A right of entry doesn't take effect in possession automatically when the condition is broken. If A allows liquor to be sold on the premises, A's action merely gives G a right to elect to take a possessory interest if G so chooses. See, e.g., Maletis, Inc. v. Schmitt Forge, Inc., 870 P.2d 865 (Or. Ct. App.), review denied, 881 P.2d 142 (Or. 1994) (classifying the reversionary interest in an easement as a right of entry and then finding that a letter indicating that the easement was extinguished served as sufficient notice of intent to terminate the easement).

---

6. *Power of termination* is the terminology used in the first Restatement of Property § 155. The Restatement 2d of Property forgoes that terminology and utilizes the older terminology, *right of entry*.

4. The Nonreversionary Future Interests: Remainders and Executory Interests

If a future interest is nonreversionary, it's either a remainder or an executory interest.

a. Remainders

A remainder is a future interest created in a transferee that becomes possessory if at all upon the *natural termination* of the preceding vested interest. The preceding vested interest (1) must have been created simultaneously with the creation of the future interest and (2) must be a particular estate. (Recall that a particular estate is a term of art that denotes any possessory interest other than a fee simple interest. See supra p. **1027**.)

Example 17.12: G transferred real property "to A for life, and upon A's death, to B." B has a remainder, not an executory interest.

b. Executory Interests

An executory interest is a future interest created in a transferee that becomes possessory if at all by *cutting short* or *divesting* the preceding vested interest. The preceding vested interest (1) need not have been created simultaneously with the creation of the future interest and (2) can be a fee simple interest or a particular estate.

Example 17.13: G transferred real property "to A and his heirs on condition that A not allow liquor to be sold on the premises, but if A allows liquor to be sold on the premises, the property is to go to B." B has an executory interest, not a remainder.

Special Case—Executory Interest Succeeds Fee Simple Determinable. In one special case, an executory interest doesn't "cut short" or "divest" the preceding vested interest but takes effect on its "natural termination." Since a remainder can't follow a fee simple interest, a fee simple must always be followed by an executory interest, even when the fee simple is subject to a special limitation.

Example 17.14: G transferred real property "to A and her heirs as long as A does not allow liquor to be sold on the premises, and upon A's allowing liquor to be sold on the premises, the property is to go to B." B has an executory interest, not a remainder.

Springing and Shifting Executory Interests. Executory interests are sometimes divided into two categories—springing and shifting. *Shifting* executory interests potentially divest an interest conferred by the grantor on a transferee. *Springing* executory interests potentially divest an interest retained by the grantor.

> *Example 17.15:* (1) G transferred real property "to A and his heirs, but if A allows liquor to be sold on the premises, to B." B's executory interest is a shifting executory interest.
>
> (2) G transferred real property "to B, to take effect in possession on B's marriage." B's executory interest is a springing executory interest.

Future Interests in Sets. When a set of nonreversionary future interests succeeds a life estate or a term of years, the first future interest will always be a remainder. The other or subsequent future interest(s), however, may be either remainders or executory interests. In determining which they are, the following rules apply:

> *Rule 1:* If the first future interest is a contingent (nonvested) remainder, the other nonreversionary future interests will also be contingent (nonvested) remainders.
>
> *Rule 2:* If the first future interest is a vested remainder subject to divestment, the other nonreversionary future interests will be executory interests.

Problems

After consulting the next section, classify the interests of B and C in the following examples:

1. G transferred real property "to A for life, remainder to B if B survives A, but if not, to C."
2. G transferred real property "to A for life, remainder to B, but if B fails to survive A, to C."

5. Vested and Contingent Future Interests

Future interests are subject to a further level of classification—classification in terms of vesting. There are four categories here: indefeasibly vested, vested subject to (complete) defeasance, vested subject to open (partial defeasance), and contingent (nonvested).

For future reference, it may be noted that UPC § 2-707 adopts a rule of construction that makes all future interests in trust contingent upon surviving the distribution date. This is a subject we take up in Chapter 18.

a. Indefeasibly Vested

An indefeasibly vested future interest is one that isn't subject to any conditions or limitations. In other words, the future interest must be certain to become a possessory fee simple *absolute* at some time in the future. See Restatement of Property § 157 comment f. Only remainders and reversions can be indefeasibly vested.

Example 17.16: G transferred real property "to A for life, remainder to B." B's remainder is indefeasibly vested. It's certain to become possessory because A is bound to die. When A dies, B's remainder will become a possessory fee simple absolute.

Note in this example that B might not be alive when A dies. Except as otherwise provided by statute,[7] B's interest isn't subject to a condition of survival of A. Therefore, the possibility of B's death before A's death has no bearing on the classification of B's interest. If B dies before A, B's indefeasibly vested remainder will pass at B's death to B's successors in interest—her devisee or, if she dies intestate, her heirs. See infra Chapter 18, Part A, for discussion of survival conditions.

Example 17.17: G conveyed real property "to A for life." G's reversion is indefeasibly vested. The comments made in the above example regarding B's remainder apply to G's reversion in this example.

Example 17.18: G conveyed real property "to A for life, remainder to B for ten years." G's reversion is indefeasibly vested. It's certain to become possessory ten years after A's death, and will at that time become a fee simple absolute.

B's remainder isn't indefeasibly vested. Although it's certain to become possessory upon A's death (a certain event), it won't become a fee simple absolute then. B's remainder is vested subject to defeasance after ten years. The comments made in Example 17.16 regarding survival apply equally here.

b. Vested Subject to Defeasance

A future interest that is vested subject to defeasance is one that is subject to one or more conditions subsequent or to one or more limitations. The precise terminology to be used will depend on whether the interest is subject to conditions subsequent, on the one hand, or to limitations, on the other hand.

If the future interest is subject to one or more *conditions subsequent*, it is called *vested subject to divestment*. Only remainders and reversions can be vested subject to divestment. Note, however, that there is an important difference between remainders and reversions. Remainders are vested subject to divestment only when they are subject to a condition subsequent. (As we shall

---

7. See, e.g., UPC § 2-707.

shortly see, remainders subject to a condition precedent are contingent.) In contrast, reversions are vested subject to divestment whenever they are subject to a condition, regardless of whether the condition is precedent or subsequent. The reason for this difference is that, by definition, reversions can never be contingent. *Reversions are always vested.*

Example 17.19: G transferred real property "to A for life, remainder to B, but if B fails to survive A, to C." B's remainder is vested subject to divestment because the condition of survival attached to her remainder is stated in condition subsequent form—"to B, but if."

C's executory interest is subject to the condition that B not survive A. This condition is stated in the form of a condition precedent—"if . . . to C." C's executory interest is contingent.

G retained no reversion.

Example 17.20: G conveyed real property "to A for life, remainder to B if B survives A, but if not, to return to me." B's remainder is subject to a condition of survival of A, but this time the condition is stated in the form of a condition precedent—"to B if." B's remainder is therefore contingent, not vested subject to divestment.

G's reversion is subject to the condition that B not survive A, and so G's reversion can't be indefeasibly vested. This condition is stated in the form of a condition precedent. Nevertheless, the rule that reversions are always vested overrides all other rules and, therefore, G's reversion is vested subject to divestment.

This analysis also applies if the phrase "but if not, to return to me" is omitted.

Example 17.21: G conveyed real property "to A for life, remainder to B if B survives A, but if not, to C." B's remainder is subject to a condition of survival of A that's stated in the form of a condition precedent—"to B if." B's remainder is therefore contingent, not vested subject to divestment.

C's remainder is subject to the condition that B not survive A. The condition is stated in the form of a condition precedent ("if [B does not survive A], to C") and, therefore, C's remainder is contingent, not vested subject to divestment.

G retained a technical reversion. (There is always a reversion when a particular estate is followed by contingent remainders. In a case such as this example, the contingencies stated with respect to the interests of B and C exhaust all the possibilities; hence, the reversion is said to be merely "technical.") The reversion is vested subject to divestment because it can't be indefeasibly vested and because it must be vested.

A future interest that is subject to one or more *limitations* is called *vested subject to limitational defeasance*. Only remainders and reversions can be vested subject to limitational defeasance.

Example 17.22: G transferred real property "to A for life, then to B for life, then to C." B's remainder is vested subject to limitational defeasance. It is sometimes referred to simply as a vested remainder for life. Note that B must survive A for his interest to become possessory. This implicit requirement of survival isn't regarded as a "condition" of survival.

C's interest is a remainder because B's interest is subject to a limitation and because it's an estate less than a fee simple. It's an indefeasibly vested remainder because it's subject to no condition or limitation.

Example 17.23: G conveyed real property "to A for life, then to return to me for life, then to C." This is the same as the example above, except that the future interest subject to limitational defeasance is a reversion in G rather than a remainder in B.

Example 17.24: G transferred real property "to A for life, then to B for 10 years, then to C." B's remainder is vested subject to limitational defeasance. In this case, the time of B's death is irrelevant. If B dies while A is still alive, B's remainder will pass to her devisees or if she died intestate to her heirs. If B dies after A's death but before the 10th anniversary thereof, the remaining portion of B's 10-year term will pass to her devisees or if she died intestate to her heirs.

c. Vested Subject to Open

The only future interest that can be vested subject to open *at inception* is the remainder. A remainder is vested subject to open when it's subject to no conditions precedent and when it's in favor of a class that contains at least one living member and that is still "open," *i.e.*, where it's possible for additional persons to become class members (typically through birth or adoption). Other and older labels for this type of interest are (i) *vested subject to partial divestment*, or (ii) *vested in quality but not in quantity*. These terms are descriptive of the phenomenon that each time a new member is added to the class the shares of the existing class members are reduced (partially divested). Whichever label is used, it's important to note that the existing class members are the ones who are regarded as having a vested remainder. The interests of the unborn or unadopted class members are contingent on being born or adopted. They are executory interests because upon birth or adoption they partially divest the interests or shares of the living class members.

Example 17.25: G transferred real property "to A for life, remainder to his children." When the transfer was made, A had two children, X and Y. X has a vested remainder subject to open in an undivided half of the property. Y has a vested remainder subject to open in the other undivided half.

Suppose a third child, Z, is born after the transfer occurred. Upon Z's birth, Z's executory interest becomes a vested remainder subject to open in an undivided third of the property, and X's and Y's interests are reduced (or partially divested) to vested remainders subject to open in an undivided third.

The executory interest, the only other nonreversionary future interest, can be in favor of a class that is subject to open, but the executory interest itself can't be called vested subject to open because executory interests are, by definition, contingent.

Reversionary interests are never subject to open at their inception because they are, by definition, retained by the transferor or the transferor's successors in interest when created. Even if a reversionary interest was originally "retained by" the transferor's successors in interest, which might be a group of people, such as the transferor's heirs, it isn't a class subject to open because the membership of this group of takers is determined at the transferor's death.

After their inception, however, reversionary future interests might be transferred to a class that contains at least one living member and that is subject to open. If the reversionary future interest is a possibility of reverter or a right of entry, a transfer to a class would still not make either one of them *vested* subject to open because these interests are regarded as contingent.[8] See infra p. 1039. A reversion, however, is always vested, and if it was subsequently transferred, it would become vested subject to open.

Example 17.26: G conveyed real property "to A for life." G later died (while A was alive), devising her indefeasibly vested reversion to A's children. Two children of A were living at G's death. These two children receive vested reversions subject to open and A's unborn children receive springing executory interests.

Example 17.27: Same as above except that A had no children at G's death. The situation at G's death would probably be viewed as follows: G carved springing executory interests (in favor of A's unborn children) out of his indefeasibly vested reversion. His indefeasibly vested reversion would thus become vested subject to divestment, and would pass to G's residuary legatee or his heirs, depending on the situation.

---

8. Although possibilities of reverter and rights of entry are classified as contingent, they are not subject to the Rule Against Perpetuities (see infra p. 1064). This anomaly was noted by John Chipman Gray in his classic treatise. Gray agreed that possibilities of reverter were, and should be, exempt from the Rule, and so he maintained that there was "no practical object" in labeling them as contingent. John Chipman Gray, The Rule Against Perpetuities 107 (4th ed. 1942). Conversely, Gray argued that rights of entry, as truly continent interests, should be subject to the Rule. Id. at 345.

d. Contingent (Nonvested)

A future interest is contingent ("nonvested")[9] if it's subject to a *condition precedent*. A condition precedent may be explicit or implicit. An explicit condition precedent exists where the language of the disposition declares that the interest is to become possessory *if* some event occurs. Implicit conditions precedent exist when the future interest is in favor of unborn or unascertained persons.

Remainders can be contingent but need not be. Executory interests are nearly always contingent.[10] Reversions can't be contingent but possibilities of reverter and rights of entry are regarded as contingent.

> *Example 17.28:* G conveyed real property "to A for life, remainder to B if B survives A." B's remainder is contingent because the condition of surviving A is stated in the form of a condition precedent—"to B if."
>
> G's reversion appears to be subject to the condition precedent that B not survive A, but G's reversion is vested subject to divestment because of the rule that reversions are always vested. This means that B's remainder in this situation acts like an executory interest because it potentially divests G's reversion. Nevertheless, it's a remainder because its predominant feature is that it takes effect in possession, if at all, on the natural termination of A's life estate.

> *Example 17.29:* G transferred real property "to A for life, remainder to A's children." When the transfer was made, A had no children. A's unborn children have contingent remainders. Their remainders, unlike B's remainder in the example above, are implicitly contingent on being born or adopted, but are not contingent on surviving A.

> *Example 17.30:* G transferred real property "to A for life, remainder to A's heirs." The remainder in favor of A's heirs is contingent because it's in favor of unascertained persons. The persons who are A's heirs can't be ascertained until A's death.

---

9. The traditional term is *contingent*, but the Restatement 2d of Property adopts the term *nonvested*.

10. The typical executory interest is subject to a condition precedent and is classified as contingent (nonvested). In rare cases, an executory interest is created that is unconditional. An example would be if G conveyed real property "to B, to take effect in possession 25 years from now." Another example would be if G conveyed real property "to B, to take effect in possession at my death." It's assumed in each case that the possessory interest retained by G is a fee simple interest, not a term of 25 years or a life estate. This means that B's future interest can't be a remainder and, therefore, it must be an executory interest. If it were a remainder, it would be classified as indefeasibly vested. The courts have been reluctant to call this type of an executory interest vested. Its classification has been perplexing because it's an executory interest. Nevertheless, it's generally assumed that, like vested interests in general, this type of an executory interest isn't subject to the Rule Against Perpetuities. See infra Chapter 19.

Nevertheless, any person who would be an heir of A if A were to die immediately is called an heir apparent or an heir expectant. The heirs expectant are regarded as having contingent remainders during A's lifetime rather than mere expectancies. Thus it's sometimes said that they take by purchase rather than by succession. Their remainders are of course implicitly contingent on their actually becoming A's heirs when A dies.

Example 17.31: G transferred real property "to A for life, remainder to B, but if B fails to survive A, to C." The condition that B survive A is a condition subsequent as to B's remainder ("to B, but if"), making it vested subject to divestment. C's executory interest is subject to the condition precedent that B not survive A and, therefore, is contingent.

Example 17.32: (1) G transferred real property "to A and her heirs on condition that A never allow liquor to be sold on the premises, but if A allows liquor to be sold on the premises, the property is to go to B."

(2) G transferred real property "to A and her heirs for as long as A never allows liquor to be sold on the premises, and upon A's allowing liquor to be sold on the premises, the property is to go to B."

B's executory interest in both cases is subject to the condition that A allow liquor to be sold on the premises. In both cases, the condition is in condition precedent form and, therefore, B's executory interest is contingent.

Example 17.33: (1) G conveyed real property "to A and his heirs on condition that A never allow liquor to be sold on the premises, but if A allows liquor to be sold on the premises, the grantor shall have the right to re-enter and take possession of the premises."

(2) G conveyed real property "to A and his heirs for as long as A never allows liquor to be sold on the premises, and upon A's allowing liquor to be sold on the premises, the premises are to revert to the grantor."

G's right of entry in the first case and G's possibility of reverter in the second case would appear to be subject to the condition precedent that A allow liquor to be sold on the premises. Most authorities do in fact classify these interests as contingent. See Am. L. Prop. §§ 4.6, 4.12; Simes & Smith on Future Interests §§ 281, 1238. The Restatement of Property § 154 comment e, at 531, classifies possibilities of reverter as contingent but doesn't classify rights of entry in terms of vesting. It is believed that both interests are properly classified as contingent.

6. Future Interests Belonging to More Than One Category

Often a future interest will be subject to open but the phrase "subject to open" won't appear in its classification because it's contingent. Or, the phrase might not appear in its classification because it's vested subject to complete defeasance. This doesn't mean that the interest isn't actually subject to open; it merely means that the fact that it's subject to open isn't formally expressed as part of its classification.

Example 17.34: G transferred real property "to A for life, remainder to A's children who survive A; but if none of A's children survives A, to B."

The remainders in A's children are contingent. They are also subject to open, but recognizing this fact by using the phrase "contingent subject to open" isn't done.

Example 17.35: G transferred real property "to A for life, remainder to her children, but if none of A's children survives A, to B." A was alive and had living children when the transfer occurred.

The remainders in A's living children are vested subject to (complete) divestment. They are also subject to open. The Restatement of Property § 157 comment c would classify the remainders as vested subject to (complete) divestment and leave it at that. Nevertheless, it's permissible to say that the interests are vested subject to (complete) divestment and to open because, unlike those in the example above, the interests are vested.

The condition subsequent of survival imposed on the interests of A's children in this example is substantively different from the condition precedent of survival imposed on A's children in the example above. If, in the above example, one or more of A's children survive A but some predecease her, only the ones who survive A take. But in this example, as long as at least one child survives A, courts can be expected to hold that the interests of those children who predeceased A are not divested. See Restatement of Property § 254 comment a, illus. 2.

TABLE SUMMARIZING THE CATEGORIES OF VESTING

Future Interest	*Permissible Categories of Vesting at Inception*
Remainder	Indefeasibly Vested Vested Subject to Defeasance (Divestment or Limitation) Vested Subject to Open Contingent
Executory Interest	Contingent
Reversion	Indefeasibly Vested Vested Subject to Defeasance (Divestment or Limitation)
Possibility of Reverter	Contingent
Right of Entry	Contingent

7. The Law Favors the Vesting of Estates

Traditionally, vested interests are preferred to contingent interests. Restatement of Property § 243, comment i. Explicit recognition of this idea is colorfully stated in Roberts v. Roberts, 2 Bulst. 123, 80 Eng. Rep. 1002 (K.B. 1613), where it was declared that "the law always delights in vesting of estates, and contingencies are odious in the law, and are the causes of troubles, and vesting and settling of estates, the cause of repose and certainty." The law delights "in preventing of contingencies, which are dangerous. . . ."

The source of the preference is complex, but it's commonly claimed that the desire to avoid certain common-law rules, such as the destructibility rule and the Rule Against Perpetuities, to promote alienability, to promote completeness of the disposition, and to promote equality of distribution among different lines of descent all played important roles.

In general, it can be said that the courts will construe a provision as not imposing a condition precedent if they can do so without contradicting the express language of the instrument, *i.e.*, where there is sufficient ambiguity in the language to permit what might be called an even choice.

Edwards v. Hammond

3 Lev. 132, 83 Eng. Rep. 614 (C.P. 1683)

Ejectment upon *not guilty,* and special verdict, the case was. A copyholder of land, burrough English, surrendered to the use of himself for life, and *after to the use of his eldest son and his heirs, if he live to the age of 21 years: provided, and upon condition, that if he die before 21, that then it shall remain to the surrenderer and his heirs.* The surrenderer died, the youngest son entered; and the eldest son being 17 brought an *ejectment*; and the sole question was, whether the devise to the eldest son be upon condition *precedent*, or if the condition be *subsequent? scil.* [an abbreviation of the Latin word *scilicet*, which means "that is to say"] that the estate in fee shall vest immediately upon the death of the father, to be divested if he die before 21. For the defendant it was argued, that the condition was *precedent*, and that the estate should descend to the youngest son in the mean time, or at least shall be in contingency and *in abeyance* 'till the first son shall attain to one and twenty; and so the eldest son has no title now, being no more than 17. On the other side it was argued, and so agreed by the Court; that though by the first words this may seem to be a condition *precedent*, yet, taking all the words together, this was not a condition *precedent*, but a present devise to the eldest son, subject to and defeasible by this condition subsequent, *scil.* his not attaining the age of 21. . . .

Notes and Question

1. *Background of Edwards v. Hammond.* The transferor in the *Edwards* case, the surrenderer, was described as a "copyholder of land, burrough English." Copyholders were free men holding land by unfree tenure. The freehold and

seisin of the copyholder's estate resided in his lord. The copyholder's evidence of title was his copy of the roll of the court of the manor; the court's roll served as a form of land registry. The rules governing the landholding of a copyholder were not uniform, but were to be found in the custom of the manor concerned. Borough English was a custom whereby the youngest son, not the eldest son, inherited lands subject to the custom. See A. W. B. Simpson, A History of Land Law 14 (2d ed. 1986).

The surrenderer in *Edwards*, engaging in a will substitute of the day, was trying to reverse this rule of inheritance by transferring (surrendering) his copyhold to his lord who would, upon the surrenderer's death, admit the grantee. The surrender would have been registered on the court rolls by the steward of the manor. The surrender didn't completely cut out the surrenderer's youngest son, for by virtue of the custom of borough English, applicable in this case, the surrenderer's youngest son was his heir and, as such, was scheduled to take the land if the eldest son failed to reach twenty-one. Apparently, however, when the surrenderer died, the youngest son was admitted immediately; at least, he entered. This precipitated the action of ejectment, which was brought by the surrenderer's seventeen-year-old eldest son.

A contingent remainder in a copyhold wasn't subject to the common-law rule of destructibility of contingent remainders. Since copyholds weren't freeholds, the seisin remained throughout in the lord of the manor.

2. *Consequences of Classification.* In *Edwards,* the direct result of holding that the remainder was vested subject to divestment was that the surrenderer's seventeen-year-old eldest son was immediately entitled to possession of the land. If the court had held that the remainder was contingent, the eldest son's right to possession would have been delayed until his twenty-first birthday, the youngest son having the right to possession in the meantime.

3. *The Mystique of Classification.* As you read the next case, Guilliams v. Koonsman, notice that the court also discussed at some length the proper classification of the future interests. Consider what consequence, if any, turns on how those future interests are classified. Is the *Guilliams* case an example of what Professor Waggoner called the "classificatory mystique"—the notion indulged by some courts that classifying the interests solves what is in fact a straightforward problem of construing the meaning of the dispositive language? See Lawrence W. Waggoner, Reformulating the Structure of Estates: A Proposal for Legislative Action, 85 Harv. L. Rev. 729, 732 (1972).

Guilliams v. Koonsman

279 S.W.2d 579 (Tex. 1955)

CALVERT, J. Our main problem involves the construction of the fourth paragraph of the will of J. J. Koonsman, deceased, which reads as follows:

> I give and devise to my son, Alvin Koonsman, all of my undivided interest in all of the remainder of my real property situated in Scurry County, Texas, which I may own at the time of my death, and to his child or children if any survive him, and in the event of Alvin's death without issue surviving him, then to my son and daughter, Jesse J. Koonsman and Mrs. Cora Guilliams, share and share alike, and to their heirs and assigns forever. . . .

The only evidence in the record before us, other than the will itself and the probate proceedings in connection therewith, is the testimony of Alvin Koonsman that J. J. Koonsman, the testator, died March 6, 1942, and that he (Alvin) has only one child, John Billy Koonsman, born October 15, 1942. From this testimony it appears that John Billy was in esse for the purpose of taking under the will on the date it became effective, that is, the date of J. J. Koonsman's death.

What is the meaning of the words "and to his child or children if any survive him" following the devise to Alvin? We have been cited to and have found no case squarely in point. If the words "if any survive him" had been omitted and we were to follow the weight of authority, heretofore noted, we would be compelled to hold that Alvin and his son, John Billy, took the first estate created as cotenants. But those words were not omitted, and we ascribe to them a two-fold effect: first, they limited the interest of Alvin Koonsman to a life estate, and secondly, they operated to make the remainder to be taken by the child or children of Alvin contingent rather than vested.

The words "if any survive him," qualifying the devise to the children of Alvin, clearly indicate that his children were not to take as cotenants with Alvin but were to take in succession to him, with the result that the devise to Alvin is limited to a life estate. No particular form of words is necessary to the creation of a life estate.

> It has been said that where the construction of a will devising property to one and his children is doubtful, the courts lean toward giving the parent a life estate, and that even a slight indication of an intention that the children shall not take jointly with the parent will give a life estate to the parent with a remainder to the children. 33 Am. Jur. 474.

The conclusion that the remainder in the child or children is contingent rather than vested is also impelled by the words "if any survive him." Survival is made a condition precedent to the vesting of the remainder rather than a condition of defeasance. While it has been said that "The law favors the vesting of estates at the earliest possible period, and will not construe a remainder as contingent where it can reasonably be taken as vested," Caples v. Ward, 107 Tex. 341, 179 S.W. 856, 858, nevertheless, when the will makes survival a condition precedent to the vesting of the remainder, it must be held to be contingent. . . .

The rule for determining whether a remainder is vested or contingent is thus stated by Gray in his work on The Rule Against Perpetuities:

> If the conditional element is incorporated into the description of, or into the gift to the remainder-man, then the remainder is contingent; but if, after words giving a vested interest, a clause is added divesting it, the remainder is vested.

3d Ed., § 108(3), page 85. The rule as thus stated has been approved and adopted by the courts of this state. Here the condition of survival is incorporated into the gift to Alvin Koonsman's child or children.

There remains to be determined the nature of the estate devised to Jesse J. Koonsman and Mrs. Cora Guilliams by the fourth paragraph of the will. They are to take the fee "in the event of Alvin's death without issue surviving him." Their estate must be held to be a contingent remainder also. It is to take effect upon Alvin's death, but only if he dies "without issue surviving him." It is an alternative contingent remainder. . . .

The judgments of the trial court and Court of Civil Appeals are reformed to . . . decree that the true meaning and effect of the fourth paragraph of the will is that the plaintiff, Alvin Koonsman, is therein and thereby given an estate for life in the property therein described, with a remainder in fee to the child or children of Alvin Koonsman, conditioned upon their surviving him, and an alternative remainder in fee to Jesse J. Koonsman and Mrs. Cora Guilliams, or their heirs and assigns, conditioned on the death of Alvin Koonsman without a child or children surviving him, and as so reformed the judgments of those courts are affirmed.

Notes and Questions

1. For the proposition that a gift "to A and A's children" presumptively creates a life estate in A and a remainder in A's children, See Restatement 2d of Property § 28.3.

2. *Reconcilable?* Can you reconcile *Edwards* and *Guilliams*? *Guilliams* is supported by the Restatement of Property § 278, but a few courts have held that a disposition such as that in *Guilliams* creates a vested remainder subject to divestment. See, e.g., Safe Deposit & Trust Co. v. Bouse, 29 A.2d 906 (Md. 1943). Do you think the testator *intends* different consequences by choosing condition precedent, condition subsequent, or even-choice language in describing contingencies? Do you think the testator's attorney might choose one form of conditional language rather than another for the purpose of accomplishing a particular legal result?

3. *Remainders for Life.* In addition to the rule of *Edwards*, another manifestation of the preference for vested interests is the rule that remainders for life are classified as vested subject to defeasance (subject to a limitation, not a condition

precedent or subsequent). The remainder for life can be viewed as presenting an even choice to the courts because they could have classified it as contingent (on surviving the primary life tenant).

Consider, now, Example 17.36:

> *Example 17.36:* G transferred real property "to A for life, then to B for life if B survives A, then to C."

This example presents a further problem for the courts because this remainder for life is expressly conditioned on survival of the primary life tenant. Does the inclusion of the phrase "if B survives A" remove this case from the even-choice category, and force a court to hold that B's remainder is contingent? A small number of courts have held that it does. Most courts, however, have held that B's remainder is vested despite the conditional language, suggesting that the preference for vesting is strong. See Simes & Smith on Future Interests § 142. Does the majority view override an obvious attempt by a drafter to rebut the preference for vested interests? Is the classification of remainders for life as vested rather than contingent likely to make any practical or legal difference? What type of interest does C take in the above example?

4. *Remainders Subject to a Power.* Frequently someone will be given a power of some sort to divert the property to someone other than the taker of the remainder. In these cases, the remainder is subject to a condition, but the condition isn't clearly stated as a condition precedent. The preference for vested estates can, therefore, be viewed as tipping the scale in favor of treating the condition as a condition subsequent.

> *Example 17.37:* G transferred real property "to A for life, empowering A to sell, consume, or otherwise dispose of the property or any part thereof as may be necessary for A's support and maintenance; at A's death the property or such part thereof as may remain unexpended is to go to B." B's remainder is vested subject to divestment in whole or in part by the exercise of the power by A.
>
> The same result would be reached in the case of a remainder interest in a trust where the settlor retained a power to revoke the trust or where the settlor conferred upon someone else (typically the trustee or the income beneficiary) a power to invade the corpus on behalf of the income beneficiary.

> *Example 17.38:* G transferred real property "to A for life, remainder to such persons as A shall by will appoint, and in default of appointment, to B." B's remainder is vested subject to divestment by the exercise of the power by A. It could be argued in this case that the language expressly imposes a condition precedent (that A will not exercise the power) on B's remainder. Nevertheless, the idea that remainders subject to a power are vested subject to divestment is so well established that B's remainder isn't regarded as contingent, even here.

5. *Remainder Subject to a Charge or a Lien.* Transferors occasionally appear to condition a remainder interest on the payment of a sum of money to a designated person. Most courts have held that the remainder is vested and that the taker is entitled to possession on the termination of the prior interest but subject to a charge or a lien on the property in the designated amount. See, e.g., Miller v. Miller, 247 N.W.2d 445 (Neb. 1976); Estate of Marra, N.Y.L.J., May 6, 1987, at 14 (Sur. Ct.). But see Allison v. Wilson, 411 S.E.2d 433 (S.C. 1991) (held that the testator intended that the requirement of a payment to the life tenant's spouse created a contingent remainder). This construction is consistent with the general preference for vested interests.

Example 17.39: G transferred real property "to A for life, remainder to B if B pays C $5,000 within one year of A's death." B hadn't paid C the $5,000 on the first anniversary of A's death. Under the majority view, if B doesn't pay the $5,000 to C within a reasonable time, C can enforce his charge or lien in that amount against the property. Had the court held B's remainder to have been contingent on B's having paid the money, B wouldn't be entitled to the property and C wouldn't receive the money.

Problems

Classify the future interests in the following problems:

1. A was childless when G made the following two transfers:

(a) G transferred real property "to A for life, then to such of A's children as survive A, but if none survives A, to C."

(b) G transferred real property "to A for life, then to A's children, but if none of A's children survives A, to C."

2. After G's transfer took place, a child (X) was born to A. Does this event alter the classifications of the future interests in G's dispositions in Problem 1(a) and Problem 1(b)? If so, how?

3. After X was born, A had another child, Y. Years later, X died, survived by A and Y. Then A died, survived by Y. Who becomes entitled to the property at the time of A's death under Problem 1(a)? Problem 1(b)?

4. In the following two cases, B dies while A is still alive. Classify the future interests at the point of their creation and at the point of B's death.

(a) G transferred real property "to A for life, remainder to B, but if B fails to survive A, to C." (It's sometimes said that an executory interest can't vest until it vests in possession. What's the meaning of this statement?)

(b) G transferred real property "to A for life, remainder to B if B survives A, but if not, to C."

5. G transferred real property "to A for life, remainder to B if B lives to attain the age of 21." The destructibility rule has been abolished by statute in the

jurisdiction. Classify the future interests at the point of their creation and at the following points:

(a) B reaches 21 while A is still alive.

(b) A dies; B is then alive but under 21.

Is All This Complexity Necessary? In a word, no. Without sacrificing the slightest degree of flexibility in the planning of family property transactions, classification and the structure of estates could be vastly simplified and the artificiality in the present system could be eradicated. A proposal for a simplified system of estates, in which classification is based on the substance of the disposition rather than the form of its wording, has been put forward in Lawrence W. Waggoner, Reformulating the Structure of Estates: A Proposal for Legislative Action, 85 Harv. L. Rev. 729, 755-56 (1972):

> [T]he reformulated structure is based on the premise that the only appropriate distinctions are between certainty and uncertainty as to the termination of possessory interests and between certainty and uncertainty as to the ultimate possession of future interests. Possessory interests, by the terms of the particular transfer, either will not terminate (fee simple absolute), will terminate (life estate or term of years), or will possibly terminate (defeasible interest). Future interests either will become possessory (indefeasibly vested), will become possessory but with a now uncertain number of takers (vested subject to open), or will possibly become possessory (contingent). The reformulated structure is shown in the accompanying chart. . . .

POSSESSORY INTERESTS	FUTURE INTERESTS
Fee Simple Absolute	None permissible
Defeasible Fee Simple	Contingent
Life Estate (may or may not be defeasible)	Contingent (not certain to become possessory); Alternative Contingent Future Interest Vested Subject to Open: Contingent (in unborn class members) Indefeasibly Vested
Term of Years	Same as with Life Estate

PART B. SELECTED CONSEQUENCES OF CLASSIFICATION

Classification in all its fine detail is far less important than it once was. This is partly because some of the rules that turned on classification have been widely abolished and partly because many of those rules applied, in any event, only to *legal* future interests in *real property,* which are less often created today. Ironically, the reduced importance of classification has played a role in keeping the complex and artificial structure in force, by reducing the pressure to reexamine and reformulate it.

At the same time, the importance of certain aspects of classification hasn't disappeared altogether. This Part examines some of the rules that turn on classification. At one time, two rules that turned on the difference between remainders and executory interests—the rule of destructibility of contingent remainders[11] and the Rule in Shelley's Case[12]—were widely followed in the United States. These rules are feudal relics, have no business being part of our law, and have been widely abolished. Their decline, in turn, makes the importance of the distinction between remainders and executory interests largely but not completely disappear. We no longer study those rules in this course.

1. Alienability of Future Interests

Voluntary Alienability. Reversions, remainders, and executory interests are descendible and devisable. If the future interest is either contingent or vested subject to defeasance, it is, of course, descendible and devisable only if the owner's death doesn't cause the interest to be extinguished.

> *Example 17.44:* G transferred real property "to A for life, remainder to B, but if B fails to survive A, to C." C dies, then B, then A. C's executory interest is contingent on B's not surviving A, but it's not contingent on C himself surviving A. Consequently, C's executory interest wasn't extinguished by his death before A, and it's descendible and devisable. B's vested remainder subject to divestment was, however, extinguished by his death before A, and so B's remainder is neither descendible nor devisable.

Reversions and vested remainders (even if defeasible) were alienable inter vivos at the common law, but contingent remainders and executory interests

11. The common-law destructibility rule provides that a legal contingent remainder in real property is destroyed if it does not vest by the time the preceding freehold estate terminates.

12. The Rule in Shelley's Case provides that a remainder interest in real property which is either in favor of the life tenant's heirs or in favor of the life tenant's heirs of the body, and which is of the same quality as that of the life estate, is held by the life tenant.

were not. Contingent remainders were at first likened to an expectancy—not an interest, but the possibility of an interest arising in the future. When executory interests were later recognized, they were regarded as sufficiently analogous to contingent remainders to warrant the same treatment.

Despite the inalienability of contingent remainders and executory interests, the common law recognizes two ways by which such "inalienable" interests can *in effect* be transferred, and equity recognizes still another. (It may be noted that these three methods of transferring inalienable future interests are also available for transferring nonexistent interests, such as expectancies.)

> *Contract to Convey.* A purported transfer, if for adequate consideration, is treated in equity as a contract to convey. The contract becomes specifically enforceable if and when all conditions precedent are satisfied so as to give the transferor an alienable interest.
>
> *Estoppel by Deed.* Even without adequate consideration—indeed, without any consideration at all—when a purported transfer is made by a deed that contains a covenant of warranty, the title inures at law by estoppel to the grantee if and when the conditions precedent are later satisfied.
>
> *Release.* At law, an inalienable future interest can be released to the holder of the interest that would be defeated by the satisfaction of the conditions precedent attached to the released interest. For example, in the case of a disposition "to A for life, remainder to B, but if B fails to survive A, to C," a release of C's executory interest to B would be enforceable at law. Releases don't have to be contained in a warranty deed, nor is consideration necessary. A writing under seal was, however, required at common law, but today where the significance of seals is abolished, an instrument capable of transferring an interest in land would probably be sufficient.

Contingent remainders and executory interests are clearly no longer thought of as mere possibilities of receiving an interest in the future. Rather, they are thought of as present interests in which the right to possession is postponed and uncertain. See Restatement of Property § 157 comment w. Even so, the states take various approaches to the inalienability rule.

In about seven states, the common-law rule of inalienability is still followed. In those states, the equitable contract to convey, the estoppel by deed, and the release methods of transferring inalienable interests are also recognized. Therefore, the inalienability rule followed in those states boils down to this: Purported transfers for inadequate consideration by quitclaim deed to someone other than a person in whose favor the interest could have been released are ineffective. See, e.g., Goodwine State Bank v. Mullins, 625 N.E.2d 1056 (Ill. App. Ct. 1993), appeal denied, 633 N.E.2d 4 (Ill. 1994).

In the other states, the inalienability rule is probably not followed, at least not strictly. By statute or case law in a few states, remainders and executory interests that are contingent as to person (interests in favor of unborn or unascertained persons) are still inalienable, but those that are contingent as to event are alienable.

> *Example 17.45:* G transferred real property "to A for life, remainder to B if B survives A; if not, to B's heirs." B's remainder is contingent as to event, and under this approach it would be alienable. However, the remainder in favor of B's heirs is inalienable under this rule because it's contingent as to person.

In the vast majority of states, mostly by statute but also in some jurisdictions by common-law decision, all contingent future interests are said to be alienable—even those that are contingent as to person. But how can a future interest contingent as to person be alienable? The answer is that these interests aren't truly alienable. While the law typically authorizes a specially appointed fiduciary called a guardian ad litem to represent the interests of unborn or unascertained persons in litigation, it's uncommon to find that this fiduciary can be appointed to join in a transfer of the property interests on behalf of these persons.

> *Example 17.46:* G transferred real property "to A for life, remainder to A's children." If A is childless, no one is authorized to transfer the remainder interest on behalf of A's unborn children. If A has living children, they can, of course, transfer their interests. A is alive, and, therefore, there is a possibility of additional children being born. No one is authorized to transfer the executory interests on their behalf. Thus, the most that A's living children can transfer is a remainder that's subject to open (partial divestment).

What, then, does it mean to say that in the vast majority of jurisdictions even future interests that are contingent as to persons are alienable? The proposition refers to future interests that are in favor of unascertained persons, rather than to those that are in favor of unborn persons as in the example above.

> *Example 17.47:* G transferred real property "to A for life, remainder to B's heirs." B is alive, but if B died now, B's sole heir would be B's daughter, C. In states in which future interests that are contingent as to persons are said to be alienable, B's heir apparent (C) would be regarded as having a transferable interest, not merely an expectancy, in the subject matter of G's disposition. See Am. L. Prop. § 4.67. If C should transfer her interest, her transferee would, however, receive an interest that's contingent on C's turning out to be B's real heir. See Restatement of Property § 162 comment c. It's thus clear that no one, not even C, can transfer the remainder interest that follows A's life estate. The remainder interest, in other words, is still not truly alienable, C's ability to transfer her interest notwithstanding. (The notion that C has a property interest in the

subject matter of the above disposition shouldn't be confused with the notion that C—as B's heir apparent—has merely an expectancy in B's own property.)

Auctioning Future Interests in England. It is reported that an organized auction is available in England to persons who want to sell their future interests, either vested or contingent. At one of these auctions, a future interest in a trust was sold for $127,000. The future interest was contingent on a woman of 37 surviving the income beneficiary, a woman of 65. The value of the corpus of the trust at the time of sale was $413,219. See Wall St. J., May 10, 1971, at 1.

Based on actuarial methods used by the Internal Revenue Service for valuing gifts made in 1971, the then-present worth of a future interest contingent on a female of 37 surviving another female age 65 was 42.08 percent of the value of the underlying property at the time of the transfer. See Letter from W. E. Wilcox, Chief, Actuarial Branch, Internal Revenue Service, April 10, 1973. On this basis, the purchaser of the future interest in the $413,219 trust got a bargain. The purchaser bought for $127,000 an interest whose actuarially computed worth was $173,882.56.

Involuntary Alienability—Creditors' Rights. Statutes in the various states provide creditors with the right to impound assets of their debtors prior to judgment and the right after judgment to subject assets to sale for its satisfaction. These statutes purport to specify the type of assets that are subject to these procedures, but the statutory language is usually so general that it's within the power of the courts to determine the extent to which the debtor's future interests can be affected.

The general principle followed by the courts under statutes is that if the future interest is voluntarily alienable, it's also subject to the claims of creditors. Indefeasibly vested remainders and reversions, since they are everywhere voluntarily alienable, are automatically available to creditors in the satisfaction of their claims. The same is true of remainders and reversions that are vested subject to defeasance.

Contingent remainders and executory interests, in states where they aren't voluntarily alienable, aren't subject to the claims of creditors. The fact that the equitable contract to convey, estoppel by deed, and release methods are available in these states does not change the result. Conversely, in states where contingent remainders and executory interests are voluntarily alienable—the vast majority of states—most courts routinely hold interests to be subject to creditors' claims. See, e.g., Everson v. Everson, 400 A.2d 887 (Pa. Super. Ct. 1979), aff'd as modified, 431 A.2d 889 (Pa. 1981). See also Restatement of Property §§ 166, 167.

When the owner of a future interest dies, the interest may be transmitted by will even if it wasn't alienable inter vivos. It may be argued that the decedent's creditors should be satisfied at this time from these assets, for otherwise they will be deprived of all chance of payment. There appears to be little law on the subject. Some statutes governing the payment of claims against decedents' estates resolve the problem by equating the creditors' rights to property that the decedent could have alienated inter vivos. Text writers and the Restatement of Property § 169 have indicated the same result would probably be reached in situations in which the controlling statute is not so explicit.

In federal bankruptcy proceedings, the rights of creditors are far reaching. The Bankruptcy Reform Act of 1978, 11 U.S.C. § 541(a)(1), treats as part of the bankrupt's estate "all legal or equitable interests" in property owned by the debtor as of the commencement of the case. This language is broad enough to include all types of future interests, even those that are immune from the claims of creditors under state law.

External Reference. Edward C. Halbach, Creditors' Rights in Future Interests, 43 Minn. L. Rev. 217 (1958).

2. Acceleration of Future Interests—Disclaimers and Other Causes

Statutory Reference: *Unif. Disclaimer of Property Interests Act § 6(b)(4)*

When property is given by way of a succession of present and future interests, a prior interest may fail in its inception for a variety of reasons. The question this Section addresses is what effect a failure of the prior interest has upon succeeding interests.

Restatement of Property

§ *233. Renunciation—Acceleration Prevented While Succeeding Interest Continues Subject to Unfulfilled Condition Precedent.* When an attempted prior interest fails because it is renounced by the person to whom it is limited, a succeeding interest is not accelerated so long as a condition precedent to such succeeding interest continues unfulfilled.

Linkous v. Candler

508 S.E.2d 657 (Ga. 1998)

THOMPSON, J. Does the language of the trust agreement in this case indicate an intent to prohibit acceleration of the trust? Because such an intent need not be express, but can be implied from the four corners of the agreement, Wetherbee v. First State Bank & Trust Co., 266 Ga. 364, 365, 466 S.E.2d 835

(1996), we hold that the trust agreement does indeed prohibit acceleration, and that the superior court erred in ruling otherwise.

On June 3, 1961, while in the midst of a pending divorce, C. Howard Candler, Jr. and Ruth O. Candler created an irrevocable trust in full settlement of Howard Candler's support obligations to Ruth Candler. Trust Company of Georgia (now SunTrust Bank) was named as trustee. The trust provided that Ruth Candler was to have a life estate in the net income of the trust assets and that, upon Ruth Candler's death, the net income of the trust was to be distributed among the then living children of Howard and Ruth Candler. The trust also provided for a per stirpes distribution to the issue of any child of Howard and Ruth Candler who pre-deceased Ruth Candler. Upon the death of the "last survivor" of Howard and Ruth Candler's children, the trust was to be divided equally among the "then living" grandchildren of Howard and Ruth Candler with the issue of any then deceased grandchild taking per stirpes its deceased parent's share.

At the time the trust was created, Howard and Ruth Candler had four living children: C.H. Candler III; Samuel O. Candler; Ruth C. Lovett; and Flora G. Candler Fuller. Howard Candler died in 1988, and Ruth Candler died on September 2, 1996. Ruth Candler was survived by three of her children: C.H. Candler III; Samuel O. Candler; and Flora G. Candler Fuller. (Ruth C. Lovett died before either one of her parents in 1964, leaving three children.)

On March 4, 1997 the surviving children of Howard and Ruth Candler filed a petition requesting the superior court to construe the 1961 trust agreement and give direction to the trustee with regard to its obligations under the agreement. The petition named the trustee, all 13 of the grandchildren of Howard and Ruth Candler, and "all otherwise unrepresented descendants, born and unborn" as respondents. The court appointed William J. Linkous, Jr., as guardian ad litem, to protect the interests of the unrepresented descendants of Howard and Ruth Candler. Thereafter, petitioners filed a written instrument, pursuant to OCGA § 53-2-115[13] seeking renunciation, release, and termination in full of their interests in the trust.

In a final order entered on September 17, 1997, the court ordered the trustee to distribute the trust to Howard and Ruth Candler's 13 grandchildren. The court reached that decision after concluding (1) that there was no language in the trust agreement which indicated an intent to prohibit acceleration; and (2) that petitioners' renunciation of their interests in the trust produced the same result as if they had predeceased Ruth Candler.

---

13. This former Code section is no longer effective as of January 1, 1998, but only to the extent that no vested rights are impaired.

The guardian ad litem appeals. Relying upon Wetherbee v. First State Bank & Trust Co., supra, he asserts that the trust agreement indicates an intent on the part of Howard and Ruth Candler to prohibit acceleration of the trust. We agree.

The common law indicates that a remainder interest can be accelerated upon the renunciation of a preceding life interest, unless the terms and circumstances of the donative instrument manifest a contrary intent.[14] Restatement (First) of Property 659 § 231 (1936). Jurisdictions have differed on what constitutes a "contrary intent." Therefore, the question must be whether, under Georgia law, the trust at issue manifests a contrary intent with respect to acceleration of the remainder interests.

In *Wetherbee*, Mr. Wetherbee created a trust for the maintenance and support of his wife for life. Upon his wife's death, a specified percentage of the trust was to be placed into a trust for each of his then living sons for their support for life. Upon the termination of the trust created for each son, the remainder was to go to his surviving wife and descendants. After Mr. Wetherbee died, his sons renounced their interests in the trust. When Mrs. Wetherbee died, the remaindermen sought to accelerate their interests. The Court observed that "the principle of acceleration of remainders is limited to those cases wherein the testator has not 'otherwise indicated' a contrary intent." *Wetherbee*, supra at 365, 466 S.E.2d 835. The Court then found a contrary intent because the testator had provided that the holder of the future interest must survive the holder of the renounced interest. In so doing, the court stated that the indication of the testator's contrary intent need not be express, but may be implied from the provisions and language of the trust.

Wetherbee controls the outcome of this case. Just as the instrument in *Wetherbee* provided that the holder of the remainder (the wife and descendants) must survive the holder of the renounced life interest (the sons), so too the instrument in this case provides that the grandchildren must survive their parents in order to take their interests in the trust. Accordingly, just as the instrument in *Wetherbee* indicated an intent to prohibit acceleration, so too the instrument in this case must be viewed as indicating an intent to prohibit acceleration.

Although other jurisdictions might take an approach which differs from *Wetherbee*, see generally Anno., 7 A.L.R.4th 1084 (1981), it cannot be said that Georgia lies outside the mainstream in this regard. Many jurisdictions hold, as does Georgia, that a substitutionary gift in a will indicates a contrary intent on the part of the testator with respect to acceleration of the remainder interests.

---

14. This common law principle was codified at OCGA § 53-2-115(c): "Unless the decedent . . . has otherwise indicated by [the terms of] his or her will, the interest renounced and any future interest which is to take effect . . . after the termination of the interest renounced shall pass as if the person renouncing had predeceased the decedent."

See, e.g., Trenton Banking Co. v. Hawley, 7 N.J.Super. 301, 70 A.2d 896 (1950) (the gift of the remainder was made to a class that would have to stay open until the death of the life beneficiary); Bass v. Moore, 229 N.C. 211, 49 S.E.2d 391 (1948) (the remaindermen's right of enjoyment was contingent upon whether they survived the life beneficiary); Compton v. Rixey's Ex'rs., 124 Va. 548, 98 S.E. 651 (1919) (acceleration of remainder would be contrary to intent of testator); and Cool v. Cool, 54 Ind. 225 (1876) (no acceleration of the remainder when widow holder of life estate elected to take against the will). This rationale is logical, for if a class of remaindermen cannot be ascertained until the death of the life beneficiary, then acceleration must not have been contemplated by the testator.

The class of remaindermen in the Candler trust is subject to open by the birth of more grandchildren. In addition, it is subject to change by the death of a grandchild, entitling that grandchild's issue to take its share. This contingency does not expire until the death of the last of Howard and Ruth Candler's children. Therefore, the remaindermen cannot be ascertained until the last child of Howard and Ruth Candler has died. To hold otherwise would be contrary to the intent of the Candlers and would deprive potential class members of their share of the trust.

JUDGMENT REVERSED.

Problems, Notes, and Questions

1. G died devising $100,000 in trust, "income to my daughter, A, for life, remainder in corpus to such of A's children as survive A; if none, to my younger brother, B." The residue of G's estate was devised to G's husband, C. What do you think should happen to the $100,000 trust in the following alternative circumstances? See 1 Restatement of Property app. at 48-79.

(a) A predeceased G. G was survived by A's two children, X and Y.

(b) A survived G, but disclaimed her income interest. At G's death, A was married and 42 years old. A's two children, X and Y, were 17-year-old twins who have just received letters of acceptance from a prestigious private university where the costs of tuition and other charges amount to about $30,000 per year. Although A hasn't passed the menopause, she certifies that the last thing on her wish list is another child.

(c) In Problem 1(b), would it make any difference if G's devise had taken the following form: "income to my daughter, A, for life, remainder in corpus to A's children, but if none of A's children survives A, to my younger brother, B"?

(d) Suppose G's devise had stated: "income to my daughter, A, for life, remainder in corpus to A's then-living children; if none, to my younger brother, B." A comment to § 233 of the Restatement of Property states:

> *Comment c. Construction problem as to existence of condition precedent.* The rule stated in [§ 233] applies only when the language of a limitation is construed to create a succeeding interest subject to a condition precedent which remains unfulfilled at the time when the creating conveyance becomes operative. . . . In resolving this preliminary problem of construction, the criterion is whether the terms and circumstances of the limitation manifest an intent to benefit persons living at the termination of the preceding interest or at the death of the person to whom such preceding interest was limited.

In Thomsen v. Thomsen, 166 P.2d 417, 164 A.L.R. 1426 (Okla. 1946), the court said:

> The doctrine of acceleration is, according to the great weight of authority, a rule of interpretation and is to be applied so as to effect and not defeat the testator's intent. . . . [T]he doctrine . . . proceeds upon the supposition that although the ultimate devise is in terms not to take effect in possession until the death of the life tenant, yet in point of fact it is to be read as a limitation of the remainder to take effect in every event which removes the prior estate out of the way and is applied in promotion of the presumed intention of the testator, and not to defeat his intention.

(e) Assume that the remainder, if stated as in Problem 1(c), can be accelerated because it's subject to a condition subsequent. Would B's interest and the mythical interests of A's unborn and unadopted children be extinguished? Or, would the interests of X and Y somehow remain subject to open and to the condition subsequent of surviving their mother, A? See Restatement of Property § 231 comments h & i (declaring that the accelerated remainder becomes indefeasible). Compare Danz v. Danz, 26 N.E.2d 872 (Ill. 1940) (holding the accelerated remainder to be indefeasible, the predominant view according to Simes & Smith on Future Interests § 798), with Hasemeier v. Welke, 141 N.E. 176 (Ill. 1923).

2. *Disclaimer Statutes.* Disclaimers, and their consequences on succeeding interests, are now widely regulated by statute. See supra Chapter 2, Part C. If the *Linkous* case had been governed by Uniform Disclaimer of Property Interests Act (UDPIA) § 6(b)(4), would there have been a different outcome? How would UDPIA § 6(b)(4) change your answers to Problem 1?

In Pate v. Ford, 376 S.E.2d 775 (S.C. 1989), William W. Pate, Sr., died in 1979, leaving an estate valued at approximately $1.6 million. Aletha F. Pate, William's wife, died in 1983, leaving an estate valued at approximately $6.78 million. William's will devised the residue of his estate in trust, with the income going to Aletha for life. At her death, the corpus was to be divided into three equal shares. Aletha's will provided that, if William didn't survive her, her estate shall also be divided into three equal shares, to be disposed of under identical terms as those contained in William's will.

Two of the three one-third shares were to continue in trust, one to pay the income to the couple's son, Billy, for life, and the other to pay the income to the couple's other son, Wallace, for life. The provisions for distribution of the corpus were identical:

> On Billy's death, [his one-third] trust shall terminate and . . . my Trustee shall distribute the assets of the trust in equal shares per stirpes to my natural born grandchildren.
>
> On Wallace's death, [his one-third] trust shall terminate and . . . my Trustee shall distribute the assets of the trust in equal shares per stirpes to my natural born grandchildren.

Wallace has five children. Billy has been thrice married, but has never had any children; Billy's wife is now 32 years old.

Wallace filed a disclaimer of his income interest in his one-third share. Under UDPIA § 6(b)(4), does the remainder interest following Wallace's income interest accelerate?

EXTERNAL REFERENCE. Patricia J. Roberts, The Acceleration of Remainders—Manipulating the Identity of Remaindermen, 42 S.C. L. Rev. 295 (1991).

Sellick v. Sellick

173 N.W. 609 (Mich. 1919)

FELLOWS, J. This case involves the construction of the will of William J. Sellick, late of Paw Paw, Van Buren county, and the effect as between certain of the legatees of the election of the widow to take [a forced share] under the statute. Mr. Sellick left real estate inventoried at $8,500 and personal property inventoried at upwards of $176,000. He left a widow, Caroline Sellick, and one son, William R. Sellick, the plaintiff, now grown to manhood, who was the child of a former wife. He also left collateral kindred, including the defendants Arthur F. Sellick, a nephew, and Gertrude Sellick, a niece. To his collateral kindred other than defendants he gave varying sums aggregating $15,000. By the second clause of his will he gave to each of the defendants $5,000. The first clause of his will is as follows:

> I give, devise and bequeath to my wife, Caroline Sellick, twenty-five thousand dollars ($25,000), to be used and enjoyed by her during her life and at her death to be equally divided between my nephew, Arthur F. Sellick, and my niece, Gertrude Sellick.

The residue of his estate he gave to his son, the plaintiff. The widow elected to take [a forced share] under the statute. The trial judge construed the first clause of the will, when taken in connection with the second clause, which gave each defendant $5,000, and the residuary clause, as giving the widow absolutely $25,000, and accordingly held that the defendants took nothing under such clause. This rendered unnecessary the determination of the other questions involved. From a decree in accordance with these views the defendants appeal, and it is here urged by their counsel that the first clause of the will gave the widow a life estate, with remainder over to them; that by the election of the widow to take under the statute her life estate is at an end, and that, applying the doctrine of acceleration of remainders, they are now entitled to said sum of $25,000. On the other hand, it is insisted by counsel for the appellee that . . . we should not apply the doctrine of acceleration of remainders, but that such life estate, given to the widow by the will, should be sequestered to reimburse the plaintiff in part for the depletion of his bequest occasioned by the payment out of it of the sums necessary to make up the widow's statutory share. In short, that he is known in the law as a disappointed legatee, and that the doctrine of acceleration of remainders should not be adopted at the expense of disappointed legatees. . . .

It must be conceded at the outset that the decisions of the court of last resort of the state of Pennsylvania sustain the contention of defendants' counsel unequivocally. Is the rule laid down by the Pennsylvania court supported by the weight of authority and by equitable principles? Should the doctrine of acceleration of remainders be applied where by its application the remainderman gets more than the will gave to him and legatees either specific or residuary get less? To these questions we shall now direct our attention.

This court has recognized the doctrine of acceleration of remainders upon the termination of the life estate of the widow by her election to take under the statute. Schulz's Estate, 113 Mich. 592, 71 N. W. 1079. But that was a case where none of the legatees were in any way harmed by the application of the doctrine. By the election of the widow to take under the statute their bequests were proportionately diminished, and by the acceleration of their remainders they were proportionately reimbursed. . . .

In the case of Jones v. Knappen, 63 Vt. 391 (22 Atl. 630, 14 L. R. a. 293), the court had before it a case quite similar to the instant case. We quote from the syllabus:

> The election of the widow, who is made life tenant of her husband's property, to take against his will does not accelerate the time for distribution so that it may be made during her lifetime; where the remainder is to be divided between specific and residuary devisees and the result of her election would work inequity by diminishing the residuary, and leaving the specific devisees to be paid in full.

In this case the court quotes the following from Woerner on Administration, 119:

> The rejection by the widow of the provisions made for her by will, generally results in the diminution or contravention of devises and legacies to other parties. The rule in such case is that the devise or legacy which the widow rejects is to be applied in compensation of those whom her election disappoints

—and then says:

> The controlling, and, we think, the more reasonable principle announced in most of these cases is the one expressed by Woerner, supra, viz. to use the renounced devises and legacies given by the will to the widow to compensate, as far as may be, the devises and legacies diminished by such renunciation. When the remaindermen are affected pro rata by such renunciation, acceleration of the enjoyment of their devises or legacies, diminished proportionally, will equitably compensate them, so far as possible for such diminution. But in this case acceleration of enjoyment would increase the specific pecuniary legacies, to the detriment of the residuary legatees, whose shares only are diminished by the renunciation. Applying the principle stated, the life use of the property given by the will to the widow, and renounced by her, should be used to compensate the residuary legatees, the next of kin of the testator and of his wife. . . .

We are persuaded that under the great weight of authority the contention of plaintiff's counsel in this regard must prevail. While the doctrine of acceleration of the time of taking effect of the remainder upon the termination of the life estate by act other than the death of the life tenant (i. e., by the election of the widow to take under the statute) must be recognized and applied in proper cases, such doctrine should not be applied where by the election a portion only of the legacies are diminished in order to make up the amount required by the statute to satisfy the widow's statutory rights. And that this should be true whether the legacy diminished be a specific or a residuary one. Under such circumstances the disappointed legatee may in a court of equity compel the sequestration of the legacy to the refractory legatee for the purpose of diminishing the amount of his disappointment.

Manifestly this is in consonance with equitable principles. In the instant case the residuary fund given to the plaintiff has been diminished by many thousand dollars in order to discharge the claim of the widow resulting from her election. To adopt defendants' claim would give to them the $25,000 many years before the time fixed by the testator for its payment. They would not only receive the amount given them by the will, but they would also receive the widow's life estate renounced by her to the disadvantage of the plaintiff. Equitable principles do not require that this should be done.

We are asked to fix the present worth of the widow's life use of the $25,000 with a view of finally closing the estate and disposing of all matters at once. The parties interested are all of age, and may make such adjustment as they may desire, but we do not feel empowered to fix the present worth of the widow's use and direct its present payment. We see no occasion, however, to longer hold the estate open. a trustee may be appointed to handle this fund of $25,000. He shall annually pay the income thereon to the plaintiff during the life of the widow, and upon her death pay the corpus to defendants in equal shares.

It follows that the decree must be reversed, and one here entered in conformity with this opinion. The defendants will recover costs of this court. Neither party will recover costs of the circuit court.

———

INTERNAL REFERENCE. For discussion of the effect of disclaimers on funding the elective share, see supra Chapter 10, Part A.

EXTERNAL REFERENCE. Restatement of Property §§ 234-35.

3. Failure of a Future Interest—Effect

A future interest can fail for a variety of reasons. The beneficiary might predecease the testator or predecease a subsequent time to which survival is required by the terms of the disposition; the future interest might be disclaimed; it might violate the Rule Against Perpetuities; and so on.

In general, a future interest that fails, regardless of the reason, is treated as if it weren't created. A particular problem exists, however, if the failed future interest is an executory interest.

Proprietors of the Church in Brattle Square v. Grant

69 Mass. (3 Gray) 142 (1855)

[Lydia Hancock, John Hancock's aunt, died in 1777, leaving a will that provided:

> I give and bequeath unto . . . the Church of Christ in Brattle Street in Boston . . . all that brick dwelling-house and land situated in Queen Street . . . to hold the same . . . upon [the] express condition and limitation . . . that the minister or eldest minister of said church shall constantly reside and dwell in said house, during such time as he is minister of said church; and in case the same is not improved for this use only, I then declare this bequest to be void and of no force, and order that said house and land then [go] to my nephew, John Hancock, Esquire, and to his heirs forever.

The residue of her estate was also devised to John Hancock, who survived her, but died fifteen years later, in 1793.

Some seventy-five or so years after Lydia Hancock's death, the Proprietors of the Church brought a bill in equity, alleging that the conditions had been continuously satisfied and that a sale of the estate had now become necessary to carry out the intent of the devise.

The court held that Lydia Hancock's will created a fee simple subject to an executory limitation in favor of the deacons of the Church; and an executory interest (executory devise) in favor of John Hancock and his heirs. The court further held that John Hancock's executory interest violated the Rule Against Perpetuities (an English invention) and was invalid. (Obviously, the Declaration of Independence had not freed the new American state of all English influence!)

The final question was how the invalidity of John Hancock's executory interest affected the church's fee simple interest.]

BIGELOW, J. . . . Upon this point we understand the rule to be, that if a limitation over is void by reason of its remoteness, it places all prior gifts in the same situation as if the devise over had been wholly omitted. Therefore a gift of the fee or the entire interest, subject to an executory limitation which is too remote, takes effect as if it had been originally limited free from any divesting gift. The general principle applicable to such cases is, that when a subsequent condition or limitation is void by reason of its being impossible, repugnant or contrary to law, the estate becomes vested in the first taker, discharged of the condition or limitation over, according to the terms in which it was granted or devised; if for life, then it takes effect as a life estate; if in fee, then as a fee simple absolute. The reason on which this rule is said to rest is, that when a party has granted or devised an estate, he shall not be allowed to fetter or defeat it, by annexing thereto impossible, illegal or repugnant conditions or limitations.

Such indeed is the necessary result which follows from the manner in which executory devises came into being and were engrafted on the stock of the common law. Originally, . . . no estate could be limited over after a limitation in fee simple, and in such case the estate became absolute in the first taker. This rule was afterwards relaxed in cases of devises, for the purpose of effectuating the intent of testators, so far as to render such gifts valid by way of executory devise, when confined within the limits prescribed to guard against perpetuities.

The result, therefore, to which we have arrived on the whole case is, that the gift over to John Hancock is an executory devise, void for remoteness; and that the estate, upon breach of the prescribed condition, would not pass to John Hancock and his heirs, by virtue of the residuary clause, nor would it vest in the heirs at law of the testatrix. But being an estate in fee in the deacons and their successors, and the gift over being void, as contrary to the policy of the law, by reason of violating the rule against perpetuities, the title became absolute, as a vested remainder in fee, after the decease of the mother of the testatrix, in the deacons and their successors, and they hold it in fee simple, free from the divesting limitation.

Notes

1. *Possibility of Reverter.* In First Universalist Society v. Boland, 29 N.E. 524 (Mass. 1892), Clark conveyed real property by deed to the First Universalist Society as follows:

> so long as said real estate shall by said society or its assigns be devoted to the uses, interests, and support of [specified] doctrines of the Christian religion; and when said real estate shall by said society or its assigns be diverted from the uses, interests and support aforesaid to any other interests, uses, or purposes than as aforesaid, then the title of said society or its assigns in the same shall forever cease, and be forever vested in the following named persons. . . .

The court held that Clark's conveyance created a fee simple determinable in the Society, and an executory interest in the persons named to take in the case of a diversion from the specified uses. The court further held that the executory interest violated the Rule Against Perpetuities and was invalid.

The court then turned to the question of the effect of that invalidity on the state of the title:

> Since the estate of the plaintiff may determine, and since there is no valid limitation over, it follows that there is a possibility of reverter in the original grantor, Clark. This is similar to, though not quite identical with, the possibility of reverter which remains in the grantor of land upon a condition subsequent. The exact nature and incidents of this right need not now be discussed, but it represents whatever is not conveyed by the deed, and it is the possibility that the land may revert to the grantor or his heirs when the granted estate determines. Clark's possibility of reverter is not invalid for remoteness. It has been expressly held by this court that such possibility of reverter . . . is not within the rule against perpetuities. Tobey v. Moore, 130 Mass. 448; French v. Old South Soc., 166 Mass. 479. If there is any distinction in this respect between such possibility of reverter and that which arises upon the determination of a qualified fee, it would seem to be in favor of the latter: but they should be governed by the same rule. If one is not held void for remoteness, the other should not be. The very many cases cited in Gray, Prop. §§ 305-312, show conclusively that the general understanding of courts and of the profession in America has been that the rule as to remoteness does not apply, though the learned author thinks this view erroneous in principle. . . . [T]he plaintiff's title must be deemed imperfect, and the entry must be, bill dismissed.

2. *State of the Authorities.* The distinction drawn by the *Grant* and *Boland* decisions has been generally followed. For more modern cases following *Grant*,

see Betts v. Snyder, 19 A.2d 82 (Pa. 1941); Standard Knitting Mills, Inc. v. Allen, 424 S.W.2d 796 (Tenn. 1967). For a case in accord with *Boland*, see City of Klamath Falls v. Bell, 490 P.2d 515 (Or. Ct. App. 1971). See William H. Agnor, A Tale of Two Cases, 17 Vand. L. Rev. 1427 (1964).

The Restatement 2d of Property § 1.5 comments b & c assert a different position, by suggesting that it might be appropriate to hold that the invalidity of an executory interest following a fee simple determinable as well as a fee simple subject to an executory limitation renders the fee interest absolute. This position was previously urged in Lawrence W. Waggoner, Reformulating the Structure of Estates: a Proposal for Legislative Action, 85 Harv. L. Rev. 729, 737-38, 757 (1972).

4. Rule Against Perpetuities As a Consequence of Classification

Before going on to Chapter 18 on construction, we should like to note one final consequence of classification: the Rule Against Perpetuities. Classification is extremely important in determining whether an interest is subject to the Rule Against Perpetuities. Reversions, possibilities of reverter, rights of entry, and vested remainders (including those that are vested subject to defeasance) aren't subject to the Rule. The Rule applies to contingent remainders and executory interests.

Once the Rule is determined to be applicable, the next inquiry is whether the particular contingent remainder or executory interest violates the Rule or not. This question is considered in Chapter 19.

Chapter 18

Construction

No greater challenge exists in estate planning practice than expressing your client's intent without ambiguity. An ability to write clearly isn't the only skill necessary. Another is the ability to anticipate, and hence clearly to provide for, the entire range of possible future events that can affect a disposition. Both of these skills can be acquired.

A first step in learning to draft without ambiguity is to examine mistakes that have been made in the past. Too often, the cases in this chapter bring into question the meaning of documents drafted by your predecessors at the bar. We've already seen evidence of this problem in Chapter 12. Whether the document was drafted by a lawyer or not, however, nearly every construction case that we've studied and that we're about to study represents someone's drafting failure.

Drafting failures tend to recur in patterns. With respect to future interests, the primary subject of this chapter, the same mistakes are made over and over again. Once you know what they are, you'll find that drafting to avoid these mistakes is surprisingly easy.

PART A. EXPRESS AND IMPLIED CONDITIONS OF SURVIVAL

Statutory References: *UPC §§ 2-701, -707*

One of the recurring problems in future interests law concerns survival: Is a future interest extinguished (terminated) if its holder dies after the creation of the interest but before the time of possession or enjoyment or before reaching a specified age? This is a question of construction, of determining the transferor's intent—not a question of lapse or of classification.

Lapse Distinguished. As we learned in Part B of Chapter 6, the rule of lapse requires a devisee under a *will* to survive the *testator*. The rule of lapse is based on the proposition that a property interest cannot be *transferred* to a deceased person. Thus, a devise to a devisee who predeceases the testator lapses, notwithstanding any contrary intent on the testator's part. The rule of lapse is not a question of construction.

The rule of lapse, however, doesn't require a beneficiary of a future interest to be alive at the distribution date—the time when a future interest becomes possessory. The distribution date arises *after*, sometimes long after, the time when the future interest was *transferred* to its recipient. To illustrate, take the simple case of "to A for life, remainder to B." Suppose that this disposition was created in G's will. The common-law rule of lapse requires both A and B to be alive when G dies because that's the time when both A and B receive their interests. Once the hurdle of surviving G is satisfied, there's no further requirement implicit in the common law necessitating B's survival of A. Consequently, an interest is not subject to a condition of survival merely because it is a *future* interest. If a condition of survival exists, it derives from a finding of the transferor's intention on the point. The survival question is therefore a question of construction, distinguishable from the rule of lapse.

1. Basic Common-Law Rule: Conditions of Survival Not Implied

Before proceeding to a discussion of the basic constructional question of survival, we digress briefly to set the matter of survival into perspective. Future interests are normally granted to persons in one or more generations *younger* than that of the income beneficiary. If the income interest is granted to the grantor's surviving spouse, the remainder interest is likely to be granted to the couple's children or descendants; if the income interest is granted to a child of the grantor, the remainder interest is likely to be granted to the child's children or descendants. It's unusual, in other words, to grant an income interest to the grantor's grandchild and follow it with a remainder interest to the grantor's parents.

Consequently, when the beneficiary of a future interest predeceases the time of possession or enjoyment, it's an unusual event, an event typically caused by the beneficiary's *premature* death. When the unusual happens, however, and a beneficiary dies before the distribution date, the first place to look to see if that event was anticipated and provided for is in the governing instrument. If the governing instrument *expressly* imposes a condition of survival—as, for example, in the disposition "to A for life, remainder to B *if B survives A*"—, then survival, of course, is required. Conversely, if the governing instrument *expressly* states that no condition of survival is imposed—as, for example, in the disposition "to A for life, remainder to B *whether or not B survives A*"—, then, of course, B need not survive A.

What happens if the governing instrument *expresses* neither intention—as, for example, in the disposition "to A for life, remainder to B"?

The basic rule of construction at common law is that a condition of survival is not implied.

Several rationales are offered in support of this rule and in favor of the product of this rule—transmissible future interests. The rule, it's said, (i) furthers the constructional preference for complete dispositions of property, (ii) furthers the constructional preference for equality of distribution among the different lines of descent, and (iii) is supported by the constructional preferences for vested over contingent interests, for vesting at the earliest possible time, and for indefeasible vesting at the earliest possible time. See Restatement of Property § 243, comments.

While it may be true that the constructional preferences set forth in (iii) played an important role in fashioning the rule against implied conditions of survival, one shouldn't equate the two questions—classification and construction.

Whether a future interest is subject to a requirement of survival is a question of construction. Whether a future interest is vested or contingent is a question of classification.

A vested future interest can be subject to a requirement of survival. A contingent future interest may be subject to conditions unrelated to survival.

The basic rule of construction against implying conditions of survival applies to individual and class gifts.

Example 18.1: G's will devised real property "to A for life, remainder to B." Both A and B survived G. Subsequently, B predeceased A.

B's property interest isn't defeated by his death before A. Upon B's death, his remainder interest passes to his successors in interest. There's no implicit condition that B survive A, even though B's remainder is a future interest.

Example 18.2: G's will devised real property "to A for life, remainder in equal shares to B and C." A, B, and C survived G.

The rule of construction against implying conditions of survival applies to gifts to more than one individual. Consequently, if either B or C (or both) predeceases A, the predeceased taker's half passes at death through the predeceased taker's estate to the predeceased taker's successors in interest.

Example 18.3: G's will devised real property "to A for life, remainder to A's children." At G's death, A and A's daughter, X, were living. During A's lifetime, a son, Y, was born to A. Both X and Y predeceased A. The rule of construction against implying conditions of survival applies to class gifts. Restatement 2d of Property § 27.3. Consequently, X's interest passed on her death to her successors in interest, and Y's interest passed on his death to his successors in interest.

External References. John L. Garvey, Drafting Wills and Trusts: Anticipating the Birth and Death of Possible Beneficiaries, 71 Or. L. Rev. 47 (1992); Edward C. Halbach, Jr. & Lawrence W. Waggoner, The UPC's New Survivorship and Antilapse Provisions, 55 Alb. L. Rev. 1091 (1992); Edward C. Halbach, Jr., Issues About Issue: Some Recurrent Class Gift Problems, 48 Mo. L. Rev. 333, 361-70 (1983); Edward C. Halbach, Jr., Future Interests: Express and Implied Conditions of Survival (pts. 1 & 2), 49 Calif. L. Rev. 297, 431 (1961).

The Discredited (?) Divide-and-Pay-Over Rule. Once upon a time, some courts recognized a rule called the divide-and-pay-over rule. The rule was this: If the only language of a disposition directs that property be divided and paid over at a future time, survival of that time is required. A trust disposition triggering this rule would be, income "to A for life, then on A's death the trustee is to divide the corpus and pay it over to A's children."

The Restatement of Property rejects this rule:

> § *260. Direction to Divide and Pay Over at a Future Date.* In a limitation purporting to create a remainder or an executory interest, the fact that the only words of gift to the intended taker thereof consist of a direction to divide and pay over, or to convert, divide and pay over, at the end of the created prior interests or at some other future date is not a material factor in determining the existence of a requirement of survival to the date of distribution.

Today, in most states, the divide-and-pay-over rule has either been overtly repudiated or appears to have fallen into disuse or never to have been followed.

See Am. L. Prop. § 21.21. Yet, the rule has not been eradicated entirely.[1] The Supreme Court of Illinois found it applicable as a "rule . . . of construction to aid courts in determining whether a gift to a class is a vested or contingent remainder." The court said: "Early vesting frequently frustrates intentions by casting property to strangers. . . . [E]arly vesting of remainders should no longer be followed in this State without question." Harris Trust & Savings Bank v. Beach, 513 N.E.2d 833, 838-39 (Ill. 1987). The Illinois Supreme Court's opinion didn't mention the rejection of the rule by the Restatement, cases in other jurisdictions, or scholarly commentary about the rule. The court did, however, pay attention to scholarly commentary demonstrating that the rule of early vesting frequently frustrates the donor's intention. See, e.g., Daniel M. Schuyler, Drafting, Tax, and Other Consequences of the Rule of Early Vesting, 46 Ill. L. Rev. 407, 437 (1951) ("Sometimes the rule of early vesting has the effect of defeating what any sensible person would assume to be the intention of a testator."); Edward H. Rabin, The Law Favors the Vesting of Estates, Why?, 65 Colum. L. Rev. 467, 479 (1965) ("[Passing] property to a dead person's estate . . . is undesirable because it raises the possibility that persons whom the testator had no intention of benefitting will become his *de facto* beneficiary.").

Conditions Unrelated to Survival. We have seen that, at common law, a future interest to which no express conditions are attached is not subject to an implied condition of survival. But what if the future interest is subject to one or more *express* conditions *unrelated* to survival? Do these express conditions automatically subject the future interest to an *implied* condition of survival? That is thc question posed in the cases below.

Bomberger's Estate

32 A.2d 729 (Pa. 1943)

[The testator's will devised $50,000 in trust, income to his niece, Mrs. Lilly Aughinbaugh, for life, corpus on Lilly's death to Lilly's children. The will continued:

> Should [niece Lilly] . . . die without leaving a child or children, I order and direct that the bequest shall be equally divided among my nephews and nieces . . . , then living, the child or children of nieces who may be deceased to have the share their mother would have been entitled to if living.

---

1. In Will of Corwith, 622 N.Y.S.2d 424 (Sur. Ct. 1995), one of the parties to the proceeding for construction of a testamentary trust urged the court to apply the divide-and-pay-over rule. The court recognized that the rule had often been criticized, but refused to consider its continuing viability because it held that the future interest was contingent on survival of the life tenant on other grounds.

Lilly died childless. All of the testator's nieces and nephews predeceased Lilly. Charles, one of the nephews, had two children, both of whom survived Lilly. The other nephews died childless. Ada, one of the nieces, had eight children: seven of them survived Lilly, but one, John, died during Ada's lifetime. Annie, the other niece, had one child, Rachel, who survived Annie but predeceased Lilly.]

STEARNE, J. . . . The language which testator used did not impose the same contingency of survivorship upon the substitutionary gift to child or children of deceased nieces that it did upon the nephews and nieces. For a nephew or niece to take required that he or she be alive when Mrs. Aughinbaugh died without issue. However, if a niece left child or children, their interest was vested. They took in precisely the same manner as if their mother, a niece, had been living at the date of the death of Mrs. Aughinbaugh. There is nothing in the substitutionary gift which expressly states that children of deceased nieces must survive Mrs. Aughinbaugh. . . . The condition of survival to a fixed time is never implied. Such condition must appear plainly, manifestly and indisputably.

"When a condition of survival to the time of distribution has been annexed to the gifts to the first takers, but not to the gifts to the substituted beneficiaries, the condition is not to be implied with respect to the latter": President Judge Van Dusen Carpenter's Estate, 42 Pa. Dist. & Co. R. 367-369. . . .

Costs to be paid from the fund.

Lawson v. Lawson

148 S.E.2d 546 (N.C. 1966)

[The testator's will devised land to his daughter Opal Lawson Long for her life, and at her death "to her children, if any, in fee simple; if none, to [Opal's] whole brothers and sisters . . . in fee simple." Fifteen years after the testator's death, Opal died without children. Four of Opal's six whole brothers and sisters survived her. Two of Opal's whole brothers survived the testator but predeceased her; each left descendants surviving Opal.]

SHARP, J. . . . Respondents contend that at the death of the testator, J. Rad Lawson, the six whole brothers and sisters of the life tenant, all of whom were then living, took a vested remainder in the land, and that they, as children of the two whole brothers who predeceased Opal Lawson Long, inherited their interest. The law, however, is otherwise.

This case presents a typical example of a contingent remainder.

> A devises to B for life, remainder to his children but if he dies without leaving children remainder over, both the remainders are contingent; but if B afterwards marries and has a child, the remainder becomes vested in that child, subject to open and let in unborn children, and the remainders over are gone forever. The remainder becomes a vested remainder in fee in the child as soon as the child is

> born, and does not wait for the parent's death, and if the child dies in the lifetime of the parent, the vested estate in remainder descends to his heirs. 4 Kent's Commentaries, p. 284 quoted in Blanchard v. Ward, 244 N.C. 142, 146, 92 S.E.2d 776, 779.

In Watson v. Smith, 110 N.C. 6, 14 S.E. 649, testator devised land to J for life, and at J's death to such child or children of his that might then be living, but should he die without issue, then to G, W, H, and O in fee. The Court held that the limitation to G, W, H, and O, was a contingent remainder. "Alternative remainders limited upon a single precedent estate are always contingent. Such remainders are created by a limitation to one for life, with remainder in fee to his children, issue, or heirs, and, in default of such children, issue, or heirs, to another or others. . . ." 33 Am. Jur., Life Estates, Remainders, etc. § 148 (1941). . . .

Clearly the interests of the whole brothers and sisters was [sic] contingent and could not vest before the death of the life tenant, for not until then could it be determined that she would leave no issue surviving. "Where those who are to take in remainder cannot be determined until the happening of a stated event, the remainder is contingent. Only those who can answer the roll immediately upon the happening of the event acquire any estate in the properties granted." Strickland v. Jackson, 259 N.C. 81, 84, 130 S.E.2d 22, 25. Respondents' parents, having predeceased the life tenant, could not answer the roll call at her death.

The judgment of the court below is Affirmed.

Notes and Questions

1. *State of the Authorities.* The decision in *Bomberger* reflects the great majority view on the question posed by *Bomberger* and *Lawson*, and the view enunciated in Restatement of Property § 261. See, e.g., Rosenthal v. First Nat'l Bank, 239 N.E.2d 826 (Ill. 1968); Bogart's Will, 308 N.Y.S.2d 594 (Sur. Ct. 1970); Am. L. Prop. § 21.25; Simes & Smith on Future Interests § 594. A few courts have adopted the *Lawson* analysis and have imposed a condition of survival on interests that were subject to conditions unrelated to survival. See, e.g., Rushing v. Mann, 910 S.W.2d 672 (Ark. 1995); Jones v. Holland, 77 S.E.2d 202 (S.C. 1953); see also Schau v. Cecil, 136 N.W.2d 515 (Iowa 1965), superseded by statute as stated in Davies v. Radford, 433 N.W.2d 704 (Iowa 1988) (*Schau* and *Davies,* along with Estate of Ruhland, 452 N.W.2d 417 (Iowa 1990), which raised similar issues, are explained and critiqued in N. William Hines, Implied Conditions of Personal Survivorship in Iowa Future Interests Law, 75 Iowa L. Rev. 941 (1990)).

Professor Patricia J. Roberts, in Class Gifts in North Carolina—When Do We "Call the Roll"?, 21 Wake Forest L. Rev. 1 (1985), noted that the *Lawson* decision seems to have been implicitly overruled by White v. Alexander, 224 S.E.2d 617 (N.C. 1976). In *White*, G devised property to S for life, "and if he shall die without heirs of his body . . . to my heirs." S died without heirs of his body, causing the gift to G's heirs to take effect. The class of G's heirs was determined at G's death. Although some of the members of that class predeceased S, the Supreme Court of North Carolina refused to imply a requirement of survival as to their interests. Unfortunately, *White* didn't expressly overrule *Lawson*. Indeed, the opinion in *White* did not even mention *Lawson*!

2. *Classification and Construction.* Did the court in *Lawson* confuse classification and construction?

Restricted and Unrestricted Conditions of Survival. Restricted conditions of survival are said to flow from language phrased in so-called *supplanting* form.

> *Example 18.4:* "To A for life, then to B, but if B predeceases A, leaving children, then to such children." B died childless before A's death. B's interest is not extinguished. See, e.g., *Krooss*, below; Restatement of Property § 254.

> *Example 18.5:* "To A for life, then to A's children, the children of any deceased child to take their deceased parents' share." Several of A's children survived A, but one child, B, died childless before A's death. B's interest is not extinguished. See, e.g., Security Trust Co. v. Irvine, 93 A.2d 528 (Del. Ct. Ch. 1953); Estate of Houston, 201 A.2d 592 (Pa. 1964); Restatement of Property § 254.

Unrestricted conditions of survival are said to flow from language phrased in *alternative* form.

> *Example 18.6:* "To A for life, then to B or B's children." B died childless before A's death. B's interest is extinguished. See, e.g., *Robertson*, below; Restatement of Property § 252.

What do you think of the distinction between supplanting and alternative language? Is it sensible? Do the two different expressions indicate that the transferors intended the different results accorded by the law?

In re Krooss

99 N.E.2d 222, 47 A.L.R.2d 894 (N.Y. 1951)

FULD, J. Herman Krooss died in 1932. He was survived by his wife Eliese and his two children, a son, John Krooss, and a married daughter, Florence Maue. By his will, he gave his residuary estate, real and personal, to his wife, "to have and to hold the same for and during the term of her natural life," with the power to use any part of it for her support and maintenance that she deemed necessary; no trust was created. The will further provided:

> Upon the death of my beloved wife, Eliese Krooss, I then give, devise and bequeath all the rest, residue and remainder of my estate, as well real as personal, and wheresoever situate, to my beloved children, John H. Krooss and Florence Maue, nee Krooss, share and share alike, to and for their own use absolutely and forever.
>
> In the event that either of my children aforesaid should die prior to the death of my beloved wife, Eliese Krooss, leaving descendants, then it is my wish and I so direct that such descendants shall take the share their parent would have taken if then living, share and share alike, to and for their own use absolutely and forever.

Florence Maue died, without having had descendants, in 1947, three years before the life beneficiary Eliese. Some months after Eliese's death, Florence's husband, as executor of his wife's estate, instituted the present proceeding in the Surrogate's Court of Bronx County to compel John Krooss, as executor under Eliese's will and as administrator c. t. a. of Herman Krooss' estate, to render and settle his respective accounts. In order to determine whether the executors of Florence's estate had status to prosecute the proceeding, the surrogate was required, initially, to construe Herman's will. He decided that the interest given to Florence was vested at the testator's death, subject to be divested only in the event of her predeceasing her mother leaving descendants, that it passed under her will, and that her husband, as executor, was entitled to bring the action.[2] The Appellate Division modified that determination. Disagreeing with the surrogate's interpretation, the Appellate Division construed the will as imposing upon each of the remaindermen a condition that he or she survive the life beneficiary; Florence having died without children before Eliese, that condition was not met, and, concluded the court, as to Florence's share in the remainder, Krooss died intestate.

---

2. In her will, Florence left her residuary estate in trust to her husband and to her brother John, as trustees, to pay the net income therefrom to the husband for life; on his death, the principal was to be distributed between Florence's two nephews, the children of her brother John, if living, and to their issue per stirpes if either should die before the termination of the trust.

The law has long favored a construction of language in deed and will that accomplishes the vesting of estates; such a result is preferred because, among other things, it enables property to be freely transferred at the earliest possible date. Accordingly, the courts are intent upon restricting defeating events to the exact circumstances specified.

The will under consideration is simple in language and simple in plan. The testator gave his widow a life estate and a power to use the principal if it proved necessary for her maintenance and support. What remained after her death he gave "absolutely and forever" in equal shares to his two children, Florence and John. Had the will stopped at that point, there would be no question that the remainders were vested. And, since that is so, additional language will not be read as qualifying or cutting down the estate unless that language is as clear and decisive as that which created the vested remainder. The further language used by the testator in this case demonstrates, not that he was rendering the vesting of the estates in his children conditional upon survival of the life beneficiary, but that he was willing to have those estates divested only upon the combined occurrences of two further events. He explicitly provided, if either of his children died before his wife, "leaving descendants," then "such descendants shall take the share the parent would have taken if then living". If the words used mean what they say, then, divestiture of the remainder estates depended upon the happening of two plainly expressed and stipulated conditions: (1) the child, Florence or John, must die before the life beneficiary, and (2) the child so dying must leave descendants. Only if both of those conditions came to pass was the remainder—by apt and unequivocal language already vested in Florence and John—to be divested and bestowed instead upon the descendants of him or her who might have died.

When a will contains language that has acquired, through judicial decision, a definite and established significance, the testator is taken to have employed that language in that sense and with that meaning in mind. . . .

Over the years, the courts have uniformly held that language such as that used by the testator here, or language substantially identical, creates a vested remainder in fee subject to be divested by the remainderman's failing to survive the life beneficiary, *if, but only if,* such remainderman leaves issue or descendants surviving. . . .

Leading commentators after reviewing the cases, have expressed themselves in similar fashion. (See 2 Powell on Real Property (1950), §§ 330-331, pp. 728-737; 2 Redfield on Law of Wills (1866), § 65, pp. 648-649; 3 Restatement, Property, § 254, Comment a, Illustration 1, particularly Example II, pp. 1284-1286.) Thus, Professor Richard R. Powell of Columbia University Law School and Reporter on Property for the American Law Institute, in his recent work on the Law of Real Property, considers the subject at some length and sums up the law in this way (op. cit., § 330, pp. 729-730):

> Supplanting limitations differ, in that some provide a taker who is to become the substitute whenever the prior taker fails to survive, while others provide a taker who is to become the substitute only under some circumstances. In cases of the second type, the constructional preference for early indefeasibility causes the requirement of survival to be strictly construed, and to operate only under the exact circumstances stipulated . . . . Similarly, in a gift "to my wife B for life, then to my children and the issue of those of my children who may be dead leaving children," the interest of a child of the testator who dies without surviving issue is indefeasible.

Turning to the will before us, we find that, at the expiration of the wife's life estate, the testator "then" gave the remainder to his children "absolutely and forever." The use of the word "then" as an "adverb of time" must be, as it long has been, construed to relate solely "to the time of enjoyment of the estate, and not to the time of its vesting in interest." Hence, the sole combination of events which could divest the "absolute" gift to the daughter Florence was her death before her mother, "leaving descendants". Only one of the specified conditions was fulfilled; although Florence did predecease her mother, she did not leave descendants. Consequently, her absolute gift remained vested and was not defeated. Not only the language employed, but the omission of any "words of survival" to indicate an intent that Florence's brother was to take if Florence died without children, illumines the testator's design to give his daughter a vested remainder. . . .

The order of the Appellate Division should be reversed and the decree of the Surrogate's Court affirmed, with costs in this court and in the Appellate Division to all parties, appearing separately and filing separate briefs, payable out of the estate. . . .

Note and Question

Restricted Condition of Survival Stated as a Condition Precedent. Would the meaning of Herman Krooss's will have been litigated if the restricted condition of survival had been stated in the form of a condition precedent?

As a general rule, clarity of expression is promoted by stating conditions in precedent form. Conditions stated in subsequent form tend to be lazily formulated and incomplete. Although it takes greater effort and discipline to state conditions in precedent form, the end product is usually worth the effort.

Robertson v. Robertson

48 N.E.2d 29 (Mass. 1943)

FIELD, C.J. This petition for partition of certain real estate, in Hudson, was brought in the Probate Court by Ralph A. Robertson and comes before us upon an appeal by Essie Pope, one of the respondents, from a decree of that court for partition.

The case arises upon the following facts which appear in the report of material facts made by the judge: Lillian G. Pope, late of Hudson, died July 12, 1931, leaving a will that has been duly allowed, which contained the following provisions:

> Fourth;—To my daughter, Grace M. Morse and her husband, Alvah W. Morse, the use, income and enjoyment of my homestead estate situated at No. 11 Felton Street, in said Hudson for the term of their natural lives or of the life of the survivor. [Grace and Alvah, or the survivor, were given a power to sell the premises.] In case that at the death of the survivor of said Grace M. Morse and said Alvah W. Morse said homestead has not then been sold then it is to go to [sic] one half part to my said son, Ernest F. Pope, one quarter part of [sic] my said daughter, Ella B. Robertson and one quarter part to my said grandson, Ralph A. Robertson, or to the issue of any that may then be dead by the right of representation.
>
> Fifth;—All the rest and residue of my estate to my children, Ella B. Robertson, Grace M. Morse and my grandchild, Ralph A. Robertson, in equal shares, or to the issue of any who may be dead by the right of representation.

The testatrix left surviving her a son, Ernest F. Pope, married to Essie Pope, a daughter Grace M. Morse, married to Alvah W. Morse, a daughter Ella B. Robertson, and a grandson, Ralph A. Robertson, who, it may be guessed, was the son of Ella B. Robertson although the fact does not appear. The son, Ernest F. Pope, died January 26, 1940, leaving a widow, Essie Pope, and no issue. The daughter Grace M. Morse died June 26, 1940, leaving no issue. Her husband, Alvah W. Morse, had predeceased her. At the time of the death of Grace M. Morse the premises described in the will of the testatrix as her "homestead estate" had not been sold. The record does not disclose what, if any, property the testatrix owned at the time of her death other than the "homestead estate."

Ralph A. Robertson, the grandson of the testatrix, brought the present petition for partition of the "homestead estate," referred to in the fourth clause of the will, and upon this petition a decree was entered that partition of the "homestead estate" be made between the petitioner, Ralph A. Robertson, and Ella B. Robertson in equal shares, and a commissioner was appointed to make such partition. The basis of this decree was that Ella B. Robertson and Ralph A. Robertson each took one quarter part of the "homestead estate" under the fourth clause of the will, but that the devise by that clause of one half part thereof to Ernest F. Pope failed by reason of his death before the death of his sister Grace M. Morse, and therefore was disposed of by the fifth or residuary clause of the will in equal shares to Ella B. Robertson, Ralph A. Robertson, and Grace M. Morse, each of whom took under said clause one sixth part of the "homestead estate," and that the one sixth part of the "homestead estate" that passed to Grace M. Morse went "by purchase from the heirs and legatees under" her will in equal shares to Ella B. Robertson and Ralph A. Robertson, so that each of them took by such transfer one twelfth part of the "homestead estate," with the result that in the aggregate Ella B. Robertson and Ralph A. Robertson each was entitled to one half part of the "homestead estate." Essie Pope, the widow of Ernest F. Pope, appealed from this decree, and contends, in substance, that the one half part of the "homestead estate" devised to her husband by the fourth clause of the will did not fail so that this part fell into the residue of the estate, but rather that it was the property of his estate in which she, as his widow, is entitled to share. The record does not show, however, to what extent she, as his widow, was entitled to share in his estate. . . .

We think that the decree of the Probate Court was based upon the correct interpretation of the will, that Ernest F. Pope took only a contingent remainder in one half part of the "homestead estate," with the result that, since the contingency upon which it depended did not happen, the appellant, Essie Pope, the widow of Ernest F. Pope, is not entitled to share in the partition of the "homestead estate." . . .

The fact that the gift to Ernest F. Pope by the provision of the fourth clause here quoted was subject to being defeated by an exercise of the power of sale . . . did not render the gift to him contingent. A remainder after a life estate is none the less vested because subject to being defeated by the exercise of a power of sale if, apart from the existence of the power, it would be a vested remainder. In these circumstances such a remainder is a vested remainder subject to being divested by the exercise of the power rather than a contingent remainder. . . . And in our opinion the conditional language with reference to the gift in default of sale under the power, "In case that at the death of the survivor of said Grace M. Morse and said Alvah W. Morse said homestead has not then been sold," does not of itself preclude this result so far as the effect of the existence of the power to sell is concerned. If the remainder in one half part of the "homestead estate" given to Ernest F. Pope was contingent rather than vested, it is for reasons other than the existence of the power of sale. . . .

We think that the language of the fourth clause of the will as a whole read in the light of the other provisions of the will discloses an intention on the part of the testatrix to postpone the acquisition by her son, Ernest F. Pope, of a vested interest in one half part of the "homestead estate" until the happening of a future event, that is, the death of the survivor of the life tenants, so that he must be deemed to have taken only a contingent interest—an interest contingent upon his surviving the life tenants, a contingency that did not happen. . . .

[T]he gift to the "issue" of Ernest F. Pope was not a gift by way of substitution in the sense of a supplanting gift. See for the distinction between an "alternative limitation" and a "supplanting limitation" Am. Law Inst. Restatement: Property, § 253, comment c. The gift to the "issue" of Ernest F. Pope ascertained as of the time of distribution, the time of the death of the surviving life tenant, is as direct a gift as the gift to Ernest F. Pope. The language of the will fixes the same time for these gifts to take effect, the time of the death of the surviving life tenant. One half part of the "homestead estate" is "then . . . to go" to Ernest F. Pope or to his "issue," and the gifts are expressly made in the alternative by reason of the use of the conjunction "or" connecting them. The canon of construction stated in Am. Law Inst. Restatement: Property, § 252, relating to an "alternative limitation employing the word 'or'," is as follows:

> In a limitation purporting to create a remainder or an executory interest, in "B or his children," or in "B or his issue," or in "B or his descendants," or by other language of similar import, the alternative form tends to establish as to the interest of B that (a) a requirement of survival to the end of all preceding interests exists; and (b) such survival is a condition precedent of such interest.

This canon of construction is clearly applicable to the language of the will here involved. And in the light of the other considerations herein stated we think that it must be followed with the result that, by reason of the death of Ernest F. Pope before the death of the surviving life tenant, the gift of an interest in one half part of the "homestead estate" to him never vested in him. . . .

The conclusion here reached may seem to rest upon a somewhat technical analysis of the language used by the testatrix. It is, however, to be assumed that this language was used by her advisedly to express her intention, and we "have to go upon slight differences." Lee v. Welch, 163 Mass. 312, 314, 39 N.E. 1112, 1113. If the testatrix had added the words "if he was then living" to the gift of an interest in one half part of the "homestead estate" to Ernest F. Pope, there could be no doubt of the correctness of the conclusion here reached. But it would be even more technical to rest a different conclusion upon the omission of these words when the same intention of the testatrix is shown by other language used by her. . . . The conclusion here reached that the vesting of this interest was intended to be postponed until the death of the surviving life tenant is not in conflict with any intention of the testatrix disclosed by her will.

Decree affirmed.

Notes and Question

1. *Restricted Condition.* Do you think Herman Krooss's intention in *Krooss* was so much different from Lillian Pope's intention in *Robertson*? Why didn't the court in *Robertson* consider whether Lillian would have preferred that the primary beneficiaries' interests fail only if they died leaving issue?

Do you think that the testator's intention in Will of Corwith, 622 N.Y.S.2d 424 (Sur. Ct. 1995), was substantially different from Herman's? In *Corwith*, the testator, Charles F. Corwith, died in 1981, leaving a will creating marital and nonmarital trusts in its residuary provisions. The issue regarding the survival condition concerned the nonmarital trust in which the testator, after providing for his wife during her life, directed that the trust property be distributed in the following manner.

> Upon the death of my wife, GRACE, if she survives me, . . . to pay over, transfer and assign two-thirds (2/3) of part B of my residuary estate, in equal portions, to (1) My aforesaid nephew, CHARLES L. CORWITH: (2) my aforesaid niece, ELAINE McDUFFIE: (3) My aforesaid nephew, VINCENT C. MARTLING; and (4) My aforesaid niece, NANCY MALINOWSKI, and one-third (1/3) of part B of my residuary estate, in equal portions, to [named charities]. If any of the aforesaid nieces or nephews do not survive to be entitled to a share of the trust or residue, then such share shall go to his or her issue, per stirpes.

Id. at 425. The testator was survived by his wife but she had since died. The testator's nephew, Charles L. Corwith, survived the testator but died without issue during the life of the testator's wife. The nephew's estate, relying on *Krooss*, argued that the testator intended to impose only a restricted condition of survival—death before the life tenant *with* issue. The court disagreed, holding that the survival language in *Krooss* was "clearly distinguishable." Id. at 427. It held that Charles's interest was a remainder subject to a condition precedent of surviving the testator's wife. The result was that Charles's interest failed and passed by intestacy to the testator's wife, as the testator's sole heir. Do you think that the survival language in *Corwith* is clearly distinguishable from the survival language in *Krooss*?

2. *Remainders Subject to a Power.* In holding that a remainder interest isn't contingent on survival of the life tenant by reason of its being subject to a power, the court in the *Robertson* case was well within existing authority. See, e.g., Walker's Estate, 121 A. 318 (Pa. 1923); Restatement of Property § 261 illus. 1. A few courts have held to the contrary, however. See, e.g., Jarrett v. McReynolds, 183 S.E.2d 343 (Va. 1971).

3. *Remainder "to B or his heirs."* Does a remainder "to B or his heirs" present the same or different problems as a remainder "to B or his issue"? The Restatement of Property § 37 comment l states that a devise of a future interest

"to B or his heirs" "normally is construed to create an estate in fee simple absolute in [B], if [B] is alive when the limited estate becomes a present interest and in [B]'s heirs if [B] is then dead." This is the result reached in Rowett v. McFarland, 394 N.W.2d 298 (S.D. 1986), and in Landmark Communications, Inc. v. Sovran Bank, 387 S.E.2d 484 (Va. 1990). But the Restatement also holds out the possibility that such a devise could be construed as creating an indefeasibly vested remainder in B, as if the devise had been "to B *and* his heirs."

2. *Special Case of Multiple-Generation Class Gifts—Class Gifts in Favor of "Issue" or "Descendants"*

Statutory References: *UPC §§ 2-708 to -709*

Remainder interests in trusts are commonly given to a class composed of the transferor's or the income beneficiary's "issue" or "descendants." A distinguishing characteristic of these class gifts is that potentially the takers reside in more than one generation. As with most other types of future interests, the recommended form for these class gifts imposes an express condition of survival to the time of possession or enjoyment. As Weller v. Sokol, below, demonstrates, a requirement of survival commonly is implied for multiple-generation class gifts, even in the absence of one expressly stated. See Restatement of Property § 249 comment i, § 296 comment g; Restatement 2d of Property § 28.2. This result is, of course, contrary to the rules of construction concerning future interests in favor of individuals and in favor of single-generation classes, such as "children," "grandchildren," "nieces and nephews," and so on. Why are class gifts in favor of "issue" or "descendants" treated differently?

A related question in the case of multiple-generation class gifts is the form of distribution among the takers. In Weller v. Sokol, below, a per-stirpes form of distribution was specified in the governing instrument. In cases in which the governing instrument doesn't specify a form of distribution, the English rule favored a per-capita form of distribution.[3] The English preference has now largely disappeared in the United States. Generally speaking, the preferred form of distribution in this country is representational. See Edward C. Halbach, Jr.,

---

3. Under a per-capita form of distribution, every member of the class takes an equal share, even those with living intervening ancestors. To illustrate, suppose G establishes a trust for A for life, remainder in corpus to A's descendants. If A had two children, one of whom had one child and the other of whom had two children, each child and grandchild would take a one-fifth share under a per-capita form of distribution. No condition of survivorship of A would be implied. See Restatement 2d of Property § 28.2 comment d, illus. 5.

Issues About Issue: Some Recurrent Class Gift Problems, 48 Mo. L. Rev. 333, 350-55 (1983).

Contrast UPC §§ 2-708 and 2-709 with the positions taken in the Restatements of Property:

> *Restatement 2d of Property § 28.2. Class Gift to "Issue" or "Descendants"*. If a gift is made to a class described as the "issue" or "descendants" of a designated person, or by a similar multigenerational class gift term, in the absence of additional language or circumstances that indicate otherwise,
>
> (1) A class member must survive to the date of distribution in order to share in the gift; and
>
> (2) such class member in order to share in the gift must have no living ancestor who is a class member; and
>
> (3) the initial division into shares will be on the basis of the number of class members, whether alive or deceased, in the first generation below the designated person.
>
> *Restatement of Property § 303. Distribution—Class Described as "Issue of B," or as "Descendants of B," or as "Family of B."* (1) When a conveyance creates a class gift by a limitation in favor of a group described as the "issue of B," or as the "descendants of B," . . . then, unless a contrary intent of the conveyor is found from additional language or circumstances, distribution is made to such members of the class as would take, and in such shares as they would receive, under the applicable law of intestate succession if B had died intestate on the date of the final ascertainment of the membership in the class, owning the subject matter of the class gift.

Although the specifics of intestate distribution among an intestate's descendants take different forms, all such forms are representational in overall approach. See supra Chapter 2, Part B. That is to say, a descendant takes only if no intervening ancestor of that descendant is alive. Any representational form of distribution, regardless of which type, would justify the rule adopted in Weller v. Sokol on the question of implying a condition of survival.

Weller v. Sokol

318 A.2d 193 (Md. 1974)

SINGLEY, J. This case combines a number of appeals from a decree of the Circuit Court of Baltimore City which construed the will of the late Arthur Nattans (Arthur Nattans I). While the appeal was originally taken to the Court of Special Appeals, we granted certiorari in order that it could be docketed in this Court.

Although the factual background and particularly the family pedigree are difficult to keep in mind, the case presents two relatively simple issues:

(i) When a will directs a distribution on the death of the testator's last surviving child among "issue and descendants" per stirpes of children of the testator who have died leaving issue surviving, where are the stocks or stirpes to be found?

(ii) Is distribution to be made only to issue and descendants living at the time of distribution?

The chancellor (Ross, J.) determined that the stocks, or stirpes, were to be found among the children of the testator, and not among the grandchildren who were the first takers of an absolute interest, and that distribution was to be made only to descendants living at the time of distribution. For reasons to be developed, we shall affirm.

Arthur Nattans I died domiciled in Baltimore on 17 April 1905, survived by his widow, Jennie Nattans; by three children of a prior marriage; Emily N. Herbert, Addie N. Bachrach, and Samuel A. Nattans, and by five children of his second marriage: Rita Nattans (later Myers), Ralph Nattans, Edith Nattans (later Hecht), Hortense Nattans (later Solomon), and Arthur Nattans (Arthur Nattans II).

The provisions of the Nattans will, executed on 3 October 1903, with which we shall here be concerned are contained in Items Sixth and Tenth. By Item Sixth, 396 shares of stock of Read Drug and Chemical Company of Baltimore City (Read's) owned by Mr. Nattans were bequeathed to trustees to pay the income from specified numbers of shares to the Nattans children, as follows:

Emily N. Herbert	40 shares
Addie N. Bachrach	29 shares
Samuel A. Nattans	29 shares
Rita Nattans (Myers)	60 shares
Ralph Nattans	40 shares
Edith Nattans (Hecht)	60 shares
Hortense Nattans (Solomon)	60 shares
Arthur Nattans II	40 shares

Item Tenth provided:

> "*Tenth*. In the event of the death of any of my children above named, during the continuance of this trust, without leaving issue him or her surviving, the income herein given to the child so dying, without issue living at his or her death, shall be divided equally among his or her surviving brothers and sisters annually during the continuance of this trust. And in case of the death of any one of my said children during the continuance of said trust, leaving issue him or her surviving, the income of the share of the one so dying shall go to and become the property of his or her child, if only one, or children, if more than one, equally, share and share alike. Upon the death of the last survivor of all my said eight children this trust shall

cease, and thereupon the entire trust property, shall be divided by my said trustees, or their successors in the trust, among the issue and descendants of such of my children as may have died leaving lawful issue him or her surviving *per stirpes and not per capita*. And the said trustees, and their successors in the trust, are authorized and directed to make, execute and deliver all such deeds and instruments of conveyance or assignment as may be necessary to make said division." (Emphasis in original.)

In Ryan v. Herbert, 186 Md. 453, 47 A.2d 360 (1946), our predecessors had occasion to review a declaratory decree which had construed the provisions of Item Tenth relating to devolution of income prior to the termination of the trust. That decree, which was affirmed on appeal, had directed that on the death of a child of Arthur Nattans I prior to the termination of the trust, leaving any issue whatsoever surviving, such issue took a vested interest in the income to which the dying child had been entitled, subject only to defeasance by the termination of the trust.

As a result, when Harold Herbert and Arthur N. Bachrach, grandsons of Arthur Nattans I, died prior to the termination of the trust without leaving descendants surviving, the income which each had been receiving was paid to his respective estate. No consideration was given to the devolution of the corpus at time of termination beyond a recognition that it would certainly pass in proportions which differed from the shares of income, and that it might well pass to persons other than those who had received income from the trust under the determination reached in Ryan. . . .

To us, however, the most compelling argument springs from the very nature of a stirpital distribution. The "issue and descendants" of the children of Arthur Nattans I could not be determined until the termination of the trust. See Restatement of Property, § 296, comment g, §§ 303(1), 304, 311(1). At that time neither Harold Herbert nor Arthur N. Bachrach was alive. While their right to receive income was found to be vested in Ryan, their right to participate in the corpus, under the terms of the will, was implicitly conditioned on survival until distribution. . . .

Decree affirmed, costs to be paid from the assets of the trust estate.

Questions

Why does a future interest in "issue per stirpes" implicitly contain a requirement of survival to the time of distribution? Should there be an implicit requirement of survival if the future interest is to "issue per capita"? In the case of issue per stirpes, should the requirement of survival be restricted or unrestricted? See Restatement of Property § 249 comment i, § 303 (unrestricted); Am. L. Prop. § 21.13, n. 10. Compare Maiorano v. Virginia

Trust Co., 219 S.E.2d 884 (Va. 1975) (unrestricted), with Elliott v. Griffin, 237 S.E.2d 396 (Va. 1977) (restricted).

Edward C. Halbach, Jr., Uniform Acts, Restatements and Other Trends in American Trust Law at Century's End

88 Calif. L. Rev. 1877, 1902-04 (2000)

VI. Clarifying and Modernizing Significant Rules of Construction

A. Remainders and Other Future Interest Problems

In recent years, legal scholarship, judicial opinions and particularly legislation have sought to refine rules of construction in our most troublesome areas of recurring uncertainties of meaning. These efforts seek better to ascertain the probable intentions of transferors—or more precisely to attribute intentions to transferors who (or whose counsel) have failed to consider these matters, or at least failed to address them in the instrument or otherwise to leave evidence of an actual intention that could be discovered through the process of interpretation.

1. Survivorship Requirements

One area where considerable progress can be recognized is in the matter of whether a condition should be implied requiring remainder beneficiaries to survive life beneficiaries, or until some other time of distribution. With better understanding of the issues and considerations involved, judicial decisions have shown considerable improvement in recent decades. With the further possibility of broader alternatives, however, significant changes are being advanced through legislation.

Reasonably revealing, and representative of a broad array of recurring situation-types, are simplified dispositions in trust: (1) "for L for life, remainder to her children;" and (2) "for L for life, remainder to his issue." Question: Are L's "children" or "issue" impliedly required to be alive at L's death for their interests to take effect? In both of these situations substantial estate planning considerations, both tax and nontax, virtually mandate that an informed drafter require class members to survive until L's death.

It would seem proper for courts to take account of this factor—that is, of what sound planning calls for. Cases have therefore recognized that in situation 2 it is appropriate to imply a survival requirement with respect to the class of "issue" (or, similarly, for a class of "descendants"). On the other hand, courts have properly been unwilling to imply such a requirement with respect to "children" (or other inflexible, one-generation classes) in cases like situation 1. This is because of an overriding concern that to do so would do even greater harm than good to the transferor's overall objectives by risking the exclusion of natural objects of his or her bounty, usually the descendants (or other family members) of a child who fails to survive, a risk that does not exist when a settlor uses the flexible term "issue" or "descendants."

The dilemma in cases of these single-generation classes (and in the case of named individuals, as in a disposition "for L for life, remainder equally to R1, R2, and R3") arises from the standard common law approach: A court is permitted to choose only between the two constructions that it is perceived the language will allow—that "children" or the like means either all of the children (i.e., including the estates of deceased children whether or not they leave issue) or only the children who survive L. The court must therefore choose the least damaging of these unfortunate alternatives, rationalizing essentially that "a court cannot write a will or trust provision" for a settlor who failed to provide for the issue of a deceased child or who, if asked, might have preferred to give a deceased child a power of appointment by which to provide more flexibly for his or her family. As judicial decisions have recognized the real considerations appropriate to their limited choices, they have at least come to provide greater certainty, and somewhat more suitability, of result, rather than continuing to fumble with such terminology as "vested" or "contingent" or inquiring whether the remainder beneficiaries are a "class" or a group of named beneficiaries.

In recent years, however, legislation has opened up a considerably better alternative. This alternative is sometimes based on analogy to antilapse statutes that apply to related beneficiaries who predecease a testator and generally supply an implied gift to a deceased child's issue (if any)—issue who may be the settlor's grandchildren where L was the settlor's spouse, or the settlor's great-grandchildren where L is the settlor's child. The trend, and most of what recent legislation exists, is based on 1990 amendments to Uniform Probate Code section 2-707.

Note and Questions

1. *Equitable Deviation: Judicial Modification of a Trust Because of Unanticipated Circumstances*. The Restatement 3d of Trusts § 66 provides that a court may modify a distributive provision of a trust if, "because of circumstances not anticipated by the settlor," the modification "will further the purposes of the trust." This doctrine is known as the equitable deviation doctrine. Comment b, illustration 5, applies the equitable deviation doctrine to a trust in which one of the beneficiaries dies prematurely:

> 5. S, who outlived her husband and her only child, left her estate in three shares, one for each of her three grandchildren. Each share was to be held in trust for the grandchild's support and education, with the property to be distributed to the grandchild "if and when he or she attains age 25." Two of the grandchildren had reached age 25 by the time of S's death and thus took their shares outright; the other grandchild, G, was 18 when S died and has now died at age 23, leaving a

widow and two very young children. Under the applicable rule of construction, G's interest fails as a result of his failure to survive until the time of distribution. Thus, unless modified, S's will has made an incomplete disposition of this share of her estate, and therefore this trust share will pass by resulting trust (see §§ 7 and 8) to S's heirs at law—that is, upon S's partial intestacy, this reversionary interest will belong equally (one-third each) to the three grandchildren. This would result ultimately in a one-ninth share of S's estate being available to G's family while the other grandchildren end up with, essentially, four-ninths of S's estate apiece (one-third via their respective trusts and one-ninth by resulting trust). These consequences of a failure of the remainder of G's trust share would produce a striking distortion of an overall testamentary trust plan that, on its face, appears to contemplate equal treatment of S's three lines of descent. Because of the unanticipated circumstances in this case and S's failure to make provision for them, the rule of this section allows the court to modify the terms of the trust if it concludes that S's probable intention and the trust purpose would be better served by doing so.

2. *Statutory Reform.* Professor Susan French proposed (but did not draft) legislation giving the beneficiary of a future interest who predeceased the distribution date a power of appointment. Susan F. French, Imposing a General Survival Requirement on Beneficiaries of Future Interests: Solving the Problem Caused by the Death of a Beneficiary Before the Time Set for Distribution, 27 Ariz. L. Rev. 801 (1985). What are the advantages and disadvantages of this approach? See Jesse Dukeminier, The Uniform Probate Code Upends the Law of Remainders, 94 Mich. L. Rev. 148, 165 (1995); Lawrence W. Waggoner, The Uniform Probate Code Extends Antilapse-Type Protection to Poorly Drafted Trusts, 94 Mich. L. Rev. 2309, 2338-42 (1996).

California amended § 6146 of its probate code in 1983 to require survival of the point of possession or enjoyment, but the amendment was ambiguous and the legislature repealed it in 1984 before it became effective.[4]

Pennsylvania and Tennessee have statutes imposing a general survival requirement for class gifts. See Pa. Cons. Stat. Ann. tit. 20, § 2514(5); Tenn. Code Ann. § 32-3-104. Illinois has a statute that imposes a survival requirement on future interests created by will given to the testator's descendants.

4. For the current version of the law, see Cal. Prob. Code §§ 21109 and 21110, neither of which requires survival until the time of possession or enjoyment.

Illinois Revised Statutes
Chapter 755

§ 5/4-11. *Legacy to a deceased legatee*. Unless the testator expressly provides otherwise in his will, (a) if a legacy of a present or future interest is to a descendant of the testator who dies before or after the testator, the descendants of the legatee living when the legacy is to take effect in possession or enjoyment, take per stirpes the estate so bequeathed; (b) if a legacy of a present or future interest is to a class and any member of the class dies before or after the testator, the members of the class living when the legacy is to take effect in possession or enjoyment take the share or shares which the deceased member would have taken if he were then living, except that if the deceased member of the class is a descendant of the testator, the descendants of the deceased member then living shall take per stirpes the share or shares which the deceased member would have taken if he were then living; and (c) except as above provided in (a) and (b), if a legacy lapses by reason of the death of the legatee before the testator, the estate so bequeathed shall be included in and pass as part of the residue under the will, and if the legacy is or becomes part of the residue, the estate so bequeathed shall pass to and be taken by the legatees or those remaining, if any, of the residue in proportions and upon estates corresponding to their respective interests in the residue. The provisions of (a) and (b) do not apply to a future interest which is or becomes indefeasibly vested at the testator's death or at any time thereafter before it takes effect in possession or enjoyment.

Note and Problems

The UPC includes a section (§ 2-707) that provides a rule of construction on survival for future interests. Section 2-707 should be read in light of § 2-701. If the following problems were controlled by UPC § 2-707 or by the Illinois statute set forth above, what result?

G was survived by his wife, W, and their son, A. G was also survived by his sister, S. G's will created the following testamentary trusts.

1. Income to my wife, W, for life, remainder in corpus to A. A died before W, leaving descendants who survived W.

2. Income to S for life, remainder in corpus to W if W is then living; if not, to A. W predeceased S. A also predeceased S, leaving descendants who survived S.

3. Income to S for life, remainder in corpus to such of her children as survive her; if none, to A. S left no children surviving her. A predeceased S.

(a) Descendants of A were living at S's death.

(b) No descendants of A were living at S's death.

4. Income to W for life, remainder in corpus to A if A is then living. G devised the residue of his estate to X-Charity. A predeceased W, leaving descendants who survived W.

External References. Section 2-707 has provoked debate. For the arguments in favor of § 2-707, see Lawrence W. Waggoner, The Uniform Probate Code Extends Antilapse-Type Protection to Poorly Drafted Trusts, 94 Mich. L. Rev. 2309 (1996); Edward C. Halbach Jr. and Lawrence W. Waggoner, The UPC's New Survivorship and Antilapse Provisions, 55 Alb. L. Rev. 1091 (1992). For critiques of § 2-707, see David M. Becker, Uniform Probate Code Section 2-707 and the Experienced Estate Planner: Unexpected Disasters and How to Avoid Them, 47 UCLA L. Rev. 339 (1999); Laura E. Cunningham, The Hazards of Tinkering with the Common Law of Future Interests: The California Experience, 48 Hastings L.J. 667 (1997); Jesse Dukeminier, The Uniform Probate Code Upends the Law of Remainders, 94 Mich. L. Rev. 148 (1995).

"Construction" of Single-Generation Class Gift to Include Descendants of Deceased Class Members. An alternative means of producing the same result as UPC § 2-707 is to construe a single-generation class gift as if it were a multiple-generation class gift. The general rule of construction is that a class gift to a single-generation class only includes members of the designated generation. Thus, the Restatement 2d of Property § 25.1 provides:

> When the donor of property describes the beneficiaries thereof as "children" of a designated person, the primary meaning of such class gift term excludes descendants of such person more remote than those of the first generation. It is assumed, in the absence of language or circumstances indicating a contrary intent, that the donor adopts such primary meaning.

Comment g, however, notes that "[t]he rule of this section is a rule of construction, and hence it yields to any finding of a contrary intent of the donor from additional language or circumstances." The next case, Cox v. Forristall, found a contrary intention.

Cox v. Forristall

640 P.2d 878 (Kan. Ct. App. 1982)

Meyer, Judge. This case involves the interpretation of a will in a partition action. . . .

The will of B. T. Freeman devised a life estate in the farm to his daughters Miranda Catherine Freeman and Alice Freeman. The will provided that in the event of marriage of either life tenant, the life interest in the farm would remain in the other tenant. Further, the will provided:

> And the life interest of both of my said daughters having terminated by marriage, the said farm shall become and be the property of my children, share and share alike, namely: Miranda Catherine Freeman, Alice Freeman, Bonnie Freeman Forrestall (sic), Nellie Freeman Hanson, Annie Freeman Cherryholmes, Grace Freeman, Frances Freeman, Enda (sic) Freeman, Sarah Freeman, Delilah Freeman Stackley, and Albert Freeman. In the event of the death of either of my said children above named prior to the expiration of the life interest of my said daughters, Miranda Catherine and Alice, the share of such child or children so dying shall descend to, become and be the property of the then living issue of their body, and in the event of their dying without issue, the share of such child or children so dying shall descend to, become and be the property of my children then living, share and share alike.

[B. T. Freeman was survived by eleven children, including Miranda and Alice. Miranda died in 1951. Alice died in 1980. Neither Miranda nor Alice ever married, and both died without issue. Only one of B. T. Freeman's eleven children, Delilah, survived Alice. Frances, Edna, and Sarah died during Alice's lifetime without issue. The other five, Bonnie, Nellie, Annie, Grace, and Albert, died during Alice's lifetime with issue (who survived Alice).]

The [trial] court interpreted the will so that the word "children" as used in the clause "my children then living" also includes, per stirpes, the grandchildren of B. T. Freeman if they are children of a deceased child of B. T. Freeman who died prior to the termination of the life estates established in the will. . . .

The basic argument is over what happened to the shares of the children who died without issue. Appellant maintains that upon the death of each child who died without issue, their remainder interest passed to B. T. Freeman's other children who were living at the time of the death of said child, thus preventing that share from passing to the issue of B. T. Freeman's children who had died prior to the children dying without issue. . . .

The Supreme Court, in Estate of Lester, 191 Kan. 83, 87, 379 P.2d 275 (1963), stated:

> [O]ther things being equal, there is a presumption against any intention on the part of a testator to disinherit his legal heirs who are favored by the policy of the law and may not be disinherited by mere conjecture. When a testator intends to disinherit those who would take under the statutes of descent he must indicate that intention clearly by plain words, express devise to others, or necessary implication. By "necessary" implication is meant one which results from so strong a probability as to the testator's meaning that an intent contrary to that imputed cannot be supposed. The presumption against disinheritance is recognized especially in the

> absence of unfriendly relations existing between the testator and his descendants. [Citations omitted.]

Appellant's interpretation states that as each child dies without issue, that share passes to the remaining children of B. T. Freeman who are alive at the time of the death of said child.

The trial court's interpretation looks to who is living at the termination of the life estate and passes the shares of the children dying without issue to the remaining children and grandchildren of B. T. Freeman living at the termination of said life estate. This divides the shares equally among the remaining interests whereas appellant's interpretation gives the last to die the biggest shares. Under appellant's interpretation, the issue of the earliest of B. T. Freeman's children to die lose part of the inheritance; if any of those children subsequently die without issue, the inheritance bypasses them and passes only to those children of B. T. Freeman who are alive.

The provision regarding the passage of the shares of children without issue is ambiguous in two respects.

First, the phrase "children then living" is ambiguous because it is not clear when "then" refers to; viz., whether one looks to the time of the successive deaths of each child without an heir, or at the death of the last life tenant.

Secondly, under the previous phrase, the share of each of B. T. Freeman's children is to pass to their issue if they die prior to the expiration of the life interest. It is difficult to harmonize the two phrases unless "children" is interpreted to mean children and grandchildren.

We have found two cases in Kansas where the word "children" was held to include "grandchildren." In Estate of Works, 168 Kan. 539, 213 P.2d 998 (1950), a will devised real estate to the testator's five children. The will further provided:

> "The above bequests and gifts of my real estate are made to my children heretofore named upon the condition that they and each of them shall hold the same during their lifetime, and at the death of any one of them the real estate herein bequeathed and devised shall descend to their legitimate children. And in case any one or more of the children above named, should die without legitimate issue, then the share above given and devised to such childless devisee shall descend to and become the property of their brothers and sisters, children of mine who shall survive, share and share alike." p. 540, 213 P.2d 998.

In *Works*, when the testator died, all of his children were living. At the time of the testator's death, his son Charles had two living children, Warren and Clark. Clark, however, predeceased his father Charles, but had three children, Charles, Paul and Mary Ella. The issue was whether Warren, the one living child of Charles, received the entire remainder in the land, or whether Warren took only one-half of the remainder and the three children of Clark took the other half. The court held that Warren took one-half and the three children of Clark took the other half, even though Clark predeceased Charles, the son of the testator.

The court stated:

> "Although the word 'children' is not ordinarily construed to include grandchildren, it is properly construed to include grandchildren when the context, or the surrounding facts and circumstances, in case of ambiguity, make it clear that the grantor so intended.
>
> "If there appears to be a doubt or uncertainty as to the grantor's intention in using the word 'children' there is a reasonable presumption against disinheritance of a grandchild whose parent is dead." 168 Kan. at 543-4, 213 P.2d 998, citing from Bennett v. Humphreys, 159 Kan. 416, Syl. PP 6, 7, 155 P.2d 431 (1945).

In Bennett v. Humphreys, 159 Kan. 416, 417, 155 P.2d 431 (1945), land was deeded to John Bell Bennett. The deed stated, in part:

> It is part of consideration of this deed that John Bell Bennett cannot sell this property during his life time and at his death is to be divided equally among his children.

At the time of the death of the life tenant, John Bennett, there was only one child living. However, another child had predeceased the life tenant, leaving a grandchild. The court held that the grandchild and the child took equally, citing the above rule.

Since certain terms of decedent's last will are ambiguous, it seems clear to us that the trial court attempted an interpretation of that will which it felt would reflect the intent of the decedent. . . . [W]e conclude the trial court was correct.

AFFIRMED.

Note

For another case construing a single-generation class gift to include the descendants of a deceased class member, see Edwards v. Bender, 25 So. 1010 (Ala. 1899). Unlike the dispositive language in *Cox*, the dispositive language in *Edwards* did not contain an express requirement of survival. The testator's will devised a tract of land to his daughter Nancy for life, remainder to Nancy's "children," without an express requirement of survival. Nancy had five children. Four of the five survived her, but one predeceased her, leaving a child, Eula, who survived her. The court held that the word "children" "may be extended to include grandchildren, when such intent appears from the whole instrument, or where otherwise the devise would fail." Although the devise would not otherwise fail (because four of Nancy's five children survived her), the court found it "evident" that the testator's intention, "though not expressly stated," was that "the issue of her children as might die before [the life tenant] should take the share which such deceased child would have taken." The court based this conclusion on the fact that the will contained a gift over in case Nancy died without issue. Nancy, of course, did not die without issue; she was survived by four of her five children.

EXTERNAL REFERENCES. Lawrence W. Waggoner, The Uniform Probate Code Extends Antilapse-Type Protection to Poorly Drafted Trusts, 94 Mich. L. Rev. 2309, 2318-2321 (1996); Annot., Word "Child" or "Children" in Will as Including Grandchild or Grandchildren, 30 A.L.R.4th 319 (1984).

3. Avoiding Ambiguity in Express Conditions of Survival

The routine procedure in estate planning practice is to impose express conditions of survival on the beneficiaries of future interests. This is done for basically the same reasons that prompt proposals for a statute imposing a survival requirement when the governing instrument fails to do so by its own terms. A future interest that passes through a beneficiary's estate is awkward, expensive, and subject to taxation under IRC § 2033. In addition, the absence of an express requirement of survival may lead to litigation concerning whether one is to be implied, litigation that may occur decades after the beneficiary's death.

The major advantage of the rule against implying conditions of survival—preserving a share of the estate for descending lines in which an ancestor predeceases the time of distribution—is easily accomplished by accompanying an express condition of survival with multiple-generation class gifts—future interests in favor of "issue" or "descendants."

If carelessly drafted, however, express conditions of survival can themselves be ambiguous and lead to litigation about their meaning.

Problem

At 9:15 p.m. yesterday evening, a tax partner in your firm came into your office, just as you were about to leave for the day. She asked you to examine a 38-page draft she prepared for an irrevocable inter vivos life insurance trust. Her client is scheduled to arrive at her office at 9:00 a.m. tomorrow morning to sign the trust.

The tax partner explained to you that the trust is a great device for this client because the client's life insurance policy that will be assigned to the trust has a face value of $6 million and a present value of $1 million. For purposes of the federal generation-skipping transfer tax, the trust will therefore have an "inclusion ratio" of 0, meaning that even though the corpus of the trust will far exceed the client's GST exemption under IRC § 2631, no generation-skipping tax will ever be incurred. You acted as if you knew what the tax partner was talking about. (To find out, see supra Chapter 7, Part A.) She left to go home. You stayed.

You began reading through the trust. You noticed that the draft provides that after the settlor's death the trustee is to collect the proceeds of the life insurance policy, invest them, and pay the income therefrom to the settlor's son, Arnold, for life. So far, so good, you thought. Then you came to the provisions for the distribution of the corpus of the trust "upon Arnold's death." These provisions state:

(a) To the surviving descendants of Arnold, by representation; or
(b) If Arnold shall leave no surviving descendants, then to the surviving descendants of the Settlor, by representation; or
(c) If the Settlor shall then have no surviving descendants, but he is survived by any of the descendants of his brother, to the descendants of his brother, by representation; or
(d) If the Settlor is not survived by any of his descendants or by any of the descendants of his brother, to the surviving descendants of his father, by representation; or
(e) If the Settlor is not then survived by any of the descendants of his father, to the Settlor's surviving heirs at law.

Finish the story. It is now 1:00 a.m.

Boone County National Bank v. Edson

760 S.W.2d 108 (Mo. 1988)

WELLIVER, J. Boone County National Bank brought this action to construc a will. They sought direction as to the proper distribution of a trust estate created by the will. Boone County National Bank is the trustee of a trust established by the Last Will and Testament of Margaret Poindexter Tello (Testatrix). The Boone County Circuit Court found the will clear and unambiguous. . . .

Appellants [Kathie E. Kalmowitz, Judith D. Edson, and Carol E. Thompson] appealed claiming the will, as written, contains a mistake creating an ambiguity. The Court of Appeals, Western District concluded that the will is ambiguous and reversed the judgment. No party disputes the awarding of costs and attorney fees to be paid out of the trust estate. . . . We affirm the trial court.

I. The Testatrix had her attorney write the will in question in 1960. The Testatrix died in 1971 and the will was probated.

The residuary clause of the will created a trust for the support of Lois Tello, Testatrix' daughter. The terms of the trust directed the trustee to pay the income of the trust to Lois and authorized the trustee to invade the corpus of the trust as necessary to properly maintain, support and educate Lois. The will provided for termination of the trust on the death of Lois.

The conditions and directions for distribution of the remaining trust corpus and any undistributed income are set out in paragraph III-G of the will. It provides as follows:

> This trust shall terminate upon the death of my said daughter. At such time my Trustee is directed to pay over all of the remaining corpus of the trust, together with any undistributed income, to the child or children of my said daughter, if she dies with children her surviving, to be divided among her said children in equal shares per stirpes and not per capita. In the event that my said daughter dies without children her surviving, I give, devise and bequeath all of the remaining corpus and undistributed income to my sisters, Jessie P. Moore, of Harlowton, Montana, and Dorothy Edson, of Harlowton, Montana, in equal shares. In the event that my sister, Jessie P. Moore, predeceases me, I desire that her share go to my other sister, Dorothy Edson. In the event that the said Dorothy Edson predeceases me, I give, devise and bequeath her share to her granddaughters, Carol Jane Edson, Kathie Margaret Edson, and Judith Dorothy Edson, or to their survivor, in equal shares.

For convenience and clarity, a diagram of the family relationships follows:

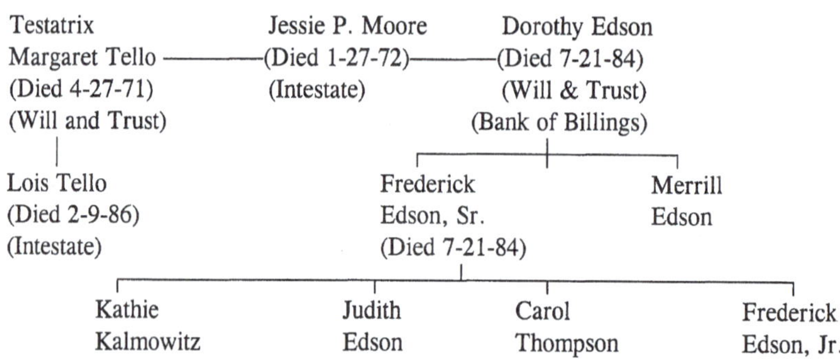

The question presented to us is whether or not the language used in the dispositive provision is ambiguous—that is, did Testatrix intend to use the pronoun "me" in the last two sentences of paragraph III-G or to use the pronoun "her" or the name "Lois."

The Testatrix died in 1971. She was survived by both of her sisters, Jessie P. Moore and Dorothy Edson, and Lois. Jessie P. Moore died intestate in 1972 leaving no spouse or children. Dorothy Edson died testate in 1984 prior to the death of Lois. Dorothy had two sons, Frederick Edson, Sr. (deceased) and Merrill Edson (respondent herein). Frederick was survived by four children, Frederick M. Edson, Jr., and appellants Kathie E. Kalmowitz, Judith D. Edson, and Carol E. Thompson.

Dorothy Edson, by her will, left all of her residuary estate to respondent First Interstate Bank in trust for the benefit of her four grandchildren. She specifically excluded her son, Merrill.

Lois Tello died intestate in 1986 and the trust for her benefit terminated. She was not survived by a spouse or any children.

The deposition of the drafting attorney was taken and offered and was ruled by the trial court to be inadmissable in this proceeding. Relying solely on his memory and not on notes or written memorandums, the attorney testified that it was his memory that the Testatrix intended that either "her" or the name "Lois" should have been used instead of the pronoun "me." He also testified that after the will was typed, it was given to Testatrix to carefully be read before signing.

II. The opposing parties each filed motions for summary judgment after discovery. Each motion incorporated by reference the deposition testimony of the attorney who drafted Testatrix' will. . . .

If the last two sentences of paragraph III-G were construed to read the pronoun "her" or the name "Lois" instead of the pronoun "me," the entire trust corpus would be distributed to appellants Kathie E. Kalmowitz, Judith D. Edson, and Carol E. Thompson, in equal shares.

Our scope of review is established by Murphy v. Carron, 536 S.W.2d 30, 32 (Mo. banc 1976). The judgment must be sustained unless there is no substantial evidence to support it, unless it is against the weight of the evidence, unless it erroneously declares the law or unless it erroneously applies the law.

III. Appellants contend that the trial court erred in overruling their motion for summary judgment. Appellants virtually assume that it was the Testatrix' intent to use the pronoun "her" or the name "Lois", either of which would tie distribution of the assets to the death of Lois instead of the death of the Testatrix. Having so assumed, appellants find the ambiguity which they assert requires construction of the will, and, they then argue that proper construction requires that the court substitute either the pronoun "her" or the name "Lois" in lieu of the pronoun "me" in the last two sentences of paragraph III-G.

One of our rights most sacredly guarded by the law is our right to dispose of our property after death by a will prepared and executed prior to death. To assure the integrity of the instrument, we require formal and verified execution of the instrument. To assure all who would make wills that their intent can and will be carried out following their death, of necessity, we must impose the most strict rules of construction. This we believe the Missouri Courts have done throughout the history of our state. . . .

If a will expresses the intention of the testatrix in clear and unequivocal language, there can be no occasion for construction of the instrument. The courts will not rewrite a will under the guise of construction.

In no case may words be transposed, supplied, substituted or otherwise omitted where the meaning is plain and unambiguous, and any alteration of the language originally employed would create a meaning different from that which it naturally had when the will was written.

The court cannot give the language used a different meaning for the purpose of carrying into effect a conjecture or hypothesis of the testatrix' intention, by supplying or rejecting words.

A. Appellants contend that the trial court misconstrued the will when it failed to substitute the intended pronoun to correct a mistake made by the draftsman. In construing a will, a court cannot correct a mistake made by the draftsman, unless the mistake appears on the face of the instrument, and unless it also appears what would have been the will if the mistake had not occurred. See Annotation, Effect of mistake of draftsman (other than testator) in drawing will, 90 A.L.R.2d 924 (1963). A mistake must be apparent on the face of the will, otherwise there can be no relief. Goode v. Goode, 22 Mo. 518, 524 (1856). Change "this doctrine, and you may as well repeal the statute requiring wills to be in writing, at once. Witnesses will then make wills and not testators." Id. We find the language used is clear and unambiguous on its face, and there is no justification for correcting possible draftsman's mistake. The trial court properly excluded the deposition of the drafting attorney.

B. The Testatrix provided for her daughter by establishing a trust for her care and support. It is clear from reading the will that Testatrix' intent was to provide for Lois. It also is clear the trust was to terminate upon Lois' death. It also is clear the Testatrix wanted the trust corpus to go to Lois' surviving children, if any, but to Testatrix' sisters if no children survived Lois.

Nothing in the will sheds light on whether Testatrix wanted further distribution tied to her death or that of her daughter, except the clear and unambiguous words which she used to tie further distribution to her own death. We can speculate that most people might have done it the other way, or that taxwise it would have been cheaper to do it the other way, but there is nothing on the face of the instrument to show an intent that it go other than by the words used, the words which she read before signing and the words which she signed.

The clear unambiguous words of the instrument mandate that the trial court be affirmed in all respects.

AFFIRMED.

In re Gustafson

547 N.E.2d 1152 (N.Y. 1989)

BELLACOSA, J. In concluding that appellants are not entitled to inherit under the relevant gift provision of this disputed will, we reaffirm two basic principles governing the adjudication of decedents' estates by courts: our primary function is to effectuate the testator's intent and the words used to express that intent are to be given their ordinary and natural meaning.

Testator executed his will in 1955 and it was admitted to probate in 1959. At issue is clause (c) of paragraph FIFTH, which bequeaths part of the residuary of one of two trusts to the "surviving child or children" of testator's brother Leonard, who predeceased the trust's life tenant, testator's widow, Elsie. A "surviving child" of Leonard, Jacqueline, is respondent before us and claims entitlement to the whole of that residuary portion. Appellants are the widow and children of Leonard's other child, Daniel (Jacqueline's brother), who, like his father, predeceased the life tenant. Daniel's children, as appellants, strive to take under paragraph FIFTH'S gift provision and urge the courts to construe the word "children" to include grandchildren so that the collateral descendants of the testator, i.e., the grandnephews and grandnieces, can partake of the testamentary plan. Since they are faced with the fundamental proposition that the word "children" will be given its ordinary and natural meaning unless the will as a whole shows an unmistakable intent that different or remoter persons or classes should be included, they argue that the one-time use of the word "issue" in a different, inoperative clause of the will creates ambiguity and warrants forsaking the general rule of construction. Daniel's widow, as separate appellant, seeks to inherit on an argument that his inchoate share vested in him prior to the death of the life tenant, Elsie, [and passed to her by intestacy from Daniel].

We affirm the order of the Appellate Division, 145 A.D.2d 979, 536 N.Y.S.2d 351, [which awarded all of Leonard's share to Jacqueline, and none of it to Daniel's widow or children,] because a construction which would substitute for the testator's chosen word a broader, judicially applied definition is unwarranted and would be unsettling to the law of descent and distribution. Further, the relevant vesting date can be only the death of the life tenant.

Carl V.E. Gustafson was 59 years old, married and childless when he died in 1959. He disposed of virtually his entire estate through two trusts of equal size with an integrated, complementary residuary plan. The trust established in paragraph SIXTH provided that testator's brothers, Leonard and Roy, were to be equal income beneficiaries, and upon the death of either of them his one-half interest in the trust (that is, a one-fourth interest in the residuary) would pass to "his child or children". When Leonard died in 1978, his children, Jacqueline and Daniel, took equally of Leonard's share in this trust. Roy continues his life tenancy in the other portion of this trust. The half of testator's estate reflected in this trust is not involved in this case.

This case and appeal revolve around the trust created in paragraph FIFTH of the will, in which Elsie, testator's widow, held a life estate. Upon her death, testator's will directed the corpus of this trust be paid as follows:

(a) One-half to my brother, E. Leonard Gustafson.

(b) One-half to my brother, Roy L. Gustafson.

(c) If a brother predeceases Elsie Warren Gustafson, then his share of this Trust shall be paid over to his surviving child or children, share and share alike.

(d) If one of my brothers shall predecease Elsie Warren Gustafson, without issue surviving, then his part of this Trust shall be paid over to his surviving brother.

Roy survived Elsie and took his share pursuant to clause (b). This, too, is not involved in the case.

At issue then is only the portion that would have been Leonard's one-quarter residuary share under clause (a), which, because of Leonard's predeceasing Elsie, must pass through clause (c). Leonard's son, Daniel, having also predeceased Elsie, leaves a widow and children who now seek to take a share of the residuary through this clause, though they are not "surviving child or children".

Courts construing donative instruments are governed by a threshold axiom: a testator's intent, as ascertained "from the words used in the will . . . according to their everyday and ordinary meaning", reigns supreme. . . . In Matter of Villalonga, 6 N.Y.2d 477, 484, 190 N.Y.S.2d 372, 160 N.E.2d 850), the natural and ordinary meaning of the word at issue here was held and applied as follows: "'[c]hildren' means immediate offspring, and we reiterate the rule of the [Matter of] Schaufele [252 N.Y. 65, 67, 168 N.E. 831] case that it will never be held to include grandchildren 'unless the will as a whole shows that unmistakable intent.'" (Emphasis added.) The will before us cannot clear that high hurdle.

The order of testator's priorities is straightforwardly expressed in paragraph FIFTH. First, he provided for his widow as long as she lived. Then, upon her death, his brothers would benefit (para FIFTH [a], [b]). If his brother(s) predeceased his widow, then the focus of testator's beneficial intent shifted to the "surviving child or children" of his brother(s) (para FIFTH [c]), a generation proximate to himself. The final subdivision of this paragraph provides that if a brother dies "without issue surviving", the surviving brother takes all. Thus, if neither issue nor children survived one brother, the other brother (or his children or his issue) would take to prevent a lapse. Accordingly, from the four corners of the will's relevant gift provision, assigning to each word its ordinary meaning, the testamentary scheme is reasonably discernible. Carl Gustafson wanted to benefit: (1) his widow while she lived; (2) his brothers who survived his widow; and (3) if a brother did not survive his widow, then the brother's child(ren) who did so survive. Those preferences of the testator as to the order and distribution of his property are not "incoherent", "inequitable", "inconsistent" or "anomalous", but even if they were, testators are privileged to act in any way they see fit to displace the State's otherwise mandated, homogenous distribution by intestacy, so long as they are compos mentis. Courts, on the other hand, are not privileged to put contrary or even additional words into a testator's actual written expression in order retrospectively to effectuate their own notions of "fair" or "equitable" distribution of estates.

Prowitt v. Rodman, 37 N.Y. 41, does not support a different result. There, an exception to the plain meaning of "children" was allowed because "the testator intended that the remote descendants should be takers . . . *if there should be a failure of the immediate offspring of [the trust life tenant]*" (id., at 54 [emphasis added]; see also, Matter of Welles, 9 N.Y.2d 277, 280, 213 N.Y.S.2d 441, 173 N.E.2d 876 ["It seems to us that the only possible occasion justifying a more inclusive meaning (of 'children') would be to avoid failure of the estate."]). There is no failure of an estate here, which is the only justification for the exception to the paramount plain meaning rule of construction.

Nor is this case about the testator's intention to disinherit unknown, collateral descendants two generations removed from him. The law of decedents' affairs recognizes no rule requiring a testator to manifest an intent to disinherit in such circumstances. Rather, our rules relate to the testator's intent to bestow a gift and to whom. In that respect, he was plain, precise and orderly, and appellants' claim to a gift in this trust remainder by implication would wrongly extend the plainly expressed and universally understood words. Our ruling, therefore, is natural, not "narrow", and a faithful application of the holding of the governing precedent, not an "extension" of it. Simply put, children means children in the judicial construction of this will. . . .

We must also address the vesting date with respect to the remainder of the trust at issue. The death of the testator's life tenant, his widow, controls. Rather than "happenstance", this is the common measuring device for the orderly transferences of decedents' assets, a rule providing specificity, not serendipity. The vesting date here is arrived at by an application of well-settled principles of the law of future interests. The language of paragraph FIFTH (c) created a requirement of survival. When the first devisee or legatee takes a life estate, words of survivorship tend to "'establish the time of the termination of all preceding interests as the time to which survival is required'" (Matter of Gautier, 3 N.Y.2d 502, 509, 169 N.Y.S.2d 4, 146 N.E.2d 771, quoting Restatement of Property § 251, at 1266). Here, the preceding interest terminated only upon the death of testator's widow, Elsie, in 1986. Daniel's predecease in 1981 is irrelevant in this respect and precludes his heirs from asserting that any entitlements inchoately vested in him before Elsie's death to accrue later to their benefit.

As we have consistently held, the plain meaning of the testamentary language itself is the surest path to the judicial discernment of a testator's donative intent.

Expanding the application of exceptions to that sound general proposition would soon swallow the rule and render less secure the effectuation of testator's relied upon, expressed intentions. Indeed, to create a new exception out of something called "paramount intent", different from the intent clearly expressed on the face of a will and in its only relevant donative provision, would be seriously unsettling because it would sacrifice predictability, an especially crucial element in the field of decedents' estates where "settled rules are necessary and necessarily relied upon. . . ."

Accordingly, the order of the Appellate Division should be affirmed, with costs to all parties filing briefs payable out of the residuary trust at issue.

HANCOCK, Judge (dissenting). I would modify the order of the Appellate Division and hold that the term "children" in paragraph FIFTH (c) of the will includes grandchildren and, therefore, that Leonard's share must be divided equally between his son Daniel's surviving children, collectively, and his daughter, Jacqueline.

In my view, construing "children" narrowly here and, thereby, disinheriting the lineal descendants of one of the testator's brothers is unwarranted and represents a distinct—and unfortunate—extension of the "unmistakable intent" rule. In Matter of Villalonga, 6 N.Y.2d 477, 190 N.Y.S.2d 372, 160 N.E.2d 850, where we applied that rule and declined to read "children" broadly, we emphasized that: (1) the will there was "a simple one . . . and not afflicted with the weakness of ambiguity" (id., at 481, 190 N.Y.S.2d 372, 160 N.E.2d 850), (2) "[t]here [was] no interchangeable use made of the terms 'children' and `issue' " (id., at 481, 190 N.Y.S.2d 372, 160 N.E.2d 850), and (3) "[n]or [did] the general distributive scheme disclose a testamentary purpose to benefit children of predeceased immediate offspring together with surviving immediate offspring" (id.). Those very factors—the absence of which led our court to construe "children" narrowly in *Villalonga*—are present in this case.

The will here is ambiguous. The ambiguity arises, in part, from the interchangeable use of the terms "children" and "issue" in paragraph FIFTH. Also, the use of "issue" in paragraph FIFTH (d) manifests a clear intention to benefit a predeceasing brother's surviving lineal descendants—not just the brother's immediate offspring as a narrow reading of "children" in paragraph FIFTH (c) suggests. Moreover, the intent of the testator as indicated by the language and structure of the entire will seems straightforward: to make gifts to his brothers or their respective family lines, treating them equally. Indeed, there is nothing in the testamentary scheme to suggest that the testator wanted to disinherit the family of his brother's son (Daniel's family), in favor of that brother's other child (Jacqueline), on the seemingly unrelated and meaningless contingency of his brother's son predeceasing his widow.

Significantly, the *Villalonga* court itself reaffirmed the well-established exception to the rule it applied, *viz.*, that where uncertainty exists, "children" should be given a broad construction to avoid an inequitable result (id., at 482-483, 190 N.Y.S.2d 372, 160 N.E.2d 850). Quoting Matter of Paton, 111 N.Y. 480, 486, 18 N.E. 625, our court reiterated that, "[o]f course, if the language employed 'is equally susceptible of one or another interpretation, we should, on every principle of right, and within the spirit of the authorities, give it that which is most equitable and consonant with the dictates of justice'" (6 N.Y.2d, at 484, 190 N.Y.S.2d 372, 160 N.E.2d 850 [emphasis added]. Accordingly, we should construe "children" in paragraph FIFTH (c) as "issue" and, thereby, avoid an incoherent interpretation of paragraph FIFTH (c) and (d) and, at the same time, avoid the patent inequity which otherwise results.

The majority's attempt to reconcile paragraph FIFTH (c) and (d) avoids neither problem. Nor does it withstand scrutiny. Paragraph FIFTH (d) cannot fairly be read—as the majority contends—as providing that, "if neither issue nor children survived one brother, the other brother (or his children or his issue) would take to prevent a lapse." Plainly, the language of paragraph FIFTH (d) does not so provide. It does no more than give the share of the estate in question to the "surviving brother" if the other dies "without issue surviving". There is no language in paragraph FIFTH (d) itself that directs or permits "issue" (or "children") to take. Only paragraph FIFTH (c) can be read as providing for that, and then, only if "children", as used by the testator, is construed to mean "issue".

Indeed, the majority's contention, that paragraph FIFTH (d) permits a devise to a brother's "issue" under certain circumstances, plainly undercuts their position and supports the view taken here. Their contention necessarily recognizes the basic point that "issue" (i.e., children of deceased children) were intended to be beneficiaries in some situations. But because, as noted, such a disposition cannot be effected under paragraph FIFTH (d), it follows that it can only be made under paragraph FIFTH (c)—i.e., by construing "children" in paragraph FIFTH (c) broadly as permitting "issue" to take.

Similarly, other provisions in the will either make little sense or run counter to the testator's over-all design if "children" is narrowly construed. For example, the distribution under paragraph SIXTH, providing for the direct gifts to the testator's two brothers, would have failed if one of them had died with grandchildren or other issue, but with no surviving immediate offspring. And the very same would be true for paragraph EIGHTH—which was explicitly intended to cover any bequest elsewhere in the will that might fail. Under that paragraph, as under paragraphs FIFTH and SIXTH, if "children" is read narrowly, there would be no provision for the very real contingency of a brother dying with no surviving sons or daughters, but with grandchildren or other lineal descendants still alive. Thus, paragraph EIGHTH, intended to avoid intestacy, would actually have permitted intestacy if read strictly.

I would resolve the ambiguities, and avoid the otherwise resulting inconsistencies and anomalies in the will, by broadly construing "children" to mean "issue". Such a construction would, in my view, yield the most reasonable and fair result—i.e., permitting Leonard's son's family (Daniel's family) as well as Leonard's daughter (Jacqueline) to share in the estate—and, thereby, avoid the certainly unintended inequity of depriving Daniel's children on the mere happenstance that their father died before their great uncle's widow. Finally, construing "children" broadly would, thus, give effect to the testator's paramount intent.

WACHTLER, C.J., and ALEXANDER and TITONE, JJ., concur with BELLACOSA, J.

HANCOCK, J., dissents in part and votes to modify in a separate opinion in which SIMONS and KAYE, JJ., concur.

Order affirmed, etc.

Notes and Questions

1. *Restatement of Property.* The court in *Gustafson* relied in part on the Restatement of Property for the proposition that words of survival relate to the time of termination of all preceding interests—the death in 1986 of Carl Gustafson's widow, Elsie. The Restatement provides:

> § *251. Time to Which Survival Is Required by Added Word, Phrase or Clause.* In a limitation purporting to create a remainder or an executory interest, a description of the intended takers as persons "who survive," or who are "living," or by other language of the same import, but which fails to designate the time to which such takers must survive, tends to establish the time of the termination of all preceding interests as the time to which survival is required.

Comment e states that this constructional preference "is a strong one," but also notes that it is opposed "by the preference for early indefeasibility." Consequently, when the preference is "reinforced by a special context indicating survival of a testator as the only survival intended, the tendency stated in this Section is overcome."

2. *Survival of the Time of Substitution?* The dissenting judge in *Gustafson*, Judge Hancock, expressed concern about the outcome of the case, as decided by the majority. Judge Hancock thought that "disinheriting the lineal descendants of one of the testator's brothers is unwarranted and represents a distinct—and unfortunate—*extension* of the 'unmistakable intent' rule." To prevent the disinheritance of Daniel's family, Judge Hancock unsuccessfully argued that "children" should be construed to mean "issue."

Is there another means of preventing the disinheritance of Daniel's family, which Judge Hancock didn't mention and possibly didn't notice? Note the order of deaths as between Daniel and his father, Leonard. Daniel died in 1981. Leonard died in 1978. Colman's Will, 33 N.W.2d 237 (Wis. 1949), is precedent for construing the word "surviving" in clause (c) as relating to Leonard's death rather than to Elsie's death.

Suppose that G's will created a trust, income to her husband, H, for life, remainder in corpus to the couple's children, but if any of the children predeceases H, that child's share to go to that child's surviving children. G and H had two children, A and B. A survived H. B predeceased H, leaving two children (X and Y) living at B's death. X predeceased H; Y survived H. In *Colman*, the court said:

> The general rule is that when a vested interest is divested by a condition subsequent, such interest immediately vests in the substitutionary legatees unless the will expressly provides otherwise. . . . Consequently then, as under the will involved herein, the substitutionary legatees are children not of the testator nor of the life tenant, but of a third person, the class is determined and the bequest vests in such class on the death of their parent, or ancestor if taking per stirpes. . . . When the interest of the parent vests in the children as a class the interest of any child then living is not divested by the death of such child prior to the termination of the life estate. . . . The law favors a vested rather than a contingent estate; and an absolute rather than a defeasible estate; and a vesting at the earliest possible period.

3. *Survival of the Testator.* Comment e to Restatement § 251, supra Note 1, states that the preference for early indefeasibility, if reinforced by a special context, can overcome the presumption that words of survival relate to the termination of all preceding interests. In such a case, words of survival can be found to relate to the death of the testator.

A case adopting this construction is Nass's Estate, 182 A. 401, 114 A.L.R. 1 (Pa. 1936). George Nass, Sr., died in 1895, leaving a will that disposed of his residuary estate in trust, the income from which was given to his wife for life. On the death of his wife, the trust was to be divided into four equal parts. One part was given to his son, George, absolutely. A half of each of the remaining three parts was given absolutely to each of his daughters, Mary, Amanda, and Julia. The other halves of the remaining three parts were continued in trust, with the income to be paid equally to each of the daughters for life. Upon the death of each daughter, the portion of the principal from which she had been receiving income was to go that daughter's child or children. Nass's will continued:

> In case of the decease of my said Daughters or either of them without leaving lawful issue then and in such case I give devise and bequeath the said part or share

> hereinbefore given, devised and bequeathed to the said Executors In Trust unto my surviving child or children absolutely and forever.

Nass's wife died in 1915. Mary, one of the daughters, died in 1913 leaving a child who survived Mary (and presumably Nass's wife, also). George died in 1924, leaving issue. Amanda died in 1934, leaving a husband but no children. Julia, the only child still living, claimed the one-eighth share of the principal from which Amanda had been receiving the income. The court rejected Julia's claim, saying:

> Our rule of construction applied to survivorship has been held to refer to the time of death of the testator unless a contrary intent appears in the will. The rule is not without sound reason, for its general effect is to distribute the property among all of testator's descendants rather than to shunt it off into one line where it may pass out of the family. It is apparent that in this case any other construction would work an inequality which would not carry out what was presumably testator's scheme. He intended to treat, not only his own children alike, but his children's children, and no other thought appears in the will. He intended an equal division of his estate among his issue, and the repeated use of the word "equal" throughout his will is a clear demonstration of this fact. "Where the will shows an intention that the descendants of deceased children shall take, and an evident intention of equality of distribution is manifested, the word "survivors" has been held to apply to the death of the testator." Page on Wills (2d Ed.) p. 1562. If testator's intent be considered otherwise, it results in giving the entire fund to one child, Julia, whose life has been prolonged beyond the lives of the other children, and would tend to prefer her and her heirs over the heirs of other children. . . . Nor is the fact that the person to whom the prior estate is given, though his death is to precede the ultimate limitation, is himself a party entitled to share, sufficient to show an unequivocal intention that he was not to take upon the happening of the contingency.

4. *Single- vs. Multiple-Generation Class Gift.* Does the Restatement's preference for construing ambiguous words of survival as relating to the termination of all preceding interests make more sense when the future interest is to a multiple-generation class such as "issue" or "descendants" than when the future interest is to a single-generation class such as "children" or "nieces and nephews"?

5. *Uniform Probate Code.* If *Gustafson* (supra), *Colman* (supra Note 2), and *Nass* (supra Note 3) had been governed by UPC § 2-707, what result?

Problem

In Smith v. Cockrill, 196 S.E. 681 (Va. 1938), Benjamin F. McConchie's will devised certain real property to his daughter, Sarah, for life, remainder in fee simple to the testator's two other children, Mary and James. The will continued:

> But should Mary . . . or James . . . die before Sarah . . . , then his or her one-half . . . is to go to their children to be divided equally amongst their children that may be living at the death of Sarah. . . . And if either Mary . . . or James . . . should die before Sarah . . . without issue, then their one-half interest is to go to my surviving child in fee simple.

First Mary died, then James. James died intestate, apparently without ever having married; he never had any children. Mary was survived by her son, Max. Max also predeceased Sarah, leaving five children, all of whom survived Sarah. It's not clear whether Max survived James. Sarah left the residue of her estate to Rosa E. Smith.

The court held that Max's five children were entitled to the property at Sarah's death:

> [Benjamin McConchie] wanted to keep it in the family, so to speak. . . .
>
> We have, therefore, arrived at the conclusion that after the death of Mary . . ., her interest passed to her son, Max . . . , and upon his death and the death of the life tenant, Sarah . . . to his children . . . ; and that upon the death of James . . . his share likewise passed to [Max's five children], they taking the share which Mary . . . would have been entitled to. Rosa E. Smith takes no share of the realty under the will of Sarah.

Does the court's conclusion deserve to be supported with any greater rigor than this? *Can* it be supported with any greater rigor than this? If the case had been governed by UPC § 2-707, what result?

Assuming the outcome reached by the court carried out Benjamin McConchies's intent, how could the disposition have been drafted so that no litigation would have been required to determine its meaning? How about "to Sarah for life, then to my descendants who survive Sarah, by representation;[5] if none of my descendants survives Sarah, to . . ."?

4. Age Specifications

Dispositions in trust frequently link a beneficiary's right to income or to possession or enjoyment of principal to reaching a specified age. According to a 1999 survey of the wealthiest one percent of Americans (defined as those with a net worth of $3 million or more or whose annual income is $225,000 or more)

5. The will should also include a definition of the term "by representation." Cf. UPC § 2-709.

commissioned by the U.S. Trust Company, and available on its website, www.ustrust.com:

> Raising a financially responsible, hard-working child could be made more difficult if that child were to be given a large inheritance or trust assets at too young an age. Just over half the parents (55%) worry about making wise inheritance decisions with regard to their children. More of the affluents (58%) believed the wiser thing to do was stipulate an age when the inheritance could be received, rather than pass on an inheritance to the child upon the death of the respondent (33%). On average, this stipulated age was 28 years old.
>
> Other steps they have taken include establishing trusts for their children. Eight of 10 respondents have or plan to set up trusts for their heirs. On average, those surveyed who have set up trusts for their children do not intend for their children to gain control of the trust assets until they are 28 years old.

As the following materials demonstrate, age specifications must be drafted with great care. If carelessly drafted, ambiguities in an age specification will probably be resolved by application of various rules of construction that sometimes conflict in a given case. The analysis is likely to begin with the rules of construction laid down in an ancient English case called Clobberie's Case, 2 Vent. 342, 86 Eng. Rep. 476 (Ch. 1677). The full report in this case appears as follows:

> In one *Clobberie's* case it was held, that where one bequeathed a sum of money to a woman, at her age of 21 years, or day of marriage, to be paid unto her with interest, and she died before either, that the money should go to her executor; and was so decreed by my Lord Chancellor Finch.
>
> But he said, if money were bequeathed to one at his age of 21 years; if he dies before that age, the money is lost.
>
> On the other side, if money be given to one, to be paid at the age of 21 years; there, if the party dies before, it shall go to the executors.

The staying power of the constructional rules established in *Clobberie's Case* is remarkable. The Restatement 2d of Property § 27.3 tells us that they are still to be followed:

> *Comment f. Age requirement specified.* . . . The language of the disposition that indicates the age requirement is not a condition but is only a description of the time to which distribution is delayed is when the gift is to the class members "to be paid to each class member at 21" or "when they attain 21 with income in the meantime." If the gift is to the class members "who attain 21," the age requirement is clearly a condition.

See also Restatement of Property §§ 257-59.

In re Parker

L.R. 16 Ch. Div. 44 (1880)

[The testator, Mary Elizabeth Parker, died in 1863, leaving a will that devised the residue of her estate in trust, the terms of which were described by the court as follows:

> upon trust to pay the dividends, interest, and income thereof, or such part thereof as my said trustees for the time being shall from time to time deem expedient, in and towards the maintenance and education of my children until my said children shall attain their respective ages of 21 years; and from and immediately after their attaining their respective ages of twenty-one years, then upon trust to pay, assign, and transfer the said stocks, funds, and securities to my said children in equal shares, if more than one, and if but one, then to such one child; and as to each daughter's share, whether original or accruing, upon trust to settle the same," for the benefit of herself and her children. And the testatrix declared "that it shall be lawful for the trustees or trustee for the time being of this my will to assign, transfer, or dispose of any component part, not exceeding one half of the presumptive share of any of my children for the preferment or advancing in life, or preparing for business, or on the marriage of any such child (being daughters) notwithstanding their minorities.

The testator was survived by her two sons and a daughter. One of the sons died in 1873, under the age of 21. The daughter and the other son both reached 21.]

JESSEL, M.R. . . . In my opinion, when a legacy is payable at a certain age, but is, in terms, contingent, the legacy becomes vested when there is a direction to pay the interest in the meantime to the person to whom the legacy is given; and not the less so when there is superadded a direction that the trustees "shall pay the whole or such part of the interest as they shall think fit." But I am not aware of any case where, the gift being of an entire fund payable to a class of persons equally on their attaining a certain age, a direction to apply the income of the whole fund in the meantime for their maintenance has been held to create a vested interest in a member of the class who does not attain that age.

The words here are plain. The trust is of residue: "to pay the dividends, interest, or income thereof, or such part thereof as my said trustees for the time being shall from time to time deem expedient, in or towards the maintenance and education of my children, until my said children shall attain their respective ages of twenty-one years"; so that there is nothing here giving an aliquot share of income to any individual child; the direction being to pay the income of the whole fund in such shares as the trustees shall think fit. I do not think you can infer anything from the direction for the settlement of the daughters' shares.

Then follows a gift of the whole fund to the children equally on attaining twenty-one. I should have felt no difficulty if it had not been for the advancement clause, which speaks of the "presumptive share of any of my children," but I do not think that clause is sufficient to alter the effect of the preceding part of the will.

That being so, I hold that the infant did not take a vested interest in his one-third share of the residue.

Clay v. Security Trust Co.

252 S.W.2d 906 (Ky. 1952)

DUNCAN, J. This Declaratory Judgment action seeks a construction of the last will and testament of James T. Clay who died a resident of Fayette County in February, 1932.

The Security Trust Company qualified as trustee and executor under the will, and on January 5, 1952, filed this action in the Fayette Circuit Court. The Bourbon Agricultural Bank and Trust Company, executor under the will of Laura Clay Macey, deceased, Matthew D. Clay, Neal McClure Clay and Charles Wylie, executor under the will of John I. Macey were named defendants. From the construction adopted by the Chancellor, Matthew D. Clay and Neal McClure Clay appeal.

The will under consideration is as follows:

> I, James T. Clay, of Lexington, Fayette County, Kentucky, do hereby make this my last will and testament.
>
> *First* I desire my just debts and funeral expenses be paid.
>
> *Second* I bequeath to Mrs. Gussie P. Rion, of Latonia, Kentucky, the sum of Ten Thousand ($10,000).
>
> *Third* All the balance of my estate of whatsoever nature and kind I give to my sister Laura Clay Macey, which is to be held by my Trustee hereinafter named during her life, and the income therefrom is to be paid to her in monthly installments. I desire my Trustee to consult with my said sister in making change of investments of the said fund. At the death of my said sister, Laura Clay Macey, I direct my Trustee to hold the said estate until my nephew John Ireland Macey, the only child of Laura Clay Macey, arrives at the age of thirty-five years, and direct that the income shall be paid to him in monthly installments until the said fund is turned over to him.
>
> I hereby give my Executor and Trustee power to sell and transfer any securities that it may hold for my estate and re-invest the proceeds in such securities or real estate as it may think proper. In the event that my Executor and Trustee should purchase any real estate, it shall have the right to sell the same for re-investment.
>
> *Fourth* I hereby nominate and appoint the Security Trust Company, Lexington, Kentucky, my Executor and Trustee.
>
> Witness my hand this 21st day of January, 1932.
>
> *James T. Clay*

At the time of testator's death he was survived by his sister, Laura Clay Macey, two half-brothers, Matthew D. Clay and Neal McClure Clay, and his nephew, John I. Macey (John Ireland Macey), the son of Laura Clay Macey. John I. Macey predeceased his mother, Laura Clay Macey and died in 1944 before he attained the age of 35. Laura Clay Macey died on February 8, 1951.

The property in question, now being held by the Security Trust Company in trust, consists entirely of personalty and amounts to approximately $42,000.

The sole question in the case is whether the remainder interest given to John I. Macey in the third clause of the will was a vested or contingent remainder. Appellees contend and the lower court found that the interest was a vested one and that the fund in question should be paid to the devisee under the will of John I. Macey. Appellants contend that the interest was contingent upon Macey attaining the age of 35 and that inasmuch as he died prior to his 35th year, the fund descends under the laws of descent and distribution and is payable to the heirs of James T. Clay.

We realize that precedent is not nearly so persuasive in cases involving construction of wills as in other cases. The paramount reason for that fact is that no two wills are exactly alike, whether phrased in the legal terminology of a trained attorney or in the simple and sometimes illiterate language of the testator. We, therefore, hesitate to say that the construction of any given will is absolutely controlled by any previous construction adopted by this court in considering some other will. Our primary concern is to determine, if possible, what the testator meant by the will under consideration.

Rules of construction are not intended as arbitrary means of fixing in every case the rights of parties under the will. However, most of the rules of modern usage are applied where the intention of the testator is otherwise obscure and because it has been determined that by their application the intention of the testator is more nearly reached.

One of the rules of construction of almost universal application is the presumption against partial intestacy. The rule is that where a will is susceptible of two constructions, the law favors that one which disposes of the entire estate. The presumption is even stronger where the will contains a residuary clause.

Another rule of equally general application is that which favors the early vesting of estates. All doubts will be resolved in favor of the construction which accomplishes an early vesting unless a contrary intention clearly appears.

Two other rules of particular applicability to the problem here presented are the following: (1) the absence of a gift or limitation over in the event of failure to attain a specified age is regarded as indicating an intention on the part of the testator that the gift should vest immediately; (2) a gift of the substance to which futurity is apparently annexed is not considered contingent upon the attainment of a specified age where there is a gift of the intermediate use.

In the case of Danforth v. Talbot's Adm'r, 46 Ky. 623, 7 B. Mon. 623, the court had before it for a construction a will the applicable portions of which were as follows:

> 7th. On the decease of my said wife, the above described farm, &x., &c., shall become the property of my son Cyrus, when arrived at the age of twenty-six years, (excepting the reservation in favor of Ann R.;) but after providing for the support and comfort of his mother, he may be entitled to all the profits arising from the same, except the reserved rights of his sister, Ann R.

In that case the court in a well-reasoned opinion held that the estate devised to Cyrus Talbot was not contingent upon his attaining the age of 26, but that the devise had the effect of merely postponing the time of enjoyment. There it was said:

> And although the event referred to, that is, the arrival of the son at the age of twenty-six, must, when abstractly and precisely considered, be regarded as uncertain and contingent, must it be assumed to have been so regarded by the testator? He evidently did not regard it as contingent. He speaks of it as a thing certainly to happen. He does not even say, "if" he shall arrive, &c., but "when" arrived at the age of twenty-six years; and he makes no devise over upon the event not happening, as he would almost certainly have done if he had regarded the happening of the event as uncertain, or its not happening as a contingency which would give a different direction to the estate. . . .

In the same case the court recognized and applied the rules of construction noted herein which arise from the omission of a devise over upon Cyrus not attaining the age of 26 and the right given him under the will to the intermediate use prior to the time of full enjoyment.

We recognize that the opinion in that case was written more than one hundred years ago. However, that fact does not militate against the weight which should be accorded it if it is sound and the reasons supporting it are valid. . . .

For the reasons indicated, we are of the opinion that the construction adopted by the Chancellor was proper and the judgment is affirmed.

Note and Questions

Drafting Age Specifications. Normally, it will be desirable expressly to require survival of the specified age and to provide for alternative takers in the event of a failure to survive. In one situation, however, there may be reason expressly to negate a requirement of survival. This arises when the donor wishes to qualify an inter vivos gift in trust to a minor child for the annual gift tax exclusion allowed by IRC § 2503(c).

To qualify for the exclusion under IRC § 2503(c), the property must "pass to the donee on his attaining the age of 21 years, and in the event the donee dies before attaining the age of 21 years, be payable to the estate of the donee or as he may appoint under a general power of appointment. . . ." The custom in estate planning practice is to use the power of appointment option. But if that option isn't chosen, then the governing instrument should clearly state that the death of the donee before reaching 21 doesn't extinguish the donee's interest. How would you draft the trust to accomplish this result? Should the instrument say "whether or not the donee lives to age 21," or should it track § 2503(c) and say "if the donee dies under 21, then the property is to be paid to the donee's estate"? See Olin L. Browder, Trusts and the Doctrine of Estates, 72 Mich. L. Rev. 1509, 1522-28 (1974); John O. Fox, Estate: A Word to be Used Cautiously, If at All, 81 Harv. L. Rev. 992 (1968); Annot., 10 A.L.R.3d 483 (1966).

5. Gifts Over on Death or on Death Without Issue

Possessory Interests. G's will devised real property as follows:

(a) To A and his heirs, but if A should die, to B.
(b) To A and his heirs, but if A should die without issue, to B.

G died and then A died without issue. B is still alive. Who is entitled to the property, B or A's successors in interest?

In Case (a), the usual construction is that the property goes through A's estate to A's successors in interest.[6] See Restatement of Property § 263.

In Case (b), the usual construction is that A's interest is divested in favor of B.[7] See Restatement of Property § 267. But see, e.g., Friedman v. Marshall, 876 S.W.2d 745 (Mo. Ct. App. 1994), where the court construed a devise of a possessory interest subject to a condition of death without issue to apply to death *before the testator* without issue.

Woods' Estate

149 A.2d 865 (N.H. 1959)

. . . . Elizabeth A. Luce . . . died in 1954. Clara E. Woods died December 30, 1956, and the administratrix was appointed January 5, 1957. Among the

---

6. In Case (a), of course, it makes no difference whether A died with or without issue.

7. The same result would be reached if B survived G but predeceased A; A's interest would be divested in favor of B's successors in interest. See, e.g., Hays v. Cole, 73 So. 2d 258 (Miss. 1954).

assets inventoried in the Woods estate was an undivided one-half interest in certain real estate in Keene.

This property was formerly owned by Mrs. Luce. In her will, after leaving $100.00 to her husband in lieu of all his rights in her estate, she provided that

> all the rest, residue and remainder of my property, whether real or personal, and wherever situated, I give, bequeath and devise in equal shares to my daughter, Jessie Evelyn Starkey, of said Keene, and my sister, Clara E. Woods, of said Keene. In case of the death of either the said Jessie Evelyn Starkey or the said Clara E. Woods, I give, bequeath and devise the share of such decedent to the survivor.

The administratrix of the Woods estate, Evelyn S. Deming, formerly Jessie Evelyn Starkey, claims that as daughter of Mrs. Luce she takes all her mother's real estate to the exclusion of Clara's heirs. In her petition, she asks us to answer the following questions: "(1) Did the said Clara E. Woods inherit in fee an undivided one-half interest in said real estate under the will of the late Elizabeth A. Starkey Luce? (2) In the event the foregoing question is answered in the negative, should the inventory be amended to exclude said one-half interest in said real estate from the estate of Clara E. Woods?"

BLANDIN, J. The basic question presented is whether Clara E. Woods took a vested interest in fee under the will of her sister, Elizabeth A. Luce, in certain real estate, so that upon her death it descended to Clara's heirs, Florence Cram and Doris Cocco, or whether it passed to Mrs. Luce's only daughter, Evelyn S. Deming. The answer depends on what the testatrix meant when, after bequeathing all the remainder of her estate in equal shares to her daughter and sister, she added the words: "In case of the death of either . . . I give, bequeath and devise the share of such decedent to the survivor." Although as administratrix of Mrs. Woods' estate, Mrs. Deming inventoried a "½ interest in Land and buildings" in the disputed real property, she presently claims this was error and that she takes it all as survivor under Mrs. Luce's will.

It is axiomatic that the law favors the early vesting of interests in the interest of certainty, the avoidance of complications, and the expeditious settlement of estates. Furthermore, the common meaning attributed to words of survivorship is that they refer to the death of the devisee in the lifetime of the testatrix. The practical difficulties of applying the construction urged by the administratrix, especially with reference to the disposition of personal estate, are obvious and militate against her claim. Furthermore, the words appear in themselves significant. Since death is certain, there seems no point in using the words "In case" unless they were intended to refer to the death of either of the devisees before that of the testatrix.

We are not unmindful of the administratrix's argument that Mrs. Luce's main concern was her sister, Clara, and her daughter, the administratrix, and that since she did not mention her brother, Samuel Luce, and another sister, Florence Cram, it must have been her intent that neither they nor their children should share in her estate. We agree that her real interest was in her daughter and her sister Clara, but had she been desirous of arranging matters so that no child of her brother or Mrs. Cram should take under her will, she could easily have done so.

In the case of Mulvanity v. Nute, 95 N.H. 526, 68 A.2d 536, cited by the administratrix, the will unequivocally expressed an intention that a joint tenancy be created. The testator gave certain property to his son and sister as "Joint Tenants" and stated that "upon the decease of one the title to vest in the survivor." 95 N.H. at page 527, 68 A.2d at page 536. He expressed the desire that his son and sister have the right to occupy the premises during their lifetime. The Court held that a joint tenancy in fee was created. It added that in order to establish the unusual estate of a life estate with remainder to the survivor, which is what the administratrix claims was created by Mrs. Luce's will, "clear and unambiguous language" would have to be used. Id. at page 528, 68 A.2d at page 537. See also RSA 477:18. We find no such language in this will indicating an intent to set up such an uncommon estate, but rather it expresses a reasonably plain purpose to make a gift in fee to two persons with the survivor taking all if, but only if, one of them died before the testatrix.

In all the circumstances, we believe the testatrix, when she said "In case of the death of either," referred to death in her lifetime. Since this did not occur, it follows that Clara E. Woods took an undivided one-half interest in fee in the disputed real property which was properly inventoried as part of her estate.

Case remanded.

Future Interests. G's will created a trust, the terms of which were:

(a) Income to L for life, remainder in corpus to A, but if A should die, to B.

(b) Income to L for life, remainder in corpus to A, but if A should die without issue, to B.

G died, then A died without issue, and then L died. B is still alive. Who is entitled to the property, B or A's successors in interest? The usual construction in both cases is that A's interest is divested in favor of B.[8] See Restatement of Property §§ 264, 269.

---

8. In Case (a), of course, it makes no difference whether A died with or without issue.

G died and then L died. A is still alive. Did A's survival of L render A's interest absolute, or does A's interest continue to be defeasible? The majority construction in both cases is that A's survival of L rendered A's interest absolute. See Restatement of Property §§ 264, 269. There is, however, division in the cases on the point, especially regarding Case (b). See Annot., 26 A.L.R.3d 407 (1969).

Definite versus Indefinite Failure of Issue. A further question exists in connection with the dispositions containing a gift over on death without issue. To reintroduce those dispositions, suppose that G disposed of property in her will as follows:

(a) To A and her heirs, but if A should die without issue, to B.
(b) To L for life, remainder to A, but if A should die without issue, to B.

After G's death, A died survived by issue. In Case (b), L was still alive when A died.

Does A's death survived by issue render her interest absolute, or does her interest continue to be defeasible? The preferred and usual construction is that A's death survived by issue renders her interest absolute. See Restatement of Property § 266. This construction, called a "definite failure of issue" construction, is codified in several states.

An older construction, now nearly universally abandoned, is called an "indefinite failure of issue" construction. Under this construction, which is the English construction carried over from the fee tail estate, A can still "die without issue" after her death. A's "death without issue" occurs if and when her last living descendant dies.

Accrued Shares. G devised a tract of land "to my three sons, A, B, and C; but if any son dies without leaving issue surviving him, the portion devised to such son shall go to my said sons then living."

After G's death, A died without issue; then B died without issue, leaving a will that devised his entire estate to his widow, W. Does C now own the entire tract of land? See Restatement of Property § 271. What happens to the ownership of the land if C dies without issue? What if C dies *with* issue?

PART B. SPECIAL PROBLEMS OF CLASS GIFTS

Class gifts are extremely useful in estate planning practice, especially multiple-generation class gifts, such as to issue, descendants, or heirs. We are already knowledgeable about many of the features that distinguish class gifts from individual gifts.

In Chapter 6, we studied the definition of a class gift—how to differentiate a class gift ("to my children") from individual gifts ("to my three children, A, B, and C;" "to my three children;" "to my children, A, B, and C"). Chapter 6 also examined the effect of the death of a potential class member before the testator's death and the applicability of anti-lapse statutes in such cases.

Chapter 2 introduced us to the different forms of representation in multiple-generation class gifts—per stirpes, per capita with representation, and per capita at each generation. In addition, Chapter 3 examined the status of adopted children and nonmarital children.

In Part A of this chapter, we studied the effect of a contingency unrelated to survival on a future interest in favor of a single-generation class, and we saw that a condition of survival is thought to be implicit in a multiple-generation class gift in which a representational form of distribution is called for.

What is left?

1. Increase in Class Membership: Class Closing and the Rule of Convenience

A unique feature of most class gifts (other than class gifts to heirs) is the ability of new entrants to join the class. Each new entrant increases the number of potential takers and partially divests the shares of the existing class members.

A class is subject to increase—subject to open—as long as it is possible for new entrants to come into the class. The ability of a class to increase ends—the class "closes"—at the *earlier* of two events: (1) the natural (or physiological) closing of the class; or (2) the artificial (or premature) closing brought about by the application of the so-called *rule of convenience.*

Natural (or Physiological) Class Closing. The natural closing of a class occurs when births (or, if adopted members are within the class description, adoptions) become physiologically impossible. A class gift in favor of a transferor's grandchildren physiologically closes upon the death of the transferor's last living child. A grandchild who is in gestation on the date the class closes is regarded as in being on the closing date.

The physiological closing of a class is traditionally predicated on the assumption that death terminates the possibility of having children. Recent medical developments have shown that the traditional assumption may not always be true. With frozen sperm, ova, and embryos on the contemporary scene, the possibility of having children can exist for years after death. See supra Chapter 3, Part B. Should a child produced after death be included as a class member? Although the law hasn't definitively solved this problem, the Introductory Note to Chapter 26 of the Restatement 2d of Property p. 131 states that such after-born children shouldn't be included in the described class "because of the practical considerations of providing assurance for an indefinite period of time that a share in the class gift will be available for such after-born persons." The Introductory Note goes on to say, however, that these after-born persons will be included if the language or circumstances of the gift indicates that the transferor intends to include them. See also UPC §§ 2-108, -701, -705.

Of course, in the vast majority of cases, no frozen sperm, ova, or embryos capable of producing a post-death child exist, and the traditional assumption about the parent's death marking the closing of the class prevails and works well. When frozen sperm, ova, or embryos capable of producing a post-death child do exist, the courts or legislatures will probably abide by the Restatement 2d and presumptively close the class under the rule of convenience (see below) no later than at the death of the parent.

Artificial (or Premature) Class Closing: The Rule of Convenience. A class may close earlier than its physiological closing. When this happens, the class has been closed artificially or prematurely. Artificial or premature closing is governed by the rule of convenience.

The rule of convenience is a rule of construction, not a rule of law. It yields to a contrary intent. Although Earle's Estate, below, illustrates this point, that case is unusual. In practice, a contrary intent can seldom be shown, and consequently the rule of convenience typically prevails.

Once a class has been closed by the rule of convenience, subsequently conceived or adopted persons are not entitled to participate in the class gift, even though they otherwise fit the class label. New entrants come into a class only if they are conceived[9] or adopted[10] while the class is still open.

Basically, the rule of convenience holds that a class closes when a class member becomes entitled to distribution of a share. This rule is founded on two basic premises. First is the premise that the use of only a group or class

---

9. As indicated above, a child in gestation when a class closes is regarded as in being at that time. In administering this principle, there is precedent suggesting a rebuttable presumption that the date of conception was nine months before the date of birth. See, e.g., Equitable Trust Co. v. McComb, 168 A. 203, 207 (Del. Ch. 1933); Wells' Will, 221 N.Y.S. 714, 724 (Sur. 1927). To enter the class, the child must be born alive and probably must be born viable. See, e.g., Ebbs v. Smith, 394 N.E.2d 1034 (Ohio C.P. 1979); Recent Developments, Torts—Wrongful Death—Unborn Child—The Estate of an Unborn Child Has a Cause of Action for Wrongful Death—O'Neill v. Morse, 70 Mich. L. Rev. 729, 735 (1972); Restatement 2d of Property §§ 26.1 comment c, 26.2 comment c.

10. With respect to an adopted child, the date of adoption, not the date of conception, is the significant date for inclusion in the class. See, e.g., Estate of Markowitz, 312 A.2d 901, 903 (N.J. Essex County Ct. 1973) ("Born when? . . . Regardless of the time when an adopted child is physically born, he or she does not come into existence as a child of the adoptive parent [in the sense that the law equates the relationship of a biological child with that of an adopted child] until the effective date of the order of adoption."); but see Restatement 2d of Property §§ 26.1 comment d, 26.2 comment d ("By analogy to a child in gestation, a child who is in the process of being adopted is regarded as an adopted child during the period the adoption is in process." To be included in the class, the adoption must be "concluded within a reasonable time" after the closing of the class.)

description indicates that *all* persons who fit the description—whenever born (or adopted)—were intended to share in the gift. In other words, the starting point is that the class wasn't intended to close until it closes naturally. Second, because of inherent difficulties or "inconveniences" in allowing participation by persons born (or adopted) after distribution, it is believed that the transferor, if the transferor had contemplated these difficulties, would have intended to exclude these persons. That is, although the basic intent of the transferor is to keep the class open until it closes naturally, if inconveniences will arise from doing so, the transferor would prefer for the class to be closed prematurely or unnaturally, so that the inconveniences will be avoided.

The inconvenience of a class being kept open after distribution is that the distributees wouldn't take an indefeasible interest. Instead, they would receive a considerably less useful defeasible one. Taking an interest that is subject to being partially divested upon the birth (or adoption) of additional class members would render the property less marketable and, if personal property, would require some device such as the posting of security to protect the interests of unborn (or unadopted) members of the class.

External Reference. Restatement 2d of Property Chapter 26, reporter's notes.

Immediate Class Gifts. As indicated, the rule of convenience comes into operation only if the class hasn't closed naturally by the time of distribution. In the absence of sperm or ova capable of producing a post-death child, an immediate testamentary devise to the children of the testator won't require premature closing. Similarly, a devise to the children of a person other than the testator won't close prematurely if the person predeceases the time of distribution. If the person is still living at the time of distribution, however, an application of the rule of convenicnce is necessary. When at least one member of the class is in existence, an immediate gift closes at the date the gift becomes effective.

> *Example 18.7:* G devised real property "to my grandchildren." When G executed his will, his only son A had a child (X). Subsequently, but before G's death, a second child (Y) was born. G was survived by his son A and by his two grandchildren, X and Y. No grandchildren were in gestation at G's death.
>
> Under the rule of convenience, the class remains open until G's death but closes at that time even though A is still alive and is therefore deemed to be capable of having more children. X and Y each take an undivided interest in one-half of the property in fee simple absolute. In other words, their interests aren't subject to partial divestment in favor of any later born (or later adopted) child of A.
>
> Suppose that at G's death, A's wife was pregnant, and that G's third grandchild (Z) was born viable. Z would be considered to have been "in being" at G's death, and consequently he would participate in the class gift. So, X, Y, and Z would

each take an undivided one-third possessory interest in the property in fee simple absolute.

In the above example, suppose that A's wife became pregnant with Z shortly after G's death, while G's estate was still in probate. Would Z be included in the class? See Restatement 2d of Property § 26.1 comment g & cases cited in reporter's note 6, at 153-54.

There is an exception to the rule that an immediate class gift by will closes at the testator's death. If there is *no* class member then "in being," the class does not close prematurely, but remains open until it closes naturally.

Example 18.8: G devised real property "to my grandchildren." At G's death, her son A was still alive, but A had no living children and none was then in gestation.

The rule of convenience doesn't close the class at G's death. The class remains open until the death of A. *All* afterborn grandchildren, if any, are entitled to participate.

Note, however, that if a child of A's had been in gestation at G's death, and if that child had been subsequently born viable, then the rule of convenience would have closed the class on G's death, resulting in that child having taken the whole property in fee simple absolute.

Specific-Sum Class Gifts. When a class gift grants a specific sum to each member of the class, as opposed to the more traditional type of class gift in which a proportional share of a fund or item of property is granted to each class member, the class closes when the gift becomes effective, whether or not any class member is then alive. If no class member is then alive, the class gift fails.

Problem

G's will created a trust, income to G's grandchildren until the death of G's last living grandchild, remainder in corpus to M-Charity. When G died, grandchild V and grandchild X were living. Subsequently, grandchild Y was conceived and born, then grandchild Z. To what portion of the income, if any, are the after-born grandchildren entitled?

It may help you in thinking about this problem to note that the Restatement 2d of Property § 26.2 comment g describes each income payment as a "postponed gift."

Postponed Class Gifts. The basic principle of the rule of convenience is that a class closes when a distribution of the property must be made. Having applied this principle to immediate class gifts, we now turn our attention to class gifts in which distribution is postponed.

Problems

When do the classes close in the following cases?

1. G devised real property "to A for life, remainder to B's children." G was survived by A, B, and B's child (X). A second child (Y) was born to B during A's lifetime. B's third child (Z) was born after A's death. B survived A.

2. In Problem 1, suppose that by the time of A's death, no children had been born to B and that none was then in gestation.

3. G devised property in trust, income to G's grandchildren, corpus to be equally divided among G's grandchildren when the youngest grandchild attains 21. When G executed her will, her first grandchild (V) had just been born. Subsequently, another grandchild (X) was born. G then died. After G's death, the following events happened, in the order stated: V became 21; another grandchild (Y) was born; X became 21; a fourth grandchild (Z) was born; Y became 21; Z became 21.

No further grandchildren had been born or were in gestation on Z's 21st birthday, but G's children were still living. G's youngest child, E, was a male, age 43; he was contemplating marriage to his 34-year-old female friend, F.

Lux v. Lux

288 A.2d 701 (R.I. 1972)

KELLEHER, J. [Philomena Lux left the residue of her estate "to my grandchildren, share and share alike." Her will further provided:

> 3. Any real estate included in said residue shall be maintained for the benefit of said grandchildren . . . until the youngest of said grandchildren has reached twenty-one years of age.

Philomena was survived by one son, Anthony John Lux, Jr., age thirty, and his five children, whose ages ranged from two to eight. The youngest grandchild was born after the will was executed but before Philomena's death.

The court held that clause 3 created a trust for the benefit of the grandchildren, the corpus of which was to be distributed when the youngest grandchild reaches 21; the class of grandchildren should remain open until then. Next, the court turned to the meaning of the term "youngest," saying:]

There are four possible distribution dates depending on the meaning of "youngest." Distribution might be made when the youngest member of the class in being when the will was executed attains twenty-one; or when the youngest in being when the will takes effect becomes twenty-one; or when the youngest of all living class members in being at any one time attains twenty-one even though it is physically possible for others to be born; or when the youngest whenever it is born attains twenty-one. This last alternative poses a question.

Should we delay distribution here and keep the class open until the possibility that Philomena's son can become a father becomes extinct? We think not.

We are conscious of the presumption in the law that a man or a woman is capable of having children so long as life lasts. A construction suit, however, has for its ultimate goal the ascertainment of the average testator's probable intent if he was aware of the problems that lead to this type of litigation. It is our belief that the average testator, when faced with the problem presented by the record before us, would endorse the view expressed in 3 Restatement, Property § 295, comment k at 1594 (1940), where in urging the adoption of the rule that calls for the closing of the class when the youngest living member reaches the age when distribution could be made, states:

> When all existent members of the class have attained the stated age, considerations of convenience . . . require that distribution shall then be made and that the property shall not be further kept from full utilization to await the uncertain and often highly improbable conception of further members of the group. The infrequency with which a parent has further children after all of his living children have attained maturity, makes this application of the rule of convenience justifiable and causes it to frustrate the unexpressed desires of a conveyor in few, if any, cases.

We hold, therefore, that distribution of the trust corpus shall be made at any time when the youngest of the then living grandchildren has attained the age of twenty-one. When this milestone is reached, there is no longer any necessity to maintain the trust to await the possible conception of additional members of the class. . . .

Problems

When do the classes close in the following cases?

1. G bequeathed $90,000 to be divided equally among those of G's grandchildren who reach the age of 21. (This type of bequest probably would be in trust, and it might provide either for the accumulation of the income until distribution, or for its payment to the grandchildren as it is earned.)

(a) One of G's grandchildren had reached 21 before G's death. Does the class close when that grandchild reached 21 or when G died?

(b) None of G's grandchildren had reached 21 before G's death. Subsequently, the first grandchild (X) reached 21; there were two other grandchildren (Y and Z) then alive. Thereafter, Y died under 21. Then Z reached 21. When did this class close? Who are the ultimate takers and what are their shares?

(c) The income from the trust was to be accumulated and added to the corpus; each grandchild was to receive a proportionate part of the corpus upon reaching 21. G was survived by a daughter, age 30, and a son, age 24, both unmarried and childless. Shortly after G's death, the son married a college classmate and the daughter married a widower, age 45, who had two children by his previous marriage. The ages of the widower's two children were 19 and 21. G's son and his bride were childless, but planned on having a family. G's daughter adopted her husband's children. Is the class closed yet? See Silberman's Will, 242 N.E.2d 736 (N.Y. 1968);[11] Nowels Estate, 339 N.W.2d 861 (Mich. Ct. App. 1983); Restatement 2d of Property § 25.4; Cal. Prob. Code § 21115(b); UPC § 2-705 (see supra Chapter 3, Part B, for further discussion).

2. G bequeathed $90,000 in trust to pay the income to A for life, then to distribute the corpus equally among those of G's nieces and nephews who reach 21. (Again, the income after A's death, but before distribution of the corpus, might be either accumulated or paid out.)

(a) Prior to A's death, one of G's nieces reached 21. Does the class close when that niece reached 21 or when A died?

(b) None of G's nieces or nephews had attained 21 by the time of A's death. Subsequently, one of the nephews, X, reached 21. Two months after X's 21st birthday, a niece was born. Another niece was born fourteen months after X's 21st birthday. Is either of these nieces included in the class?

3. G devised land "to my grandchildren, but if any grandchild should die before attaining 21, his or her share to go to my then surviving grandchildren." G was survived by children and grandchildren. All of the grandchildren were under 21. Additional grandchildren were born after G's death. How many class gifts are created here? When do they close?

2. *Class Gifts to Heirs or Next of Kin*

Statutory References: *UPC §§ 2-701, -711*

The terms "heirs" and "next of kin" have primary meanings that are fixed by statute. Historically, and technically, the two terms have different meanings. *Heirs* are identified by the statute of descent—the term refers to those to whom a decedent's *real property* descends on the decedent's death intestate. *Next of kin* are identified by the statute of distribution—the term refers to those to whom a decedent's *personal property* is distributed upon the decedent's death intestate. A few states still provide for different patterns of takers for real and personal property, but most states, by far, have consolidated the two patterns into a single statute, called a statute of descent and distribution. Consequently, in the

11. Discussed in Samuel M. Fetters, The Determination of Maximum Membership in Class Gifts in Relation to Adopted Children, Silberman's Will Examined, 21 Syracuse L. Rev. 1 (1969).

vast majority of states, the pattern of intestate succession is the same for real and personal property.

The term "heirs" or "next of kin" is sometimes used in a nontechnical sense, to mean children or issue. This usually arises when one or the other term is used interchangeably with children or issue, such as in the disposition "to A for life, remainder to A's heirs, but if A dies without issue, to B." See, e.g., Connor v. Biard, 232 S.W. 885 (Tex. Civ. App. 1921); Restatement 2d of Property § 29.1 comment d. By statute in Georgia, all "limitations over" to "heirs" presumptively mean children and the descendants of deceased children. See Ga. Code Ann. § 44-6-23, interpreted in Dodson v. Trust Co. of Georgia, 117 S.E.2d 331 (Ga. 1960). See also N.C. Gen. Stat. § 41-6.

Suppose a future interest is given to the "representatives" of a deceased person. Does the term "representatives" mean "issue"? Or, does it mean "heirs"? In Boston Safe Deposit & Tr. Co. v. Wilbur, 728 N.E.2d 264 (Mass. 2000), the court held that the term meant "heirs."[12]

When the term "heirs" or "next of kin" is used in a technical sense, the class gift so created isn't subject to open. Once the takers are determined, by application of the relevant intestacy statute, new entrants can't later join the class.

Dodge Testamentary Trust

330 N.W.2d 72 (Mich. Ct. App. 1982)

BEASLEY, P.J. This appeal is taken by various interested parties from an order of the Wayne County Probate Court directing distribution of the trust corpus of a testamentary trust arising under the will of John F. Dodge, deceased. The order was entered pursuant to a thorough and carefully drawn opinion prepared by Judge Willis F. Ward of the Wayne County Probate Court, in which he made findings of fact, conclusions of law and determination of claims.

John F. Dodge, an early and highly successful automobile manufacturer, died testate on January 14, 1920.[13] His will, which was dated April 4, 1918, was

---

12. The court used the term "statutory distributees" instead of "heirs," but the meaning is the same.

13. John F. Dodge died in New York, while on a trip with Horace Dodge, his brother and co-founder of the Dodge Brothers machine shop, which later produced the Dodge automobile. The Dodge brothers were on a trip to the National Automobile Show where Dodge cars were on display. John was an early victim on an influenza epidemic that swept New York. Horace also contracted influenza, as did John's wife Matilda, who upon learning of John's illness took the first train to New York to be at his bedside. Matilda was so sick that she was unable to attend her husband's funeral back in Detroit. Horace died in Palm Beach later that year of a relapse. See Jean Maddern Pitrone, Tangled Web: Legacy of Auto Pioneer John F. Dodge 94-98 (1989). Eds.

admitted to probate in the Wayne County Probate Court. In his will, John F. Dodge created a residuary trust which [set forth comprehensive and lengthy provisions governing the distribution of the income among the testator's widow and four of his six children and their "issue." With respect to the corpus of the trust, Paragraph 20:14(h) of the will provided:]

> [U]pon the death of all of my said children, Winifred Dodge Gray, Isabella Cleves Dodge, Frances Matilda Dodge and Daniel George Dodge, then I direct my said trustees to convey my said estate to the heirs of my said children, Winifred Dodge Gray, Isabella Cleves Dodge, Frances Matilda Dodge and Daniel George Dodge, in such proportion as by law such heirs shall be entitled to receive same.
>
> The provisions I have made in this Will for my son John Duval Dodge, have been made after careful thought and deliberation on my part, un-influenced by any person or persons whomsoever, and I believe these provisions to be the most wise I can make for my said son, John Duval Dodge. I make this explanation in order that it may be known that I have given careful thought to the claims of my said son, John Duval Dodge, and in order that neither my wife, nor any of my children may be accused of having influenced me in reference to the provisions that I have herein made in regard to my said son.

John F. Dodge left surviving him his widow, Matilda R. Dodge (Wilson), and six children, John Duval Dodge, Winifred Dodge Gray (Seyburn), Isabella Cleves Dodge (Sloane), Frances Matilda Dodge (Van Lennep), Daniel George Dodge, and Anna Margaret Dodge. The first three children were born of testator's marriage to Ivy Dodge, who died in 1900, and the second three were born of his marriage to Matilda R. Dodge (Wilson). His widow, Matilda, remarried in 1925 to Alfred Wilson, and they adopted two children, Richard S. Wilson and Barbara Wilson (Eccles). Matilda, who died in 1967, is perhaps best known for her generous bequests which have become the site of Oakland University and the various Meadowbrook cultural events.

Winifred Dodge Gray (Seyburn) was the first-born offspring of John F. Dodge and the last to die in 1980. Her death in 1980 operated to terminate the residuary trust created under the will. Winifred Dodge Gray (Seyburn) had two children as issue of the Gray marriage, Winifred Gray Seyburn Cheston, born in 1917, and Suzanne Gray Seyburn Meyer, born in 1920. Winifred Dodge Gray (Seyburn) also had two children as issue of the Seyburn marriage, Edith Seyburn Quintana, born in 1923, and Isabel Seyburn Harte, born in 1924. These four children of Winifred Dodge Gray (Seyburn) survive.

Isabella Cleves Dodge (Sloane) died March 9, 1962, without issue, while a resident of Florida.

John Duval Dodge, who was substantially disinherited in his father's will, died in 1942, leaving a widow, Dora Dodge, who died in 1950, and a daughter, Mary Ann Dodge (Danaher), who survives.[14]

Anna Margaret Dodge was born June 14, 1919, subsequent to execution of her father's will in 1918. She died intestate on April 13, 1924.

Daniel George Dodge died August 15, 1938, leaving surviving him his widow, Annie Laurine Dodge (Van Etten), and his mother, Matilda R. Dodge (Wilson).

Frances Matilda Dodge (Van Lennep) died in 1971, survived by her husband, Frederick L. Van Lennep, whom she had married in 1949. Also, she left surviving her three children, Judith Frances Johnson (McClung), born in 1941 as issue of Frances' first marriage to James P. Johnson, Jr., whom she divorced in 1948, Fredericka Van Lennep (Caldwell), born in 1951, and John Francis Van Lennep, born in 1952, all of which children survive.

Not mentioned in the will was testator's infant daughter, Anna Margaret Dodge, she having been born June 14, 1919, a year after execution of the will. She took as a pretermitted heir, i.e., the same share she would have received if the testator died intestate. However, she died intestate at age five in 1924, and the devolution of her property was affirmed in Dodge's Estate, 242 Mich. 156, 218 N.W. 798 (1928).

John Duval Dodge attacked the validity of his father's will, which case was settled under a then newly-enacted statute authorizing such settlements, which statute was enacted largely as a result of this subject situation.[15] Subsequently, in 1939, John Duval Dodge renewed his will contest and attempted to set aside the settlement agreement. The decision of the circuit court upholding the settlement agreement and rejecting the claim that the will and trust were invalid was affirmed in Dodge v. Detroit Trust Co., 300 Mich. 575, 2 N.W.2d 509 (1942).

In the within proceedings, a guardian ad litem was appointed to represent all unknown claimants to the trust and, after extensive discovery procedures, he reported that there were not any additional interested parties. On this appeal, we

---

14. John Duval Dodge was reportedly a rebellious son, who was expelled from boarding school more than once for truancy. When, at age nineteen, he secretly married eighteen-year-old Marie O'Connor, and when word of the marriage was reported in a newspaper, John F. Dodge instructed his lawyer to draw up a new will, essentially disinheriting John Duval. See Jean Maddern Pitrone, supra note 13, at 58, 77-78, 84-85. Eds.

15. The testator's will gave his son, John Duval Dodge, only a monthly stipend of $150 for life so that he "would never be a public charge." The testator's widow, Matilda, wanted to settle her stepson's suit, but state law did not then permit out-of-court settlements. At her direction, her attorneys pressured the state legislature to change the law to allow such settlements. The result was the "Dodge Law" to which the court alluded. Once the statute became effective, John Duval's suit was settled for $1.6 million. See Jean Maddern Pitrone, supra note 13, at 100, 111. Eds.

consolidate seven separate appeals (files), in some of which there are cross-appeals. We have reviewed at least 30 briefs which have been filed, varying in length from five pages to more than 80 pages.

At the outset, we hold that since the probate court order, which is the subject of all these appeals, affects the rights of the parties with finality, it is a final order, directly appealable to this Court.

In his splendid opinion, the probate judge discussed four issues of law and made detailed rulings cited to authority. First, he dealt with the meaning of the word "heirs" as used in paragraph 20:14(h) of the last will and testament of John F. Dodge, deceased. The issue arises because, in the termination provision of the testamentary trust, the testator said:

> . . . then I direct my said trustees to convey my said estate to the heirs of my said children, Winifred Dodge Gray, Isabella Cleves Dodge, Frances Matilda Dodge and Daniel George Dodge, in such proportion as by law such heirs shall be entitled to receive same.

The question is whether the word "heirs" was used in the will in its technical sense to denote those persons who inherit under the intestacy laws or whether "heirs" as used in the will was intended to designate only the "issue" or "children" of testator's children.

The cardinal rule of law and the predominant rule in the construction and interpretation of testamentary instruments is that the intent of the testator governs if it is lawful and if it can be discovered. This legal proposition finds support in many cases. Unless the will is ambiguous on its face, the testator's intention is derived from the language of the will.

In Brooks v. Parks,[16] which was decided in 1915, about three years prior to the date of execution of the Dodge will, the will in question provided in the residuary clause that one-half would go to a daughter during her lifetime and after her decease to her children and that the other half would go to another daughter during her lifetime and after her decease *to her heirs*. The Court upheld an interpretation that provided that the residue left to the second daughter would pass to her husband, saying that he was an heir of his wife and, as such, would inherit her half. In so holding, the Court declined to interpret the entire will as evidencing a contrary intent. Brooks is authority for defining the word "heir" as designating the persons appointed by law to succeed in case of intestacy and for holding that wherever the word "heir" occurs in a will, unaccompanied by qualifying or explanatory expressions, it must be allowed the meaning the law gives it.

---

16. 189 Mich. 490, 155 N.W. 573 (1915).

We are satisfied that, in 1918 when the will of John F. Dodge was drawn and signed, the word "heirs" was a technical term with a well and clearly defined meaning, namely, those designated by the statutes of intestate succession to receive one's estate on death and that "heirs" included the spouse of the decedent.[17]

We note that the attorney drawing John F. Dodge's will appears to have been able and experienced in the practice of probate law. He was not a mere tyro, unfamiliar with common and accepted usage in legal circles of words used in the descent and distribution of property upon death.[18]

Thus, we ascribe to the word "heirs", as used in the subject will, its technical meaning as it existed in 1918 when the will was drafted and executed. We decline to conclude that the draftsman of the will made a "mistake" when he used in the will two different words, "issue" and "heirs". On the contrary, we believe that the attorney drawing the will used these two different words in their known, technical legal sense with the intention that the trust corpus descend differently than the trust income.

We acknowledge that a strong, visceral countering argument is made that the testator never intended that any part of his estate, either corpus or income from the testamentary trust, would pass outside of his bloodlines and that the testator intended that the natural objects of his bounty were those in the bloodlines, not spouses of his children, e.g. a son-in-law. At the outset, in weighing the merits of this argument, we note that the law does not permit that we indulge in speculation regarding the testator's intention. We look first to the will and only go beyond the language of the will if convinced that ambiguity is present. The fact that the testator named only his children and their issue to receive trust income, while leaving the residue of the trust corpus upon final termination to the heirs of his children, is not an indication of an ambiguity in the will. . . .

Thus, we conclude that John F. Dodge did employ a skilled attorney in the preparation of his will, and that the words employed must be given their accustomed technical meaning according to common legal usage. In its legal and technical sense, the word "heir" is understood under established rules of decision as designating persons appointed by law to succeed in the case of intestacy. Wherever the word is employed unaccompanied by qualifying or explanatory expressions, it must be allowed the meaning the law gives it. We hold that the term "heirs", as used in the will, means those persons designated by statute to receive that class of property under the laws of intestate succession.

---

17. Brooks v. Parks, supra; Shumway's Estate, 194 Mich. 245, 160 N.W. 595 (1916); Menard v. Campbell, 180 Mich. 583, 147 N.W. 556 (1914).

18. 61 Supreme Court Records and Briefs, pp. 346-361 (October Term, 1941).

The second issue decided by the probate court was when should the remainder (corpus) interests of the heirs of the testator's named children vest. Should it be the time of each child's death, or should it be later at the termination of the trust upon the death of the last surviving child?

Unless a testator clearly and unambiguously states to the contrary, vesting of contingent remainders shall be determined as of the date of death of the ancestor. We decline to hold that testator's will in this case clearly and unambiguously established the time of vesting at the date of the termination of the trust. Consequently, we conclude that the date of death of the ancestor is the time of vesting of the contingent remainder interests in this trust.

This conclusion finds support in the case law. Jamieson Estate[19] is the leading case and is express authority for Michigan's preference for early vesting, the Court saying:

> [I]t has long been the law in Michigan that vested estates are to be favored, and that conditions of survivorship will not lightly be implied. . . . Indeed, we have characterized as a rule of property not to be disturbed the rule that when ambiguity exists whether a testator intended to condition a remainderman's taking of an estate merely upon survival of the testator or upon survival of the holder of a precedent estate, the latter condition should not be implied. (Citation omitted.)

In Jamieson, the Court rejected the argument that vesting should be postponed until the time of distribution, saying:

> In the accurate use of language, only those entitled to inherit at the death of another can be called his heirs. Accordingly, unless a contrary intention appears, a gift in a will to the heirs of a person, whether he be the testator or a life tenant or another, will be construed as a gift to such heirs determined as of the time of death of that person.[20]

Shortly before decedent's will was drafted in 1918, the Court in Shumway's Estate,[21] stated that only the clearest expression of a preference for delayed vesting would justify a departure from the rule favoring early vesting. In Jamieson, supra, the Court quoted Shumway with approval, saying:

---

19. 374 Mich. 231, 237-238, 132 N.W.2d 1 (1965). See also, 3 Restatement of Property, § 308, p. 1706, which states that where there is a gift to "heirs", then the statute is applied as of the death of the designated ancestor absent evidence of an intent to the contrary.

20. Jamieson, supra, 374 Mich. at p. 251, 132 N.W.2d 1, citing New England Trust Co. v. Watson, 330 Mass. 265, 267, 112 N.E.2d 799 (1953).

21. 194 Mich. 245, 160 N.W. 595.

> We conclude that unless a contrary intent is manifested, when a testator disposes of property to heirs, the heirs are to be determined upon the death of their ancestor. Such contrary intent will not be deduced from the bare fact that the heirs are secondary remaindermen. Nor will such contrary intent be found to exist simply because some of the testator's language may be strained into ambiguity, but rather "only plain, unambiguous language by the testator will prevent application of that rule [favoring early vesting] in construing a will."[22]

Shumway also indicates that there is nothing particularly unusual about giving trust income to certain life tenants and a non-possessory (remainder) interest to a class of heirs that could include the life tenants themselves.

In the within case, it is contended that the following circumstances suggest that the deceased would have preferred to postpone vesting until termination of the trust: (1) the deceased's express desire to postpone vesting beyond the date of his own death; (2) the indications that the deceased would not have wanted John Duval Dodge to take as an heir of the named life tenants; and (3) the potential for greater federal estate taxation under a theory of successive vesting. These speculations, while interesting, do not justify departure from the established rule favoring early vesting.

As indicated in Shumway, supra, the intention to postpone vesting must be manifested and tangibly expressed in such language as plainly conveys the thought beyond mere surmise, conjecture or supposition. We do not find such clear language in the will, plainly expressing a preference to postpone vesting until the termination of the trust. Postponing vesting beyond the date of his own death is no indication by the testator that he wanted to put it off as long as possible, until the death of his last surviving child which, in fact, turned out to be a period of approximately 60 years.

This is not a circumstance indicating any preference for vesting at the termination of the trust, as opposed to vesting on the dates of the respective deaths of the named children. Neither does the intention of the testator to exclude his son John Duval Dodge from significant[23] trust income during the life of the trust establish any intention to postpone vesting until the termination of the trust.

The argument in this regard is based on the very questionable assumption that the deceased did not even want John Duval Dodge to acquire any vested interest in the corpus of the trust as a possible heir of the four named children. The probate court properly rejected this argument that the deceased meant to prohibit John Duval Dodge from inheriting through his brothers and sisters as

---

22. Jamieson, supra, 374 Mich. at p. 252, 132 N.W.2d 1.

23. The will directed the trustees to pay $150 per month to John Duval Dodge during his lifetime.

a contention based entirely upon speculation. The probate court correctly noted that "no language in the will expressly establishes this intention". Even if it were assumed that the testator did intend to preclude John Duval Dodge from taking as an heir of his siblings, the desire was not so plainly expressed as to warrant a departure from the established rule favoring early vesting.

Finally, the idea that the deceased planned to postpone vesting in order to avoid federal estate taxes is without merit. The will does not even refer to federal estate taxes and does not appear to show any concern for them. The federal estate tax was newly enacted in 1918, was quite modest by today's standards, and would hardly have played a major role in the drafting of the will.

In any case, if tax consequences led the testator to prefer to postpone vesting, he should have expressed this preference in clear language in the will. As previously indicated, we do not find error in the conclusion of the probate court favoring vesting as of the time of the death of each ancestor named in the will, i.e., the four named children of the testator.

The third issue discussed and decided by the probate court was whether the word "heirs", as used in the testator's will, should be defined according to the statutes of distribution in effect at the time of the death of each named life income beneficiary, rather than according to the statute of descent in effect at the testator's death. The probate court held that the statutes of distribution in effect at the date of death of the immediate ancestor should be applied in determining the heirs of the children named in the testator's will and in determining the share to which each such heir was entitled. The probate court recited three reasons for this conclusion.

First, the court said that the testator expressed a clear wish in his will that the heirs of his children should take "in such proportion as by law such heirs shall be entitled to receive same". The probate court interpreted this phrase to mean that the testator did not intend that the law at the time of his death would govern determinations to be made many years into the unpredictable future.

Second, the probate court noted that the trust corpus presently in question consists entirely of personal property. No evidence was presented to refute this or to establish that real estate ever was intended to be included in the trust. See Dodge v. Detroit Trust Co., supra, 300 Mich. at p. 598, 2 N.W.2d 509.

Third, the probate court seemed to believe that, since it had already decided that "heirs" is to be defined by reference to the statute in existence at the date of death of the immediate ancestor, it would create a dilemma if it held that the statute was modified by the statute in effect at the date of the execution of the will, citing Brooks v. Parks, supra.

The significance of this issue is that the statute of descent in effect at the time of the testator's death, 1917 P.A. 341; 1915 CL 11795,[24] left nothing to the husband of an intestate woman who died leaving issue to inherit her real estate. However, the statute of descent was amended by 1931 P.A. 79; 1929 CL 13440[25] to allow one-third of any real estate to descend to the surviving husband and the remaining two-thirds to go to the woman's issue. Furthermore, the statute of distribution gave the husband one-third of the woman's personal property.[26]

Thus, if the probate court applied the statute of distribution or the amended statute of descent to determine the "heirs" of the testator's daughter Frances, then it would properly find her surviving husband, Frederick L. Van Lennep, to be entitled to a one-third share of the quarter of trust corpus reserved for her (Frances's) heirs.

On the other hand, if the probate court should have applied the statute of descent in effect at the time of the deceased's death, then Van Lennep was not entitled to take at all, and the entire quarter of the corpus passing to Frances's heirs would go to her children, including appellant, Judith Johnson McClung.

Therefore, in order for appellant McClung to prevail, she must prevail in both of the following propositions: first, that the deceased intended the statutes in effect at the date of his (testator's) death to apply to the determination of his children's heirs, and, second, that he intended the statute of descent, rather than the statute of distribution, to apply.

We reject both of these contentions. The language of the will reveals a clear intention to apply future intestacy laws, rather than those in effect at the time the will was drafted. The will provides specifically that the heirs of the testator's

---

24. 1915 CL 11795, provides in part:

If such intestate shall die under the age of twenty-one years, and not having been married, all the estate that came to such intestate by inheritance from a parent, which has not been lawfully disposed of, shall descend to the other children and the issue of deceased children of the same parent, if there be such children or issue, and if such persons are in the same degree of kindred to said intestate they shall take equally, otherwise they shall take by right of representation.

25. 1929 CL 13440, provides in part:

If the intestate shall leave a husband or widow and no issue, one-half of the estate of such intestate shall descend to such husband or widow. . . .

If the intestate shall leave a husband or wife and no issue, nor father, mother, brother nor sister, and there be no child of brother or sister, the estate of such intestate shall descend to the husband or wife of such intestate, as the case may be.

26. 1915 P.A. 314; 1915 CL 13913, provides in part:

In any other case the residue, if any, of the personal estate shall be distributed in the same proportion and to the same persons, and for the same purposes, as prescribed for the descent and disposition of the real estate.

four named children should take "in proportion as by law such heirs *shall* be entitled to receive same". Furthermore, since the vesting of the heirs' interests should occur upon the death of each of the four named children, the application of any statutes other than those in effect on the dates of the four named children's respective deaths would be inconsistent and would create a kind of legal dilemma.

As indicated in Brooks v. Parks, supra, there is nothing improper about applying a statute of distribution or descent enacted after the death of the testator. We are satisfied that the inclusion of a single piece of real estate, namely, the boat house, appraised at $40,000 in the inventory of the estate, was an obvious oversight. Thus, we do not believe that those cases which depend for decision on a conclusion that the property involved is "mixed" with both real and personal property are here applicable.

We would not believe that the testator intended to have a trust which had been so painstakingly prepared for the benefit of his named children be invalidated on account of the presence of any real estate. It would appear that the parcel of real estate, which we believe was included only by oversight, amounted to only about one-thousandth of the total value of the trust property. See Dodge v. Detroit Trust Co., supra, 3 Mich. at p. 598, 2 N.W.2d 509. We are not inclined to believe that this "blend" of realty and personalty is the type that was before the courts in the cases cited by appellant[27] and upon which those cases depended for decision.

Furthermore, the real estate parcel included was sold in 1929 and, by the time the first of the four named children who were beneficiaries (Daniel) died in 1938, the trust property consisted entirely of personal property. It was well established at the time the will was drafted and executed that when a devise of personal property is made to the heirs of a given person, the heirs should be identified by application of the statutes in effect at the time of that person's death.[28] Therefore, we conclude that in determining the heirs of each of the four named life income beneficiaries of the trust, it was not error to apply the statute of distribution in effect at the date of each child's death.

The fourth issue considered and determined by the probate court was whether the statutes of the State of Michigan or of the state of domicile of the ancestor determine the "heirs". The issue, which presents a close and difficult question, relates to Isabella Cleves Dodge (Sloane), who died in 1962 while a resident of the State of Florida.

---

27. Lyons v. Yerex, 100 Mich. 214, 58 N.W. 1112 (1894); Allison v. Allison's Executors, 101 Va. 537, 44 S.E. 904 (1903).

28. Hascall v. Cox, 49 Mich. 435, 13 N.W. 807 (1882); Turner v. Burr, 141 Mich. 106, 104 N.W. 379 (1905).

The significance of which state's law controls results from the fact that, in 1962, Florida law[29] provided that collateral kindred of the half blood would inherit only half as much as those of the whole blood while Michigan law[30] provided that heirs of the half blood in these circumstances would take equally with heirs of the whole blood. Thus, under Florida law the heirs of Isabella Cleves Dodge (Sloane) would take as follows: two-fifths to Winifred Dodge Seyburn, two-fifths to Mary Ann Dodge Danaher, and one-fifth to Frances Dodge Van Lennep, the latter being a half-sister because Isabella and Frances had different mothers. Under Michigan law, Winifred Dodge Seyburn, Mary Ann Dodge Danaher and Frances Dodge Van Lennep would each take one-third.

As previously indicated, the Dodge will provided in paragraph 20:14(h) that, upon termination, the residue of the trust be conveyed to the heirs of the four named children. In Colvin v. Jones,[31] the Court said:

> It is the rule that where the owner of property dies, intestate, . . . his personal property is distributed according to the law of his domicile.

Since Isabella Dodge Sloane died in 1962 domiciled in Florida, it is claimed that technically her heirs should be decided under Florida law. In this connection, 3 Restatement of Property, § 305, pp. 1674-1675 provides as follows:

> When a conveyor describes his conveyees as the "heirs" of a designated person, it is primarily the same as if he had said "those persons who would have succeeded to the property of the named ancestor if he had died intestate." Thus, unless a contrary intent of the conveyor is found from additional language or circumstances, the applicable local law which is used to determine the persons who come within the term "heirs" is the law which would be used to ascertain the heirs of the designated ancestor if he had owned the property in question and had died intestate (see §§ 251 and 308 of the Restatement of Conflict of Laws).

The encyclopedia American Law of Property provides:[32]

> Suppose the subject matter of a devise is located in one state, the testator was domiciled in another state, and the ancestor whose heirs are designated as the beneficiaries is domiciled in still another state. The statute of which state is to be applied? Assuming that the average testator makes a disposition in favor of

---

29. 1945 Fla.Laws 731.24.

30. 1948 CL 702.84.

31. 194 Mich. 670, 677, 161 N.W. 847 (1917).

32. 5 American Law of Property, § 22.58(a), which is cited in 53 Harvard L. Rev. 207, 212-213, 228 (1937).

"heirs", etc., only after he has exhausted his specific desires so that in effect he is saying "Now let the law take its course," the solution in the ordinary case of this conflict of laws problem becomes relatively simple. If the subject matter of the gift is land, the statute is the one in the state in which the land is located, *and if the subject matter is personal property, then the statute should be the one in the state in which the ancestor is domiciled. This seems the desirable resolution of the conflict of laws problem.* (Emphasis added.)

Where personal property is involved, the normal and technical meaning of "heirs" requires the use of the statute of intestacy of the state of the last domicile of the decedent whose heirs are being determined. In holding to the contrary, the probate court placed heavy reliance on Sewart Estate,[33] where the Court said:

> [T]he basic question in construing the will is the intention of the testatrix. Such intention is to be determined, if possible, from the language of the instrument.

In this case, the testator, John F. Dodge, created a testamentary trust which provided for payment of trust income to four named children, the oldest of whom was under 25 at the time of execution of the will. By its terms, the trust terminated upon the death of the last survivor of the four named children. We assume that the testator contemplated that the trust would continue for many years and that there was nothing in the circumstances to indicate where each named child would die.

The Dodge will does not expressly say that in determining residuary heirs of the four named children, resort should be had to the state of domicile at the time of death of the deceased child. Neither does the Dodge will expressly say that residuary heirs of the four named children should be determined under Michigan law. Under these circumstances, we believe the Sewart decision is controlling.

In 52 A.L.R.2d 482, 495, Sewart is described as illustrative of the general rule that in the absence of anything to indicate a contrary intention on the part of the testator, the "heirs" are ascertained by reference to the law of the testator's domicile.

In Sewart, the Court said, among other things:

> In passing on controversies of this nature courts have repeatedly recognized that the maker of the will was presumably familiar with the laws of his own State and ordinarily without specific information as to statutes in force in other States. Such situation may not be ignored in the construction of the language of a will.[34]

---

33. 342 Mich. 491, 497, 70 N.W.2d 732; 52 A.L.R.2d 482 (1955).

34. 342 Mich. 497, 70 N.W.2d 732.

In Sewart, the Court also stated:

> A decision of the supreme court of Kansas in Keith v Eaton, 58 Kan 732; 51 P 271 (1897), is also in point. . . . In holding that the will must be construed in accordance with the law of the domicile of the testator, it was said . . . :
>
> > In the absence of a contrary meaning, to be gathered from the circumstances surrounding a testator or from the instrument as a whole, the sense of the words used by him is to be ascertained in the light of the law of his domicile. Presumptively, he is more familiar with that law than with the law of other jurisdictions. That is the law which is constantly with him, controlling his actions and defining his rights, and more naturally than any other law would be present to his mind in the drafting of an instrument dispository of his property.[35]

We are aware that there are factual differences between Sewart and the within case, but we do not believe they are of a nature to require a different result than that reached by the probate court here. Consequently, we find that, in accordance with Sewart, the intention of the testator was that the heirs of his four named children be determined under the laws of the State of Michigan. This intention is controlling.

In summary, giving effect to our rulings concerning these four issues discussed by the probate court, we hold that: (1) "heirs" as used in paragraph 20:14(h) of the will means those persons designated by statute to whom the law would give that class of property under the laws of intestate succession; (2) the contingent remainder interest of such "heirs" in the trust corpus vested at the date of death of the respective four named children of the testator; (3) the word "heirs" is defined as of the date of death of each of the four named children of the testator; and (4) in determining the "heirs" of each of the four named children of the testator, we look to the laws of the State of Michigan. However, these rulings do not resolve all of the claims and counter-claims made by the parties on appeal.

[The court then disposed of several claims of individuals who had entered into assignments, agreements, or made elections of various sorts, or had been adopted, and continued:]

Consistent with this opinion, we approve the probate court's conclusion regarding disposition of the trust corpus, the cited fractions representing the fractional interests of the total trust corpus as follows:

1. The "heirs" of Daniel George Dodge (entitled to one-quarter of the trust corpus).

---

35. 342 Mich. 499-500, 70 N.W.2d 732.

a. Annie Laurine Dodge (Van Etten), the surviving spouse, assigned her one-half share equally to:

Winifred Dodge Gray (Seyburn) 1/24
Isabella Cleves Dodge (Sloane) 1/24
Frances Matilda Dodge (Van Lennep) 1/24

b. The surviving brothers and sisters each shared the remaining half equally as follows:

Winifred Dodge Gray (Seyburn) 1/32
Isabella Cleves Dodge (Sloane) 1/32
Frances Matilda Dodge (Van Lennep) 1/32
(John Duval Dodge) . . . . (1/32)

c. However, the one-thirty-second share which was to go to John Duval Dodge was assigned by him to the following:

Matilda R. Dodge Wilson Fund 1/128
Winifred Dodge Gray (Seyburn) 1/128
Isabella Cleves Dodge (Sloane) 1/128
Frances Matilda Dodge (Van Lennep) 1/128

2. The "heirs" of Isabella Cleves Dodge Sloane (entitled to one-quarter of the trust corpus).

a. The surviving sisters and child of deceased brother, entitled to share equally by right of representation are:

Winifred Dodge Gray (Seyburn) 1/12
Frances Matilda Dodge (Van Lennep) 1/12
Mary Ann Dodge Danaher (daughter of
John Duval Dodge) 1/12

3. The "heirs" of Frances Matilda Dodge Van Lennep (entitled to one-quarter of the trust corpus).

a. The surviving spouse entitled to a one-third share is:

Frederick L. Van Lennep 1/12

b. The surviving issue entitled to share equally in the remaining two-thirds are:

Judith Johnson McClung 1/18
Fredericka Van Lennep Caldwell 1/18
John F. Van Lennep 1/18

4. The "heirs" of Winifred Dodge Gray Seyburn (entitled to one-quarter of the trust corpus).

a. The surviving issue entitled to share equally are:

Winifred Seyburn Cheston	1/16
Suzanne Seyburn Meyer	1/16
Edith Seyburn Quintana	1/16
Isabel Seyburn Harte	1/16

AFFIRMED.

Notes and Questions

1. *Quality of Legal Services.* If nothing else, the will of John F. Dodge disproves the theory that the wealthy need not worry about the quality of legal services provided them. Every litigated question could and should have been anticipated and unambiguously provided for in the will. A lawyer's job is to anticipate such questions, bring them to the client's attention for decision, and effectuate the client's intention without ambiguity.

2. *Uniform Probate Code.* If UPC §§ 2-701 and 2-711 had governed John F. Dodge's trust, would the case have been litigated? Would the outcome have differed?

3. *Controlling Statute.* In drafting a class gift to a designated person's heirs, the statute to be applied to determine the takers should be expressly identified in the governing instrument. See UPC § 2-703; Restatement 2d of Property § 29.2 comment c. Failing an express identification, the *Dodge* case held that the controlling statute is: (i) the statute of distribution (ii) of the testator's domicile (iii) in existence when the designated person died.

Using the intestacy statute of the testator's domicile is in line with predominant authority, but the Restatement 2d of Property § 29.2 follows the Restatement of Property § 305 in taking the position that the takers should be governed by the statute that would be used to determine the designated person's actual takers if the designated person had died intestate, owning the subject matter of the gift. In the case of personal property, the position of the Restatements would be that the controlling statute is the statute of distribution of the designated person's domicile. Real property would normally be governed by the statute of descent of the situs.

Using the statute of distribution, when the subject matter is personal property, is also in line with existing authority. When the subject matter is a mixture of real and personal property, the position of the Restatement 2d of Property § 29.3 is that the takers of the personal property are determined under the statute of distribution and the takers of the real property are determined under the statute of descent. There is authority, however, some of which is cited in the

Dodge case, to the effect that the statute of descent controls the takers of both the real and personal property, in cases of mixtures.

Using the statute in existence at the designated person's death is also the predominant view. See Restatement 2d of Property § 29.4. There is some authority, however, for the view that the statute to be used is the one in existence when the transfer occurred. See Samuel M. Fetters, Future Interests, 23 Syracuse L. Rev. 219, 224-25 (1972), for a discussion of New York cases to this effect.

4. *No Condition of Survival.* Once the takers are determined, class gifts to heirs follow the normal rule that no condition of survival is imposed unless one is expressly stated. In so holding, the *Dodge* case is consistent with existing authority and the Restatement 2d of Property § 29.5. As is the case with respect to other types of class gifts (see Lawson v. Lawson, supra p. 1070, there is a minority view that a class gift to heirs that is contingent on an event unrelated to survival is also subject to a condition of survival. See, e.g., Continental Illinois Nat'l Bank & Tr. Co. v. Eliel, 161 N.E.2d 107 (Ill. 1959). But see Hofing v. Willis, 201 N.E.2d 852 (Ill. 1964).

5. *Spouse as an Heir.* Although a person's spouse wasn't an heir under the common-law canons of descent, modern intestacy statutes include the spouse as an heir. Consequently, as the *Dodge* case illustrates, the designated person's spouse is entitled to participate in a class gift to the designated person's heirs, in the absence of a manifested intent to the contrary on the part of the transferor. See Thomas v. Higginbotham, 318 S.W.2d 234 (Mo. 1958); Restatement 2d of Property § 29.1 comment j.

6. *Can the State Be an "Heir"?* If, at the time the heirs are to be ascertained, the only claimant is the state by virtue of its right to escheat, § 2-711 of the UPC takes the position that the state takes. The Restatement of Property § 305 comment n and the Restatement 2d of Property § 29.1 comment k take the position that the class gift fails for want of a taker. Which position do you favor?

Problems

1. *Division Among Classes and Class Members.* In the *Dodge* case, the class gift was in favor of the heirs of John F. Dodge's four named children. The court assumed that this meant that the trust corpus was to be divided into four equal shares, the heirs of each named child to get a one-fourth share. This position is supported by the Restatement 2d of Property § 29.8. Also, as held in *Dodge*, the division of each share among the takers within each class is normally determined in accordance with the relevant intestacy statute, rather than on a per capita or some other basis. See Restatement 2d of Property § 29.6.

Although the will of John F. Dodge could certainly have been drafted more clearly on these points, there have been cases exhibiting even poorer drafting. Consider the following:

(a) To A for life, remainder to B and the heirs of A.

(b) To A for life, remainder to A's heirs in equal shares, per stirpes.[36]

(c) To A for life, remainder in equal shares to my heirs and the children of A and the children of B.

2. *Time When Heirs Are Ascertained.* As the *Dodge* case illustrates, the general rule of construction is that heirs or next of kin of a designated person are ascertained at the time of the person's death. See Restatement 2d of Property § 29.4. There are several circumstances, however, in which the general rule of construction doesn't hold. Ascertainment is often *postponed* if ascertainment at the person's death could result in a complete failure of the gift or in depriving one or more descending lines of a share. To avoid a gap in possession, ascertainment is often *accelerated* or *postponed* if the person is still alive or has predeceased the time when the gift to that person's heirs is to take effect in possession or enjoyment. Consider the following dispositions in the light of the common law and of UPC §§ 2-701 and 2-711:

(a) G devised real property "to A's heirs." A survived G.

(b) G devised real property "to L for life, remainder to A's heirs." A survived both G and L.

(c) G devised real property "to A's heirs." Or, G devised real property "to L for life, remainder to A's heirs." In both cases, A predeceased G. At A's death, A's heirs are her two children, X and Y. X predeceased G. G was survived by Y and X's child, Z.

(d) G devised real property "to A for life, remainder to my (G's) heirs."

(1) G, a widower, was survived by his only descendant, A. Compare Restatement 2d of Property § 29.4 comment f; Restatement of Property § 308 comment k; Hanley v. Craven, 263 N.W.2d 79 (Neb. 1978), with Gross v. Hartford-Connecticut Trust Co., 123 A. 907 (Conn. 1924).

(2) G, a widower, is survived by his three children, A, B, and C.

(e) G devised real property "to A for life, remainder to the persons who would be my (G's) heirs if my (G's) death occurred at the time of A's death."

(f) G devised real property "to A for life, remainder to my (G's) then heirs."

---

36. In Estate of Pistor, 146 A.2d 685 (N.J. Super. Ct. App. Div. 1958), aff'd, 154 A.2d 721 (N.J. 1959), the court held that the word "equally" indicated that the transferor intended the takers to be the life tenant's descendants (with each descending line receiving an equal share), to the exclusion of the life tenant's surviving spouse, who was among his actual heirs. See also Post's Trust, 304 N.Y.S.2d 954 (Sur. Ct. 1969). Contra, e.g., Eiten v. Eiten, 357 N.E.2d 810 (Ill. App. Ct. 1976); Gustafson v. Svenson, 366 N.E.2d 761 (Mass. 1977); Wright v. Brandon, 863 S.W.2d 400 (Tenn. 1993).

(g) G devised real property "to A for life, then to my (G's) heirs."

(h) G devised real property "to A for life, remainder to my (G's) heirs who survive A." See Love's Estate, 66 A.2d 238 (Pa. 1949).

EXTERNAL REFERENCES. Restatement 2d of Property § 29.4, comments, reporter's note; Restatement of Property § 308, comments.

3. Inter Vivos Transfers to the Grantor's Heirs: The Doctrine of Worthier Title

Statutory Reference: *UPC § 2-710*

Problem

After substantial revision, an irrevocable inter vivos life insurance trust provided that after the Settlor's death and the $6 million life insurance proceeds are collected and invested by the trustee, the income is to be paid to the Settlor's son, Arnold, for life. See supra p. 1092. Upon Arnold's death, the corpus of the trust is to be distributed as follows:

(a) To the descendants of Arnold who survive Arnold, to be divided among them by representation; or

(b) If Arnold is not survived by any descendants of his own, then to the descendants of the Settlor who survive Arnold, to be divided among them by representation; or

(c) If Arnold is not survived by any descendants of the Settlor, then to the descendants of the Settlor's brother [name of brother] who survive Arnold, to be divided among them by representation; or

(d) If Arnold is not survived by any descendants of the settlor's brother [name of brother], then to the descendants of the Settlor's father [name of father] who survive Arnold, to be divided among them by representation; or

(e) If Arnold is not survived by any descendants of the Settlor's father, then to Arnold's heirs at law.

(f) If the Settlor is not survived by his son, Arnold, then upon the Settlor's death the corpus of the trust is to be distributed to the Settlor's heirs at law.

In the light of the *Dodge* case, it might occur to you that subparagraphs (e) and (f) still need work. Apart from the general need to clarify the term "heirs at law," would it ever have occurred to you that subparagraph (f) was drafted by the settlor's lawyers with the *actual* intention that it constitute a *reversion* in the settlor himself, so that in the unlikely event that subparagraph (f) becomes effective the corpus of the trust would go to the settlor's residuary legatees named in the settlor's will?

One of the tax purposes of this irrevocable inter vivos life insurance trust is to avoid the inclusion of the policy proceeds in the settlor's gross estate. Would that purpose be jeopardized in this case if subparagraph (f) is interpreted as a reversion in the settlor rather than a remainder in the settlor's heirs? See IRC § 2042.

Doctor v. Hughes

122 N.E. 221 (N.Y. 1919)

CARDOZO, J. The action is brought by judgment creditors to subject what is alleged to be an interest in real property to the lien of a judgment.

In January, 1899, James J. Hanigan conveyed to a trustee a house and lot in the city of New York. The conveyance was in trust to pay from the rents and profits to the use of the grantor the yearly sum of $1,500. The payments might, however, exceed that sum in the discretion of the trustee. Direction was also made for the payment of some debts, and for the payment of two mortgages, then liens upon the property. The trustee was empowered to mortgage, in order to pay existing liens, or to carry into effect the other provisions of the deed. He was also empowered to sell. Upon the death of the grantor, he was to "convey the said premises (if not sold) to the heirs at law of the party of the first part." In case of a sale, he was to pay to the heirs at law "the balance of the avails of sale remaining unexpended." He was authorized at any time, if he so desired, to reconvey the premises to the grantor, and thus terminate the trust.

At the trial of this action, the grantor was still alive. His sole descendants were two daughters. By deed executed in June, 1902, one of the daughters, Mrs. Hughes, conveyed to her husband all her interest in this real estate. Judgment against Mr. and Mrs. Hughes for upwards of $4,000 was afterwards recovered by the plaintiffs. The question to be determined is whether either judgment debtor has any interest in the land. The Special Term held that there passed to Mr. Hughes under the conveyance from his wife an estate in remainder which was subject to the claims of creditors. The Appellate Division held that the creator of the trust did not intend to give a remainder to any one; that his heirs at law, if they receive anything on his death, will take by descent, and not by purchase; and hence that there is nothing that creditors can seize.

We reach the same conclusion. The direction to the trustee is the superfluous expression of a duty imposed by law. "Where an express trust is created, every legal estate and interest not embraced in the trust, and not otherwise disposed of, shall remain in or revert to, the person creating the trust or his heirs." Real Property Law, § 102. (Consol. Laws, c. 50). What is left is not a remainder (Real Property Law, § 38), but a reversion (Real Property Law, § 39). To such a situation neither the rule in Shelley's Case (1 Coke Rep. 104), nor the statute abrogating the rule (Real Property Law, § 54), applies. The heirs mentioned in this deed are not "the heirs . . . of a person to whom a life estate in the same premises is given." Real Property Law, § 54. The life estate belongs to the trustee. The heirs are the heirs of the grantor. . . . The question is whether there is any remainder at all. In the solution of that problem, the distinction is vital between gifts to the heirs of the holder of a particular estate, and gifts or attempted gifts to the heirs of the grantor. "A man cannot, either by conveyance at the common law, by limitation of uses, or devise, make his right heir a purchaser." Pilus v. Milford, 1674, 1 Vent. 372; Read v. Erington, 1594, Cro. Eliz. 322; Bingham's Case, 2 Co. Rep. 91a., 91b; Cholmondaley v. Maxey, 12 East, 589, 603, 604. "It is a positive rule of our law." Hargrave's Law Tracts (1787) p. 571. "If a man make a gift in taile, or a lease for life, the remainder to his own right heirs, this remainder is void, and he hath the reversion in him; for the ancestor during his life beareth in his body (in judgment of law) all his heirs, and therefore, it is truly said that haeres est pars antecessoris." Co. Litt. 22b. To the same effect are all the commentators. 1 Fearne, Contingent Rem. 21; 2 Fearne, 205 (section 389); 2 Washburn on Real Prop. (6th Ed.) § 1525; Vin. Abr. Rem. A, p. 11; Bacon, Abr. Uses, B2; Gilbert, Uses, 20; Preston on Estates, 291; 24 Halsbury's Laws of England, pp. 213, 214. The heirs have a mere expectancy, spes successionis, which may be barred by deed or will. This rule, that a reservation to the heirs of the grantor is equivalent to the reservation of a reversion to the grantor himself, is not to be confused with the rule in Shelley's Case. The two are quite distinct. The one "applies only to the acts of an ancestor as between him and his own heirs." The other is confined to the limitation of estate of inheritance to the heirs of a person who has taken under the same instrument a prior estate of freehold.

At common law, therefore, and under common-law conveyances, this direction to transfer the estate to the heirs of the grantor would indubitably have been equivalent to the reservation of a reversion. In England, the rule has been changed by statute. The Inheritance Act of 1833 provides (3 & 4 Wm. IV, c. 106, § 3) that—

> When any land shall have been limited by any assurance . . . to the person or to the heirs of the person who shall thereby have conveyed the same land, such person shall be considered to have acquired the same as a purchaser by virtue of such assurance, and shall not be considered to be entitled thereto as his former estate or part thereof.

But in the absence of modifying statute, the rule persists to-day, at least as a rule of construction, if not as one of property. There are modern instances of its application to facts hardly to be distinguished from those of the case at bar. Alexander v. De Kermel, 81 Ky. 345; Akers v. Clark, 184 Ill. 136, 56 N. E. 296, 75 Am. St. Rep. 152; Hobbie v. Ogden, 178 Ill. 357, 53 N. E. 104; Robinson v. Blankenship, 116 Tenn. 394, 92 S. W. 854. The reservation of a reversion is not inconsistent with the creation of a trust to continue until the death of the reversioner. We do not say that the ancient rule survives as an absolute prohibition limiting the power of a grantor. At the outset, probably, like the rule in Shelley's Case, it was a rule, not of construction, but of property. But it was never applied in all its rigor to executory trusts, which were "molded by the court as best to answer the intent of the person creating them." We may assume that this is the principle that would control the courts to-day. Executory limitations are no longer distinguished from remainders, but are grouped with them as future estates (Real Prop. Law, §§ 36, 37; Tilden v. Green, 130 N. Y. 29, 47, 28 N. E. 880, 14 L. R. A. 33, 27 Am. St. Rep. 487), and deeds, like wills, must be so construed as to effectuate the purpose of the grantor (Real Property Law, § 240, subd. 3). There may be times, therefore, when a reference to the heirs of the grantor will be regarded as the gift of a remainder, and will vest title in the heirs presumptive as upon a gift to the heirs of others. But at least the ancient rule survives to this extent: That, to transform into a remainder what would ordinarily be a reversion, the intention to work the transformation must be clearly expressed. Here there is no clear expression of such a purpose. No doubt there are circumstances on which it is possible to build an argument. The grantor instructs the trustee, at the end of the life estate, to convey the land (if unsold) to the heirs, and if there has been a sale to pay the proceeds to the heirs. The more appropriate direction, if the grantor retained a reversion, would have been for payment of the proceeds of any sale to the executors or next of kin. "If the ancestor devises his estate to his heir at law by will, with other limitations, or in any other shape than the course of descents would direct, such heir shall take by purchase." 2 Bl. Comm. 241. But the words "heirs" and "next of kin" are often employed as interchangeable. In this instance, the two classes are in fact identical. Nothing in the surrounding circumstances suggests a purpose to vary the course of descent or distribution as it would be regulated by law. If that is so, the courts are not to be controlled by mere inaccuracies of expression. Such slips of speech might be significant if we were construing an admitted remainder. They do not turn into a remainder what would otherwise be a reversion. There is no adequate disclosure of a purpose in the mind of this grantor to vest his presumptive heirs with rights which it would be beyond his power to defeat. No one is heir to the living, and seldom do the living mean to forego the power of disposition during life by the direction that upon death there shall be a transfer to their heirs. This grant by its terms was subject to destruction at the will of the trustee. We think it was also subject to destruction, as against the heirs at law, at the will of the grantor. They had an expectancy, but no estate.

The judgment should be affirmed, with costs. . . .

Note

Post-Doctor v. Hughes Case Authority. In Burchell's Estate, 87 N.E.2d 293 (N.Y. 1949), the terms of an irrevocable inter vivos trust of real property were that the income was to be paid to the grantor for her life. Upon her death, the principal of the trust estate was to go to such persons as the grantor appoints by will; in default of appointment, to the grantor's next of kin as in intestacy.

In an opinion written by Judge Bromley, the court held that the gift in default created a remainder interest in the grantor's heirs, not a reversion in the grantor:

> Confusion as to the nature of an estate when that estate is limited to heirs of the grantor arises because of the existence in our modern jurisprudence of remnants of the ancient doctrine of worthier title (46 Harv. L. Rev. 993). Prior to our decision in Doctor v. Hughes (225 N.Y. 305 . . .), a conveyance by a grantor with a limitation over to his heirs was said to be governed by that doctrine, under which a limitation over to a grantor's heirs resulted in an automatic reversion in the grantor and nullified the limitation over. . . .
>
> It is clear from the cases in this State since Doctor v. Hughes . . . , as admirably analyzed in Richardson v. Richardson [81 N.E.2d 54 (N.Y. 1948)], that, despite the language in that opinion that a reversion exists unless there is clear evidence to the contrary, the rule has been less limited in application. Where a clear intent exists, there is no problem in construing the instrument, since the doctrine no longer exists as a rule of property. But where the grantor's intent is not expressed in unmistakable language, the rule comes into play. Then we look to the instrument for those indicia deemed significant in arriving at the intent of the grantor. In the first of the line of cases following Doctor v. Hughes (supra), (Whittemore v. Equitable Trust Co., 250 N.Y. 298), we applied the rule of construction in the manner indicated in the second interpretation above. We discovered the intent of the grantor from other factors, as shown by the instrument, in order to give full effect to the words of limitation.
>
> While we have not yet adopted a rule, either by statute or judicial construction, under which language limiting an interest to heirs is unequivocally given its full effect, the presumption which exists from the use of the common-law doctrine as a rule of construction has lost much of its force since Doctor v. Hughes (supra). Evidence of intent need not be overwhelming in order to allow the remainder to stand. Whether the rule should be abrogated completely is a matter for the Legislature.
>
> The instant cases furnish sufficient additional indications of the settlor's intent to justify our giving effect to the language of the instrument limiting an estate to the grantor's heirs. Not the least among those indications was the reservation of a testamentary power of appointment as the sole control over the subsequent disposition of the corpus of the trust estate. . . . The fact that the trust agreement reserved a power of appointment is evidence that the settlor believed she had created an interest in the property on the part of others and reserved the power in order to defeat that interest or to postpone until a later date the naming of specific

takers. Where we have held that a reversion was intended although a testamentary power of appointment was reserved, the instruments have provided that the trust principal would revert to the grantor upon some contingency or that the grantor retained control over the principal.

In analyzing an instrument and attempting to explore the almost ephemeral qualities which go to prove the necessary intent, many single factors may be considered. Some considered significant in one case may be deemed minimal in another, since their effect may be counteracted by the presence of other factors. It is impossible to set up absolute criteria to serve as a measuring standard for all cases. In the last analysis, the ultimate determination rests on the particular instrument under consideration, aided by the rule which has grown out of the old common-law doctrine and developed over a long line of cases as a rule which allows the language of the instrument creating a remainder to take effect provided some additional evidence pointing the intent of the grantor is present to buttress the language which would create the remainder.

Hatch v. Riggs National Bank

361 F.2d 559 (D.C. Cir. 1966)

LEVENTHAL, C.J. Appellant seeks in this action to obtain modification of a trust she created in 1923. The income terms of the trust instrument are of a spendthrift character, directing the trustees to pay to the settlor for life all the income from the trust estate "for her own use and benefit, without the power to her to anticipate, alienate or charge the same. . . ." Upon the death of the settlor-life tenant, the trustees are to pay over the corpus as the settlor may appoint by will; if she fails to exercise this testamentary power of appointment, the corpus is to go to "such of her next of kin . . . as by the law in force in the District of Columbia at the death of the . . . [settlor] shall be provided for in the distribution of an intestate's personal property therein." No power to appoint the corpus by deed, nor any power to revoke, alter, amend or modify the trust, was expressly retained by appellant, and the instrument states that she conveys the property to the trustees "irrevocably."

Appellant does not claim that the declaration of trust itself authorizes her to revoke or modify the trust. In effect she invokes the doctrine of worthier title, which teaches that a grant of trust corpus to the heirs of the settlor creates a reversion in the settlor rather than a remainder in his heirs. She claims that since she is the sole beneficiary of the trust under this doctrine, and is also the settlor, she may revoke or modify under accepted principles of trust law.

The District Court, while sympathizing with appellant's desire to obtain an additional stipend of $5000 a year, out of corpus, "to accommodate recently incurred expenses, and to live more nearly in accordance with her refined but yet modest tastes,"[37] felt that denial of the requested relief was required by this court's decision in Liberty National Bank v. Hicks, 84 U.S.App.D.C. 198, 173 F.2d 631, 9 A.L.R.2d 1355 (1948). Summary judgment was granted for appellees. We affirm.

I. . . . The doctrine of worthier title had its origins in the feudal system which to a large extent molded the English common law which we inherited. In its common law form, the doctrine provided that a conveyance of land by a grantor with a limitation over to his own heirs resulted in a reversion in the grantor rather than creating a remainder interest in the heirs. It was a rule of law distinct from, though motivated largely by the same policies as, the Rule in Shelley's Case. Apparently the feudal overlord was entitled to certain valuable incidents when property held by one of his feoffees passed by "descent" to an heir rather than by "purchase" to a transferee. The doctrine of worthier title—whereby descent is deemed "worthier" than purchase—remained ensconced in English law, notwithstanding the passing of the feudal system, until abrogated by statute in 1833.[38]

The doctrine has survived in many American jurisdictions, with respect to inter vivos conveyances of both land and personalty, as a common law "rule of construction" rather than a "rule of law." In Doctor v. Hughes, 225 N.Y. 305, 122 N.E. 221 (1919), Judge Cardozo's landmark opinion reviewed the common-law history of the doctrine and concluded that its modern relevance was as a rule of construction, a rebuttable presumption that the grantor's likely intent, in referring to his own heirs, was to reserve a reversion in his estate rather than create a remainder interest in the heirs. Evidence might be introduced to show that the grantor really meant what he said when he spoke of creating a remainder in his heirs.

In the decades that followed, the worthier title doctrine as a rule of construction with respect to inter vivos transfers won widespread acceptance.[39]

---

37. In her complaint, appellant also sought an additional $50,000 from corpus to purchase a residence, but dropped this request at the hearing. The District Court found that there was "no suggestion of extravagance" in appellant's way of life or in her request for additional funds. She now lives in a one-bedroom apartment in a modest residential section of Long Beach, California, and has no assets except limited jewelry, furniture, personal effects, and a medium-priced automobile.

38. 3 & 4 Wm. IV, ch. 106, § 3. For more detailed discussion of the evolution of the doctrine of worthier title at common law, see Annot., 125 A.L.R. 548, 549-550 (1940); Doctor v. Hughes, 225 N.Y. 305, 122 N.E. 221 (1919); Burchell's Estate, 299 N.Y. 351, 87 N.E.2d 293, 296 (1949).

39. See Restatement, Property, 314(1) (1940); Restatement (Second), Trusts, 127 comment b (1959); Annot., 16 A.L.R.2d 691 (1951).

The "modern" rationale for the rule is well stated in an opinion of the Supreme Court of California:

> It is said that where a person creates a life estate in himself with a gift over to his heirs he ordinarily intends the same thing as if he had given the property to his estate; that he does not intend to make a gift to any particular person but indicates only that upon his death the residue of the trust property shall be distributed according to the general laws governing succession; and that he does not intend to create in any persons an interest which would prevent him from exercising control over the beneficial interest. . . . Moreover, this rule of construction is in accord with the general policy in favor of the free alienability of property, since its operation tends to make property more readily transferable.[40]

While the weight of authority, as just indicated, supports the retention of the doctrine of worthier title (unlike its common-law brother, the Rule in Shelley's Case) as a rule of construction, there has been substantial and increasing opposition to the doctrine.[41]

The views of the critics of the doctrine, which we find persuasive against its adoption, and borne out by the experience of the New York courts in the series of cases which have followed Doctor v. Hughes, supra, may be summarized as follows. The common-law reasons for the doctrine are as obsolete as those behind the Rule in Shelley's Case.[42] Retention of the doctrine as a rule of construction is pernicious in several respects.

First, it is questionable whether it accords with the intent of the average settlor. It is perhaps tempting to say that the settlor intended to create no beneficial interest in his heirs when he said "to myself for life, remainder to my heirs" when the question is revocation of the trust, or whether creditors of the settlor's heirs should be able to reach their interest. But the same result is far from appealing if the settlor-life beneficiary dies without revoking the trust and leaves a will which makes no provision for his heirs-at-law (whom he supposed to be taken care of by the trust). In short, while the dominant intent of most such trusts may well be to benefit the life tenant during his life, a subsidiary but

---

40. Bixby v. California Trust Co., 33 Cal.2d 495, 202 P.2d 1018, 1019 (1949). See also McKenna v. Seattle-First Nat'l Bank, 35 Wash.2d 662, 214 P.2d 664, 16 A.L.R.2d 679 (1950).

41. See. e.g., Simes, Fifty Years of Future Interests, 50 Harv. L. Rev. 749, 756 (1937); Note, 48 Yale L. J. 874 (1939); Note, 39 Colum. L. Rev. 628, 656 (1939); Comment, 34 Ill. L. Rev. 835, 850-51 (1940). A recent study of the subject by Professor Verrall of the University of California, under the auspices of the California Law Revision Commission, resulted in a strong condemnation of the doctrine. Verrall, The Doctrine of Worthier Title: A Questionable Rule of Construction, 6 U.C.L.A. L. Rev. 371 (1959).

42. The Rule in Shelley's Case (1 Coke Rep. 104) has been abolished by statute in the District of Columbia. D.C. Code 45-203 (1961 ed.).

nevertheless significant purpose of many such trusts may be to satisfy a natural desire to benefit one's heirs or next of kin. In the normal case an adult has a pretty good idea who his heirs will be at death, and probably means exactly what he says when he states in the trust instrument, "remainder to my heirs."

It is said that the cases in which such is the grantor's intent can be discerned by an examination into his intent; the presumption that a gift over to one's heirs creates a reversion can thereby be rebutted in appropriate cases. But the only repository of the settlor's intent, in most cases, will be the trust instrument itself. Nor would it be fruitful or conducive to orderly and prompt resolution of litigation to engage in searches for other sources of intent. In the typical case of this genre—a stark, unqualified "to myself for life, remainder to my heirs"—the instrument will send forth no signals of contrary intent to overcome the presumption that only a reversion was intended. Yet this is precisely the class of cases in which settlors are likely to have intended to create beneficial interests in their heirs.

A lengthier document may send forth more signals, but they may well be murky. Where other indicia of intent can be discovered in the trust instrument, with the aid of ingenious counsel, the result, as the New York cases have demonstrated, is a shower of strained decisions difficult to reconcile with one another and generative of considerable confusion in the law.[43] After three decades of observing the New York courts administer the rule of construction announced in Doctor v. Hughes, supra, Professor Powell of Columbia observed that "there were literally scores of cases, many of which reached the Appellate Division, and no case involving a substantial sum could be fairly regarded as closed until its language and circumstances had been passed upon by the Court of Appeals. . . . This state of uncertainty was the product of changing an inflexible rule of law into a rule of construction."[44]

An excellent example of this confusion is the effect to be given the fact that, as in the case at bar, the settlor has reserved the power to defeat the heirs' interest by appointing the taker of the remainder by will. One might well think that the reservation of a power of appointment was an index of intent which buttressed the presumption of a reversion by demonstrating that the settlor did not wish to create firm interests or expectations among his heirs, but intended to retain control over the property. Most courts, including the New York Court of Appeals in its most recent pronouncement on the subject, have disagreed,

43. The New York cases are admirably summarized and discussed in Verrall, op. cit. supra note 38, at 374-387.

44. Powell, Cases On Future Interests 88 n. 14 (3d ed. 1961).

albeit over the voice of dissent.[45] They have reasoned that the retention of the testamentary power of appointment confirms the intent to create a remainder in the heirs, since the settlor would not have retained the power had he not thought he was creating a remainder interest in the heirs.

We see no reason to plunge the District of Columbia into the ranks of those jurisdictions bogged in the morass of exploring, under the modern doctrine of worthier title, "the almost ephemeral qualities which go to prove the necessary intent."[46] The alleged benefit of effectuating intent must be balanced against the resulting volume of litigation and the diversity and difficulty of decision.[47] We are not persuaded that the policy of upholding the intention of creators of trusts is best effectuated by such a rule of construction, with its accompanying uncertainty.

The rule we adopt, which treats the settlor's heirs like any other remaindermen, although possibly defeating the intention of some settlors, is overall, we think, an intent-effectuating rule. It contributes to certainty of written expression and conceptual integrity in the law of trusts. It allows heirs to take as remaindermen when so named, and promises less litigation, greater predictability, and easier drafting. These considerations are no small element of justice.

We hold, then, that the doctrine of worthier title is no part of the law of trusts in the District of Columbia, either as a rule of law or as a rule of construction. Any act or words of the settlor of a trust which would validly create a remainder interest in a named third party -ay create a valid remainder interest in the settlor's heirs. It follows that the District Court was correct in granting summary judgment for appellees in this case, since appellant's action is based on the theory that she was the sole beneficiary and hence could revoke the "irrevocable" trust she had created. . . .

Affirmed.

Notes and Questions

1. *Legislative Abolition of the Worthier Title Doctrine.* The New York court in *Burchell* seemed to favor complete abrogation of the doctrine of worthier title but declined to take that step because the court thought abrogation was a matter exclusively for the legislature. Whatever the merits of that idea in New York

---

45. Burchell's Estate, 299 N.Y. 351, 361, 87 N.E.2d 293, 297 (1949); see Comment, 34 Ill. L. Rev. 834, 844-45 (1940).

46. Burchell's Estate, supra, 299 N.Y. at 361, 87 N.E.2d at 297 (1949).

47. These results led Judge Fuld to call for "clarifying legislation." Dissent in Burchell's Estate, supra note 45.

when *Burchell* was decided, with the experience of Doctor v. Hughes and its progeny, the *Hatch* case shows that abrogation isn't necessarily restricted to legislation in jurisdictions that have no such history. In any event, the New York legislature stepped in and abolished the worthier title doctrine in 1966. Over twenty other states also have abrogating legislation—Alaska, Arizona, Arkansas, California, Colorado, Hawaii, Illinois,[48] Indiana, Kansas, Massachusetts, Michigan, Minnesota, Montana, Nebraska, New Mexico, North Carolina, North Dakota, Pennsylvania, South Dakota, Tennessee, Texas, Utah, Washington, West Virginia, and Wisconsin. A statute in Georgia makes application of the doctrine unlikely, by declaring that the word "heirs" is presumed to mean children, unless a contrary intention appears. Ga. Code Ann. § 44-6-23.

Section 2-710 of the UPC abolishes the worthier title doctrine.[49]

2. *Post-Hatch Case Authority*. Since 1966, when the *Hatch* case was decided, no state supreme court authority recognizing the validity of the doctrine exists.

3. *Analysis of the Doctrine*. Professor Waggoner has criticized the transformation of the worthier title doctrine into a rule of construction:

> In shifting the inter-vivos branch of the doctrine to a rule of construction, Judge Cardozo may have desired to soften the old rule of law by allowing it to yield to the grantor's contrary intention. But shifting a rule of law to a rule of construction is not a natural evolutionary step in legal development. Rules of law and rules of construction are based on entirely different premises. Rules of law are intent-defeating; rules of construction are intent-effecting. Defeating intention is only justified to vindicate goals of sound public policy; the proper function of rules of law is therefore to prohibit individual choices that are deemed to be unduly harmful to society as a whole. Rules of construction, on the other hand, operate in areas in which society as a whole is indifferent to the result. The only public policy goal that rules of construction vindicate is giving effect to private intention in areas of societal indifference. Rules of construction seek to facilitate this intent-effecting goal by providing a presumptive meaning—one designed to accord with common intention—to words that have failed to express the actual intention of the parties clearly.
>
> When the policy reasons that underlie a rule of law disappear, as they have with respect to the worthier title doctrine, the normal course is for the legislature to

48. But see Stewart v. Merchants Nat'l Bank, 278 N.E.2d 10 (Ill. App. Ct. 1972), where the court seems to have held that the statute only abrogates the worthier title doctrine as a rule of law, not as a rule of construction. See Note, The Doctrine of Worthier Title as a Rule of Construction in Illinois, 67 Nw. U. L. Rev. 773 (1973). Harris Trust & Savings Bank v. Beach, 513 N.E.2d 833 (Ill. 1987), however, referred to Illinois' "1955 statutory abolition of the doctrine."

49. The states of Alaska, Arizona, Colorado, Hawaii, Michigan, Montana, New Mexico, North Dakota, South Dakota, and Utah abolished the worthier title doctrine as part of their enactment of Article II of the revised version of the UPC.

> repeal the rule (as the English legislature did in 1833) or for the courts to abrogate it or at least to nibble away at its scope until it eventually ceases to operate. The shifting of the worthier title doctrine from a rule of law to one of construction is therefore not a normal step in the evolutionary process of law. It has done more harm than good.

Lawrence W. Waggoner, Estates in Land and Future Interests in a Nutshell 166-67 (2d ed. 1993). The doctrine was condemned in vehement terms in W. Barton Leach, Property Law Indicted! 56 (1967).

4. *Resurrection of the Doctrine?* The Restatement 2d of Property § 30.2(1) states that the doctrine continues as a rule of construction. Comment a states:

> The continuation of the [inter-vivos branch of the worthier title doctrine] as a rule of construction may be justified on the basis that it represents the probable intention of the average transferor. . . .
>
> The increased alienability of the subject matter of the transfer which results from the application of the [doctrine] is also a justification for it.

This comment prompted the inclusion of § 2-710 in the UPC.

5. *Drafting Procedures to Avoid the Doctrine.* Consider again subparagraph (f) of the irrevocable life insurance trust found in the problem supra p. 1139. Remember, the federal government has considerable revenue to gain if the worthier title doctrine is applied.[50] If it is applied, and if the life insurance proceeds are included in the settlor's gross estate, the possibility exists of attorney liability in malpractice. See generally Gerald P. Johnston, Legal Malpractice in Estate Planning—Perilous Times Ahead for the Practitioner, 67 Iowa L. Rev. 629 (1982).

Assuming that the settlor's lawyer notices the worthier title problem before the irrevocable (and unamendable) trust is signed, the better course is to redraft subparagraph (f) so that it leaves no doubt that it creates a remainder interest in the settlor's heirs. In a world in which the phrase "remainder to my heirs" presumptively means "reversion in myself," how can the settlor's lawyer make it beyond dispute that subparagraph (f) means what it says? Should subparagraph (f) be redrafted to say "to my heirs at law, and I really mean it—no kidding!"? A more lawyerly way of saying it might be:

> . . . to my heirs at law, such persons to take as purchasers, my intention being to create a remainder interest in favor of my heirs at law; I do not intend to retain a reversion in myself.

---

50. On the tax consequences in general of application of the worthier title doctrine, see Stanley M. Johanson, Reversions, Remainders, and the Doctrine of Worthier Title, 45 Tex. L. Rev. 1, 16-27 (1966).

Suppose the worthier title problem in subparagraph (f) wasn't noticed until *after* the trust was signed and the $6 million life insurance policy was irrevocably assigned to the trustee. Could the settlor's lawyer successfully petition for reformation of subparagraph (f), to add language making it clear that a remainder was intended? See Palmer on Restitution ch. 18; John H. Langbein & Lawrence W. Waggoner, Reformation of Wills on the Ground of Mistake: Change of Direction in American Law?, 130 U. Pa. L. Rev. 521, 524-28 (1982). Would this reformation be controlling for federal tax purposes? See supra Chapter 7, Part B. Would it make any difference if the reformation occurred before or after the settlor's death? See Rev. Rul. 73-142, 1973-1 C.B. 405 (the decree, which was finalized before the decedent's death, was controlling because it effectively extinguished the power that would have brought the value of the trust corpus within the provisions of IRC §§ 2036 and 2038).

6. *Testamentary Branch of the Doctrine.* At common law, the worthier title doctrine had two branches—the inter vivos branch and the testamentary branch. The above materials relate solely to the inter vivos branch, which as its name implies, applies only to inter vivos transfers.

The testamentary branch provided that a *devise* of *land* to the testator's heirs was a nullity if the interest devised to them was identical to the interest they would take in intestacy. Like the inter vivos branch, this was a rule of law, not of construction. See Joseph W. Morris, The Wills Branch of the Worthier Title Doctrine, 54 Mich. L. Rev. 451 (1956). No decision in this country has prolonged the existence of the testamentary branch by holding that it "persists today, at least as a rule of construction, if not as one of property." The Restatement of Property § 314(2) and the Restatement 2d of Property § 30.2(2) declare the testamentary branch not to exist as either a rule of law or of construction. Most recently, in two states in which no abrogating legislation exists, the rule was abolished by court decision (City Nat'l Bank v. Andrews, 355 S.2d 341 (Ala. 1978); In re Campbell, 319 N.W.2d 275 (Iowa 1982); Estate of Kern, 274 N.W.2d 325 (Iowa 1979)) and it's doubtful that it remains in effect anywhere today.[51] See Restatement 2d of Property § 30.2 reporter's note 6, at 471-75.

7. *Continuation of the Inter Vivos Branch as a Rule of Law?* In a few states that haven't enacted abrogating legislation, older cases exist applying the inter vivos branch of the worthier title doctrine as a rule of law, not of construction.

---

51. But see Estate of Grulke, 546 N.W.2d 626 (Iowa Ct. App. 1996) (court applied worthier title doctrine to a devise in a will executed in 1973 because *Kern* decision, decided in 1979, applied prospectively only).

See Restatement 2d of Property § 30.2 reporter's note 4, at 470. Whether these decisions would be followed today is uncertain.

PART C. INCOMPLETE DISPOSITIONS

Theoretically, the calculus of estates does not admit of a disposition that is incomplete: A transferor is considered to have retained by way of a reversionary interest any interest not expressly transferred. For example, in the simple disposition "to A for life," it would be assumed that a reversion in the transferor takes effect upon the death of the life tenant. As we shall see, however, courts sometimes find that a disposition creates a future interest by implication. This process is commonly illustrated by the disposition "to A for life, remainder to B if A dies without issue." If A dies with issue, this disposition has been found to contain an implied remainder interest in their favor. See Restatement of Property § 272.

1. Implication of Interests in Principal

In Hilton v. Kinsey, 185 F.2d 885 (D.C. Cir. 1950), James H. Hilton died in 1919, devising his estate in trust, income to his children, J. Franklin Hilton and Catharine Hilton, for life; a cross remainder in the income was provided to the survivor for life. As to the corpus, the will stated:

> In case my son, J. Franklin Hilton, or my daughter, Catharine S. Hilton, should have any [children], such [children], if of J. Franklin Hilton, shall be entitled to his [share] after his death, and if my daughter, Catharine S. Hilton, should have any [children], said [children] shall be entitled to her [share] after her death. . . . Should [they] have no children, then the money of the estate [should be paid to specified charities].

J. Franklin died in 1941, without children; Catharine died in 1947, survived by her daughter, Mary.

The court held that Mary, not the charities or the testator's heirs, was entitled to the half of the corpus from which J. Franklin had been receiving the income prior to his death:

> [W]hen the general plan of the testator for the disposition of his property is considered . . . it is clear that . . . the children of J. Franklin and Catharine, if any, were to be the ultimate beneficiaries of the residuary estate. Under similar circumstances it has been held that although testator's plan is incompletely expressed, it may be implied from the contents of the will as a whole and a cross-remainder of the corpus read into the will. In Boston Safe-Deposit & Trust Co. v. Coffin, [152 Mass. 95, 25 N.E. 30,] the testator, as to one portion of his estate, made the following disposition: The income to grandchildren A, B, and C for life; upon the death of A, or B, or C without issue, the income to be divided among the

survivors; upon the death of A, or B, or C with issue, that issue to take the portion of the estate of which the grandchild had enjoyed the interest and income; if A, B, and C all die without issue, the principal to go to the other children of the testator. Both A and B predeceased C, dying without issue. C enjoyed the entire income until his death. He died with issue. It was argued that the issue of C was entitled to the original amount from which C received the income, namely, one-third of the corpus, the remaining two-thirds passing by intestacy. The court rejected this contention, holding that there was an implied cross-remainder of the two-thirds to the issue of C, and, accordingly, that C's children took the entire corpus.

There is a striking similarity between that case and the present one. Franklin predeceased Catharine. Subsequent to his death she was clearly entitled to, and actually received for a period of six years until her death, the income from the entire corpus of the estate. Prior to her death her interest in the estate was not the life income from half the corpus, but the income from the whole. And the gift to the children was to be not a half, but the whole interest of the parent. Therefore, we hold that the provision for a cross-remainder as to the income between the parents had the effect of increasing the share of the children of one should the other die without children.

Warner v. Warner

237 F.2d 561 (D.C. Cir. 1956)

BURGER, C.J. This is an appeal from a decision of the District Court instructing a trustee, on his petition for instructions, as to the distribution of the corpus of a trust created by the will of Brainard Warner, Sr. The pertinent trust provisions are as follows:

> All the rest, residue and remainder of my estate, . . . I give, . . . unto The Washington Loan and Trust Company, . . . in trust . . . ; third, to divide the remainder of the net income from this trust estate among my wife, Mary H. Warner and my nine children in equal shares, such payments to commence as soon as practicable after my decease and to continue for and during the term of the life of my said wife.[52] On the death of my said wife, I direct my said trustee to divide the entire residuum of my estate into nine (9) equal parts paying one part thereof unto each of my said children.[53] In the event of the death of any of said children before the decease of my said wife, with issue him or her surviving, then such issue shall take the share of its deceased parent in the income and on the death of my wife the share of the deceased parent in the principal, but if there be no such

52. By the time of testator's death in 1916 one child, Southard Parker Warner, had predeceased him, unmarried and without issue.

53. The wife died in 1954 and during the period from the death of the testator until the death of the wife, three more of his children had died as follows: (a) Brainard H. Warner, Jr., who died leaving issue who still survive; (b) Rebecca P. Warner, who died testate and without issue; and (c) Andrew Parker Warner, who died testate and without issue.

issue, then the share of the deceased child in the income shall be paid to the survivor or survivors of my said wife and children as the case may be, share and share alike until the death of my said wife, when the final division shall take place.

Five of testator's nine children survived him and the life tenant; one child predeceased testator without issue; three children survived testator but predeceased the life tenant, one leaving issue and two leaving no issue. Plaintiff joined as parties defendant the five surviving children, the three children of the child who died before the life tenant and with issue, and the two sole beneficiaries[54] of the estates of the two children who survived testator but predeceased the life tenant without issue. The plaintiff-trustee asked for instructions on the following questions:

1. Did the testator intend that the interest of those children who survived him and died without issue before the death of the life tenant pass under their respective wills to the distributees thereunder, or

2. Did the testator intend that the interests of those children who survived him and died without issue before the death of the life tenant be divested on death and follow the provision for the payment of income and vest per stirpes in the surviving children or the issue of a deceased child and be distributed accordingly?

The District Court ruled that an examination of the entire will revealed that testator intended to provide primarily both income and principal for his children and their issue, thereby retaining his estate in the "blood line." The Court stated it was "satisfied that the testator intended to divest the share of the child dying without issue in the principal as well as the income, and the proper construction is that there are cross-remainders both as to the income and principal to surviving children, although the will, being ineptly drawn, fails to include the word 'principal'." In other words the trial court has read the will as though it contained provisions for final division of principal in substantially the same terms as testator used with respect to income.

Jennie M. Warner appealed from this decision, contending that her husband, Andrew Parker Warner, having survived the testator, received a vested remainder which could be divested *only* if he died *with issue* and since Andrew died without issue, Jennie, sole beneficiary under his will, was entitled to his share of the principal. Thus, the issues before us are:

(a) Did Andrew acquire a vested remainder in the principal?

(b) If so, what provision of the will, if any, operates to *divest* Andrew's remainder?

---

54. Jennie M. Warner, widow of Andrew Parker Warner, and Anna Parker Warner, sister of Rebecca P. Warner.

As to the first issue, there is little dispute. The law favors early vesting unless testator manifests a contrary intent. Since Andrew Parker Warner was in being at the death of the testator and had an immediate right to possession upon the expiration of his mother's life tenancy, his remainder interest became vested at the death of the testator.

The second question, then, is what provision of the will, if any, divested Andrew's remainder interest in the principal. Divestiture is not accomplished by the provision that "In the event of the death of any of said children before the decease of my said wife, with issue him or her surviving, then such issue shall take the share of its deceased parent . . . in the principal." A provision, such as this, that the children of deceased remaindermen shall take their parents' share is not sufficient to prevent the remainder from being vested; divestiture occurs only upon death leaving issue—there is no divestiture by death alone without issue.

If divestiture of Andrew's share of the principal is to be accomplished, it must be by implication based on the fact that the will provides for divestment of the interest *in income* of those children dying without issue. Appellees contended, and the District Court held, that since the testator provided for the divestiture of the *income interests* of children dying without issue and set up cross-remainders of such interests in the survivors of his wife and children, similar cross-remainders must be implied as to the interest in principal of children dying without issue, even though the will does not so state.

Appellees rely on two cases[55] in which a cross-remainder of principal was implied when there was a cross-remainder of income. It is clear, however, that these cases do not establish a rule that a cross-remainder of principal *must* be implied in such circumstances. In Boston Safe-Deposit & Trust Co. v. Coffin, the court found that the testator intended each branch of his family to have 1/7th of his estate. Therefore, rather than declare two-thirds of one of the 1/7th interests intestate property, thus taking it away from that branch of the family, the court implied a cross-remainder of principal as to the two-thirds. This was done to prevent partial intestacy and to maintain equality of treatment between different branches of the family. Furthermore, since the will had never made any disposition of the principal interest in suit there was no divestment of a vested interest by implication—i.e., the court supplied a disposition where the will was silent; it did not change a disposition already made.

Hilton v. Kinsey concerned the construction of an extremely "ineptly drawn" will. It was necessary for this court to make certain interpretations; e.g., the word "off-spring" was limited by interpretation to mean "children" in order to

55. Boston Safe-Deposit & Trust Co. v. Coffin, 1890, 152 Mass. 95, 25 N.E. 30, 8 L.R.A. 740; Hilton v. Kinsey, 1950, 88 U.S. App. D.C. 14, 185 F.2d 885, 23 A.L.R.2d 830.

prevent the will from violating the rule against perpetuities, and the phrase "his . . . and . . . her interest" was interpreted to mean "share of the corpus." The court then found the general plan of testator was that his grandchildren were to be the ultimate beneficiaries and a cross-remainder of a share of the principal was implied in the surviving grand-child. The alternative interpretation, aside from finding an intestacy, would have resulted in a charity taking, and the court stated that an interpretation was favored which prefers the family and kindred to "utter strangers."[56]

In both of these cases the remainder interest in income, provided by the will, went to a person other than the one in whom the remainder interest in principal was implied. In neither case did the court indicate it was implying the remainder in principal simply because of the existence of the income remainder; both courts relied on other factors which they considered indicative of testators' intent.

Appellant relies on De Korwin v. First Nat. Bank of Chicago, 7th Cir., 1949, 179 F.2d 347, which involved a problem similar to that presented by the Warner will. The court there had to construe the following testamentary provision:

> Sixth:—When the last survivor of my daughters shall have deceased and the youngest surviving child of my daughters shall have attained the age of twenty-one (21) years all of said trust estate then remaining in the hands of said trustee shall be divided in equal shares between my grand-children, the surviving issue of any deceased grand-child to stand in the place of and receive the share which such deceased grand-child would have been entitled to receive if then living.

The court concluded that the words following "grand-children" do not prevent the remainders from vesting on the death of the testator but instead fix the conditions upon which *divestiture* will occur and the gift to the descendants of the deceased remaindermen will take effect. It was argued in this case, as here, that testator's central purpose was to keep his estate in the hands of his lineal descendants *because he limited the enjoyment of the trust income to his lineal descendants*. The court held, however:

> But to argue that the testator, because he limited the enjoyment of the trust income to his lineal descendants, intended to follow the same pattern in disposing of the corpus is to indulge, we think, in a non sequitur. Indeed, the clarity of the language with which the testator expressed his intention to restrict to his lineal descendants the enjoyment of the trust income, in contrast with the language employed by him in disposing of the trust corpus, weighs against appellants'

56. We do not regard a son's wife as an "utter stranger" to the family and in a position comparable to a charity, even when the son married her after the death of the father.

> contention that he was attempting to follow the same scheme in both instances. And finally, it must be remembered that the best guide to the testator's intent is the particular dispositive language used by him. Here, that language, though perhaps not as plain as some might desire, is substantially equivalent to that which Illinois construes as creating a vested remainder, subject to divestiture only by death with issue in the period prior to distribution.

Since in the case of one of the grand-children (Stanley) the event upon which divestiture was conditioned—death with issue—did not occur, his interest in the corpus passed intestate to his heirs at law.[57]

We cannot agree with the District Court that an examination of the entire will demonstrates testator intended to retain his estate in the blood line and that the will was "ineptly drawn." Standing alone, the fact that testator explicitly provided for the divestiture of the *income* interest of children dying without issue is not the kind of evidence of testator's intent on which courts should rely to divest such children's vested remainder in the *principal*. Furthermore, while it is true that the testator provided for the divestment of a deceased parent's share of the *principal* when the parent was survived by issue, this provision alone does not establish that testator wanted all his property to remain in the blood line. If such *were* testator's intent he would more likely have made entirely different provisions—e.g., he might have set up a trust, with his wife and nine children as income beneficiaries, and the trust to terminate when the last one of this group died; at that time the issue of the nine children would take their parents' share of the corpus plus one-ninth of the wife's share; there would be appropriate provisions for the issue of a deceased parent taking the parent's share of the income and cross-remainders of income interests of those parents dying without issue; it would also be provided that the share of principal of a child dying without issue would go to the issue of the other children. Such a provision would have assured that the estate was kept in the blood line for a longer period of time than was possible under the disposition testator did make. For under the will as *written* any child who survived the wife received the corpus absolutely and could dispose of it in any way he chose—he could leave it in toto to his spouse, charities, etc., by testamentary or inter vivos grants, thus taking it out of the blood line completely. This, it seems to us, tends

57. Plaintiff in this case was the executrix of Joseph De Korwin who had married testator's oldest daughter and was the father of testator's grandchild, Stanley. Stanley's other heirs were a widow and half-sister. Another grandchild, Otto, died without issue and leaving as heirs a widow, father, sister and half-brother. Thus, the court was not impressed by the fact that the estate would pass out of testator's blood line. De Korwin v. First Nat'l Bank of Chicago, D.C.N.D. Ill.1949, 84 F.Supp. 918, 923.

substantially to neutralize if not entirely negate the "blood line" argument.[58] Contrary to the conclusion of the court below, we feel the will *does not* show an intent to keep the estate in the blood line.

An analysis of the controlling provisions of the will also suggests it was not "ineptly drawn" and that, on the contrary, the will uses the pertinent terms artfully. Testator, with discriminating use of the terms "income" and "principal," specifically provided that issue shall take the share of a deceased parent in the *income* and on death of the life tenant a share in the *principal*. He next provided for a cross-remainder of the *income* interest of a child who predeceased the life tenant without issue and then refers to the "final division." The crucial words he used are all words of art contained in a single sentence and we find it difficult to assume that a testator who was presumably trained and experienced in probate and trust work[59] would make such specific provisions, employing the words "income" and "principal", and intend something *other* than what he said. We are impressed by the fact that if testator *intended* to say what he did in fact say, he chose the simplest way of doing so, even to the point of a terseness which gave rise to the seeming need for judicial instruction. To find for appellees we must rule that, assuming testator meant just what he said, he should have explicitly stated, "Furthermore, there are to be no cross-remainders of principal." We cannot expect testators to rebut, in this fashion, possible interpretations of their words.

To sustain the trial court's holding we must at least do one of two things:

(a) *read out* of the will the words "in the income." or

(b) *read into* the will a whole new clause dealing with "the final division" of *principal* in the event of the death of any of testator's children without issue.

The trial court felt that the testator merely omitted the word "principal." However, the problem is more than a matter of simply supplying the words "and principal" to the phrase dealing with disposition of income. The "income provision" concerns the wife and surviving children and *only* during the life of the wife. The problem of "principal" disposition commences only on the death of the wife and would apply (on the trial court's theory) only to the children then surviving or, if deceased, to their issue. The suggestion that the simple insertion of the words "and principal" after "in the income" solves all over-looks the fact that the first problem involves the wife *and* the children and the second involves only the children and their issue *after* the wife's death.

---

58. That testator was not concerned that all his property stay in the "blood line" is further evidenced by the fact that he bequeathed $6000 to each of his nine children absolutely, to be paid when they became 21.

59. Testator was president of the Washington Loan and Trust Company, Washington, D.C., for some years prior to making this will.

It seems to us to be beyond the powers of judicial interpretation to say that the last inclusion of the phrase "in the income" was inadvertent or that the testator intended, but omitted to provide, that the principal be disposed of in a pattern similar to the disposition of the income. We must conclude that the will is "ineptly drawn" only if we start with the premise that the testator intended to confine his bounty to "blood relatives" and to eliminate "in-laws."[60] We can find nothing in the will which supports such a premise.

Appellees' final argument in support of an interpretation implying cross-mainders [sic] of principal is that if the court finds the will creates vested remainders subject to divestiture only as to children dying *with* issue, there will be an intestacy as to the share of Southard Parker Warner who predeceased testator without issue. This point was not relied on or discussed by the District Court.

This court has held that the provision in the District of Columbia lapse statute[61] that a devise or bequest which fails shall be deemed included in the residuary clause of the will is inapplicable to devises and bequests *in the residuum* and that as to such devises and bequests there is an intestacy. Appellees argue that since the bequest to Southard was in the residuary clause of the will there will be an intestacy as to a 1/9th share of the principal unless there is implied a cross-remainder of the principal interest of a child dying without issue. Appellees, therefore, contend that we must adopt their interpretation in order to avoid intestacy as to a 1/9th share.

Generally speaking if there are two permissible interpretations of a will courts prefer to adopt the one which will avoid intestacy. However, we do not believe that on the facts of this case, in order to avoid intestacy[62] only as to a 1/9th share of the residuum, we should read precise and controlling words into this will when there is no showing that the testator intended them to be there, especially when the result would be a divestiture of a vested remainder.

It is where the words of an instrument as written produce no rational result whatever that courts, faced with an obligation to resolve the problem by

---

60. As we pointed out above, all parties concede that if testator's son survived the life tenant, the 1/9th share could be given to "in-laws" or any others selected by the son.

61. This statute provides:

> If a devisee or legatee die [sic] before the testator, leaving issue who survive the testator, such issue shall take the estate devised or bequeathed as the devisee or legatee would have done if he had survived the testator, unless a different disposition be made or required by the will. Unless a contrary intention appear [sic] by the will, such property as shall be comprised in any devise or bequest in such will which shall fail or be void or otherwise incapable of taking effect shall be deemed included in the residuary devise or bequest, if any, contained in such will. § 19-110, D.C.Code 1951.

62. We do not decide here whether or not there is an intestacy, but only rule that our decision is not affected by such an assumption.

decision, can and do interpret the instrument to produce a result which they regard as consistent with the whole. But where the words as written produce a result which is not irrational or inconsistent with the evident intent of the instrument then courts should refrain from reading controlling words into or out of the instrument. That this may lead to a partial intestacy is not sufficient to warrant rewriting this will on the basis of the scant evidence we have as to testator's unexpressed intent, since the document can be rationally interpreted and applied without adding or excising words.

Therefore, we hold that this instrument gave testator's children vested remainders in the principal subject to being divested only on death with issue and that the interests of Rebecca P. Warner and Andrew Parker Warner were transmissible by their respective wills to their distributees, Anna Parker Warner and Jennie M. Warner. Since the parties have never explicitly considered the question of the effect of this ruling on Southard's 1/9th share and the trial court did not reach or rule on this point, we shall remand the case for further proceedings not inconsistent with this opinion.

Reversed and remanded.

Estate of Thall

219 N.E.2d 397 (N.Y. 1966)

FULD, J. Solomon Thall died in September, 1943, survived by his wife, a sister and issue of a deceased brother. By a will executed in 1941, he left his residuary estate in trust for the life of his wife with the income to be shared by her and by the testator's sister Sophie Levitsky and Sophie's two sons, Emanuel Landis and Ben Ami Landis. Upon the death of the widow, the corpus of the trust, after payment of certain legacies, was to go to Sophie, Emanuel and Ben Ami, "share and share alike". There then follow these clauses pertaining to the corpus:

> In the event that my sister Sophie Levitsky shall predecease me or surviving me shall predecease my said wife, I give and bequeath her share to her sons Emanuel Landis and Ben Ami Landis, share and share alike.
>
> Should either Emanuel Landis or Ben Ami Landis predecease me or predecease my said wife, I give and bequeath the share of the one so dying to his surviving child or children, and if more than one, share and share alike.
>
> If either of my said nephews Emanuel Landis or Ben Ami Landis should predecease me or surviving me shall predecease my said wife without leaving any child or children him surviving, I direct that his share shall be paid to his surviving brother.

The testator's widow is still alive. Ben Ami Landis died in 1956 survived by his daughter Barbara Ann. Sophie Levitsky died in 1961, and Emanuel Landis died without issue in 1962.

The will makes no provision for disposition of the income provided for Sophie and her two sons in the event which actually occurred, the death of all of them before that of the testator's widow, and this hiatus renders a construction of the will necessary at this time. The will likewise fails to provide for disposition of the corpus under the circumstance which in fact came to pass, namely, the death of one of Sophie's sons without issue *after* the death of the other son who was survived by a child.

The Surrogate decided that both the net income (after deduction of the widow's interest) and the entire corpus (excluding certain specific bequests) should be equally divided, one half to Ben Ami's daughter, Barbara Ann, and one half to those persons who were the testator's distributees on the date of his death. On appeal, the Appellate Division modified the Surrogate's decree by providing (1) that all of the net *income* was payable to the testator's distributees and (2) that, upon the death of the testator's widow, the entire corpus should be paid to Barbara Ann Landis. In our view, Barbara Ann is entitled to all of that portion of the net income not payable to the widow and, upon the latter's death, is to receive the whole of the corpus, except for the specific bequests.

The first rule of testamentary construction, of course, is that a will be interpreted to reflect the actual intention of the testator and the second that this intention be ascertained from a reading of the document as a whole. If a "general scheme" be found, it is the duty of the courts to carry out the testator's purpose, notwithstanding that "general rules of interpretation" might point to a different result.

Corollary to these broad principles is the doctrine that a court may "give effect to an intention or purpose, indicated *by implication*, where the express language of the entire will manifests such an intention or purpose" and the testator has simply neglected to provide for the exact contingency which occurred. As the Appellate Division wrote [Matter of Selner's Estate,] (261 App.Div. [618,] at pp. 620-621, 26 N.Y.S. [783] at p. 786, supra),

> If . . . the property or estate claimed to be bequeathed or devised by implication, in a contingency which has occurred, has been made the subject of an express bequest or devise in another contingency, which did not occur, then effect may be given to such bequest or devise by implication, in the contingency which did occur, if a reading of the entire will makes manifest that such was the intention of the testator.

In the case before us, the testator's intent, as manifested in his will, is plain. Outside of assuring his wife a minimum income during her lifetime, his paramount concern was for his sister and her two sons. His widow and his collateral relatives were left no part of the bulk of his estate. Indeed, in his bequests to the latter, token $1,000 gifts, he repeated more than once his direction that their legacies were to lapse if they predeceased him—or his widow, in the case of gifts from the trust corpus. Quite different were the provisions of the testator's will for his sister and her sons. In addition to receiving that portion of the trust income not bequeathed to his wife, they were to have the entire trust corpus—except for small gifts to collaterals—upon the wife's death. The testator's interest in his sister and her sons also appears in other parts of his will, for instance, in his bequests of personal property to them.

In disposing of his residuary estate, it is evident that the testator inadvertently neglected to foresee every eventuality. As indicated, he provided that Sophie's share, if she predeceased his widow, was to be divided between Emanuel and Ben Ami; that, if either Emanuel or Ben Ami predeceased the widow, the share of the one so dying was to pass to his surviving children, unless he died without issue, in which event his share was to be paid to his surviving brother. Manifestly, the testator expected that Sophie would die before her sons and that each of the sons thereafter dying would be survived by either a child or a brother. However, he failed to anticipate—what actually came to pass—that the second of the sons would die without issue, survived not by his brother but by the latter's child. Quite obviously, what the testator most desired was that his estate should ultimately go to, and remain within, a particular branch of his family. He could not have intended the descendants of Sophie to be deprived of any portion of his estate by the happenstance that the son (of hers) who was without children died *after*, rather than *before*, the son who left offspring. In short, since the testator desired his sister's descendants to take, there is a necessary "implication" that he did not intend any interest of a grandchild of hers to be defeated by the deaths of Emanuel and Ben Ami, as it were, in the wrong order.

Quite dissimilar are the cases in which the court has decreed an intestacy where the intent of the testator is not sufficiently clear to permit a bequest or devise by implication. [In Matter of Jay's Will, 1 N.Y.2d 897, 154 N.Y.S.2d 649, 136 N.E.2d 720,] for instance, the testator left his residuary estate to his wife for life and upon her death to his issue and, if she died without issue, to his mother or sister or the "survivor". We held that the death of the mother and sister prior to the testator's widow resulted in intestacy. In that case, however, unlike the present, there was no manifest intention by the testator to preserve for a particular branch of his family the interests of the remaindermen who might predecease the life tenant.

It is our conclusion, then, that upon the death of the testator's widow the corpus of the trust, except for specific bequests, is to be turned over to Barbara Ann Landis. It is also our conclusion that she is presently entitled, by reason of section 63 of the Real Property Law, Consol.Laws, c. 50, to the income other than the portion payable to the widow. That section provides that,

> When, in consequence of a valid limitation of a future estate, there is a suspension of the power of alienation, or of the ownership, during the continuance of which the rents and profits are undisposed of, and no valid direction for their accumulation is given, such rents and profits shall belong to the persons presumptively entitled to the next eventual estate.

It is clear that Barbara Ann Landis is the person "presumptively entitled to the next eventual estate", and, consequently, all of the income not otherwise disposed of belongs to her.

We have considered the other arguments advanced by the several parties and agree with the Appellate Division's resolution of them.

The order of the Appellate Division should be modified as herein indicated, with costs to all parties filing briefs payable out of the income of the trust in the same manner as the Surrogate's decree directs the payment of counsel fees and allowances, and, as so modified, affirmed.

Notes and Questions

1. *Death in the "Wrong Order."* In stating that the testator "did not intend any interest of a grandchild of [Sophie's] to be defeated by the deaths of Emanuel and Ben Ami, as it were, in the wrong order," the court seemed to be under the impression that if Emanuel's death without issue had occurred before, rather than after, Ben Ami's death, Emanuel's share of the corpus would have gone to Ben Ami's issue, Barbara Ann. Does the language of the will support the court's assumption?

2. *Comparison With Krooss.* Judge Fuld, who wrote the opinion of the court in *Thall*, also wrote the opinion of the court in In re Krooss, supra p. 1073. *Krooss* wasn't cited or discussed in *Thall*. Is *Krooss* relevant to the disposition of Emanuel's share of the corpus? Are *Krooss* and *Thall* reconcilable?

3. *Income to the Persons Entitled to the Next Eventual Estate.* With respect to the trust income, the court invoked § 63 of the New York Real Property Law,[63] which directs that undisposed-of income belongs "to the persons presumptively entitled to the next eventual estate." The application of this section, however, is dependent on the instrument not disposing of the income. Did the instrument dispose of the income? See Olin L. Browder, Jr., Trusts and the Doctrine of Estates, 72 Mich. L. Rev. 1509, 1560-61 (1974).

---

63. This section now appears, in somewhat modified form, as N.Y. Est. Powers & Trusts Law § 9-2.3.

2. Incomplete or Ambiguous Dispositions of Income

Dewire[64] v. Haveles[65]

534 N.E.2d 782 (Mass. 1989)

WILKINS, Justice. This petition for a declaration of rights seeks answers to questions arising from an artlessly drafted will that, among its many inadequacies, includes a blatant violation of the rule against perpetuities. . . .

Thomas A. Dewire died in January, 1941, survived by his widow, his son Thomas, Jr., and three grandchildren (Thomas, III, Paula, and Deborah, all children of Thomas, Jr.). His will placed substantially all his estate in a residuary trust. The income of the trust was payable to his widow for life and, on her death, the income was payable to his son Thomas, Jr., the widow of Thomas, Jr., and Thomas Jr.'s children.[66] After the testator's death, Thomas, Jr., had three more children by a second wife. Thomas, Jr., died on May 28, 1978, a widower, survived by all six of his children. Thomas, III, who had served as trustee since 1978, died on March 19, 1987, leaving a widow and one child, Jennifer. Among the questions presented, and the most important one for present purposes, is to whom the one-sixth share of the trust income, once payable to Thomas, III, is now payable.

In his will, the testator stated: "It is my will, except as hereinabove provided, that my grandchildren, under guidance and discretion of my Trustee, shall share equally in the net income of my said estate." At another point, he referred to the trust income being "divided equally amongst my grandchildren." The rule against perpetuities violation occurred because the will provided for the trust's termination "twenty-one years after the death of the last surviving child of my

---

64. Sheila Dewire, executrix of the estate of Thomas A. Dewire, III, and mother of Jennifer.

65. Paula Dewire Haveles, Deborah Dewire, Stephen Dewire, Andrew Dewire, and Constance Dewire. Paula Dewire Haveles is the current trustee of the testamentary trust under the will of her grandfather, Thomas A. Dewire.

66. The language of the will directing this distribution appears in article third of the will and reads as follows:

> Third: To my wife, Mabel G. Dewire, I give, devise and bequeath all the rest, residue and remainder of all the estate of which I shall die seized, for and during the term of her natural life, and upon her decease to my son, Thomas A. Dewire, Jr., and his heirs and assigns, but in trust nevertheless upon the following trusts and for the following purposes:
>
> A. To hold, direct, manage and conserve the trust estate, so given, for the benefit of himself, his wife and children in the manner following, that is to say:
>
> To expend out of the net income so much as may be necessary for the proper care, maintenance of himself and wife conformable to their station in life, and for the care maintenance and education of his children born to him in his lifetime, in such manner as in his judgment and discretion shall seem proper, and his judgment and discretion shall be final.

said son, Thomas A. Dewire, Jr., when the property of the trust shall be equally divided amongst the lineal descendants of my grandchildren."[67]

There is no explicit provision in the will concerning the distribution of income on the death of a grandchild while the gift of income to grandchildren continues . . . .

Our task is to discern the testator's intention concerning the distribution of a grandchild's share of the trust income on his death. As a practical matter, in cases of this sort, where there is no express intention, we must resort to reasonable inferences in the particular circumstances which on occasion shade into rules of construction that are applied when no intention at all can be inferred on the issue. In this case, the reasonable inference as to the testator's intention is that Jennifer should take her father's share in the income.

Certain points are not in serious controversy and are relatively easy to resolve. The gift of net income to the testator's grandchildren, divided equally or to be shared equally, is a class gift. . . . The class includes all six grandchildren, three of whom were born before and three of whom were born after the testator's death. . . . Because there is a gift over at the end of the class gift, the testator intended the class gift to his grandchildren only to be a gift of a life interest in the income of the trust. The general rule is that, in the absence of a contrary intent expressed in the will or a controlling statute stating otherwise, members of a class are joint tenants with rights of survivorship.

This last stated principle becomes important in deciding whether Jennifer, the child of the deceased grandson, takes her deceased father's share in the trust income or whether the remaining class members, the other five grandchildren, take that income share equally by right of survivorship. Jennifer argues, under the general rule, that the will manifests an intent contrary to a class gift with rights of survivorship. We agree with this conclusion. Thus we need not decide, as Jennifer further argues, whether the rule of construction presuming a right of survivorship in class members should be rejected in the circumstances and replaced by a rule based on principles similar to those expressed in the antilapse statute.[68]

---

67. As we shall explain, the possibility that Thomas, Jr., would have a child born after the testator's death was sufficient to cause the violation of the rule against perpetuities. The fact that Thomas, Jr., had children born after the testator's death makes possible a violation of the rule in actual fact.

68. The Massachusetts antilapse statute applies only to testamentary gifts to a child or other relation of a testator who predeceased the testator leaving issue surviving the testator and to class gifts to children or other relations where one or more class member predeceased the testator (even if the class member had died before the will was executed). G.L. c. 191, § 22. The rule of construction of § 22 is that the issue of a deceased relation take his share by right of representation "unless a different disposition is made or required by the will."

In this case, no class member predeceased the testator and, therefore, § 22 does not explicitly

Before we explain why the will expresses an intention that, during the term of the class gift, Jennifer, while living, should take her father's share in the income, we discuss the rule against perpetuities problem.[69] The prospect that interests under this will may vest beyond the permissible limit of the rule against perpetuities is not only theoretically possible, it is actuarially likely. The interests of the grandchildren in the trust income vested at their father's death (if not sooner) and, because he was a life in being at the testator's death, those interests vested within the period of the rule. The gift over at the end of the class gift of income to the grandchildren, however, might not vest seasonably because another grandchild could have been born after the testator's death and could be the surviving grandchild. In this case, in fact, the three youngest grandchildren were born after the death of the testator but they are measuring lives for the term of the class gift. The parties agree that the purported gift of the remainder to the lineal descendants of the testator's grandchildren "twenty-one years after the death of the last surviving" grandchild violates the rule against perpetuities in its traditional form and would be void. See Second Bank-State St. Trust Co. v. Second Bank-State St. Trust Co., 335 Mass. 407, 410-411, 140 N.E.2d 201 (1957). There is no need at this time to decide the question of the proper distribution of trust income or assets at the death of the last grandchild. The question will be acute at the death of the last grandchild, when the class gift of income from the trust will terminate.[70]

---

aid Jennifer. The policy underlying § 22 might fairly be seen as supporting, as a rule of construction (absent a contrary intent), the substitution of a class member's surviving issue for a deceased class member if the class is made up of children or other relations of the testator. See Bigelow v. Clap, 166 Mass. 88, 91, 43 N.E. 1037 (1896). It has been suggested that "[t]he policy of [antilapse] statutes [dealing with the death of a class member after the testator's death] commends itself to decisional law." Restatement (Second) of Property, Donative Transfers § 27.3 comment i (Tent. Draft No. 9, 1986). If the antilapse statute protects the interests of the issue of a relation who predeceases a testator, there is good reason why we should adopt, as a rule of construction, the same principle as to a relation of a testator who survives the testator but dies before an interest comes into possession. In the case of a class gift of income from a trust, the interest could be viewed as coming into possession on each income distribution date.

69. In its classic formulation, the rule against perpetuities declares that: "No interest is good unless it must vest, if at all, not later than twenty-one years after some life in being at the creation of the interest." J.C. Gray, The Rule Against Perpetuities § 201, at 191 (4th ed. 1942).

70. The common law rule against perpetuities has been modified by statute. See G.L. c. 184A, § 1 (1986 ed.), applicable to wills of persons dying after January 1, 1955 (St.1954, c. 641, § 2) and thus not directly applicable in this case. The second look or wait-and-see principle of G.L. c. 184A, § 1, has been applied as a matter of decisional law to an instrument to which § 1 did not apply. See Warner v. Whitman, 353 Mass. 468, 472, 233 N.E.2d 14 (1968). If a wait-and-see approach is applicable here, and if the last surviving grandchild were to be one of the grandchildren alive at the death of the testator, there would be no violation of the rule against perpetuities. We might even decide that there was no violation of the rule if all the grandchildren were to die within twenty-one years of the death of the last grandchild who was living at the

The rule against perpetuities problem need not be resolved at this time. It has some bearing, however, on what should be done during the term of the class gift with the one-sixth share of the trust income that is in dispute. We reject the argument that, because of the violation of the rule against perpetuities, the income interests should be treated as being more than life interests. There is no authority for such a proposition. Although the gift over violates the rule against perpetuities in its traditional form and in time may prove to violate it in actual fact, the language providing for such a distribution may properly be considered in determining a testator's intention with respect to other aspects of his will. . . . For the purposes of distribution of assets, a will is to be construed as if a provision violating the rule against perpetuities is not contained in it, but we have never said that the language of a void clause cannot be used to determine the testator's intention as to dispositions that do not violate the rule.

We are now in a position to discuss the question whether the class gift of income to grandchildren calls for the payment of income equally to those grandchildren living from time to time (as joint tenants with rights of survivorship) or whether the issue of any deceased grandchild succeeds by right of representation to his income interest. The latter result better conforms with the testator's intentions.

The testator provided that the trust should terminate twenty-one years after the death of his last grandchild. It is unlikely that the testator intended that trust income should be accumulated for twenty-one years, and we would tend to avoid such a construction. Certainly, we should not presume that he intended an intestacy as to that twenty-one year period. He must have expected that someone would receive distributions of income during those years.[71] The only logical recipients of that income would be the issue (by right of representation) of deceased grandchildren, the same group of people who would take the trust assets on termination of the trust (assuming no violation of the rule against perpetuities). If these people were intended to receive income during the last twenty-one years of the trust as well as the trust assets on its termination, it is logical that they should also receive income during the term of the class gift if their ancestor (one of the grandchildren) should die. Such a pattern treats each grandchild and his issue equally throughout the intended term of the trust. Where, among other things, every other provision in the will concerning the distribution of trust income and principal (after the death of the testator and his wife) points to equal treatment of the testator's issue per stirpes, there is a

---

testator's death. See Restatement (Second) of Property, Donative Transfers § 1.4 (1983).

71. At one point in his will, the testator says that the trust income is payable "to [Thomas, Jr.] and his children and their heirs at law."

sufficient contrary intent shown to overcome the rule of construction that the class gift of income to grandchildren is given to them as joint tenants with the right of survivorship. . . .

Judgment shall be entered declaring that . . . Jennifer Ann Dewire in her lifetime is entitled to one-sixth of the net income of the trust during the period of the class gift of income, that is, until the death of the last grandchild (and a proportionate share of the income of any grandchild who dies leaving no issue) . . .

SO ORDERED.

Notes and Questions

1. *Rejection of the Cross-Remainder Doctrine.* The Restatement 3d of Trusts § 49 comment c supports the *Dewire* case by providing:

> *c. . . . Multiple life beneficiaries: income share(s) not expressly disposed of.* . . . Where the income of a trust is payable to two or more life beneficiaries with a gift over on the death of the survivor, and an income beneficiary dies, the disposition of the income share [that] the deceased beneficiary had been receiving depends on the terms of the trust. Where the terms of the trust make no express provision for the situation, the normal inference is that the settlor intended the income share to be paid to the issue (if any) of the deceased income beneficiary in the typical case in which the remainder is to pass to the descendants of the beneficiaries upon the survivor's death.

This provision of the Restatement 3d is discussed by the Reporter in Edward C. Halbach, Jr., Uniform Acts, Restatements, and Trends in American Trust Law at Century's End, 88 Calif. L. Rev. 1877, 1906 (2000).

2. *UPC § 2-707.* Would UPC § 2-707 produce the result reached by the court in *Dewire*? Professor Waggoner argues that it would. See Lawrence W. Waggoner, The Uniform Probate Code Extends Antilapse-type Protection to Poorly Drafted Trusts, 94 Mich. L. Rev. 2309, 2332-33 (1996).

3. *Question.* Suppose that G devised property in trust, to "pay one-third of the income to my son, A, for life, one-third to my daughter, B, for life, and one-third to my son, C, for life; upon the death of the survivor of my children, corpus to my then-living descendants, by representation; if none, to X-Charity." A died first, survived by descendants. Then B died without surviving descendants. Under the Restatement 3d, who would take B's share of the income? Cf. Cox v. Forristall, supra p. 1088.

Problems

Consider the proper disposition of the trust income or corpus in the following cases:

1. G transferred property in trust, to pay the income from the trust "to A." A died, devising all of her estate to B. See Restatement 2d of Trusts § 128 comment b; Scott on Trusts § 128.2; Olin L. Browder, Jr., Trusts and the Doctrine of Estates, 72 Mich. L. Rev. 1509, 1532-42 (1974). Compare Estate of Bowles, 764 P.2d 510 (N.M. Ct. App. 1988) (will devising income from Blackacre to testator's sister and residue of estate, including Blackacre, to testator's children; held, the will gave the sister only a *life estate* in income from Blackacre).

2. G devised property in trust, to pay the income "to my children, A and B, for their respective lives; corpus upon their deaths to their descendants, by representation; if none, to X-Charity." A died without issue, survived by B.

3. G devised property in trust, to pay the income "to A and B for 21 years; at the expiration of 21 years, corpus to my then-living descendants, by representation; if none, to X-Charity." A died five years after G's death, devising all of her estate to C.

4. G devised property in trust, directing the trustee to pay to A during A's lifetime so much of the income as the trustee determines is necessary for A's support and education, corpus on A's death to A's then-living descendants, by representation; if none, to X-Charity. During A's lifetime, the income was more than sufficient to pay for A's support and education. What happens to the surplus income?

5. G devised property in trust, directing the trustee to pay $50,000 per year to A for A's lifetime, corpus on A's death to A's then-living descendants, by representation; if none, to X-Charity. What happens to the surplus income if the income exceeds $50,000 in any one year?

6. G devised $600,000 in trust, granting the trustee the discretionary power to spray the income among G's surviving spouse, H, and G's descendants; the trust terminates upon H's death, with the corpus then going to G's then-living descendants, by representation; if none, to X-Charity.

G's descendants are her two adult children, A and B, and three young grandchildren, X, Y, and Z. X and Y are A's children; Z is B's child.

Since neither H nor the children, A and B, need any of the income from the trust, they all agree with the trustee that the trustee's discretionary power should be exercised in favor of the grandchildren, who are minors.

How should the trustee divide the income among X, Y, and Z? Should half of the income be divided between X and Y, with the other half going to Z; or should the income be divided among X, Y, and Z equally? A and B have different views on the matter. Can the trustee allocate any of the income to the grandchildren, given the fact that they have living ancestors (A and B)?

EXTERNAL REFERENCES. Olin L. Browder, Trusts and the Doctrine of Estates, 72 Mich. L. Rev. 1509, 1542-75 (1974); Edward C. Halbach, Jr., Issues About Issue: Some Recurrent Class Gift Problems, 48 Mo. L. Rev. 333, 355-57 (1983).

Chapter 19

The Rule Against Perpetuities And Related Rules

WE now make an abrupt shift from matters of construction, the purposes of which are to carry out intent, to rules of law that defeat intent for reasons of overriding social policy. Specifically, the main subject of this chapter is the Rule Against Perpetuities. The Rule Against Perpetuities was originally designed to prevent the dead hand from indirectly curtailing the alienability of property for too long a period—in perpetuity. The indirect curtailment of alienability was said to arise from attaching contingencies to future interests in property.

A rule that developed, step by step over time, into the rule known today as the Rule Against Perpetuities was initiated in the much-celebrated Duke of Norfolk's Case, 3 Ch. Cas. 1, 22 Eng. Rep. 931 (1682). The so-called *modern* Rule Against Perpetuities was formulated by Professor John Chipman Gray in the second edition of his book, The Rule Against Perpetuities (2d ed. 1906):

RAP

No [nonvested property] interest is good unless it must vest, if at all, not later than 21 years after some life in being at the creation of the interest.[1]

Nothing resembling this mechanically precise "rule" was stated by the judge in the Duke of Norfolk's Case, the Lord Chancellor, the First Earl of Nottingham. His pronouncements about prohibiting perpetuities appear to be mere musings:

---

1. This formulation was carried forward, word for word, in subsequent editions of his book. Gray on Perpetuities § 201. A similar formulation was set forth in the first edition of the book published in 1886.

> But what Time? And where are the Bounds of that Contingency? You may limit, it seems, upon a Contingency to happen in a Life: What if it be limited, if such a one die without Issue within twenty-one Years, or 100 Years, or while Westminster-Hall stands? Where will you stop, if you do not stop here? I will tell you where I will stop: I will stop wherever any visible Inconvenience doth appear; . . . .

Despite the appearance of imprecision, even casualness, of the Lord Chancellor's statement,[2] the Duke of Norfolk's Case was an exceedingly important case at the time. But not in the way that might at first be imagined: The decision apparently served less as a judicial warning that perpetuities would not be tolerated than as an approval of conveyancers' practices current at the time. The future interest challenged in the Duke of Norfolk's Case was an executory interest. Although the destructibility rule had earlier been held inapplicable to executory interests in Pells v. Brown, Cro. Jac. 590, 79 Eng. Rep. 504 (K.B. 1620), that decision was a sudden and unexpected departure from prior law. Also, a later decision, Purefoy v. Rogers, 2 Wm. Saund. 380, 85 Eng. Rep. 1181 (K.B. 1670), cast some doubt on the continuing validity of *Pells*, by holding that a contingent remainder could not avoid destruction by changing into an executory interest after it was created. The Duke of Norfolk's Case assured the practicing bar that *Pells* remained solid law.

Gradually, over the 150 or so years following the Duke of Norfolk's Case, the pronouncement that a contingency limited to "happen in a Life" was valid, but beyond that, an invalidity would arise "wherever any visible Inconvenience doth appear," grew step by step into the Rule Against Perpetuities stated by Professor Gray, above. The period of a life was enlarged to multiple lives, which in effect is but a single life, the choice being postponed to turn upon which of several is the survivor. Scatterwood v. Edge, 1 Salk. 229, 91 Eng. Rep. 203 (K.B. 1697). To this period was added the period of an actual minority of a beneficiary; and also an actual period of gestation. Some considerable time later, in Cadell v. Palmer, 1 Cl. & F. 372, 6 Eng. Rep. 956 (1833), the minority period was disengaged from an actual minority and allowed as a 21-year period in gross.

Although Professor Gray's book solidified the common-law Rule Against Perpetuities, stunting its further evolution throughout much of the twentieth century, the Rule Against Perpetuities is again undergoing change. These changes are mainly in the form of perpetuity-reform legislation, though there have also been some developments at common law. Among the most important reforms was the promulgation in 1986 of the Uniform Statutory Rule Against

---

2. Although Nottingham, the Lord Chancellor, did not define a perpetuity, he apparently felt that he would know one if he saw it.

Perpetuities (USRAP or Uniform Rule). The Uniform Rule was revised modestly and incorporated into the UPC in 1990. See UPC §§ 2-901 to -906. The perpetuity-reform movement is discussed infra Part D.

External References. On the Duke of Norfolk's Case, see George L. Haskins, Extending the Grasp of the Dead Hand: Reflections on the Origins of the Rule Against Perpetuities, 126 U. Pa. L. Rev. 19 (1977); George L. Haskins, "Inconvenience" and the Rule For Perpetuities, 48 Mo. L. Rev. 451 (1983). On Professor Gray's influence, see Stephen A. Siegel, John Chipman Gray, Legal Formalism, and the Transformation of Perpetuities Law, 36 U. Miami L. Rev. 439 (1982). On the mechanics of the common-law Rule, see W. Barton Leach, Perpetuities in a Nutshell, 51 Harv. L. Rev. 638 (1938); W. Barton Leach, The Nutshell Revisited, 78 Harv. L. Rev. 973 (1965).

PART A. MECHANICS OF THE COMMON-LAW RULE AGAINST PERPETUITIES

Interests to Which the Rule Applies. The Rule Against Perpetuities applies to future interests in property, whether legal or equitable, but only if they are nonvested (contingent). Classification of the interests in a disposition is, therefore, a preliminary but crucial step to solving perpetuity questions. Specifically, the Rule applies to contingent remainders and to executory interests, both of which are nonvested future interests. The Rule does not apply to vested remainders, not even to those that are vested subject to defeasance; nor does the Rule apply to reversions, which are always vested.[3] The other two reversionary future interests—possibilities of reverter and rights of entry—are also considered exempt from the Rule Against Perpetuities.

Class gifts are also subject to the Rule, and in fact are treated specially. The early English decision of Leake v. Robinson, 2 Mer. 363, 35 Eng. Rep. 979 (Ch. 1817), laid down the proposition that *if the interest of any potential class member might vest too remotely, the entire class gift is invalid*. This is the so-called all-or-nothing rule, by which it is meant that a class gift is either *completely* valid or *completely* invalid. It is not permissible to treat the interest of each class member separately and say that some class members have valid interests and other class members have invalid interests. More extensive consideration of the special case of class gifts is presented in Part E, infra.

The "Perpetuity Period." The common-law perpetuity period is defined as a life in being plus 21 years. The period can be extended by one or more

---

3. "A vested interest is not subject to the Rule against Perpetuities." Gray on Perpetuities § 205.

periods of gestation, *but only when an actual pregnancy makes the extension necessary.*[4] In other words, the period of gestation is not a formal part of the perpetuity period. Cadell v. Palmer, 1 Cl. & F. 372 (H.L. 1883).

The life in being, often called the *measuring life*, must be the life of a person "in being at the creation of the interest." This means that the person whose life is the measuring life must be alive or in gestation when the perpetuity period begins to run. The measuring life must also be a human life—the life of a corporation, an animal, or a plant cannot be used. But there are no further restrictions. Theoretically, anyone in the world who was alive or in gestation when the interest was created can be the measuring life. As a practical matter, though, it is not that simple, as we shall see, when one gets down to the problem of identifying the measuring life in actual cases.

Although the 21-year part of the perpetuity period is described by Gray as coming *after* the death of the person who is the measuring life, and we often refer to it as the *tack-on* 21-year period, the 21-year part need not be preceded by a measuring life; it can stand on its own. A testamentary transfer "to such of my grandchildren as are living on the 21st anniversary of my death" would be valid without the necessity of locating a measuring life.

While authority on the question is sparse, it seems to be agreed that the 21-year part cannot come first, followed by a life that is in being 21 years *after* the creation of the interest. This is a consequence of the requirement that the measuring life must be in being *at* the creation of the interest.

> *Example 19.1:* G bequeathed property in trust "to pay the income to G's children for 21 years, then to pay the income to such of G's grandchildren as may then be living for life, and on the death of the survivor to pay the corpus of the trust to G's descendants then living by representation."
>
> If G is survived by one or more children, the remainder interest in the corpus of the trust violates the Rule and is invalid.

As noted above, a child in gestation at the commencement of the perpetuity period can be a measuring life because the child is considered then to be "in being." So also the perpetuity period is expandable at the end to account for an actual period of gestation, if necessary.

---

4. UPC § 2-901(d) (USRAP § 1(d)) takes a different approach. It provides that, "in determining whether a nonvested property interest [is valid under the common-law Rule], the possibility that a child will be born to an individual after the individual's death is disregarded."

1. The Requirement of Initial Certainty

Requirement of Initial Certainty. Implicit in Professor Gray's formulation is the *requirement of initial certainty*, which is that *a nonvested future interest is invalid if, at the creation of the interest, there exists any possible chain of events that might subsequently arise that would allow the interest to remain nonvested beyond a life in being plus 21 years.*

Measuring Life. The "perpetuity period" is a life in being plus 21 years plus, if needed for validity, one or more periods of gestation. The life in being is traditionally called the "measuring life." This suggests that one must identify a particular person as *the* measuring life in *each* case and then test the interest to determine whether or not the interest might remain nonvested beyond 21 years following such person's death. This is *not* the procedure, however. It is wrong to speak as if there is a definite perpetuity period tied into the lifetime of a particular person in the case of both valid and invalid interests. For a life in being to be a "measuring life," the person must satisfy the requirement of initial certainty, which means that *there must be a causal connection between the person's death and the vesting or termination*[5] *of the interest no later than 21 years thereafter.*

Only *valid* dispositions produce a particular life who has the requisite causal connection and is identified as the so-called *measuring* life. An invalid interest is invalid because there is *no* measuring life that makes it valid—not because it might remain nonvested beyond 21 years after the death of an *identifiable* measuring life. This is what is meant when it is said that invalidity under the common-law Rule depends upon the existence, as of the interest's creation, of an invalidating chain of possible postcreation events. *The search for a "measuring life," therefore, turns out in reality to be a search for a "validating life."*

In Truth, There Is No "Perpetuity Period" at Common Law. The requirement of initial certainty is a mechanism for testing the validity of an interest *in advance* of its actual vesting or termination. With the decision made in advance, the common law has no need to mark off a "perpetuity period" in the case of invalid interests,[6] and no common-law decision has ever declared or

---

5. An interest terminates when vesting becomes impossible. In the following example, B's interest terminates if and when B predeceases A: "to A for life, remainder to B if B survives A."

6. See Lawrence W. Waggoner, Perpetuities: A Perspective on Wait-and-See, 85 Colum. L. Rev. 1714, 1714-17 (1985); Lawrence W. Waggoner, Perpetuity Reform, 81 Mich. L. Rev. 1718, 1720-24 (1983). Professor Dukeminier disputes this. Jesse Dukeminier, A Modern Guide to Perpetuities, 74 Calif. L. Rev. 1867, 1868-76 (1986); Jesse Dukeminier, Perpetuities: The Measuring Lives, 85 Colum. L. Rev. 1648, 1649-54 (1985). The dispute is in reality a by-product of a different controversy concerning the wait-and-see method of perpetuity reform (see infra Part D); it has no bearing on the solution of perpetuity problems under the common-law Rule, a point

even intimated that it does. Here is why: A "perpetuity period" would be necessary only if *actual* postcreation events were to be taken into account to see if an interest for which there is *no* validating life *actually* vests or terminates within that period of time. But the common-law Rule does not permit actual postcreation events to be considered. For interests for which there *is* a validating life, there is no need to trace the actual longevity of that person, for the time of that person's death is immaterial. By definition, the interest *cannot possibly* vest or terminate beyond 21 years after that person's death; the actual time of that person's death does not matter. For valid interests, in other words, the common law uses the life-in-being-plus-21-years "period" in a way that does not require an actual period of time to be marked off by the tracing of the lives of so-called "measuring lives."

2. *How to Search for a Validating Life*

Goal of the Search: To Find One Person for Whom There Is No Invalidating Chain of Possible Postcreation Events. The Official Comment to § 1 of the Uniform Rule sets forth the following guidance for solving a perpetuities problem:

> The process for determining whether a validating life exists is to postulate the death of each individual connected in some way to the transaction, and ask the question: Is there with respect to this individual an invalidating chain of possible [postcreation] events? If one individual can be found for whom the answer is No, that individual can serve as the validating life. As to that individual there will be the requisite causal connection between his or her death and the questioned interest's vesting or terminating no later than 21 years thereafter.

Note that the converse is also true: If no person can be found for whom there is no invalidating chain of possible postcreation events, there is no validating life; an interest for which there is no validating life is invalid.

Only Insiders Need to Be Considered. In searching for a validating life, there is no formal rule forbidding the testing of anyone in the world to see if that person has the causal connection demanded by the requirement of initial certainty. There is, for example, no law against testing your favorite movie star or rock star in each case, if you want to do that. But experience has shown that no outsider will pass the test.

What we mean to say is that you can safely limit the persons you test to insiders—those who are connected in some way to the transaction. Only insiders have a chance of supplying the requisite causal connection demanded by the

---

that corroborates the position that there is no "perpetuity period" as such at common law.

requirement of initial certainty. The insiders to be tested vary from situation to situation, but would always include the transferor, if living, the beneficiaries of the disposition, including but not restricted to the taker or takers of the challenged interest, the objects and donee of a power of appointment, persons related to the foregoing by blood or adoption, especially in the ascending and descending lines, and anyone else who has any connection to the transaction. If there is any doubt about a particular person, no harm is done by subjecting that person to the test. Usually it takes no more than an instant to resolve whether or not a person arguably on the fringe of the transaction has the requisite causal connection demanded by the requirement of initial certainty.

There is, however, no point in even considering the life of a complete outsider who is clearly unconnected to the transaction—a person selected at random from the world at large—just because the outsider happened to be in being at the creation of the interest. Outsiders in that category have already been tested and found *always* to be wanting. No outsider can possibly fulfill the requirement of initial certainty because there will always be an invalidating chain of possible postcreation events as to every outsider who might be proposed: Any outsider can immediately die after the creation of the interest without having any effect whatsoever on the time when the interest will vest or terminate.

Survivor of a Group. In appropriate cases the validating life need not be individuated. Rather, if we view the situation as of the date of the interest's creation, the life can be an unidentified member of a group of individuals. It is common in these cases to say that the members of the group are the validating *lives*. This is acceptable, as long as it is recognized that the true meaning of the statement is that the validating *life* is the life of the member of the group who turns out to live the longest. As the court said in Scatterwood v. Edge, 1 Salk. 229, 91 Eng. Rep. 203 (K.B. 1697), "for let the lives be never so many, there must be a survivor, and so it is but the length of that life; for [Justice] Twisden [in Love v. Wyndham, 1 Mod. 50, 54 Eng. Rep. 724, 726 (K.B. 1681)] used to say, the candles were all lighted at once."

Recipient of the Interest as the Validating Life. A well established but sometimes overlooked point is that the recipient of an interest might be the validating life. See, e.g., Rand v. Bank of California, 388 P.2d 437 (Or. 1964). This point is especially useful in cases in which an interest is contingent on the recipient's reaching an age in excess of 21 or is contingent on the recipient's survival of a particular point in time that is or may be in excess of 21 years after the interest was created or after the death of a person in being at the date of creation.

Problems

Consider the validity of the remainder interest in the following cases:

1. G devised property "to A for life, remainder to B."
2. G devised property "to A for life, remainder to B if B survives A."
3. G devised property "to A for life, remainder to A's children."

Problems

All the nonvested property interests in the following cases satisfy the requirement of initial certainty and are therefore valid. Using the above text as a guide, identify the validating life for each interest.

1. G devised property "to A for life, remainder to such of A's children as attain 21." G was survived by his son (A), his daughter (B), A's wife (W), and A's two children (X and Y).

2. Take the same facts as in Problem 1, but change the disposition to read "to B for life, remainder to such of A's children as attain 21."

3. G devised real property "to such of my grandchildren as attain 21." Some of G's children are living at G's death.

4. (a) G devised real property "to such of A's children as attain 25;" or,

(b) G devised real property "to such of A's children as are living on the 25th anniversary of my death."

A predeceased G. At G's death, A had three living children, all of whom were under 25.

Multiple Interests. Dispositions of property sometimes create more than one interest that is subject to the Rule. When this happens, the validity of each interest must be tested separately. A validating life that validates one interest might or might not validate the other interests. Consequently, one must search for a validating life for each interest.

Problems

1. G devised property "to A for life, then to A's children for their lives, and on the death of each of them to the survivor or survivors of them for life, and on the death of the survivor of them, to B and her heirs."

Do any of the interests created in this disposition violate the common-law Rule Against Perpetuities? See Dodge v. Bennett, 102 N.E. 916 (Mass. 1913); Gray on Perpetuities § 207. Suppose the remainder interest to B had been contingent on survival of A's last surviving child—that is, suppose it had said "to B if B is then living"?

2. All but one of the future interests in the following cases fail the requirement of initial certainty and are therefore invalid. Explain why there is no validating life in each case. Which future interest is valid and why?

(a)(1) G devised real property "to A and her heirs so long as liquor is not sold on the premises, and upon liquor's being sold on the premises, the property is to go to B;" or

(2) G devised real property "to A and her heirs on condition that no liquor be sold on the premises, but if liquor is sold on the premises, the property is to go to B."

In both cases, G was survived by A and B.

(b) G devised property in trust, directing the trustee to pay the net income therefrom "to A for life, then to A's children for the life of the survivor, and upon the death of A's last surviving child, to pay the corpus of the trust to A's grandchildren." G was survived by A and A's two children, X and Y.

Interests That Must Vest or Terminate Within 21 Years. As noted above, there is no need to search for a validating life for interests that are certain to vest or terminate within 21 years after their creation; the 21-year part of the period validates such interests.

In Green v. Green, 221 N.E.2d 388 (Ohio P. Ct. 1966), an action for a declaratory judgment was brought to construe the will of Roy C. Green, who died on July 24, 1955. Roy was survived by his only child Richard, his sister Helen, Richard's wife Elsie, and their three children, William, Judith, and Betsy. William was born on February 1, 1941, Judith on May 21, 1942, and Betsy on July 28, 1947. Roy's will established a trust that provided:

> (6) The trust shall terminate upon the last to happen of the following counts:
>
> (a) The death of my son, Richard C. Green.
>
> (b) The death or remarriage of Elsie L. Green.
>
> (c) The day the youngest living child of my son, Richard C. Green, in being on the date of my death, attains twenty-five (25) years of age.
>
> (d) The death of my sister, Helen Green.
>
> Upon the termination of the trust, the Trustee shall assign, transfer, convey and deliver all of the property then comprising the trust to the lineal descendants of my son, Richard C. Green, per stirpes.

To a contention that the interest in the corpus violated the Rule Against Perpetuities, the court responded:

> Where a trust is to terminate at the time when a designated person attains a specified age, courts have construed this to mean that if the person dies before attaining the required age, the trust terminates immediately upon his death.

Fishberg's Will, 158 Misc. 3, 285 N.Y.S. 303 (Sur. Ct. 1936); Sammis v. Sammis, 14 R.I. 123 (1883); Butler v. Butler, 40 R.I. 425, 101 A. 115 (1917).

Other courts have held that the trust terminates when the designated person would have attained the specified age had he lived that long. Clark's Estate, 13 N.J. Misc. 393, 178 A. 574 (Orphans' Court 1935); Stein v. United States National Bank of Portland, 165 Or. 518, 108 P.2d 1016 (1941).

Basically, the court is trying to find the intention of the testator, and this is reflected in the authorities cited.

Fortunately, we need not analyze the cases to see whether they can be reconciled, nor need we choose between the two views, for under either view the trust in the present case will terminate, the class will close, and the remainders will vest within twenty-one years after lives in being at the date of the testator's death. . . .

What feature of the case allowed the court to declare the interests valid without choosing "between the two views"?

3. Time of Creation

Statutory References: *UPC § 2-902 (USRAP § 2)*

The time when a property interest is created is important because it fixes the time when the validating life must be "in being." It is also important because it demarks the facts that can be taken into account in determining the validity of an interest. Under the common-law Rule, an interest is valid only if at the time when the interest is created, with the facts *then existing* taken into account, the interest is certain to vest or terminate within a life in being plus 21 years. The facts that *actually* occur from that time forward, with one exception concerning interests created by the exercise of certain powers of appointment (see infra Part E), are irrelevant; all that counts thereafter is what *might* happen.

Property interests created by will are created when the testator dies, not when the testator signs the will. Thus the validating life for testamentary transfers must be a person who was alive (or in gestation) when the testator died, and the facts that can be taken into account in determining the validity of an interest created by will are those existing at the testator's death.

Property interests created by inter vivos transfers are created when the transfers become effective for purposes of property law generally. This would ordinarily be the date of delivery of the deed or the funding of the trust. Thus the validating life for inter vivos transfers must be a person who was alive (or in gestation) when the transfer became effective, and the facts that can be taken into account in determining the validity of an interest created by inter vivos transfer are those existing at that time.

Problem

G conveyed property to a trustee, directing the trustee to pay the net income to herself (G) for life, then to G's son A for his life, then to A's children who are living at G's death for their respective lives, and upon the death of the last survivor of such children, the corpus of the trust is to be distributed among A's then-living descendants, by representation. Are any interests in this trust invalid? Suppose:

1. The trust was irrevocable.
2. G retained the power to revoke the trust.

The Postponement Principle. For purposes of the Rule Against Perpetuities, the time of creation of a property interest is postponed in certain cases. One of the leading decisions on the postponement principle is Cook v. Horn, 104 S.E.2d 461 (Ga. 1958). In the course of its opinion, the court explained the principle in these terms:

> While there is a scarcity of authority on this question, and none that we have found in Georgia, the prevailing opinion by both the courts of other jurisdictions and recognized text writers is that, when a settlor has the power during his lifetime to revoke or destroy the trust estate for his own exclusive personal benefit, the question whether interests, or any of them, created by an instrument or deed of trust are void because in violation of the rule against perpetuities, is to be determined as of the date of the settlor's death and not as of the date the instrument is executed and delivered. See Ryan v. Ward, 192 Md. 342, 64 A.2d 258, 7 A.L.R.2d 1078; Mifflin's Appeal, 121 Pa. 205, 15 A. 525, 1 L.R.A. 453; Goesele v. Bimeler, 14 How. 589, 14 L.Ed. 554; Manufacturers Life Insurance Company v. von Hamm-Young Co., 34 Haw. 288; Pulitzer v. Livingston, 89 Me. 359, 36 A. 635; City Bank Farmers Trust Company v. Cannon, 291 N.Y. 125, 51 N.E.2d 674, 157 A.L.R. 1424; Equitable Trust Co. v. Pratt, 117 Misc. 708, 190 N.Y.S. 152, affirmed on opinion below 206 App. Div. 689, 199 N.Y.S. 921; Gray, Rule Against Perpetuities, (4th Ed.) 510, par. 524; 45 Harv. L. Rev. 896; 51 Harv. L. Rev. 638; 86 Univ. of Pa. L. Rev. 221; Restatement of Property, § 373, comments (c), (d), and Ryan v. Ward, 192 Md. 342, 64 A.2d 258, 7 A.L.R.2d 1078.
>
> While none of these authorities is binding upon this court, the conclusion reached by them is in accord with the aim of and reason for the rule against perpetuities, which is to prevent the tying up of property for an unreasonable length of time and to prohibit unreasonable restraint upon the alienation of property. So long as the settlor of an inter vivos trust has the absolute right to revoke or terminate the trust for his own exclusive personal benefit, there is no tying up of property and no restraint upon the alienability of the property in the trust fund, and thus no reason to include this time during which the trust is so

destructible in determining whether a limitation is violative of the rule against perpetuities. Restatement, Property, sec. 373 states:

> The period of time during which an interest is destructible, pursuant to the uncontrolled volition, and for the exclusive personal benefit of the person having such a power of destruction is not included in determining whether the limitation is invalid under the rule against perpetuities.

We conclude that this rule is a sound one, which does no violence to the rule against perpetuities, but is in complete accord with its aim and purpose.

Does the postponement principle extend to cases other than revocable trusts? Court authority on this question is sparse, if not nonexistent, but the commentators believe that it does. See Simes & Smith on Future Interests § 1252. The Restatement of Property § 373 also declares the principle to be broader: For purposes of the Rule Against Perpetuities, the creation of an interest is postponed so long as the interest "is destructible, pursuant to the uncontrolled volition, and for the exclusive personal benefit of the person having such a power of destruction."

Under this statement of the principle, the power need not be a power to revoke and it need not be held by the settlor or transferor. An *unqualified* and *currently exercisable* power held by *any* person *acting alone* to become the beneficial owner of the questioned interest is sufficient. Accord Restatement 2d of Property § 1.2; UPC § 2-902(b) (USRAP § 2(b)).

An example of a power that should cause a postponement of the time of creation of the remainder interest under the postponement principle would be a presently exercisable general power of appointment over the remainder interest. Another example would be a power, held by any person who could act alone, to invade the corpus of a trust.

Be sure to notice an important consequence of the idea that a power need not be held by the settlor to postpone the time of creation: It makes postponement available even in cases of testamentary transfers.

Example 19.2: G devised property in trust, directing the trustee to pay the income "to A for life, remainder to such persons as A shall appoint; in default of appointment, the property to remain in trust to pay the income to A's children for the life of the survivor, and upon the death of A's last surviving child, to divide the corpus equally among A's grandchildren." A survived G.

If the perpetuity period commences running on G's death, the remainder interest in favor of A's grandchildren is invalid. But if the Restatement view is followed, thus postponing the running of the period to the expiration (at A's death assuming that A does not relinquish the power before death) of A's presently exercisable general power, the interest is valid. The substance of this transaction is the equivalent of G's having devised the property to A in fee simple absolute and of A's having in turn devised the property at his death in accordance with G's gift in default clause. The Restatement view ought therefore to be followed. Note, however, that if G had conferred on A a *nongeneral* power or a general *testamentary* power, the perpetuity period would clearly commence running on G's death, causing the grandchildren's interest to be invalid. For more discussion of powers of appointment, see infra Part E.

Problem

In Year One, G created an irrevocable inter vivos trust, funding it with $20,000 cash. In Year Five, when the value of the investments in which the original $20,000 contribution was placed had risen to a value of $30,000, G added $10,000 cash to the trust. G died in Year Ten. G's will poured the residue of his estate into the trust. G's residuary estate consisted of Blackacre (worth $20,000) and securities (worth $80,000). At G's death, the value of the investments in which the original $20,000 contribution and the subsequent $10,000 contribution were placed had risen to a value of $50,000. G's trust created property interests that are subject to the Rule Against Perpetuities. When are those interests "created" for purposes of determining whether or not they are valid? Cf. UPC § 2-902(c) (USRAP § 2(c)).

The Rule of Convenience. As noted, in determining whether a nonvested property interest is valid or invalid, the facts existing at the creation of the interest are to be taken into account. This refers not only to the facts as such, but also to the rules of law or construction that those facts trigger. A rule of construction that figures prominently in many perpetuity cases is the rule of convenience.

Problems

Determine the validity of the property interests in the following cases:

1. G devised property in trust, directing the trustee to pay the net income therefrom "to A for life, then to A's children for the life of the survivor, and upon the death of A's last surviving child, to pay the corpus of the trust to A's grandchildren." A predeceased G. G was survived by A's two children, X and Y.

2. G devised real property "to such of A's children as attain 25." At G's death, A (who was then alive) had three living children, all of whom were under 25.

3. In Problem 2, suppose that A's eldest child had reached 25 by the time of G's death.

4. G devised real property "to A for life, then to such of A's children as reach 25." A survived G. By the time of G's death, A's eldest child had reached 25.

4. Constructional Preference for Validity

Gray stated that a will or deed is to be construed without regard to the Rule Against Perpetuities, and then the Rule is to be "remorselessly" applied to the provisions so construed. Gray on Perpetuities § 629. Some courts may still adhere to this proposition. See Colorado Nat'l Bank v. McCabe, 353 P.2d 385 (Colo. 1960); Continental Illinois Nat'l Bank & Trust Co. v. Llewellyn, 214 N.E.2d 471 (Ill. App. Ct. 1966).

Most courts, we believe, would now be inclined to adopt the proposition put forward by the Restatement of Property § 375, which is that where an instrument is ambiguous—that is, where it is fairly susceptible to two or more constructions, one of which causes a Rule violation and the other of which does not—the construction that does not result in a Rule violation should be adopted. Cases supporting this view include First Nat'l Bank v. Jenkins, 345 S.E.2d 829 (Ga. 1986); In re Damon, 896 P.2d 1339 (Haw. 1994); Southern Bank & Trust Co. v. Brown, 246 S.E.2d 598 (S.C. 1978); Davis v. Rossi, 34 S.W.2d 8 (Mo. 1930).

Does Rust v. Rust, which follows, also represent an application of the constructional preference for validity?

Rust v. Rust

211 S.W.2d 262 (Tex. Civ. App.), aff'd, 214 S.W.2d 462 (Tex. 1948)

McCLENDON, C.J. Suit to construe the will of John Y. Rust, Jr. The controlling question is whether the provisions of the will disposing of the residuary estate violates Art. I, Sec. 26, Texas Constitution, Vernon's Ann.St., condemning perpetuities. The trial court upheld all provisions of the will, rendered judgment accordingly, and defendant Mrs. Margene Welch Rust, surviving wife of testator, has appealed in her individual capacity, and as guardian of the estate of Margene A. Rust (a minor), the only child of herself and testator.

The pertinent portions of the will (after a $1,000 legacy to Mrs. Rust) read:

> Four. All the remainder of my property of every kind and character, real, personal, mixed or choses in action of which I may die seized or possessed and wheresoever situated, I will, give, devise and bequeath in trust to my executors and trustees hereinafter named and to the survivor thereof and the substitute trustee hereinafter named to hold, manage, use and control for the use and benefit of my daughter, Margene A. Rust.

> The property here left for the use and benefit of my daughter, Margene, shall be held in trust by my trustees, the survivor thereof and the substitute trustee until the 17th day of October, 1967, upon which date the trust shall terminate and the property here left in trust shall vest in fee simple in my daughter, Margene A. Rust, free of any restrictions whatsoever.
>
> If my daughter, Margene A. Rust, dies before October 17, 1967, the date upon which the trust herein created terminates, and leaves surviving her issue of her body, then such issue of her body shall become the beneficiary or beneficiaries of this trust and upon the date of its termination the fee simple title to all the property here left in trust shall vest share and share alike in such issue of her body then surviving.
>
> If my daughter, Margene A. Rust, dies before October 17, 1967, the date upon which the trust herein created terminates and does not leave surviving her any issue of her body, then upon her death, all of the property here left in trust shall pass in fee simple share and share alike unto my then living brothers and sister with the child or children of any brother or sister who then may be deceased, taking the share of the parent per stirpes . . . .

Testator's two brothers George Foster and Armistead Dudley Rust were named independent executors without bond. They, and the survivor of them, were also named as trustees; a bank in San Angelo was named substitute trustee.

The facts are without dispute. They show:

John Y. Rust, Jr., died May 6, 1942. His will was probated May 26, 1942, and his executors promptly qualified and took charge of his estate. His only heirs at law were his surviving wife and daughter. His father, John Y. Rust, Sr., was living. His mother, Agnes B. Rust, died in 1941. The only other children of his father and mother were the two brothers and a sister, Sarah Agnes Rust Gordon. George Foster Rust was married to Minnie Rust. They had no children. Armistead Dudley Rust was married to Sarah J. Rust. They had one child, Nancy Rust, a minor. Mrs. Gordon's husband was Charles R. Gordon. Their only child was a daughter, Jean, married to Charles R. Rainey. Her only child was a three-month old son.

Testator's estate consisted principally of a 1/4 undivided interest in ranch lands—20,394.9 acres in Kimble County, known as Bear Creek Ranch, and 20,895.1 acres in Tom Green County, known as Campbell Ranch. His interest therein was appraised at $116,284.44. The rest of his estate was personalty, appraised at $10,533.05. His total indebtedness was listed at $81,547.75, $73,520.75 of which was in a note to his father for advances to cover excessive living expenses, secured by trust deed upon his interest in the two ranch properties. Net value of his estate was appraised at $45,289.94. The other 3/4 interest in these ranches was owned by his brothers and sister. We give these details regarding his family and estate for whatever light they may shed upon a proper interpretation of the will.

The executors have paid Mrs. Rust's legacy; have renewed the trust deed (now held by a bank); and together with the other joint owners have executed two oil and gas leases upon the ranch properties.

The suit was brought by the two brothers, as executors and trustees, as well as individually, joined in by all the other contingent beneficiaries under the will and the owner of the mineral leases, against Margene W. Rust, individually and as guardian of Margene A. Rust, and against the latter individually. In view of a possible conflict of interest between Margene W. Rust and her ward, the court appointed a guardian ad litem for the latter, who sought to uphold the will, and appears here as an appellee in support of the judgment. . . .

Since, on May 6, 1942 (the date of testator's death) it was within the range of possibilities that Margene A. Rust (born October 17, 1932) might die before October 17, 1946, (21 years prior to the termination of the trust period) and leave a surviving child, the controlling issue is whether, on the one hand, her interest in the property constituted a vested (base) fee subject to defeasance in case of her death prior to October 17, 1967, or, on the other hand, no title would vest in her unless and until she was living on that date. Stated differently, the issue is whether (a) her living until October 17, 1946, constitutes a condition precedent to the vesting of any title in her (appellants' contention), or (b) her death prior to that date constitutes a condition subsequent divesting the title vested in her as of the date of her father's death. . . .

It is, of course, essential to immediate vesting (possession or enjoyment being postponed) that the person to take be presently in existence and of certain identity. See 2 A.L.I. Rest. Property, § 157, com. q. And it is also well established that the fact that the legal title is vested in trustees, with full discretion as to the application of the income or corpus to the uses of the beneficiary during the trust period, does not militate against the immediate vesting of the beneficial (equitable) title in the beneficiary. . . .

Furthermore, if the beneficial title vested in Margene A. Rust, "it is immaterial that full possession and enjoyment of the property is postponed beyond the period of a life or lives in being and 21 years thereafter with the ordinary period of gestation added." Anderson v. Menefee [Tex. Civ. App., 174 S.W. 907]. . . .

Applying these rules to the bequest to Margene A. Rust, clearly and without substantial doubt, we think, the fee title to the residuary estate vested in her immediately upon the death of her father, defeasible upon the condition subsequent of her death prior to October 17, 1967, and subject to the trust provisions.

The first paragraph of clause Four, standing alone, would vest a fee simple absolute title in her, subject to the trust, since in so many words it unconditionally vests the legal title in the trustees for her "use and benefit." The second paragraph puts a time limit for the duration of the trust, upon expiration of which her title is to be "free of any restrictions whatsoever." The language, "the trust shall terminate and the property . . . shall vest in fee simple in" her, "free of any restrictions whatsoever," is not reasonably susceptible of the construction that her title had not theretofore vested but was to vest initially as of that date. The words, "free of any restrictions whatsoever," can have no other meaning than that her title should thenceforth be free of the restrictions imposed by the trust, otherwise they would be pure surplusage. The vesting at that time was to be free of these restrictions. Even without this last clause, the language employed is that usually found in instruments creating remainders universally held to be vested, and not contingent. A devise by A to B for life with remainder at his death to C creates a vested remainder in C upon the death of A, subject to B's life estate. The use of "at his death" or words of similar import denote the time when the right of possession and enjoyment of the estate begins, and not the time when the estate in remainder vests.

The third and fourth paragraphs are clearly conditional clauses of defeasance, and as such conditions subsequent. The remaining paragraphs merely detail the powers and duties of the trustees. We find nothing in the language of the will, "read as an entirety and in the light of the circumstances of its formulation," which would call for a construction other than that the contingency of the daughter's dying before October 17, 1967, constituted a condition subsequent divesting her title, and that her living until then was not a condition precedent to its vesting. . . .

The fourth clause vests the fee simple title in the named contingent remaindermen immediately upon the death of the daughter prior to October 17, 1967, without bodily issue. Under no possible contingency could this paragraph create a perpetuity.

The third is the only paragraph which presents any constructional doubt. A doubt which we resolve in favor of a vested remainder upon the death of the daughter prior to October 17, 1967, leaving bodily issue, for reasons we now discuss.

The general plan of the testator seems clear. His primary solicitude was for his daughter, his only child. His principal estate was in extensive ranch property, held in undivided interests, and heavily incumbered. To preserve the estate to his daughter would necessitate wise business management over an extended period of years. He fixed this period as terminating on the daughter's 35th birthday. For obvious reasons he intrusted this management to his two brothers, who owned 2/3 of the remaining interest in the property. The only limitations imposed upon the daughter's otherwise complete fee simple title to the property were (1) the trust provisions which merely postponed her possession and untrammeled enjoyment of the property, and (2) defeasance of her title upon the contingency of her death during the trust period.

His secondary solicitude, should this contingency eventuate, was for his daughter's "bodily heirs", if any, giving them the identical status with reference to the property as that of his daughter. He substitutes them as beneficiaries of the trust and vests complete title at the end of the trust period. The same considerations favoring immediate vesting in the bodily issue and continuing the trust exist in this contingency as originally as to the daughter's title. The considerations as to the trust provisions would not apply in the contingency of the daughter's death without bodily issue.

The only doubt cast upon this immediate vesting is the use of the word "then" before the last word "surviving." In addition to the presumption of early vesting of title, and the general scheme of the testator, there are other considerations which favor construing "then" as referring to the death of the daughter and not the termination of the trust. "Issue of her body," we think, were clearly used in the sense of "children." This appears from use of the words, "share and share alike." As said by the great Oran M. Roberts, in the leading case of Hancock v. Butler, 21 Tex. 804:

> It is presumed it would be difficult to find one case where a man had expressly given his property, to all his descendants, to take per capita—children, grandchildren, great-grandchildren, etc. The general sense of American mind, as exhibited in deeds, wills, and in statutes of descent and distribution, is that it is proper to give property to children, grandchildren, etc., they taking per stirpes.

The possibility of the daughter having any grandchild, the child of a deceased child, prior to 1967, was exceedingly remote.

Another applicable presumption is that against intestacy. "A construction which would render the decedent intestate as to any part of his estate is not favored." 44 Tex. Jur., p. 707, § 148. In case of the death of the daughter before October 17, 1967, leaving a surviving child or children, all of whom including any descendants should die prior to that date, there would be no one to take under the will, if the title had not previously vested in the daughter's "bodily heirs." The only other limitation over (par. 4) was contingent exclusively upon the daughter's dying before October 17, 1967, without leaving any "issue of her body."

Additionally, it is well settled that: ". . . the rule against perpetuities is a rule of property and not one of construction; and where the instrument is capable of two constructions, "one of which would give effect to the whole . . . and the other result in defeating (it) . . . , in whole or in part, preference will be accorded to the construction which will uphold" it. 41 Am.Jur., p. 58, § 12. . . .

If, however, we be mistaken in this construction, and the limitation over to the bodily heirs of the daughter is void as creating a perpetuity, the other provisions of the will would not thereby be affected. In that case the title of the daughter would be defeasible only in case of her death before October 17, 1967, without leaving any heir of her body. A.L.I. Rest. Property, § 229, com. e. Under this construction the surviving bodily heirs of the daughter would take the same title from her by inheritance that they would under the will, construed as valid, subject only to the contingency that the daughter should make no different disposition by will, or otherwise part with her title. . . .

The trial court's judgment is affirmed.

5. Consequences Of Invalidity

When an interest is invalid because it violates the common-law Rule Against Perpetuities, the invalid interest is stricken from the disposition. Unless the doctrine of infectious invalidity applies, see infra p. 1193, the other interests created by the disposition (assuming that none of them violates the Rule) take effect as if the invalid interest had never been created.

Example 19.3: G devised real property "to A for life, then to A's children for the life of the survivor, and upon the death of A's last surviving child, to A's grandchildren." G devised her residuary estate to her husband, H.

Due to the invalidity of the remainder to A's grandchildren, the disposition reads as if *that* remainder interest had never been created: "to A for life, then to A's children for the life of the survivor." Since G's devise did not validly dispose of all interests in the parcel of real property, the undisposed-of interest passes under G's residuary clause to H. This testamentary transfer of the remainder interest to H is deemed to have occurred at G's death. Thus when A's last surviving child dies, the property goes to H (or H's successor in interest).

Note that if G's original devise had been in her residuary clause, the undisposed-of interest would have been intestate property and would have passed at G's death to her heirs at law.

Example 19.4: G devised real property "to A for life, then for life to such of A's children as reach 25, then to B."

The remainder for life to A's children is invalid. The effect of striking it is not to create a gap that must be filled by the residuary clause. Rather it is to accelerate B's remainder: The devise now reads "to A for life, then to B."

In preparation for reading the *Brown* decision, below, consider again the *Grant* and *Boland* cases, supra Chapter 17, Part B.

Brown v. Independent Baptist Church

91 N.E.2d 922 (Mass. 1950)

QUA, C.J. The object of this suit in equity, originally brought in this court, is to determine the ownership of a parcel of land in Woburn and the persons entitled to share in the proceeds of its sale by a receiver.

Sarah Converse died seised of the land on July 19, 1849, leaving a will in which she specifically devised it

> to the Independent Baptist Church of Woburn, to be holden and enjoyed by them so long as they shall maintain and promulgate their present religious belief and faith and shall continue a Church; and if the said Church shall be dissolved, or if its religious sentiments shall be changed or abandoned, then my will is that this real estate shall go to my legatees hereinafter named, to be divided in equal portions between them. And my will further is, that if my beloved husband, Jesse Converse, shall survive me, that then this devise to the aforesaid Independent Church of Woburn, shall not take effect till from and after his decease; and that so long as he shall live he may enjoy and use the said real estate, and take the rents and profits thereof to his own use.

Then followed ten money legacies in varying amounts to different named persons, after which there was a residuary clause in these words,

> The rest and residue of my estate I give and bequeath to my legatees above named, saving and except therefrom the Independent Baptist Church; this devise to take effect from and after the decease of my husband; I do hereby direct and will that he shall have the use and this rest and residue during his life.

The husband of the testatrix died in 1864. The church named by the testatrix ceased to "continue a church" on October 19, 1939.

The parties apparently are in agreement, and the single justice ruled, that the estate of the church in the land was a determinable fee. We concur. The estate was a fee, since it might last forever, but it was not an absolute fee, since it might (and did) "automatically expire upon the occurrence of a stated event." Restatement: Property, § 44. It is also conceded, and was ruled, that the specific executory devise over to the persons "hereinafter named" as legatees was void for remoteness. The reason is . . . that the determinable fee might not come to an end until long after any life or lives in being and twenty-one years, and in theory at least might never come to an end, and for an indefinite period no clear title to the entire estate could be given.

Since the limitation over failed, it next becomes our duty to consider what became of the possibility of reverter which under our decisions remained after the failure of the limitation. First Universalist Society of North Adams v. Boland, 155 Mass. 171, 175, 29 N.E. 524, 15 L.R.A. 231 [supra Chapter 17,

Part B]; Restatement: Property, § 228, illustration 2, and Appendix to Volume II, at pages 35-36, including note 2. A possibility of reverter seems, by the better authority, to be assignable inter vivos (Restatement: Property, § 159) and must be at least as readily devisable as the other similar reversionary interest known as a right of entry for condition broken, which is devisable, though not assignable. It follows that the possibility of reverter passed under the residuary clause of the will to the same persons designated in the invalid executory devise. It is of no consequence that the persons designated in the two provisions were the same. The same result must be reached as if they were different.

The single justice ruled that the residuary clause was void for remoteness, apparently for the same reason that rendered the executory devise void. With this we cannot agree, since we consider it settled that the rule against perpetuities does not apply to reversionary interests of this general type, including possibilities of reverter. Proprietors of the Church in Brattle Square v. Grant, 3 Gray, 142, 148, 63 Am. Dec. 725 [supra Chapter 17, Part B]; First Universalist Society of North Adams v. Boland, 155 Mass. 171, 175-176, 29 N.E. 524, 15 L.R.A. 231 [supra Chapter 17, Part B]; Restatement: Property, § 372. See Gray, Rule Against Perpetuities, 4th Ed., §§ 41, 312, 313. For a full understanding of the situation here presented it is necessary to keep in mind the fundamental difference in character between the attempted executory devise to the legatees later named in the will and the residuary gift to the same persons. The executory devise was in form and substance an attempt to limit or create a new future interest which might not arise or vest in anyone until long after the permissible period. It was obviously not intended to pass such a residuum of the testatrix's existing estate as a possibility of reverter, and indeed if the executory devise had been valid according to its terms the whole estate would have passed from the testatrix and no possibility of reverter could have been left to her or her devisees. The residuary devise, on the other hand, was in terms and purpose exactly adapted to carry any interest which might otherwise remain in the testatrix, whether or not she had it in mind or knew it would exist.

We cannot accept the contention made in behalf of Mrs. Converse's heirs that the words of the residuary clause "saving and except therefrom the Independent Baptist Church" were meant to exclude from the operation of that clause any possible rights in the land previously given to the church. We construe these words as intended merely to render the will consistent by excluding the church which also had been "above named" from the list of "legatees" who were to take the residue.

The interlocutory decree entered December 16, 1947, is reversed, and a new decree is to be entered providing that the land in question or the proceeds of any sale thereof by the receiver shall go to the persons named as legatees in the will, other than the Independent Baptist Church of Woburn, or their successors in interest. Further proceedings are to be in accord with the new decree. Costs and expenses are to be at the discretion of the single justice.

So ordered.

Question and Problem

1. *Criticism of Brown.* The *Brown* decision has been criticized on the ground that the testator "did not die twice." Lewis M. Simes, Is the Rule Against Perpetuities Doomed?, 52 Mich. L. Rev. 179 n.4 (1953). What is Simes' point?

2. *Problem.* G devised real property "to A for life, remainder to A's children, but if none of A's children reaches 25, to B." G was survived by A, who had two children, X and Y, neither of whom had reached 25 at G's death. What is the consequence of the invalidity of B's executory interest?

Infectious Invalidity. In appropriate cases, the invalidity of an interest may, under the *doctrine of infectious invalidity*, be held to invalidate one or more otherwise valid interests created by the disposition, or even invalidate the entire will. The question turns on whether the general dispositive scheme of the transferor will be better carried out by elimination of only the invalid interest or by elimination of other interests as well.

This is a question that must be answered on a case by case basis. Several items are relevant to the question, including who takes the stricken interests in place of those designated to take by the transferor. Some jurisdictions have become noted for a greater willingness to apply infectious invalidity than others. See Simes & Smith on Future Interests § 1262; Am. L. Prop. § 24.48 et seq.; Restatement of Property § 402.

6. Separability

When an interest is expressly subject to alternative contingencies, the courts treat the situation as if two interests were created in the same person or class, so that the invalidity of one of the interests does not invalidate the other. This principle was established in Longhead v. Phelps, 2 Wm. Bl. 704, 96 Eng. Rep. 414 (K.B. 1770), and has been followed in this country. See Simes & Smith on Future Interests § 1257; Am. L. Prop. § 24.54; Restatement of Property § 376.

To illustrate, suppose property is devised "to B if X-event or Y-event happens." B in effect has two interests, one contingent on X-event happening and the other contingent on Y-event happening. If X-event might occur too remotely, the consequence of separating B's interest into two is that only one of them, the one contingent on X-event, is invalid. B still has a valid interest—the one contingent on the occurrence of Y-event. Another way of viewing it is to say that the invalid contingency is stricken or excised. Thus the devise is altered to read "to B if Y-event happens." The following examples further illustrate this principle.

> *Example 19.5:* G devised real property "to A for life, then to such of A's children as survive her and reach 25, but if none of A's children survives her or if none of A's children who survives her reaches 25, then to B."
>
> B takes only if none of A's children survives A; his interest that is contingent on that event is valid. If one or more of A's children survives A, B cannot take even if none of them lives to 25. B's interest that is contingent on none of A's surviving children reaching 25 is invalid. The language "or if none of A's children who survive him reaches 25" is in effect stricken from the devise.
>
> The interest of A's children is invalid and replaced by a reversion.

The principle of separability is applicable only when the transferor has *expressly* stated the contingencies in the alternative. Where alternative contingencies are merely implicit, no separation will be recognized. See Proctor v. Bishop of Bath and Wells, 2 H. Bl. 358, 126 Eng. Rep. 594 (C.P. 1794).

> *Example 19.6:* G devised real property "to A for life, then to such of A's children as survive him and reach 25, but if none of A's children does so, then to B."
>
> B has only one interest, and it is invalid. B cannot take even if none of A's children survives A.

PART B. MODERN POLICY OF THE RULE AGAINST PERPETUITIES

Lewis M. Simes, The Policy Against Perpetuities[7]

103 U. Pa. L. Rev. 707, 708, 710, 712-15, 721-24 (1955)

What public policy actuates this rule? If we are to content ourselves with the terse and sometimes superficial pronouncements on the subject scattered through the books, the policy of the Rule has never been in doubt. Ever since it first emerged in the *Duke of Norfolk's Case*, it has been declared to be a rule in furtherance of the alienability of property. . . . [I]f it were not for this Rule, property would be unproductive and society would have less income.

But why should a future interest make property inalienable, and why does inalienability make property unproductive? In answering these questions we must recall that the Rule against Perpetuities developed as a rule restricting future interests in specific land. Viewed thus, the rationale of the Rule is not

7. Also published in Lewis M. Simes, Public Policy and the Dead Hand (1955).

difficult to perceive. In order to make a profit from land, one must have a type of ownership which insures enjoyment forever or for a fixed and determinable period of time. People who purchase land, whether for profit or for their own use and enjoyment, are not likely to buy unless they can secure either a fee simple absolute or a lease for a fixed term of years. . . .

Now, if the policy of the Rule against Perpetuities is to make property productive, just how far is this policy advanced in the application of the Rule today? Is property still taken out of commerce by remote contingent future interests? *I believe it is no exaggeration to say that, at the present time, due to changes both in the nature of capital investments and in the law, the proposition that contingent future interests make property unproductive is rarely true in the United States and almost never true in England.* I should like to discuss at some length my reasons for this belief.

In the first place, the future interest with which the Rule against Perpetuities is concerned is nearly always an equitable interest in a trust. The modern trust instrument, if well drawn, will contain broad powers of sale and reinvestment. While the beneficiary who has an equitable estate subject to a future interest may have difficulty in selling his property, that does not make it unproductive. As a practical matter, the trustee will have an absolute legal estate which he can sell, and will be empowered to reinvest the proceeds. While at one time in the history of the law, in the absence of express authorization in the trust instrument, the trustee's powers of reinvestments were extremely limited, today the rapidly extending "prudent man rule" gives the trustee a wide field of selection in making trust investments productive.

Moreover, not only is the trustee empowered by the terms of any well-drawn trust instrument to sell and reinvest in productive property; the law requires him to do so. One of the duties imposed by law upon trustees is to use reasonable care in making the trust property productive.

Suppose, however, that the trust instrument is not well drawn, and no express powers of alienation are given to the trustee. Still the trust property is not necessarily taken out of commerce. The law recognizes that, when circumstances change in a matter unforeseen by the settlor, the trustee may secure permission of the court to sell. . . .

Statutes in several states have gone even further in permitting the trustee to sell and reinvest in the absence of a power to do so expressed in the trust instrument. . . .

Of course, it must be recognized that, so far as the common law is concerned, it is perfectly clear that the existence of a power in a trustee to sell and reinvest does not take the case out of the Rule against Perpetuities. Though courts have rarely discussed the position . . . when they have done so, they have generally dismissed the matter without adequate rationalization.

There is a second reason why future interests do not make property unproductive. Not only is there commonly a power of sale in a trustee where future interests arise in American family settlements; the subject matter of the trust is commonly corporate shares and government or corporate bonds. In the case of corporate shares, the economic value is neither in the interest owned by the beneficiary of the trust, nor is it in the shares in the hand of the trustees. It is the property of the corporation. Certainly that is freely alienable. . . .

There is, moreover, a third situation where, according to American law, the existence of future interests does not render property unproductive. Let us assume that somewhat unusual case where the trust device is not used, and legal future interests in land are created. A devises a particular piece of land to B for life, remainder to B's issue who survive him, in fee simple. Beginning with the case of Bofl v. Fisher,[8] decided in 1850, the American courts have developed a doctrine to this effect: where land is affected with a future interest, a court of equity has power to order a sale and to set up a trust in the proceeds, when this is necessary for the preservation of all interests in the land. . . .

If alienability for purposes of productivity is not the justification of the modern Rule against Perpetuities, then what is the public policy which justifies it?

Before suggesting what I believe to be the true answer, I should like to take a moment to mention two other explanations of the Rule which are sometimes made. First, it is said that the Rule is designed to prevent an undue concentration of wealth in the hands of a few. Professor Leach has indicated that the Rule is intended to remove the "threat to the public welfare from family dynasties built either on great landed estates or on great capital wealth." But, as he points out, that threat is rather effectively removed by our income and estate taxes. I am disposed to agree with him. Indeed, I feel that undue concentration of wealth is an evil which can best be combated by tax legislation, rather than by perpetuity rules.

A second reason sometimes given for the Rule is as follows: it is socially undesirable for some members of society to have assured incomes and be protected from the economic struggle for existence; the principle of survival of the fittest should apply, so that those who are unable to maintain themselves in the economic struggle for existence should not survive. The American Law Institute, without giving its blessing to this particular rationale, states it as follows: "It is obvious that limitations unalterably effective over a long period of time would hamper the normal operation of the competitive struggle. Persons

---

8. 3 Rich. Eq. 1 (S.C. 1850). [See also Am. L. Prop. §§ 4.98-.99; Simes & Smith on Future Interests §§ 1941-46; Lewis M. Simes & Clarence B. Taylor, Improvement of Conveyancing by Legislation 235-38 (1960); Restatement of Property § 179 at pp. 485-95. Eds.]

less fit, less keen in the social struggle, might be thereby enabled to retain property disproportionate to their skills in the competitive struggle." Several answers may be made to this argument. The Rule against Perpetuities does permit economic provision for the unfit for one generation, indeed for one generation and during the minority of the next. It would seem almost as bad to permit this sort of thing for the first generation as for succeeding generations. If it be answered that there is a social objection to the continuation of a line of weaklings, the answer is that a restriction on the tying up of property does not eliminate that objection. Modern society, with its elaborate welfare machinery, is not organized on a theory of survival of the fittest, but of survival of the weak. Moreover, if human experience means anything, we may well conclude that the progeny of weaklings are likely to be more numerous in a state of poverty than in a state of wealth.

Thus I believe that neither of these explanations for the Rule is adequate. There are in my opinion, however, two other bases for the social policy of the Rule, the force of which can scarcely be denied.

First, the Rule against Perpetuities strikes a fair balance between the desires of members of the present generation, and similar desires of succeeding generations, to do what they wish with the property which they enjoy. It is almost axiomatic that one of the most common human wants is the desire to distribute one's property at death without restriction in whatever manner he desires. Indeed, we can go farther and say that there is a policy in favor of permitting people to create future interests by will, as well as present interests, because that also accords with human desires. The difficulty here is that, if we give free rein to the desires of one generation to create future interests, the members of succeeding generations will receive the property in a restricted state. They will thus be unable to create all the future interests they wish. Perhaps, they may not even be able to devise it at all. Hence, to come most nearly to satisfying the desires of peoples of all generations, we must strike a fair balance between unrestricted testamentary disposition of property by the present generation and unrestricted disposition by future generations. In a sense this is a policy of alienability, but it is not alienability for productivity. It is alienability to enable people to do what they please at death with the property which they enjoy in life. As Kohler says in his treatise on the philosophy of law: "The far-reaching hand of a testator who would enforce his will in distant future generations destroys the liberty of other individuals, and presumes to make rules for distant times."

But, in my opinion, a second and even more important reason for the Rule is this: it is socially desirable that the wealth of the world be controlled by its living members and not by the dead. I know of no better statement of that doctrine than the language of Thomas Jefferson, contained in a letter to James

Madison, when he said: "The earth belongs always to the living generation. They may manage it then, and what proceeds from it, as they please, during their usufruct." Sidgwick, in his *Elements of Politics*, also discusses the problem in the following words: "... it rather follows from the fundamental assumption of individualism, that any such posthumous restraint on the use of bequeathed wealth will tend to make it less useful to the living, as it will interfere with their freedom in dealing with it. Individualism, in short, is in a dilemma. . . . Of this difficulty there is, I think, no general theoretical solution: it can only be reduced by some practical compromise."

EXTERNAL REFERENCE. For a critique of Professor Simes's argument, see T.P. Gallanis, The Rule Against Perpetuities and the Law Commission's Flawed Philosophy, 59 Camb. L. J. 284 (2000).

The Know-and-See Theory. Professor Simes said that the Rule "strikes a fair balance between the desires of members of the present generation, and similar desires of succeeding generations, to do what they wish with the property which they enjoy." Where, specifically, is that "fair balance" to be drawn?

Hobhouse suggested a know-and-see theory: "A clear, obvious, natural line is drawn for us between those persons and events which the Settlor knows and sees, and those which he cannot know or see." Sir A. Hobhouse, The Dead Hand 188 (1880).

Leach and Tudor expanded on the know-and-see test:

> The Rule against Perpetuities came into being as a means of preventing inordinate family pride from tying up the soil of England in a manner which would produce undesirable economic and social consequences. In establishing the balance between private right and public interest the courts arrived at a solution which permitted the following: . . . In a will a man of property could provide for all of those in his family whom he personally knew and the first generation after them upon attaining majority.

W. Barton Leach & Owen Davies Tudor, The Common Law Rule Against Perpetuities, in Am. L. Prop. § 24.16, at 51. The authors went on to muse that it might have been better if the tack-on, 21-year part of the period were not a period in gross, but instead were treated like the period of gestation—allowed only if needed to take account of an actual minority. The fact is, however, that it is now beyond dispute that the tack-on, 21-year part of the period is a period in gross; that point was settled long ago in Cadell v. Palmer, 1 Cl. & F. 372, 6 Eng. Rep. 956 (1833).

Professor Waggoner has suggested a further refinement of the theory:

> [T]he [know-and-see] standard [arguably means] that donors should be allowed to exert control through the youngest generation of descendants they knew and saw, or at least one or more but not necessarily all of whom they knew and saw. . . .

Lawrence W. Waggoner, The Uniform Statutory Rule Against Perpetuities, 21 Real Prop. Prob. & Tr. J. 569, 587 (1986). Professor Waggoner went on to suggest that the tack-on, 21-year part of the period performs a desirable function, especially in a wait-and-see system (see infra Part D), for it allows the inclusion of the afterborn members of a generation with respect to which one or more members were "in being"—known and seen by G—at the creation of the interest.

To help us think about and visualize the "know-and-see" theory in action, we think it is useful to present the following charts of four hypothetical four-generation families.[9] Each family is a rather typical two-child family.[10] In each case, G has two children, A and B, four grandchildren (V, X, Y, and Z), eight great-grandchildren (K, L, M, N, P, Q, R, and S), and so on.[11] G's descending line looks the same in each family, as follows:

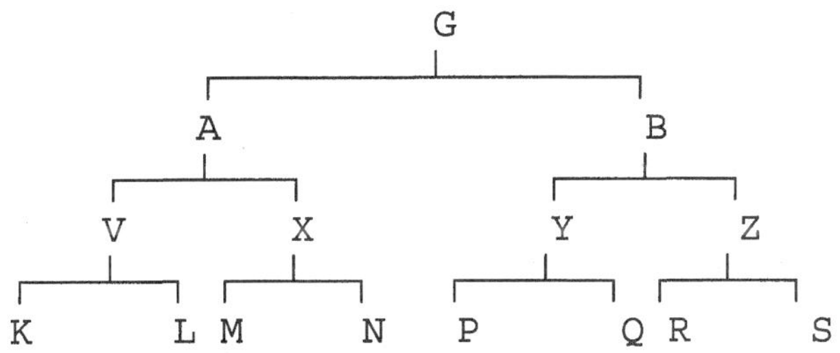

The families differ from one another on when child-bearing takes place. In Family I, the children are born when the parents are 20 and 25, respectively; in Family II, the parents are 25 and 30 when their children are born; in Family III, the parents are 30 and 35; and in Family IV, childbearing has been deferred until the parents are 35 and 40.

We make no claim that these hypothetical families are frequently duplicated in real life; they are too symmetrical. Nevertheless, in various combinations, and taking due account of the fact that the number of offspring and the timing

---

9. Four-generation families are not unusual. See supra Chapter 1, Part B.

10. Census Bureau statistics on fertility rates indicate an average number of children per woman of about 2.04. This is down from the average of 2.48 in 1970 and considerably down from 3.45 in 1960-64. See U.S. Bureau of the Census, Statistical Abstract of the United States: 1999, table 96, at 78 (119th ed. 1999).

11. For the sake of simplicity, the charts do not depict G's spouse or the spouses of G's descendants.

of childbearing will vary widely from one family to another and within the same family at each generation and from one descending line to another, we believe that these hypothetical families do, in the aggregate, sufficiently resemble actual families to make the charts illuminating for our purposes.

We present these charts now, and will frequently refer to them as we proceed, for a straightforward reason: As courts and others get absorbed with atypical postcreation events, we think that typical postcreation events should not be ignored.

FAMILY I: PARENTS ARE 20 AND 25 WHEN CHILDREN ARE BORN

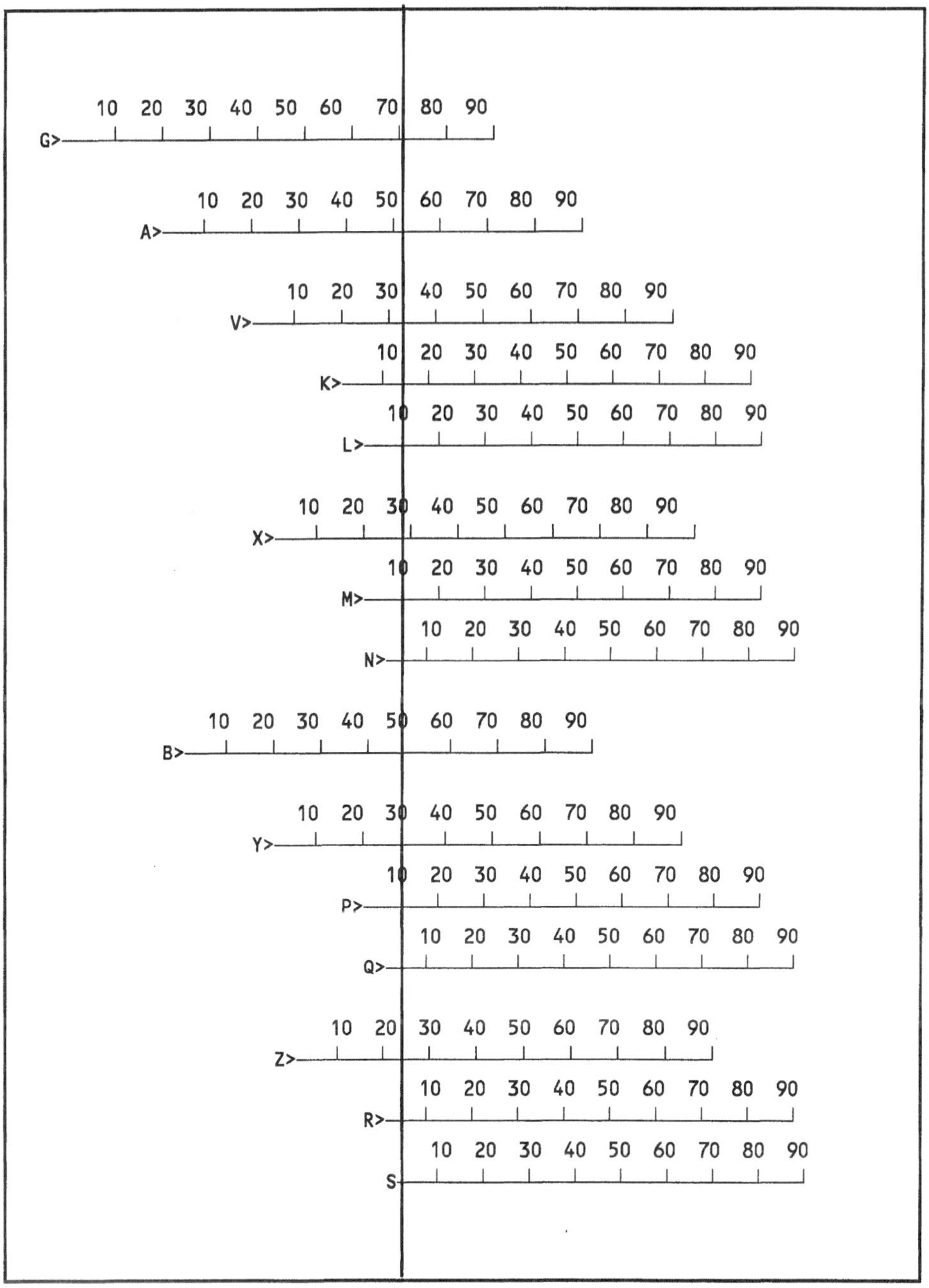

FAMILY II: PARENTS ARE 25 AND 30 WHEN CHILDREN ARE BORN

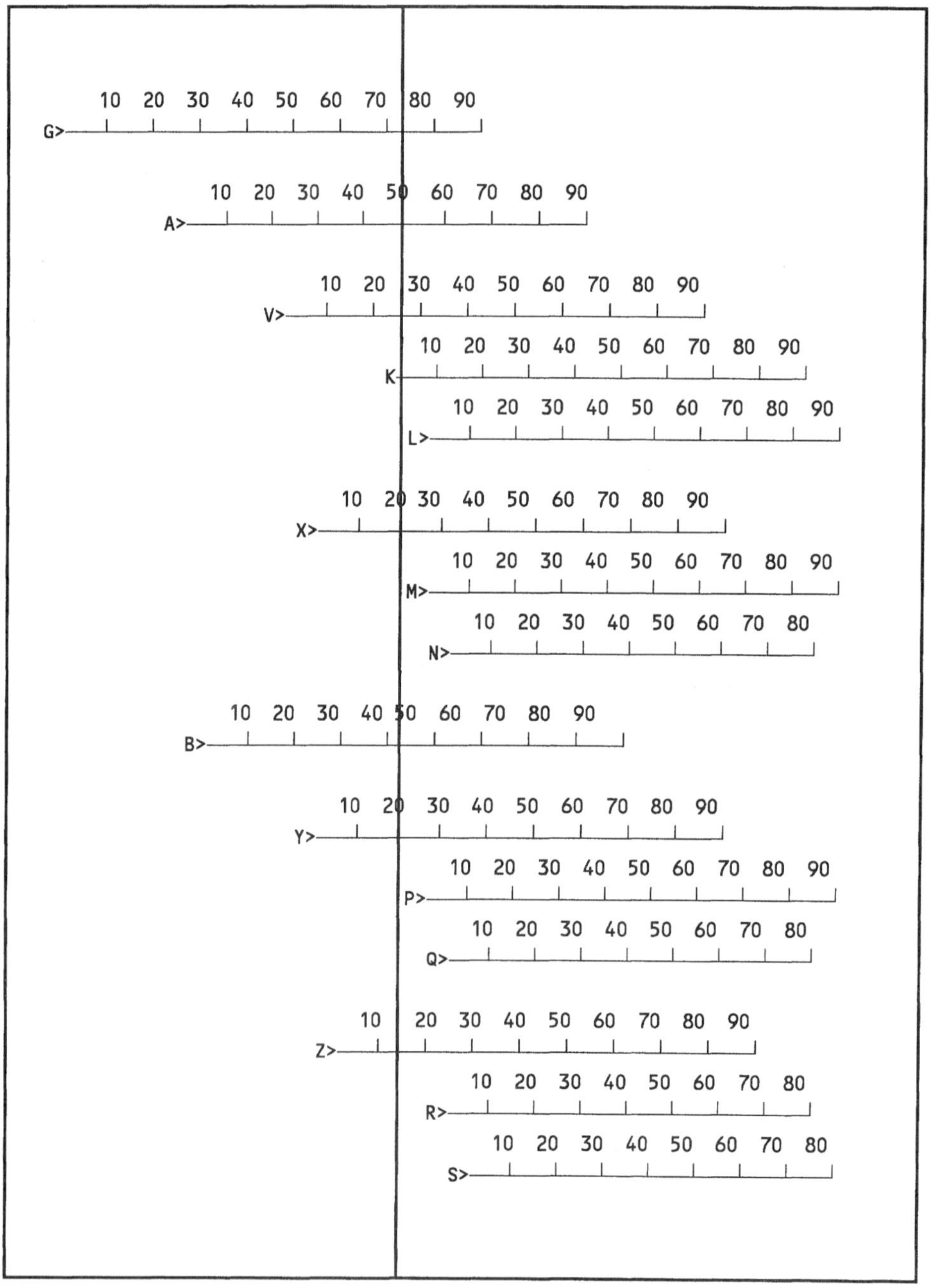

FAMILY III: PARENTS ARE 30 AND 35 WHEN CHILDREN ARE BORN

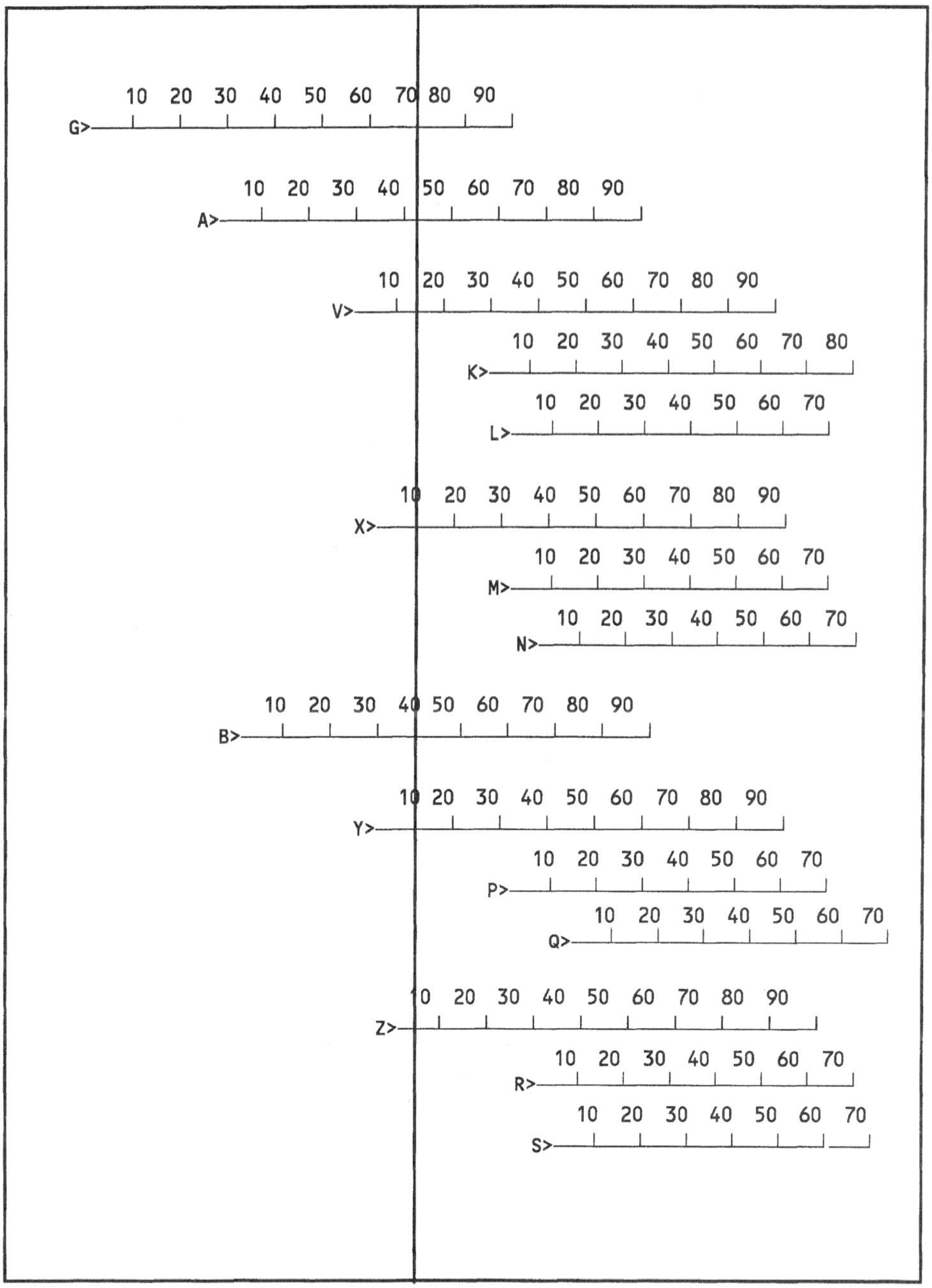

FAMILY IV: PARENTS ARE 35 AND 40 WHEN CHILDREN ARE BORN

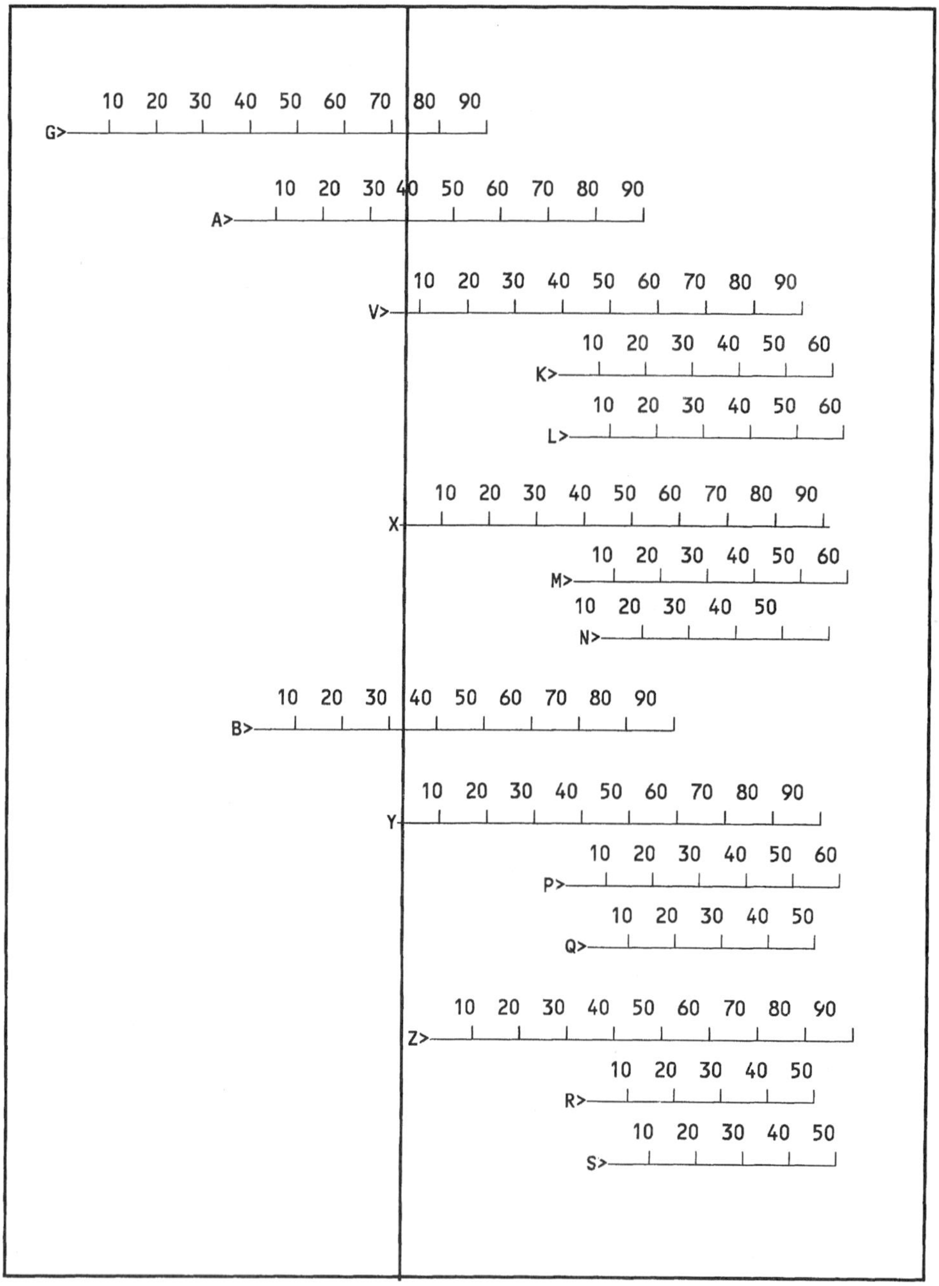

In thinking about the significance of these four charts as they relate to the idea that—in policy—the Rule Against Perpetuities should allow donors to tie up their property through the youngest generation of descendants that the donors knew and saw, keep in mind that statistical life expectancy has now reached a little over 75 years, on average.[12] As shown by the vertical line drawn on each chart, G's hypothesized death at age 75 would mean that the youngest descendant G will have known and seen—the youngest descendant "in being" at G's death, and thus the youngest descendant potentially qualifying as a measuring or validating life for purposes of the Rule Against Perpetuities—is a newborn great-grandchild (S) in Family I, a newborn great-grandchild (K) in Family II, a 5-year-old grandchild (Z) in Family III, and a pair of newborn grandchildren (X and Y) in Family IV. Notice, too, that for G's youngest descendant in being at G's death to be a child, rather than a grandchild or more remote descendant, G would have to die prematurely—35 or more years prematurely in Family I, 25 or more years prematurely in Family II, 15 or more years prematurely in Family III, and 5 or more years prematurely in Family IV.

Technical Violations of the Rule. How well is the "fair balance"—the "know-and-see" theory—actually served by the common-law Rule Against Perpetuities? In thinking about this question, observe that the requirement of initial certainty makes validity dependent on the full array of *possible* postcreation events, not on the events that *actually* happen. In the world of the common-law Rule, every chain of possible postcreation events that can be imagined, no matter how fanciful, is taken seriously—even those that have become impossible by the time of the lawsuit. As stated by Sir Lloyd Kenyon, the Master of the Rolls, in the immensely influential case of Jee v. Audley, 1 Cox 324, 29 Eng. Rep. 1186 (Ch. 1787):

> Another thing pressed upon me, is to decide on the events which have happened; but I cannot do this without overturning very many cases. The single question before me is, not whether the limitation is good in the events which have happened, but whether it was good in its creation; and if it were not, I cannot make it so.

---

12. A dramatic rise in life expectancy has occurred across this century. In 1900, life expectancy at birth was 47 years; in 1910 it was 50 years; in 1930 it was 60 years; and in 1970 it reached 70 years. (The low life expectancies in the earlier half of this century were primarily caused by a high rate of infant mortality, which has now dramatically declined.) Since 1970, life expectancy has been inching up rather more slowly. Recent figures show that it reached 75.1 years in 1989 and 76.5 years in 1997 and is projected to be 76.9 in 2005 (80.2 for women, 73.5 for men). See U.S. Bureau of the Census, Statistical Abstract of the United States: 1999, table 127, at 93 (119th ed. 1999); U.S. Bureau of the Census, Statistical Abstract of the United States: 1990, tables 103, 106, at 72, 74 (110th ed. 1990); U.S. Bureau of the Census, Historical Statistics of the United States, table B107-115, at 55 (part 1, 1975). For the sake of arithmetic simplicity, we use 75 as the life expectancy of our transferor, G.

Translation: A *single* chain of imagined events that can postpone vesting (or termination) beyond a life in being plus 21 years spoils the transferor's disposition.

In consequence of the requirement of initial certainty, validity is withheld from interests that are likely to, and in fact would (if given the chance), vest well within the period of a life in being plus 21 years. Reasonable dispositions can be rendered invalid because of exceedingly remote possibilities, such as women who have passed the menopause giving birth to (or adopting) additional children, married individuals in their middle or late years later remarrying persons who were born after the transfers, or the probate of estates taking more than 21 years to complete. Professor Leach called these, respectively, the fertile octogenarian, the unborn widow (we call this case the afterborn spouse), and the administrative contingency. See W. Barton Leach, Perpetuities in a Nutshell, 51 Harv. L. Rev. 638, 643-44 (1938).[13] None of these dispositions offends the public policy of preventing transferors from tying up property in long-term or even perpetual family trusts. On its face, each disposition seems quite reasonable, violating the common-law Rule on technical grounds only.

1. The Case of the Fertile "Octogenarian"[14]

Fertile-Octogenarian Example. Consider G, a member of Family I, supra. G died at age 75, survived by his 55-year-old daughter A, who had passed the menopause, and by A's adult children, V (age 35) and X (age 30). G's will devised property in trust, income "to A for life, then to A's children for the life of the survivor, and upon the death of A's last surviving child, corpus to A's grandchildren."

In thinking about the full array of possible postcreation events, consider the one that seems most likely: A has no more children and V and X live to, but not beyond, their remaining life expectancies of 42 and 47 more years, respectively.[15] If this happens, the remainder interest in the corpus in favor of A's grandchildren will vest on X's death 47 years after G's death. G knew and saw both V and X. G also knew and saw all four of A's grandchildren (K, L, M, and N), who will succeed to the corpus of the trust when X dies. Even if V

---

13. See also W. Barton Leach, Perpetuities in Perspective: Ending the Rule's Reign of Terror, 65 Harv. L. Rev. 721 (1952); W. Barton Leach, Perpetuities: Staying the Slaughter of the Innocents, 68 L.Q. Rev. 35 (1952).

14. The term "octogenarian" is not to be taken literally; it refers to persons who are infertile, young or old, male or female.

15. It is important to notice the distinction between "life expectancy at birth" and "remaining life expectancy." Even if life expectancy at birth is 75 years, the remaining life expectancy of persons who have lived beyond birth is somewhat greater than 75 years minus their current ages.

or X lives well beyond V's or X's life expectancy, the remainder in the corpus of the trust still will vest on the death of either V or X, who were "in being" at the creation of G's trust.

Among the array of "possible" postcreation events exists one that is extremely unlikely: A becomes pregnant and has a third child[16] or A adopts a child and that third child outlives by more than 21 years A, V, X, K, L, M, N, and anybody else one can think of who has any connection to this transaction. Under this chain of events, the interest in the corpus in favor of A's grandchildren vests beyond a life in being plus 21 years.

Jee v. Audley. Jee v. Audley, the early and famous English decision quoted earlier, laid down for perpetuity law the conclusive presumption of lifetime fertility. Again, we quote the words of the judge in that case, Sir Lloyd Kenyon, the Master of the Rolls:

> I am desired to do in this case something which I do not feel myself at liberty to do, namely to suppose it impossible for persons in so advanced an age as John and Elizabeth Jee [both age 70] to have children; but if this can be done in one case it may in another, and it is a very dangerous experiment, and introductive of the greatest inconvenience to give a latitude to such sort of conjecture.

The conclusive presumption of Jee v. Audley has stuck and, due to reported advances in reproductive technology, is perhaps justified:[17] A is conclusively presumed capable of bearing children until she dies. Consequently, the grandchildren's remainder interest in the corpus of G's trust is invalid.

Only one American common-law decision, Will of Lattouf, 208 A.2d 411 (N.J. Super. Ct. App. Div. 1965), has squarely rejected Jee v. Audley and held in a perpetuity case that the presumption is rebuttable, not conclusive. The Restatement of Property § 377 (1944) squarely supports the conclusive presumption, and there are many perpetuity cases, recent as well as not so recent, that have adhered to it. See, e.g., Abram v. Wilson, 220 N.E.2d 739, 742 (Ohio P. Ct. 1966) ("Obviously, . . . it is clearly possible for the testator's 75-year-old brother to have children . . . ."); Turner v. Turner, 196 S.E.2d 498, 501 (S.C. 1973) ("The possibility of childbirth is never extinct."[18])

The *Lattouf* case is discussed in Samuel M. Fetters, The Perpetuities Period in Gross and the Child *En Ventre Sa Mere* in Relation to the Determination of Common-law and Wait-and-see Measuring Lives: A Minor Heresy Stated and

16. Reported advances in reproductive technology have apparently made this possible. See supra Chapter 3, Part B; Chapter 14, Part B.

17. See supra note 16.

18. In 1987, South Carolina became the first state to enact the Uniform Rule, under which a disposition such as the one in *Turner* would most likely not be invalid.

Defended, 62 Iowa L. Rev. 309 (1976); Lawrence W. Waggoner, *In re Lattouf's Will* and the Presumption of Lifetime Fertility in Perpetuity Law, 20 San Diego L. Rev. 763 (1983).

Possibility of Adoption. Professor Leach was an outspoken critic of the conclusive presumption of lifetime fertility, and wrote extensively in favor of making it rebuttable, as the *Lattouf* court did. See, e.g., W. Barton Leach, Perpetuities: New Hampshire Defertilizes the Octogenarians, 77 Harv. L. Rev. 279 (1963); W. Barton Leach & Owen Davies Tudor, The Common Law Rule Against Perpetuities, in Am. L. Prop. § 24.22. Professor Leach argued that perpetuity law should get into step with two other areas of the law in which the presumption was rebuttable—trust termination cases[19] and charitable deduction cases under the federal tax laws.[20] What has happened, however, is that the law in these two areas has more recently moved in the direction of perpetuity law, rather than the other way around. The reason is the same for all three areas: Although it might be possible in a given case, such as *Lattouf*, to establish that the birth of biological children is impossible,[21] it can almost never be established that it is *impossible* for a woman or man to have additional children by adoption. See Clark v. Citizens & S. Nat'l Bank, 257 S.E.2d 244 (Ga. 1979) (possibility of adoption would not allow the presumption to be rebutted even it were rebuttable in trust termination cases); Rev. Rul. 74-410, 1974-2 C.B. 187 (possibility of a 60-year-old woman adopting one or more children is not so remote as to be negligible; charitable deduction denied); Rev. Rul. 71-442, 1971-2 C.B. 336 (possibility of a 56-year-old man adopting a child is not so remote as to be negligible; charitable deduction denied); Priv. Ltr. Rul. 80-10-011 (possibility of 60-year-old man adopting a child is not so remote as to be negligible; charitable deduction denied despite medical evidence that man's age and physical condition were such that his ability to father a child was "near zero").

Constructional Preference for Validity. If shifting the presumption of lifetime fertility to a rebuttable presumption holds out little hope for overcoming invalidity in cases in which future children are extremely unlikely (though not strictly impossible), another approach seems more promising. This approach is to apply the constructional preference for validity and hold that the possibility of future children was so remote that the transferor never contemplated it and so did not intend to include such children in the class gift language even if—against the odds—one or more ultimately materializes. So construed, the

---

19. See Scott on Trusts § 340.1.

20. See Waggoner, Perpetuity Reform, supra note 6, at 1730 n.28.

21. Reported advances in reproductive technology cast doubt even on this proposition. See supra note 16.

requirement of initial certainty *is* met, and the interest is valid.[22] See, e.g., Bankers Trust Co. v. Pearson, 99 A.2d 224 (Conn. 1953) (testator was held to have meant children in being when he spoke of the children of his brother, age 55, and sisters, ages 52 and 57); Joyner v. Duncan, 264 S.E.2d 76 (N.C. 1980) (testator was held to have meant children in being when he spoke of the children of his 47-year-old son). Since the relevant time for determining the intent of a testator is the time of execution of the will—not the time of death—this construction is ordinarily available to a court only if at the time the testator executed the will there was reason to expect that the person in question would not have additional children.

Surprisingly, the Supreme Judicial Court of Massachusetts has seemed unwilling to adopt such a construction even in apparently appropriate cases. See Second Bank-State St. Trust Co. v. Second Bank-State St. Trust Co., 140 N.E.2d 201 (Mass. 1957); Sears v. Coolidge, 108 N.E.2d 563 (Mass. 1952). In neither case did the court articulate reasons for denying the construction. It may be significant that other ways of upholding the gifts were found,[23] which allows us to speculate that the construction might have been adopted had another validating method not been available. Is there a different explanation? Although facts known to the testators suggested that they never contemplated the possibility of the birth or adoption of additional children, the court might have sensed that these facts, by themselves, do not show that the testators arrived at a specific intent to exclude such children in the unlikely event of their birth or adoption. If this is the explanation for the refusal to apply the construction in the *Second Bank-State St. Trust Co.* or *Sears* cases, it is not entirely persuasive, however: If the testators had been apprized of the fact that the children's inclusion would cause an invalidity, it is all but certain that they *would* have arrived at a specific intent to exclude them. The application of the constructional preference for validity therefore seems justified in those two cases and cases like them.

The Case of the "Precocious Toddler"[24]—Young Children and the Presumption of Fertility. If an elderly person or a person whose physical

---

22. This procedure has been rejected outright in England on the ground that class gifts are unambiguous and therefore extrinsic evidence is inadmissible for the purpose sought. See Ward v. Van Der Loeff, [1924] App. Cas. 653 (Visc. Cave); cf. Estate of Kalouse, 282 N.W.2d 98 (Iowa 1979). The Restatement of Property § 377 comment c, which supports the procedure, answers this point by asserting that it is proper in this situation to utilize the Rule itself as a basis for finding an ambiguity. Cf. Simes & Smith on Future Interests § 1289.

23. In the *Second Bank-State St. Trust Co.* case, the court saved the gift under the subclass doctrine; see infra Part E; in the *Sears* case, the court saved the gift under the second-look doctrine; see infra Part E.

24. Professor Leach's term, again: He cornered the market!

condition prevents the birth of children is conclusively presumed to be able to have children, are children who have not yet reached puberty subject to the same conclusive presumption? Cases raising this problem are rare. The best known is Re Gaite's Will Trusts, [1949] 1 All Eng. Rep. 459 (Ch.), the facts of which form the basis of Example 19.7.

> *Example 19.7:* G devised property in trust, directing the trustee to pay the net income "to A for life, corpus to such of A's grandchildren living at my death or born within five years thereafter who shall attain the age of 21 years." G was survived by A (a 65-year-old widow) and by A's two children and one grandchild.
>
> If a child under the age of 5 is conclusively presumed to be capable of having a child, the remainder in favor of A's grandchildren who reach 21 is invalid. Although any grandchild of A's born to A's two children who were living at G's death will either reach 21 or die before reaching that age no later than 21 years after the death of the survivor of these two children (who were "in being" at G's death), the conclusive presumption if applicable would say that it is possible that A will conceive and bear a child who will in turn conceive a child, all within five years of G's death. Such grandchild therefore might reach 21 more than 21 years after the death of the survivor of A and A's two children and one grandchild who were living when G died.

There have been American cases in which a child shortly after (probable) puberty was conclusively presumed capable of having children. An example is Rust v. Rust, supra p. 1185, where the testator's daughter, Margene, who was 9.5 years old when the testator died, was presumed to be able to have a child before her 14th birthday. (Recall that the court found a way to uphold the gift anyway.) This presumption may, of course, be well justified. In early July 1979, a widely published United Press International newspaper article reported that "a 10-year-old girl gave birth to twin girls at Indiana University Medical Center last week. . . ." According to the report, "Hospital officials . . . said the multiple birth for a mother so young was 'extremely unusual.'"

Age Contingencies Exceeding 21. G devised $100,000 in trust, "income to my son B for life, remainder to such of B's children as reach 30; if none reaches 30, to B's descendants who survive B, by representation; if none, to X-Charity." Appropriate provisions for the distribution of the income are made if one or more of B's children is still under 30 when B dies.

Consider how this disposition would play out in all four of the hypothetical families charted supra pp. 1201-04, if G died at his life expectancy of age 75. Consider Family I, first, where B is 50 years old at G's death and his youngest child, Z, is 25 years old; it is, of course, possible—but nevertheless unlikely—that B will have more children. The same prediction is appropriate for

Family II, where B is 45 at G's death and Z is 15; concededly, though, the probabilities make it a degree or two less unlikely that additional children will be born to B. Family III is an even closer call, for B is 40 at G's death and Z is 5. Regardless of the possibilities and probabilities, if the charts of Families I, II, and III hold, the *actual* postcreation events are that B will have no more children after G's death. Family IV is different, however, and we will address that family below.

Under the assumption that in Families I, II, and III there will be no more children, B's children would be Y and Z in each family. Z is the younger of the two and therefore will reach 30 later. Z will reach 30 five years after G's death in Family I; fifteen years after G's death in Family II; and twenty-five years after G's death in Family III. In all three families, Z will reach 30 before B's death, if B lives out a normal life expectancy. Both B and Z (and Y, as well) were "in being" at G's death.

Now consider Family IV. There, when G dies, B is 35 and Z's birth is five years away. The postcreation events, if they play out as charted, include an afterborn child. That afterborn child, Z, will reach 30 thirty-five years after G's death, when B is 70 and Y is 35. What would it take for Z's interest to vest more than 21 years after the death of B and Y (B's only descendant who was "in being" at G's death)? *Both* B and Y would have to die *very* prematurely: They would both have to die before Z's ninth birthday, which means that B would have to die under the age of 49 *and* Y would have to die under the age of 14.

We now wish to shift away from the reality of the situation and turn to how the common-law Rule Against Perpetuities looks at it. In the world of the common-law Rule, G's disposition flunks the requirement of initial certainty. At common law, it is assumed that B can have another child after G's death and that this afterborn child can outlive B, Y, and, in Families I, II, and III, Z (and anyone else you might think of) by more than 21 years. There is no validating life—no one beyond 21 years of whose death the afterborn grandchild's interest *cannot* remain nonvested. Under the all-or-nothing rule for class gifts, that possibility makes the interest of *all* the class members invalid—including the interest of Y, who was "in being" at G's death in all four families, and the interest of Z, who was "in being" in Families I, II, and III. In addition, the alternative remainders in favor of A's descendants and in favor of X-Charity are invalid because there is no validating life for either of them.

Before you ponder this example further on your own, we wish to bring you back specifically to the "know-and-see" *policy* of the Rule Against Perpetuities: Despite the fact that G knew and saw both Y and Z in Families I, II, and III, and despite the fact that G knew and saw Y in Family IV and that Y was in the same generation as that of the afterborn Z, G's gifts to them are invalid! In the case of the common-law Rule Against Perpetuities, there plainly is a gap between policy and operation.

Age Contingencies Not Exceeding 21—The Fertile Decedent and the Child En Ventre Sa Frigidaire![25] G devised $100,000 in trust, "income to my son B for life, remainder to such of B's children as reach 21; if none reaches 21, to B's descendants who survive B, by representation; if none, to X-Charity." Appropriate provisions for the distribution of the income are made if one or more of B's children is still under the age of 21 when B dies.

G's residuary devisees challenge the validity of G's disposition. They argue that the requirement of initial certainty is not met because it is possible that when B dies he will leave sperm on deposit in a sperm bank, and that after B's death B's widow—who could be someone not "in being" at G's death—will become pregnant with that sperm and give birth to a child of B's; B's postdeath child cannot reach 21 within 21 years after B's death and will not *necessarily* reach 21 within 21 years after the death of anyone else you might put forward. G's residuary devisees argue that there is no validating life and the remainder interests after B's life estate are invalid.

Do the remainder interests flunk the requirement of initial certainty? How would you answer the argument advanced by G's residuary devisees? See supra Chapter 3, Part B. For a legislative solution to this problem, see USRAP § 1(d) and its UPC counterpart, UPC § 2-901(d).

2. *The Case of the Afterborn Spouse*

Pound v. Shorter

377 S.E.2d 854 (Ga. 1989)

WELTNER, J. When Elizabeth Shorter died in 1929, her will created a trust that provided for her one unmarried son as follows:

> In trust further, should my son die, either before or after my death, leaving neither child, nor children of a deceased wife surviving him, but leaving a wife surviving him, to pay over the annual net income arising each year from said trust property, in quarterly installments each year, to the wife of my said son, during her life, and upon the death of the wife of my said son, to thereupon pay over, deliver and convey, in fee simple, the corpus of said trust property to the children and descendants of children of my brother . . . and sister. . . .

The son married in 1953 and died in 1987, survived by his widow. He left no descendants. After his death, the trustee bank filed a petition to determine the validity of the trust item. The trial court found that the item created a perpetuity

25. Professor Leach's term: See W. Barton Leach, Perpetuities in the Atomic Age: The Sperm Bank and the Fertile Decedent, 48 A.B.A.J. 942 (1962).

and decreed that the trust be terminated and that the son's widow have fee ownership. Fifty-two lineal descendants of Elizabeth Shorter appeal.

1. The Rule against Perpetuities, adopted first by the legislature in 1863, provides:

> Limitations of estates may extend through any number of lives in being at the time when the limitations commence, and 21 years, and the usual period of gestation added thereafter. The law terms a limitation beyond that period a perpetuity and forbids its creation. When an attempt is made to create a perpetuity, the law will give effect to the limitations which are not too remote and will declare the other limitations void, thereby vesting the fee in the last taker under the legal limitations. OCGA § 44-6-1.

2. We have undertaken a study of both the rule against perpetuities and an alternative approach, commonly called "wait and see." Fifteen states have adopted some form of the "wait-and-see" approach and all have done so through legislation. We conclude:

(1) that the traditional rule against perpetuities has been effective so far in Georgia, judging by the few cases brought to invalidate grants, and the even fewer invalidations; and

(2) that the alternative "wait-and-see" approach has many problems, including initial uncertainty (which is avoided by the traditional rule) and the necessity for selecting a method by which to determine the length of the waiting period.[26]

3. We are not convinced that the goals of certainty and early vesting will be served by adopting the alternative, and accordingly decline to do so.

4. As the will encompasses the possibilities that the son might marry a woman who was unborn in 1929 (a life *not* "in being") and then predecease her, it violated the rule against perpetuities.

Judgment affirmed.

All the Justices concur.

---

26. The problems may be summarized as follows: (1) there is actually no severe problem of grants being invalidated due to a violation of the rule against perpetuities; (2) technical violations of the rule can be avoided by competent drafting, so only unwary counsel is trapped by the rule; (3) there is a big problem of expense and inconvenience during the waiting period; (4) there is an increase in litigation due to the alternative doctrine; (5) much of the testator's estate is diverted to lawyers' fees; (6) most alternative statutes provide for cy pres litigation at the end of the waiting period if the interest has neither vested nor failed, and that litigation is difficult and expensive due to the passage of time; and (7) the alternative does not simplify the perpetuities law. Ira Mark Bloom, Perpetuities Refinement: There is an Alternative, 62 Wash. L. Rev. 23 (1987).

Notes

1. *Reality*. Not disclosed but known by the court was the fact that Mildred Shorter, the son's widow, was in being in 1929 when Elizabeth Shorter died.[27] In direct response to the *Pound* decision, the Georgia legislature the following year enacted the Uniform Rule, which adopts the wait-and-see method of perpetuity reform.

2. *State of the Authorities*. In accord with Pound v. Shorter are Easton v. Hall, 154 N.E. 216 (Ill. 1926); Chenoweth v. Bullit, 6 S.W.2d 1061 (Ky. Ct. App. 1928); Restatement of Property § 370 comment k, illus. 3.

3. *No Violation If Devisees Can Be Their Own Validating Lives*. The possibility of an afterborn spouse does not always create a perpetuity violation. In an appropriate case, the devisees of the remainder interest following the spouse's death are their own validating lives. This would be the case if the contingent remainder were in favor of named individuals (Y and Z perhaps) or a class that was closed at G's death (for example, the children of G's predeceased daughter, A).

Furthermore, if the remainder was not contingent on survival, the fact that it was still subject to open at G's death would not invalidate it if the class could not increase beyond lives in being. For example, in the absence of a condition precedent of survival, a remainder in favor of G's grandchildren would be valid in the above example. See Lanier v. Lanier, 126 S.E.2d 776 (Ga. 1962). But one in favor of G's great-grandchildren would be invalid.

4. *Constructional Preference for Validity*. Even when no other validating lives can be located, the principle of construction favoring validity can often be used to avoid the afterborn-spouse problem. When the language of the instrument fairly allows, some courts have construed G's reference to a child's spouse as referring only to the person to whom the child was married when the will was executed or when G died. See Willis v. Hendry, 20 A.2d 375 (Conn. 1941) (G's will referred to "the wife of my said son"); Friend's Will, 28 N.E.2d 377 (N.Y. 1940) (G's will referred to "the widow of my said son Sol"). This procedure, however, is not always available to courts, as the *Pound* case demonstrates.

---

27. This is not to suggest that there never are "afterborn spouses." Pablo Casals, the famous cellist, was around 80 when he married his 20-year old student Martita. Of the marriage, Casals wrote: "I was aware at the time that some people noted a certain discrepancy in our ages—a bridegroom of course is not usually thirty years older than his father-in-law." Pablo Casals, Joys and Sorrows 277 (1970).

3. The Case of the Administrative Contingency

This technical violation can occur where a disposition involves the performance by a fiduciary (an executor, a trustee) of some administrative function, the completion of which might, but is extremely unlikely to, take more than 21 years.

Typical examples are the completion of the probate of a will, the settlement of an estate, the payment of debts or taxes, the sale of estate assets, or the delivery of trust corpus on the termination of a trust.

Administrative Contingency Example. Consider G, again, in Family I, II, III, or IV. G died at age 75, devising real property "to such of my grandchildren, born before or after my death, as may be living upon final distribution of my estate." G is survived by her children (A and B) and her grandchildren (V, X, Y, and Z in Families I, II, and III; V, X, and Y in Family IV).

The grandchildren's interest is invalid, by the majority view. Though unlikely, there is a possibility that the final distribution of G's estate will not occur within 21 years after G's death.[28] This possibility eliminates validating the interest on the basis of the 21-year part of the period. In addition, there are no lives in being that can validate it. As always, not only are afterborn grandchildren presumed, but also presumed is the possibility that final distribution of G's estate will occur when such afterborn grandchildren have outlived by more than 21 years the deaths of A, B, V, X, Y, and, in Families I, II, and III, Z.

As the above example illustrates, the term "administrative contingency" is somewhat misleading. It does not refer to the possibility that the administrative task will never be completed. If it did, all interests that are to take effect in possession upon the completion of an administrative task would be contingent and invalid. But in fact, such gifts are upheld. See cases collected in Am. L. Prop. § 24.23 n.2. Rather, it is accepted as certain that the task will be completed, presumably because of the fiduciary's legal obligation to do so;[29] the uncertainty is that the task might not be completed within the perpetuity period. Thus, the administrative contingency problem commonly arises because the

---

28. There have been rare instances of distribution of an estate being delayed for a very long time. See, e.g., Richards v. Tolbert, 208 S.E.2d 486 (Ga. 1974) (57 years between death and probate of the will); Hostetter v. Estate of Hostetter, 394 N.E.2d 77 (Ill. App. Ct. 1979) (25 years); Haddock v. Boston & Me. R.R., 15 N.E. 495 (Mass. 1888) (63 years); Garrett Estate, 94 A.2d 357 (1953), cert. denied, 345 U.S. 996 (1953) (23 years).

29. But see Miller v. Weston, 189 P. 610 (Colo. 1920) (en banc), where the court held that a devise to A "on the admission of this will to probate" is contingent on the probate of the will and invalid because probate "may never happen." The court was unwilling to accept probate as a certainty even if "probate is required by law to be made." In effect, the perpetuity requirement of initial certainty did not allow the possibility of the law's being disobeyed to be ignored!

interest is contingent on survival of the administrative function. These dispositions have the completely rational objective of preventing the actual distribution of property to the estate of a dead person, thereby avoiding unnecessary expenses of administration and possible double estate taxation.[30]

Survival of a Period That Might Exceed 21 Years. At bottom, the administrative contingency problem is often one of survival of a period of time that might exceed 21 years. Interests that are contingent on survival of a period that might exceed 21 years, however, are not always invalid. They will be valid if the devisees can themselves be the validating lives, which requires that the questioned interest either be in favor of one or more individual takers or a class that is closed at the testator's death.

Example 19.8: G devised real property "to such of my children as may be living upon final distribution of my estate." G is survived by children.

The children's interest is valid. Since no children will be born to G after her death, her children are their own validating lives.

Class Subject to Open for More Than 21 Years. When the interest is in favor of a class that is not closed at the testator's death, the administrative contingency problem can also arise even if there is no condition of survival.

Example 19.9: G devised real property "to such of my great-grandchildren, born before or after my death, as may be living upon final distribution of my estate." G is survived by children and grandchildren.

The interest would be invalid even if the phrase "as may be living" were omitted. A great-grandchild could be conceived and born before the completion of the probate of G's estate and more than 21 years after the death of the survivor of G's children and those of G's grandchildren that were living at G's death. Note, however, that the invalidity here is due to the fact that the class of great-grandchildren could not only increase after the testator's death, but also increase after the death of lives in being at his death.

If the class cannot increase after lives in being, the absence of a condition of survival will save a gift in favor of a class even though it is not closed at the testator's death. To illustrate this point, suppose the gift in Example 19.9 were

---

30. Concerns about double estate taxation, under the federal estate tax at least, may be somewhat overdrawn. The reason is that IRC § 2013 provides for a credit against the estate tax of a second decedent in the amount of the estate tax imposed on the estate of the prior decedent. If the two decedents die within two years of one another, the amount of the credit is 100 percent of the prior decedent's estate tax attributable to the inclusion of the transferred property. The credit is 80 percent of this amount if the second decedent dies between two and four years after the death of the prior decedent, 60 percent if the second death occurs between four and six years, 40 percent for deaths between six and eight years, and 20 percent for deaths between eight and ten years.

in favor of G's grandchildren. Now suppose that the phrase "as may be living" were omitted. This would make the grandchildren's interest valid because no new members could join the class after the death of the survivor of G's children, all of whom were, of course, "in being" at G's death.

The Fiduciary's Obligation. A minority of courts has devised an escape from the administrative contingency problem. Since the administrative function is to be performed by a fiduciary, the procedure is to hold that the fiduciary's obligation is not only to complete the task, but to do so within a reasonable time, and to hold further that a reasonable time is something less than 21 years. See Belfield v. Booth, 27 A. 585 (Conn. 1893); Asche v. Asche, 216 A.2d 272 (Del. 1966); Brandenburg v. Thorndike, 28 N.E. 575 (Mass. 1885); cf. Estate of Taylor, 428 P.2d 301 (Cal. 1967) (vesting occurs at time distribution *should* have been made). There is a difficulty with this minority view: Although there may be an obligation to complete fiduciary tasks expeditiously, it is a fiction to say that there is *always* a violation of a fiduciary duty when the settlement of an estate takes more than 21 years. While rare, there can be cases where protracted and successive litigation over a multitude of issues legitimately ties up an estate for a very long time. Even on a case-by-case basis, it would seem to be impossible to conclude with the certainty required by the Rule that no such delay will properly arise.

Constructional Preference for Validity. Depending on the language employed, the principle of construction favoring validity may be available as a method of avoiding invalidity. For example, if a condition of survival is ambiguous on the point, it would probably be construed to relate to the death of the testator or of the life tenant rather than to the completion of the administrative task, such as the final distribution of the estate.[31] Indeed, this construction has on occasion been adopted even when the language unambiguously related to the estate's final distribution.[32]

Despite precedents supporting one or the other of these two salvage devices, the administrative contingency problem has not been solved. Most courts would

---

31. See First Nat'l Bank v. Jenkins, 345 S.E.2d 829 (Ga. 1986) (Will provided that "upon the death of [the life tenant], and after [paying hospital and medical expenses incurred by the life tenant during his life time and at his death paying for his funeral and grave marker], my trustee is directed to divide all the remaining trust property [among various beneficiaries] then living;" held, the remainder interests vested at the life tenant's death, with "only possession or actual payment . . . delayed until his estate is settled, including payments for funeral expenses and the grave marker."); Restatement of Property § 374 comment f.

32. See Malone v. Herndon, 168 P.2d 272 (Okla. 1945), where a will providing that on the death of the life tenant leaving issue surviving him, the "trust estate shall be paid over, delivered and conveyed to such issue living at the time of said payment, delivery and conveyance" was construed to require survivorship of the life tenant.

probably still conclude that devises, such as G's in the first example given above, violate the Rule and are therefore invalid.[33]

PART C. PERPETUITY SAVING CLAUSES—THE PRACTITIONER'S FRIEND

The common-law Rule Against Perpetuities should be and for the most part is less fearsome to practicing estate planning lawyers than it is to law students and law graduates studying for the bar examination. This is not because estate planning lawyers have found that the Rule becomes more understandable with experience, but because they have discovered a secret: They need not be greatly concerned about the technicalities of the Rule because they use perpetuity saving clauses.

Formulated and used properly, perpetuity saving clauses mean that lawyers need not ever fear that the trusts or other property arrangements they draft will violate the common-law Rule. In addition, unless the trust or other property arrangement is unreasonable—for example, unless it is to continue beyond the death of the last living member of the transferor's youngest descendant living when the trust or other arrangement was created—the practicing lawyer need not fear that the perpetuity saving clause will have any practical effect other than to save the disposition from a Rule violation. Trusts are routinely created that would violate the Rule, were it not for the perpetuity saving clause; essentially a technicality, a perpetuity saving clause is nevertheless essential in such trusts.

In Re Villar

[1929] 1 Ch. 243 (C.A.)

[The testator died on September 6, 1926, survived by his widow, five children (three sons and two daughters), and two infant grandchildren (children of one of his daughters). The testator's will created a residuary trust, the terms of which basically were that an annuity of a specified amount was to be paid to his widow and the remaining part of the income was to be paid to his children and their descendants. All interests in the trust were to vest in the testator's descendants living at the expiration of the "period of restriction." According to the terms of the testator's will, the "period of restriction" was to expire "20 years from the day of the death of the last survivor of all the lineal descendants

33. See Prime v. Hyne, 67 Cal. Rptr. 170 (Ct. App. 1968), for an example of a decision that rejected the notion that the fiduciary's duty guarantees that an estate will be distributed within 21 years of the decedent's death.

of Her Late Majesty Queen Victoria who shall be living at the time of my death."]

LORD HANWORTH, M.R. This is an appeal from Astbury J., who had to determine whether or not in the main the will of the testator ought to be declared ineffective. . . . The terms of the residuary gift which are easy to carry out as regards the payment of income at the present time are to be treated as invalid, because of the period of restriction to the end of which distribution of the capital was postponed. The argument is that as the ascertainment of the end of this period will create serious difficulty in time to come, the residuary gift ought to be set aside as invalid. The period of restriction is defined as "the period ending at the expiration of 20 years from the day of the death of the last survivor of all the lineal descendants of Her Late Majesty Queen Victoria who shall be living at the time of my death." We have the evidence of a member of the College of Arms, who says the descendants of Queen Victoria numbered not less than 120 in 1922, and that they might have increased in number by 1926. On the other hand I suppose they might have decreased in number, for I do not know whether the births of new descendants between 1922 and 1926 were sufficient to fill the vacancies among the descendants caused by death. However, it is quite clear that there were a large number of the descendants of Queen Victoria in being on September 6, 1926, and obviously there may be great difficulty in ascertaining whether and when the last of these lineal descendants had passed away. That is what has to be ascertained, and it depends on the existence of one single life out of many others. I recognize that serious difficulty might well arise in the future in ascertaining the date when that life ceased. . . .

But it is said that the Courts ought to take into consideration the difficulty that will arise in the future when, it may be 100 years hence, their successors will be faced with the problem of finding out who is the last survivor of this body of 120 or 130 persons and when he died. That is a difficulty which may arise by reason of the vicissitudes of life, but it may not. It is possible that 120 years hence the Court may find a number of problems relating to the births, marriages and deaths of various persons; but they appear to me to be matters which we ought not to take into account. The difficulties are not insurmountable, and they may in fact never arise. Therefore I return to the view that the only matter I have to consider is whether the residuary gift of the testator can be declared invalid on the ground that it has transgressed some rule of law at the present time. The answer must be that it has not so transgressed, and, if so, we cannot by reference to difficulties that may arise hereafter make a new will for the testator.

I regret the decision, as there is no reason for such a fanciful disposition; but testing it by the rules which have to be applied, I can find no breach of the existing law, and the will must therefore stand. The appellant has suggested that the whole residuary gift should be set aside, but at the present time there is no difficulty in dealing with the estate as directed by the testator. It seems impossible to set aside a gift which works well in the present but which may in the future cause difficulty. I think that the decision of Astbury, J., was right, and that the appeal must be dismissed.

LAWRENCE, L.J., concurring. . . . In my judgment the decision in Thellusson v. Woodford, [11 Ves. Jr. 112, 32 Eng. Rep. 1030 (H.L. 1805)], which is binding on this Court, affords a complete answer to the contention of the appellants that the testator's residuary gift is void, as infringing the rule against perpetuities. In that case Lord Eldon . . . states that "the language of all the cases is, that property may be so limited as to make it unalienable during any number of lives, not exceeding that, to which testimony can be applied, to determine, when the survivor of them drops."

Much stress has been rightly laid by the appellants in the present case on the words "not exceeding that to which testimony can be applied," but in my opinion these words were intended to apply to cases such as In re Moore, [[1901] 1 Ch. 936,] where it is obviously impossible to ascertain the lives specified.[34]

Moreover I think that in cases of that kind the question is not whether the rule against perpetuities has or has not been infringed, but whether the gift is void for uncertainty. If it be impossible to ascertain the lives upon the death of the survivor of which vesting of the capital is to take effect, such vesting is not in fact postponed beyond the permitted limit, but the gift is void for uncertainty. . . .

In the present case there is in my opinion no infringement of the rule against perpetuities. . . . [Nor is the gift void for uncertainty, for] the evidence shows at most that it is difficult at the present time to ascertain who are the lineal descendants in question. . . . In my judgment the evidence falls far short of proving that the number of lives exceeds that to which testimony can be applied to determine when the survivor of them drops. . . .

[The concurring opinion of RUSSELL, L.J. is omitted.]

Perpetuity Saving Clauses. The principle of *Villar* provides the platform for the modern perpetuity saving clause. These clauses are a variation of the language in cases like *Villar*, in which the transferor directly links the term of the trust to a period of time measured by the life of the survivor of a group of designated persons in being at the time of the transfer plus 21 years (20 years,

34. In In re Moore, the testator created a trust to endure until "twenty-one years from the death of the last survivor of all persons who shall be living at my death." Eds.

in *Villar* itself). Although perpetuity saving clauses also establish a period of time measured by the life of the survivor of a group of designated persons in being at the time of the transfer plus 21 years, the difference is that saving clauses do not directly govern the term of the trust; they operate as a backstop just in case the actual term of the trust exceeds the time allotted by the saving clause. That part of a perpetuity saving clause that establishes this period of time is called the *perpetuity-period component*. Saving clauses contain another component, called the *gift-over component*. This component expressly creates a gift over that is guaranteed to vest at the termination of the period established in the perpetuity-period component but only if the interests in the trust or other arrangement have neither vested nor terminated earlier in accordance with their primary terms.

It is important to note that regardless of what group of persons is designated in the perpetuity-period component of the saving clause, the survivor of the group is not necessarily the person who would be the validating life for the questioned interest in the absence of the saving clause. Without the saving clause, the questioned interest might in fact have been invalid because of the existence of an invalidating chain of possible postcreation events with respect to every person who might be proposed as a validating life. The persons designated in the saving clause, however, become validating lives for all interests in the trust or other property arrangement. The saving clause confers on the last surviving member of the group the requisite causal connection demanded by the requirement of initial certainty. See Norton v. Georgia R.R. Bank & Trust, 322 S.E.2d 870 (Ga. 1984) (upholding the validity of a traditional perpetuity saving clause).

In most cases, the saving clause does more than avoid a violation of the common-law Rule; it also, in a sense, overinsures the client's disposition against the possibility that the gift over will ever take effect. The period of time established by the perpetuity-period component of the clause provides a margin of safety. Almost always, the length of time is sufficient to exceed—usually by a substantial margin—the time when the interests in the trust or other arrangement actually vest (or terminate) by their own terms. The clause, therefore, is usually a formality that validates the disposition without affecting the substance of the disposition at all.

Royal Lives and Other Ploys. As noted in *Villar*, Thellusson v. Woodford, 11 Ves. Jr. 112, 32 Eng. Rep. 1030 (Ch. 1805), is the source of the so-called uncertainty rule. American authorities take a somewhat stricter view about the matter of uncertainty than was exhibited in *Villar*. The Restatement of Property § 374 comment l declares that a clause like that in *Villar*—called a royal-lives clause—would be found invalid by an American court, as would specified similar periods such as one measured by the lives of "those persons whose names appear in the City Directory of the City of X." Accord Restatement 2d of Property § 1.3 comment a; USRAP § 1 comment, part B (designation of group is invalid if the group is such "that would cause it to be impracticable to determine the death of the survivor"). Although *Villar* is perhaps the widest group that has ever been upheld, even by an English court,[35] cases of a trust actually being declared invalid are few.[36]

Validity is one thing; discretion and practicability are another. Lord Hanworth said that "there is no reason for such a fanciful disposition" as that in *Villar*, and he was certainly correct. A device sometimes mentioned by commentators is the dozen-healthy-babies ploy, under which the transferor designates a period governed by the life of the survivor of a number of newborn babies in the maternity ward of a specified hospital. A 21-year period is then tacked on after the death of the survivor. Writing in the early 1950s, when life expectancy at birth was about 68 years, Professor Leach said that the period resulting from this device would "add up to about a century."[37] Although it would seem at first glance that his mathematics were a little off (68 + 21 = 89, not 100), Professor Leach undoubtedly understood that a group of newborns will almost certainly include several persons who will live beyond their life expectancies. Professor Leach apparently estimated that an additional 11 years or so would account for this.

With the current life expectancy at birth standing at about 75 years, the total period of time produced by this device today would average out to a period well in excess of the 96 years calculated by adding 21 to 75. In fact, it would yield an average period of about 115 years.[38] Professor Leach rightly condemned the

---

35. Another candidate for the prize comes from Warren's Will, 105 Sol. J. 511 (1961), where the period was measured by the life of the survivor of 194 marital issue of Queen Victoria.

36. In In re Moore, [1901] 1 Ch. 936, the testator created a trust to endure until "twenty-one years from the death of the last survivor of all persons who shall be living at my death." In a short opinion, the court held the gift void for uncertainty. "It is impossible to ascertain when the last life will be extinguished," the court said. Cases are collected in Restatement 2d of Property § 1.3 reporter's note 3.

37. W. Barton Leach & Owen Davies Tudor, The Common Law Rule Against Perpetuities, in Am. L. Prop. § 24.16, at 52.

38. The average life expectancy of the longest-living member of a group of twelve newborn babies, selected at random, is 94.2 years. With the 21-year tack-on period, the twelve-healthy-babies ploy would produce, on average, a period of about 115 years (94 + 21).

The 94-year life expectancy was computed by applying a complicated actuarial formula to the data set forth in Table 80CNSMT, in Fed. Est. & Gift Tax Rep. (CCH) ¶ 6415.301 (1989). Starting with an original cohort of 100,000 newborns, Table 80CNSMT gives the number of people who live to age one (98,740), age two (98,648), and so on to ages 109 (33) and 110 (0).

We would like to express our gratitude to Dr. Cecil Nesbitt, professor emeritus of mathematics at the University of Michigan, for deriving the actuarial formula used in the computation; he derived the formula from the principles set forth in Newton L. Bowers, Jr. et al., Actuarial Mathematics ch. 16 (1986).

healthy-babies ploy,[39] but he was probably poking at a strawman. To our knowledge, this device is not used by practicing lawyers. What lawyers actually do is depicted below.

Prototype Trusts Saved by Prototype Perpetuity Saving Clause. We present below two types of trusts as prototypical of trusts that are actually created in practice; we also give you a sample of a type of saving clause frequently used. Were it not for the inclusion of a perpetuity saving clause, the remainder interests in both trusts would flunk the requirement of initial certainty and be invalid. (The first type of trust is more frequently created than the second, but the second type is also used in practice.)

As before, we place G in the families we charted earlier. Assuming that G dies at age 75, G is survived by G's children (A and B) and grandchildren (V, X, Y, and Z). (In Family IV, however, Z is not "in being" at G's death but is born five years later.)

> *Example 19.10: Corpus to Grandchildren Contingent on Reaching an Age Exceeding 21.* G devised property in trust, income in equal shares to G's children for the life of the survivor, then in equal shares to G's grandchildren, remainder in corpus to G's grandchildren who reach age 30; if none reaches 30, to G's descendants who survive G's last surviving child, by representation; if none, to X-Charity.

> *Example 19.11: Corpus to Descendants Contingent on Surviving Last Living Grandchild.* G devised property in trust, income in equal shares to G's children for the life of the survivor, then in equal shares to G's grandchildren for the life of the survivor, and on the death of G's last living grandchild, corpus to G's descendants then living, by representation; if none, to X-Charity.

G's lawyer inserted a perpetuity saving clause in both dispositions. Specifically, the saving clause selected by G's lawyer says:

> The trust hereby created shall terminate in any event not later than 21 years after the death of the last survivor of my descendants who are in being at the time this instrument becomes effective, and unless sooner terminated by the terms hereof, the trustee shall, at the termination of such period, make distribution to the persons then entitled to the income of this trust, and in the same shares and proportions as they are so entitled.

Does the use of a saving clause to validate the dispositions in Examples 19.10 and 19.11 extend dead-hand control beyond that which the common-law Rule allows or should allow, or does it vindicate the know-and-see policy of the common-law Rule?

39. See J.H.C. Morris & W. Barton Leach, The Rule Against Perpetuities 13 (2d ed. 1962).

Consider each of the four charted families and work out how long ultimate vesting in Example 19.10 will likely take. As for Example 19.11, the time of likely final vesting can be projected by determining the number of years after G's death it will be until G's youngest grandchild, Z, will reach the end of Z's remaining life expectancy.[40] That will be 51 years after G's death in Family I; 61 years after G's death in Family II; 71 years after G's death in Family III; and 80 years after G's death in Family IV.

Will the period of time marked off by the perpetuity-period component of the saving clause exceed the time of projected actual vesting? If so, by how much? To work this out, you need to add 21 years to the remaining life expectancy of G's youngest descendant in being at G's death: G's youngest descendant in Family I is S, a newborn greatgrandchild whose life expectancy is 75 years; in Family II, the youngest descendant is K, a newborn greatgrandchild whose life expectancy is 75 years; in Family III, G's youngest descendant is Z, a 5-year-old grandchild whose remaining life expectancy is 71 years; and in Family IV, the youngest descendants are X and Y, newborn grandchildren whose life expectancies are 75 years.

Malpractice Liability. Would G's lawyer be liable in malpractice if the lawyer had failed to insert a perpetuity saving clause in the above dispositions? In the technical violation cases studied earlier, would a lawyer drafting an irrevocable inter vivos trust be liable in malpractice if the lawyer inserts a perpetuity saving clause that gears the perpetuity-period component to a group of persons living at the settlor's death?

Lucas v. Hamm

364 P.2d 685 (Cal. 1961), cert. denied, 368 U.S. 987 (1962)

[After the death of the testator, the attorney who drew the will, in his capacity as counsel of record for the executors, advised the residuary devisees in writing that the residuary trust provision was invalid. The devisees subsequently entered into a settlement agreement with the testator's blood relatives under which the devisees received $75,000 less than they would have received had the trust provision been valid.

In an action for damages brought by the devisees against the drafting attorney, the trial court dismissed the complaint, and the plaintiffs appealed.]

GIBSON, C.J. . . . [The court held that lack of privity does not insulate an attorney who negligently draws a will from liability in tort to the devisees who lose their testamentary rights because of the attorney's negligence, nor does it insulate the attorney from liability in contract to such devisees as third party

---

40. On remaining life expectancies, see supra note 15.

beneficiaries if the attorney fails properly to fulfill his or her obligations under the contract with the testator. See supra Chapter 12, Part D. The court then took up the question whether the attorney had been negligent or had breached the contract.]

The complaint, as we have seen, alleges that defendant drafted the will in such a manner that the trust was invalid because it violated the rules relating to perpetuities and restraints on alienation. These closely akin subjects have long perplexed the courts and the bar. Professor Gray, a leading authority in the field, stated: "There is something in the subject which seems to facilitate error. Perhaps it is because the mode of reasoning is unlike that with which lawyers are most familiar. . . . A long list might be formed of the demonstrable blunders with regard to its questions made by eminent men, blunders which they themselves have been sometimes the first to acknowledge; and there are few lawyers of any practice in drawing wills and settlements who have not at some time either fallen into the net which the Rule spreads for the unwary, or at least shuddered to think how narrowly they have escaped it." Gray, The Rule Against Perpetuities (4th ed. 1942) p. xi; see also Leach, Perpetuities Legislation (1954) 67 Harv. L. Rev. 1349 (describing the rule as a "technicality-ridden legal nightmare" and a "dangerous instrumentality in the hands of most members of the bar"). Of the California law on perpetuities and restraints it has been said that few, if any, areas of the law have been fraught with more confusion or concealed more traps for the unwary draftsman; that members of the bar, probate courts, and title insurance companies make errors in these matters; that the code provisions adopted in 1872 created a situation worse than if the matter had been left to the common law, and that the legislation adopted in 1951 (under which the will involved here was drawn), despite the best of intentions, added further complexities. (See 38 Cal. Jur. 2d 443; Coil, Perpetuities and Restraints; A Needed Reform (1955) 30 State Bar J. 87, 88-90.)

In view of the state of the law relating to perpetuities and restraints on alienation and the nature of the error, if any, assertedly made by defendant in preparing the instrument, it would not be proper to hold that defendant failed to use such skill, prudence, and diligence as lawyers of ordinary skill and capacity commonly exercise. The provision of the will quoted in the complaint, namely, that the trust was to terminate five years after the order of the probate court distributing the property to the trustee, could cause the trust to be invalid only because of the remote possibility that the order of distribution would be delayed for a period longer than a life in being at the creation of the interest plus 16 years (the 21-year statutory period less the five years specified in the will). Although it has been held that a possibility of this type could result in invalidity of a bequest (Estate of Johnston, 47 Cal. 2d 265, 269-270, 303 P.2d 1; Estate of Campbell, 28 Cal. App. 2d 102, 103 et seq., 82 P.2d 22), the possible occurrence of such a delay was so remote and unlikely that an attorney of ordinary skill acting under the same circumstances might well have "fallen into the net which the Rule spreads for the unwary" and failed to recognize the danger. We need not decide whether the trust provision of the will was actually invalid or whether, as defendant asserts, the complaint fails to allege facts necessary to enable such a determination, because we have concluded that in any event an error of the type relied on by plaintiffs does not show negligence or breach of contract on the part of defendant. . . .

The judgment is affirmed.

Notes

1. *Criticism.* R. E. Megarry, in 81 L.Q. Rev. 478, 481 (1965), commented on the *Lucas* decision:

> An Englishman's comment on the decision must perforce observe a proper restraint. Doubtless the Supreme Court of California is the best judge of the standard of competence which is to be expected of California lawyers of ordinary skill and capacity. Let it be accepted that [it] is highly unlikely that it would take longer than the perpetuity period for the estate to be distributed. The question then becomes whether an ordinary lawyer who undertakes to draft a will should be expected to know that a gift will be void for perpetuity if there is any possibility, however unlikely, that the perpetuity period will be exceeded. This part of the rule is so fundamental, and so highly stressed by all the books and teachers, that he who does not know it must be expected to know little or nothing of the rest of the rule. The standard of competence in California thus seems to be that it is not negligent for lawyers to draft wills knowing little or nothing of the rule against perpetuities, and without consulting anyone skilled in the rule (a point mentioned by the Court of Appeal but ignored in the judgment of the Supreme Court). If the rule against perpetuities is in this category, what other fundamentals of the law are there of which the California attorney may be ignorant without culpability? How does California translate and apply *spondet peritiam artis?* However bright the future of Lucas v. Hamm may be in England on the score of privity, it is to be hoped that on the standard of professional competence it will prove to be a slur on the profession which, like the mule, will display neither pride of ancestry nor hope of posterity.

See also Murray T. Bloom, The Trouble with Lawyers 72-75 (1968).

2. *Continuing Validity of Lucas?* In Wright v. Williams, 121 Cal. Rptr. 194, 199 n.2 (Ct. App. 1975), the court said: "There is reason to doubt that the ultimate conclusion of Lucas v. Hamm is valid in today's state of the art. Draftsmanship to avoid the rule against perpetuities seems no longer esoteric." See also Millwright v. Romer, 322 N.W.2d 30 (Iowa 1982). Cf. Bucquet v. Livingston, 129 Cal. Rptr. 514 (Ct. App. 1976); Smith v. Lewis, 530 P.2d 589, 605 (Cal. 1975) (Clark J., dissenting).

3. *Model Rules of Professional Conduct,* Rule 1.1 (1983): "A lawyer shall provide competent representation to a client. Competent representation requires the legal knowledge, skill, thoroughness and preparation reasonably necessary for the representation."

EXTERNAL REFERENCE. Gerald P. Johnston, Legal Malpractice in Estate Planning—Perilous Times Ahead for the Practitioner, 67 Iowa L. Rev. 629 (1982).

PART D. WAIT-AND-SEE AND OTHER METHODS OF PERPETUITY REFORM

The need for perpetuity reform is not much in doubt, but controversy persists about the method. Three basic methods have been advanced: (i) discrete statutory repair of the fertile octogenarian, afterborn spouse, and administrative contingency problem areas, along with reduction of age contingencies to 21; (ii) immediately available reformation; and (iii) wait-and-see, with deferred reformation (reformation only if an interest remains contingent at the expiration of the permissible vesting period).

We believe we are accurate in reporting that the only realistic hope for widespread perpetuity reform today is in legislative adoption of the third method—wait-and-see with deferred reformation. This is the approach of the Uniform Rule. The Uniform Rule has been approved by the House of Delegates of the American Bar Association, on the unanimous recommendation of the Council of the A.B.A. Section of Real Property, Probate and Trust Law. The Uniform Rule has also been unanimously endorsed by the Joint Editorial Board for the Uniform Probate Code, the Board of Regents of the American College of Probate Counsel, and the Board of Governors of the American College of Real Estate Lawyers. The Uniform Rule has been incorporated into the Uniform Probate Code as Part 9 of Article II, has been enacted in 46 percent of the states, making it the single most widely enacted method of perpetuity reform to date, and seems to be on its way to additional enactments. There is also a chance that a common-law court, without the benefit of legislation, might adopt the similar approach of the Restatement 2d of Property (1983), infra p. 1242.

1. Specific-Statutory-Repair Method

The specific-statutory-repair method is in effect in two jurisdictions—Illinois[41] and New York.[42] Until 1988, this method was also in effect in Florida;[43] it was repealed when Florida enacted the Uniform Rule. Until 1991, California had a statute aimed at the afterborn spouse category, but not the other categories of technical violation;[44] this provision was repealed when California enacted the Uniform Rule.

Although these statutes differ slightly in detail,[45] we present the Illinois provisions as illustrative of the specific-statutory-repair approach to perpetuity reform.

Illinois Revised Statutes
Chapter 765

§ *305/4. Application of the Rule Against Perpetuities*. . . . (c) In determining whether an interest violates the rule against perpetuities:

(1) it shall be presumed (A) that the interest was intended to be valid, (B) in the case of an interest conditioned upon the probate of a will, the appointment of an executor, administrator or trustee, the completion of the administration of an estate, the payment of debts, the sale or distribution of property, the determination of federal or state tax liabilities or the happening of any administrative contingency, that the contingency must occur, if at all, within the period of the rule against perpetuities, and (C) where the instrument creates an interest in the "widow," "widower," or "spouse" of another person, that the maker of the instrument intended to refer to a person who was living at the date that the period of the rule against perpetuities commences to run;

(2) where any interest, but for this subparagraph (c)(2), would be invalid because it is made to depend upon any person attaining or failing to attain an age in excess of 21 years, the age specified shall be reduced to 21 years as to every person to whom the age contingency applies;

---

41. See Ill. Rev. Stat. ch. 765, § 305/4(c). The Illinois statute also contains a wait-and-see element applicable only to trusts. See id. § 305/5. The statute is explained by its drafter in Daniel M. Schuyler, The Statute Concerning Perpetuities, 65 Nw. U.L. Rev. 3 (1970).

42. See N.Y. Est. Powers & Trusts Law §§ 9-1.2, -1.3.

43. See Fla. Stat. § 689.22(5)(a)-(d) (repealed).

44. See Cal. Civ. Code § 715.7 (repealed).

45. The differences are recounted and analyzed in Waggoner, Perpetuity Reform, supra note 6, at 1726-50.

(3) if, notwithstanding the provisions of subparagraphs (c)(1) and (2) of this Section, the validity of any interest depends upon the possibility of the birth or adoption of a child, (A) no person shall be deemed capable of having a child until he has attained the age of 13 years, (B) any person who has attained the age of 65 years shall be deemed incapable of having a child, (C) evidence shall be admissible as to the incapacity of having a child by a living person who has not attained the age of 65 years, and (D) the possibility of having a child or more remote descendants by adoption shall be disregarded.

2. Proper Scope of Perpetuity Reform—The Prevention-of-Unjust-Enrichment Theory

The specific-statutory-repair method of perpetuity reform saves the technical violation cases from invalidity, but leaves other perpetuity violations untouched. The two methods we are about to study—reformation and wait-and-see (with deferred reformation)—affect all perpetuity violations. A theoretical case for this wider scope of perpetuity reform was set forth in Lawrence W. Waggoner, Perpetuity Reform, 81 Mich. L. Rev. 1718, 1719-29, 1785 (1983), as follows:

> The original case for perpetuity reform, indeed the only case for reform that has been systematically presented, argues from the technical violation categories and rests on the Rule's "harshness" or "illogicality" in defeating such reasonable dispositions. This case is an argument for reversing the invalidity in the technical violation categories, but not for interfering with the normal operation of the Rule in all cases of perpetuity violation. . . .
>
> The theme of this Article is that there is a respectable case for intercession in all cases of perpetuity violation. The case is grounded upon and is in fact an application of the theme of another article that John Langbein and I recently co-authored, entitled *Reformation of Wills on the Ground of Mistake: Change of Direction in American Law?,* [130 U. Pa. L. Rev. 521 (1982)]. Pointing to the long-recognized reformation doctrine for nonprobate transfers, that article advocates the forthright adoption of a similar doctrine for wills. Cases of well-proven mistake of law or fact in the formulation of the terms of gratuitous transfers invoke the fundamental principle of equity jurisprudence: preventing unjust enrichment. If mistakes are not corrected, unintended takers are enriched at the expense of the intended beneficiaries. In one respect, the application of this idea to the perpetuity area is easier than in the generalized cases of mistake that are the main focus of attention in the earlier article. Extrinsic evidence is hardly necessary to show that a perpetuity violation is the product of a mistake, but such evidence is frequently necessary to prove a mistake in other cases.
>
> The application of the prevention-of-unjust-enrichment idea to the perpetuity area is easier, though more subtle, in another respect. Preventing unjust enrichment in generalized cases of mistake requires an open-ended remedy of reformation, to be applied by courts on an ad hoc basis. Because perpetuity

violations are relatively homogeneous, the method to be applied in the correction of the mistake can take a common and hence more automatic form. It need not, in fact, be framed overtly as a method of correcting a mistake but can be cast as a legislative reformulation of the Rule Against Perpetuities itself. This approach will be effective as long as it is understood that correction of mistake is the underlying objective of the reformulation, so that the reformulation is shaped by the legislature and administered by the courts in accordance with that objective. . . .

The objective of reform, then, should be to prevent such unjust enrichment, so far as would have been legally possible at the drafting stage of the disposition. . . .

With the theory of reform properly focused on the prevention of unjust enrichment, courts in jurisdictions that have adopted the reformation method should reform offending dispositions by injecting a saving clause into the instrument. And legislatures contemplating perpetuity reform should . . . enact wait-and-see statutes modeled on the [saving-clause principle].

3. *Immediately Available Reformation*

Statutory References: *UPC § 2-905(b) (USRAP § 5(b))*

Berry v. Union National Bank

262 S.E.2d 766 (W. Va. 1980)

HARSHBARGER, J. This case presents the issue whether a private testamentary trust which violates the rule against perpetuities should be modified to effectuate a testatrix' intent or should fail.

Clara Clayton Post died on June 20, 1975, in Harrison County. Her will and codicil were admitted to probate on June 23, 1975, at which time Josephine H. Berry, appellant, qualified as executrix. After a series of specific bequests to her heirs at law, appellees Ellen Clayton and Arthur Clayton, and to other parties, Ms. Post created a private educational trust for the descendants of her late husband's brothers and sisters, giving her trustee absolute discretion to provide educational expenses for [the descendants of her late husband's brothers and sisters] meeting certain criteria. The trust was to endure for twenty-five years after testatrix' death or until the principal was reduced to less than $5,000.00, whichever should first occur. At the termination of the trust the principal and interest were to be distributed per stirpes to the then living descendants of her husband's brothers and sisters. The Union National Bank of Clarksburg, appellee, was named trustee.

Executrix Berry recognized that the trust potentially violated the rule against perpetuities and entered into a trust termination agreement with the trustee. The agreement amended the twenty-five year provision to twenty-one years and required the executrix to initiate a declaratory judgment action in the Circuit Court of Harrison County to determine *inter alia*, whether the trust violated the rule against perpetuities and whether it was proper for the executrix and trustee to enter into a trust termination agreement. A guardian ad litem was appointed for the unborn beneficiaries on April 26, 1977. The trial court granted summary judgment for the heirs at law, finding that the trust provision violated the rule against perpetuities and was therefore void and without force. The court additionally ruled that the executrix and trustee were not authorized to enter into the trust termination agreement. Executrix Berry appealed. . . .

The analysis of any problem concerning a will must begin with the fundamental principle that a testator's intent shall be ascertained and followed to the extent possible. . . .

The rule against perpetuities is a common law rule which reflects the public policy that a testator or trustor cannot control the devolution of his property for an inordinate period of time. . . .

If a testator creates an estate which vests or has the possibility of vesting after a life in being plus twenty-one years and a period of gestation, the estate violates the rule against perpetuities and the testator's intent will be defeated. . . .

It is here that principles of law collide: a testator may not indefinitely control the devolution of his property; but a testator's intent should be honored and intestacy avoided whenever feasible. To remedy this apparent conflict, we adopt a doctrine of equitable modification which courts should apply to certain devises that on their face appear to violate the rule against perpetuities but meet the conditions enumerated below. Our action accords with a developing trend to ameliorate the harsh consequences of "remorseless application" of the rule. The theory which we endorse today is akin to the doctrine of *cy-pres* which was initially developed in the area of charitable trusts and was legislatively enacted in West Virginia in 1931 for that purpose. W.Va.Code, 35-2-2.

The purpose of equitable modification is to revise an instrument in a fashion that effectuates a testator's general intent within the limitations established by the rule.

We support the underlying policies of the rule against perpetuities and will deny validity to an interest which vests beyond the time limitations provided in the rule. However, before a testamentary scheme is totally obliterated by application of the rule, we will determine whether the testamentary disposition can be equitably modified to comport with the rule's underlying policy.

A non-charitable devise or bequest which violates the rule will be modified if the following conditions are met:

(1) The testator's intent is expressed in the instrument or can be readily determined by a court;
(2) The testator's general intent does not violate the rule against perpetuities;
(3) The testator's particular intent, which does violate the rule, is not a critical aspect of the testamentary scheme; and

(4) The proposed modification will effectuate the testator's general intent, will avoid the consequences of intestacy, and will conform to the policy considerations underlying the rule.

The testamentary trust here meets all these criteria for application of the equitable modification doctrine.

Testatrix clearly expressed her general intent in Section IX of her will when she stated:

> I believe it was the desire of my husband that such funds as I might have at my death should be used to help such persons (who are later defined in this section) obtain educations. This is the only expression I ever heard him make relative to the disposition of such funds.

Her general intention to provide funds for education of her husband's nieces, nephews and their families does not contravene the rule. Her particular intention to have the trust continue for twenty-five years after her death or until the principal was less than $5,000.00 violates the rule. There is no indication that the twenty-five year period is a critical aspect of her testamentary scheme. If the trust is modified to reduce that twenty-five year period to twenty-one years before distribution of the remaining principal to the then living descendants of her husband's siblings, the general intent to provide for their education will be effectuated, intestacy for that portion of her estate will be avoided, and property will not be controlled by her beyond the perpetuities' limitation. . . .

It is not necessary for us to address the other issues raised in the parties' briefs due to our disposition of the main question. We hold, therefore, that the will of Clara Clayton Post should be equitably modified to reduce the duration of the trust from twenty-five years to twenty-one years. The ruling of the circuit court is reversed and the cause remanded for appointment of additional guardians ad litem and further proceedings consistent with this opinion.

Reversed and remanded.

Notes

1. *State of the Authorities*. In 1992, West Virginia enacted the Uniform Rule effectively displacing *Berry* for posteffective-date transfers. In decisions antedating *Berry*, the courts in Hawaii, Mississippi, and New Hampshire had adopted the immediately available reformation approach. See In re Chun Quan Yee Hop, 469 P.2d 183 (Haw. 1970) (period in gross lowered from 30 to 21; in 1992, Hawaii enacted the Uniform Rule effectively displacing the rule of this case for posteffective-date transfers); Carter v. Berry, 140 So. 2d 843 (Miss. 1962) (age contingency lowered from 25 to 21); Edgerly v. Barker, 31 A. 900 (N.H. 1891) (age contingency lowered from 40 to 21).

Legislation in Missouri, Oklahoma, and Texas authorizes or directs the courts to reform defective instruments. See Tex. Rev. Stat. § 5.043; see also Idaho Code § 55-111. Until 1991, California had an immediate-reformation statute, but it was repealed when California enacted the Uniform Rule.[46]

Although these judicial decisions and statutes authorize or direct reformation of the defective instrument in a way that comes as close as possible to the transferor's intent without violating the common-law Rule, the cases have all been of a similar type to *Berry* and in each case the courts have reformed the disposition by lowering the period in gross or age contingency to 21. A method of reformation more faithful to the transferor's intention would have been to insert a saving clause into the governing instrument. See Olin L. Browder, Construction, Reformation, and the Rule Against Perpetuities, 62 Mich. L. Rev. 1 (1963); Waggoner, Perpetuity Reform, supra, at 1755-59; John H. Langbein & Lawrence W. Waggoner, Reformation of Wills on the Ground of Mistake: Change of Direction in American Law?, 130 U. Pa. L. Rev. 521, 546-49 (1982). The Supreme Court of New Hampshire came close to adopting this method of reformation in Richardson Trust, 634 A.2d 1005 (N.H. 1993) (the trust in essence provided that income was to be distributed to the testator's issue and, upon a failure of issue, the income was to be distributed to a named charity; the probate court ruled and the supreme court affirmed, relying on *Edgerly,* that the income should be distributed to the testator's issue until either no issue remain or the "trust violates the rule against perpetuities" at which time the principal should be distributed in accordance with the intestate succession statute). The Supreme Court of Mississippi adopted this method of reformation but revealed a degree of misunderstanding by also purporting to adopt the wait-and-see method of perpetuity reform without seeming to realize that immediate reformation and wait-and-see are mutually inconsistent methods of perpetuity reform. Estate of Anderson v. Deposit Guaranty Nat'l Bank, 541 So. 2d 423 (Miss. 1989) (the court upheld the testamentary trust, which was to last for 25 years from the date of admission of the will to probate, the income to be used for the education of the descendants of the testator's father, and the corpus at the end of the 25-year period to be paid over to testator's nephew, Howard Davis, or if Howard was not then living, to the heirs of Howard's body; by inserting a saving clause but also by adopting the wait-and-see method).

In another case, Merrill v. Wimmer, 481 N.E.2d 1294 (Ind. 1985), the Supreme Court of Indiana held that judicial reformation to correct a perpetuity violation is forbidden by reason of the fact that in Indiana the common-law Rule

46. See Cal. Civ. Code § 715.5 (repealed), applied in Estate of Ghiglia, 42 Cal. App. 3d 433, 116 Cal. Rptr. 827 (1974) (age contingency lowered from 35 to 21).

was then codified. Do you agree that codification of the common-law Rule precludes the reformation method of perpetuity reform?[47]

2. *Reformation Authorized by the Uniform Rule.* Although the Uniform Rule adopts the wait-and-see method of perpetuity reform, reformation also plays an important role under the Uniform Rule. Section 3 establishes a deferred-reformation rule by directing a court to reform a disposition if, after exhaustion of the permissible vesting period, it violates the Statutory Rule Against Perpetuities. More significant for our purpose here, however, is § 5 of the Uniform Rule. Under that section, the wait-and-see rule adopted by the Uniform Rule applies only prospectively; as to pre-existing interests, § 5(b) authorizes immediate reformation. In line with the law review articles listed above, *Richardson,* and *Anderson*, the Official Comment to § 5(b) urges courts to consider reforming a pre-existing perpetuity violation by judicially inserting an appropriate saving clause rather than by lowering an age contingency or period in gross to 21. The comment notes that a saving clause would probably have been used at the drafting stage of the disposition had it been drafted competently. In addition, the comment notes that the period of time marked off by the perpetuity-period component of an appropriate saving clause would ordinarily be more than sufficient to give the contingencies attached to the nonvested interest to work themselves out to a final resolution under the terms set forth by the transferor. See Abrams v. Templeton, 466 S.E.2d 117 (S.C. Ct. App. 1995) (the state had adopted the Uniform Rule; the court inserted a saving clause in accordance with the state statute that required, rather than merely authorized, a court to reform a pre-enactment trust containing invalid interests).

4. Wait-and-See/Deferred Reformation

Statutory References: *UPC §§ 2-901, -903 (USRAP §§ 1, 3)*

We know that the basis upon which validity or invalidity depends is the full array of possible postcreation events. In its early stages, the perpetuity-reform movement focused on the technical-violation categories. Because the postcreation chains of possible events that invalidate those interests are so unlikely to happen, it was rather natural to propose that the requirement of initial certainty be abandoned in favor of taking actual postcreation events into account. Instead of invalidating an interest because of what *might* happen, waiting to see what *does* happen seemed then and still seems now to be more

47. "[T]he reformation method . . . does not alter the [common-law] Rule at all. The Rule is left intact, and the disposition is altered to conform to it." Waggoner, Perpetuity Reform, supra note 6, at 1755-56. In any event, Indiana subsequently enacted the Uniform Rule, which specifically authorizes reformation of pre-effective date interests.

sensible. Known as the wait-and-see method of perpetuity reform, this approach is the approach recently promulgated by the two preeminent national organizations concerned with law reform—the American Law Institute and the National Conference of Commissioners on Uniform State Laws.

Neither the ALI's Restatement 2d of Property (1983) nor the NCCUSL's Uniform Rule (1990) alters what may be called the *validating* side of the common-law Rule. Dispositions that would have been valid under the common-law Rule remain valid. Practitioners under either wait-and-see regime can and should continue to use a traditional perpetuity saving clause. The wait-and-see element is applied only to interests that fall prey to the *invalidating* side of the common-law Rule. Interests that would be invalid at common law are saved from being rendered *initially invalid*. To prevent the unjust enrichment of unintended takers caused by a drafter's mistake in failing to insert an appropriate perpetuity saving clause, otherwise invalid interests are, as it were, given a second chance: These interests are valid if they actually vest within the permissible vesting period and become invalid only if they remain in existence but still nonvested at the expiration of that period.

Shifting the focus from possible to actual postcreation events has great attraction, and wait-and-see has been widely adopted, though still opposed by a few academics. The greatest controversy over wait-and-see concerns how the permissible vesting period is to be marked off—the permissible period of time for the contingencies attached to an otherwise invalid interest to be finally resolved.

Until recently, the conventional assumption was that the permissible vesting period must be marked off in time by reference to so-called measuring lives who are in being at the creation of the interest; the permissible vesting period under this assumption expires 21 years after the death of the last surviving measuring life. Controversies raged over who the measuring lives should be and how the law should identify them.

Saving-Clause Principle of Wait-and-See. It now seems understood that wait-and-see is nothing more mysterious than a perpetuity saving clause injected by the law when the governing instrument fails to include one. In effect, the perpetuity-period component of a standard saving clause constitutes a privately established wait-and-see rule. The permissible vesting period under wait-and-see is, or should be, the equivalent of the perpetuity-period component of a well-conceived saving clause.

The saving clause is rounded out by providing the near-equivalent of a gift-over component via a provision for judicial reformation of a disposition in case the interest is still in existence and nonvested when the permissible vesting period expires.

Title in Abeyance. One of the early objections to wait-and-see should be mentioned at this point. It was once widely argued and still occasionally is argued that wait-and-see can cause harm because it puts the validity of property interests in abeyance—no one can determine whether an interest is valid or not. This argument has been shown to be false. Keep in mind that the wait-and-see element is applied only to interests that would be invalid were it not for wait-and-see. These otherwise invalid interests are always nonvested future interests. It is now well understood that wait-and-see does nothing more than subject that type of future interest to an *additional* contingency. For the interest to vest, the original contingencies must be satisfied within a certain period of time. If that period of time—the permissible vesting period—is easily determined, then the additional contingency causes no more uncertainty in the state of the title than would have been the case had it been explicitly placed in the governing instrument itself. It should also be noted that only the status of the affected future interest in the trust or other property arrangement is deferred. In the interim, the other interests, such as the interests of current income beneficiaries, are carried out in the normal course without obstruction.

The Permissible Vesting Period. As indicated above, the greatest controversy has been over how to mark off the permissible vesting period. This is the subject to which we now turn. The problem arises because the common-law Rule contained no mechanism for marking off an actual period of time to wait to see if an otherwise invalid interest vests or terminates in "due time." The only mechanism the common law provided is the requirement of initial certainty, which as noted supra p. 1176, is a mechanism for testing the validity of an interest at the point of its creation. The decision is made at the point of creation, with postcreation events disregarded and, therefore, the common law had no cause to mark off a "perpetuity period" during which postcreation events are allowed to be taken into account. At common law, there either is a validating life or there is no validating life. There is no validating life for invalid interests, hence there is no common-law "perpetuity period" to wait out. A permissible vesting period is necessary only under the wait-and-see method of perpetuity reform.

a. Early Forms of Wait-and-See Legislation

Pennsylvania-Style Statutes. Enacted in 1947, the Pennsylvania statute (20 Pa. Cons. Stat. Ann. § 6104(b)) was the first wait-and-see statute. The statute mistakenly presupposes that there is a common-law perpetuity period, and therefore it contains no method of marking that period off. The statute provides:

> Upon the expiration of the period allowed by the common law rule against perpetuities as measured by actual rather than possible events, any interest not then vested and any interest in members of a class the membership of which is then subject to increase shall be void.

Pennsylvania-style statutes are also in effect in Ohio,[48] South Dakota,[49] Vermont,[50] and Virginia.[51] The only case ever to apply the Pennsylvania statute or a Pennsylvania-style statute is Estate of Pearson, 275 A.2d 336 (Pa. 1971), a decision universally condemned for not explaining who the measuring lives were and how they are to be identified under the statute.[52]

Massachusetts-Style Statutes. First enacted in Massachusetts in 1954, the Massachusetts-style statute expressly measures the permissible vesting period by the length of one or more life estates in persons in being at the creation of the interest:

> In applying the rule against perpetuities to an interest in real or personal property limited to take effect at or after the termination of one or more life estates in, or lives of, persons in being when the period of said rule commences to run, the validity of the interest shall be determined on the basis of facts existing at the termination of such one or more life estates or lives. In this section an interest which must terminate not later than the death of one or more persons is a "life estate" even though it may terminate at an earlier time.

Massachusetts-style statutes are in effect in Maine[53] and Maryland.[54] Until 1989, this type of statute was also in effect in Connecticut[55] and Massachusetts;[56] it was repealed when Connecticut and Massachusetts enacted the Uniform Rule.

Choosing to restrict the permissible vesting period to the length of one or more life estates in persons in being at the creation of the interest does not even reverse the invalidity in a standard administrative-contingency case,[57] nor does it provide appropriate relief in age-contingency-in-excess-of-21 cases. The

48. See Ohio Rev. Code Ann. § 2131.08(c).

49. See S.D. Codified Laws Ann. § 43-5-6.

50. See Vt. Stat. Ann. tit. 27, § 501.

51. See Va. Code § 55-13.3.

52. See, e.g., Waggoner, Perpetuity Reform, supra note 6, at 1762-76.

53. See Me. Rev. Stat. Ann. tit. 33, § 101.

54. See Md. Est. & Trusts Code Ann. § 11-103(a).

55. See Conn. Gen. Stat. § 45-95 (repealed).

56. See Mass. Gen. Laws Ann. Ch. 184A, § 1 (repealed).

57. Note, however, that in the two states that had such statutes but repealed them, there was a decision upholding a standard administrative contingency disposition under the common-law Rule, on the theory that the fiduciary has an obligation to complete the administrative task within a period of time less than 21 years. See Belfield v. Booth, 27 A. 585 (Conn. 1893); Brandenburg v. Thorndike, 28 N.E. 575 (Mass. 1885).

statutes, in fact, further provide that if at the end of the restricted vesting period, an interest would be invalid because it is "contingent upon any person attaining or failing to attain an age in excess of twenty-one, the age contingency shall be reduced to twenty-one as to all persons subject to the same age contingency." See Foley v. Evans, 570 N.E.2d 179 (Mass. App. Ct.), rev. denied, 573 N.E.2d 985 (Mass. 1991) (considering both the wait-and-see reform and the age-contingency reform). In Second Nat'l Bank v. Harris Trust & Savings Bank, 283 A.2d 226 (Conn. Super. Ct. 1971), this latter provision was held inapplicable to a trust that was created by the exercise of a general testamentary power of appointment and that provided for the income to go to the testator-donee's daughter, Mary, for 30 years, remainder to Mary, but if she was not then living, to her descendants, per stirpes. The court held that the executory interest in favor of Mary's descendants violated the Rule Against Perpetuities and was invalid; the effect was to render Mary's remainder interest absolute. As for the age-contingency provision of the statute, the court said: "It seems too clear for argument that the remainder to Mary's children is not 'contingent upon any person attaining or failing to attain an age in excess of twenty-one.'" Id. at 232.

Clearly, Massachusetts-style statutes fall markedly short of fulfilling the goal of preventing unjust enrichment of unintended takers.

Kentucky-Style Statutes. Enacted in 1960, the Kentucky statute (Ky. Rev. Stat. § 381.216) adopts a permissible vesting period measured by the life of persons who have a "causal relationship" to the vesting or failure of the interest in question:

> In determining whether an interest would violate the rule against perpetuities the period of perpetuities shall be measured by actual rather than possible events; Provided, however, the period shall not be measured by any lives whose continuance does not have a causal relationship to the vesting or failure of the interest.

Until 1996, 1987, 1992, and 1999, respectively, this type of statute was also in effect in Alaska,[58] Nevada,[59] New Mexico,[60] and Rhode Island[61]; it was repealed when Alaska, Nevada and New Mexico enacted the Uniform Rule, and when Rhode Island abolished the Rule entirely.

---

58. See Alaska Stat. § 34.27.010 (repealed).

59. See Nev. Rev. Stat. § 111.103 (repealed).

60. See N.M. Stat. Ann. § 47-1-17.1 (repealed).

61. See 1999 R.I. Laws, ch. 99-403 § 1 (repealing former version of R.I. Gen Laws § 34-11-38).

As we shall see, the meaning of "causal relationship to the vesting or failure of the interest" is much in dispute. One commentator recently concluded: "It is apparent that the 'causal relationship' test does little to clarify the problem of measuring lives under wait-and-see."[62]

Nevertheless, the Supreme Court of Mississippi judicially adopted the wait-and-see method of reform using "causal-relationship" lives. Estate of Anderson v. Deposit Guaranty Nat'l Bank, supra p. 1233.

Problems and Note

In the following cases, by whose life or lives is the permissible vesting period measured under a Kentucky-style statute?

1. G deeded real property "to A and his heirs, but if the property is used for nonresidential purposes, to X and his heirs."

2. G died, survived by his child, A, and by A's children, X (age 26) and Y (age 21). G's will devised property "to A for life, then to A's children who attain 25."

The architect of the causal-relationship formula and the principal drafter of the Kentucky statute believes that X is the only causal-relationship measuring life in Problem 1 and that X and Y are among the causal-relationship measuring lives in Problem 2. See Jesse Dukeminier, Perpetuities: The Measuring Lives, 85 Colum. L. Rev. 1648, 1666-67 (Case 6, which is essentially the same as Problem 2), 1705-06 (Case 18, which is essentially the same as Problem 1) (1985).

In a debate centering partially on these examples, Professor Waggoner argued that A, not X, should properly be regarded as the only causal-relationship measuring life in Problem 1; that Y but not X should properly be regarded as a causal-relationship measuring life in Problem 2; and that disputes of this sort demonstrate that the causal-relationship-to-vesting formula is not a useful method of identifying the measuring lives for wait-and-see. See Lawrence W. Waggoner, Perpetuities: A Perspective on Wait-and-See, 85 Colum. L. Rev. 1714, 1719-24 (1985).

---

62. Paul G. Haskell, A Proposal for a Simple and Socially Effective Rule Against Perpetuities, 66 N.C. L. Rev. 545, 554 (1988).

Fleet National Bank v. Colt

529 A.2d 122 (R.I. 1987)

[The testator, Samuel P. Colt, died in 1921, survived by his son Roswell and Roswell's daughter, Elizabeth.[63] The testator left a will that created a testamentary trust, under which a one-sixth share of his residuary estate was to pay income to Roswell for life, then to Roswell's children for life, and on the death of each of Roswell's children, to pay to "the child or children of such deceased child . . . , per stirpes and not per capita, his [or] her proportionate share of this trust estate, as an estate vested in fee simple, discharged of all trust."

After the testator's death, several additional descendants were born. Among them were Roswell's son, Caldwell, and Elizabeth's three children and Caldwell's two children. After Roswell's death in 1935, each of his children began receiving a proportionate share of the trust income. Caldwell died in 1985, survived by his two children and by his sister, Elizabeth, and her three children.]

SHEA, J. This case is before the court following a Superior Court granting of a joint motion for certification. . . .

The orthodox rule against perpetuities . . . has been the subject of much criticism and debate by legal scholars and writers. See W. Leach, Perpetuities in Perspective: Ending The Rule's Reign of Terror 65 Harv. L. Rev. 721 (1952). The major criticism of the rule is that it often serves to totally defeat the intent of the testator by invalidating a gift due to remote contingencies based upon improbable happenings. Id. at 723.

In answer to these criticisms Rhode Island, among other states, has enacted a statute to modify the rule. General Laws 1956 (1984 Reenactment) § 34-11-38 modifies the rule against perpetuities by directing that "the period of perpetuities . . . be measured by actual rather than possible events." Our statute requires, however, that the possible measuring lives bear a causal relationship to the vesting or failure of an interest. If, after applying the rule as modified by the statute, a gifted interest is still violative of it, the statute directs that the interest be reformed "to approximate most closely the intention of the creator of the interest." Through this statute, our Legislature has adopted both the "wait-and-see" approach and the "cy pres doctrine" as reformation of the rule against perpetuities. Although the statute embodies this state's present method

---

63. The testator was also survived by another son, Russell, and by his brother, LeBaron. Also living at the testator's death were Russell's three children, Lebaron's three children, and LeBaron's five grandchildren. These other relatives were beneficiaries of other shares of the testamentary trust created by the testator's will, but those other shares and these other relatives did not figure in the perpetuity question raised by the case.

of application of the rule against perpetuities, unfortunately, the statute itself may not be retroactively applied in the case before us because, by its terms, it "shall not be construed to invalidate or modify the terms of any interest which would have been valid prior to May 17, 1983."

We believe § 34-11-38 is a codification of a policy employed by this court prior to the statutory adoption of rule-against-perpetuities reform by the Legislature. . . .

The facts of the case before us present a particularly appropriate situation in which to apply the rule in terms of "wait-and-see actualities" rather than "orthodox possibilities." There is no question that the property at issue in Caldwell's estate is now distributable in fee simple. The only question is who will receive the distribution. Notwithstanding the identity of the persons to inherit, the property will no longer be held unalienable; its transferability is no longer controlled. The purpose of the rule therefore, that of preventing lengthy restraints on the alienation of property, will be fulfilled at this time regardless of who we decide may inherit.

Applying the wait-and-see approach to the rule against perpetuities, we examine the vesting of an interest at the time the contingency upon which it depends occurs. If the facts as they exist at that time allow for vesting within a life or lives in being plus twenty-one years, the gift is valid and the various possibilities that may have prevented vesting when viewed at the death of the testator are irrelevant. Restatement (Second) Property § 1.4 (1983); Note, Understanding the Measuring Life in the Rule Against Perpetuities, 1974 Wash. U.L.Q. 265, 287. Examining the facts, therefore, as they exist at the death of Caldwell rather than at the death of the testator, we must determine whether his shares vest in his children's possession within a life in being plus twenty-one years. This life in being must bear a causal relationship to the vesting of interests under the Will because although the orthodox rule against perpetuities defines a measuring life to be any life whatsoever in being at the death of the testator and requires no causal relationship, the wait-and-see doctrine limits the range of possible measuring lives by requiring that they bear a causal relationship to the vesting of the future interest in question. Note at 290; 61 Am.Jur.2d Perpetuities § 29 at 37 (1981). "The meaning of the causal relationship principle . . . encompasses every relationship that any validating life at common law bears to vesting. It embraces every person who, in the particular situation, can affect vesting." J. Dukeminier, Perpetuities: The Measuring Lives, 85 Col. L. Rev. 1648, 1648 (1985).

At the time of Caldwell's death, his sister Elizabeth . . . [was] the only one of Roswell's . . . children who was alive at the testator's death. . . . She is thus a life in being and an acceptable measuring life. She is causally connected not only to the vesting of the remainder in her own children, but also to the life estate of her siblings and thus to the remainder in her sibling's children. If, for example, Elizabeth had predeceased her father Roswell, the income that Roswell had been receiving as a first life tenant would have been divided [into fewer shares]. Thus, the amount of Caldwell's share, and consequently the amounts of his children's shares, were dependent upon the survival of Elizabeth.

Since Elizabeth is still living today, it is clear that the remainder interests of Caldwell's children have vested within the time period set by the rule against perpetuities. The testator's gift to them, therefore, is valid.

Note and Question

1. *The "Elementary Logic" of the Causal-Relationship Formula.* Commenting on the *Colt* decision, Professor Fletcher said:

> At most, Elizabeth was related to the resolution of only the first uncertainty—the division of shares at Roswell's death. Even here, Roswell's life, not Elizabeth's, is the defensive life. The fact that a class member, such as Elizabeth, happened to be alive at the effective date, is not significant. If, however, we see Elizabeth as significant at Roswell's death, nevertheless she serves no useful function thereafter, and her continued life thereafter should be unusable.
>
> Professor Dukeminier should disapprove of the court's disposition of this case. With respect to the uncertainty in identifying Caldwell's children, Elizabeth is totally useless and should not get on Professor Dukeminier's list; even if he should let her on, he surely would strike her from it the moment Roswell dies.

Robert L. Fletcher, Perpetuities: Basic Clarity, Muddled Reform, 63 Wash. L. Rev. 791, 832 n.57 (1988).

2. *Retroactivity of the Rhode Island Causal-Relationship Statute.* Are you convinced that application of the Rhode Island causal-relationship wait-and-see statute to the *Colt* case was prevented by the statutory provision that said that the statute "shall not be construed to invalidate or modify the terms of any interest which would have been valid prior to May 17, 1983"?

b. Restatement 2d of Property (1983)

In adopting the wait-and-see method of perpetuity reform, the Restatement 2d of Property rejected the causal-relationship formula for determining the measuring lives and chose instead to use a predetermined list of lives. Under § 1.3(2) of the Restatement 2d of Property, the permissible vesting period expires 21 years after the death of the survivor of:

> (a) The transferor if the period of the rule begins to run in the transferor's lifetime; and
>
> (b) Those individuals alive when the period of the rule begins to run, if reasonable in number, who have beneficial interests vested or contingent in the

property in which the non-vested interest in question exists and the parents and grandparents alive when the period of the rule begins to run of all beneficiaries of the property in which the non-vested interest exists, and

(c) The donee of a nonfiduciary power of appointment alive when the period of the rule begins to run if the exercise of such power could affect the non-vested interest in question.

If a property interest is still in existence but nonvested at the expiration of the permissible vesting period, § 1.5 provides that "the transferred property shall be disposed of in the manner which most closely effectuates the transferor's manifested plan of distribution and which is within the limits of the rule against perpetuities."

So far, the Restatement 2d's version of wait-and-see has not been directly adopted by any common-law court,[64] nor has it been legislatively enacted by any state. A statute enacted in Iowa, however, was influenced by the Restatement 2d; the Iowa statute designates as the measuring lives the beneficiaries and "the grandparents of all such beneficiaries and the issue of such grandparents. . . ." Iowa Code § 558.68(2)(b)(2) (enacted in 1983). See Estate of Keenan, 519 N.W.2d 373 (Iowa 1994) (reformed the trust after finding that the trust would be certain to violate the wait-and-see time period).

Professor Dukeminier expressed displeasure that the Restatement 2d did not adopt the causal-relationship formula and assailed the Restatement's predetermined list by arguing that it "does not faithfully adhere to any principle at all," is drafted so ambiguously that its words "are like quicksilver" that "slip and slide and elude our grasp," and "may take years of learned analysis and litigation to solve its sphinxine riddles." Jesse Dukeminier, Perpetuities: The Measuring Lives, 85 Colum. L. Rev. 1648, 1675, 1681, 1701 (1985).

---

64. It has received favorable comment in a few cases, however. See Hansen v. Stoecker, 699 P.2d 871, 874-75 (Alaska 1985) ("We are persuaded [by the Restatement 2d and other authorities] that the wait-and-see approach should be adopted as the common law rule against perpetuities in Alaska.") The Alaska wait-and-see statute using the causal-relationship standard for identifying measuring lives was not applicable in *Hansen* because the interest in question was created before the effective date of the statute. As indicated in the text, that statute was repealed when Alaska enacted the Uniform Rule in its place.

See also DeWire v. Haveles, 534 N.E.2d 782, 785-86 n.7 (Mass. 1989) (the court suggested that it might follow the Restatement 2d; note, however, that Massachusetts subsequently enacted the Uniform Rule); Nantt v. Pucket Energy Co., 382 N.W.2d 655, 661 (N.D. 1986) (citing the Restatement 2d of Property, the court said that the wait-and-see rule "is a basic common sense approach to 'perpetuities' today").

But see Pound v. Shorter, supra p. 1212 (without mentioning the Restatement 2d, the court rejected wait-and-see as a common-law concept; note, however, that Georgia subsequently enacted the Uniform Rule).

c. Uniform Statutory Rule Against Perpetuities [Uniform Probate Code Article II Part 9]

Statutory References: *UPC §§ 2-901 to -906 (USRAP)*

Introduction. The National Conference of Commissioners on Uniform State Laws promulgated the Uniform Rule in 1986, amended it modestly in 1990,[65] and brought it into the Uniform Probate Code. The general contour of the Uniform Rule is similar to that of the Restatement 2d of Property. The validating side of the common-law Rule is retained but the invalidating side is replaced with wait-and-see and deferred-reformation elements. The major departure from the Restatement approach is that the Uniform Rule uses a flat 90-year permissible vesting period under its wait-and-see element rather than a period ending 21 years after the death of the survivor of a predetermined list of measuring lives.

Enactments. The Uniform Rule is currently in effect in California, Colorado, Connecticut, the District of Columbia, Georgia, Hawaii, Indiana, Kansas, Massachusetts, Michigan, Minnesota, Montana, Nebraska, Nevada, New Mexico, North Carolina, North Dakota, Oregon, South Carolina, Tennessee, Utah, Virginia,[66] and West Virginia.

Rationale of the 90-Year Permissible Vesting Period. The most striking feature of the Uniform Rule is its use of a flat period of 90 years as the permissible vesting period in its wait-and-see element. The rationale for this step was explained by the Professor Waggoner, the reporter for the Uniform Rule, as follows:

> [T]he philosophy behind the 90-year period was to fix a period of time that approximates the average period of time that would traditionally be allowed by the wait-and-see doctrine. There was no intention to use the flat-period-of-years method as a means of lengthening the [permissible vesting] period beyond its traditional boundaries. The fact that the traditional period roughly averages out to a longish-sounding 90 years is a reflection of a quite different phenomenon: the dramatic increase in longevity that society as a whole has experienced in the course of the twentieth century. Seen in this light, the 90-year period is an evolutionary step in the development of the wait-and-see doctrine.
>
> [T]he traditional method of delimiting the [permissible vesting] period is to use actual measuring lives plus 21 years. Specifically, under this method, a group of persons—called the measuring lives—is identified. Once the group is identified, the

---

65. The 1990 amendment added subsection (e) to § 1 (UPC § 2-901(e)).

66. Virginia adopted the Uniform Rule on April 8, 2000. See Va. Code §§ 55-12.1 - 12.6. On the same day, Virginia also made the Rule Against Perpetuities optional. See Va. Code § 55-13.3(e); infra p. 1252.

lives of all its members are traced to see which one outlives all the others and when that survivor dies. The [permissible vesting] period extends 21 years beyond the death of that last surviving measuring life.

From its inception, the actual-measuring-lives approach has been plagued by two problems: identification and tracing. The identification problem concerns the method by which the measuring lives are to be chosen. Rival methods have been advanced. Under one method . . . , the measuring lives are identified by testing each disposition to determine the persons whose lives have a "causal relationship" to the vesting or failure of the future interest in question. The actual meaning of causal relationship is in dispute, and the adoption of that method could require front-end litigation to determine the identity of the measuring lives in a given case. Neither the Restatement nor [the Uniform Rule] adopted the causal-relationship method. The Restatement specifies the measuring lives in a different way. The Restatement uses a list composed, generally speaking, of the transferor, the beneficiaries of the disposition, the parents and grandparents of the beneficiaries, and, in certain cases, the donee of a nonfiduciary power of appointment; of the foregoing, those who are in being at the creation of the interest are the measuring lives. It soon became apparent that the Restatement's list contained ambiguities, at least at the fringes, which could also require front-end litigation to determine the full complement of measuring lives in a given case. The framers of [the Uniform Rule] concluded that an ambiguity-free formulation of the specified-list method would necessitate a complex set of statutory provisions. . . .

The second problem plaguing the actual-measuring-lives approach is that of tracing. No matter how the measuring lives are identified, the lives of those actual individuals must be traced to determine which one is the longest survivor and when he or she died.

The tracing and identification problems are exacerbated by the premise, seemingly accepted under both methods, that the measuring lives cannot always remain a static group, assembled once and for all at the beginning. Instead, individuals who were once measuring lives must be dropped from the group if certain events happen (such as the individual's divorce, adoption out of the family, or assignment of his or her beneficial interest to another); conversely, individuals who were not among the initial group of measuring lives must be included later if certain events happen (such as marriage, adoption into the family, or receipt of another's beneficial interest by assignment or succession) and if they were living when the interest in question was created. This instability within the group of measuring lives heightens the potential for a further round of litigation at one point or another during the running of the [permissible vesting] period.

By opting for a flat period of years, the framers of [the Uniform Rule] eliminated the clutter that has heretofore plagued the wait-and-see strategy—the problems of identifying, tracing, and possibly litigating the make-up of a sometimes-fluctuating group of measuring lives. The expiration of a [permissible vesting] period measured by a flat period of years is litigation free, easy to determine, and unmistakable.

The framers of [the Uniform Rule] considered objections to replacing the actual-measuring-lives approach with a flat period of years, despite the gain in administrative simplicity that would result. One such objection was the idea that the use of actual measuring lives—especially if determined by the causal-relationship method—generates a [permissible vesting] period that self-adjusts to each situation, somehow extending the dead hand no further than necessary in each case. A flat period of years obviously cannot replicate a self-adjusting function. This objection proved unfounded, however, for the actual-measuring-lives approach also fails to perform a self-adjusting function. Although that approach produces [permissible vesting] periods of different lengths from one case to another, it does *not* generate a [permissible vesting] period that expires at a natural or logical stopping point along the continuum of each disposition, thereby pinpointing the time before which actual vesting ought to be allowed and beyond which it ought not to be permitted. Instead, the actual-measuring-lives approach—under either the specified-list or causal-relationship method—generates a [permissible vesting] period whose length almost always *exceeds* by some arbitrary period of time the point of actual vesting in cases that are traditionally validated by the wait-and-see strategy. The actual-measuring-lives approach, therefore, performs a margin-of-safety function, a function that *can* be replicated by the use of a proxy such as the flat 90-year period under [the Uniform Rule].

In standard cases, the rivalry between the causal-relationship and the specified-list methods of identifying actual measuring lives is very little concerned with the length of the [permissible vesting] period. Often, the specified-list method will produce a greater number of measuring lives than the causal-relationship method. In the normal course of events, however, the [permissible vesting] period is not governed by the number of measuring lives, but by the lifetime of the youngest. Unless the additional measuring lives are younger than the others or are clustered in very young age groups, such as under the twelve-healthy-babies ploy, a greater number of measuring lives seldom adds to the length of the [permissible vesting] period. In the normal course of events, the youngest measuring life is the key to the length of the [permissible vesting] period, and no matter which method is used for determining the identity of the measuring lives, the youngest measuring life, in standard trusts, is likely to be the transferor's youngest descendant living when the trust was created. The 90-year period of [the Uniform Rule] is premised on this proposition. Using four hypothetical families deemed to be representative of actual families, the framers determined that, on average, the transferor's youngest descendant in being at the transferor's death—assuming the transferor's death to occur between ages 60 and 90, which is when 73 percent of the population die—is about 6 years old. The remaining life expectancy of a 6-year old is about 69 years. The 69 years, plus the 21-year tack-on period, gives [a permissible vesting] period of 90 years. Although this method may not be scientifically accurate to the nth degree, the Drafting Committee considered it reliable enough to support a [permissible vesting] period of 90 years, given the margin-of-safety function that it performs.

Lawrence W. Waggoner, The Uniform Statutory Rule Against Perpetuities: The Rationale of the 90-Year Waiting Period, 73 Cornell L. Rev. 157, 162-68 (1988).

Acceptance of the 90-Year Period under the Federal Generation-Skipping Transfer Tax. In general terms, trusts that were irrevocable on September 25, 1985, are exempt from the federal generation-skipping transfer tax. See Tax Reform Act of 1986 § 433(b)(2). These trusts are called "grandfathered trusts." Under Treasury Regulations, "grandfathered trusts" can become ungrandfathered if a nongeneral power of appointment is exercised so as to postpone the vesting of an interest beyond the perpetuity period. See Treas. Reg. § 26.2601-1(b)(1)(v)(B)(2), (D) ex. 6-7. Acting in ignorance of the 90-year period of the Uniform Rule, the original version of this regulation defined the perpetuity period solely in terms of a life in being plus 21 years. After the 90-year period of the Uniform Rule was brought to the attention of Treasury Department officials, the Department amended the regulation to accommodate the Uniform Rule's 90-year period.

A related issue concerns the exercise of a nongeneral power of appointment in a manner that postpones the vesting of an interest beyond the perpetuity period for trusts that have qualified for the GST exemption. The Treasury Regulation addressing this issue also accommodates the Uniform Rule's 90-year period. Treas. Reg. § 26.2652-1(a)(5) ex. 9.

***Deferred Reformation—the Approach of the Uniform Rule*.** Section 3 of the Uniform Rule directs a court, upon the petition of an interested person, to reform a disposition within the limits of the 90-year permissible vesting period, in the manner deemed by the court most closely to approximate the transferor's manifested plan of distribution, in any one of three circumstances. The "interested person" who would frequently bring the reformation suit would be the trustee.

Seldom will this section become operative. Of the fraction of trusts and other property arrangements that are incompetently drafted, and thus fail to meet the requirement of initial validity under the codified version of the validating side of the common-law Rule, almost all of them will have terminated by their own terms long before any of the circumstances requisite to reformation under § 3 arise.

If, against the odds, the right to reformation does arise, it will be found easier than perhaps anticipated to determine how best to reform the disposition.[67] The court is given two reformation criteria: (i) the transferor's manifested plan of distribution, and (ii) the 90-year permissible vesting period. Because governing instruments are where transferors manifest their plans of distribution, the

---

67. Note that reformation under § 3 is mandatory, not subject to the discretion of the court. Consequently, as noted in the comment to § 3, the common-law doctrine of infectious invalidity is superseded by the Uniform Rule.

imaginary horrible of courts being forced to probe the minds of long-dead transferors will not materialize.

The theory of § 3 is to defer the right to reformation until reformation becomes truly necessary. Thus, the basic rule of § 3(1) is that the right to reformation does not arise until a nonvested property interest or a power of appointment becomes invalid; under § 1, this does not occur until the expiration of the 90-year permissible vesting period. By confining perpetuity litigation to those few cases in which the permissible vesting period actually is exceeded, perpetuity litigation is limited to purposive cases. In contrast to the immediately available reformation approach of Berry v. Union Nat'l Bank, supra p. 1230, which encourages nonpurposive or wasteful perpetuity litigation, the Uniform Rule's 90-year wait-and-see and deferred-reformation approach adopts a judicial hands-off policy. See Lawrence W. Waggoner, The Uniform Statutory Rule Against Perpetuities: Oregon Joins Up, 26 Willamette L. Rev. 259 (1990).

The deferred-reformation approach has additional advantages beyond working more efficiently by greatly minimizing the number of reformation suits. In the few cases where perpetuity reformation becomes necessary, the deferred-reformation approach minimizes the risk of judicial error by postponing judicial intervention until the time when more information about family circumstances existing at the time of distribution of the trust corpus is known. In addition, any concern that deferring the right to reformation deprives the courts of valuable extrinsic evidence that would be available under the immediate-reformation approach is groundless. Under the immediate-reformation rule, exemplified by the *Berry* case, the courts have not relied on extrinsic evidence of the transferor's intent. The reason is obvious: The transferors never entertained the possibility that the governing instruments contained perpetuity violations in the first place. Hence, the transferors never formed an intent as to what they would have wanted done had they been informed of the violations. As expected, therefore, the courts operating under the immediate-reformation rule have not determined the transferor's intent by reference to extrinsic evidence but by reference to the governing instrument. Deferring the right to reformation until after the permissible vesting period has run its course does not deprive the courts of valuable extrinsic evidence. See Mary Louise Fellows, Testing Perpetuity Reforms: A Study of Perpetuity Cases 1984-89, 25 Real Prop. Prob. & Tr. J. 597 (1991).

The deferred-reformation approach is also consistent with the saving-clause principle embraced by the Uniform Rule. Deferring the right to reformation until the permissible vesting period expires is the only way to grant every reasonable opportunity for the donor's disposition to work itself out without premature interference. One of the reasons why the Uniform Rule specifically rejects the idea of granting a right to reformation at any time on a showing of a violation of the common-law Rule is that the experience under these statutorily or judicially established reformation principles has not been satisfactory. As in *Berry*, the courts have lowered periods in gross or age contingencies to 21. This is a step that amounts to an unwarranted distortion of the donor's intention, a distortion that is avoided by deferring the right to reformation until the contingencies as originally written by the donor have been given a chance to be fulfilled.

To be sure, if the courts utilize the immediate-reformation approach to insert a perpetuity saving clause rather than to lower a period in gross or an age contingency to 21, as in Richardson Trust, supra p. 1233 and Estate of Anderson v. Deposit Guaranty Nat'l Bank, supra p. 1233, frustration of the donor's intention is avoided, but this comes at the expense of a reformation suit. The insertion-of-a-saving-clause approach is therefore less efficient than wait-and-see with deferred reformation. The period of time produced by a judicially inserted perpetuity saving clause would be about the same in length as that which is automatically granted by the Uniform Rule without front-end litigation. The more efficient course is to defer the right to reformation until after the permissible vesting period has run its course. Deferring the right to reformation reduces the necessity and cost of litigation because, as noted, the contingencies attached to most future interests that would otherwise have fallen victim of the common-law Rule will be resolved well within the permissible vesting period. Litigation to reform an offending disposition will seldom become necessary. The Restatement 2d is in accord with this approach. Reformation is provided for in the Restatement only if the nonvested property interest becomes invalid after waiting out the permissible vesting period. See Restatement 2d of Property § 1.5.

At the same time, the Uniform Rule is not inflexible, for it grants the right to reformation before the expiration of the 90-year permissible vesting period when it becomes necessary to do so or when there is no point in waiting that period out. Thus subsection (2), which pertains to class gifts that are not yet but still might become invalid under the wait-and-see element, grants a right to reformation whenever the share of any class member is entitled to take effect in possession or enjoyment. Were it not for this subsection, a great inconvenience and possibly injustice could arise, for class members whose shares have vested within the period might otherwise have to wait out the remaining part of the 90 years before obtaining their shares. Reformation under this subsection will seldom be needed, however, because of the common practice of structuring trusts to split into separate shares or separate trusts at the death of each income beneficiary, one separate share or separate trust for each of the income beneficiary's then-living descendants; when this pattern is followed, the circumstances described in subsection (2) will not arise.

Subsection (3) also grants the right to reformation before the 90-year permissible vesting period expires. The circumstance giving rise to the right to reformation under subsection (3) occurs if a nonvested property interest can vest but not before the 90-year period has expired. Though unlikely, such a case can theoretically arise. If it does, the interest—unless it terminates by its own terms earlier—is bound to become invalid under § 1 eventually. There is no point in deferring the right to reformation until the inevitable happens. The Uniform Rule provides for early reformation in such a case, just in case it arises.

Problems

Consider how G's disposition might appropriately be reformed in the following cases.

1. G devised property in trust, directing the trustee to pay the income "to A for life, then to A's children for the life of the survivor, then to A's grandchildren for the life of the survivor, and on the death of A's last surviving grandchild, the corpus of the trust is to be divided among A's then-living descendants by representation; if none, to" a specified charity. G was survived by her child (A) and by A's two minor children (X and Y). After G's death, another child (Z) was born to A. Subsequently, A died, survived by her children (X, Y, and Z) and by three grandchildren (M, N, and O). X, Y, and Z died within the 90-year period following G's death, but some of A's grandchildren were still living at the expiration of the 90-year period.

2. G devised property in trust, directing the trustee to pay the income "to A for life, then to A's children"; the corpus of the trust is to be equally divided among A's children who reach the age of 30. G was survived by A, by A's spouse (H), and by A's two children (X and Y), both of whom were under the age of 30 when G died. After G's death, another child (Z) was born to A. Although unlikely, suppose that at A's death (prior to the expiration of the 90-year period), Z's age was such that he could be alive but under the age of 30 on the 90th anniversary of G's death. Suppose further that at A's death X and Y were over the age of 30.

EXTERNAL REFERENCES. The Uniform Rule has sparked a lively academic debate. See e.g., Ira M. Bloom, Perpetuities Refinement: There Is an Alternative, 62 Wash. L. Rev. 23 (1987) (arguing that the Uniform Rule is unnecessary because of infrequency of appellate-level perpetuity cases; author proposes own version of perpetuity-reform statute); Jesse Dukeminier, The Uniform Statutory Rule Against Perpetuities: Ninety Years in Limbo, 34 UCLA L. Rev. 1023 (1987) (labeling the Uniform Rule as "an extraordinarily risky venture" (at 1024), "so bizarre that the mind boggles" (at 1025), "Waggoner's phantom ship" (at 1068), an idea that gives "a bizarre turn to perpetuities reform" (at 1069), and an act that "is deserving of oblivion" (at 1079)); Mary

Louise Fellows, Testing Perpetuity Reforms: A Study of Perpetuity Cases 1984-89, 25 Real Prop. Prob & Tr. J. 597 (1991) (testing the various types of perpetuity reform measures and concluding, on the basis of empirical evidence, that the Uniform Rule is the best opportunity offered to date for a uniform perpetuity law that efficiently and effectively achieves a fair balance between present and future property owners); Paul G. Haskell, A Proposal for a Simple and Socially Effective Rule Against Perpetuities, 66 N.C. L. Rev. 545 (1988) (arguing for replacement of both the validating and invalidating sides of the common-law Rule with a statutory rule requiring vesting in possession no later than 125 years after creation); Amy Morris Hess, Freeing Property Owners from the RAP Trap: Tennessee Adopts the Uniform Statutory Rule Against Perpetuities, 62 Tenn. L. Rev. 267, 283 (1995) (arguing that if the common-law Rule is to remain part of the law of Tennessee, then the Uniform Rule is "a highly desirable and long overdue reform"); Ronald C. Link & Kimberly A. Licata, Perpetuities Reform in North Carolina: The Uniform Statutory Rule Against Perpetuities, Nondonative Transfers, and Honorary Trusts, 74 N.C. L. Rev. 1783, 1783 (1996) (explaining the Uniform Rule and demonstrating through recent North Carolina cases how it will "greatly simplify" the law); John D. Moore, Comment, The Uniform Statutory Rule Against Perpetuities: Taming the "Technicality-Ridden Legal Nightmare," 95 W. Va. L. Rev. 193 (1992) (reviewing pre-Uniform Rule perpetuities law in West Virginia, analyzing the Uniform Rule, and comparing the Uniform Rule to other alternative reforms).

5. Abolition of the Rule—The Dynasty Trust

Restated in 1986, but scheduled to be repealed in 2010, the federal generation-skipping transfer tax (GSTT), with its unusually stiff rates (see supra Chapter 7), has spurred a growing movement for states to abolish the Rule Against Perpetuities. A few states had already abolished the Rule before 1986—including Wisconsin,[68] South Dakota,[69] and Idaho[70]—but the number of states abolishing the Rule in the years after 1986 has grown rapidly. Why is this so, given that the GSTT imposes high taxes on trusts that persist through more than one generation? The answer is that the GSTT also contains a large exemption—over $1 million per donor, and over $2 million for married donors acting together. This exemption relies only on state perpetuity law to control the length of exempt trusts. Furthermore, despite the growing movement to abolish

68. Wis. Stat. § 700.16(5).

69. S.D. Codified Laws § 43-5-8.

70. Idaho Code § 55-111; Locklear v. Tucker, 203 P.2d 380 (Idaho 1949).

the Rule, Congress continues to rely on state perpetuity law to control the length of exempt trusts. Indeed, not only has Congress allowed the GST exemption to remain in existence despite the Rule abolition movement, but Congress recently increased the amount of the exemption to reflect inflation. Previously, the exemption amount was fixed at $1 million, but beginning in 1999 the amount has been rising in increments of $10,000 as inflation increases, and beginning in 2004, the amount will be equal to the estate tax exclusion amount. See IRC § 2631(c). Because of the commercial interests of banks and local attorneys, states are beginning to compete with one another for true dynasty trusts—trusts that last perpetually (or as long as the settlor wants), not for a mere ninety years or for the length of lives in being plus 21 years.

States jumping on the dynasty trust bandwagon fall into two broad groups. States in the first group have abolished the Rule Against Perpetuities entirely. Other than Wisconsin, South Dakota, and Idaho, already mentioned, this group also includes New Jersey and Rhode Island. See N.J. Laws § 46:2F-9; R.I. Gen. Laws § 34-11-38. States in the second group have made the Rule Against Perpetuities optional, meaning that the settlor may provide in the trust instrument that the Rule does not apply. Examples here include Illinois, Maine, Maryland, Ohio, and Virginia. See Ill. Comp. Stat., ch. 765, §§ 305/3, 305/4; Me. Rev. Stat., ch. 33, § 101-A; Md. Est. & Trusts Code § 11-102; Ohio Rev. Code § 2131.09; Va. Code § 55-13.3. In all of these states except Virginia, the trust must also provide some mechanism for the sale of trust assets, either by the trustee or by a third party.

In addition, three states have taken idiosyncratic approaches to dynasty trusts. Delaware abolished the Rule with respect to trusts of personal property only. See Del. Code, tit. 25, § 503. (The Virginia statute likewise seems designed to be limited to personal property in trust, but it is poorly drafted and, as written, applies to "any trust." See Va. Code § 55-13.3(e).) Florida, which had previously enacted the Uniform Rule, adopted legislation extending the wait-and-see period from 90 years to 360 years. See Fla. Stat. § 689.225. Last but not least, Alaska abolished the Rule except with respect to the creation or exercise of certain powers of appointment. See Alaska Stat. §§ 34.27.051, 34.27.075.[71]

It remains to be seen what effect the repeal of the GSTT, slated to go into effect in 2010 (see supra Chapter 7), will have on the abolition movement.

---

71. The principal purpose of retaining some perpetuity rule for powers of appointment was to avoid the so-called "Delaware Tax Trap." For background, see Jonathan Blattmachr & Jeffrey Pennell, Adventures in Generation-Skipping, or How We Learned to Love the "Delaware Tax Trap," 24 Real Prop., Prob. & Tr. J. 75 (1989).

External Reference: Verner F. Chaffin, Georgia's Proposed Dynasty Trust: Giving the Dead Too Much Control, 35 Ga. L. Rev. 1 (2000).

PART E. SPECIAL APPLICATIONS OF AND EXCLUSIONS FROM THE RULE AGAINST PERPETUITIES

1. Class Gifts

a. General Rule: "All or Nothing"

Under the Rule Against Perpetuities, a class gift stands or falls as a whole. This all-or-nothing rule, usually attributed to Leake v. Robinson, 2 Mer. 363, 35 Eng. Rep. 979 (Ch. 1817), is commonly stated as follows:

> ***If the interest of any potential class member might vest "too remotely," the entire class gift is invalid.***

Another way of stating the same rule, which you may find more or less helpful, is set forth in the Restatement of Property §§ 371, 383, 384:

> ***A class gift is entirely invalid if its membership might continue either to increase or decrease (or both) beyond 21 years after the death of a life in being at the creation of the interest.***

(The word "decrease" refers to a class gift that is subject to a condition *precedent* of survival.)

Although strongly condemned by some (but not all) commentators, the all-or-nothing rule has been squarely rejected by only one American decision, Carter v. Berry, 140 So. 2d 843 (Miss. 1962).[72] The rationale of the

72. In the *Carter* case, G's will (executed in 1955) created a trust that was to terminate at the earlier of "35 years from the date [of execution] of this will" or "when my youngest grandchild (whether now living or hereafter born) shall become 25 years of age." G was survived by a 22-year-old married daughter who was then childless and by a 24-year-old married daughter who then had three young children. Since the remainder interest in favor of the grandchildren wasn't subject to an express condition of survivorship of the termination of the trust, the obvious solution to the perpetuity problem was to hold that the gift to the grandchildren was valid in its entirety even under the all-or-nothing rule. In other words, the class wasn't subject to decrease at all and couldn't increase after the deaths of G's daughters, who were "in being" at the creation of the interest.

While this possible solution was noted, the court inexplicably thought it "necessary and proper to deal also with the issues in this case on a second basis, namely, that . . . the gift is contingent [on survivorship of the termination of the trust]." This made the class gift one that would be entirely invalid under the all-or-nothing rule.

all-or-nothing rule is discussed in Lawrence W. Waggoner, Estates in Land and Future Interests in a Nutshell 296-98 (2d ed. 1993).

The rule has been upheld and applied in numerous cases, including recent ones. See, e.g., Beverlin v. First Nat'l Bank, 98 P.2d 200 (Kan. 1940); Thomas v. Citizens & Southern Nat'l Bank, 163 S.E.2d 823 (Ga. 1968); Will of Lattouf, 208 A.2d 411 (N.J. Super. Ct. App. Div. 1965). Also, no American statute reverses the rule.

The following three examples illustrate the all-or-nothing rule: Example 19.12 illustrates a class gift that is invalid because it is subject to decrease "too long," Example 19.13 illustrates a class gift that is invalid because it is subject to increase "too long," and Example 19.14 illustrates a class gift that is invalid because it is subject to both increase and decrease "too long."

Example 19.12: G devised real property "to A for life, then to such of A's children as reach 25." G was survived by A and by A's two children, V and X. V had reached 25 at G's death, but X was under 25.

The class gift in favor of A's children is invalid. There is no validating life because the membership of the class might decrease, though not increase, beyond 21 years after the death of A, V, X, and anyone else who was in being at G's death.

Example 19.13: G devised property in trust, directing the trustee to pay the net income therefrom "to A for life, then to A's children for the life of the survivor, and upon the death of A's last surviving child to pay the corpus of the trust to A's grandchildren." G was survived by A and by A's two children, V and X.

The court then went on to reject the all-or-nothing rule, the result of which was that the only valid interests were those of the three grandchildren who were living at G's death. This result, the court conceded, wouldn't carry out G's intent because he "wanted all of his grandchildren to take, not just those living at the time of his death." The court nevertheless said that "if this were the only choice, we would not hesitate to take it." But the Mississippi court felt that another choice was available, which was to hold that the cy-pres (reformation) power could be invoked to reduce the latest time of trust termination to the time when G's youngest grandchild should reach *21*, rather than 25 as G had stipulated. This way, the entire class gift was made valid because the court eliminated the possibility of a decrease in class membership beyond 21 years after the deaths of G's two daughters.

In sum, the Mississippi court began with a disposition that was entirely valid, under ordinary precepts of construction. Nevertheless, citing academic criticisms of the all-or-nothing rule, the court proceeded to reject the all-or-nothing rule on the ground that "it is not good logic or sound law," found that the result of rejecting the "ill-considered doctrine of Leake v. Robinson" didn't carry out G's intention because of the real prospect of afterborn class members, and so changed G's disposition by lowering the age from 25 to 21.

Two fairly important points the court didn't note are: changing the age from 25 to 21 didn't carry out G's intention either and it made the rejection of the all-or-nothing rule of no consequence because, as altered by the court, the class gift was *entirely valid* even *under* the all-or-nothing rule.

The remainder interest in the corpus in favor of A's grandchildren is invalid. There is no validating life because the membership of the class might increase, though not decrease, beyond 21 years after the death of A, V, X, and any one else who was in being at G's death you might care to propose.

Example 19.14: Same facts and disposition as the above example, except that the remainder upon the death of A's last surviving child was in favor of "A's then-living grandchildren."

The remainder interest in the corpus in favor of A's grandchildren is invalid. The class might increase "too long" and, due to the addition of the condition precedent of survival of A's last surviving child, it might also decrease "too long."

Class Gifts under Wait-and-See. The above discussion relates to the treatment of class gifts under the common-law Rule Against Perpetuities, under which the requirement of initial certainty still reigns. As for the all-or-nothing rule itself, perpetuity reformers haven't seen fit to change it. The rule isn't reversed in the Uniform Rule or under the Restatement 2d of Property. The sting of the all-or-nothing rule, however, is substantially eliminated by the application of the wait-and-see element.[73]

Consider how the above examples would be treated under the wait-and-see element of USRAP (UPC § 2-901(a)(2)). If you place G in one of our four charted families, supra pp. 1201-04, and if you posit G's death at around age 75, you will see that it's extremely unlikely that the class gift in Example 19.12 will *actually* decrease beyond the 90-year permissible vesting period after G's death.[74] You will also see that the class gift in Example 19.13 is unlikely to increase beyond the 90-year period and the class gift in Example 19.14 is unlikely to increase or decrease beyond that period.[75] Should the unlikely happen in any of these cases, G's disposition would become subject to reformation under USRAP § 3 (UPC § 2-903), the application of which is explained and illustrated in the official comment to § 3.

Specific-Sum Class Gifts; Gifts to Subclasses. The English courts held the all-or-nothing rule to be inapplicable to specific-sum class gifts and gifts to subclasses; the American courts have followed suit, sometimes describing the two situations as "exceptions." The two situations are in fact distinguishable from the one to which the all-or-nothing rule applies. See Lawrence W.

---

73. See USRAP § 1 comment part G.

74. Or beyond the period allowed by the Restatement 2d, measured by 21 years after the deaths of A, V, and X.

75. Or beyond the period allowed by the Restatement 2d, measured by 21 years after the deaths of A, V, and X.

Waggoner, Estates in Land and Future Interests in a Nutshell § 15.3 (2d ed. 1993).

b. Specific-Sum Class Gifts

Storrs v. Benbow

3 DeG. M. & G. 390, 43 Eng. Rep. 153 (Ch. 1853)

THE LORD CHANCELLOR. . . . The question arises upon a clause in a codicil which is in these words, —

> Item. I direct my executors to pay by and out of my personal estate exclusively the sum £500 a-piece to each child that may be born to either of the children of either of my brothers lawfully begotten to be paid to each of them on his or her attaining the age of twenty-one years without benefit of survivorship.

This is a money legacy to each child of any nephew the testator had or might have. The testator had brothers living, but there might be legacies too remote, because the gift included legacies to children of a child not yet born.

The bill was filed twenty or thirty years ago; and the cause was heard before Sir John Leach. The argument then was, that the gift was too remote, but Sir John Leach thought that, according to the true construction of the clause children born in the lifetime of the testator were meant, and therefore he said the gift could not be too remote, for it only let in children that might be born between the date of the will and the death. A decree was accordingly made declaring that the children *in esse* only at the time of the death of the testator were entitled to the legacies, and it was referred to the Master to inquire. &c. The Master found that the Plaintiff was *in esse* in this sense, namely that the testator died in October and the Plaintiff was born six months afterwards; and I think he was so. The question then is whether he is entitled; I am of opinion that he certainly is, for he was a child *in esse* within the meaning put upon the clause by Sir John Leach.

There are three ways in which this gift might be interpreted; it might mean children that were *in esse* at the date of the will; it might mean children that might come into *esse* in the lifetime of the testator; and it might mean children born at any time. I own it seems to me that this gentlemen is entitled *quacunque via*. If it was to the children then in being, he would I think be probably within the meaning of such description; but if it was to children to come *in esse* in his lifetime and afterwards to be born, it seems to me that a child *in ventre sa mere* at the death of the testator was a child "hereafter to be born" within the meaning of the provision.

The rule that makes a limitation of this kind mean children at the death of the testator is one of convenience: a line must be drawn somewhere, otherwise the distribution of the testator's estate would be stopped, and executors would not know how to act; but that rule of convenience cannot be applied to exclude a child certainly within the meaning of the limitation in the absence of any contrary expressed intention of the testator. I think therefore that Sir John Leach was right, supposing the interpretation of the will to be what I have stated, and that this child certainly comes within the description. I must add however that I do not say that the gift was at all remote if it meant a child to be born at any time, because this is not the case of a class: it is gift of a pecuniary legacy of a particular amount to every child of every nephew which the testator then had, or of every nephew that might be born after his death, and is therefore good as to the children of the nephews he then had, and bad as to the children of nephews to be born after his death.

It would be a mistake to compare this with Leake v. Robinson, [2 Mer. 363, 35 Eng. Rep. 979 (Ch. 1817),] and other cases where the parties take as a class, for the difficulty which there arises as to giving it to some and not giving it to others does not apply here. The question of whether or not the children of afterborn nephews shall or shall not take, has no bearing at all upon the question of whether the child of an existing nephew takes: the legacy given to him cannot be bad because there is a legacy given under a similar description to a person who would not be able to take because the gift would be too remote. I give therefore no positive opinion upon the point of remoteness generally in this case, because I think that *quacunque via*, on the construction of the will, there is nothing to justify the exclusion from taking of a child who was conceived at the death of the testator and born six or seven months afterwards. If the words in question meant children who though not then in existence should be in existence at the death, the Plaintiff was in existence at the death; and if they meant children born at any time, he was born and must have been born if at all within such a time as made his legacy not remote. I am therefore of opinion that in any way he is entitled.

c. *Gifts to Subclasses*

American Security & Trust Co. v. Cramer

175 F. Supp. 367 (D.D.C. 1959)

YOUNGDAHL, J. Six of the eleven defendants before the Court have moved for summary judgment. A hearing has been held and memoranda of points and authorities have been submitted. Plaintiff, trustee of a testamentary trust, is a stakeholder in this controversy among competing heirs. Since all the material facts have been stipulated, the Court is free to render summary judgment.

Abraham D. Hazen, a resident of the District of Columbia, died in the District on December 4, 1901. His will, executed on October 16, 1900, was admitted to probate on March 11, 1902.

Testator was survived by Hannah E. Duffey, who is referred to in his will as his "adopted daughter". At the time of the testator's death, Hannah had two children: Mary Hazen Duffey (now Cramer), born November 12, 1897, and Hugh Clarence Duffey, born July 11, 1899. After the testator's death, Hannah gave birth to two more children: Depue Hazen Duffey, born October 9, 1903, and Horace Duffey, born July 8, 1908.

The will provided for the payment of debts and certain specific bequests and then provided that the residue of the estate be put in trust for the benefit of testator's wife for life. At her death, one-half of the corpus was to be, and has been, given to testator's sister and brothers; the other half, composed of realty, remained in trust for Hannah for life. At Hannah's death, the income was to go to the children of Hannah "then living or the issue of such of them as may then be dead leaving issue surviving" Hannah, and then "upon the death of each the share of the one so dying shall go absolutely to the persons who shall then be his or her heirs at law according to the laws of descent now in force in the said District of Columbia".

Testator's widow died on October 31, 1916; Hannah died on May 21, 1915.

On October 5, 1917, the heirs of the testator brought an action in equity to have the provisions of the seventh paragraph of the will stricken as being in violation of the rule against perpetuities. The Supreme Court of the District of Columbia held that the interests of Hannah's children under the will were valid and the Court of Appeals affirmed. Hazen v. American Security & Trust Co., 1920, 49 App.D.C. 297, 265 F. 447. The validity of the remainders over, after the death of each child, was expressly not ruled upon as the life estates were not "so intimately connected with the gift over as to require us now to determine the validity of such gifts."

Hugh, one of the four life tenants after the death of the widow and Hannah, died on December 19, 1928 and shortly thereafter the trustee brought a bill for instructions; this time the validity of the remainder over to Hugh's heirs was in issue. On January 2, 1930, Judge Bailey ruled that "the remainder provided by the will after his (Hugh's) death to the persons who shall then be his heirs at law became vested within the period prescribed by law and is valid."

On December 13, 1954, Depue died and for the fourth time a suit concerning this trust was started in this court. The trustees desired instructions as to the disposition of Depue's one-sixth share. While this action was pending, on December 18, 1957, Horace died. A supplemental bill was then filed, asking for instructions as to the disposition of this one-sixth share as well. The remainder over after the death of the sole living life tenant, Mary, cannot yet take effect; however, due to the request of all the parties concerned, and in order to save both the time of this court and the needless expense it would otherwise cost the estate, the Court will also pass on the validity of this remainder.

The law that governs the questions here involved is the law in effect at the time of the testator's death: December 4, 1901.

The . . . effect of the [common-law] rule [against perpetuities] is to invalidate *ab initio* certain future interests that might otherwise remain in existence for a period of time considered inimicable to society's interest in having reasonable limits to dead-hand control and in facilitating the marketability of property. The policy of the law is to permit a person to control the devolution of his property but only for a human lifetime plus twenty-one years and actual periods of gestation. With careful planning, this period could be as long as one hundred years—and this is long enough.

A gift to a class is a gift of an aggregate amount of property to persons who are collectively described and whose individual share will depend upon the number of persons ultimately constituting the class. The members of the class must be finally determined within a life or lives in being plus twenty-one years and actual periods of gestation, or the gift will fail. Put another way, the class must close within the period of the rule against perpetuities, if the class gift is to be valid. Unless a contrary intent is indicated by the testator, the class will close when any member of the class is entitled to immediate possession and enjoyment of his share of the class gift. Applying these basic principles to the trust here involved, it is seen that the life estates to Hannah's children had to vest, if at all, at the termination of the preceding life estates of the widow and Hannah. Since Hannah's children had to be born within Hannah's lifetime, and since Hannah was a life in being, the class (Hannah's children) physiologically had to close within the period of the rule. This has already been so held. Hazen v. American Security & Trust Co., supra, at note 6. Furthermore, the remainder over at Hugh's death has been held valid. The Court now holds that the remainder limited to the heirs of Mary is valid. Both Hugh and Mary were lives in being at the testator's death; the remainders limited to their heirs had to vest, if at all, within the period of the rule. Horace and Depue were born after the testator died; the remainders over at their deaths are invalid.

In applying the rule against perpetuities, it does not help to show that the rule might be complied with or that, the way things turned out, it actually was complied with. After the testator's death, Hannah might have had more children; one of these might have lived more than twenty-one years after the death of all the lives in being at the testator's death. The vesting of the remainder in this after-born's heirs would take place after the expiration of lives in being and twenty-one years, since the heirs could not be ascertained until the after-born's death and an interest cannot be vested until the interest holder is ascertained. Consequently, because of the possibility that this could happen, even though, in fact, it did not, the remainders limited to the heirs of Horace and Depue (both after-borns) are invalid as a violation of the rule against perpetuities.

Counsel have not argued the point of whether the invalidity of the remainders to the heirs of Horace and Depue serves to taint the otherwise valid remainders to the heirs of Mary and Hugh. Of course, the remainder after Hugh's life estate has already been distributed and is not properly in issue. Nevertheless, as shall be demonstrated, it (and the remainder to the heirs of Mary) are not affected by the two invalid remainders, since the four remainders are to subclasses and stand (or fall) separately.

Beginning with Jee v. Audley, 1 Cox Eq.Cas. 324 (1787) and flowering with Leake v. Robinson, 2 Mer. 363, 35 Eng. Rep. 979 (Chancery 1817), there has been the curious anomaly in future interests law that if the interest of any potential member of a class can possibly vest too remotely, the interests of all the members of the class fails [sic]. In other words, the rule is that a class gift is inseparable. For example, T creates a trust to pay the income to A for life and then to pay the corpus over to such of A's children as attain the age of twenty-five. When A dies he might have a child who is not yet four years of age and who was not in being at T's death; this child would not take a vested interest until he satisfied the contingency of reaching the age of twenty-five; since a child under four could not become twenty-five within twenty-one years, the child's interest is void by virtue of the rule against perpetuities. While this much may be sound, the rule in Leake v. Robinson goes on to invalidate the entire class gift. That is, even if the child under four has two brothers who are over twenty-five when A dies, these two brothers take nothing because the invalid interest of their little brother (who, remember, may only be imagined) is contagious—so says *Leake*. Unless the testator intended to have all of the twenty-five-year-old sons take, or none at all (and this is difficult to imagine in the absence of an express provision in the will), the rule is a dubious one. Fortunately, the Court need not apply it in this case because of the limitation put on it by a long line of cases beginning with Catlin v. Brown, 11 Hare 372, 68 Eng.Rep. 1318 (Chancery, 1853).

In *Catlin*, the devise was of mortgaged property to A for life, then to the children of A in equal shares during their lives, and after the death of any such child, his share to his children and their heirs. Some of A's children were in being at the time that the testator died; some were born after his death. Counsel conceded that the remainders over to the heirs of those children of A born after the testator's death were invalid. The question was whether those concededly invalid remainders tainted the otherwise valid remainders and rendered them invalid. The Court held that they did not; the remainders to the heirs of the children in being at the testator's death were valid. *Leake* was distinguished on the ground that it concerned remainders to one class (A's children that reach twenty-five) while the remainders involved in *Catlin* were to a group of subclasses (the heirs of each of A's children was a subclass). In other words, the limitation placed on *Leake* by *Catlin* is that if the ultimate takers are not described as a single class but rather as a group of subclasses, and if the share to which each separate subclass is entitled will finally be determined within the period of the rule, the gifts to the different subclasses are separable for the purpose of the rule.

In the instant case, the language of the will compels the Court to read it as a devise of remainders to subclasses and within the rule of Catlin. The provision in issue reads, in part:

> . . . and *each* of the children of said adopted daughter shall take only for and during the terms of their *respective* lives and upon the death of *each* the share of the *one* so dying shall go absolutely to the persons who shall then be *his or her* heirs at law . . . (Emphasis supplied). . . .

When a remainder in fee after a life estate fails, there is no enlargement or diminution of the life estate; rather there is then a reversion in the heirs of the testator. The two one-sixth shares held invalid shall pass to the successors in interest to the heirs of Abraham D. Hazen. . . .

Notes and Questions

1. *Authority*. The specific-sum and subclass rules of Storrs v. Benbow and Catlin v. Brown are supported by the Restatement of Property §§ 385, 389.

2. *Infectious Invalidity*. Even though the remainder interests to the heirs of Mary and the heirs of Hugh were valid, would it have been appropriate for the court to have held that the invalidity of the remainder interests to the heirs of Horace and the heirs of Depue so "infected" the testator's overall scheme that the remainders to the heirs of Mary and the heirs of Hugh should also have been held invalid? The court didn't discuss the issue because "counsel have not argued the point." Compare Estate of Morton, 312 A.2d 26 (Pa. 1973); Restatement of Property § 389 comment f; see also Will of Shehan, 597 N.Y.S.2d 1017 (Sur. Ct. 1993) (as an alternative reason to finding the subclass rule inapplicable, the court held that it would be contrary to the testator's intent to treat the families equally to uphold some, but not all, of the trusts).

3. *Wait-and-See*. As under the common-law Rule, the remainder interests to the heirs of Mary and the heirs of Hugh would be initially valid under § 1(a)(1) of the Uniform Rule (UPC § 2-901(a)(1)). The remainder interests to the heirs of Horace and the heirs of Depue would not be initially invalid, however, but would instead be subject to the wait-and-see element contained in § 1(a)(2) (UPC § 2-901(a)(2)). If neither Horace nor Depue outlive the 90-year period, the remainder interests to their heirs will be valid, also. If one or the other outlives the 90-year period, an unlikely event, the court would reform the testator's disposition under USRAP § 3 (UPC § 2-903). The provision for man-

datory reformation has the effect of abolishing the doctrine of infectious invalidity. See USRAP § 1, comment part G.

2. *Powers of Appointment*

Statutory References: *UPC §§ 2-901(b), -901(c) (USRAP §§ 1(b), 1(c))*

If a power of appointment violates the Rule Against Perpetuities, the power is invalid, and the disposition takes effect as if the power had never been created. If the power itself is valid, some or all of the interests created by its exercise may violate the Rule and be invalid.

a. General Powers Presently Exercisable

Validity of the Power at Common Law. Under the common-law Rule, a general power that is presently exercisable is treated as the equivalent of a *vested* property interest and is therefore not subject to the Rule Against Perpetuities.

If the exercisability of a general power is subject to a condition precedent, the power is treated as the equivalent of a *nonvested* property interest for purposes of the Rule. Although a mouthful, this type of power might be called a *general power not presently exercisable because of a condition precedent*. This is the term used in USRAP § 1(b) (UPC § 2-901(b)). The term signifies that once the condition precedent is satisfied, the power becomes presently exercisable. (Note that a power of appointment expires on the donee's death. A deferral of a power's exercisability until a future time (even a time certain), therefore, imposes a condition precedent on the power's exercisability—the condition precedent being that the donee must be alive at that future time.)

A general power not presently exercisable because of a condition precedent must satisfy the requirement of initial certainty to be valid, which requires a certainty, when the power is created, that the *condition precedent* to its exercise will be resolved one way or the other no later than 21 years after the death of an individual then alive.

Consequently, although (as we shall see) neither a nongeneral power nor a testamentary power can validly be conferred on an unborn person (unless some special restriction is imposed on it forbidding its exercise beyond a life in being plus 21 years), an unborn person can be the recipient of a valid general power that becomes presently exercisable upon the donee's birth. To be valid, of course, the donee's birth must be certain to occur within a life in being plus 21 years.

Example 19.15: G devised real property "to A for life, then to A's first born child for life, then to such persons as A's first born child shall appoint." G is survived by A, who is childless.

The general power conferred on A's first born child is valid. The condition precedent—that A have a child—is certain to be resolved one way or the other within A's lifetime; A is the validating life. If, however, the relevant language had been "then to such persons as A's first born child shall appoint after reaching the age of 25," the additional contingency of reaching 25 would have invalidated the general power, at common law.

Validity of the Power under Wait-and-See. Under the Uniform Rule, the validity of powers of appointment is governed by §§ 1(b) and (c).[76] Under § 1(b)(1), a general power of appointment not exercisable because of a condition precedent is initially valid if it satisfies the requirement of initial certainty. If the requirement of initial certainty isn't satisfied, the power isn't automatically invalid but instead is subject to the wait-and-see element contained in § 1(b)(2). The power is valid if the condition precedent actually occurs within the 90-year period; if it doesn't, the disposition is subject to reformation under § 3.

Validity of the Exercise at Common Law. In determining the validity of an exercise of a general power presently exercisable, the power is treated as the equivalent of ownership of the property subject to the power. Accordingly, donees are considered to have created the appointed interests. Exercises are treated as if donees first exercised the powers in their own favor and then created the appointed interests out of the property. Consequently the appointed interests are created, for purposes of the Rule, when the exercises of the powers become effective, with the possibility of postponement in certain cases under the principles outlined supra p. 1182.

Example 19.16: G was the life income beneficiary of a trust and the donee of a presently exercisable general power over the succeeding remainder interest. G exercised the power by deed, directing the trustee after her death to pay the income to G's children in equal shares for the life of the survivor, and upon the death of her last surviving child to pay the corpus of the trust to her grandchildren.

The validity of the appointed interests depends on whether or not G's appointment was irrevocable. If it was irrevocable, the remainder interest in favor of G's grandchildren is invalid. The appointed interests were created when the deed was delivered or otherwise became effective. If G reserved a power to revoke her appointment, the remainder interest is valid. The appointed interests are created at G's death.

Validity of the Exercise under Wait-and-See. The only change under the Uniform Rule is that an exercise that would have been invalid at common law isn't initially invalid but instead is subject to the wait-and-see element of the

76. A general power presently exercisable is not subject to the Uniform Rule.

Uniform Rule. The 90-year period applies in determining the validity of appointed interests that would have been invalid at common law.

b. Nongeneral Powers and Testamentary Powers

Validity of the Power. A nongeneral power (whether testamentary or presently exercisable) or a general testamentary power is invalid if, when the power is created, it is possible for the power to be *exercised* later than 21 years after the death of an individual then alive.

> *Example 19.17:* (1) G devised real property "to A for life, then to A's first born child for life, then to such persons as A's first born child shall by will appoint;" or
>
> (2) G devised real property "to A for life, then to A's first born child for life, then to such of A's grandchildren as A's first born child shall appoint."
>
> G is survived by A, who is childless.
>
> The power of appointment conferred on A's first born child—a general testamentary power in Case (1), a nongeneral power presently exercisable in Case (2)—is invalid. The latest possible time of exercise is at the death of A's first born child, who can't be the validating life because that child wasn't "in being" at the creation of the power.

The lesson is that a nongeneral or testamentary power conferred on an unborn person is invalid.

Problem

G devised property in trust, directing the trustee to pay the income "to A for life, then in equal shares to A's children for their respective lives; on the death of each child, the proportionate share of corpus of the one so dying shall go to such persons as the one so dying shall by will appoint." G was survived by A and A's two children, X and Y. After G's death, another child (Z) was born to A.

1. Are the powers conferred on A's children valid under the common-law Rule? See Restatement of Property § 390 comment f; Am. L. Prop. § 24.32; J.H.C. Morris & W. Barton Leach, The Rule Against Perpetuities 141-42 (2d ed. 1962). Cf. Slark v. Darkyns, L.R. 10 Ch. App. 35 (C.A. 1874). But see Camden Safe Deposit & Trust Co. v. Scott, 189 A. 653 (N.J. 1937); Re Phillips, 11 D.L.R. 500 (Ont. 1913).

2. How would the situation be treated under the Uniform Rule? Assume that Z was born five years after G's death and that Z died at age 75, leaving a will that purported to exercise Z's power of appointment. See USRAP § 1 comment part H, ex. 25.

Fiduciary Powers. Discretionary powers held by fiduciaries are nongeneral powers of appointment, for purposes of the Rule Against Perpetuities. Discretionary fiduciary powers include a trustee's power to invade the corpus of the trust for the benefit of the income beneficiary or a trustee's power to accumulate the income or pay it out or to spray it among a group of beneficiaries. Purely administrative fiduciary powers, however, aren't subject to the Rule Against Perpetuities.

Consider the validity of the fiduciary powers in the following cases, first under the common-law Rule and then under USRAP §§ 1(c), 4(2)-(4) (UPC § 2-901(c), 2-904(2)-(4)).

1. G devised property in trust, directing the trustee to pay the income to A for life, then to A's children for the life of the survivor, and on the death of A's last surviving child to pay the corpus to B. The trustee is granted the discretionary power to sell and reinvest the trust assets and to invade the corpus of the trust on behalf of the income beneficiary or beneficiaries. G was survived by A and by A's two children, X and Y.

2. G devised property in trust, directing the trustee to pay the income to A for life, then to A's children; each child's share of principal is to be paid to the child when the child reaches 40; if any child dies under 40, the child's share is to be paid to the child's estate as a property interest owned by such child. The trustee is given the discretionary power to advance all or a portion of a child's share before the child reaches 40. G was survived by A, who was then childless.

3. G devised property in trust, the terms of which authorized the trustee to accumulate the income or pay it or a portion of it to A during A's lifetime; after A's death, the trustee was authorized to accumulate the income or to distribute it in equal or unequal shares among A's children until the death of the survivor; and on the death of A's last surviving child to pay the corpus and accumulated income (if any) to B. The trustee was also granted the discretionary power to invade the corpus on behalf of the permissible recipient or recipients of the income. G was survived by A, B, and A's two children, X and Y. Compare John Chipman Gray on Perpetuities §§ 410.1-.5; Lyons v. Bradley, 53 So. 244 (Ala. 1910); Woodruff Oil & Fertilizer Co. v. Yarborough's Estate, 142 S.E. 50 (S.C. 1928), with Andrews v. Lincoln, 50 A. 898 (Me. 1901); Bundy v. United States Trust Co., 153 N.E. 337 (Mass. 1926); Thomas v. Harrison, 191 N.E.2d 862 (Ohio P. Ct. 1962).

Validity of the Exercise—Nongeneral and Testamentary Powers. If a nongeneral or testamentary power passes the appropriate test for validity as set forth above, it can validly be exercised. Whether or not such a power has in fact been validly exercised is the next question.

For the most part, the Rule Against Perpetuities applies to appointed interests (and appointed powers) in the same way it applies to interests (and powers) created by an owner of property. At common law, the requirement of initial certainty applies. Under the Uniform Rule, interests (or powers) that don't satisfy the requirement of initial certainty and are therefore not validated by § 1(a)(1) (or, in the case of appointed powers, §§ 1(b)(1) or 1(c)(1)), are entitled to a 90-year period to determine their validity. See USRAP § 1(a)(2), (b)(2), (c)(2) (UPC § 2-901(a)(2), (b)(2), (c)(2)). Nevertheless, in the case of nongeneral and testamentary powers, there are some perpetuity questions and doctrines peculiar to appointments.

Industrial National Bank v. Barrett

220 A.2d 517 (R.I. 1966)

PAOLINO, J. This is a bill in equity brought by the Industrial National Bank of Rhode Island, executor and trustee, and Aline C. Lathan, co-executor, under the will of Mary M. Tilley, deceased, for construction of the latter's will and for instructions to the executors and trustee thereunder. . . .

It appears that Arthur H. Tilley, husband of the deceased, died January 28, 1959. Under the eighth clause of his will, admitted to probate February 5, 1959, he devised the property, which qualified for the full marital deduction, to the Industrial National Bank, in trust, with directions to pay the net income at least quarterly to his wife for life and such amounts of the corpus annually or at more frequent intervals as she should in writing request, for her comfort and support, and without being accountable to any court or remainderman therefor. He also conferred upon her a general testamentary power of appointment over the corpus remaining at her death. Mary M. Tilley died October 28, 1963. Under the fourth clause of her will, admitted to probate November 7, 1963, she exercised her general testamentary power of appointment to the Industrial National Bank, in trust "to pay over the net income thereof to and for the use and benefit of my granddaughters, Aline C. Lathan and Evelyn M. Barrett . . . equally for and during the term of their natural lives, and upon the death of either of them, to pay over said net income to her issue, per stirpes and not per capita." The trustee was also given uncontrolled discretion to pay over to either of said grandchildren, or the issue of any deceased grandchild, for specific purposes, portions of the principal. Finally, the testatrix provided the trust would terminate "twenty one (21) years after the death of the last survivor of the younger grandchild or issue of either grandchild of mine living at my death. . . ."

On the date of Arthur H. Tilley's death, Aline C. Lathan and Evelyn M. Barrett and one great-grandchild were in being. On the date of Mary M. Tilley's death the aforesaid respondents plus six additional great-grandchildren were in being. One great-grandchild was born subsequent to her death. . . .

The complainants contend that Mrs. Tilley's exercise of the power of appointment created under her husband's will does not violate the rule against perpetuities. . . .

The complainants . . . contend that . . . the better-reasoned authorities hold the perpetuity period should be counted from the date of the power's exercise rather than its creation, which would make the gift here vest within the prescribed time. . . .

It is fundamental law that when the free alienation of a future interest in property is limited, the interest must vest within lives in being plus twenty-one years from the date of the creating instrument. When the persons who will take or the extent of their interests are to be determined by the exercise of a subsequent power of appointment, the rule against perpetuities requires that the vesting time be computed as if the appointment were a part of the instrument creating the limitation, because until it is exercised the limitation is incomplete.

Nevertheless as the primary concern behind the rule is to prevent restraint on alienation, a distinction is made between general and special powers. In the case of a general power of appointment by deed and will, all courts hold that since the donee has absolute disposing power over the property and may bring it into the market place at any time, he has what is tantamount to a fee. Therefore, since whatever estates may be created by one seized in fee may be also created under a general power, the commencement of the limitation is computed from the time of the power's exercise and not its creation.

In the case of a general power of appointment by will, however, the weight of authority counts the perpetuity period from the date of creation on the ground that since the donee cannot freely alienate the property during his life, he is not the practical owner thereof. A minority view disagrees with this position on the theory that the concept of actual ownership clouds the substance of the matter, which is that if the person having the power without the ownership may appoint to whomsoever he pleases at the time he exercises it, he is in the same position in respect to the perpetuity as if he were actually the owner. Thorndike, General Powers And Perpetuities, 27 Harv. L. Rev., pp. 705, 717. Also see Northern Trust Co. v. Porter, 368 Ill. 256, 13 N.E.2d 487, for leading citations on both positions.

Since this is a case of first impression, we have read with interest the authorities supporting the above positions. See Gray, General Testamentary Powers And The Rule Against Perpetuities, 26 Harv. L. Rev., p. 720; Thorndike, General Powers And Perpetuities, supra; Annot., 1 A.L.R. 374; and Northern Trust Co. v. Porter, supra. From this reading it appears that the early English cases in counting the perpetuity period did not distinguish between a general power to appoint by deed and will and a general power to appoint by will only and we think the cases following this position are the more persuasive.

In essence the majority jurisdictions characterize a general power of appointment by will as being in the nature of a special power, and, as such, a part of the creating instrument of the donor. They reach this result solely on the ground that because the donor has tied up ownership of the property until the donee's death, the restraint on alienation is sufficient to count the perpetuity period from the power's creation.

We think that this position misapprehends the fundamental concepts involved here. The law does not prohibit an estate being tied up for the life of any one individual, but prohibits only restraint beyond lives in being plus twenty-one years. See Thorndike, supra. When the donee exercises his power, he is at that time the practical owner thereof, for the purposes of the rule, as he can appoint to anyone of his choice as well as his own estate. Furthermore when he exercises the power he can create, unlike the case of a special power, estates entirely independent from those created or controlled by the donor, and so, as to the donee, the power is a general one. See Perpetuities In Perspective: Ending The Rule's Reign Of Terror, by W. Barton Leach, 65 Harv. L. Rev. 721.

Consequently, we hold the trust created by clause fourth of Mrs. Tilley's will pursuant to her general testamentary power of appointment is valid. We arrive at this conclusion not only because logic favors its adoption but also because we believe it is in line with the trend to obviate the technical harshness of the rule against perpetuities and decide cases on the substance of things. 6 American Law of Property § 24.45 (1952), p. 118; 3 Restatement, Property § 343 (1940), p. 1913; Union & New Haven Trust Co. v. Taylor, 133 Conn. 221, 50 A.2d 168. For a learned discussion of this problem, see Perpetuities In A Nutshell, 51 Harv. L. Rev. 638, and Perpetuities: The Nutshell Revisited, 78 Harv. L. Rev. 973, both being articles by W. Barton Leach. . . .

On July 6, 1966, the parties may present to this court for approval a form of decree, in accordance with this opinion, to be entered in the superior court.

Notes

1. *State of the Authorities.* The position taken by the court in the *Barrett* case is supported by legislation enacted in a few American states.[77] This is also the

---

77. See Del. Code Ann. tit. 25, § 501; S.D. Codified. Laws § 43-5-5; Wis. Stat. Ann. § 700.16(c). The Delaware and South Dakota statutes apply the same rule to the exercise of nongeneral powers as well as the exercise of general testamentary powers, a position that's responsible for the enactment of IRC § 2041(a)(3). Section 2041(a)(3) was construed in the light of the Wisconsin statute in Estate of Murphy v. Commissioner, 71 T.C. 671 (1979). See Jeffrey N. Pennell & Jonathan G. Blattmachr, Adventures in Generation Skipping, Or How We Learned to Love the "Delaware Tax Trap," 24 Real Prop. Prob. & Tr. J. 75 (1989). Any exercise of a nongeneral power (and, in certain circumstances, the mere possibility of any such exercise) in a

English view, as first enunciated in Rous v. Jackson, L.R. 29 Ch. 521 (1885) and now codified in the Perpetuities and Accumulations Act, § 7. The vast majority view, however, is to the contrary. The Restatement 2d of Property § 1.2 comment d, illus. 12 rejects the reasoning of the *Barrett* case and supports the majority view, on the ground that the "complete freedom of transfer by will that opens up momentarily on [the donee's] death is not enough to eliminate the interference with unqualified control of beneficial rights . . . that is caused . . . during [the donee's] lifetime." The Uniform Rule also supports the majority view. See USRAP § 2(a), comment (UPC § 2-902(a)).

2. *Special Principle for Transition to Uniform Rule.* As just noted, the Uniform Rule adopts the majority view of relation back, namely that the validity of the exercise of a nongeneral or testamentary power must be decided with reference to the date of the power's original creation by the donor. However, a different date determines whether the applicable law on perpetuities is the Uniform Rule or pre-existing law. Section 5(a) of the Uniform Rule (UPC § 2-905(a)) provides: "this [Act] applies to a nonvested property interest or a power of appointment that is created on or after the effective date of this [Act]. For purposes of this section, a nonvested property interest or a power of appointment created by the exercise of a power of appointment is created when the power is irrevocably exercised or when a revocable exercise becomes irrevocable." In other words, one must engage in a two-step inquiry. The first step is to determine whether the Uniform Rule or the state's pre-existing perpetuity law applies. The second step is to evaluate the validity of the nongeneral or testamentary power under that applicable law.

Consider the following hypothetical, based upon the facts of Matter of Wold, 708 A.2d 787 (N.J. Super. 1998). In 1944, G established a trust providing for income to A for life, remainder to such of A's spouse or descendants as A may by will appoint. In 1987, the state adopted the Uniform Rule. A now wishes to execute a will, exercising her power to create nonvested interests in her descendants, and she wishes to avail herself of the Uniform Rule's 90-year wait-and-see period. May she? The answer is yes. Although the validity of A's exercise of the power will be determined with reference to the 1944 date of creation under the doctrine of relation back, the governing perpetuities law will be the Uniform Rule, because A's exercise of the power will become irrevocable at her death, which is well past the 1987 effective date of the Uniform Rule in this jurisdiction.

3. *Marital Deduction.* Note that general testamentary powers are typically conferred on the donor's surviving spouse in a trust that qualifies for the federal

"grandfathered" trust under the federal generation-skipping transfer tax would cause the trust to lose "grandfathered" status.

estate tax marital deduction under IRC § 2056(b)(5). See supra Chapter 7. If the surviving spouse exercises the power by creating a trust, the lawyer drafting the donee-client's will must be especially alert to the fact that the appointed interests and powers are treated in the majority of states as if they were created when the donee-client's power was created. If a perpetuity saving clause is used, the clause must tie the perpetuity-period component into the lives of persons in being at the creation of the donee-client's power, not at the exercise of the donee-client's power.

Estate of Bird

225 Cal. App. 2d 196, 37 Cal. Rptr. 288 (1964)

STONE, J. Jeannette Miller Bird and Geoffrey Andrew Bird, her husband, executed their wills simultaneously February 17, 1961.

Jeannette died June 16, 1961, and her will, which was admitted to probate, provided, insofar as here pertinent: "2. This trust shall exist and continue for and during the life of my said husband, GEOFFREY ANDREW BIRD, and shall cease and terminate upon his death. I give and grant to my husband the exclusive power to dispose of the corpus, and undistributed income, under the terms of his Last Will and Testament. . . ."

Geoffrey Bird died just three months later, September 16, 1961. He exercised the power of appointment created by Jeannette's will, by the following provisions in his will:

> FIFTH: I will, devise and bequeath to CITIZENS NATIONAL BANK, in trust, all of the rest, residue and remainder of my property of every nature, kind and description, including the property and assets which are included in the Marital Deduction Trust as set forth in my wife's Will, and I do now specifically exercise my power of testamentary disposition by including such assets in this trust.
>
> (a) Said property is to be held by the Trustee for the following purposes:
>
> 1. The net income shall be distributed in monthly or other convenient installments to or for the benefit of my said children in equal shares for life. . . .
>
> 3. This trust shall terminate on the death of the last survivor of my children and my grandchildren living at the time of my death, and the entire corpus and undistributed net income shall go and be distributed to the children of my grandchildren per capita.

Counsel for both appellant and respondent agree that the matter is one of first impression in California, and they pose two questions: First, whether the period prescribed by the rule against perpetuities . . . is determined as of the time the power was created, that is, at Jeannette's death, or at Geoffrey's death when the power was exercised. Second, if the time the power is created governs, is the determination made according to the facts existing at the time of creation of the power, or are the circumstances existing at the time the power is exercised, controlling? We hold that the period is counted from the time the power of appointment is created, but that the facts and circumstances are considered as of the time of its exercise. This holding disposes of both questions raised. . . .

Simes and Smith, in their work, The Law of Future Interests, section 1276, page 214, tell us that the common law rule is:

> . . . in determining the validity of an appointment under a special power or a general testamentary power, though the period is counted from the creation of the power, facts and circumstances are considered as of the time of its exercise. . . .

The Restatement of Property adopted the common law rule applicable to general testamentary powers of appointment. . . . The rule is expressed in section 392 as follows:

> . . . an appointment under either a general testamentary power or a special power is invalid, because of the rule against perpetuities, only to the extent that its limitations, (a) construed in the light of the circumstances existent when the power is exercised, but (b) measured, for the purpose of applying the rule against perpetuities, from the time when the power was created, violate that rule.

In commenting upon the rationale of the rule, the Restatement points out that:

> The element of the stated rule embodied in Clause (a), mitigates the destructive effect of the doctrine of "relation back." In applying the rule against perpetuities to the limitations of an attempted appointment made under either a general testamentary power or a special power, no useful end would be served by finding an invalidity because of some possible uncertainty, present when the power was created, but actually and definitively excluded by the course of events which has already occurred and which is known at the time of the exercise of the power. By the part of the rule embodied in Clause (a) the fiction of "relation back" is prevented from having destructive effects greater than those required for the reasonable effectuation of the underlying social policy of the rule against perpetuities.

This is in accord with the liberal approach toward the rule against perpetuities taken by the California Supreme Court in the recent case of Wong v. Di Grazia, 60 A.C. 505, [35 Cal.Rptr. 241, 386 P.2d 817]. . . .

The facts of this case demonstrate the reasonableness of the common law rule embodied in section 392 of the Restatement of Property, supra. By reason of the proximate deaths of Jeannette and Geoffrey, only three months elapsed between creation of the power and its exercise. There was no factual change during that short interval. The lives in being at the time the power was exercised were in being when the power was created, so that the power of appointment did not, in fact, violate the rule against perpetuities. To defeat the purposes and the wishes of Jeannette and Geoffrey because a violation of the rule against perpetuities was theoretically possible, but in fact did not occur, seems to us to be unnecessarily restrictive. It is the sort of rigid mechanistic application of the rule which the Supreme Court decried in Wong v. Di Grazia, supra.

In any event, we find Civil Code section 715.2 and the common law rule to which it refers, controlling. Applying his test, there was no violation of the rule against perpetuities at the time the power of appointment was created, when considered in the light of the facts and circumstances as of the time the power of appointment was exercised.

The judgment is reversed.

Notes and Questions

1. *Supporting Authority*. Taking a "second look" at the facts existing at the date of the exercise of a nongeneral or testamentary power is a well established procedure. See Restatement of Property § 392; Am. L. Prop. § 24.35.

2. *Second Look for Gifts in Default*. Can a second look at the facts also be taken in determining the validity of a gift in default in cases in which the power isn't exercised? Am. L. Prop. § 24.36, written by W. Barton Leach and Owen Davies Tudor, supports a second look for gifts in default. Shortly after this treatise was published, this position was adopted in apparently the first American case to consider the question, Sears v. Coolidge, 108 N.E.2d 563 (Mass. 1952). Four years later, Simes & Smith on Future Interest § 1276 came out against the decision in *Sears*. Not long after, however, a Canadian court upheld a gift in default by applying the second-look doctrine. See Re Edwards, 20 D.L.R.2d 755 (Ont. 1959). Later, the Pennsylvania court did the same thing but did so without discussing the issue, except to assert that it was "the better view." See In re Frank, 389 A.2d 536 (Pa. 1978). The authority of this decision is undercut by the fact that the Pennsylvania wait-and-see statute was applicable to the case and required the same result, and the court so noted.

Problems

G devised property in trust, income to A for life, remainder in corpus to such persons as A shall by will appoint. A's will appointed the property in a further trust, the terms of which were that the income was to go to A's children in equal shares for their lives; on each child's death, the share of corpus proportionate to the child's share of income was to go to the child's then-living descendants, by representation.

Consider the validity of A's appointment under the common-law Rule and under the Uniform Rule in the following circumstances:

1. A died, survived by her two children, X and Y, both of whom were also in being at G's death.

2. A died, survived by her two children, X and Y; X was in being at G's death but Y was born after G's death.

Amerige v. Attorney General

88 N.E.2d 126 (Mass. 1949)

[Timothy Leeds left property by will in trust for his brother, James Leeds, for life and then for such persons as James should by will appoint.

James by will expressly blended his own property with that over which he had the power conferred by Timothy, and gave a part of the combined estates in trust for the benefit of his daughter, Mary Elizabeth Williams, for life and then for such persons as she should by will appoint.

Mary Elizabeth by her will also blended her own estate with that over which she had the power conferred by James and left the residue thereof in trust for her two children for life, then to his or her issue, but in default of issue to hold for the life of the survivor, then to his or her issue, but if then there should be no issue of either, to certain charities.

The court held that Mary Elizabeth's appointment violated the common-law Rule Against Perpetuities to the extent it included property from the estate of Timothy.

Among others, James was survived by his daughter Mary Elizabeth, who was also living at Timothy's death, and by Mary Elizabeth's two children, Mary and Edward, neither of whom was living at Timothy's death.]

SPALDING, J. This is a petition for instructions by the trustees under the will of Mary Elizabeth Williams, late of Hopkinton. The case was heard in the Probate Court on a statement of agreed facts and was reserved and reported to this court without decision. . . .

The charities . . . advance the argument that none of the property appointed by Mary Elizabeth Williams is derived from property of Timothy. They invoke the principle that where the donee of a general power of appointment disposes of owned and appointive property as a single fund the appointive property is allocated to the various dispositions of such fund in such manner as to give the maximum effect to such dispositions. That principle is recognized by our decisions, Stone v. Forbes, 189 Mass. 163, 170-171, 75 N.E. 141; Minot v. Paine, 230 Mass. 514, 525, 120 N.E. 167, 1 A.L.R. 365, and by the American Law Institute in § 363 of the Restatement of Property. Thus, it is argued, James Leeds dealt with his own and the appointive property as a single fund and to give the maximum effect to his dispositions the debts, expenses, legacies and residuary gifts must be charged against the appointive property and if this is done that property is exhausted and there is no property of Timothy remaining which Mary Elizabeth Williams could appoint. But that principle is not applicable here. In the case at bar there were successive donees of the power created by Timothy, James Leeds and Mary Elizabeth Williams. The appointments which violate the rule against perpetuities were made by Mary Elizabeth Williams, the second donee. None of the appointments made by James is invalid and no contention is made to the contrary. In all of the cases we have seen where the principle of allocation has been applied the valid and invalid dispositions have been made by the same person in the same will. To give the maximum effect to such dispositions under the principle of allocation the law is attempting to carry out the presumed intent of the testator. The doctrine ought not to be applied in the case of successive donees where the dispositions of the first donee are valid and those of the second invalid. It cannot reasonably be said that James contemplated that Mary Elizabeth Williams would exercise the power improperly with the result that he must be presumed to have intended that his dispositions be charged against the appointive property.

The case is remanded to the Probate Court for further proceedings in conformance with this opinion. . . .

3. Charitable Gifts

With one exception, future interests given to charities are subject to the Rule Against Perpetuities. The Rule applies to charitable interests in the same way it applies to future interests given to private parties. At common law, if there is a condition precedent attached to the interest, and if there is no validating life, the charitable interest fails.

> *Example 19.18:* G devised real property "to A for life, then to such of A's children as reach 25, but if none of A's children reaches 25, to X Charity."
>
> The remainder in favor of X Charity is invalid. So is the remainder in favor of A's children. Under the wait-and-see modification of the common-law Rule, these interests wouldn't be initially invalid, but would be given a chance to vest or terminate on their own terms within the allowable waiting period.

Constructional Preference for Vested Charitable Interests. Charitable interests, like private interests, aren't subject to the Rule if they are vested. There is a pronounced tendency in the decisions to construe charitable interests as vested if the language of the instrument permits this classification. Many charitable gifts, which if contingent would have been invalid, have been saved by this device.

Charitable Interests Excluded if Preceded by Another Charitable Interest. As noted above, there is one formal exception to the principle that charitable future interests receive no preferential treatment under the common-law Rule. A future interest held by a charity is excluded from the application of the Rule if the interest was preceded by an interest that is also held by a charity. See Restatement 2d of Property § 1.6; USRAP § 4(5) (UPC § 2-904(5)).

The rationale for this exclusion is that, because the law allows a perpetual tying up of property for a single charity, it ought to do so when the transferor provides for a shift from one charity to another, even though the shift might take place beyond the perpetuity period.

Example 19.19: G devised real property "to the X School District so long as the premises are used for school purposes, and upon the cessation of such use, to Y City."

The executory interest in favor of Y City is valid.

4. Contracts

Owing to its roots as a means by which to curb remotely vesting future interests that made *property* inalienable, especially indestructible executory interests, the Rule Against Perpetuities is inapplicable to legal relationships that do not create property interests. Contracts—even long-term contracts—are generally exempt. It has been held that optional modes of settlement for the payment of life insurance proceeds cannot violate the Rule, nor can annuity contracts, even though future payments may be subject to uncertainties that might not be resolved within a life in being plus 21 years. Doyle v. Massachusetts Mutual Life Ins. Co., 377 F.2d 19 (6th Cir. 1967); Holmes v. John Hancock Mutual Life Ins. Co., 41 N.E.2d 909 (N.Y. 1942).

5. Commercial Transactions

As noted above, legal relationships that do not create property interests are not subject to the Rule Against Perpetuities. Although this exempts most contracts from the Rule, some contractual arrangements do create property interests under our classificatory scheme of estates. Many of these legal relationships arise out of commercial transactions.

The Rule Against Perpetuities would seem to be a wholly inappropriate instrument of social policy to use as a control over these arrangements. The period of the Rule—a life in being plus 21 years—may be suitable as a limit on gratuitous transfers of property, but it is not suitable for bargained-for exchanges. Nevertheless, the common-law Rule has been applied to certain types of commercial transactions. The Rule Against Perpetuities argument is usually raised by the party seeking to avoid performance of the contract.

a. Commercial Transactions under the Uniform Rule

In recognition of the point that the life-in-being-plus-21-year period has no relevance to commercial transactions, the Uniform Rule broke new ground by excluding all commercial transactions from the Rule Against Perpetuities. See USRAP § 4(1) (UPC § 2-904(1)). Consequently, under the Uniform Rule, none of the transactions we are about to consider would be subject to the Rule. The drafting committee of the Uniform Rule took notice of the fact that some of these commercial transactions do restrain the alienability of property, but thought that their control was not, strictly speaking, a Rule Against Perpetuities question and hence was beyond the scope of the project. The official comment notes, however, that these transactions are subject to the common-law rules regarding unreasonable restraints on alienation and, in some cases, marketable title acts.

Another approach is to enact a separate set of statutory provisions limiting the duration of certain commercial transactions to a flat period of years, such as 30, as has been done in Illinois (Ill. Rev. Stat. ch. 765, § 305/4(a)) and Massachusetts (Mass. Gen. Laws Ann. ch. 184A, § 5).

b. Options In Gross

A contract right to purchase property is an option in gross if the optionee has no possessory interest in the property, such as a leasehold interest. If the subject of an option is land or a unique chattel, the option is specifically enforceable. Specifically enforceable contracts are treated as creating equitable property interests. Because equitable property interests are subject to the Rule Against Perpetuities, the prevailing view is that options in gross are invalid if they are exercisable beyond a life in being plus 21 years. See Symphony Space v. Pergola Properties, Inc., 669 N.E.2d 799 (N.Y. 1996). But see Pathmark Stores, Inc. v. 3821 Associates, L.P., 663 A.2d 1189 (Del. Ch. Ct. 1995) (held that 30-year option contract did not violate the common-law Rule).

Example 19.20: (1) A, the owner of Blackacre, sells an option to B under which A obligates himself, his heirs and assigns at any time in the future to convey Blackacre to B, his heirs and assigns for $X.

(2) A, the owner of Blackacre, sells Blackacre to B. As part of the transaction, B obligates himself, his heirs and assigns at any time in the future to reconvey Blackacre to A, his heirs and assigns for $X.

Both options are invalid by the great majority view. They are neither specifically enforceable nor are damages for their breach recoverable. Case (2) deserves a special comment. There the option was reserved by the transferor of the property. Although reversionary interests aren't subject to the Rule, reserved options aren't accorded the same immunity. See Woodall v. Bruen, 85 S.E. 170 (W. Va. 1915). Yet the difference between a reserved option and a right of entry may be only a matter of form. For example, suppose the grant of Blackacre in the variation had read: "to B and his heirs, but if the grantor or his heirs should ever tender $X to B, his heirs or assigns, the grantor or his heirs shall have the right to re-enter and retake the premises." Presumably this change in form would transform A's invalid option into a valid right of entry.

Options that are limited to expire if they aren't exercised within a life in being plus 21 years are valid. The options in the above example would have been valid if the obligation hadn't been to convey Blackacre "at any time in the future," but rather had been to do so "during the lifetime of the survivor of A and B," or "during the next 21 years." Even without so explicit a limitation, a court might construe the language of the option as being so limited. The absence of language such as "his heirs and assigns," for example, might lead a court to hold that the option was to last only during the lifetime of either party or only during their joint lives.

c. Rights of First Refusal (Preemptive Rights)

Unlike options to purchase, rights of first refusal do not obligate the owners of property to sell the property whether they want to or not. Instead, they obligate the owners to offer the property first to the preemptioners only if the owners decide to sell. The preemptioners can buy the property, but if they decline, the owners are then free to sell to anyone else.

Rights of first refusal have been held to be subject to the Rule Against Perpetuities and void if they are exercisable beyond a life in being plus 21 years. See, e.g., Joseph v. Pollack, 795 F. Supp. 163 (E.D. Va. 1992).

It has been suggested that preemptive rights that require merely an offer at the prevailing *market price*, as opposed to a fixed price, ought to be valid even if they are of unlimited duration. See Am. L. Prop. § 26.67. The argument is that this type of a right of first refusal effects no restraint on alienation, direct or indirect. This idea was rejected, however, in Atchison v. City of Englewood, 463 P.2d 297, 303 (Colo. 1969), where the court held that the difficulty of ascertaining and locating the owner of the preemptive right at some indefinite time in the future constituted a "sufficiently unreasonable restraint upon the transferability of the property as to justify imposition of the rule against perpetuities." Accord Lake of the Woods Ass'n, Inc. v. McHugh, 380 S.E.2d 872 (Va. 1989); see also Buck v. Banks, 668 N.E.2d 1259 (Ind. Ct. App. 1996) (held Uniform Rule inapplicable to a commercial contract, leaving the common-law Rule intact, which resulted in the preemptive right being held void). But see Juliano & Sons v. Chevron, U.S.A., 593 A.2d 814 (N.J. Super. Ct. 1991) (found no justification for applying the common-law Rule to a right of first refusal after the legislature adopted the Uniform Rule). Other courts have also upheld preemptive rights of limited duration permitting purchase at market price. See, e.g., Swartz v. Bianco Family Trust, 874 P.2d 430 (Colo. Ct. App. 1993); Hare v. McClellan, 662 A.2d 1242 (Conn. 1995); Wildenstein & Co. v. Wallis, 595 N.E.2d 828 (N.Y. 1992); Robroy Land Co., Inc. v. Prather, 622 P.2d 367 (Wash. 1980).

In Estate of Royer v. Wineland Equipment, Inc., 663 A.2d 780 (Pa. Super. Ct. 1995), the court upheld a preemptive right as a reasonable restraint on alienation, even though it permitted the holder of the right to acquire the property at a fixed price that was below the market price. In Continental Cablevision, Inc. v. United Broadcasting Co., 873 F.2d 717 (4th Cir. 1989), the court saved a market-price right of first refusal from invalidity by imposing a 21-year limit on its duration, even though the actual language of the document creating the right of first refusal didn't specify an expiration date. Accord Peterson v. Tremain, 621 N.E.2d 385 (Mass. App. Ct. 1993).

Metropolitan Transportation Authority v. Bruken Realty Corp.

492 N.E.2d 379 (N.Y. 1986)

SIMONS, J. In 1966 the State of New York, acting through the Metropolitan Commuter Transportation Authority (now plaintiff Metropolitan Transportation Authority [MTA]) bought all the capital stock of plaintiff Long Island Railroad from the Pennsylvania Railroad for $65 million. Included among the assets acquired were 65 acres of real property in Queens which had been used by the Long Island Railroad as a freight yard. As part of the consideration, to reduce the purchase price, the State conveyed air rights above this property to Delbay Corporation, a subsidiary of Pennsylvania, together with an easement permitting it to erect columns, piers or foundations and to install utility services necessary to support and service improvements within the air rights. It also executed an "option agreement" granting Delbay the right to purchase 12 lots in the freight yard at market value if MTA subsequently determined that the property was "no longer necessary for [its] transportation operations." The option expired if Delbay, or its successors or assigns, did not exercise it within 99 years. The issue presented on this appeal is whether that option agreement violated the prohibition against remote vesting stated in New York's Rule against Perpetuities (see, EPTL 9-1.1[b]).

On April 16, 1982 MTA notified Delbay that it no longer required six of the lots and that Delbay could acquire them. Delbay thereafter assigned its right to two of the lots to a real estate developer, defendant Bruken Realty Corporation, and Bruken, by letter dated July 13, 1982, notified MTA of its election to purchase them. Although the original agreement provided for arbitration of the market value, the parties agreed to attempt to negotiate the price after obtaining separate appraisals. The air rights conveyed to Delbay had since been acquired by the City of New York in a tax foreclosure proceeding, however, and, with the air rights and the ground rights in separate ownership, the parties were unable to reach agreement. Accordingly, they selected arbitrators and submitted the determination of market value to them. Before hearings could start, plaintiffs instituted this action requesting that the court enjoin the arbitration proceeding and declare that the conveyance to Delbay of the right to acquire the freight yard lots was void. Plaintiffs subsequently moved for summary judgment and Supreme Court denied the motion on alternative legal grounds (125 Misc.2d 497, 479 N.Y.S.2d 646). The Appellate Division affirmed, without opinion, 112 A.D.2d 508, 492 N.Y.S.2d 508, and the matter is before us on a certified question by its leave. We now affirm.

I. The rules limiting the right of owners to indefinitely control title to property developed because of the natural antagonism between society's interest in promoting the free and ready transfer of property and the desire of property owners to control the future disposition of their holdings. Originally intended to restrict family dispositions, usually dispositions by royalty or the landed gentry, the rules have antecedents as old as any known to the common law. Their purpose is to ensure the productive use and development of property by its current beneficial owners by simplifying ownership, facilitating exchange and freeing property from unknown or embarrassing impediments to alienability. The rules are legal prohibitions, based on the public policy of the State. They may not be waived, as could rules enacted for the benefit of the parties alone. When an owner attempts to exert control over the transferability of his property for too long a time, the courts will step in, invalidate the restricting provisions, and permit transfer to take effect uninhibited by the restraint.

In New York an owner's power to dispose of property is limited by three rules. The first two, known as the Rule against Perpetuities, are found in subdivisions (a) and (b) of EPTL 9-1.1. The Rule declares that no estate in property shall be valid (1) if the instrument conveying it suspends the power of alienation for a period longer than lives in being at the creation of the estate plus 21 years[78] and (2) unless it must vest, if at all, before expiration of the same period. Although the statutory period is lives in being plus 21 years, in this case the parties to the agreement were corporations and, inasmuch as no measuring life or lives were stated in the instruments, the permissible period is 21 years. The third rule regulating dispositions is established by common law and invalidates conveyances which impose unreasonable restraints on alienation.

The statutory rule prohibiting remote vesting and the common-law rule against unreasonable restraints serve the same general purpose by limiting the power of an owner to create uncertain future estates. The statutory rule does so indirectly by limiting the time when future interests must vest. The rule against unreasonable restraints on alienation does so directly by forbidding owners to impose conditions on conveyances which block the grantee from freely disposing of the property. While the statutory rule is inflexible, measured solely

78. The suspension of the power of alienation rule is discussed infra Part F. Eds.

by the passage of time, the common-law rule is applied by considering the reasonableness of the restraint. Whether a restraint on the disposition of property is unreasonable is a question of fact depending upon its purpose, duration and, where applicable, the designated method for fixing the purchase price. It is generally said that the reason for the common-law rule is that ownership of property cannot exist in one person and the right of alienation in another, but the same general policy concerns underlying the rule against perpetuities also favor a rule against unreasonable restraints.

II. Plaintiff contends that the State's agreement gave Delbay an option to buy the freight yard lots, that options are subject to the rule against remote vesting under the holding of Buffalo Seminary v. McCarthy, 86 A.D.2d 435, 451 N.Y.S.2d 457, aff'd. on opn. below 58 N.Y.2d 867, 460 N.Y.S.2d 528, 447 N.E.2d 76) and that since Delbay's option might not be exercised within the statutory period, it is void. Whether the provision is void or not requires a determination first of the nature of the interest created—whether it is an option or, as Bruken claims, a preemptive right—and, second, if it is a preemptive right, whether the rule applies to it.

[The court held that options in gross are subject to EPTL § 9-1.1, and continued.] Preemptive rights differ significantly from options, however, and we have not yet decided whether they are subject to that rule.

A. The right acquired by Delbay, though called an option by the parties, was a preemptive right to buy the freight yard property. An option grants to the holder the power to compel the owner of property to sell it whether the owner is willing to part with ownership or not. A preemptive right, or right of first refusal, does not give its holder the power to compel an unwilling owner to sell; it merely requires the owner, when and if he decides to sell, to offer the property first to the party holding the preemptive right so that he may meet a third-party offer or buy the property at some other price set by a previously stipulated method. Once the owner decides to sell the property, the holder of the preemptive right may choose to buy it or not, but the choice exists only after he receives an offer from the owner. If the holder decides not to buy, then the owner may sell to anyone. . . .

B. We turn then to whether the rule against remote vesting applies to preemptive rights.

The New York courts which have considered the question have reached different results as have courts from other jurisdictions.

The courts which have declined to apply the rule have tried to distinguish preemptive rights from other interests in property by determining either (1) that the holder of a preemptive right has an interest which vests immediately, not remotely or (2) that the holder acquires only a contract right exercisable at some future date, not an interest in property. Commentators, and this court as well, have criticized both analyses as contrary to established principles of law and have urged that the courts might better concede that although preemptive rights offend the basic policy of the rule against remote vesting, the offense is properly offset by their utility in modern legal transactions and that usefulness justifies excepting them from the operation of the rule (see, 5A Powell, op. cit. ¶771[1], at 72-68, 72-70; Simes and Smith, Future Interests § 1154, at 64 [2d ed. 1956]; Leach, Perpetuities: New Absurdity, Judicial and Statutory Correctives, 73 Harv. L. Rev. 1318, 1320).

The courts have reached this conclusion in a number of circumstances involving options and preemptive rights, e.g., for options appurtenant to leases or to mineral rights or to franchise rights or for options to expand an easement or to acquire an interest in a party wall if the optionee decided to build adjacent to the optionor's land (Beloit Bldg. Co. v. Quinn, 145 Kan. 507, 66 P.2d 549). The holder's rights have been recognized because enforcement did not violate the underlying purposes of the rule against remote vesting. Quite the contrary, enforcement of the preemptive right in such cases encouraged the holder to develop the property by insuring his opportunity to benefit from development and to recapture his investment in it. For similar reasons recent decisions have held that, because the management of condominium developments has a valid interest not only in securing the occupancy of the units but also in protecting the ownership of the common areas and the underlying fee, its preemptive rights to repurchase units before sale to third parties should be excepted from the operation of the rule. . . . Finally, Bruken claims that there is a "public interest" exception to the rule prohibiting remote vesting and it urges us to adopt that exception and apply it here (see, Southeastern Pa. Transp. Auth. v. Philadelphia Transp. Co., 426 Pa. 377, 233 A.2d 15). In the Southeastern Pa. Transp. Auth. case, the court enforced an otherwise invalid option to permit a municipal agency to acquire facilities to insure continued mass transportation services in the Philadelphia area. The holding is said to rest upon the rationale that government is similar to a charity and thus not subject to the rule against remote vesting (see, Note, Southeastern Pennsylvania Transportation Authority v. Philadelphia Transportation Co., The Rule Against Perpetuities—Does the Rule Apply to an Option to Purchase Held by a Municipality, 72 Dick. L. Rev. 651, 660, 661).

Implicit in these decisions is a recognition that although preemptive rights unlimited in duration violate the rule against remote vesting they do so only marginally and that application of the rule, because of its inflexibility, may operate to invalidate legitimate transactions. This is so particularly in commercial and governmental activities because neither "lives in being" nor "twenty one years" are periods which are relevant to business or governmental affairs. In such cases the need to insure free alienability is served more effectively if the validity of the preemptive right is assessed by applying the common-law rule prohibiting unreasonable restraints (see, Leach, Perpetuities in a Nutshell, 51 Harv. L. Rev. 638, 660-661; Leach, op. cit., 73 Harv. L. Rev., at 1320; Berg, Long-Term Options and the Rule Against Perpetuities, 37 Cal. L. Rev. 1, 21-22; Simes and Smith, op. cit. § 1154, at 64).

This case illustrates the point. Application of the rule against remote vesting here would defeat the policies underlying the rule because it would invalidate an agreement which promoted the use and development of the property while, at the same time, imposing only a minor impediment to free transferability. Through its agreement with Pennsylvania Railroad, the State advanced its objective, to obtain a substantial reduction in the price it paid to acquire the assets of the Long Island Railroad property, assets the State needed to maintain commuter service to the approximately 260,000 passengers of the New York City and Long Island area who used the transportation facilities of the Long Island Railroad daily. It had no long-term interest in the freight yard property or in the air rights conveyed to Pennsylvania Railroad; it was confronted with the possibility that the Long Island Railroad, previously bankrupt, subsequently reorganized, and in serious financial condition in 1966, might shortly be dissolved. The State's interest was preservation of the passenger transportation facility and it intended to keep the freight yard property only long enough to evaluate the need for the lots in conjunction with operating the commuter service. This agreement gave MTA the opportunity to do so. In the meantime the State conveyed the air rights to Pennsylvania, granting it the necessary easements to develop those rights, and a preemptive right for the future acquisition of the ground rights, so that the interests in air and ground rights could eventually be reunited. The transfer permitted the parties to put both properties, the railroad and the freight yard, to their maximum productive use, a benefit which far outweighed any public interest served by automatic invalidation of the preemptive right to the lots solely because of remote vesting of Delbay's interest. Moreover, because the parties were a State authority and a national transportation corporation engaged in a widely publicized transaction—not private citizens whose interest might never be discovered with the passage of time—it did so without unknown limitations on the title which could inhibit future property transfers. Manifestly whatever obstacles there are to the disposition of property by restrictions such as this are best regulated by the rule against unreasonable restraints on alienation so that the utility of the restriction may be considered, rather than by the inflexible rule against remote vesting.

III. Under the rule prohibiting unreasonable restraints on alienation, the validity of the preemptive right rests on its reasonableness, judged by its duration, price and purpose. The duration of the restraint is not measured by the life of the preemptive right. The rule does not condemn restrictions on transfer, i.e., provisions which postpone sale during the option period; it condemns only the "effective prohibition against transferability itself" (Allen v. Biltmore Tissue

Corp., 2 N.Y.2d 534, 542, 161 N.Y.S.2d 418, 141 N.E.2d 812, supra [emphasis in original]). Indeed, dusty New York authority holds that preemptive rights may be perpetual (see, De Peyster v. Michael, 6 N.Y. 467, supra; Jackson ex dem. Lewis v. Schutz, 18 Johns 174 [Spencer, Ch. J., concurring]; Overbagh v. Patrie, 8 Barb. 28, affd. 6 N.Y. 510; see also, Schnebly, Restraints Upon the Alienation of Legal Interests: III, 44 Yale L. J. 1380, 1392-1394). Thus, the reasonableness of Delbay's preemptive right must be determined not by considering the 99-year term, but by considering the 90-day period during which the right could be exercised after the MTA decided to sell.

Reasonableness also depends on price, for the method by which the price is set can be critical in determining whether a preemptive right unlawfully restrains transfers. When the holder has a right to purchase at a fixed price, or at a price less than that offered in the market, it is likely to involve a sacrifice by the owner if he wishes to transfer the property, thus becoming a far more serious interference with alienability (see, Simes and Smith, op. cit. § 1154, at 62-63). A preemptive right, however, usually will not be unlawful when conditioned on payment of market value or a sum equal to a third-party offer (see, Restatement of Property § 413 [1944]; and see generally, Ann., 40 A.L.R.3d 920 § 4). Market value, in some instances, may be less than sale price, but a market value fixed by arbitrators compelled to consider the price a willing seller would accept from a willing buyer at the time of sale can hardly be unreasonable, as a matter of law, notwithstanding the separate ownership of air and ground rights.

Finally, as we have stated, the preemptive right in this case clearly served a beneficial purpose and given its reasonableness in terms of duration and price, it should be enforced.

In sum, we hold that the rule against remote vesting does not apply to preemptive rights in commercial and governmental transactions, that their validity is to be judged by applying the rule against unreasonable restraints and that the preemptive right granted Delbay by the State was under all the circumstances a reasonable restriction on the alienability of the freight yard lots.

Accordingly, the order of the Appellate Division should be affirmed. Question certified answered in the affirmative.

d. Options Appurtenant to Leasehold Interests

Options to renew a lease are not subject to the Rule Against Perpetuities. By the majority American view, options to purchase the property are also immune when held by the lessee of the premises. Thus options appurtenant to leaseholds, even those that are exercisable beyond a life in being plus 21 years, are valid.

e. Leases to Commence in the Future

A lease that is to commence at a fixed time in the future is valid even if the fixed time is or might be beyond a life in being plus 21 years. This is the view of the small handful of cases in which the issue has been decided. These leases are analogous to springing executory interests that aren't subject to any contingency.

Example 19.21: (1) A, the owner of Blackacre, leases the premises to B for 30 years. Shortly thereafter A leases the premises to C for 10 years commencing on the expiration of B's term.

(2) A, the owner of Blackacre, leases the premises to C for 10 years commencing 30 years from date.

C's lease is valid in both cases.

A lease to commence in the future, if subject to a contingency, is invalid if the contingency might occur beyond a life in being plus 21 years. There has been considerable litigation concerning the validity of so-called "on completion" leases—leases to commence on the completion of a building. These leases would be clearly valid if the lessor was obligated to complete the building within 21 years, but in the absence of an explicit obligation of this sort, some courts have held the lease to be invalid. See, e.g., Southern Airways Co. v. DeKalb County, 115 S.E.2d 207 (Ga. Ct. App.), rev'd on other grounds, 116 S.E.2d 602 (Ga. 1960). Other courts, however, have upheld these leases on the theory that the lessee's interest was vested from the beginning (see Isen v. Giant Foods, Inc., 295 F.2d 136 (D.C. Cir. 1960)), or on the theory that there was an implicit obligation to complete the building within a reasonable time (see Wong v. DiGrazia, 386 P.2d 817 (Cal. 1963); Singer Co. v. Makad, Inc., 518 P.2d 493 (Kan. 1974); Coulter & Smith, Ltd. v. Russell, 966 P.2d 852 (Utah 1998)).

f. Top Leases and Top Deeds

A common practice in the oil and gas industry is for the owner of land to lease or deed to another, usually an oil company, a working interest or a royalty interest that is to last for a period of a time certain *and* as long thereafter as oil, gas, or other minerals are produced in paying quantities. See 2 Howard R. Williams & Charles J. Meyers, Oil and Gas Law § 322 (1985). The landowner's retained interest in either type of arrangement has been held to be a possibility of reverter, with the lessee or grantee taking a defeasible estate—a fee simple determinable. See Caruthers v. Leonard, 254 S.W. 779 (Tex. Comm'n App. 1923) (lease); York v. Kenilworth Oil Co., 614 S.W.2d 468 (Tex. Civ. App. 1981) (lease); Peveto v. Starkey, 645 S.W.2d 770 (Tex. 1982) (deed; see infra p. 1285). Possibilities of reverter are excluded from the common-law Rule Against Perpetuities. See, e.g., Bagby v. Bredthauer, 627 S.W.2d 190 (Tex.

Civ. App. 1981). They are also assignable in many states. See Bagby v. Bredthauer, supra; York v. Kenilworth Oil Co., supra. Because the interest remains a possibility of reverter in the hands of the assignee, the exclusion from the common-law Rule continues even after the assignment. See Bagby v. Bredthauer, supra; Murphy v. Jamison, 117 S.W.2d 127 (Tex. Civ. App. 1938).

A common commercial practice in the oil and gas industry is to create so-called top leases and top deeds. This type of a lease or deed takes effect on the expiration of a bottom lease or a bottom deed. A bottom lease or a bottom deed is a lease or a deed of the type described in the preceding paragraph. Like the bottom lease or bottom deed, the top lease or top deed is also defeasible—*i.e.*, it is also for the period of a time certain *and* as long thereafter as oil, gas, or other minerals are produced in paying quantities. The validity of this type of an arrangement was the subject of the following case.

Peveto v. Starkey

645 S.W.2d 770 (Tex. 1982)

SONDOCK, J. . . . A.G. Jones and his wife conveyed an undivided three-fourths term royalty interest[79] in several tracts of land to Peveto. The primary term of the royalty deed was "for a period of fifteen years" from April 23, 1960, and "as long thereafter as oil, gas or other minerals, or either of them is produced . . . in paying commercial quantities." . . .

In November of 1973, Jones conveyed to Starkey, by top deed, a three-fourths term royalty interest. This royalty deed was for a primary term of ten years and "as long thereafter as oil, gas or other minerals, or either of them, is produced . . . in paying commercial quantities." The deed contained the following typed provision:

> This grant shall become effective only on the expiration of the above described Royalty Deed to R.L. Peveyto [sic] dated April 23, 1960.

Four months before Peveto's deed was to expire, Jones and Peveto executed another instrument. This instrument purported to extend the primary term of Peveto's deed from fifteen years to twenty-five years. . . .

Peveto . . . argues the royalty deed to Starkey violates the Rule against Perpetuities. Article I, section 26 of the Texas Constitution expressly provides: "Perpetuities . . . are contrary to the genius of a free government and shall never be allowed. . . ." Tex.Const. Art. I, § 26. The Rule states that no interest

79. The three-fourths term royalty interest was conveyed by two identical deeds. One was for an undivided one-fourth and the other for an undivided one-half interest. Reference to "the deed" includes both instruments.

is valid unless it must vest, if at all, within twenty-one years after the death of some life or lives in being at the time of the conveyance. The Rule requires that a challenged conveyance be viewed as of the date the instrument is executed, and it is void if by any possible contingency the grant or devise could violate the Rule.

The deed from Jones conveying the term royalty interest to Starkey was a standard form nonparticipating royalty deed. The printed portion of the granting clause conveyed a presently vested three-fourths royalty interest. However, following the property description, the parties inserted: "this grant shall become effective only upon the expiration of [Peveto's] . . . Deed. . . ." This additional clause causes the Jones-Starkey deed to violate the Rule.

The interest Jones conveyed to Peveto by the first term royalty deed was a determinable fee. This Court defined a determinable fee to be "an interest which may continue forever, but the estate is liable to be determined, without the aid of a conveyance, by some act or event circumscribing its continuance or extent." Stephens County v. Mid-Kansas Oil & Gas Co., 113 Tex. 160, 254 S.W. 290, 295 (1923).

All parties agree the deed from Jones to Starkey is unambiguous. Thus, the intent of the parties must be determined from the four corners of the instrument. The rights of the parties are governed by the language used and the choice of designating words is of controlling importance. The words used here postpone the vesting of Starkey's interest until some uncertain future date. A grant "effective only upon" the termination of a determinable fee cannot vest until the prior interest has terminated. A determinable fee could continue forever, and may not terminate within the time period prescribed by the Rule. The words "effective only upon" created a springing executory interest in Starkey which may not vest within the period of the Rule; therefore, the deed is void.

Because the restrictive language used in the Jones-Starkey deed prevented the grant of the interest from Jones to Starkey from vesting in interest until after Peveto's interest terminated, and since this might not occur within the period prescribed by the Rule, we hold that the instrument violates the Rule against Perpetuities.

Accordingly, we reverse the judgment of the courts below. Judgment is here rendered that the deed from Jones to Starkey is void.

6. Possibilities of Reverter and Rights of Entry

Possibilities of reverter and rights of entry (also known as rights of re-entry, rights of entry for condition broken, and powers of termination) are generally exempt from the common-law Rule Against Perpetuities. See Brown v. Independent Baptist Church, supra p. 1191. As rather vividly demonstrated by

Peveto v. Starkey,[80] above, their nonreversionary counterpart—the executory interest that follows either a fee simple determinable or a fee simple subject to an executory limitation—*is* subject to the common-law Rule. When the grantor, Jones, conveyed the royalty deed to Peveto, Jones retained a possibility of reverter; hence, Jones's retained interest was exempt from the Rule. What interest did Jones subsequently convey, by top deed, to Starkey? The classification of Starkey's interest was crucial to its validity. If, as some commentators have urged, Jones's conveyance to Starkey was part of Jones's possibility of reverter—a partial conveyance of a possibility of reverter—Starkey's interest should have been upheld. The Supreme Court of Texas, however, held that the second conveyance created a springing executory interest, which violated the Rule. It would appear that the Supreme Court of Texas made a correct judgment, for when owners of possibilities of reverter carve out and transfer to others interests that can divest their possibilities of reverter, the interests carved out and transferred are springing executory interests.

By statute in some states, possibilities of reverter and rights of entry expire if they don't vest within a specified period of years (such as 30 years).

Although the Uniform Rule doesn't subject possibilities of reverter and rights of entry to the Uniform Rule or impose a time limit on the duration of these interests, the Official Comment to § 4 urges states enacting the Uniform Rule to consider enacting a provision limiting the duration of these interests to a certain period of years, such as 30, if the state has not already done so.

PART F. A DIVERGENT "RULE AGAINST PERPETUITIES"—PROHIBITION OF THE SUSPENSION OF THE POWER OF ALIENATION

The rule we have been thinking of as the Rule Against Perpetuities is a rule against remotely vesting future interests. Prior to the turn of this century, it wasn't altogether clear that rule was *the* rule against perpetuities. A divergent form of the rule existed, called the rule against the suspension of the power of alienation (the antisuspension rule). In Avern v. Lloyd, L.R. 5 Eq. 383 (1868), the court held that if living persons can together convey a fee, the disposition can't be invalid, regardless of the time of possible vesting; validity merely required that the power of alienation not be suspended beyond a life in being plus 21 years. To illustrate the difference, consider these dispositions, which would violate the rule against remotely vesting future interests:

---

80. See also Proprietors of the Church in Brattle Square v. Grant and First Universalist Society v. Boland, supra Chapter 17, Part B.

Example 19.22: G conveys land "to A and his heirs, but if the land ever ceases to be used for residential purposes, to B and her heirs."

Because A and B can join together and convey a fee in the land, the power of alienation isn't suspended, and the disposition is valid.

Example 19.23: G conveys land "to A and her heirs, but if the land ever ceases to be used for residential purposes, to B and his heirs if B is then living; if not, to B's heirs at law."

Because B's heirs at law have an interest in the land, an unascertained class, A and B can't join together and convey a fee in the land. However, B's heirs at law will be ascertained no later than at B's death, a life in being, so this disposition also is valid under the suspension rule.

Professor John Chipman Gray, in his book on the Rule Against Perpetuities that was first published in 1886, argued strongly that the antisuspension rule was not *the* rule against perpetuities—the rule against perpetuities was the rule against remotely vesting future interests. Gray won the battle, for the *Avern* decision was disapproved in In re Hargreaves, 43 Ch. Div. 401 (C.A. 1890), and henceforth the rule against remotely vesting future interests became *the* Rule Against Perpetuities in both the United States and England.

Nevertheless, in the United States, statutory support for the antisuspension rule was already in place, and therefore that rule wasn't obliterated altogether; in fact, even today, this is the rule in a few states, as we shall see.

The source of the legislative antisuspension rule was the New York property reform legislation of 1830. That legislation, including its antisuspension provision, spread to a number of other states (in some instances with significant modifications). Experience with the antisuspension provision, however, wasn't a happy one. The original New York legislation was quite restrictive; it allowed no tack-on 21-year period, and it allowed the power of alienation to be suspended only "during the continuance of not more than two lives in being," not multiple lives.

The quantity of litigation in New York, produced by the necessity for construction of the original statute and efforts to avoid the severity of the perpetuities period it imposed, reflects against the practicability of the legislative doctrine. It has long been the consensus of opinion that the New York effort at perpetuities reform was misguided. As indicated below, a retreat is in full progress, which takes the form either of a reenactment of the common-law Rule in some states that had copied the New York legislation, or in amendments, as in New York itself, which have substantially the same effect.

The current New York legislation is set forth below. You will note that the current statute codifies both the common-law Rule Against Perpetuities and a much-liberalized version of the antisuspension rule, under which the common-law period of multiple lives plus a 21-year tack-on period is allowed.

In effect, the antisuspension rule has been rendered nearly meaningless, since almost any disposition that violates the antisuspension rule also violates the common-law Rule.

New York Estates, Powers & Trusts Law

§ *9-1.1. Rule against perpetuities.*

(a) (1) The absolute power of alienation is suspended when there are no persons in being by whom an absolute fee or estate in possession can be conveyed or transferred.

(2) Every present or future estate shall be void in its creation which shall suspend the absolute power of alienation by any limitation or condition for a longer period than lives in being at the creation of the estate and a term of not more than twenty-one years. Lives in being shall include a child conceived before the creation of the estate but born thereafter. In no case shall the lives measuring the permissible period be so designated or so numerous as to make proof of their end unreasonably difficult.

(b) No estate in property shall be valid unless it must vest, if at all, not later than twenty-one years after one or more lives in being at the creation of the estate and any period of gestation involved. In no case shall lives measuring the permissible period of vesting be so designated or so numerous as to make proof of their end unreasonably difficult.

Suspension Legislation In Other States. As noted above, the original New York legislation spread to other states, in some instances with only minor amendments, in other instances with rather significant changes. The principal difference in this regard was between those states that adopted the "two-lives" period for suspension (Arizona, Michigan, Minnesota, and Wisconsin) and those that substituted a "multiple-lives" period like that under the common-law Rule (California, Idaho, Indiana, Montana, North Dakota, Oklahoma, and South Dakota).

The antisuspension rule has been repealed or in effect abrogated in all the above states except Idaho (suspension must be restricted to lives in being plus 25 years, modified by a provision allowing reformation of dispositions that violate the suspension rule), South Dakota (suspension must be restricted to lives in being plus 30 years, modified by a wait-and-see element and a provision that declares that there is no suspension of the power of alienation if the trustee has a power of sale), and Wisconsin (suspension must be restricted to lives in being plus 30 years, modified by a provision that declares that there is no suspension of the power of alienation if the trustee has a power of sale). The latter have the antisuspension rule as their only restriction on perpetuities. In these states, the Rule Against Perpetuities does not exist.

EXTERNAL REFERENCES. See Restatement 2d of Property, Statutory Note to § 1.1; Am. L. Prop. chs. 6 & 7; Simes & Smith on Future Interests ch. 41.

PART G. USE OF THE PERPETUITY PERIOD TO CONTROL TRUST INDESTRUCTIBILITY AND INCOME ACCUMULATION

The type of vesting required by the Rule Against Perpetuities is vesting *in interest*, not vesting *in possession*. Consequently, the Rule doesn't directly limit the *duration* of a trust. A trust can, theoretically, endure beyond the 21-year period following the death of the validating life or, if the wait-and-see modification has been adopted and applies, beyond the permissible vesting period. In effect, however, because of the application of a related rule, the continuance of a trust beyond the perpetuity period can occur only by inaction of the beneficiaries. And, should the beneficiaries allow the trust to continue, another related rule requires the trustee to disgorge the trust's income; no income can therefore be accumulated for future distribution.

1. Permissible Duration of Indestructibility of Trusts

The beneficiaries of a trust can join together to compel the trust's termination and the distribution of its assets, unless the trust is an indestructible trust. An indestructible trust is a trust in which the settlor has expressly or impliedly restrained its premature termination. See supra Chapter 14.

Restatement 2d of Property

§ *2.1. Duration of Trust.* A trust created in a donative transfer, which has not terminated within the period of the rule against perpetuities as applied to such trust, shall continue until the trust terminates in accordance with its terms, except that a trust, other than a charitable trust, may be terminated at any time after the period of the rule against perpetuities expires by a written agreement of all of the beneficiaries of the trust delivered to the trustee, which agreement informs the trustee that the trust is terminated and gives the trustee directions as to the distribution of the trust property.

Duration of Indestructibility under the Uniform Rule. Under the Uniform Rule, the applicable perpetuity period is 90 years with respect to trusts whose validity is governed by the wait-and-see element of § 1(a)(2), (b)(2), or (c)(2). See USRAP § 1 comment part G.

External References. Restatement 2d of Trusts § 62 comment o; Restatement 2d of Property, Legislative Note & Reporter's Note; Gray on Perpetuities § 121; Scott on Trusts § 62.10(2); Simes & Smith on Future Interests §§ 1391-93.

2. Accumulations of Income

Restatement 2d of Property

§ *2.2 Accumulation of Trust Income.*

(1) An accumulation of trust income under a noncharitable trust created in a donative transfer is valid until the period of the rule against perpetuities expires with respect to such trust and any accumulation thereafter is invalid.

(2) An accumulation of trust income under a charitable trust created in a donative transfer is valid to the extent the accumulation is reasonable in the light of the purposes, facts and circumstances of the particular trust.

(3) The trust income released by an invalid accumulation shall be paid to such recipients and in such shares and in such manner as most closely effectuates the transferor's manifested plan of distribution.

(4) An accumulation of trust income occurs when part or all of the current income of the trust can be and is retained in the trust, or can be and is so applied by the trustee as to increase the fund subject to the trust, and such retention or application is not found to be merely in the course of judicious management of the trust.

Comment:

a. Historical Note: Prior to the death of Peter Thellusson in July, 1797, directions or authorizations to accumulate income were seldom involved in litigation. Probably they were seldom made. Certainly such provisions were not frequently made so as to call for an accumulation of long duration. Thus, the necessity for any rule specifically regulating their creation had not arisen. The will of Peter Thellusson raised the problem in a dramatic manner. He had devised the major part of his very large estate to his eldest male lineal descendant to be ascertained at the end of a period measured by nine lives in being and had directed that the income of his assets should be accumulated from the time of his death to the time of the ascertainment of such ultimate taker. This will was held valid by the House of Lords in Thellusson v. Woodford [11 Ves.Jr. 112, 32 Eng. Reg. 1030 (1805)] and the opinions rendered by the lower and higher courts in this case laid the foundation for what has since been the rule against accumulations. In the House of Lords it was declared that "a testator can direct the rents and profits to be accumulated for that period during which he may direct that the title shall not vest, and the property shall remain unalienable." In England, the presentation of this case in the lower courts had led to the enactment of a statute [39 and 40 Geo. III c. 98 (1800)] considerably more restrictive than the rule affirmed in the Thellusson case. The subsequent English decisions are largely based on the modifications introduced by this statute. In most of the jurisdictions in the United States the law concerning accumulations is still found only in court decisions. The statutory ingredient in the American law of accumulations is set forth in the Statutory Note to § 2.2. Since the statutes deal only with some aspects of the problem, such as the permissible period, the allowable exceptions to the statute's applicability, and the disposition of released income, a large part of the law of accumulations is nonstatutory.

b. Tax considerations. The widespread use of accumulation trusts has been encouraged by the federal income tax advantage of having trust income taxed to the trust as a separate income tax entity in years when the tax rate applicable to the trust was lower than the tax rate applicable to trust beneficiaries to whom the income might be distributed. Also, income accumulated in the trust could be made available to future generations without a federal gift tax or federal estate tax being imposed on the current generation of beneficiaries under the trust. The development of the so-called throwback rule and the extension of its reach by the Tax Reform Act of 1969, with some modifications thereof in the Tax Reform Act of 1976, have undermined the utilization of accumulation trusts to effect significantly, in the long run, federal income tax savings. The introduction in the Tax Reform Act of 1976 of a generation-skipping tax has curtailed to some extent the avoidance of federal gift and estate taxes as the beneficial enjoyment of the trust property moves from one generation of trust beneficiaries to another. Nevertheless, trusts under which the trustee has discretion to pay out or accumulate trust income continue to have substantial attractions for use in estate planning.

c. Tax accounting income contrasted with trust accounting income. Income from a tax accounting standpoint is a broader concept than income from a trust accounting standpoint. Realized capital gain is income from a tax accounting standpoint, but is principal from a trust accounting standpoint. Income in respect of a decedent collected by a trust becomes principal of the trust, but is income for tax purposes. There can be an accumulation of income for the purposes of this section only if income from a trust accounting standpoint is retained in the trust.

d. Discretionary accumulations compared with mandatory accumulations. Most accumulation trusts give the trustee discretion to accumulate the income or pay it out to some trust beneficiary. The discretion will usually relate not only to current income, but also to income accumulated in past years. A mandatory accumulation trust does not provide the desirable flexibility to meet changing conditions that may affect the needs of the beneficiaries. Its use is most appropriate when the trust fund has to be built up to some larger amount to effectuate the purpose the trust is designed to accomplish.

e. Undesirable social consequences provided by accumulations of trust income. Accumulations of trust income do not keep the trust income from use in the economy because such income will be invested in some manner and not taken completely out of circulation. The fiduciary restrictions on trust investments, however, mean that there is not the same freedom of the use of such income in the economy in the hands of the trustee as there would be in the hands of the trust beneficiary.

Accumulations of trust income tend to build up the control of increased amounts of wealth in fewer and fewer people. However, the impact of the higher income tax rates slows down substantially the build-up process referred to.

Accumulations do tend to perpetuate the policies of the transferor who may have established the trust and, as in the case of the rule against perpetuities in relation to vesting, some limit on the period of time such policies should remain in control is desirable.

PART H. RELATED RULES OF SOCIAL POLICY—VALIDITY OF RESTRAINTS ON PERSONAL CONDUCT

In addition to the Rule Against Perpetuities and the rules relating to the duration of the indestructibility of trusts and the duration of accumulations of income, there are a variety of other rules that limit the dead hand. These rules prevent transferors of property from conditioning their largesse on certain types of personal conduct of the beneficiaries. We quote below this series of rules, as set forth in the Restatement 2d of Property.

Restatement 2d of Property

§ *5.1. Basis for Determining Validity of Restraints on Personal Conduct.* Unless contrary to public policy or violative of some rule of law, a provision in a donative transfer which is designed to prevent the acquisition or retention of an interest in property in the event of any failure on the part of the transferee to comply with a restraint on personal conduct is valid.

§ *5.2 Effect of Impossibility of Performance.* Impossibility of performance of the terms of a provision in a donative transfer, otherwise valid under the general rule stated in § 5.1, excuses lack of performance if, and only if, this result is the appropriately ascertained intent of the person imposing the restraint.

§ *6.1 Restraints on Any First Marriage.*

(1) Except as stated in subsection (2), an otherwise effective restriction in a donative transfer which is designed to prevent the acquisition or retention of an interest in property by the transferee in the event of any first marriage of the transferee is invalid. If the restriction is invalid, the donative transfer takes effect as though the restriction had not been imposed.

(2) If the dominant motive of the transferor is to provide support until marriage, the restraint is normally valid.

§ *6.2 Restraints on Some First Marriages.* An otherwise effective restriction in a donative transfer designed to prevent the acquisition or retention of an interest in the event of some, but not all, first marriages of the transferee is valid if, and only if, under the circumstances, the restraint does not unreasonably limit the transferee's opportunity to marry. If the restriction is invalid, the donative transfer takes effect as though the restriction had not been imposed.

§ *6.3 Restraints on Remarriage.* An otherwise effective restriction in a donative transfer which is designed to prevent the acquisition or retention of an interest in property by the transferee in the event of the remarriage of the transferee is valid only if:

(1) The transferee was the spouse of the transferor, or

(2) The restraint is reasonable under all the circumstances.

§ *7.1 Provisions Encouraging Separation or Divorce.* An otherwise effective restriction in a donative transfer which is designed to permit the acquisition or retention of an interest in property by the transferee only in the event of a separation or divorce from the transferee's spouse is invalid, unless the dominant motive of the transferor is to provide support in the event of separation or divorce, in which case the restraint is valid.

§ *7.2 Provisions Detrimentally Affecting Family Relationship.* An otherwise effective provision in a donative transfer which is designed to permit the acquisition or retention of an interest in property only in the event of either the continuance of an existing separation or the creation of a future separation of a family relationship, other than that of husband and wife, is invalid where the dominant motive of the transferor was to promote such a separation.

§ *8.1 Provisions Concerning Religion.* An otherwise effective provision in a donative transfer which is designed to prevent the acquisition or retention of property on account of adherence to or rejection of certain religious beliefs or practices on the part of the transferee is valid.

§ *8.2 Restraints Against Personal Habits.* An otherwise effective provision in a donative transfer which is designed to prevent the acquisition or retention of an interest in property on account of the transferee acquiring or persisting in specified personal habits is valid.

§ *8.3 Restraints Concerning Education or Occupation.* An otherwise effective provision in a donative transfer which is designed to prevent the acquisition or retention of an interest in property on account of a failure on the part of the beneficiary to acquire or continue an education or occupation is valid.

§ *9.1 Restraints on Contests.* An otherwise effective provision in a will or other donative transfer, which is designed to prevent the acquisition or retention of an interest in property in the event there is a contest of the validity of the document transferring the interest or an attack on a particular provision of the document, is valid, unless there was probable cause for making the contest or attack.

§ *9.2 Restraints on Attacks on Fiduciaries.* An otherwise effective provision in a will or other donative transfer, which is designed to prevent the acquisition or retention of an interest in property in the event the propriety of the performance of the fiduciary with respect to the administration of the transferred property is questioned in a legal proceeding, is valid, unless the beneficiary had probable cause for questioning the fiduciary's performance.

§ *10.1 Restraints on Enforcing Obligations of Transferor or Transferor's Estate.* An otherwise effective provision in a will or other donative transfer, which is designed to prevent the acquisition or retention of an interest in property if there is an attempt to enforce an independent obligation of the transferor or the transferor's estate, is valid.

§ *10.2 Restraints on Asserting Right to Other Property Owned or Disposed of by Transferor.* An otherwise effective provision in a will or other donative transfer which imposes a condition precedent to the interest of a beneficiary that the transfer, if accepted, is in lieu of an interest in other property owned or disposed of by the transferor, is valid.

DIVISION FOUR
ADMINISTRATION

Chapter 20

Fiduciary Administration

IN this Chapter, we discuss selected aspects of fiduciary administration. We concentrate on the fiduciary relationships created when a person becomes a property fiduciary—a personal representative of a decedent's estate, a conservator or guardian of an incapacitated person's estate, or a trustee. While other relationships, such as attorney and client, principal and agent, corporate officer and stockholder, partner and joint venturer, are also conventionally labeled "fiduciary,"[1] the legal responsibilities imposed on property fiduciaries tend to be more specific and more onerous. Another difference between the fiduciary roles examined here and others is that non-corporate property fiduciaries are more likely to be unaware of the legal implications of the positions they have accepted. Friends and relatives often agree to act as executor or trustee simply to be helpful.

PART A. INTRODUCTION: FIDUCIARY ADMINISTRATION OF ESTATES AND TRUSTS

By way of background to the substantive rules regulating property fiduciaries, we first survey the process of administering estates and trusts, focusing particularly on judicial supervision of the three types of property fiduciaries: estate personal representatives, guardians and conservators, and trustees.

---

1. For general discussions of fiduciary law and obligations, see Tamar Frankel, Fiduciary Law, 71 Calif. L. Rev. 795 (1983); Ernest J. Weinrib, The Fiduciary Obligation, 25 U. Tor. L.J. 1 (1975).

1. Personal Representatives

Statutory References: *UPC §§ 1-403, 3-107, -108, -701, -714, -715, -801, -803, -909, -1004, -1006*

Historical Background. After the 1540 Statute of Wills made devises of land possible, testate and intestate devolution of land occurred without special procedures. Title to land passed at death directly to the devisee or heir. The devisee or heir took free of the decedent's debts. Disputes over succession were resolved in actions at law.

As to personal property, there was an office resembling a probate court called the "ordinary" (a judge of the ecclesiastical court), which had authority to accept proof of due execution of wills of personal property and to appoint administrators of intestate personal assets. Executors and administrators were supposed to collect the assets, pay just claims against the decedent, and distribute whatever remained to legatees or distributees. In the absence of controversy, there were no further proceedings once the ordinary had approved a will or appointed an administrator.

American Probate Systems. In the American colonies, the authority of the English ordinary was disbursed among various officials, including courts, legislative creations, and governors' designees. Gradually, these various offices evolved into special courts.

Today, specialized probate courts typically are inferior courts. Appeals usually take the form of de novo proceedings in trial courts of general jurisdiction. In some states, these courts are staffed by elected persons who need not be lawyers. The trend in the states east of the Rockies has been toward more powerful, lawyer-staffed, separate tribunals of restricted subject-matter jurisdiction that includes the probate functions of the English ordinary and chancellor. The California model, widely emulated in the West, makes probate jurisdiction the business of a special docket or division of the trial court of general jurisdiction. In Pennsylvania, a probate official known as the Register of Wills issues papers opening estates, while a court known as the Orphans Court handles other aspects of probate jurisdiction. In New York, the specialized court handling probate matters is called the Surrogate's Court and the judge is called the Surrogate.

Over time, American probate courts have tended to exercise a style of supervision over decedents' estates that is overly formal. A fully adjudicated distribution order is probably unnecessary in most cases. Most estates pass without controversy to a sole surviving heir or a small group of adults who are eager to expedite estate settlement and to release the fiduciary.[2] Nevertheless, personal representatives can't shortcut mandatory closing procedures. If they do, they're subject to possible sanction by the probate court. The resulting costs and delays may explain the popularity of probate avoidance devices we studied supra Chapter 8.

The Uniform Probate Code was originally drafted in 1969 in response to widely publicized criticisms of typical probate systems. See Richard V. Wellman, The Uniform Probate Code: A Possible Answer to Probate Avoidance, 44 Ind. L.J. 191 (1969). Article III of the Code, covering probate of wills and administration of decedents' estates, was designed to permit estates of all sizes and asset mixes to be settled with as little procedure as possible. Article IV, devoted to estates located in two or more jurisdictions, permits personal representatives appointed in the decedent's domicile to unify estates[3] for administration purposes merely by filing copies of the domiciliary probate and appointment orders in the local probate office, thereby gaining the powers of a locally appointed personal representative.

UPC Procedures. Under the UPC, probate jurisdiction is assigned to a court that has the stature of a trial court of general jurisdiction, in terms of the qualifications of the judge, the finality of its orders, and the range of matters it may consider. The Code establishes the office of "registrar," to be occupied by

---

2. The probate procedures in a few states permit individuals to avoid court supervised estate administration. The first Texas constitution expressly gave testators the ability to direct that their executors be independent of probate court control after opening of the estate. The "independent executor" device appears to be used routinely by knowledgeable estate planners in Texas. The independent executor device also exists in Washington. In New York, it exists by custom. In Georgia, a statute permitting testators to direct that their executors be excused from "making inventory or returns" allows testate estates to be administered independently of probate court supervision. Independent administration also exists in practice for testate and intestate estates in some areas where officials who control probates and appointments lack the stature, inclination, or tradition of supervising estates.

3. Non-uniform probate laws tend to force separate administrations in each state where land or other assets belonging to the decedent may be located. Succession to land is governed by the law of situs, meaning that local probate procedures are virtually unavoidable in each state where the decedent owned land. Succession to personal and intangible assets is controlled by the law of the decedent's domicile, but procedural rules protect local creditors, and possessors and controllers of out-of-state assets of a decedent may insist on local appointment of an administrator to whom they can make safe payment or delivery. Enactment of Articles III and IV of the UPC by the situs state means that the domiciliary personal representatives from other states can avoid local administrations in the UPC state by filing copies of letters of authority from domicile and copies of duly probated wills with a probate office at the location of the assets. Following these steps, a personal representative can give marketable title by deed in a sale or distribution without court involvement. For a brief discussion of ancillary administrations with and without the UPC, see Richard V. Wellman, How the Uniform Probate Code Deals with Estates that Cross State Lines, 5 Real Prop. Prob. & Tr. J. 159 (1970).

an official who is empowered to probate wills and open estates in "informal" (nonadjudicative) proceedings. Informal proceedings don't involve advance notice to interested persons, hearing, or the presentation of testimony. The registrar responds to a detailed application for probate by an interested person.

An estate is opened by the appointment of a personal representative. The statute directs the personal representative to administer and distribute the estate without further contact with the public probate office. Whether the estate is testate or intestate, the personal representative's powers are the same. Persons interested in estates may request "formal" (adjudicated) proceedings as an alternative to informal probate.

In the absence of binding court orders, estates are settled and titles cleared through UPC limitations and purchaser-protection provisions. Under § 3-108, wills may be probated or contested and estates may be opened within three years after death. Section 3-803 provides that claims against an estate, if not otherwise barred by "non-claim" procedures, are barred one year after the decedent's death. Persons to whom estate assets have been wrongfully distributed remain liable to restore the property or its equivalent value. Under § 3-1006, distributee liability to heirs and devisees ends at the later of three years after the decedent's death or one year after distribution.[4] Purchasers and other third persons who assist or deal with a personal representative for value and in good faith are protected by § 3-714. Personal representatives, acting in good faith and in the best interests of those apparently interested in estates, are protected from liability for acts taken in reliance on informal orders of probate and appointment. Section 3-108 gives a remedy "[w]henever fraud has been perpetrated in connection with any proceeding or in any statement filed under this Code or if fraud is used to avoid or circumvent the provisions or purposes of this Code." Action must be commenced against the perpetrator within two years following discovery of the fraud. Innocent beneficiaries of another's fraud are also liable for restitution, but an action against an innocent recipient must be initiated within five years after commission of the fraudulent act.[5]

The view underlying UPC procedures is that state statutes creating and defining rights in decedents' creditors and successors may impose valid qualifications on such rights as necessary to support a system for prompt settlement of estates without binding adjudications by the courts. The decision in Tulsa Professional Collection Services, Inc. v. Pope, 485 U.S. 478 (1988),

---

4. Distributee liability to decedents' creditors ends no later than one year after death, a period which may be shortened by use of the short non-claim procedure described infra p. 1303.

5. For a more detailed discussion of UPC's informal proceedings and associated safeguards, see Richard V. Wellman & James W. Gordon, The Uniform Probate Code: Article III Analyzed in Relation to Changes in the First Nine Enactments, 1975 Ariz. St. L.J. 477.

tested the distinction between limitations in probate statutes that may bar claimants without notice and state action in the form of probate court orders. In Mullane v. Central Hanover Bank & Trust Co., 339 U.S. 306 (1949), the Court held that due process in probate court proceedings required notice reasonably calculated to apprise persons whose interests are affected and that, as to known persons, notice by publication doesn't meet this requirement. In *Pope*, an Oklahoma law and implementing court order purported to bar unsecured creditors of an estate if they failed to perfect their claims within a statutory period of two months after publication of notice of the opening of the estate to claims. The procedure was held ineffective to bar a decedent's creditor who was known to, or reasonably ascertainable by, the estate fiduciary. The Court conceded that enactment and enforcement of a "self-executing" statute of limitation doesn't constitute state action implicating the protections of the due process clause. The Court then observed:

> Here, in contrast, there is significant state action. The probate court is intimately involved throughout, and without that involvement the time bar is never activated. The nonclaim statute becomes operative only after probate proceedings have been commenced in state court. The court must appoint the executor or executrix before notice, which triggers the time bar, can be given. Only after this court appointment is made does the statute provide for any notice. . . . Indeed, in this case, the District Court reinforced the statutory command with an order expressly requiring appellee to "immediately give notice to creditors." The form of the order indicates that such orders are routine. . . . Finally, copies of the notice and an affidavit of publication must be filed with the court. . . . It is only after all of these actions take place that the time period begins to run, and in every one of these actions, the court is intimately involved. This involvement is so pervasive and substantial that it must be considered state action subject to the restrictions of the Fourteenth Amendment.

Prior to *Pope*, most probate codes included "short" non-claim time bars allowing creditors from two to six months after the opening of an estate to present in writing claims for allowance or disallowance. In general, pre-*Pope* codes reflected the view that creditors need not be given actual notice of a pending estate administration, but were on their own to ascertain a debtor's death. Most codes also contain "long" non-claim provisions barring claims against unadministered assets after periods ranging from one to several years after the decedent's death. See Debra A. Falender, Notice to Creditors on Estate Proceedings: What Process is Due?, 63 N.C.L. Rev. 659 (1985).

Are UPC non-claim provisions subject to the *Pope* decision? The Code's short non-claim provisions are keyed to published notice to creditors, who are given four months after first publication to present claims. See UPC § 3-803. Professor Sarajane Love has argued that the UPC's "short" non-claim statute, unlike the statute involved in *Pope*, does not constitute state action for due process purposes.[6] She points out that "the principal actor in administering an estate, the decedent's personal representative, does not become a state actor for all constitutional purposes merely because he or she is appointed by a probate court."[7] It's also arguable that UPC's "long" non-claim statute, which is unrelated to any notice to creditors and was shortened in 1989 from three years to one year after death, is safe from a *Pope* challenge on the ground that since it begins to run at death, there is an insufficient nexus between termination of creditors' claims and court proceedings to constitute state action.[8]

Publication of notice by the personal representative is mandatory. The duty to do so arises upon acceptance of appointment (§§ 3-701, 3-801), but an informal proceeding seeking issuance of letters ends with an order making or declining to make an appointment (§ 3-107(4)). The appointing office has no power to sanction a personal representative who neglects to publish. As a result, personal representatives control whether publication and the start of the four-month non-claim period will occur. Claims not barred because of a personal representative's failure to publish notice may be barred by limitations running prior to death (§ 3-802) or by the long non-claim period running from death. Until barred, a claim may be pursued against an estate or its distributees (§ 3-1004).

Because of uncertainty regarding the state action question posed by *Pope* as applied to the UPC,[9] the Uniform Law Commissioners approved two modest amendments to the UPC in 1989. One shortened the "long" non-claim period from three years to one year after death. This amendment benefits persons interested in unadministered estates and estates administered without the use of the short non-claim procedure; it hastens the elimination of undischarged claims against a decedent. The other amendment expressly authorizes the use of an

---

6. Sarajane Love, Estate Creditors, the Constitution, and the Uniform Probate Code, 30 U. Rich. L. Rev. 411 (1996).

7. Id. at 431 (footnote omitted). For an opposing view, see Mark Reutlinger, State Action, Due Process, and the New Non-claim Statutes: Can No Notice Be Good Notice If Some Notice is Not?, 24 Real Prop. Prob. & Tr. J. 433 (1990).

8. See Love, supra note 6, at 425.

9. A court considering extending the "state action" test to the UPC's short non-claim provision should take account of data indicating that creditors in general are disinterested in the procedural protections traditionally extended to them by probate legislation. See Allison Dunham, The Method, Process and Frequency of Wealth Transmission at Death, 30 U. Chi. L. Rev. 241 (1963); John H. Langbein, The Nonprobate Revolution and the Future of the Law of Succession, 97 Harv. L. Rev. 108 (1984). Hence, costs incurred by imposing new responsibilities upon personal representatives to search for creditors to notify would likely exceed any resulting benefits.

optional short non-claim bar operating no earlier than sixty days following actual notice to present claims. The changes don't affect pre-*Pope* Code language purporting to bar known and unknown creditors who are unaware of an administration or fail for other reasons to respond to a published notice to present claims within four months.

If the fact that a state official appoints the personal representative renders the UPC subject to *Pope*, are all acts of a personal representative acts of the state? If so, are UPC's no-notice procedures to secure probate of a will or appointment of a personal representative and related limitations likely to withstand constitutional challenge by an overlooked heir or a devisee claiming under a recently discovered will?

The UPC's basic limitation period expiring three years after death appears to be "self-executing" under *Pope*. Hence, the operation of the Code's informal proceedings may withstand due process challenge.[10]

2. Guardians and Conservators

Statutory References: *UPC §§ 5-102, -208, 310, -315, -425*

Because minor children and incapacitated adults lack competency, they must depend on others for care and property management. All states have judicial procedures for appointing persons to perform these functions. In non-UPC states, the laws providing protective proceedings contemplate two types of guardians: guardian of the person, a fiduciary who is judicially charged with the care and custody of the minor or incapacitated adult, and guardian of the property (or estate), a fiduciary who is responsible for managing assets that a minor or incapacitated adult owns.

Under the UPC (which now incorporates the recent Uniform Guardianship and Protective Proceedings Act), a court-appointed "guardian" of a minor or an incapacitated person is essentially a guardian of the person only (§ 5-102(3)), but §§ 5-208 and 5-315 confer limited authority on a guardian to receive and expend funds on behalf of the person under his or her protection. The UPC uses the term "conservator" to refer to a fiduciary who is responsible for "manag[ing] the estate of a protected person" § 5-102(1). (A "protected person" means a minor or an adult for whom a conservator has been appointed. § 5-102(8)). A UPC conservator has no control of the protected person's custody,

---

10. For opposing views concerning the constitutional validity of the UPC's informal probate procedures, see Roger A. Manlin & Richard A Martens, Informal Proceedings Under the Uniform Probate Code: Notice and Due Process, 3 U. Mich. J. L. Ref. 38 (1969)(concluding that UPC procedures are constitutional); Note, The Constitutionality of the No-Notice Provisions of the Uniform Probate Code, 60 Minn. L. Rev. 317 (1976).

but a conservator may seek formal appointment to the office of guardian of the same individual (§ 5-425 comment).

The UPC and the Uniform Guardianship and Protective Proceedings Act allow a parent or spouse to appoint a guardian by will "or other signed writing." The latter phrase includes durable powers of attorney, trust instruments, and specific documents for guardianship appointments. Judicial confirmation of such appointments is required. In addition to parental and spousal appointment, the traditional method of appointment by court is also continued.

Professional Guardians. In recent years, courts have frequently appointed professional guardians, including public agencies or nonprofit corporations. Professional guardians are not subject to any licensing requirements or other legal regulations. They are required to submit periodic accountings to the court, but the ability of courts to supervise guardians is limited. As a result, there have been increasing allegations of financial misfeasance by professional guardians. See Dean Starkman, Guardians May Need Someone to Watch over Them, Wall St. J., May 8, 1998, at B 1. Preferring to limit guardians to persons with whom the ward has a close relationship, the UPC and the Uniform Guardianship and Protective Proceedings Act do not list professional guardians priority for appointment as guardian (§§ 5-310). Professional guardian are not disqualified from appointment but may be appointed only if persons with priority are not available or decline or if a court, acting in the ward's best interest, declines to appoint a person with statutory priority (§ 5-310 comment).

3. Trustees

Statutory References: *UPC §§ 7-101, -102, -103*

Inter vivos trusts aren't subject to judicial involvement until and unless there is litigation between the fiduciary and beneficiaries. However, legislation in a few states permits any person interested in a trust to require that the trust be administered under the continuing supervision of a court. More commonly, legislation requires testamentary trustees to qualify with the court having control of the testator's probate estate before undertaking the office. Qualification may or may not involve submission of the trust administration to continuing court supervision. To qualify, the trustee may be required to post bond unless the trust instrument excuses the requirement. Some statutes provide that nonresidents of the state of probate and foreign corporations not qualified to engage in local trust business can't qualify for appointment as trustee.

Once qualified, a supervised testamentary trustee may be required to submit periodic accountings to the court. Judicial orders settling the accounts of a fiduciary may or may not be binding on all beneficiaries. The scope of the review may indicate a different effect for a regular, periodic accounting to a supervising court as well as for a final accounting seeking discharge of the fiduciary. In both cases, an accounting purporting to bind is ineffective against the interest of a beneficiary to whom inadequate notice has been accorded. In the case of minor or unascertainable beneficiaries, the propriety of any claimed representation other than by a duly appointed guardian ad litem is likely to be governed by legislation, or by equitable principles in the absence of statute. Judicial orders favoring fiduciaries over beneficiaries may be avoided or modified by collateral attack for extrinsic fraud if the fiduciary was guilty of actual or constructive fraud for failure to inform beneficiaries adequately of matters affecting their rights.

UPC Article VII eliminates many of the problems involving court qualification and supervision of testamentary trustees. Article VII identifies a passive, jurisdictional relationship between every trust and a court of the state of principal administration of the trust. It permits mailed notice and provides for representation of unborn or unascertained interests. Furthermore, the UPC neither requires court qualification of trustees nor the posting of bond, filing of inventories, or judicial approval of accounts periodically or at any other time.

UPC § 7-101 requires trustees to register trusts in the court of the principal place of administration. The purpose of trust registration is to assure that a particular court will be available to the parties on a permissive basis, rather than to subject the trust to compulsory continuing court supervision. A trustee registers a trust by filing a short statement acknowledging acceptance of a trust. The statement must identify the trust by the name of the settlor, date of the trust instrument, and the place of probate of the will if the trust is testamentary. Except for trusts created without a writing, the names of the beneficiaries, the nature and value of the assets, and the terms of the trust need not be disclosed. No sanctions for non-registration are provided except that a trustee who refuses to register a trust within thirty days after receipt of a written demand for its registration by a settlor or beneficiary is subject to removal if an interested person petitions for removal. Trust registration has been a controversial innovation. Several states adopting the UPC have omitted the trust registration provisions.

PART B. THE DUTY OF LOYALTY

Statutory References: *UTC §§ 703, 802, 808, 810, 1002, 1008, 1009*

Matter of Green Charitable Trust

431 N.W.2d 492 (Mich. Ct. App. 1988)

HOOD, J. Respondents, Comerica Bank and Miles Jaffe, appeal as of right from an order of visiting Oakland County Probate Judge George E. Benko which removed respondents as trustees of the Leslie H. Green and Edith C. Green Charitable Trust, removed Comerica as personal representative of the estate of Edith C. Green, deceased, and surcharged respondents in the amount of $1,900,000. The petitioners are the Michigan Attorney General, St. Peter's Home for Boys, Bishop of the Episcopal Church—Diocese of Michigan, Dean of the Cathedral Church of St. Paul, and the Cathedral Church of St. Paul. This case is based on the petitioners' objections to respondents' sale of real property owned by the estate and charitable trust to Maurice Cohen, a client of respondent Jaffe.

Leslie and Edith Green owned and maintained a residence on 315 acres in Bloomfield Township, Oakland County, known as Turtle Lake Farms.

In 1969, Leslie and Edith Green created a charitable trust funded in part by a grant of an interest in Turtle Lake Farms. As finally amended, the beneficiaries of this trust are St. Peter's Home for Boys, the Cathedral Church of St. Paul and the Cathedral of the Episcopal Church, Diocese of Michigan. The named trustees were the Greens, Comerica and Miles Jaffe.

Mr. Green died in 1973. His will gave Mrs. Green a life estate in the portion of Turtle Lake Farms including their residence and created a marital trust for the benefit of his wife during her lifetime. The charitable trust was made the residuary beneficiary of the marital trust and would receive the marital trust's interest in Turtle Lake Farms upon Mrs. Green's death. Comerica was named sole trustee of the marital trust.

Mrs. Green died in March, 1983. Her will made specific bequests totaling $320,000 and directed the establishment of a million dollar trust fund for her granddaughter. The residue of her estate was left to the charitable trust. Mrs. Green's estate consisted of cash and securities valued at $1,340,000, plus her interest in Turtle Lake Farms. Comerica was designated personal representative of the estate.

Upon Mrs. Green's death, Bishop McGehee and Dean Herlong of the Episcopal Church became co-trustees of the charitable trust as provided for under the trust. Under the trust, only Comerica and Jaffe were empowered to make decisions regarding the disposition of the real property.

According to respondents, soon after Mrs. Green's death they determined that the liquid assets of the estate were insufficient to satisfy the cash bequests, the funding of the $1,000,000 trust fund for the granddaughter, the estate taxes and the administrative expenses. After reviewing the options, Comerica and Jaffe concluded that the interests of the estate and its beneficiaries would best be served by the sale of the Turtle Lake property.

At Mrs. Green's death, three entities owned undivided interests in Turtle Lake: the Edith Green estate, the marital trust, and the charitable trust. For the sale, Comerica acted in three capacities: as executor of the estate, as sole trustee of the marital trust, and as one of the trustees of the charitable trust. Jaffe also acted in several capacities. He was a trustee of the charitable trust. Also, Jaffe and his firm, Honigman, Miller, Schwartz & Cohn, were attorneys for the estate, for Comerica as executor, for Comerica as trustee of the marital trust, and for Comerica as trustee of the charitable trust. The record also contains testimony of Dean Herlong to the effect that Jaffe, at least on one occasion, provided legal advice to him in his role as trustee. Jaffe had been a personal friend of the Greens, as well as their attorney. He drafted their wills and the trust instruments.

During the time between Leslie Green's death and the death of his wife, Comerica's trust department received inquiries from individuals interested in purchasing Turtle Lake Farms. Since the intent was for Mrs. Green to live out her life on the property, Comerica informed inquiring developers that the property was not on the market and that they would be notified when it became available. The parties' briefs describe in detail the events following Mrs. Green's death and leading up to the sale of the Homestead, the real property concerned in this action. The Homestead is the western portion of the Turtle Lake property, consisting of 211 acres and including the Green's mansion and other buildings, Turtle Lake, and lakefront property on Upper Long Lake.

On September 15, 1983, Comerica accepted an offer from Maurice Cohen for the Homestead. The sale was closed on November 1, 1983, by execution of a land contract for $3,250,000, with $1,500,000 down payment and the balance over two years at twelve percent interest. Maurice Cohen is a successful real estate developer and was represented by the Honigman firm.

This case concerns the objections by the charitable trust beneficiaries to Jaffe's and his law firm's conflicts of interest in representing both buyer and seller, to Comerica's management of the sale of the property, and to the adequacy of the price received for the Homestead ....

Testifying for Comerica were Gari Kersten and Cleveland Thurber. Kersten was vice president of Comerica's trust real estate department which supervised the management of trust real estate and the Comerica representative who apparently worked most closely with Jaffe on the sale of property. Thurber was in charge of Comerica's trust department, which generally oversaw the trust, and one of the trust officers who participated in decisions to sell the property to and accept the Cohen offer. Another Comerica employee, the sales manager, Mr. Keating, apparently supplied information to Kersten on the value of the property. David Wind was another trust officer involved in various decisions. Neither of these two men testified.

Leo Majzels, who had done an appraisal of the property in 1973, was retained by Comerica following Mrs. Green's death as part of the efforts to prepare a marketing plan and as a consultant to assist in evaluating the value of the property. Calvin Hall was retained to submit a development plan on the possible uses of the land. Donald Tilton was retained to study possible environmental problems caused by the wetlands on the property.

Also testifying was Paul C. Robertson, a local land developer and builder, who had expressed interest in developing the property prior to Mrs. Green's death and who contacted Comerica regarding the property again in May, 1983.

The Attorney General is a petitioner as a necessary party in interest to estate proceedings involving charitable trusts. . . . .

Maurice Cohen visited the Homestead in April, 1983, and expressed an interest in purchasing the Green residence and a few surrounding acres. Kersten told Cohen that the sale of such a small parcel was not desirable because it would reduce the marketability of the balance of the property. Jaffe put Cohen in touch with Calvin Hall and showed Cohen Hall's development plan to encourage Cohen's interest in a larger parcel. Throughout the summer, Jaffe continued to meet with Cohen to encourage him to make a suitable offer for the entire parcel.

According to Jaffe, when he realized in August that Cohen was interested in making "a hard offer" on the entire Homestead, he informed Thurber that there was a potential conflict of interest because his law firm represented Cohen. In a letter of August 12 to Thurber, Jaffe requested the consent of Comerica, Bishop McGehee and Dean Herlong, as trustees, to the Honigman firm's dual representation and indicated that, in any event, Jaffe would not act as co-trustee with respect to any offer by Cohen. It does not appear that Jaffe sent copies of the letter directly to Bishop McGehee or Dean Heriong.

On August 18, at a meeting of Comerica representatives and Honigman attorneys, Majzels expressed his opinion that the Homestead should sell for between $3 and $3.5 million.

On August 22, all of the trustees of the charitable trust met to discuss the possible sale of the land and the question of dual representation. Dean Herlong testified that Thurber informed them of the estate's cash needs and Jaffe discussed the various problems with development of the property. Jaffe, Thurber and Kersten also informed Bishop McGehee and Dean Herlong that they expected Cohen to make an offer for the western portion of the property. Jaffe explained the conflict of interest.

Former Chief Justice G. Mennen Williams was also present at this meeting in his capacity as Senior Warden of the Vestry of the Cathedral Church of St. Paul but he did not testify at trial. Dean Herlong testified that the Chief Justice was present at the Dean's request. The Senior Warden is the representative of the cathedral to whom Dean Herlong is ultimately responsible, and Dean Herlong felt it was in the best interest of the cathedral for the Chief Justice to be present. The Chief Justice . . . was precluded from practicing law, and we find no indication in the record that he was present as or in any way acted as a legal advisor . . . .

On August 23, Cohen made an offer for the Homestead of $3 million. Neither the price nor the conditions were acceptable to Jaffe or Comerica, and Kersten directed Jaffe to go back to Cohen and see what could be done to better the offer.

On August 26, a one-page circular describing generally the land and its availability was sent to people who had expressed an interest in the property and to local real estate people. Kersten authorized the mailing against the advice of Jaffe.

On August 31, 1983, Bishop McGehee and Dean Herlong sent a letter to Jaffe consenting to the dual representation "subject to the satisfactory demonstration by the Comerica Bank after reasonable investigation that the offer is indeed suitable, appropriate, and in keeping with the present market situation."

On September 6, Kersten met with Robertson. Kersten apparently attempted to secure an offer on the entire parcel from Robertson, indicating that the asking price was $10 million, with $4 million down. Kersten met with Cohen on September 12, apparently in an attempt to secure a better offer and to obtain an extension of Cohen's offer, both of which Cohen refused. A revised offer at $3.25 million was prepared by the Honigman attorneys and accepted on September 15.

On September 19, Dean Herlong was informed of the sale. On September 26, Wind, Kersten, and Jaffe met with Dean Herlong, Bishop McGehee and Chief Justice Williams. Dean Herlong testified that he expressed at this meeting his concerns regarding the sale and Comerica's marketing of the property. The Cohen deal was closed on November 1, 1983. Bishop McGehee and Dean Herlong signed the land contract as trustees of the charitable trust. Dean Herlong testified that Jaffe told them that the sale was a "fait accompli" and that their signatures were a legal formality.

On December 29, Jaffe wrote to Bishop McGehee and Dean Herlong advising them that another Honigman client was interested in another part of the property and requesting their consent to the multiple representation. In a letter dated March 5, 1984, Dean Herlong consented to the multiple representation, but asked for a written appraisal of the property before sale. According to Jaffe, Dean Herlong indicated for the first time that he was dissatisfied with the way in which the Cohen sale had been handled. Dean Herlong testified that he had orally conveyed his dissatisfaction earlier.

After the present controversy arose, appraisals of the market value of the Homestead as of September 15, 1983, were prepared by Majzels, who was selected by Jaffe, and by Proctor, who was selected by Dean Herlong from a list of appraisers submitted by Jaffe. Over Dean Herlong's objection, the instructions to the appraisers included information on the Cohen sale. The appraisals were completed in 1985, with Majzels indicating a value of $3.35 million and Proctor arriving at a value of $5.15 million for the Homestead.

On September 9, 1984, Comerica filed its first account on the estate of Edith Green. On October 29, 1985, St. Peter's Home for Boys filed a petition and objection to the account. On December 2, 1985, the Attorney General filed a similar petition. On November 12, 1986, Bishop McGehee and Dean Herlong filed petitions in the probate court pursuant to M.C.L. § 700.805, to surcharge Comerica and Jaffe as trustees of the charitable trust, and the Attorney General filed a petition to surcharge and remove Comerica as executor of the Edith Green estate, as trustee of the marital trust, and as trustee of the charitable trust.

On November 13, 1986, Judge Benko began hearings on all of these petitions, excluding issues related to the marital trust because Comerica had been discharged as trustee when the Leslie Green estate had been closed in 1984. Following several days of testimony, the probate court issued its thirty-four page opinion, finding that Jaffe and Comerica violated their obligations as trustees to the settlors and beneficiaries of the charitable trust and that Comerica violated its obligation as personal representative to the Edith Green estate. As to Comerica, the court found that it had negligently handled the sale of the property, as evidenced by its inadequate efforts to determine the property's value and its failure to adequately market the property. Furthermore, the court found that Comerica was negligent in its response to Jaffe's acknowledged conflict of interest and in allowing Jaffe and his firm to control the negotiations. As to Jaffe, the court found that his conflict of interest, although acknowledged, tainted the sale because there was not full disclosure of the extent of his prior representation of Cohen on personal tax matters, because Jaffe actively participated in the negotiations and because his course of conduct insured that his client, Cohen, obtained the property at an inadequate price. The court found that both parties had failed in their duty to keep the beneficiaries reasonably informed and to fulfill a self-imposed duty to keep their co-trustees fully advised of developments. . . . .

We now turn to the substantive issue of whether Jaffe and Comerica violated their duties to the trust. As a preliminary matter, we note that, while Jaffe maintains that he declined to act as a trustee with respect to any offer by Cohen, he did not resign his position as trustee. Therefore, his duties to the beneficiaries and the trust as to matters related to the valuation and marketing of the property did not end when he chose to decline to act on the offer. . . .

Paragraph VII of the trust gives the trustees broad powers "to do everything they in good faith deem advisable even though it would not be authorized or appropriate for fiduciaries (but for this power) under any statutory or other rule of law . . . ." Paragraph V empowers Comerica and Jaffe "in their sole discretion" to determine the timing of any sale of the real property so as to realize its "full value."

Giving trustees discretionary or broad powers does not mean that there are no limits to those powers. Trustees' actions will be reviewed for abuse of that discretion. The trustee is bound to exercise his discretion honestly and in good faith. . . .

As noted by the parties, the liability of the trustee may be limited by the terms of the trust instrument. Comerica's and Jaffe's liability for error, negligence, mistake of judgment, act or omission as trustees of the charitable trust was limited to actions done in bad faith. This provision is consistent with the common law principle that trustees may not be liable for mere mistakes or errors of judgment where they have acted in good faith and within the limits of the law and of the trust.

The exculpatory clause does not preclude judicial review or application of the required standard of care . . . .

An exculpatory clause generally is not considered to reduce or enlarge the standard of care required of the trustee in administering the trust, but acts to relieve the trustee of personal liability under the stated circumstances. It will not generally be construed to mean that the trustee is not accountable to anyone for his actions. A trust implies an equitable duty to act for the benefit of the beneficiary and an all-inclusive exculpatory clause would connote either that there was no enforceable duty owed the beneficiary or that there was no remedy for a breach of duty even if the breach was found to be unconscionable.

The "bad faith" standard used in the Green trust has not been defined in the trust context in Michigan. However, the principle has been applied in trust situations in evaluating a trustee's diligence, honesty, and good faith. In the insurance context, bad faith has been defined as "arbitrary, reckless, indifferent, or intentional disregard of the interests of the person owed a duty." Commercial Union Ins. Co. v. Liberty Mutual Ins. Co., 426 Mich. 127, 136, 393 N.W.2d 161 (1986).

Bad faith is not a specific act in itself, but defines the character or quality of a party's actions. Its presence, as with a determination that a trustee has violated his duty to the trust, depends on the facts of the individual case. . . .

Specific duties of trustees include keeping the beneficiaries "reasonably informed of the trust and its administration." M.C.L. § 700.814. In the context of the sale of real property, there is an obligation to seek the highest price obtainable. The entire circumstances of the case will be considered in reviewing a contested sale. That the price realized at the sale was at or above the appraised value does not necessarily indicate that the best price was obtained.

The duty to obtain the best price has been expanded upon in other jurisdictions to specifically include consideration of those factors noted by the probate court: the determination of fair market value, the proper marketing of the property, and the adequacy of the price obtained. The parties have referred us to a number of cases from other courts, one of which, Allard v. Pacific National Bank, 99 Wash.2d 394, 663 P.2d 104 (1983), is strikingly similar to our situation. In *Allard*, the Supreme Court of Washington affirmed a finding that the trustee had breached its fiduciary duties in its management of the sale of real property located in downtown Seattle, the sole asset of the trust. The beneficiaries argued a breach of duty based on the trustee's failure to inform them of the sale and failure to either obtain an independent appraisal or place the property on the open market prior to the sale.

The Washington court found that the trustee "must inform beneficiaries . . . of all material facts in connection with a nonroutine transaction which significantly affects the trust estate and the interest of the beneficiaries prior to the transaction taking place." *Allard*, supra, 99 Wash.2d at 404-405, 663 P.2d 104. This duty is based on the generally recognized principle that the beneficiaries must know how the estate is being managed in order that they may hold the trustee to proper standards of care and honesty and obtain the benefits to which they are entitled. Id. . . . In *Allard*, there was one offer made for the property by a leaseholder who had a right of first refusal. The court found that, at a minimum, the beneficiaries had a right to know of the offer prior to the sale to give them the opportunity to outbid the leaseholder.

We agree with the *Allard* court that this duty, especially in the instant case where the single most valuable asset was the real property, imposed on Jaffe and Comerica the responsibility of informing all the beneficiaries of the impending sale. It is not clear in what capacity, as co- trustees or as representatives of the beneficiaries, Dean Herlong and Bishop McGehee were first contacted. However, it is clear that Jaffe and Comerica had made a specific commitment to keep Dean Herlong and Bishop McGehee informed, and that commitment should also have been kept. The probate court did not err in finding that Jaffe and Comerica breached this duty.

We now turn to whether the trustees fulfilled their duties in the sale of the property. *Allard's* second issue requiring an appraisal or testing the market has been considered in other jurisdictions as part of the trustee's duty to establish the value of the property offered for sale. Knowledge of value is the basic assurance that any sale price is fair and just.

Factors which have been considered in determining whether adequate efforts were taken to determine value include the existence of a "sound" appraisal and consultation with competent local real estate people to obtain their expert advice. In general, the question is whether the trustee has done its homework.

In the absence of a thorough appraisal, the trustee may establish value by "testing the market." "Testing the market" is not limited to consideration of offers volunteered by actual potential buyers. It includes whatever actions may be available to encourage fair, legitimate and seasonable competition.

In *Allard*, the leaseholder made an initial offer of $139,000. The trustees demanded at least $200,000, and the leaseholder eventually met that price. The trustees' price was apparently based on an internal appraisal by the trustee bank's trust department. However, the court found that, by failing to obtain an independent outside appraisal or testing the market to determine what a willing buyer would pay, the trustees had breached their fiduciary duty.

In our case, respondents argue that they had two appraisals to guide them, Majzels' and Kersten's. But Jaffe, Kersten and Majzels testified that Majzels was not engaged as an appraiser, but as a consultant supplying his input on an appropriate asking price. Jaffe specifically testified that they did not want an appraisal "early on" for fear that it would establish a ceiling on the price that could deleteriously affect the manner of selling the property. That Kersten and Comerica's real estate department had an opinion regarding the value is relevant but not determinative. No evidence was presented by Keating as to the basis for his input, nor is there any indication that Kersten's opinion is equal to a sound and thorough independent appraisal. The last full appraisal on the property was done in 1973. The passage of time, as well as the duty of the trustees, indicated that obtaining a sound and thorough appraisal would have been prudent.

Nor do the facts indicate that the trustees, in the alternative, had "tested the market." Jaffe's reference to not wanting the appraisal "early on" highlights the weakness in crediting the contacts with local developers in early 1983 as part of "testing the market." Jaffe testified that these contacts were not for the purpose of soliciting offers, which might have helped establish value. There is no indication that these contacts were part of an organized effort to "test the market" in a manner which would reasonably take the place of a sound and thorough appraisal. The record does not indicate that the trial court clearly erred in finding that the trustees did not fulfill their duty of establishing the value of the property.

The probate court's next concern was the inadequate marketing of the property. Marketing means taking action to bring the property's "availability to the attention of a wide spectrum of potential purchasers." Lockwood v. OFB Corp., 305 A.2d 636, 639 (Del Ch, 1973). There is no one set method of marketing, rather the cases indicate that all the circumstances surrounding the sale are considered to determine adequacy. We agree with the Chancery Court of Delaware, that what we are looking for is "a reasonably aggressive program which men of prudence and intelligence would have followed." Id. Factors which have been considered include advertisement in appropriate publications, contact with local developers, listing with a local broker, use of "For Sale" signs, showing the property to prospective customers, consultation with local sources on whether the offer price was the best offer obtainable, canvassing for possible purchasers, wide circulation of brochures and taking advantage of events—such as free publicity—to give notice of the sale. In short, we are looking to see if the trustees adopted and followed "a comprehensive and thorough plan to assure that the reasonable and intelligent steps necessary to secure the best possible market price were taken." Lockwood, supra, 305 A.2d 640.

[T]he record indicates that, whatever early contacts with local developers occurred, they were not for the purpose of marketing the property. The indications from Jaffe and Kersten are that these early contacts, along with the information received from Hall and Tilton, were an attempt to formulate a plan for the orderly marketing of the property. According to Jaffe and Kersten, it was not until August that the trustees decided on the standard to be applied in selling the property. The distribution of the circular was their only marketing effort.

Even assuming that sending out a circular could be sufficient, this method of marketing is suspect in these circumstances. While the trustees were actively considering an offer on less than all of the property and for an initial cash payment of $1.5 million, the property was being marketed to the rest of the world in its entirety. At least one potential buyer was told that he needed an initial cash outlay of $4 million. Furthermore, the entire extent of the marketing effort encompassed approximately twenty days—the time between the mailing and the acceptance of the Cohen offer.

The testimony of Dean Herlong is that he was informed on August 22 that interested parties would be given thirty days to respond. However, the circular did not indicate a time limit or that time was of the essence. The record indicates that potential purchasers such as Robertson, who had previously expressed an interest, were originally told it would be nine months to a year before offers would be accepted. Other purchasers could easily have accepted the circular as the first step in the long-awaited offering. The general impression we are left with is that the trustees were basically dormant, waiting for offers to be brought to them. Such lack of activity does not indicate that they fulfilled their duty to the trust.

The third area considered was the adequacy of the price obtained. While an accurate determination of value gives the trustees a good idea of where the bidding should begin, it does not mean that a higher price may not be available. The entire range of activities and surrounding circumstances are examined to see if the trustees took steps to understand the value and qualities of the property, as well as the nature of the market, and then took appropriate steps to secure the maximum price available.

A review of the record indicates that the trustees took a number of actions similar to those mentioned in the cases above. Prior to the Cohen offer, there were phone calls to local developers, there was consultation with an appraiser regarding value, other experts—Hall and Tilton—were consulted as to the use and potential problems, and at least two prospective purchasers—Robertson and Johnson—were contacted. Following the offer, a flyer was widely circulated among those local entities apparently most likely to be interested. If this were a simple matter of checking off an appropriate number of boxes, it could be argued that the trustees fulfilled their duty. However, in viewing these actions as a whole, we cannot say that these actions amounted to any actual concerted effort to determine or obtain the highest price available. This is not to say that a written or established plan is required, but rather it is to say that individual actions which do not indicate a concerted effort towards understanding and achieving the maximum price are not enough.

In the absence of some contemporaneous evidence on the value of the property, the court was forced to consider the appraisals made in 1985 in determining what an adequate price might have been. Both Majzels and Proctor testified; both appraisals were available. Both respondents and petitioners were diligent in pointing out to the court the respective strengths and weaknesses of the appraisals.

We find that, as with any other means for the assessment of damages, an appraisal must establish with a reasonable degree of certainty what an adequate price would have been; however, the law does not require a higher degree of certainty than the nature of the case permits. Given the facts of this case regarding the inadequacies of the trustees' actions with regard to the sale, it is not logical to require proof of a known purchaser or the existence of another offer to establish a price. The inadequate marketing in this case virtually precludes such a finding.

The court's finding that Proctor's appraisal, which included consideration of the development potential of the property, was more compelling as an indicator of price than Majzels' appraisal is not clearly erroneous. That the probate court found the development potential relevant to the worth of the property is not the same as Comerica's argument that the court was requiring the fiduciaries to speculate in risky land ventures.

The remaining issue concerning the trustees involves the court's finding that Jaffe was involved in a conflict of interest situation which tainted the sale and established his bad faith and self-dealing. We agree . . . that this is not a case of self-dealing because there was no evidence that Jaffe was actually a party or that he directly profited from the sale. We have been given no authority for the proposition that whatever indirect interest Jaffe may have had in his firm's fees amounts to self-dealing. However . . . there is evidence of a potential conflict of interest or conflicting loyalties which must be considered. . . .

As a trustee, Jaffe was bound to consider the interests of the trust as paramount to all others. If other interests would prevent him from making a sound decision from the point of view of the trust, a potential conflict of interest exists. It is a fundamental principle that the trustee must display complete loyalty to the interests of the beneficiary, to the exclusion of all selfish interests or consideration of the interests of third parties. This principle is based on the understanding that a person acting in two capacities or in behalf of two interests may consciously or unconsciously favor one side over the other. It is not necessary that the trustee gain from the transaction to find disloyalty. Bogert, [Trusts and Trustees] § 543, p 204. "In its desire to guard the highly valuable fiduciary relationship against improper administration, equity deems it better to forbid disloyalty and strike down all disloyal acts, rather than to attempt to separate the harmless and the harmful by permitting the trustee to justify his representation of two interests." Id., p 207.

As an attorney, Jaffe also had an obligation to use his skills and judgment in representing his client, thereby assuming a position of the highest trust and confidence. "A lawyer who is also a fiduciary bears a doubly high degree of responsibility and accountability." State Bar Grievance Administrator v. Estes, 392 Mich. 645, 653, 221 N.W.2d 322 (1974). While the Code of Professional Responsibility is not directly in issue in this case, it is relevant as expressing a standard of professional conduct expected of lawyers by which Jaffe may be measured. At the very least, the Code puts the attorney on notice that he is to be sensitive to the potential problems accompanying the representation of multiple clients, Canon 5, and that it is his duty to avoid even the appearance of impropriety.

The cases cited by Jaffe for his proposition that multiple representation may be valid are not determinative, since in those cases the parties were fully informed of the nature of the conflict. As noted by the probate court, Dean Herlong and Bishop McGehee, as co-trustees, were not fully informed of the extent of Jaffe's past representations of Cohen. Nor is it clear that they were kept apprised of the extent of his involvement in the Cohen negotiations and eventual sale. Similarly, the beneficiaries were not fully informed.

The fact is that Jaffe, as a named trustee, as the agent of Comerica and as an attorney with the law firm representing both the buyer and the seller, had a responsibility to avoid even the appearance of a conflict. The record indicates that the multiplicity of his roles created a situation fraught with conflict that could not be avoided by simply withdrawing as trustee for purposes of approving the Cohen offer. Jaffe's own testimony indicates the difficulty of the position in which he found himself "It's very difficult in these kinds of situations, . . . to differentiate the head that you're using as trustee from the head that you're using as counsel. After all, you only have one. You have a lot of hats but you only have one head." The record indicates that, even after he committed not to act as a trustee, he was actively involved in the negotiations, and yet he testified that he had declined to act as both attorney for the estate and trustee for the charitable trust. The only party left to represent was Cohen, but Jaffe maintains that his firm's representation of the buyer was kept separate from him.

We know that Jaffe was involved in meetings regarding the adequacy of the offer and that he indicated approval of it to Comerica. As noted by the trial court:

> Even had the one page circular been designed to expose the property in its most favorable light to the market, there obviously was no time for any developer to investigate the property, perform soil borings, conduct environmental studies, prepare site plans, have the property appraised and study development costs, let alone prepare a bid. Cohen, on the other hand, had the benefit of the Calvin Hall site plans and Tilton materials and had spent five months studying the property before he had Honigman lawyers submit his bid.

At the very least, the short time span between the mailing of the circular and the acceptance of the Cohen offer gives the appearance that matters had been manipulated to assure that no other offers would be submitted or considered. Given our earlier finding on the inadequacy of the sale efforts, we cannot say that Jaffe's actions were the fair and adequate dealings of the loyal fiduciary. The court did not clearly err in finding a conflict or in finding that the conflict resulted in a breach of Jaffe's fiduciary duties.

However, while it was appropriate for the probate court to consider the Code of Professional Responsibility as indicative of the standard to which Jaffe should be held, we find that its holding that he violated the Disciplinary Rules must be vacated. The appropriate context for consideration of this type of attorney misconduct appears to be proceedings by the attorney discipline board or an action brought by an aggrieved client. The probate court's holding on this issue was not a necessary part of this adjudication and, to the extent it may be considered a holding of the court, we vacate it.

We further agree, given the facts of this case, that it is clear that Comerica had a responsibility to monitor or in some way react to Jaffe's conflict. Comerica's duty of loyalty applied to Jaffe and his firm as Comerica's employees or agents. Where a trustee allows its agents to pursue their own interests while carrying on trust work, the trustee may be liable to the same extent as the agent.

On the basis of all of the above, we affirm the trial court's holding that Jaffe and Comerica failed in their duties as trustees. Their actions and inactions were not mere negligence or errors in judgment. Their actions, clearly in violation of their duties and done with reckless or indifferent disregard of the beneficiaries' interests, indicate they acted in bad faith and preclude any insulation from liability under the trust's exculpatory clause.

As to Comerica's liability as personal representative, by statute the personal representative stands in a position of confidence and trust with respect to the beneficiaries. Edith Green's will gave Comerica, as personal representative, the same broad powers it enjoyed as a trustee. But the similar limitation of liability, excluding negligence and mistake of judgment, was specifically made not applicable to a corporate fiduciary such as Comerica. As a fiduciary, Comerica is liable for loss resulting from its negligence in handling the estate and for any misfeasance, malfeasance, or other breach of duty.

As a fiduciary, Comerica is held to the same standards regarding the sale of the property as were discussed above. Furthermore, the loyalty rule considered above with regard to Jaffe applies to all fiduciaries and their agents, not just trustees. The reasons discussed above also support the court's finding that Comerica is liable for its failure to fulfill its duties as the personal representative. . . .

As to whether Dean Herlong and Bishop McGehee were estopped to complain . . . , the general rule is that ratification occurs only where the beneficiary acted with full knowledge of all the facts and not under the influence of misrepresentation, concealment or other wrongful conduct of the trustee. The record supports the probate court's finding that there is no estoppel because their qualified consent was not based on a full disclosure of the facts or the extent of the Jaffe-Cohen dealings. Nor were they fully informed when they signed the Cohen land contract.

On the issue of damages . . . , [t]he probate court found Comerica, as personal representative and trustee, and Jaffe, as trustee, jointly and severally liable for their activities in the amount of $1,900,000. There was no finding concerning the marital trust, nor did there need to be. Comerica's liability was based on an evaluation of its activities. That Comerica was not found liable for its role as trustee of the marital trust does not make its liability in its other roles any the less. The same is true for Jaffe. That Jaffe was not a trustee or personal representative of the estate is irrelevant to the liability imposed because of his own breach of duty as a trustee of the charitable trust. To carve out identities and liabilities at this stage of the proceedings smacks of the artificial and appears to be an effort to avoid liability rather than define the limits of liability.

. . . .

Finally, both Jaffe and Comerica ask that they be reinstated as co-trustees and personal representative. Removing a fiduciary is a question entrusted to the discretion of the probate court, and that court's decision will not be reversed absent an abuse of discretion. Given the facts of this case, we find no abuse of discretion.

With the exception of the finding regarding Jaffe's violation of the Code of Professional Responsibility, which is vacated, the probate court's order is affirmed.

Notes and Questions

1. *Aftermath*. The facts of *Green* make it an especially interesting case. Miles Jaffe, whom the court found had violated his duty of loyalty, was a highly respected Detroit lawyer who specialized in estate planning. Following the court's decision, he lost his law practice and eventually died a broken man. How could a sophisticated lawyer like Jaffe allow himself to be placed in a situation where the conflict of interest is so apparent? Are there any particular factors that might explain why he let his guard down as trustee of the Green trust?

2. *Exoneration Clauses*. One factor that may have entered into Jaffe's thinking was the existence of an exoneration clause in the trust instrument. Why didn't the clause relieve Jaffe of all liability? Should these clauses be enforceable as written? Should parties be able contractually to waive all legally recognized trustee duties, or are these duties (or some of them) mandatory?

Consistent with the standard adopted in paragraph VII of the trust instrument in *Green*, the UTC §1008(a) provides that an exoneration clause is unenforceable to the extent that it (1) relieves the trustee of liability for breach of trust committed in bad faith or with reckless indifference to the purposes of the trust or the interest of the beneficiaries; or (2) was inserted as a result of an abuse by the trustee of a fiduciary or confidential relationship to the settlor." Was Miles Jaffe guilty of acting in bad faith? If so, exactly in what respect?

Subsection (b) of UTC § 1008 goes on to create a presumption that an exoneration clause drafted or caused to be drafted by the trustee is invalid as an abuse of the fiduciary relationship unless the trustee proves that the term was fair under the circumstances and that its contents were adequately communicated to the settlor. What effect would this provision have had if applied in the *Green* case?

In Marsman v. Nasca, 573 N.E.2d 1025 (Mass. App. Ct), appeal denied, 579 N.E.2d 1361 (Mass. 1991), the testator's will created a discretionary trust in favor of her husband, Cappy. The will stated that "after having considered the various available sources of support for him, my trustees shall . . . in their sole and uncontrolled discretion, pay over to him, or use, apply and/or expend for his direct or indirect benefit such amount or amounts or principal thereof as they shall deem advisable for his comfortable support and maintenance." The will also included the following exculpatory clause: "No trustee hereunder shall ever be liable except for his own willful neglect or default." The will was prepared and drafted by James F. Farr, Esq.,[11] and it named him sole trustee. A few years after the testator's death, Cappy wrote to Farr that his business was at a standstill and requested some funds from the trust. Farr replied that he thought the trust terms were broad enough to permit a distribution of principal and enclosed a check for $300, but he also asked Cappy to state in writing the need for support and why the need had arisen. Cappy did not reply and never again asked for distributions from the trust. Farr made no investigation of Cappy's situation or of his available sources of support. Cappy's financial difficulties intensified to the point that his checks were bouncing, and his step-daughter agreed to take over his finances. Cappy died a few years later. The court found that Farr had breached his fiduciary duties by failing to inquire into Cappy's available sources of support, and Farr raised the exculpatory clause as a defense. The court held that the clause was enforceable, stating that there was no evidence that Farr's insertion of the clause was an abuse of his fiduciary relationship with the testator. Regarding the fact that the clause was inserted by Farr, the trustee, the court simply stated, "The fact that the trustee drew the instrument and suggested the insertion of exculpatory clause does not necessarily make the provision ineffective." Would this response be adequate under the approach adopted in UTC § 1008(b), referred to above?

3. *Sales Based on Appraisal Price and the Trustee's Disclosure Obligation.* In both *Green* and the *Washington* case discussed in the court's opinion, Allard v. Pacific National Bank, the trustees sold land, which constituted the sole or major asset in the trust, at appraisal prices without testing the market. Real estate appraisal is a notoriously inexact process. Its weakness makes the trustee's duty to keep the beneficiaries informed all the more important. In what

---

11. James F. Farr, who died in 1993, was a prominent trusts and estates lawyer in Boston and a trustee of many private trusts. His book, An Estate Planner's Handbook (4th ed. 1979) (coauthored with Jackson W. Wright, Jr.) was widely considered the leading practitioner's guide for many years.

respects did Jaffe's and Comerica's actions fall short of meeting that duty? What more should Jaffe in particular have done to satisfy his fiduciary duty?

4. *Self-Dealing and the "No-Further-Inquiry" Rule*. The court in *Green* concluded that Jaffe's actions, while tainted by a conflict of interest, did not constitute self-dealing. Self-dealing exists when the trustee sells trust property to itself individually or sells individual property to the trust. In these circumstances, courts have applied a prophylactic rule known as the "no-further-inquiry" rule. The beneficiaries may set the transaction aside even though it was made in good faith and for a reasonable price. See UTC § 802(b). Moreover, the trustee is chargeable with any profit the trustee realized through the breach of trust. See UTC § 1002(a)(2). If it has made no profit, the trustee is chargeable with any loss to the trust estate resulting from the breach of trust or any profit that would have accrued to the trust estate if there had been no breach of trust. See UTC § 1002(a)(1). See also Charles B. Baron, Self-Dealing Trustees and the Exoneration Clause: Can Trustees Ever Profit from Transactions Involving Trust Property?, 72 St. John's L. Rev. 43 (1998).

There is no self-dealing if a corporate trustee retains for the trust or purchases from others its own shares as trust property.[12] Nevertheless, the practice has been condemned both in the Restatement 2d and 3d of Trusts § 170 comment n on the basis of the possibility of conflict of interest. The Section 802(b) of the Uniform Trust Code provides that a beneficiary may void a "transaction involving the investment or management of trust property" which is "affected by a conflict between's the trustee's fiduciary and personal interests . . . ." Subsection (c)(4) goes on to create a presumption that a transaction is so affected by a conflict of interest where it involves "a corporation or other person or enterprise in which the trustee . . . has an interest that might affect the trustee's best judgment." Presumably, this would include a corporate trustee's retention in a trust portfolio of shares of its own stock. The Restatement 3d of Trusts relaxes the stricture somewhat by providing that it is "ordinarily permissible for a modest amount of the trustee's stock to be held indirectly through an otherwise appropriate purchase of shares in a pooled investment vehicle."

Does the fact that the purchase or sale of trust assets was made on behalf of the trustees but not by them directly mean that the transaction is not self dealing? For a case answering no, see Stegemeier v. Magness, 728 A.2d 557 (Del. 1999). In *Stegemeier*, the court expressly stated that in reviewing allegations of self-dealing the standard for trust law is higher than that fog corporate law. Specifically, corporate law provides a safe harbor for corporate

---

12. Self dealing would exist, however, if a corporate trustee purchased for inclusion in the trust other assets, including securities, that the trustee owned.

directors if the tainted transaction was approved by a majority of disinterested directors. Trust law provides no analogous safe harbor for self-dealing trustees.

The rationale for the no-further-inquiry rule can be explained in economic terms. In Robert Cooter & Bradley J. Freedman, The Fiduciary Relationship: Its Economic Character and Legal Consequences, 68 N.Y.U. L. Rev. 1045 (1991), the authors state, "The duty of loyalty must be understood as the law's attempt to create an incentive structure in which the fiduciary's self-interest directs her to act in the best interest of the beneficiary." Id. at 1074. The no-further-inquiry rule is justified, they argue, as a means of overcoming proof problems and increasing the probability that the fiduciary's duties will be enforced: "To overcome difficulties in proof, the law infers disloyalty from its appearance, presuming that a fiduciary will appropriate the principal's [i.e., beneficiary's] asset when it is in her self-interest to do so." Id. at 1055.

5. *Ratification of Breaches of Fiduciary Duties*. Trustee actions that would otherwise constitute a breach of the duty of loyalty may be ratified, thereby relieving the trustee of liability. If the settlor holds the power to revoke the trust, he may ratify the breach without the beneficiaries' consent. See UTC § 808(a). Lacking such a power, the settlor's ratification will not be binding on the beneficiaries. The beneficiaries, however, may ratify a breach. Uniform Trust Code § 1009 provides that a trustee is not liable to a beneficiary for a breach of trust "if the beneficiary consented to the conduct constituting the breach, released the trustee from liability, or ratified the transaction constituting the breach, unless: (1) the consent, release, or ratification of the beneficiary was induced by improper conduct of the trustee; or (2) at the time of the consent release, or ratification, the beneficiary did not know of the beneficiary's rights or of the material facts relating to the breach."

6. *Authorization of Actions Otherwise Constituting Breaches of Trust*. To be distinguished from ratification is prior authorization of trustee actions that would otherwise constitute a breach of trust. Uniform Trust Code § 802(b) permits the trust instrument or a court to authorize transactions that would otherwise violate the trustee's duty of loyalty.

7. *Duty to Earmark*. Suppose a trustee causes trust assets to be registered in its name without any indication that the asset is subject to the trust. If the asset falls in value due to unforeseeable market developments beyond the control of the trustee, should the trustee be able to avoid liability for the loss by explaining away any inference of intentional wrongdoing? Though arguably prohibited by the rule against self-dealing, a distinct duty to earmark a trust investment so as to distinguish it from individual assets of the trustee is recognized by the authorities. See UTC § 810(c); Restatement 2d of Trusts § 179. A breach of the duty to earmark is likely to be treated as a "technical" breach for which the trustee isn't chargeable in the absence of bad faith, negligence, or loss causally

related to the appearance of an individual holding. See Restatement 2d of Trusts § 205 comment f.

One might question why a purchase transaction between a trust and its trustee acting as an individual should subject the fiduciary to an insurer's liability at the option of beneficiaries, when a loss of a non-earmarked asset may be explained by the fiduciary so as to remain a trust estate loss. A partial answer is that rules formerly governing the liability of securities issuers and transfer agents controlling registrations of securities known to be held in trust produced high transaction costs for transfers involving earmarked securities. As a result, trust instruments commonly relieve trustees from the duty to earmark and non-earmarking is now the order of the day. In the meantime, the old transfer agent problem has been substantially eliminated by enactments in 39 states of the Uniform Act for Simplification of Fiduciary Security Transfers. Section 3 of the act provides: "a corporation or transfer agent making a transfer of a security pursuant to an assignment by a fiduciary . . . may assume without inquiry that the assignment, even though to the fiduciary himself or his nominee, is within his authority and capacity and is not in breach of his fiduciary duties."

The question remains whether a fiduciary who can establish complete good faith, absence of any personal gain, and lack of any realistic causal connection between conduct labeled "breach of trust" and financial harm to the estate should be made an insurer of trust assets. What are the costs and benefits of using this strict liability rule as a deterrent?

Estate of Rothko

372 N.E.2d 291 (N.Y. 1977)

COOKE, J. Mark Rothko, an abstract expressionist painter whose works through the years gained for him an international reputation of greatness, died testate on February 25, 1970. The principal asset of his estate consisted of 798 paintings of tremendous value, and the dispute underlying this appeal involves the conduct of his three executors in their disposition of these works of art. In sum, that conduct as portrayed in the record and sketched in the opinions was manifestly wrongful and indeed shocking.

Rothko's will was admitted to probate on April 27, 1970 and letters testamentary were issued to Bernard J. Reis, Theodoros Stamos and Morton Levine. Hastily and within a period of only about three weeks and by virtue of two contracts each dated May 21, 1970, the executors dealt with all 798 paintings.

By a contract of sale, the estate executors agreed to sell to Marlborough A.G., a Liechtenstein corporation (hereinafter MAG), 100 Rothko paintings as listed for $1,800,000, $200,000 to be paid on execution of the agreement and the balance of $1,600,000 in 12 equal interest-free installments over a 12 year period. Under the second agreement, the executors consigned to Marlborough Gallery, Inc. a domestic corporation (hereinafter MNY), "approximately 700 paintings listed on a Schedule to be prepared", the consignee to be responsible for costs covering items such as insurance, storage restoration and promotion. By its provisos, MNY could sell up to 35 paintings a year from each of two groups, pre-1947 and post-1947, for 12 years at the best price obtainable but not less than the appraised estate value, and it would receive a 50% commission on each painting sold, except for a commission of 40% on those sold to or through other dealers.

Petitioner Kate Rothko, decedent's daughter and a person entitled to share in his estate by virtue of an election under EPTL 5-3.3,[13] instituted this proceeding to remove the executors, to enjoin MNY and MAG from disposing of the paintings, to rescind the aforesaid agreements between the executors and said corporations, for a return of the paintings still in possession of those corporations, and for damages. . . . The Attorney-General of the State, as the representative of the ultimate beneficiaries of the Mark Rothko Foundation, Inc., a charitable corporation and the residuary legatee under decedent's will, joined in requesting relief substantially similar to that prayed for by petitioner. On June 26, 1972 the Surrogate issued a temporary restraining order and on September 26, 1972 a preliminary injunction enjoining MAG, MNY, and the three executors from selling or otherwise disposing of the paintings referred to in the agreements dated May 21, 1970, except for sales or dispositions made with court permission. . . . By a 1974 petition, the Attorney-General, on behalf of the ultimate charitable beneficiaries of the Mark Rothko Foundation, sought the punishment of MNY, MAG, Lloyd and Reis for contempt and other relief.

Following a nonjury trial covering 89 days and in a thorough opinion, the Surrogate found: that Reis was a director, secretary and treasury of MNY, the

---

13. The statutory reference is to New York's mortmain legislation, since repealed. Under this law, the excess over 50% of an estate included in a charitable devise could be claimed by a spouse or children if the objectors, under all other terms of the will and applicable intestacy law, would be beneficiaries of the assets denied to the charity. Thus, the legislation invited will draftsmen to avoid the statute by including a devise to one outside the statutory beneficiary class conditioned to take effect to the extent that the charitable devise failed for any reason. Rothko's will, prepared by co-executor Reis who had a law degree but had never practiced law, contained no such saving clause. It included a devise of certain paintings to the Tate Gallery in London, a devise to the artist's wife of the home and contents plus $250,000, and a residuary devise to the Mark Rothko Foundation which had been previously formed and was controlled by Rothko and the three persons named as his executors. Rothko's two children exercised the mortmain election and became entitled to a quarter of the residue. Estate of Rothko, 71 Misc.2d 74, 335 N.Y.2d 666 (1972), affirmed, 43 A.D.2d 819, 351 N.Y.S.2d 940 (1974). This aspect of the *Rothko* case is discussed in John H. Merryman, The Straw Man in the Rothko Case, Art News, Dec. 1976, p. 32. Also, see Lee Seldes, The Legacy of Mark Rothko (1978) for a description of the artist and the post-mortem scramble for his estate that began with his 1970 suicide. Eds.

consignee art gallery, in addition to being a coexecutor of the estate; that the testator had a 1969 *inter vivos* contract with MNY to sell Rothko's work at a commission of only 10% and whether that agreement survived testator's death was a problem that a fiduciary in a dual position could not have impartially faced; that Reis was in a position of serious conflict of interest with respect to the contracts of May 21, 1970 and that his dual role and planned purpose benefited the Marlborough interests to the detriment of the estate; that it was to the advantage of coexecutor Stamos as a "not-too-successful artist, financially", to curry favor with Marlborough and that the contract made by him with MNY within months after signing the estate contracts placed him in a position where his personal interests conflicted with those of the estate, especially leading to lax contract enforcement efforts by Stamos; that Stamos acted negligently and improvidently in view of his own knowledge of the conflict of interest of Reis; that the third coexecutor, Levine, while not acting in self-interest or with bad faith, nonetheless failed to exercise ordinary prudence in the performance of his assumed fiduciary obligations since he was aware of Reis' divided loyalty, believed that Stamos was also seeking personal advantage, possessed personal opinions as to the value of the paintings and yet followed the leadership of his coexecutors without investigation of essential facts or consultation with competent and disinterested appraisers, and that the business transactions of the two Marlborough corporations were admittedly controlled and directed by Francis K. Lloyd. It was concluded that the acts and failures of the three executors were clearly improper to such a substantial extent as to mandate their removal under SCPA 711 as estate fiduciaries. The Surrogate also found that MNY, MAG and Lloyd were guilty of contempt in shipping, disposing of and selling 57 paintings in violation of the temporary restraining order dated June 26, 1972 and of the injunction dated September 26, 1972; that the contracts for sale and consignment of paintings between the executors and MNY and MAG provided inadequate value to the estate, amounting to a lack of mutuality and fairness resulting from conflicts on the part of Reis and Stamos and improvidence on the part of all executors; that said contracts were voidable and were set aside by reason of violation of the duty of loyalty and improvidence of the executors, knowingly participated in and induced by MNY and MAG; that the fact that these agreements were voidable did not revive the 1969 *inter vivos* agreements since the parties by their conduct evinced an intent to abandon and abrogate these compacts. The Surrogate held that the present value at the time of trial of the paintings sold is the proper measure of damages as to MNY, MAG, Lloyd, Reis and Stamos. He imposed a civil fine of $3,332,000 upon MNY, MAG and Lloyd, same being the appreciated value at the time of trial of the 57 paintings sold in violation of the temporary restraining order and injunction. It was held that Levine was liable for $6,464,880 in damages, as he was not in a dual position acting for his own interest and was thus liable only for the actual value of paintings sold MNY and MAG as of the dates of sale, and that Reis, Stamos, MNY and MAG, apart from being jointly and severally liable for the same damages as Levine for negligence, were liable for the greater sum of $9,252,000 "as appreciation damages less amounts previously paid to the estate with regard to sales of paintings." . . . The liabilities were held to be congruent so that payment of the highest sum would satisfy all lesser liabilities including the civil fines and the liabilities for damages were to be reduced by payment of the fine levied or by return of any of the 57 paintings disposed of, the new fiduciary to have the option in the first instance to specify which paintings the fiduciary would accept.

The Appellate Division . . . modified to the extent of deleting the option given the new fiduciary to specify which paintings he would accept. Except for this modification, the majority affirmed the opinion of Surrogate Midonick, with additional comments. Among others, it was stated that the entire court agreed that executors Reis and Stamos had a conflict of interest and divided loyalty in view of their nexus to MNY and that a majority were in agreement with the Surrogate's assessment of liability as to executor Levine and his findings of liability against MNY, MAG and Lloyd. The majority agreed with the Surrogate's analysis awarding "appreciation damages" and found further support for his rationale in Menzel v. List, 24 N.Y.2d 91, 298 N.Y.S.2d 979, 246 N.E.2d 742. . . .

In seeking a reversal, it is urged that an improper legal standard was applied in voiding the estate contracts of May, 1970, that the "no further inquiry" rule applies only to self-dealing and that in case of a conflict of interest, absent self-dealing, a challenged transaction must be shown to be unfair. The subject of fairness of the contracts is intertwined with the issue of whether Reis and Stamos were guilty of conflicts of interest. Scott is quoted to the effect that "[a] trustee does not necessarily incur liability merely because he has an individual interest in the transaction . . . In Bullivant v. First Nat. Bank [246 Mass. 324, 141 N.E. 41] it was held that . . . the fact that the bank was also a creditor of the corporation did not make its assent valid, *if it acted in good faith and the plan was fair*" (2 Scott, Trusts, § 170.24, p. 1384 [emphasis added]) . . .

These contentions should be rejected. First, a review of the opinions of the Surrogate and the Appellate Division manifests that they did not rely solely on a "no further inquiry rule", and secondly, there is more than an adequate basis to conclude that the agreements between the Marlborough corporations and the estate were neither fair nor in the best interests of the estate. . . . The opinions under review demonstrate that neither the Surrogate nor the Appellate Division set aside the contracts by merely applying the no further inquiry rule without regard to fairness. Rather they determined, quite properly indeed, that these agreements were neither fair nor in the best interests of the estate.

To be sure, the assertions that there were no conflicts of interest on the part of Reis or Stamos indulge in sheer fantasy. Besides being a director and officer of MNY, for which there was financial remuneration, however slight, Reis, as noted by the Surrogate, had different inducements to favor the Marlborough interests, including his own aggrandizement of status and financial advantage through sales of almost one million dollars for items from his own and his family's extensive private art collection by the Marlborough interests. . . . Similarly, Stamos benefited as an artist under contract with Marlborough and, interestingly, Marlborough purchased a Stamos painting from a third party for $4,000 during the week in May, 1970 when the estate contract negotiations were pending. . . . The conflicts are manifest. Further, as noted in Bogert, Trusts and Trustees (2d ed.), "The duty of loyalty imposed on the fiduciary prevents him from accepting employment from a third party who is entering into a business transaction with the trust" (§ 543, subd. [S], p. 573). "While he [a trustee] is administering the trust he must refrain from placing himself in a position where his personal interest or that of a third person does or may conflict with the interest of the beneficiaries" (Bogert, Trusts [Hornbook Series—5th ed.], p. 343). Here, Reis was employed and Stamos benefited in a manner contemplated by Bogert. In short, one must strain the law rather than follow it to reach the result suggested on behalf of Reis and Stamos.

Levine contends that, having acted prudently and upon the advice of counsel, a complete defense was established.[14] Suffice it to say, an executor who knows that his coexecutor is committing breaches of trust and not only fails to exert efforts directed towards prevention but accedes to them is legally accountable even though he was acting on the advice of counsel. When confronted with the question of whether to enter into the Marlborough contracts, Levine was acting in a business capacity, not a legal one, in which he was required as an executor primarily to employ such diligence and prudence to the care and management of the estate assets and affairs as would prudent persons of discretion and intelligence accented by "[n]ot honesty alone, but the punctilio of an honor the most sensitive" (Meinhard v. Salmon, 249 N.Y. 458, 464, 164 N.E. 545, 546,

14. Counsel advised all three executors that Reis had a conflict of interest. In the same letter, though, the law firm advised them that the Surrogate wouldn't entertain a petition for advance approval of any contracts for liquidating the estate through Marlborough. Surrogate Midonick's opinion stated: "While it is true . . . that Surrogates do not usually give advance approval concerning matters of business judgment which are within the province of executors, no indication was given that the opposite rule governs when a fiduciary faces a conflict of interest." In re Rothko, 84 Misc. 2d 830, 840, 379 N.Y.S.2d 923, 936 (Surr. Ct. 1975). Should the law firm be liable to Levine for negligence? See Peter S. Cremer, Should the Fiduciary Trust His Lawyer?, 19 Real Prop. Prob. & Tr. J. 786 (1984). Eds.

supra). Alleged good faith on the part of a fiduciary forgetful of his duty is not enough. He could not close his eyes, remain passive or move with unconcern in the face of the obvious loss to be visited upon the estate by participation in those business arrangements and then shelter himself behind the claimed counsel of an attorney.

Further there is no merit to the argument that MNY and MAG lacked notice of the breach of trust. The record amply supports the determination that they are chargeable with notice of the executors' breach of duty.

The measure of damages was the issue that divided the Appellate Division. The contention of Reis, Stamos, MNY and MAG, that the award of appreciation damages was legally erroneous and impermissible, is based on a principle that an executor authorized to sell is not liable for an increase in value if the breach consists only in selling for a figure less than that for which the executor should have sold. For example, Scott states:

> The beneficiaries are not entitled to the value of the property at the time of the decree if it was not the duty of the trustee to retain the property in the trust and the breach of trust consisted *merely* in selling the property for too low a price (3 Scott, Trusts [3d ed.], § 208.3, p. 1687 [emphasis added]).
>
> If the trustee is guilty of a breach of trust in selling trust property for an inadequate price, he is liable for the difference between the amount he should have received and the amount which he did receive. He is not liable, however, for any subsequent rise in value of the property sold. (Id., § 208.6, pp. 1689-1690).

A recitation of similar import appears in comment d under Restatement, Trusts, § 205:

> *d. Sale for less than value.* If the trustee is authorized to sell trust property, but in breach of trust he sells it for less than he should receive, he is liable for the value of the property at the time of the sale less the amount which he received. If the breach of trust consists *only* in selling it for too little, he is not chargeable with the amount of any subsequent increase in value of the property under the rule stated in Clause (c), as he would be if he were not authorized to sell the property. See § 208. (Emphasis added).

However, employment of "merely" and "only" as limiting words suggests that where the breach consists of some misfeasance, other than solely for selling "for too low a price" or "for too little", appreciation damages may be appropriate. According to Scott (§ 208.3) and the Restatement (§ 208), the trustee may be held liable for appreciation damages if it was his or her duty to retain the property, the theory being that the beneficiaries are entitled to be placed in the same position they would have been in had the breach not consisted of a sale of property that should have been retained. The same rule should apply where the breach of trust consists of a serious conflict of interest—which is more than merely selling for too little.

The reason for allowing appreciation damages, where there is a duty to retain, and only date of sale damages, where there is authorization to sell, is policy oriented. If a trustee authorized to sell were subjected to a greater measure of damages he might be reluctant to sell (in which event he might run a risk if depreciation ensued). On the other hand, if there is a duty to retain and the trustee sells, there is no policy reason to protect the trustee. He has not simply acted imprudently; he has violated an integral condition of the trust.

"If a trustee in breach of trust transfers trust property to a person who takes with notice of the breach of trust, and the transferee has disposed of the property . . . [i]t seems proper to charge him with the value at the time of the decree, since if it had not been for the breach of trust the property would still have been a part of the trust estate." (4 Scott, Trusts [3d ed.], § 291.2; see, also, United States v. Dunn, 268 U.S. 121, 132, 45 S. Ct. 451, 69 L.Ed. 876). This rule of law which applies to the transferees MNY and MAG also supports the imposition of appreciation damages against Reis and Stamos, since if the Marlborough corporations are liable for such damages either as purchaser or consignees with notice, from one in breach of trust, it is only logical to hold that said executors, as sellers and consignors, are liable also *pro tanto*.

Contrary to assertions of appellants and the dissenters at the Appellate Division, Menzel v. List, 24 N.Y.2d 91, 298 N.Y.S.2d 979, 246 N.E.2d 742, supra is authority for the allowance of appreciation damages. There, the damages involved a breach of warranty of title to a painting which at one time had been stolen from plaintiff and her husband and ultimately sold to defendant. Here, the executors, though authorized to sell, did not merely err in the amount they accepted but sold to one with whom Reis and Stamos had a self-interest. To make the injured party whole, in both instances the quantum of damages should be the same. In other words, since the paintings cannot be returned, the estate is therefore entitled to their value at the time of the decree, i.e., appreciation damages. These are not punitive damages in a true sense, rather they are damages intended to make the estate whole. Of course, as to Reis, Stamos, MNY and MAG, these damages might be considered by some to be exemplary in a sense, in that they serve as a warning to others, but their true character is ascertained when viewed in the light of overriding policy considerations and in the realization that the sale and consignment were not merely sales below value but inherently wrongful transfers which should allow the owner to be made whole. . . .

[The balance of the opinion is omitted. It dealt with the trial court's handling of conflicting evidence as to present value of unrecovered paintings, the question of revival of the 1969 contract between MNY and Rothko, and the time of sales held to violate the restraining order and temporary injunction.]

Accordingly, the order of the Appellate Division should be affirmed, with costs to the prevailing parties against appellants, and the question certified answered in the affirmative.

Notes and Questions

1. *Sequel.* In a subsequent proceeding, the surrogate allowed the four law firms involved in the case a total recovery of $3.2 million. By far the largest portion, $2.6 million, went to the firm that represented Kate Rothko. In re Rothko, 414 N.Y.S.2d 444 (Surr. Ct. 1079).

Marlborough Gallery bore most of the burden of the $9.2 million damage award. The gallery's owner, Frank Lloyd, was indicted and later convicted for tampering with evidence in the case, specifically by altering purchase and sale prices of Rothko paintings in the gallery's stock books. N.Y. Times, Jan.7, 1983, at A1.

For a fascinating retrospective on the Rothko estate dispute and its effects on the lives of the individuals involved in it, see Judith H. Dobrzynski, A Betrayal the Art World Can't Forget, N.Y. Times, Nov. 2, 1998, at B 1.

2. *Appreciation Damages.* The portion of the majority opinion dealing with the justification for "appreciation damages" merits close scrutiny. Are these damages compensatory, as the court stated, or punitive? Beneficiaries of a trustee's obligation to get a fair price for trust properties that the trustee is required to sell plainly have legitimate expectations to the property's fair market value as of a time when a legitimate sale should have occurred. Isn't recovery in excess of such fair market value punitive rather than compensatory?

Professor Wellman has criticized the award of "appreciation damages" as a form of punishment for fiduciary misconduct:

> The costs of penalty awards in cases where a fiduciary's conduct is not obviously wrongful are most severe for estates consisting of unique assets where potential conflicts of interest are common. Testators and settlors whose estates include real property, closely held corporate stock, stamps, books, automobiles, coins, or art understandably select as fiduciaries persons knowledgeable about those assets. As these persons accept fiduciary positions or deal with associates or potential associates who are fiduciaries, conflicts or potential conflicts of interest must arise. A rule which discourages the selection of persons who are experienced and successful in the handling of the testator's kind of assets is clearly unwise.
>
> *Rothko* will increase the complexity of these trusteeships. As a precedent, it will encourage fiduciaries to consult their attorneys prior to any transaction possibly tainted with conflict of interest. And, if the attorneys read Surrogate Midonick's opinion carefully, the fiduciaries will be advised to seek a court proceeding with

notice for and an opportunity to be heard by all persons interested in the estate, including appropriate state officials if charitable bequests are involved. What could be more wasteful? . . .

Against the argument that *Rothko* may increase a fiduciary's legal costs, it might be argued that a fiduciary faced with possible conflicts of interest will incur these legal costs whether or not *Rothko* penalties are assessed. That is, the standard remedies for disloyalty may induce fiduciaries, before every transaction, to seek legal advice or court instructions concerning possible conflicts of interest. If that is true, the argument runs, the additional risk of liability for appreciation damages will not increase the legal costs of a fiduciary who may have a personal interest in conflict with that of the estate.

This argument is unpersuasive. First, those honest and able fiduciaries in a position of possible conflict may well be willing to administer the estate without extraordinary legal advice or court instructions if they know that the estate's fair market value at the time of its disposition will provide a ceiling on their liability. Honest fiduciaries will be overly cautious only when threatened with surcharges they can neither estimate nor control. Second, if costs will be the same without regard to the fiduciary's honesty, there is absolutely no justification for the award of any penalty surcharge in the name of deterrence. . . .

Finally, as *Rothko* vividly illustrated, disguising appreciation damages as a form of compensation may lead to shattering liabilities that would never be levied in the name of pure punishment. Few if any courts or juries in the land would have assessed a two-million dollar fine against executor Stamos. Stamos was a close friend of Rothko, a fellow artist and the guardian of Rothko's minor children. His disloyalty was simply that he wanted to favor the gallery because the gallery might help him gain recognition for his own works.

Richard V. Wellman, Punitive Surcharges Against Disloyal Fiduciaries—Is Rothko Right?, 77 Mich. L. Rev. 95, 114-17 (1978).

In Robert Cooter & Bradley J. Freedman, The Fiduciary Relationship: Its Economic Character and Legal Consequences, 66 N.Y.U. L. Rev. 1045 (1991), the authors argue that punitive damages for breaches of fiduciary duties *should* be more common in order effectively to deter wrongdoing. "[T]he strongest case for punitive damages," they contend, "can be made when the enforcement error is large—where there is a significant failure to sanction wrongdoing." Id. at 1070.

For an argument that, owing to cognitive biases, property fiduciaries face greater risks of liability than do non-fiduciary contracting parties, see Gregory S. Alexander, A Cognitive Theory of Fiduciary Relationships, 85 Cornell L. Rev. 767 (2000).

3. *Co-fiduciaries*. If a private, non-charitable trust has multiple trustees, the default rule requires that they act unanimously, although the trust instrument can provide otherwise. (Some states have statutes providing that for private trusts with three or more trustees, a majority may act.) The rule is different for

charitable trusts. A simple majority of trustees are permitted to act. Uniform Trust Code § 703(a) changes the default rule for private, non-charitable trusts by allowing a majority of the trustees to act.

Given Reis' relationship with Marlborough Gallery, what should Levine have done? How would you have advised him? In this connection, consider Restatement 2d of Trusts § 258, which provides:

> (1) Except as stated in Subsection (2), where two trustees are liable to the beneficiary for breach of trust, each of them is entitled to contribution from the other, except that
>
> (a) if one of them is substantially more at fault than the other, he is not entitled to contribution from the other but the other is entitled to indemnity from him; or
>
> (b) if one of them receives a benefit from the breach of trust, the other is entitled to indemnity from him to the extent of the benefit; and for any further liability, if neither is more at fault than the other, each is entitled to contribution.
>
> (2) A trustee who commits a breach of trust in bad faith is not entitled to contribution or indemnity from his co-trustee.

4. *Commercial Banks as Trustees*. Some conflict of interest questions are virtually unavoidable when the same corporation operates a trust department and engages in commercial lending. Bank regulations create so-called "Chinese walls" to prevent material insider information from flowing between commercial loan and trust departments in violation of SEC Rule 10b-5, as well as to minimize the likelihood of charges of divided loyalties. See Report, Problems of Fiduciaries Under the Securities Laws, 9 Real Prop. Prob. & Tr. J. 292 (1974).

PART C. REGULATION OF TRUST INVESTMENTS: THE PRUDENT INVESTOR RULE

Statutory Reference: *UPC § 7-302*
Uniform Prudent Investor Act
UTC § 804

Estate of Janes

681 N.E.2d 332 (N.Y. 1997)

LEVINE, J. Former State Senator and businessman Rodney B. Janes (testator) died on May 26, 1973, survived solely by his wife, Cynthia W. Janes, who was then 72 years of age. Testator's $3,500,000 estate consisted of a $2,500,000 stock portfolio, approximately 71% of which consisted of 13,232 shares of common stock of the Eastman Kodak Company. The Kodak stock had a date-of-death value of $1,786,733, or approximately $135 per share.

Testator's 1963 will and a 1969 codicil bequeathed most of his estate to three trusts. First, the testator created a marital deduction trust consisting of approximately 50% of the estate's assets, the income of which was to be paid to Mrs. Janes for her life. In addition, it contained a generous provision for invasion of the principal for Mrs. Janes's benefit and gave her testamentary power of appointment over the remaining principal. The testator also established a charitable trust of approximately 25% of the estate's assets which directed annual distributions to selected charities. A third trust comprised the balance of the estate's assets and directed that the income therefrom be paid to Mrs. Janes for her life, with the remainder pouring over into the charitable trust upon her death.

On June 6, 1973, the testator's will and codicil were admitted to probate. Letters testamentary issued to petitioner's predecessor, Lincoln Rochester Trust Company, and Mrs. Janes, as coexecutors, on July 3, 1973. Letters of trusteeship issued to petitioner alone. By early August 1973, petitioner's trust and estate officers, Ellison Patterson and Richard Young had ascertained the estate's assets and the amount of cash needed for taxes, commissions, attorneys' fees, and specific bequests.

In an August 9, 1973 memorandum, Patterson recommended raising the necessary cash for the foregoing administrative expenses by selling certain assets, including 800 shares of Kodak stock, and holding "the remaining issues ... until the [t]rusts [were] funded." The memorandum did not otherwise address investment strategy in light of the evident primary objective of the testator to provide for his widow during her lifetime. In a September 5, 1973 meeting with Patterson and Young, Mrs. Janes, who had a high school education, no business training or experience, and who had never been employed, consented to the sale of some 1,200 additional shares of Kodak stock. Although Mrs. Janes was informed at the meeting that petitioner intended to retain the balance of the Kodak shares, none of the factors that would lead to an informed investment decision was discussed. At that time, the Kodak stock traded for about $139 per share; thus, the estate's 13,232 shares of the stock were worth almost $1,840,000. The September 5 meeting was the only occasion where retention of the Kodak stock or any other investment issues were taken up with Mrs. Janes.

By the end of 1973, the price of Kodak stock had fallen to about $109 per share. One year later, it had fallen to about $63 per share and, by the end of 1977, to about $51 per share. In March 1978, the price had dropped even further, to about $40 per share. When petitioner filed its initial accounting in February 1980, the remaining 11,320 shares were worth approximately

$530,000, or about $47 per share. Most of the shares were used to fund the trusts in 1986 and 1987.

In addition to its initial accounting in 1980, petitioner filed a series of supplemental accountings that together covered the period from July 1973 through June 1994. In August 1981, petitioner sought judicial settlement of its account. Objections to the accounts were originally filed by Mrs. Janes in 1982, and subsequently by the Attorney-General on behalf of the charitable beneficiaries (collectively, "objectants"). In seeking to surcharge petitioner for losses incurred by the estate due to petitioner's imprudent retention of a high concentration of Kodak stock in the estate from July 1973 to February 1980, during which time the value of the stock had dropped to about one third of its date-of-death value, objectants asserted that petitioner's conduct violated EPTL 11-2.2(a)(1), the so-called "prudent person rule" of investment. When Mrs. Janes died in 1986, the personal representative of her estate was substituted as an objectant.

Following a trial on the objections, the Surrogate found that petitioner, under the circumstances, had acted imprudently and should have divested the estate of the high concentration of Kodak stock by August 9, 1973. The court imposed a $6,080,269 surcharge against petitioner and ordered petitioner to forfeit its commissions and attorneys' fees. In calculating the amount of the surcharge, the court adopted a "lost profits" or "market index" measure of damages espoused by objectants' expert--what the proceeds of the Kodak stock would have yielded, up to the time of trial, had they been invested in petitioner's own diversified equity fund on August 9, 1973.

The Appellate Division modified solely as to damages, holding that "the Surrogate properly found [petitioner] liable for its negligent failure to diversify and for its inattentiveness, inaction, and lack of disclosure, but that the Surrogate adopted an improper measure of damages" (Matter of Janes, 223 A.D.2d 20, 22, 643 N.Y.S.2d 972). [T]he Court held that the Surrogate's finding of imprudence, as well as its selection of August 9, 1973 as the date by which petitioner should have divested the estate of its concentration of Kodak stock, were "well supported" by the record. The Court rejected the Surrogate's "lost profits" or "market index" measure of damages, however, holding that the proper measure of damages was "the value of the capital that was lost"—the difference between the value of the stock at the time it should have been sold and its value when ultimately sold. Applying this measure, the Court reduced the surcharge to $4,065,029. We granted petitioner and objectants leave to appeal, and now affirm.

I. Petitioner's Liability

Petitioner argues that New York law does not permit a fiduciary to be surcharged for imprudent management of a trust for failure to diversify in the absence of additional elements of hazard, and that it relied upon, and complied with, this rule in administering the estate. [P]etitioner claims that elements of hazard can be capsulized into deficiencies in the following investment quality factors: "(i) the capital structure of the company; (ii) the competency of its management; (iii) whether the company is a seasoned issuer of stock with a history of profitability; (iv) whether the company has a history of paying dividends; (v) whether the company is an industry leader; (vi) the expected future direction of the company's business; and (vii) the opinion of investment bankers and analysts who follow the company's stock." Evaluated under these criteria, petitioner asserts, the concentration of Kodak stock at issue in this case, that is, of an acknowledged "blue chip" security popular with investment advisors and many mutual funds, cannot be found an imprudent investment on August 9, 1973 as a matter of law. In our view, a fiduciary's duty of investment prudence in holding a concentration of one security may not be so rigidly limited.

New York followed the prudent person rule of investment during the period of petitioner's administration of the instant estate. This rule provides that "[a] fiduciary holding funds for investment may invest the same in such securities as would be acquired by prudent [persons] of discretion and intelligence in such matters who are seeking a reasonable income and the preservation of their capital" (EPTL 11-2.2[a][1]).[15] Codified in 1970, the prudent person rule's New York common-law antecedents can be traced to King v. Talbot, 40 N.Y. 76, wherein this Court stated:

> [T]he trustee is bound to employ such diligence and such prudence in the care and management [of the trust], as in general, prudent men of discretion and intelligence in such matters, employ in their own like affairs.
>
> This necessarily excludes all speculation, all investments for an uncertain and doubtful rise in the market, and, of course, *everything that does not take into view the nature and object of the trust, and the consequences of a mistake in the selection of the investment to be made* . . . .
>
> *[T]he preservation of the fund, and the procurement of a just income therefrom, are primary objects* of the creation of the trust itself, and are to be primarily regarded" (id., at 85-86 [emphasis supplied]).

---

15. The recently enacted Prudent Investor Act requires a trustee "to diversify assets unless the trustee reasonably determines that it is in the interests of the beneficiaries not to diversify, taking into account the purposes and terms and provisions of the governing instrument" (EPTL 11-2.3[b][3][C]). The act applies to investments "made or held" by a trustee on or after January 1, 1995 and, thus, does not apply to the matter before us (EPTL 11-2.3 [a]).

No precise formula exists for determining whether the prudent person standard has been violated in a particular situation; rather, the determination depends on an examination of the facts and circumstances of each case. In undertaking this inquiry, the court should engage in "'a balanced and perceptive analysis of [the fiduciary's] consideration and action in light of the history of each individual investment, viewed at the time of its action or its omission to act'" (Matterof Donner, 82 N.Y.2d 574, 585, 606 N.Y.S.2d 137, 626 N.E.2d 922 [quoting Matter of Bank of MY, 35 N.Y.2d 512, 519, 364 N.Y.S.2d 164, 323 N.E.2d 700]). And, while a court should not view each act or omission aided or enlightened by hindsight, a court may, nevertheless, examine the fiduciary's conduct over the entire course of the investment in determining whether it has acted prudently. Generally, whether a fiduciary has acted prudently is a factual determination to be made by the trial court.

As the foregoing demonstrates, the very nature of the prudent person standard dictates against any absolute rule that a fiduciary's failure to diversify, in and of itself, constitutes imprudence, as well as against a rule invariably immunizing a fiduciary from its failure to diversify in the absence of some selective list of elements of hazard, such as those identified by petitioner. Indeed, in various cases, courts have determined that a fiduciary's retention of a high concentration of one asset in a trust or estate was imprudent without reference to those elements of hazard. The inquiry is simply whether, under all the facts and circumstances of the particular case, the fiduciary violated the prudent person standard in maintaining a concentration of a particular stock in the estate's portfolio of investments.

Moreover, no court has stated that the limited elements of hazard outlined by petitioner are the only factors that may be considered in determining whether a fiduciary has acted prudently in maintaining a concentrated portfolio. Again, as commentators have noted, one of the primary virtues of the prudent person rule "lies in its lack of specificity, as this permits the propriety of the trustee's investment decisions to be measured in light of the business and economic circumstances existing at the time they were made" (Laurino, Investment Responsibility of Professional Trustees, 51 St John's L Rev 717, 723 [1977] [emphasis supplied]).

Petitioner's restrictive list of hazards omits such additional factors to be considered under the prudent person rule by a trustee in weighing the propriety of any investment decision, as: "the amount of the trust estate, the situation of the beneficiaries, the trend of prices and of the cost of living, the prospect of inflation and of deflation" (Restatement [Second] of Trusts § 227, comment e). Other pertinent factors are the marketability of the investment and possible tax consequences (id., comment o). The trustee must weigh all of these investment factors as they affect the principal objects of the testator's or settlor's bounty, as between income beneficiaries and remainder persons, including decisions regarding "whether to apportion the investments between high-yield or high-growth securities" (Turano and Radigan, New York Estate Administration ch. 14, § P, at 409 [1986]).

Moreover, and especially relevant to the instant case, the various factors affecting the prudence of any particular investment must be considered in the light of the "circumstances of the trust itself rather than [merely] the integrity of the particular investment" (9C Rohan, N.Y. Civ. Prac-EPTL I 11- 2.2[5], at 11-513, n.106 [1996]). As stated in a leading treatise:

> [t]he trustee should take into consideration the circumstances of the particular trust that he is administering, both as to the size of the trust estate and the requirements of the beneficiaries. He should consider each investment not as an isolated transaction but in its relation to the whole of the trust estate (3 Scott, Trusts § 227.12, at 477 [4th ed]).

Our case law is entirely consistent with the foregoing authorities. Thus, in Matter of Bank of N.Y, although we held that a trustee remains responsible for imprudence as to each individual investment in a trust portfolio, we stated:

> *The record of any individual investment is not to be viewed exclusively, of course, as though it were in its own water-tight compartment*, since to some extent individual investment decisions may properly be affected by considerations of the performance of the fund as an entity, as in the instance, for example, of individual security decisions based in part on considerations of diversification of the fund or of capital transactions to achieve sound tax planning for the fund as a whole. The focus of inquiry, however, is nonetheless on the individual security as such and factors relating to the entire portfolio are to be weighed only along with others in reviewing the prudence of the particular investment decisions" (35 N.Y.2d, at 517, 364, N.Y.S.2d 164, 323 N.E.2d 700, supra [emphasis supplied]).

Thus, the elements of hazard petitioner relies upon as demonstrating that, as a matter of law, it had no duty to diversify, suffer from two major deficiencies under the prudent person rule. First, petitioner's risk elements too narrowly and strictly define the scope of a fiduciary's responsibility in making any individual investment decision, and the factors a fiduciary must consider in determining the propriety of a given investment.

A second deficiency in petitioner's elements of hazard list is that all of the factors relied upon by petitioner go to the propriety of an individual investment "exclusively . . . as though it were in its own water-tight compartment" (Matter of Bank of N.Y., supra, at 517, 364 N.Y.S.2d 164, 323 N.E.2d 700), which would encourage a fiduciary to treat each investment as an isolated transaction rather than "in its relation to the whole of the trust estate" (3 Scott, op. cit., at 477). Thus, petitioner's criteria for elements of hazard would apply irrespective of the concentration of the investment security under consideration in the portfolio. That is, the existence of any of the elements of risk specified by petitioner in a given corporate security would militate against the investment even in a diversified portfolio, obviating any need to consider concentration as a reason to divest or refrain from investing. This ignores the market reality that, with respect to some investment vehicles, concentration itself may create or add to risk, and essentially takes lack of diversification out of the prudent person equation altogether.

Likewise, contrary to petitioner's alternative attack on the decisions below, neither the Surrogate nor the Appellate Division based their respective rulings holding petitioner liable on any absolute duty of a fiduciary to diversify. Rather, those courts determined that a surcharge was appropriate because maintaining a concentration in Kodak stock, under the circumstances presented, violated certain critical obligations of a fiduciary in making investment decisions under the prudent person rule. First, petitioner failed to consider the investment in Kodak stock in relation to the entire portfolio of the estate, i.e., whether the Kodak concentration itself created or added to investment risk. The objectants' experts testified that even high quality growth stocks, such as Kodak, possess some degree of volatility because their market value is tied so closely to earnings projections. They further opined that the investment risk arising from that volatility is significantly exacerbated when a portfolio is heavily concentrated in one such growth stock.

Second, the evidence revealed that, in maintaining an investment portfolio in which Kodak represented 71 % of the estate's stock holdings, and the balance was largely in other growth stocks, petitioner paid insufficient attention to the needs and interests of the testator's 72-year-old widow, the life beneficiary of three quarters of his estate, for whose comfort, support and anticipated increased medical expenses the testamentary trusts were evidently created. Testimony by petitioner's investment manager, and by the objectants' experts, disclosed that the annual yield on Kodak stock in 1973 was approximately 1.06%, and that the aggregate annual income from all estate stockholdings was $43,961, a scant 1.7% of the $2.5 million estate securities portfolio. Thus, retention of a high concentration of Kodak jeopardized the interests of the primary income beneficiary of the estate and led to the eventual need to substantially invade the principal of the marital testamentary trust.

Lastly, there was evidence in the record to support the findings below that, in managing the estate's investments, petitioner failed to exercise due care and the skill it held itself out as possessing as a corporate fiduciary. Notably, there was proof that petitioner (1) failed initially to undertake a formal analysis of the estate and establish an investment plan consistent with the testator's primary objectives; (2) failed to follow petitioner's own internal trustee review protocol during the administration of the estate, which advised special caution and attention in cases of portfolio concentration of as little as 20%; and (3) failed to conduct more than routine reviews of the Kodak holdings in this estate, without considering alternative investment choices, over a seven-year period of steady decline in the value of the stock.

Since, thus, there was evidence in the record to support the foregoing affirmed findings of imprudence on the part of petitioner, the determination of liability must be affirmed.

II. Date of Divestiture

As we have noted, in determining whether a fiduciary has acted prudently, a court may examine a fiduciary's conduct throughout the entire period during which the investment at issue was held. The court may then determine, within that period, the "reasonable time" within which divesture of the imprudently held investment should have occurred. What constitutes a reasonable time will vary from case to case and is not fixed or arbitrary. The test remains "the diligence and prudence of prudent and intelligent [persons] in the management of their own affairs." . . .

Again, there is evidentiary support in the record for the trial court's finding, affirmed by the Appellate Division, that a prudent fiduciary would have divested the estate's stock portfolio of its high concentration of Kodak stock by August 9, 1973, thereby exhausting our review powers on this issue. Petitioner's own internal documents and correspondence, as well as the testimony of Patterson, Young, and objectants' experts, establish that by that date, petitioner had all the information a prudent investor would have needed to conclude that the percentage of Kodak stock in the estate's stock portfolio was excessive and should have been reduced significantly, particularly in light of the estate's over-all investment portfolio and the financial requirements of Mrs. Janes and the charitable beneficiaries.

III. Damages

Finally, as to the calculation of the surcharge, we conclude that the Appellate Division correctly rejected the Surrogate's "lost profits" or "market index" measure of damages. Where, as here, a fiduciary's imprudence consists solely of negligent retention of assets it should have sold, the measure of damages is the value of the lost capital . . . .

In imposing liability upon a fiduciary on the basis of the capital lost, the court should determine the value of the stock on the date it should have been sold, and subtract from that figure the proceeds from the sale of the stock or, if the stock is still retained by the estate, the value of the stock at the time of the accounting. Whether interest is awarded, and at what rate, is a matter within the discretion of the trial court. Dividends and other income attributable to the retained assets should offset any interest awarded.

Here, uncontradicted expert testimony established that application of this measure of damages resulted in a figure of $4,065,029, which includes prejudgment interest at the legal rate, compounded from August 9, 1973 to October 1, 1994. The Appellate Division did not abuse its discretion in adding to that figure prejudgment interest from October 1, 1994 through August 17, 1995, $326,302.66 previously received by petitioner for commissions and attorneys' fees, plus postjudgment interest, costs, and disbursements.

Accordingly, the order of the Appellate Division should be affirmed, without costs.

Notes

1. *Diversification and the Market Risk/Specific Risk Distinction.* As part of its portfolio-wide perspective, both the Restatement 3d of Trusts and the Uniform Prudent Investor Act, which the Uniform Trust Code incorporates, expressly provide that trustees are normally under a duty to diversify trust investments. See Restatement 3d of Trusts § 227(b); Uniform Prudent Investor Act § 3. Understanding the scope of this duty and its rationale requires some background regarding investment risk management.

Because all investments involve some risk in the sense of possible loss of real, inflation-adjusted value, modern portfolio theory (MPT) defines caution as the prudent management of risk rather than avoidance of risk. In defining prudent risk management the new Restatement draws upon a conceptual distinction made in MPT between uncompensated, or "specific," risk and compensated, or "market" (or "systemic") risk. Investors care about return and risk. Generally, they want the greatest return for the least risk, and they want to be compensated in proportion to the risk they assume. Risk is the probable variability of future returns in relation to the expected rate of return (meaning total return). The greater the risk, the greater the expected return the investor will demand to compensate the risk.

The market doesn't compensate all types of risk, only that type that affects the market generally. An example is the risk of change in general economic conditions. Almost all investments are affected by this risk the same way, although in different degrees. Another type of risk (loosely called "specific" risk) is that which specifically affects a particular investment or industry but not the market as a whole. The federal defense budget has particular effects on the aerospace industry, while the threat of terrorism affects the travel industry differently than it affects other sectors of the economy. The market doesn't compensate investors for assuming specific risk, but investors can reduce specific risk through diversification. Investors reduce specific risk by acquiring assets that react in opposite ways to the same events (e.g., the effect of rain on the value of shares in firms manufacturing umbrellas versus those manufacturing suntan lotion). Market risks, by contrast, aren't diversifiable because they are systemic. At the same time, there is no reason to diversify them since the market has already rewarded investors for taking them. MPT holds that the investor should hold a broad portfolio in order to reduce specific risk to a low level.

The Restatement 3d's position on diversification of trust investments is consistent with MPT. Comment g to § 227 states that "a trustee's duty of prudent investing normally calls for reasonable efforts to reduce diversifiable risks, while no such generalization can be made with respect to market risk." The appropriate level of market risk for any particular trust depends on that trust's purposes and the relevant trust and beneficiary circumstances. Comment e to the same section also provides that "[f]ailure to diversify on a reasonable basis in order to reduce uncompensated [i.e., specific] risk is ordinarily a violation of both the duty of caution and the duties of care and skill."

The shift to emphasizing total portfolio risk reduction leads the new Restatement to abandon the traditional view that trustees must avoid "speculative" investments. Accordingly, § 227 comment g rejects the rule that treats specific classes of investments or techniques as per se imprudent. An investment that has a high specific risk may be permissible if, as part of a strategy of diversification, it contributes to reducing total portfolio risk.

2. *Delegation of Fiduciary Duties*. It is well settled that trustees may not delegate to others those responsibilities that they can reasonably be required to perform themselves. The line between delegable and non-delegable functions isn't always clear. The courts usually articulate the line in terms of an equally uncertain distinction between discretionary and ministerial acts. It is clear, though, that while a trustee may employ investment advisors, delegating the power to select trust investments to an agent is a breach of the duty not to delegate. Restatement 2d of Trusts § 171 comment h. Commentators have criticized this rule on the ground that it inhibits trustees from taking advantage of specialized expertise in an industry that increasingly has become specialized. The question, they argue, shouldn't be whether to delegate but how to delegate in the way most effective for the trust. See John H. Langbein, Reversing the Non-Delegation Rule of Trust-Investment Law, 59 Mo. L. Rev. 105 (1994).

The Restatement 3d of Trusts, responding to these criticisms, abandons the traditional non-delegation rule. Section 171 provides that"[a] trustee has duty personally to perform the responsibilities of the trusteeship except as a prudent person might delegate those responsibilities to others." Section 227, comment j sheds further light on the subject, stating that "the trustee has power, and may sometimes have a duty, to delegate [investment] functions . . . ."It requires that the power to delegate be exercised reasonably and with due care, eschewing any simple objective test for determining whether the delegation power has been properly exercised. Similarly, both the Uniform Prudent Investor Act § 9 and Uniform Trust Code § 807 abrogate the non-delegation rule.

Section 227.1 of the Restatement 2d of Trusts provides that reliance on counsel's advice is no defense to a breach of trust. What implications does the Restatement 3d of Trust's repeal of the non-delegation rule have for § 227.1?

3. *Index Mutual Funds and the Prudent Investor Rule.* Related to the question about the duty not to delegate is the widespread practice of trust investment in mutual funds. Restatement 3d of Trusts § 227 comment m approves of a strategy of achieving diversification through investing trust assets in mutual funds. In John H. Langbein & Richard A. Posner, Market Funds and Trust Investment Law, 1976 Am. Bar Found. Res. J. 1, 19-24 (1976), the authors argue that not only are mutual funds an appropriate trust investment vehicle but that "index" or "market" funds are especially effective in achieving optimal levels of diversification with minimal transaction costs. Index funds are mutual or other investment funds comprised of a securities portfolio that's designed to approximate market indexes like the Dow Jones or NASDAQ.

4. *Uniform Federal Standards of Care for National Banks?* Federal law allows national banks to exercise the same fiduciary powers that the relevant state law permits state banks and trust companies to exercise. 12 U.S.C. § 92a. The federal administrative agency that is responsible for regulating national banks is the Office of the Comptroller of the Currency (OCC). The OCC recently issued a notice of proposed rulemaking inviting comments on whether uniform standards of care generally applicable to national bank trustees' administration of trusts and investment of trust property should be enacted. 65 Fed. Reg. 75872 (Dec. 5, 2000). What prompted this inquiry is the fact that while all states impose the duties of care, impartiality, and prudence on trustees, states have interpreted these duties differently, as we have seen. This is especially true of the duty of prudence in trust investments. The OCC has not thus far proposed specific standards but is merely inviting comments on whether it should adopt uniform federal standards of care regulating the fiduciary activities of national banks. If such uniform federal standards are adopted, they would preempt inconsistent state law but could be modified by the terms of the trust instrument.

5. *Social Investing.* Can trustees, consistent with their fiduciary duties, take social or political considerations into account in making investment decisions? The question has been much debated, but there is little case law directly dealing with the issue. Compare Blankenship v. Boyle, 329 F. Supp. 1089 (D.D.C. 1971) (purchase by union pension fund of shares in certain electric utilities to induce them to buy union-mined coal held a breach of duty of loyalty) with Bd.

of Trustees of Employees Retirement System v. Mayor of Baltimore, 562 A.2d 720 (Md. 1989) (holding that a city ordinance which divested public employees pension plan from South Africa-related investments did not violate the duty of loyalty). Restatement 3d of Trusts § 277, comment c takes the following position:

> [T]he trustee's [investment] decisions ordinarily must not be motivated by a purpose of advancing or expressing the trustee's personal views concerning social or political issues or causes. Such considerations, however, may properly influence the investment decisions of a trustee to the extent permitted by the terms of the trust or by the consent of the beneficiaries . . . . In addition, social considerations may be taken into account in investing the funds of charitable trusts to the extent the charitable purposes would justify an expenditure of trust funds for the social issue or cause in question or to the extent the investment decision can be justified on grounds of advancing, financially or operationally, a charitable activity conducted by the trust.

EXTERNAL REFERENCES. Edward C. Halbach, Jr., Trust Investment Law in the Third Restatement, 77 Iowa L. Rev. 1151 (1992); John H. Langbein, The Uniform Prudent Investor Act and the Future of Trust Investing, 81 Iowa L. Rev. 641 (1996).

PART D. THE DUTY OF IMPARTIALITY: ALLOCATIONS BETWEEN INCOME AND PRINCIPAL BENEFICIARIES

Statutory References: *Uniform Principal and Income Act*
UTC § 803

Trusts typically have multiple beneficiaries who have differing interests in income and principal. This situation creates the potential for conflicting preferences among beneficiaries. For example, beneficiaries who have a remainder interest in principal usually prefer that the trustee emphasize capital appreciation in making investment decisions, while life income beneficiaries prefer an investment strategy that emphasizes income-production. Conflicts also frequently exist among concurrent beneficiaries. Concurrent life beneficiaries, for example, may have different tax positions or different preferences between income and growth. Responding to these problems, trust law has long recognized a duty on the trustee to act impartially between income and principal beneficiaries. The duty of impartiality is involved in decisions about how to allocate receipts and expenditures between income and principal. It also applies in the context of decisions concerning trust investments. The case that follows illustrates the relationship between trust duties of investment and the duty of impartiality.

Dennis v. Rhode Island Hospital Trust National Bank

744 F.2d 893 (1st Cir. 1984)

BREYER, C.J. The plaintiffs are the great-grandchildren of Alice M. Sullivan and beneficiaries of a trust created under her will. They claimed in the district court that the Bank trustee had breached various fiduciary obligations owed them as beneficiaries of that trust. The trust came into existence in 1920. It will cease to exist in 1991 (twenty-one years after the 1970 death of Alice Sullivan's last surviving child). The trust distributes all its income for the benefit of Alice Sullivan's living issue; the principal is to go to her issue surviving in 1991. Evidently, since the death of their mother, the two plaintiffs are the sole surviving issue, entitled to the trust's income until 1991, and then, as remaindermen, entitled to the principal.

The controversy arises out of the trustee's handling of the most important trust assets, undivided interests in three multi-story commercial buildings in downtown Providence. The buildings (the Jones, Wheaton-Anthony, and Alice Buildings) were all constructed before the beginning of the century, in an area where the value of the property has declined markedly over the last thirty years. During the period that the trust held these interests the buildings were leased to a number of different tenants, including corporations which subsequently subleased the premises. Income distribution from the trust to the life tenants has averaged over $34,000 annually.

At the time of the creation of the trust in 1920, its interests in the three buildings were worth more than $300,000. The trustee was authorized by the will to sell real estate. When the trustee finally sold the buildings in 1945, 1970, and 1979, respectively, it did so at or near the lowest point of their value; the trust received a total of only $185,000 for its interests in them. These losses, in plaintiffs' view, reflect a serious mishandling of assets over the years.

The district court . . . while rejecting many of plaintiffs' arguments, nonetheless found that the trustee had failed to act impartially, as between the trust's income beneficiaries and the remaindermen; it had favored the former over the latter, and, in doing so, it had reduced the value of the trust assets. To avoid improper favoritism, the trustee should have sold the real estate interests, at least by 1950, and reinvested the proceeds elsewhere. By 1950 the trustee must have, or should have, known that the buildings' value to the remaindermen would be small; the character of downtown commercial Providence was beginning to change; retention of the buildings would work to the disadvantage of the remaindermen. The court ordered a surcharge of $365,000, apparently designed to restore the real value of the trust's principal to its 1950 level.

On appeal, plaintiffs and defendants attack different aspects of the district court's judgment. [The court then announced that it affirmed the district court's judgment.]

I. a. The trustee first argues that the district court's conclusions rest on "hindsight." It points out that Rhode Island law requires a trustee to be "prudent and vigilant and exercise sound judgment," Rhode Island Trust Co. v. Copeland, 39 R.I. 193, 98 A. 273, 279 (1916), but "[n]either prophecy nor prescience is expected." Stark v. United States Trust Co. of New York, 445 F.Supp. 670, 678 (S.D.N.Y.1978). It adds that a trustee can indulge a preference for keeping the trust's "inception assets," those placed in trust by the settlor and commended to the trustee for retention. How then, the trustee asks, can the court have found that it should have sold these property interests in 1950?

The trustee's claim might be persuasive had the district court found that it had acted *imprudently* in 1950, in retaining the buildings. If that were the case, one might note that every 1950 sale involved both a pessimistic seller and an optimistic buyer; and one might ask how the court could expect the trustee to have known then (in 1950) whose prediction would turn out to be correct. The trustee's argument is less plausible, however, where, as here, the district court basically found that in 1950 the trustee had acted not imprudently, but *unfairly*, between income beneficiaries and remaindermen.

Suppose, for example, that a trustee of farmland over a number of years overplants the land, thereby increasing short run income, but ruining the soil and making the farm worthless in the long run. The trustee's duty to take corrective action would arise from the fact that he knows (or plainly ought to know) that his present course of action will injure the remaindermen; settled law requires him to act impartially, "with due regard" for the "respective interests" of both the life tenant and the remainderman. Restatement (Second) of Trusts § 232 (1959). See also A. Scott, The Law of Trusts § 183 (1967); G.G. Bogert & G.T. Bogert, The Law of Trusts and Trustees § 612 (1980). The district court here found that a sale in 1950 would have represented one way (perhaps the only practical way) to correct this type of favoritism. It held that instead of correcting the problem, the trustee continued to favor the life tenant to the "very real disadvantage" of the remainder interests, in violation of Rhode Island law.

To be more specific, in the court's view the problem arose out of the trustee's failure to keep up the buildings, to renovate them, to modernize them, or to take other reasonably obvious steps that might have given the remaindermen property roughly capable of continuing to produce a reasonable income. This failure allowed the trustee to make larger income payments during the life of the trust; but the size of those payments reflected the trustee's acquiescence in the gradual deterioration of the property. In a sense, the payments ate away the trust's capital.

The trustee correctly points out that it did take certain steps to keep up the buildings; and events beyond its control made it difficult to do more. In the 1920's, the trustee, with court approval, entered into very longterm leases on the Alice and Wheaton-Anthony buildings. The lessees and the subtenants were supposed to keep the buildings in good repair; some improvements were made. Moreover, the depression made it difficult during the 1930's to find tenants who would pay a high rent and keep up the buildings. After World War II the neighborhood enjoyed a brief renaissance; but, then, with the 1950's flight to the suburbs, it simply deteriorated.

Even if we accept these trustee claims, however, the record provides adequate support for the district court's conclusions. There is considerable evidence indicating that, at least by 1950, the trustee should have been aware of the way in which the buildings' high rents, the upkeep problem, the changing neighborhood, the buildings' age, the failure to modernize, all together were consuming the buildings' value. There is evidence that the trustee did not come to grips with the problem. Indeed, the trustee did not appraise the properties periodically, and it did not keep proper records. It made no formal or informal accounting in 55 years. There is no indication in the record that the trust's officers focused upon the problem or consulted real estate experts about it or made any further rehabilitation efforts. Rather, there is evidence that the trustee did little more than routinely agree to the requests of the trust's income beneficiaries that it manage the trust corpus to produce the largest possible income. The New Jersey courts have pointed out that an impartial trustee

> must view the overall picture as it is presented from all the facts, and not close its eyes to any relevant facts which might result in excessive burden to the one class in preference to the other.

Pennsylvania Co. v. Gillmore, 137 N.J.Eq. 51, 43 A.2d 667, 672 (1945). The record supports a conclusion of failure to satisfy that duty.

The district court also found that the trustee had at least one practical solution available. It might have sold the property in 1950 and reinvested the proceeds in other assets of roughly equivalent total value that did not create a "partiality" problem. The Restatement of Trusts foresees such a solution, for it says that

> the trustee is under a duty to the beneficiary who is ultimately entitled to the principal not to . . . retain property which is certain or likely to depreciate in value, although the property yields a large income, unless he makes adequate provision for amortizing the depreciation.

Restatement (Second) of Trusts § 232, comment b. Rhode Island case law also allows the court considerable discretion, in cases of fiduciary breach, to fashion a remedy, including a remedy based on a hypothetical, earlier sale. In, for example, Industrial Trust Co. v. Parks, 190 A. at 42, the court apportioned payments between income and principal "in the same way as they would have been apportioned if (certain) rights had been sold by the trustees immediately after the death of the testator" for a specified hypothetical value, to which the court added hypothetical interest. In the absence of a showing that such a sale and reinvestment would have been impractical or that some equivalent or better curative steps might have been taken, the district court's use of a 1950 sale as a remedial measure of what the trustee ought to have done is within the scope of its lawful powers.

In reaching this conclusion, we have taken account of the trustee's argument that the buildings' values were especially high in 1950 (though not as high as in the late 1920's). As the trustee argues, this fact would make 1950 an unreasonable remedial choice, other things being equal. But the record indicates that other things were not equal. For one thing, the district court chose 1950, not because of then-existing property values, but because that date marks a reasonable outer bound of the time the trustee could plead ignorance of the serious fairness problem. And, this conclusion, as we have noted, has adequate record support. For another thing, the district court could properly understand plaintiffs' expert witness as stating that the suburban flight that led to mid-1950's downtown decline began before 1950; its causes (increased household income; more cars; more mobility) were apparent before 1950. Thus, the court might reasonably have felt that a brief (1948-52) downtown "renaissance" should not have appeared (to the expert eye) to have been permanent or longlasting; it did not relieve the trustee of its obligation to do something about the fairness problem, nor did it make simple "building retention" a plausible cure. Finally, another expert testified that the trustee should have asked for power to sell the property "sometime between 1947 and 1952" when institutional investors generally began to diversify portfolios. For these reasons, reading the record, as we must, simply to see if it contains adequate support for the district court's conclusion as to remedy (as to which its powers are broad), we find that its choice of 1950 as a remedial base year is lawful.

Contrary to the trustee's contention, the case law it cites does not give it an absolute right under Rhode Island law to keep the trust's "inception assets" in disregard of the likely effect of retention on classes of trust beneficiaries. The district court's conclusion that the trustee should have sold the assets if necessary to prevent the trust corpus from being consumed by the income beneficiaries is reasonable and therefore lawful.

c. The trustee challenges the district court's calculation of the surcharge. The court assumed, for purposes of making the trust principal whole, that the trustee had hypothetically sold the trust's interests in the Wheaton-Anthony and the Alice buildings in 1950, at their 1950 values (about $70,000 and $220,000, respectively). It subtracted, from that sum of about $290,000, the $130,000 the trust actually received when the buildings were in fact sold (about $40,000 for the Wheaton-Anthony interest in 1970 and about $90,000 for the Alice interest in 1979). The court considered the difference of $160,000 to be a loss in the value of the principal, suffered as a result of the trustee's failure to prevent the principal from eroding. The court then assumed that, had the trustee sold the buildings in 1950 and reinvested the proceeds, the trustee would have been able to preserve the real value of the principal. It therefore multiplied the $160,000 by 3.6 percent, the average annual increase in the consumer price index from 1950 to 1982, and multiplied again by 32, the number of full years since 1950. Finally, the court multiplied again by an annual 0.4 percent, designed to reflect an "allowance for appreciation." It added the result ($160,000 X 4 percent X 32), about $205,000, to the $160,000 loss and surcharged the trustee $365,000. We are aware of a number of mathematical problems with this calculation. (Why, for example, was no account taken of inflation when subtracting sale receipts from 1950 values?) But, in the context of this specific litigation, fairness as between the parties requires us to restrict our examination to the two particular challenges that the trustee raises.

First, the trustee claims that the court improperly ascertained the 1950 values of the trust's interests because it simply took a proportionate share of the buildings' values. That is to say, it divided the total value of the Alice Building by four to reflect the fact that the trust owned a 1/4 undivided interest. The trustee argues that the building's values should have been discounted further to reflect the facts that the trust owned a fractional interest in the buildings and that fractional interests (with their consequent problems of divided control) typically sell at a discount.

This particular matter in this case, however, was the subject of conflicting evidence. On the one hand, the trustee showed that the marketplace ordinarily discounted the value of fractional interests. On the other hand, the plaintiffs introduced an expert study giving the 1950 values of the trust's interests at precisely the figure shown by the district court. When the trustee finally sold the trust's interests (in 1970 and 1979), their value was *not* significantly discounted. And, since the trustee also controlled (as a trustee) other fractional interests in the same building, the trustee arguably could have arranged to sell the entire building in 1950 as it did in 1970 and 1979. Evaluating this evidence and the merits of these arguments is a matter for the district court. We see no abuse of the district court's powers to make reasonable judgments as to hypothetical values in its efforts to devise an appropriate remedy for the trustee's breach of duty.

Second, the trustee argues that the district court should not have applied to the 1950 hypothetical sales value a 4 percent interest factor—a factor designed to compensate for 3.6 percent average annual inflation and for 0.4 percent "appreciation." We do not agree with the trustee in respect to the 3.6 percent.

Rhode Island law simply requires that the court's approach be reasonable and its calculations grounded in the record's facts. See generally Industrial Trust Co. v. Parks, supra. The trustee does not claim that it requires the court to follow any one particular calculation method, such as that, for example, contained in Restatement (Second) of Trusts § 241. And, we believe the inflation adjustment meets Rhode Island's broader requirements.

For one thing, it seems reasonable for the court—in devising a remedy for the trustee's violation of its duty of impartiality—to assume that a fair trustee would have maintained the property's real value from 1950 through 1982. Such an assumption is consistent with basic trust law policies of providing income to income beneficiaries while preserving principal for the remaindermen, and, consequently, of avoiding investment in wasting assets. Moreover, it is consistent with readily ascertainable general economic facts that wages and many asset values as well as prices have on average kept pace with inflation. See generally K. Hirsch, Inflation and the Law of Trusts, 18 Real Prop., Prob. & Tr. J. 601 (Win.1983); Comment, Investment and Management of Trust Funds in an Inflationary Economy, 126 U. of Pa.L.R. 1171, 1197 (1978). While the value of long term bonds has fallen, the value of common stocks and much property has risen. See generally R. Ibbotson & R. Sinqucfield, Stocks, Bonds, Bills and Inflation: The Past and the Future (1982); J. Wiedemer, Real Estate Investment (1979). Where a court is trying to create, not a measure of the trustee's duty, but simply a plausible reconstruction of what would have occurred to a hypothetical 1950 reinvestment, we see nothing unreasonable in assuming that the value of the corpus would have kept pace with inflation.

We reach a different conclusion, however, in respect to the additional 0.4 percent, designed to reflect "appreciation." Neither the court nor the parties have provided us with any reason to believe that the trustee would have outperformed inflation. There is no evidence in the record suggesting that a hypothetical reinvestment of hypothetical proceeds from a hypothetical 1950 property sale would have yielded real appreciation over and above inflation's nominal increase. We have found no information about the performance of an average, or typical, trust. And the general publicly available sources offer insufficient support for a claim of likely real increase. See R. Ibbotson & R. Sinquefield, supra. Moreover, one can imagine reasonable disagreement about whether any such hypothetical real appreciation would belong to the life tenant or to the remainderman. These factors lead us to conclude that, in adding 0.4 percent interest for real appreciation, the district court exceeded its broad remedial powers. Our recalculation, omitting the 0.4 percent, reduces the surcharge from $365,781.67 to $345,246.56.

d. The trustee objects to the court's having removed it as trustee. The removal of a trustee, however, is primarily a matter for the district court. A trustee can be removed even if "the charges of his misconduct" are "not made out." Petition of Slatter, 108 R.I. 326, 275 A.2d 272, 276 (1971). The issue here is whether "ill feeling" might interfere with the administration of the trust. The district court concluded that the course of the litigation in this case itself demonstrated such ill feeling. Nothing in the record shows that the court abused its powers in reaching that conclusion. [The balance of the opinion, rejecting the plaintiff's contentions that (1) pre-judgment interest should have been awarded, and (2) that defendant should have been charged personally with plaintiff's attorneys fees, is omitted.]

The judgment of the district court is modified and as modified affirmed.

Note

1. *The Traditional Rules of Income and Principal.* Prior to 1997, nearly all states had enacted one of two versions of the Uniform Principal and Income Act (UPIA), the original 1931 act or the 1962 act. These acts operate as default rules. They yield to a contrary provision in the trust instrument.

Both acts set out detailed rules regarding the allocation of receipts and expenditures between income and principal. Both sets of rules tended to rely on form over substance. For example, with respect to corporate distributions, it was well settled that income beneficiaries receive ordinary cash dividends and that principal beneficiaries receive any capital gains if the stock is sold. The states differed over allocation of stock dividends, but the two competing rules (the so-called "Pennsylvania" and "Massachusetts" rules) both emphasized form over substance.

The emphasis on form also appeared in rules concerning other sorts of receipts. The 1962 UPIA, for example, allocated to income receipts like rent and interest on bonds and loans, while allocating to principal sale proceeds and payment of bond principal. For assets like natural resources, patents, and copyrights, the Act took a somewhat less rigid approach, allocating for natural resources, for example, royalties to income except for 27 ½ percent allocated to principal.

2. *The Duty of Impartiality under Modern Portfolio Theory.* Recall that Modern Portfolio Theory (MPT), which is the foundation for the Uniform Prudent Investor Act and similar provisions concerning trust investments, instructs that trustees should invest in ways designed to maximize overall return

and not be controlled by the form of a particular investment. At the same time trust law's duty of impartiality seems to require that trustee pay attention to the form of specific investments to the extent that certain types of investments do not benefit all of the beneficiaries evenly. Suppose, for example, that from the perspective of overall return and diversification, prudence favors investing in the stock of a company that pays no dividends because the firm plows all of its earnings back into the company. How can the trustee invest in such a company without breaching its duty of impartiality by disfavoring the income beneficiary? Under the traditional rules regarding allocations between income and principal, trustees frequently faced such dilemmas.

In recent years, MPT has changed not only trust law's thinking about prudence but also its approach to income and principal matters. The 1997 Uniform Principal and Income Act, revised by the Uniform Law Commissioners in 2000, sets out an approach that is expressly predicated on the principles of MPT. The 1997 Act, as revised, continues many of the 1962 Act's rules. However, to enable trustees to invest from a portfolio-maximizing perspective, Section 104 of the Act authorizes the trustee depart from the traditional principal-and-income rules and make equitable adjustments between income and principal. Specifically, § 104(a) states:

> A trustee may adjust between principal and income to the extent the trustee considers necessary if the trustee invests and manages trust assets as a prudent investor, the terms of the trust describe the amount that may or must be distributed to a beneficiary by referring to the trust's income, and the trustee determines ... that the trust is [otherwise] unable to [administer the trust impartially].

For a discussion of this provision and the 1997 Act generally, see Joel C. Dobris, Why Trustee Investors Often Prefer Dividends to Capital Gain and Debt Investments to Equity—A Daunting Principal and Income Problem, 32 Real Prop., Prob. & Tr. J. 255 (1997).

3. *Unproductive Assets*. Unproductive (and underproductive) assets present the opposite problem from that involved in *Dennis*. The income generated by unproductive assets is less rather than more than a return provided by normal trust investments. The trustee's duty of impartiality usually means that such assets must be sold. See Restatement 3d of Trusts § 240. If sale of the asset is delayed, the proceeds must be allocated between income and principal. Restatement 3d of Trusts § 241(2) provides the following formula to determine how much should be allocated to principal:

> The net proceeds from the sale of the property are apportioned by ascertaining the sum that, together with simple interest at the current rate of income on trust investments from the time the duty arose to the time of sale, would equal the net proceeds; the sum so ascertained is to be treated as principal and the rest of the

> proceeds as income. The net proceeds are determined either by adding to the net sale price the net income received or by deducting from the net sale price the net deficit incurred in carrying the property prior to the sale.

The Restatement's formula can be expressed algebraically by the following equation: Principal = net proceeds ÷ (1 + [period of years held multiplied by the interest rate]).

If the settlor directs that the trustee retain an unproductive asset, the apportionment rules usually don't apply. There is disagreement about what to do, however, where unproductive property is an original trust asset but the settlor doesn't expressly direct its retention. Some courts have refused to order apportionment under these circumstances (see, e.g., Creed v. Connolly, 172 N.E. 106 (Mass. 1930)), while other courts imply both a duty to dispose of unproductive assets and a duty to apportion upon sale (see, e.g., Rowland's Estate, 6 N.E.2d 393 (N.Y. 1937)).

4. *Allocation Rules for Not-for-Profit Institutions*. Unlike private trusts, which are subject to the allocation rules just studied, particularly the Revised Uniform Principal and Income Act, most charitable institutions are subject to a statute that permits them to implement a total return approach. The Uniform Management of Institutional Funds Act (UMIFA) allows charitable trustees and directors of nonprofit institutions to count appreciation, realized and unrealized, in the value of a fund for purposes of establishing an income stream that balances corpus and operating needs. See Joel C. Dobris, Real Return, Modern Portfolio Theory, and College, University, and Foundation Decisions on Annual Spending From Endowments: A Visit to the World of Spending Rules, 28 Real Prop., Prob & Tr. J. 49 (1993).

5. *Total Return Unitrusts*. More recently, states have been moving to enact statutes permitting trustees of private trusts to apply the total return approach to a conventional income trust. Under these statutes, a trustee may convert an income trust to a total return unitrust (TRU), or vice versa, after giving notice to current and remainder beneficiaries. The statutes vary regarding the extent of the trustee's discretion over important issues like rate of return. New York's statute, for example, adopts a fixed rate of return of 4%, with a smoothing rule after the first three years, while Delaware's statute gives the trustee a choice to set the rate between 3 and 5%, taking into account the settlor's expressed intentions, general economic conditions, projected earnings and capital appreciation, and projected inflation. Another difference among states concerns the relationship between the TRU approach and the adjustment approach of the 1997 UPIA. The Delaware statute, for example, does not include a trustee adjustment power, while New York and other states include both the power to adjust and a separate TRU provision. For an example of a TRU-only statute, see Del. Code § 3527 (enacted June 21, 2001), and for an example of a statute

containing both the UPIA adjustment power and a separate TRU provision, see N.Y. Est. Powers & Trusts Law §§ 11-2.3(5), -2.4 (enacted Sept. 5, 2001). The UPIA's adjustment power and the TRU approach got a boost when the Treasury Department issued proposed regulations (REG-106513-00 (2/15/01)) giving them the green light for various tax purposes, including the income requirement of the federal estate tax marital deduction (see supra Chapter 7, Part A.4).

E. THE DUTY TO ACCOUNT

Statutory References: *UTC § 813*
UPC §§ 7-303, -307

As mentioned at the outset of this Chapter, property fiduciaries are required to file an accounting with the court prior to their discharge from office. For trustees, this will normally occur upon termination of the trust. For estate representatives, the accounting occurs at the end of administration. In addition, estate representatives must make earlier periodic accountings beginning, immediately upon their appointment. Many statutes also require that trustees of testamentary trusts make intermediate accountings. Even where they do not, trustees often find it advantageous to file periodic accountings with the supervising court as a means of gaining judicial approval of their actions with respect to the trust proper.

Traditionally, the accounting takes a form of a detailed description of the fiduciary's actions during the period covered by the accounting. The accounting must describe property received, income earned, disbursements made, taxes paid, and all distributions of income and/or principal made during the covered period. Under the traditional rules the fiduciary must provide notice of an accounting to all persons having an interest in the estate or trust.

The Uniform Trust Code changes the traditional rules in various ways. Section 813, for example, limits the trustee's duty to inform to the trust's "qualified beneficiaries," defined in § 103(12) as "a distributee or permissible distributee of trust income or principal" as of specified dates. Remote remainder beneficiaries are not entitled to information about the trust's administration unless they have filed a specific request with the trustee.

Upon settlement of the final accounting, the fiduciary makes final distribution and is then discharged by the supervising court. Normally, if beneficiaries have received proper notice of an accounting and failed to object, the fiduciary is protected against subsequent objections, absent fraud, of course. The case that follows illustrates the potential breadth of the term "fraud."

National Academy of Sciences v. Cambridge Trust Company

346 N.E.2d 879 (Mass. 1976)

REARDON, J. This matter is before us for further appellate review, the Appeals Court having promulgated an opinion.

The facts which give rise to the case are essentially as follows. Leonard T. Troland died a resident of Cambridge in 1932 survived by his widow, Florence R. Troland. By his will executed in April, 1931, he left all of his real and personal property to be held in trust by the Cambridge Trust Company (bank) with the net income of the trust, after expenses, 'to be paid to, or deposited to the account of (his wife) Florence R. Troland' during her lifetime so long as she remained unmarried. He further provided that '(k)nowing my wife, Florence's, generosity and unselfishness as I do, I wish to record it as my intention that she should not devote any major portion of her income under the provisions of this will, to the support or for the benefit of people other than herself. It is particularly contrary to my will that any part of the principal or income of my estate should revert to members of my wife's family, other than herself, and I instruct the trustees to bear this point definitely in mind in making decisions under any of the options of this will.' The testator went on to provide in part that on his wife's death or second marriage the bank would transfer the trusteeship to The National Research Council of Washington, D.C., which the petition alleged to be an agency of the National Academy of Sciences (academy), to constitute a trust to be known as the Troland Foundation for Research in Psychophysics. He directed that income be accumulated and added to principal until sufficient to produce an annual income of $50,000 or the 1931 purchasing power equivalent of that amount of money, at which time the income was to be applied by the academy within certain specific guidelines set out in the will. The testator further provided instructions to the academy as successor trustee concerning his wife's support should she he widowed again after a second marriage or should her second husband fail to support her.

The will was allowed, the trust was established as provided by the testator, and the bank paid the income thereof to the widow until her death in 1967. During the period from 1932 to 1945 the widow provided eighteen different mailing addresses for income checks to be transmitted to her by the bank. On February 13, 1945, she married Edward D. Flynn in West Palm Beach, Florida, and failed to advise the bank of her remarriage. Following her remarriage she lived in Perth Amboy, New Jersey. Commencing on April 14, 1944, she directed the bank to forward all her monthly checks to her in care of Kenneth D. Custance, her brother-in-law through marriage to her sister. Over the years these checks were forwarded to two Boston addresses and were made payable to 'Florence R. Troland.' Custance in turn forwarded the checks to Florence R. Flynn who indorsed them in blank 'Florence R. Troland' and returned them to Custance who also indorsed them prior to depositing them in bank accounts in his name maintained at the State Street Bank and Trust Company in Boston and the National Bank of Wareham, Massachusetts. After Florence R. Flynn's death on December 25, 1967, the bank for the first time learned of her remarriage. Throughout her second marriage Florence R. Flynn lived with her husband who was able to provide support for her and who, although aware that she was receiving payments from the trust, was ignorant of the limitation on her rights to receive such payments. In March, 1968, the bank brought a suit in equity in the Superior Court, Suffolk County, against Custance, the National Bank of Wareham, the State Street Bank and Trust Company, and Edward D. Flynn for recovery of amounts 'represented by checks made payable to Florence R. Troland and collected by Florence R. Flynn subsequent to the date of her marriage.' In this litigation the bank recovered $41,416.64 from which it paid legal fees and disbursements of $14,475.49. The total of all checks collected by Florence R. Flynn following her marriage in 1945 up to the date of her death is $106,013.41. The twelfth through thirty-third accounts of the bank covering that period between her remarriage and October 8, 1966, were presented to the Probate Court for Middlesex County in separate proceedings and allowed. The academy had formal notice prior to the presentation of the twelfth through fourteenth accounts and the eighteenth through thirty-third accounts, and with respect to the fifteenth through seventeenth accounts assented in writing to their allowance. The academy, unaware of the widow's remarriage, did not challenge any of the accounts and they were duly allowed.

The petition brought in the Probate Court by the academy seeks revocation of the seven decrees allowing the twelfth through thirty-third accounts of the bank, the excision from those accounts of 'all entries purporting to evidence distributions to or for the benefit of 'Florence R. Troland' . . . subsequent to February 13, 1945,' the restoration by the bank to the trust of the amounts of those distributions with interest at the rate of six per cent, a final account reflecting the repayments and adjustments, appointment of the academy as trustee, and payment by the bank of the costs and expenses of the academy's counsel.

Following hearing a judge of the Probate Court revoked the seven decrees allowing the twelfth through thirty-third accounts, ordered restoration to the trust of $114,314.18, representing amounts erroneously distributed to Florence R. Flynn plus Massachusetts income taxes paid on those amounts from trust funds, together with interest thereon in the sum of $104,847.17 through March 31, 1973, and interest thereafter at the rate of six per cent per annum to the date of restoration in full. . . .

The issues before us have to do with the power of the Probate Court judge to order the revocation of the decrees allowing the twelfth through thirty-third accounts, and the propriety of charging the bank for the amounts erroneously disbursed, as well as the disposition of the several claims for counsel fees, interest and disbursements.

The bank recited in the heading of each of the challenged accounts that the trust was 'for the benefit of Florence R. Troland,' and stated in schedule E of each account (in the first four accounts specifically as 'Distributions to Beneficiary') that monthly payments of $225 or more were made to 'Florence R. Troland.' The Appeals Court held that these recitals and statements 'constituted a continuing representation by the bank to the academy and to the court that the widow remained 'Florence R. Troland' despite her (then unknown) remarriage to Flynn, and that she remained the sole income beneficiary of the trust.' . . . The court further held that those representations were technically fraudulent in that '(t)hey were made as of the bank's own knowledge when the bank had no such knowledge and had made absolutely no effort to obtain it.' . . .

The doctrine of constructive or technical fraud in this Commonwealth is of venerable origin. As we pointed out in Powell v. Rasmussen, 355 Mass. 117, 118-119, 243 N.E.2d 167 (1969), the doctrine here was developed in two opinions by Chief Justice Shaw. In Hazard v. Irwin, 18 Pick. 95, 109 (1836), it was defined in the following terms: '(W)here the subject matter is one of fact, in respect to which a person can have precise and accurate knowledge, and . . . he speaks as of his own knowledge, and has no such knowledge, his affirmation is essentially false.' This rule was reiterated by Chief Justice Shaw in Page v. Bent, 2 Met. 371, 374 (1841): 'The principle is well settled, that if a person make a representation of a fact, as of his own knowledge, in relation to a subject matter susceptible of knowledge, and such representation is not true; if the party to whom it is made relies and acts upon it, as true, and sustains damage by it, it is fraud and deceit, for which the party making it is responsible.' In this case the marital status of Mrs. Troland/Flynn was a fact susceptible of precise knowledge, the bank made representations concerning this fact of its own knowledge when it had no such knowledge, and the academy to whom the representations were made relied on them to its detriment. While this standard of fraud in law has been developed primarily in the context of actions seeking rescission of contracts and of tort actions for deceit, we have indicated in past decisions that an analogous standard might be applicable to misrepresentations in the accounts of fiduciaries. We hold today that 'fraud' as used in G.L. c. 206, § 24, contemplates this standard of constructive fraud at least to the extent that the fiduciary has made no reasonable efforts to ascertain the true state of the facts it has misrepresented in the accounts. This rule is not a strict liability standard, nor does it make a trustee an insurer against the active fraud of all parties dealing with the trust. Entries in the accounts honestly made, after reasonable efforts to determine the truth or falsity of the representations therein have failed through no fault of the trustee, will not be deemed fraudulent or provide grounds for reopening otherwise properly allowed accounts. However, in the instant case the probate judge found that the bank, through the twenty-two years covered by the disputed accounts, exerted 'no effort at all . . . to ascertain if Florence R. Troland had remarried even to the extent of annually requesting a statement or certificate from her to that effect' and that 'in administering the trust acted primarily in a ministerial manner and in disregard of its duties as a trustee to protect the terms of the trust.' In these circumstances we have little trouble in concluding that the bank's representations as to the marital status of the testator's widow fully justified the reopening of the accounts.

Cases relied on by the bank in which this court refused to allow previously allowed accounts to be reopened are distinguishable in that either they did not involve representations of fact susceptible of precise knowledge but rather questions of judgment and discretion as to matters fully and frankly disclosed in the accounts, or that the alleged wrongful acts or mistakes of the trustee were discernible from an examination of the accounts, the trust documents and the law. We adhere to our decisions that it is the duty of beneficiaries 'to study the account presented to the Probate Court by the trustee, and to make their objections at the hearing.' Greene v. Springfield Safe Deposit & Trust Co., supra, 295 Mass. at 154, 3 N.E.2d at 257. However, in this case the fact of the widow's remarriage was not discernible from the most scrupulous examination of the accounts, the trust documents and the relevant law, and the bank cannot avoid responsibility here for its misrepresentations by alleging a breach of duty on the part of the academy.

As to the propriety of surcharging the bank for the amounts erroneously disbursed, when a trustee makes payment to a person other than the beneficiary entitled to receive the money, he is liable to the proper beneficiary to make restitution unless the payment was authorized by a proper court. Since, as we have held, the decrees allowing the twelfth through thirty-third accounts were revoked properly, the bank thus became liable to the academy to restore to the trust corpus the payments it made to Mrs. Troland/Flynn when she was not entitled to receive them. In addition to the amounts erroneously disbursed, the bank was also properly charged by the Probate Court judge with simple interest on those payments at the legal rate of six per cent per annum. . . .

[T]he decree is affirmed.

[The dissenting opinion of WILKINS, J. is omitted.]

Note

"No Judicial Accounting" Provisions. Settlors who wish to relieve their trustees of the burden of making repeated accountings often insert in the trust instrument a so-called "no judicial accounting" provision. These provisions require only that the trustee make periodic accounting to the adult beneficiaries and not to the court. Some jurisdictions have been unwilling to enforce such clauses in the case of testamentary trusts and, in a few instances, inter vivos trusts as well. New York courts have been especially hostile to these clauses. See, e.g., Estates of Brush, 46 Misc.2d 277, 259 N.Y.S.2d 390 (Sur. Ct. 1965).

PART F. SELECTION, REMOVAL, AND COMPENSATION OF FIDUCIARIES

Statutory References: *UPC §§ 3-203, 3-608, 3-611, 3-719, -721*
UTC §§ 705, 706, 708

Selecting Personal Representatives and Trustees. Selecting property fiduciaries can be a tricky business. Often the persons) whom the client wants to serve as estate personal representative are not prepared to carry out the sometime onerous responsibilities of the job. Most people want their property fiduciary to be people whom they know well and trust. Those are, obviously, important criteria, but they should be the only factors that the client takes into account. Estate personal representatives should be individuals or institutions that have the wherewithal to liquidate a person's estate. This means that they should possess some degree of financial sophistication or at least be able to supervise someone else who is financially sophisticated. Financial sophistication is even more important when selecting trustees. A trustee must be knowledgeable about investments, including tax implications.

Clients often wish, initially at least, to select family members to serve as personal representative and/or trustee. While there is nothing inherently wrong with this, the client should be made aware of several potential issues. First, family members often do not possess the degree of financial sophistication that property fiduciaries usually need. Second, the family member whom the client wishes to act as fiduciary may well also be a beneficiary. The problem here is not one of merger but potential conflicts of interest or at least the potential for disputes between the fiduciary-beneficiary and other beneficiaries. Finally, fiduciaries, even those who are family members, are always vulnerable to the possibility of liability for breach of fiduciary duties, and family members, once they are made aware of the issue, may not be financially able or willing to bear the risk of legal liability. Corporate fiduciaries are usually much better able to bear the risk through a variety of risk-spreading techniques.

The mention of corporate fiduciaries raises another issue that is likely to occur to the client, namely, whether there should be two (or more) co-trustees, with at least one being a corporate entity. Here again, multiple considerations compete. On the one hand, there is the matter of cost. Family members may, and often do, waive the fiduciary's right to receive a fee; corporate fiduciaries, obviously, will not do so. On the other hand, corporate fiduciaries are more likely than family members or friends of the client to possess the desirable degree of financial sophistication. It is possible, however, for a personal fiduciary to obtain the benefits of such sophistication if the fiduciary is given the authority to retain accountants, investment advisors, and others who are in a position to provide the personal fiduciary with specialized assistance.

Where there are multiple fiduciaries, problems may arise in their relationship with each other. Not infrequently, disputes arise over such questions as the division of responsibilities among them, custody of assets, and fees. Corporate fiduciary usually want to have custody over all assets and receive the full fee to which they are entitled. (We discuss below the amount to which a fiduciary is entitled to receive as a commission.)

A final, and very important, matter concerning the selection of fiduciaries involves appointment of the drafting attorney as estate representative and/or trustee. We raised this topic in Chapter 4 when we discussed the interrelationship between undue influence and the professional responsibilities of drafting attorneys. Briefly to summarize what we said there, while no per se rule bans lawyers from preparing documents that name the lawyer as a fiduciary, special disclosure and counseling is strongly advisable.

Family Offices. The tremendous growth in family wealth during the past decade has led to growing popularity of a new institution for managing family wealth, the "family office." The central purpose of the family office is to provide coordinated management of family fortunes of substantial proportions over several generations. It often originates in a family-owned business, handling shareholder record-keeping and legal compliance requirements for family members. As the business becomes more complex, these responsibilities are shifted to an entity that operates outside of, but complementary to the family business.

Family offices typically serve multiple functions. Primary among these are asset-preservation and enhancement, financial education for younger generation family members, and fulfilling family philanthropic goals. The functions and organization of any family office change over time as the family grows larger and its needs become more diverse. See Sara Hamilton, Wealth Management: Keeping It in the Family, 136 Tr. & Est., August 1997, at 28.

The executives of family offices may be trustees of family trusts or occupy other positions within the family firm. Even if they are not trustees, however, family office executives are fiduciaries, subject to all the usual duties of property fiduciaries. As such, they are subject to the risk of liability for failure to comply with duties of care, loyalty, prudence, and other customary fiduciary responsibilities. Not surprisingly, then, family office executives frequently require that exculpation and indemnification provisions be included in their employment contracts. They may also request liability insurance policies to provide more protection in the event of litigation brought against them.

Disgruntled Beneficiaries and Removal of Fiduciaries. By one estimate, over the next twenty years eight trillion dollars will pass from one generation to the next. As part of this enormous transfer of wealth, over one million Americans are expected to inherit over one million dollars each.[16] Much of this wealth will be transferred into private trusts and managed by professional trustees. Even that which is not will be managed for some period of time by estate fiduciaries. The transfer and management of such vast sums of wealth by fiduciaries has already begun to generate closer scrutiny of fiduciaries by entitled recipients. Beneficiaries are increasingly objecting to fiduciary practices ranging from investment decisions to commissions. Indeed, organizations such as Heirs Inc. and Fiduciary Solutions have been formed for the purpose of providing advice to estate and trust beneficiaries who believe that estate representatives or trustees are mishandling fiduciary assets or charging excessive fees.[17]

One option available to disgruntled beneficiaries is removal of the fiduciary. As the old saying goes, however, "Easier said than done." Courts view removal as a drastic action, one to be taken only under exceptional circumstances. UPC § 3-611 provides that an estate personal representative may be removed at the request of an interested person only for cause. Cause exists if "removal would be in the best interests of the estate, or if it is shown that the personal representative . . . intentionally misrepresented material facts in the proceedings leading to his appointment, or that the personal representative has disregarded an order of the Court, has become incapable of discharging the duties of his office, or has mismanaged the estate or failed to perform any duty pertaining to the office." For trustees, UTC § 706 provides that a court may remove a trustee, either at the request of a beneficiary, co-trustee or the settlor or on its own motion, only under four limited circumstances: (1) the trustee has committed a "serious breach of trust"; (2) lack of cooperation among the trustees "substantially impairs" trust administration; (3) removal would serve the best interests of the beneficiaries because the trustee is unable or unwilling

16. Davidson Gighotti, Pity the Poor Heir, Sarasota, March 1996, at 64.

17. Brigid McMenamin, Don't Count Your Chickens, Forbes, March 6, 2000, at 104.

to administer the trust effectively; or (4) because of a "substantial change of circumstances" or upon the request of all the beneficiaries, the court finds that removal "best serves the interests of all the beneficiaries and is not inconsistent with a material purpose of the trust."

Fiduciary Compensation Practices. It goes without saying that clients are keenly interested in the fees charged by fiduciaries, including trustees and estate personal representatives. In the past, many states statutorily set the personal representative's fee. The typical statute provided a schedule of fees based on a percentage of the estate. The UPC abandons the fee schedule approach and provides that the estate personal representative and the attorney representing the estate are entitled to "reasonable compensation." UPC §§ 3-719, 3-721. The UPC permits personal representatives to establish their fees and those of estate attorneys with formal court approval. Because this is a marked departure from the conventional practice,§ 3-721 emphasizes that any interested person can require court review of these fees.

For inter vivos trusts, the trustee's fee is usually established by the terms of the trust agreement. In the absence of any explicit agreement, the reasonable compensation standard is applied. See Bogert on Trusts § 975. UTC § 708 adopts the reasonable compensation standard as the default rule and goes on to provide that if the trust instrument specifies the compensation level, the court may allow more or less in either of two circumstances: (1) the trustee's duties were "substantially different" from those initially contemplated; or (2) the specified compensation is "unreasonably low or high."

Clients are especially likely to be concerned about fees if the fiduciary is a corporate fiduciary (i. e., a bank or trust company). Corporate fiduciaries typically recommend including in wills or trust instruments compensation provisions that permit them to be paid without prior court approval. In addition, the suggested compensation provisions might state that the testator or grantor "recognizes that such compensation may exceed the compensation for [fiduciary] services in effect from time to time under applicable law."

Corporate fiduciaries' commission policies vary, of course, but to illustrate these policies we have taken the following information from the January 1991 commission policy statement of a major firm, United States Trust Company. Acting as estate personal representative, the company applies the rates currently permitted by New York law:

5% on the first $100,000
4% on the next $200,000
3% on the next $700,000
2 1/2% on the next $4,000,000
2% on the balance.

The company charges a minimum fee of $25,000.

For trusts, the company charges an annual fee consisting of two parts, a base fee of $2,000 per trust plus a variable fee. The variable fee is:

1 % on the first $3,000,000 of principal
3/4 of 1 % on the next $2,000,000 of principal
½ of 1 % on the next $5,000,000 of principal
3/8 of 1% on the balance.

Additional compensation is required for acquisition of special investments, for closely-held companies, and for certain other estates and trusts services.

G. THE TRUST AND OUTSIDERS: CREDITORS AND THE EPA

Statutory References: *UPC 003-808, 5-429, 7-306*
UTC § 1010

Creditors' Claims. The common-law rule is that a trustee is personally liable on any contract that the trustee makes regardless of whether the trustee had the power to enter into the contract. One with whom the trustee contracts can't obtain a legal judgment against the trustee as trustee so as to collect the judgment against trust assets. The trustee doesn't avoid personal liability merely by signing in its fiduciary role. See, e.g., Dolben v. Gleason, 198 N.E. 762 (Mass. 1935). The trustee is entitled to be indemnified out of trust assets, but if the contract is beyond the trustee's powers there is no right to indemnity. Moreover, the trustee is personally liable to the extent that the trust estate is insufficient to indemnify the trustee.

The contract may expressly relieve the trustee of personal liability if the trustee had authority to enter into the contract. Under these circumstances, the creditor does have recourse against trust assets on the theory that the creditor is enforcing the trustee's right to indemnity (but only to the extent of the trustee's right of indemnification). The other theory upon which creditors may recover against trust assets is unjust enrichment. If the creditor has conferred a benefit upon the trust estate, the trustee is entitled to recover directly from the trust estate to that extent.

The trustee's tort liability follows the same general approach. The trustee is personally liable for torts committed by the trustee or the trustees employee in the course of trust administration. The trustee, if not personally at fault, is entitled to indemnification from trust assets. See, e.g., Matter of Lathers, 137 Misc. 226, 243 N.Y.S. 366 (1930). It's likely that a court that permits a contract creditor to reach trust assets through substitution of the creditor for the trustee's right to indemnity will reach the same result when a tort claimant tries to reach trust assets, but courts have been somewhat cautious in committing themselves to this position. See, e.g., Johnston v. Long, 181 P.2d 645 (Cal. 1947).

Commentators have criticized the traditional rules as unfair to both creditors and the trustee where the trustee isn't personally at fault and trust assets are insufficient to indemnify the trustee. See John D. Johnston, Jr., Development in Contract Liability of Trusts and Trustees, 42 N.Y.U. L. Rev. 483 (1966). Reacting to these criticisms, recent statutes have reversed the traditional rules. Section 7-306 of the Uniform Probate Code is an example. It permits both tort and contract creditors to proceed against the trustee in his or her representative capacity whether or not the trustee is personally liable. Comparable provisions apply to the liability of estate personal representatives (§ 3-808) and conservators of an incompetent's property (§ 5-429). The Uniform Trust Code takes a somewhat different approach. For contract creditors, section 1010 provides a default rule of no personal liability if the trustee properly entered into the contract and if the contract disclosed the fiduciary status. For tort creditors, it provides that the trustee is personally liable only if the trustee was personally at fault.

Fiduciary Liability Under CERCLA. Perhaps the most controversial basis of fiduciary liability in recent years has been the federal "Superfund" act, the Comprehensive Environmental Response, Compensation, and Liability Act, 42 U.S.C. § 9601-75, usually called "CERCLA." CERCLA imposes liability for the costs of cleaning up toxic waste sites on any "owner" of land on which hazardous substances are found. It is clear that a trustee can be an "owner" under CERCLA, but the statute does not say whether a trustee is personally liable or liable only in its fiduciary capacity, that is, only to the extent of the trust's assets. Obviously, personal liability has much greater financial ramifications for trustees than fiduciary liability.

The widely-discussed decision in City of Phoenix v. Garbage Service Co., 827 F. Supp. 600 (D. Ariz. 1993), raised for fiduciaries great fear that they would be held personally liable under CERCLA any time land that they owned in trust was found to be contaminated with a hazardous substance. In that case, Valley National Bank (VNB) acquired in 1965, as an original trust asset of a testamentary trust, an option to repurchase a landfill site in Phoenix, Arizona, that the settlor had previously owned. VNB exercised the option. At the time it did so, Garbage Services, Inc., which the decedent settlor had completely owned and which VNB now owned, was managing the site. After exercising the option, VNB leased the land to Garbage Services, which managed the site until it was closed in 1972.

In 1980, the city of Phoenix acquired title to the site by condemnation. Later, in 1989, it sued VNB to recover the cleanup costs under CERCLA. VNB argued that because it owned the landfill as trustee, it was not personally liable and that its liability was limited to the amount of the assets held in the trust. The court held that VNB was personally liable.

In response to fiduciaries' fears of broad personal liability under CERCLA after City of Phoenix, Congress in 1996 enacted a new statute limiting trustees liability. The Asset Conservation, Lender Liability, and Deposit Insurance Protection Act of 1996 amends CERCLA to provide that the liability of a fiduciary is limited to the assets held in a fiduciary capacity. The Act made two major changes. First, it confined fiduciary personal liability to circumstances where the fiduciary is liable "independently of [its] ownership as a fiduciary or actions taken in a fiduciary capacity." 42 U.S.C. § 9607(n)(2) (1996). Second, it created certain safe harbors for fiduciaries to avoid personal liability. These include undertaking or directing others to undertake a clean-up or "any other lawful means of addressing hazardous substances" on the site, including in the trust instrument a term or condition that "relates to compliance with an environmental law" or monitoring or enforcing such a term, providing "financial or other advice . . . to other parties to the fiduciary relationship, including the settlor or beneficiary"; and administering, as a fiduciary, a facility that was contaminated before the fiduciary relationship began. 42 U.S.C. § 9607(n).

The 1996 statute mollifies many of the concerns that grew out of the City of Phoenix decision. It does not, however, apply to possible fiduciary liability under federal environmental legislation other than CERCLA.

Index

References are to Pages

ISBN 1-58778-070-4

90000

9 781587 780707